Commercial Agreements and Competition Law

Practice and Procedure in the UK and EC

Second edition

Commercial Agreements and Competition Law

Practice and Procedure in the UK and EC

Second edition

Nicholas Green, LLB, LLM, PhD

of the Inner Temple, Barrister

and

Aidan Robertson, MA, LLM

of the Middle Temple, Barrister
Fellow, Wadham College, Oxford

KLUWER LAW INTERNATIONAL
LONDON – THE HAGUE – BOSTON

Published by
Kluwer Law International Ltd
Sterling House
66 Wilton Road
London SW1V 1DE
United Kingdom

Kluwer Law International Ltd incorporates
the publishing programmes of
Graham & Trotman Ltd,
Kluwer Law & Taxation Publishers
and Martinus Nijhoff Publishers

Sold and distributed in
the USA and Canada by
Kluwer Law International
675 Massachusetts Avenue
Cambridge MA 02139
USA

In all other countries, sold and distributed by
Kluwer Law International
P.O. Box 322
3300 AH Dordrecht
The Netherlands

ISBN 90-411-0868-8

First published 1986

Second edition 1997

British Library Cataloguing in Publication Data
A catalogue record for this book is available from the British Library

Library of Congress Cataloging-in-Publication Data is available

Typeset in Bembo 10/11½ by On Screen, West Hanney, Oxfordshire
Printed and bound in Great Britain by Hartnolls Ltd, Bodmin, Cornwall

Contents

PART I PROCEDURE

Tables of Cases

English Decisions

Cases on the Register of Restrictive Trade Practices

Cases on the Exempt Register of Restrictive Trade Practices

Informal OFT Investigations

OFT Investigations under the Competition Act 1980

Cases Considered by the DTI under ICTA 1988, s.568

Reports of the Monopolies and Mergers Commission

Decisions in Other National Courts

Australia

Belgium

Germany

Holland

Hong Kong

Ireland

United States

European Decisions–EC Commission, CFI and ECJ

Tables of Primary Legislation

UK Statutes

Treaty of Rome

Treaty of Paris

Berne Convention for the Protection of Literary and Artistic Works

Tables of Secondary Legislation

Statutory Instruments

EEC Directives and Decisions

EEC Regulations

Select Bibliography

The bibliography below provides a selection of the major texts used in this area. Other more specialised articles and documents of relevance are referred to as appropriate in each chapter.

General Texts: United Kingdom

Allen, *Monopoly and Restrictive Practices* (Unwin University Books, 1968)
Brock, *The Control of Restrictive Practices from 1956* (McGraw-Hill, 1966)
Butterworths, *Competition Law Encyclopaedia*, ed. Freeman and Whish, looseleaf
Chitty on Contracts, Volume II (Sweet and Maxwell, 27th edn. 1994)
Cornish, *Intellectual Property, Patents, Copyright, Trade Marks and Allied Rights* (Sweet and Maxwell, 3rd edn. 1996)
Cunningham, *The Fair Trading Act 1973* (Sweet and Maxwell, 1974 and Supplement 1978)
Everton, *Trade Winds: An Introduction to the UK's Law of Competition* (Alan Osborne, 1978)
George and Joll (eds.), *Competition Policy in the United Kingdom and EEC* (Cambridge, 1975)
Korah, *Competition Law of Britain and the Common Market* (Martinus Nijhoff, 3rd edn. 1982)
Livingston, *Competition Law and Practice* (FT Law and Tax, 1995)
Macdonald, *Resale Price Maintenance* (Butterworths, 1964)
O'Brien and Swann, *Information Agreements, Competition and Efficiency* (Macmillan, 1968)
Pickering, *Resale Price Maintenance in Practice* (George Allen and Unwin, 1966)
Stevens and Yamey, *The Restrictive Practices Court: A Study of the Judicial Process and Economic Policy* (Weidenfeld and Nicolson, 1965)
Summerfield and Stanbrook, *The Resale Prices Act* (Charles Knight and Co, 1964)
Swann, O'Brien, Maunder and Howe, *Competition in British Industry* (Unwin University Books, 1974)
Whish, *Competition law* (Butterworths, 3rd edn. 1993)
Wilberforce, Campbell and Elles, *Restrictive Trade Practices and Monopolies* (Sweet and Maxwell, 2nd edn. 1965 and Supplement 1971)

General Texts: EC Law

In addition to the texts above which deal with UK and EC law the following may be noted:

Bellamy and Child, *Competition Law of the EEC* (Sweet and Maxwell, 4th edn. 1994, 1st supplement 1996)
Goyder, *EC Competition Law* (OUP, 2nd edn. 1992)
Guy and Leigh, *The EEC and Intellectual Property* (Sweet and Maxwell, 1981)
Kerse, *EC Antitrust Procedure* (Sweet and Maxwell, 3rd edn. 1994)
Korah, *An Introductory Guide to EEC Competition Law and Practice* (ESC, 4th edn. 1995)
Ortiz Blanco, *EC Competition Procedure* (OUP, 1996)
Ritter, Braun and Rawlinson, *EEC Competition Law* (Kluwer, 1991)
Rowe, Jacobs, Joelson (eds.) *Enterprise Law of the 80s: European and American perspectives on Competition and Industrial Organisation* (ABA, 1980)
Slot and McDonnell (eds.) *Procedure and Enforcement in EC and US Law* (Sweet and Maxwell, 1993)
Swann, *Competition and Industrial Policy in the European Community* (Methuen, 1983)
Van Bael and Bellis, *Competition Law of the European Community* (CCH, 3rd edn. 1994)
Wyatt and Dashwood, *European Community Law* (Sweet and Maxwell, 3rd edn. 1993), Chapters 13–20

Governmental and other Texts: UK and EC

A Review of Monopolies and Mergers Policy: A Consultative Document (1978) Cmnd 7198 (The Liesner Committee Report)
A Review of Restrictive Trade Practices Policy: A Consultative Document (1979) Cmnd 7512 (The Liesner Committee Report)
Opening Markets: New Policy on Restrictive Trade Practices (1989), Cm 727
Abuse of Market Power: A Consultative Document on Possible Legislative Options (1992) published by the Department for Trade and Industry
Tackling Cartels and the Abuse of Market Power: Implementing the Government's Policy for Competition Law Reform. A Consultation Document (1996) published by the Department for Trade and Industry
Tackling Cartels and the Abuse of Market Power: A Draft Bill. An Explanatory Document (1996) published by the Department for Trade and Industry
CBI, *The Competition Act 1980* (1980)
EC Commission, Annual Reports on Competition Policy. Detailed account of policy and developments in Commission thinking during relevant year. An important source of information
EC Commission, *Competition Policy Newsletter.* A quarterly bulletin on latest Commission developments in enforcement, law and policy. Also available on the World Wide Web at http://europa.eu.int/en/comm/dg04/dg4home.htm
National Economic Development Office Report, *Competition Policy* (1978)
OECD, *Concentration and Competition Policy* (1979)
OECD, *Buying Power* (1981)
OECD, *Collusive Tendering* (1976)
OECD, *Refusal to Sell* (1968)

OFT, Annual Report of the Director General of Fair Trading. Annual reports outlining the work of the OFT in the particular year. The Report also contains lists of cases given dispensation under section 21(2) during that year

OFT, *Fair Trading*, a quarterly bulletin reporting OFT activity. Contains lists of cases given section 21(2) dispensation during the previous quarter. Information is also available on the World Wide Web at http://www.open.gov.uk/oft/ofthome.htm

OFT, *An Outline of United Kingdom Competition Policy* (1995)

OFT, *Cartels: Detection and Remedies: A Guide for Purchasers* (1995)

OFT, *Monopolies and Anti-competitive Practices* (1995)

OFT, *Restrictive Agreements (a Basic Guide)* (1997)

OFT, *Restrictive Trade Practices (a Detailed Guide)* (1997)

OFT, *Restrictive Trade Practices in the Bus Industry* (1995)

OFT Research Paper No. 1 (author: NERA) *Market Definition in UK Competition Policy* (1992)

OFT Research Paper No. 2 (author: London Economics) *Barriers to Entry and Exit in UK Competition Policy* (1994)

OFT Research Paper No. 5 (author: Myers) *Predatory Behaviour in UK Competition Policy* (1994)

OFT Research Paper No. 12 (authors: Dobson and Waterson) *Vertical Restraints and Competition Policy* (1996)

General Texts: United States of America

Relevant legal *and* economic texts are noted below:

Austin, *Antitrust Law, Economics, Policy* (Matthew Bender, 1976)

Gellhorn, *Antitrust Law and Economics* (West, 4th edn. 1994)

Hawk, *United States, Common Market and International Antitrust* (Law and Business Inc/Harcourt Brace Jovanovich, 1980)

Kaysen and Turner, *Antitrust Policy* (Harvard University Press, 1959)

Lamb and Shields, *Trade Association Law and Practice* (Little Brown, 1971)

Neale and Goyder, *The Antitrust Laws of the USA* (NIESR, 1980)

Posner, *Antitrust Law* (Chicago, 1978)

Raybould and Firth, *Comparative Law of Monopolies* (1988, revised 1991) – covers EC, US, UK and German law

Scherer and Ross, *Industrial Market Structure and Economic Performance* (Rand McNally, 3rd edn. 1990)

Principal Statutory Provisions

The provisions below are of central importance to the text and are referred to throughout. They are laid out here to aid easy reference.

1 Article 85 Treaty of Rome: Restrictive Agreements in EC Law

ART. 85.1. The following shall be prohibited as incompatible with the common market: all agreements between undertakings, decisions by associations of undertakings and concerted practices which may affect trade between Member States and which have as their object or effect the prevention restriction or distortion of competition within the common market, and in particular those which:

(a) directly or indirectly fix purchase or selling prices or any other trading conditions;
(b) limit or control production, markets, technical development, or investment;
(c) share markets or sources of supply;
(d) apply dissimilar conditions to equivalent transactions with other trading parties, thereby placing them at a competitive disadvantage;
(e) make the conclusion of contracts subject to acceptance by the other parties of supplementary obligations which, by their nature or according to commercial usage, have no connection with the subject of such contracts.

2. Any agreements or decisions prohibited pursuant to this Article shall be automatically void.

3. The provisions of paragraph 1 may, however, be declared inapplicable in the case of:

– any agreement or category of agreements between undertakings;
– any decision or category of decisions by associations and undertakings;
– any concerted practice or category of concerted practices;

which contributes to improving the production or distribution of goods or to promoting technical or economic progress, while allowing consumers a fair share of the resulting benefit, and which does not:

(a) impose on the undertakings concerned restrictions which are not indispensable to the attainment of these objectives;
(b) afford such undertakings the possibility of eliminating competition in respect of a substantial part of the products in question.

2 Article 86 Treaty of Rome: Abuse of a Dominant Position in EC Law

ART. 86. Any abuse by one or more undertakings of a dominant position within the common market or in a substantial part of it shall be prohibited as incompatible with the common market in so far as it may affect trade between Member States. Such abuse may, in particular, consist in:

(a) directly or indirectly imposing unfair purchase or selling prices or unfair trading conditions;
(b) limiting production, markets or technical development to the prejudice of consumers;
(c) applying dissimilar conditions to equivalent transactions with other trading parties, thereby placing them at a competitive disadvantage;
(d) making the conclusion of contracts subject to acceptance by the other parties of supplementary obligations which, by their nature or according to commercial usage, have no connection with the subject of such contracts.

3 Sections 6 and 11 Restrictive Trade Practices Act 1976: Application of Act to Goods and Services Agreements

6.–(1) This Act applies to agreements (whenever made) between two or more persons carrying on business within the United Kingdom in the production or supply of goods, or in the application to goods of any process of manufacture, whether with or without other parties, being agreements under which restrictions are accepted by two or more parties in respect of any of the following matters –

(a) the prices to be charged, quoted, or paid for goods supplied, offered or acquired, or for the application of any process of manufacture to goods;
(b) the prices to be recommended or suggested as the prices to be charged or quoted in respect of the resale of goods supplied;
(c) the terms or conditions on or subject to which goods are to be supplied or acquired or any such process is to be applied to goods;
(d) the quantities or descriptions of goods to be produced, supplied or acquired;

(e) the process of manufacture to be applied to any goods, or the quantities or descriptions of goods to which any such process is to be applied; or

(f) the persons or classes of persons to, for or from whom, or the areas or places in or from which, goods are to be supplied or acquired, or any such process applied.

(2) For the purposes of subsection (1) above it is immaterial–

(a) whether any restrictions accepted by parties to an agreement relate to the same or different matters specified in that subsection, or have the same or different effect in relation to any matter so specified, and

(b) whether the parties accepting any restrictions carry on the same class or different classes of business.

(3) For the purposes of this Part of this Act an agreement which–

(a) confers privileges or benefits only upon such parties as comply with conditions as to any such matters as are described in subsection (1) *(a)* to *(f)* above; or

(b) imposes obligations upon parties who do not comply with such conditions;

shall be treated as an agreement under which restrictions are accepted by each of the parties in respect of those matters.

(4) Without prejudice to subsection (3) above, an obligation on the part of any party to an agreement to make payments calculated by reference–

(a) to the quantity of goods produced or supplied by him, or to which any process of manufacture is applied by him; or

(b) to the quantity of materials acquired or used by him for the purpose of or in the production of any goods or the application of any such process to goods;

being payments calculated, or calculated at an increased rate, in respect of quantities of goods or materials exceeding any quantity specified in or ascertained in accordance with the agreement, shall be treated for the purposes of this Act as a restriction in respect of the quantities of those goods to be produced or supplied, or to which that process is to be applied.

This subsection does not apply to any obligation on the part of any person to make payments to a trade association of which he is a member, if the payments are to consist only of bona fide subscriptions for membership of the association.

11.–(1) The Secretary of State may by statutory instrument make an order in respect of a class of services described in the order (in this Act referred to, in relation to an order under this section, as "services brought under control by the order") and direct by the order that this Act shall apply to agreements (whenever made) which –

(a) are agreements between two or more persons carrying on business within the United Kingdom in the supply of services brought under control by the order, or between two or more such persons together with one or more other parties; and

(b) are agreements under which restrictions, in respect of matters specified in the order for the purposes of this paragraph, are accepted by two or more parties.

(2) The matters which may be specified in such an order for the purposes of subsection (1) *(b)* above are any of the following –

(a) the charges to be made, quoted or paid for designated services supplied, offered or obtained;

(b) the terms or conditions on or subject to which designated services are to be supplied or obtained;

(c) the extent (if any) to which, or the scale (if any) on which, designated services are to be made available, supplied or obtained;

(d) the form or manner in which designated services are to be made available, supplied or obtained;

(e) the persons or classes of persons for whom or from whom, or the areas or places in or from which, designated services are to be made available or supplied or are to be obtained.

Note: services agreement are now subject to registration having been called up by the Restrictive Trade Practices (services) Order 1976 S.I. 1976 No. 98.

4 Section 10 Restrictive Trade Practices Act 1976: Public Interest (Gateways) Provisions for Goods Agreements

10.–(1) For the purposes of any proceedings before the Court under Part I of this Act, a restriction accepted or information provision made in pursuance of an agreement to which this Act applies by virtue of this Part shall be deemed to be contrary to the public interest unless the Court is satisfied of any one or more of the following circumstances–

(a) that the restriction or information provision is reasonably necessary, having regard to the character of the goods to which it applies, to protect the public against injury (whether to persons or to premises) in connection with the consumption, installation or use of those goods;

(b) that the removal of the restriction or information provision would deny to the public as purchases, consumers or users of any goods other specific and substantial benefits or advantages enjoyed or likely to be enjoyed by them as such, whether by virtue of the restriction or information provision itself or of any arrangements or operations resulting therefrom;

(c) that the restriction or information provision is reasonably necessary to counteract measures taken by any one person not party to the agreement with a view to preventing or restricting competition in or in relation to the trade or business in which the persons party thereto are engaged;

(d) that the restriction or information provision is reasonably necessary to enable the persons party to the agreement to negotiate fair terms for the supply of goods to, or the acquisition of goods from, any one person not party thereto who controls a preponderant part of the trade or business of acquiring or supplying such goods, or for the supply of goods to any person not party of the agreement and not carrying on such a trade or business who, either alone or in combination with any other such person, controls a preponderant part of the market for such goods;

(e) that, having regard to the conditions actually obtaining or reasonably foreseen at the time of the application, the removal of the restriction or information provision would be likely to have a serious and persistent adverse effect on the general level or unemployment in an area, or in areas taken together, in which a substantial proportion of the trade or industry to which the agreement relates is situated;

(f) that, having regard to the conditions actually obtaining or reasonably foreseen at the time of the application, the removal of the restriction or information provision would be likely to cause a reduction in the volume or earnings of the export business which is substantial either in relation to the whole export business of the United Kingdom or in relation to the whole business (including export business) of the said trade or industry;

(g) that the restriction or information provision is reasonably required for purposes connected with the maintenance of any other restriction accepted or information provision made by the parties, whether under the same agreement or under any other agreement between them, being a restriction or information provision which is found by the Court not to be contrary to the public interest upon grounds other than those specified in this paragraph, or has been so found in previous proceedings before the Court; or

(h) that the restriction or information provision does not directly or indirectly restrict or discourage competition to any material degree in any relevant trade or industry and is not likely to do so;

and is further satisfied (in any such case) that the restriction or information provision is not unreasonable having regard to the balance between those circumstances and any detriment to the public or to persons not parties to the agreement (being purchasers, consumers or users of goods produced or sold by such parties, or persons engaged or seeking become engaged in the trade or business of selling such goods or of producing or selling similar goods) resulting or likely to result from the operation of the restriction or the information provision.

(2) In this section–

(a) "purchasers", "consumers" and "users" include persons purchasing, consuming or using for the purpose or in the course of trade or business or for public purposes;

and

(b) references to any one person include references to any two or more persons being interconnected bodes corporate or individuals carrying on business in partnership with each other.

Note: Section 19 for services is *mutatis mutandis* in the same terms as section 10.

5 Section 21 Restrictive Trade Practices Act 1976: Main Provision for Exempting Registered Agreement from Reference to the Restrictive Practices Court

21.–(1) The Director may refrain from taking proceedings before the Court –

(a) in respect of an agreement if and for so long as he thinks it appropriate so to do having regard to the operation of any directly applicable Community provision and to the purpose and effect of any authorisation or exemption granted in relation to such a provision;

(b) where an agreement–

(i) of which particulars are entered or filed in the register pursuant to this Act has been determined (whether by effluxion of time or otherwise); or

(ii) has been so determined in respect of all restrictions accepted or information provisions made under that agreement.

(2) If it appears to the Secretary of State, upon the Director's representation, that the restrictions accepted or information provisions made under an agreement of which particulars are so entered or filed are not of such significance as to call for investigation by the Court, the Secretary of State may give directions discharging the Director from taking proceedings in the Court in respect of that agreement during the continuance in force of the directions.

(3) The Secretary of State may at any time upon the Director's representation withdraw any directions given by him under subsection (2) above if satisfied that there has been a material change of circumstances since the directions were given.

6 Section 29 Restrictive Trade Practices Act 1976: Exemption from Registration for Agreements Important to the National Economy

Agreements important to the national economy

29.–(1) If it appears to the Secretary of State, on consideration of an agreement proposed to be made by any parties, that the conditions set out in subsection (2) below are complied with in respect of the proposed agreement, he may, by order made on or before the conclusion of the agreement, approve the agreement for the purposes of this section; any agreement so approved shall be exempt from registration under this Act during the continuance in force of the order.

(2) The conditions for the making of an order under subsection (1) above in respect of an agreement (in this section referred to as the conditions of exemption) are–

(a) that the agreement is calculated to promote the carrying out of an industrial or commercial project or scheme of substantial importance to the national economy;

(b) that its object or main object is to promote efficiency in a trade or industry or to create or improve productive capacity in an industry;

(c) that the object cannot be achieved or achieved within a reasonable time except by means of the agreement or of an agreement for similar purposes;

(d) that no restrictions are accepted or information provisions made under the agreement other than such as are reasonably necessary to achieve that object; and

(e) that the agreement is on balance expedient in the national interest.

(3) In considering the national interest for the purposes of subsection (2)*(e)* above the Secretary of State shall take into account any effects which an agreement is likely to have on persons not parties thereto as purchasers, consumers or users of any relevant goods or, in relation to an agreement to which this Act applies by virtue of an order under section 11 or section 12 above, as users of any relevant services.

(4) An order under this section shall continue in force for such period as may be specified therein, which may be extended by subsequent order of the Secretary of State: but the period so specified or extended shall not exceed the period which appears to the Secretary of State sufficient for the purposes for which the order was made.

(5) An order under this section approving an agreement may be revoked by order of the Secretary of State at any time after the expiry of one year from the day on which the first-mentioned order was made if it appears to him–

(a) that the object or main object of the agreement has not been or is not likely to be achieved, or that any other condition or exemption is no longer satisfied in respect of the agreement; or

(b) that the agreement is used for purposes other than those for which it was approved;

and may be so revoked at any time if the Secretary of State becomes aware of circumstances by reason of which, if known to him at the material time, the agreement would not have been approved.

The Secretary of State shall not make an order by virtue of paragraph *(a)* or paragraph *(b)* of this subsection unless he has given to each of the parties at least 28 days' notice of his intention to make the order.

(6) The Secretary of State shall–

(a) lay before each House of Parliament a copy of any order made under this section and of the agreement to which the order relates; and

(b) made available for public inspection a copy of any such agreement.

(7) Subsection (6) above shall not apply–

(a) to an agreement which varies an agreement previously approved under this section; or

(b) to an order approving such an agreement;

if in the Secretary of State's opinion the variation does not substantially affect the operation of restrictions accepted or information provisions made under the agreement previously approved.

7 Section 2 Competition Act 1980: Provision Defining Anti-competitive Practices

Anti-competitive practices

2.–(1) The provisions of sections 2 to 10 below have effect with a view to the control of anti-competitive practices, and for the purposes of this Act a person engages in an anti-competitive practice if, in the course of business, that person pursues a course of conduct which, of itself or when taken together with a course of conduct pursued by persons associated with him, has or is intended to have or is likely to have the effect of restricting, distorting or preventing competition in connection with the production, supply or acquisition of goods in the United Kingdom or any part of it or the supply or securing of services in the United Kingdom or any part of it.

(2) To the extent that a course of conduct is required or envisaged by a material provision of, or a material recommendation in, an agreement which is registered or subject to registration constituting an anti-competitive practice for the purposes of this Act; and for the purposes of this subsection–

(a) a provision of an agreement is a material provision if, by virtue of the existence of the provision (taken alone or together with other provisions) the agreement is one to which that Act applies; and

(b) a recommendation is a material recommendation in an agreement if it is one to which a term implied into the agreement by any provision of section 8 or section 16 of that Act (terms implied into trade association agreements and services supply association agreements) applies.

(3) For the purposes of this Act, a course of conduct does not constitute an anti-competitive practice if it is excluded for those purposes by an order made by the Secretary of State; and any such order may limit the exclusion conferred by it by reference to a particular class of persons or to particular circumstances.

(4) Without prejudice to the generality of subsection (3) above, an order under that subsection may exclude the conduct of any person by reference to the size of his business, whether expressed by reference to turnover, as defined in the order, or to his share of a market, as so defined, or in any other matter.

(5) [Repealed by the Deregulation and Contracting Out Act 1994.]

(6) For the purposes of this section any two persons are to be treated as associated –

(a) If one is a body corporate of which the other directly or indirectly has control either alone or with other members of a group of interconnected bodies corporate of which he is a member, or

(b) if both are bodies corporate of which one and the same person or group of persons directly or indirectly has control;

and for the purposes of this subsection a person or group of persons able directly or indirectly to control or materially to influence the policy of a body corporate, but without having a controlling interest in that body corporate, may be treated as having control of it.

(7) In this section "the supply or securing of services" includes providing a place or securing that a place is provided other than on a highway, or in Scotland a public right of way, for the parking of a motor vehicle (within the meaning of the Road Traffic Act 1988).

(8) For the purposes of this Act any question whether, by pursuing any course of conduct in connection with the acquisition of goods or the securing of services by it, a local authority is engaging in anti-competitive practice shall be determined as if the words "in the course of business" were omitted from subsection (1) above; and in this subsection "local authority" means –

(a) in England and Wales, a local authority within the meaning of the Local Government Act 1972, the Common Council of the City of London or the Council of the Isles of Scilly,

(b) in Scotland, a local authority within the meaning of the Local Government (Scotland) Act 1973, and

(c) in Northern Ireland, a district council established under the Local Government Act (Northern Ireland) 1972.

8 Section 84 Fair Trading Act 1973: Meaning of "public interest" – Relevant to Cases before the Monopolies and Mergers Commission under the Competition Act 1980

84.–(1) In determining for any purposes to which this section applies whether any particular matter operates, or may be expected to operate, against the public interest, the Commission shall take into account all matters which appear to them in the particular circumstances to be relevant and, among other things, shall have regard to the desirability–

(a) of maintaining and promoting effective competition between persons supplying goods and services in the United Kingdom;

(b) of promoting the interests of consumers, purchasers and other users of goods and services in the United Kingdom in respect of the prices charged for them and in respect of their quality and the variety of goods and services supplied;

(c) of promoting, through competition, the reduction of costs and the development and use of new techniques and new products, and of facilitating the entry of new competitors into existing markets;

(d) of maintaining and promoting the balanced distribution of industry and employment in the United Kingdom; and

(e) of maintaining and promoting competitive activity in markets outside the United Kingdom on the part of producers of goods, and of suppliers of goods and services, in the United Kingdom.

(2) This section applies to the purpose of any functions of the Commission under this Act other than functions to which section 59(3) of this Act applies.

Foreword

It is over ten years since the first edition of this work. Every time it seemed appropriate to embark upon a revision the government announced a review of UK competition law and this proved an excellent excuse to delay commencing the project.

It must also be confessed that the task represented by rewriting the first edition appeared so daunting that the excuse for delay presented by threatened law reform was seized upon with undue enthusiasm. A second edition might therefore have remained a pious aspiration on my part had I not been able to persuade Aidan Robertson to share in the task of co-authoring this work, and I am immensely grateful to him for agreeing to add his name to the front page. This edition has taken over four years to prepare. We have stuck to the remit of the first edition and have concentrated on the impact of competition law on commercial agreements. The ever burgeoning growth of the law in this area has meant that we have also stuck to concentrating on those core areas of competition law which practitioners are likely to confront most regularly in their everyday practices. Even keeping within these parameters has resulted in a book of 1,100 pages.

UK competition law is in the throes of reform. We contemplated delaying publication until the proposals became law. However, on reflection, we believe that the new law will be some time in preparation and hence the present UK regime will remain on the statute books for a period, which will give the UK parts of this book continued utility. There will also, no doubt, be transitional arrangements in the new legislation which will mean that practitioners will not be able to forget the Restrictive Trade Practices Act 1976 for some considerable time to come. None the less, it is our intention to produce a third edition when the new law comes into force.

It has taken more early mornings, late nights and weekends than either of us care to recall to revise this work. Along the way we have had assistance from many practitioners, students, pupils and others. In this connection, we would like to record special thanks to Marie Demetriou who spent a considerable amount of time scouring the Official Journal and other sources on our behalf and preparing drafts of text. The final text is, of course, the sole responsibility of the authors.

Nicholas Green
Brick Court Chambers

Part I

Procedure

1 Agreements Registrable under the RTPA 1976

A. Introduction

1.1 The Restrictive Trade Practices Act 1976 ("RTPA 1976" hereafter) is a highly complex statute. Although the government proposed its abolition and replacement with legislation modelled on EC law in a White Paper in 1989 and subsequently in 1996,[1] this has not yet happened, and there is no obligation under EC law for the government so to do, as the European Commission confirmed in its *Twenty-third Report on Competition Policy*.[2] Instead, there has been piecemeal reform, most importantly under the Deregulation and Contracting Out Act 1994.

In this chapter the agreements to which the RTPA 1976 applies are examined. Analysis of agreements excluded from the Act may be found in Chapter 2.

1.2 Essentially the RTPA 1976 creates rules for four types of agreement:

(i) agreements concerning goods;
(ii) agreements concerning services;
(iii) information agreements concerning goods;
(iv) information agreements concerning services.

[1] The Department of Trade and Industry issued two documents in 1996, both entitled *Tackling Cartels and the Abuse of Market Power*. The first document, sub-headed "Implementing the Government's Policy for Competition Law Reform" published in March, followed on from a series of earlier Green and White Papers. *Opening Markets: New Policy on Restrictive Trade Practices* (Cm 727, 1989), was in turn preceded by a Green Paper *Review of Restrictive Trade Practices Policy* (Cm 331, 1988), whose criticisms of the current legislation in Chapter 2 remain pertinent today. See also, in relation to reform of the Fair Trading Act 1973, the 1992 Green Paper *Abuse of Market Power* (Cm 2100) and the Department of Trade and Industry Press Release in response 14 April 1993. The second document was published by the DTI in August 1996. Sub-headed " A Draft Bill", it contained draft legislation for the repeal of the RTPA and the Resale Prices Act 1976. However, although it remains government policy to introduce competition law reform, no legislation was announced in the Queen's Speech in October 1996. Reform was announced in the Queen's Speech in May 1997.

[2] (1993), para. 81.

It should be stressed at the outset that these categories are completely separate from each other. At present only categories (i), (ii) and (iii) are actually controlled by law and even then numerous exceptions exist to each category. Category (iv) may at some future date become subject to the law but this could only be achieved by a statutory Order issued by a competent minister.

1.3 The following matters are discussed in this chapter:

Section B. Agreements caught by the legislation. Analysis of the width of sections 6 and 11 RTPA 1976 being the provisions determining which restrictive goods and services agreements must be registered. A detailed analysis of the statutory wording is provided.
Section C. Goods agreements which must be registered (s. 6 RTPA 1976).
Section D. Services agreements which must be registered (s. 11 RTPA 1976 and S.I. 1976 No. 98—the "Services Order").
Section E. Provisions in agreements which may be disregarded when determining whether the Act applies (ss. 9 and 18 RTPA 1976).
Section F. Note on information agreements.
Section G. The impact upon trade associations.
Section H. Informal, parallel behaviour between major firms: "complex monopolies".
Section I. Check list for determining registrability.

B. Agreements Caught by the Legislation

1.4 If the RTPA 1976 applies to an agreement then particulars of that agreement must be furnished to the Office of Fair Trading[3] who are then statutorily bound to place the particulars on the Register of Restrictive Trade Practices. All agreements registered must be referred to the Restrictive Practices Court (RPC or "the Court" hereafter) for assessment whether the restrictions therein operate against the public interest in which case they are prohibited. However, the Director General of Fair Trading may, often following discussions with the parties to the agreement, obtain a dispensation for the agreement from the Secretary of State which saves the agreement from reference to the Court. Such dispensations are given when the restrictions in the agreement in question are not "significant". (This procedure is examined in Chapter 4.)

1. Sections 6 and 11 RTPA 1976—Words and Phrases Defined

1.5 Section 6 brings *goods* agreements within the control procedure outlined above. Section 6 commences with the following:

> "This Act applies to agreements (whenever made) between two or more persons carrying on business within the United Kingdom in the production or supply of goods, or in the application to goods of any process of manufacture, whether with or without other parties, being agreements under which restrictions are accepted by two or more parties in respect of any of the following matters ..."

[3] Throughout this book where statutory reference is made to the Director General of Fair Trading (DGFT) reference in the text is to the Office of Fair Trading (OFT) since in practice it is officials of that office who undertake the tasks entrusted to the DGFT. It is usually only where wider public issue points arise that the DGFT personally takes a part in the case.

1.6 Section 6 follows with a list of restriction types to which the Act applies. Section 11 repeats, with minor differences, section 6 but applies the Act to *services* agreements. The only significant difference is that *services* agreements are registrable with the OFT only to the extent that specific types of restrictive agreement have been expressly called up for registration by a statutory instrument issued by the Secretary of State. In 1976 the Minister enacted the Restrictive Trade Practices (Services) Order S.I. 1976 No. 98 which prima facie brought under control all types of services agreement. The only excluded agreements are those listed in Schedule 1 to the Act (examined in Chapter 2). The relevant part of section 11 provides that the Act applies to "agreements (whenever made) which ... are agreements between two or more persons carrying on business within the United Kingdom in the supply of services brought under control by the Order, or between two or more such persons together with one or more other parties" and are agreements containing restrictions listed in section 11 (2)(a)–(e).

Details of the types of restriction actually specified in sections 6 and 11 are given later in the chapter. The following discussion elaborates upon the meaning of the various words and phrases in the portions of sections 6 and 11 quoted above.

(1) "Agreements" and "arrangements"

1.7 To be registrable parties must be in an "agreement". The term "agreement" is nowhere in the Act given a precise definition. This has led the Court of Appeal to conclude that the word must be given its ordinary and popular meaning.[4] The *Oxford English Dictionary* (2nd edn. 1989) defines an agreement as: "A coming into accord; an arrangement between two or more persons as to a course of action; a mutual understanding; a covenant, or treaty." Of some help is section 43(1) RTPA 1976 according to which "agreement" includes "any agreement or arrangement, whether or not it is intended to be enforceable (apart from any provision of this Act) by legal proceedings, and references in this Act to restrictions accepted or information provisions made under an agreement shall be construed accordingly". Hence the scope of the legislation covers not only agreements but also the vaguer concept of "arrangements". In *MD Foods plc* v *Baines*[5] Lord Nicholls, giving the judgment of the House stated:

> "At the outset it should be noted that the Act applies to agreements and arrangements, however made ('any agreement or arrangement'), and whether legally enforceable or not: see Section 43(1). An agreement may be made in writing in a single document or in more than one document, or by correspondence, or by word of mouth, or partly in one way and partly in another. An agreement may be inferred from a course of conduct. A restriction may be accepted expressly or impliedly (see Section 43(1)). An agreement which provides encouragement to comply with conditions regarding price and so forth is treated as an agreement under which restrictions are accepted in respect of those conditions (Section 6(3))."

As a preliminary point it should be stressed that not all agreements or arrangements need be registered. It is only those containing restrictions caught by the Act which are subject to control. Thus, for example, a simple conveyance or lease is an agreement but since it would contain restrictions of a type covered by the Act only in exceptional circumstances is rarely registrable.[6]

[4] *per* Willmer LJ in *British Basic Slag Ltd's Application* (1963) LR 4 RP 116 at pp. 145, 146; [1963] 1 WLR 727 (CA).

[5] [1997] 2 WLR 364, 370.

[6] See *Ravenseft Properties* v *Director General of Fair Trading* [1977] 1 All ER 47 (QBD) examined in detail at paras. 2.26–2.75.

1.8 While the commercial concept of an "agreement" is readily understandable, that of "arrangement" is less certain and has given rise to much debate and litigation. Despite early cases which suggested a narrow meaning to the word[7] subsequent case law has made it clear that a wide meaning is to be accorded the phrase. Thus, in *British Basic Slag Ltd* Cross J held that, "all that is required to constitute an arrangement not enforceable in law is that the parties to it shall have communicated with one another in some way, and that as a result of that communication each has intentionally aroused in the other an expectation that he will act in a certain way".[8] Lord Justice Diplock in the *British Basic Slag* case when on appeal affirmed the formulation of Cross J in the lower court when he stated that an arrangement, "involves mutuality in that each party, assuming he is a reasonable and conscientious man, would regard himself as being in some degree under a duty, whether moral or legal, to conduct himself in a particular way as the case may be, at any rate so long as the other party or parties conducted themselves in the way contemplated by the arrangement".[9] The definitions given above, however, are somewhat imprecise and are in practice of limited value to businessmen seeking a predictable basis upon which to conduct relationships with other businessmen. The following is a non-exhaustive list of examples about which a view may be expressed.

(a) Formal agreements

1.9 Formal, written agreements between two or more parties to accept restrictions listed in the Act are clearly caught by the Act. This would include the articles of association of an incorporated trade association which constitutes an agreement between the shareholders. Although restrictive clauses are rarely present in the articles of association, if a clause exists binding members to decisions of the board or of some other designated body the members will be in "agreement" as to decisions of that board or designated body: sections 8(1) (for goods) and 16(2) (for services) RTPA 1976.

1.10 Agreements embodied in settlements reached by parties to litigation may be registrable. Frequently parties to commercial litigation settle their disagreements with a settlement which may be approved by the judge. Approved settlements, Tomlin orders[10] and other forms of compromised litigation may all form registrable agreements if they include, among their terms, registrable restrictions.

(b) Trade association agreements

1.11 Agreements entered into by trade associations operate according to section 8(1) RTPA 1976, "as if the agreement were made between all persons who are members

[7] e.g. *Re Austin Motor Co Ltd's Agreement* (1957) LR 1 RP 6 at p. 19: "It seems to me that an arrangement must at least connote an arrangement whereby the parties to it accept mutual rights and obligations." This *dictum* of Upjohn J was construed by the Registrar of Restrictive Trading Agreements (the predecessor of the Director General of Fair Trading) narrowly as excluding informal gentlemen's agreements (Second Report (1962) Cmnd 1603). Subsequent case law has viewed the *Austin Motors* definition with more of a liberal eye. See in this respect *British Basic Slag Ltd's Application* (1962) LR 3 RP 178 at p. 197 (RPC) and *Fisher* v *Director General of Fair Trading* [1982] I CR 71 at p. 78.

[8] (1962) LR 3 RP 178 at p. 196. See *Aberdeen Solicitors Property Centre Ltd* v *DGFT, The Times*, 20 February 1996.

[9] (1963) LR 4 RP 116 at p. 154. The Court of Appeal encountered obvious difficulties with the concept of an arrangement. Dankwerts LJ stated (*ibid.* at p. 149): "the provisions of the Act ... seem to me to be calculated to drive any accurately minded lawyer to despair. Once the ascertainable ambit of arrangements, rights or obligations, which are legally enforceable is left behind, one flounders in a morass of inexactitudes." He added: "heaven help the lawyer who has to advise a client".

[10] *Topliss Showers Ltd* v *Gessey & Son Ltd* [1989] ICR 5010.

of the association or are represented on it by such members". If restrictions are contained in that agreement they operate "as if the ... restriction or information provision ... were accepted or made by each of those persons". Thus, agreements between trade associations *inter se* are caught as are agreements between an association and a company or private person. (See section G of this chapter for further details.) Trade association is defined in section 43(1) as "a body of persons (whether incorporated or not) which is formed for the purpose of furthering the trade interests of its members, or of persons represented by its members".

(c) Trade association recommendations

1.12 Under sections 8(2) and (3) (goods) and 16(3) and (4) (services) RTPA 1976, recommendations, whether implied or express, of a trade association to its members are registrable by virtue of a fictitious provision which is deemed by the Act to exist in the association's constitution, whereby members agree to abide by the recommendation. Many trade association officials find difficulty in accepting that non-binding recommendations are registrable equally with mandatory rules, yet this is the clear consequence of sections 8 and 16. It is premised upon the basis that recommendations can influence members' behaviour to a significant degree and can lead to harmonised behaviour. The meaning of "recommendation" is not defined in the Act but may be construed to include, among others, express and implied recommendations, guidance notes, advice in the form of circulars, exhortations at association meetings as to the "wisest" course to follow, etc. It is irrelevant, for purposes of registration, that the recommendation might not be followed.

(d) Constitutions of unincorporated associations

1.13 In the case of unincorporated associations, the constitution, whether it consists of a brief enumeration of objectives or is a complex series of documents, will comprise an agreement between the current members and, if it contains registrable restrictions, must be furnished to the OFT. Rarely, however, in practice are restrictions of any significance incorporated into such documents. Sections 8 and 16, discussed above, apply to unincorporated associations as well as to incorporated associations; the definition of trade association in section 43(1) includes both varieties.

(e) Oral agreements

1.14 Oral agreements containing registrable restrictions are caught. So-called "gentlemen's agreements" where the parties claim to be honour bound only are "arrangements" within the meaning of the Act and are accordingly registrable.

(f) Collateral undertakings

1.15 Written contracts with ancillary or collateral, orally agreed, restrictive terms or an "understanding" between the parties to comply with certain restrictions are caught. In this case the combined agreement and arrangement would be registrable. Thus for example, X, Y and Z set up, by a written agreement, a joint buying pool which by the terms of the agreement allows the parties to purchase from the group or from other sources. However, they orally agree to purchase only from the pool thereby restricting their freedom to purchase from independent sources. In this case irrespective of whether the written agreement is on its own registrable the oral agreement certainly is. The OFT would almost certainly view the written and oral agreement as one agreement containing written and oral terms.

(g) Conditional agreements

1.16 An agreement the coming into effect of which is conditional upon the conclusion of other agreements is to be viewed as an agreement in conjunction with the said other agreements. A common example is to be found in the case of directors' service agreements which are entered into in conjunction with the sales of businesses. Thus, for example, in *Donald Storrie Estate Agency Ltd* v *Adams*[11] the Defendants were formerly partners in an estate agency business. They sold the business to the Nationwide Building Society for about £800,000. The business was sold pursuant to a sale agreement between the former partners (a husband and wife), as vendors, the firm itself, and the Building Society as purchaser. It was envisaged by the Building Society that it would, in due course, assign the agreement to a wholly owned subsidiary which would thereafter operate the estate agency business sold to its parent company. However, the sale agreement was expressly stated to be conditional upon the completion of certain events including the delivery by the vendors (the partners) to the purchaser (the Building Society) of a new executed contract of employment with the purchaser in certain approved terms, and, that the purchaser would procure that the said contracts of employment were executed on its behalf or, if the agreement had been assigned to its subsidiary, on behalf of the assignee. One issue the judge had to decide was whether the sale agreement and the service agreements constituted a single, integral agreement, or two separate agreements. The judge stated that it was quite correct to conclude that the service agreements and the sales agreement were not between the same parties but he observed "completion of the latter was dependent, *inter alia*, on completion of the service agreement".[12] Thus "one could not be effective without the other, nor could the other without the one".[13] Accordingly, the two agreements were to be viewed as a single overall agreement for the purposes of the RTPA 1976.[14]

(h) Unilateral dissemination of price lists

1.17 If X unilaterally sends his price list to Y who subsequently reciprocates by forwarding his to X, then an arrangement has almost certainly come into being despite the absence of formal communication between X and Y. An "arrangement" or understanding may be inferred from the conduct of the parties in such a case.[15] If X and Y continue to exchange price lists upon the evolved understanding that each will refrain from undercutting the other then the parties are again almost certainly in a registrable arrangement. If the OFT suspect an unregistered arrangement but have no tangible proof thereof, they may send an informal, inquiring letter asking the parties whether they have accepted registrable restrictions and requesting details of such arrangements or agreements if they exist.

(i) Unilateral no-poaching

1.18 X, with the hope of influencing Y's behaviour, unilaterally refrains from selling in Y's primary marketing area; Y, on appreciating the fact, reciprocates by refraining from sell-

[11] (1989) SLT 305.
[12] *ibid.*, p. 309, col. 1.
[13] *ibid.*
[14] This conclusion was followed in *Sterling Financial Services Ltd* v *Johnston* (1990) SLT 111.
[15] See *Mileage Conference Group of the Tyre Manufacturer's Conference Ltd's Agreement* (1966) LR 6 RP 49, [1966] 1 WLR 1137 (RPC). See also *Schweppes Ltd* v *Registrar of Restrictive Trading Agreements* (1964) LR 5 RP 103; [1965] 1 WLR 157 (CA); and *Telephones* (1964) LR 5 RP 135; [1965] 1 WLR 174 (CA). In the two Court of Appeal cases it was held that the Registrar was entitled to request, from parties, documents pertaining to the circumstances surrounding the entering of the alleged agreements. This was allowed because the

ing in X's primary marketing area. This is almost certainly another example of an arrangement which may be inferred by the conduct of the parties. As with (g) above, there is no formal agreement. The binding factor is an understanding derived from conduct entailing an expectation about each other's conduct or a moral obligation to refrain from selling in each other's territories. As with (g) above, such an "arrangement" is almost certainly registrable. Should *any* form of communication between X and Y as to this conduct exist the case for registration will be even more compelling. An arrangement of this nature is, however, on the very fringe of the concept of an "arrangement" and falls within the Act because of the precise, premeditated conduct of X and the calculated response of Y. If, conversely X refrains from selling in Y's territory for reasons unrelated to any possible response by Y then no arrangement has evolved and any market division which emerges will constitute a natural and not a contrived result. The fact that this result is to the mutual benefit of both X and Y is immaterial.

(j) Arrangement through conduct of agents

1.19 If X sends to his solicitor or accountant or other agent a price list or other document expressing X's future corporate plans for transmission to the solicitor or accountant or other agent of Y, this would amount to an arrangement if Y in any way responds positively by accepting restrictions, since X is attempting to induce Y to act in a particular manner listed in section 6 RTPA 1976 and Y has indicated concurrence.[16]

(k) Conduct in oligopolistic markets

1.20 The raising of prices by firms in an oligopolistic market or in a market in which competitors monitor closely each other's price moves and react accordingly by matching such price moves does not necessarily involve a registrable agreement or arrangement. Although X might know or expect rivals to follow his price moves because of the particular market circumstances, an arrangement between X and his rivals does not exist. X has simply assumed the role of price leader; the RTPA does not apply simply because rivals fall into line behind him. However, if there is any communication whatsoever, whether it consists of a discussion over a quiet drink or a simple "nod and a wink" at a trade association meeting, then this may well be sufficient to turn innocent price leadership into an "arrangement".[17] During counsel's submissions in *Galvanised Tank Manufacturers*, Buckley J commented: "There must surely be a difference between a price leader who says that he will increase his prices and then waits for other manufacturers to follow before he makes his increase effective, and one who puts up his price, irrespective of whether others follow and without waiting for them to do so."[18]

cont.
Registrar necessarily required evidence of whether mutual expectations had been aroused or gentlemen's agreements concluded.

16 For an analogous tax case on the word arrangement in s. 411 Income Tax Act 1952 (now s. 670 Income and Corporation Taxes Act 1988) see *Crossland* v *Hawkins* [1961] Ch 537, [1961] 3 WLR 202 (CA); cf. *Pogson (Inspector of Taxes)* v *Lowe* [1981] STC 400; and *Halifax Society* v *Registry of Friendly Societies* [1978] 1 WLR 1544.

17 But see *British Basic Slag Ltd's Application* (1963) LR 4 RP 116, where Counsel for the company pointed out that the definition of "arrangement" given at first instance by Cross J was wide enough to embrace innocent price leadership. For the reasons given in the text this is probably incorrect. Korah, *Competition Law of Britain and the Common Market* (1982) notes, at p. 110: "Price leadership does not amount to an 'arrangement' unless the firms have communicated with each other, in words or conduct, before publishing a price change, and have not only led each other to expect certain action but have also done something to encourage the others to rely on it occurring."

18 (1965) LR 5 RP 315 at p. 338. See paras. 8.35–8.38.

(l) Professional bodies

1.21 In the case of professional bodies which are incorporated and which exercise a quasi-judicial function (for example with regard to licensing and the conduct and discipline of traders) members abiding by the rules of the professional body may constitute an arrangement with each other as to the terms upon which they supply goods or services. An illustration is *Fisher* v *DGFT* concerning the National Greyhound Racing Club which licenses greyhound racecourse executives and trainers and performs disciplinary functions. The Court of Appeal held, with respect to the inter-relationship of licensees in this organisation: "There was here an independent party making rules and granting licences. There was no evidence of any meeting of minds of the licensees who provided services. There was no evidence of any obligation being undertaken by one licensee to another. It is impossible to find either a multilateral agreement or a multilateral arrangement."[19] The following general rule may thus be assumed to apply:

> "The mere fact that persons voluntarily engaged in activities whereby they become subject to a regime of rules is not in itself any manifestation of their will also to agree or arrange *inter se* to abide by those rules, so that any infraction of the rules carries with it a breach of at least a moral obligation undertaken by each of such persons towards all other persons bound by the rules. All that can be inferred from this commonplace situation, taken by itself, is that each such person binds himself to the rules *vis-à-vis* the rule-making body, and accepts whatever sanctions may be vested in the rule making body in the event of breach of the rules.
>
> Of course, the position is different if the persons who engage in the restrictive practices in question do so under a regime of rules which they themselves have set up ... Admittedly even in such a situation, where the rules are made and imposed from outside, one could conceive of additional facts which might show that there was not merely an imposition of rules on the persons who are bound by them, but also an additional agreement or arrangement between those persons *inter se* to abide by the rules. For this to exist, however, there must be some further evidence of a manifestation of will on their part to this effect."[20]

1.22 This approach was applied by the Court of Appeal in *Re Royal Institution of Chartered Surveyors' Application*,[21] where it was held that the RICS constitution did constitute an arrangement caught by the Act. The element of reciprocity or mutuality was found to exist in the fact that as a matter of professional practice within this profession, members of the institution regarded themselves bound, though in honour only, to comply with the RICS's charter, bye-laws and regulations. Thus membership of the RICS involved the mutual acceptance of obligations to fellow members. In *Fisher* on the other hand, the fact of obtaining a licence to participate in the sport on the club's licensed tracks did not itself provide evidence of the acceptance by licensees of mutual obligations to each other.

(m) Negotiations

1.23 If X, Y and Z are in the process of negotiating an agreement which would contain restrictions of a type listed in sections 6 or 11 RTPA 1976 there is no arrangement or agreement until the contract is concluded. If no agreement is ever reached but, sub-

19 See *Fisher* v *Director General of Fair Trading* [1982] ICR 71 at p. 80 per Waller LJ. Noted in DGFT Annual Report 1982, at pp. 35, 108, 109. (This case concerned services.)

20 *ibid. Fisher* v *Director General of Fair Trading* at p. 82 per Kerr LJ. See also *Royal Institution of Chartered Surveyors' Application* [1985] ICR 330 where there was held to be an agreement between the members *inter se*, judgment affirmed by the Court of Appeal [1986] ICR 550.

21 [1986] ICR 550, affirming McNeill J [1985] ICR 330.

sequently, the parties adhere to goals and aims discussed during negotiation this will represent strong (if not compelling) evidence of an informal arrangement.[22] The RPC has held that participation in the making of standard form contracts is not a restriction within the meaning of the Act. Rather, it is the agreement to use such standard forms or the pressing for their use which constitutes a relevant restriction.[23]

(n) Groups of agreements considered collectively

1.24 If X and Y conclude a series of agreements which individually are not registrable but together are registrable the OFT may take a collective view of the contracts when determining registrability. It has been held that where contracts are made in expectation, and in the light, of each other then there is a subsisting arrangement interlinking the contracts together.[24] Thus for example, bearing in mind that two parties must accept registrable restrictions, if X negotiates an agreement with Y and then X and Y conclude two formal agreements with all of the restrictions accepted by X in one agreement and the registrable restrictions accepted by Y in the other then the OFT will almost certainly view this as a series of linked agreements which should be viewed collectively. This list of examples is not exhaustive. If in doubt about registration the businessman who seeks a safe path to pursue may seek the view of the OFT. In such cases documents should be furnished to the OFT with the express proviso that the parties do not necessarily accept the registrability of the agreement or arrangement.

For details of the registration process see paras. 4.2 and following. Independent legal advice can of course be taken if this is preferred.

(o) The difference between hope and expectation

1.25 In *Southern Co-operative* v *Shearman*[25] it was held that a mere hope that someone would do something was insufficient to found an "arrangement" within the meaning of section 43 RTPA 1976 and that, at the very least, a mutual expectation that, as a result of discussions, some mutual obligation would be fulfilled was required. The case turns upon its own facts. However, it is a useful illustration of the difference between registrable and unregistrable arrangements and of the degree of factual and evidential certainty that the courts will require before satisfied that mutual obligations have *de facto* been accepted. For this reason the case warrants some consideration.

1.26 The Defendant was a dairy roundsman who in March 1990 entered a formal written agreement with Churchfields Dairies ("Churchfields") whereby he purchased from Churchfields part of the goodwill of that company in relation to the activities of a dairyman and purveyor of milk products in the area of Andover. Pursuant to the agreement the Defendant agreed to purchase milk exclusively from Churchfields. The Defendant carried on thereafter the business under the name Sunrise Dairies. Under the agreement the consideration was £45,000 of which £5,000 was payable forthwith and the remainder by ten annual instalments of £4,000 each. The agreement was therefore of ten years' duration. Churchfields had an option to repurchase the business at the end of the ten-year period or before that date upon the occurrence of certain events. At the trial, the Defendant gave evidence that he was not a paper-

[22] See *Schweppes No. 2* (1971) LR 7 RP 336, [1971] 1 WLR 1148 (Ch D).

[23] See *Birmingham Association of Building Trades Employers' Agreement* LR4 RP54, where the RPC (*ibid.*, p. 101) saw no reason to dissent from the submissions of the Registrar as to the non-application of the Act to the making of standard form contracts (see also *ibid.*, p. 78).

[24] *ibid.*

[25] Collins J, 6 February 1995 (unreported).

work man and regarded written agreements as "perhaps an evil". He did not regard himself bound by their terms. For example, he would persuade roundsmen to come to work for him notwithstanding that they were subject to covenants not to compete in favour of their then employers. The Defendant was by this and other means effective in taking customers away from the Plaintiff in the Andover area. The Plaintiff accordingly retaliated by starting to compete in Salisbury through a company called Buttercup, where the Defendant operated. The Plaintiff also commenced action against the Defendant's employees who had breached their restrictive covenants to the Plaintiff. After a time, the Plaintiff decided that "war" was not its best interests so sought to conclude an agreement with the Defendant which ensured that the Plaintiff would continue to supply milk but through the Defendant. To achieve this, Churchfields had to relax the exclusivity provisions in its agreement with the Defendant. Accordingly, a meeting was held between the Plaintiff, the Defendant and a representative of Churchfields to discuss the situation.

1.27 It is clear from the judgment that views differed as to what was or was not agreed at the aforesaid meeting. The Defendant contended that agreement was reached under which Churchfields would not insist on their exclusive supply obligations, the Defendant would take over some of the Plaintiff's rounds which would mean that the Defendant acquired 20 per cent of his requirements from milk from the Plaintiff and the remaining 80 per cent from Churchfields. Further, it was contended that the Plaintiff would cease to trade by means of Buttercup in Salisbury and would cease to compete with Churchfields.

1.28 Conversely, the Plaintiff and Churchfields denied that an agreement was ever reached. Churchfields had negotiated upon the basis that it would sell a minimum of 600 gallons to the Defendant and the Plaintiff would, pull out of Salisbury. However, realising the unlikelihood of Churchfields being able to achieve this position, the company's fallback was to permit the Defendant to enter an agreement with the Plaintiff which gave the Defendant the rounds in Andover. The judge rationalised Churchfields's negotiation position upon the basis that the cessation of hostilities would enable the Defendant to trade in peace (to the advantage of Churchfields) without constant risk of litigation and its attendant costs.

1.29 The Plaintiff's negotiating position was to "string" Churchfields along, to find a way to make the Defendant trade more reasonably and to stop him inducing the Plaintiff's employees to move over to the Defendant, thereby eroding the Plaintiff's goodwill in its rounds.

1.30 Approximately one month after the meeting the Plaintiff concluded a formal agreement with the Defendant. The recitals to the agreement stated as follows:

> "Whereas,
>
> A. The customer carries on the business of a dairyman and wishes to act as distributor for the society's products as certain of its own and the society's customers;
>
> B. The customer is party to an agreement with Churchfields Dairies Limited dated March 1990 which prohibits the customer from obtaining supplies of milk otherwise than from Churchfields.
>
> C. The customer has obtained confirmation from Churchfields that his compliance with his obligations set out in this agreement shall not be treated as a breach of the said agreement."

1.31 After the agreement was signed Churchfields—apparently unaware of the agreement between the Plaintiff and the Defendant—wrote to the Plaintiff. He referred to a "proposed agreement". The company confirmed that it was prepared to waive its exclusive supply agreement with the Defendant. It emphasised that the trading dispute in Salisbury had to be resolved within two months from the date the proposed agreement was signed.

1.32 Under the formal agreement between the Plaintiff and Defendant, the Plaintiff agreed to transfer certain customers representing a stipulated gallonage of milk to the Defendant for the Defendant to supply. A formula was included in the agreement to assess the percentage of the Defendant's total business represented by the transferred customers and this percentage of milk was required to be purchased from the Plaintiff. The agreement was for five years. The percentage started at about 17 per cent and was planned to increase to about 22 per cent. At the end of five years it was to revert to the Plaintiff.

1.33 Not long after the agreement was signed, the Defendant was failing to purchase the requisite percentage of milk from the Plaintiff. Over the ensuing two years the Defendant's purchases dwindled until, in about June 1994, they had ceased altogether. In February 1994 proceedings were commenced by the Plaintiff. The defence was, *inter alia*, that the agreement between the Plaintiff and Defendant was in fact part of a wider tripartite arrangement between the Plaintiff, the Defendant and Churchfields which contained restrictions excepted by at least two persons in relation to the supply of goods, particulars of which had not been furnished as required by the RTPA 1976 and, accordingly, the restrictions therein were void pursuant to section 35 RTPA 1976.

1.34 The judge did not specify what restrictions within the meaning of the RTPA 1976 were alleged by the Defendant to exist. However, the restrictions are set out in the pleaded Defence and Further and Better Particulars thereof, to which reference has been made, and they were as follows: that the Plaintiff would not sell milk products in the areas to be supplied by the Defendant; the Defendant would purchase certain quantities of milk from the Plaintiff; and the Plaintiff would not compete with Churchfields in Salisbury.

1.35 The defence was dependent upon a supposed matrix of fact, namely the existence of an alleged tripartite agreement subject to the RTPA 1976. In the event the Defendant was unable to prove the facts to support the "arrangement". The judge stated in this respect:

> "I am quite satisfied that no agreement was concluded at that meeting. There was never in terms any agreement between the three parties, nor do I believe that any such tripartite agreement had ever came into being.
>
> The relevance of all this is to a defence which is raised that depends upon the Restrictive Trade Practices Act of 1976 and asserts that there was such a tripartite agreement or arrangement which ought to have been registered under the Act and because it was not so registered is unenforceable.
>
> It is necessary for any such arrangement to exist so as to be registrable that at the very least there should have been some mutual obligations between the parties. It may be that it is even sufficient that the parties expected as a result of their discussions that such mutual obligations would be fulfilled, but it seems to me that the highest it could be put on the facts of this case is that there was a hope by Churchfields that Southern Co-Operative would pull out of Salisbury as a result of their agreeing to release Mr Shearman [the Defendant] from the obligations that he had under his agreement with them to receive his supplies exclusively from them.
>
> It never in my view went further than that, and as a matter of fact Southern Co-Operative did not cease in competition in Salisbury from some two years after January 1992 by which time Mr Shearman had effectively ceased to purchase most of his supplies from Southern Co-Operative and it was plain that the relationship between Southern Co-Operative and Mr Shearman had all but broken down. Accordingly in my judgment the defence based upon the Restrictive Trade Practices Act does not succeed."

(2) Meaning of "between two or more persons"

1.36 The word "persons" is not defined but its normal legal meaning of natural or legal persons must be assumed. Legal persons include companies, statutory undertakings and all other bodies endowed with legal personality by operation of law, for example co-operative societies.[26] Section 43(2) RTPA 1976 provides that for the purposes of, *inter alia*, sections 6 and 11 RTPA 1976, "any two or more inter-connected bodies corporate, or any two or more individuals carrying on business in partnership with each other, shall be treated as a single person". Examples will be used to demonstrate the width of the phrase.

(a) Partnerships comprising natural persons may be counted as one person

1.37 Section 43(2), above, uses the word "individuals", which indicates that partnerships between companies must be treated as agreements between separate parties. This is logical since otherwise inter-company agreements would only have to be dressed up as partnerships to avoid registration. An agreement between Mr A, Mr B and Mr C is a single-person partnership; conversely an agreement between A Ltd, B Ltd and C Ltd, is a tripartite agreement. The statute indicates the status of an agreement between A Ltd, Mr B and Mr C. Such a situation could arise where a company enters an agreement with two consultants for a fixed period of time and rather than pay the consultants a fee enters a profit-sharing scheme with them. Since there are *de facto* two sets of parties with A Ltd, on the one hand, and Mr B and C on the other this would be viewed as a registrable bipartite agreement. In *Donald Storrie Estate Agency Ltd* v *Adams*,[27] it was held that section 43(2) is dealing with the case of two or more individuals carrying on business in partnership. Such individuals fall to be treated as a single person but *not* the same person as the firm of which they are partners. The judge stated: "the firm is a separate person (see section 4(2) of the Partnership Act 1890). The Act does not say that two or more individuals carrying on business in partnership, and the firm itself, shall be treated as one person for the purpose of the exempting provisions of the 1976 Act."[28] It is conceivable that a situation could occur where A Ltd, Mr B and Mr C were in a permanent commercial and legal relationship with each other, in which case there may exist *de facto* only one economic unit and accordingly it would be reasonable to treat them as one person. Such might be the case where a company has a permanent relationship with an external firm of lawyers or accountants whose sole client is the company. Such firms occur in particular in continental Europe where legal privilege entailing confidentiality of documentary correspondence is only accorded to external legal advisers and not in-house lawyers.[29]

(b) Joint tenants

1.38 In *Ravenseft Properties* v *Director General of Fair Trading*,[30] Mocatta J held that joint tenants were to be considered as separate persons unless carrying on business in partnership in which case, in accordance with section 43(2) RTPA 1976, they are

[26] e.g. *Doncaster and Retford Co-operative Societies' Agreement* (1960) LR 2 RP 105.
[27] (1989) SLT 305.
[28] *ibid.*, p. 309H. The learned judge cited with approval the opinion of Stamp J in *Registrar of Restrictive Trading Agreements* v *Schweppes Ltd* [1971] 1 WLR 1148, 1168, 1169.
[29] A similar rule applies to European Commission competition investigations under Reg. 17/62, OJ 1959-62 Spec Ed 87 under the Court of Justice's ruling in Case 155/79 *AM&S* v *Commission* [1982] ECR 1575, [1982] 2 CMLR 264.
[30] [1978] QB52, [1977] 1 All ER 47 (QBD).

treated as one party. The relevance of this point primarily lies in the question of the registrability of leases. Most leases are outside the scope of the legislation; the question of registrability is discussed at paras. 2.226–2.235.

(c) Inter-connected bodies corporate: parents and subsidiaries

1.39 An agreement between a parent and a wholly owned subsidiary does not count as an agreement for the purposes of the Act since the agreement is between members of the same body. Section 43(1) defines "inter-connected bodies corporate" as "bodies corporate which are members of the same group, and for the purposes of this definition 'group' means a body corporate and all other bodies corporate which are its subsidiaries". Subsidiaries are as defined in section 736 Companies Act 1985[31] or in the case of an Industrial and Provident Society, section 15 of the Friendly and Industrial and Provident Societies Act 1968. It will be a question of fact, in a given case, whether a company holding shares in another company is to be treated as an interconnected body corporate. For example, if X and Y form a joint venture company, XY Ltd, in which both hold 50 per cent of the shares, then neither X nor Y will be treated as an inter-connected body corporate with XY Ltd. Conversely, even in a 50:50 joint venture, if one or other of the shareholders is able, as a result of the particular clauses in joint venture agreement, to exercise *de facto* or *de jure* control over XY Ltd, that partner together with XY Ltd may constitute an inter-connected body corporate for the purposes of section 43 RTPA 1976.

1.40 Inter-connected bodies corporate are *not*, however, treated as being one and the same economic entity. Section 43 RTPA 1976 only concerns itself with counting heads and not with treating the persons to which it relates as one and the same persons. Thus if P is a foreign, non-resident company with a subsidiary S in the UK then an agreement between S and Y, another resident UK company, is registrable, S and P are counted as one person resident in the UK. The alternative (and judicially rejected) interpretation would be that S and P are one and the same and that since P (as opposed to S) does not carry on business within the UK the agreement with Y is an agreement between a resident and a non-resident company and is hence excluded from the Act which requires that at least two parties be carrying on business within the UK. To take another perhaps less obvious example: where two companies agree to accept registrable restrictions on the supply of goods to a third party which is a subsidiary of one of them, according to *Schweppes No. 2* parent and subsidiary are treated as separate entities.[32] Another example of a possibly non-registrable agreement is as follows. P is a United Kingdom company which has a subsidiary in France. P wishes to enter a non-registrable agreement with a United Kingdom company. P therefore procures that its French subsidiary (FS) enters agreement with the United Kingdom company. The agreement is not registrable provided that there is no overarching "arrangement" between P, FS and the United Kingdom company.

1.41 One commentator has suggested that in the following situation there is no registrable agreement: A and B are subsidiaries respectively of C and D; C and D agree

[31] s. 736 Companies Act 1985 was substituted for the original s. 736 by s. 144(1) Companies Act 1989. A company is a subsidiary if (a) another company, the holding company, holds a majority of the voting rights in it; (b) if the holding company is a member of the subsidiary and has the right to appoint or remove a majority of the board of directors; or, (c) if the holding company is a member of the subsidiary and controls either alone or through an agreement with other members or shareholders a majority of the voting rights in it. S. 736A explains and supplements s. 736.

[32] See *Schweppes No. 2* (1971) LR 7 RP 336 at pp. 370–372.

that A and B shall not sell their goods for less than X. C and D control A and B by power of shareholding alone since they are neither agents for A and B nor have they appointed directors to the boards of A and B. C and D do not supply goods. Arguably, A and C cannot be regarded as one and the same person; nor can D and B. As C and D are not carrying on business in the supply of goods their agreement is not registrable—moreover A and B are not parties to the agreement.[33] It is suggested that not to register such an agreement would be dangerous and that the safest course is to register on a fail-safe basis (see paras. 4.43–4.46); the situation can equally be analysed as the controlling shareholder of A Ltd agreeing with the controlling shareholder of B that their companies will fix prices. It seems artificial to say that A and B have not agreed to fix prices simply because the meeting of minds arises through majority members and not directors or managers.

1.42 If X incorporates his business in XX Ltd, X can enter a registrable agreement with the business (XX Ltd) despite the fact that X and XX Ltd are factually and economically indistinguishable. The following example exemplifies how the RTPA 1976 may intervene so as to render an otherwise non-registrable agreement, registrable. A franchisor (F) enters a franchise agreement with the franchisee XX Ltd. In order to secure or protect the solvency of the franchisee, the franchisor demands that the shareholders (including X) in the franchisee company enter a covenant not to compete with the franchisee company during the currency of the franchise agreement and for a period thereafter. These covenants will be similar to covenants accepted by XX Ltd. There will be two persons accepting restrictions within the meaning of the Act. Had the covenantors not given the undertakings the agreement may well have been non-registrable as a result of the franchisor not having accepted any relevant restrictions or section 9(3) RTPA 1976 and/or Schedule 3(2) RTPA 1976. It will matter not that X might not carry on business in the UK since there will be two persons who do so carry on business (XX Ltd and F).

(3) Meaning of "restrictions are accepted by two or more parties"

1.43 It is sometimes possible to draft agreements so that registrable restrictions are only accepted by one party. If this can be managed the agreement need not be registered since the Act requires that restrictions be accepted by two or more parties. The government, in 1956 when the requirement of two parties accepting restrictions was first introduced into legislation, refused to extend the duty to furnish particulars to agreements whereby only one of the parties accepted restrictions, on the basis that to so extend would draw exclusive dealing contracts into the registration net which was considered undesirable as a question of policy. For example, if X and Y enter an agreement under which X can sell wherever he pleases in the UK but Y may not sell in Wales which is X's main selling area then no registrable agreement exists—only one party has accepted restrictions. For another example, if A, B and C sign a contract whereby A shall supply his services at a price higher than that of B and C but where B and C shall set prices independently and may supply the service at any price they wish, there is no registrable agreement. Again, if X, Y and Z enter a contract whereby X must not grant discounts of more than 5 per cent but where Y and Z can arrange discounts as and at whatever rate when they please, then again, no registrable agreement arises since only one party accepts restrictions.

[33] Cunningham, *The Fair Trading Act 1973* (1974), p. 218.

1.44 It is further important to appreciate that the provisions relating to goods in the Act are entirely separate from those relating to services. Thus in considering the registrability of an agreement, parties must scrutinise their agreements twice: once to see whether the Act applies by virtue of the goods restrictions and a second time to see whether the Act applies by virtue of the services agreements. A "mixed" agreement between a supplier of goods *and* a provider of services is hence outside the scope of the Act: there must be two or more goods suppliers or producers or two or more services providers. It follows that an agreement in which suppliers of goods accept restrictions relating exclusively to services is not registrable. Nor are agreements under which suppliers of services accept restrictions relating exclusively to goods. Thus, if X, Y and Z who are manufacturers of goods agree that they will only pay a haulier a specified mileage rate for the service of handling their goods, this agreement falls outside of the legislation. Though an agreement between hauliers over the mileage rate charges they will demand for hauling the manufacturers goods is registrable as an agreement by services providers to fix prices.[34]

1.45 *Multi-sided agreements* In a multipartite agreement involving more than two parties the duty to furnish particulars applies even though the condition of "two or more persons carrying on business within the United Kingdom" and the condition of restrictions which "are accepted by two or more parties" are satisfied by different firms: X is an English manufacturer, Y is an English dealer, A is a Swedish manufacturer and B is a Swedish dealer. An agreement concluded between X, Y, A and B which contains restrictions between X and A for example, to fix prices, control output and share markets, is a registrable agreement. The condition of two parties is satisfied by X and Y—albeit that Y accepts no registrable restrictions. Furthermore, the restrictions are accepted by parties to an agreement in which there are two persons carrying on business within the UK, it does not matter that A is not a UK company. Were Y to depart from the agreement or relinquish the restrictions this would render the agreement non-registrable.

(4) Meaning of "carrying on business within the United Kingdom"

1.46 The statute defines neither "business" nor "carrying on". The Court has considered the term "business" on a number of occasions and apparently considers that whether a body is carrying on business is a question of fact to be decided in each case. In one case a federation of trade associations which was not itself a party to the referred agreement—which was however between certain associations who held membership in the Federation—was held not to be carrying on business in the UK.[35] However, in later cases the Court has held that trade associations may carry on business within the UK and that the term is not related exclusively to the types of business mentioned in sections 6 and 11 RTPA 1976.[36] Hence the term "business" is construed widely and evidently may include general trade association activities.

[34] This example was given in the Liesner Committee *Review of Restrictive Trade Practices Policy* (1979) Cmnd 7512, para. 5.20. In the DGFT Annual Report 1977, p. 38 it is indicated that fee fixing agreements concerning road haulage were largely abandoned during 1976–77, freeing the OFT thereby from the obligation to take Court action.

[35] See *Wholesale Confectioners Alliance's Agreement (No. 2)* (1961) LR 2 RP 231 at p. 239.

[36] See *Newspaper Proprietors' Association Ltd's and National Federation of Retail Newsagents' Booksellers and Stationers' Agreement* (1961) LR 2 RP 435 at pp. 498, 499; and *Japan Canned Food Exporters' Agreement* (1971) LR 7 RP 474.

1.47 A UK company which is a party to an international market-sharing agreement whereby foreign undertakings refrain from selling in the UK is not party to a registrable agreement since there are not two parties carrying on business *within the UK*. This is not to say of course that other provisions, for example, Articles 85 and 86 EC must not apply. The carrying on of business in the UK requirement is relevant also to joint ventures. An agreement between an English company X and a French company Y to form an equal partnership joint venture company—XY Ltd—will not escape the legislation upon the basis that only one party is carrying on business within the UK. This will be because, if XY Ltd is incorporated in the UK, there will be two parties conducting business within the jurisdiction when that company comes into being (though not before). If XY Ltd were incorporated in France this would avoid the Act, though, if the commercial operations of XY Ltd related to the UK market the fact that it was incorporated abroad will not prevent it from being categorised as a party "carrying on" business in the UK. As was stated earlier, the test of where business is being carried out is a factual one, though place of incorporation will in practice generally be strong evidence of the place of business. It follows from the above that the fact that a company has its registered offices or headquarters abroad does not of itself mean that the company does not carry on business in the UK. An agreement influencing trade between EC Member States will of course be vulnerable to EC competition law.

1.48 The precise meaning of "carrying on" is far from clear. The phrase is an important one for foreign companies with agencies in the UK. Section 43(4) RTPA 1976 provides that "a person shall not be deemed to carry on a business within the United Kingdom by reason only of the fact he is represented for the purposes of that business by an agent within the United Kingdom". "Agent" may be given its usual legal meaning of one who has authority to bind in legal relations his principal to a third party. Hence, simply by having a representative or other commercial agent in the UK, a foreign company is not necessarily carrying on business within the UK. Precisely when the agent stops being merely a representative and commences to do something more substantial on behalf of the foreign company so as to turn "agent" into a branch or subsidiary which carries on business on behalf of the parent is not clear. If the "agent" produces or manufactures goods on behalf of his "principal" this presumably goes beyond mere agency-like activities and begins to resemble "carrying on business" activities. A rule of thumb might be that anything greater than merely negotiating, entering and concluding contracts on behalf of the principal (or anything necessarily ancillary to that) would amount to "carrying on" business within the UK.[37]

[37] This is some support for the proposition that the test whether a company carries on business in the United Kingdom is to be construed by reference to the policy of the Act in question. In *Re Companies Numbers 007816 to 007822 of 1994*, 31 June 1995, Parker J was required to decide whether certain offshore insurance companies, agents and brokers were carrying on or had been carrying on business in the United Kingdom contrary to s. 2(1) Insurance Companies Act 1982 (ICA 1982). The judge held that the section in question had to be given a narrow construction since breach thereof carried with it the possibility of penal sanctions. He held that in approaching the question whether a person was carrying on business within the United Kingdom, at least within the meaning of s. 2(1) ICA 1982, the Court was concerned with the question whether what was done in the United Kingdom amounted in all the circumstances to the carrying on of insurance business in the United Kingdom. On the facts the judge held that business was not conducted in the United Kingdom notwithstanding the presence of two so-called UK wholesale brokers (the UK companies) who acted as agents for the offshore companies and the offshore agents. The UK companies did not make underwriting decisions since these decisions were at all material times taken by the offshore companies, and although the UK companies were active in the UK in offering the insurance services of the offshore insurers, the terms of the policies issued by the latter were not negotiated by the UK companies. In the context of the RTPA 1976, which is not penal, it may be that a less restrictive approach should be adopted.

1.49 The European Commission, in 1962, issued a notice on distribution contracts with commercial agents, in which they listed factors which distinguished an independent trader from one who was in reality no more than an extension of his principal. UK law appears not to be dissimilar to EC law.[38] The relationship between principal and commercial agent is clearly analogous to that of principal and agent in the section 43(4) context and, accordingly, the criteria stipulated by the Commission may be informative. If one applies the criteria of the notice to section 43 the following conclusions emerge: a person who is simply an "agent" and who does not carry on business within the UK will accept none of the risks attached to the transaction in question (though he may assume the usual *del credere* guarantees); he will not keep as his own property a considerable stock of the contract products; he will not maintain or ensure at his own expense a substantial service to customers free of charge; he will not determine contract prices or terms and conditions.

1.50 The above commentary on "agents" does not define the meaning of "carrying on". The test is essentially one of fact. In merchant businesses the place of sale is a telling factor;[39] in the case of provision of services the place at which the service is rendered will be an important feature. In cases unrelated to restrictive practices where the question has been discussed, the place where the operations take place from which the profits arise has been a central factor.[40] An important question is whether a foreign parent company—X—with a subsidiary—Y—incorporated and trading in the UK is carrying on business in the UK. It is fundamental in UK company law that a company, once incorporated, has legal personality discreet from that of its promoter or incorporator.[41] Hence X and Y would be separate companies for purposes of English law; X would not carry on business within the UK but Y would. This rule is not to be confused with the provisions of section 43(2) RTPA which, as noted above, renders inter-connected bodies corporate "one person" for the purposes of the definition of agreement. Thus, a parent and subsidiary do not agree with each other. However, this does not mean they are one and the same economic entity. It should be stressed that different rules apply under EC law, these are dealt with at paras. 6.16–6.22.

(5) "Restriction"

1.51 The word restriction is nowhere exactly defined though may safely be assumed to refer to restrictions of a type listed in sections 6 and 11 RTPA 1976. According to section 43(1) RTPA 1976 restriction "includes a negative obligation, whether express or implied and whether absolute or not". Thus a negatively framed agreement between X and Y not to undercut each other is as equally registrable as a positively framed one between X and Y to match each other's prices.[42] In most cases it is possible to identify a relevant restriction by reference to the express terms of a contract or other docu-

[38] JO 1962 139/2921 (24 December 1962) for the EC law. For the UK position see OFT Investigation into *British Telecommunications* (*Pricing Policy for the Placing of Advertisements in Yellow Pages Directories*) (10 October 1984) under the Competition Act 1980 at p. 44, para. 7.4.

[39] See *Saccharin Corporation* v *Chemische Werke Von Heyden AG* [1911] 2 KB 516; *Smidth* v *Greenwood* [1921] 3 KB 583; *Firestone Tyre and Rubber Co* v *Lewellin* [1957] 1 All ER 561; *Dunlop Pneumatic Tyre Co* v *AG für Motor* [1902] 1 KB 342.

[40] e.g. *Smidth* v *Greenwood* [1921] 3 KB 583 at p. 593.

[41] *Salomon* v *Salomon* [1897] AC 22 (HL).

[42] See for examples of restrictions judicially defined as "negative", *Mileage Conference Group of the Tyre Manufacturers' Conference Agreement* (1966) LR 6 RP 49; [1966] 1 WLR 1137, parties accepted mutual restriction not to tender at a price lower than the one circulated to them by their central co-ordinating office; *Electrical Installations at the Exeter Hospital Agreement* (1970) LR 7 RP 102, parties agreed not to tender in response to an invitation until after "discussions" with other interested parties.

ment. However, given the breadth of the concept of a restriction, including, as it does, implied and negative obligations, the process of determining the existence of a relevant restriction may entail a complex forensic exercise. As a matter of contract law it should first be determined whether the agreement contains any implied terms since, of course, an implied term may constitute a relevant restriction within the meaning of the RTPA 1976. In this regard attention may need to be paid to whether the agreement contains an "entire agreement" clause which purports, or seeks to purport, to exclude any implied terms. As a matter of contract law the courts have been reluctant to concede that entire agreements clauses necessarily serve to effectively exclude all implied terms. Moreover, it should not be overlooked that, even where no separate clause or term is implied, it may be possible to deduce relevant restrictions by necessary implication from the express terms of an agreement. Thus, for example, where X and Y agree to abide by an agreed price list in the sale of their products, the express contractual duty to sell at those particular prices will also lead to the acceptance of a negative restriction not to sell otherwise than at the prices in question.[43] To be registrable there does not have to be a proven harmful *effect* upon competition; all that need exist is an agreement containing restrictions listed by the Act. It should be appreciated that registrability turns on the form of an agreement and not its effect. Nor is the motive or purpose behind a clause relevant in determining whether it constitutes a restriction for the purposes of the Act.[44] The OFT will take the economic "significance" of the restriction into consideration when the question of dispensation from the obligation to refer the restrictive agreement to the RPC is discussed. Section 21(2) RTPA 1976 (discussed in depth at paras 4.77 and following) permits the Director General of Fair Trading to make representations to the Secretary of State for a direction that the agreement in question need not be referred to the RPC on the basis that a restriction therein is not "significant".

1.52 The restriction apparently must go further than is allowed by general law. If the parties agree to a restriction in respect of something that the law forbids then the restriction is not registrable. This is so even though the restrictive agreement contains sanctions.[45] Thus, for illustration, it would not be a registrable restriction for parties to agree, or a trade association to recommend to members: that goods should not be produced below a certain quality where that quality is prescribed by law; that contracts should not unreasonably exclude liability since that is the legal effect of the Unfair Contract Terms Act 1977; or, that goods should never be produced that are not of a merchantable quality since that is an obligation incumbent upon vendors by virtue of Sale of Goods legislation.

1.53 Another possible example of a restriction upon the conduct of a party which might not constitute a relevant restriction for the purposes of the RTPA 1976 as a result of the fact that the restriction would, in any event, be imposed by the common law is a restrictive covenant accepted by the vendor of land or other property not to compete

[43] See e.g. *Re: Phenol Producers' Agreement* (1960) LR2 RP1.

[44] *Sterling Financial Services Ltd* v *Johnston* [1990] SLT 111.

[45] See *British Waste Paper Association's Agreement* [1963] 1 WLR 540 at p. 548 (RPC): "It is not a restriction within the Act of 1956 to impose by agreement a term which goes no further than is already provided by general statute" (*per* Megaw J). See also No. 5130 Register of Restrictive Trade Practices *British Soft Drinks Council* (1985). The Association made recommendations to members as to the best way to comply with EC legislation on labelling and minimum durability of retail packs of food and drink. The recommendation was registrable under s. 8 but was bound to be given s. 21(2) exemption on the basis that it sought compliance with legal obligations. It may none the less be asked why the recommendation was registrable if it could not be defined as a restriction under s. 6.

with the purchaser. Prima facie, a non-compete covenant accepted by a vendor would constitute a classic restriction for the purposes of section 6 (Goods) and 11 (Services) RTPA 1976. However, in *Herbert Morris Ltd* v *Saxelby*[46] the Court was concerned with a case whereby the Plaintiff company was the leading manufacturer of hoisting machinery in the UK and the Defendant had been in the Plaintiff's employment as a draftsman. After a number of years service the Defendant was engaged by the company upon a two-year contract and thereafter, subject to four months' notice of either side, upon the terms of an agreement which contained a restriction accepted by the Defendant that he would not during a period of seven years from his ceasing to be employed by the Plaintiff, either in the United Kingdom or the Republic of Ireland, carry on either as principal, agent, servant or otherwise alone or jointly or in connection with any other person firm or company, or be concerned or assist directly or indirectly, whether for reward or otherwise, in the sale or manufacture of pulley blocks, hand overhead runways, electric overhead runways, or hand overhead travelling trains. It was held that the covenant was wider than was required for the protection of the Plaintiff company and was not enforceable under the doctrine of restraint of trade. In this regard the House of Lords affirmed the decision of the Court of Appeal.[47] In the course of giving judgment, Lord Shaw stated, when addressing an argument distinguishing between restrictive covenants in relation to the sale of a business, on the one hand, and restrictive covenants in the case of contracts of service on the other:

> "When a business is sold, the vendor, who, it may be, has inherited it or built it up, seeks to realise this piece of property, and obtains a purchaser upon a condition without which the whole transaction would be valueless. He sells, he himself agreeing not to compete; and the law upholds such a bargain, and declines to permit a vendor to derogate from his own grant. Public interest cannot be invoked to render such a bargain nugatory: to do so would be to use public interest for the destruction of property. Nothing could be a more sure deterrent to commercial energy and activity than a principle that its accumulated results could not be transferred save under conditions which would make its buyer insecure."[48]

1.54 Lord Shaw was of the view that a restriction accepted by a vendor of a business not to compete would, even in the absence of an express covenant, be imposed by virtue of the common law doctrine of non-derogation from grant. It was for this reason that he stated that "the law upholds such a bargain and declines to permit a vendor to derogate his own grant". The "law" referred to is not the law of contract but the common law of non-derogation from grant. Accordingly, it is arguable that a vendor accepting a non-compete covenant does not accept a relevant restriction since, even in the absence of an express restrictive vendor. However, it must be observed also that the *dictum* of Lord Shaw was *obiter*. Further, for whatever reason vendor covenants have long been treated, whether correctly or otherwise, as relevant restrictions for the purposes of the Act. It should not therefore be assumed without more ado that reasonable vendor covenants, otherwise consistent with the law of non-derogation from grant, do not constitute a relevant restriction. In all the circumstances a "fail-safe" furnishing of particulars is advisable.[49]

[46] [1916] AC 688 (HL).
[47] [1915] 2 Ch 57.
[48] [1916] AC 688, 713, 714.
[49] In this regard attention will need to be paid to the Restrictive Trade Practices (Sale and Purchase and Share Subscription) (Goods) Order 1989 (S.I. 1989 No. 1081), which provides exemptions from the RTPA 1976 for certain categories of sale and purchase and share subscription agreements. Though see *Donald Storrie Estate Agency Ltd* v *Adams* (1989) SLT 305. In that case Counsel chose to rely upon non-

1.55 An unusual example from decided case law may be found in *Telephone Apparatus Manufacturers' Application*.[50] In this case an agreement between the Postmaster General and eight manufacturers of telephone apparatus which allocated contract work between the manufacturers was deemed to be free from the duty to register, albeit that the agreement operated a market-sharing system. The traditional and legally protected freedom to enter contracts without constraint enjoyed by the Crown is a liberty that the RTPA does not affect. Under general law, therefore, the restrictive agreement between the Crown and the manufacturers was free from registration. The Court of Appeal held that a second agreement entered into between all of the manufacturers which simply regulated the conduct of the parties with respect to the first agreement with the Postmaster General was likewise free from the duty to register. Lord Justice Harman stated: "The ... agreement ... is merely a regulation of the method by which the eight contractors carry out their contractual obligations, and is exempt from registration along with the Crown agreement."[51]

1.56 Section 6(3) RTPA adds a gloss to the meaning of restriction, which in view of the wide definition of "arrangement", is somewhat superfluous. It makes it clear that to be a registrable restriction the restraint on conduct need not be formal. Section 6(2)(a) and (b) provides that an agreement is none the less registrable even though it only: (a) confers privileges or benefits upon such parties as comply with conditions as to any of such matters as are described in section 6(1) RTPA 1976; or (b) imposes obligations upon parties who do not comply with such conditions.

1.57 For example, if in a specialisation agreement X and Y agree that they will both refrain from selling at below a certain price provided that, and for as long as, they supply each other with their own brand of product at a preferential rate neither have accepted a restriction not to sell at below a certain price though there would, none the less, be a strong inducement not to do so. Section 6(3)(a) indicates that for the purposes of the legislation X and Y are presumed to have accepted restrictions as to the price of goods. A similar effect in respect of services agreements is brought about by virtue of section 17(1) RTPA 1976.

1.58 An important issue which vexes some businessmen and advisers is whether restrictive covenants in commercial leases are registrable restrictions. Following *Ravenseft Properties* v *Director General of Fair Trading*[52] most leases may be assumed to fall outside the scope of the legislation. However, this is not an absolute rule and the registrability of leases and restrictive covenants contained therein is discussed at paras. 2.226–2.235.

1.59 It has been doubted (though not expressly decided) that an agreement does not contain a relevant restriction if the parties can escape from the obligation it ostensibly imposes at their own option and at any time.[53] Though, if the parties considered themselves morally bound not to release themselves from an obligation an "arrangement" might very well have risen within the meaning of section 43 RTPA 1976. It should follow, however, that a contract clause expressing a reservation of right does not constitute a restriction, for example the supplier reserving the right at all times to

cont.
compete clauses in service contracts the vendors of the business concluded with the purchasers instead of non-compete clause accepted by the same persons qua vendors. See also *Sterling Financial Services Ltd* v *Johnston* (1990) SLT 11.

50 [1963] 1 WLR 463; (1963) LR 3 RP 462.

51 *ibid.*, at p. 478.

52 [1977] 1 All ER 47 (QBD).

53 *Net Book Agreement* (1963) LR 3 RP 246, 298.

(say) sell in the territory of the customer, sell at any price it wishes, vary the terms and conditions upon which it has hitherto traditionally supplied, etc.

(6) Registrability: minimum degree of contractual certainty

1.60 In *J. Bibby Agriculture Ltd* v *C.D. North and Sons*[54] the Court of Appeal (Sir Stephen Brown, President, Stocker LJ, Scott LJ) was required to consider, *inter alia*, whether a right of first refusal constituted a restriction within the meaning of the RTPA 1976. The litigation arose out of an agreement between the Plaintiff and the Defendants under which the latter became retailers in relation to the Plaintiff's animal feed products. The agreement in question, however, described the Defendant as agents rather than retailers. Pursuant to the agreement, the Plaintiff undertook not to sell animal feed direct to farmers west of a map line in Cornwall save as might from time to time be agreed in writing between the parties (clause 1); the Plaintiff undertook further not to appoint any other agents to supply their full range of animal feeds in this area during the period of the agreement (clause 2); the agents (Defendants) undertook not to purchase or sell animal feeds from any source other than the Plaintiff during the period of the agreement save that the agent was entitled "English Grain for the purpose of processing and selling their own rolled oats and provender products" (clause 3). Clause 4 of the Agreement provided as follows: "Except for English Grain purchased locally for their own use as in clause 3 above, the Agents shall give the Company first refusal on all Grain offered to or purchased by them."

1.61 The Plaintiff commenced proceedings for the unpaid price of animal feed products supplied by the Plaintiff pursuant to the agreement. The Defendant pleaded a set-off based upon a counterclaim which alleged a breach by the Plaintiff to the restrictions contained in clause 1 of the agreement requiring the Plaintiff not to sell animal feed direct to farmers west of the specified geographical line in Cornwall. The Plaintiffs, thereafter, served a Reply and Defence to Counterclaim. Paragraph 3 of the Defence pleaded that the agreement was registrable pursuant to the RTPA 1976 particulars of which had not been furnished. The Plaintiff pleaded further that by virtue of section 35(1) the restrictions upon which the Defendants relied in the Counterclaim were void and/or unenforceable. A preliminary issue was ordered to be tried of the following question: "whether or not the terms relied on in paragraphs 3 and 8 of the Counterclaim are void and/or unenforceable by virtue of the provisions of section 35 of the Restrictive Trade Practices Act 1976". At first instance it was held that the agreement was not registrable. The Plaintiff appealed from that ruling. On appeal an issue was whether clause 4 of the agreement constituted a relevant restriction and, if it did, whether it was capable of amounting to an exempt restriction under Schedule 3(2) of the Act. Lord Justice Scott stated:

> "If 'English Grain' could be regarded as goods of the same description as animal feeds, then the restrictions in Clause 4 would, it is accepted, be covered, as the restrictions in clause 3 are covered, by sub-paragraph (b) of paragraph 2 of the Third Schedule. On that footing, the agreement would not require registration."

1.62 The court observed that the task of discerning what the parties intended by use of the word "English Grain" was not assisted by the fact that the matter had been dealt with, at first instance, as a preliminary issue wherein evidence of the parties' trading practices and the factual matrix to the agreement was not adduced. The Court was therefore strug-

[54] Court of Appeal, unreported, 18 November 1991.

gling to find a proper interpretation of those words. While the Court was prepared to endeavour to analyse the clause, they also considered whether the clause was sufficiently certain in contractual terms to give rise to a relevant, registrable restriction:

> "I would not for my part wish to leave my judgment simply on the basis of Mr Mowbray's second point, with which I have just been dealing. It must be the case that, for a restriction in an agreement to render the agreement registrable, the restriction must reach the minimum test of certainty of any contractual term. In my opinion, clause 4 lacks the requisite certainty to be enforceable at all. It refers to 'first refusal'. That expression is well known in some contexts. It is generally thought to confer the right to purchase the property in question, if the owner of it desires to sell. There is implicit, generally, the requirement that the owner, if he does require to sell, must inform the person who has the right of first refusal of that desire and of the prices; and the person with the right of first refusal then has some period to make up his or her mind whether or not to exercise the right to purchase. If the right is not exercised, the owner of the property is free to sell to whoever he wishes. But that meaning cannot be attributed to the expression 'first refusal' in clause 4, because the clause 4 right of first refusal is expressed to apply to '... all Grain offered to [the Defendants] or purchased by [the Defendants]'. So what obligation, one may ask, is imposed on the Defendants and when? Suppose an offer of grain, not being English grain purchased locally, is received by the Defendants from some third party. What are the Defendants supposed to do? Mr Oliver has contended that it is then their contractual obligation to inform the Plaintiff of the offer so as to enable the Plaintiff to accept the third parties' offer, if the Plaintiff wants to do so. That is a recognisable contractual obligation but it can hardly be described as a right of first refusal. If grain is actually purchased by the Defendants, what obligation then arises under clause 4? The Defendants may not want to sell the grain at all. They may want to incorporate it into their own provender products. Is there to be any obligation in those circumstances for them to offer the grain to the Plaintiff at some and, if so, what price? Mr Oliver's answer was that clause 4 would require the Defendants, on purchasing any grain not being English grain purchased locally, to offer that grain for purchase by the Plaintiff at the price at which the Defendants had bought it. That would not be a right of first refusal. That would be an option to purchase. If the parties had intended the Plaintiffs to have an option to purchase, they could, by appropriate language, have produced that result. They would not have referred to a right of first refusal. I do not think it is possible to come to a certain conclusion as to what right the parties intended to grant the Plaintiff under clause 4, as to what obligations the parties intended to impose on the Defendants under clause 4. I do not think it is possible, with any certainty, to identify the restrictions that clause 4 was intended to place on the Defendants. I would hold that clause 4 is bad for uncertainty, and for that reason is to be left out of account in considering whether or not the agreement is registrable."

C. Section 6 RTPA 1976: Goods Agreements which Must be Registered

1.63 It is necessary at this stage only to outline the types of restrictions which if incorporated in goods agreements render the agreement registrable. Detailed analysis of each restriction type is given in subsequent chapters and reference to those chapters should be made for further guidance. There is no comprehensive definition of the term "goods", which must therefore be given its ordinary and natural meaning. Section 43(1) RTPA 1976 gives some assistance in providing that "goods" includes "ships and aircraft, minerals, substances and animals (including fish), and references to the getting of minerals and the taking of such animals". Section 100 (1) of the Electricity Act 1989 further provided that electricity is to be treated as goods under the RTPA.[55] An agreement is not registrable if

[55] s. 100 Electricity Act sets out transitional provisions relating to the registrability and procedures for registration of agreements for the generation, transmission or supply of electricity. These were necessary as

the subject matter of an agreement is not goods or services as defined by the RTPA 1976.[56] Section 6(1)(a)–(f) RTPA requires the following types of restrictive goods agreement to be registered—Agreements containing:

(a) Restrictions in respect of "the prices to be charged, quoted or paid for goods supplied, offered or acquired, or for the application of any process of manufacture to goods". This provision is examined in Chapter 8. Price fixing agreements whether concluded between suppliers or purchasers are caught as are collusive tendering agreements and many other forms of agreement.

(b) Restrictions in respect of "the prices to be recommended or suggested as the prices to be charged or quoted in respect of the resale of goods supplied." This provision supports section 6(1)(a) and is also examined in Chapter 8.

(c) Restrictions in respect of "the terms or conditions on or subject to which goods are to be supplied or acquired or any such process as is to be applied to goods." This provision includes all of the myriad types of agreement covering terms and conditions of trade. These are examined in Chapter 9.

(d) Restrictions relating to "the quantities or descriptions of goods to be produced, supplied or acquired". "Description" mean "kinds" of goods and hence restrictive agreements over quantities of goods or kinds of goods are registrable. Among others, specialisation agreements, quota schemes, joint research and development agreements, joint selling and purchasing agreement, will fall under this provision. These are primarily examined in Chapter 12 on Joint Ventures and Co-operation.

(e) Restrictions relating to "the processes of manufacture to be applied to any goods, or the quantities or descriptions of goods to which any such process is to be applied". In conjunction with (d) above, collective agreements limiting production or processing are registrable. In *Scottish Master Monumental Sculptors Association's Agreement*[57] the RPC held that the lettering of gravestones constituted the application of a process of manufacture thereby bringing the provision of certain services within the provisions of the RTPA 1976 applicable to goods.

(f) Restrictions relating to "the persons or classes of persons to, for or from whom, or the areas or places in or from which, goods are to be supplied or acquired, or any such process applied". Under section 6(1)(f) market-sharing agreements are caught as are collective boycotts by groups of persons of other parties. Section 6(2) and (4) RTPA 1976 elaborate upon aspects of these restrictions and are examined separately below. Section 6(2)(a) RTPA 1976 provides that in determining whether an agreement is registrable or not, it does not matter that the parties do not accept identical restrictions. Thus, if X accepts a restriction as to the price at which he sells and Y a restriction as to the geographical territories in which he will sell, then the agreement between X and Y is registrable. Section 6(2)(b) simply provides that it is immaterial that parties might be at different levels of business or even be in different businesses. Thus, a wholesaler may enter a registrable agreement with a retailer, or a butcher may enter a reg-

cont.
a consequence of privatisation of the electricity industry, as previously these agreements existed between different parts of the same nationalised entity. For the application of competition legislation to the electricity industry, see para. 2.124.

56 See for example *WAC Ltd* v *Whillock* [1990] IRLR 23, where the Scottish Court of Session held that a shareholders' agreement relating to the rights and obligations attaching to those shares was not registrable.

57 (1965) LR 5 RP 437.

istrable agreement with a baker. Though in the latter case, it may well be that since the parties are in different occupations there is no real competition between them for the restriction to harm. This factor will not, it should be stressed, affect registrability.

1.64 Section 6(4) RTPA 1976 extends the restrictions noted in (d) and (e) above and reads:

> "an obligation on the part of any party to an agreement to make payments calculated by reference—(a) to the quantity of goods produced or supplied by him, or to which any process of manufacture is applied by him; or (b) to the quantity of materials acquired or used by him for the purpose of or in the production of any goods or the application of any such process to goods; being payments calculated, or calculated at an increased rate, in respect of quantities of goods or materials exceeding any quantity specified in or ascertained in accordance with the agreements, shall be treated for the purpose of this Act as a restriction in respect of the quantities of those goods to be produced or supplied, or to which that process is to be applied."

1.65 Thus, in a quota agreement, where competitors wish to devise a mechanism whereby each adheres to his given market share (the quota), it might be arranged that parties exceeding the quota pay a sum, calculated by reference to the extent the quota is exceeded, into a common fund which is then used to compensate those who have lost trade as a result of the party exceeding his quota taking their sales. Such an agreement would be registrable under section 6(1)(d) even in the absence of section 6(4). If there is no formally fixed quota for each party who may produce or supply at will, but there none the less exists a proviso that those producing more than a stipulated amount pay a compensatory sum into a central fund, then although the effect is the same as in the first example there is no market-sharing or quota agreement caught by section 6(1)(d). Section 6(4) hence makes it clear that this less formal variety of quota scheme is registrable. There seems little doubt that such a scheme would have been a registrable "arrangement" in any event.

1.66 Fees paid by members of trade associations by way of bona fide subscription do not need to be registered. The last paragraph of section 6(4) makes specific exemption for such payments. Payments other than by way of bona fide subscription may amount to registrable agreements between the member and the association.[58]

D. Section 11 RTPA 1976: Services Agreements which Must be Registered: S.I. 1976 No. 98, the "Services Order"

1.67 Under the Act restrictive agreements relating to services are not automatically registrable. Only those classes or categories of agreement that have been expressly made the subject of an Order of the Secretary of State—a "calling up" order—need be registered. Moreover, the Secretary of State does not have *carte blanche* to call up for

[58] This subscription to trade associations' exemption was introduced into the legislation by s. 96 Fair Trading Act 1973. It was introduced to cope with the numerous agreements which were being furnished to the OFT for registration and which entailed the OFT wasting time in making individual representations to the Secretary of State for directions not to refer such innocuous agreements to the RPC under what is now s. 21(2) RTPA 1976. See further paras. 14.9–14.18.

registration any service agreement he sees fit. Rather, he may only call up for registration services only those agreements containing restrictions of a type listed in section 11(2)(a)–(e) RTPA 1976. A class of service described by a statutory instrument is called a "designated service". Accordingly, the Secretary of State may call up for registration any of the following restrictive services agreements:

(a) Agreements concerning, "the charges to be made, quoted or paid for designated services supplied, offered or obtained". Price fixing agreements are thus contemplated as registrable.
(b) Agreements concerning, "the terms or conditions on or subject to which designated services are to be supplied or obtained". Agreements concerning terms and conditions of trade are registrable.
(c) Agreements concerning, "the extent (if any) to which, or the scale (if any) on which, designated services are to be made available, supplied or obtained". Quota schemes for the provision of services fall under this provision.
(d) Agreements concerning, "the form or manner in which designated services are to be made available, supplied or obtained". The OFT view this as a wide provision which arguably catches, *inter alia*, agreements involving restrictions on advertising. Section 6 for goods does not appear wide enough to catch advertising restrictions.
(e) Agreements concerning, "the persons or classes of persons for whom or from whom, or the areas or places in or from which, designated services are to be made available or supplied or are to be obtained".

1.68 In 1976 the Secretary of State issued an Order—S.I. 1976 No. 98—calling up for registration the classes of service agreement listed above. The Order however makes provision for a large number of exemptions. These are examined in Section G of Chapter 2 on agreements not subject to registration. However, in the explanatory note appended to the Order the categories of exemption are listed and it is convenient to at least repeat them here. Thus some service agreements (though not all) in the following sectors may be exempted from registration: international sea transport services; carriage by air; road passenger transport; the raising of funds and making of loans by building societies; the exercise of financial control by the Treasury or the Bank of England; banking services in Northern Ireland; the provision of insurance services; unit trust schemes; and the implementation of decisions of the Panel on Take-Overs and Mergers.

1.69 The structure of control for services is clearly similar to that for goods agreements. The notion of "services" is defined so as to exclude all agreements relating to goods. Section 20 RTPA 1976 defines "services" as follows:

> "'Services'—
> (a) does not include the application to goods of any process of manufacture or any services rendered to an employer under a contract of employment (that is, a contract of service or of apprenticeship, whether it is express or implied, and, if it is express, whether it is oral or in writing), but, with those exceptions,
> (b) includes agreements (whether professional or other) which for gain or reward are undertaken and performed for any matter other than the production or supply of goods, and, (c) includes arrangements for the use by public service vehicles (within the meaning of the Public Passenger Vehicles Act 1981) of a parking place which is used as a point at which passengers on services provided by means of such vehicles may be taken up or set down, and any reference to the supply of services or to supplying, obtaining or offering services or to making services available shall be construed accordingly."

The New Roads and Street Works Act 1991 further defines services as including the provision of a facility to use a toll road.[59]

1.70 In addition to the exclusions in (a) above, it is important to note that in all but the most exceptional case the grant of a lease is not the supply of a service. This was the effect of the ruling in *Ravenseft Properties Ltd* v *Director General of Fair Trading*[60] and is concurred in by the OFT which has stated that it considers the *Ravenseft* decision to apply also to the grant of licences of proprietary interests:

> "The case is clear authority for the view that a landlord engaged in only letting property is not to be regarded as carrying on business in the supply of services within the meaning of the legislation. It would also appear from the case that only in extremely rare cases do the covenants in leases amount to the acceptance of restrictions within the meaning of the legislation.
>
> It may be helpful to add that the Office has taken the view that the principles laid down in the judgment in this case are of general application to proprietary rights and the grant of an industrial property licence including, e.g. a copyright licence does not constitute the supply of a service within the meaning of the legislation."[61]

1.71 The *Ravenseft* decision is of some importance and is examined in depth at paras 2.201–2.202 and 2.228–2.231 on non-registrable agreements. Section 17 RTPA 1976 applies to all services agreements called up for registration. Section 17(1) has the same effect as section 6(3) with respect to an agreement whereby benefits or privileges are conferred upon parties complying with conditions as to any restriction, or imposes obligations on those who do not (section 6(3) is discussed above, in connection with the word "restriction"). Such an agreement will be treated as an agreement under which parties accept restrictions in respect of those conditions. Section 17(2) has the same effect as section 6(4) in respect of quota schemes and general commentary on that goods section applies, *mutatis mutandis*, to services.

E. Provisions to be Disregarded in Determining Registrability: sections 9 and 18 RTPA 1976

1.72 When parties to agreements are deciding whether their agreements must be furnished to the OFT for registration, they may disregard certain features and clauses of their agreement from consideration. Thus, if in an agreement between X and Y, the restrictions accepted by Y are disregardable restrictions, then the only restrictions left will be those accepted by X and the agreement will not be registrable because only one party, X, will have accepted registrable restrictions: Section 9 RTPA 1976 indicates provisions in *goods* agreements which may be disregarded; section 18 does likewise for *services agreements*. These two provisions will be examined separately. It should be noted at the outset that the RPC adopted a very narrow view of a provision in these sections: in *Association of British Travel Agents Ltd's Agreement* (*ABTA*)[62] Lincoln J seemed to suggest that sections 9 and 18 were intended only to exclude from the Act certain restrictions which were either innocuous or which, for well-established policy reasons, were considered to be inappropriate for such a regulatory

[59] s. 10(1) New Roads and Street Works Act 1991.
[60] [1977] 1 All ER 47 (QBD).
[61] DGFT Annual Report 1976, p. 36.
[62] [1984] ICR 12 at p. 51 D (RPC).

system of control. Accordingly, where it was claimed that a clearly anti-competitive restriction was exempt from control because of these provisions, the Court made the assumption that Parliament had not intended to exempt the restriction from the Act:

> "It is unthinkable that in section 18(6) of the Act of 1976 Parliament intended to leave intact a restriction which appears, in the light of that evidence, to be harmful to the public interest."[63]

1.73 It appears to be the case that argument over whether restrictions may be disregarded may occur not only at the time of the decision as to registrability but also during judicial analysis of the restriction.[64] Though, given the highly technical and mechanistic procedures laid down by the Act for determining registrability it must be seriously doubted whether the effect of an agreement has any part whatever in determining that question.

1. Section 9 RTPA 1976: Goods

(1) Section 9(1) and (2): coal and steel agreements

1.74 Restrictive agreements in the coal and steel industry are subject to the provisions of the European Coal and Steel Community Treaty (ECSC). Articles 65 and 66 thereof provide competition rules which are applied by the European Commission. It is arguable that these provisions exclude the operation of national laws in the Member States, although some legal doubt hangs over this proposition since the precise interrelationship between EC and national law in this field is uncertain.[65] Section 9(1) and (2) provides that in deciding upon the registrability of an agreement no account is to be taken of restrictions relating to coal and steel between parties to which the ECSC Treaty applies. Parties to which the ECSC rules of competition apply are defined in Article 80 ECSC as "undertakings". An "undertaking", in this context, means "any undertaking engaged in the coal or the steel industries ... and ... any undertaking or agency regularly engaged in distribution other than sale to domestic customers or small craft industries". In discussing the question of Community law and its overlap mention should be made of section 34 RTPA 1976 which reads: "An agreement is exempt from registration under this Act so long as there is in force in relation to that agreement an authorisation given for the purpose of any provision of the ECSC Treaty relating to restrictive trade practices." Thus an exempted agreement need not be registered nor can it be referred to the RPC. Arguably, it follows that since the Act, technically, applies to it, it cannot be referred to the Monopolies and Mergers Commission under the monopolies provisions of the Fair Trading Act 1973 since the RTPA 1976 is mutually exclusive of that legislation, though not of the mergers provisions of the 1976 Act.

(2) Section 9(3): terms relating exclusively to goods supplied

1.75 Section 9(3) RTPA 1976 is an extremely important provision and allows certain terms in agreements to be ignored when considering whether the agreement is registrable. Section 9(3) is subject to section 9(4) and reference thereto should be made. Section 9(3) reads: "In determining whether an agreement for the supply of goods or for the application of any process of manufacture to goods is an agreement to which

63 *ibid.*, at pp. 48–51 esp. at pp. 50D–51F.
64 *ibid.*, at pp. 50, 51.
65 See on the interaction of EC and UK competition law paras. 6.114–6.119.

the Act applies by virtue of this Part, no account shall be taken of any term which relates exclusively to the goods supplied, or to which the process is applied, in pursuance of the agreement." This phrase has given rise to much speculation as to its scope. Its importance is that if the restrictive terms in an agreement can be fitted within its terms it need not be registered. It is clear that section 9(3) exempts certain basic categories of agreement. Thus, many simple contracts for sale (or for processing) of goods and long-term supply agreements need not be registered. A contract between X and Y whereby X agrees to supply Y with a specified amount of a certain product over the following year at a fixed price is a restrictive agreement under which Y is restricted as to the amount he may acquire and the price he pays. In *J. Bibby Agriculture Ltd* v *C.D. North and Sons*[66] Lord Justice Scott stated, having recited section 9(3) RTPA 1976: "So, to take the simplest case, an agreement which provides for goods to be sold at a specified price excludes any other prices. But since the price relates exclusively to the goods supplied, the restriction can be ignored." Similarly in an agreement whereby X—who lacks manufacturing capacity—entrusts the application of a process to Y (a competitor), section 9(3) may free the agreement from registration because terms such as the price to be paid for the processing and the obligation on Y to undertake the processing may be ignored. The phrase "the application to goods of any process of manufacture" has been judicially described as "curious". The phrase apparently applies to processes such as rust proofing or plating and does not embrace the initial manufacture of the goods.[67]

The House of Lords has clarified the way in which section 9(3) is to be construed. In *MD Foods plc* v *Baines*[68] Lord Nicholls, expressing the judgment of the House, criticised the judgment of the Court of Appeal which adopted a formalistic and mechanical approach to the construction of section 9(3) which led to artificial and in some instances absurd results. Lord Nicholls, having commented on the extreme breadth of the concepts of "agreement" and "arrangement", stated:

> "Section 9(3) which must be seen against this background, cuts down the width of Section 6. As I read the Act, the purpose of Section 9(3) is to provide that in the case of every agreement for the supply of goods, however the agreement was made, there should be left out of the count that part of its content which relates exclusively to goods supplied. In determining whether the Act applies account should be taken only of the remainder of the content of the agreement. Similarly, in respect of agreements the application of any process of manufacture to goods, which are also within the scope of Section 9(3) a corresponding approach is applicable to the equivalent provision in Section 18(2), regarding agreements as to services.
>
> Thus Section 9(3) calls for an examination of the provision of an agreement, not in a formalistic way akin to a blue pencil test, but having regard to the substance of their content. A restriction which applies both to goods supplied and to other goods is to be disregarded so far as it relates only to goods supplied: so far as it relates to other goods the restriction is outside the scope of the Section 9(3) exemption, and the statutory provisions of the Act are to be applied accordingly. If Stamp J intended to suggest otherwise in his passing observations in *Registrar of Restrictive Trading Agreements* v *Schweppes Limited (No. 2)* (1971) L.R. 7 R.P. 336, C-D, I am unable to agree with him.
>
> Any other approach would lead to frankly absurd results. It would mean that in a statute concerned with competition policy in the public interest, registrability and scrutiny by the

[66] Court of Appeal, unreported, 18 November 1991: Sir Steven Brown, President; Lord Justice Scott, Lord Justice Stocker.

[67] *Vernon Pulp* v *UPC* [1980] FSR 179 at p.189 *per* Megarry VC.

[68] [1997] 2 WLR 364.

Court would depend on the form in which a restriction was framed and not upon the substance of the restriction. Two agreements could contain exactly the same restrictions: one would be registrable and the other not. It would mean that an agreement, entered into in one form, would not be registrable, but it would become registrable if at a later date the drafting were tidied up and two restraints were telescoped into a single clause in an amended agreement. Parliament cannot have intended this. These distinctions without a difference would bring the Act into disrepute."

1.76 The word "term" can be problematic. A single term may contain two restrictions. Thus, if X and Y agree in a single term of an agreement to market a product exclusively through a joint venture company two restrictive obligations exist: (i) obligation to sell only through the joint company; and (ii) obligation to refuse to fulfil orders placed by third parties with the individual parties. Section 9(3), however, does not operate to exclude restrictions from consideration, it operates to exclude "any term" which relates exclusively to the goods supplied or to which the process is supplied. What section 9(3) thus provides is that one examines a term and if that term relates exclusively to the goods, then, irrespective of the number of restrictions inherent within it, that term may be ignored. It would appear that each restriction which is inferred from a "term" must itself relate exclusively to the goods else the "term" will not, in turn, relate exclusively to the goods supplied. The difficulties and attendant perils of drafting arising out of this word were clearly highlighted by the ruling of the Court of Appeal in *Associated Diaries Ltd* v *Andrew Baines*[69] but were conclusively dismissed subsequently by the House of Lords. In order to understand the case it is necessary to set out the facts in a little detail. The Plaintiff was a large wholesale distributor of milk and other commodities. The Defendant was a milk roundsman selling and delivering milk for domestic consumers on his milkround. The Defendant was not employed by the Plaintiff but was an independent contractor. The Plaintiff and Defendant entered an agreement dated the 10 August 1989 pursuant to which the Defendant agreed to supply the Plaintiff's milk in a defined territory. The agreement contained a number of restrictions which were either clearly within the scope of section 9(3) or were otherwise exemptible pursuant to Schedule 3(2). The "problem" was clause 4(iii) which was in the following terms:

"In consideration of the undertaking and agreement on the part of the company [namely to supply the Defendant with milk, not to sell milk by way of retail to the customers of the Defendant, and to use all reasonable endeavours to persuade its bottled milk buyer customers not to sell milk by way of retail to the Defendants customers] the [Defendant] hereby undertakes and agrees with the company:
(iii) during the continuance of this agreement ... not to sell milk by way of retail to any customers of the company."

Lord Justice Schiemann described in the Court of Appeal the dilemma in the following terms:

"The critical question, therefore, is whether because of the application of the shearing provisions in section 9(3), clause 4(iii) is to be disregarded in determining whether the RTPA applies to the Agreement. If it is to be disregarded, the Agreement falls entirely within Schedule 3 para. 2, and the RTPA does not apply. If it is not to be disregarded, the Agreement includes a relevant restriction that is not covered by Schedule 3, para. 2 and is subject to registration."

[69] [1996] ICR 183 (CA); [1997] 2 WLR 364 HL.

1.77 In the High Court, the judge had held that clause 4(3) was not a relevant restriction. The judge had set out the Plaintiff's submission with approval:

> "The case for the Company is that clause 4(3) imposes more than one restrictions. To the extent that it restricts the sale of milk supplied by the Company pursuant to its obligation under clause 2(i)[70] that is while the Company is not absolved from its obligation by clause 3,[71] it relates exclusively to that milk. To the extent that it relates to milk supplied by third parties while the Company is absolved from its obligations to supply Mr Baines or for the purposes of another business the restriction is one relating to other goods of the same description as the milk supplied under the Supply Agreement within paragraph 2(b) of Schedule 3."

1.78 The Court of Appeal, however, rejected the submission. The Court acknowledged the drafting pitfalls inherent in the concept of a "term". The Court stated:

> "It is common ground that the agreement could have been drafted so as to impose precisely the same obligations on each party as the agreement under consideration and so as to result in an agreement which was not registrable. All that would have been necessary would have been to substitute for the existing clause 4(iii) two clauses: one clause which provided 'the customer undertakes during the continuance of this agreement not to sell by way of retail milk supplied by the Company to any customers of the Company'; and another clause which provided 'the customer undertakes during the continuance of this agreement not to sell by way of retail milk obtained from sources other than the Company to any customers of the Company'."

1.79 In such an agreement the first clause would be disregarded pursuant to section 9(3) because it would relate exclusively to the goods supplied in pursuance of the Agreement. That agreement, notionally shorn of the first clause, would then be one to which Schedule 3(2) applied and, the net effect would be that the RTPA 1976 would not apply because all of the restriction would either be disregardable pursuant to section 9(3) or exempted pursuant to Schedule 3(2).

1.80 The Court of Appeal accepted that its construction of the word "term" was technical and could lead to unsatisfactory results. However, they were not minded to avoid such unsatisfactory results by reading the word "term" in section 9(3) as if it meant "restriction". The Court clearly had some sympathy with the argument advanced to it that there was no conceivable policy which could be served by providing that an agreement in the form agreed by the parties should be registrable whereas the same agreement (*mutatis mutandis*) drafted with the two substitute clauses would not be registrable. They further accepted that if the agreement had been drafted in a way *more* restrictive to the Defendant by requiring him to purchase all milk from the Plaintiff, rather than in a way less restrictive to the Defendant allowing him in certain circumstances to acquire it from third parties, then undoubtedly, clause 4(3) would have fallen within section 9(3) and been disregardable. They recited, in this regard, the argument put to them by the Plaintiff that it was absurd to deny a party the right to sue on an agreement which was less favourable to a

[70] Clause 2(1) provided as follows: "The Company undertakes and agrees with the customer that the customer complying with the obligations on its part herein contained: (i) subject to the provisions of clause 3 hereof to supply the customer with all milk for sale in the business."

[71] Clause 3 provides as follows: "If and to the extent that the company shall be hindered or prevented from supplying the customer with part or all of the customers requirements of milk by reason of any court whatsoever beyond the reasonable control of the company ... (i) the company shall to that extent only be free from all obligations to supply milk to the customer and (ii) the customer shall to that extent only and notwithstanding the provisions of sub-clause 4(1) hereof be entitled to purchase milk from other sources."

Defendant while not allowing the same party the right to sue in respect of an agreement which was more favourable. In response to these arguments the Court reiterated that the question whether an agreement was registrable (as opposed to whether it was contrary to the public interest) was a mechanistic one which differed in the approach adopted, for instance, under Article 85 EC. As a matter of analysis the Court emphasised that throughout the Act the draftsman had used the expressions "term" and "restriction" deliberately in different contexts. Accordingly, it was not possible to equate one with the other.

1.81 The judgment of the Court of Appeal was decisively rejected by the House of Lords in this regard. In particular, the House of Lords was highly critical of the adoption of an approach to construction which would lead to absurd, inconsistent and arbitrary results. In this regard the quotation from the judgment set out above is relevant. The judgment of the Court of Appeal had the potential to cause consternation amongst lawyers who had long assumed that "term" meant the same as "restriction". This was, after all, the approach adopted by Warner J in *Diazo Copying*.

1.82 Of the word "term", Lord Nicholls stated:

> "I do not believe that the interpretation of the Act which I prefer does any violence to the statutory language. 'Term', used in relation to an agreement, is a loose expression. Its meaning is not confined to a linguistically discrete provision. In ordinary usage one refers to the 'terms' of an agreement when referring generally to the provisions of the agreement. In ordinary usage one states that a particular obligation is a 'term' of an agreement, meaning thereby simply that it is a contractual obligation. This is so even if the obligation expressed in the agreement as part of a larger, linguistically indivisible obligation.
>
> The context supports this usage of 'term'. This meaning produces a workable and sensible result, the suggested alternative does not. Section 9(3) is intended to be applicable to all agreements, and terms must bear a meaning capable of being applied across the range of different forms in which an agreement, as widely defined in the Act, can come into being. Mr Baines' interpretation of Section 9(3), which involves looking at the form in which the provision is expressed, could not be applied to implied agreements or implied terms where, *ex hypothesi*, a restriction was accepted without its being expressed in any form. In such cases the substance of the restriction is capable of being identified in Section 9(3) applied accordingly, but there could be no criteria for deciding which of several possible forms in which the restriction might be expressed is the form to be adopted for the purposes of Section 9(3). Further, an attempt to apply the 'form' interpretation to an oral agreement could involve a bizarre analysis of precisely what words were used and by whom in the course of a discussion at a meeting or over the telephone. There remain express terms of written agreements. In such cases Mr Baines' interpretation could be applied, for the reason already given, with an arbitrariness of result which would bemuse a businessman.
>
> In Mr Baines' submissions and in the Court of Appeal Judgments reliance was placed on the contrast in language in Section 9 between 'term' and 'restriction'. This was seen as supporting the view that term is not synonymous with, or co-extensive with, restriction. Linguistic arguments of this character should be handled warily. They are a legitimate and useful aid in statutory interpretation, but they are no more than this. Sometimes a difference in language is revealing and therefore important, other times not. In the process of statutory interpretation there always comes a stage, before reaching a final decision, when one should stand back and view a suggested interpretation in the wider context of the scheme and purpose of the Act. After all, the object of the exercise is to elucidate the intention fairly and reasonably attributable to Parliament when using the language under consideration. It is wrong to rely upon linguistic dissimilarities as indicative of an intended meaning with far reaching consequences when those consequences, seen in the wider context of the Act as a whole, lack all rhyme and reason."

1.83 The word "agreement" is likewise to be widely construed. Agreement means, according to section 43(1), "any agreement or arrangement, whether or not it is intended to be enforceable by legal proceedings". In *Diazo Copying Materials*, Warner J thus stated: "So an unenforceable arrangement can be an 'agreement for the supply of goods' for the purposes of section 9(3) and restrictions accepted under such an arrangement may fall to be left out of account by virtue of that subsection."[72] Thus, if X, Y and Z are rivals and develop an informal, unwritten understanding that they will supply each other in the event of any of them experiencing a shortfall in stocks, then the vague arrangement is counted as an agreement and the moral obligation on each of them to supply each other in a crisis rather than take advantage of a competitor's problems is an agreement for the supply of goods and is exempt under section 9(3), subject to the possible application of section 9(4) discussed below. From *Diazo Copying Materials* it is now clear that where there is a master agreement between two parties for the supply of goods by one to the other and where this is followed by specific individualised agreements implementing the master agreement, section 9(3) can apply. Warner J held in respect of such situations:

> "Granted that such a 'master' agreement may take the form of an unenforceable arrangement, its implementation would, in most commercial situations, require that the parties should enter into individual contracts of sale (or of hire) in respect of the goods actually supplied in pursuance of it. To hold that in such a situation a restriction relating exclusively to the goods supplied may be left out of account by virtue of section 9(3) if accepted under an implementing contract, but not if accepted under the 'master' agreement, would seem to us unwarranted by anything in the terms of the subsection or by its discernible purpose."[73]

1.84 In *Diazo Copying Materials* two restrictions in a joint venture agreement were held to be exempted by section 9(3) and accordingly are informative. The case concerned the production of photocopiers by HTL and MSL. Under an agreement HTL would produce photocopiers to MSL's order. MSL would market the product throughout the world but HTL would have a right to purchase back at a significant discount on the retail price such of the products as it required for sale in the UK or in any other territory where MSL was unable to exploit its exclusive right to market the product. In this agreement there were two important restrictions. First, a restriction on MSL requiring that company to supply HTL at a discount in such quantities as HTL should require. Secondly, a restriction on HTL in the areas in which it could sell since it could only market the product in the UK, or, abroad in areas that MSL had relinquished. With respect to the first restriction it was held that this was a restriction in an agreement for the supply of goods and that the restriction as to the second territories where HTL could sell was a restriction which related "exclusively to the goods supplied".[74] The judgment of Warner J certainly indicates a wide view of section 9(3). It would have been possible for the Court in that case to have defined the restrictions imposed on HTL not to sell outside the UK not in terms of a restriction relating exclusively to the *goods* supplied but in terms of a restriction relating to the territory in which the goods could be supplied. If this had been the case it is hard to see how section 9(3) would have applied. However, on the basis of this judgment export restrictions in joint venture contracts are not registrable. Moreover, in terms of the drafting of such contracts it may be possible for various forms of market sharing between joint venture parties to be worded so as to conform with section 9(3). Thus if X, Y and Z combine in order to manufacture a complex piece of

[72] [1984] ICR 429.
[73] *ibid.*, at pp. 438, 439.
[74] *ibid.*, at pp. 436–438.

technical equipment and seek to divide up the market between them as regards its sales the contract may be drafted to grant to X, Y and Z an "exclusive assignable and divisible right to sell use and exploit the subject product throughout the territory as defined and shall grant an exclusive assignable and divisible right to use and exploit the technical data made available to it pursuant to this agreement".[75] Although the wording simply gives to X, Y and Z exclusive territories it implies negative restrictions on X, Y and Z not to sell in each other's territories. It seems probable that this conclusion applies only in the context of joint venture agreements whereby the parties jointly develop and produce a product and then individually sell it. An agreement between A, B and C who each produce different, competing goods to share the market geographically between them is expressly registrable under section 6(1)(f) RTPA 1976 and would further not benefit from section 9(3) as a result of section 9(4) discussed below.

1.85 It is a moot question whether the following benefits from section 9(3): X entrusts the processing of his goods to Y and promises Y that he will not have another person process his goods. Is this restriction on not going elsewhere one relating "exclusively to the goods supplied or to which the process is supplied" or is it a restriction as to persons who may process the goods? If it is the former then it can be ignored when determining registration. If the restriction "not to go elsewhere" cannot realistically be described as a term relating exclusively to the product or the process, such a restriction is in relation to the persons who may process X's goods and hence falls within section 6(1)(f). The latter (narrower) view is probably correct though there is no judicial guidance on point.

1.86 Finally, in respect of section 9(3) it may be commented that the wording is lamentably vague. The original intention was simply to exclude from registration various, everyday supply contracts. However, the provision is drafted so loosely that potentially it provides an escape route for a wide range of restrictive agreements.[76]

(3) Section 9(4): proviso to section 9(3)

1.87 Section 9(4) reads:

> "Where any such restrictions as are described in section 6(1) above are accepted or any such information provisions as are described in section 7(1) above are made as between two or more persons by whom, or two or more persons to or from whom, goods are to be supplied, or the process applied, in pursuance of the agreement, subsection (3) above shall not apply to those restrictions or to those information provisions unless accepted or made in pursuance of a previous agreement—(a) in respect of which particulars have been registered under this Act; or (b) which is exempt from registration by virtue of an order under section 29 (agreements important to the national economy) or section 30 (agreements holding down prices) ..."

1.88 There are two aspects to section 9(4) RTPA 1976. The first question concerns the interpretation of the words up to "unless" in the middle of the provision. The second

[75] These were, *mutatis mutandis*, the words used by HTI and MSL in the *Diazo Copying Materials* case.

[76] In *Diazo Copying Materials* it is possible that the apparently liberal approach to s. 9(3) of the Court was, to an extent, conditioned by the fact that if the Court held that s. 9(3) did not exempt the restrictions they would have been forced to have held the Defendant to be in contempt of court. HTL was in Court as a consequence of an application by the Director General for leave to issue writs of sequestration against HTL. The Director General alleged that the agreement between HTL and MSL was registrable and hence in breach of an earlier Court order imposed against HTL not to enter into any other unregistered agreements. The Court was apparently of the view that HTL had not been wilful or deliberate in seeking to undermine the Court order and was thus perhaps loathe to find contempt of court. (See [1984] ICR 429 at pp. 434H–436F which chronicles how the parties took legal advice as to registrability and finally notified the OFT when their legal advisers reconsidered their views upon registrability.)

question concerns the remainder of section 9(4). The first part of the provision says that the exemption in section 9(3) does *not* apply where restrictions are accepted between two persons who are at the same level of trade, i.e. all suppliers, or all persons supplied. For the exemption in section 9(3) to apply, the restrictions which relate exclusively to the goods must be in agreements between parties at different levels of trade. Thus on the facts of *Diazo Copying Materials*,[77] discussed above, it was sufficient for purposes of section 9(3) that MSL supplied HTL with photocopiers for sale by HTL in the United Kingdom. The Court concentrated on the functions allocated to the parties under the contract rather than the everyday functions of the parties. Thus MSL was treated as a supplier and HTL as a dealer. There was no discussion of the fact that the territory restriction, which was held to be a restriction which related "exclusively to the goods supplied" (and hence excludable under section 9(3)), was in an agreement between HTL and MSL in their capacity as suppliers, i.e. it *was* arguably an agreement between persons at the same level of trade. In *Topliss Showers Ltd* v *Gessey* Neill J stated: "It is clear that section 9(4) only applies where the restrictions are accepted as between two or more persons who are either suppliers or persons supplied; in other words there have to be two or more persons in the same class. Furthermore, the persons in that class have to be persons who supply or are supplied with goods 'in pursuance of the agreement'."[78]

1.89 Guidance as the scope of section 9(4) is given by the ruling of the Court of Appeal in *Express Dairies Ltd* v *Sidhu and Others*.[79] In that case a Supply Agreement relating to the sale of milk and dairy products (which included fruit juice) was concluded between the Plaintiff and the Defendants. The Supply Agreement was also associated with a transaction of sale of November 1988 under which the Defendants purchased from the Plaintiff a milk depot located on the Great West Road, Hounslow, Middlesex. The parties were the Plaintiff and the Defendants and another company in the Defendant's group in which the legal estate to be conveyed was at that time vested. Completion of the conveyance was expressed to be "conditional" upon the Defendants entering into the Supply Agreement. The sale was completed and the Supply Agreement was entered into. Pursuant to the Supply Agreement which was expressed to continue for a period of five years from 18 November 1988 the Plaintiff agreed to supply and keep supplied the Defendants with milk and dairy products as set out more specifically in a Schedule to the Agreement. Under the Supply Agreement it was provided, first, that the Defendants would pay the Plaintiff for the milk supplied at prices for the time being specified in the National Dairymen's Association Wholesale Price List and, second, that the Defendants would pay to the Plaintiff for the dairy products the prices "which [the Plaintiff] shall from time to time charge". The price for the milk was thus not under the direct control of the Plaintiff, whereas the price for the dairy products was under the control and discretion of the Plaintiff. The Agreement provided further that the milk and dairy products would be delivered by the Plaintiff to the Defendants' milk depot in the Great West Road and that such delivery would be at no extra charge. Clause 4 of the Agreement provided as follows:

[77] [1984] ICR 429 at pp. 437–439.

[78] [1982] ICR 501 at p. 517G. See also *Cadbury Schweppes and J. Lyons Agreement* [1975] ICR 240: X and Y agreed to supply goods to Z, a marketing subsidiary of X in order to achieve output quotas between them. Mr Justice Stamp held: (a) X and Z did *not* constitute one person, they were separate legal entities; (b) the agreement between X and Y prima facie fell within s. 9(3); and (c), however, X and Y were both manufacturers, i.e. at the same level of trade and s. 9(4) rendered inapplicable the sanctuary in s. 9(3) and thus rendered the Act generally applicable.

[79] 30 October 1991, unreported, Farquharson LJ; Scott LJ.

> "Subject to Clause 5 hereof the Retailer [the Defendants] shall not during the currency of the Agreement purchase Milk and Dairy products from any person, firm or company other than Express [the Plaintiff] or such subsidiary or associated companies of Express as it may nominate."

1.90 Clause 5 contained exceptions concerning such matters as government restrictions, strikes, lock outs. Lord Justice Scott described the agreement in the following terms:

> "The Agreement has been described as a solus agreement, and in a sense that is what it is. But it is not a solus agreement in the sense in which that expression may be understood in the petrol trade or in the beer trade. It does not tie the [Defendants] to the sale of Express products from specific premises, such as 443 to 447 Great West Road, Hounslow."

1.91 Clause 4 did not contain any geographical limit. It was not therefore confined to the business carried on by the Defendants from the premises at the Great West Road. The Plaintiffs contended that the clause covered and restricted the Defendants in any business relating to milk and dairy products that they might carry on anywhere in the United Kingdom. The Defendants were always, it was contended, obliged, pursuant to Clause 4, to purchase their milk and dairy products from the Plaintiff. Clause 8 of the Agreement contained another restriction in the following terms:

> "During the currency of this Agreement, the Retailer shall not solicit or canvass the sale of milk or dairy products to retail customers, semi-retail customers, bottled milk buyers or agents of Express in any area."

1.92 Despite the use of the word "retailer" in clause 8 the Defendants were, in fact, wholesalers selling milk and dairy products to various retail outlets. The Plaintiffs were also wholesalers of milk. The Plaintiffs acquired their milk from the Milk Marketing Board and then distributed it either to smaller wholesalers such as the Defendants, or to retail outlets. Lord Justice Scott held expressly:

> "So, in so far as their trade consists of the supply of milk or dairy products to retail outlets Express is in potential competition with the [Defendants]; and [clause] 8 of the Supply Agreement prevents the [Defendants] from soliciting or canvassing the sale of milk or dairy products to customers of Express in any area."

1.93 The dispute between the parties arose when the Plaintiffs discovered that the Defendants had been purchasing milk and dairy products more cheaply from other large wholesalers, in competition with the Plaintiffs. The Plaintiffs commenced proceedings against the Defendants and sought summary judgment for breach of contract. Mr Justice Vinelott at first instance granted summary judgment having concluded that the Defendants had no triable defence. The Defendants did not at that stage raise a defence based upon the RTPA 1976. Prior to the hearing before the Court of Appeal the Defendants amended the draft defence to raise, *inter alia*, a defence based upon the RTPA 1976. The Court of Appeal were able to deal with this defence peremptorily:

> "an amended version of the draft defence has been prepared which raises two additional defences and to these two defences we have given our attention. One of these alleges that the Agreement between [the Plaintiff] and the [Defendants] (the Supply Agreement) is an agreement registrable under the provisions of the Restrictive Trade Practices Act 1976. It is said that the Agreement comes within section 6(1)(a) and (f) and that although section 9(3) would appear to remove the agreement from those requiring registration, sub-section (4) of section 9 brings the agreement back again into the cat-

egory of those which ought to be registered. As to that, I would say only that I can see no substance at all in the proposition that this is an agreement which is covered by section 9(4) of the 1976 Act."

1.94 It was thus clear that the Court concluded (without difficulty) that the restrictions (in particular in clauses 4 and 8) were restrictions to which section 9(3) applied. However, they did not consider that section 9(3) was dis-applied as a result of the operation of section 9(4). This is notwithstanding that, as the Court emphasised, the Plaintiffs and Defendants were both wholesalers operating at the same level of market in competition with each other. The agreement in question was in short an exclusive distribution agreement between competing wholesalers. Usually, of course, distribution agreements are between a person operating at different levels of the market (e.g. manufacturer/wholesaler; wholesaler/retailer). this case provides support for the conclusion that section 9(4) applies to classic horizontal agreements whereby the parties thereto agree restrictions in relation to *different* goods. In the *Express Dairies* case the agreement concerned the *same* goods. Notwithstanding the absence of reasoning in the judgment, it remains authority for the proposition that section 9(4) does not apply to distribution agreements whether vertical or horizontal.

1.95 The second question relates to the second half of section 9(4). This lays down the principle that a parent or master agreement which is registered or exempted from registration, covers and exempts any later affiliated or subordinate agreement made "in pursuance" of it. Thus, for example, if X, Y and Z agree to supply goods to certain distributors or upon certain standard terms and they duly register this agreement, then, if X subsequently enters an agreement with a distributor on the terms laid out in the main agreement this subsidiary agreement is not registrable.

(4) Section 9(5): agreements to abide by standards set by British Standards Institution (BSI) and others

1.96 Agreements between parties to abide by standards set by the BSI may be discounted in determining registrability. The BSI, which is government sponsored, sets standards following discussions with suppliers and consumers and such standards are presumed to be within the public interest. Section 9(5) accordingly allows the disregard, for registration purposes, of terms in agreements between producers or suppliers to comply with, or between purchasers only to acquire goods complying with, "(a) standards of dimension, design, quality or performance, or (b) arrangements as to the provision of information or advice to purchasers, consumers or users". The proposition described above in connection with section 9(3) RTPA 1976 that an implied negative obligation is inherent in a positive restrictive term is relevant here also. As with section 9(3) such an implied negative term, since it is in reality the reverse side of the positive restrictive term, may be treated as one and the same as the disregardable, positive, restrictive term. Thus, a restriction between producers, for example, to produce exclusively goods which accord to BSI standards is also an implied negative restriction not to manufacture goods below or differing from that standard. Alternatively an agreement between purchasers only to acquire goods according to BSI standards contains the implied negative restriction not to acquire goods differing from the standard. In both examples the positive restriction and the implied negative restriction are integral ingredients of the same "term" and may thus be disregarded. In drafting an agreement to fall within the exception care should be taken to ensure that the "term" to be disregarded contains *only* restrictions which fall within section 9(5) since, if the "term" in question contains (even inferentially) restrictions relating to *other* matters, section 9 will not apply. See in this regard the discussion of the word "term" under section 9(3) RTPA 1976 and the ruling of the House of Lords in *Associated Dairies Ltd* v *Baines,* paras. 1.75 and following.

1.97 The leniency shown the BSI is extended to other trade associations or organisations who set standards and whose standards have been approved by the Secretary of State by statutory instrument. This form of dispensation has been exercised on a number of occasions. Thus, for example, standards concerning safety precautions for veterinary products drawn up following discussions between the Ministry of Agriculture, Fisheries and Food, the Ministry of Health and the representatives of professional and commercial organisations have been formally approved.[80] Approval has also been given to standards for safety precautions for pesticides.[81]

1.98 Agreements to abide by standards differing from those set by the BSI or other approved bodies are not exempt from registration. An agreement whereby an association sets a high product quality standard could be used to harm the sales of smaller, lesser producers who manufacture lower quality goods to satisfy the cheaper end of the market. Standard setting can clearly have a pronounced effect upon the market and hence warrants control.

(5) Section 9(6): industrial relations agreements

1.99 In common with restrictive practices laws in other industrialised states, restrictive agreements relating to labour and employment are excluded from control. Collective employer–employee agreements are hence beyond the pale of the legislation. Section 9(6) reads, in pertinent part, that in determining registrability, "no account shall be taken of any restriction or information provision which affects or otherwise relates to the workers to be employed or not employed by any person, or as to the remuneration, conditions of employment, hours of work or working conditions of such workers". As expressed above, the section is prima facie of considerable breadth: many commercial agreements can, and do, exert a secondary affect upon labour conditions and terms of pay. An agreement between X and Y to set up a joint venture company in another part of the country and concentrate their joint efforts there can mean that employment prospects at X and Y's existing factories may suffer as work is diverted to the joint venture. Thus, section 9(6) must be construed narrowly so as to exempt from registration only those agreements *specifically* affecting or relating to the matters noted in section 9(6). The RPC has held that an agreement between manufacturers to halt production in order to combat a strike is not exempt from registration even though the agreement was specifically to deal with labour problems and not to restrain competition between the parties. It is noteworthy that in that case the agreement was ultimately adjudged by the Court not to restrain competition—the restrictions in question were very short lived.[82]

80 Restrictive Trade Practices (Approval of Standards and Arrangements) Order 1983, S.I. 1983 No. 382, as amended by S.I. 1984 No. 1269 and S.I. 1986 No. 614, relating to tobacco products; Restrictive Trade Practices (Approval of Standards and Arrangements) Order 1984, S.I. 1984 No. 2031, relating to proof marks for small arms. The following Orders all arise out of the privatisation of the electricity industry and the creation of Electricity Association Services Ltd on 6 April 1990, which is owned by the privatised electricity companies and which *inter alia* provides standards information and advice to the electricity industry: Restrictive Trade Practices (Standards and Arrangements) Order 1990, S.I. 1990 No. 888, Restrictive Trade Practices (Standards and Arrangements) (Goods) Order S.I. 1990 No. 1986 and (Services) Order S.I. 1991 No. 1897 (made under s. 18(5) RTPA), Restrictive Trade Practices (Standards and Arrangements) (Goods) Order 1993, S.I. 1993 No. 2473, and (Services) Order 1993, S.I. 1993 No. 2453.

81 *op. cit.* S.I. 1969 No. 226, Sch., Art. 2.

82 See *Scottish Daily Newspaper Society's Agreement No. 1* (1971) LR 7 RP 379.

1.100 Section 9(6) is expressed to cover agreements relating to the workers to be employed. Presumably an agreement between X and Y not to employ certain specified individuals is not registrable. Equally, an agreement between X and Y that they would only employ workers with a certain skill or qualification would not be registrable. An agreement between X and Y whereby each will employ different, and agreed upon, types of worker is also not registrable. Though an agreement not to "employ" certain specified individuals as consultants or agents would be registrable. Such individuals would not be "workers". The agreement would be registrable under section 18 as an agreement as to the persons from whom (consultancy and/or agency) services will be acquired. "Worker" for the purposes of section 9(6) is defined as "a person who has entered into or works under a contract with an employer whether the contract be by way of manual labour, clerical work, or otherwise, be express or implied, oral or in writing, and whether it be a contract of service or of apprenticeship or a contract personally to execute any work or labour".

1.101 For relevant judicial analysis of the industrial relations exemption see the commentary on section 18(6), at paras. 1.105–1.106. See also paras. 11.135 and following on staffing restrictions for discussion of section 79 FTA 1973, which may also be relevant in this area.

2. *Section 18 RTPA 1976: Services*

(1) Section 18(1)–(4): terms relating exclusively to services supplied

1.102 Section 18(2)–(4) provides in effect that no term relating exclusively to the services supplied shall be considered in determining registrability. The analysis of "term" in relation to section 9(3) applies here equally (see paras. 1.75 and 1.82). Section 9(3), it will be recalled, allows suppliers to impose certain restrictions on dealers. Section 18 permits the equivalent in relation to services. The "equivalent" in the services context can be complex. Retailers may equate to agents who, rather than sell the suppliers' goods to consumers, arrange contracts of service or for services between supplier and consumer. Restrictions imposed upon the authority of the agent to conclude contracts are apparently not registrable. Since an agent contracts on behalf of his principal restrictions imposed on the agent's authority represent restrictions accepted by the principal. Thus a principal prevents his agent from advertising his services in a form other than that prescribed by the principal or if the principal requires the agent to sell the service subject to certain price conditions stipulated by the principal these are terms which relate exclusively to the service supplied and are accordingly not registrable. The principal in such cases is merely limiting his agent's authority. It is thought that section 18(2) will have very limited application; very few services (as opposed to goods) are sold by an agent to the consumer. More commonly the provider of services is the agent who operates as middleman between vendor and purchaser of goods, e.g. an estate agent or auctioneer. The only notable suppliers of services who act through an agent are tour operators who sell through travel agents, insurance and financial services companies who may sell through brokers. Conversely, if a principal requires the agent to act *only* for that principal and for no other this would be a restriction accepted by the *agent* as to the persons to whom agency services can be provided i.e. to the one principal and no other.

1.103 The same proviso relating to agreements between persons at the same level of trade as is specified in section 9(4) applies to services by virtue of section 18(3). Thus the recommendations of a service supply association to its service supplier members of restrictive terms for adoption by agents would not be exempt from registration. In such cases the members who are all suppliers are deemed to have accepted *inter se* the restriction in the recommendation.

(2) Section 18(5): agreements to abide by standards set by the BSI and others

1.104 This provision follows, *mutatis mutandis*, section 9(5) and reference may be made thereto for commentary.

(3) Section 18(6): industrial relations agreements

1.105 This provision follows, *mutatis mutandis*, section 9(6) and reference may be made thereto for commentary. The provision was considered by the RPC in *Association of British Travel Agents Ltd Agreement*[83] (the *ABTA* case). In that case ABTA had imposed various staffing restrictions on tour operators and travel agents as preconditions of ABTA membership. For example, ABTA required travel agent members to employ throughout the year at least two full-time employees with certain specified training or practical experience. The Director General challenged this restriction on the obvious basis that it prevented travel agents who could not afford two full-time employees from being members of ABTA. Non-membership of ABTA entailed the serious consequence that tour operators who were ABTA members would not deal with the firm since they were bound only to deal with other members. ABTA argued that the staffing requirement was exempt under section 18(6) as relating to matters of employment and terms and conditions of employment. The RPC, in a judgment read by Lincoln J, adopted a narrow view of the exception in section 18(6). The Court was of the evident conclusion that the staffing requirements were against the public interest: "It is unthinkable that in section 18(6) ... Parliament intended the Court to leave intact a restriction which appears, in the light of the evidence, to be harmful to the public interest, especially where it is a member of a family of restrictions, simply because it relates to certain aspects of employment."[84] Lincoln J made it implicitly clear that section 18(6) was intended primarily to exclude from the Act restrictions contained in the terms and conditions of collective agreements. He thus added the important qualification to section 18(6): "it does not enjoin the Court to disregard employment or staffing restrictions where they are a component of a cluster of restrictions all constituting a manner of trading".[85] In the event the staffing requirement was associated with premises requirements and financial soundness requirements.

1.106 In *Donald Storrie Estate Agency Ltd* v *Adams,*[86] it was held that section 18(6) was not "apt" to cover persons such as directors of companies who, previously, had been the owners of a business sold to the director's employer in circumstances where the director operated under a service contract. In the contract in question the director had given certain covenants coming into operation post-termination. The judge held that section 18(6) did *not* apply to a "period when the [director] had ceased to be in the [employer's] employment".[87]

83 [1984] ICR 12.
84 *ibid.*, at p. 51D.
85 *ibid.*, at p. 51E.
86 [1989] SLT 305.
87 *ibid.*, pp. 309, 310.

F. The Registrability of Information Agreements

1.107 In all of the provisions mentioned and quoted in this chapter when the notion of a restriction is discussed, reference is also made to information provisions. This could give the impression that all agreements between parties to exchange information are registrable to the same extent as supply agreements. This is not so. Information agreements relating to goods are only registrable to the extent specified in S.I. 1969 No. 1842 which calls up for registration information agreements concerning certain prices and terms and conditions. Information agreements relating to services are *not* as of yet registrable. For detailed analysis of information agreements see Chapter 9.

G. Trade Associations and Registrability

1.108 Since the RTPA 1976 specifically draws within its enforcement net trade association–member relations, it is worth clarifying precisely how the legislation achieves this goal. A trade association is defined in section 43(1) RTPA 1976 to mean "a body of persons (whether incorporated or not) which is formed for the purpose of furthering the trade interests of its members, or of persons represented by its members". This definition applies only for goods associations. Where services are concerned the definition is slightly different. Section 16(1) RTPA 1976 defines a services supply association as one, "whether incorporated or otherwise ... whose membership consists wholly or mainly of persons ... who are either engaged in the supply of services brought under control by [an] order or are employed by or represent persons so engaged; and, its objects or activities include the promotion of the interests of persons engaged in the supply of those services who are either members affected by the order or are persons represented by such members". An association to which the Act applies need not comprise exclusively of services suppliers, it need only comprise "mainly" of such suppliers. "Mainly" presumably means more than half, though nowhere in the Act is guidance given on this. It is pertinent to note that the word "mainly" is linked to and follows the word "wholly" thereby implying that something rather more than 51 per cent might be what is sought.

Other than the definitions above, the provisions of sections 8 (goods) and 16 (services) operate in like fashion.

1.109 (i) Under sections 8(1) and 16(2) RTPA 1976 agreements made by trade associations are deemed to be agreements entered into by the members. Thus, if an association concludes an agreement on behalf of its member with another association or person it is registrable; it cannot be argued that the members were not party to the agreement and the trade associations were not carrying on business. Thus an agreement between a supply association and a purchasing association is an agreement between the suppliers who belong to the association and the purchasers who belong to the association. An agreement concluded by a federation of trade associations is treated as an agreement between the trade associations who belong to the federation and, *a fortiori*, the individual members of that association. These provisions which deem trade association agreements to have been concluded by individual members are in practice largely irrelevant since almost all association constitutions provide that members authorise the association to enter agreements upon their behalf.

1.110 (ii) Under sections 8(2) and (3) (goods) and 16(3) and (4) (services) RTPA 1976 a term is implied into the constitutions of associations caught by the Act which provides that recommendations (whether express or implied) made to members by or on behalf of the association are deemed to have been accepted by members of the association. Thus association recommendations are registrable in so far as they relate to matters (restrictions) listed in section 6 for goods and section 11 for services. The term deemed into the association's constitution is impliedly incorporated irrespective of any existing constitutional clause to the contrary. According to sections 8 and 16 the wording of the deemed clause would be as follows:

> "Each member, and any person represented on the association by any member, agrees to comply with those recommendations and with any subsequent recommendations made to them by or on behalf of the association as to the action to be taken by them in relation to the same class of goods or services or processes of manufacture and in respect of the same matters."

1.111 The word "recommendation" implies the existence of some form of active behaviour by the association. The association must, directly or indirectly, encourage some "specific" course of conduct. Thus, if a trade association circular simply said: "Our market research demonstrates that average costs have risen by 3 per cent over the last 3 months" this could not be taken as a recommendation. If, however, the association added to that circular the additional words "and members should rethink their prices accordingly" then this will count as a recommendation. Similarly the issue by an association of a standard form contract for use by members may represent an implied recommendation to members to use the contract even though no express recommendation to use its terms exists.

1.112 Under these provisions members are deemed to be bound by the recommendation and by any subsequent recommendation in relation to "any particular class of goods or process of manufacture" (section 8(2)(b)). This phrase is relevant since it affects the approach that is likely to be adopted by the OFT to a trade association recommendation. If an association suggests to its members in a circular that they refuse to supply X who runs a dubious retail outlet selling hi-fi equipment but heads the circular "Re Terms to Retail Shops in Electrical Business" then the recommendation may be viewed widely as a specific recommendation concerning the electrical business and not, more narrowly, as a recommendation concerning an individual hi-fi seller. The "particular class of goods" is electrical equipment not hi-fi. Clearly, the more widely framed the recommendation the more serious its restrictive effect. In framing recommendations, association officials might consider ensuring that its terms are as narrow as possible.[88] Though it should be stressed that many registrable recommendations are highly desirable and registration should not necessarily be feared.

H. Informal, Parallel Behaviour: Complex Monopolies

1.113 It will be appreciated that although the definition of an arrangement is wide there will be forms of parallel conduct between competing firms which fall short of being described as an arrangement and hence do not fall under the RTPA 1976. Such parallel

[88] See *National Federation of Retail Newsagents, Booksellers and Stationers' Agreement (Nos. 3 and 4)* (1972) LR 7 RP 425; [1972] 1 WLR 1162 (HL) noted, Cunningham, *op. cit.*, n. 41 at pp. 251, 252; Korah (1972) JBL 326 at p. 329.

conduct may however be investigated under the Fair Trading Act 1973 (FTA 1973) which permits the Monopolies and Mergers Commission (MMC) to examine what are known as "complex monopolies". A complex monopoly exists under sections 6 (goods) and 7 (services) FTA 1973 where at least 25 per cent of the goods and/or services are supplied by or supplied to, two or more firms conducting their business in a parallel fashion with anticompetitive consequences. Though where this "parallelism" results from an agreement or arrangement which is registrable the MMC has no jurisdiction to examine the case which must be dealt with under the RTPA 1976.[89]

1.114 Almost all parallel conduct can result in a complex monopoly. For example: X controls 16 per cent of the market and sells at 10 per unit, Y controls 8 per cent of the market, and likewise sells at 10 per unit in order not to lose trade to X. Z controls 10 per cent of the market and after studying the pricing policies of X and Y decides to lower his prices from £10.50 per unit to £10 per unit in order not to lose sales to X and Y. In this example no agreement exists yet firms who between them control 34 per cent of the total market act as if they had fixed prices together. In such a situation less powerful suppliers would probably align their prices to the 10 per unit mark. The MMC has investigated complex monopolies in respect of parallel conduct other than simply price policy though pricing matters have often been in focus.[90] Other conduct examined has concerned restrictions on advertising,[91] standard contractual terms,[92] quality standardisation between products,[93] and no poaching in respect of competitors customers.[94]

1.115 An example concerned the exclusive purchasing arrangements operated by manufacturers and importers of spare parts for motor cars. The MMC concluded that 24 car manufacturers and importers together supplied about 37 per cent of the UK market and that they should be required to exclude from their franchise agreements any clause requiring franchisees to buy car parts exclusively from them. The MMC commented that: "One of the likely effects on competition of exclusive buying requirements is that they may lead to a restriction of competition in that, if a supplier imposes exclusivity on any person, other suppliers and potential customers may be prevented from competing for that person's custom and part of the market may thus be closed to them."[95] Thus, despite the absence of an agreement between the manufacturers and the importers the fact that they all operated similar franchising agreements (and hence operated as if there were an agreement) resulted in the MMC recommending that the government take action against the manufacturers and importers. Such action was taken in August 1982 with the enactment of the Restriction of Agreements (Manufacturers and Importers of Motor Cars) Order 1982[96] which prohibited manufacturers and importers requiring franchisees to take all or part of their requirements of spare parts from that single supplier. Exceptions were made in the case of parts to be provided under warranty and supplies of parties in pursuance of a recall campaign.

[89] See s. 10(2) FTA 1973. See also ss. 54(5) FTA 1973 and Sch. 3(8) FTA 1973.
[90] See e.g. *Ceramic Sanitaryware* (1978) Cmnd 7327 concerning whether the parallel prices were reasonable in the context of the countervailing power of customers.
[91] See for examples the investigation of the MMC into certain professions: *Solicitors* (1975–76) HC 557; *Barristers* (1975–76) HC 512; *Accountants* (1976) Cmnd 6573.
[92] e.g. *Credit Card Franchising Services* (1982) Cmnd 8034.
[93] *Electrical Lamps No. 2* (1968–69) HC 4.
[94] *Films for Exhibition in Cinemas No. 2* (1983) Cmnd 8858.
[95] *Car Parts* (1982) HC 318 was then considered in *New Motor Cars* Cm 1808.
[96] S.I. 1982 No. 1146.

I. Check List for Determining Registrability

1.116 The following is an outline guide for determining whether an agreement falls within the duty to register under the RTPA 1976. This outline is not a substitute for a proper analysis of the language of the Act. Once prima facie registrability is determined the question of exemption arises. In this regard the positions is remarkably complex. However, regard should be paid, in particular, to the threshold exemption in S.I. 1996 No. 348 (£20 million) and the EC block exemption Order (S.I. 1996 No. 349).

(1) Goods agreements

Questions

1. Is there an agreement or arrangement whether written or oral between the parties or a trade association agreement or recommendation? If there is then question (2) should be considered. If there is not the Act does not apply.
2. Are two or more of the parties carrying on business within the UK in the supply of goods? If the answer is yes then question (3) must be answered. If not the Act does not apply.
3. Does the agreement, arrangement or trade association agreement or recommendation contain restrictions listed in section 6 RTPA 1976? If the answer is yes then question (4) must be answered. If not the Act does not apply.
4. Does the agreement, etc. contain any terms which may be "disregarded" by virtue of section 9 RTPA 1976? When considering registration these terms may be ignored. Question (5) must be answered.
5. Do the restrictions that remain bind at least two parties? If the remaining restrictions bind only one party then the agreement is not registrable. An agreement is still registrable if parties accept different restrictions listed in section 6 RTPA 1976.
6. If the agreement, etc. has reached this stage it is prima facie registrable. The final question to ask is whether the agreement fits into one of the exempt categories of agreement specified in Schedule 3 RTPA 1976.

(2) Services agreements

Questions

1. Is there an agreement or arrangement whether written or oral between the parties or a service supply association agreement or recommendation? If there is question (2) should be considered. If there is not the Act does not apply.
2. Are two or more of the parties carrying on business within the UK in the provision of services? If the answer is yes then question (3) must be answered. If not the Act does not apply.
3. Is the agreement, etc. taken outside of the scope of the duty to register by either Schedule 1 RTPA 1976 or by the Schedule to the Services Order (paras 2.60 and following)? If the agreement falls within these provisions it is not registrable. If the agreement is *not* exempt question (4) must be considered.
4. Does the agreement, etc. contain any restrictions listed in Article 3 of the Services Order (which lays down registrable restrictions and repeats the wording of section 11 RTPA 1976 which may be referred to in the absence of the Services Order)? If the agreement, etc., contains registrable restrictions question (5) must be considered. If not the Act does not apply.

5. Does the agreement, etc. contain any restrictions which may be "disregarded" by virtue of section 18 RTPA 1976? When considering registration these terms may be ignored. Question (6) must be answered.
6. Do the restrictions that remain bind at least two parties? If the remaining restrictions bind only one party then the agreement is not registrable. An agreement is still registrable if parties accept different restrictions listed in section 11 RTPA 1976. If two or more parties accept restrictions question (7) must be considered.
7. Does the agreement which is now prima facie registrable fit into one of the exempt categories of agreement specified in Schedule 3 RTPA 1976 or into one of the categories of non-notifiable agreements introduced by Order under section 27A RTRA 1976 or into one of the categories of non-notifiable agreements introduced by Order under section 27A RTPA 1976?

(3) Information agreements

Notes

1. Only information agreements concerning goods are registrable (services agreements have not as yet been called up for registration).
2. Only those agreements containing restrictions of a type described in the Restrictive Trade Practices (Information Agreements) Order 1969 S.I. 1969 No. 1842 need be registered. For detailed analysis see Chapter 9.

(4) Summary

The above questions seek to outline the salient features of a registrable agreement. A summary of these features would be as follows:

(i) There must be an agreement or trade association recommendation.
(ii) There must be at least two parties trading within the UK.
(iii) The agreement must contain a restriction of a sort listed in the Act.
(iv) The agreement must not be exempt for any reason.
(v) The agreement must have at least two parties who accept restrictions that are not exempt and are registrable.

The various categories of exemptions and of non-notifiable agreements referred to above are discussed in Chapter 2.

2 Agreements not Registrable under the RTPA 1976

A. Introduction

2.1 The system of control as laid down in the RTPA 1976 for restrictive agreements is highly complex. It is also selective; not all agreements are caught. In this chapter agreements excluded from control whether by virtue of the RTPA 1976 or by other statutes will be discussed. The following is a summary of the content of this chapter and may be used as a guide to exemptions.

Section B.	Exemption for agreements important to the national economy under section 29 RTPA 1976.
Section C.	Exemption of agreements holding down prices under section 30 RTPA 1976.
Section D.	Exemption for wholesale co-operative societies under section 32 RTPA 1976.
Section E.	Exemption for agricultural and forestry associations under section 33 RTPA 1976.
Section F.	Exemption for agreements authorised under the European Coal and Steel Community Treaty under section 34 RTPA 1976.
Section G.	Exemption for certain categories and types of service agreement under Schedule 1 RTPA 1976 and the Schedule to S.I. 1976 No. 98 The Restrictive Trade Practices (Services) Order 1976.
Section H.	Exemption for agreements for statutory purposes and rationalisation schemes under Schedule 3, para. 1 RTPA 1976.
Section I.	Exemption for exclusive dealing agreements and exclusive service supply agreements under Schedule 3, paras. 2 and 7 RTPA 1976.
Section J.	Exemption for know-how agreements concerning goods and services under Schedule 3, paras. 3 and 8 RTPA 1976.

Section K. Exemption for trade mark agreements under Schedule 3, para. 4 RTPA 1976.

Section L. Exemption for patent, registered design, and copyright agreements under Schedule 3, paras. 5 and 5A RTPA 1976.

Section M. Exemption for agreements relating to the supply of goods and services where the agreement has overseas operation only under Schedule 3, paras. 6 and 9 RTPA 1976.

Section N. Exemption for agreements involving the Crown.

Section O. Exemption for leasehold agreements and other property related contracts.

Section P. Exemption for agreements whose restrictions may be disregarded under sections 9 and 18 RTPA 1976.

Section Q. Exemption for certain non-competition covenants taken on change of ownership of a business under S.I. 1989 No. 1081, the Restrictive Trade Practices (Sale and Purchase and Share Subscription Agreements) (Goods) Order 1989, and S.I. 1989 No. 1082, the Restrictive Trade Practices (Services) (Amendment) Order 1989.

Section R. Agreements subject to the RTPA 1976 but non-notifiable as being below specified turnover thresholds: the Restrictive Trade Practices (Non-notifiable Agreements) (Turnover Threshold) Order 1996 (S.I. 1996 No. 348).[1]

Section S. Agreements subject to the RTPA 1976 but non-notifiable as being covered by an applicable EC block exemption: the Restrictive Trade Practices (Non-notifiable Agreements) (EC Block Exemptions) Order 1996 (S.I. 1996 No. 349).[2]

2.2 These exemptions cover a wide variety of goods and services. Knowledge and understanding of these provisions, therefore, is important to parties wishing to avoid competition problems, or, to parties who wish to know how to modify existing registrable agreements so as to bring them within an exemption and render them not subject to registration. Knowledge of these provisions is of course always relevant in discussions as to registrability with the OFT.

B. Agreements Important to the National Economy: section 29 RTPA 1976

2.3 Potential exists for the Secretary of State to exempt from the RTPA certain goods or services agreements deemed to be important to the national economy. Power to grant this exemption lies under section 29 RTPA 1976. This power can only be exercised in respect of an agreement submitted in draft form; the Department of Trade and Industry (DTI) which administers section 29 has no power to grant exemption to an agreement which has already been concluded.[3] Particulars of an agreement exempted need not be furnished. Failure to obtain exemption entails registration and possible reference to the Court for evaluation. Though an agreement only requires section 29

[1] Adopted pursuant to s. 27A RTPA 1976 itself inserted by s. 10 Deregulation and Contracting Out Act 1994.

[2] *ibid.*

[3] Competition Policy Division, Department of Trade and Industry, 1 Victoria Street, London SW1H 0ET.

treatment if it is not subject, in form, to an EC block exemption in which case it is, in any event, exempt from the duty to furnish particulars (see paras 2.250 and following). To obtain exemption parties to the draft agreement must persuade the DTI that it satisfies the conditions for exemption laid down in section 29(2)(a)–(e). It is important to note that section 29 is an exceptional provision applying to exceptional agreements. In appropriate circumstances parties subject to tight time constraints may negotiate exemption with the DTI in only a few weeks. The DTI has in the past accorded high priority to section 29 applications and seeks to expedite their passage, if appropriate, through the Act. Occasionally, the OFT refers an agreement to the DTI for consideration though more usually parties make direct representations to the DTI.

1. The Conditions for Exemption: section 29(2)

2.4 Parties to a proposed agreement must satisfy the DTI as to the conditions outlined in section 29(2)(a)–(e). The DTI views these criteria pragmatically while ensuring that they are properly complied with before exemption is granted. The criteria for exemption are examined below.

(1) "(a) that the agreement is calculated to promote the carrying out of an industrial or commercial project or scheme of substantial importance to the economy"

2.5 A number of agreements have passed through section 29; almost all of these successes have been since 1982. The agreements have concerned such matters as research and development in the agricultural biotechnology field; sub-contracting of production and marketing of the System X telephone system; joint research; development and marketing of gas turbine powered generating sets; and the construction of the Channel Tunnel. A specialisation agreement in the paper industry was exempted in 1969. In a set of guidelines issued jointly by the DTI and the OFT on the operation of the Restrictive Trade Practices Act 1976, it is stated that examples of the sorts of industrial or commercial projects envisaged by section 29 would be specialisation and standardisation agreements; agreements concerning the creation of new capacity or significant new employment prospects; and joint ventures to create industrial units large enough to compete in world markets.[4] No definition is given of the meaning of "substantial importance to the national economy". The DTI adopts a fairly pragmatic view of what is in the interests of the national economy which is more sophisticated than simply some positive impact on the balance of trade, so that enhancement of exports, although relevant, will not be the sole criterion. An agreement with employment enhancement prospects should fit the definition; an agreement of wider political importance might also be justifiable, for example the agreements in respect of the Channel Tunnel which helps improve intra-EC commercial trade links.[5] An agreement in a field of technological importance where the parties are engaged in international competition is of clear importance to the national economy.

2.6 There is doubt as to the word "substantial"; where this has arisen elsewhere in the RTPA 1976 the Court has refused to attach a specific meaning or value to the word

[4] *Guidelines on the Operation of the Restrictive Trade Practices Act 1976* (DTI and OFT, 1984).

[5] Exempt Register Nos CT/20/ER/151-161 (1988 and 1989). See also s. 33(5) Channel Tunnel Act 1987 and Orders made thereunder allowing the Secretary of State power to designate parties to the Tunnel Concession Agreement as inter-connected bodies corporate for the purposes of obtaining approval under s. 29 RTPA.

preferring to avoid a "strictly quantitative or proportional assessment".[6] The extent of the importance of the agreement to the national economy may thus be taken as a matter for the submission of economic and statistic data showing such factors as employment prospects; domestic and export potential; technological advances; spin-off effects for other products and markets; effect on distribution patterns in the market, etc.

(2) "(b) that its object or main object is to promote efficiency in a trade or industry or to create or improve productive capacity in an industry"

2.7 The agreement in question must have one or more of three objectives. First, it must promote efficiency; secondly, it must create productive capacity; and thirdly, it must improve productive capacity. It should be noted that these three objectives are not necessarily mutually exclusive.

2.8 *Promotion of efficiency* A joint research and development venture in the high-technology field might promote efficiency.[7] "Efficiency" is a vague term but economists would consider such factors as: (a) innovation, which means basic inventiveness and the ability to improve basic inventions; (b) production and entrepreneurial efficiency, which implies the ability to manufacture at the correct output to obtain economies of scale, the ability to deploy an effective distribution system to facilitate market penetration, the ability to meet sudden changes in demand pattern; and (c) effective use of resources, which includes full exploitation of management and expert skills, proper exploitation and licensing of intellectual property rights, and optimal use of plant to meet consumer needs.

2.9 *Creation of productive capacity* This objective was satisfied in an agreement between Rolls-Royce and GEC concerning the joint production and marketing of gas turbine generating sets.[8] Rolls-Royce are, of course, experts in the production and maintenance of gas-turbine engines; GEC had expertise in the manufacture of generating sets (a set of equipment powered by a gas turbine drive, the principal function of which is to generate electricity). The parties agreed to form a joint venture company for the joint production and marketing of gas turbine driven electricity generating sets. Neither of the parties separately would easily have been able to manufacture the product. However, jointly they could combine their complementary skills and create a new product. The generating set created could operate either in connection with or

[6] *Net Book Agreement No. 1* (1962) LR 3 RP 246 at p. 310; [1962] 1 WLR 1347. See also *R* v *MMC ex parte South Yorkshire Transport* [1993] 1 WLR 597 for a definition of "substantial" in the context of the merger provisions of the Fair Trading Act 1973.

[7] e.g. Exempt Register No. 149, Agreement concerning *Research and Development into Agricultural Biotechnology*. See *Black Bolt and Nut Association's Agreement* (1960) LR 2 RP 50 where Mr Justice Diplock (as he then was) when commenting on an agreement which entailed the fixing of prices, pointed out the value of the exchange of technical data and know-how between the parties and accepted that this exchange improved the efficiency of smaller firms. Moreover, he considered that the beneficial co-operation which took place could only have occurred in the absence of price competition: "It is only human nature to be more reluctant to impart 'know-how' to a competitor who may use it to, undercut one's own prices and take away one's own customers than to a competitor who can only use it to benefit himself and his product." There seems no reason why, had a s. 29 type provision been available in 1960 (which it was not) such a case might not have passed under it. Though, for criticism of the case, see Yamey (1961) 24 MLR 488.

[8] Exempt Register No. 148, *Agreement between Rolls-Royce Ltd, The General Electric Company plc and Lathetronic Ltd* (June 1984) (*The Gas Turbine Powered Generating Sets Agreement*).

independently of ancillary equipment and thus had the ability to be used in many contexts. Since it needed no connection to a national grid, it could be used, for example, on oil rigs or at power stations or in other isolated areas.

2.10 It seems that creating new capacity in the provision of a service would satisfy this requirement. Thus in the agreements exempted under section 29 for the construction of the Channel Tunnel,[9] the creation of new capacity in cross Channel transport services was considered to meet this requirement.

2.11 The relevant "capacity" here is productive capacity. It is a point for debate whether, for example, an agreement to provide extra storage capacity for raw materials needed in production is an exemptible agreement.

2.12 *Improvement of productive capacity* While a joint venture which combines complementary talents into the manufacture of a new products involves an element of creativity, many agreements have as their objective simply the improvement of existing capacity. A specialisation agreement whereby X and Y are competitors but agree to concentrate their efforts on the research, development and marketing of different products would be an example. As a result of this agreement X and Y will limit substantially the extent of competition between them. However, they improve significantly their capacity in the product they have specialised in and (hopefully) they will also have increased their product quality through the intensified effort. In one exempted agreement the parties entered a specialisation agreement for coated paper with the objective of avoiding duplication of capacity and wasting scale economics. The parties were anxious to increase capacity in order to meet the expected upturn in the demand for coated paper which would arise with the increased use of colour photography.[10] A draft agreement between British Telecommunications (BT), Plessey Telecommunications and Office Systems (P), and, GEC (G) concerning System X (the new BT telecommunication system) has also been cleared under section 29. The electrical equipment needed for System X was manufactured by third parties for BT. Under the agreement P were to be main contractors and G the principal sub-contractor. There was also provision for competitive tendering between P and G but only after a certain date. An express object of the agreement was "to achieve changes in the procurement and supply of System X to allow more effective production of equipment in higher volume at lower cost, with progressively improved features and facilities. This objective would permit GEC and Plessey to achieve their aim of expansion of export activity."[11]

2.13 It appears to be the case that an agreement to increase existing capacity in order to meet expected or potential demand is as equally exemptible as an agreement to increase capacity to meet existing demand. The specialisation agreement and other cases noted above certainly suggest this.

2.14 According to the wording of this exemption condition, the objectives listed above do not have to be the sole aim of the agreement. An agreement may entertain other

[9] See note 5.

[10] See e.g. Exempt Register No. 2, *Specialisation Agreement between Bowater Paper Corporation and Reed Paper Group Ltd* (1969) agreement terminated December 1977.

[11] Exempt Register No. 147, *Agreement between British Telecommunications, Plessey Telecommunications and Office Systems Ltd and The General Electricity Company plc* (October 1982) (*the System X Agreement*). See also No. 4036 Register of Restrictive Trade Practices, *Agreement between GEC and Standard Telephone and Cable concerning joint supply arrangement to the Post Office of digital line and multiplex systems equipment*. The agreement gained s. 21(2) exemption.

objects and still earn exemption so long as the objectives specified in the statute are, at least, the "main" objects.

(3) "(c) that the object cannot be achieved or achieved within a reasonable time except by means of the agreement or of an agreement for similar purposes"

2.15 This requirement is a common one for the assessment of joint ventures and simply means that restrictive agreements for beneficial ends should not be allowed if it can be established that the parties could achieve those ends individually without the artificial benefit of an agreement. It is thus incumbent upon the parties to convince the DTI that an agreement is essential to success. This might entail showing that the parties do not have adequate capital to "go it alone". Further, parties might show that they do not have adequate technology to act alone and that only in combination with another party could they succeed. Thus in the Rolls-Royce–GEC agreement concerning gas turbine powered electricity generators, an important element was the complementary nature of the respective companies' expertise. Indeed, in the preamble to the actual joint venture agreement it was recorded:

> "(A) each of GEC and RR possesses specialist expertise, which is technically complementary, in the development and construction of gas turbine powered equipment for the generation of electrical power, and they wish to establish a joint company to use that complementary expertise for applications above ten megawatts in unit output. (B) GEC and RR intend that such complementary expertise should encourage orderly technical research and development to establish a more effective product range than one which either GEC or RR acting separately could support."

2.16 Similarly in the coated paper specialisation agreement, had the parties not agreed to concentrate their research, development and production on different types of paper then they might have failed to be in a position to take advantage of the upswing in demand for such paper which arose when colour photography became popular. In that case the object of the agreement was an increase in capacity; the agreement was the means to achieve it.

2.17 It appears clear that the word "object" refers to the three objects outlined in section 29(2)(b), viz. promotion of efficiency, creation of productive capacity and, improvement of productive capacity.

2.18 Section 29(2)(c) provides another negotiating counter for the parties, who may argue that whilst it is possible that they could achieve the objective individually, the agreement is none the less necessary in order for the parties to achieve the object "within a reasonable time". Thus if X and Y combine in a joint venture company to increase their capacity and output in the expectation of an imminent increase in demand they may argue that the agreement enables them to fully meet demand from the very moment it increases. It might have been that alone they would, over an extended period of time, have increased output to match demand. However, this would have entailed lost sales during the period in which they were in the process of increasing the capacity. Alternatively, X and Y could be manufacturers of high-technology products who need to combine and pool technical skill in order to be able to produce a patentable article before international rivals. Again, the same product could have been produced individually, given time. However, the agreement was necessary for there to be realistic chance of winning the patent race.

2.19 In the final analysis the word "reasonable" depends on the circumstances of each case and will be a subject for discussion and negotiation with the DTI.

(4) "(d) that no restrictions are accepted or information provisions made under the agreement other than such as are reasonably necessary to achieve that object"

2.20 This lays down a rule of minimum restrictiveness. Similar rules, which require the parties to show that the restrictions in question are "indispensable" to success exist under Article 85(3) EC (the exempting formula for agreements prohibited by Article 85(1) EC).[12] All that the parties must do under the section is show that the restrictions are "reasonably necessary". Thus, parties need *not* show that in the absence of the restrictions the agreement would not have been entered by the parties. Parties need only show that the restrictions positively facilitate achievement of the objectives in question. Thus, for example, X and Y might argue that in the absence of a non-competition clause between them there would not have been a strong incentive on the parties to pool the know-how and technical information they needed for effective joint production. Alternatively, X and Y might argue that in the absence of a specialisation agreement between them with both parties agreeing to concentrate production on different products (e.g. different types of coated paper)[13] they would not be able to compete as effectively on the international market. Certainly they could have competed in the absence of the restriction but the restriction enables them to be better prepared for that market and facilitates its penetration.

2.21 It should be acceptable to argue about the utility of restrictions both collectively and individually, i.e. the individual effect of each restriction and the collective effect of all the restrictions together.[14] Though, it should not be expected that the DTI will accept repugnant restrictions upon the basis that the other restrictions are acceptable.

(5) "(e) that the agreement is on balance expedient in the national interest"

2.22 Section 29(2)(e) is elaborated upon by section 29(3) which provides that in considering the "national interest" the DTI "shall take into account any effects which an agreement is likely to have on persons not parties thereto as purchasers, consumers or users of any relevant goods ... or, as users of any relevant services". Section 29(3) is curious in that where the agreement concerns goods, the DTI must consider its effects on purchasers, consumers or users, but, where the agreement concerns services only the interests of users are to be considered. Section 29(3) provides that these categories of vested interest must be considered, the section is by no means an exhaustive definition of section 29(2)(e). The provision does not, therefore, exclude other factors being taken into account when the national interest is being considered. Clearly it would be absurd to equate the "national interest" with the parochial interests of purchasers, consumers and users (but apparently not suppliers to the parties) of that product or service. The "national interest" as a concept is undefined. It is unclear whether, given the economic nature of section 29, the national interest means the national economic interest or whether political and social factors may also be weighed in the balance. It is certainly arguable that "national interest" is far wider

[12] See e.g. *Thirteenth Commission Competition Report* (1983), para. 55; *Sixth Commission Competition Report* (1976), paras. 53–59; *Fourth Commission Competition Report* (1974), paras. 37–42. See e.g. Case 61/80 *Co-operative Stremzel* v *Commission* [1981] ECR 851. See also *Transocean Marine Paint* [1967] CMLR D9; [1974] 1 CMLR D11; [1975] 2 CMLR D75; [1980] CMLR 694.

[13] e.g. Exempt Register No. 2, *Specialisation Agreement between Bowater Paper Corporation and Reed Paper Group Ltd* (1969), agreement terminated 1977.

[14] cf. *ABTA's Agreement* [1984] ICR 12 at p. 24D "We propose to consider and test the restrictions not only in relation to each other but also against the total backcloth of the circumstances of the case."

than "national economy" (the words used in the heading to section 29) and that if the draftsman had intended "national interest" to mean the national economic interest then section 29(2)(e) would have been reworded as simply "national economy". Section 29(2)(e) is, at base, a get-out device for the government to avoid exempting an agreement that prima facie appears to justify exemption. It will be appreciated that the Secretary of State has discretion whether to grant exemption under the provision. This derives from the opening words of section 29(1): "*If it appears* to the Secretary of State ... that the conditions ... are complied with ... *he may* ..."[15]

2. *Types of Exemptible Agreement*

2.23 The application of section 29 to various types of agreement and the relevant cases will be discussed in subsequent chapters. None the less a brief survey of possible agreement types may be given here for purposes of quick reference: joint production and marketing; joint research and development; specialisation agreements; exchange of assets agreements; exchange of know-how and information; patent pooling; and, product standardisation. The list is obviously non-exhaustive.[16]

3. *Form and Extent of the Exemption*

2.24 Exemption is made in the form of a statutory Order made by the Secretary of State (though it will usually be signed on his behalf by a senior DTI civil servant).[17] The exemption will be for a period specified in the Order, say five years. This period may be extended by subsequent Order. The time period, or extension thereof, will in any event only be for a period long enough to allow the parties to achieve their objective. Accordingly, parties must be prepared for negotiations concerning the length of the exemption. An Order may be revoked at any time after the expiry of one year from the issue of the first Order.[18] Such a revocation, however, may only be made where it appears:

> "(a) that the object or main object of the agreement has not been or is not likely to be achieved, or that any other condition or exemption is no longer satisfied in respect of the agreement; or (b) that the agreement is used for purposes other than those for which it was approved."[19]

2.25 Exemption may also be withdrawn if facts come to the attention of the DTI which, had they been available earlier, would have induced them to refuse exemption.[20] In all cases of withdrawal of exemption 28 days' notice must be given to the parties. Current DTI policy appears to be to grant five-year exemptions which might not be considered a very long period.[21] Although, in the very first case on section 29, initial exemption was granted for six years and was later extended for four years more.[22]

[15] Emphasis not in original.

[16] See OFT and DTI publication, *Guidelines on the Operation of the Restrictive Trade Practices Act 1976* (1984), para. 6; Liesner Committee, *A Review of Restrictive Trade Practices Policy* (1979) Cmnd 7512, pp. 46, 47. The Channel Tunnel Agreements referred to in note 5 are clearly *sui generis*.

[17] s. 29(4) RTPA 1976.

[18] s. 29(5) RTPA 1976.

[19] s. 29(5)(a) and (b) RTPA 1976.

[20] s. 29(5) RTPA 1976.

[21] As in Exempt Register No. 147 (1982) (*System X*); Exempt Register No. 148 (1984) (*Gas-Turbine Powered Generating Sets*); Exempt Register No. 149 (1984) (*Agricultural Biotechnology*).

[22] Exempt Register No. 2, *Specialisation Agreement between Bowater Paper Corporation and Reed Paper Group Ltd*—exemption given in 1969, extension given in 1975 for a further four years. The agreement was terminated by the parties in 1977.

2.26 All agreements may only become exempt after they have been laid before each House of Parliament together with the Order proposed to be made exempting them from registration. All agreements are public documents and may be inspected at the Register of Restrictive Trade Practices compiled and supervised by the OFT. The agreements are placed on a public register entitled the Exempt Register.[23] Variations to agreements made by the parties do not require parliamentary approval, nor need they be placed on the register if the variation does not substantially affect the operation of the restrictions or information provisions accepted under the exempted agreement.[24]

2.27 A variation to an agreement must be notified to the Secretary of State within 21 days of being made. The Secretary of State has the power to revoke the original exemption.[25]

4. Section 29 Agreements and EC Law

2.28 Any agreement definable as important to the national economy will usually be of substantial proportions. Almost inevitably the agreement will have export ramifications. It seems certain, therefore, that such an agreement will require the approval not only of the DTI but also of the European Commission. Parties submitting a draft to the DTI for approval must therefore consider notifying their agreement to the Commission. Indeed the DTI as a rule request the parties to "clear the lines" with Brussels. It will be appreciated that an agreement that has approval under English law but which is unacceptable in European law will be of limited value;[26] this is a view held by the DTI. This is of course the case in relation to agreements *not* exempted by applicable block exemptions (for which see paras 2.250 and following).

An agreement falling foul of Article 85(1) is void under Article 85(2) EC. If a joint production venture seeks to sell in Europe then there is little point in seeking section 29 clearance if clearance under Article 85(3) is not forthcoming. Parties should thus ensure that they have the acceptance of the Commission of their agreement if it will have any significant effect on inter-state trade, a condition satisfied in the case of agreements providing for all but insignificant exports to Community countries.[27] An agreement whose market is the UK only may, none the less, restrict inter-Member State trade if it hinders the chances for other EC companies to compete in the UK. An agreement whose focus is exclusively outside of the EC should be free from EC competition law. Where the agreement concerns non-EC markets exclusively and has no impact on even the UK market, then it should not even require section 29 clearance, being exempt from control under Schedule 3(6) and (9) RTPA 1976 (agreements with overseas operation). Finally, the application of Article 85 EC is something that should be discussed with the DTI which under Article 5 EC are under a "duty of co-operation" to ensure the fulfilment of Community objectives. Theoretically, European law should be taken into consideration under section 29

[23] s. 29(6) RTPA 1976.

[24] s. 29(7) RTPA 1976.

[25] See paras. 2.30–2.35. For the relationship between EC and UK law, see paras. 6.114–6.119.

[26] In *Eurotunnel* OJ 1988 L311/36, the Commission granted negative clearance to agreements for the construction of the Channel Tunnel.

[27] The authority for this under UK law could be s. 29(2)(e) which requires the DTI to consider whether the agreement, on balance, is expedient to the national interest. It is certainly arguable as a matter of UK law that the national interest must be compatible with the European Community interest. As for the position from the point of view of EC law, Member States are required by Art. 5 EC to co-operate with the Community in achieving the objectives of the Treaty, and thus it would seem that Member States are required to bear in mind the Community's interest.

RTPA 1976.[28] In this respect the DTI does *not* require as a *pre-condition* of section 29 exemption the approval of the Commission. Formal exemption under Article 85(3) EC can take many months or even years to obtain. Exemption under section 29 can arise in a matter of only weeks. Obviously, therefore, the DTI cannot wait upon the results of Commission deliberations before making a decision.

5. Beneficial Agreements not Large Enough to Gain section 29 Exemption

2.29 If parties to an agreement decide that the agreement is not of large enough proportions to stand a realistic chance of section 29 exemption, then details of that agreement must either be furnished to the OFT or modified to avoid the statutory duty to furnish particulars.[29] If parties decide to furnish the agreement the OFT will have to assess the significance of the restrictions in it. Where the OFT is satisfied that the agreement has no significant restrictive consequences, it might seek dispensation from reference to the RPC under section 21(2) RTPA 1976. Details of this provision are given in at paras. 4.77 and following. Where the OFT identifies "significant" restrictions in an agreement which render usage of the section 21(2) procedure inappropriate, parties face a defence of their agreement before the RPC. In practice, parties usually modify agreements so as to avoid a Court hearing.

6. Variation of Agreements approved under section 29 RTPA 1976: section 29(5A)–(5H) and (6A) and (6B)[30]

2.30 An Order amending section 29 was made on 19 February 1996 and came into force on 19 March 1996. The Order creates a form of "opposition procedure" in respect of variations to agreements which have already been made the subject of exemption orders pursuant to section 29 RTPA 1976. The substance of the new provisions are as set out below.

2.31 In relation to an agreement approved by an Order under section 29 which is varied, the approval is treated as extending to the variation provided the Secretary of State receives particulars of the variation before the end of the period of 21 days from the day of the variation.[31] The "particulars" to be given to the Secretary of State are

[28] The problem of beneficial agreements that are too substantial to benefit from s. 21(2) RTPA 1976 but too small to fit within s. 29 RTPA 1976 was noted by the Liesner Committee, *A Review of Restrictive Trade Practices Policy* (1979) Cmnd 7512, paras. 5.44–5.46. They concluded that the word "substantial" should be withdrawn from s. 29(2)(a). The government has not amended s. 29 to implement this recommendation.

[29] See No. 4036 Register of Restrictive Trade Practices, *Agreement between GEC and Standard Telephone and Cable concerning a joint supply arrangement to the Post Office of digital line and multiplex systems equipment*. The agreement was given s. 21(2) clearance although, in 1982 the draft *Agreement between GEC, Plessey and BT concerning System X* was given s. 29 clearance.

[30] Introduced by virtue of the De-regulation (Restrictive Trade Practices Act 1976) (Amendment) (Variation of Exempt Agreements) Order 1996 (S.I. 1996 No.346) into s. 29 RTPA 1976. The Order was made in exercise of the powers conferred upon the Secretary of State s. 1 of the Deregulation and Contracting Out Act 1994. The Order was introduced to remove or reduce certain burdens affecting persons in the carrying on of a trade, business, profession or otherwise by the RTPA 1976 without removing any necessary protection afforded by that Act (Order Recital (a)). The Order was adopted following consultation with representative organisations and after a document setting out the Secretary of State's proposals had been laid before Parliament pursuant to s. (3) of the Deregulation and Contracting Out Act 1994 (Order Recitals (b) and (d)).

[31] s. 29(5A).

either the original or a true copy of the instrument varying the approved agreement, or in other cases, a memorandum in writing setting out the variation signed by at least one party to the agreement. Upon receipt of such particulars the Secretary of State is required to consider whether the agreement should cease to be approved under section 29 as a result of the variation. He is required to give notice of his decision (whether for or against) to *each* of the parties to the agreement (and not just the party notifying, if only one) within 28 days of receipt of the particulars.[32] Where the Secretary of State decides that approval should lapse and where he has given notice to the parties of his decision he is empowered (but not obliged) to revoke the Order, by a second Order. However, he may adopt an Order to revocation only upon expiry of a period of 28 days beginning with the date of the notice.

2.32 In the event that the Secretary of State is furnished with particulars of successive variations (for example the parties furnish to the Secretary of State particulars of a new variation, fourteen days after having furnished particulars of a first variation) then the duty of the Secretary of State is to abandon his existing assessment of the variation and to consider the combined effect of the variations when deciding whether or not the approval should lapse.[33]

2.33 It may well occur that, the Secretary of State having given notice to the parties of his decision that an approval should cease, the parties seek further to amend the agreement to overcome the objections of the Secretary of State. The parties might, for example, rescind their earlier variation or amend the same so as to remove the vices identified by the Secretary of State. Section 29(5F) provides that when the Secretary of State received particulars of a variation in circumstances where he has already given to the parties a notice that the agreement should cease to be approved but where he has not yet revoked the Order granting the approval under section 29, then the power[34] to adopt an Order of revocation should not become exercisable or shall cease to be exercisable. Instead, the Secretary of State is required to consider the combined effect of the variation which was the subject of the prior notice and the variation to which the subsequent particulars relate. In other words he, once again, examines the merits in the round.

2.34 In circumstances where the Secretary of State is required to reconsider a variation of an approved agreement as a result of the furnishing of particulars of a *second* variation, the time limit for the exercise of the power to adopt an Order of revocation changes from the 28-day period provided for in section 29(5D). The time limit which *now* applies depends upon whether the Secretary of State has hitherto adopted a decision[35] and a notice thereof has been served upon the parties to the agreement. Where such a decision has been taken the time limit is either: (a) 56 days from the date particulars were first furnished of a variation which is the subject matter of the decision; alternatively (b) if the date is earlier then the time period is the end of the period of 28 days beginning with the date of notice of the decision. In cases where the variation to which the Secretary of State's decision relates has already been the subject of a prior decision then the time limit is the ordinary time limit set out in section 29(5D), namely upon the expiry of 28 days beginning with the date of the notice.

[32] s. 29(5C).
[33] s. 29(5E).
[34] Conferred by s. 29(5D).
[35] Under s. 29(5D).

2.35 Under section 29(5C) the Secretary of State is required to decide whether or not the Order of approval should cease as a result of the variation. He is required to give notice of his decision to each of the parties within 28 days of receipt of the particulars. The decision in question may be positive or negative; it might indicate that approval is to cease or it might indicate that approval is to continue. In the latter case the Secretary of State is required[36] to lay before each House of Parliament a copy of the Notice and of the variation to which the Notice relates; and make available for public inspection a copy of the variation. The Secretary of State may dis-apply the publication requirement in relation to variations which the Secretary of State con-siders insignificant.[37]

2.36 In the event that an approval Order lapses, for example because particulars of a variation are not furnished to the Secretary of State within 28 days of their having been made, or because the Secretary of State adopts an Order of revocation, the agreement falls back into the general provisions of the RTPA 1976 and becomes subject to registration. If particulars of the agreement will already have been furnished to the DGFT as part of the initial application for section 29 clearance, the losing of section 29 exemption will not, without more, result in the agreement becoming unlawful pursuant to section 35 RTPA 1976 for failure to furnish particulars. It is to be noted that the obligation to furnish particulars of variations applies regardless of whether or not the variation constitutes a relevant restriction for the purposes of the Act. If the variation does give rise to a relevant restriction the Order of approval lapses because particulars were not furnished to the Secretary of State within 21 days thereof, section 35 is not thereby engaged. The parties will still have sufficient time in which to furnish particulars under the normal provisions of the Act.[38]

C. Section 30 RTPA 1976: Agreements Holding Prices Down

2.37 The Secretary of State and the Minister for Agriculture, Fisheries and Food may make orders of a fixed duration, approving agreements made at their request which relate exclusively to the prices or charges to be made in connection with transactions of any description and which are designed to either prevent or restrict increases or to secure reductions in prices. Such approved agreements are exempt from registration. An identical power is granted to those authorities in respect of any term included in an agreement at their request. In determining whether an agreement is to be registered, terms so incorporated are to be disregarded. Approval orders may not be of more than two years in duration though they may subsequently be extended for further periods of two years maximum. Orders may be revoked without notice to the parties (contrast under section 29) if it appears to the authority that the agreement is being

[36] s. 29(6B).
[37] s. 29(7) RTPA 1976 as amended by Art. 2(4) of the Order.
[38] para. 2 of the Explanatory Note states: "this Order amends the Restrictive Trade Practices Act 1976 which requires that restrictive agreements between two or more persons carrying on business in the United Kingdom in the production or supply of goods or supply or services be furnished to the Director General of Fair Trading for registration. This Order changes the procedure for dealing with variation agreements which are exempt from registration by virtue of Orders made under ss. 29 or 30 of the Act. At present, if variations are not approved by a further Order before they are made, the original Order made under ss. 29 or 30 ceases to have effect and the agreement becomes subject to registration."

used for non-approved purposes. As with section 29, copies of the agreements must be made public. Confidential and/or secret information contained in contracts need not be made public. Parties should make submissions to the relevant authorities if they wish to have data held back from the public register.

2.38 It should be fully appreciated that the authorities cannot, *ex post facto*, approve agreements or terms. The agreement or term must be made at the authorities' request. There is presumably, however, nothing to prevent parties from requesting the authorities to request them to enter an agreement or incorporate a term which keeps prices down. It has been common practice hitherto for price agreements to be concluded on the initiative of the government.

2.39 Section 30 is rarely if ever used today, though prior to 1980 there were nearly 150 agreements approved by this procedure. Many of these cases concerned the Secretary of State for Prices and Consumer Protection in requesting trade associations to recommend restrictions on price increases for staple products over an often short period of time. Although the section has received little attention over recent years due to a reluctance on the part of government to intervene in price mechanisms it could theoretically enjoy a revival. A factor which influences its usage will be the rate of inflation since curbs on price rises would represent an unnecessary control whilst the annual rate of inflation is low. Clearly, inflation rates need not always remain happily low and hence the potential for section 30 Orders remains. A number of (now historical) cases are outlined below which show up characteristic features of section 30 price control schemes.

2.40 If an agreement, or term of an agreement which is approved by an Order under section 30 is subsequently varied the approval extends to the agreement or term as varied.[39] However, the Order ceases to have effect if particulars of the variation are not received by the competent authority which made the Order before the end of the period of 21 days from the date of the variation. When the variation is made by a written instrument the original of the variation or a true copy thereof are to be produced to the competent authority. Where the variation is in any other form a memorandum in writing must be given signed by one of the parties to the agreement. Where a competent authority receives such particulars, that authority may by Order revoke the approval Order if it appeals to the authority that as a result of the variation the agreement or term should no longer be approved for the purposes of section 30. Unlike in relation to agreements exempt pursuant to section 29 RTPA 1976 there are no provisions whereby the competent authority must take a decision upon a variation, give notice of its decision to the affected parties, or exercise its power or revocation within a fixed period of time. Under section 39(4A) the competent authority appears not to be fettered in the manner or timing of any Order of revocation.

(1) Case study I: bread prices (1978): strikes and prices[40]

2.41 During a bakery workers' strike in November 1978, the Secretary of State for Prices and Consumer Protection requested the National Association of Master Bakers, Confectioners and Caterers to recommend to its members that, should the strike not end before the end of the month, they restrict their prices for a period of 12 days or,

[39] s. 30 was amended by the Deregulation (Restrictive Trade Practices Act 1976) (Amendment) (Variation of Exempt Agreements) Order 1996, S.I. 1996 No. 346 made on 19 February 1996, coming into force on 19 March 1996 which introduced the new s. 30(4H) and amended s. 30(5).

[40] Exempt Register No. 146, *National Association of Master Bakers, Confectioners and Caterers (bread prices)* (1978).

if the strike ended before expiry of that period, until the strike ended. The trade association duly made the recommendation to members and exemption from registration under section 30 was granted. It is interesting to note: (a) that the section 30 exemption derived from the initiative of the government and not the parties; (b) the very short period of time for which the exemption was to last; and (c), that the procedure was used as a means of strategically controlling prices during a strike.

(2) Case study II: coffee prices (1978): regulated price increases[41]

2.42 This case, which concerned increases in coffee prices, was typical of many others. The Secretary of State requested retail trade organisations to recommend to members of the group that they restrict increases for specified categories of coffee during a six-month period in 1977. Depending on size of retail outlet the permissible increases in gross margin were from up to 5 per cent to up to 7 per cent. "Gross margin" meant the difference between the buying price and the selling price measured as a percentage of the selling price. The trade organisation proposed that its retailer members co-operate with the government. Thus, they recommended that members be prepared to show any relevant records to authorised officials in the event of a complaint. Members were asked to identify the special categories of price controlled products by use of the phrase "low margin" at the point of sale. There was a review of the scheme after six months and an agreement whereby, if the Secretary of State considered renewing his request beyond the initial six months, there would be consultations with the retail trade. The Department of Prices and Consumer Protection prepared a draft letter to be sent to members by the trade organisation. Similar schemes were effected at the same time by the Scottish Grocers Federations and other symbol groups (Mace and Spar).

(3) Case study III: shoes: price freezes[42]

2.43 During 1978 and 1979 the government sought to control shoe prices; they hence encouraged traders to accede to requests to voluntarily regulate price increases. The agreements in question, which were given section 30 clearance, were between major shoe retailers (for example K Shoe Shops Ltd accepted the regulation) who gave undertakings to freeze prices. Thus, for illustration, K Shoe Shops Ltd agreed to restrict its prices so that in the 1978 and 1979 accounting periods its gross margin would not exceed its gross margin for its 1977 accounting period. "Gross margin" was defined by the government to mean "the difference, expressed as a percentage of the value of sales, between the value of sales (excluding VAT) of all goods sold by retail by the company, and the cost (excluding VAT) to it of these goods". It is instructive to note that here the price control was based on a freeze in increases. This maintained the price differentials prevailing between brands and, accordingly, did not dramatically effect the competitive relationship between traders *inter se*.

(4) Case study IV: Selective Price Restraint Scheme 1976 and the Retail Consortium: elements in schemes to ensure flexibility[43]

2.44 During 1976 the government embarked upon an ambitious price restraint scheme whereby price increases of only 5 per cent would be accepted by suppliers of a wide

[41] Exempt Register No. 144, *Retail Margins on Coffee* (1977).
[42] Exempt Register No. 145, *Shoes* (1978).
[43] Exempt Register No. 105, *Selective Price Restraint Scheme* (1976). For other interesting examples see Exempt Register No. 56, exemption by the Minister of Technology for *Early Warning Systems* (1969); Exempt Register No. 65, exemption by Ministry of Agriculture Fisheries and Food for *Beer Prices* (1969).

range of products to the scheme over a six-month period. Following discussions the Retail Consortium agreed to recommend to its retail members that they freeze selling prices of products in the scheme unless the suppliers price was increased. Where supplier prices did increase more than 5 per cent retailers were requested to keep their price increases to 5 per cent. Retailers were further exhorted to refrain from altering price differentials between competitive products. Suppliers would be free from the obligation to restrain selling price to a retailer who distorted price differentials to the detriment of the suppliers product. One interesting aspect of this scheme was contained in paragraphs 4(b) and (c) of the letter sent to a retail consortium. These read:

> "(b) if as a consequence of rising costs or falling volume the maintenance of the 5 per cent limit on scheme items would result in a significant reduction in a retailers over-all net profit margin he will be free to withdraw one or more, or all, items from the schemes as necessary; (c) the Government will be prepared to endorse a retailer's withdrawal in part or in whole form the scheme, and to explain and defend it in public as necessary, if the retailer has been able to show to the satisfaction of the Government (who will consult the appropriate trade associations as necessary) that its action was necessary for the reasons above."

2.45 The government in fact undertook intensive media advertising of the scheme to explain to the public the efforts being made by retailers and suppliers of staple foods. The scheme, moreover, was introduced despite the fact that at the period profit margins of manufacturers, of services and of the distributive trades were at very low levels, putting at risk both employment and investment prospects. The express purpose of the scheme, according to the government letter sent to the Retail Consortium, was to assist in the battle against the raging inflation then prevailing.

(5) Case study V: recommendations of CBI 1972: staggering of price increases[44]

2.46 Under this scheme the Secretary of State requested the CBI to propose to members that they should agree to certain terms for the prices to be charged for goods and services being terms designed to prevent or restrict price increases. As with other section 30 cases on trade associations, the recommendations to be made to members in implementation of the scheme were exempted from registration. Members who complied with the scheme signed an undertaking (specimens of which were provided by the government for the purpose) to the effect that they undertook to do their utmost to: (a) avoid raising prices for products or services supplied in the United Kingdom; (b) to limit unavoidable price increases to 5 per cent or less; (c) to time price increases to be at least twelve months distant from previous increases or where impossible at least eight months and at a maximum rate proportional to an annual rate of 5 per cent; (d) where, exceptionally, larger increases were imperative to limit the weighted average of price changes over the whole range of products or services to 5 per cent or less.

D. Section 32 RTPA 1976: Wholesale Co-operative Societies

2.47 Under section 32 RTPA 1976 the Secretary of State may approve certain Wholesale Co-operative Societies so that they are not treated as trade associations or services

[44] Exempt Register No. 67, *Recommendations of CBI* (1972).

supply associations under the Act. To be "approved" under this section the Society must satisfy the DTI:

> "(a) that it carries on business in the production or supply of goods or in the supply of services or in the application to goods of any process of manufacture;
> (b) that its shares are wholly or mainly held by industrial and provident societies; and
> (c) that those societies are retail societies or societies whose shares are wholly or mainly held by retail societies."[45]

2.48 Once approved the Society is not treated under the Act as a trade/service supply association. Accordingly, any recommendation, for example as to bargain offers, made by the Society to its members would not be registrable. This approval runs for a two-year period which may on subsequent occasions be extended for further two-year periods.[46] The approval may, however, be withdrawn at any time by the Secretary of State in the case of any agreement or recommendation made by the Society that would, in the absence of this exempting approval, have rendered that agreement or recommendation registrable. However, such an approval will only be withdrawn if it appears to the Secretary of State that, "the agreement or recommendation has such adverse effects on competition that it should not be precluded from being investigated by the Court under the provisions of this Act".[47] Once withdrawal of approval occurs the Society in question is subject to the normal rigours of the Act.[48]

E. Section 33 RTPA 1976: Agricultural, Forestry and Fisheries Associations

1. Section 33: Details

2.49 Under section 33 RTPA 1976, the duty to register does not apply to agricultural, forestry and fisheries associations carrying out certain functions and exhibiting certain characteristics. The exemption applies to associations, associations of associations (federations), and co-operative associations.[49]

2.50 Association, and associations of associations, obtain exemption if they satisfy certain conditions.[50] Co-operative associations on the other hand need not satisfy the conditions to enjoy exemption.[51] The "conditions" are laid out in section 33(3) and may be summarised as follows:

[45] s. 32(1)(a)–(c) RTPA 1976. An industrial and provident society is a society registered or deemed to be registered under the Industrial and Provident Societies Act 1965–78 or under the Industrial and Provident Societies (Northern Ireland) Act 1969—s. 32(7) RTPA 1976. A "retail society" means a society which carries on business in the sale by retail of goods for the domestic or personal use of individuals dealing with the Society, or in the provision of services for such individuals.
[46] s. 32(3), (4) RTPA 1976.
[47] s. 32(4)(b) RTPA 1976.
[48] s. 32(6) RTPA 1976.
[49] s. 33 re-enacts *mutatis mutandis* s. 1(2) Agriculture and Forestry Associations Act 1962. The provisions for fisheries were added by s. 44 Agriculture (Miscellaneous Provisions) Act 1968.
[50] s. 33(2)(a) and (b).
[51] s. 33(2)(c).

(a) the association is, or is deemed to be, registered under the Industrial and Provident Societies Acts 1965 to 1978 or under the Industrial and Provident Societies Act (Northern Ireland) 1969 or, if a company within the meaning of the Companies Act 1985, contains in its constitution such provisions as may be prescribed by order of the Ministers with respect to numbers of members, numbers of shares held by members, profits distribution, voting rights or other matters;[52]
(b) at least 90 per cent of the voting power is attached to shares held by persons occupying land used for agriculture and or forestry or by persons engaged in fishing;
(c) the only business, or the principal business, carried on by the association is essentially concerned with the marketing or preparation for marketing of agricultural or forestry or fisheries produce produced or caught by members of the associations. The association may be concerned with the supply of goods to members required for the production of produce or the catching of fish or the performance of forestry tasks without losing exemption from the Act.

2.51 Associations and associations of associations which satisfy these conditions and co-operative associations are exempt from the legislation only to the extent laid down in section 33(1). This provides that the Act does not apply to these bodies for the purposes of or in connection with the marketing or preparation for market of produce produced or caught by members, or, the supply by the association to the members of goods required in production or fishing, or, for the production or supply of produce or the catching or supply of fish by members themselves.

2.52 Clearly the exemption is very broad taking out of the scope of the legislation many agricultural or fisheries activities of associations, co-operative associations or their members. However, the relevant ministers may by statutory instrument withdraw this exemption from any class of agreement they see fit.[53]

2. *Other Relevant Statutory Exemptions and Provisions in Agriculture*

2.53 While considering agricultural provisions a number of other statutory provisions warrant mention.

(1) Section 8 Plant Varieties and Seeds Act 1964[54]

2.54 This provides that the RTPA 1976 does not apply—(a) to any licence granted by a holder of plant breeders' rights or by any other person authorised to grant a licence in respect of such rights; (b) to any assignment of plant breeders' rights or of the title to apply for the grant of such rights; or (c) to any agreement for such a licence or assignment. The licence, assignment or agreement so exempted is one under which restrictions are accepted only in respect of goods which are plants or parts of plants of the plant variety which is the subject of those plant breeders' rights or will be the subject of them if granted. Consequently, an agreement is only exempted if it relates

[52] For the detailed rules concerning implementation of s. 33(3)(a) see Art. 4 of Agricultural and Forestry Association Order 1982 S.I. 1982 No. 569.

[53] s. 33(4). This power has been exercised in respect of the Order described above. S.I. 1982 No. 569 contains six articles concerning: citation and commencement—Art. 1; revocation—Art. 2; interpretation—Art. 3; provisions to be contained in the memorandum or articles of association—Art. 4; application of s. 33(1) RTPA 1976, i.e. types of agreement that are exempt—Art. 5; amount of business to be done with members by certain associations if the exemption in s. 33(1) is to remain—Art. 6.

[54] The 1964 Act refers to the RTPA 1956. Sch. 5, para. 3 RTPA 1976 amends reference to the 1956 Act to reference to the RTPA 1976.

exclusively to plant breeders' rights. An agreement containing additional restrictions is not exempt. If additional restrictions are included then the whole of the agreement becomes registrable and not just the additional restrictive elements. This exemption follows the basic pattern of the general exemption for patents and registered designs and licences, assignments and agreements relating thereto. Reference should be made to section 1 of this chapter for analysis. This exemption, however, will be of limited value to any firm with export aspirations. The Court of Justice has made it patently clear that licences of plant breeder rights are subject to EC competition laws where the licence extends beyond simply granting a use right (see para. 13.17).

(2) Section 45 Agriculture (Miscellaneous Provisions) Act 1968

2.55 This permits agricultural marketing boards to notify their agreements to the appropriate minister and to obtain exemption from the RTPA 1976 if the minister does not object. Only certain agreements, however, are exempted in this way, these being agreements entered into by marketing boards in the exercise of their powers under sections 20(1) and 36 of the Agricultural Marketing Act 1958. It is interesting to note that in section 20(2) of this Act powers exercised by the boards are, in some circumstances, subject to control by the minister whose function it is to safeguard the public interest. Correspondingly, the minister is statutorily required to consider the competition law aspects of the agreement and make appropriate directions to cure any harmful aspects of the agreement.

(3) Section 9(11) Agriculture Act 1967

2.56 This permits the relevant minister to grant exemptions to agreements entered into by the Meat and Livestock Commission in connection with a development scheme.

(4) Schedule 1(3) Cereals Marketing Act 1965

2.57 This provision simply provides that the Home Grown Cereals Authority shall not be treated as a trade association for the purpose of the RTPA 1976.[55] Consequently, recommendations of the Authority will not be registrable in the same way as recommendations of ordinary trade associations are.

F. Section 34 RTPA 1976: Authorisations under the ECSC Treaty: Coal and Steel Agreements

2.58 Section 34 RTPA 1976 reads, simply: "An agreement is exempt from registration under this Act so long as there is in force in relation to that agreement an authorisation given for the purpose of any provision of ECSC Treaty relating to restrictive trade practices." The principal article of the ECSC Treaty by which restrictive agreements may be authorised is Article 65 ECSC. Under this article the European Commission has exclusive competence (i.e. to the exclusion of national courts) to grant authorisations.[56] Section 34 does not say that restrictive agreements authorised under the ECSC Treaty are excluded from the Act. It says rather that such agreements are caught by the Act but exempt from registration. This has important consequences. Since the agree-

[55] Amended from RTPA 1956 by Sch. 5, para. 4 RTPA 1976.

[56] cf. Case C-128/92 *H.J. Banks* v *British Coal Corporations* [1993] ECR I-1209.

ment is caught by the RTPA 1976 it cannot be referred to the Monopolies and Mergers Commission under the monopoly provisions of the Fair Trading Act 1973 (see section 10(2)), though there is nothing in the FTA 1973 to preclude the merger provisions of the FTA. Thus, a coal and steel agreement may be referred to the MMC under the merger provisions. This was illustrated in the MMC investigation into *British Steel plc/C Walker and Sons (Holdings) Ltd*, where a steel merger came within the exclusive jurisdiction of the EC Commission under the ECSC, while those products not covered by the ECSC remained the subject of a merger reference to the MMC under the Fair Trading Act 1973.[57] Conduct relating to such an agreement might not technically be excluded from the Competition Act 1980. Section 2(2) of that Act only excludes from its ambit a course of conduct that is required or envisaged by a material provision of, or a material recommendation in, "an agreement which is registered or subject to registration under the Restrictive Trade Practices Act 1976 ..."

2.59 Coal and steel agreements are also excluded from the RTPA 1976 by section 9(1) and (2) of the Act. These have already been discussed at para. 1.74 and reference thereto may be made for further details.

G. Service Agreements Exempt from Control

2.60 Details of exempt services agreements may be found in either the Schedule to the Restrictive Trade Practices (Services) Order 1976 S.I. 1976 No. 98, or Schedule 1, Restrictive Trade Practices Act 1976. The OFT deals with a significant number of cases each year in which exemption under one of the above mentioned two instruments is under debate.[58]

2.61 On interpretation, it should be noted that the wording and style of various exemptions differs and no common rules of construction can apply. The exemptions use various techniques, for example: limiting general words by reference to specific, bracketed words; limiting activities by reference to statutory provisions elsewhere; limiting activities by use of the words "in their capacity as such". Each provision must be examined individually and, where appropriate, expert evidence adduced to clarify its meaning.

1. Schedule 1, RTPA 1976: Professional Services Exempt from Registration[59]

2.62 The following types of services agreement fall outside of the RTPA 1976. It should be stressed that agreements entered into by such parties are not immune from challenge by the European Commission under EC law if the agreement affects trade between Member States of the Community.

(1) Legal services

2.63 "Legal services (that is to say, the services of barristers, advocates or solicitors in their capacity as such". Thus, an agreement between three local solicitors to fix conveyancing fees is not registrable. An agreement by solicitors to fix fees for acting as

[57] The MMC concluded that the proposed merger might be expected not to operate against the public interest. The European Commission also authorised that part of the merger which came within its jurisdiction, see *Twentieth Report on Competition Policy* (1990), para. 132.

[58] DGFT Annual Report 1983, p. 43.

[59] See for a critical view of the professions, MMC Report *Supply of Professional Services* (1970) Cmnd 4463. See paras. 11.191–11.192

advisers on house and garden improvements would not be exempt since such activities could hardly be said to relate to the services of lawyers "in their capacity as such". More equivocal would be whether solicitors fixing fees for offering estate agency services would remain within Schedule 1. On the basis that exceptions are to be construed narrowly, it seems safer to assume that Schedule 1 would not apply to such an agreement, as there is authority for arguing that one looks at the extent of a profession's ordinary activities in practice.[60]

2.64 However, the position may be different in Scotland. In *Aberdeen Solicitors Property Centre Ltd and Anor* v *DTFT*[61] the RPC (Scotland) held that the long tradition within Scotland that heritable property had been largely marketed by solicitors meant that estate agency services provided by solicitors in Scotland constituted legal services. Accordingly, an agreement whereby a number of solicitors' firms regularly used the services of a company to advertise properties being sold by them, which services were provided subject to rules made by the company after consultation with the regular users, among which was a rule against the advertisement of properties which were being marketed jointly by a solicitors' firm and an estate agents' firm, constituted a restriction falling within the exempt category of restrictions set out in Schedule 1 RTPA 1976.

(2) Medical services

2.65 "Medical Services (that is to say the provision of medical or surgical advice or attendance and the performance of surgical operations)". The words in brackets define what is meant by medical services. They appear to be widely drafted to include all form of advisory work and all forms of surgery. The word attendance presumably implies attending to the needs of patients and this would include the provision of drugs and other forms of medical aid.

(3) Dental services

2.66 "Dental services (that is to say, any services falling within the practice of dentistry within the meaning of the Dentists Act 1984)". The definition of the practice of dentistry in section 37 of the Dentists Act, while vague, is none the less broad:

> "the practice of dentistry shall be deemed to include the performance of any such operation and the giving of any such treatment, advice or attendance as is usually performed or given by dentists, and any person who performs any operation or gives any treatment, advice or attendance on or to any person as preparatory to or for the purpose of or in connection with the fitting, insertion or fixing of dentures, artificial teeth or other dental appliances shall be deemed to have practiced dentistry within the meaning of this Act."

2.67 It is important to note that the enumeration of dental functions in section 37 is expressed to be non-exhaustive: the practice of dentistry simply includes, among other things, those functions. Factual evidence given by experts would have to be submitted to the OFT to prove the ambit of a dentist's functions if an agreement was entered into between dentists which concerned matters not mentioned in section 37.

[60] The point was raised but not decided in a motion to strike out in *Royal Institution of Chartered Surveyors* v *DGFT* [1981] ECC 587, discussed in para 2.79 below.

[61] *The Times*, 20 February 1996. See also *Aberdeen Solicitors Property Centre* DGFT Annual Report 1993, p. 40; and *Edinburgh Solicitors Property Centre* DGFT Annual Report 1994, p. 48.

(4) Ophthalmic services

2.68 "Ophthalmic Services (that is to say, the testing of sight)". An agreement between opticians concerning the sale price of eye glass frames or contact lenses not relating to the "testing" or sight is accordingly not exempt under the RTPA 1976.

(5) Veterinary services

2.69 "Veterinary Services (that is to say, any services which constitute veterinary surgery within the meaning of the Veterinary Surgeons Act 1966)". Under section 27 (interpretation) of the Veterinary Surgeons Act 1966, "veterinary surgery" means: "the art and science of veterinary surgery and medicine and, without prejudice to the generality of the foregoing, shall be taken to include—(a) the diagnosis of diseases in, and injuries to, animals including tests performed on animals for diagnostic purposes; (b) the giving of advice based upon such diagnosis; (c) the medical or surgical treatment of animals; and (d) the performance of surgical operation on animals". The functions in (a)–(d) are only examples of a veterinary surgeons functions. Section 27 simply gives as a definition—"the art and science of veterinary surgery and medicine". Consequently, if an agreement in this profession does not clearly fit within the categories of (a)–(d) then it might be necessary to adduce expert evidence as to the precise scope of a veterinary surgeon's functions.

(6) Nursing services

2.70 "The services of nurses". Schedule 1(6) is amended by Schedule 7(27) Nurses, Midwives and Health Visitors Act 1979. This Act repeals the Nurses Act 1957 and the Nurses and Midwives Act (Northern Ireland) 1970 and part repeals the Nurses (Scotland) Act 1957. These latter three are specifically mentioned in the unamended version of Schedule 1(6) RTPA 1976. No definition of nursing is given in the 1979 Act. However, some assistance might be obtained by examining the rules for admission to the register of qualified nurses. One thing is clear, the definition of "nurse" includes a person qualified in another Member State of the EC as a nurse and who holds qualifications designated by the Secretary of State by order as having "Community equivalence" for purposes of registration (section 11 (3)(b) of the 1979 Act).

(7) Midwives, physiotherapists and chiropodists

2.71 "The services of midwives, physiotherapists of chiropodists in their capacity as such". The words "in their capacity as such" are used throughout the Schedule.[62] It will require factual expert evidence to be submitted to the OFT (or the Court) in order that the ambit of these services be determined. It is doubtful (or at best a question for argument) whether the sale of accessories connected with those professions can be described as being within the services provided. Sales of accessories constitute the supply of goods and agreements in connection with such sales may be registrable.

(8) Architects

2.72 "The services of architects in their capacity as such". Since no guidance is given as to interpretation nor any statute referred to for a definition the services of architect can only be determined in any case of doubt by the submission of relevant evidence.[63]

[62] See para. 2.84.
[63] For definition of "as such", see para. 2.84.

(9) Accountants and auditors, and insolvency services

2.73 "Accounting and auditing services (that is to say, the making or preparation of accounts or accounting records and the examination, verification and auditing of financial statements)". This paragraph is problematic. The central question is whether the bracketed words define the meaning of "auditing services" or "accounting and auditing services". If the bracketed words define the latter then the exemption is narrow; if the former then it is wide. The bracketed words describe very narrow activities: accountants commonly advise on tax, financial policy, international trade, management policy, marketing and a plethora of other commercial and consultancy issues. However, the bracketed words refer only to book-keeping activities and not to general non-book-keeping accountancy matters. It would seem the better view that the bracketed words limit only the meaning of "auditing services". Thus, an agreement between accountants as to fees to be charged for tax advisory services is probably not registrable. This conclusion, however, is by no means free from doubt.

2.74 Under s. 439(2) Insolvency Act 1986 a new paragraph 9A is added to the Schedule 1 exemptions.[64] The new para. 9A reads: "9A. Insolvency services within the meaning of section 428 of the Insolvency Act 1986".

2.75 Section 428(3) defines insolvency services as: "the services of persons acting as insolvency practitioners or carrying out under the law of Northern Ireland functions corresponding to those mentioned in section 388(1) or (2) in Part XIII, in their capacity as such". This is a somewhat unhelpful definition. However, sections 388 (1) and (2) of the 1986 Act define in detail the functions of an insolvency practitioner. These are as follows and may be divided into two separate categories: (i) insolvency practitioners in relation to companies; and (ii) insolvency practitioners in relation to individuals. As regards category (i) such a practitioner acts in relation to a company as either its liquidator, provisional liquidator, administrator or administrative receiver, or, as its supervisor of a composition or scheme approved by it under Part I of the Insolvency Act 1986 (i.e. voluntary arrangements). As regards category (ii) such a practitioner acts in relation to an individual by acting as that individual's: trustee in bankruptcy or interim receiver of his property or as permanent or interim trustee in the sequestration of his estate; trustee under a deed which is a deed of arrangement made for the benefit of his creditors or, in Scotland, a trust deed for his creditors; supervisor of a voluntary arrangement proposed by him and approved under Part VIII of the Insolvency Act 1986; or, as administrator of the estate of a deceased person whose estate is subject to an Order issued by the Lord Chancellor under section 421 of the 1986 Act (orders in respect of insolvent estates of deceased persons).

2.76 The definition of "insolvency practitioner" is thus defined by section 1 of the 1986 Act. Paragraph 9A excludes the RTPA 1976 from agreements made by such practitioners but only where they are acting "in their capacity as such". This, it will be appreciated is the standard proviso to Schedule 1 exemptions.[65] Section 428(2) of the 1986 Act is explicit as to which restrictive agreements are exempt from the RTPA 1976. These, it will be noted, repeat section 11 RTPA, *mutatis mutandis*. For the sake of clarity these exempt restrictions are given below. Thus agreements containing restrictions on the following matters need not be registered:

> "(a) the charges to be made, quoted or paid for insolvency services supplied, offered or obtained;

[64] Originally added by s. 217 Insolvency Act 1985.

[65] For definition of "as such", see para. 2.84.

(b) the terms or conditions on or subject to which insolvency services are to be supplied or obtained;
(c) the extent (if any) to which, or the scale (if any) on which, insolvency services are to be made available, supplied or obtained;
(d) the form or manner in which insolvency services are to be made available, supplied or obtained;
(e) the persons or classes of persons for whom or from whom, or the areas or places in or from which, insolvency services are to be made available or supplied or are to be obtained."

(10) Patent agents

2.77 "The services of regulated patent agents (within the meaning of Part V of the Copyright Designs and Patents Act 1988), in their capacity as such". The Secretary of State maintains a register pursuant to section 275(1) Copyright Designs and Patents Act 1988 of registered patent agents. Thus agreements relating to applications for patents are exempt, the business of applying presumably involves the complex tasks undertaken in researching and preparing the formal application. Agreements concerning all subsequent activities presumably fall within the phrase "in their capacity as such".[66] It is immaterial that the agreement concerns a patent application for territory other than the UK.

Schedule 10(A)[67] further exempts:

> "10A. The services of persons carrying on for gain in the United Kingdom the business of acting as agents or other representatives of other persons for the purpose of applying for or obtaining European patents or for the purpose of conducting proceedings in relation to applications for or otherwise in connection with such patents before the European Patent Office or the Comptroller and whose names appear on the European list (within the meaning of Part V of the Copyright Design and Patents Act 1977) in their capacity as such persons."

(11) Parliamentary agents

2.78 "The services of parliamentary agents entered in the Register in either House of Parliament as agents entitled to practice both in promoting and in opposing Bills, in their capacity as such parliamentary agents". Agreements concerning all peripheral matters relating to promotion or opposition may be assumed to be included in those verbs. Thus an agreement between agents concerning the types of Bills they will promote or oppose (i.e. a form of specialisation or market-sharing) will be exempt from registration.

(12) Surveyors

2.79 "The services of surveyors (that is to say, of surveyors of land, of quantity surveyors, of surveyors of buildings or other structures and of surveyors of ships) in their capacity as such surveyors". This paragraph was cursorily examined by the Court in *Royal Institution of Chartered Surveyors* v *Director General of Fair Trading*.[68] In that case the Royal Institution (RICS) published two booklets entitled *The Rules of Conduct, Disciplinary Powers and Procedures*, and *Professional Charges*. They also published sheets containing scales of charges. The documents formed, in the OFT's view, a registrable

[66] For definition of "as such", see para. 2.84.
[67] Added by Sch. 5, para. 7 Patents Act 1977, amended by s. 60(6) Administration of Justice Act 1985 and Sch. 8, para. 18(1) and (2) Copyright Designs and Patents Act 1988.
[68] [1981] ECC 587. For an explanation of why the OFT sought to adopt a strict attitude see, MMC Report on the *Supply of Surveyors Services* with reference to scale fees (1977) HC 5. The MMC criticised the adoption of *ad valorem* scales on the basis that they were not related to costs. Interestingly, the Royal Institution of Chartered Surveyors were unable, in view of the disparate work carried on, to describe the functions of a surveyor accurately.

agreement and were duly registered. The OFT viewed the agreement as price fixing and referred the case to the RPC. The RICS applied to the Court to have the register rectified under section 26(1) RTPA on the basis that the restrictions fell within Schedule 1, para. (xii) (above). The Director General sought to strike out the application upon the grounds that the notice of application and supporting affidavits disclosed no reasonable cause of action. The Court refused the application to strike out and held that the claim of the RICS was not unarguable. The Director General had contended that members of the RICS provided services related to the sale and valuation of various types of personal property and that these valuation activities were not within the wording of the exemption. This was so *even* though such valuation activities were within the ordinary practice of the chartered surveyor. Mr Justice Slade considered this to be an argument of some force, however, he refused to give a definitive ruling before full evidence as to the nature of a surveyor's functions was submitted:

> "We think it arguable that in many cases the question posed ... will not be capable of being answered without evidence as to the activities commonly carried on in the course of their work by persons who, according to the common parlance, fall within the relevant description. Similarly, we think it at least arguable (though we say no more than this) that the nature and extent of the meaning of the phrase 'in their capacity as such surveyors' can only be satisfactorily determined by admitting evidence of the activities commonly carried on in the course of their work by persons who, according to common parlance, fall within the broad description 'surveyor of land', 'quantity surveyor', or 'surveyor of land and buildings', as the case may be."[69]

2.80 Although, as noted above, no definitive answer was given, it would appear to be the case that the words in brackets do limit the general words expressed outside the brackets. Thus, restrictive agreements relating to activities of surveyors relating to types of valuations not within the brackets are, it is submitted, registrable. This question is not entirely free from doubt, given that Slade J stated that the converse was at least arguable.

(13) Engineers and technologists

2.81 "The services of professional engineers or technologists (that is to say, of persons practising or employed as consultants in the field of—(a) civil engineering; (b) mechanical, aeronautical, marine, electrical or electronic engineering; (c) mining, quarrying, soil analysis or other forms of mineralogy or geology; (d) agronomy, forestry, livestock rearing or ecology; (e) metallurgy, chemistry, biochemistry or physics; or (f) any other form of engineering or technology analogous to those mentioned in the preceding sub-paragraphs); in their capacity as such engineers or technologists". This exemption is very wide since in addition to exempting agreements listed in the specific fields (a)–(e), it also excludes (in (f)) all fields of activity "analogous" to those listed in (a)–(e). Precisely what is an "analogous" field would have to be negotiated over with the OFT by reference to expert evidence.

(14) Education

2.82 "Services consisting of the provision—(a) of primary, secondary or further education within the meaning of the Education Act 1944, The Education (Scotland) Acts 1939–71 or the Education and Libraries (Northern Ireland) Order 1972, or (b) of University or other higher education not falling within the preceding subparagraph".

[69] [1981] ECC 587, 604. The point was not raised in the course of the subsequent proceedings: *Re Royal Institution of Chartered Surveyors' Application* [1985] ICR 330, 334–335.

(15) Ministers of religion

2.83 "The services of ministers of religion in their capacity as such ministers".

(16) General points on interpretation

2.84 The most problematic phrase in these exemptions is "in their capacity as such". Thus, when is a surveyor acting in his capacity as such? If a surveyor gives advice on the price at which to sell a car he is not acting in his capacity as a surveyor. But, if a surveyor advises on the valuation of a property this is much closer to the line. Surveyors clearly do more than simply value buildings. The precise ambit of what a surveyor does therefore can only be tested by reference to expert evidence. This was a point accepted by Slade J in the *Royal Institution of Chartered Surveyors* case.[70]

2.85 An interesting point to arise from the *Surveyors* case derives from the dictum of Slade J that:

> "We think it arguable that, if all the services to be supplied by members of the RICS in respect of which they accept restrictions are exempt services, the agreement does not become registrable merely because the members have agreed not to supply 'designated services' of a nature quite outside the ordinary course of their professional work."[71]

This *dictum* concerns the following type of fact situation: X, Y and Z are surveyors who enter a restrictive agreement exempt under Schedule 1(12). They also agree not to provide advisory services relating to the hire of luxury holiday dwellings abroad. The Court in the dictum above concluded that it was arguable that such an ancillary restraint did not render an otherwise exempt agreement subject to the Act and even permits the otherwise registrable element to escape. This conclusion—if arguable—is probably suspect. This should not be seen as necessarily justifying non-registration. A total restriction on supplying a service at all is a registrable restriction under section 11 (2)(c) which requires registration of restrictions concerning "the extent (if any) to which, or the scale (if any) on which, designated services are to be made available, supplied or obtained".

2. Paras. 2–10, Schedule to the Restrictive Trade Practices (Services) Order 1976 S.I. 1976 No. 98

2.86 This statutory instrument has the principal function of calling up for registration all services agreements excepting those laid down in the Schedule which itemises a number of activities that are not covered. For purposes of clarity it may be noted that according to para. 1(a) of the Schedule to the S.I. a service supply association which does not belong to the relevant category of person or which does not carry out the relevant activity is none the less deemed so to do if it represents persons who do.

[70] If an architect agreed with another architect to fix prices for quantity surveying services they sought to provide, then (irrespective of any question of professional qualification) the agreement would presumably not be exempt from registration on the basis that, although quantity surveying agreements were exempt when concluded by surveyors, the architects were not surveyors and hence it was not an agreement they entered into in their capacity as architects. As a rule it would seem to be the case that an agreement entered into between an exempt category of service provider (e.g. an engineer) concerning subject matter exempt in another category (e.g. patent agents) is not exempt. See generally, *MMC Report on the Supply of Architect Services with Reference to Scale Fees* (1977) HC 4.

[71] [1981] ECC 587, 607.

(1) International carriage of goods by sea

2.87 Paragraph 2 exempts international carriage of goods by sea. A number of agreement types are envisaged in this paragraph: (a) agreements between operators only whereby the *only* restrictions accepted concern the service of the international carriage of goods or passengers by sea. Thus, *no* exemption exists if non-operators are also present, if the carriage is not international, or if restrictions exist in the agreement which are unrelated to the carriage itself;[72] (b) agreements between operators and clients of the operators services where the only restrictions are in respect of carriage services for goods; (c) agreements between operators of international sea transport services and one other person supplying services in respect of the operation of the international sea transport function where the restrictions accepted relate to the supply or acquisition of that other service. In this paragraph "international sea transport services" means the international carriage of passengers or goods wholly or partly by sea. This exemption is buttressed by section 11 of the Merchant Shipping (Liner Conference) Act 1982 which exempts corporate participation in the conference system from the RTPA 1976.

2.88 The scope of para. 2 has been considered briefly by the High Court in the context of an appeal under the Arbitration Acts 1950–79 from the final award of a panel of arbitrators in *Compagnie Maritime Belge and Others* v *Compagnia de Navigazione Merzario and Others.*[73] The application for leave to appeal concerned an agreement between two groups of shipping lines who, collectively, formed the SUNAG Agreement. That agreement concerned the multi-modal (i.e. by road and sea) transport of goods between Northern Europe and certain destinations in the Middle East. Carryings were divided and shared between the respective groups within the Agreement. Certain provisions of the agreement provided for over- and under-carriage payments. If one group over- or under-carried in relation to its allotted share it would respectively be liable for or entitled to a compensatory payment to be paid to or to be received from the other group. The arbitration concerned the legality of the agreement under EC and UK competition law. The arbitrators held in favour of the Claimants and concluded that the agreement constituted a "liner conference" within the meaning of Article 1 of Council Regulation 4056/86/EEC and that the block exemption for such liner conferences contained in Article 3 therein applied. Further, they held that the agreement fell within the scope of para. 2 of the Schedule to the RTPA Services Order. The Respondents to the arbitration sought leave to appeal from the High Court upon the basis that the arbitrators plainly misdirected themselves in law as to both EC and UK competition law. Mr Justice Gatehouse granted leave to appeal on all the EC questions and referred the same to the European Court of Justice pursuant to Article 177 EC. However, he refused leave in relation to the UK grounds of appeal. In his brief judgment he indicated that the arbitrators' award should be appended to his judgment and included as part of the documents to be referred to the ECJ. Since the judgment was given in open court and the award

[72] An example of an exempt agreement would be an agreement between carriers X, Y and Z whereby they will concentrate for 70 per cent of their trade on certain agreed lines and routes thereby limiting the extent to which they competed with each other. A non-exempt agreement would be between shipowners and tugowners concerning standard terms and conditions for the provision of tug services in and out of UK ports. This agreement is not exclusively between carriers, it is not international, nor are any restrictions contained in the standard terms and conditions directly related to the carrier's job of transportation. See for an example of a registrable agreement along these lines No. S161 Register of Restrictive Trade Practices, *British Tugowners Association Standard Terms and Conditions* (1984).

[73] 18 January 1995, Gatehouse J, unreported.

formed a part thereof it unusually falls into the public domain. In their award the arbitrators accepted that in relation to the RTPA 1976 the SUNAG Agreement was an agreement between two or more persons carrying on business in the United Kingdom in the supply of services; and that pursuant to the agreement two or more persons accepted relevant restrictions. The Respondents had submitted that the SUNAG Agreement was a registrable agreement particulars of which had not been furnished to the OFT and that, accordingly, the restrictions which the Claimants sought to enforce (the over-carriage penalty) were void and could not lawfully be enforced. As a preliminary point the arbitrators stated that it was "obvious" that "in an appropriate case, the words 'international sea transport services' embrace through transport services partly undertaken otherwise than by sea, and ... in the case of the parties to the SUNAG Agreement, inland haulage in which they were involved was undertaken only as part of through transportation. So, the fact that the parties to the SUNAG Agreement accepted restrictions in respect of inland haulage did not put them or their agreement outside the scope of the Schedule". The Respondents had submitted that on the evidence the SUNAG Agreement extended to restrictions covering freight-forwarding, port-handling and groupage (the consolidation of cargoes) and these were not restrictions "in respect of" international sea transport services. The arbitrators dealt with this submission in the following terms:

> "The Claimants' report was that, particular in relation to containerised traffic (with which the SUNAG was concerned), it would be absurd to divorce such ancillary services and operations from the overall transport service that was the subject-matter of the SUNAG Agreement. We agree with that view and regarded the Respondents' contrary arguments as commercially insupportable and not ones that we were driven to accept by reason of the wording of the Schedule to the 1976 Order. However, in case the matter should go further, we find the following facts on the evidence before us:
>
> (i) as to freight-forwarding, that the only restrictions accepted by the parties to the SUNAG Agreement were as to the commission that would be payable to freight-forwarders, the amount of which was based on the amount of ocean freight. It is, we consider, indisputable that these restrictions were, so far as the parties to SUNAG were concerned, in respect of the provisions of international sea transport services;
>
> (ii) as to port-handling, whether the service being offered is 'port-to-port' or 'door-to-door', that port-handling of containerised traffic and, where appropriate (viz in 'port-to-port' traffic), equivalent handover, is an integral part of the sea transport provided; and
>
> (iii) as to groupage, that restrictions accepted by the members of the SUNAG Agreement in relation to groupage would fall within the description 'restrictions ... in respect of international sea transport services'."

2.89 As noted above Mr Justice Gatehouse did not grant leave to appeal upon the arbitrators' findings in this regard. This is not, however, to say that the learned judge endorsed unequivocally the findings of the arbitrators but only that his refusal reflects the normal practice under the Arbitration Acts that leave to appeal from an arbitral award should be granted only where it is plain that the abitrators misdirected themselves. This formula leaves open the possibility that an arguable but ultimately incorrect arbitral finding remains undisturbed by the courts.

(2) Carriage by air

2.90 Paragraph 3 exempts an agreement to which only air transport undertaking are party and in which the only restrictions relate to carriage by air. This wide exemption extends to agreements made between an air transport undertaking[74] and its agent where the only restrictions accepted are in pursuance of the main agreement between the operators.[75] For example, carrier X might agree with carrier Y the precise quantities of freight they should transport to Norway from the UK. In pursuance of this agreement X might instruct his agent to only accept a certain, lower than usual, volume of orders. The restriction in the carrier/agent agreement as to the volume of trade is thus in pursuance of the main carrier/carrier agreement which contains restrictions in the form of quotas. Adherence by a UK operator to air-freight rates recommended by the International Air Transport Association or to a recommendation by that Association not to discount would be outside the scope of the RTPA 1976. As with other exemptions in the Schedule to the Order, the exemptions exist by virtue of the international nature of the excluded sector. Thus, it would hinder the competitiveness of the UK firms if they were subject to regulatory rules that their competitors were free from. International charter flights are however subject to the Competition Act 1980.[76]

(3) Carriage of passengers by road

2.91 Paragraph 4 has now been amended by section 115 of the Transport Act 1985 which effectively renders agreements for carriage of passengers by road subject to the main part of the Services Order which itself brings services agreements under the control of the RTPA 1976. For the sake of clarity paragraph 4 now reads:

> "An agreement to which the only parties are road passenger transport operators, and the only restrictions accepted thereunder relate to the provision in Northern Ireland and the Republic of Ireland, of services, using one or more public service vehicles (within the meaning of the Public Passenger Vehicles Act 1981),[77] for the carriage of passengers by road at separate fares."

Thus, after the Transport Act 1985, only agreements between road passenger transport operators (e.g. buses, coaches) relating to Northern Ireland or the Republic of Ireland are exempt from registration. Agreements relating to the remainder of the UK *are* registrable.

(4) Agreements between the government and building societies in respect of the raising of funds or the making of loans

2.92 Paragraph 5 of the Schedule has now been repealed by S.I. 1986 No. 2204. Formerly it exempted agreements between building societies and either or both of the Treasury or the Secretary of State which contain restrictions relating to fund raising or the making of loans, agreements between building societies inter se made in pursuance of a master agreement concluded with the government, agreements between the building societies which contain restrictions as to the interest rates charged or to be charged for loans, and inter-building society agreements containing restrictions on interest rates paid or to be paid to shareholders or depositors. This exemption was withdrawn by the Restrictive Trade Practices (Services) (Amendment) Order 1986.[78]

[74] "Air transport undertaking" is defined in accordance with the Air Navigation Order 1974 S.I. 1974 No. 1114.
[75] para. 3(2).
[76] Anti-Competitive Practices (Exclusions) (Amendment) Order 1984, S.I. 1984 No. 1919.
[77] See s. 1(1)(a) and (b) of that Act.
[78] S.I. 1986 No. 2204.

Deliberations by members of the Building Societies Association as to mortgage rates and interest rates for lenders are not forms of price-fixing agreements subject to registration. There are further exemptions for building societies in sections 454 and 455 Housing Act 1985 and section 84 of the Housing Associations Act 1985. These are discussed at paras. 2.102–2.105.

(5) Governmental control over the general monetary system

2.93 Paragraph 6 exempts agreements to which either or both of the Bank of England or the Treasury are party and which relate exclusively to the exercise of control by the Bank of England and/or the Treasury over financial institutions or over the monetary system generally or to the conduct of the money markets, public sector debt instruments or foreign currencies. The obvious function of this paragraph is to ensure that the RTPA 1976 does not interfere in the implementation of government economic policy. However, where an agreement which controls the economic issues mentioned is not related "exclusively" to those issues but contains other matters in addition, then, according to the paragraph, the agreement is subject to control.

(6) Banking agreements concerning Ireland

2.94 Paragraph 7 has now been repealed by S.I. 1985 No. 2044. Formerly it exempted agreements between banks in which restrictions were accepted between the parties as to the supply of bank services in Northern Ireland and the Republic of Ireland. Thus an agreement between Lloyds and National Westminster, for example, to issue a limited number of personal loans each in those territories would not be registrable. Likewise an agreement not to open for service on Saturdays in those territories would not be registrable. However, an agreement between Lloyds and National Westminster to the same effect as these two example agreements would be registrable if applicable to England. This exemption was withdrawn by the Restrictive Trade Practices (Services) (Amendment) Order 1985, S.I. 1985 No. 2044. Agreements pertaining to Northern Ireland or Northern Ireland and the Republic of Ireland are now prone to registration under the RTPA 1976.

(7) Agreements between insurance companies

2.95 Paragraph 8 exempts agreements between insurance companies which contain restrictions relating to the provision of insurance services. Thus, restrictive agreements as to premiums or as to poaching of other companies' clients are not registrable. It should be noted, however, that the European Commission have taken a strict approach to premium fixing and other restrictions imposed in agreements between insurers even where imposed for the protection of policy holders and/or investors. Hence, if the agreements in question is likely to affect trade between Member States, the value of the exemption from the RTPA 1976 will be reduced since the threat of Article 85(1) remains. In *Fire Insurance D* the Commission stressed that restrictive conduct confined to one Member State (Germany) could affect inter-state trade. This was confirmed by the Court of Justice on appeal.[79] An agreement which is subject to block exemption under Commission Regulation 3932/92/EEC will not, in any event, require to be furnished since it will be a non-notifiable agreement under S.I. 1996, No. 349, as to which see paras. 2.250 and following.

[79] [1985] CMLR 246 at pp. 254, 255 (Commission); Case 45/85 *Verband der Sachversicherer* [1987] ECR 405 (ECJ).

(8) Agreements between trustees or managers of unit trust schemes

2.96 Paragraph 9 exempts agreements between trustees or managers of unit trust funds authorised under the Prevention of Fraud (Investments) Act 1958 or the Prevention of Fraud (Investments) Act (Northern Ireland) 1940, where the only restrictions found in the agreement relate to the management of, or sale and purchase of units of, authorised unit trust schemes. It should be noted that if the agreement in addition to containing exemptible restrictions (i.e. those relating to the management, sale and purchase of units) contains other restrictions then the whole agreement becomes registrable. The exemption in para. 9 exists in respect of agreements containing exempted restrictions only.

(9) Implementation of decisions of the Panel on Take-overs and Mergers, Compliance with the City Code on Take-overs and Mergers

2.97 Paragraph 10 exempts recommendations by trade associations to comply with the provisions of the City Code on Take-overs and Mergers and recommendations implementing a decision of the Panel on Take-overs and Mergers. For exemption to exist the trade association must be represented on the Panel on Take-overs and Mergers or be a member of an association that is so represented. Trade association is as described in section 16 RTPA 1976.

H. Schedule 3, para. 1: Rationalisation Schemes and Agreements for Statutory Purposes

1. Rationalisation Schemes

2.98 Schedule 3, para. 1 excludes from the RTPA 1976 any agreement expressly authorised by an enactment or by any scheme, Order or other instrument made under an enactment. Furthermore, agreements constituting or forming part of a scheme certified by the Secretary of State under Chapter V of Part XIII of the Income and Corporation Taxes Act 1988 relating to schemes for rationalising industry are likewise excluded from the Act. See paras. 12.260–12.292 for details. A brief description suffices at this stage in order to demonstrate the ambit of this exemption. Such agreements seek to facilitate attempts by industry to rationalise production and thereby avoid the creation or maintenance of excess capacity during a recession: by agreement certain firms leave the market with compensation while remaining firms share the residual demand. Rationalisation arrangements have been put into effect by major companies in old mature industries on an EC-wide basis and indeed have had their schemes accepted by the European Commission. It is debatable whether or not a rationalisation scheme could gain exemption under section 29 RTPA 1976 (agreements important to the national economy) since, although the orderly reduction of capacity may be in the long- term best interests of the UK economy, for section 29 to operate the parties to the agreement must prove that their scheme has as its object or main object the promotion of efficiency or the creation or improvement of productive capacity. A rationalisation agreement obviously does not improve or increase capacity. However, it may be argued that it promotes efficiency which is an alternative criterion to promotion of capacity. In a National Economic Development Office (NEDO) Report in 1978 the example of man-made fibres was given as an example for possible section 29 exemption. Man-made fibres is a declining industry in the UK and the EC due to the effects of cheap imports. During 1978 it was estimated that less than 75 per cent of EC capacity was being used. The NEDO report suggested that the restructuring and down grading of capacity that was necessary could be undertaken by agreement which should be exempted under section 29.[80]

2.99 If parties to a proposed rationalisation agreement decide against the section 29 route then they must satisfy the conditions of Chapter V of the Income and Corporation Taxes Act 1988. Section 568 of that Act permits rationalisation schemes to be certified by the Secretary of State where the latter is satisfied:

> "(a) that the primary object of the scheme is the elimination of redundant works or machinery or plant from use in an industry in the United Kingdom; and
> (b) that the scheme is in the national interest and in the interest of that industry as a whole; and
> (c) that such number of persons engaged in that industry as are substantially representative of the industry are liable to pay contributions in furtherance of the primary object of the scheme by agreement between them and the body of persons carrying out the scheme."

2.100 Parties seeking exemption for their scheme will hence have to undertake negotiations with the DTI on the three factors quoted above. In preparing arguments reference may be made to cases decided by the European Commission under Article 85(1) and (3) EC where economic assessment of the pros and cons have been made.[81] Most cases under section 568 have historically concerned rationalisation agreements in the steel industry.[82]

2. Restrictive Agreements Expressly Authorised by an Enactment, Scheme or Order

2.101 A number of statutes contain provisions relating to the application of the RTPA 1976, and these are examined in the following order:

Housing

1. Housing Act 1985

Transport

2. Merchant Shipping (Liner Conferences) Act 1982
3. Airports Act 1986
4. Channel Tunnel Act 1987

[80] NEDO, *Competition Policy* (1978), pp. 14, 15. In the guidelines issued jointly by the OFT and the Department of Trade and Industry, *Guidelines on the Operation of the Restrictive Trade Practices Act 1976* (September 1984) rationalisation schemes are not mentioned in the brief section on s. 29 though the details given of s. 29 in those guidelines represent only a cursory summary of the section. Interestingly, the Liesner Committee, *op. cit.*, at para. 3.6 seems to accept that the NEDO report might be acceptable as regards rationalisation. A restructuring scheme for the ten biggest European Companies in the synthetic fibres sector aimed at closing down parts of their capacity (on average 18 per cent) by certain dates was approved in 1984 by the Commission. See Commission Competition Report 1983, para. 59. See also, OJ 1983 C 314 (19 November 1983) for a summary of the agreement, and [1985] CMLR 787 for the Commission decision.

[81] See *Twenty-third Commission Competition Report* (1993), paras. 82–89; *Thirteenth Commission Competition Report* (1983), paras. 56–61; and *Twelfth Commission Competition Report* (1982), paras. 38–41 for details of the Commission philosophy on restructuring and rationalisation.

[82] Under its predecessor, s. 406 Income and Corporation Taxes Act 1970.

5. New Roads and Street Works Act 1991
6. Railways Act 1993

Utilities

7. Energy Act 1976
8. Participation Agreements Act 1978
9. Telecommunications Act 1984
10. Gas Act 1986
11. Electricity Act 1989
12. Water Industry Act 1991

Financial services

13. Restrictive Trade Practices Act 1977
14. Financial Services Act 1986
15. Companies Act 1989

Broadcasting

16. Broadcasting Act 1990

(1) Housing Act 1985

2.102 The commercial realities of inner city property and housing generally dissuade building societies from lending on property in areas renowned to be run-down or declining. Section 442 provides that a local authority may enter into an agreement with a building society or other recognised body[83] under which the authority indemnifies against default by the mortgagor of such property. An indemnity agreement of this nature must obtain the approval of the Secretary of State which may be specific or general. General approvals will only be given by the Secretary of State following consultations with the Chief Registrar of Friendly Societies and such organisations representative of building societies and local authorities as the Secretary of State thinks expedient. Sections 445–449 seek to assist first time buyers of houses. Section 445 authorises the Secretary of State to make advances to recognised lending institutions enabling them to assist first-time buyers. Under section 449, advances to lending institutions under section 445 are to be on terms settled by the Secretary of State, with the Treasury's consent, after consultation with lending and savings institutions or their representative organisations. Recommendations by those organisations will of course be equivalent to recommendations by service supply associations.

2.103 Section 454 excludes the RTPA in both of these cases. It reads:

> "Section 16(3) and (5) of the Restrictive Trade Practices Act 1976 (recommendations by services supply associations to members) do not apply to—
> (a) recommendations made to building societies or recognised bodies about the making of agreements under section 442 (local authority agreements to indemnify mortgagees) or the corresponding Northern Ireland provisions, or
> (b) recommendations made to lending institutions and savings institutions about the manner of implementing sections 445 to 449 (assistance for first time buyers) or to the corresponding Scottish or Northern Ireland provisions,

[83] Financial institutions may be recognised under s. 444(1) Housing Act 1985.

provided that the recommendations are made with the approval of the Secretary of State, or as the case may be, the Department of the Environment for Northern Ireland, which may be withdrawn at any time on one month's notice."

2.104 Section 445(1) of the Act excludes certain agreements made between building societies from the RTPA 1976. It reads:

> "In determining for the purposes of the Restrictive Trade Practices Act 1976 whether an agreement between building societies is one to which that Act applies by virtue of an order made, or having effect as if made, under section 11 of that Act (restrictive agreements as to services) no account shall be taken of any term (whether or not subject to exceptions) by which the parties or any of them agree not to grant loans on the security of new houses unless they have been built by or at the direction of a person who is registered with, or has agreed to comply with standards of house building laid down or approved by, an appropriate body."

2.105 An "appropriate body" is one concerned with the specification and control of standards of house building and which has as its chairman a person appointed by the Secretary of State and which promotes or administers schemes conferring rights in respect of defects in the condition of houses on persons having or acquiring interests in them. This section exempts from the RTPA 1976 the recommendation by the Building Societies' Association that mortgages only be granted on new houses registered with the National House Building Council.[84] This recommendation was withdrawn on 1 August 1989, upon which date the functions of the Association were transferred to the newly established Council of Mortgage Lenders.[85] Following the MMC's Report into *Structural Warranty Services in Relation to New Homes*,[86] the Secretary of State did not accept the MMC's recommendations designed to remove barriers to entry into the supply of structural warranty services, but sought comments as to ways other than those set out in the Report in which this could be done.[87]

(2) Merchant Shipping (Liner Conferences) Act 1982

2.106 This Act enables the UK to accede to the Geneva Convention on a Code of Conduct for Liner Conferences 1974[88] negotiated under the aegis of the United Nations Conference on Trade and Development (UNCTAD), and, also abide by the requirements of Council Regulation 954/79/EEC[89] which seeks to ensure that no discrimination arises between EC shipping lines. Section 2(1) of the Act empowers the Secretary of State to make regulations to give effect to the Code. The Code confers rights and duties on shippers, shipping conferences and their members. Conferences are under a general duty to police themselves but must notify the Secretary of State of disciplinary measures taken. Given that conferences comprise groups of shipping companies who combine to determine terms and conditions of trade, competition law questions are bound to be raised. The policy of the government, in line with that of other nations, is that the conferences should be exempt

[84] See MMC Report into *Structural Warranty Services in Relation to New Homes* (Cm 1439, 1991), paras. 2.16 *et seq.* for the background to this.
[85] para. 2.47, MMC Report into *Structural Warranty Services in Relation to New Homes* (Cm 1439, 1991).
[86] Cm 1439, 1991. The MMC successfully resisted a judicial review application brought by the NHBC to quash the finding against the public interest contained in the Report: *R* v *MMC ex parte NHBC* [1994] *The Times*, 25 January.
[87] DTI Press Release, 6 March 1991.
[88] See the Schedule to the Act for the text of the code. For Commencement Order see S.I. 1985 No. 406.
[89] OJ 1979 1121/11.

from orthodox antitrust control.[90] Section 11 of the Act provides that the RTPA 1976 and the common law doctrine of restraint of trade shall not apply to any restrictions on trade[91] between states which are Contracting Parties to the Code and which are accepted within the framework of a conference.

2.107 Section 11(2)(a)–(c) outlines the exempted restrictions. These are: (a) restrictions in respect of the provision of international liner services accepted by the operators of such services under which an agreement to which two or more such operators are parties; (b) restrictions in respect of international liner services accepted by operators of such services or persons for whom such services are provided under an agreement to which one or more such operator(s) and one or more such person(s) are party; (c) restrictions in respect of the supply or acquisition of any service in connection with the operation of international liner services accepted by operators of such services or persons in the business of supplying such a service under an agreement to which one or more such operators and one such supplier are parties. Under section 11(3) where a restriction relates in part only to matters mentioned in section 11(2) the exemption is applicable only in so far as the restrictions relate to those matters. Under section 11(4) it is stated that it is immaterial for the purposes of section 11(2) that there are additional parties to an agreement mentioned in section 11 (2) except that section 11(2)(c) does not apply where the parties to an agreement include more than one such supplier as is mentioned in that paragraph. It is implicit from section 11(5) that the Secretary of State may, if he sees fit, call up for registration and apply the RTPA 1976 to services agreements of categories mentioned in section 11(2). In relation to the meaning of "international sea transport services" see the discussion under para. 2 of the Schedule to the RTPA 1976.

(3) Airports Act 1986

2.108 Regulation of competition in the aviation sector is primarily carried out by the Civil Aviation Authority. The OFT's powers are limited under both the RTPA 1976[92] and the Competition Act 1980.[93] Hence a concordat was reached in 1985 between the CAA and OFT[94] giving the CAA the principal and the OFT the subsidiary role in regulation. The Airports Act 1986 privatised airport operators and subjected them to regulation by the CAA. The MMC may be required by the CAA to investigate whether and airport is carrying on a course of conduct against the public interest.[95] In making its report, the MMC is required not to consider whether any agreement which is registrable under the RTPA 1976 operates against the public interest.[96]

(4) Channel Tunnel Act 1987

2.109 The Channel Tunnel raises competition law issues as it could be argued that it forms a natural monopoly, and certainly can be regarded as an essential facility. Competition

[90] Liner conferences benefit from a block exemption under EC law, Council Regulation 4056/86. This is strictly interpreted by the Commission, see *French-West African Shipowners' Committee* [1993] 5 CMLR 446 and *Cewal* OJ 1993 L34/20.

[91] cf. *Mogul Steamship* v *McGregor Gow* [1892] AC 25.

[92] para. 3, Sch. 1 Services Order S.I. 1976 No. 98, see para 2.90.

[93] para. 4, Sch. 1, Anti-Competitive Practices (Exclusions) Order 1980, S.I. 1980 No. 979; see paras. 3.40–3.52.

[94] Airlines and competition—An agreed statement by the CAA and OFT (21 May 1985).

[95] s. 43 Airports Act 1986.

[96] s. 45(3) Airports Act 1986. There is also provision in s. 74 Airports Act 1986 regarding the disclosure of confidential information to enable the regulatory bodies to perform their allotted tasks.

legislation is modified in two ways by the Channel Tunnel Act 1987. First, the RTPA 1976 is excluded from applying to the Concession Agreement under which the Tunnel was constructed and is operated.[97] Secondly, joint concessionaires may be treated as inter-connected bodies corporate for the purpose of both a monopoly reference under the FTA 1973 and an investigation under the Competition Act 1980.[98]

(5) New Roads and Street Works Act 1991

2.110 This Act sets up a statutory framework within which new roads may be constructed by way of a concession agreement with a private sector concessionaire. The concessionaire agrees to design, construct and operate a new road in return for the right to collect tolls. The facility to use the road in return for the toll charged is deemed by this Act to be a service for the purposes of the RTPA 1976.[99] Therefore such agreements may be caught by the Services Order.[100]

(6) Railways Act 1993

2.111 The privatisation of British Rail is provided for under the Railways Act 1993. This includes the establishment of an Office of Rail Regulation, headed by a Regulator, which will perform similar functions to the other regulatory offices set up under privatisation laws.[101] This has three main implications from a competition law point of view. First, the Regulator may refer to the MMC for report upon the compatibility with the public interest any matter relating to the provision of a railway service by a licensed operator.[102] The MMC will report to the Regulator on whether any of the matters referred have effects adverse to the public interest, but in so doing are required to assess the compatibility with the public interest of any agreement to which the holder of a licence is a party which is subject to the RTPA 1976.[103] Second is the relationship between the Regulator and the DGFT which is set out in section 67 Railways Act 1993. The Act envisages a concurrent jurisdiction with respect to both monopoly investigations under the Fair Trading Act 1973 and investigations into anti-competitive course of conduct under the Competition Act 1980. Before either exercises powers in these areas, it is required to consult the other.[104] Thirdly, section 131(1) Railways Act 1993 excludes the application of the RTPA 1976 if an agreement is registrable as a consequence of a provision being included at the behest of the Regulator or Secretary of State. Section 131(3) goes on to give the Secretary of State the power to direct the DGFT not to refer to the RPC any other agreement for the provision of railway services which, despite section 131(1), is caught by the RTPA 1976. This power may only be exercised if it appears to the Secretary of State that either the effect on competition is insignificant or, if there is a significant effect, it is not greater than is necessary to achieve one of four specified objectives. These are: the protection of users' interests; the promotion of the use of railways; the promotion of

[97] s. 33(1) Channel Tunnel Act 1987.
[98] s. 33(2) Channel Tunnel Act 1987.
[99] s. 10 New Roads and Street Works Act 1991. It is also deemed to be a service for the purposes of the FTA 1973 and the Competition Act 1980.
[100] cf. paras. 1.67–1.69.
[101] e.g. OFTEL for telecommunications, see paras. 2.117–2.118.
[102] s. 13(1) Railways Act 1993.
[103] s. 14(2) Railways Act 1993.
[104] There are also confidentiality provisions in s. 145 Railways Act 1993, which are subject to exceptions in the event of either the DGFT exercising his powers under RTPA 1976 or a MMC investigation.

efficiency and economy by service providers; or the promotion of measures designed to enable passengers to use more than one passenger service operator's service.

(7) Energy Act 1976

2.112 Section 5 provision exempts certain restrictive agreements between petroleum suppliers from the RTPA 1976 when certain market or political circumstances arise. The Act generally makes provision with regard to resources in the UK and the use of energy. Much of the Act has now been repealed or amended but certain operative parts remain. Section 1 empowers the Secretary of State to make orders regulating the production, supply, acquisition and use of crude liquid petroleum, natural gas and petroleum products, electricity or other fuel substances whether solid, liquid or gaseous used as fuel. Section 2 empowers the Secretary of State to give directions to undertaking in respect of their production, supply or use of substances mentioned in section 1. Section 3 provides that the Secretary of State shall only exercise the powers in section 1 and 2 after making an Order in Council declaring that the powers are necessary either for the UK to meet its EC obligations or its obligations as members of the International Energy Agency (a sub-body of the OECD) or its obligations as party to an International Energy Agreement, to take emergency measures in connection with the reduction or threatened reduction of fuel supplies. The power may also be exercised where there exists or is imminent in the UK an actual or threatened emergency affecting fuel or electricity supplies rendering governmental control necessary.

2.113 Section 5 provides limited exemption from the RTPA 1976. To be so exempt agreements must satisfy various conditions: (i) it must be in writing and be between two or more persons carrying on business in the supply of petroleum, and, is made by them with the Secretary of State and each other, and, contains a power for the Secretary of State to terminate it on the ground that its continuance is no longer in the national interest; (ii) the agreement must contain no restrictions otherwise registrable under the RTPA 1976 other than restrictions mentioned in section 6(1)(a)–(c) RTPA 1976, viz. restrictions on prices and terms and conditions of sale; (iii) the agreement must relate exclusively to petroleum; (iv) the agreement must contain a clause stating that the restrictions contained within the contract are operative only during the currency of an Order in Council under section 3 of the Act. Even in the absence of this provision such an agreement would almost certainly be exempt under the doctrine of Crown immunity. Moreover, it would probably fall within the exemption provided by section 29 RTPA 1976—agreements of importance to the national economy.

2.114 Section 5(2) provides an additional exemption for agreements entered at a time when there is in force an Order in Council and which satisfy certain conditions laid down in section 5(3) but which do not involve the Secretary of State. The conditions are: (i) that the agreements is made exclusively between persons carrying on business in the production or supply of petroleum and that at least two of the parties carry on business in the UK; (ii) that restrictions in the agreement relate only to matters listed in section 6(1)(d), (e) and (f) RTPA 1976 (viz. restrictions on the quantities of goods to be supplied, to whom and for what purpose, etc); and (iii) that the agreement is not to the like effect as another agreement made while the Order in Council is in force in respect of which exemption has been withdrawn unless none of the parties to the new agreement were parties to the old (now non-exempt) agreement or the Secretary of State has affirmed the new agreement. Agreements exempt in this matter may become re-subject to the RTPA upon written notice being given to the parties by the Secretary of State that the agreement is no longer necessary in the national interest having regard to the fuel emergency.[105] Where an agreement ceases to be exempt it must be registered with the OFT. All of the normal statutory penalties and consequences result from non-registration.[106]

(8) Participation Agreements Act 1978[107]

2.115 The substance of the whole Act is contained in section 1. The purpose of the section is to enable the Secretary of State for Energy to exempt from the RTPA 1976, agreements providing for majority state participation in the disposition of UK offshore petroleum. Agreements subject to this Act might well be exemptible under section 29 RTPA 1976 which excludes from the registration duty agreements important to the national economy. The Participation Agreements Act 1978 does, however, have the virtue of making certain the exemption. The Participation Agreements Act excludes from the Act various agreements. The agreements so exempted are termed certified participation agreements.[108] A certified participation agreement is one between the Secretary of State the Oil and Pipelines Agency (the successor to the British National Oil Corporation (BNOC)) or a wholly owned subsidiary of the Agency and which is, or supplements, an agreement entered into with a view to securing participation by the government or a body on its behalf (e.g. British Gas Corporation) or the Agency, in activities connected with petroleum existing in its natural condition in strata in the UK or beneath waters which form part of the territorial sea adjacent to the UK or are in a designated area within the meaning of the Continental Shelf Act 1965.[109]

Exemption is not provided for agreements relating to dealings by the Agency in any substance other than petroleum or petroleum products.[110]

The Act has retroactive effect exempting certified participation agreements from the RTPA 1976.[111]

2.116 In March 1985 the government announced the abolition of BNOC replacing it with the Oil and Pipelines Agency (OPA). The Participation Agreements Act specifically refers to BNOC as a principal party. However, under section 7 of the Oil and Pipelines Act 1985 references in the Participation Agreements Act to BNOC are to be taken to refer to the OPA. Under section 1(3) of the 1985 Act the OPA will *not* be regarded as a servant or agent of the crown. Nor will it enjoy any status, privilege or immunity of the crown.

(9) Telecommunications Act 1984

2.117 Under section 13 of the Telecommunications Act 1984, the Director General of Telecommunications (DGT) may make to the Monopolies and Mergers Commission (MMC), a reference requiring the latter to investigate and report on whether any matters, relating to the provision of telecommunication services or the supply of

[105] s. 5(5).
[106] s. 6.
[107] As amended by the Oil and Pipelines Act 1985.
[108] "Agreement" is, by virtue of s. 1(6) given the same meaning as it has in the RTPA 1976.
[109] The extension of the exemption to petroleum existing in its natural conditions in strata in the UK is achieved by s. 31; Continental Shelf Act 1965. The definition of "participation agreement" is the same as that in ss. 2(1)(e) and 20 Petroleum and Submarine Pipe-Lines Act 1975.
[110] s. 1(3) Participation Agreements Act 1978.
[111] s. 1(2). When the Act was introduced the government gave an undertaking that the Secretary of State would consult with and take the advice of the Department of Prices and Consumer Protection which was, at that time, partly responsible for the administration of competition policy. Today consultation would presumably be had with, and the advice taken of, the Department of Trade and Industry and the OFT (See Official Report, Standing Committee A, 29 November 1977: C.28).

telecommunication equipment by a person authorised by a licence under section 7 of the Act to run a telecommunications system, operates or may be expected to operate against the public interest. Moreover, the MMC may consider whether adverse effects of such a licence may be remedied by modification to the conditions therein. Section 14 of the Act lays down rules for the making of a report by the MMC. Section 14(2) states:

> "Where, on a reference under this section, the Commission conclude that any person who is authorised by the licence to run a telecommunication system is a party to an agreement to which the Restrictive Trade Practices Act 1976 applies, the Commission, in making their report on that reference, shall exclude from their consideration the question whether the provisions of that agreement, in so far as they are provisions by virtue of which it is an agreement to which the Act applies, operate, or may be expected to operate, against the public interest ..."

Thus such an agreement would fall to be considered in accordance with the ordinary provisions of the RTPA 1976.[112]

2.118 Given that the DGT is the telecommunications partner of the Director General of Fair Trading in so far as competition is concerned, a brief note on his position is warranted. From 1912 until 1982 telecommunications was a state run monopoly. Licences were granted to other operators only in so far as their systems were for private use. The British Telecommunications Act 1981 opened the door to the licensing of competing suppliers to the public. However, British Telecom (BT) enjoyed the right to be consulted prior to the licensing of a potential rival. The 1984 Act places BT on the same legal footing as any other potential provider of telecommunication services, viz. it must be licensed in the same way as any other and derives its rights and powers from the licence. The DGT is not a civil servant, he is the holder of a statutory position in the same way as is the Director General of Fair Trading. The DGT presides over the Office of Telecommunications (OFTEL) which equates to the OFT and which is staffed by civil servants predominantly on secondment from the Department of Trade and Industry.[113] Under the Act the DGT has functions related both to licensing and to general industry supervision. The 1984 Act extends to the DGT the functions of the Director General of Fair Trading under Part III of the Fair Trading Act 1973 (courses of conduct detrimental to consumer interests), under the monopoly provisions of that Act and under the Competition Act 1980. These transfers of course relate only to telecommunications. Persons wishing to complain of anti-competitive conduct under the Competition Act may now therefore complain to either OFTEL or the OFT, each of which is required to consult the other before exercising any of their concurrent powers.[114]

2.119 A brief summary of the licensing rules indicates the ambit of the Act. Section 7 imposes a duty on any person wishing to run a telecommunication service to obtain a licence. It is an offence to run an unauthorised system or to run an authorised system in an unauthorised manner. The licence may be imposed subject to conditions regulating every

[112] For an example of an agreement relating to telecommunications being referred to the RTPA, the agreement between *Race-Course Association Ltd and Satellite Information Services Ltd* dated 21 October 1987. The parties gave undertakings to the RPC on 11 January 1994.

[113] The address of OFTEL is: 50 Ludgate Hill London EC4M 7JJ. Telephone (0171) 634 8700.

[114] s. 50(4) Telecommunications Act 1984. The extent of the DGT's powers, and their interaction with those of the DGFT and other competition authorities, was considered by the Divisional Court (Phillips LJ, Hooper J) on judicial review in *R* v *Director General of Telecommunications ex p British Telecommunications plc* (20 December 1996). The case has a wider significance for the powers of other industry regulators, each of whom enjoys similar statutory powers to those of the DGT.

aspect of a company's operation. Conditions may be modified either by agreement between the licensee and the DGT or by the DGT following a reference to the MMC and a report by the latter finding that the activities of the licensee may be expected to operate against the pubic interest. There is no statutory power to revoke a licence so that the only other method of review will be by revocation of the licence as a whole which will depend upon provisions providing for revocation in the licence itself. Contravention of a condition is not an offence but may result in the DGT issuing an enforcement order which may be final or provisional (section 16). Enforcement of the order is by proceedings for injunction in the High Court. Moreover any person suffering loss for anothers failure to comply with an order may sue the licensee for damages.[115]

(10) Gas Act 1986

2.120 The Gas Act 1986 created and governs the functions of Director General of Gas Supply ("DGGS").[116] The DGGS's powers are concurrent with those of the DGFT, in so far as they overlap. The DGGS may refer to the MMC the issue of whether the supply of gas to tariff (i.e. non-large user) consumers is compatible with the public interest.[117] The MMC, when reporting, may not take into account whether any agreement to which the RTPA 1976 applies is in the public interest.[118] The RTPA 1976 is excluded by section 62 Gas Act 1986 from applying to agreements entered into prior to 28 November 1985 for the supply of gas as defined in that section or otherwise specified in an Order.[119] The gas supply industry in the UK has been extensively investigated by the MMC. Reports were issued in 1988 under the Fair Trading Act 1973[120] and in 1993, the latter comprising concurrent reports under the Fair Trading Act 1973[121] and the Gas Act 1986.[122]

2.121 The 1988 Report recommended measures designed to introduce more competition for British Gas plc in the supply of larger industrial and commercial customers, called the non-tariff market. Undertakings given to the DGFT by British Gas consequent to the report included an agreement to limit the share of British Gas of this market to 40 per cent by 1995, to release gas to other shippers to enable them to supply the remain-

[115] Compare this with s. 35(2) RTPA. This provision was presumably introduced by the government in order to give a cause of action to a plaintiff such as Mercury Communication who were forced to commence proceedings alleging inducement of breach of contract as the means to have the Post Office Engineering Union lift its "blacking" of the inter-connection between BT and Mercury. Under s. 18(6) trade unions have no immunity from such civil actions.

[116] The DGGS's office is known as OFGAS, the Office of Gas Supply. Its address is Stockley House, 130 Wilton Road, London SW1V 1LQ, Telephone 0171 828 0898.

[117] s. 24 Gas Act 1986. The MMC recommended in its Report on the *Supply within Great Britain of Gas through Pipes to Tariff and Non-tariff Customers, and the Supply within Great Britain of the Conveyance or Storage of Gas by Public Gas Suppliers* (Cm 2314, 1993), para 2.225, and MMC Report on the *Conveyance and Storage of Gas and the Fixing of Tariffs for the Supply of Gas by British Gas plc* (Cm 2315, 1993), para. 2.175, that the DGGS be given full concurrent power with the DGFT to refer issues of supply of gas to the non-tariff as well as the tariff market.

[118] s. 25(2) Gas Act 1986. There are also provisions in s. 42 Gas Act 1986 regarding the disclosure of confidential information to enable the regulatory bodies to perform their allotted tasks.

[119] There has been one Order under this section, the Restrictive Trade Practices (Gas Supply and Connected Activities) Order 1986, S.I. 1986 No. 1810.

[120] *Gas: A Report on the Matter of the Existence or Possible Existence of a Monopoly Situation in relation to the Supply in Great Britain of Gas through Pipes to Persons other than Tariff Customers* (Cm 500, 1988).

[121] MMC Report, *The Supply within Great Britain of Gas through Pipes to Tariff and Non-tariff Customers,* see note 117; supporting material in vols. 2 and 3, Cm 2316 and 2317 respectively. The only authorised public gas supplier in Great Britain at this time was British Gas plc.

[122] MMC Report on the *Conveyance and Storage of Gas and the Fixing of Tariffs for the Supply of Gas by British Gas plc* (Cm 2315, 1993, supporting material in vols. 2 and 3, Cm 2316 and 2317 respectively).

ing share of this market, and to establish a separate gas transport and storage unit. The idea behind this unit was to provide a non-discriminatory system for the supply of transportation of gas and storage services to all shippers, including British Gas.

2.122 The 1993 reports concluded that the objective of creating self-sustaining competition had not been successfully put into practice. It recommended that British Gas be split into its constituent parts, divesting the trading from the transport systems and reducing its monopoly of supply to the largely domestic tariff market, with the aim of its eventual removal. It rejected British Gas's submission that the objective of instilling competition into the market could be done by way of establishing separate transport and trading units remaining under the ownership of British Gas.

2.123 In the event, the Secretary of State was not persuaded that divestment of trading activities by British Gas was necessary, although he did accept that the operation of its trading and transport businesses should be fully separated. He also decided that British Gas's tariff monopoly should end in April 1996 with competition being phased in over the two years to April 1998.[123]

(11) Electricity Act 1989

2.124 The Electricity Act 1989 created and governs the Director General of Electricity Supply ("DGES").[124] the DGES's powers are concurrent with those of the DGFT, in so far as they overlap.[125] The DGES may investigate under section 43(1) of the 1989 Act courses of conduct which may be detrimental to electricity consumers' interests, be they economic, health, safety or other interests. The DGES may refer to the MMC either a monopoly situation under the FTA 1973 or an anti-competitive course of conduct under the Competition Act 1980.[126] The MMC in making a report is required to disregard whether any agreement registrable under the RTPA 1976 operates against the public interest,[127] this being considered to be a matter for the DGFT or DGES. The RTPA is applied to the electricity industry by the simple expedient of section 100 which specifies that electricity is to be treated as "goods" for the purposes of the RTPA.[128] The Secretary of State is given powers under section 100(2) to exempt pre-existing agreements, this being done by a series of Orders.[129] The effect of these Orders is to exempt most of the inherited arrangements in the electricity industry from the application of the RTPA 1976, but future agreements will require scrutiny to ensure compliance with the Act.

[123] DTI Press Release, 21 December 1993.

[124] The DGES's office is known as OFFER, the Office of Electricity Regulation. Its address is Hagley House, Hagley Road, Birmingham B16 8QG, telephone 0121 456 2100. In Scotland, the address is Regent Court, 70 West Regent Street, Glasgow G2 2QZ, telephone 0141 331 2678. In Northern Ireland, its address is Brookmount Buildings, 42 Fountain Street, Belfast BT1 5EE, telephone 01232 311575.

[125] s. 43(2) Electricity Act 1989.

[126] ss. 43(2) and 43(3) Electricity Act 1989. There is also provision in s. 57 Electricity Act 1989 regarding the disclosure of confidential information to enable the regulatory bodies to perform their allotted tasks.

[127] s. 12(2) Electricity Act 1989.

[128] cf. para. 1.63. for the definition of goods. S. 100(1) also specifies that electricity is to be regarded as goods for the purposes of the FTA 1973 and the Competition Act 1980.

[129] Electricity (Restrictive Trade Practices Act 1976) (Exemptions) Orders, Nos. 1–4, 1990, respectively S.I. 1990 No. 759, S.I. 1990 No. 1319, S.I. 1990 No. 1490, S.I. 1990 No. 2348; Electricity (Restrictive Trade Practices Act 1976) (Exemptions) (Amendment) Order 1991, S.I. 1991 No. 88; Electricity (Restrictive Trade Practices Act 1976) (Exemptions) Order 1992, S.I. 1992 No. 1024; Electricity (Restrictive Trade Practices Act 1976) (Exemptions) Order 1993, S.I. 1993 No. 912.

(12) Water Industry Act 1991

2.125 The Water Act 1989 which regulated the water industry in the UK at the time of privatisation and immediately after has been replaced by a number of statutes, principally the Water Industry Act 1991. This statute governs the Director General of Water Services' (DGWS) powers,[130] which in so far as they overlap with the DGFT's powers, are enjoyed concurrently. The DGWS may investigate under section 31 of the 1991 Act courses of conduct relating to the supply of water and sewerage services which may be detrimental to consumers and to refer them to the MMC, either under the relevant provisions of the FTA 1973 or under the Competition Act 1980.[131] The MMC in making a report is required to disregard whether any agreement registrable under the RTPA 1976 operates against the public interest,[132] this being considered to be a matter for the DGFT or DGWS.

(13) Restrictive Trade Practices Act 1977 (loan finance and credit facilities agreements)

2.126 When service agreements were called up for registration by S.I. 1976 No. 98 (see paras. 1.67–1.71 for analysis) it was quickly appreciated that certain finance agreements concerning both goods and services would have to be given specific exemption from the Act. In the Annual Report for 1977 the OFT stated:[133]

> "During 1977 it was found that, because of the application of the ... legislation to commercial services, a large number of loan-financing agreements fell within the scope of the legislation in that they contained restrictions on the freedom of action of borrowers, lenders or guarantors which were accepted by at least two parties to such agreements. The purpose of these restrictions was not to restrict competition but to protect the security of loans and the ability of borrowers to repay. Accordingly, the Restrictive Trade Practices Act 1977 made provision for the disregard of restrictions in such agreements with the object of removing them from the scope of the legislation under which restrictions are accepted only by overseas parties and which relate to activities outside the UK. In addition, the order-making powers of the Secretary of State were extended so that if any harmful agreements had been exempted inadvertently they might be restored to control."

2.127 The RTPA 1977 effectively expands the category of restrictions to be disregarded when considering registration. As a result, agreements, for instance, between banks and financial institutions for the provision of loan finance and credit facilities by way of consortium lending, are exempt from the RTPA 1976.

2.128 Section 1(3) coupled with Part 1 of the Schedule to the Act adds a new Article 4 to the 1976 Services Order. This Order (S.I. 1976 No. 98) it will be recalled requires services agreements to be registered. The Schedule to the Order provides for exemptions from the duty to register. The RTPA 1977 thus provides a new exempt category of agreements. The following must be read in this light.

2.129 The new article of the Order provides that if an agreement as to services contains certain "financing terms" as defined in the article, no account shall be taken of any restriction in the agreement which is solely concerned with securing the loan or maintaining a persons ability to discharge it when considering the registrability of the

[130] The DGWS's office is known as Ofwat, the Office of Water Services. Its address is Centre City Tower, 7 Hill Street, Birmingham B5 4UA, telephone 0121-625 1300.

[131] There are provisions enabling the disclosure of confidential information for these purposes contained in s. 174 Water Act 1989, s. 206 Water Industry Act 1991 and s. 204 Water Resources Act 1991.

[132] s. 15(2) Water Industry Act 1991.

[133] At pp. 34, 35.

agreement. Thus the catalyst for allowing such terms to be disregarded is the existence of "financing terms" in the agreement.

"Financing terms" means according to Article 4(1):

> "(a) the making or continuation of a loan; (b) the granting or continuation of any form of credit or of facilities for credit; (c) the supply of any property by way of lease or hire (with or without the option to acquire the ownership of the property); (d) the assumption of any liability in the event of a person's default; and (e) the granting of any right to resort to any property in the event of a person's default."

Thus, where an agreement contains "financing terms" no account is to be taken under Article 4(3) of restrictions whose "sole purpose" relates to one or both of the following: "(a) to maintain a persons ability to discharge any liability incurred by him under or in connection with the financing term; and (b) to protect a person against the consequences of another person's default in discharging such a liability".

2.130 The RTPA 1977 will not be needed very often. Usually in such arrangements restrictions are only imposed upon one party, the purchaser. Thus, a supplier of goods on extended credit terms might impose a restriction on purchasers that they do not resell the goods on hire purchase or other credit terms. The restriction is only accepted by the purchaser and hence the agreement would not be registrable since two parties do not accept registrable restrictions. Likewise restrictions imposed in romalpa clauses might fall only on one party. Thus, a clause in an agreement for the sale of goods whereby the supplier retains title in the goods until such time as the goods have been paid for (the *Romalpa* clause) may also contain a restriction on the price the purchaser may resell at pending full payment for the goods.[134] This price restriction would fall only on one party thus the agreement would not be registrable. However, in both examples above, had the supplier accepted registrable restrictions the agreement would still have been exempt since the restrictions on the purchaser are exempt under the RTPA 1977. If a trade association recommends adoption of loan finance security clauses, such as are described above, to its members for inclusion in contracts with purchasers, then such a recommendation need not be registered. The recommendation would not be in respect of any matter described in section 6 RTPA 1976 (i.e. registrable restrictions).

2.131 The 1977 Act might have some use in respect of complicated joint ventures. If a financial institution lends investment capital to a joint venture company—Joint Co Ltd—-which has been set up and incorporated by A Co, B Co and C Co and the finance company imposes a restriction in a collateral contract with A, B and C that they purchase all or a given percentage of their requirements from Joint Co Ltd, then such a restriction would be exempt under the RTPA 1977. It need not matter that the restriction is drafted into an agreement that is different from the actual loan agreement since the two agreements can be viewed as a single arrangement. Thus, since the finance company's object with the restriction is to ensure the profitability of Joint Co Ltd and, in turn, safeguard its own loan to Joint Co Ltd it should benefit from the exemption.

2.132 Where there is an overseas element to the agreement Article 4(4) of the Schedule to the Services Order applies. This reads:

[134] See *Aluminium Industrie Vaassen BV* v *Romalpa Aluminium Ltd* [1976] 1 WLR 676 (CA). See generally on the 1977 Act (1978) LSGaz. (5 April 1978) for a comment on the legislative history; and Hansard HL Vol. 384, col. 1042 and HC Vol. 933, col. 1589 for parliamentary history.

"If the financing terms relate to the doing of anything outside the United Kingdom by a person who neither resides nor carries on a business within the United Kingdom, no account shall be taken of any restriction which is accepted only (a) by him; or (b) by one or more other such persons; or (c) by him and one or other such persons—"

2.133 Thus, taking the Joint Co Ltd example above and imagining that Joint Co Ltd is incorporated outside the UK, that the finance institution is outside the UK; but that A, B and C are resident in the UK. If one further imagines that the finance company imposes restrictions on Joint Co Ltd with regard to terms and conditions of sale and credit, then, the overall arrangements would not be registrable. Any restrictions accepted by the finance house or by Joint Co Ltd would be exempt under Article 4(4) above. Restrictions accepted by A, B and C would be exempt under Article 4(1) and (3).

The Act has retroactive effect thus exempting agreements entered into pre-1977.

(14) Financial Services Act 1986

The conduct of investment business[135] in the UK is regulated under the regime set up by the Financial Services Act 1986 ("FSA 1986"). Under the FSA 1986, the Securities and Investments Board together with recognised self-regulating organisations, investment exchanges and clearing houses are exempt in several ways from ordinary competition legislation,[136] control of restrictive trade practices being in the hands of the Secretary of State.[137]

2.134 The DGFT's role in matters covered by the FSA 1986 is advisory. The Secretary of State is required not to recognise a self-regulating organisation, investment exchange or clearing house unless satisfied that its rulebook[138] does not restrict competition any more than is necessary for the protection of investors.[139] Under section 122, the DGFT is required to advise by report to the Secretary of State on this test,[140] although this advice is non-binding, and to keep those rulebooks under review. The DGFT has investigative powers under section 123 to carry out the functions under section 122.

2.135 Section 125(1) provides that the RTPA 1976 is not to apply to any agreement for the constitution of a recognised self-regulating organisation, investment exchange or clearing house. Nor, under section 125(2), does the RTPA 1976 apply to any agreement between such an organisation, exchange or clearing house and a person subject to any of their rulebooks. The Secretary of State can also direct the DGFT under section 127 not to refer the constitutions of or agreements involving recognised professional bodies under the FSA 1986 to the RPC if satisfied that any restriction of competition is for investor protection.

2.136 The DGFT continues to have a role in the regulation of financial services as a consequence of three limitations in the ambit of the FSA 1986. First, the FSA's definition of investment business does not extend to the provision of all financial services. for example, agreements between banks and building societies are not within the FSA

135 Defined by Sch. 1, Financial Services Act 1986.

136 The background to this exemption is that the DGFT had referred aspects of the Stock Exchange rules to the RPC in 1979. Although the hearing was due in 1984, the case was adjourned in 1983 following an agreement between the Secretary of State and the Stock Exchange, leading to the enactment of the Restrictive Trade Practices (Stock Exchange) Act 1984 exempting the Stock Exchange from the RTPA 1976. The 1984 Act is superseded by the FSA 1986: see s. 125(8) FSA 1986.

137 The Transfer of Functions (Financial Services) Order 1992, S.I. 1992 No. 1315, vests these powers in the Treasury.

138 i.e. as defined by s. 122(4)(a), its "rules, statements of principle, regulations, codes of practice, guidance and arrangements".

139 ss. 119,120 FSA 1986.

140 Under s. 122(8) the reports may be published. They are summarised in the DGFT's Annual Reports.

if not relating to investment business. Thus in *American Express Gold Card*,[141] an agreement between several banks concerning terms and conditions of encashment of the personal cheques of American Express Gold Card holders was given section 21(2) directions under the RTPA 1976. Nor does non-life insurance come within the definition of investment business, so the threatened collective boycott of General Accident car insurance by the Institute of Independent Insurance Brokers was properly within the powers of the DGFT to deal with under section 3 RTPA.[142]

2.137 Secondly, agreements made by businesses regulated by the rulebooks of recognised self-regulatory organisations, investment exchanges and clearing houses are only exempt from the RTPA 1976 if the agreement is required or contemplated by those rulebooks. So any agreement outside the framework of regulatory control under the FSA 1986 remains subject to registration under the RTPA 1976. Thus in *Globex*[143] some aspects of an agreement between the Chicago Mercantile Exchange and Reuters, restricting Reuters' ability to supply business information to other parties, were considered to fall outside section 122(2) FSA and thus fell within the Services Order.

2.138 Thirdly, the provisions of the FTA 1973 and the Competition Act 1980 are not completely excluded. The DGFT retains power to make a monopoly reference under the FTA 1973, though rulebooks cannot be taken into account in establishing whether a complex monopoly exists.[144] The MMC cannot in making their report comment on whether any rulebook operates against the public interest.[145] Under section 126 FSA 1986, no course of conduct required to contemplated by any rulebook shall constitute an anti-competitive practice for the purpose of the Competition Act 1980, thus retaining the DGFT's powers to investigate other courses of conduct within the financial services sector.[146]

(15) Companies Act 1989

2.139 The 1989 Act regulates the auditing profession in the UK. It applies to supervisory bodies which maintain and enforce rules as to eligibility for appointment as a company auditor and the way in which such work is conducted.[147] It also applies to qualifying bodies which govern professional qualifications in this area.[148] By section 47(1) the Secretary of State is given the powers under Schedule 14 of the 1989 Act to prevent restrictive trade practices by such bodies.[149] Consequently, supervisory and qualifying bodies are granted certain limited exceptions from competition legislation. The RTPA 1976 is stated not to apply to an agreement for the constitution of a recognised supervisory or qualifying body in so far as it relates to rules of or guidance issued by that body, for so long as that body remains recognised.[150] Should there be a monopoly reference under the FTA 1973, the MMC is required not to report on

[141] No. S. 1945 (1986).
[142] *Re Institute of Independent Insurance Brokers* [1991] ICR 822; see further paras. 5.10–5.15.
[143] DGFT's Annual Report 1989, p. 44.
[144] s. 124(1) FSA 1986. For example in *Credit Card Services* Cm 718 (1989), the MMC found that there was a complex monopoly consisting of Visa International and banks and building societies operating the Visa system.
[145] s. 14(3) FSA 1986.
[146] Thus the DGFT investigated the treatment by banks of small businesses in 1991 under the Competition Act 1980, Annual Report 1991, p. 36.
[147] s. 30(1) Companies Act 1989.
[148] s. 32(1) Companies Act 1989.
[149] There is provision for continuing scrutiny by the DGFT under para. 3(4), Sch. 14, Companies Act 1989.
[150] para. 9(1), Sch. 14, Companies Act 1989.

whether rules or guidance of such a body operate against the public interest.[151] It is also provided that such rules or guidance shall not constitute an anti-competitive practice for the purposes of the Competition Act 1980.

(16) Broadcasting Act 1990

2.140 Independent television and radio in the UK are now governed by the Broadcasting Acts 1990 and 1996. The 1990 Act set up an Independent Television Commission ("ITC"), among whose duties is to ensure fair and effective competition in the provision of television programme services in the UK. Section 2(3) of the 1990 Act states that this does not affect the discharge by the DGFT, the Secretary of State of the MMC of any of their functions in connection with competition.[152] However, section 194 gives the Secretary of State power to withdraw by Order certain networking arrangements for the newly created Channel 3[153] from the application of the RTPA 1976. Networking agreements (under section 39) are inter-company agreements for the mutual production and supply of programmes to enable the participating companies (being Channel 3 (ITV) franchisees) to provide a national network. Under Schedule 4 the OFT and MMC assess the agreement by reference to Article 85(3) type criteria.[154] There are also provisions enabling the Secretary of State to modify networking arrangements in the event of an adverse report by the MMC under the monopoly or merger provisions under the FTA 1973 or under the Competition Act 1980.[155]

I. Exclusive Dealing and Purchasing Agreements: Schedule 3, paras. 2 and 7 RTPA 1976

1. Interpretation

2.141 Exclusive dealing and purchasing agreements are examined in Chapter 10 so that detailed discussion is unnecessary here. The exemption in the Act is *only* needed if and in so far as the agreement in question is not in any event exempted under Commission Regulation 1983/83/EEC, i.e. is a non-notifiable agreement under S.I. 1996 No. 349 (see paras. 2.250 and following). In this section the scope of the exemption afforded such agreements will be discussed. It should be noted that exclusive dealing contracts are subject to the Competition Act 1980 and, where one of the parties is a monopoly, to the monopoly provisions of the Fair Trading Act 1973. Moreover, the Court of Justice has held that simply because an exclusive dealing contract is made between parties who are situate in one Member State only, this does not necessarily mean that they avoid EC competition law. An agreement between an English supplier and various

[151] para. 8(3), Sch. 14, Companies Act 1989.

[152] There is also provision in s. 197 Broadcasting Act 1990 regarding the disclosure of confidential information to enable the regulatory bodies to perform their allotted tasks.

[153] The Secretary of State exercised his powers by the Broadcasting (Restrictive Trade Practices Act 1976) (Exemption for Networking Arrangements) Order 1994, S.I. 1994 No. 2540.

[154] See for the application of the Art. 85(3) criteria to the actual networking agreements being considered and ultimately concluded by the companies granted Channel 3 (ITV) franchises under the 1990 Act: *Channel 3 Networking Arrangements* (DGFT Consultative Paper—August 1992); DGFT Report on *Networking Arrangements* (3 December 1992); MMC Report, *Channel 3 Networking Arrangements* (April 1993).

[155] s. 193 Broadcasting Act 1990.

exclusive dealers can affect trade between the Member States by making it more difficult for continental exporters to obtain representation in the United Kingdom.[156]

2.142 Schedule 3, para. 2 reads

> "This Act does not apply to an agreement for the supply of goods between two persons, neither of whom is a trade association, being an agreement to which no other person is party and under which no restrictions as are described in section 6(1) above are accepted or no such information provisions as are described in section 7(1) above are made other than restrictions accepted or provision made for the furnishing of information—
> (a) by the party supplying the goods, in respect of the supply of goods of the same description to other persons; or (b) by the party acquiring the goods, in respect of the sale, or acquisition for sale, of other goods of the same description."

2.143 Schedule 3, para. 2 for goods has its counterpart in Schedule 3, para. 7 for services which, although worded slightly differently, is to the same effect. The exemption permits two types of restriction to exist: (a) restrictions on the supply of goods by supplier to dealer; and (b) restrictions on the dealer with regard to the holding for sale of additional goods competing with those of the supplier. Thus the following common restrictions will be exempted: (i) that the supplier will not supply (or will limit supplies to) any other dealer within the territory granted to the dealer; (ii) that the dealer will not purchase for resale or sell goods that compete with those of the supplier.

2.144 The exemption does have a number of limitations (but see below for the effect of section 9(3) RTPA 1976 on this Schedule). First, no exemption exists for agreements where either of the parties is a trade associations, e.g. supply association X agrees with dealer association Y that members of X will only supply to members of Y. Such agreements are not necessarily bad but they must be furnished to the OFT and negotiated over on an individual basis. Secondly, the phrase "for the supply of" implies any agreement "whereby one party agrees to supply goods [or services] to another, notwithstanding that it may contain agreement on other related or other related matters".[157] It should be noted that although the contract may cover other matters it may *not* contain other restrictions. If other restrictions are included it must be furnished. Thirdly, only bilateral agreements are exempt, if more than two persons exist particulars of the agreement must be furnished. "Person" includes inter-connected companies. Thus if X is a wholly owned subsidiary of Y and both X and Y acting as suppliers enter an exclusive dealing agreement with Z, as dealer, then this is treated as a bilateral agreement since X and Y are one person being inter-connected bodies corporate under section 43(2) RTPA 1976.

2.145 The wording of the Schedule does *not* allow the supplier to prevent the dealer from manufacturing goods which compete with those of the supplier. However, this is rarely a problem since the dealer can be prevented from selling those goods and accordingly there would be little incentive for him to manufacture.

2.146 Sections 9(3) and 18(2) RTPA 1976 permit the parties to disregard certain restrictions when determining registrability. Section 9(3) for goods permits the disregard of any term which relates "exclusively to the goods supplied". Section 18(2) for services permits disregard of any term which relates exclusively to the services supplied (for detailed analysis of section 9 and 18 RTPA see paras. 1.75–1.86). Frequently exclusive dealing contracts contain restrictions which do relate exclusively to the goods or

[156] See Case 23/67 *Brasserie de Haecht* v *Wilkin (No. 1)* [1968] CMLR 26; [1967] ECR 407; Case 234(89) *Delimitis* v *Henninger Bray* [1991] ECR I-935 [1992] 5 CMLR 210.

[157] *Schweppes* v *Registrar of Restrictive Trading Agreements No. 2* (1971) LR 7 RP 336 at p. 375 *per* Stamp J [1971] 1 WLR 1148 (ChD).

services supplied. Thus, for example, the following would appear to be exempt restrictions: (a) that the dealer will not sell the goods or provide the service outside of his allotted exclusive territory into the territory of another dealer; (b) that the dealer will sell the goods in specified packages or under specified trade mark; (c) that the dealer hold a specified quantity in stock of the contract product.

2.147 In *Associated Dairies Ltd* v *Baines*[158] the Court of Appeal was concerned with an agreement between Associated Dairies (the Plaintiff) and Mr Baines (the Defendant). The Plaintiff was a large wholesale distributor of milk and other commodities. The Defendant was a milk roundsman selling and delivering milk to domestic consumers on his "milk round". The Agreement contained the following contractual clauses:

(i) "... not to sell milk by way of retail to the customer of the business" (clause 2(2)—obligation accepted by Plaintiff);
(ii) "To use all reasonable endeavours to persuade its bottled milk buyer customers not to sell milk by way of retail to the customers of the business" (clause 2(3)—obligation accepted by the Plaintiff);
(iii) "... for a period of five years from the date hereof ... to purchase from the company all milk to be sold in the business" (clause 4(1)—obligation accepted by Defendant);
(iv) "... during the continuance of this Agreement ... not to sell the milk by way of retail to any customers of the company" (clause 4(3)—obligation accepted by Defendant).

2.148 The case went to House of Lords who rejected the ruling of the Court of Appeal. However (whilst getting the result wrong) the Court of Appeal none the less found the questions to be posed correctly. The Court of Appeal were required, *inter alia*, to consider the scope of Schedule 3(2) as it applied to the relevant restrictions taking due account of section 9(3) RTPA 1976. In this regard the Court stated:

"The ... Defendant contends that the following relevant restrictions are accepted under the Agreement:
(i) a supplier's non-competition clause imposed by clause 2(2), being a restriction on the Plaintiff in respect of the persons to whom it can supply milk: Section 6(1)(f);
(ii) a supplier's reasonable endeavours clause imposed by clause 2(3), being a restriction on the Plaintiff in respect of the terms or conditions on or subject to which it can supply milk to other purchasers: Section 6(1)(c);
(iii) a exclusive purchase obligation imposed by clause 4(1), being a restriction on the ... Defendant as to the persons from whom he can acquire milk: Section 6(1)(f);
(iv) a purchaser's non-competition obligation imposed by clause 4(3) being a restriction on the ... Defendant in respect of the persons to whom he can supply milk: Section 6(1)(f).

It is not in dispute that clause 2(2) and 4(1) are relevant restrictions. Without more, however, the agreement would come within the exemption for exclusive dealing agreements in Schedule 3 paragraph 2.

There was a dispute whether clause 2(3), because it is a 'reasonable endeavours' obligation, is as a matter of law a relevant restriction within Section 6(1)(c). However, if it is a relevant restriction, it comes within Schedule 3 paragraph 2 and so does not affect the answer to the question before the Court.

The critical question, therefore, is whether because of the application of the shearing provisions in Section 9(3), clause 4(3) is to be disregarded in determining whether the RTPA applies to the Agreement. If it is to be disregarded, the agreement falls entirely within Schedule 3, paragraph 2, and the RTPA does not apply. If it is not to be disregarded, the agreement includes a relevant restriction that is not covered by Schedule 3, paragraph 2 and is subject to registration."

[158] [1996] ICR 183 (CA); [1997] 2 WLR 364 (HL).

2.149 Accordingly, the Court of Appeal identified these three clauses which fell within the scope of Schedule 3(2). However, the Court was of the view that clause 4(3) of the relevant agreement was not capable of falling within the scope of the exemption. In this regard it is important to observe that the Court stated that one applied section 9(3) as a preliminary step in considering whether Schedule 3(2) applies. If a term can be disregarded pursuant to section 9(3) then no account will be taken of it when the operation of Schedule 3(2) is being considered. In short, one applies section 9 first and Schedule 3 subsequently. Lord Justice Schiemann expressed the order of analysis in the following terms:

> "The Act employs as a matter of legislative drafting technique, a complicated three stage method of identifying agreements which need not be registered.
>
> The first of these stages is contained in Section 9 and provides that no account is to be taken of certain restrictions and certain terms in the agreements under consideration. The agreement is notionally shorn of the restrictions and terms identified in Section 9. I refer to this as the shearing stage.
>
> The second stage in identifying registrable agreements is to see whether they are exempted by virtue of the provisions of Schedule 3 to the Act. In carrying out the second stage one is looking at the agreement as shorn. I refer to this second stage as the exemption stage. If the agreement in the second stage is found to be exempted matters stop there.
>
> If it is not exempted one goes through the third stage and examines whether the agreements comes within the concept of a restrictive agreement as defined in Section 6."

The error into which the Court of Appeal fell was to treat the word "term" as different from "restriction". The House of Lords corrected this error. Lord Nicholls, expressing the judgment of the House, stated:

> "Taken by itself [Schedule 3 paragraph 2] does not operate to exempt Mr Baines' agreement from the Act. Some of the restrictions in the agreement fall within sub-paragraphs (a) and (b). The company's obligation not to sell milk to Mr Baines' customers is within sub-paragraph (a). Mr Baines' obligation to buy all his milk from the company is an obligation not to buy milk elsewhere. This falls within sub-paragraph (b). So also does his obligation under Clause 4(3) so far as it relates to milk not supplied by the company. Mr Baines' obligation not to sell milk to customers of the company is within sub-paragraph (b) so far as it relates to milk not bought from the company because that is a restriction accepted by him, as the person acquiring goods under the agreement, in respect of the sale of other goods of the same description.
>
> However, Mr Baines' obligation not to sell to companies customers milk supplied to him by the company is outside sub-paragraph (b). This obligation is a restriction accepted in respect of the sale of the very goods acquired under the agreement, not a restriction in the respect of sale of other goods of the same description. This being so, the agreement is not within the paragraph 2 exemption, if the paragraph is taken by itself, because to be within the paragraph the agreement must be one under which no relevant restrictions are accepted beyond those falling within sub-paragraphs (a) and (b)."

Lord Nicholls completed the process by concluding that the part of the clause in question which related to the goods supplied by the company was capable of being disregarded pursuant to Section 9(3) such that, once disregarded, Schedule 3 paragraph 2 was capable of applying to the residue so as to take the entire agreement outwith the scope of the Act.

2.150 Schedule 3 para. 2 was considered in a different context in *Vernon Company (Pulp Products) Ltd* v *Universal Pulp Containers Ltd.*[159] Vernon (V) were manufacturers of disposable bed pans made of treated paper pulp. The patent rights for these items had

[159] [1980] FSR 179 (ChD).

expired in 1976. The design and production drawings were owned by V and were copyright protected. Since 1964 V had subcontracted part of its production to UPC and V had supplied UPC with the moulds for making the bed pans. In 1967 V installed a new vacuum moulding machine which increased production output fourfold. Subsequently, two of these machines were sold to UPC in order to increase their capacity in line with that of V. Under the oral agreement between V and UPC the latter was free to use the machines to produce other items which did not compete with the products they produced for V. V claimed that during the initial stages of production they furnished UPC with related confidential advice and assistance. The oral agreement between the parties was formalised in 1971 and under the written agreement V appointed UPC as its sole sub-contractor and UPC agreed to supply V with a specified number of bed pans per week. The price of the supply of bed pans by UPC to V was based upon the resale price by UPC. UPC agreed to only supply V and not to manufacture competing products during the currency of the agreement and for a period of two years subsequent to termination. This agreement ended in 1979 and V decided against renewal. They informed UPC who then indicated to V that they intended to tender for contracts to supply disposable bed pans to hospitals in competition with V. V sought an interlocutory injunction restraining UPC from producing and selling disposable bed pans which competed with those of V. UPC brought a cross-motion to restrain V from trying to enforce the clause of the contract which prevented them from supplying products which competed with V. The basis of this argument was that the agreement between V and UPC was a registrable one under the RTPA 1976 and since it was unregistered restrictions in it were void and unenforceable and hence illegal for V to seek to enforce. V argued against this that the agreement was not registrable and was exempt by virtue of Schedule 3, para. 2 RTPA 1976.[160] McGarry VC refused to determine either of the parties claims at an interlocutory hearing on the basis that a full trial was needed for proper argument on the points. The question of interest is whether, for the purposes of Schedule 3(2), V could be said to have been supplying UPC with the contract goods, viz. bed pans. In reality V simply sub-contracted UPC to produce the goods for him. V did not supply UPC with bed pans, indeed, the reverse applied with UPC producing bed pans for supply to V. Schedule 3, para. 2 envisages that there be a supply of goods between the parties. In this case the only supply of goods was by UPC to V but there was clearly no exclusive dealing arrangement in force with UPC as supplier and V as dealer; that would be a reversal of the true relationship between the parties. Consequently, it would seem therefore unlikely that Schedule 3, para. 2 was relevant.

2.151 See paras. 2.212–2.214 for details of agreements containing restrictions fitting into more than one exemption.

2. *Clarification of Meaning of "Description" in Schedule 3, para. 2(b)*

2.152 Schedule 3, para. 2(b) quoted and discussed above contains a latent ambiguity. It is intended at this point simply to clarify the ambiguity. The provision allows restrictions to be imposed upon a dealer in respect of the sale or acquisition for sale of other goods of the same "description". What are other goods of the same "description"? There are two alternative interpretations. First, goods of the same description are

[160] The parties notified their agreement to the OFT in November 1979 but, so it was alleged, only as a precautionary measure. The OFT contended that the agreement was registrable (see *ibid.*, at p. 186).

those which are of the same brand description, e.g. all washing machines made by X Co; all clothes manufactured by Y using Y's trade mark. Secondly, it could additionally mean all goods of the same generic description, e.g. *all* vacuum cleaners of *whatever* brand, *all cutlery of whatever* make. For the purposes of Schedule 3, para. 2(b), the latter interpretation is generally assumed to be correct. Businessmen will find comfort in that this is the wider of the two alternatives. Thus, Schedule 3, para. 2(b) allows the supplier to prohibit the dealer from carrying *competing* goods, i.e. goods of the same generic description.[161]

2.153 If this wider interpretation were not accepted Schedule 3, para. 2 would have little value or significance. It would not allow suppliers to prevent their dealers from stocking and selling goods which compete with the contract goods. A supplier is far less likely to give a dealer the boon of an exclusive territory if he knows that the dealer is promoting and selling goods which compete with his. This logic has been fully accepted by the European Commission who have exempted in Regulation 1983/83/EEC exclusive dealing agreements containing no-dualling clauses from the prohibition in Article 85(1).

3. *Mutual Exclusive Dealing: Whether Excluded or Not?*

2.154 Does Schedule 3, para. 2 exclude mutual exclusive dealing? This covers the situation whereby X agrees to supply Y exclusively with kitchen knives and Y agrees to supply X exclusively with pen-knives and other non-domestic cutting edges. X and Y are thus made dealers for each other. Ostensibly such an agreement fits the criteria for exclusion: first, it is an agreement between two parties; secondly, neither party is a trade association; thirdly, the only restrictions are on the supplier(s) in respect of the supply of goods of the same description to other persons in the dealer's territory (Sch. 3, para. 2(a)). The question now arising is whether the exclusion lapses because X and Y are both suppliers and dealers. It is noteworthy that Schedule 3, para. 2(a) and (b) both use the singular phrase "the party" supplying, and, "the party" acquiring, i.e. the Schedule seems to envisage only one of the parties as dealer and only one of the parties as supplier. To meet this argument it is notable that under section 6(c) Interpretation Act 1978 singular implies plural and vice versa.

2.155 Moreover, it is arguable that such an agreement may involve each supplier accepting restrictions in respect of goods that they do not supply. This would be the case where, in respect of the other party's goods, each party, for example, agrees not to sell goods which compete with those goods. Thus, X who takes Y's knives will not also take goods which compete with Y's knives. Is this excluded? It is probable that Schedule 3(2) does not embrace mutual exclusive dealing because such agreements do not entail the parties accepting *only* the restrictions as described in this Schedule. Thus suppliers would also accept purchasing restrictions and purchasers would accept supplier restrictions. The Schedule assumes that only one type of restriction is accepted by either party and that one of the parties accepts supplier restrictions, and the other purchasing restrictions.

2.156 If doubtful parties should furnish particulars of mutual exclusive dealing restrictions on a fail-safe basis (see paras. 4.43–4.46). In terms of economic policy mutual exclusive dealing can be anti-competitive. If X makes Y his exclusive dealer and Y

[161] This conclusion is in line with the rulings of the RPC to the effect that "descriptions of goods" (s. 6(1)(d) RTPA 1976) means "kinds of goods": *British Waste Paper Association's Agreement* (1963) LR 4 RP 29 at p. 50; *British Furniture Manufacturers Federated Association's Agreement* (1966) LR 6 RP 185.

makes X his exclusive dealer where X and Y are rival manufacturers, then the parties can effectively divide the market between them. X, in his own territory, will be able to control the sale of Y's goods; Y in his own territory may control the sale of X's goods. In EC law mutual exclusive dealing is not exempt as are most ordinary exclusive dealing contracts. For details see Chapter 10.

4. *Examples of Exempt Restrictions*

2.157 It is implicit from the above that the combination of section 9(3) and Schedule 3, para. 2 provides a fairly wide exemption for exclusive dealing systems. The following are examples of negatively and positively drafted restrictions commonly found which should benefit from the exemption. In relation to section 9(3) reference should be made to the commentary on the word "term" in that provision at paras. 1.75–1.82.

2.158 (a) Exemption under Schedule 3, para. (2)(a) (restrictions on supplier in respect of supply to persons other than the dealer):

- supplier agrees to inform dealer of all sales made by the supplier to other dealers;
- supplier agrees to inform dealer of the price and other terms and conditions of sale relating to sales by the supplier to other persons or dealers;
- supplier agrees not to supply goods to other dealers or persons in the territory exclusively granted to the contract dealer;
- supplier agrees to supply persons other than the contract dealer only to a specified extent, e.g. a fixed number or volume per annum; or only up to a fixed percentage of the total sales made by the dealer in the previous year;
- supplier agrees to supply dealers or persons other than exclusive dealer on specified terms and conditions only, e.g. at a fixed price with a no-discount policy;
- on no-credit terms; on no-delivery, customer must collect terms etc. This enables the contract dealer to supply on more favourable terms than other dealers;
- supplier agrees not to actively market the contract goods but will satisfy unsolicited orders from persons other than the exclusive dealer.

2.159 However, care should be taken when considering these clauses. Where the supplier supplies the contract dealer on terms and conditions that are more favourable than those offered other buyers, the supplier may be vulnerable to a charge of price discrimination under the Competition Act 1980. This however will only be a major problem for suppliers who are either dominant or who enjoy significant economic power.

2.160 (b) Exemption under Schedule 3, para. 2(b) (restrictions on dealer in respect of sale or purchase for resale of goods other than those supplied by contract dealer):

- dealer agrees to purchase contract goods only from contract supplier, i.e. dealer agrees not to purchase the suppliers brand of goods from a person (e.g. a wholesaler) other than the supplier;
- dealer agrees to purchase a fixed percentage of his requirements from the contract supplier, i.e. dealer restricts his purchases of other goods;
- dealer agrees to purchase and sell only goods of the brand manufactured or supplied by the contract supplier (i.e. a no "dualling" clause whereby the dealer holds one brand only, common in motor industry for example);

- dealer agrees to purchase and sell only a fixed percentage of goods of a brand not manufactured or supplied by the supplier;
- dealer agrees not to sell goods of the description and brand manufactured by the contract supplier but that he acquires from another supplier through mail-order methods.

2.161 (c) Exemption under section 9(3) RTPA 1976 (terms relating exclusively to goods supplied):
- dealer agrees to sell the contract goods under a specified trade mark;
- dealer agrees to sell the contract goods packed and presented as specified by supplier;
- dealer agrees to advertise goods as specified by supplier;
- dealer agrees to maintain a sales network or stock of goods as specified by supplier;
- dealer agrees to provide after sales and guarantee services in respect of contract goods as specified by the supplier;
- dealer agrees not to sell contract goods by mail order methods.

2.162 (d) Section 9(6) RTPA 1976 (restrictions relating to workers to be employed). Reference should be made to paras. 1.99–1.100 for detailed analysis of this provision and the apparent judicial attitude towards it following the *ABTA* case:
- supplier requires dealer to employ only staff with X years experience in handling and marketing of the contract goods;
- supplier requires dealer to employ staff with specific qualifications which render them experienced in the contract goods.

2.163 In drafting distribution contracts where the distribution system covers all or a large part of the UK then parties would be wise to concentrate on drafting their agreement so as to fit within the block exemption for exclusive dealing in regulation 1983/83/EEC. It is now orthodox wisdom that widely spread purely national distribution networks may affect trade between EC Member States so as to activate Article 85 EC. See paras. 10.13–10.21 for analysis.

5. Overlapping Exemptions and Drafting Problems: Possible Solutions

2.164 Many businessmen and legal advisers find difficulty in drafting distribution agreements so as to avoid the duty to register. The decision of the House of Lords in *Associated Dairies* v *Baines*[162] has substantially eased the path of legal advisers seeking to draft exclusive distribution (or indeed other) agreements falling within section 9(3) and/or Schedule 3(2). The problems have, to a degree, been alleviated by S.I. 1996 No. 349 which renders non-notifiable agreements subject to EC block exemptions. See paras. 2.250 and following. Commission Regulations 1983/83/EEC and 1984/83 EEC exempt exclusive dealing and exclusive purchasing agreements.

J. Know-How Agreements Concerning Goods and Services: Schedule 3, paras. 3 and 8 RTPA 1976

2.165 This exemption is only required to the extent that an agreement is not already exempt under Commission Regulation 240/96/EC concerning technology transfer

[162] [1997] 2 WLR 364.

agreements. An agreement covered by that Regulation is non-notifiable: see paras. 2.250 and following. The same applies in relation to know how licensing agreements still exempt under Commission Regulation 556/89 by virtue of the transitional provisions in Article 11 of Regulation 240/96/EC. Schedule 3, paras. 3 and 8 exempts certain forms of know-how agreement. Schedule 3, para. 3 for goods reads:

> "This Act does not apply to an agreement between two persons (neither of whom is a trade association) for the exchange of information relating to the operation of processes of manufacture (whether patented or not) where—
> (a) no other person is party to the agreement; and
> (b) no such restrictions as are described in section 6(1) above are accepted or no such information provisions as are described in section 7(1) above are made under the agreement except in respect of the descriptions of goods to be produced by those processes or to which those processes are to be applied."

2.166 Schedule 3, para. 8 with appropriate modifications provides the same for services. The only significant difference is in the wording of subparagraph (b) which reads: "(b) all such restrictions as are mentioned in section 11(1)(b) above which are accepted under the agreement relate exclusively to the form or manner in which services incorporating those techniques or processes are to be made available or supplied".

2.167 Know-how or technical information of industrial relevance can take many forms, for example, research results, drawings and technical plans, formulae, techniques, commercial reports, etc. When a person applies for a patent much of this valuable information will not need to be submitted unless it is central to the operation of the patent.[163] However, when a patentee licenses his patent to another person he will probably wish to include this know-how information. The licensee may be restrained from disclosing this information by a clause in the licence or by the common law remedy of breach of confidence. What is clear is that agreements concerning know-how are commercially valuable and that possessors of such information may wish to restrict its dissemination.

2.168 The exemption in Schedule 3, paras. 3 and 8 is narrow and its wording obscure. The following points will be relevant to interpretation. First, there must be two parties only to the agreement. Though, under section 43(2) RTPA 1976 any two or more inter-connected bodies corporate may be treated as a single person. The same applies to two or more individuals carrying on business in partnership with each other. Secondly, no exemption exists if any of the parties are trade associations. Thirdly, the exemption only applies where there is an agreement for the *exchange* of information. The exchange of information agreement must concern processes for the manufacture of goods or techniques or processes to be applied in the provision of services. Thus, exchange of information concerning for example product design or characteristics and innovative packing methods do not qualify for exemption since the agreement is not for the exchange of information on processes of manufacture. The concept of "processes of manufacture" (Schedule 3, para. 3 goods) and "techniques or processes to be applied" (Schedule 3, para. 8 services) are not defined in the Act. "Processes of manufacture" was discussed by the Court in *Scottish Master Monumental Sculptors Association's Agreement*[164] where guidance was drawn from the *Shorter Oxford Dictionary*. Accordingly, a process of manufacture implied, for example, the processing or making by hand, physical labour or mechanical power, the working up into suitable forms for

[163] s. 14(3) Patents Act 1977.

[164] (1965) LR 5 RP 437 at p. 463, but see for a narrower view of the concept of "manufacture" in a different context, *Commissioners of Customs and Excise* v *Savoy Hotel* [1966] 1 WLR 948 at pp. 952, 953.

use. In the final analysis the concept was to be determined by reference to the facts of the case. A similar conclusion may be assumed to apply to "techniques or processes to be applied in the provision of" services. Thus, special dry-cleaning services of a laundry and dry-cleaning firm might not represent a process but they almost certainly entail a technique to be applied in the provision of the service.

2.169 There must be an "exchange of information" implying a two-sided flow of information. Thus, if X licenses a patent to Y and also agrees on a dissemination of information to Y concerning know-how connected to the patent no exemption exists because there is no "exchange" of information. It would, however, appear to be fairly easy to overcome this problem. If, in the know-how agreement between X and Y, there is included a clause requiring Y to inform X of any improvement he makes to the patented invention, this should be sufficient since the data being supplied by Y to X do concern the process of manufacture. It is relevant to note that according to the strict wording of the exemption in Schedule 3, paras. 3 and 8, all that is apparently necessary is for the agreement itself to provide for the exchange of information; there is nothing to say that in pursuance of the agreement, information necessarily must actually be exchanged. Thus, if X agrees to provide Y with know-how and includes a clause in the agreement requiring Y to notify X of improvements in the patented invention, then the agreement should be exempt even though Y makes no improvements to the invention and hence does not report back improvements to X. The important factor is that the agreement provides for the potential of a bilateral exchange of information.[165]

2.170 Fifthly, the exemption will exist if all of the factors in (a)–(d) above are satisfied and where the only restrictions contained in an agreement relating to goods are "in respect of the descriptions of goods to be produced by those processes or to which those processes are to be applied". Where the agreement concerns services, the only acceptable restrictions are those which, "relate exclusively to the form or manner in which services incorporating those techniques or processes are to be made available or supplied". The word "descriptions" in the goods exemption means "kinds".[166] Thus, where X agrees to disseminate know-how to Y, restrictions may be included in the agreement limiting the goods Y will make with the information or the goods that Y will subject to the process he has learned of by virtue of the information he has acquired from X. Restrictions as to the price at which the products produced by Y may be sold or as to the terms of their supply are not restrictions as to description and, if included in the agreement, entail withdrawal of the exemption.

2.171 Exemption will not lie for an agreement which contains restrictions which would be exempt under more than one provision of Schedule 3. See paras. 2.212–2.214 for details.

2.172 Given that know-how is not a proprietary interest protected by law in the same way that a patent or copyright is, it is uncertain whether the *Ravenseft* doctrine and the OFT interpretation of that doctrine apply. See paras. 2.201–2.203. If they do not apply then know-how licences can only be exempted under this provision of the RTPA; they would not additionally benefit from the common law exemptions.

[165] But see Korah, *Competition Law of Britain and the Common Market*, 3rd edn. (1982), p. 120, who doubts this conclusion though gives no reasons for such doubts.

[166] See *British Waste Paper Association's Agreement* [1963] LR 4 RP 29 at p. 50; and also *British Furniture Manufacturers Federated Association's Agreement* (1966) LR 6 RP 185.

K. Trade Mark Agreements: Schedule 3(4) RTPA 1976[167]

2.173 Schedule 3, para. 4 deals with both certification trade marks and trade mark licences. These will be dealt with separately.

1. Certification Trade Marks[168]

2.174 Under section 50 and Schedule 2 of the Trade Marks Act 1994 groups of manufacturers supplying goods or services of the same description may apply for a certification trade mark from the registrar of trade marks. To obtain such a mark the relevant goods or services must as a result of their "origin, material, mode of manufacture of goods or performance of services, quality accuracy or other characteristics" be distinguishable from other goods or services.[169] The proprietor of the mark cannot be a supplier so will generally be a trade association. Registration of the mark entitles authorised users to proceed against non-authorised users. This right of action to protect against unauthorised use is recognised as giving holders of the mark significant potential economic power. To curtail possible abuse of this power the usage and licensing of the mark used to be subject to regulation by the Fair Trading Division of the Department of Trade and Industry. However, these regulatory powers have now been entrusted by the new legislation to the Trade Marks Registrar, who it is thought will continue to follow the same practice. Therefore, the system is designed to prevent anti-competitive abuse of the trade mark, in particular its use as an unjustified barrier to entry against potential competitors. Provided a licence permitting use by a licensee of a certification trade mark goes no further than permitted by Schedule 3, para. 4(2) RTPA 1976,[170] it is not subject to registration. On the other hand, the inclusion of non-approved restrictions necessarily entails registration under the RTPA 1976.

2. Collective Trade Marks

2.175 Collective trade marks were introduced to UK law by the Trade Marks Act 1994.[171] A collective trade mark is one which distinguishes goods or services of members of an association which is the proprietor of the mark. As with certification trade marks, the Registrar of Trade Marks must approve regulations adopted by the association setting

[167] As substituted by Sch. 4, para. 7 Trade Marks Act 1994.

[168] See Annand and Norman *Guide to the Trade Marks Act 1994*, Chapter 13.

[169] For examples under s. 37 Trade Marks Act 1938 which preceded the current legislation see, "*Stilton*" *T. M.* [1967] RPC 173; *Union Nationale Inter-Syndicate's Application* [1922] 2 Ch 653 (CA). Most certification marks today are used in connection with specific qualities such as technical and safety standards or composition. The BSI "Kite Mark" is a well known example.

[170] As substituted by Sch. 4, para. 7 Trade Marks Act 1994.

[171] A restriction in an agreement between the proprietor of such a certification mark and a licensee requiring the latter to employ the mark only in respect of goods conforming to the certificate is not registrable. Neither is an agreement whereby the parties agree to incorporate such a clause in contracts with third parties. Both restrictions simply permit what the law already requires. In terms of the RTPA, the rule is that there is no registrable restriction if the alleged restriction simply requires a party to do what he is already bound to do by law— *British Waste Paper Association's Agreement* (1963) LR 4 RP 29; [1963] 1 WLR 540.

out the criteria for a licence to use such a mark. Accordingly, the same exemption is granted to collective trade marks by Schedule 3, para. 4(2) RTPA 1976[172] as applies for certification trade marks.

3. *Trade Mark Licences*

2.176 Schedule 3, para. 4(1) RTPA 1976, [173] provides an exemption for certain trade mark licensing agreements, other than certification or collective trade mark licences, which are dealt with under Schedule 3, para. 4(2) RTPA 1976, noted above. It states that an exemption is given to agreements authorising the use of a registered trade mark, provided that no registrable restrictions are accepted other than in respect of:

> "(a) the descriptions of goods bearing the mark which are to be produced or supplied, or the processes of manufacture to be applied to such goods or to goods to which the mark is to be applied, or
> (b) the kinds of services in relation to such the mark is to be used which are to be made available or supplied, or the form or manner in which such services are to be made available or supplied, or
> (c) the descriptions of goods which are to be produced or supplied in connection with the supply of services in relation to which the mark is to be used, or the process of manufacture to be applied to such goods."

2.177 Thus a restriction on the proprietor not to use the trade mark on goods which compete with the registered user's would be exempt as a restriction concerning the description of goods to be produced or supplied. For example, if a trade mark was registered covering goods made of high quality wool from a specific type of sheep from a specific locality, then an agreement could exist between the proprietor of the mark who manufactured jumpers and the licensee who manufactured woollen gloves whereby the proprietor agrees not to use the mark on any gloves he decides to manufacture. Alternatively, the licensee could agree not to supply goods bearing the trade mark which competed with the proprietor (e.g. jumpers).

2.178 As with other exemptions provided for in the Schedule the effect of Schedule 3(4), para. 1 is non-cumulative. If the agreement contains restrictions which would be exempt under Schedule 3(4), para. 1 and restrictions which would be exempt under another Schedule, then, no exemption lies. Schedule 3(4), para. 1 states, as do the other schedules, that exemption is granted only if all the restrictions contained in the agreement can be exempted under Schedule 3(4), para. 1. The existence of any other restrictions in the agreement, even if exemptible under other schedules, hence renders the exemption in Schedule 3(4), para. 1 inapplicable. This is often problematic because trade mark licences and grants are frequently accompanied by production (patent or know-how or both) agreements and licences which would need to be considered as part of an overall agreement or arrangement with the trade mark agreement. The exemption does not apply in the case of unregistered trade marks. This is a point which those advising on franchise law might bear in mind. A franchisor exploits the goodwill and reputation developed over a trade mark by licensing it to franchisees in different locations who offer goods using the trade mark. The franchisee will be subject to controls as to the quality and variety of the goods.

[172] s. 49 and Sch. 1, Trade Marks Act 1994
[173] As substituted by Sch. 4, para. 7 Trade Marks Act 1994. This replaces previous provisions relating to trade mark registered user agreements, since the new Act does not adopt a system of registered users.

Many restrictions in these contracts will be disregardable under section 9(3) RTPA as relating exclusively to the goods supplied. Where the franchise is based around a non-registered trade mark and the agreement should be furnished to the OFT for registration on the Register; dispensation may be obtained under section 21(2) RTPA following negotiations with the OFT.

2.179 Finally, the important question of whether the grant of an intellectual property right can ever legally be viewed as a restriction and whether such a grant is the supply of goods or services arises. These questions are examined in depth in the section on patent licenses and reference should be made to in the next section of this chapter for discussion.

2.180 See under paras. 2.212–2.214 for details of agreements containing restrictions fitting into more than one exemption.

L. Patents, Copyright and Design Right: Schedule 3, paras. 5, 5A and 5B

2.181 An agreement is only required to be furnished if it is not a non-notifiable agreement. Commission Regulation 240/96/EC exempts technology transfer agreements and therefore, under S.I. 1996 No. 349 (see paras. 2.250 and following), an exempt patent licence is non-notifiable and the exemption is not required. Schedule 3, para. 5 exempts agreements concerning patent rights and registered designs Schedule 3, para. 5A, which was introduced by section 30 Competition Act 1980, concerns exemption for copyright agreements. There is *no* EC block exemption existing for copyright licences *unless* they are ancillary to other IP rights and are covered by Commission Regulation 240/96/EC (technology transfer licences). Schedule 3, para. 5B, was added by the Copyright, Designs and Patents Act 1988.[174] It should be noted at the outset that the Schedule does not provide exemption from the Competition Act 1980. The usual question that will be asked under that Act will concern the economic effects of a patent or copyright holder's refusal to license.

1. Patents and Registered Designs: Schedule 3, para. 5(1)–(3)[175]

2.182 Schedule 3, para. 5 provides a broad exemption from the RTPA 1976. It is expressed to cover a wide range of agreements:

(i) licences granted by proprietors of patents;
(ii) licences granted by proprietors of registered designs;
(iii) licences granted by a licensee of a patent;
(iv) licences granted by a licensee of a registered design;
(v) licences granted by a person who has applied for a patent;
(vi) licences granted by a person who has applied for the registration of a design;
(vii) assignments of patents;
(viii) assignments of registered designs;
(ix) assignments of the right to apply for a patent;
(x) assignment of the right to apply for the registration of design;
(xi) an agreement for any such licence or assignment as is mentioned above.

[174] s. 303(1), Sch. 7, paras. 18(1) and (3), Copyright, Designs and Patents Act 1988.

[175] For licensing of plant breeders' rights see s. 8 Plant Varieties and Seeds Act 1964. This section is similar to Sch. 5 and provides exemption for such agreements.

2.183 Bare licences imposing no restrictions do not require registration. Such an agreement simply allows the licensee to do what would otherwise be unlawful as a violation of the patentee's rights. Schedule 3, para. 5(2) and (3) outlines the restrictions which may be incorporated into the licences, sublicences and assignments etc. above and which will not threaten the exemption from registration under the RTPA 1976. Schedule 3, para. 5(2) sets out permissible restrictions in goods licences, assignments and agreements. These are those in respect of:

> "(a) the invention to which the patent or application for a patent relates, or articles made by the use of that invention; or (b) articles in respect of which the design is or is proposed to be registered and to which it is applied."

For services licences, assignments and agreements the permissible restrictions will all be,

> "in respect of the invention to which the patent or application for a patent relates."

2.184 Although, as will be seen, the exemption is very wide it only applies to agreements between two parties. Where there are three or more parties the exemption does not exist because Schedule 3, para. 5(4)–(8) provides that patent pools must be registered if at least two of the parties to the pool accept registrable restrictions. Patent pools are discussed below.

2.185 The notion of a restriction on the invention or the articles for which the design is registered is wide ranging. It covers, for example: (i) restrictions on price (each party agrees to charge a standard price); (ii) restrictions on the number of the product manufactured or the extent of the provision of the service; (iii) restrictions requiring use of the patented invention upon only certain kinds of article or in certain, specified forms of service; and (iv) restrictions on the areas the parties will sell the patented product in. An agreement becomes registrable if it contains restrictions not relating to the invention. Thus, tying restrictions whereby the licensee is required to take a non-patented product from the proprietor as a condition of being allowed to take the patented product is not a restriction relating to the invention.[176] Similarly, if in a licence between a proprietor and a licensee there were additional restrictions relating to non-patented products or non-registered designs (e.g. relating to prices or markets in which they could be sold) then, again, the agreement would be registrable.[177]

2.186 Provided that there are two parties only the exemption continues to apply where each has a patent or registered design which he cross-licenses to each other. Thus, in *Automatic Telephone and Electric Co Ltd*[178] two producers of traffic operated traffic lights held different patents in respect of that product. They agreed to cross-license each other on a royalty free basis and also to divide the UK into territories, each party being restricted from selling outside his territory. The agreement further imposed restrictions on price. The case concerned the rights of the government to discovery of documents and not the patent licensing question. None the less, it appears that it was accepted that the cross-licensing was prima facie exempt.

176 But see s. 44 Patents Act 1977 which seeks to prohibit such tying clauses and hence makes registration under the RTPA 1976 somewhat hollow. See *Huntoon* v *Kolynos* (1930) 47 RPC 403.

177 See *Flushing Cistern Makers Ltd's Agreement* [1973] ICR 654 where price restrictions were imposed in licences covering both patented products and registered designs and non-patented or registered products—it was accepted that no exemption applied.

178 (1964) LR 5 RP 1; (1965) LR 5 RP 135 (CA). For an interesting sequel to the case when the firms in question were fined for offences relating to registration see *DPP* v *Automatic Telephone and Electric Co Ltd* (1968) 112 SJ 109.

2.187 Although the question is not free from all doubt, the exemption in Schedule 3, para. 5 appears to lapse when the relevant patent expires. The wording of Schedule 3, para. 5 does seem to imply that the licence or assignment, etc. relates to an *existing patent or registered design*.[179] Subsequent to expiry of the patent an agreement between a holder of a former patent and a licensee fixing prices or dividing markets will be registrable. Where an agreement concerns a number of different patents or registered designs then care must be taken to ensure that, prior to expiration of the patent or design, the agreement is modified. If it is not modified then the whole agreement will become registrable since it will now contain restrictions on non-exempt products as well as restrictions on exempt products and to obtain exemption under Schedule 3, para. 5 there must be no restrictions in the agreement at all other than exempt ones.

2. Patent Pools and Registered Design Pools: Schedule 3, para. 5(4)–(8)

2.188 The exemption in Schedule 3, para. 5(1)–(3) does not exist for patent pools or registered design pools. Note that Commission Regulation 240/96/EC does not apply either to all patent pools (see Article 5). Accordingly a pool is not a non-notifiable agreement if not within the scope of a relevant block exemption. Nor is there exemption for agreements, licences or assignments made pursuant to the pool agreement. Under Schedule 3, para. 5(5) a "patent or design pooling agreement" means an agreement:

> "(a) to which the parties are or include at least three persons (in this and the following subparagraph the 'principal parties') each of whom has an interest in one or more patents or registered designs, and
> (b) by which each of the principal parties agrees, in respect of patents or registered designs in which he has an interest, or in respect of patents or registered designs in which he has or may during the currency of the agreement acquire an interest, to grant such an interest as is mentioned in subparagraph (6) below."

2.189 The grant of interests referred to in Schedule 3, para. 5(6) concern the grant:

> "(a) of an interest in one or more such patents or registered designs to one or more of the other principal parties, or to one or more of those parties and to other persons; or
> (b) of an interest in at least one such patent or registered design to a third person for the purpose of enabling that person to grant an interest in it to one or more of the other principal parties, or to one or more of those parties and to other persons."

2.190 While the language of these provisions is verbose the message is clear. No exemption exists for owners of patents and registered designs who have pooled their respective rights by granting rights to each other or to one or more of the members of the pool. It makes no difference that the rights are granted indirectly. This might be the case where proprietors assign their rights to a trade association which then grants rights to the other members of the association. A set up of this nature arose in *Flushing Cistern Makers Ltd's Agreement* where members of the association granted to the association

[179] This is the implication that may be drawn from the critical comment of the Court in *Flushing Cistern Makers Ltd's Agreement* [1973] ICR 654 at p. 658 that: "In some cases agreed prices continued to be issued despite the expiration of patents or copyrights relating to them." In terms of the common law doctrine of restraint of trade a restraint on the licensee on competing with the patent holder after expiration of the patent may well be an unreasonable restraint of trade: *Mouchel* v *William Cubitt* (1907) 24 RPC 194.

royalty-free licences under their patents. The association subsequently granted sub-licences to other members. The pooling arrangement in this case would fall outside the exemption in Schedule 3, para. 5 RTPA 1976.[180]

2.191 A problem lies in deciding who is a "principal party" to use the wording of Schedule 3 para. 5(5). Joint holders of patent rights, registered design rights, or licences relating to patents or registered designs are to be treated as one party. Thus, if X, Y and Z jointly purchase rights in a patent and form a joint venture partnership to exploit the licence, the grant by the proprietor is deemed to be to a single person and the licence is treated as a bilateral agreement which may accordingly benefit from the exemption in Schedule 3, para. 5(1)–(3).[181] A patent pooling scheme or registered design pool between three or more subsidiaries of a single patent company counts as a patent pool between three independent principal parties and must be registered. This runs counter to the general policy of the RTPA 1976 which treats inter-connected companies as a single person. Indeed, such is the case for the remainder of the Schedule 3 exemptions, including design right pooling agreements under para. 5(2)–(6) RTPA. However, section 43(2)(a) RTPA 1976 expressly provides that this is not to be the case for Schedule 3, para. 5(4)–(8).

2.192 Exemption used to exist for patent pools up until 1973 when they were excluded from the exemption by section 101 Fair Trading Act 1973. There is no reason to suppose that patent pools will not be appropriate for dispensation from reference to the Court under section 21(2) RTPA 1976. When such agreements were considered by the Court they seemed to adopt a liberal attitude. In *Permanent Magnet Association's Agreement No. 1*[182] a pooling of patents and technical data was in operation between the parties who also fixed prices. The government contended that the pool which was accepted as beneficial could exist independently of the price fixing which was objected to. The Court was sufficiently impressed with the pooling arrangement to hold that it justified the price fixing on the basis that without it the pool would operate less efficiently. Accordingly, the benefits to the public in terms of the improved technical capacity of the industry and the better service thus provided to customers existed by virtue of the price restrictions in the agreements.[183]

2.193 Doubt exists over the general registrability of patent pools. These doubts are discussed in relation to the *Ravenseft* doctrine below.

3. *Copyright Agreements: Schedule 3, para. 5A RTPA 1976*

2.194 Schedule 3, para. 5A was introduced into the RTPA 1976 by section 30 Competition Act 1980 and exempts a wide range of copyright licensing agreements from registration. The provision exempts four types of agreement:

[180] That case was decided prior to entry into force of the Fair Trading Act 1973 when patent pools could still obtain exemption under s. 8 RTPA 1956. The withdrawal of the exemption for patent pools derives from s. 101 Fair Trading Act 1973 which inserted a s. 8A into the RTPA 1976. S. 8A became Sch. 3, para. 5(4)–(8) RTPA 1976. The *Flushing Cistern* case turned not on the existence of a pool but on the existence of restrictions in the sub-licences granted by the association concerning products that were not covered by patent or registered design, i.e. the sub-licences contained both exempt and non-exempt restrictions.

[181] Sch. 3, para. 5(8) RTPA 1976.

[182] (1969) LR 3 RP 119 at p. 168.

[183] See MMC Report on the *Supply of Electric Lamps* (1951) HC 287 where the MMC were critical of the patent pooling activities of a trade association but were not forced to scrutinise every aspect of the case since the parties voluntarily modified their agreement by granting licences to non-members and by refraining from fixing the prices under which non-patented articles could be sold.

(i) licences granted by the owner of copyright;
(ii) sub-licences granted by licensees of copyright;
(iii) assignments of any copyright;
(iv) agreements for the assignment or licence of any copyright.

This exemption is retroactive so that any agreement already registered may be taken off the register. Furthermore, it should follow that no private damages action may be taken against parties to an unregistered agreement under section 35(2) RTPA 1976 (discussed at paras 5.98 and following).

2.195 The restrictions that may be incorporated safely into agreements without invoking the duty to register fall within the category of restrictions described in the Act as being, "in respect of the work or other subject matter in which the copyright subsists or will subsist".[184]

2.196 Thus restrictions relating only to the subject matter of the copyright are allowed. Given the intensely competitive book and music industries it is considered that this exemption will not lead to significant competition problems.[185] In any event copyright licences are subject to the Competition Act 1980 and the monopoly provisions of the Fair Trading Act 1973.[186] The sorts of exempted restrictions will be similar to those exempt for patent licences, viz. restrictions on quantity produced, price, marketing territories, etc.

2.197 The Schedule was examined in *Academy Sound and Vision* v *WEA Records*.[187] Under a written agreement WEA assigned the copyright in certain master recordings to Academy. The nub of the agreement stipulated that WEA had a right for three months from the date of the agreement to sell its existing stocks of records made from the master recording in the UK and Eire. Additionally, Academy agreed during this period solely to manufacture records from the master and not therefore to sell them. For Academy this period was called the "inaction period". Academy sued WEA for allegedly selling a substantial number of records and cassettes after expiration of the three-month period in breach of the copyright now belonging to Academy and in breach of the contract concluded between Academy and WEA. WEA argued, among other things, that the agreement was one to which the RTPA 1976 applied and that, since it had not been duly registered, the restrictions therein were void and unenforceable under section 35 RTPA 1976. Thus, the restriction preventing sale after the three-month period was unenforceable. It was argued by counsel for WEA that:

> "the phrase, 'in respect of the subject matter in which the copyright subsists' in its application to the present case covers only the assignment of the copyright in the master recordings and to matters directly related to that assignment, for instance matters relating

[184] It was suggested by counsel in, *Academy Sound and Vision* v *WEA Records* [1983] ICR 586 at pp. 593, 594, that the word "work" referred to an original work within the meaning of Part I of the Copyright Act 1956 and the phrase "other subject matter" referred to sound recordings, films, broadcasts, etc. which were subject to distinct copyright under Part II *et seq.* of the same Act. Vinelott J considered this to be too narrow a construction (*ibid.* at p. 594C). See also No. 2514 Register of Restrictive Trade Practices, *Publishers Association* (1976).

[185] See Merkin and Williams, *Competition Law: Anti-trust Policy in the United Kingdom and the EC* (1984), pp. 342 *et seq.*

[186] See Investigation into *Ford Motor Company* (OFT March 1984) refusal to grant copyright licences; see the report of the MMC (February 1985) Cmnd 9437, pp. 36, 37. See also Investigation into *BBC and ITV: publication of programme information* (OFT December 1984) also on refusal to license, see the report of the MMC (September 1985) Cmnd 9614—all of these concerned the Competition Act 1980. See paras. 13.363–13.383 for details.

[187] [1983] ICR 586 (Ch D).

to licences and consultancy agreements in force, and does not cover the provisions dealing with copies made from the master recordings and in existence at the date of the agreement or to be made by Academy during the inaction period."[188]

Mr Justice Vinelott disagreed:

"The phrase 'in respect of' is not one ... which should be narrowly construed. In other statutory contexts, including the Restrictive Trade Practices Act 1976 and its predecessor, a wide scope has been attributed to it. In the context of paragraph 5A, which was clearly designed to exclude from the Act of 1976 agreements relating to copyright protected by the Copyright Act itself, the legislative intention must, I think, have been to except provisions fairly incidental to an assignment of any copyright within the Copyright Act, including the disposal of copies made by the owner of the copyright in a sound recording."[189]

Example: software licensing restrictions

2.198 A common situation in which copyright restrictions are in question is the licensing of computer software. By virtue of section 3(1)(b) the Copyright Design and Patents Act 1988 applies to computer programs which are treated as literary works. The type of restrictions actually incorporated will depend upon such factors as: (i) the degree of specialisation of the software; (ii) the nature of the market and whether sold in the High Street or by high technology, reputable companies; and (iii) the nature of the sale or licensing transaction since different considerations apply if the licensed product is mass produced and sold in computer stores or if the licensing agreement is individually negotiated and provides the licensor with an opportunity to enforce the restrictions. Given the above considerations the following may be included in software licensing agreements and RTPA 1976 problems still avoided. Restrictions on:

- use of the software only on designated computers;
- use of software in processing licensees data only thereby preventing use of the software on a time-share basis or on a consortium basis;
- use of the software at a designated physical location;
- use of the software on any computer system which can be accessed by remote controls;
- copying of the software for anything but adoption and archival purposes;
- reverse engineering in order to determine the contents of the software;
- modification of the software;
- assignment or transfer of the licence without prior written authorisation of the licensor such authorisation not to be unreasonably withheld;
- sublicensing of the software to third parties;
- use of any proprietary information contained in the software.

All of these restrictions may if it is submitted reasonably be defined as restrictions in "respect of the work or other subject-matter in which the copyright subsists or will subsist" and should hence fall within the scope of the exemption.

4. Design Right Agreements: Schedule 3, para. 5B RTPA 1976

2.199 Schedule 3, para. 5B was introduced into the RTPA 1976 by section 303(1) Copyright, Designs and Patents Act 1988. It exempts from registration a range of

[188] *ibid.*, at p. 594.
[189] *ibid.*

agreements relating to design rights equivalent to those exempted under para. 5A. Design right is created by Part III Copyright, Designs and Patents Act 1988,[190] and is intended to be complementary to registered design protection. Para. 5B exempts four types of agreements:

(i) licences granted by the owner of design right;
(ii) sub-licences granted by licensees of design right;
(iii) assignments of design right;
(iv) agreements for the assignment or licence of any design right.

Exemption is granted provided that the only restrictions in the agreement which would otherwise be registrable under sections 6(1) or 7(1) RTPA are in respect of articles made to the design.

2.200 However, under para. 5B(2)–(6) exemption is not granted to agreements made as part of a design pooling agreement or for consequential licences, assignments or agreements. This exclusion from exemption of design pooling agreements is similar to that for patent and registered design pooling agreements under para. 5(4)–(8) considered above. A design pooling agreement is defined as an agreement to which there are at least three parties having an interest as owner or licensee in design rights, where each grants an interest in a design right to at least one of the others. One point of difference from the treatment of patent and registered design pooling agreements is that in determining whether there are three persons party to the design pooling agreement, a parent and its subsidiaries are counted as one person under section 43(2) RTPA 1976.

5. The Ravenseft Doctrine: Licensing Agreements may not be Restrictive

2.201 The schedules concerning trade marks, patents and copyright all concern the grant of rights by a proprietor to a licensee. Thus a patent holder may license a person to exploit the patent subject to certain conditions and restrictions. The owner of a trade mark may license a person to use that mark for certain uses only and not others. A fundamental question arises: when a proprietor licenses a right to a licensee subject to limitations imposed upon the right has the licensee accepted restrictions? The licensee starts with no rights at all to use the intellectual property; if he sought to manufacture a product patented by the proprietor the latter could obtain an injunction to prevent that violation of his patent and damages. Similar conclusions hold true for other rights such as copyright or trade marks. Thus, when the licensee is granted a licence, albeit a licence subject to limitations, he is still gaining rights; the limitations do not take away anything he had before he entered the contract. They solely define the boundaries of the rights he has attained. It may thus be asked whether *any* limited licence of a proprietorial right imposes a restriction on the licensee. The answer to this question differs in UK law and EC law.

(1) Position in UK law

2.202 The accepted position in UK law is that a limitation or restriction imposed on the licensee by virtue of the proprietorial right itself is not a registrable restriction. Thus, a restriction on a patent licensee derives from the patent itself and not from a

[190] s. 213 Copyright, Designs and Patents Act 1988 defines a design right as subsisting in designs for "any aspect of the shape or configuration (whether internal or external) of the whole or part of an article". Part III of the Act sets out the criteria for design right protection.

restriction existing purely by virtue of the agreement. For example: X is the patentee of a process for strengthening glass and he uses this patent to manufacture especially strong glass for industrial use in factories. X licenses Y to use the patent but under the licence Y may only manufacture strengthened glass for greenhouses. This restriction on Y derives from the patent itself. If Y breaches the licence X can sue him for infringement of his patent rights; Y has no right to use the process for anything other than greenhouses and X need not rely on breach of the agreement to enforce the restriction. In the Court of Appeal in *Automatic Telephone and Electric Co Ltd* Wilmer LJ elucidated upon this principle. He stated that the agreements in question: "in the picturesque phrase used by [counsel] did not have the effect of closing any door which was previously open to the contractors; its effect was merely to open a door through which the selected contractor might pass."[191] This principle has been accepted by the House of Lords in restraint of trade cases. In *Esso Petroleum Co Ltd* v *Harper's Garage (Stourport)*,[192] Lord Reid stated: "A person buying or leasing land had no previous right to be there at all, let alone trade there, and, when he takes possession of that land subject to a negative restrictive covenant, he gives up no right or freedom which he previously had."[193] The most important confirmation of the principle in the context of the restrictive trade practices legislation arose in *Ravenseft Properties* v *Director General of Fair Trading*[194] where the question was asked, "to what extent can a covenant in a lease properly be said to involve restrictions for the purposes of the relevant Acts?"[195] The answer of the Court was based upon the two authorities cited above and was that, "only in very exceptional cases can the limitation of freedom of trade effected by covenants in a lease constitute restrictions for the purposes of the relevant Act".[196] Equally important to this question was the conclusion of the Court that the supply of a lease by a landlord did not amount to the provision of a service for the purposes of the RTP legislation. The provisions of services implied "doing things for people".[197] Simply granting a lease was not doing something for the tenant.

2.203 Subsequent to *Ravenseft* the OFT issued the following statement:

> "It may be helpful to add that the Office has taken the view that the principles laid down in the judgment in this case are of general application to proprietary rights and the grant of an industrial property licence including, e.g. a copyright licence does not constitute the supply of a service within the meaning of the legislation."[198]

Thus, proprietary licences do not restrict the licensee in the opinion of the OFT. If this is so the holder of the right can accept any restrictions he pleases and still avoid registering the agreement since only one person will be accepting registrable restrictions (in accepting the restrictions the holder clearly limits *his* freedom to exploit the right as he wishes).

2.204 The OFT further accepts as the above statement reveals, that the grant of a licence is not the supply of services. It should be clear that it is, in principle, only restrictions upon

[191] (1963) LR 3 RP 462 at p. 483.

[192] [1967] 1 All ER 699 at pp. 707, 714, 719, 724, 725; [1968] AC 269 at pp. 298, 309, 316, 325. Followed in *Cleveland Petroleum* v *Dartstone* [1969] 1 All ER 201; [1969] 1 WLR 116 (CA).

[193] *Esso Petroleum* v *Harper op. cit.*, at pp. 707, 708; and [1968] AC at p. 298.

[194] [1977] 1 All ER 47 (QBD).

[195] *ibid.*, at p. 53(g), (h).

[196] *ibid.*

[197] *ibid.*, at p. 53(C).

[198] DGFT Annual Report 1976, p. 36.

the *licensees*, through the licence, has an otherwise closed door opened for it. Equally, the licensor; if it accepts restrictions has a hitherto *open* door shut or part-closed. The conclusion that, to this extent, licensors cannot benefit from the open and shut door principle is without prejudice to the second rationale in the *Ravenseft* case, namely whether a licensor accepting a restriction in relation to goods or services. If granting a lease is not the provision of a service then, arguably, agreeing not to license (say) third parties is, likewise, not a restriction concerning a service. Licensors cannot, however, assume that every restriction accepted escapes the RTPA 1976. For example, a restriction accepted by the licensor as to the prices charged or customers or areas supplied with products manufactured under a patent is plainly a restriction as to goods.

2.205 There is a third argument which suggests that such licensing agreements are not registrable. A restriction in an agreement which merely restrains the parties from doing something they are already bound not to do in general law cannot be a restriction for RTPA 1976 purposes.[199] Thus, a trade association which recommends members to refrain from exempting themselves from liability for death or personal injury caused by their breach of contract or negligence in contracts with customers is not a restriction since section 2(1) Unfair Contact Terms Act 1977 already prohibits such clauses.[200] Thus, a person is prohibited at law from infringing another person's patent rights. If a patent licence defines, through limitations imposed on the licensee, the latter's legal right to use the patent, then an action by the holder to enforce the agreement and prevent its breach is an action to enforce the general law, i.e. his general legal right to prevent patent infringements.

2.206 The arguments given above suggest that the Schedule exemptions for intellectual property discussed above serve little or no purpose. Though since the Act expressly exempts certain licences this might imply that Parliament intended non-exempt agreements to be registered. These arguments suggest that the extent of the application of the RTPA 1976 to intellectual property licences is uncertain.[201] In view of these doubts the following practical consequences should be considered:

(a) the OFT adopts a sympathetic approach to intellectual property licences;
(b) parties should furnish agreements to the OFT that do not fall within the exemptions including with the documents a letter expressing the view that the parties do not consider the agreements to be registrable for the reasons given above but that they are none the less furnishing the OFT with the agreement on a precautionary "fail-safe" basis;
(c) furnishing protects the parties from the dramatic consequences of section 35(1) RTPA 1976 which renders void and unenforceable restrictions in unregistered agreements;[202]
(d) furnishing protects against any third party who considers himself to have suffered damage from the agreement and who could, in the absence of furnishing,

[199] See, e.g. *British Waste Paper Association's Agreement* (1963) LR 4 RP 29.
[200] Any trade association recommendation allowing or encouraging a clause prohibited by the Unfair Contract Terms Act 1977 or the Unfair Terms in Consumer Contracts Regulations S.I. 1994 No. 3159 would not obtain s. 21 (2) dispensation from reference to the Court.
[201] See Korah (1977), JBL 79n. 19; Korah, *Competition Law of Britain and the Common Market*, 3rd edn. (1982), pp. 126, 127; Cunningham, *The Fair Trading Act 1973* (1974), pp. 257, 258.
[202] Thus notification will prevent one party to the agreement subsequently trying to escape obligations under the agreement by arguing that the agreement should have been registered and that accordingly it is void and unenforceable under s. 35(1) RTPA. See, e.g. *Academy Sound and Vision v WEA Records* [1983] ICR 586 (Ch D).

bring a private damages action under section 35(2) RTPA 1976 against the parties for failure to furnish a registrable agreement;

(e) the OFT might not register the agreement. Alternatively, if they do register the agreement it may be treated leniently and given section 21(2) RTPA 1976 dispensation from reference to the Court.[203]

2.207 An important point to consider is whether it is possible for both proprietor of the right and the licensee to accept restrictions which are registrable even given the cases discussed above, i.e. does the statutory exemption extend to cover cases that would not be covered by the *Ravenseft* doctrine? The answer is "yes", and this may be demonstrated by reference to certain cross-licensing agreements which entail registrable restrictions being accepted by both parties. If X grants to Y an exclusive licence to use his patented process for strengthening glass but limits Y's licence to use in respect of glass for greenhouse then Y has not—on the *Ravenseft* principle—accepted restrictions. X, however, has accepted a restriction not to use his process in connection with glass for greenhouses (i.e. this derives from the exclusivity clause granted to Y). If Y now grants to X an exclusive licence in connection with a different patent for glass and limits X to use of this process for industrial purposes, then X is not restricted under the agreement but Y is since he has accepted a restriction on the use of his patent for industrial purposes. In this agreement both X and Y have accepted restrictions. Both of these restrictions relate exclusively to the invention itself and hence are exempt under Schedule 3(5) and the cross-licensing agreement need not be registered. This example shows that the Schedule 3 exemptions do have a use and do not totally overlap with the *Ravenseft* principle.[204] Finally, it may be asked whether the *Ravenseft* principle affects patent pools? The discussion on cross-licensing suggests that patent pools may fall outside the *Ravenseft* principle. A patent holder licenses two licensees who are limited as to permissible uses of the patent. Neither licensee therefore accept restrictions on the *Ravenseft* basis. However, the licensees agree to grant back to the holder exclusive licences of improvement patents they come to own. In such a case both licensees have accepted restrictions since neither may use the improvement patents they own. The agreement between the three parties thus contains two parties who accept restrictions (i.e. the two licensees). Where, in a patent pool, more than one holder of a patent right limits his freedom in any way then the agreement falls outside of *Ravenseft*. Restrictions on the licensees can be ignored; it is restrictions on holders that must be counted since these are not exempt under the *Ravenseft* open and shut door principle.

2.208 It may be questioned whether these sundry exemptions apply to know-how agreements. The OFT consider that the *Ravenseft* doctrine applies to "proprietary" rights, for example patents, copyright, trade marks. However, know-how is not generally considered to fit within this category of rights. Know-how is a contractual right that is protected not by express statute but by contractual remedies, and by principles of confidentiality, unfair competition and equity. In practice know-how may comprise the services of engineers or experts provided by the supplying/licensing company, the supply of manuals, guidance notes etc. Know-how often, in practice, entails the provision of

[203] See e.g. No. 5044, Register of Restrictive Trade Practices, *Agreement between Croda International and Manox Ltd* under which the parties shared know-how and other technology for the production of pigments used in the UK in the manufacture of printing inks, paints and cosmetics. S. 21(2) dispensation was given.

[204] For another hypothetical example, see Cunningham, *op. cit.*, at pp. 257, 258.

services and even the supply of goods. On this basis, and according to the OFT view of the *Ravenseft* doctrine, know- how is not clearly covered. However, there are a number of reasons for considering that know-how *is* exempted by the common law rule.

2.209 First, the OFT view, as represented by the quote above, only clarifies their position as regards standard intellectual property rights, it does not state that all other rights are excluded from the *Ravenseft* doctrine. Secondly, *Ravenseft* re-affirmed the "open and closed door" theory; it did not invent it (see the cases cited above). Thus applying the open and closed door theory to know-how, a person who is allowed by the owner of confidential know-how to use that know-how, had in a practical sense no pre-existing right or ability to use the know-how. If the user had covertly and illicitly obtained the know-how, the owner could have evoked common law and equitable rights to restrain its illicit use. The contract granting the user his rights thus creates rights, it does not take any away. In this sense such a contract is not restrictive even though it may contain limits imposed on the user's exploitation of the know-how. There is, however, a contrary view which is that since any person may by their own efforts create the know-how, a contract granting a person a use right forecloses that option. Thus, before the contract the person had an unfettered right to create and exploit the know-how (however economically and technically unlikely that might be) whereas after the contract that right evaporated and was replaced by a fettered contractual right. In this somewhat hypothetical sense (since the user is most unlikely to be able to avail himself of the potential to create the know-how) the user is restricted.

2.210 Thirdly, the Court in *Ravenseft* held that the grant of a lease was not within the Act because it did not entail the provision of services or the supply of goods. Know-how is an amorphous concept: it may consist of documents, it may entail the grantor assisting the user in instituting facilities to exploit the know-how, it may necessitate the grantor providing goods which the user will need in connection with the know-how. If, on the facts, the know-how is unrelated to any assistance given by the grantor or any related goods provided by the know-how owner, then it may be argued that the communication of know-how does not involve the supply of goods or the provision of services. The simple fact that the know-how will almost certainly be reduced to documentary form does not mean that the contract is for the supply of goods, i.e. the papers containing the information. In *Ravenseft* the fact that the leases, naturally enough, were reduced to documentary form did not mean that the lessor supplied goods to the tenants.

(2) Position in EC law

2.211 The position under EC law has been that limitations on licensees are restrictive and may at least where the technology is not new infringe Article 85(1) EC.[205] The Commission has issued separate block exemptions for patent and know-how licences laying down their policy towards certain types of clause now to be replaced by a combined technology transfer block exemption.[206] Where an agreement between two UK parties is likely to affect trade between the Member States of the EC then the agreement must comply with EC policy and reference to the block exemptions is essential. Indeed reference to the regulation is probably essential for any patent

[205] See Case 258/78 *LC Nungesser KG and Eisele* v *EC Commission* (the *Maize Seed* case) [1982] ECR 2015; [1983] CMLR 278.
[206] Reg. 240/96 OJ 1996 L31/2, 9 February 1996.

and/or know-how licence system which covers all or a substantial part of the UK market. In such cases intra-Community trade may well be affected.

6. *Position where Agreement Overlaps two Different Exemptions in Schedule 3*

2.212 An agreement which has restrictions which are exempted by more than one provision of Schedule 3 is *not* exempt from the Act. The exemptions in Schedule 3 are mutually exclusive of each other. Thus, if in an exclusive dealing agreement there are restrictions which would enable it to be exempt under Schedule 3, para. 2 and also restrictions that would fit with Schedule 3, para. 4 (for example imposing restrictions on the dealer as to the types of goods the suppliers trade mark may be affixed to) then no exemption exists.[207] The exemptions in Schedule 3 each provide that to earn exemption the agreement in question must contain no restrictions "other than", or "except in respect of", restrictions permitted by that specific provision.

2.213 This rule does have the effect of limiting the value of the exemptions. Parties to agreements have a number of options: (a) redraft the agreement to ensure that the restrictions fit within only one provision of the schedule; (b) redraft the agreement so as to fit the restrictions into one of the wider exemptions. For example, it is common practice in cases where a holder of patent rights wishes to license that patent to a licensee and also licence relevant know-how to him, to fit all of the restrictions in one agreement exempt under Schedule 3, para. 5 (patents). Thus, X licenses a patent to Y and concludes in the agreement provisions for the transfer of know-how concerning the patent to Y and restrictions on its use. It might be arguable that the know-how restriction can be equally well described as an information provision in respect of the invention to which the patent relates. If this is so then it fits under Schedule 3, para. 5 along with the basic grant of the patent licence. In such a case know-how and patent licence restrictions may be drafted so as to fit within one exemption; (c) draft more than one agreement and ensure that each individual agreement is exempt. The difficulty with this approach is that the OFT will probably view the agreements as part of a larger single arrangement and hence non-exempt.

2.214 In cases where an agreement unavoidably contains restrictions exempt under more than one provision, the best course is to furnish particulars of the agreement to the OFT with an accompanying letter stating that (if the agreement contains only intellectual property restrictions) the parties do not consider the agreement to impose restrictions. If the OFT do decide to register it, dispensation under section 21 (2) may well be available.

M. Agreements with Overseas Operation Only: Schedule 3, paras. 6 and 9

2.215 Schedule 3, paras. 6 and 9 exclude from the RTPA 1976 agreements and trade association recommendations whose restrictions relate exclusively to:

(a) the supply of goods by export outside the UK;
(b) the production of goods outside the UK;
(c) the application of any process of manufacture to goods outside the UK;

[207] See e.g. *Schweppes* v *Registrar of Restrictive Trading Agreements No. 2* (1970–71) LR 7 RP 336; [1971] 1 WLR 1148 *per* Stamp J.

(d) the acquisition of goods to be delivered outside the UK and not imported into the UK for home use;
(e) the supply of goods to be delivered outside the UK otherwise than by export from the UK;
(f) the supply of services to persons outside the UK;
(g) the supply of services in relation to property of any description (whether movable or immovable) outside of the UK.

2.216 It is to be noted that in relation to Schedule 3(9), in relation to supplying services with overseas operation, the wording is inexplicably different from that used in Schedule 3(6) in relation to goods. Schedule 3(9) does not concern the acquisition of services whereas Schedule 3(6) does concern the acquisition of goods. Thus, for example, if X agrees to appoint Y as his sole agent in France and accepts a further obligation to appoint no one else, X has accepted a restriction as to the acquisition of agency services. X will obtain those services from Y and from no other person. The service in question will relate to the function attributed to the agent in France. The fact that the agreement has overseas operation only would not bring it within the scope of Schedule 3(9). If the agreement concerned goods and X agreed to acquire goods only from Z in France for use in France this would constitute a restriction as to the acquisition of goods to be delivered outside the United Kingdom and would amount to an acquisition which had overseas operation and which fell within the scope of Schedule 3(6).

2.217 Schedule 3, paras. 6 and 9, thus provides a broad exemption for agreements relating to the supply, acquisition and production and processing of goods for export. Exemption is also provided for the supply of services. The word export is not defined in the Act. Presumably it simply implies the transfer of goods or services across frontiers. It will be a question of fact in each case whether this occurs. An agreement whereby a UK company purchases supplies in the UK on behalf of subsidiaries or branches abroad is almost certainly an export sale. Concerning acquisition of goods, the exemption applies where goods are obtained domestically for delivery abroad. Where the goods are imported into the UK for re-export in the same state the exemption remains. If the goods are imported into the UK and some of them are used in the UK and some are re-exported then no exemption will lie.

2.218 Thus, agreements between exporters under which, for example, the parties fix the prices or share the export market geographically or by quota will be exempt. Agreements between firms whose operations are overseas concerning buying prices are likewise free from registration so long as the relevant goods are to be made or processed outside the UK. It does not matter in such a case that the goods are, at a later date, imported into the UK.

2.219 Under section 25 RTPA 1976 export agreements exempt under the Act must be notified to the OFT. However, in practice many firms do not bother and the OFT has no powers to enforce compliance.

2.220 Although export agreements need not be registered they may be referred to the MMC under the monopoly provisions. The MMC has in the past adopted something of a patriotic view of such cartels. In a report on the supply and export of wire rope and fibre rope and cordage,[208] the MMC noted that while price fixing tends towards higher home prices and the reduction of incentives between firms to be efficient, such detriments were less acute where the export market was concerned. The view

[208] MMC Report HC 2 (November 1973).

adopted apparently favours the UK balance of payments over the consumers welfare abroad. Such a view would, of course, be entirely unacceptable to the European Commission. It may no longer be attractive even to the MMC. Where an export agreement focuses attentions on Community markets then clearance must be obtained from the Commission. Failure to obtain clearance or exemption can result in the agreement becoming void and the Commission fining the parties.

2.221 If an export agreement contains restrictions affecting the domestic market as well as the export market it becomes registrable in normal manner. To fit within the exemption *all* restrictions must relate exclusively to the foreign market. See paras. 2.212–2.214 for details of agreements containing restrictions fitting into more than one exemption.

N. Crown Agreements

2.222 Acts of Parliament are presumed not to bind the Crown in the absence of express provision or necessary implication.[209] This long-standing rule of statutory interpretation is independent of the royal prerogative. Where, as is frequently the case, it is necessary that the Crown be bound then each statute will make the necessary provision. If an Act is silent, however, and there is no necessary implication to the contrary, then the Crown and its numerous agents and servants are exempt.

2.223 The RTPA accordingly does not bind the Crown, its agents or servants. The underlying basis of the doctrine is that the Act would hamper the conduct of government business or prejudice its interests. An agreement between the Crown and, say, X, Y and Z is not registrable even though two or more persons might accept restrictions. Thus in *Telephone Apparatus Manufacturers Application*[210] an otherwise restrictive agreement between telephone producers and the Postmaster General was not subject to registration. Crown immunity can have wider implications. In the *Telephone* case cited above, manufacturers of telephones entered into agreements *inter se* setting out a machinery for satisfying their contractual duties to the Postmaster General. Under the agreement with the Crown (in the form of the Postmaster General) the manufacturers were to supply telephones. The agreement between the manufacturers *inter se* was designed to share out this work on a quota basis. The Court of Appeal held that this secondary agreement was not registrable since it was necessary in order to implement the agreement with the Crown. Registration and assessment of the agreement by the RPC would have harmed the interests of the Postmaster General.

2.224 Simply because an institution is incorporated by the Crown exercising prerogative powers and its powers are subject to the control of the Queen in Council and the Privy Council does not mean that the institution itself enjoys Crown privilege.[211]

2.225 The Crown, conversely, is not excluded from employing the RTPA against third parties. In 1978 the Post Office retrieved £9 million in settlement from suppliers of

[209] See e.g. *Province of Bombay* v *Municipal Corporation of Bombay* [1974] AC 58; *Attorney General for Ceylon* v *A. D. Silva* [1953] AC 461; *Madras Electric Supply Co Ltd* v *Boarland* [1955] AC 667; *BBC* v *Johns* [1965] Ch 32; *Lord Advocate* v *Dumbarton DC* [1990] AC 521, in which Lord Keith stated that the Crown would be bound by a statute if otherwise the legislation would be frustrated in a "material respect". See generally, Wade, *Administrative Law*, 7th edn. (1994), p. 839 *et seq.*; Hogg, *Liability of the Crown* (1971), Chapter 7.

[210] (1963) LR 3 RP 462.

[211] e.g. *Royal Institution of Chartered Surveyors Application* [1985] ICR 330 affirmed by the CA [1986] ICR 550, 562 applying *Dickson* v *Pharmaceutical Society of Great Britain* [1970] AC 403.

cables to them who had clandestinely colluded to fix tender prices. These collusive tendering agreements came to light as a result of enquiries arising from Monopolies and Mergers Commission investigations into insulated wires and cables. In 1975 the Director General successfully applied to the RPC for injunctions against the parties further restraining them from giving effect to other like agreements.[212] Under section 35(2) RTPA 1976 private individuals may sue in damages, for breach of statutory duty, any person who has failed to furnish particulars of their agreement in due time. The Post Office successfully used this provision as the major bargaining counter against the cable producers in settling out of court for, as stated above, £9 million.

O. Restrictive Covenants in Leases and Other Property Agreements: The *Ravenseft* Doctrine

2.226 The decision in *Ravenseft Properties* v *Director General of Fair Trading*[213] indicates that only in exceptional cases will restrictive covenants in leases constitute restrictions for the purposes of the RTPA 1976. In that case the plaintiffs applied to the Court for a declaration that certain restrictive covenants in commercial property leases were not registrable. The plaintiffs owned and managed a very large number of properties in the UK. When services agreements were brought under control in 1976 it was feared that commercial leases would fall to be registered if they incorporated restrictive covenants. Mr Justice Mocatta commented at the outset of the case:

> "If as a result of the [legislation] leases are brought under control ... this would clearly be a very serious matter for the applicants and for other companies in a comparable position in that the applicants may well have current hundreds if not thousands of leases and ... each of these would have to be examined in order to make certain whether or not there was an obligation under the ... Act ... to register such leases as agreements between two or more persons carrying on business within the United Kingdom in the supply of services brought under control by the [legislation]."[214]

2.227 The types of restrictive covenant being examined by the Court were varied. They included covenant on the lessee:

- not to effect alterations to the premises;
- to use the property exclusively for the restricted purposes laid down in the lease;
- not to assign, transfer, underlet or part with or share the possession or occupation of the premises or any part thereof;
- to insure against risks specified in the lease with an insurer nominated by the lessor.

In one case where the lessee was a limited company the lessor further required the managing director and owner to provide a surety that his company would abide by the restrictions in the lease.[215]

[212] cf. *Agreement Relating to Tenders for the Supply of Telephone Cables* (20 November 1975) unreported, noted in some detail in DGFT Annual Report 1975, p. 91. For the actual agreements see Nos. 3850, 3851, 3852, Register of Restrictive Trade Practices. For details of the case see para. 5.101.

[213] [1977] 1 All ER 47 (QBD).

[214] *ibid.*, at p. 49.

[215] *ibid.*, at p. 55(d)(e): "There is nothing in the Acts to convert a guarantor's obligations to pay the creditor on default by the principal debtor into a restriction. On the other hand there is in cl. 6(2) of this underlease an exceptional provision containing a covenant by the surety with the lessor that, if the lessee should go into liquidation and the liquidator should disclaim the underlease, the lessor might, within three months after any such disclaimer in writing, require the surety to accept an underlease of the premises for a term equivalent to

1. *Basis of the Ravenseft Doctrine*

2.228 The Court held that in none of the leases in question were the restrictive covenants registrable. The principles used by the Court to arrive at this conclusion are of importance to anyone considering the registrability of a restrictive property agreement:

2.229 (a) The provision of services entails "doing things for people".[216] Thus, where a lessor was only involved in letting property he was not carrying on a business in the provision of services. However, this is not an absolute rule. If the landlord provides services in connection with the property he lets then he may be in the business of providing services. Cleaning and porterage services provided by the landlord would fit into this category.[217]

2.230 (b) Restrictive covenants in a lease do not amount to restrictions on the tenant. The principles behind this conclusion were discussed at paras 2.201–2.210 in respect of intellectual property licences. Lord Reid in *Esso Petroleum Co Ltd* v *Harper's Garage (Stourport) Ltd* stated: "A person buying or leasing land had no previous right to be there at all, let alone to trade there, and, when he takes possession of the land subject to a negative restrictive covenant, he gives up no right or freedom which be previously had."[218] Thus a tenant subject to restrictive covenant gives up no freedom, since he had none to start with, and hence cannot be subject to a restriction.

2.231 (c) There must be a trading nexus between the lessor and lessee for, exceptionally, the Act to apply. Mr Justice Mocatta stated: "a lease ... would only fall within the scope of the Act if there were some trading nexus between the parties alleged to have accepted restrictions and the subject matter of the agreement."[219] The formula given by Mocatta J is far from clear. Its object is to exclude from consideration agreements between providers of services and the recipients where there is no commercial or trading link between them. Thus a landlord who leases commercial property to a travel agent and who provides cleaning services for

cont.
the residue of the original term had there been no disclaimer, at the same rent and subject to the like covenants and conditions as were reserved by and contained in the underlease. This covenant by the surety would, however, not come into play until after the original lessee was in liquidation." This situation, held Mocatta J, was covered by the *Esso Petroleum* rule. The fact that it came into operation only after the original lessee was in liquidation was also apparently relevant.

216 *ibid.*, at p. 53C.

217 *ibid.*

218 [1967] 1 All ER 699 at p. 707; [1968] AC 269 at p. 298. See also *Automatic Telephone and Electric Co Ltd's Application* (1963) LR 3 RP 462 at p. 483; [1963] 2 All ER 302 at p. 307; *Cleveland Petroleum Co Ltd* v *Dartstone Ltd* [1969] 1 All ER 201 at p. 203; [1969] 1 WLR 116 at p. 119. Both cases were cited with approval on this point in *Ravenseft*. But see *Stephens* v *Gulf Oil Canada Ltd* (1974) 45 DLR 161 *per* Henry J.

219 [1977] 1 All ER 47 at p. 53. There is no legal justification for this trading nexus rule in the Act. It seems to have been adopted as a result of various concerns expressed by Counsel for the OFT: "The Director did not wish to argue, however, that in the case where both the lessor and the lessee provided services this was a state of fact sufficient to require the lease to be registered. If that were the case, there would be extraordinary anomalies between leases granted to a tenant who was going to provide a service on the premises, such as using the premises for the purposes of a betting shop, and a tenant who was going to use the premises for the purposes of selling greengroceries." (*ibid.*, at p. 53(e)(f)). Rather curiously the "nexus" spoken of by Mocatta J was expressed to be between the parties, one the one hand, and the subject matter of the lease, on the other hand. Precisely what is envisaged in this nexus is unclear. The subject matter of the lease is the estate demised by the lessor and it is, accordingly, difficult to imagine what trading nexus could exist between parties and estate. The most logical interpretation of this dictum is the one given in the text, i.e. a commercial trading link between the parties themselves which is in some way affected by the agreement between them.

the travel agent on the premises can hardly be said to have a "trading nexus" with the travel agent. They certainly do not compete with each other. The commercial link or nexus in question will almost certainly be one of competition between the parties. The OFT is unlikely to be interested in an agreement in which the parties are not in a position to affect competition.[220]

2. *Conditions for Determining Registrability*

2.232 From the *Ravenseft* decision for a lease or other property agreement to be registrable it is submitted the following conditions must be satisfied:

(a) There must be two parties carrying on business within the United Kingdom. Thus, leases of residential homes are outside the scope of the Act.
(b) Both parties (i.e. lessor and lessee) must be providers of services albeit that the services may be different.
(c) There must be a trading nexus between the services in question, based in some way upon competition.
(d) The lease must contain restrictions on both parties that fall within section 11(2)(a)–(e) RTPA 1976. These restrictions must derive from the agreement itself and not from the right of occupation; restrictive covenants in a lease limiting the lessees use of the premises are not restrictions since the limitations derive from the right of occupation. Most likely the restrictions will relate to a limitation on the lessees activities which have no bearing on how he uses the demised property.

3. *Agreement Likely to be Registrable*

2.233 The Court held in *Ravenseft* that, "it is only the most exceptional circumstances of collateral agreements or of a sale and lease-back plus very special circumstances that restrictions contained in lease could possibly fall within the ambit of the" legislation. The Court did not fully explain what was intended by the citation of these examples.[221]

(1) Collateral agreements

2.234 The Court gave an example of a lease involving an agreement which might be registrable:

> "A lessor carries on business in both Brighton and Eastbourne in separate premises in those towns as a travel agent; in other words he provides services to the public. He then leases the Eastbourne premises to two joint tenants each of whom enters into a collateral undertaking not to open up a travel agency business in Brighton. The landlord, by letting the premises he previously used as a travel agency will be giving up that business in

[220] In terms of policy if the lessor and lessee are direct rivals then the agreement may have anti-competitive effects. If the lessor and lessee are supplier and customer then, again, the agreement can effect competition. In this latter case competition is not effected between the parties themselves since they do not compete; competition may be effected in the lessee's market if the lease gives the lessee some advantage over his rivals. Again, competition might be affected where manufacturer X, who has excess capacity, leases factory space and plant to rival manufacturer Y. X could use the lease to restrict Y in a manner advantageous to X.

[221] [1977] 1 All ER 47 at p. 55(j).

Eastbourne. In such a case there would be a sufficient nexus between the subject matter of the leases and the restrictions entered into which would be in respect of services."[222]

Essentially such an agreement would be a no-poaching or market-sharing agreement.

(2) Sale and lease back agreements

2.235 The Court intimated that sale and lease back arrangements when coupled to other circumstances might be registrable.[223] A common sale and lease back situation concerns the tied house pub or tied petrol filling station. In a typical sale and lease back X sells the fee-simple in land to Y subject to a lease hold interest; Y purchases the property subject to the lease which is to be granted to X. The sale to Y of the property and the lease back to X all occur within one transaction. Thus, X through the conveyance, has translated his freehold interest into a leasehold interest. The sale and lease back arrangement involves X in giving up rights he held before the contract. It does not therefore satisfy the open and shut door *Esso Petroleum* principle. Lord Denning MR in a later case explained why: "We should hold that when a person takes possession of premises under a lease, *not having been in possession*, previously; and on taking possession, he enters into a restrictive covenant tying him to take all his supplies from the lessor, prima facie, the tie is valid. It is not an unreasonable restraint of trade."[224] Since X has been in possession prior to his obtaining the leasehold interest he has given up freedom and accepted a restriction. Thus, in a sale and lease back one party will accept restrictions on use. However, to be registrable there must still exist all of the *other* conditions for registrability noted above. Thus, the other party must also accept registrable restrictions. In sale and lease backs there is invariably a trading nexus between the parties, e.g. petrol company and filling-station owner; brewery and publican. These two examples concern suppliers of goods, though there is no reason why a restrictive sale and lease back agreement between providers of services should not be registrable. Indeed, the example given by Mocatta J in *Ravenseft* (above) concerns services. It appears to be the case that such agreements are safe from registration so long as the only person accepting restrictions is the party whose freehold has been turned into a leasehold, i.e. the original owner.[225]

[222] *ibid.*, at pp. 54, 55.

[223] *ibid.*, at p. 55(j).

[224] *Cleveland Petroleum Co Ltd* v *Dartstone Ltd* [1969] 1 All ER 201 at p. 203; [1969] 1 WLR 116 at p. 119 (emphasis added).

[225] Assignment and lease back agreements might also be registrable. Such agreements are common in local authority land development schemes. A local authority wishes a plot of land developed, it leases the land on a 999-year lease to a property developer. The developer in order to obtain finance enters into a lease and lease back agreement with an investment company or other financial institution. Under this agreement the developer assigns or transfers for consideration the 999-year lease to the investment company who leases back the property for a smaller period (e.g. 99 years). The developer now pays the investment company a rent based upon and variable with certain factors (e.g. the expected profits of the developer). This assignment and lease back is intended to operate as a mortgage substitute: the developer assigns the land for a large consideration (the loan); he pays rent on the lease he takes (the repayment). Clearly under this agreement there are two parties providing services in the UK. There is a trading nexus between the parties in that they both have a financial interest in the development venture. The developer gives up a freedom he previously enjoyed. In such situations care must be taken to ensure that any restrictions entered are all accepted by the developer. If all the restrictions are heaped on one side then there are not two parties accepting restrictions and registration is avoided. While the OFT have no real interest in seeing such agreements the danger is s. 35(1) RTPA 1976 which renders void restrictions in unregistered, registrable agreements. Restrictions in the finance agreement between the financier and the developer may, irrespective of any other rules, be exempt under the RTPA 1977 (exemption for loan finance and credit facilities agreements). See paras. 2.126–2.132.

4. *Competition Act 1980: Overlap*

2.236 Finally, it should be noted that although most agreements will be outside the scope of the RTPA 1976, they may still be caught by the Competition Act 1980. Thus, a powerful property company who controls competition in a locality by restricting the numbers of commercial tenants of a particular class he leases to, might be conducting an anti-competitive course of conduct. If one company owned all or a large part of the leasehold property in a particular area and granted leases to only one butcher and one travel agent and one greengrocer, etc. then, since other traders of the same class can only compete if they can purchase the freehold of a property in the area, the effect of the landlord's selective approach may be to preclude competition in the locality. For the landlord, of course, it might be possible to justify a higher rent by being able to grant his tenants a cushion from competitors. To be susceptible to challenge under the Competition Act 1980, however, the lessor would have to control the nature of outlets over a very large relative area. Hence competition problems are unlikely. It is conceivable that a property company might purchase all or most of the sites bearing special characteristics needed by certain industries (e.g. access to a raw material, limited source of power, communication route, etc.). In such a case the property company would gain sufficient economic power over the supply of a rare commodity, i.e. the land. Indeed ownership of a port which dominates traffic routes to certain destinations would be a good example of control over property conferring significant market power. It is pertinent to note, in this respect, that activities relating to the provision of land are expressly contemplated as being subject to the Competition Act 1980, section 2(7) CA 1980 provides that the provision of car parking facilities constitutes a service; section 23 CA 1980 provides that the making of arrangements for a person to put or keep on land a caravan constitutes a supply of services.

P. Agreements with Disregardable Restrictions

2.237 Sections 9 and 18 RTPA 1976 were discussed at paras. 1.74–1.100. When assessing whether an agreement is registrable or not certain terms in the agreement may be disregarded. In negotiations with the OFT or in mounting a defence before the Court the irrelevance of such terms may also be asserted. These disregardable terms cover: coal and steel agreements; agreements relating exclusively to the goods or services sup plied; agreements concerning standards; agreements concerning industrial relations. Reference to Chapter 1 should be made for further details.

Q. Sale of Business Agreements: Non-Competition Clauses

2.238 Agreements for the change of ownership of a business, either by share or assets transfer, or for the subscription for shares in a company, in which only certain typical types of non-competition covenants taken are now exempt from registration. This is as a consequence of S.I. 1989 No. 1081, the Restrictive Trade Practices (Sale and Purchase and Share Subscription Agreements) (Goods) Order 1989, and S.I. 1989 No. 1082, the Restrictive Trade Practices (Services) (Amendment) Order 1989. Reference should be made to paras. 11.105–11.114 for further details.

R. Restrictive Trade Practices (Non-Notifiable Agreements) (Turnover Threshold) Order 1996: the £20 million aggregate turnover threshold

2.239 Pursuant to the Restrictive Trade Practices (Non-Notifiable Agreements) (Turnover Threshold) Order 1996[226] an agreement is a non-notifiable agreement where the aggregate annual turnover of the respective groups to which the parties belong does not exceed £20 million upon the day on which the agreement is made. If this condition is met particulars of the agreement (save for a price fixing agreement) although in principle registrable need not be furnished to the OFT for registration. Being subject to the Act the agreement is exempt from the Competition Act 1980. The operative part of the Order[227] provides as follows:

> "(1) For the purposes of Section 27A of the Act, and subject to the provisions of that Section, an agreement is a non-notifiable agreement if the parties to it are persons whose aggregate relevant annual turnover in the United Kingdom does not exceed £20 million on the date on which it is made.
> (2) For the purposes of paragraph (1) above the relevant annual turnover in the United Kingdom of a person party to an agreement shall include the relevant annual turnover in the United Kingdom of any person which on the date the agreement is made is a member of the same group of interconnected bodies corporate as that party."

"Agreement" includes arrangements[228] and therefore the "parties" are the parties to the agreement or the arrangement. Article 3(4) of the Order states that in relation to an agreement to which the Act has effect by virtue of Sections 8 and 16 RTPA 1976 as if it were an agreement between members of a goods or services trade association or persons represented on the trade association by such members, references in Article 3 to the "parties to an agreement" include references to those members or persons. It will be recalled that both sections 8 and 16 RTPA 1976 contain a deeming provision whereby the constitution of the association is deemed to contain a term pursuant to which each member (and any person represented on the association by any such member) agrees to comply with such recommendations (and subsequent recommendations) made to them by or on behalf of the associations as to the action to be taken by them in relation to certain classes of goods or services, or processes of manufacture.[229]

2.240 Pursuant to Article 3(2) the relevant annual turnover of the parties to the agreement is deemed to include the relevant turnover of any person which on the date the agreement is made is a member of the same group of inter-connected bodies corporate as that party. In relation to trade associations, the decisions and recommendations will be non-notifiable (provided that they do not entail price fixing) if the aggregate turnover of *all* of the members of the associations and the groups to which they belong does not exceed £20 million.

2.241 If the relevant turnover in the United Kingdom of the group in question is under £20 million *at the outset* then it matters not that thereafter (or even immediately after signature of the agreement) turnover exceeds £20 million. The agreement, if non-notifiable upon signature, remains non-notifiable, in principle, *ad infinitum*. It matters

[226] S.I. 1996 No. 348 made pursuant to s. 27A RTPA 1976.
[227] Art. 3(1).
[228] See 43(1) RTPA 1976.
[229] See ss. 8(3) (Goods), and 16(4) (Services).

not that the turnover might be exceeded by a very substantial margin. In such circumstances the Director General might (assuming the agreement comes to his attention) conclude that any restrictions or information provisions contained within the agreement "are of such significance as to call for investigation by the Court"[230] and enter or file on the register particulars of the agreement. In such circumstances, the agreement ceases to be a non-notifiable agreement and the Director General is bound to give notice of that fact to each of the parties to the agreement.[231]

2.242 The threshold criteria set out in the Order do not operate in the same way as the European Commission Notice on Agreements of Minor Importance. For example, the turnover of the parties to the agreements might be only £5 million and the turnover of the other members of the respective groups might be only £10 million on the day the agreement is signed. However the day after signature the parent company of one of the parties may be acquired (or indeed may acquire) another group with a turnover of £250 million. The agreement is non-notifiable. In this regard the position is different under EC competition law. Under the EC Commission Notice (and setting aside considerations of market share) where parties and their respective groups have an aggregate worldwide turnover of less than 300 million ECU prima facie the agreement is deemed to be *de minimis*. However, under the Notice if the threshold is exceeded, at a future point in time, the presumption that the agreement is *de minimis* lapses and the parties would need to consider notifying the agreement to the Commission, if it were not otherwise subject to a block exemption. Under the Order, conversely, an agreement is a non-notifiable agreement if the turnover does not exceed £20 million "on the date upon which it is made". The Order does not say that an agreement is non-notifiable "if the turnover does not exceed £20 million", or "to the extent that turnover does not exceed £20 million". The Order may lead to some inconsistent results. For example, A and B share markets on a geographical basis for certain new technologies within the United Kingdom. Upon the day the agreement is made the turnover of A and B and their respective groups, in aggregate, is £19 million. Eighteen months later it is (because the market sharing successfully stifles competition and increases the profits of A and B) £100 million and turnover is expanding month by month. In such circumstances the agreement between A and B remains non-notifiable. New entrants—C and D—come into the market and conclude a market sharing agreement in a form similar to that concluded between A and B. The aggregate turnover of C and D is £21 million. Unlike the agreement between A and B (which now accounts for a turnover of circa £120 million) that between C and D *is* subject to the duty to furnish particulars to the Director General.

2.243 The *only* category of agreement which is notifiable even where the aggregate turnover of the parties and their respective groups in the United Kingdom does not exceed £20 million is price fixing agreements. All other forms of agreement, including market sharing, are in principle non-notifiable.

2.244 It is to be emphasised that the relevant turnover is the turnover *in* the United Kingdom. Accordingly, it does not matter that the turnover of the parties and/or their respective groups outside the United Kingdom may be very substantial. Article 2 of the Schedule to the Order defines "turnover in the United Kingdom". The definition is of some complexity and for the sake of convenience is set out in full below:

[230] s. 1(2A) RTPA 1976, inserted by the Deregulation and Contracting Out Act 1994, s. 10(4), Sch. 3 paras. 1 and 2.

[231] s. 25A(1) RTPA 1976.

"2. 'Turnover in the United Kingdom' during any particular period means the total amount charged for the supply of goods and services in the United Kingdom during that period in the ordinary course of a person's business after deduction—

(a) Of trade discounts, rebates and other allowances;
(b) Of Value Added Tax and other taxes related directly to turnover; and
(c) Of any amount charged or any such supply where both the person supplying both the goods and services and the person to whom they were supplied were members of one and the same group of inter-connected bodies corporate at the time of the supply:

Provided that in a case in which the total amount of revenue receivable by a person during any particular period in the ordinary course of his business in the United Kingdom, after deduction—

(i) Of amounts receivable in respect of the supply by him of goods or services;
(ii) Of trade discounts, rebates and other allowances;
(iii) Of Value Added Tax and other taxes directly related to turnover; and
(iv) Of any amount receivable from any other person where both he and that other person were members of one and the same group of interconnected bodies corporate when payment fell due,

equals one third or more of the total amount charged for the supply of goods and services in the United Kingdom during the said period in the ordinary course of his business, after the deductions mentioned in sub-paragraphs (a), (b) and (c) above.

'Turnover in the United Kingdom' during that period means the aggregate of the two said total amounts after the above mentioned respective deductions."

2.245 The best way to understand the definition is by way of example. Before considering an example a number of observations may be made. First, the definition contains two parties: a basic test and a proviso. The starting point for calculating turnover in the United Kingdom is different in each part. Under the basic test the starting point is the total amount charged for the supply of goods and services. In the proviso it is the total amount of revenue receivable by the person in the relevant period. In the latter case one thus takes into consideration revenue over and above that received from the supply of goods and services, for example, rents, dividends, returns on other investments, etc. An example demonstrates how the definition operates. In a given year X has a total revenue of £17 million. This is derived from rents, dividends from subsidiaries, returns on other investments, and receipts from the supply of goods and services. In the year in question of this total revenue X has receipts from supplies of goods and services amounting to £10 million. For the purposes of the basic test under the Order X must first deduct from £10 million: trade discounts; rebates and other allowances (£1 million); VAT and other turnover related taxes (£2 million); and revenue from intra-groups supplies of goods and services (£1 million). The total amount to be deducted is therefore £6 million (i.e. £10 million minus £4 million). X must now carry out a second calculation under the proviso in order to determine its turnover in the United Kingdom for the purposes of the Order. X now deducts from its *total* revenue (i.e. £17 million) the following deductions: sums received for the supply of goods and services (£10 million); trade discounts rebates and other allowances (£1 million); VAT and other turnover related taxes (£2 million); and revenue from intra-group supplies of goods and services (£1 million),[232] The turnover calculated by

[232] Note that in relation to revenue from intra-group supplies of goods and services the amounts in relation to the basic provisions and in relation to the proviso are calculated at different *times*. in relation to the basic provision the amount is calculated "at the time of the supply". In the case of the proviso, however, the amount is calculated "when payment fell due". It is clear that repayment may fall due at a considerable period of time after the time of the supply.

reference to the proviso is £3 million (£17 million minus £14 million). X now calculates whether the proviso turnover equals one-third or more of the basic turnover. On this basis £3 million is more than one-third of £6 million and, accordingly, upon the basis of the text in the proviso, "turnover in the United Kingdom" means the aggregate of £3 million and £6 million i.e. £9 million.

2.246 The purpose of the somewhat convoluted text is to arrive at a turnover figure which reflects the company as a whole and not only of the revenue derived from the goods and services supplied. It takes account of the fact that a substantial amount of the parties' financial muscle may be derived from sources other than the supply of goods or services, the subject of the agreement in question.

2.247 For the purposes of the Order the turnover is calculated upon an annual basis. There is no problem in making such calculation where the parties have been operating in the United Kingdom for a number of years and have prepared annual accounts.

2.248 However, where the persons in question have not been operating for a full 12-month period the calculation is more difficult. Article 3(3) of the Order states:

> "For the purposes of this Article, the relevant annual turnover in the United Kingdom of a person in a particular case is:–
> (a) Where the relevant period equals 12 months, the turnover in the United Kingdom of that person during that period, and
> (b) Where the relevant period does not equal 12 months, the amounts which bears the same proportion to the turnover in the United Kingdom of that person during that period as 12 months does to that period."

"Relevant period" is defined in Article 1 of the Schedule. Three alternative definitions are set out in that provision: (i) where the person in question has within the two years ending immediately before the date on which the agreement in question was made, completed an accounting period of more than 6 months, the last such period so completed constituted a relevant period; or, (ii) where the person in question has not completed such a period but has, within the six months ending immediately before the date on which the agreement in question was made, completed an accounting period of six months or less, so much of the period of 12 months ending on the last day of the last such period to be completed as during which that person was carrying on business of supplying goods or services in the United Kingdom or otherwise carrying on business in the United Kingdom; or, (iii) in any other case, so much of the period of 12 months ending immediately before the date on which the agreement in question was made as during which that person was carrying on a business of supplying goods or services in the United Kingdom or otherwise carrying on business in the United Kingdom.

2.249 It is notable that the Order does not condition the non-notifiable status of an agreement upon the market share of the parties, as does the European Commission Notice on Agreements of Minor Importance. This means that parties with modest turnovers but very high shares in niche markets may conclude non-notifiable agreements simply because, upon the date the agreement was signed, the aggregate turnover of the parties did not exceed £20 million. Such a scenario would not be exceptional in the case of small, high technology companies engaged in exploiting patented technology or technology protected by secret know-how. The companies may be small at the outset of the period of exploitation of the technology but, if it is successful, grow very rapidly thereafter. So far as the Order is concerned the market share of the parties is simply irrelevant provided that, when the agreement was signed, the aggregate turnover did not exceed £20 million.

S. Restrictive Trade Practices (Non-Notifiable Agreements) (EC Block Exemptions) Order 1996

2.250 Pursuant to the Restrictive Trade Practices (Non-Notifiable Agreements) (EC Block Exemptions) Order 1996[233] certain categories of agreement subject to exemption pursuant to block exemption regulations of the EC Council or EC Commission constitute non-notifiable agreements for the purposes of section 27A RTPA 1976.

Accordingly, particulars need not be furnished to the DGFT for registration. The Order was adopted by the Secretary of State in the exercise of powers conferred upon him by section 27A RTPA 1976. The Order was made on the 19 February 1996. It was laid before Parliament on the 20 February 1996 and it came into force on the 19 March 1996. It applies only to agreements made on or after the 19 March 1996.[234]

2.251 Section 27A(1) RTPA 1976[235] defines non-notifiable agreements. A non-notifiable agreement is one which:

> "(a) is subject to registration under [the RTPA 1976],
> (b) is, and has always been, of a description specified for the purposes of this section by order made by the Secretary of State,
> (c) is not, and has never been, a price-fixing agreement, and
> (d) is not an agreement in respect of which the Director has entered or filed particulars under section 1(2)(b) above."

The Order was made for the purpose of specifying a description of non-notifiable agreement as referred to in section 27A(1)(b). Article 3 of the Order states:

> "An agreement is of a description specified for the purposes of Section 27(a) of the Act (which defines non-notifiable agreements) if:
> (a) it is an agreement which is exempt from Article 85.1 of the EC Treaty by virtue of the application to it of a block exemption regulation; or
> (b) it is an agreement which does not fall within the prohibition contained in Article 85.1 of the EC Treaty but which, if it did so fall, would be exempt from that provision by virtue of the application to it of a block exemption regulation."

In effect, the Order provides that an agreement (other than a price-fixing agreement) which, in *form* complies with the provision of a block exemption regulation of the Council of Ministers or the European Commission, will be a non-notifiable agreement and particulars of such an agreement will not have to be furnished to the Director General unless he requires them by serving a notice on the parties pursuant to Section 25A(1) RTPA 1976. A non-notifiable agreement it still an agreement subject to the RTPA 1976; the parties are merely exempt from the duty to furnish particulars and the OFT cannot, whilst particulars are un-registered, refer the agreement to the RPC. Being subject, in principle, to the Act, a non-notifiable agreement is exempt from the Competition Act 1980.

2.252 The purpose of the Order is to bring the position under UK restrictive practices law into line with EC competition law, but without altering the substantive provisions of the RTPA 1976. The Order thus describes two categories of agreement the particulars of which need not be furnished to the Director General, notwithstanding that they contain relevant restrictions accepted by at least two persons carrying on business in the United Kingdom within the meaning of the Act. The first category is

[233] S.I. 1996 No. 349.
[234] Reg. 1(2).
[235] Inserted by the Deregulation and Contracting Out Act s. 10(1).

agreements exempt from the prohibition in Article 85(1) by virtue of the application of a block exemption regulation adopted pursuant to Article 85(3)EC. The second category is agreements which in form are consistent with block exemption regulations but which for *other* reasons do not fall within Article 85(1) in particular because they either do not affect trade between the Member States of the EC to an appreciable degree or because the clauses or terms of the agreement in question, although drafted in a form giving the appearance of restrictions, none the less have only a *de minimis* impact upon competition or otherwise constitute ancillary restraints within the "rule of reason" doctrine and for that reason do not constitute restrictions within the meaning of Article 85(1). A number of observations may be made about the Order.

2.253 First, the reference to "agreement" in Article 3 is a reference to the concept of an agreement within the meaning of the RTPA 1976 to include "arrangement" within the meaning of section 43(1).The reference is, therefore, not a reference to agreements, concerted practices or decisions of associations of undertakings within the meaning of Article 85(1) even though, given the extended meaning attributed to "agreement" by section 43(1) there may, in practice, be no, or only a minor, difference between the RTPA 1976 and Article 85(1).

2.254 Secondly, agreements are only non-notifiable if they do not constitute a "price-fixing" agreement within the meaning of section 27A(1)(c), nor have *ever* been price fixing agreements. Price fixing agreements are defined as agreements to which the RTPA 1976 applies by virtue of sections 6(1)(a) or (b), or 11(2)(a) of that Act. "Price fixing" also includes information provisions in respect of any of the matters set out in section 7(1)(a) or (b) or 12(2)(a). Section 6(1)(a) and (b) refer respectively to agreements in respect of which restrictions are accepted in respect of "the prices to be charged, quoted or paid for goods supplied, offered or acquired, or for the application of any process of manufacture to goods" and, "the prices to be recommended or suggested as the prices to be charged or quoted in respect of the resale or goods supplied". Thus horizontal price fixing agreements or arrangements and agreements or arrangements as to resale prices *cannot* amount to non-notifiable agreements. Section 7(1)(a) refers to statutory instruments adopted by the Secretary of State directing that the Acts shall apply to information agreements covering "the prices charged, quoted or paid to be charged, quoted or paid for goods which have been, or are to be supplied, offered or required or for the application of the process of manufacture to goods". Section 12(2)(a) refers to information agreements as to services and empowers the Secretary of State, by statutory instrument, to make Orders in relation to agreements which relate to "the charges made, quoted or paid or to be made, quoted or paid for designated services which have been or are to be supplied, offered or obtained". It should be noted that the Secretary of State has not, to date, exercised the power available to him under section 12 to adopt a statutory instrument bringing under control exchange of information agreements as to *services*. In respect of goods agreements these were brought under control of the Act by the Restrictive Trade Practices (Information Agreements) Order 1969.[236] Services agreements do not therefore fall within the scope of the RTPA 1976 and, in any event, particulars of the same are not required to be notified to the Director General. Article 85(1)(a) prohibits price fixing agreements. It is only in highly exceptional circumstances that a price fixing agreement could ever be subject to the exemption in Article 85(3) EC. One such block exemption regulation does however

[236] S.I. 1969 No. 1842.

exist. Council Regulation 4056/86/EEC[237] concerning the application of Articles 85 and 86 to maritime transport services, applies the competition rules to "liner conferences" within the meaning of Article 1(3)(b). Pursuant to that provision a liner conference constitutes an agreement between vessel operating carriers pursuant to which, *inter alia*, the parties apply "uniform or common freight rates". The Regulation is intended to implement and make more precise the UNCTAD Code on Liner Conferences.[238]

2.255 Thirdly, it is to be observed that an agreement which obtains *individual* exemption after having been notified is *not* a non-notifiable agreement. Such an agreement may however be treated leniently by the Court under the terms of Section 5 RTPA 1976 pursuant to which the Court may only act if and insofar as it considers it right to do so having regard to the operation of a directly applicable Community measure such as a block exemption regulation. Somewhat inconsistently the position *vis-à-vis* agreements authorised upon a individual basis by the Commission under the ECSC Treaty (in particular Article 65 thereof) is different in that such agreements are not subject to the Act.

2.256 Fourthly, the Order, in effect, makes redundant a number of the exemptions to the Act contained in Schedule 3. That Schedule sets out descriptions of categories of agreement which, although they might contain restrictions rendering them subject to the duty to furnish particulars, are noen the less exempted from the Act. Pursuant to Schedule 3(2) an exemption exists for exclusive dealing agreements. A similar exemption exists pursuant to Schedule 3(3) for know-how agreements in relation to goods. Schedule 3(5) concerns patents and registered designs. Such agreements would now most likely be exempted pursuant to Commission Regulation 1983/83/EEC (exclusive distribution agreements); Commission Regulation 1984/83/EEC (exclusive purchasing agreements; and/or Commission Regulation 240/96/EC (technology transfer agreements).

2.257 Fifthly, it is clear from section 27(A) that for an agreement to be non-notifiable it must, at all times since its inception, have been in a form which is consistent with a relevant block exemption. In this regard the status of an agreement as non-notifiable will not however be prejudiced by an agreement growing in size so as to be more than *de minimis* in terms of its effect on trade between Member States, or, its impact upon competition. This is clear from Regulation 3 which states that an agreement is non-notifiable if it is exempt from Article 85(1) by virtue of an applicable block exemption; *or* is an agreement which does not fall within the prohibition (because for example of its insignificant effect on trade or upon competition)[239] in Article 85(1) but which, if it did, would none the less be exempt. It does not matter that an agreement changes in form over time, through amendment, *provided* that the changes or amendments do not entail loss of block exemption. The position in relation to agreements which, when concluded, are not within the strict confines of a block exemption but which *become* block exempt by virtue of the operation of an opposition procedure contained within a block exemption regulation is problematic. For example Article 4 of Regulation 240/96/EC (technology transfer agreements)[240] provides an opposition procedure in relation to restrictions of competition not expressly permitted by Articles 1 and 2 *and* not expressly prohibited in the black-list in Article

[237] OJ 1986 L378/4, 31 December 1986.

[238] cf. Council Directive 954/79/EEC, OJ 1979 L 121/1 concerning ratification by Member States of the United Nations Convention on a Code of Conduct for Liner Conferences (the UNCTAD Code). See also recital 3 of Regulation 4056/86/EEC (*ibid.*).

[239] See Order, Explanatory Note.

[240] OJ 1986 L31/2.

3. Article 6 gives, as examples, ties and no-challenge clauses. An agreement is *only* non-notifiable under section 27A if (*inter alia*) it "... has always been" within the block exemption (section 27A(1)(b)). An agreement which is block exempt by operation of a opposition procedure will not necessarily have *always* been block exempt. For instance, if the parties lodge the notification *after* (even the day after) the agreement is signed then, since exemption can only be granted as from the date of notification,[241] when the exemption is ultimately granted under the opposition procedure it will *not* cover the entire lifespan of the agreement and it will not be possible to say that the agreement "has always been" block exempt. The exemption granted under an opposition procedure, provided it covers the *entire* duration of the agreement in question, should qualify the agreement for non-notifiable status since the agreement is still exempt "... by virtue of the application to it of a block exemption legislation" (Order, Article 3) in the sense that it is the regulation which provides the mechanism (the opposition procedure) by which the agreement becomes exempt.

2.258 Sixthly, most block exemption regulations expressly state that they are exhaustive of the restrictions of competition which may be included.[242] However, some regulations are ambiguous and do not state expressly that they are exhaustive of the restrictions which may be permitted.[243] In the case of most block exemptions the inclusion of even one additional restriction not permitted by the Regulation will result in the Regulation being inapplicable in its entirety. Accordingly, the inclusion of even one restriction of competition within the meaning of Article 85(1) could result in an agreement, otherwise non-notifiable, being subject to the normal duty under the RTPA 19796 to furnish particulars. The position is not uniform across all block exemption regulations. For example Regulation 1475/95/EC[244] (motor vehicle selective distribution) expressly provides in Article 6 that the inclusion of certain black-listed clauses does *not* inevitably entail complete loss of block exemption.

2.259 Seventhly, section 27A(1)(d) states that an agreement is not a non-notifiable agreement if it is an agreement in respect of which the Director General has entered or filed particulars under section 1(2)(b) of the Act upon the register. The Director General has the power to file particulars of otherwise non-notifiable agreements which are of such significance as to warrant investigation by the Court. [245] It may arise that parties furnish particulars of an agreement because, for example, they are unsure whether it falls, four square, within the terms of an applicable block exemption regulation. If the Director General (perhaps mistakenly) files particulars of the agreement upon the register, it becomes non-notifiable. It will, in such circumstances, be open to the parties to apply to the Restrictive Practices Court pursuant to section 26 for an Order rectifying the register on the basis that it was non-notifiable.

[241] *Ibid.* Art. 4(7) and see Recital 25 of the Regulation.

[242] See e.g. Art. 2 Reg. 1983/83/EEC (exclusive dealing); Art. 7 Reg. 1984/83/EEC (exclusive purchasing).

[243] Reg. 4056/86/EEC on liner conferences is an example – see Art. 3 thereof. Though since the block exemption involves price-fixing it would not be non-notifiable in any event.

[244] OJ 1995 L145/25.

[245] s. 1(2A) RTPA 1976.

3 Anti-competitive Practices: Practice and Procedure under the Competition Act 1980

A. Introduction

3.1 The RTPA 1976 applies only to agreements and trade association practices; it excludes practices by individual firms which might be anti-competitive or agreements where (often due to the economic power of one side) only one party accepts restrictions. The monopoly control provisions of the Fair Trading Act 1973 do focus on this behaviour but only where performed by "monopoly" firms (meaning control of 25 per cent of the market).[1] In the gap between these two pieces of legislation the Competition Act 1980 (CA 1980 hereafter) operates. It also significantly overlaps with the monopoly provisions, as will be demonstrated. The CA 1980 developed out of, *inter alia*, the Liesner Committee Report, *Review of Restrictive Trade Practices Policy*, which highlighted the need for legislation to stop the gap and to provide a more rapid and less cumbersome machinery for the analysis of the conduct of economically powerful single firms.[2] It has been amended in some important respects by the Deregulation and Contracting Out Act 1994.

3.2 The 1980 Competition Act provides for three regulatory procedures: (i) under sections 2–10 whereby the Director General may investigate and subsequently refer to the MMC anti-competitive practices; (ii) under sections 11 and 12 whereby the Secretary of State may refer certain public undertakings to the MMC for "efficiency audits" concerning costs, general efficiency and abuses of monopoly power; and (iii) under section 13 whereby the Secretary of State may require the Director General to investigate any price specified to be "of major public concern".

[1] s. 6 Fair Trading Act 1973.

[2] (1979) Cmnd 7512. See also Liesner Report *A Review of Monopolies and Mergers Policy* (1978) Cmnd 7198, Annex B, paras. 9–17. See also Cunningham and Tinnion, *The Competition Act 1980* (1980); Merkin and Williams (1980) 43 MLR 429 J; Kay and Sharpe (1982) *Fiscal Studies* 191; Kirkbride, "Anti-Competitive Practices Under The Competition Act 1980—The Real Meaning And Approach" [1991] JBL 245; A.R. Everton, "Discrimination and Predation in the United Kingdom: Small Grocers and Small Bus Companies—A Decade of Domestic Competition Policy" [1993] ECLR 6.

It is with the first of these three procedures that this chapter is concerned. However, a brief overview of procedures (ii) and (iii) is given at the end of the chapter.

3.3 The following may be found in this chapter.

Section B. Anti-competitive practices: summary of regulatory procedure. In this section an overview of procedure under the CA 1980 is given.

Section C. Anti-competitive practices: definitions, examples. In this section a detailed analysis of statutory wording is given.

Section D. Anti-competitive practices: exclusions from the Act. This Section examines the scope of the exemptions from the CA 1980.

Section E. Anti-competitive practices: the investigation procedure. This section gives a detailed analysis of law and practice relating to the procedural steps as outlined in Section B.

Section F. Investigation of public bodies: brief overview of provisions in Act empowering OFT to investigate public bodies.

Section G. Investigation of prices of major public concern: brief overview of provisions in Act empowering OFT to investigate prices in the market.

Section H. Confidentiality in OFT and MMC reports: brief analysis of provisions covering confidentiality of information.

Section I. Assessment of competition by OFT and MMC.

Section J. Summary: check list for determining whether CA 1980 applies.

B. "Anti-Competitive Practices": Summary of Regulatory Procedure

3.4 It is useful at this early stage to provide a sketch of the regulatory system. The details are examined later. It suffices therefore to summarise the main stages of the procedure:

Stage 1. Complaints to the OFT of "anti-competitive practices". Complaints may be made by competitors, customers or others.

Stage 2. Investigation: the OFT investigate conduct to see whether a quick solution may be found and to verify the facts. Parties may negotiate the giving of assurances to the OFT at this stage.

Stage 3. The OFT may embark upon a more detailed investigation to determine whether the conduct is anti-competitive and whether it is adverse to the public interest, and may then accept undertakings from the complained of parties as a solution.

Stage 4. The "competition reference": the OFT may refer the case to the MMC for further analysis by way of investigation.

Stage 5. Monopolies and Mergers Commission investigation: the MMC investigate and report within six months on the allegedly anti-competitive conduct and its compatibility with the public interest.

Stage 6. Post-MMC undertakings: following an adverse report, the OFT may again accept appropriate undertakings. Alternatively, in certain situations, the Secretary of State may exercise wide powers of statutory Order against the person whose conduct is complained of.

An additional stage, requiring the OFT to produce a formal report at the end of its formal preliminary investigation in stage 3, was removed by section 12(3) Deregulation and Contracting Out Act 1994.[3]

C. Anti-Competitive Practices: Definitions, Examples

3.5 Section 2(1) CA 1980 reads:

> "a person engages in an anti-competitive practice if, in the course of business, that person pursues a course of conduct which, of itself or when taken together with a course of conduct pursued by persons associated with him, has or is intended to have or is likely to have the effect of restricting, distorting or preventing competition in connection with the production, supply or acquisition of goods in the United Kingdom or any part of it or the supply or securing of services in the United Kingdom or any part of it."

The following seeks to explain the meaning of certain key words and phrases in section 2(1). That provision is central to the CA 1980 since only "anti-competitive practice" so defined is subject to the regulatory procedure in sections 2–10 of the Act.

1. "Business"

3.6 "Business" is defined in section 33(2) CA 1980 as "a professional practice and includes any other undertaking which is carried on for gain or reward or which is an undertaking in the course of which goods or services are supplied otherwise than free of charge".[4] This definition is non-definitive; it simply provides that "business" includes certain things. The proviso words "otherwise than free of charge" are hard to construe. On ordinary rules of statutory interpretation the meaning of words and phrases may be gleaned by reference to surrounding words and phrases. Accordingly, "business" excludes activities not carried on for profit, gain or reward. However, many non-profit making bodies are intimately connected with the commercial world and may exercise considerable economic power, e.g. in trade associations. It is likely, therefore, that the word business will be construed widely and the proviso words construed narrowly. Thus, a non-profit making body which is intimately connected with a market and which therefore (albeit indirectly) influences others' profits should be considered to be in "business". This interpretation is in line with the analogous judgment of the House of Lords in *Town Investment Ltd* v *Department of the Environment*[5] which concerned the Counter Inflation (Business Rents) Order 1972. This instrument was designed as a counter-inflationary measure. The House of Lords construed "business" by reference to the mischief of the Order and, by so doing, held the activities of a non-profit making body (*in casu* a government department) to be business activities within the meaning of the Order.[6]

[3] Reports issued by the OFT under this earlier procedure are referred to in the text where relevant in understanding the OFT's policy in the application of the Act.

[4] s. 33(2) CA 1980 applies the definition in s. 137(2) Fair Trading Act 1973.

[5] [1978] AC 359 at pp. 383H–384B, 401B–D, 402E–H, 403A.

[6] However, there is an implication to be taken from s. 2(8) CA 1980 that the narrow view prevails. This provision requires that in considering the conduct of local authorities the section is construed as if the words "in the course of business" were omitted. Thus the Act applies to local authorities even though they may not be conducting business. s. 2(8) seems to imply that the words "in the course of business"

3.7 In the Committee stage of the Competition Bill it was pointed out that an investment policy could be viewed as a policy "in the course of business" which restricted competition. The Minister for Consumer Affairs gave an assurance that the Act was not intended to be used to investigate investment planning.[7]

2. *"Course of conduct"*

3.8 This term implies continuity or repetitiveness. Single, isolated or unconnected acts would not fall within the Act. The MMC, and hence presumably the OFT, takes a liberal view of the phrase and construes it so as to catch a wide range of anti-competitive behaviour. A course of conduct might include repetition of the same act. It might also include a series of different acts which have an economic connection (e.g. they are performed in the same market). It is an equivocal question whether a firm X who has interests in various markets and which perpetrates isolated, anti-competitive acts in each separate market, is engaged in a "course of conduct" or is simply performing a series of unconnected acts. It is certainly arguable that a policy of perpetrating, disparate anti-competitive acts is a course of conduct designed to improve by anti-competitive means that person's general standing in the market. The phrase presumably includes the behaviour of one person who pursues several courses of conduct. These can all be investigated simultaneously provided they are all specified in the statutory notices.[8] The OFT may find a course of conduct in cases which at first sight appear to be one-off transactions. In *Unichem Ltd*,[9] an offer of shares in a co-operative was held to be a course of conduct, as it was intended to be an incentive for offerees to continue doing business with it. Thus the offer *per se* did not constitute a course of conduct, but the incentive did.

3.9 The Secretary of State may exclude by order under section 2(3) and (4) CA 1980 categories of practice from the definition of "course of conduct". The exclusion may refer to specific practices or to particular categories of circumstance. This power has already been exercised. The Anti-Competitive Practices (Exclusion) Order 1980 excludes specific categories of activity from control, as amended by the Anti-Competitive Practices (Exclusions) (Amendment) Order 1994. Excluded categories of conduct are examined later at paras. 3.40–3.56.

3.10 A course of conduct subject to investigation may be past, present or future. Past practices are included so as to prevent companies escaping control by suspending a practice as soon as they become aware of OFT interest. Furthermore, many practices may be related to seasonal factors and hence periodic.

cont.
exclude the activities of local authorities who are administrators not traders. However it is arguable that s. 2(8) was merely making it clear in an equivocal section that local authorities were not excluded from the Act. This latter interpretation is, it is submitted, the preferable one in terms of policy and likely OFT application in the light of an uncertain s. 2(1). Moreover local authorities are very different organisations from, for example, trade associations. With regard to local authorities, the OFT accept that although the practice of selective competitive tendering is theoretically subject to the Act, the CA 1980 is not an appropriate method of analysis provided tendering systems are operated in accordance with government principles. Tendering procedures may, however, be subject to express statutory provisions—for example the provisions of Part v of the Transport Act 1985 in respect of tendering for subsidised bus services. See, HL Deb. Vol. 405, No. 83, 19 February 1980, Col. 610.

7 Following the House of Lords decision in *Pepper* v *Hart* [1993] AC 593, it is likely that a court would regard this statement as binding in the interpretation of this term.

8 See *Anti-Competitive Practices: A Guide to the Provisions of the Competition Act 1980* (OFT publication, 1986), p. 35.

9 OFT Report, 15 September 1988; MMC Report Cm 691, 1989; Competition: the Unichem Ltd (Allotment of Shares) Order 1989, S.I. 1989 No. 1061.

3. "Restricting, distorting or preventing competition"

3.11 By stark contrast with the RTPA 1976 which regulates agreements of a specified *form*, the CA 1980 regulates practices and conduct which exert a particular, anti-competitive *effect*. These words are prefaced by "has or intended or is likely to have the effect of". Thus, it is clear that the OFT may intervene pre-emptively to prevent economic harm, during the currency of a practice to curtail it, or, subsequent to the end of a practice to cure it. The words "restrict", "distort" or "prevent" are not necessarily substitutes for each other. An exclusive dealing contract, for example, can restrict competition between supplier and dealer (e.g. no poaching by supplier on dealer's territory; non-own-production by dealer), but because such agreements may increase penetration of a market and reduce capital entry barriers (since the supplier need not own his own retail outlet) they may increase competition generally in the market rather than prevent it.[10]

3.12 It is important to appreciate that whether a practice has anti-competitive effects will depend largely upon the nature of the market. The OFT have commented:

> "whether or not a firm's practice is anti-competitive will depend, to a large extent, upon the market position of that firm. The Act is not directed specifically at firms in dominant market positions. However, it is more likely that a firm can restrict, distort or prevent competition if it has some degree of market power.
>
> Where a firm is only one among a host of small traders in a market, it is unlikely that it will be able to engage in an anti-competitive practice since, if it attempts to impose restrictive terms on its customers, all that will happen is that it will lose business to its competitors. It follows that, though the Act does not require a monopoly situation to be identified, an important consideration in assessing whether a practice is anti-competitive is the extent to which the firm responsible enjoys market power, whether on a local or national level."[11]

Thus, for example, if X with 4 per cent of the market share refuses to supply a customer, that customer may obtain goods elsewhere. If Y with 75 per cent of the market refuses to supply that customer, then he may find it more difficult to obtain alternative supplies since Y might be dominant in his locality. In the latter case Y's market power might render his conduct anti-competitive. The question of assessing competition in a market is one of some complexity. Accordingly, it is considered separately at greater length below at paras. 3.21–3.36.

3.13 The phrase inferentially implies a *de minimis* rule whereby ostensibly anti-competitive practices turn out to be innocuous when the extent of relevant competition affected is measured. The OFT have adhered to this *de minimis* principle. Thus in *British Railways Board*[12] (*Allocation of Facilities on Motorail*) the OFT examined allegedly serious discriminatory conduct by BRB who operated a system called Motorail which was a facility available to private passengers wishing to use train services and take a car with them. BRB decided to restrict the use of Motorail to private passengers so, accordingly, re-

[10] In *Sealink Harbours Ltd*, charges for customs clearance services and port exit permits at Fishguard and Holyhead, 14 October 1987, the OFT concluded that a practice of charging unrealistically low prices for customs clearance services was a distortion of competition though it did not prevent or exclude competition. In MMC Report into *Ford Motor Company* (February 1985) Cmnd 9437 the MMC stated: "We do not accept Ford's argument that a practice cannot be found to be anti-competitive unless it is shown that stopping it would increase competition. It is sufficient that stopping the practice would provide an opportunity for competition" (*ibid.*, at p. 38, para. 6.25).

[11] *Anti-Competitive Practices: A Guide to the Provisions of the Competition Act 1980* (OFT publication, 1982), *op. cit.*, at p. 7. See also the OFT comments in the second edition (1986) of the guidelines, *op. cit.*, n. 8, pp. 9, 10. See also Kirkbride, *op. cit.*, note 2.

[12] 9 February 1983.

fused to make the facility available to companies (e.g. parcel carriers and motor-car dealers) who wished to use the facility for commercial purposes. The OFT concluded that this refusal to supply the service was reasonable given that BRB wished to reserve the facility for non-commercial usage. The interesting point for current purposes concerns BRB's practice of refusing absolutely to grant access to Motorail to companies expressing a desire to use the service on a regular basis, whereas companies seeking irregular use of the service were not inevitably barred from its use. The OFT accepted that there was discrimination here. They also noted that, "BRB's policy of refusing access to Motorail to companies carrying parcels for reward (a policy applied in fact only to those companies which had indicated that they wished to use Motorail regularly) was linked to its perception of the competition offered by such companies to its Red Star Parcels service. In making this link, BRB was intending to restrict competition with Red Star."[13] Despite this finding that there was prima facie, anti-competitive conduct, they concluded that the conduct had an insignificant effect upon competition in the market. This was because: (a) there was a number of alternative competitive modes of inter-city transport for commercial goods and parcels including alternative facilities offered by BRB; (b) the space available on Motorail would, in any event, have been far too small in overall terms to have had any effect on the parcel carrying market; and (c) the incidence of use of Motorail by commercial carriers was too small for the restricting of access to the service to have had an appreciable effect on the market.

3.14 A second case on *de minimis*, again involving the British Railways Board, concerned *British Railways Board*[14] (*Facilities for Car Hire and Advertising of Self-Drive Vehicle Hire at Railway Stations*). In this case the OFT apparently applied a test of substantiality, i.e. did the practices in question affect competition substantially? BRB granted an exclusive right in respect of the provision of self-drive car hire facilities to Godfrey Davis Ltd and its subsidiary Godfrey Davis (Car Hire) Ltd. The OFT decided that this was potentially anti-competitive since it precluded other car hire firms operating in railway stations. The second course of conduct examined by the OFT concerned advertising. BRB restricted car hire advertising in railway stations so as to cushion Godfrey Davis Ltd from advertising competition at those locations. This course of conduct was also prima facie considered anti-competitive. However, with respect to both courses of conduct, the OFT found that the practices had but small significance in the market. With regard to the exclusive franchise the OFT concluded that the total amount of business diverted to Godfrey Davis Ltd was very small in proportion to the total car hire market. With regard to the advertising restriction, the OFT found that there was little demand for railway station sites for strategic advertising. Further, the restriction could not cushion Godfrey Davis from external advertising. Consequently, the restriction had minimal effect upon competition; the effect of either practice on competition was not "substantial".[15] It is clear from the facts of this case that "substantial" means anything more than insignificant.[16]

[13] *ibid.*, at p. 30.

[14] 18 May 1983.

[15] *ibid.*, at p. 40. See *Sheffield Newspapers* (October 1981) OFT Report of Investigation under s. 3 CA 1980 tying discounts considered by OFT to be too small to be significant: *Sheffield Newspaper* required estate agents to advertise for 48 weeks prior to being granted a 5 per cent discount. See also *British Telecommunications* (*Pricing Policy for the Placing of Advertisements in Yellow Pages Directories*) (10 October 1984) tying of advertising space to advertising agency services too limited in its exclusionary effects on other advertising agents to have anti-competitive consequences. In *British Coal Corporation* (9 October 1991), para 6.28 of the Report, the OFT concluded that a loyalty rebate scheme was anti-competitive, but unlikely to have a significant effect in the market and therefore did not justify a competition reference to the MMC.

[16] For example, see the definition of "substantial" in s. 64(3) FTA 1973, discussed by the House of Lords in *R* v *MMC ex parte South Yorkshire Transport* [1993] 1 WLR 23, and noted by Robertson [1993] ECLR

3.15 Conduct which is anti-competitive may none the less be unsuitable for investigation by the OFT because of its international scope over which the OFT has no jurisdiction. In *De Beers Central Selling Organisation*[17] the OFT concluded that although there were aspects of the Central Selling Organisation (CSO) which had monopolistic characteristics any ill effects which might have flown from the operation of that monopoly would have been negligible so far as the UK was concerned and since the OFT had jurisdiction only over the state of competition within the UK the Director General decided not to pursue the matter. The OFT investigation had revealed that the CSO was responsible for marketing up to 80 per cent of the world production of rough diamonds. Some 40 per cent were produced in De Beers' mines and the CSO had arrangements with many other producers to market their production. The diamonds were sold under tightly controlled arrangements limiting the number of purchasers able to purchase direct from the CSO. The CSO sorts and grades the rough diamonds and sells them at regular sales ("sights") held every five weeks in London, Lucerne and Kimberley. Only approved purchasers ("sight holders") could attend the sales. The greater part of the world's supply of rough diamonds were sold through the five-weekly London sights. There were only three UK-based sight holders and they, as with their foreign counterparts, largely sold rough diamonds they purchased to overseas buyers. The diamond cutting industry in the UK was very small with most cutting and polishing also taking place abroad.

3.16 It is further important to know precisely where the competition restrictive, distortive or preventive effects of a course of conduct may be felt since a practice which operates only locally may be as anti-competitive as one operating nationally (hence the words—"in the United Kingdom or any part of it") In this context the OFT have stated:

> "An essential step in identifying an anti-competitive practice is to locate the market in which competition might be affected. The effects of the practice may influence competition at several different levels where a firm is using an anti-competitive practice as a device for improving its own market position at the expense of others, the effect of the practice will be felt in the market in which the firm is operating. But, less obviously, an anti-competitive practice may also have effects on markets which are only partly related to, or even wholly divorced from, the firm's main market. Thus, a cosmetic manufacturer's practice may influence competition between cosmetic retailers; or a finance house may influence the vehicle market by tying leasing facilities to a certain make of car.
>
> The competition affected may be at any of the different stages of the production and distribution of goods, as well as in the different stages of the supply or securing of services. Buying power as well as selling power can have anti-competitive effects."[18]

3.17 The OFT, in many investigations, have examined conduct affecting only a very localised market. In Scottish and Universal Newspapers Ltd, SUNL, a newspaper company, set up a free newspaper called the *Lanarkshire World* which they used to restrict the amount of advertising revenue available to rivals by giving away large amounts of advertising space free of charge over an unreasonable period of time. The company also imposed a condition on advertisers in the *Lanarkshire World* that they would not advertise in any other free newspaper in the region. The existence of the *Lanarkshire World*, the cheapness of advertising space therein and the condition attached to advertising in the paper were all

cont.
217 "Substantial: what's in a word?". A similar meaning is given to "substantial" in EC law. See Case 19/77 *Miller International Shallplatten GmbH* v *Commission* [1978] ECR 131, [1978] 2 CMLR 334; Case 107/82 *AEG Telefunken* v *Commission* [1983] ECR 3151. These cases indicate *inter alia* that a firm with only 5 per cent of the market may be considered a "significant firm".

17 OFT press release 17 August 1989, noted DGFT Annual Report, 1989, p. 100.

18 *Anti-Competitive Practices* (1982 edn.), *op. cit.*, note 11, at p. 7. See also at pp. 10, 11 in the 1986 edition.

part of a policy designed to harm a rival free newspaper called the *Hamilton and Motherwell People*. Indeed, this predatory conduct included SUNL selling its advertising space at a level below the marginal cost of production and distribution. The OFT concluded that the conduct was anti-competitive. What is of interest is the fact that the investigation focused upon a small market within which SUNL was dominant. The OFT defined in their report the goods and services market as local newspaper advertising and the geographical market as the Lanarkshire region of Scotland which included the district council area of Motherwell and Hamilton and adjacent parts of the old county of Lanark. Accordingly, only a limited number of firms were providing the services in question within that area; of these SUNL was dominant.[19] It is thus clear that the OFT may, and will, define a market quite narrowly such that an individual firm, insignificant against the setting of the national market, is dominant on its own "patch".

4. *"Person", and "Of itself or when taken together with a course of conduct pursued by persons associated with him"*

3.18 An investigation may delve into a single course of conduct or it may cast its net far wider examining a series of courses of conduct pursued by associated persons. A course of conduct pursued by a single person may not be anti-competitive; however, the same conduct when viewed in the context of the behaviour of an associated person may be anti-competitive. For the OFT to "aggregate" two separate courses of conduct they must be "associated"; (i) one must be a corporate body of which the other directly or indirectly has control, either alone or with other members of a group of inter-connected bodies corporate of which he is a member; or (ii) both are corporate bodies of which one and the same person or group of persons directly or indirectly has control.

3.19 For the purposes of the definition of "anti-competitive practice" a person or group of persons able directly or indirectly to control or materially influence the policies of a company can be treated as having control of it, even though they do not have a controlling interest in it.

3.20 "Person" includes bodies whether incorporated or otherwise, partnerships and individuals. Thus both "horizontal" and "vertical" association is caught. "Horizontal" association includes associations between parties at the same level of distribution. It would comprise further the situation whereby the behaviour of two rival and unconnected firms have their behaviour co-ordinated by a third party, for example a trade association. "Vertical" association includes the case where the company controls another which is at a different level of distribution (e.g. wholesaler–retailer).

5. *"Anti-competitive practice"*

3.21 The Act refrains from defining "anti-competitive practices" and hence any conduct whatsoever that has an undesirable effect upon competition may fit the definition. In each case the surrounding economic circumstances will need to be assessed. To be anti-competitive the behaviour in question need not have to amount to "misconduct" in the

[19] 11 January 1983. See also, *Essex County Newspapers Ltd* (14 July 1983); *British Airports Authority/Gatwick Airport* (22 February 1984); *Southern Vectis Omnibus Company Ltd* (17 February 1988); *West Yorkshire Road Car Company Ltd* (15 August 1989); *Highland Scottish Omnibuses Ltd* (22 September 1989); *South Yorkshire Transport Ltd* (13 October 1989); *Kingston-Upon-Hull City Transport Ltd* (12 February 1990); *South Down Motor Services Ltd* (15 July 1992). It will not escape notice that most of these investigations are concerned with either local newspapers or local bus services.

sense of unlawful behaviour, though, unlawful behaviour might also be anti-competitive because of its surrounding circumstances.[20]

3.22 It is impossible to give an exhaustive list of possible anti-competitive practices. The following are examples of practices which may, in appropriate circumstances, be anti-competitive:

3.23 (a) Price discrimination: the discriminatory treatment of different customers may restrict competition as between those customers, after discounts or other allowances have been taken into account. The competitive effects of such conduct occur at two levels. First, competition between supplies may be distorted.[21] Secondly, competition between customers may be distorted.

3.24 (b) Predatory pricing and predatory conduct:[22] the OFT have stated

> "Predatory behaviour involves a company deliberately accepting losses in the short term, with the intention of eliminating a competitor, so that it may earn larger profits in the long time. Companies that are 'diversified' (involved in a number of different unconnected activities) or 'vertically integrated' (carrying out different stages in the production or distribution of the same product) may behave in a predatory fashion by cross-subsidising their loss-making activities, and by reducing the price of output at late stages in a vertically integrated production process. Predatory behaviour is not limited to pricing policy. It often involves increases in capacity."[23]

3.25 In recent years the OFT has investigated many complaints of predatory conduct particularly in the bus sector. For example, in *Grey-Green Coaches*[24] when a competing commuter coach service was introduced between the Isle of Grain and London, Grey-Green offered free travel until further notice to passengers travelling between certain points on its services. The OFT concluded that the effect of such free travel could be to eliminate new competition, and following discussions with the company concerned, procured an agreement from the company to withdraw the free travel offer. In *Becton Dickinson*[25] a supplier of hypodermic needles and sy-

20 MMC Report, *Sheffield Newspapers Ltd* (1982) Cmnd 8664, para. 7.8: "The operation of s. 2(1) cannot be limited to illegal conduct, for clearly the Act is intended to make possible control of conduct which, unless prohibited by the exercise of powers under this Act, is perfectly legal. It is true that the section refers only to conduct restricting, distorting or preventing competition, but to interpret 'conduct' as meaning 'misconduct' in the sense of conduct producing that effect is to reduce the definition to a tautology." In the 1986 guidelines (*op. cit.*, n. 8, p. 12) the OFT define an anti-competitive practice as: "one which in some way frustrates or inhibits the effective working of the competitive process." See also the *Wrigley Company Ltd* (DGFT Annual Report 1994, p. 44). The OFT accepted assurances from Wrigley, *inter alia*, that it would not remove competitors' chewing gum or display stands without written authorisation from the person controlling the premises.

21 An example of price discrimination directed at excluding entry to the market is found in *Healthcall* (DGFT Annual Report 1994, p. 45). In October 1994 the OFT concluded an enquiry into allegations that Healthcall, which provides deputising services for general medical practitioners, had, on certain occasions, withdrawn its services from general practitioners who were intended to establish their own deputising co-operatives. The OFT further received complaints that Healthcall had selectively lowered its fees to certain general practitioners in order to deter the initiation of competing deputising services. Healthcall gave the OFT an assurance that this was not company policy and that it would not enter into selective price cutting for the purpose of preventing the establishment or maintenance of competing services. It also accepted that it would take appropriate steps to ensure that its policy was recognised and implemented at all levels of management.

22 See OFT Research Paper (No. 5), *Predatory Behaviour in UK Competition Policy*, Geoffrey Myers (November 1994).

23 *Monopolies and Anti-Competitive Practices: A Guide to the Provisions of the Fair Trading Act 1973 and the Competition Act 1980* (1994), p. 19.

24 OFT Press Notice 24 January 1985.

25 OFT Report 15 June 1988.

ringes was alleged to be adopting a predatory pricing policy. Following an investigation by the OFT of the company's prices profits and market circumstances the OFT concluded that the company's pricing policy was not anti-competitive and no further action was required. When investigating a complaint of predatory conduct the OFT focus its analysis upon three categories of evidence: (i) whether the structure and characteristics of the market are such as to make predation a sensible and feasible business strategy; (ii) whether the alleged predatory incurs losses arising from the course of conduct; (iii) what the intention of the alleged predatory are, taking into account any relevant evidence of its behaviour in other markets.

3.26 (c) Vertical price control practices: attempts by supplies to control of influence the prices or discounts applied on resale by purchasers may fall within the scope of the Act. The relationship with the Resale Prices Act 1976 will need to be taken account of. Though, given that this Act is aimed at a different object to that of the CA 1980, its applicability in a given case cannot serve to exclude the CA 1980.[26]

3.27 (d) Transfer pricing: in *First-Day Covers*[27] the Royal Mail amended its pricing structure in order to avoid criticism that it was under-charging its in-house operation which was in competition with certain independent companies. In October 1994 the Royal Mail announced that it would introduce a scheme early in 1995 to enable independent producers of first-day covers to claim a rebate on stamps affixed and cancelled on such covers. This followed complaints from certain independent producers that they suffered a competitive disadvantage because the Royal Mail charged its in-house operations, the Philatelic Bureau, only the production cost of stamps, while charging them almost the full face value thereof. The rebate scheme reflected a more appropriate allocation of the costs incurred by Royal Mail in handling its own first-day cover business and that of the independent producers. The OFT welcomed the development as enabling independent producers to compete on a more equal basis with the Philatelic Bureau in the production and sale of first-day covers.

3.28 (e) Exclusive supply and purchasing agreements: under an exclusive supply agreement the supplier agrees to supply only one customer invariably in a defined geographical territory. The customer, in turn, might agree not to compete with the suppliers' other customers in that territory. Sometimes suppliers exert pressure (including making supply conditional upon the customer not dealing in competing goods) to achieve sales exclusivity.[28] In an exclusive purchasing agreement the customer agrees to purchase exclusively from a single supplier. Variations exist on this particular theme in contracts not specifying exclusivity but, otherwise, requiring customers to buy a defined portion of their requirements from the supplier, or even requiring customers to take a specified quantity in a defined period. All of the above contracts may, in certain circumstances and especially where the supplier has market power, have anti-competitive effects.

[26] See *Black and Decker* OFT Report (8 March 1989); MMC Report Cm 805 (1989).

[27] DGFT Annual Report, p. 45.

[28] The OFT has investigated many cases where suppliers have used different commercial strategies in order to persuade their distributors not to deal in competing products. Often, at an early stage of an informal OFT investigation, the company has resolved the matter by the giving of assurances to the OFT. In *Dolby Laboratories Inc* (OFT press notice, 6 July 1990), DGFT Annual Report 1990 (p. 116) Dolby Laboratories Inc changes its distribution policy following discussions with the OFT. Dolby was a major supplier in the UK of stereo sound processors for use in cinemas. Following discussions with the OFT it amended its previous policy of stipulating that distributors of stereo sound processors should not also deal in competitors' products. In *Reed Business Publishing Ltd* (OFT press notice, 12 October 1990, DGFT Annual Report 1990, p. 117), Reed Business Publishing gave a written assurance to the OFT that for three years it would not seek to impose exclusive advertising arrangements on recruitment advertisers in

3.29 (f) Tie-in sales and full line forcing: a tie-in exists when a supplier of a product or service (the tying product/service) requires customers to purchase all or part of their requirements of another product or service (the tied product/service) from the same source, or from a nominated supplier. Customers might find such "ties" convenient since it might enable them to buy or obtain several products or services from one supplier. Equally they might consider that being "forced" to acquire the tied product or service was an unreasonable fettering of their commercial freedom.[29] However, where the supplier has market power competition for the tied product/services may be restricted since third parties are, by the tie, precluded from supplying that product or service. In addition, customers are often required as a condition of supply of certain items in a particular range, to buy all or even other items in the range. This practice is known as "full-line forcing" and may restrict competition between the supplier and competitors who offer a more limited number of items.

3.30 (g) Selective distribution systems: pursuance to such systems the supplier deals only with a certain number of distributors or only with those which can satisfy certain criteria premised upon such matters as stockholding levels of pre- or post-sales service. The criteria may be qualitative (based on the dealer, his staff and premises) and/or quantitative (designed to limit the number of dealers to be supplied). Such systems may restrict competition between distributors though, conversely, they may en-

cont.
its magazine *Computer Talk* by offering discounted advertising rates for exclusive contracts. The OFT had been concerned that such contracts could frustrate competition from rival publications given the dominant position of *Computer Talk* in the market for advertising computer operations vacancies. Upon Reed amending its practices and giving the aforesaid assurances, the DGFT stated: "I have no objection to discounts which reflect price competition or cost savings. However, where they are conditional upon exclusive dealing by the customer, the discount can have a detrimental effect upon competition, or upon potential competition."

In *Roof Unit Group Ltd* (DGFT Annual Report 1991, p. 36), Roof Unit Group gave the OFT assurances that it would not refuse to supply distributors simply because they had sold or were selling or were intending to sell competing manufacturers' products. The company subsequently produced a new set of documentation specifying both its own and its distributors' rights and duties to reflect the terms of the assurances. The documentation and the assurances formed the basis of future distribution agreements to be concluded by the company. In *Scotsman Communications Ltd* (DGFT Annual Report 1991, p. 36) Scotsman Communications gave an assurance to the OFT that it would not offer advertisers discounts off advertising rates in return for exclusive advertising contracts in its publication *Accountancy Age*.

[29] In *British Equestrian Trade Association (BETA)* (DGFT Annual Report 1992, p. 30), the BETA agreed, following complaints, to change its body protector scheme so that manufacturers of body protectors were no longer obliged to become members of BETA in order to obtain the approval of that body for their products. Prior to this change the BETA operated a form of tie whereby it would only provide approval services to manufacturers in the even that they accepted membership of the association. This was a form of tying of different services (namely approval and membership) one to the other. In *Ferham Products: The Tanks and Drums Group* (DGFT Press Release 12 December 1989; DGFT Annual Report 189, p. 101) the OFT received complaints from an insulation manufacturer and from plumbers and builders merchants that Ferham Products and the Tanks and Drums Group had announced that in future only complete water tank kits would be supplied. Hitherto the component items were supplied separately. A recent law change had required that water storage tanks be installed with insulation and other specified components. However, it did not require that suppliers refuse to sell tanks and those items separately. The two companies were the largest supplies of water storage tanks in the UK. Accordingly, the OFT concluded that their refusal to continue supplying tanks without insulation etc. could have amounted to an anti-competitive practice within the meaning of the CA 1980. The OFT also concluded that limiting supply to the complete kit could adversely affect competition from independent component manufacturers and be detrimental to purchasers who could no longer shop around for the best package. Following correspondence with the OFT the companies indicated that they would resume supplying tank components separately as well as in combined units. In the light of such assurances the DGFT decided not to commence an investigation under the Act.

hance the efficiency with which a product is distributed and consumers' requirements satisfied. The principal criteria relied upon by the OFT to determine whether selective distribution systems might be anti-competitive turns upon the degree of competition between the suppliers of the product (i.e. the degree of inter-brand as opposed to intra-brand competition). The market power of the supplier is, accordingly, critical.

3.31 (h) Refusals to deal: a refusal to deal by a supplier with market power may severely restrict and distort competition downstream. The problem usually arises where a vertically integrated company refused to supply items needed by a rival who is not engaged in the complete production process or agrees to supply such items only at prices which are uneconomical thereby making it difficult for the rival to compete in the end-product market on a competitive basis.[30] In *Eschmann Bros and Walsh Ltd*,[31] the company agreed to supply suitably qualified third-party services with spare parts for its sterilising equipment used in hospitals and surgeries (autoclaves). The company had hitherto adopted a policy of not supplying independent servicing engineers. The OFT identified an important point of principle which, had the company not amended its policy, could well have led to a reference to the MMC. The OFT stated:

> "Whether spare parts should be made available to third parties is a question that has been frequently raised with the Office. The Director General recognises that manufacturers may be reluctant to have their products serviced by independents, particularly if these products involve specialised or advanced technology or need to be maintained to exacting standards. On the other hand, independent servicing can provide healthy competition to the manufacturers' own servicing network to the benefit of users of the equipment. In the present case, the company has decided to supply independents who meet the standards of skill and servicing practice which the company requires of its own personnel. Access to training facilities and manuals, for an appropriate fee, will be on a similar basis."

In deciding whether or not to accept undertakings the Director General will have regard to reports of the MMC and his own prior investigations. In *Gallaher*[32] the DGFT announced that it would not be investigating Gallaher's discount policy under the CA 1980. Nurdin and Peacock and the Federation of Wholesale Distributors had complained to the OFT that Gallaher granted more favourable terms to multiple retailers than it offered to cash and carry wholesalers and that the company acted against retailers receiving special terms if they sold on to other traders. In considering the complaint, the Director General considered the 1981 MMC Report into such discounts which concluded that the grant of discriminatory discounts

[30] See e.g. OFT Report (17 February 1988) *The Southern Vectis Omnibus Company Ltd*. The OFT investigated the refusal by the main supplier of local bus services on the Isle of Wight to grant competitors access to the main bus station in Newport and concluded that such refusal was anti-competitive. The company gave undertakings with a view to remedying the problem thereby avoiding the need for an MMC investigation. See also OFT Report (8 March 1989) and MMC Report (11 October 1989, Cm 805) *Black and Decker*. In this investigation the OFT concluded that Black and Decker's policy of refusing to supply retailers believed to be loss leading on the company's products was anti-competitive. The practice was referred to the MMC who concluded that the adoption of a single test, applied to all retailers, to adjudge whether their loss leading was anti-competitive and contrary to the public interest. This was notwithstanding that the practice of refusal to supply loss-leaders was permitted by the Resale Prices Act 1976. The company gave undertakings that it would determine loss-leading by reference to individual circumstances and that it would not indicate to dealers that it would withhold supplies by reference to any standard criteria on price or promotion.

[31] OFT Press Notice 24 August 1989, DGFT Annual Report 1989, p. 100.

[32] OFT Press Notice 14 September 1989, DGFT Report 1989, p. 100.

was not against the public interest when there was competition both among suppliers and among retailers and where, as a result of that competition, the benefits were passed on to consumers in one form or another. Further, the Director General took account of his own report, *Competition and Retailing* (1985), wherein the OFT updated the information contained in the MMC report and concluded that its findings were still valid. The Director General, in relation to the Gallaher complaint, concluded that the latter's policy sought to ensure that the special discounts it gave to multiples were passed on to consumers in the form of lower prices, which was a policy the MMC found acceptable. The DGFT saw nothing in Gallaher's conduct which would invalidate the MMC conclusions.

3.32 (i) Discriminatory licensing or refusals to license: the refusal by an intellectual or physical property right holder to license third parties to use or obtain access to the right in question might, in certain circumstances restrict competition and be contrary to the public interest.[33] Restrictive licensing policies may also arise in relation to the licensing of technology and know-how. The OFT states generally:

> "invention, innovation and other creative activity would clearly be discouraged without some restriction on competition in the granting of intellectual property rights. Consequently, a refusal to license such rights, or the inclusion of restrictive terms in licences of such rights. Nevertheless, where the company enjoying those rights has considerable market power, the effects of the restriction of competition may, in some circumstances, suggest that its licensing policy should be regarded as anti-competitive practice. Similarly with the licensing of technology: while a company need not license its technology to all applicants, there may be occasions when a refusal to licence reinforces its market power to such an extent that it should be regarded as anti-competitive."[34]

3.33 The OFT has taken the view that conduct is likely to be anti-competitive only where there is some degree of market power. Market power may exist in local markets and is not, therefore, necessarily the preserve of large undertakings. However, in all cases the minimum statutory qualifying criteria must be satisfied. The OFT has identified three broad categories of possible anti-competitive conduct:

> "– practices which do, or could, eliminate the competition a company faces in a market in which it is engaged;
> – practices which do, or could, prevent the emergence of new competitors or restrict competition in a market in which a company is engaged, by making it difficult for existing competitors to expand; and
> – practices which have such an affect on the terms and conditions of supply in some market—though not necessarily one in which the company under scrutiny is engaged—that they distort competition between companies engaged in that market."[35]

3.34 It is important to understand the difference between conduct which harms other parties because it is anti-competitive and conduct that harms other parties because it is economically efficient. A vigorous and innovative firm may deter new firms from entering the market not because it consciously seeks to exclude new firms but simply because new firms are scared of competing. Indeed, the pioneer firm in a market may enjoy scale economies and technological advances that leave subsequent entrants floundering in its wake. While

[33] See e.g. OFT Report, 21 March 1984; MMC Report 28 February 1985 Cmnd 9437, *Ford Motor Company*. The OFT have concluded, particularly in their report into *The Southern Vectis Omnibus Company Ltd* (OFT Report, 17 February 1988, para. 7.4) that the exercise of property rights (*in casu* access to a bus station to competitors) may be investigated under the CA 1980.

[34] *Monopolies and Anti-Competitive Practices: A Guide to the Provisions of the Fair Trading Act 1973 and the Competition Act 1980* (1994), p. 22.

[35] *ibid.*, p. 19.

the ill fortune of followers can be attributed to the efficiency of the pioneer it cannot be attributed to anti-competitive behaviour by the pioneer. The MMC have confirmed this obvious distinction between efficiency and anti-competitiveness in general reports under the Fair Trading Act 1973.[36] They have also re-affirmed the principle in respect of the Competition Act 1980. In *Sheffield Newspapers* they stated:

> "It is a feature of competition that it may lead to the failure and disappearance of an unsuccessful competitor. Nevertheless, to fail in competition is not the same thing as to be excluded from competing because competition is restricted, distorted or prevented."[37]

The OFT has recognised the difference. It has thus stated:

> "Nevertheless, the Competition Act is not intended to deal with every cause of market failure, and competition may fail to work effectively for reasons other than the abuse of market power—for example, because of deficiencies in the information available to customers, clearly, too, a company may adopt practices basically in order to approve its own efficiency—with no deliberate intention of behaving anti-competitively."[38]

3.35 The concept of anti-competitive conduct is an economic one; it contains no element of public interest within it. Thus, arguments to the effect that a practice is not anti-competitive because it has a beneficial effect upon employment or because it allows the perpetrator to compete effectively in the international market are not relevant to a determination of anti-competitiveness. Such arguments relate to the public interest and should be identified separately. Following the changes to the 1980 Act brought about by the Deregulation and Contracting Out Act 1994, however, the OFT may consider both the question of whether conduct is anti-competitive and whether it may operate against the public interest.[39] The question of public interest thus goes to the justification or exculpation of an otherwise restrictive agreement or practice. Of course, certain economic elements in the assessment of anti-competitive effect are also relevant to the public interest. The most important would appear to be that agreements or practices which prima facie appear restrictive may not be so when the extent of their effects are considered. This *de minimis* argument has been accepted by the OFT as relevant and the relevant cases have already been discussed in connection with the words "restricting, distorting or preventing competition", above.

3.36 Another important factor to note is that conduct which is economically "disruptive" need not necessarily be anti-competitive. An action taken as a legitimate response to a commercial situation may well cause damage to competitors; it is not, simply by virtue of that damage, anti-competitive. In *British Telecommunications (Pricing Policy for the Placing of Advertisements in Yellow Pages Directories)* 10 October 1984, the OFT examined the policy of British Telecommunications (BT) in suddenly withdrawing a discount which had hitherto been granted to advertising agents who placed adverts in *Yellow Pages* on

[36] e.g. MMC Report into the *Supply of Metal Containers* (1970) HC 6 where the MMC considered whether the discounts offered by Metal Box were over and above those justified by cost economies; MMC Report on the *Supply and Processing of Colour Film* (1966) HC 1 where the MMC stated (at para. 260) that a monopoly can benefit the public if it can effectively exploit scale economies which lead to cost savings which are passed on to the consumer. They accepted that this can strengthen the dominance of the monopoly but added that so long as the benefits of the monopoly were passed on to customers it was justified; see also MMC Report on the *Supply of Primary Batteries* (1974) HC 1, para. 429.

[37] MMC Report, *Sheffield Newspapers Ltd* (1982) Cmnd 8664, para. 7.13.

[38] *Monopolies and Anti-Competitive Practices: A Guide to the Provisions of the Fair Trading Act 1973 and the Competition Act 1980* (1994), p. 19.

[39] s. 4(1) Competition Act 1980.

behalf of advertisers. The agents complained, among other things, that the refusal to grant a discount overnight forced them to raise their prices to advertisers. The OFT on this point recognised that BT's action was disruptive. However, given certain other circumstances they concluded that the action was commercially justified and was not anti-competitive.

3.37 As noted above, prior to the changes brought about by section 12 Deregulation and Contracting Out Act 1994, amending section 4 of the Competition Act 1980, the OFT was statutorily prohibited from considering issues of the public interest, which were specified by the 1980 Act to be only a matter for consideration by the MMC. This separation of functions was removed by the 1994 Act and so public interest arguments to the OFT can be presented as such, not needing to be presented in the guise of competition arguments.

6. *"Services"*[40]

3.38 The supply or securing of services does not include services provided under a contract of employment. "Services" does include: (i) the undertaking and performance for gain or reward of engagements (whether professional or other) for any matter other than the supply of goods. Clearly the performance of a service with respect to (rather than in the supply of) goods is a service; thus plant valuation, quality control services, and, engineering consultancy services, *inter alia*, are included; (ii) the rendering of services to order; (iii) the provision of services by making them available to potential users; (iv) the making of arrangements for a person to put or keep on land a caravan, other than arrangements by which a person may occupy the caravan as his only or main residence;[41] (v) the provision of car parking facilities;[42] and, (vi) the charging of a toll for use of a toll road.[43] The need to expressly provide for car parking and caravan sites is thought to be due to doubts as to the extent of which the granting of leases is subject to control as a supply of services following *Ravenseft* v *Director General of Fair Trading*.[44] However, it seems likely following that decision that certain abusive practices by commercial landlords may in any event be anti-competitive (see para. 2.232). Leasing or indeed property licensing practices are not immune from investigation. See for instance the OFT Report into the refusal by Southern Vectis Bus Company to grant access to its rivals to its bus depot.[45] Equally, the licensing of intellectual property rights could constitute a service under the CA 1980 notwithstanding the statement made by the OFT in 1976 that they do not consider the grant of intellectual property rights to constitute the supply of services under the RTPA 1976.[46] Indeed, the OFT have investigated, and concluded to be an anti-competitive practice, the refusal by Ford Motors to license other persons to manufacture or sell in the

[40] Defined as *per* s. 137(3), (4) Fair Trading Act 1973.
[41] s. 23 CA 1980. For definition of caravan see s. 29(1) Caravan Sites and Control of Development Act 1960. Holiday caravan sites are expressly subject to control by both the CA 1980 and the Fair Trading Act 1973 by this provision.
[42] s. 2(7) CA 1980. This brings car parking under the control of the Act but it remains excluded from the 1973 Fair Trading Act. Thus, "parking practices" cannot be reviewed as abuses of monopoly power but can be as anti-competitive practices.
[43] s. 10(1) New Roads and Street Works Act 1991.
[44] [1977] 1 All ER 47 (QBD).
[45] 17 February 1988.
[46] DGFT Report 1976, p. 36.

UK any replacement Ford motor body part. Ford claimed to be entitled to prohibit such manufacture or sale by virtue of the copyright subsisting in the drawings of body parts registered under the Registered Designs Act 1949. This practice, stated the OFT, enabled Ford Motors to control the spare parts market and also "control the supply of replacement body parts to the garage trade through its dealer network, and ... this would be likely to have effects on the ability of independent factors to compete with that network for the distribution and supply of replacement body parts for Ford vehicles, and on the ability of the independent repairers to compete with that network for repair of Ford vehicles".[47] The OFT's view was confirmed by the MMC.[48] The licensing of patent rights moreover was recognised as being prone to investigation as an anti-competitive practice by section 14 CA 1980, which amended section 51 Patents Act 1977.[49]

7. *"Goods"*[50]

3.39 This includes, *inter alia*, buildings and other structures, ships, aircraft and hovercraft. The word supply as in "supply of goods" includes, *inter alia*, supply by way of sale, lease, hire, hire purchase and construction. The supply of electricity is of services and not of goods though electricity itself is to be treated as goods for the purposes of the CA 1980.[51] This only seems to duplicate the ways in which electricity is treated under the CA 1980. No meaningful distinction seems to turn on the difference between the electricity as such and the electricity as supplied.

D. Anti-Competitive Practices: Exclusions from the Act

3.40 As with the RTPA 1976 various exclusions from control are listed in the Act. First are exclusions now contained in the Anti-Competitive Practices (Exclusions) Order 1980, as amended.[52] Secondly, courses of conduct required or envisaged by agreements subject to registration under the RTPA 1976 are excluded by virtue of section 2(2) Competition Act 1980. Thirdly, there are exclusions provided in other statutory enactments.

These categories of exclusion are described below. It should be clearly understood that these exclusions are of variable extent. Some are very narrowly drafted indeed and provide but scant shelter from investigation.

47 *Ford Motor Company: Licensing for the Manufacture or Sale of Replacement Body Parts* (21 March 1984), p. 41, para. 8.17. See also, *British Broadcasting and Independent Television Publications Ltd: Publication of Programme Information* (13 December 1984)—in respect of copyright licensing.

48 MMC Report, *Ford Motor Company* (February 1985) Cmnd 9437, pp. 34-37, paras. 6.14-6.26. See also MMC Report *BBC and ITP* (September 1985) Cmnd 9614, paras. 6.8 and 6.9 which confirms the point. In the case of motor spare parts, licensing powers are now conferred following an adverse MMC Report upon the Secretary of State by s. 144 Copyright, Designs and Patents Act 1988. In the case of programme listings, publishers may use listings under s. 176 and Sch. 17 Broadcasting Act 1990, licensing terms to be settled in default of agreement by the Copyright Tribunal.

49 Now substituted by s. 295, Sch. 5, para. 14, Copyright, Designs and Patents Act 1988.

50 Defined by s. 137(3), (4) Fair Trading Act 1973.

51 s. 100(1) Electricity Act 1989.

52 The 1980 Order has been amended by Amendment Orders in 1984, S.I. 1984 No. 1919, and 1994, S.I. 1994 No. 1557.

1. *Anti-Competitive Practices (Exclusion) Order 1980*[53]

3.41 Under Article 2 of the Order two categories of conduct are excluded from the Act. These are, first, conduct listed in Schedule 1 to the Order, and, secondly, conduct pursued by persons defined in Article 2(b) to the Order. These will be examined in turn.

(1) Schedule 1, para. 1: export contracts

3.42 Conduct comprising the incorporation in contracts for the supply of goods of conditions which relate exclusively to the supply of those goods outside of the UK, is excluded from control. Moreover, the refusal to supply goods except on those terms is also excluded. Where the export market is the EC, businessmen should assume that the European Commission will be interested under Articles 85 or 86 EC if it is considered that the conduct in question affects inter-state trade.

(2) Schedule 1, para. 2: Transport Acts agreements and conduct

3.43 Any course of conduct required or envisaged by agreements made between bus operators and local authorities under section 24 of the Transport Act 1968 or sections 1–3 of the Transport Act 1978 is excluded. The former provision establishes the National Bus Company and the Scottish Transport Group and imposes duties (not enforceable by individuals) on the bodies to co-ordinate passenger transport services. The latter provisions empower local authorities to enter agreements with carriers with respect to financing and facilities. Thus, for example, local authority bus subsidies are not anti-competitive practices even though the buses might as a result sell their services below cost thereby competitively affecting competing road and rail passenger services. This exclusion is narrowly drafted and does not protect ordinary commercial carriers. This exclusion is now effectively redundant following the Transport Act 1985, which provides for the repeal of these statutory provisions and hence no new agreements can be made thereunder.

(3) Schedule 1, para. 3: international sea transport

3.44 Any course of conduct pursued by an operator of international sea transport services in relation to such services is excluded. This includes the acquisition of any goods or any other services in connection with the operation of the international sea transport services. The exclusion extends further to any person securing international sea transport services. Similar exclusions to these for liner conference agreements exists under section 11 Merchant Shipping (Liner Conferences) Act 1982 which excludes operation of the RTPA 1976 (see paras. 2.106–2.107). Similar general exclusions lie under the RTPA 1976 (see paras. 2.87–2.89).

(4) Schedule 1, para. 4: aviation

3.45 This excludes any course of conduct pursued by an air transport undertaking or required or envisaged by a restriction accepted under an agreement described in para. 3(2) of the Schedule to the RTPA (Services) Order 1976, being a course of conduct pursued solely in respect of international carriage by air. However, Schedule 1, para. 4 has now been amended by the Anti-Competitive Practices (Exclusions) (Amendment) Order 1984 S.I. No. 1919 which amends the Exclusion Order so as to bring charter flights within the Act.[54]

[53] S.I. 1980 No. 979 came into operation 12 August 1980. It has been amended by the Anti-Competitive Practices (Exclusions) (Amendment) Order 1984, S.I. 1984 No. 1919 and the Anti-Competitive Practices (Exclusions) (Amendment) Order 1994, S.I. 1994 No. 1557.

[54] See *Civil Aviation Authority*, Official Journal, 21 May 1985. In an agreed statement the CAA and OFT have agreed that the CAA will assume primary investigative responsibility. However, the OFT will

A charter flight is defined as "a flight on which the whole capacity of the aircraft is available for purchase by one or more charterers for his or their own use or for resale". (The same now applies under the FTA 1973 under S.I. 1984 No. 1887 in respect of domestic and international charter flights.)

(5) Schedule 1, para. 5: building societies

3.46 Any course of conduct required or envisaged by an agreement entered into between the Treasury and the building societies concerning the raising of funds or the making of loans is excluded from control. Note that this gives only a limited exemption to the building societies.

(6) Schedule 1, para. 6: Bank of England and Treasury

3.47 Any course of conduct required or envisaged by an agreement described in para. 6 of the 1976 Services Order to which the Bank of England or the Treasury, or both, are parties, and which relates exclusively to their control over financial institutions, over the money market generally, or to the conduct of markets in money, in public sector debt instruments or in foreign currencies, is excluded from control.

(7) Schedule 1, para. 7: agricultural and forestry associations

3.48 This excludes any course of conduct pursued by a member of an agricultural and forestry association or of a fishery association as defined in section 33 RTPA 1976 (for commentary see paras. 2.49–2.52) or pursued by such an association and being required or envisaged by an agreement described in that section, not being an agreement between the association and someone who is a member neither of the association nor of a constituent association.

(8) Schedule 1, para. 8: parish and community councils

3.49 Any course of conduct pursued by a parish or community council within the meaning of the Local Government Act 1972 or the Local Government (Scotland) Act 1973 respectively is excluded.

(9) Article 2 exceptions: exclusions based on size[55]

3.50 This excludes from control persons of below a certain size measured by reference to specified, quantitative criteria. Thus, a course of conduct is not within control if pursued by a person who meets one of two alternative tests.[56] The tests are that the person either: (i) has a relevant annual turnover in the UK of less than £10 million[57] and who is not a member of a group of interconnected bodies corporate which has an aggregate annual turnover in the UK of £10 million[58] or more; or, (ii) enjoys less than one quarter of the relevant market and who is not a member of a group of interconnected bodies corporate which enjoys one quarter or more of a relevant market. For the purposes of these criteria Schedule 2 to the Order assists with certain elaborations. "Turnover in

cont.
intervene where: (a) requested so to do by the CAA; (b) the CAA or Secretary of State identify matters outside the scope of civil aviation law and within the confines of competition policy; (c) a complainant, dissatisfied with the response of the CAA, requests the OFT to consider the competition implications.

55 The criteria laid down in Art. 2 were amended by the Anti-Competitive Practices (Exclusions) (Amendment) Order 1994, S.I. 1994 No. 1557.

56 Under the original 1980 Order, these tests were cumulative.

57 Under the original 1980 Order, this figure was £5 million.

58 Under the original 1980 Order, this figure was £5 million.

the UK" means the total amount charged for the supply of goods and services in the UK during that period in the ordinary course of a person's business after deduction of: trade discounts, rebates and other allowances; value added tax and other taxes directly related to turnover; and any amount charged for any supply where both the person supplying the goods or services and the person to whom they were supplied were members of one and the same group of inter-connected bodies corporate at the time of supply. Turnover periods are generally 12 months.[59] A person's share of a market for purposes of calculating a quarter may be described in terms of value, cost, price or by quantity.[60] In determining this market share no account is taken of transactions concluded between members of one and the same group of inter-connected bodies corporate at the time of supply.[61] Where the "person" is in a group then the £10 million and the quarter market share requirements apply to the whole group.[62]

3.51 With respect to the quantitative requirements above, it must be stressed that for the exclusion from the Act to apply *either* of the criteria may be satisfied. Thus a firm with a market share of 75 per cent but with turnover of £9 million is excluded. Although it has a dominant market share, its turnover entitles it to take the benefit of Article 2(b)(i) of the amended Order and escape investigation under the CA 1980. It may, however, come within the scope of the monopoly provisions of the Fair Trading Act 1973, which is concerned only with market share.

3.52 Finally, where local authorities are concerned there are no exclusions based quantitatively upon turnover or market share. Such factors are very clearly inadequate as reflections of their economic power and influence. Local authorities are subject to control in so far as their conduct amounts to a "course of business".

2. *Courses of Conduct Caught by RTPA 1976*

3.53 Section 2(2) CA 1980 states that a course of conduct required or envisaged by a "material" provision in a registrable agreement under the RTPA 1976 is not to be regarded as an anti-competitive practice under the CA 1980. The same applies to "material" recommendations of trade associations. Section 2(2) thus makes the CA 1980 and the RTPA 1976 mutually exclusive. The word "material" used in section 2(2) CA 1980 simply means that the provision of the agreement or the trade association recommendation which requires or envisages the course of conduct under the spotlight is one to which the RTPA 1976 applies. Thus, if a trade association recommended that its members refuse to deal with categories of firms not meeting certain creditworthiness criteria, or adopt a particular course of discriminatory pricing or employ a very strict exclusion of liability clause in standard form contracts with customers, then such collective conduct and all those who pursue it are regulated under the RTPA 1976 and not the CA 1980. A course of conduct complained of by a single, unhappy purchaser in pursuance of the trade association recommendation, will only relate to the conduct of one supplier implying perhaps that investigation of the single supplier's behaviour by the OFT under the CA 1980 is called

[59] But cf. Sch. 2, para. 2(b) for determining turnover where the relevant period is less than 12 months. This states: "Where the relevant period does not equal twelve months, the amount which bears the same proportion to the turnover in the UK of that person during that period as twelve months does to that period", is to be considered.

[60] Sch. 2, para. 3.

[61] *ibid.*

[62] Sch. 2, paras. 5, 6.

for. However, the course of conduct emanates from a registrable trade association recommendation. Accordingly, the complained of course of conduct is not subject to the CA 1980. This defining of boundaries between the CA 1980 and the RTPA 1976 is logical. The conduct described in the above example is common to all the trade association members: the RTPA 1976 focuses upon the collective nature of the practice and the OFT can use their powers under that Act to enjoin the behaviour of *all* participant firms. This leads to more effective regulation than under the CA 1980 which allows the OFT to investigate only those firms named in the notice: it militates against the collective analysis of conduct.

3.54 Agreements that are excluded from the RTPA 1976 (see Chapter 2) may none the less fall within the CA 1980. Thus exclusive dealing contracts are reviewable under that Act, as are exclusive purchasing agreements, exchanges of know-how and patent or other intellectual property licensing practices, etc. In investigations under the CA 1980, the examination and analysis of the OFT will be different from that under the RTPA 1976. Thus, whereas under the RTPA 1976 the OFT will assess the collective effect of an agreement on competition (i.e. both parties will be investigated) under the CA 1980 the OFT will be examining the conduct of the single party whose conduct has been complained of. If the parties who are being investigated under the CA 1980 can establish that they have an agreement that is registrable under the RTPA 1976 then the OFT have no jurisdiction under the CA 1980 though they may of course take action under the RTPA 1976.

3. *Courses of Conduct Excluded by other Statutes*

3.55 Some anti-competitive courses of conduct in relation to the financial services sector are excluded by other statutes from being investigated under the CA 1980, there being other means of regulation in place. With respect to the auditing profession, the Secretary of State is given the powers under Schedule 14 of the Companies Act 1989 to prevent restrictive trade practices by recognised supervisory or qualifying bodies,[63] which consequently are granted certain limited exceptions from competition legislation, both RTPA 1976[64] and CA 1980.[65]

3.56 The rules, guidance, codes, principles and practices of recognised self-regulating organisations, investment exchanges or clearing houses under the Financial Services Act 1986 are excluded from being considered as anti-competitive courses of conduct for the purposes of the CA 1980.[66]

4. *Exercise of OFT's CA 1980 powers by other regulators*

3.57 The powers of the OFT under the CA 1980 are specified by a number of statutes to be exercisable concurrently with a sectoral regulator. Thus the Rail Regulator,[67] the Director General of Water Services,[68] the Director General of Electricity Supply,[69] the Civil

[63] There is provision for continuing scrutiny by the DGFT under para. 3(4), Sch. 14, Companies Act 1989.
[64] See paras. 2.73–2.76 above.
[65] Sch. 14, para. 10, Companies Act 1989.
[66] s. 126 Financial Services Act 1986.
[67] s. 67 Railways Act 1993.
[68] s. 31 Water Industry Act 1991
[69] s. 43 Electricity Act 1989.

Aviation Authority[70] and the Director General of Telecommunications[71] each enjoy powers under the CA 1980 concurrently with the OFT.

3.58 In addition, under the Gas Act 1986 the Gas Consumers' Council is required to refer to the OFT any matter which it investigates under its duties under that Act and which would be appropriately investigated under the CA 1980.[72]

5. Government Bodies (Crown Immunity) and Local Authorities (Tendering Practices)

3.59 Governmental departments and agencies generally enjoy Crown immunity and, therefore, are not subject to the competition legislation. This is not to say that such bodies may not engage in distinctly anti-competitive conduct effect since such bodies often do engage in commercial activities in vigorous competition with the private sector. Following a ministerial agreement concluded in 1990 to the effect that such bodies should comply with all relevant regulatory requirements even though not strictly bound so to do, and that they should ensure that their immunity does not lead to a distortion of competition in markets in which they do business, the OFT will pursue complaints against Crown immune bodies. Where the OFT concludes that an anti-competitive course of conduct is being pursued it will draw its preliminary finding together with any remedy which it may consider appropriate to the attention of the body concerned or, in the case of an agency, to that of the "parent" department. Pursuant to the ministerial agreement, it is the OFT's expectation that its findings will be accepted and its remedies implemented.

3.60 Anti-competitive practices may be carried out by local authorities. There are no particular exceptions for local authorities. There are no exclusions for such authorities based quantitatively upon turnover or market share in the Act. Such factors are clearly inadequate as reflections of the economic power and influence of an authority. Local authorities are subject to control insofar as their conduct amounts to a "course of business". Such authorities are often engaged in the acquisition of goods or the securing of services. Anti-competitive conduct can also arise where local authorities supply goods or services otherwise than free of charge. For example, the purchasing and public-procurement activities of local authorities could be included within the ambit of the Act. However, during the passage of the Competition Bill through Parliament, the government made it clear that it had "no intention of undermining the widely recognised practice of selective competitive tendering, because the reasonable application of such procedures by local authorities does offer very real benefits both to authorities and to their suppliers". Further, the government spokesman stated that the government would not consider it appropriate for there "to be investigations into tendering systems by local authorities when these are operated in accordance with principles accepted by the government".[73] Tender procedures may, however, be subject to express statutory requirements. Thus for example Part V of the Transport Act 1985 deals with tendering for subsidised bus services. Schedule 2, Part II of the Environmental Protection Act 1990 deals with tendering of waste disposal contracts by waste disposal authorities. Furthermore, local authorities might well be subject to EC rules on public procurement.

[70] s. 56 Airports Act 1986. A concordat was reached in 1985 between the CAA and OFT giving the CAA the principal and the OFT the subsidiary role in regulation; see note 54 above.

[71] s. 50(3) Telecommunications Act 1984. See, on the relationship between these Acts, *R v Director General of Telecommunications ex p British Telecommunications plc*, 20 December 1996; see para. 2.118, note 114.

[72] s. 32(5) Gas Act 1986.

[73] House of Lords Parliamentary Debate, Vol. 405, No. 83, 19 February 1980, col. 610.

E. Anti-Competitive Practices: The Investigation Procedure

3.61 At the beginning of this chapter six stages were identified as relevant in an anti-competitive practice investigation.[74] These will now be discussed in greater depth.

1. *Stage 1: Complaints to the OFT*

3.62 The OFT rely for information of anti-competitive conduct upon, *inter alia*, the financial press, upon evidence obtained via economic analysis and research undertaken in house, and upon complaints made by competitors or customers who feel threatened by another's behaviour. Most investigations commence using data obtained through a complaint. Complaints may be made in any form either orally or in writing. If requested and where this is compatible with the rights of the complained of party, the OFT will keep the identity of the complainant confidential.[75] Alternatively, a complainant may prepare a brief for submission to the OFT outlining his grievance. There are no rules governing the form of a complaint. The following is a suggested outline structure for a complaint based upon the sort of information the OFT might need to know: (a) the relationship of the complainant to the person pursuing the alleged anti-competitive conduct; the OFT will want to know whether the complainant is a supplier, purchaser or rival, etc. of the complained of person. This enables them to assess the legal and economic relevance of the data furnished to them in the complaint. (b) The nature of the complained of conduct, whether it is a selling or buying practice, whether it entails control over vertical prices, discrimination, predation and any evidence to support the complaint, for example, texts of agreements, minutes of negotiations or meetings, terms of transactions, business documents, circulars, etc. (c) The alleged anti-competitive effects specifying in as much detail as possible how the practice has affected trade. This might entail statistical evidence showing trends in price, market share, turnover, profit levels, other factors in price formation, data demonstrating that the complained of conduct is curbing entry to the market or is deterring the investment or development plans of existing firms. The practice might, for example, be shown to have necessitated the shedding of labour or specialised personnel. The more acute the evidence of unfair economic consequence the more likely it is that OFT action will be forthcoming. The OFT do not have the resources to investigate every complaint in great depth; they naturally must concentrate most thoroughly upon those which appear to be most economically serious. (d) The market share of the complainant and an estimate (since accurate data might not be available to the complainant) of the market share of the complained of person(s). The greater the market share of the complained of person the more serious the potential anti-competitive consequences. (e) The duration of the conduct in terms of the length of time that it was in operation, or the number of times the complained of conduct was repeated. It appears to be the case that single, isolated acts are not reviewable by the OFT, some element of continuity or repetition being required by the Act. In practical terms, the longer the du-

[74] An additional stage, requiring the OFT to produce a formal report at the end of its formal preliminary investigation, was removed by s. 12 Deregulation and Contracting Out Act 1994. A total of 35 reports had been issued by the end of 1994, thus only averaging less than three a year.

[75] s. 19(1) CA 1980 which forbids disclosure of information obtained during the CA 1980 procedure without the complainant's consent. This is subject to s. 19(2) which provides exceptions where disclosure is necessary for the performance of other statutory obligations.

ration or the greater the number of times the complained of conduct has been repeated, the more likely there is to be an anti-competitive effect. (f) Whether the conduct complained of is carried on in conjunction with any other person and if so what the relationship is between the parties. (g) General details of the geographical market, the products or services in question, and customer profiles. While the complainant will be familiar with his market this cannot be reasonably expected of the OFT. Accordingly, background information concerning the product, its substitutes, method of pricing, the extent and nature of competition, the extent of overseas competition, etc. is of value. (h) If the subject of the complaint is known to seek to justify the conduct complained of as being in the public interest, then it should be possible to present a rebuttal at this early stage, thus presenting the complainant's public interest case in the best possible light from the outset. Since the changes brought in by the Deregulation and Contracting Out Act 1994, an assessment of the public interest is now within the OFT's jurisdiction. A considerable amount of background information may be needed by the OFT before they can make a considered judgment of the facts.

3.63 While some businessmen may be wary of such an extensive approach to a complaint, it should not be overlooked that in commercial litigation it is a salutary rule that the party who has the first opportunity to lay the factual and legal ground can predispose the judge to use their interpretation of events as the framework for further analysis. As an alternative businessmen may persuade their trade association to make the complaint. This would be appropriate, for example, where a major supplier was using coercive selling tactics against a number of smaller purchasers who could utilise the collective muscle power a trade association possesses to present a complaint to the OFT. Complaints may, of course, be made by the legal advisers of the complainant. Other possible methods of complaint may be via a local MP or as a result of lobbying the Secretary of State who may request the OFT to investigate. Neither has a legal right to demand an investigation but it is hardly likely that the OFT would not, at least, consider such a request seriously. A direct complaint to the OFT is invariably the most effective way to proceed.

2. *Stage 2: Investigation*

3.64 Prior to the amendments made to the Competition Act 1980 by the Deregulation and Contracting-out Act 1994, an investigation under the 1980 Act was divided into two parts. A preliminary investigation was initiated which might, should the OFT decide to take matters further, lead to a formally constituted investigation and official report. This procedure was cumbersome and could tie the hands of the OFT should it decide that the MMC should investigate an anti-competitive practice in a wider context.[76] Moreover, the OFT was statutorily barred from considering issues of the public interest. It could only assess whether a course of conduct was anti-competitive.

3.65 Hence the distinction between preliminary and formal investigation was removed,[77] to be replaced by a system giving the OFT power to investigate alleged anti-competitive practices and their compatibility with the public interest.[78]

[76] See *R* v *DGFT ex parte Southdown Motor Services* (1993) 12 Tr Law 90, where a reference to the MMC on more than just the practice investigated under the formal investigative procedure was held by the Divisional Court to be *ultra vires*.

[77] s. 12(3) Deregulation and Contracting Out Act 1994.

[78] s. 4(1) Competition Act 1980, as amended by s. 12(4) Deregulation and Contracting Out Act 1994.

3.66 Such inquiries are not necessarily confined to anti-competitive practices; the OFT might decide, following an inquiry, that the conduct complained of is properly dealt with under the RTPA 1976 or under the monopoly provisions of the Fair Trading Act 1973.

3.67 In practice, there is a two-stage approach to the conduct of an investigation. The first is to see if there is substance to the complaint together with supporting evidence; the second is to analyse potentially justifiable complaints in more depth. But no clear demarcation line can be drawn.

3.68 Many complaints are found by the OFT to have no real substance. For example there are the "disgruntled" or "sacked employee" cases where an employee or ex-employee complains (sometimes anonymously) of his firm or ex-firm. Such complaints are often groundless. In many situations the OFT are in something of an adjudicatory position between a complainant and a complained of firm. Care is always taken in such cases to give both sides the opportunity to be fully heard and to submit their arguments. This routinely entails contacting the complained of party first to gauge that person's reactions. It should be appreciated that at this informal stage the OFT has no power to demand information or to expedite matters, and considerable delays can sometimes result while parties seek legal advice, ponder their responses, or, simply stall for time. Some informal investigations can proceed for up to 12 months because of such delays.

3.69 As the OFT receive up to 1,000 general complaints each year, the informal procedure thus provides an expedient means for the OFT to assess a practice. The OFT view this informal procedure as an opportunity to test the water:

> "The object of these inquiries is to check that there is evidence to support the complaint, to give the firm complained about the chance to give its side of the story, and to obtain more information so that the Director General can have a better understanding of the complaint and its surrounding circumstances. Many complaints prove on further examination to include matters which are not the Director General's responsibility, but if further action is appropriate, the Director General will have to decide which of his powers to use. In the case of a possible anti-competitive practice, it may also be necessary to find out whether or not the firm or practice complained of is exempt from the legislation."[79]

At this stage the OFT often manage to obtain "assurances" from parties to complained of practices that they will terminate the conduct or otherwise "cure" the ill. Many examples of internal assurances have been referred to in this chapter in particular with regard to the meaning of "anti-competitive practices" above. The informal inquiry is thus something of a carrot and stick: parties who provide assurances to the OFT save themselves the expense, time and general inconvenience of a full OFT investigation which might ultimately develop into a full-blown MMC inquiry. Examples of assurances obtained at this pre-formal stage are given in the discussion of negotiation of undertakings in stage 3 and in relation to the discussion of the phrase "anti-competitive practice". Where the OFT consider further investigation necessary, a team of investigators will be appointed to undertake a detailed inquiry. This team may be different from that which conducted the initial inquiry. Though, some specialist economists and accountants may be involved at both stages.

[79] *Anti-Competitive Practices: A Guide to the Provisions of the Competition Act* 1980 (1982 edn.), p. 14. See also DGFT Report 1980, p. 43.

3. *Conduct by OFT of Investigation*

(1) Form of investigation, OFT powers to compel disclosure of documents

3.70 To assist them in their inquiry the OFT may require any person to disclose any documents specified in the notice which are under that person's control and relate to matters under investigation.[80] The OFT may further compel disclosure of estimates, returns or such other information as may be specified in the notice. Failure to disclose properly is a criminal offence. The OFT may specify, further, the form in which such data is to be furnished.[81] The OFT may not compel production of data that could not be compelled in civil proceedings before the High Court.[82] The normal rules as to legal privilege for documents are thus incorporated. It is arguable that investigated parties may refuse to deliver up documents that may expose them to penalties. The House of Lords has, at least, gone this far in respect of Articles 85 and 86 EC when fines may be imposed.[83] Fines, however, are not an option under the CA 1980 and accordingly there seems limited scope for refusing to disclose documents on this basis.

3.71 The OFT may terminate an investigation at any time prior to its conclusion. Where the OFT is investigating a practice which is also the subject of a European Commission investigation liaison between the authorities may be necessary. Although no formal statutory exchange of data between the authorities is provided for, the OFT does keep lines open with the Commission. In cases of overlap the OFT, usually, makes way for the Commission, though this is not inevitable.

(2) Importance of market analysis

3.72 In discussions and negotiations with the OFT parties should be prepared to submit evidence on economic factors relating exclusively to the complained of conduct and its effects. Thus, evidence as to the product market and geographical market will be very important. As regards product market, parties will wish to show that their product or service is subject to competition from a wide range of similar goods and services or substitutes which are to some degree in competition; thus, for example, if the complained of party manufactures beer it may be arguable that cheap wine is a competing product.[84] If the product in question is apples then the product market might be pears, other hard fruits, and some soft fruits.[85] In *Scottish and Universal Newspapers* the OFT defined the product

[80] s. 3(7)(a) CA 1980. See statement of Under Secretary of State for Trade, HC Comm. Rep. Deb. 27 November 1979, col. 430: "Nothing can be done under the sub-sections of Clause 3 unless it is done with a view to establishing: 'that a person is pursuing a course of conduct, which does amount to such a practice'."

[81] s. 3(7)(b) CA 1980. In an interview given by Sir Gordon Borrie, Director General of Fair Trading, to the *Sunday Times*, 6 April 1980, it was stated: Q: "The Confederation of British Industry secured an amendment in the Act laying down that the OFT must give its reasons before making a reference to the Monopolies Commission. Will this be a limiting factor from the start? A: It's not a fishing expedition. I'm not entitled to go rampaging round the place. I've got to specify what I'm looking for, the kind of anti-competitive practice that appears to me to exist."

[82] s. 3(7) CA 1980. See s. 3(8) which applies s. 85(5)–(8) Fair Trading Act 1973 (enforcement provisions relating to production of documents) which renders failure to comply or the provision of false information a criminal offence punishable by fine or summary conviction. A court may make any order it sees fit to cure the infringement.

[83] See *Rio Tinto Zinc* v *Westinghouse* [1978] AC 547 (HL) construing s. 14, Civil Evidence Act 1968.

[84] See Case 170/78*Commission* v *UK* [1983] 3 CMLR 512 in which the European Court of Justice held that beer and imported cheap, still white wine were competing products so that for the UK to maintain a large tax differential between the two products gave beer a competitive advantage over the imported wine which was protectionist in effect and was in breach of Art. 95 EC (prohibiting discriminatory taxation).

[85] See e.g. Case 22/76 *United Brands Continental BV* v *Commission* [1978] ECR 207; [1978] 1 CMLR 429 noted Baden Fuller (1979) 4 ELRev 423; Korah (1980) 17 CMLRev 395; Bishop (1981) 44 MLR 282;

market in an investigation into newspaper company advertising practices as: daily papers; local radio; posters; cinema; direct mail; directories and prestel. The more widely complained of party can define the product market, the less significant will become his conduct. Such a company will invariably plead that it is a little fish in a big pond. A complainant, on the other hand, will base his evidence on the narrowest product market in order to suggest that the complained of party is in reality a big fish in a small pond.

3.73 As regards geographical market exactly the same principle applies. The complained of party will suggest that the geographical market is wide; the complainant will suggest that it is narrow. A party will seek to show that many distant rival suppliers can get their products or services to the location where the complained of party sells or provides services without difficulty. This will entail, in goods cases, showing that there are readily available and economic forms of transport. The complainant will by contrast seek to show that the geographical market is small, that there is no effective competition outside of the local market and that the potential for penetration by outsiders is small.

3.74 The OFT have conducted a number of investigations into the practices of newspaper companies and bus companies. In each the geographical market has been important, although the arguments of parties in such investigations have sometimes tended to ignore the importance of market definition. How does one decide whether a newspaper in Wolverhampton, for example, competes with one in Birmingham which is only 10-20 miles away? One essential factor will be the location of readers. This will primarily be determined by the extent to which the paper views itself as a local paper covering local news and containing local advertising. Thus, a local newspaper may not be subject to strong competitive pressures from Birmingham newspapers.

3.75 In the final analysis the OFT has its own economists who are experienced in this form of market analysis. Parties, in making representations over such factors, must thus remain realistic if their submissions are to remain credible.

4. *Stage 3: Negotiation of Undertakings and Assurances*

(1) Informal assurances

3.76 The Act provides for "undertakings" to be given by parties to the OFT. However, many cases are dealt with on the basis of "assurances" given to the OFT by parties to the complained of conduct. Prior to the changes made by the Deregulation and Contracting Out Act 1994, informal assurances were more important to the OFT since it could only accept undertakings after a full formal investigation and report into the anti-competitive course of conduct. Since the changes to the CA 1980 entailed in the 1994 Act, the OFT may take undertakings without the necessity of producing a fully reasoned report, though it is required to issue a notice publicising the proposed undertaking for comment.[86] However, informal assurances remain an option for the OFT where it is considered that the case can be satisfactorily dealt with without the necessity of publishing a notice. The OFT's practice in accepting informal assurances under the procedure prior to the changes in the CA 1980 thus remains relevant. Many examples of informal assurances have already been given. In *Permutit-Boby Ltd's Spare Parts Policy*[87] the OFT persuaded PBL, specialists in water treatment equipment, to modify its spare-parts supply policy. Com-

cont.
Zanon (1982) 31 ICLQ 36, where the European court considered that branded bananas could be a discrete product market.

86 s. 4(2) CA 1980, as substituted by s. 12(4) Deregulation and Contracting Out Act 1994.

87 14 February 1983, DGFT Annual Report 1983, p. 106.

plaints had been received from independent service companies who had been refused supplies of spare parts direct from PBL; this denied them the chance to compete on equal terms with PBL's own service engineers for repair and servicing work. Following OFT pressure, PBL agreed to supply spare parts to all prospective customers for a 12-month trial period. In lieu of this the OFT agreed not to commence a formal investigation.

3.77 In *Boosey and Hawkes plc Franchise Agreements*[88] Boosey and Hawkes, who are manufacturers, importers and distributors of musical instruments, agreed to amend their franchise agreements. The amendment consisted of the deletion of a clause in the agreement designed to prevent a franchised dealer from obtaining foreign-made musical instruments which competed with those of Boosey and Hawkes. The OFT agreed to halt inquiries following this amendment by the company.

3.78 In *Halifax Building Society and Property Insurance*[89] the Halifax Building Society agreed, following discussions with the OFT, to no longer insist on its borrowers taking out property insurance through the Society. Subject to certain new conditions borrowers were thereafter able to arrange their own property insurance. Under the new arrangement accepted by the OFT where the borrower desired to arrange his own insurance the Society's administrative costs would be borne by the borrower; these included a small charge for contingency insurance to cover against the possibility of any breakdown in the independent insurance arrangements. Following this development the Director General wrote to other building societies which continued to tie mortgages to insurance agency services requesting them to say what changes they proposed to make in the light of the Halifax relaxation.

3.79 In *Wadham Stringer*[90] the company agreed to reinstate credit and discount facilities to Mr Merson, a car dealer, following discussions with the OFT. Mr Merson operated a business importing left-hand drive British made cars from the continent for conversion to right-hand drive. He complained to the OFT that Wadham Stringer had withdrawn credit and discount facilities for the supply of necessary parts on the ground that Mr Merson was undercutting their own retail trade. Following OFT pressure Wadham Stringer reinstated credit and discount facilities and assured the OFT that this had not been company policy but was unilateral action taken by a local branch manager.

3.80 In *Scottish Milk Marketing Board's Cattle Breeding Service*[91] the OFT intervened following a complaint about the dominant position of the SMMB and its pricing policy for delivery of semen to farms and provision of an artificial insemination service. Following discussions the SMMB: (a) assured the OFT that its cattle breeding services were not subsidised out of revenues from other activities and that it did not therefore gain an unfair advantage in those parts of the market where private companies competed; (b) changed the accounting and pricing policy of its cattle breeding services division to ensure that administrative costs were more closely related to activities which would enable the prices charged for different services to reflect more accurately underlying costs; (c) discontinued the practice of charging a higher insemination service fee for using bought-in rather than SMMB-supplied semen, in order to avoid discrimination against private bull breed-

[88] 1 September 1983, DGFT Annual Report 1983, p. 107. See also *Kango Wolf Power Tools* DGFT Annual Report 1984, p. 108 the company agreed not to prevent its dealers from supplying goods which competed with the Kango "task force" range of goods following informal OFT discussions.

[89] 15 June 1982, DGFT Annual Report 1982, p. 102. For detailed analysis of related cases and their context see para. 11.234 on the *Building Societies Association* case.

[90] 11 August 1982, DGFT Annual Report 1982, pp. 102, 103.

[91] 1 December 1982, DGFT Annual Report 1982, p. 103. For other examples see, *Grey-Green Coaches* DGFT Annual Report 1985 p. 64; *British Gas Corporation* DGFT Annual Report 198,5 p. 64; *Enfield Advertiser and Enfield Independent* DGFT Annual Report 1985, p. 64.

ers; (d) reduced the handling charge for delivery of bought-in semen to farms from 50p to 30p and the handling charge for the artificial insemination service using bought-in semen from £1.50 to £1.10. This had the effect of relating the fee for delivery and use of bought-in semen more closely to its handling costs, plus a small contribution to overheads. This case demonstrates clearly the value of informal OFT intervention. The case could easily, given the economic position of the SMMB, have led to full reference to the MMC.

(2) Undertakings

3.81 The OFT may accept an undertaking from a person as an alternative to making a reference to the MMC. It can do so if it appears to the OFT that three criteria are satisfied.[92] First, that there are reasonable grounds for believing that any person has pursued an anti-competitive course of conduct. Second, that the practice may operate against the public interest, now or in the future, or may have done so in the past. Third, that an undertaking offered by that person (or associated person,[93] to enable a parent to undertake on behalf of a subsidiary) would remedy or prevent adverse effects to the public interest now or in the future.

3.82 Before accepting such an undertaking, the OFT must first publish a notice covering certain specified matters and second consider representations made following publication of that notice.[94]

The notice must (a) state that the OFT is proposing to accept an undertaking under section 4(1) CA 1980; (b) identify the course of conduct under investigation; (c) identify the person pursuing it; (d) identify the goods or services involved; (e) specify the effects adverse to the public interest; (f) set out the terms of the proposed undertaking; (g) identify who is proposing to give the undertaking; and, (h) set a deadline for third parties to make representations to the OFT.[95] Publication is to be made in such a way as to bring the notice to the attention of persons who would be affected or have an interest were the matter to be referred to the MMC.[96] When the OFT receives representations, it may seek modifications to the undertaking, but when it does so, it is not required to re-publish the modified undertaking in the form set out.[97]

3.83 Note that the onus is on the parties to proffer undertakings. The written representations should contain proposals as to what should be done to remedy the adverse effect on the public interest specified in the notice.[98] It would appear from the statutory language that the OFT has no jurisdiction to accept an undertaking unless and until it has complied with all the statutory conditions precedent.[99]

(3) The scope for negotiations

3.84 The scope for negotiation of undertakings will depend upon the number of options existing that may cure the complained of conduct of its anti-competitive effects. Parties should thus consider the OFT views carefully and draw up a list of possible options ranging from the most extreme option (usually total abrogation of the practice) to less

92 s. 4(1) CA 1980, as substituted by s. 12(4) Deregulation and Contracting Out Act 1994.
93 As defined by s. 2(6) CA 1980: see s. 4(10) CA 1980, as substituted by s. 12(5) Deregulation and Contracting Out Act 1994.
94 s. 4(2) CA 1980, as substituted by s. 12(4) Deregulation and Contracting Out Act 1994.
95 s. 4(3A) CA 1980, as substituted by s. 12(4) Deregulation and Contracting Out Act 1994.
96 s 4(3) CA 1980, as substituted by s. 12(4) Deregulation and Contracting Out Act 1994.
97 s. 4(3B) CA 1980, as substituted by s. 12(4) Deregulation and Contracting Out Act 1994.
98 s. 4(1)(C) CA 1980.
99 For the importance attached to the giving of statutory notices under the CA 1980 see *R* v *DGFT ex parte Southdown Motor Services* (1993) 12 Tr Law 90.

extreme options (involving modification of the practice). Parties must be realistic in this; the OFT will expect the parties to suggest effective curative measures, though there may be scope for negotiation over some of the finer detail. Thus, if the OFT upholds a complaint that a party has operated a below-cost selling predatory campaign the OFT may seek an undertaking from the party that it will not sell below cost. In such a case discussions may well occur over the precise meaning of cost. In a case involving discriminatory discounts there may be scope for negotiation over when a discount is discriminatory and when it is justified as a response to competitive and other ordinary commercial pressures.

3.85 An interesting example of an undertaking given by a firm in order to avoid reference to the MMC is that given by Scottish and Universal Newspapers Ltd (SUNL) following an OFT report concluding that SUNL were predatory pricing in respect of advertising space in one of their newspapers (the *Lanarkshire World*).[100] The undertakings finally given contained built in provision enabling the OFT to monitor the future conduct of the parties. Essentially the undertaking accepted by the OFT required SUNL:

- not to supply or offer to supply advertising space in the *Lanarkshire World* free of charge to any person. This undertaking did not prohibit SUNL from publishing free of charge details of the publishing activities of SUNL itself or corrections to any advertisement which had previously appeared in *Lanarkshire World* free of charge;
- not to supply or offer to supply any advertising space in *Lanarkshire World* upon condition that that person does not acquire or offer to acquire advertising space in any competing publication;
- not to supply or offer to supply any advertising space in *Lanarkshire World* to any person on a charge which does not equal or exceed that part of the marginal cost of producing and distributing the *Lanarkshire World* attributable to that advertising space.

3.86 The OFT had SUNL incorporate in the undertaking various monitoring provisions entitling the OFT to call on SUNL to furnish information on: (i) size, content and circulation of *Lanarkshire World*; (ii) costs incurred in production and circulation; (iii) charges made for the supply of advertising space in the paper; and (iv) revenue attributed to the paper. The undertakings were stated to be effective for a five-year period.[101] Undertakings in several other cases have been given for ten years and in *Black and Decker*[102] the undertaking was not limited in duration.

(4) Variations and release of undertakings

3.87 Where circumstances change the OFT may release the person from the undertakings or, conversely, draft a new undertaking to take account of the changes.[103] In such cases the OFT must notify the persons concerned of the release or the changes stating the nature of the changed circumstances.[104] Parties subject to undertakings should thus discuss with the OFT what the latter consider to represent a change of circumstances likely to lead to release from or variation of undertakings. Thereafter parties should be ready to make suitable representations to the OFT in respect of release.

[100] *Scottish and Universal Newspapers Ltd* (11 January 1983).
[101] A copy of the undertaking is given in (1983) 11 *British Business*, p. 58. The wording used in the text to this note is a reasonable copy of the precise wording used.
[102] Press release 11 May 1990.
[103] s. 4(4)(b) CA 1980.
[104] s. 4(5) CA 1980.

3.88 The OFT, in monitoring undertakings will also notify persons whom they consider are failing to comply with the undertaking. Failure to comply with either an undertaking *per se* or a variation thereof can lead to full MMC investigation.[105]

3.89 Under section 5(3) no reference may be made to the MMC within a period of four weeks commencing from either the date of the OFT concluding that there are reasonable grounds for believing that a person is pursuing or has pursued an anti-competitive course of conduct[106] or the date of a notice of a breach[107] or variation of an undertaking, or a new undertaking,[108] whichever is relevant. Nor may a reference be made to the MMC more than eight weeks *after* those dates. It is during this short period of eight weeks from date of report or notice until the last date for the making of a reference that the OFT will consider undertakings. This relatively short period imposes pressure upon firms to give an immediate undertaking. The eight-week period may be extended for a further four weeks by the Secretary of State if the latter considers it necessary in order to allow the OFT to continue negotiating undertakings. An extension can only result from a representation by the OFT; the Secretary of State cannot extend the period unilaterally. There is hence no scope for lobbying the Secretary of State,[109] though a request to the OFT to have the period extended is, of course, feasible. If no reference is made within the specified period or extension thereof the inquiry lapses. Upon the evidence of the negotiation of undertakings in monopoly cases this is a very tight time schedule; firms will need to respond rapidly and with conviction.[110] For other forms of lobbying see under stage 4, below.

5. Stage 4: The "Competition Reference"

(1) Form of the reference

3.90 Following publication of a report, and within the specified time limits, the OFT *may* make a "competition reference" to the MMC. There are three situations in which such references may be made: (i) where, the OFT has concluded that there are reasonable grounds for belief that a person is pursuing or has pursued a course of conduct which constitutes an anti-competitive practice and the OFT has not accepted satisfactory undertakings from the relevant parties—this is termed a "report reference";[111] (ii) where the OFT has given notice under section 4(4)(c) to a person who has hitherto given undertakings but who has subsequently failed to carry out those undertakings—a reference here is termed a "notice reference";[112] (iii) where the OFT has given notice under section 4(5) to a person who has hitherto given undertakings but who, in the opinion of the OFT taking into account changing circumstance, should now accept new, varied or extended undertakings, and where such persons refuse to accept the new, varied or extended undertakings, this also is termed a "notice reference".[113]

The OFT may not refer conduct which is covered by an undertaking.[114]

[105] s. 4(4)(c) and s. 5(1)(b) CA 1980.
[106] s. 5(1)(a) CA 1980, as substituted by s. 12(1) Deregulation and Contracting Out Act 1994.
[107] s. 5(1)(b) CA 1980.
[108] s. 5(1)(c) CA 1980.
[109] s. 5(4) CA 1980.
[110] See s. 29 CA 1980 which exempts from the RTPA 1976 undertakings given under s. 88 Fair Trading Act 1973 in consequence of an adverse MMC report following a monopoly or merger reference or a competition reference under the CA 1980. This section clears up doubts that such undertakings fell within the broad definition of agreement in s. 43(1) RTPA 1976. The section is retroactive.
[111] s. 5(1)(a) CA 1980 as substituted by s. 12(1) Deregulation and Contracting Out Act 1994.
[112] s. 5(1)(b) and s. 5(2)(b) CA 1980.
[113] s. 5(1)(c) and s. 5(2)(b) CA 1980.
[114] s. 6(3) CA 1980, as substituted by s. 12(6) Deregulation and Contracting Out Act 1994.

3.91 The OFT is not required to refer an anti-competitive practice to the MMC. In *British Coal Corporation*,[115] the OFT concluded that a loyalty rebate scheme was anti-competitive, but unlikely to have a significant effect in the market and therefore did not justify a competition reference.

(2) Informal representations to the Secretary of State

3.92 Following an adverse OFT investigation parties will have to decide whether to negotiate undertakings or whether to stand by their public interest arguments and seek to defend the practices before the MMC. At this stage an opportunity for making representations to the Secretary of State exists. Under section 7(2) CA 1980 the Secretary of State may, before the end of a two-week period commencing with the day on which he receives a copy of the competition reference sent to him by the Director General of Fair Trading, direct the MMC not to proceed with a reference. The Secretary of State may also, within the same time constraints, direct the MMC not to proceed with a variation to a competition reference made by the Director General. The period of two weeks sounds very brief. In practice the scope for submissions is longer since the competition reference may not be made until after four weeks following the date of the OFT's conclusion under section 5(1)(a) CA 1980 that there is an anti-competitive course of conduct. Thus, representations may be made for six weeks from that earlier date. The scope for such submissions will vary from case to case. Some parties for example have argued on the basis of evidence to be found in Hansard of parliamentary debates on the Competition Bill and have suggested that, according to the ministerial statements made at the time, certain practices were outside the scope of the Act. This has been the case, for example, with respect to the licensing of copyright. Parliamentary statements differed as to whether such licensing practices could be regulated under the Act. Parties therefore considered that the Secretary of State might feel constrained to follow the statements of earlier ministers and succumb to their requests to stop a reference to the MMC. Such attempts have to date uniformly failed. The Secretary of State apparently considers that he is not bound by parliamentary statements;[116] that the scope of the power of review under section 2(1) CA 1980 is unlimited; and that the proper place for an effective and thorough examination of the merits is the MMC itself. As a result although the possibility of successful submissions is not ruled out current practice is to refrain from interfering with OFT decisions to refer cases to the MMC. If submissions are to succeed they will almost certainly be on the basis that a reference to the MMC is against the public interest. The Secretary of State and supporting DTI staff will not readily wish to second guess *economic* decisions made by the OFT, which is in a much better position to assess the market. As regards public interest arguments the Secretary of State will probably be of the view that the MMC is a more appropriate forum for their exposition since that body has the personnel and experience to weigh up in an effective manner public interest arguments. Moreover, the Secretary of State is inclined to point out that he is not bound to follow MMC recommendation made in a report at the conclusion of proceedings. The Secretary of State for Trade and Industry did however in 1994 direct that an investigation into a bus operator's alleged predatory conduct on the Isle of Arran be halted as being an unnecessary burden on business.[117] The OFT's Press Release pointedly remarked that the MMC had

[115] 9 October 1991. See para. 6.28 of the Report. See also *Sealink Harbours* (14 October 1987).

[116] It is, however, now the case, following the House of Lords decision in *Pepper* v *Hart* [1993] AC 593, that ministerial statements can be taken into account in interpreting ambiguities to be found within a statute.

[117] *Arran Transport and Trading Co Ltd*, DGFT Annual Report 1994, p. 44.

previously condemned the type of practices being alleged in the present case. It may well be that this is an isolated case, stemming from the fact that the Secretary of State was launching his deregulation initiative at the time with the declared aim of reducing burdens on business, which culminated in the Deregulation and Contracting Out Act 1994, and thus was thus a politically expedient decision. In view of the changes to the Anti-Competitive Practices (Exclusions) Order brought about by the 1994 Amendment Order discussed at paras. 3.51–3.52 above, the company concerned would fall below the new £10 million threshold and thus not be susceptible to investigation under this Act.

It should be stressed that any representations made to the Secretary of State are outside of the formal procedure as envisaged by the CA 1980.

6. *Stage 5: Monopolies and Mergers Commission: Investigation and Report*

(1) Duty of the MMC

3.93 Few investigations ever reach this stage since most companies prefer to give undertakings rather than devote resources to further battle.

The scope of the remit for the MMC is determined by the "competition reference". In the reference the OFT specify: the person(s) to be investigated; the goods and services concerned; and, the course of conduct to be investigated.[118] If, however, a satisfactory undertaking is obtained from X out of a group of associated persons then X and his behaviour need not be referred. Alternatively, X might give undertakings in respect of one activity but not in respect of another; in such a case only the latter practice might be referred. Prior to the changes made by the 1994 Act the OFT could not refer persons, goods and services, or conduct not outlined in the OFT's report of its conclusions under section 5(1)(a).[119] Conversely, it was not obliged to refer for investigation every person or piece of conduct mentioned in that report.[120] In effect the reference had to be related to the report.

3.94 In *R* v *DGFT ex parte Southdown Motor Services*,[121] Auld J quashed a competition reference made by the OFT of "local bus services in the Bognor Regis area" on the basis that the OFT had only investigated and reported upon[122] two particular services thus limiting a competition reference to the MMC to these services.[123] He held that "the only course or courses of conduct which the [OFT] is entitled to specify in a reference are courses of conduct described in [its] report as anti-competitive and in connection with services specified in the report".[124] It was observed that "the mere mention in a report of a course of conduct as part of the trading background or by way of comparison or in some other incidental manner, would not qualify"[125] to bring that conduct within the ambit of matters which could then be referred to the MMC. The implication of the judgment for the current procedure appears to be that a person investigated must be able to deal with the matters raised by the OFT in its reference, without the risk that the MMC could then be used as a means of widening the scope of the investigation. If the OFT does wish to widen the scope of an

118 s. 6(1) CA 1980. Though the MMC may investigate conduct not mentioned in the reference if it appears to them to be similar in form and effect to that specified; see s. 6(5)(a) CA 1980.
119 s. 6(2) CA 1980, now repeated by the Deregulation and Contracting Out Act 1994.
120 *ibid.*
121 (1993) 12 Tr Law 90.
122 OFT Report of 15 July 1992.
123 The resulting MMC Report, Cm 2248, is thus pithily entitled *Southdown Motor Services. A report on the conduct of Southdown Motor Services Limited in respect of its operation of local bus services on routes 262 and 242 in Bognor Regis* (June 1993).
124 (1993) 12 Tr Law 90, 102.
125 (1993) 12 Tr Law 90, 100.

investigation, it may do so under the 1980 Act by starting another wider investigation or it may instead make a monopoly reference under the Fair Trading Act 1973.[126] The Director may refer a practice to the MMC even though it has been abandoned on the basis that it may be resumed at a future date.[127] Simply because an undertaking has been given to the OFT this does not necessarily entail escape from investigation by the MMC; the OFT can, as noted above, make a reference covering a situation about which unfulfilled or unsatisfactory undertakings have been given.[128] Thus, X cannot simply give an undertaking to avoid reference to the MMC if he has no intention of complying with it since, as described under Stage 4, a competition reference may derive from a breached undertaking.

3.95 The duty of the MMC is to, "investigate and report" on:

> "(a) whether any person subject to the reference was at any time during the period of twelve months ending on the date of the reference pursuing, in relation to goods or services specified in the reference, a course of conduct so specified or any other course of conduct which appears to be similar in form and effect to the one so specified; and (b) whether, by pursuing any such course of conduct, a person subject to the reference was at any time during that period engaging in an anti-competitive practice; and (c) whether, if any person was so engaging in an anti-competitive practice, the practice operated or might be expected to operate against the public interest."[129]

The public interest is defined by section 84 Fair Trading Act 1973, which is quoted below at para. 3.101.

3.96 The OFT may (but in practice does not) influence proceedings before the MMC since they may, *at any time*, by notice to the MMC, restrict the scope of the latter's investigation by excluding from the investigation: some or all of the activities of the person subject to the reference; any goods or services specified in the reference; or, any course of conduct specified in the reference. On the receipt of such a notice the MMC must discontinue their investigation into those matters and must make no reference to them in their report.[130] This power of control exercisable by the OFT is subject to veto powers held by the Secretary of State.[131] Where the OFT exercises its power of control over the MMC a copy of the variation reference must be sent to the Secretary of State. The Secretary of State may, within a two-week period commencing from the date on which he receives notice of the variation, direct the MMC not to proceed with the particular investigation. Alternatively, the Secretary of State may direct the MMC to ignore the variation to the reference made by the OFT.

(2) MMC procedure

3.97 The rules for MMC proceedings are essentially the same as those under the Fair Trading Act 1973 for mergers.[132] Thus, the time limit for a report is six months beginning on the

[126] This was done in the case of *Holmes McDougall* (*Restrictions of Advertisements Containing Prices*), OFT Report dated 3 October 1985, which prompted an industry-wide investigation under the Fair Trading Act 1973, resulting in the MMC Report *Specialised Advertising Services*, Cm 280 (1988). This in turn led to the Secretary of State enjoining certain types of price advertising restrictions in mountaineering and hill-walking magazines by the Restriction on Conduct (Specialist Advertising Services) Order 1988, S.I. 1988 No. 1017.

[127] As in *WM Still and Sons Ltd* (22 July 1982), p. 38.

[128] s. 5(1) CA 1980 and s. 4(4)(c) CA 1980.

[129] s. 6(5) CA 1980.

[130] s. 6(6) CA 1980.

[131] s. 7(2) CA 1980.

[132] s. 7(6) CA 1980 which provides that ss. 70 (time limits for report on merger reference), 84 (public interest) and 85 (attendance of witnesses and production of documents) of the Fair Trading Act 1973 and Pt II of that Act (performance of functions of the Commission) shall apply.

date of the reference, though the period can be extended by a further three months at the discretion of the Secretary of State on receiving representations from the MMC.

3.98 On the basis that a case takes six months from complaint to OFT conclusions; two months thereafter before the competition reference, and a six further months for the MMC to investigate and report; a 15-month period can elapse prior to a final report. The period may, even then, be longer where post MMC undertakings have to be negotiated or decided. By contrast, as the *Wadham Stringer* case discussed under Stage 3 reveals, an informal solution may arise in under four weeks.

3.99 As noted above, the actual procedure before the MMC is the same as that for ordinary references under the Fair Trading Act 1973. The MMC determines its own procedure.[133] In practice the MMC are inquisitorial and not adversarial. They avoid confrontations between the parties, preferring rather to invite oral and written submission from the parties and other interested persons in private hearings which are not open to the public. The OFT generally meet with the MMC at an early stage in order for the former to present their views and the results of their investigations. The MMC take efforts to independently collect empirical and other data. Thus the MMC might employ consultant market research organisations, accountancy firms or bodies such as the Consumers Association to undertake empirical spade work on its behalf. The MMC usually devote about five staff to CA 1980 investigations, although back up teams of lawyers, economists, accountants and other civil servants within the MMC administration may be involved in analysis of evidence.

(3) Submissions by parties

3.100 The MMC may specify the nature of the information they require from the parties. Frequently parties are asked for submissions relating to the following matters and questions:

(a) whether the parties agree with the factual analysis as described by the OFT;
(b) whether the parties agree that the course of conduct specified by the OFT has been carried on;
(c) whether there are any additional facts that the parties wish to be taken into account;
(d) whether the parties agree that the course of conduct specified constitutes an anti-competitive practice;
(e) what the view of the parties is to the effects of the course of conduct specified in the reference on the public interest.

The MMC are under a duty to act fairly in the conduct of an investigation, but this does not mean that it is to be carried out as if it were a trial in court. In particular, as Mann J stressed in *R* v *MMC ex parte Elders IXL*,[134] "there is no general rule that one party to an investigation should be given all the material submitted by another". It is sufficient that each party be given the opportunity to make its submissions on the relevant issues.[135]

133 s. 81(2) Fair Trading Act 1973. Under s. 81(3) the Secretary of State may give general guidance on the conduct of proceedings. However, to date, no such guidance has been given.

134 [1987] 1 All ER 451, 461. The investigation in question arose out a merger reference under the Fair Trading Act 1973, but the principle is of general application to all MMC investigations. See also paras. 5.142–5.145.

135 *R* v *MMC ex parte Matthew Brown plc* [1987] 1 All ER 463.

(4) The public interest: section 84 Fair Trading Act 1973

3.101 By the time parties arrive before the MMC they will be familiar with the arguments concerning the anti-competitive practice and its effects on the public interest. These arguments will have been rehearsed before the OFT. The MMC's inquiry into whether an anti-competitive practice operated or might be expected to operate against the public interest consists of two analytical requirements: the finding of an anti-competitive practice and a finding on the public interest. For the second part of the analysis, section 84 Fair Trading Act 1973 reads as follows:

> "In determining for any purposes to which this section applies whether any particular matter operates, or may be expected to operate, against the public interest, the Commission shall take into account all matters which appear to them in the particular circumstances to be relevant and, among other things, shall have regard to the desirability—.
> (a) of maintaining and promoting effective competition between persons supplying goods and services in the United Kingdom; (b) of promoting the interests of consumers, purchasers and other users of goods and services in the United Kingdom in respect of the prices charged for them and in respect of their quality and the variety of goods and services supplied; (c) of promoting, through competition, the reduction of costs and the development and use of new techniques and new products, and of facilitating the entry of new competitors into existing markets; (d) of maintaining and promoting the balanced distribution of industry and employment in the United Kingdom; and (e) of maintaining and promoting competitive activity in markets outside the United Kingdom on the part of producers of goods, and of suppliers of goods and services, in the United Kingdom."

3.102 The factors in section 84(1)(a)–(e) are only examples of particular circumstances the MMC must consider. Parties may present any other arguments they so desire. In the investigation into *Sheffield Newspapers*[136] the MMC appeared to accept that in their style and economic philosophy section 2(1) CA 1980 (definition of anti-competitive practice) and Article 85(1) EC were similar. They rejected, however, an argument based upon the similarity between Article 86 EC (abuse of a dominant position) and section 2(1), that the latter provision could only be operative against parties who had "misconducted" themselves. The MMC replied that while Article 86 EC may involve misconduct, section 2(1) certainly did not. The importance of this point lies not so much in the misconduct argument as in the relevance of EC law as a guide to MMC policy. Article 85 EC is broad enough to catch agreements whereby suppliers enter agreements with dealers or other purchasers and which contain anti-competitive and restrictive clauses. Much of the work of the OFT under the CA 1980 concerns restrictive clauses in contracts between persons at different distributional levels. Consequently the two provisions have points of similarity. Given this fact the MMC seemed prepared to accept that had Article 85 EC cases been cited to them which were relevant to the analysis then the MMC would have considered them:

> "By contrast, the wording of the opening part of Article 85 does seem to us to reflect a concept very similar to that embodied in section 2(1) of the Competition Act, and if SNL had been able to point to decisions of the European Court interpreting Article 85(1) in the restricted sense contended for, we might have had to consider to what extent the similarity of language should incline us towards a like interpretation."[137]

[136] MMC Report *Sheffield Newspapers Ltd* (1983) Cmnd 8664.

[137] *ibid.* at para. 7.12. Arguably, by virtue of Art. 5 EC and the legal doctrine of "supremacy" of EC law over domestic law, the MMC is bound to take into account the provisions of European law and in particular Arts. 85 and 86 in so far as those provisions may apply to the facts of the case. In *Tate and Lyle plc* and *Feruzzi, Berisford* (Cmnd 89) para. 16.20, the MMC, in a merger case, took into consideration EC case law.

In the light of this statement parties may seek support for their arguments from EC decisions on competition. Decisions of the European Commission as well as judgments of the European Court should be relevant in this respect.

(5) Pre-publication inspection of the report

3.103 As with the OFT reports companies concerned are given an opportunity to verify the factual part of the report which is relevant to them prior to its publication thereby enabling them to comment on and correct its factual content if necessary. This is not intended to represent an opportunity for the parties to make further submissions. The parties will not usually be given the conclusions to the report. Under section 17(2) CA 1980 the Secretary of State must give at least 24 hours' notice of formal publication to those named in the reference.

7. *Stage 6: Post-MMC Undertakings and Orders*

(1) Procedure and undertakings, section 10 CA 1980

3.104 In the event of an adverse report of the MMC a number of options arise. The MMC, in their report, *must* consider what action (if any) should be taken for the purpose of remedying or preventing the adverse effects of that practice.[138] Moreover, they *may*, recommend suitable curative action.[139] Following this adverse report the Secretary of State *may*, by notice in writing, request the Director to seek to obtain from the person(s) concerned an undertaking to, "take or refrain from taking any action with a view to remedying or preventing those adverse effects".[140] Thus, the OFT may seek positive (i.e. obligation to act—e.g. restore trading links or supplies) or negative (i.e. obligation not to act—e.g. refrain from selling below cost or discriminating between customers) undertakings. Despite use of the non-mandatory word "request" to describe the Secretary of State's communication to the Director General the latter is under a duty to seek undertakings.[141] Undertakings may only be enforced by the Secretary of State. Third parties have neither *locus standi* to enforce nor any remedy for breach of such an undertaking.[142]

3.105 Where the OFT fails to obtain a satisfactory undertaking it may advise the Secretary of State about the appropriate action to take. The Secretary of State must take account of this advice when considering whether or not to make a formal Order against the party in question under the Order making powers in section 10 CA 1980. If such an Order is made it may take a number of forms: (a) it may be prohibitive enjoining a person engaging in an anti-competitive practice specified in the MMC report or any other practice which is similar in form and effect; (b) alternatively or additionally, the Order might involve the exercise of any of the powers specified in Part I of Schedule 8 to the Fair Trading Act 1973. These are very wide ranging and can render unlawful the performance of behaviour reported as anti-competitive by the MMC. The wide Order making powers in (a) may only be exercised in a number of situations. These are: where the person concerned has refused to give the OFT an undertaking following an adverse MMC report in pursuance of a request by the latter, or, where the OFT were not requested to seek an undertaking and the Secretary of State thought it appropriate to proceed immediately

[138] s. 8(4)(a) CA 1980.
[139] s. 8(4)(b) CA 1980.
[140] s. 9(1) CA 1980.
[141] s. 9(2)(b) CA 1980.
[142] *Fogg* v *Esso Petroleum* [1990] *The Independent*, 23 April; *Mid Kent Holdings plc* v *General Utilities plc* [1996] 3 All ER 132.

with an Order; or where the OFT notify the Secretary of State that an undertaking given to them following an adverse MMC report is not or has not been fulfilled.[143]

(2) The Order

3.106 The relevant Order making powers referred to in Part I of Schedule 8 to the Fair Trading Act 1973 include the power to:

- s. 4(1)(C) CA 1980 make it unlawful to make or perform any agreement;
- require the termination of any agreement;
- make it unlawful for a person to withhold supplies of goods or services from any specified firm or person;
- make it unlawful to require, as a condition of supplying goods or services, the buying of other goods, or any payment for services other than the goods or services supplied;
- make it unlawful to discriminate between persons or firms on the prices charged for goods or services;
- make it unlawful to give any preference in the supply of goods or services;
- make it unlawful to charge prices for goods or services differing from those in any published list;
- require publication of price lists;
- regulate prices to be charged for any goods or services;
- make it unlawful to notify recommended or suggested prices to persons supplying goods or services; and,
- prohibit or restrict the acquisition of a business or the assets of another business.

3.107 Before the Secretary of State makes an Order he must publish a notice expressing his intention so to do and containing information of the contents of the Order. The notice must, according to section 10(4), afford at least a 30 day period to enable written representations to be made during that period. This period thus allows parties to submit arguments to the Minister commenting upon the effects the proposed Order may have upon the market and their trade. An Order will be effected by statutory instrument which may be annulled by a vote in either House of Parliament.

F. Investigation of Public Bodies

3.108 While the competition reference and preceding investigation of anti-competitive practices is the central part of the Act, also provided for is a machinery for the investigation of public authorities. The OFT do not have an involvement in this procedure. Under sections 11 and 12 CA 1980 the Secretary of State may refer for investigation to the MMC any question relating to: (a) the efficiency and costs of; (b) the service provided by; or (c) possible abuse of a monopoly situation by, public bodies. A public body is defined in section 11(3) CA 1980 as any body corporate which supplies goods or services by way of business, the affairs of which are managed by its members and the members of which hold office as such by virtue of their appointment to that or another office by a minister under any enactment. This mechanism for investigating and scrutinising the performance of nationalised industries and other public bodies is, of course, additional to existing con-

[143] s. 10(3) CA 1980.

trols of public accountability and responsibility to Parliament through the agencies of Ministerial and Select Committee control. Well over thirty references have been made to date under this procedure. The MMC must report on any questions referred to them but they are excluded from commenting on the appropriateness of any financial obligations or guidance as to financial objectives given under statute (or in any other enactment) by a minister; the MMC may, however, comment upon the way such objectives are being achieved. Nor can the MMC report on whether a course of conduct registrable under the RTPA 1976 is contrary to the public interest. Following an adverse MMC report which concludes that the body has operated against the public interest the Secretary of State shall give a copy of the report to the minister(s) responsible for that body. The relevant minister(s) may, thereafter, require the body to submit proposals outlining how they would remedy or prevent the adverse results specified.

3.109 Following an adverse report the Secretary of State may exercise any of the Order making powers contained in Schedule 8 to the Fair Trading Act 1973. Those powers do not, however, extend to exercising the power in para. 10 thereof. This is the power to regulate the prices to be charged for any goods or services.

3.110 The Secretary of State may under section 11 (4) CA 1980 exclude by Order various persons from control. This power has been exercised once to date. In the Competition (Exclusion of Bus Operators) Order 1980[144] the Secretary of State excluded from the risk of reference to the MMC any person whose annual turnover from the provision of bus services is less than £1 million. This exclusion does not apply if the annual turnover of the bus service provider and any other associated person(s) is £1 million or more. A person's annual turnover means the total of the amounts received during the 12 months ending on the last day of the period in respect of which returns have most recently been made under section 157 of the Road Traffic Act 1960. The amounts to be counted are those in respect of the carriage of passengers in the course of the provision of bus services by the carrier in question. When the carrier is a local authority the relevant turnover amount is the greater of either the total cost of providing the service or the total amount determined by reference for the test of non-local authority carriers.

3.111 The powers under section 11(1) may be exercised in connection with person as defined in section 11(3). This latter provision covers:

(i) any body corporate which supplies goods or services by way of business, the affairs of which are managed by its members and the members of which hold office as such by virtue of their appointment to that or another office by a Minister under any enactment;

(ii) any person not falling within (i) who provides in Northern Ireland a bus service within the meaning of section 14 of the Finance Act (Northern Ireland) 1966 (this is the effect of section 114(1)(a) Transport Act 1985 which amends section 11);

(iii) any person who provides a railway passenger service in pursuance of an agreement entered into by London Regional Transport by virtue of section 3(2) of the London Regional Transport Act 1984 (this is the effect of section 14(1)(b) Transport Act 1985 which amends section 15(1) of Schedule 6 to the London Regional Transport Act 1984 which added section 11(3)(b) Competition Act 1980);

(iv) any statutory water undertaker within the meaning of the Water Act 1973;

(v) any board administering a scheme under the Agricultural Marketing Act 1958 or the Agricultural Marketing Act (Northern Ireland) 1964;

[144] S.I. 1980 No. 980 (came into force on 12 August 1980).

(vi) any body corporate with a statutory duty to promote and assist the maintenance and development of the efficient supply of any goods or services by a body as described above;

(vii) any subsidiary within the meaning of the Companies Act 1985 of a body as described above.

3.112 Section 11 investigations, by their very nature, tend to be wide ranging and the conclusions somewhat unspecific. An illustration of such an investigation demonstrates their scope. In *British Airports Authority*[145] the DTI, acting for the Secretary of State, requested the MMC to investigate certain aspects relating to the efficiency and costs of, and the service provided by the British Airports Authority (BAA) in its commercial activities. "Commercial activities" was defined in effect as: (a) the making of arrangements by concession and otherwise for persons other than the BAA to arrange for the sale of goods and the provision of services at airports (e.g. catering, car-hire services, public car parks, etc); (b) the making of arrangements whether by licence, contract or otherwise, by persons other than the BAA, for the provision of services to airlines, including the provision of services by one airline to another; (c) the granting of leases of land including the grant of consents to assignments of leases and the general administration of such leases.

3.113 As will be immediately apparent section 11 investigations are very different creatures to those under section 2. In the latter case the MMC places under an analytical microscope an isolated, identifiable commercial practice; in the former case the MMC casts a roving, critical eye over a wide gamut of activities. The DTI will, admittedly, narrow the scope of a section 11 investigation by posing a limited number of questions for the MMC to consider. Thus in *British Airports Authority* the DTI required the MMC to consider whether the BAA could improve its efficiency, or reduce its costs or improve the service provided having particular regard to: (a) the scope for increasing competition at the point of sale, bearing in mind security and safety requirements and the need to ensure the comfort and convenience of passengers and the efficient operation of the airport; (b) the methods adopted by the BAA in selecting concessionaires, for example the methods of putting out to tender, the terms imposed upon successful tenderers, and, the award and renewal of contracts; (c) the monitoring of standards of concessionaires; and (d) the administration and management of leases of land owned by the BAA.

3.114 On conclusion of the investigation the MMC reported and made recommendations, most of which were of a very general nature, concerning:[146] the role of the BAA board; planning guidelines; targets for commercial performance; internal organisation of BAA; information and computing; finance and government targets; budgetary projections; presentation of results; internal auditing of staff; investment appraisal; concessions; property management; aircraft fuel supply; extent of competition; basis of tendering; air traffic services; manpower efficiency; staff training; industrial relations; quality of service; and, performance indicators. With respect to many of these categories the MMC's conclusions and recommendations were perfunctory. Thus, concerning targets for commercial performance the MMC suggested that they be made more "challenging"; with regard to budgetary projections the MMC similarly recommended they be made more "vigorous and challenging". In some areas the MMC were more specific and constructive. For example, with regard to the presentation of financial results and the allocation of expenditure to particular activities, the MMC recommended an alteration in the methods of con-

[145] *British Airports Authority, a report on the efficiency and costs of, and the service provided by, the British Airports Authority in its commercial activities* (December 1985) Cmnd 9644.

[146] *ibid.*, at pp. 128–134.

structing the published accounts. Not surprisingly, the most detailed recommendations concerned the extent of competition in airports. The MMC noted and accepted that point of sale competition was largely prevented by lack of space. However, they noted also that BAA believed the concessionaires deserved some degree of protection from competition and that they could be effectively regulated by price supervision imposed by BAA. The MMC were critical of the system used by BAA to ensure that concessionaires did not abuse their economic power and made 11 recommendations for improving the system. BAA was subsequently privatised under the terms of the Airports Act 1986.

3.115 From the above it will be seen that section 11 investigations serve different ends to section 2, anti-competitive practices, investigations. Their remit is wider and the conclusions reached and recommendations made, inevitably given the increased number of subjects for examination, generally are less precise.

G. Investigation of Prices of "Major Public Concern"

3.116 The government in section 1 CA 1980 abolished the Price Commission. This body played an important role in the regulation of prices. The power to so regulate, following abolition of the Commission, transferred to the Secretary of State who may order the OFT to undertake *ad hoc* investigations into particular prices of public concern. This power is now contained in section 13 CA 1980. In deciding whether a price is one of major public concern the Secretary of State is required to consider if: (i) the provision or acquisition of the good or service is of general economic importance, or (ii) whether customers are significantly affected directly or indirectly by the price. The Secretary of State must specify a time period in which the OFT must make a report. The report must contain the OFT's findings of fact in addition to other observations the OFT wish to bring to the attention of the Secretary of State. The report must be published. No penalties attach to this investigatory power. None the less, it should be borne in mind that evidence of monopoly abuse may emerge in which case further investigation might result. Additionally, the OFT may, in the light of the investigation, commence an anti-competitive practices investigation under sections 2 and 3. Further, it is conceivable that the Secretary of State might negotiate a section 30 RTPA 1976 agreement with the industry whose prices were investigated (section 30 RTPA 1976—agreements to keep prices down, see paras 2.37–2.46; section 30, however, has not been used since the late 1970s.

H. Confidentiality in OFT and MMC Reports

3.117 Section 16(1) CA 1980 imposes a duty of confidentiality on the OFT and the MMC. It provides that in reporting both bodies shall:

> "have regard to the need for excluding, so far as that is practicable—(a) any matter which relates to the private affairs of an individual, where the publication of that matter would or might, in the opinion of the Commission or the Director, as the case may be, seriously and prejudicially affect the interests of that individual, and (b) any matter which relates specifically to the affairs of a body of persons, whether corporate or unincorporate, where publication of that matter would or might, in the opinion of the Commission or the Director, as the case may be, seriously and prejudicially affect the interests of that body, unless in the opinion of the Commission or the Director, as the case may be, the inclusion of that matter relating specifically to that body is necessary for the purposes of the report."

It will be by no means easy to challenge the reasonableness of the inclusion in a report of material an individual or firm would prefer was kept confidential. The discretion accorded both the OFT and MMC here is very wide. They may even include information seriously and prejudicially affecting a firm if they consider it necessary for purposes of the report; though presumably the duty to consider excluding information deleterious to the position of an individual is of a higher standard than where the information does not relate to an individual.

3.118 Absolute privilege attaches to any report of the OFT or the MMC who are therefore completely safeguarded from actions for defamation. This derives from section 16(2).

3.119 Section 17 CA 1980, relevant only to MMC reports, provides further that the Secretary of State may exclude material from the MMC report as laid before Parliament and as published. This power of exclusion will be exercised where the Secretary of State considers that disclosure of certain information would seriously and prejudicially affect the private affairs and interests of an individual or where the same harm would occur to other firms or legal persons. The Secretary of State has an over-riding obligation to exclude matters from the report where publication would be against the public interest.

3.120 It follows from the above that a certain scope for exclusion arises in respect of material to be incorporated in a report. Representations may be made to the OFT in respect of their reports and to the Secretary of State in respect of MMC reports. To succeed with such representations parties must marshal their evidence and arguments so as to convince the Director General or Secretary of State that serious and prejudicial harm would follow from disclosure. Individuals must establish likewise though the tenor of the Act implies that they will receive a more sympathetic hearing. It is, however, clear that such arguments will succeed only in exceptional cases.

I. Assessment of Competition by OFT and MMC

3.121 Throughout this chapter, examples have been given of cases where the OFT and MMC have concluded that conduct does or does not restrict competition. It may be helpful, therefore, to describe in greater detail how the OFT and MMC set about assessing competition in a given case.[147] The test below sets out what would represent, in a particular case, an exhaustive analysis of competition in the market. It is not intended to be suggested that the OFT or MMC would engage in such an inquiry in every case. There are four principal factors which the authorities take into account when assessing competition:

(i) the structure of the market and the strength of existing competition;
(ii) the scope for substitution between goods by consumers and producers;
(iii) the bargaining power of buyers and suppliers; and
(iv) the threat of entry and the growth of competitors.

It is appropriate to examine each one of the above, in brief, in turn.

[147] See *Monopolies and Anti-Competitive Practices: A Guide to the Provisions of the Fair Trading Act 1973 and the Competition Act 1980* (1994); *Market Definition in UK Competition Policy*, Research Paper No. 1 (February 1992) undertaking by NERA for the OFT; *Barriers to Entry and Exit in UK Competition Policy*, Research Paper No. 2 (March 1994) undertaken by London Economics for the OFT; *Assessing Competition, Monopolies and Mergers Commission Guidelines* (October 1993).

3.122 Turning first to the structure of the market and the strength of competitors. In this regard a number of different facets will be examined. These would include:

(a) The number, size and market share of competitors: a market may have a large number of firms but, none the less, be dominated by one. Conversely, a market which has a relatively small number of evenly balanced companies may be very competitive.[148]

(b) International trade and openness of the market: the level of competition in a given market will usually be affected by the degree of its accessibility to international trade. Barriers to import (including regulatory, legal or institutional barriers of a tariff or non-tariff nature), transport costs and cultural barriers such as preferences for nationality produced produce may serve to insulate producers in the United Kingdom. When examining import penetration it is important to consider the source of the import since imports originating from foreign subsidiaries of the same group as domestic companies may not always be treated as true or fully effective substitutes for domestic production.

(c) The nature of competition which may not always depend upon price. The authorities will invariably review how prices are determined, for instance, whether they are based on list prices or individually negotiated, whether they are discounted heavily and if so upon what basis, etc. Competition may also be based upon product quality, brand loyalty, after-sales services, the development of new products. It has been accepted at the EC level that price competition is not necessarily the sole determinant of competition in selective distribution systems.

(d) The relative financial strength of companies in a market may be important since some companies may have access to financial resources within a group whereas other companies may be more reliant upon the external financial markets. Further, the current and past profitability of companies is likely to be a significant factor.

(e) The rate of growth in the market is also important. Markets which are growing sluggishly or declining may be unattractive to new entrants with the effect of insulating the incumbents to a degree. Such incumbents will need to compete for market share to maintain or expand output. Conversely, in a market which is growing rapidly a company may expand turnover simply by maintaining its market share, or may even do so where its market share is reducing.

(f) Product strategies to develop consumer loyalty can also serve to reduce competition in some markets. This occurs particularly where consumers have developed preferences and loyalties to particular products or suppliers. Such companies may operate in a host of different niche segments of the market insulating one from the other. The companies in question may maintain their position by intensive advertising, which is designed more to sustained the company's market position than to benefit the consumer.

(g) Exit costs from an industry may be significant since they will be taken into account, as part of the assessment of the risks of failure, by a company considering entry to the market. Exist costs may also be such that companies, once in the market, are deterred from making rational economic decisions (i.e. exiting) and continued to compete even when they earn low or negative returns. Such cases may

[148] See OFT investigation into household detergents (DGFT Annual Report 1992, p. 31) where OFT concluded that there was active competition between two dominant companies Proctor and Gamble and Lever Brothers.

arise where companies have particular assets, developed at very high cost, which have, however, a low resale value. Alternatively, regulatory obligations such as the obligation to pay compensation to employees may deter exit.

3.123 Turning, secondly, to the scope for substitution between goods by consumers and producers, the process of assessing competition entails determining the extent of the relevant market. The "market" is generally defined by reference to demand-side substitutability criteria. In particular the authorities consider whether (say) product A is a substitute for product B by reference to its price, quality, and intended use. Sometimes, however, a market may be identified by reference to characteristics of its production (supply-side substitutability). The MMC in their Guidelines *Assessing Competition* state as follows:

> "In considering the scope of substitutability between different products, it will be necessary to collect evidence from buyers and sellers of the products. Weight may be given to such factors as:
> (a) buyers' perceptions about whether or not the products are substitutes, particularly if those buyers have considered shifting purchases between the products;
> (b) the relative price, quality and performance of the various products;
> (c) similarities of differences in the price movements of the products over time and that are not explained by common or parallel changes in factors such as the cost of inputs;
> (d) the costs that the purchaser may have to pay to switch from one product to another;
> (e) complementary fixed investments which commit purchasers to one product;
> (f) sellers' perceptions about whether or not the products are substitutes; and
> (g) the ability and speed with which producers of substitute products can meet increased demand."

3.124 In a report commissioned by the OFT[149] the following conclusion is drawn about the practice of the OFT and MMC in product market definition:

> "We found that many report do not deal explicitly with definition of the relevant product market, and reports frequently take a relaxed approach to terminology when talking about 'markets', 'market sectors', 'market segments', 'sub-markets' and so on. In carrying out the case studies, we did not find a consistent thread to the approach taken on market definition, not any indication that this was in principle regarded as an activity on which a vigorous approach needed to be taken. In some cases, this informal approach can be justified on this basis that the report's conclusion would stand on any one of the number of plausible definitions of the relevant market. However, in any cases we felt that insufficient attention had been taken in defining the market when to do so might have improved the direction of the enquiry itself."[150]

3.125 Turning, thirdly, to the bargaining power of buyers and suppliers, it is common sense that the market strength of a major producers may be countered or even negatived by the countervailing power of buyers of the finished product or of suppliers of raw materials and other imports. The power of buyers and suppliers may thus keep in check the putative power of the company under investigation and indeed lead to the conclusion that the investigated company has no real ability to abuse its market position. The actual strength of the bargaining power of a buyer or supplier depends upon the characteristics of the market. Whether a buyer can exert sufficient power to discipline its supplier may depend upon such factors as:

149 *Market Definition in UK Competition Policy*, OFT Research Paper No. 1 (February 1992), NERA for the OFT.
150 *ibid.*, p. 18.

(a) whether the buyer is an important customer of the produced because it purchases large volumes relative to the producer's output;
(b) whether the buyer's purchases from its suppliers represent a significant part of its own input costs in which case it is likely to be very sensitive to price and devote time and resources to shopping around;
(c) whether there is little brand differentiation;
(d) whether switching costs (i.e. the cost the purchaser may have to pay to change from one product to another) are low relative to produced switching costs. Switching costs can, conversely, strengthen the buyer's hand if the producer faces costs in switching to alternative customers. Equally, the buyer's bargaining strength may be diminished to alternative suppliers and it thereby becomes dependent upon one supplier;
(e) whether the purchaser represents a potential competitor to its supplier by reverse integration, i.e. by producing the inputs in-house. Equally, a company may be disciplined by a powerful supplier. The circumstances in which a supplier could successfully discipline its customer would be similar to those identified above in relation to a buyer. A supplier's bargaining strength is likely to be significant if the product it sells is a major input to its customer's business and there are no or few close substitute products available. A supplier will have bargaining strength if it is flexible and able to switch at low cost to supplying alternative purchasers or to producing different products or, even, integrating downstream into its customer's market.

3.126 Turning, fourthly, to the threat of entry and the growth of competitors we are now concerned with whether a market is "contestable".[151] A major company may refrain from abusing its market power as a result of the threat of new entry into the market or the expansion of existing firms. Whether such threats do, in fact, constrain the conduct of an existing company with a substantial market share will depend upon the nature and extent of the barriers to entry and expansion in the market. The MMC thus states:

> "Whether the threat of entry is an important constraint on existing firms depends upon whether there are barriers to entry which present obstacles to the development of competition. Of course, there will always be some barriers to entry to any market. Entry into a market cannot be costless and a new entrant is likely at least initially to face higher costs than incumbents. What is relevant here is an assessment of the extent to which barriers to entry in practice limit actual or potential competition. For example, while there may be no legal obstacles, entry barriers may make market entry based on reasonable commercial considerations and motives unlikely. Such barriers need not preclude entry entirely nor need they exist indefinitely to limit competition. It may be enough if they delay of impede entry for a significant period of time."[152]

3.127 The following are examples of entry barriers which may, in given circumstances, be relevant:

(a) Governmental restrictions: governmental regulation may inhibit entry by imposing (say) high safety and quality standards or the payment of high compensation

[151] See for a brief but helpful discussion of the literature on contestability and its application in cases before the UK competition authorities Ridyard, "Contestability Theory and its Practical Impact on Competition Policy Decisions" (1995) *The Business Economist*, Vol. 26, No. 2. For examples of cases where contestability expressly or inferentially played a part see *Tampons* MMC 1986 Cmnd 9705 especially para. 8.35; *Highland Scottish Omnibuses* OFT Report 1989; MMC 1990 Cm 1129.

[152] *Assessing Competition* (*ibid.*) p. 9, para. 21.

awards to employees made redundant. Equally, the government may restrict entry by imposing quotas upon participation in an industry. Further, government regulation may control the terms and conditions upon which goods or services are supplied which new entrants would view as denying them the ability to maximise their investment.

(b) Upstream shortages: shortages in the availability of raw materials or facilities or appropriate technology may make entry difficult or even impossible.

(c) Economies of scale and scope: scale economies can deter entry if a new entrant is forced to choose between entering on a large scale, which increases the risk of entry, alternatively, entering on a small scale but suffer a cost disadvantage. Economies of scale may be a particularly important barrier to entry where participation in the market necessarily involves entry on a particular scale. Thus, an entrant may be deterred from entering if, upon entering, it must obtain a large market share in order to be able to operate at the minimum efficient size. Further, where there are joint costs in producing two or more products this may give a company competing in both products an advantage over entrants competing in only one product. Such economies (of "scope") may deter entry into one market if there are barriers to entry into the other related market, or if the putative entrant is simply uninterested in entering the other related market. Further, there may be economies of scale in a company operating in successive stages of the production process. If a new entrant must enter as a vertically integrated undertaking or face a cost advantage, this may deter entry in the first place. Entry is made more difficult if there are problems of entering the market at any one stage in the chain of production.

(d) Exit costs: the presence of "sunk costs" may act as a major deterrent to entry. If these costs are unrecoverable, on exiting, this may deter entry in the first place. Such costs may arise in relation to specialised assets which are relevant to a particular business or location. Another example of a sunk cost is advertising.[153]

(e) Excess capacity: if an incumbent company maintains excess capacity with which it may react to or discourage new competitors, this may deter all new entry. The mere existence of excess capacity can send a red light signal to a putative entrant signifying that the incumbent may increase output in the short term as a deterrent to entry.

(f) Product differentiation and brand loyalty: incumbent companies may, over a period of time, develop loyalty to their brands and it may be difficult for new entrants to counter such loyalty with consumers. Alternatively, the cost of developing a competing brand may be very high. As noted above, advertising is a sunk cost which is non-recoupable in the event that the new entrant fails and exits the market.

(g) Predictions of the conduct of incumbents: entry may be deterred if the potential entrant believes or supplies that the incumbent will react viciously to new entry. The reputation of the incumbent for successful retaliation, its ability to finance price wars, and the extent to which the incumbent has invested heavily in the industry and must remain there in order to recoup its investment will all be relevant in estimating whether an incumbent is likely to act in a manner such as to pose a realistic threat to entry.

[153] See e.g. Sutton, *Sunk Costs and Market Structure: Price Competition, Advertising and the Evaluation of Concentration* (1991), MIT Press.

J. Summary: Check List for Determining whether Competition Act 1980 Applies

3.128 The following is an outline guide to the main features of the Act. It is not a substitute for proper examination of the Act itself in a given situation. Each of the conditions below is discussed in depth in the text above.

Condition 1 The conduct or practice in question must be one that the Act applies to. The Act excludes from its scope the following:

(i) agreements which are registrable under the RTPA 1976 and therefore assessed under that legislation (s. 2(2) CA 1980);
(ii) conduct or practices carried out by a person either with a turnover of less than £10m or, alternatively, with less than 25 per cent market share in the relevant market. Person for these purposes includes any group of companies of which that person is part (Article 2 S.I. 1980 No. 979, as amended by S.I. 1994 No. 1557);
(iii) certain defined types of conduct in certain defined circumstances relating to: export sales; local authority and bus operator agreements; international sea transport; aviation; building societies agreements with the Treasury; Bank of England agreements with the Treasury; agricultural and forestry associations; parish and community councils (Schedule 1, S.I. 1980 No. 979.)

The course of conduct need not cover the whole of the UK, a fairly small area therein suffices.

Condition 2 Does the person alleged to have acted anti-competitively possess sufficient economic power? Conduct will have a harmful economic effect only if the perpetrator of the conduct enjoys economic power. Determining such power necessitates consideration of the geographical and product markets as well as assessing the state of competition in the market.

Condition 3 Is the practice or conduct in question an isolated instance or a series of acts? Section 2(1) CA 1980 refers to a "course of conduct". It is generally considered that the phrase implies more than one act.

Condition 4 Does the course of conduct in question concern at least one of the following?

(i) "the production, supply or acquisition of goods in the United Kingdom";

and/or

(ii) "the supply or securing of services in the United Kingdom".

Condition 5 The course of conduct must (a) have; or (b) be intended to have; or (c) be likely to have, the effect of restricting, distorting or preventing competition in the UK or a part thereof.

4 Registration and Negotiation of Restrictive Trading Agreements

A. Introduction

4.1 In this chapter the procedures which must be followed in order to furnish particulars and negotiate an agreement will be discussed. The emphasis of this chapter lies in explaining the procedural and legal basis of furnishing, registration and negotiations under the Act. The following subjects are discussed:

Section B. Registration of agreements: procedure and practice. This section examines the duty to register; consequences of non-registration; provisional validity; details of the registration process; variation of agreements; time limits; strategy in event of failure to register; the "fail-safe" method of furnishing particulars of agreements.

Section C. The register: problems with confidential information. This section examines the contents of the register; protecting confidential and secret information.

Section D. Powers of the OFT to obtain information. This section examines: OFT notices sent to parties requesting information; when a notice may be issued; examination of parties on oath before the Court; failure to furnish correct information and penalties.

Section E. The section 21 RTPA 1976 procedure: negotiations with the OFT. This section examines the legal context of negotiations with the OFT; statistics showing trends in negotiations; the relationship with EC law.

Section F. Modification and abandonment of agreements; options available to parties. This section examines the termination and abandonment of agreements; the termination, registration and novation of agreements; agreements filleted of all registrable restrictions; effluxion of time and expired agreements.

Section G. Negotiations under section 21(2): dispensation from reference to the Court. This section examines the criteria employed by the OFT in conducting negotiations with parties. In particular the section discusses the relevance or otherwise of public interest arguments; the *de minimis* principle for small-scale agreements; the notion of "reasonableness" and the Unfair Contract Terms Act 1977, and the Unfair Terms in Consumer Contracts Regulations 1994; the tests of discrimination and unfairness; the meaning of a material effect on competition; whether the OFT assess the whole agreement or simply the restrictions in the agreement.

Section H. OFT procedure for evaluation of agreements. This section examines the steps taken by the OFT and Secretary of State in evaluating agreements.

B. Registration of Agreements: Procedure and Practice[1]

1. *The Duty to Register*

(1) Consequences of non-registration, provisional validity

4.2 Agreements and association recommendations caught by the Act must be registered.[2] As a general rule, particulars must be furnished within three months of the agreement being made. Time limits are discussed in detail at paras. 4.35–4.37. Prior to furnishing of particulars, the restrictions remain valid but unenforceable.[3] Furnishing details of agreements to the OFT is in many respects a neutral process; it does not in any way signify the end of the agreement. Once furnished, a process of negotiation and discussion with the OFT commences.

4.3 Failure to register within three months results in all of the registrable restrictions in the agreement becoming void and unenforceable.[4] Moreover, it is unlawful (though not a criminal offence) to give effect to, enforce or purport to enforce the restrictions in an unregistered agreement.[5] Parties might decide to continue informally the agreement but in the event of dispute the agreement cannot be enforced in a court of law or in arbitration.[6] Furthermore, the OFT upon discovering an agreement it considers to be seriously anti-competitive might consider seeking injunctive relief against the agreement.

[1] The rules for registration are set down in S.I. 1984 No. 392 Registration of Restrictive Trading Agreements Regulations 1984.

[2] s. 24 RTPA 1976 elaborated upon by Sch. 2 RTPA 1976 Furnishing of Particulars of Agreements.

[3] This was not the case until the Deregulation (Restrictive Trade Practices Act (1976)) (Amendment) (Time Limits) Order 1996, No. 347, made pursuant to s. 1 Deregulation and Contracting Out Act 1994. Prior to this Order, failure to notify before the registrable restrictions came into effect was fatal to the enforceability of those restrictions at any time thereafter (Sch. 2, para. 5(1) RTPA 1976). Any application for an extension of time for furnishing particulars must be made within this three month time limit in accordance with Art. 12, Registration of Restrictive Trading Agreements Regulations 1984 (S.I. 1984 No. 392); see para. 4.38.

[4] s. 35(1)(a) RTPA 1976. Mackinnon J held that s. 35(1)(a) RTPA only applied to registrable restrictions, not all restrictions in *Snushalls Team Ltd* v *Marcus*, judgment of 21 March 1990, unreported, but noted by Tulley, Law Society's Gazette 22 August 1990. See also para. 5.97.

[5] s. 35(1)(b) RTPA 1976.

[6] s. 35(3) RTPA 1976. For the effects in law of "unenforceable" agreements see *Boddington* v *Lawton* [1994] ICR 478 (in relation to the willingness of the courts to lend assistance to the enforcement of agreements or covenants in restraint of trade).

4.4 Proper furnishing of particulars of the agreement gives the parties a right to enforce the agreement until such time as the Court declares it against the public interest and enjoins its continuance. In *British Concrete Pipe Association's Agreement*,[7] in 1983, Sir John Donaldson MR stated:

> "price fixing is not inherently bad—it can be justified in some circumstances—-and accordingly the restrictive practices legislation provides that, so long as you do not do it secretly and you register your agreement, you may go on with the agreement unless and until the Court has examined it and has come to the conclusion that it is not one of the exceptional agreements which should be permitted ..."[8]

Thus furnished agreement enjoys a "provisional validity" until such time as it is judicially condemned. However, it is not certain what effect this judgment will have on two earlier cases in which courts were unwilling to enforce registered agreements pending a decision of the RPC. Indeed, there was a clear inclination to preempt the RPC's decision. In *Daily Mirror Newspapers* v *Gardner*,[9] Lord Denning MR stated of a trade association recommendation to boycott the *Daily Mirror* newspaper:

> "Prima facie, therefore, the recommendation is unlawful. No doubt the final decision will rest with the Restrictive Practices Court. But I think that it comes within the purview of this court also. If the federation makes a recommendation which is unlawful, as being prohibited by the Restrictive Trade Practices Act, I think it ranks as 'unlawful means'. As such, this court can intervene [by injunction] to stop it."[10]

4.5 It is submitted that if Lord Denning was indicating that any court could enjoin a duly furnished agreement as being, without more ado, unlawful this is incorrect. To so hold strips section 35—which renders unenforceable only agreements particulars of which are not furnished—of its meaning. It is submitted, following *British Concrete Pipe*, that the validity is absolute until the RPC decides otherwise, However, some doubts might remain in relation to agreements that appear to have little chance of success before the RPC.

4.6 Failure to register also leaves a company vulnerable to the "disenchanted employee" problem. It has been held that an employee who discloses to a newspaper the fact that his company is operating an unregistered agreement and provides supporting documentary evidence of that fact to the newspaper may not be in breach of his duty to protect the confidential nature of his employers business secrets. The Court of Appeal in *Initial Services* v *Putterill*[11] held that the duty of confidentiality was subject to exceptions where the disclosure was justified in the public interest (e.g. in cases of crime or fraud). Disclosure of the fact of non-registration may well be in the public interest and it apparently does not matter that disclosure is not made to the relevant authorities.

(2) The transfer of property and money under void restrictions

4.7 Pursuant to section 35(1)(a) RTPA 1976 if particulars of an agreement which is subject to registration are not duly furnished within the requisite time the agreement is "void"

7 [1983] ICR 215.
8 *ibid.*, at p. 218.
9 [1968] 2 QB 762 (CA) followed in *Brekkes* v *Cattel* (1972) LR 7 RP 150 at p. 167 *per* Pennycuick VC.
10 *ibid.*, at pp. 782, 783. See *per* Davies LJ at p. 784 and *per* Russell LJ at p. 785. Counsel for the Defendants apparently argued that the agreement could not be unlawful until found to be so by the RPC (*ibid.*, at pp. 776, 777).
11 [1968] 1 QB 396: newspaper informed by laundry manager who had resigned that his ex-company and others were conspiring to fix the price of laundry services. See also *BSC* v *Granada Television* [1981] AC 1096; *Lion Laboratories* v *Evans* [1984] 2 All ER417.

in respect of all restrictions accepted or information provisions made thereunder. Pursuant to section 35(1)(b) it is "unlawful" for any person party to the agreement who carries on business within the United Kingdom to give effect to, or enforce or purport to enforce, the agreement in respect of any such restrictions or information provisions. It is clear from section 35(2) that a person party to the agreement carrying on business within the United Kingdom who gives effect to, or enforces or purposes to enforce the agreement in respect of the restrictions does *not* commit a criminal offence. However, the obligation not to give effect to, enforce or purport to enforce the restrictions represents a duty actionable under the tort of breach of statutory duty and is owned to "any person" who may be affected by a contravention of that duty.

4.8 The question arises as to the enforceability of money or goods passing under void restrictions. For example, X belong to a group of firms operating a profit pooling cartel pursuant to which each firm is assigned a sales territory. Each party pays part of their profits into a central fund for distribution to other parties in less profitable territories. X pays £10,000 into the pool at the end of a particular year. Particulars of the agreement are not furnished to the OFT in accordance with the RTPA 1976. The agreement is therefore void in respect of the restrictions pursuant to section 35. Can X recover the money paid under the Agreement?

4.9 Two recent cases, neither concerning the RTPA 1976, shed some light upon the vexed question of property and money passing under an unlawful or illegal agreement.

4.10 In *Boddington* v *Lawton*,[12] the Vice Chancellor, Sir Donald Nicholls (as he then was) gave judgment in a most unusual restraint of trade case. It will be helpful to recite the facts briefly. The staff at a special hospital for persons detained under the Mental Health Act 1983 engaged in industrial action as a result of discontent over working conditions. In the course of the action the patients were locked up to an extent greater than usual and certain medical treatments were interrupted. The patients initiated legal proceedings against the staff claiming damages, *inter alia*, for trespass, false imprisonment and breach of duty. The staff were members of the Prison Officers' Association which provided funds for the conduct of their defence pursuant the Association's rules. Following judgment in an unrelated matter it was held that the Prison Officers' Association was not a trade union and did not therefore enjoy the protection of legislation which rendered lawful and enforceable rules of a trade union otherwise unlawful and enforceable as restraints of trade. The trustees of the Association sought a declaration in the Chancery Division that, none the less, they could continue to finance the defence of the staff without fear of claims by other members of the Association who might object to such use of funds provided in part by their own contributions.

4.11 The Vice Chancellor observed that agreements in restraint of trade were often described as "illegal" or "unlawful" and were therefore "unenforceable" and "void". However, he drew a distinction between different degrees of illegality or unlawfulness:

> "These expressions need to be handled with great care. Agreements can be vitiated and struck down by the law for widely differing reasons, and questions regarding them arise in widely differing circumstances. An agreement to commit a murder is unlawful. The same may be said of an agreement unreasonably restricting the activities of a former employee who wishes to set up a competing business. But the law is not so crude as to treat these two instances as identical in all respects when faced with questions arising out of such agreement."[13]

[12] [1994] ICR 478.
[13] *ibid.*, p. 490G, H.

The Vice Chancellor stated that the approach of the law to an agreement in unreasonable restraint of trade was to decline to assist the parties to enforce it. The agreement did not give rise to legally binding obligations and was, in that sense, void. However, he stated that because a contract in unreasonable restraint of trade was void did it not mean that the agreement would be disregarded for all purposes and that the law would proceed as though there had never been an agreement between the parties.[14] The Vice Chancellor noted that the law would countenance the existence of such an agreement and if the parties wished to implement it they were at liberty so to do. In so doing they would not be acting illegally or unlawfully. However, if either party chose to withdraw, the Court would not assist the other to enforce the agreement or award him damages for breach.[15]

4.12 The Vice Chancellor proceeded to set out a number of hypothetical situations in which parties to agreements in unreasonable restraint of trade, might seek to move the Court for relief. The hypothetical situation upon which the Vice Chancellor based his conclusions was as follows:

> "Two people, A and B, pay money to T. Under the agreement between the three of them, T is subsequently required to pay some of the money to B. The agreement is an unreasonable restraint of trade, and A resiles from it."

4.13 The Vice Chancellor then considered the question of relief the Court would grant arising out of permutations of the above factual situation, as follows:

(i) T pays B without objection from A. Can T afterwards recover the payment from B: "The answer must be no. T has carried out an unenforceable contract. There can be no foundation, at law or in equity, entitling him to recover the payment. In the absence of fraud or mistake or something of that character no one would say that B has been unjustly enriched. What has happened is simply that, although not legally compellable to do so, T has made to B a payment he agree to make. The payment was accord with the parties' expectations and intentions under the contract, albeit that in law the contract was unenforceable. In this way, although the contract is unenforceable and in that sense void, the law takes cognisance of the existence of the contract and its terms to the extend of looking to them for an explanation of how the payment came to be made. That explanation negatives T's claim that he 'ought' to have a restitutionary remedy and recover the money. If the law were otherwise, and if T could recovery the money from B, the law would effectively be preventing parties from carrying out an unenforceable contract, because if one of them subsequently changed his mind he could get his money back".[16]

(ii) A resiles from the agreement. He objects to T making the payment to B. Will the Court, at A's request, intervene to prevent T paying B? According to the Vice Chancellor A cannot sue T for having made payment to B. T has disposed of the money

[14] It would appear that the Vice Chancellor was confining his comments to agreements in restraint of trade since he expressly excluded from his analysis "the position regarding contracts of which the law disapproves for other reasons" (*ibid.*, p. 491A). This caveat may be very relevant in relation to agreements in breach of the duty to furnish particulars under the RTPA 1976.

[15] *ibid.*, p. 491B citing *Esso Petroleum Company Ltd* v *Harper's Garage (Southport) Ltd* [1968] AC 269, 297 *per* Lord Reid; *Mogul Steamship Company* v *McGregor Gower and Co* [1892] AC 25, 39 *per* Lord Halsbury LC; *Attorney General of the Commonwealth of Australia* v *Adelaide Steamship Company Ltd* [1913] AC 781, 797 *per* Lord Parker of Waddington. See also *Bank of India* v *TransContinental Commodity Merchants Ltd and J. N. Patel* [1982] 1 Lloyds Reports 427, 429 *per* Bingham J.

[16] *ibid.*, p. 492E–G.

in a manner the parties agreed and A cannot complain of this in course. T did nothing more than carry out an unenforceable agreement. Cognisance of the agreement is taken to the extent of explaining how A came to pay T, and how T came to pay B. The payment by T to B was in accordance with A's expectations.[17]

(iii) Will the Court assist B in obtaining performance of an agreement which is unenforceable? The answer is no. B cannot sue T for payment.[18]

(iv) Is the position in relation to A, different if A's intervention and objection occurred *before* T paid B? The Vice Chancellor stated: "I do not think this can make a difference. A cannot, by unilaterally withdrawing, prevent T from implementing the agreement is he chooses to do so, or obtain legal redress if T goes ahead and makes payment despite A's objections. The law will not enforce the agreement. Nor, in my view, will it intervene and afford restitutional remedies in the circumstances I have postulated."[19]

(v) Can either B or T compel A to discharge any unperformed obligations still resting on him under the (unenforceable) agreement? The answer is "no".[20]

(vi) If T has the means enabling him to perform his (unenforceable) obligations without the assistance of A, will the Court intervene at A's request to prevent T performing his (unenforceable) obligations? The Vice Chancellor stated: "I can see no compelling reason why the Court should intervene at A's request to stop [B]. B is not being enriched unjustly."[21]

4.14 The basis underlying the observations of the Vice Chancellor was that the Court, in not lending its assistance to any of the parties, would *not* be countenancing unjust enrichment. The Vice Chancellor thus concluded his analysis of the hypothetical examples by stating:

> "To avoid any misunderstanding, I add that my observations assumed that, for his part, T remains willing to carry out his obligations under the unenforceable agreement. Nothing I have said is directed at a situation where T declines to pay B and seeks, contrary to the agreement, to keep the money for himself. Nor are my remarks directed at the situation where T or B declined to carry out some other obligation they undertook. Those are very different positions, and I am not to be taken as suggesting that in such cases A would be without a remedy."[22]

4.15 The question arises whether the position as set out by the Vice Chancellor in *Boddington* would apply to agreements void and unlawful pursuant to section 35 RTPA 1976. It is to be observed that the Vice Chancellor expressly recognised that the principles he was enunciating were confined to the doctrine of agreements in unreasonable restraint of trade. He acknowledged that the position might be different in relation to "contracts of which the law disapproves for other reasons".[23] Section 35(2) and (3) RTPA 1976 confer the express right upon any person affected by a contravention to bring an action for breach of statutory duty. Thus a third party might obtain an injunction to restrain parties to a registrable but unregistered agreement performing the restrictions thereunder. Moreover,

[17] *ibid.*, pp. 492H, 493A.
[18] *ibid.*, p. 492C, D.
[19] *ibid.*, p. 493B.
[20] *ibid.*, p. 493B.
[21] *ibid.*, p. 493C.
[22] *ibid.*, p. 493E. The Vice Chancellor gave, as an example of the latter situation, the position regarding oral contracts for the sale of land which, under the pre-1989 law, were unenforceable by action in the absence of a written memorandum in writing (s. 40 Law of Property Act 1925) (*ibid.*, pp. 493F, 494A).
[23] *ibid.*, p. 491A.

since the *policy* of the RTPA 1976 as evidenced by section 35(1)(b) is to prevent an unregistered agreement having any effect upon the market it is well arguable that the courts would respect that statutory purpose and prevent by injunction a party to the agreement endeavouring to enforce, even voluntarily, restrictions in an agreement in breach of the duty to furnish particulars. It is thus arguable that the position in relation to the RTPA 1976 is stricter than that under the doctrine of restraint of trade. Whether the position under the RTPA 1976 is the same as, or more stringent than, that under the doctrine of restraint of trade is an open question.

4.16 The position in relation to property passing under an illegal contract has been further clarified by the House of Lords in *Tinsley* v *Milligan*.[24] In that case, the Plaintiff and the Defendant, two single women, formed a joint business venture to run lodging houses. Using funds generated by the business they purchased a house in which they lived together and which was vested in the sole name of the Plaintiff upon the understanding that the Plaintiff and Defendant were jointly beneficial owners of the property. The purpose of that arrangement was to assist in the perpetration of frauds upon the Department of Social Security and over a number of years the Defendant, with the connivance of the Plaintiff, made false benefit claims on the Department. The Plaintiff did likewise. The money thus obtained helped the parties meet their bills but did not represent a substantial part of their income and contributed only in a small way to their acquisition of the equity in the property. Subsequently, the Defendant repented of the frauds and disclosed them to the Department. A dispute between the parties led to the Plaintiff moving out leaving the Defendant in occupation. The Plaintiff thereafter gave the Defendant notice to quit and in due course brought proceedings against the Defendant claiming possession and asserting sole ownership of the property. The Defendant counterclaimed for an Order for sale and for a declaration that the property was held by the Plaintiff on trust for the parties in equal shares. At first instance the judge dismissed the Plaintiff's claim and allowed the counterclaim. The Court of Appeal dismissed the Plaintiff's appeal. The House of Lords also dismissed the Plaintiff's appeal. The leading judgment was given by Lord Browne-Wilkinson[25] who expressed the following propositions. (i) First, property in chattels and land can pass under the contract which is illegal and therefore would have been unenforceable as a contract. (ii) Second, a Plaintiff can at law enforce property rights so acquired provided that he does not need to rely on the illegal contract for any purpose other than providing the basis of his claim to a property right. (iii) Third, it is irrelevant that the illegality of the underlying agreement was either pleaded or emerged in evidence: if the Plaintiff has acquired legal title under the illegal contract that is enough.[26] Lord Browne-Wilkinson stated:

> "Neither at law nor in equity will the Court enforce an illegal agreement which has been partially, but not fully, performed. However, it does not follow that all acts done under a partially performed contract are of no effect. In particular it is now clearly established that at law (as opposed to in equity), property in goods or land can pass under, or pursuant to, such a contract. If so, the rights of the owner of the legal title thereby acquired will be in force, provided that the Plaintiff can establish such title without pleading or leading evi-

[24] [1993] 3 WLR 126. See also, on the more arcane question of availability of compound interest on payments made under *ultra vires* transactions *Westdeutsche Landesbank Girozentrale* v *Islington LBC*, HL [1996], AC 669.

[25] The leading judgment of the majority was given by Lord Browne-Wilkinson. Lord Jauncey gave a shorter judgment to the same effect. Lord Lowry agreed with both judgments. Lord Keith and Lord Goff dissented.

[26] *ibid.*, p. 147C.

dence of the illegality. It is said that property lies where it falls, even though legal title to the property was acquired as a result of the property passing under the illegal contract itself."[27]

4.17 The position is only different where the Plaintiff (or Defendant upon a Counterclaim) is forced to plead or rely upon an illegality in order to assert his or her claim to the property.[28] Lord Browne-Wilkinson thus concluded that:

> "In my judgment the time has come to decide clearly that the rule is the same whether a Plaintiff founds himself on a legal or equitable title: he is entitled to recover if he is not forced to plead or rely on the illegality, even if it emerges that the title on which he relied was acquired in the course of carrying through an illegal transaction."

Put another way:

> "The Court is only entitled and bound to dismiss a claim on the basis that it is founded on an illegality in those cases where the illegality is of a kind which would have provided a good defence if raised by the Defendant. In a case where the Plaintiff is not seeking to enforce an unlawful contract but founds his case on collateral rights acquired under the contract (such as a right of property) the Court is neither bound nor entitled to reject the claim unless the illegality of necessity forms part of the Plaintiff's case."[29]

4.18 As noted above, the application of the above principles to the RTPA 1976 remains subject to some doubt. It may well be that the position under the RTPA 1976 is slightly stricter than that pertaining in relation to restraint of trade. Under the latter doctrine, the agreement is unenforceable but it is now unlawful for the parties voluntarily to give effect to it. In relation to the RTPA 1976 the Court may take the view that not only is the agreement unenforceable so far as the restrictions are concerned but, as a matter of policy, it should enjoin its *voluntary* furtherance by the parties.

4.19 It is submitted (tentatively) that the following represents the position under the RTPA 1976:

(a) The Courts will not allow parties to enforce a void restriction to an agreement. The Court will not enforce an illegal restriction which has been partially but not fully performed. Illegality may be pleaded as a defence.[30]
(b) The Court will enforce any *other* obligation contained in the agreement which is unrelated to the restriction provided it is severable therefrom.
(c) The Court will not permit a party to sue for damages for breach of a restriction by another party nor will the Court permit a party to obtain restitution of money paid under a void restriction.
(d) The Court will not grant an injunction to prevent a party from breaching a restriction.[31]

[27] *ibid.*, p. 146D. Lord Browne-Wilkinson cited, as examples of this proposition *Bowmakers Ltd* v *Barnet Instruments Ltd* [1945] KB 65; *Ferret* v *Hill* (1854) 15 CB 207; *Taylor* v *Chester* (1869) LR 4 QB 309; *Alexander* v *Rayson* [1936] 1 KB 169. These authorities were discussed by Lord Browne-Wilkinson at pp. 146E–H, 147A–B. He also concluded that equity would not lead to any different result (*ibid.*, pp. 147H–148A).

[28] It was upon this basis that Lord Browne-Wilkinson thus explained cases such as *Singh* v *Ali* [1960] AC 167 (*ibid.*, pp. 151H-152H).

[29] *ibid.*, p. 153A, B, F.

[30] See e.g. *Topliss Showers* v *Gessey* [1982] ICR 501; *Vernon* v *Universal Pulp Containers* [1980] FSR 179; *Academy Sound and Vision* v *WEA Records* [1983] ICR 589. For commentary see para. 5.97.

[31] See e.g. *Donald Storrie Estate Agency Ltd* v *Adams* [1989] SLT 305; *Sterling Financial Services* v *Johnston* [1990] SLT 111 (Court will not grant injunctive relief if the clause to be enforced is an unregistered restriction).

(e) The Court probably will grant an injunction at the behest of a party to prevent the voluntary enforcement of a restriction.
(f) Property may pass under an illegal restriction.
(g) The transferee of property under an illegal restriction may found a claim in respect of that property provided that in so doing the claimant is not forced to plead or rely upon the illegality.

(3) Vulnerability to private damages actions

4.20 Under section 35(2) RTPA 1976, any third person who suffers damage as a consequence of an improperly unregistered agreement may sue those parties for damages in the common law tort of breach of a statutory duty. Thus, a local authority could sue building contractors who supply to it under a collusive tendering arrangement.

2. *Details of Registration Process*

(1) Documents, common form agreements

4.21 Under section 24 RTPA 1976, the OFT must be furnished with the names and addresses of parties to the agreement.[32] Further, it must be furnished with the terms of the whole agreement and not just the restrictions in the agreement. This can give rise to considerable logistical problems in the case of complex agreements involving many parties. For example, it is not uncommon in corporate reconstructions for bankers and other financiers (often involved in a debt–equity swap) to extract restrictive covenants from companies within the group and even some of its trading partners. Not infrequently the documentation runs to hundreds of thousands of pages which represents dozens of different agreements. The restrictions might be located in any number of agreements. In these cases it is very difficult to determine the exact scope of the "agreement" when bearing in mind that "agreement" includes "arrangement" (section 43 RTPA 1976). It may be that virtually very individual agreement represents the "arrangement" in which particulars of everything must be furnished. In practice parties tend to furnish the core documents only thereby "taking a view" that other agreements in the matrix of documents do not form part of the "arrangement". Two copies (at least one of which is signed) of the terms of any written agreement must be sent to the OFT.[33] Where the agreement or part of it is not in writing, two copies of a written memorandum (signed by the person furnishing details of the agreement) setting out the relevant terms of the oral agreement must be sent to the OFT.[34] Where a person enters multiple agreements (described as "common-form agreements") which are all subject to registration and which are identical except for the identity of the other party or the date, it is sufficient to furnish one copy of the agreement and, in respect of the others, to furnish to the OFT two copies of a memorandum (at least one of which is signed by the person furnishing the details) which: (a)

[32] Reg. 2(3) S.I. 1984 No. 392, Registration of Restrictive Trading Agreement Regulations: "Where the documents sent out or delivered ... do not disclose the name and address of any person party to the agreement, there shall also be sent or delivered therewith two copies of a document indicating that person's name and address: Provided that this paragraph shall not require the name or address of any of them to be provided if their number exceeds 100 and there is sent or delivered with the documents sent or delivered ... two copies of a document indicating their number or their approximate number."

[33] Reg. 2(2)(a) S.I. 1984 No. 392.

[34] Reg. 2(2)(b) S.I. 1984 No. 392. When documents are being furnished to the OFT they must be accompanied by a Certificate (available from the OFT entitled Form RTP(C)) signed by the person furnishing the documents which declares that to the best of the signatory's knowledge proper details have been furnished. All documents have to be listed on the certificate (Reg. 7 S.I. 1984 No. 392).

refers to the agreement of which the particulars are being or have been furnished; (b) indicates the dates of the other agreements and the names and addresses of the parties thereto; and (c) states that those agreements are otherwise identical to the agreement of which particulars are being or have been furnished.[35]

4.22 The OFT provides a form for registration, Form RTP(C). Originally this comprised only the certificate required by the person submitting the documents for registration.[36] As well as ensuring that statutory requirements for registration are complied with, this Form now includes two further parts, an Annex and a Request for Fast Track Registration Procedure, neither of which stipulated by statute; there is thus no legal obligation to complete either of these two additional parts.

(2) The Annex

4.23 First is an Annex to Form RTP(C). This is a request by the OFT for further information to assist it in determining whether the agreement is registrable and whether it needs to be referred to the Restrictive Practices Court. In practice, the OFT is seeking information to enable it to consider how to evaluate restrictions contained in furnished agreements. Therefore, if the Annex is not completed, it is likely that the OFT will respond with a request for the information. Failure to complete the Annex will usually lead to delay. Moreover, the Fast Track Registration Procedure is only available to those who have submitted an Annex.

4.24 The Annex sets out nine requests for further information:[37]

1. *Has specific exemption from Article 85 of the EC Treaty been sought or received or is the agreement covered by a block exemption?* The interaction between EC and UK law is dealt with in more detail at paras. 6.114–6.119. At this point, it is sufficient to appreciate that exemption from Article 85(3) will almost invariably lead to the OFT advising the Secretary of State to exercise section 21(1) powers not to refer an agreement to the Restrictive Practices Court.
2. *Give a brief description of the nature, purpose, date(s) and duration of the arrangement.* There is scope here for influencing the OFT's view of an agreement. Parties submitting an agreement should not include as a statement of purpose anything which may be expected to raise competition concerns.[38]
3. *Give information about the business and corporate structure of the parties to the agreements.* An agreement may take on a different significance if it is known that it is entered into by a subsidiary of a much larger company. Alternatively, what might look like a restriction by a large company might in fact only apply to one part of it. Though there is no reference to a divisional structure on the Annex, it would be relevant to include this if it affects the application of the restriction.
4. *What in your opinion are the relevant restrictions in the agreement and the persons who accept them?* This request is similar to the requirement in the Annex to Form A/B (notification of agreements to the European Commission) that restrictions of competition be listed. The obligation is frequently satisfied by a mere recitation of clause numbers. Clearly this list binds no one. In the context of the RTPA parties can set out why they consider borderline cases might fall within (say) section 9(3) and therefore be disregardable.

[35] Reg. 4(1)(a)–(c).
[36] See note 34 above.
[37] The requests have been edited and rephrased here.
[38] i.e. those matters covered specifically in Part II of this book.

5. *What is the UK turnover of the parties to the agreement in the goods or services affected, the total business turnover and total group turnover (if relevant)?* This does not request turnovers relative to other firms in the market and is restricted just to the UK. Further turnover information relevant to market structure should be included in response to requests 7 and 8. Clearly absolute turnover figures by themselves are of little use to the OFT in assessing market structure.
6. *Please explain the nature of the goods or services affected by the agreement. Include the 1992 Standard Industrial Classification (SIC) code if possible.* This is somewhat ambiguous. It could be taken as merely requesting information about the intrinsic characteristics of the goods or services concerned. A wider view is that it also requires explanation of the market for those goods or services: the product market. Opportunity should be taken at this point to give this information, as it is also relevant to request (7), in which information is requested about substitute products for the goods or services concerned. Care should be taken in defining the product market affected by the agreement. The smaller the market share of the parties to the agreement, the less likely it is to cause OFT concern, and thus thought should be given to providing the widest plausible definition of the product market, hence showing that the agreement is of significance only to a small portion of that market.
7. *Give a description of the structure of the market for the goods or services concerned, in particular the geographical extent of the market, the main competitors and their market share, total market turnover, ease of entry for new competitors, substitute products for the goods or services affected, and other points about market structure.* This information is not limited to the UK; if the market is transnational, then all relevant information should be given. Where information is not available, estimates should be submitted provided these are indicated as such. As with request (6), it will be in the interests of the submitting parties to emphasise that they have a small share in a large market, and that they are subject to full competitive pressures. Information about potential competitors from other industries who might switch into this product market can show that what appears to be a market characterised by few competitors is in fact one in which competitive pressure is exercised by the threat of entry by potential competitors.
8. *What are the market shares of each of the parties to the agreement (group market share if part of a group) in the goods or services affected?* Although only the parties' market shares are asked for, information should be given about other competitors' market shares if it shows that these parties are subject to competition from larger players in the market. But this information would assist if it showed that these parties in fact dominated the market with the largest market shares. So discretion should be exercised.
9. *Comment on the purpose of the restrictions.* This gives an opportunity to set the restrictions within their business context and explain why they are required for business, not anti-competitive, purposes.

4.25 The Annex gives parties to an agreement considerable scope for setting their case out in advance to the OFT. Although it might be thought to be a time consuming exercise, it gives the parties the opportunity to take the initiative in the registration process. Although OFT officials are experienced in market definition, they may be more prepared to accept the parties' analysis if it is clearly set out and reasoned than if it appears to be a superficial attempt at manipulation with the obvious aim of downplaying the anti-competitive impact of the agreement.

(3) Request for fast track registration

4.26 Second is a Form of Request for "Fast Track" Registration Procedure. This encapsulates an undertaking from the OFT to adopt a quick procedure to deal with some applications for registration under the RTPA. This undertaking is only a statement of policy, pursuant to the Code for Enforcement Agencies, and the OFT reserves its right not to adhere to the timetable if it is necessary to refer back any issue of registrability to the parties. The onus is thus on the parties to have analysed the agreement correctly in advance and to supply full information in the Annex. The undertaking is to give a response to a furnishing of particulars within two months provided the agreement meets certain criteria.

4.27 The response to be given is whether the agreement is registrable and if it is, how it is to be dealt with. The three means of dealing with the agreement are the OFT making representations to the Secretary of State not to refer the agreement to the Restrictive Practices Court under either section 21(1)(a) or section 21(2),[39] or the OFT deciding to refer the agreement to the Restrictive Practices Court.[40]

4.28 The criteria to be satisfied before an agreement can take the benefit of this fast track procedure are set out below. They are aimed at agreements between small and medium sized companies with small market shares, in a similar way to the way in which practices by such companies are excluded from the Competition Act 1980 by the Anti-Competitive Practices (Exclusions) Order 1980,41 though the market share threshold is lower in this case. As only limited guidance is given in the Fast Track procedure as to market share and turnover calculation, it would seem sensible to have regard to the 1980 Order where doubt arises.

4.29 The criteria are cumulative. They are that:

(a) the aggregate turnover of the parties to the agreement in their business activities as a whole is less than £5 million or the market share of the parties in the goods or services the subject of the agreement is less than 5 per cent. (It is possible to read the guidance as meaning that 5 per cent is to be measured in terms of the goods or services supplied under the particular agreement in question, but this would be economically irrational and is not supported by the 1980 Order, so it would not be safe to rely upon such an interpretation); or, the agreement has specific exemption under Article 85(3) EC (to be attached to the request), or is block exempt (otherwise than through use of an opposition procedure);[42]

(b) the agreement contains no price-fixing restrictions or information provisions as to the prices of goods;

(c) the parties are not applying for any part of the agreement to be placed on the special section of the register under section 23(3);[43]

(d) the parties do actually consider the agreement registrable and are not just furnishing on a "fail-safe basis";[44] and,

(e) an Annex to Form RTP(C) has been completed.

The request for Fast Track Registration Procedure must contain a declaration by the person submitting the particulars that these criteria are met.

39 See paras. 4.77–4.85.
40 See Chapter 5.
41 See paras. 3.41–3.52.
42 See paras. 7.167–7.173.
43 See paras. 4.60–4.65.
44 See paras. 4.43–4.46.

(4) Furnishing of trade association recommendations

4.30 Where the agreement in question is a trade association recommendation then the documents that will have to be furnished may be numerous. Under sections 8 and 16 RTPA 1976 restrictive agreements may emerge in a number of forms:

(a) Where an association enters an agreement with another person or association, the members and persons represented on the association are deemed to be parties to the main agreement and are deemed to accept its restrictions. Particulars of the names and addresses of the members and persons represented by members must therefore be furnished (except when they exceed 100 when a statement of that fact suffices). All of the terms of the agreement must be furnished.

(b) Where the agreement comes about by virtue of the constitution, memorandum and articles of association, rules, regulations, bylaws and resolutions of the association or a sub-committee thereof. Particulars to be furnished in such cases may be numerous. Parties must furnish the documents comprising the relevant restrictions *and* any further documents by virtue of which the restrictions arose. Thus, where the restrictive agreement is a schedule of fees or charges to be complied with by a group of members and the schedule has been calculated by a sub-committee of the association whose authority derives from the articles of association or other constitutional document, the following would have to be furnished: names of the members of the group; the schedule of charges or fees; the articles or other constitutional document of the association; and a list of all the members of the association (if it does not exceed 100). If the sub-committee was constituted by resolutions then these would also have to be furnished. Other resolutions not affecting any restriction or merely varying the membership of the sub-committee without altering its functions would not be required.

(c) Where a trade association makes specific recommendations about registrable matters the recommendation must be registered. In such a case the documents to be furnished are: the constitution of the association; a list of all members whether or not the recommendation was made to them (unless they exceed 100); and copies of the recommendations issued to members. The actual recommendation will usually be in the form of a circular in which case the circular must be furnished. Further, any extracts from minutes of meetings authorising the recommendation should be furnished. An indication of the problems faced by the OFT when confronted with documents is given in the 1976 Annual Report of the Director General where the difficulties encountered following the calling up for registration of service agreements led to the following commentary:[45]

"The first task of the Division is to enter registrable services agreements in the public register of restrictive trading agreements. This calls for careful examination of the documents, in a number of cases copious and complex, which have been submitted in order to determine whether the agreement is in fact registrable. In some cases it proved possible to establish this by prima facie examination which disclosed the acceptance of at least one restriction and in these cases the agreement can be entered in the register pending a full examination of all the restrictions which is, of course, necessary at a later stage. In other cases this did not prove a practicable way to proceed and often further discussion and correspondence with the parties was required. It frequently involves as much time and effort, if not more, to determine that a particular agreement is not registrable as to reach a conclusion that it is. The indica-

[45] *ibid.*, at p. 36.

tions are that between one fifth and one third of the agreements initially furnished may turn out not to be registrable."

4.31 In fact, more recent figures show the number of unregistrable agreements submitted to comprise about half of all those furnished for registration.[46] No doubt this reflects both the practice of fail-safe furnishing and a more general confusion about the interpretation of the legislation.

3. *Variation and Termination of Agreement*

4.32 Section 24(2)(b) requires that the OFT be furnished with details of variations and determinations of agreements. This duty applies only to variations whereby: (a) a further restriction to which the Act applies is accepted by one or more of the parties; (b) a restriction ceases to have effect; (c) the application of an existing restriction is extended or reduced as regards the areas or places or the classes of persons, goods, processes of manufacture or service to which it relates; or (d), so far as restrictions are accepted as to the terms or conditions on which goods are to be supplied or acquired or any process of manufacture is to be applied to goods or any designated service is to be supplied or obtained, the terms or conditions as varied.[47]

4.33 Parties to varied agreements must furnish the OFT with two copies (at least one of which is signed) of any written instrument which either terminates or varies (as above) the agreement.[48] Where the variation or determination is decided upon orally by the parties then two copies of a memorandum (at least one of which is signed) laying down the complete details of the termination or variation must be furnished.[49]

4.34 The furnishing of variations poses a constant headache for the OFT. Many variations to trade association recommendations are innocuous. For example, if an association recommends to its members the adoption of an improvement in a production technique, or recommends that certain cost adjustment formulae be incorporated into contracts, or recommends that standard form contracts be adopted, then these may well, after due consideration, earn dispensation under section 21(2) RTPA 1976 from reference to the Court. However, the OFT will often not be in a position to make a proper section 21(2) assessment if there is a steady flow of variations to the recommendation since they can never be certain that having obtained a section 21(2) dispensation for a recommendation or agreement, a variation will not be furnished which causes them to reconsider the position. Trade association officials might thus bear in mind, when considering non-essential variations, that they must be furnished and that this could reduce the chances of the section 21(2) procedure being used in their favour. Lack of a section 21(2) dispensation need not prove fatal. The OFT may simply leave a recommendation or agreement on the register and justify non-reference to the Court on the basis that given the steady flow of variations they are not in a position to properly assess it but that they are, none the less, monitoring developments.

46 In the five-year period 1987–91, out of 7,831 agreements submitted, 4,005 were registrable: see figures in DGFT's Annual Report for 1991 at p. 37.

47 Reg. 5(a)–(d).

48 Reg. 6(2)(a). See Art. 3 of the Order for details of registration of agreements that have become newly registrable as a result of the commencement of either an Order concerning goods information agreements or an Order concerning services generally and which agreements have been varied before the end of three months following commencement of the relevant Order.

49 Reg. 6(2)(b) S.I. 1984 No. 392.

4. *Time Limits for Registration*

4.35 The various time limits for registration are given in Schedule 2, para. 5 RTPA 1976.[50] The time limits below apply even where an agreement is temporary or very short-lived (e.g. a couple of days or less) or made in an emergency. Where a registered agreement is ended details must be provided within three months. The terminated agreement will remain on the register. Compliance with these time limits is essential if the legal consequences of non-registration are to be avoided. The following table sets out the various time periods. The table opposite is adapted and expanded from Schedule 2, para. 5.

4.36 The time limits within which particulars of agreements must be furnished has been significantly modified, and eased, by terms of the Deregulation (Restrictive Trade Practices Act) 1967 (Amendment) (Times Limits) Order 1996: S.I. 1996 No. 347. This Order was made pursuant to the Deregulation and Contracting Out Act 1994 which permits statutory provisions to be amended by statutory instrument in order to reduce burdens said to affect to persons carrying on business. The Order amends the RTPA 1976 which, prior the amendment, required restrictive agreements between two or more persons carrying on business in the UK in the production or supply of goods or supply of services to be furnished to the OFT. Prior the Order the Act required that particulars of certain categories of agreement be furnished *before* the restrictions in them took effect or within three months from the date of the agreement whichever first occurred. If particulars were not furnished as required the restrictions in the agreement were void and it was unlawful to give effect to them pursuant to section 35 RTPA 1976. The Order removed the requirement to furnish particulars of agreements before the restrictions took effect. The time limits for furnishing particulars in the relevant categories concerned came three months from the date of the agreement. The Order makes it unlawful for the parties to operate the restrictions in relation to the categories of agreement concerned in the period prior to the particulars being furnished. The new provision applies in respect of the period before the time for furnishing has expired. If the time for furnishing expires without the agreement having been furnished the existing provision in section 35 RTPA applies, as it did prior to the Order. The Order makes a number of consequential amendments to the Act to give effect to the changes referred to above.

4.37 The principal consequential amendment brought about by the Order is the insertion into section 27 RTPA 1976 of a new section 27ZA. The side note to this new section is: "Certain provisions not to be acted upon before registration". Pursuant to section 27ZA(2) in the case of agreements covered by categories (a) (agreements made on or after 25 November 1968 other than agreements to which categories (b)–(j) apply) and (f) (agreements whether made before or after 25 November 1968 which becomes subject to registration by virtue of variation on or after that date) in the Table it is unlawful, before particulars of the agreement concerned have been duly furnished to the Director, for any person who carries on business within the United Kingdom and is a party to the agreement to give effect to, or enforce or purport to enforce, the agreement in respect of the restrictions accepted or information provisions made under the agreement. In the case of particulars required to be furnished by virtue of category (i) in the table (variations on or after 25 November 1968 of an agreement whether made before or after the date being a variation which extends or adds to the restrictions accepted or information

[50] These time limits have been varied by the Restrictive Trade Practices (Non-notifiable Agreements) (Turnover Threshold) Order S.I. 1996 No. 348; see paras. 2.239–2.249, made pursuant to s. 1 Deregulation and Contracting Out Act 1994.

Description of agreement	Time for registering particulars
(a) Agreement made on or after 25 November 1968, other than an agreement to which (b) to (j) below apply.	Within 3 months from the day on which the agreement is made.
(b) Agreement approved by order under section 29 or section 30 above which becomes subject to registration by virtue of the expiry or revocation of that order.	Within 1 month from the day on which the agreement becomes so subject.
(c) Agreement which becomes subject to registration by virtue of the revocation of an order under section 9(5) above.	Within 1 month from the day on which the agreement becomes so subject.
(ca) Agreement which ceases to be a non-notifiable agreement.	Within 1 month from the day on which the agreement so ceases.
(d) Agreement which becomes subject to registration by virtue of an order under section 7 above coming into force after the making of the agreement.	Within 3 months from the day on which the agreement becomes so subject.
(e) Agreement which becomes subject to registration by virtue of an order under section 11 or section 12 above coming into force after the making of the agreement.	Within 3 months from the day on which the agreement becomes so subject.
(f) Agreement whether made before on or after 25 November 1968 which becomes subject to registration by virtue of a variation on or after that date (not being a variation which becomes subject to registration by virtue of an order under section 11 or 12 above).	Within 3 months from the day on which the agreement becomes so subject.
(g) Agreement which becomes subject to registration by virtue of the expiry or withdrawal of an approval given under section 32 above.	Within 3 months from the day on which the agreement becomes so subject.
(h) Agreement which was subject to registration on 25 November 1968, of which particulars had not been duly furnished.	Within 3 months from 25 November 1968.
(i) Variation on or after 25 November 1968 of an agreement (whether made before or after that date) being a variation which extends or adds to the restrictions accepted or information provisions made under the agreement [other than a variation to which (ii) below applies].	Within 3 months from the day of the variation.
(ii) Variation of an agreement being a variation which extends or adds to the restrictions accepted or information provisions made under the agreement and which becomes subject to registration by virtue of the revocation or variation of an order made under section 11 or 12 above.	Within 1 month from the day on which the variation becomes so subject.
(j) Any other variation of an agreement, and the determination of an agreement.	Within 3 months from the day of the variation or determination.

Note: Any references in the second column of the table in this paragraph to a period calculated from a specified day is a reference to the period in question inclusive of that day.

provisions made under the agreement) it is unlawful for particulars of the variation concerned have been duly furnished for any person who carries on business within the United Kingdom and is a party to the agreement concerned to give effect to or enforce or purport to enforce the extensions or additions to the restrictions excepted or information provisions made under the agreement. Pursuant to section 27ZA(4) and (5), section 35(2)–(7) RTPA 1976 applies in relation to the enforcement of the obligation (i.e. to furnish particulars) imposed by section 27ZA(2) and (3).

5. Extensions of Time for Registration

4.38 If parties to an agreement require additional time in order to register their agreement they may apply in writing to the OFT for an extension.[51] Such an application will only be considered if it is made within the normal period for registration (see table on page 191). The OFT may not grant an extension if the application is made outside of the period. In making an application parties must: (a) identify the agreement to which the application relates. This would entail, at least, giving the names and addresses of parties and a summary of the contents of the agreement; (b) indicate the amount of time requested; and (c) state why it is impracticable to furnish particulars within the statutory required period.[52] A common reason for not being able to furnish details on time is that the parties have only just discovered that the Act applies and the end of the registration period is imminent. Another reason might be that the agreement or part of it is oral and the parties are having difficulties in agreeing upon what should be included in the written memorandum of the oral terms. Difficulties might arise, in the case of a series of complex multipartite transaction, in determining precisely the scope of the agreement or arrangement.

6. Strategy in Respect of Failure to Register

4.39 Parties who fail to register their agreements in proper time will find that the tenor of negotiations with the OFT will depend upon the latter's view of the parties reasons for failing to register. Non-registration can be the result of wilful avoidance of the law; a misconceived belief that the agreement was exempt from registration (perhaps after having taken legal advice); or simply, unawareness of the need to register. Many businessmen who are party to relatively small-scale agreements are oblivious to the obligation to register which the RTPA 1976 imposes on them. Accordingly, how the OFT responds will largely depend upon such factors as: the explanations for non-registration given by the parties; the period of time during which the agreement has been unlawfully unregistered; the seriousness of the restrictions in question (if it is a price fixing or market sharing agreement a strict attitude may be expected); the likelihood of the restrictions being continued with by the parties if the OFT does not seek a prohibitive order from the Court, etc. The onus in such cases is on the parties to persuade the OFT that the failure to register is not a wilful or serious breach of the Act.

4.40 If the OFT adopts a lenient view then it may adopt the procedure laid down in section 21(1) RTPA 1976. This empowers the OFT to refrain from taking Court action where an agreement that has been registered has been determined or where all of the restrictions in an agreement have been determined. To benefit from this procedure parties

[51] s. 35(1) RTPA 1976.

[52] Reg. 12(2)(a)–(c) S.I. 1984 No. 392.

should: (a) terminate the agreement altogether; (b) furnish particulars of an agreement on the same terms as the old agreement; (c) re-adopt the new agreement. The OFT will advise parties to pursue this course where they are satisfied that the parties acted innocently and where the agreement in question appears not to be unduly restrictive. Where trade associations are concerned, the OFT often sends a letter to a senior officer of the association which incorporates suitable wording for a circular that may be sent round to members explaining the situation.[53]

4.41 If the OFT considers the failure to notify to be wilful, it might simply demand immediate termination of the agreement if it considers this adequate to prevent its perpetuation. If, however, it considers that the parties may seek to revive the agreement informally, or if the agreement is unacceptably restrictive, it might seek an injunctive order of the Court prohibiting the agreement and any other unregistered agreement.

7. *Informal Consultations with the OFT*

4.42 The OFT used to be willing to consider draft agreements and advise upon their registrability. However, due to excessive use of this facility, the OFT has for some years preferred parties to furnish the details of the agreement in accordance with the normal rules on registration and *then* to discuss whether the agreement is registrable or not. The OFT, despite the above change in procedure, remains willing to discuss general points about application of the legislation. Such information may be obtained by letter or over the phone. The identity of the person (client) requesting the information need not be disclosed and hence anonymity poses no problems.

8. *Registration of Dubious Agreements*

(1) The fail-safe method

4.43 As the discussion of registrable agreements in Chapter 1 demonstrates, the criteria for registration are exceptionally complex. Likewise, the criteria for determining whether restrictions in a clause are disregardable, or exempt, or whether the parties to an agree-

[53] See e.g. No. S892 Register of Restrictive Trade Practices, *Master Photographers Association*. The Association issued standard terms and conditions for the supply of photographic services to the public at weddings. The Secretary of the Association, when informed by the OFT that the standard terms and conditions were registrable sent a letter to the members of the association which stated: "Dear Members, that quasi quango dedicated to the permanent employment of unnecessary civil servants primed by Parliament to make complicated as much of nothing as possible (the Office of Fair Trading) have advised me that our Model Release Form is not legal because we did not tell them first! So we withdraw it today, tell them tomorrow and use it again, unchanged, the next day. To think we pay good taxes for such laws! Yours sincerely—Secretary." The association were apparently unsympathetic to the lenient attitude of the OFT. See also, No. 3769 Register of Restrictive Trade Practices, *Hard Non-ionic Detergents*. The Association sought to obtain an undertaking from its members to abstain from the use of siliceous materials and hard ionics on health and environmental grounds. They appreciated that a general ban on "hard" ionics would cause practical difficulties, extra cost and process problems for some users of the materials. "Hard" ionics can cause foaming in sewage works and water courses; siliceous materials when used in the manufacture of scouring products can cause health hazards for workers. Clearly bans on the use of these ingredients could have economic repercussions, especially for firms who would find it expensive to adapt to non-use of them. The undertakings were not registered. The Association was advised that the undertakings were registrable and at a Council meeting it was decided to transform the undertakings into an association recommendation on the basis that it would be more likely to earn s. 21(2) dispensation in that form. The recommendation was sent to members on 6 March 1973. On 20 March 1973 the Council had to revoke the recommendation, submit it to the OFT, and then re-issue it.

ment are exempt, or whether the agreement is exempt because it concerns a particular activity, are equally of considerable complexity. There may certainly exist reasonable doubt in many instances. The obvious difficulty for parties to such agreements is that failure to register can lead to unwelcome consequences. The restrictions in the agreement will be void and unenforceable, the parties vulnerable to damages suits by third parties, and the OFT might decide to seek a court order prohibiting the agreement. Conversely, the parties might decide that in their opinion the agreement is not registrable and that even if it is the chances of detection by the OFT slim. Parties must weigh pros and cons and assess risks in coming to a decision.

4.44 One course of action that is commonly used is to furnish particulars of the agreement on a fail-safe basis. Under this procedure parties furnish details of their agreement to the OFT but accompany the documents with a letter expressly reserving the right to argue at a later date that the agreement is exempt. Frequently, the parties include in the letter reasons indicating why they consider the agreement non-registrable. The Courts have long emphasised that, notwithstanding the immense complexity of the RTPA 1976, there is, in fact, a straightforward and simple solution for those advisers wishing to ensure that their arrangements do not fall foul of the automatic voidness imposed by section 35 in relation to registrable but unregistered agreements. In *Re Flushing Cistern Makers Limited Agreement*[54] the RPC stated:

> "We heard much in argument of the difficulty that companies have in discovering the law in this still novel field. There is a short and not very difficult solution available to those who are wondering whether they are sailing too close to the wind. They should confide in the Registrar, so that they will at least have the benefit of experience and learning of his department. If, on the other hand, they prefer to construct and operate for years an elaborate machinery such as this agreement, which is solely designed to restrict competition and agree prices which the public have to pay for their goods, they should not be too surprised if this Court decides that it is high time that sanctions are brought to bear on them, and to lay on their necks a yoke designed to press continuously on them of their obligations to comply with the 1968 Act."

4.45 In *Associated Dairies Ltd* v *Baines*,[55] Lord Justice Schiemann stated:

> "It should not be forgotten that the Act proceeds from the assumption that restrictive agreements can be against the public interest. There is no significant hardship involved in furnishing particulars of an agreement which any layman can see is what may loosely be described as restrictive and leaving it to the Registrar to sort out with the aid of the Court if need be whether the agreement is registrable. There is a public potential advantage and no significant public or private disadvantage in furnishing information on borderline cases whereas there is a significant public potential disadvantage in allowing the borderline cases to go unexamined because of lack of notification."

4.46 If the OFT accepts that the agreement is exempt it will not be placed on the register. If it is considered to be registrable it will be placed on the register and negotiations will be commenced as to whether it can be given section 21(2) dispensation. If the parties consider the agreement non-registrable and either seek a definitive ruling on the question, or wish to challenge the view of the OFT that the agreement is registrable, they may apply to the Court for a declaration under section 26(2) RTPA 1976 that the agreement is exempt from registration. Conversely, the OFT might likewise apply for an order that the

[54] [1973] 3 All ER 817, 824.

[55] [1996] ICR 183. (Reversed on appeal to the House of Lords on a different basis [1997] 2 WLR 364.)

agreement is registrable. Given that the time periods allowed for registration are very short (three months maximum) parties will have to make such an application quickly. In *Ravenseft* v *Director of General Fair Trading*[56] the applicants, with the co-operation of the OFT, applied for a declaration and because of the imminence of the end of the registration period, obtained a hearing and judgment within just a few weeks. The OFT agreed since this was a test case on an important point of law, to shorten proceedings, to submit evidence by way of affidavit only, and to accept the judgment of the Court as if it were a final hearing. Under section 26(1) any person aggrieved may apply to the Court for an order to have the register rectified by variation or removal of details. This course of action is, of course, only feasible following registration by the OFT.[57] In such a case, the OFT may respond with an application for an order striking out the application, on the grounds *inter alia* that the notice of application and the supporting affidavit disclose no reasonable cause of action and that the claim is an abuse of court procedure.[58]

9. Summary of Registration Rules

4.47 The following is a check list of the salient points concerning registration. The details of registration policy are found in S.I. 1984 No. 392.

4.48 (i) How to register

- Details must be furnished by or on behalf of any one party to an agreement. Two copies of each document must be furnished.
- One copy of each document furnished must be signed by the person providing them.
- The person providing the documents must sign the statutory certificate declaring that the details are accurate and complete; copies of the certificate are obtainable from the OFT.
- The Annex to the statutory certificate and the Request for Fast Track Registration Procedure, if appropriate, should be submitted; copies of these are available from the OFT.
- There is no charge for registration.
- Documents should be sent to: OFT (RTP), Field House, 15–25 Bream's Buildings, London EC4A 1PR. Telephone (0171) 242-2858.

4.49 (ii) What must be provided

- Names and addresses of all persons who are party to the agreement. In the case of trade associations, the names and addresses of members. Where there are more than 100 members an indication of the approximate number of members may be substituted for all the names and addresses.

[56] [1977] 1 All ER 47 Mocatta J.

[57] This approach was employed in *Royal Institution of Chartered Surveyors* v *Director General of Fair Trading* [1981] ECC 587; see also, Usher (1980) JBL 453.

[58] See s. 9(3) Restrictive Practices Court Act 1976 which endows the RPC with powers of jurisdiction equivalent to those of the High Court (or the Court of Session in Scotland or the High Court of Northern Ireland). See also RSC Ord. 18, r. 9. In the *Chartered Surveyors* case (above note 56) Slade J, delivering the judgment of the Court, cited *Metropolitan Bank* v *Pooley* (1885) 10 AC 210 at p. 214 as authority for the view that striking out should only occur in respect of a proceeding which is "on the face of it manifestly groundless". A striking out action will, one might reasonably conclude, rarely succeed.

- All of the terms of the agreement and *not* just those restrictive clauses which render the agreement registrable. Two copies of the documents should be provided. Where the agreement is unwritten two copies of a memorandum setting out all the terms of the agreement must be provided.
- The Annex to the statutory certificate and Request for Fast Track Procedure, if appropriate.

4.50 (iii) Trade associations

- Where an agreement is contained in the constitution, rules, regulations, bylaws or resolutions of the association or a committee or sub-committee thereof all of these documents must be provided.
- Where specific recommendations are made by an association to members the following must be furnished: the agreement by which the association is formed; the details of members unless the number exceeds 100 (see above); copies of recommendations (usually in the form of circular letters); and, minutes, if any, authorising recommendations.

4.51 (iv) Standard form or common form contracts

The following should be furnished to the OFT:

- copies of the agreement;
- names of the different parties to the agreements;
- the date the agreement is made;
- the geographical coverage of agreements and other minor differences between contracts;
- a statement that the agreements are otherwise identical to the specimen actually furnished;
- where parties wish to furnish details of an up-date to the agreement, a memorandum identifying the new parties to and the dates of each agreement should be provided together with a statement that these are the only respects in which the agreements differ from that previously provided.

4.52 (v) Variations

Details of variations should be furnished where:

- the change entails the acceptance of a new restriction by one or more of the parties;
- the change eliminates or reduces the impact of a restriction, e.g. it excludes from its application some person, good or service, or some area or place;
- the change relates to the terms and conditions on which goods or services are to be supplied or obtained;
- the registrable restrictions are all brought to an end;
- two copies of the revision together with a completed statutory certificate must be provided.

10. Registration of Orders of the RPC

4.53 Pursuant to section 23 RTPA 1976 the Director is required to maintain the Register at such premises within the United Kingdom and in such form as he may determine. Pursuant to section 23(2) the Director is under a duty to cause notice of any declaration made under section 1(3) and any Order made under section 2 to be entered in the register. It is notable that orders made pursuant to section 35 are not the subject of the duty in section 23(2). There is no definition in section 23 of "the register". The register contains two sections. First, the public section, secondly, the special section. Section 23(2) does not distinguish between the two parts of the Register and, on one view, empowers the Director to place declarations and orders on any one of the two parts of the register. However, it is known that the Director and the Secretary of State take the view that the duty in section 23(2) relates only to the public section of the register.

4.54 Pursuant to section 23(3), regulations made under section 27 shall provide for the maintenance of a special section of the register and for the entry or filing in that section of such particulars as the Secretary of State may direct. The Secretary of State takes the view that "particulars" includes orders and declarations made by the RPC notwithstanding that, elsewhere in the Act, particulars refers to particulars of agreements, arrangements and decisions of associations of undertakings. It is the view of the Director and the Secretary of State that the special section of the register is under the control of the Secretary of State alone. If the Secretary of State decides not to place an Order, in a given case, upon the special section of the register he does not have the power to place it upon the public section. In such circumstances he simply decides not to place an Order on the special section and it is left to the Director to cause notice of the Order or declaration in question to be entered into the public section of the register. There is no authoritative guidance of the RPC as to the precise allocation of responsibility between the Director and the Secretary of State in relation to the filing of orders and declarations on the register. Moreover, there is no guidance in the Act as to whether or not orders and declarations made pursuant to section 35 may, in any event, be placed upon the register or any part thereof.

C. The Register: Problems with Confidential Information

4.55 The OFT are legally bound to place on a public register all agreements caught by the Act.[59] The register is kept at Field House, 15–25 Bream's Buildings, London EC4A 1PR.[60] It is open for inspection between 10 a.m. and 4.30 p.m. on Mondays to Fridays. There is a small fee for inspection of files. Copies will be made on payment of a photocopying fee.

4.56 The register is a treasure trove of information. Many businessmen and legal advisers are unaware of the potential value of the registered information. For example, a businessman who wished to set up a franchise operation in the furniture business might find a selection of contract precedents registered which provide him with valuable information about setting up a franchise network. He will also be able to find out about any other restrictive agreements operated in the furniture industry. This may provide him with

[59] s. 1(2) RTPA 1976.
[60] Enquiries may be made by phone, (0171) 242 2858, or by fax, (0171) 269 8800.

useful information about competitors and their agreements. Lawyers may find that agreements given dispensation under section 21(2) RTPA 1976 are useful guides and precedents though it should be borne in mind that copyright in an agreement almost certainly remains with the parties' lawyers. Brief details of the agreement and the registration number are given of all cases granted section 21(2) dispensation in the Annual Report of the DGFT. This provides a useful catalogue of precedents. The DGFT Report, however, does *not* list cases that have been resolved by termination of the restriction, termination of the agreement itself, or, expiration of the agreement through effluxion of time.

4.57 An additional source of information may be found in *Fair Trading* (the quarterly journal of the OFT) who publish an update of agreements registered. From this source one can discover the registry number of the agreement (if given the register number, or the name of a party, OFT staff can locate an agreement within minutes); the subject matter of the agreement; the outcome of the negotiations with the OFT; and the month and year the negotiations reached a conclusion. Various symbols are used on the index to the register kept at the OFT.[61] These symbols are: (a) "B" indicating that a section 21(2) dispensation has been given; (b) "D" indicating that the agreement has been determined by the parties other than by effluxion of time; and (c) "F" indicating that the agreement has been modified so as to bring it outside the scope of the legislation. Thus for example on the index one would find:

"S.186 optical dispensing services D 11/82"

This would indicate that a services agreement is registered as 186 on the register, it concerns optical dispensing services and was determined by the parties in November 1982.

1. *Contents of the Register*

4.58 The OFT will place on the register copies of the documents sent to them.[62] They will also place on the register copies of documents or other information obtained by them following the sending of a statutory notice issued under section 36 RTPA 1976 which requires the parties to furnish details of agreements subject to the Act. This notice may be sent to parties who have registered their agreement in order to elicit further information or to parties the OFT has reasonable cause to believe are party to an unregistered agreement. In extreme cases the OFT may apply to the Court to have a person attend before the Court and give evidence on oath concerning the matters of which the OFT has given notice to him under section 36. Any documents or information deriving from this hearing may be registered.[63]

4.59 The OFT may also register any documents or information furnished to the OFT by the parties which it considers is appropriate to place on the register. Often the memorandum and articles of association of trade associations are included. Correspondence

[61] Agreement on the register can be traced by use of an index system kept in the waiting room at the registry. Agreements are classified by reference to the Standard Industrial Classification (SIC) for services agreements or the Commodity Indices for the Standard International Trade Classification (SITC) for goods agreements. For service agreements there is also an index of the parties to the agreement. A computerised index system is now also available.

[62] Reg. 8 S.I. 1984 No. 392.

[63] s. 37 RTPA 1976. Under s. 37(2) notes of the examination must be taken and shall be read over and signed by the person being examined. They may thereafter be used in evidence against that person. The Court may require that person to disclose any documents or other information in his possession or control specified in the notice given by the Director. Confidential information protected by legal privilege may not be required to be disclosed, e.g. communications between party to agreement and legal adviser.

between trade associations and members incorporating a recommendation, newspaper or journal articles where they refer to the parties and the agreement, minutes of association meetings, etc. may also be placed on the register. However, regulation 8(2) of S.I. 1984 No. 392 (Registration of Restrictive Trading Agreements Regulations) states that the OFT need *not* include on the register:

> "any details as to parties or other persons, prices, terms or other matters as are material for the purpose only of defining the particular application from time to time of a continuing restriction accepted under an agreement of which particulars are entered or filed in the register, being details which the Director considers it unnecessary to enter or file therein."

Regulation 8(2) is of limited application since it only applies to information which has the sole purpose of defining a restriction. The OFT view this provision as an administrative tool designed to prevent the register becoming swamped by superfluous detail. Thus, if X and Y enter an agreement whereby X will provide a service to Y's customers as identified in a customer list then the agreement and the customer list will be registered. If the agreement also provides that Y will keep the customer list up to date then the OFT may refrain from registering a stream of amendments and changes to the list.

2. The Special Section

4.60 The OFT also maintain a "special section" to the register. Details placed upon this register are not available for public inspection. The contents of the special section are at the discretion of the Secretary of State. Under section 23(3) (a) and (b) RTPA 1976 the special section may contain:

(a) any information subject to registration that in the Secretary of State's opinion it would not be in the public interest to have made public;
(b) any information whose publication would, in the Secretary of State's opinion, substantially damage the legitimate business interests of any person, though the Secretary of State may refuse to place information on the special section if of the opinion that publication would be in the public interest.[64]

When the Secretary of State directs that particulars of an agreement be placed upon the special register it is normal practice for the OFT to include an abbreviated reference in the public register which merely refers to the subject matter of the agreement and the names of the parties. A third party seeking to inspect that part of the register would be denied access. However, the Secretary of State may decide that the entire agreement (including details of the parties to the agreement itself) should be placed upon the special section of the register. In such circumstances the Secretary of State will inform the OFT, in writing, of the necessity to exclude such information from the index of the public register.

3. Protecting Confidential and Secret Information

4.61 The presumption concerning registration is full disclosure of documents. Parties enjoy no right to withhold confidential or commercially sensitive data even though the data might bear no relevance to the restrictions in the agreement. Registration thus exposes

[64] s. 23(3)(b) was substituted by s. 11 Deregulation and Contracting Out Act 1994. The earlier version restricted non-publication to information about secret processes of manufacture of goods or provision of services, or information concerning the presence absence or situation of any mineral or other deposits.

the possibility of firms being able to examine confidential documents of their rivals. The "special section" of the register provides some comfort. However, to qualify for exemption from the ordinary register parties must persuade the Secretary of State that publication of the information would either harm the public interest, or, would substantially damage legitimate business interests.

(1) Scope of special section

4.62 The scope of the special section is limited to information, the publication of which may be contrary to the public interest or information the publication of which may substantially damage legitimate business interests. It follows that ordinary commercially sensitive data *cannot* be placed on the special section unless it can be shown that publication would *substantially* damage legitimate business interests. It is possible to persuade the DTI that commercially sensitive pricing data may be omitted from the register under this provision,[65] though it has to be shown that it would in some way cause substantial damage, over and above ordinary damage.[66] The phrase "information the publication of which would ... be contrary to the public interest" does not provide great scope to retain the confidentiality of registrable agreements. Agreements relating to defence matters or international commercial relations might fall within this category.[67]

(2) Procedure

4.63 The procedure for claiming exemption is that parties must submit a memorandum to the OFT indicating the particulars of the information they wish placed on the special section. Moreover, they must lay out their reasons for seeking inclusion in the special section. With respect to specific pieces of information parties should bear in mind, that included on the ordinary register, may be copies of agreements *and* minutes of meetings referring to the agreement, Thus, for example, an agreement between X and Y concerning mineral rights might be referred to in the minutes of a board meeting. Since implications flowing from the minutes may give important information it may, not unreasonably, be considered as confidential, With regard to reasons, parties should seek to demonstrate not only how the information is commercially sensitive but also how it affects their "legitimate" business interests, and how disclosure could cause "substantial" damage to those interests.

4.64 One other possibility arises which might be of use to parties. Regulation 8(2) of S.I. 1984 No. 392 (discussed above) allows the OFT to refrain from registering information which simply defines the application of a restriction. As noted above, the scope of this provision is limited and the OFT view it primarily as an administrative convenience. How-

[65] See e.g. No. 10659 Register of Restrictive Trading Agreements, *Merlin/Ajax* (registered 23 February 1993, s. 21(2) directions given 16 March 1993), where information about price and payment terms, as well as technical information about circuit breakers, was omitted from the register under the earlier version of s. 23(3)(b) RTPA 1976 referred to in note 64 above, despite the fact that the earlier version seemed inapt for such a purpose. See also No. CT/23/ER/154 on the exempt register under s. 29, where usage charges for the Channel Tunnel negotiated between the tunnel owners and the two national railways using it were omitted under s. 31(4) and CT/33/ER/160 where payment and price terms for trains as well as penalty clauses for late delivery were omitted under s. 31(4). S. 31(4) allows particulars referred to in 31(5) to be omitted; s. 31(5) states that those particulars are the ones provided in s. 23(3).

[66] "Substantial" was partially defined by the House of Lords in *R* v *MMC ex parte South Yorkshire Transport Ltd* [1993] 1 WLR 23 in the context of s. 64(3) Fair Trading Act 1973, as meaning "something greater than" as opposed to more than *de minimis*. See Robertson, "Substantial: what's in a word?" [1993] ECLR 217.

[67] In *Aluminium Imports from Eastern Europe* OJ 1985 192/1 at p. 98, para, 10.2, the European Commission noted in respect of British corporate involvement in an international aluminium agreement that the UK government directed the Registrar of Restrictive Trading Practices (as he then was) to place details of the agreement on the special section of the Register.

ever, it might be arguable that commercially sensitive data that is superfluous to the restrictions in question might none the less be perceivable as defining the application of the restriction. The notion of defining the application of a restriction is not defined and, could, with liberal construction be taken in some cases as including a wide range of materials. Parties might consider drafting a memorandum for submission to the OFT outlining which information is superfluous to the restriction, how it is commercially sensitive and how it defines the application of the restriction(s).

4.65 Memoranda seeking to justify exemption from the ordinary register are made to the OFT who will consider the memorandum and give their advice on it to the Secretary of State who will then, with the assistance of his staff at the DTI, decide how best to exercise his discretion. The DTI often go back to the parties for clarification of their submissions.

D. Powers of the OFT to Obtain Information

1. *OFT Notices*

4.66 Where the OFT has "reasonable cause to believe" that a person is or may be party to a registrable agreement it might give to the relevant person(s) a notice requiring them to notify the OFT whether they are party to a registrable agreement and, if they are, to furnish such particulars of the agreement as are specified in the notice. The notice invariably specifies a time limit for compliance.[68] Where the person suspected of being party to an agreement is a trade association, notice may be given either to the association generally, or to the secretary, manager or other similar officer of the association.[69] Notices may be sent to parties to services or goods export agreements.[70] These are exempt from the Act but, none the less, must be registered with the OFT.[71]

4.67 The OFT may also issue a notice to a person who has furnished information with the OFT for registration purposes. The notice will specify such extra information as the OFT considers "expedient" in connection with registration. A notice may also be sent to a person who is party to an agreement, the details of which have been furnished by someone else. Thus, if X, Y and Z are in an agreement the details of which have been furnished by X the OFT might issue notices to Y and Z requiring them to furnish information.[72]

2. *When a Notice may be Issued: "Reasonable Cause", OFT Practice*[73]

4.68 The OFT may only issue a notice when they have "reasonable cause" to believe that an agreement is being operated. The Director General must be able to establish that there ex-

[68] s. 36(1) and (2) RTPA 1976. In 1992, a typical year, the OFT sent out s. 36 Notices in 15 investigations, as well as a number of less formal letters of enquiry: DGFT's Annual Report 1992, p. 32.

[69] s. 36(4) RTPA 1976.

[70] s. 36(5) and (6) RTPA 1976.

[71] Sch. 3, paras. 6 and 9 RTPA 1976 excludes from operation of the Act goods and services agreements which have exclusively overseas operation. These agreements are, however, registrable under s. 25 RTPA 1976.

[72] s. 36(3) RTPA 1976. These notices can have spectacular results. In 1978 the OFT unearthed 199 agreements in which 111 companies concerned mainly with the supply of construction materials such as hot rolled asphalt, coated macadam, surface dressing chippings, coated stone, sand, gravel and limestone had "unwritten understandings" with each other.

[73] For an explanation of how the OFT exercises its powers illustrated with actual case studies, see Walker-Smith, "Collusion: its detection and investigation" [1991] ECLR 71.

ists a strong prima facie case as to the existence of an agreement or arrangement.[74] This means that the OFT cannot issue a statutory notice in response to a hunch. The OFT may however send out a notice where they have reasonable cause to suspect that a registrable agreement *might* exist. In that sense, the OFT does have authority to issue notices in response to strong suspicions.

4.69 The "reasonable cause" requirement causes problems for the OFT who, in some circumstances, might believe that an agreement exists but have no or little tangible evidence to prove it. This is sometimes the case where the OFT observe unexpected patterns of corporate behaviour. For example X, Y and Z might, after a period of intense price competition, suddenly harmonise their prices to an unexpected degree. The OFT, as observers of this conduct, might suspect collusion as the cause of the harmonisation. In such a case it is hard to argue that it has "reasonable cause" to believe that an agreement exists. It is possible that the price co-ordination emerged through natural market forces, i.e. the companies became more consciously sensitive to each other's pricing patterns. In "observed conduct" cases such as this the OFT will probably not issue a statutory notice. Rather, it might send an informal letter to the parties asking them whether they are party to a registrable agreement and reminding them of the duty to register and the consequences of non-compliance. Such a letter invariably proves effective; it indicates to the parties that their activities are being scrutinised and that continuation with an unregistered, clandestine, agreement would be futile.

4.70 Notices issued pursuant to section 36(3) RTPA 1976 are susceptible to judicial review pursuant to RSC Order 53. The Act provides that documents or information may be required "as the Director considers expedient for the purposes of or in connection with the registration or the agreement". This does not give an unfettered discretion to the DGFT. During the course of 1992, as part of the on-going investigations conducted by the DGFT into alleged unregistered but registrable price fixing and market sharing agreements in the ready mixed concrete sector operating throughout the 1980s, the DGFT issued notices pursuant to section 36(3) RTPA 1976 to a number of companies in the ready mixed concrete sector. The companies pursuant to section 36(3) notices enquiring whether they were party to unregistered registrable agreements had furnished memoranda to the OFT setting out particulars of price fixing and market sharing agreements. These memoranda had been duly placed upon the Register by the DGFT. These subsequent notices were largely in identical form. They stated that the DGFT in exercise of his powers pursuant to section 36(3) and considering that the furnishing of the documents and information specified in the Notice was expedient for the purposes of or in connection with the registration of agreements hereby required the addressee company to furnish all documents and information in its possession or control relevant to: (i) the names and addresses of any employees or agents of the company who were involved in the formation of and/or any variation in the scope or terms of certain agreements which were defined in the notice by reference to their numbers on the register of restrictive trading agreements; (ii) the position and status of each of the individuals with respect of the company at the time of their said involvement and at present; and (iii) the dates of the said involvement on each of the individuals. None of the companies to whom the registered agreements related had issued proceedings pursuant to section 26 RTPA 1976 for rectification of the register. A number of companies in the ready mixed concrete

[74] It was stated by Lord Denning MR in the Court of Appeal in *Registrar of Restrictive Trading Agreements* v *W.H. Smiths* (1969) LR 7 RP 122, 147 to be an objective test reviewable by the court.

sector commenced proceedings for judicial review.[75] The companies sought leave to move for judicial review of the notices. The grounds relied upon by the Applicants may be summarised as follows: (a) that the notices were not issued in furtherance of the task of the DGFT in deciding whether or not an agreement was registrable since the agreements in question in respect of which details were sought pursuant the notices had *already* been placed upon the register; (b) the true purpose of the notices was to further the investigation of the DGFT into possible contempt of court by the ready mixed concrete producers concerned which was not a proper exercise of the power under section 36(3); and (c) in any event, the Applicants were not bound to reply to the notices since so to do would infringe the right against self-incrimination. On 14 October 1992 Mr Justice Brooke in the Divisional Court granted leave to the Applicant to move for judicial review against the notices. Further, he granted, pursuant to RSC Order 53 rule 3(10), a stay of the notices pending the hearing of the applications for judicial review.[76] Thereafter, the Applicants served their respective Notices of Motion. The principal relief sought was an order of *certiorari* to remove into the Court and quash the notices issued by the DGFT and/or the relevant decision or decisions by or on behalf of the DGFT to issue the said notices; further or alternatively, declarations that the notices and/or decision or decisions by or on behalf of the DGFT to issue the notices were *ultra vires* and void and of no effect. The merits of the Applicant's submissions were not ultimately tested by the Divisional Court since, shortly before the hearing of the substantive motion, the DGFT withdrew the disputed notices and paid the Applicants' costs. It is correct to say that notwithstanding the withdrawal of the notices by the DGFT and the payment of costs, no admissions whatever were made as to the merits of the Applicants case. The DGFT claimed that the purpose for withdrawing the notices was that the OFT had obtained the information in question from other sources.

4.71 The arguments that would have been advanced by the DGFT at the substantive hearing were set out in affidavit evidence served prior to the hearing. Essentially, the DGFT considered that it was expedient for him to be provided with details of certain of the individuals who had been involved in the cartel agreements and that such details were relevant to the question whether or not those individuals could be said to have had the authority to enter into the said agreements on behalf of their employers or to have had ostensible authority so to do. Further, the DGFT considered that such information would have enabled his officials to trace the individuals in question who could then have been approached for relevant information. The argument advanced by the DGFT is not an argument that he would have to advance today. However, at that particular point in time the Court of Appeal in *Re Supply of Ready Mixed Concrete*[77] had indicated that a company would not be party to a registrable agreement under the Act if those of its employees who actually participated in the agreements in question did not have the authority of their employer so to do. That particular test of whether an agreement registrable under the RTPA 1976 had come into being was rejected, subsequently, by the House of Lords.[78] However, at the time when the judicial review would have been heard it was the applicable law. It is worth mentioning, in passing, that in relation to one of the Applicants

[75] The Companies and the Crown Office case reference number were *Joseph Adshead and Son Ltd* (CO-1391-92; CO-1048-92); *Tarmac Topmix Ltd* (CO-1390-92); *Pioneer Concrete (UK) Ltd, Mixconcrete Ltd* (CO-1271-92); and, ten companies in the RMC Group (CO-1305-92).

[76] The stays were in the following terms: "It is ordered that ... all further proceedings in respect of which this application relates be stayed until the determination of the aforesaid Motion or further Order."

[77] [1992] QB 213.

[78] [1995] 1AC 456. The House of Lords ruled that the acts of employees were attributable to employers whether authorised or not.

(Joseph Adshead and Son Ltd) the DGFT had in February 1992 issued a notice pursuant to section 36(3) RTPA 1976 which sought details relating to the detailed enforcement of the various agreements particulars of which had been furnished to the DGFT and already placed upon the register. In relation to *these* notices the DGFT accepted that they were wider in scope than permitted under section 36(3) and they were withdrawn.

4.72 A number of additional points may be made as to the powers of the DGFT pursuant to section 36(3) which arose in the course of the above proceedings. First, the DGFT took the view that his responsibilities under the Act, so far as they concerned registration, did not cease in relation to a particular agreement once all of the details prescribed by the Registration of Restrictive Trading Agreements Regulations 1984 were entered on the Register. They duty of the DGFT, as set out in section 1(2)(a) RTPA 1976, was to compile and *maintain* a register which duty was additional to the duty to enter and file particulars of such agreements under section 1(2)(b) RTPA 1976. The DGFT understood his duty as being to satisfy himself that the details entered on the register were accurate and this entailed the making of subsequent enquiries. The DGFT considered that he had the power, of his own motion, to place on the register additional material amending existing particulars and, where he was satisfied that an agreement was improperly placed on the register to remove those particulars. Second, in relation to the Applicants argument that the DGFT was not entitled to use the power under section 36 for the purposes of furthering contempt proceedings, the DGFT accepted that a major (though not sole) consideration behind the issuing of the disputed notices was the need to determine the question of the registrability of the agreements disclosed by the memorandum furnished by the parties to enable the DGFT to decide whether it was appropriate to commence contempt of court proceedings. The question whether there was a breach of a court order entailed deciding whether a subsequent agreement was registrable. Accordingly, section 36 could be used as a precursor to contempt proceedings since it was, none the less, being used to decide whether an agreement was registrable.

3. Examination on Oath before the Court

4.73 Under section 37 RTPA 1976 the OFT may, where they have issued a notice under section 36 RTPA 1976 (see above), apply to the Court for an order that a person specified in a notice, attend the Court to give evidence under oath. Such a person may be represented by a solicitor or by counsel who may put to him such questions as the Court allows for the purpose of enabling him to explain or qualify any answers given by him. Notes of the examination are taken and are read over and signed by the person under examination. These notes may be used in evidence against him. The Court may require such a person to disclose any documents or other particulars in his possession or control as may be specified in the notice. Where the notice specifies a company as the person to be examined, a Court order may be made requiring the attendance of any director, manager, secretary or other officer of the company or person likely to have relevant knowledge.[79] For the purposes of the section, unincorporated trade associations are treated as companies (i.e. as if they were incorporated).[80] Information that is privileged because it is a communication between a person examined and his legal adviser may not be required to be disclosed by the Court.[81]

[79] s. 37(3) RTPA 1976. The power to compel the appearance of other relevant persons was introduced by the Fair Trading Act 1973 as a response to the case of *Registrar of Restrictive Trading Agreements* v *W.H. Smiths* (1969) LR 7 RP 122 where the Court of Appeal upheld the RPC's refusal to compel attendance of a local branch manager. The Court said that local branch managers were not managers in the sense of the Act.

[80] s. 37(5) RTPA 1976.

[81] s. 37(6) RTPA 1976.

4.74 Refusal to comply with a Court order brings the person refusing into contempt of court. The giving of incorrect information to the Court may be perjury which is a criminal offence. The procedure under section 37 is considered by the OFT in exceptional cases only. See further paras. 5.107–5.111.

4. *Failure to Furnish Correct Information: Penalties*

4.75 If any person knowingly or recklessly furnishes false information or wilfully alters, suppresses or destroys any relevant document he may commit a criminal offence. If found guilty he may be liable on summary conviction to a fine. If convicted on indictment such a person may face gaol for up to two years or to a fine or both.[82] In *DPP* v *Automatic Telephone and Electric Co*[83] two companies were fined £500 and had to pay costs between them of 750 guineas. Periodic daily fines may be imposed after a conviction up until such time as the documents have been properly furnished.[84] Where the OFT issues a notice to any person under section 36 RTPA 1976 (see above) failure to comply constitutes a criminal offence for which offenders may be liable on summary conviction to a fine.[85] Where an offence under section 37 has been committed by a company, its directors, managers, secretary or any other relevant person acting on the company's behalf, it may also be liable to a fine where the offence has been committed with their consent or connivance or is attributed to their neglect.

4.76 The *Automatic Telephone* case noted above reveals the dangers inherent in failure to monitor junior management. In 1959 a major agreement between the parties involving, *inter alia*, market sharing and price fixing was abandoned leaving an agreement involving simply the exchange of patents which was not registrable. In 1962 certain middle management, unbeknown to senior management, exchanged price lists and acted to fix price levels. The parties were prosecuted upon the basis that they had suppressed information when registering their agreements. Thus, the actions of the middle management superseded the good faith of the senior management in abandoning the earlier restrictive agreement. If such actions are carried out in disobedience of earlier orders of or undertakings to the RPC, the company may be held liable in contempt of court.[86]

E. The section 21 RTPA 1976 Procedure: Negotiations with the OFT

1. *Legal Context*

4.77 Section 21 is, in practical terms, at the very heart of the RTPA 1976. Many businessmen and lawyers, however, when considering this area of the law view the Restrictive Practices Court to be its central pillar. This is in practical terms a misconception since only a minute percentage of registered cases (under 1 per cent) reach the Court. In vir-

82 s. 38 RTPA 1976.
83 (1968) 112 SJ. 109.
84 s. 38(4) RTPA 1976.
85 s. 38(1) RTPA 1976.
86 *DGFT* v *Pioneer Concrete (UK) Ltd (Ready Mixed Concrete No. 2)* [1995] 1AC 456. Liability for contempt of court is discussed at paras. 5.69–5.86.

tually every case a result is reached as a consequence of discussions between the parties and the OFT and not as a consequence of judicial deliberation.

4.78 Section 21 RTPA 1976 is given below in full:

"(1) The Director may refrain from taking proceedings before the Court ...
(a) in respect of an agreement if and for so long as he thinks it appropriate so to do having regard to the operation of any directly applicable Community provision and to the purpose and effect of any authorisation or exemption granted in relation to such a provision;
(b) where an agreement ...
(i) of which particulars are entered or filed in the register pursuant to this Act has been determined (whether by effluxion of time or otherwise); or
(ii) has been so determined in respect of all restrictions accepted or information provisions made under that agreement.
(2) If it appears to the Secretary of State, upon the Director's representation, that the restrictions accepted or information provisions made under an agreement of which particulars are so entered or filed are not of such significance as to call for investigation by the Court, the Secretary of State may give directions discharging the Director from taking proceedings in the Court in respect of that agreement during the continuance in force of the directions.
(3) The Secretary of State may at any time upon the Director's representation withdraw any directions given by him under subsection (2) above if satisfied that there has been a material change of circumstances since the directions were given."

4.79 Thus in three situations the presumption expressed in section 1(2) RTPA 1976 that all registered agreements will be referred to the Court may be rebutted. In practice, reference to the Court is generally reserved for those cases where the OFT wish to enforce the ban on unregistered agreements with an injunctive order, or where a registered agreement exhibits clearly objectionable characteristics (for example, price fixing or collusive tendering). In the latter case, it might refer agreements to the Court even though the parties have either terminated all the restrictions or abandoned the agreement altogether.[87]

4.80 The three situations mentioned above are:

(i) where the OFT makes a representation to the Secretary of State under section 21(2) and the latter directs the OFT not to refer the agreement to the Court;
(ii) where, before any proceedings have begun, the parties have terminated the agreement or it has expired or, though it continues in force, all the registrable restrictions have been eliminated or have ceased to have effect (these are called "determined agreements"); and,
(iii) where the OFT considers it appropriate to refrain from proceedings as a result of directly applicable EC law. Thus an agreement exempt under Article 85(3) EC or an applicable block exemption may well be (and inevitably is) spared a reference to the Court. Indeed, now such block exempt agreements are likely to be non-notifiable.[88]

Situations (i) and (ii) are of greatest significance and are examined at paras. 4.86–4.114. Situation (iii) is considered at paras. 4.82–4.85.

[87] See paras. 5.2–5.20 and 5.65–5.68 respectively.
[88] Restrictive Trade Practices (Non-notifiable Agreements) EC Block Exemptions Order 1996, S.I. 1996 No. 349; see paras. 2.250 and following.

2. *Relevant Statistics: Enforcement Trends*

4.81 The figures below show that only about half of all agreements submitted for registration are indeed registrable, a reflection as much on the complexity of the legislation as on the use of fail-safe furnishing of particular. Of those agreements which prove to be registrable about half are given the benefit of a section 21(2) direction. Of the others, some are dealt with either by the parties removing the restrictions or terminating the agreement. In theory, the OFT might refer an agreement containing registrable restrictions to the Restrictive Practices Court, but in practice this would be exceptional. Although there have been a large number of Court hearings (over 1000 since 1956) in less than sixty of these have the parties actually disputed the merits of the agreement in full trial. The vast majority of the cases concern enforcement actions by the OFT for injunctions in undisputed proceedings.

The figures given below are based on the total number of agreements registered during the specified year.

Year	*No. agreements submitted*	*No. reg*	*No. 21(2)*[89]
1990	1,230	676	467
1991	1,327	619	321
1992	1,249	689	503
1993	1,251	686	711
1994	1,280	581	1,261
1995	1,393	602	1,406

3. *The Application of EC Rules: Partial Safety for Parties*

4.82 Many businesses obtain exemption for their agreements under EC law. This might be because they have received a formal exemption decision under Article 85(3) EC, or because the Commission has sent them a "comfort letter" saying that as things stand the Commission see no grounds for taking further action, or because the Commission have issued to them a "negative clearance" which is a statement to the effect that on the facts available to the Commission it does not consider the agreement to fall within Article 85(1) EC. Alternatively, parties may have drafted their agreement so as to ensure that it complies with the terms of a "block exemption". These enactments provide parties with an automatic exemption from the ban—on restrictive agreement in Article 85(1). Further details of these exemptions may be found in Chapters 6 and 7. The importance in UK terms is that the OFT may refrain from referring to the Court an agreement which benefits from EC exemption.

4.83 However, falling within the scope of an EC exemption, does not guarantee smooth passage under UK rules. An agreement may not be within the EC net if it does not "affect trade between Member States". Such might be the case with an agreement between two purely UK parties which has no international repercussions. Even though an agreement is not subject to Article 85 EC it will of course remain subject to the RTPA 1976. The parties may find it of no avail to present to the OFT a negative clearance in which the Commission state that there are no grounds for applying Article 85. Further, there might be excep-

[89] This figure includes agreements submitted in previous years.

tional cases where although a restrictive agreement has beneficial effects on the EC market, and accordingly the Commission grant an exemption under Article 85(3) EC, it has harmful effects on the UK market. In such a case the OFT would intervene. The OFT and the Commission in Brussels keep reasonably close contact and invariably an exemption from the EC Commission is honoured by the OFT.[90]

4.84 The Restrictive Practices Court may, under section 5 RTPA 1976, decline or postpone application of its powers under the Act if it sees fit having regard to EC law. It is under no obligation to do so however.[91]

4.85 Particulars of an agreement exempted under EC law must still be furnished under the RTPA 1976, unless it comes within the category of non-notifiable agreements discussed at paras. 2.250 and following.[92] Indeed, under the Registration of Restrictive Trading Agreements (EC Documents) Regulation 1973 (S.1. 1973 No. 950) parties should furnish copies of decisions granting negative clearance or exemption to the OFT. This will enable the latter to consider exercising its power under section 21(1) RTPA 1976 and refrain from referring the registered agreement to the RPC. In practical terms parties should notify the OFT of a comfort letter or other form of EC clearance (e.g. good faith undertaking) in so far as these relate to a registered agreement since these clearances may equally be persuasive under section 21 (1).

F. Modification and Abandonment of Agreements: Options Available to Parties

4.86 Under section 21(1)(b) the OFT may refrain from referring an agreement to the Court in four situations.

1. *Termination and Abandonment*

4.87 Parties to unregistered agreements that have been operated clandestinely invariably terminate and abandon agreements once light is thrown upon them. In such cases the OFT, in response to the underhand method of their operation, invariably refer such agreements to the Court for an order under section 35(3) RTPA 1976 restraining the parties from continuing with the agreement or any other unregistered agreement on similar terms.[93] References to the Court may be justified, not on the grounds that the restric-

[90] See e.g. No. S1083 Register of Restrictive Trade Practices, *Society of Motor Manufacturers and Traders (SMMT)* (1984). OFT refrained from taking proceedings against the SMMT trade fair rules on the basis that the Commission granted Art. 85(3) exemption—see *SMMT* OJ 1983 1376/1. The OFT did not give s. 21(2) exemption but simply closed the file on the basis of s. 21(1)(a) RTPA 1976.

[91] In *Mallaig and North-west Fishermen's Association (No. 2)* unreported, noted DGFT Annual Report 1975, pp. 90, 91, the RPC released parties to a price fixing agreement from a previous prohibitive order. This was done because the parties wished to fix minimum prices in accordance with EC Regulation 2142/70/EEC on the common organisation of a market in fish products. Regulations are directly applicable in Member States and take precedence over contradictory national law. The Court viewed this as a "material change" in the circumstances of the case justifying release from the Order. Conversely, the Commission is not bound to follow prohibitory decisions imposed by national authorities: Case 298/83 *CICCE* v *Commission* [1985] ECR 1105; [1986] 1 CMLR 486.

[92] Restrictive Trade Practices (Non-notifiable Agreements) (EC Block Exemptions) Order 1996, S.I. 1996 No. 349.

[93] In the DGFT Annual Report 1992, p. 32, it is reiterated that it is "almost invariably" the practice to seek such orders. See also DGFT Annual Report 1994, p. 45 which is to the same effect.

tions are unduly serious (though often they are as otherwise they would have been registered) but on the basis that the parties blatantly ignored the registration laws. Where the OFT is satisfied that the parties will not continue with the agreement, it might refrain from referring the agreement.

4.88 Where an agreement has been registered but the OFT indicates that its restrictions are unacceptable, parties have little option but to terminate and abandon or face a full-scale battle to defend the agreement before the Court. Invariably parties choose to abandon or negotiate. Agreements which for example seek to set prices, share markets, fix methods of trading in a rigid manner, tender for contracts on an agreed basis, or impose unreasonable exclusion or limitation clauses in contracts with consumers, will rarely be acceptable and will have to be modified or, more likely, abandoned, if a reference to the Court is to be avoided.[94] Parties thus face the dilemma of deciding upon a course of action involving modification or abandonment if an agreement cannot be considered for a section 21(2) exemption. Negotiations concerning modification or outright abandonment would thus occur *after* the OFT have decided that a section 21(2) exemption is inappropriate. In cases of agreements containing restrictions of the type noted above the OFT will discard the section 21(2) option almost immediately. Where the OFT takes a strict line on a registered restriction, for example because it seeks to set prices or fees, reference to the Court is not as likely as it would be in respect of an unregistered agreement.[95] If parties can persuade the OFT of their firm intention not to revive the agreement, the OFT may well decide not to refer. Parties should consider positively giving such assurances.

4.89 It would, however, be rare for the DGFT to accept assurances in lieu of orders of the RPC. One example where assurances *were* accepted occurred in June 1992 when the DGFT announced that he had received assurances from a number of major milk retailers by which they undertook not to make agreements to fix the price of milk and other products sold by milk roundsmen and not to collude in tendering for the supply of milk. The assurances were given following discovery in the 1980s of a large number of unlawful price fixing and collusive tendering agreements. The agreements had, by 1992, all been ended. The then DGFT (Sir Gordon Borrie) stated:

> "I will not tolerate unlawful price fixing agreements. In this case I am pleased that I have been able to secure undertaking not to make such arrangements without myself or the retailers incurring a great expense of time and money on Court action. These undertakings are generally given by the companies now operating in the business, some of whom would not have been bound by Court orders. The companies have agreed to consult my Office about the arrangements that they will make to ensure compliance with the undertakings."

One factor which affected the decision of the DGFT to accept assurances was that there had been a number of changes of ownership in the milk retailing and wholesaling business as concerned since the agreements were made and a number of the companies who gave assurances were thus not parties to those agreements. The assurances committed the parties: (a) not to make any agreements registrable under the RTPA 1976 which restricted the prices to be charged for liquid milk or other products sold by milk roundsmen; (b) not to make any agreements registrable under the RTPA 1976 which constituted collusive tendering in relation to the supply of liquid milk or other products through milk roundsmen; (c) not to make any other registrable agreements affecting liquid milk

[94] See DGFT Annual Report 1979, p. 45.

[95] References in respect of registered agreements are made under s. 1(2) RTPA 1976 and Court orders are made under s. 2(2) RTPA 1976. For discussion see paras. 5.2–5.20.

or other products sold through milk roundsmen without first providing particulars to the DGFT; (d) to institute a programme to ensure employees complied with the undertakings; (e) to supply details of the compliance programmes to the DGFT and to give due weight to any comments or suggestions made by the DGFT with a view to improving the effectiveness of such programmes. In the light of these undertakings the DGFT decided not to refer the agreements to the RPC.[96]

4.90 If they are referred to the Court and an order is made against them such an order can hang like an administrative millstone around the necks of responsible directors and managers of the firms subject to the order. Breach of the order, however innocuous or unintentional, may result in the parties being in contempt of court, with the serious repercussions that entails. A Court order places a severe and continuous administrative onus on parties to institute monitoring and compliance systems to avoid contempt.[97]

2. *Termination, Registration and Novation*

4.91 As has already been discussed (see para. 4.87) where parties have unwittingly entered and failed to register a relatively innocuous restrictive agreement, an escape route does exist which enables them to avoid the potentially serious consequences of non-registration. Parties must immediately terminate the agreement, thus allowing the OFT to exercise its discretion not to refer determined agreements to the Court. Subsequently, they must furnish the details of the agreement to the OFT for registration, and finally, they must create an entirely new agreement on the terms of the old. It is not enough simply to reactivate the old agreement (by ratification) since this would be simply to revive an unlawful, unregistered agreement. It is, legally speaking, a wiser course to novate the old agreement; that is to say, to create a new agreement on the terms of the old. This involves re-signing and re-dating the contract. Parties who wish to adopt this course should ensure that the OFT concurs in it.

3. *Agreements Filleted of all Relevant Restrictions*

4.92 Many businessmen decide that rather than conduct lengthy negotiations with the OFT about registrable restrictions they will fillet out of their agreements all of the restrictions. In this respect three broad categories of agreement are to be found:

(i) Agreements where the restrictions are the central part of the agreement and are its *raison d'être*. In such cases filleting of restrictions berefts the agreement of all utility and parties must decide how important the agreement is to them and whether it is worth arguing over with the OFT.

(ii) Agreements containing restrictions that are peripheral to the central purpose of the agreement. Often trade associations recommend to their members that they adopt a standard form contract in their dealings with consumers. Such contracts may contain a substantial number of restrictions. If the OFT object to any of the restrictions the parties should consider seriously how valuable that particular restriction is to their business and whether it is worth defending in Court. Indeed, be-

[96] OFT Press Notice (11 June 1992). The agreements covered most of England and Wales and parts of Scotland. The OFT investigation occurred in the early 1980s. The agreements were terminated on or shortly after discovery by the OFT. Particulars of 158 agreements were entered on the register. A copy of the actual undertakings given by the companies concerned is set out in an annex to the Press Notice.

[97] See paras. 5.69–5.88.

fore entering into negotiations with the OFT, parties should, perhaps in conjunction with legal advisers, undertake a searching inventory and evaluation of the utility of every registrable restriction in the agreement. Further, they should have in their minds an idea of the relative value of each restriction to their trade. This will enable parties to know how far to go in making concessions or in agreeing to modifications. In the *Association of British Travel Agents*[98] case, for example, ABTA refused, in the face of OFT opposition, to terminate its collective exclusive dealing arrangement whereby travel agents who were ABTA members could only deal with tour operators who were ABTA members and vice versa. ABTA decided to defend this agreement before the Court and, although it was ordered to relinquish certain other restrictions, the Court accepted ABTA's public interest arguments concerning this collective exclusive dealing agreement which ABTA had termed the "stabiliser".

(iii) Agreements where the restrictions exist for historical reasons and have little or no bearing on the contract. In a number of cases parties include, as a matter of tradition, certain restrictions in contracts. The OFT when confronted with such clauses encourages the parties to assess the worth of the restriction and fillet where possible. Many trade associations have taken the opportunity to reassess their standard form contracts and modify them so as to either avoid registration altogether or render them suitable to a section 21 (2) direction.[99]

4.93 As an illustration, during 1978–80 various service supply associations of media owners undertook detailed reviews of their marketing practices. In particular, they reconsidered the methods of payment of commission to advertising agencies and further, they reviewed the criteria employed in deciding whether or not to recognise a particular agency. The associations had accepted a number of restrictions as to the agencies to whom, and the terms on which, commission and credit should be given. In January 1979 the Newspaper Publishers Association and the Newspaper Society recommended to members revised rules whereby each member company would grant credit to listed advertising agencies who satisfied certain basic financial criteria. Recommendations concerning the competence or experience of agencies were dropped following OFT pressure. Moreover, no recommendations were in future to be made as to commission and members would be free to offer credit to non-listed agencies. In his Annual Report for 1980 the DGFT commented: "The modified agreements involve major changes and the Director General will need to have experience of the working of any new scheme and its effects before he can come to a final conclusion as to the significance of the remaining restrictions."[100]

4.94 Companies undertaking revisions and reviews of existing practices may submit draft variations of registered agreements to the OFT for the latter's opinion. In such cases the OFT, in accordance with standard practice, will usually seek the views of concerned third parties before making any final assessment of the significance of the restrictions.[101]

98 [1984] ICR 12.

99 See e.g. DGFT Annual Report 1979, p. 42.

100 DGFT Annual Report 1980, p. 44. Other service supply associations followed suit in 1980, for example, the Periodical Publishers Association, the Scottish Daily Newspapers Society, the Association of Independent Radio Contractors, and the Independent Television Companies Association. In 1984 the OFT undertook a detailed investigation into the practices of British Telecommunications pricing policy for the placing of advertisement in Yellow Pages Directories, under the Competition Act 1980. The conclusion was that there was no anti-competitive practice in operation. See OFT Report, 10 October 1984.

101 DGFT Annual Report 1979, p. 43. Though in the light of recent changes in administrative procedure the OFT might request parties to register the variations before the OFT assess them.

4. *Effluxion of Time: Expired Agreements*

4.95 Many agreements lapse because they have run their allotted contractual time and have no further relevance. A typical example of such cases are sale of assets agreements. Where a business is sold the agreement for the sale of assets may sometimes be registrable. For example, a parent company may sell off a subsidiary under a contract which requires the former parent not to engage for a stipulated period of time (for example 12 months) in any business which would compete with that of the subsidiary which was sold. Such an agreement might be registrable (subject of course to applicable exemptions for certain categories of vendor covenants under the Restrictive Trade Practices (Sale and Purchase and Share Subscription Agreements) (Goods) Order 1989 S.I. 1989 No. 1081) if the subsidiary also accepts restrictions.

G. Negotiations under section 21(2): Dispensation from Reference to the Court

4.96 Parties to agreements may obtain dispensation from reference to the Court. Section 21(2) RTPA 1976 empowers the OFT to make representations to the Secretary of State for the latter to direct the OFT to refrain from referring an agreement to the Court. The OFT may only make such a representation upon the basis that the restrictions "are not of such significance as to call for investigation by the Court". A central question therefore is what is meant by "significance". Other important issues for businessmen and advisers to note are the stages through which section 21(2) cases will proceed.

1. *The Relevance of Public Interest Arguments in Determining Significance*

4.97 The concept of "significance" is by no means an easy one to define. In 1975 the OFT stated:

> "Broadly speaking the criteria now adopted in deciding whether or not a representation can be made is whether the agreement appears capable of causing detriment of the kind which the Court might take into account if the agreement came before it. Thus a primary consideration is whether the agreement is likely to reduce competition between those affected in any material respect which would be disadvantageous to consumers or customers or whether it is likely to produce discriminatory or other unfair results."

4.98 There is an implication in this statement[102] that the OFT undertake a preliminary assessment of the public interest. This derives from the words in the statement that they assess restrictions for "detriment of the kind which the Court might take into account if the agreement came before it". Such an implication is wrong and misleading. The word "detriment" is a key word in Court proceedings to assess restrictive agreement. A restrictive agreement referred to the Court must satisfy various public interest criteria laid down in the RTPA 1976 (in section 10(1)(a)–(h) for goods and section 19(1)(a)–(h) for services). If an agreement satisfies these criteria (known as the gateways; see paras. 5.21–5.64) it must also pass muster under what is known as the "balancing tailpiece" test. Under this test of

[102] DGFT Annual Report 1973, p. 35. An almost identical definition was given in the 1975 Report (at p. 49) except that the word "disadvantageous" in the 1973 statement inexplicably changed to "advantageous". This discrepancy must have been an error.

restrictive agreements (which is laid out at the end of sections 10(1) and 19(1) RTPA 1976) parties must prove that the public interest points in their favour outweigh "any detriment to the public or to persons not parties to the agreement". This rather oblique reference to detriment, not surprisingly, has given rise to some confusion. Accordingly, OFT statements clarified the use of the word. In 1979, the OFT stated:

> "Previous reports have explained the use of section 21(2) of the Act and the powers and responsibilities of the Director General in relation to those of the Court, but experience has shown that there is still room for mis-understanding and the following points bear repeating. The Office forms a considered view of the significance of restrictions. They may be significant because, for example, they limit suppliers freedom to make their own decisions about prices, charges or methods of trading. Any restriction which appears capable of causing detriments either to consumers or to other traders as a consequence, for example, of a reduction in competition or because it has discriminatory of unfair results, is in principle a matter a significance. It is then up to the parties to decide whether they wish to defend any such restriction before the Court, to modify it, or to abandon it. If any restriction is to be defended, the whole of the agreement must be referred to the Court. In considering the question of significance, the Office needs to take into account the views of interested parties and users of the services. Most associations continue to show considerable willingness to co-operate in reducing the constraints on their members and in achieving more equitable and reasonable agreements. In several cases they have welcomed the opportunity to review long-standing provisions which are no longer apposite."[103]

4.99 Thus the OFT focuses its analysis on the economic consequences of a restriction especially as it affects the parties. Economists can play a role in the evaluation of restrictions. The OFT is aware that the scheme of the RTPA is against allowing an administrative body, such as the OFT, the right to decide upon public policy matters. The OFT has publicly accepted this limitation upon its discretion under section 21(2):

> "It is not always appreciated that the Director General's concern is with the question whether or not a restriction is of significance for the Court; if it is, he must refer it, if it is not, he may make a representation to the Secretary of State. Wider considerations of the public interest which may justify a restriction are for the Court only to decide and the legislation specifies various grounds ('gateways') on which the parties to an agreement may argue that the restrictions in it are not on balance against the public interest."[104]

4.100 It follows that in negotiating with the OFT the sorts of matters laid down in sections 10(1) and 19(1) RTPA 1976 (the "gateways") are immaterial. This at least is the tenor of the statements made by the OFT and is largely correct. Thus, for example, arguments to the effect that the restriction is needed: to protect the public against injury; to prevent serious unemployment; or to maintain export earnings, will be rejected by the OFT. However, some of the gateways do apply economic criteria of a nature that would be relevant in determining "significance". In particular, sections 10(1)(h) and 19(1)(h) provide that restrictive agreements might be acceptable where they do not "directly or indirectly restrict or discourage competition to any material degree". This applies a *de minimis* rule to restrictions such that where they have no significant effect upon competition they may be acceptable. The word "significance" in section 21(2) can be equated with an assessment of effect of a restriction on competition. The Liesner Committee, *Review of Restrictive Trade Practices Policy* in 1979 expressly recognised the relationship between sec-

[103] DGFT Annual Report 1979, p. 45.

[104] DGFT Annual Report 1977, p. 38. Though, the DGFT does now have powers to consider public interest arguments under the Competition Act 1980 following the amendments brought about by the Deregulation and Contracting Out Act 1994.

tion 21(2) and sections 10(1)(h) and 19(1)(h) RTPA 1976 when it stated of those sections: "one possible application would be to challenge before the Court the Director General of Fair Trading's refusal to make a section 21 (2) representation to the Secretary of State, or the latter's refusal to discharge the Director General of Fair Trading from taking an insignificant agreement before the Court".[105]

4.101 From the above it is clear that the concept of significance (or insignificance) is essentially an economic concept. It does not embrace *broad* public policy considerations but does appear to include public policy considerations where these are *narrowly* grounded in economic principle and relate specifically to the parties own circumstances. Therefore, simply because a negotiating factor under section 21(2) has a counterpart in the "gateways" in sections 10 and 19 RTPA 1976 does not mean that it must necessarily be excluded as a submission to the OFT. Nonetheless, it should be clearly understood that whilst parties may submit economic arguments, the OFT may reject them if it considers them to have a public interest grounding.

2. *De Minimis: Small-Scale Agreements and Significance*

4.102 Agreements whose economic effect is marginal may now be exempted from notification under the Restrictive Trade Practices (Non-notifiable Agreements) (Turnover Threshold) Order 1996.[106]

3. *Reasonableness, the Unfair Contract Terms Act 1977: the Unfair Terms in Consumer Contracts Regulations 1994 and Significance*

4.103 The OFT hold that restrictions that injure the consumer's interests are significant:

> "The recommendation of standard terms and conditions by an association is not regarded as necessarily having a significant effect on competition but, to ensure there is no likely detriment, the terms should be fair and reasonable to all concerned, not likely to mislead those who will use them, and not unnecessarily exclude variations to meet special circumstances and requirements. The benefit to customers of having standard conditions must be balanced against any detriment to them of being deprived of the freedom to secure more favourable terms than those likely to result from the restrictions imposed by them. In general, mandatory standard terms and conditions are not regarded as suitable for section 21(2) since they are not variable to meet special circumstances. In all cases the recommended terms and conditions are looked at clause by clause."[107]

4.104 Trade associations registering recommended standard form contracts often encounter the criticism that the terms of the agreement are not fair and reasonable. The OFT applies the broad test of reasonableness laid down in the Unfair Contract Terms Act 1977. That Act prohibits absolutely certain types of contract clause but, in the main, renders exclusion and limitation of liability clauses valid only if "reasonable". Although the Act provides no precise definition of the meaning of "reasonable", it does provide some detailed guidelines for use. The OFT justifies application of this Act on the basis that an "unreasonable" restriction cannot be insignificant. Moreover, an agreement that is unreasonable would, when referred to the Court (no section 21(2) dispensation being available)

[105] Cmnd 7512, annex D, para. 10.
[106] S.I. 1996 No. 348, issued under s. 27A(1)(b) and 27A(2)(a) RTPA 1976, as inserted by s. 10 Deregulation and Contracting Out Act 1994. See paras. 2.239–2.249.
[107] Cmnd 7512, Annex C(4) and DGFT Annual Report 1980, p. 51.

be struck down under the balancing tailpiece even if it managed to pass through the public interest gateways. The balancing tailpiece provides that for an agreement to be acceptable it must be established that a restriction "is not unreasonable having regard to the balance between those [public interest] circumstances and any detriment to the public or to persons not parties to the agreements". Thus, the Court must itself apply a test of reasonableness.

4.105 What is or what is not a reasonable clause is a matter for debate (see paras. 11.9–11.26 on terms and conditions of trade). Where standard form contracts are concerned reference may be made to the Unfair Contract Terms Act 1977 and to cases on the meaning of "reasonableness" under that Act. The OFT considers that the Act is difficult for individuals and small companies to enforce and litigate and therefore it seeks to ensure that trade associations in drafting standard form contracts do not exploit any superior bargaining strength they might possess. Where parties are of equal or roughly equal strength and a standard form contract has been freely negotiated the OFT is more likely to adopt a laissez-faire attitude on the basis that a clause freely agreed upon will only in exceptional circumstances be unfair. The same analysis should apply to unfair terms under the Unfair Terms in Consumer Contracts Regulations.[108] The intent of the legislation is to prevent exploitation of consumers. In 1995 the OFT set up a Unfair Contract Terms Unit within the office to enable the DGFT to exercise his power to enforce the Regulations. This will clearly affect the view taken of significance under section 21(2).[109]

4.106 In *British Bottle Association's Agreement* the Court condemned an exclusion of liability clause in a standard form contract used by members of the British Bottle Association. This strict approach was adopted even though the clause was rarely if ever enforced against purchasers of bottles:

> "No purchaser, who gave evidence and who was asked the question, was aware of the existence of this clause as a part of his contract for the purchase of bottles. We would only say this: we would have had no hesitation whatever in declaring this restriction to be against the public interest, even if all the other restrictions had been in the public interest."[110]

4.107 A number of points may be extracted from the decision in *British Bottle Association* which may be cited as justification for the OFT approach. First, simply because the purchaser under a standard form contract may be a company rather than an ultimate individual consumer does not necessarily mean that a restrictive clause will be presumed to be freely agreed to. Second, restrictive clauses that exist for historical reasons alone and which are not commonly applied in practice should be reviewed and where possible removed.[111] Third, the Court adopts a strict approach to limitation and exclusion clauses thereby justifying an equally vigorous approach by the OFT.

4. Discrimination, Unfairness and Significance

4.108 The OFT have consistently repeated the view that an agreement which leads to discriminatory or unfair consequences is significant and no section 21(2) representation

108 S.I. 1994 No. 3159. These regulations implement the Unfair Terms in Consumer Contracts Directive, OJ 1993 L95/29.
109 See *Fair Trading* Vol. 10 (Summer 1995), pp. 16, 17.
110 [1961] 1 WLR 760 at p. 792.
111 Given that the Act contains a presumption that restrictions are against the public interest one that has no practical effect or value must necessarily succumb to the presumption. If no arguments may be argued for its retention then it should be filleted.

may be made. A not uncommon example derives from "approved lists" whereby an association recommend to its members that they only deal with either firms approved by the association or who satisfy certain criteria. Approval systems *per se* are not necessarily objectionable so long as the criteria employed for granting approved status are fair and non-discriminatory. Thus approval by reference to commercially justifiable standards of financial liquidity or creditworthiness might be permissible. However, where an association recommends quality or competence criteria, discriminatory results may well result. The OFT contend, for example, that for a trade association to deter its members from dealing with customers who do not meet quality standards is to unfairly prejudice firms who serve the lower end of the market. Further, it denies consumers the choice of buying cheaper, lower quality goods or services.[112]

4.109 Likewise if an association recommends that members provide better discounts to members of a purchasers organisation than to independents this discriminates against independents *vis-à-vis* competing aligned firms. A common problem that might lead to discriminatory or unfair results is the maintenance of credit lists where associations or groups of companies operate credit assessment schemes under which the creditworthiness of customers is assessed and members of the scheme advised accordingly. If the scheme runs on anything other than totally objective data it runs a risk of unfairly labelling a person a bad credit risk. The criteria adopted for assessment will be carefully scrutinised by the OFT.[113]

5. Consumer Choice and Significance

4.110 Any agreement having a material effect upon competition cannot be treated as insignificant as the *LWT–Football League agreement*[114] shows. In 1979 the OFT threatened to apply to the Court for an interim order under section 3 RTPA 1976 against London Weekend Television Limited (LWT) and the Football League. The latter granted LWT exclusive rights to televise football matches played under the League's jurisdiction for a three-year period commencing 1 July 1979. This agreement superseded arrangements existing between the League, the BBC and the independent companies. The OFT complained that this would reduce choice for consumers and limit coverage. The agreement was exclusionary in that the BBC was effectively precluded from covering football. In response to such pressures the parties abandoned the agreement and entered a new one which brought in the BBC. The OFT has over the years dealt with literally hundreds of sports coverage agreements of this nature. The longer the period of exclusivity the more likely it is that the OFT will view the agreement as restrictive of competition. The size of the parties and the length of the exclusivity period meant that the effects of the agreement would inevitably be material.

4.111 Choice is an essential ingredient in competition; hence the standardisation of contract terms between suppliers can reduce an important part of that competition. There are certainly benefits for supplier and consumer to be derived from standard form contracts. None the less, the OFT adopts a thorough clause by clause approach to standard form contracts recommended by associations. The standardisation, for example, of credit periods can eradicate an important factor that customers look to when choosing between firms.

112 See e.g. the approved advertising agency systems operated by the various associations of media owners. DGFT Annual Report 1979, p. 44.

113 See e.g. No. 3669 Restrictive Trade Practices Register, *Agreement between Members of Aberdeen Fish Salesmen Association Ltd*, s. 21(2) dispensation given.

114 DGFT Annual Report 1979, p. 46. The OFT has referred broadcasting arrangements for Premier League football matches to the RPC; no date for hearing had been set at the time of writing.

Similarly, the harmonisation of even mundane clauses can, *in extremis*, be relevant, though usually the harmonisation of non-essential contract matters is suitable on a *de minimis* basis (see above) for section 21(2) representation. For example in the *Association of Domestic Laundry and Cleaning Services Code of Practice* (drawn up with OFT assistance) guideline 10 for implementing the code exhorted that: "Members accept liability for loss or damage arising out of fire or burglary even when they are not negligent (when the customer has no insurance himself)... Members are therefore strongly recommended to check that their insurance cover is adequate to indemnify them (i.e. Members) in such circumstances." Members of the association thus refrained from exempting liability even though they might legally have been entitled to do so when it was "reasonable" under the Unfair Contract Terms Act 1977. It is possible that in the absence of the Code some laundry firms might have legally excluded liability and passed on the savings they made (from not being liable) in insurance costs to the consumer in the form of lower charges. Thus the standardised term might marginally have affected competition. The OFT, none the less, obtained section 21(2) dispensation for the code, upon the basis that there was no material effect on competition.[115]

6. *Section 21(2) Applies to the Significance of the Restriction and not the Agreement*

4.112 In evaluating a registered agreement the OFT assess only the restrictions in the agreement *not* the agreement as a whole. In 1980 the OFT stated: "It is important to note that it is not the significance of the agreement as a whole which has to be considered, but that of the restrictions in it. Agreements significant in themselves, but in which all the restrictions are insignificant, are acceptable for a representation." For example in 1980, section 21(2) dispensation was given to an agreement between two large corporations to set up a joint venture company to produce starch and gluten. The two parents—Reed International Ltd and Rank Hovis McDougal—agreed not to compete with the joint venture company and Rank Hovis McDougal agreed to supply the company's requirements of wheat flour. The restrictions were agreed in the context of a venture between two substantial companies and involved large sums of money. However, they were insignificant in their effect upon competition because of the limited extent to which the two companies competed with each other.[116]

4.113 It is not therefore the turnover of the parties which is relevant. Nor is it the monetary value of the contract. The principal question is whether the restrictions in the agreement are significant. Any other conclusion would, of course, be commercially unrealistic since otherwise agreements between large companies would always be unsuitable for section 21(2) representation and would either have to be modified or face referral to the Court.

7. *Summary of "Significance" in Section 21(2)*

4.114 In conclusion the following points may be reiterated:

[115] No. S12 Register of Restrictive Trade Practices. See also Nos. S572 and S13 Register of Restrictive Trade Practices, *Agreement between St. Crispins Boot Trade Association and Members of the National Association of Shoe Repair Factories* concerning a code of practice for shoe repairs. Members were made aware that the council of the Association recommended both the Code and the guide to the Code to members. The Code contains a clause under which members refrained from limiting their legal liability for repairs they carried out.

[116] No. 3785 Register of Restrictive Trade Practices (1980).

(a) Significance is an economic concept which does not incorporate public interest considerations such as those laid out in the "gateways" in sections 10 and 19 RTPA 1976.
(b) A *de minimis* rule applies such that restrictions whose effect upon competition is insubstantial or insignificant are suitable for section 21(2) treatment despite the fact that prima facie the restriction takes an objectionable form. Section 21(2) is one of the few instances in the RTPA 1976 where effect is more important than form.[117]
(c) Trade association recommendations and recommended standard form contracts must ensure that their terms are reasonable taking into account the meaning of reasonableness in the Unfair Contract Terms Act 1977 and in the Unfair Terms and Consumer Contracts Regulations.[118]
(d) Trade association recommendations and recommended standard form contracts should ensure that their terms are not discriminatory or unfair, i.e. that like categories of customer are treated alike. Discriminatory terms will be considered "significant" in section 21(2) terms.
(e) Agreements, trade association recommendations, and, recommended standard form contracts should not unduly limit consumer choice.
(f) In assessing "significance" under section 21(2) the OFT examine the registrable restrictions and *not* the overall agreement.

H. OFT Procedure for Evaluation of Agreements

1. *Prima Facie Examination to Determine Registrability*

4.115 On receipt of an agreement the OFT must determine whether it is registrable. Usually the OFT first checks that the documents furnished sufficiently and accurately record the provisions of the agreement. The OFT might request clarification or further documents from the parties. The mere fact that parties have furnished documents is not of course relevant given that many parties furnish on a fail-safe basis when uncertain of an agreement's registrability. In complex agreements, for example, standard form contracts recommended by service supply associations involving financial restrictions, the OFT might adopt a "prima-facie examination" approach whereby they examine the agreement to check whether the minimum requirements for registrability are satisfied leaving aside other matters for future considerations. This approach was common during the period 1976–78 when services agreements were being furnished in large numbers following the calling up Order of 1976 requiring services agreements to be registered.[119] Nearly 600 agreements were furnished to the OFT between the commencement of the Order and the end of 1976.[120] Sometimes the registrability of an agreement cannot be dealt with on this basis, and in such circumstances, negotiations by correspondence and discussion might occur over a lengthy time period in order to determine whether the Act applies.[121] For instance an agreement fixing the fees to be charged by two firms of mapping and ocean

[117] The Restrictive Trade Practices (Non-notifiable Agreements) (Turnover Threshold) Order S.I. 1996 No. 348 also takes effect into consideration, see paras. 2.239–2.249.
[118] S.I. 1994 No. 3159.
[119] Restrictive Trade Practices (Services) Order 1976 S.I. 1976 No. 98.
[120] DGFT Annual Report 1976, p. 36.
[121] *ibid.*

surveillance consultants might well be exempt from the Act under Schedule 1, para. 13 RTPA 1976 which exempts from the Act professional services including services of professional engineers and technologists. The provision gives a long elaboration of categories of engineer and technologist. Whether the fee fixing agreement described above fell within the exemption would depend upon factual information defining the scope of mapping and ocean surveillance activities. The OFT might decide that, on the facts, the agreement was exempt as relating to (say) "mining, quarrying, soil analysis or other forms of mineralogy or geology" (Schedule 1, para. 13(c)) or "mechanical, aeronautical, marine, electrical or electronic engineering" (Schedule 1, para. 13(b)). The OFT has commented: "It frequently involves as much time and effort, if not more, to determine that a particular agreement is not registrable as to reach a conclusion that it is."[122]

2. *Worst Restrictions First*

4.116 When services agreement first became registrable the OFT adopted a selective approach to agreements tackling the most blatant and obviously significant restrictions first leaving others until time allowed a more detailed examination. According to the OFT this approach achieved the rapid abandonment of major restrictions in many agreements albeit that some lesser restrictions remained to be negotiated over.[123] Given that certain categories of agreement are as yet unregistrable, principally services information agreements (see para. 1.107), it is possible that this approach will be redeployed if a sudden flush of such agreements were to become registrable by virtue of an Order of the Secretary of State.

3. *Negotiations and Third Parties' Submissions*

4.117 It will be recalled that when considering any "detriment" that results from a restriction the OFT looks to the consequences for consumers and other third parties. The OFT requests these parties to submit their comments. There are no rules as to who may submit comments, though the OFT gives considerable weight to the comments of those who are, or may be, affected by the restrictions. Thus, the views of customers and consumers are important, or users where services are concerned. Collecting this information can be a lengthy process spanning many months. Interested parties may present their submissions to the OFT at a meeting, or in writing. Where the person submitting information to the OFT so desires confidentiality may be secured. Some third parties are clearly concerned that in submitting information to the OFT they are damaging their commercial relations with the parties to the agreement, or even inviting retaliatory action.

4.118 When the OFT consults third parties it sometimes discovers that such persons have already been influential in the shape of the agreement. In such cases, what at first sight might have appeared unduly restrictive might turn out to be perfectly acceptable to third parties. For illustration, in *Tugowners Association Standard Towage Conditions* the OFT examined a variation of a standard form contract used by providers of towage services which sought to exclude liability for every type of imaginable liability howsoever caused. The contract operated in the context of agreements between tug owners and owners of ships which were to be towed in and out of port. Ostensibly the clauses were patently unreasonable throwing all of the risk on to ship owners. Section 21(2) dispensation however was given in 1984 following the

[122] *ibid*. Initial estimates in 1976–77 of agreements furnished but found not to be registrable suggested that up to one third of furnished agreements were outside of the Act. Later statistics suggest that nearly half of all furnished agreements are not registrable. See paras. 4.30–4.31.

[123] DGFT Annual Report 1977, p. 37.

submissions of third parties. The British Maritime Law Association (BMLA) wrote to the OFT stating that it had already examined the agreement and given its approval. It noted further that membership of the BMLA included: the General Council of British Shipping; the British Tugowners Association; Lloyds of London; and the P&I. Clubs (shipping insurers). The major insurers of shipping—the P&I. Clubs—also wrote individually to the OFT explaining how the exclusion clauses were not unreasonable when viewed in the overall context of insurance which counterbalanced the benefits and burdens of the exclusion clauses.[124]

4. *Negotiating Modifications to Agreements*

4.119 The options open to parties once agreements have been registered have already been discussed. Essentially, parties may: terminate and abandon the agreement; fillet the agreement of all the registrable terms; fillet the agreement of such terms as render it unsuitable for representation; refuse to negotiate modifications and seek to defend the agreement before the RPC. The OFT might be involved in processing as many as 200 plus agreements at any one time. Negotiations can take many months to complete, well over one year can sometimes elapse before a result is reached. Though if the parties invoke the Fast Track Procedure (see paras. 4.26–4.29) the response time may be more rapid. The OFT refuses to redraft agreements for parties. It will however make known their objections to a restriction but then it falls to parties to suggest amendments which will overcome those objections.

4.120 In terms of actual procedure, the OFT notifies the parties of its initial identification of restrictions giving them a preliminary view of their significance. After it has consulted third parties it will give to the parties to the agreement a more detailed, considered view of the restrictions.[125]

5. *Representation by the OFT to the Secretary of State*

4.121 When the OFT is satisfied that an agreement is suitable for a representation, a representation is drafted for submission to the Secretary of State. The representation is not simply a letter requesting a direction to refrain from taking court proceedings. It usually takes the form of an analysis of the legal and economic considerations which make the agreement suitable for representation. It has been very loosely described as a "mini-MMC report". Thus depending on circumstances the submission may contain details of such factors as:

(a) the parties and their backgrounds for example their size, market-share, turnover etc.;
(b) why the agreement is registrable and full details of its terms;
(c) the history of negotiations with the company and the extent (if any) of the subsequent modifications;
(d) why the agreement as it stands is acceptable and what the economic consequences and characteristics of the agreement are;
(e) the identities of third parties and what their views were including OFT appraisal of these views;
(f) the nature of the geographical and product market.

[124] No. S161 Register of Restrictive Trade practices, *British Tugowners Association Standard Towage Conditions* (s. 21(2) dispensation given in 1984).
[125] DGFT Annual Report 1978, p. 42.

4.122 The length and detail of the representation varies. Easier cases, for example sale of asset cases, require relatively short reports. Complex cases, for example concerning standard form contracts drafted by services supply associations, may require detailed, lengthy reports. Both lawyers and economists play a part in preparation of these reports.

4.123 Parties have no right to inspect the representation. Nor is it otherwise published at any point. Clearly, if the parties to a furnishing of particulars provide the information requested in the Annex to form RTP(C) then the OFT is able to prepare its section 21(2) report more rapidly and fully.

6. *Directions Given by the Secretary of State*

4.124 If the OFT representation is accepted by the Secretary of State the Director General will be notified that he need not refer the restrictive agreement to the Restrictive Practices Court. In practice staff at the Department of Trade and Industry (DTI) review the representations. Only very rarely do they query a representation made by the OFT. Occasionally a request for further data is made or an enquiry as to the views of a third party who does not seem to have been consulted is made.

4.125 If the Secretary of State accepts that restrictions in an agreement are not of significance he is not bound to give a direction discharging the Director General from commencing proceedings. Section 21(2) merely states that if it appears to the Secretary of State that a restriction is not of significance he "may" direct the Director General to refrain from taking court proceedings. There might be delicate circumstances relevant to the agreement known to the Secretary of State which convince him that a full examination of the case by the Court is desirable. Consultation by the DTI with other governmental departments is sometimes made.

7. *Post-Direction Monitoring by the OFT: section 21(3)*

4.126 Once a direction has been given to the OFT permitting it to refrain from referring an agreement to the Court, the OFT may at any time apply to the Secretary of State under section 21(3) RTPA 1976 for the directions given by him to be withdrawn. The criteria for such a withdrawal is that there has been, "a material change of circumstances" since the directions were given. The Director General is not bound to seek withdrawal of a direction simply because of a material change of circumstance. Certainly a direction by the Secretary of State for withdrawal of a direction could in principle be subject to judicial review on the basis that there was not a "material change of circumstances" justifying withdrawal of a direction. Such an action has never been commenced. However, the Court has heard actions on the meaning of the words "prima facie evidence of a material change in the relevant circumstances" under section 4(4) RTPA 1976. This permits the parties to apply to the Court to be relieved from a previous Court order made against them. To succeed they must establish "prima facie evidence of a material, change in the relevant circumstances". In *Cement Makers Federation Agreement No. 2*[126] the Court accepted the arguments of counsel for the Director General that this phrase meant that the applicant had to show that by reason of new facts there was a prima facie change in an essential part of the reasoning by which the Court had come to its previous conclusions. If this applies to section 21(3) then the Secretary of State may only with-

[126] [1974] ICR 445, noted DGFT Annual Report 1973, pp. 68-70. See also *Mallaig and North-west Fishermen's Association No. 2* (unreported) noted DGFT Annual Report 1975, pp. 90, 91.

draw a direction where satisfied that a material change in circumstances has arisen such as to effect an essential part of the reasoning which led him to grant the initial application made by the OFT. When comparing section 4(4) with section 21(3) two differences should be borne in mind. First, the words from section 4(4) noted above apply to *applications* by parties to the Court for the variation of an order, they do not relate to the making of the decision by the Court. Section 21(3) conversely uses the words to refer to the actual *making* of the decision to withdraw directions.[127] Second, the evidentiary burden appears different in both sections. In section 4(4) the parties may act by making an application where they have "prima facie evidence". In section 21(3) the Secretary of State may act by withdrawing a direction only where "satisfied" that a material change in circumstances has occurred. The latter appears to be the stricter burden of proof of the two provisions which should be some comfort to parties. None the less, these differences alone should not be sufficient to alter the basic conclusion above concerning the *Cement Makers* case and its relevance to section 21(3).

4.127 There is little doubt but that the Secretary of State may also review a direction and withdraw it where there is evidence of fraud or misrepresentation by the parties, for instance in furnishing inaccurate data or documents for registration.[128] However, it is less clear whether a direction can be revoked where the Secretary of State made an error in granting a direction or where there is a material error in the representation of the OFT which persuaded the Secretary of State to grant the direction but where the parties correctly and in good faith furnished details of their agreement. Is discovery of such an error by the authorities a material change in circumstances justifying withdrawal of the direction? Under normal circumstances section 21(3) would be used in respect of the behaviour of the firms themselves. For example, an agreement given a section 21(2) direction on *de minimis* grounds may become significant because one of the parties is taken over and its economic power overnight increases dramatically changing it from a minor to a major participant in the market. It might also be used where for political (e.g. EC) reasons the market structure changes.[129]

4.128 In administrative law a decision by a competent authority once made is prima facie irrevocable.[130] However, many powers conferred by statute are subject to ancillary powers to entertain fresh proceedings and make a different decision. An example would be planning applications which may be varied at any time if a fresh application is made. Often the power to review expressly includes cases of mistake.[131] Even where express powers are not conferred it has been strongly argued that statutory tribunals have inherent juris-

[127] Under s. 4(1) RTPA 1976 the Court may discharge or vary a previous Order where it "appears to the Court to be proper at the time of the hearing" to do so. The Court is thus apparently not bound by any evidentiary burden.

[128] See e.g. *Lazarus Estates Ltd* v *Beasley* [1956] 1 QB 702 at p. 712 *per* Lord Denning MR: "No judgment of a Court, no order of a Minister, can be allowed to stand if it has been obtained by fraud. Fraud unravels everything."

[129] See *Mallaig and North-west Fishermen's Association No. 2* (unreported), noted DGFT Annual Report 1975, pp. 90, 91—Common Agricultural Policy of EC required parties to do things they were prohibited from doing by a court order. Court accordingly changed its order under s. 4 RTPA 1976.

[130] See Wade, *Administrative Law* (7th edn. 1994), pp. 263–264. For cases see: *Gould* v *Bacup Local Board* (1881) 50 LJMC 44—local authority unable to change its policy when it has already informed affected parties by notice that it intended to rely upon a different policy. Wade (*ibid.*, at p. 263) comments on this case: "Although the Court said that the authority's notice would estop it, the true ground of decision was probably that the election, once formally made, was a legal act which there was no power to undo"; see also *Livingstone* v *Westminster Corp* [1904] 2 KB 109.

[131] See Wade, *op. cit.*, at p. 262.

diction to set aside judgments obtained by fraud and to review decisions where facts subsequently discovered reveal a miscarriage of justice.[132] Case law on whether mistake justifies vitiating a previous decision is scant. One judgment suggests that the power to review on grounds of mistake does exist. In *Rootkin* v *Kent CC*[133] a local authority agreed to pay the travel costs to school of a girl who the authorities believed lived more than three miles away from school. The authority thus considered themselves under a statutory duty to pay. When they subsequently discovered that the girl lived within a three-mile radius of school they sought to withhold payment. The Court of Appeal held that the first decision was not irrevocable and that the decision was not taken in the exercise of any power to determine a legal right and hence could not affect the duty to exercise the discretion when the true facts materialised.

4.129 Although section 21(3) seems only to envisage withdrawal of a direction, in practice it has been used by the OFT as a lever to obtain variations of agreements as well. In 1979 the OFT stated:

> "The work also involves examining variations to agreements already subject to directions, so as to decide whether or not it is necessary to seek the withdrawal of the directions on the ground that there has been a material change of circumstances since the directions were given. So far it has not been necessary to seek the withdrawal of directions on any varied agreement, but it has been necessary to seek amendments to some in order to allow the directions to stand."[134]

8. *Time*

4.130 The negotiation and analysis of registered agreements is not a rapid process. The briefest and easiest of cases (for example codes of practice drafted with OFT assistance under the Fair Trading Act 1973) may take six months from furnishing of documents to granting of section 21(2) directions. A "fast track procedure" is available under which the OFT will deal with certain agreements within two months. Details are set out at paras. 4.26–4.29. The period of time between OFT representation and Secretary of State grant of direction is approximately two to three months.

4.131 Some agreements take between one and two years to reach a result. An exceptionally difficult case may take up to three years. The causes of these delays are diverse. Though an agreement furnished to the OFT is at least safe from the potentially serious consequences of failure to register under section 35 RTPA 1976 (restrictions void; parties vulnerable to damages actions by affected third parties; reference to Court for injunctive order possible). Moreover, once furnished the agreement may continue until a final decision on it has been reached by the Court itself. It is thus not necessarily always in the parties best interests to expedite the process. The incentive to stall is the greater if parties are aware that the agreement is likely to be unacceptable to the OFT. In complex cases delay tactics are not the only problem. The OFT has to undertake detailed market analysis;[135] collect information from interested third parties; and of course negotiate modifications

132 See RSC Ord. 20, r. 11; *Hip Foong Hong* v *H. Neotia and Co* [1918] AC 888 (PC), and see Wade, *op. cit.*, at p. 262.

133 [1981] 1 WLR 1186 (CA).

134 DGFT Annual Report 1979, p. 47.

135 In one case the OFT had to look through piles of telephone books in order to be able to compile lists of growers of an agricultural product. This exercise was necessary in order to be able to assess how great the competition was to the parties to the agreement. This would indicate to them how much market power the parties possessed. See No. 4336 Register of Restrictive Trade Practices, *Banbury Marketing Services (Mushrooms)*.

to agreements with the parties. In cases where the agreement is anti-competitive but the effects are not readily identifiable from a simple reading of the agreement, some legal advisers take the view that the Annex to RTP(C) should not be filled in or done so only sparingly. The cynical hope is that this will delay the OFT's inevitable objections.

5 Court Proceedings in UK Law

A. Introduction

5.1 In this chapter proceedings before the United Kingdom courts will be examined. The following summarises the contents of the chapter.

Section B. Proceedings brought by the Director General: general survey of court orders.

Section C. Defending restrictive agreements before the Restrictive Practices Court.

Section D. Restraining orders under section 35(3) RTPA 1976: proceedings commenced by the Director General against unregistered agreements.

Section E. Proceedings for contempt of court against parties to agreements who breach court orders.

Section F. Action commenced by parties or the Director General for a declaration concerning the registrability of an agreement.

Section G. Action by parties to an agreement for a declaration that an agreement is registrable: using the consequences of failure to register.

Section H. Private actions for damages: failure to register agreements; resale price maintenance; breach of Competition Act ministerial Orders.

Section I. Criminal law proceedings for conspiracy to defraud.

Section J. Enforcement of section 36 Notices: section 37— Court's power to order examination on oath.

Section K. Offences in connection with registration under section 36.

Section L. Stays of Proceedings of the RPC: inter-relationship of UK and EC Competition Law.

Section M. Judicial review of decisions of the Director General of Fair Trading, the MMC and the Secretary of State.

The related issue of when proceedings may be brought in UK courts for breaches of EC law is dealt with at paras. 6.115–6.119.

B. Proceedings Brought by the Director General: General Survey of Court Orders

1. Persons Subject to Court Orders

5.2 If parties to a registered agreement cannot arrive at a satisfactory, negotiated conclusion with the OFT leading to dispensation under section 21(2), the Director General may refer the agreement to the Restrictive Practices Court for assessment of its compatibility with the public interest.[1] In practice very few such agreements furnished in due time are referred, the vast majority of cases being negotiated to a conclusion. Any restriction or information provision that *is* declared to be against the public interest is void; the agreement itself in which the restrictions exist remains valid.[2] If the Director General so decides he may further apply to the Court for the Court to make a restraining order against the parties. On such an application the Court has a discretion whether or not to make an order.[3] Orders may be made against: the parties to the agreement who carry on business within the UK; any trade association of which any party is a member; and any person acting on behalf of such an association.[4] When an order is made it may be for all or any of the purposes listed in section 2(2)(a)–(c) RTPA 1976. Thus, the Court may make an order restraining the relevant persons:

> "(a) from giving effect to, or enforcing or purporting to enforce, the agreement in respect of those restrictions or those information provisions;
> (b) from making any other agreement (whether with the same parties or with other parties) to the like effect; or
> (c) where such an agreement as is mentioned in paragraph (b) above has already been made, from giving effect to that agreement of enforcing or purporting to enforce it."[5]

5.3 Where an order is made against a member of a trade association, the order may include provisions for restraining the association and its agents from "procuring or assisting" that person to do anything which would entail a contravention of the order.[6] Where the association has made a recommendation to its members which is subject to the Act there

[1] s. 1(2)(c) and (3) RTPA 1976. This jurisdiction is subject to paras. 6(2) and 9(2) of Sch. 3 RTPA 1976 relating to agreements for supplying goods and services with overseas operation; see Cunningham, *The Fair Trading Act 1973* (1974), Chapter 16, for a detailed analysis of the statutory language.

[2] s. 2(1) RTPA 1976. The consequences of an agreement being declared void are discussed at paras. 4.3-4.19 and reference thereto should be made for details. Many agreements are valueless to the parties once the restrictions have been struck down. A declaration is not a coercive judgment and refusal by a party to comply with its terms does not amount to a contempt of court: *Webster* v *Southwark LBC* [1983] QB 678.

[3] s. 2(2) RTPA 1976.

[4] s. 2(3) RTPA 1976. The words, "any person acting on behalf of" were introduced into the law by s. 104(1) Fair Trading Act 1973, where a trade association is unincorporated it has no legal personality or existence separate from that of its members. However, since the order can be made against "any person acting on behalf of" the trade association this includes, *inter alia*, the personnel and officers of the association.

[5] s. 2(2)(c) RTPA 1976 was introduced by s. 104(1) Fair Trading Act 1973 to prevent parties to agreements from entering new agreements prior to the Court's order, registering it with the OFT and thereby circumventing the Order.

[6] s. 2(4) RTPA 1976. Thus, for example: the Court order restrains X, Y and Z from fixing prices. The order may also restrain the trade association of X, Y and Z from requiring from them statistical data which could be used, when exchange through the agency of the association, to lead to price uniformity between X, Y and Z. However, the Court will not make an order against a foreign trade association which does not carry on any business in the UK: *Japan Canned Food Exporters' Association's Agreement* (1971) LR 7 RP 474 at p. 481.

is deemed to be a "term" (the deeming term) in the constitution of that association providing that all members to whom the recommendation is made will abide by it and by any other recommendations on the same matter.[7] Any order made against an association could, for this reason, be made against its members as well. However, the necessity for this is negated by section 2(5) which allows the Court to make an order against the association restraining it from making any recommendation to which the deeming term would apply. Thus, if the Court had condemned a price recommendation, the order against the association would be in respect of subsequent recommendations on price. Section 2(4), however, does not apply to future recommendations on different subject matter. Thus, the same association could lawfully make recommendations concerning standard terms and conditions or a code of practice, etc.[8] It should be noted that the powers of the Court are not made by determination of the agreement effected after commencement of proceedings. Where, subsequent to commencement, the agreement is varied the Court may deal with the original agreement or the agreement as varied or both as it sees fit.[9]

2. *Nature of the Court Order: Injunctions and Undertakings*

5.4 The Court does not necessarily impose an injunction on the parties. It is usually prepared to accept an undertaking from those concerned that they will not proceed with the condemned conduct. The Court is perhaps a little more liberal here than with unregistered agreements. This is understandable since an unregistered agreement is void and it is unlawful to seek to enforce it, whereas registered agreements may be continued with up until an adverse court declaration. None the less the Court, even in respect of unfurnished agreements, has frequently been prepared to accept undertakings. It will be a question for argument in Court whether an undertaking is accepted or formal injunction made. Breach of either is contempt of court and punishable as such. The order (whether it incorporates an injunction or an undertaking) will restrain the parties from continuing with the original agreement. The order may also be accompanied by a reasoned judgment, even though the matter has been dealt with by consent, but although the jurisdiction for the Court to act in such a way has been established[10] the Court has not yet exercised its jurisdiction to do so (see para. 5.75). If parties should breach the order through ignorance and where no "wilful defiance" is present the Court might take a lenient view of the contempt. "Lenient" has meant imposition of a small fine and an order that the contemnor (the defendant alleged to be in contempt of court) pay the costs of the Director General on a standard basis, the usual order is for costs to be paid on an indemnity basis.[11] Practical problems may arise where a trade association gives an undertaking to terminate restrictive recommendations. Thus, if the order restrains the association from recommending a standard profit margin of 7.5 per cent, would a *member* of the association be in contempt if he continued to add a 7.5 per cent margin subsequent to the order on the basis that it was the commercially realistic figure? Would the Court react differently if the margin was changed just slightly to 7.25 per cent? Provided that

[7] ss. 8 and 16 RTPA 1976.

[8] See for examples: *National Federation of Retail Newsagents Agreement Nos. 3 and 4* [1972] 1 WLR 1162; (1972) LR 7 RP 425 noted by Korah (1972) JBL 326 at p. 329; *National Federation of Retail Newsagents Agreement No. 5* [1973] ICR 649 at p. 653.

[9] s. 2(6) RTPA 1976.

[10] *Re: Agreements relating to the supply of freight forwarding services between the UK and Australasia* [1997] *The Times*, 24 January (RPC).

[11] See e.g. *National Federation Electrical Association's Agreement* (1961) LR 2 RP 447 at p. 452 *per* Diplock J. See also *Garage Equipment Association Agreement* (1964) LR 4 RP 491.

the member bona fides sets his prices without reference to any other party and by reference to market forces then he could not be said to have entered an "agreement" to the like effect as the original agreement. For a detailed analysis of the contempt issue see paras. 5.69–5.89.

3. Nature of the Court Order: Prohibition of Agreements to the "like effect"

5.5 In addition to restraining continuance of the original agreement the order will usually also restrain agreements "to the like effect". Parties may not, in order to circumvent the Court order, abandon the condemned agreement and start again with a similar but, none the less, new and different agreement. In certain early cases the Court, in deciding whether the parties had entered an agreement to "like effect", concentrated on the *form* of the new agreement to see if it adopted a similar machinery to the old, condemned agreements. The question asked was: "Do the parties by the new agreement agree that one or more of them shall do or refrain from doing acts like those which it was agreed should be done or not done by those provisions of that other agreement which contained restrictions declared to be contrary to the public interest?"[12] Where the original agreement has been scrutinised by the Court and a detailed analysis undertaken of the restrictions declared contrary to the public interest, it will be relatively straightforward for the parties (and a subsequent Court hearing a contempt action) to work out what a "like" agreement would be. However, in many past cases, where the Court rejected arguments put to it concerning the advantages of the agreement for the public interest, it has not given detailed reasons in its judgment. In such cases deciding what is to the "like effect" is more difficult since little Court guidance in the form of analysis is at hand. Furthermore, since today the vast majority of cases before the Court concern undefended agreements which are referred by the Director General simply as an enforcement mechanism to ensure against their continuance, no judgment is given and hence no analysis of the restrictions occurs. In such cases there is no judicial guidance about what to avoid in any new agreement entered into by the parties.[13] Few businessmen today bother to defend price-fixing agreements, for example, yet OFT policy with many such cases is to refer them to the Court for a restraining order or for the giving of appropriate undertakings.

5.6 Where a subsequent agreement is to the "like effect" as a prior restriction subject to orders made by or undertakings given to the Court depends upon whether the new restriction achieves the same end result as the earlier restriction. Pursuant to this "achievement test" the Court will look at the new restriction in order to determine what, according to its language and terms, if made effective, it would do or achieve and then the Court will ask the question: are those things done or achieved the same as those which the old agreement, if operative, would have done or achieved?[14] Thus, for example, in relation

[12] *Black Bolt and Nut Association's Agreements* (1961) LR 3 RP 433 at p. 442; [1962] 1 WLR 75. On the word "like" the Court stated: "How like is like? The word 'like' is imprecise. At one extreme it can be said that the earth is like an orange; at the other that one pea is like the other proverbial pea in the pod. To say that one thing is 'like' another means no more than that the one thing bears to the other a resemblance relevant to the comparison sought to be made" (*ibid.*, at p. 443). See *British Concrete Pipe Association's Agreement* [1982] ICR 183 at p. 188E *per* Mocatta J: "'to the like effect' has a different meaning from 'to the same effect'. 'Like' does not mean 'the same' or 'identical with'; the nearest synonym is 'similar'."

[13] See *National Daily and Sunday Newspapers Proprietors Agreement* [1986] ICR 44 at p. 50. The RPC held that the defendants were not in contempt of an earlier court order where the earlier order was made in unopposed proceedings and was not sufficiently clear, precise and particularised.

[14] *Re: Black Bolt and Nut Associations Agreement* (1962) LR 3 RP 43, 61 at *per* Lord Evershed MR.

to a trade association recommendation it would not be enough to say merely "the old recommendation was as to price and so is the new and therefore it is to like effect". In analysing the resemblance between the old and new restrictions the comparison required to be made is in those characteristics of the restrictions which caused the Court instance to declare them contrary to the public interest.[15] In this respect the Court seised of contempt proceedings would necessarily analyse the reasoning of the Court which first declared the restrictions contrary to the public interest. It is recognised that there is substantial difficulty in applying this test where no attempt has been made to justify the original agreement or recommendation under any of the relevant gateways and there has been no judgment.[16] In *Associated Transformer Manufacturers Agreement*[17] the Court identified a similar difficulty where a reasoned judgment could not, having regard to the terms of the new agreement or recommendation, have had any application to it.[18]

5.7 In *British Concrete Pipes Association Agreement*,[19] the Court adopted a test of the like effect which incorporated economic evidence. Thus, an agreement which had a different mechanism and form from the first agreement but which achieved the same purpose and commercial effect as the first could constitute an agreement of "like effect" to the first. If the Court made an order restraining X, Y and Z from formally fixing prices it could well be contempt of court for those parties subsequently to exchange price lists. In both cases the aim is to control prices yet in both the mechanism by which that object is achieved may be very different. The *British Concrete Pipes* case suggests that this wider "achievement" or "economic effects" based test is now accepted by both the Restrictive Practices Court and the Court of Appeal. In that case, the question was whether an informal oral arrangement was to the "like effect" as a formal collusive tendering and price-fixing agreement abandoned voluntarily in 1959 and in respect of which undertakings had been given to the Court in 1965. The informal oral arrangement again allocated tenders between the parties but this time by a different mechanism and in respect of a narrower range of products than was the case in the first agreement. The Court, none the less, held that the 1974 agreement was to the "like effect" as the earlier versions and the parties were accordingly fined for contempt of court. In summary, a number of rules of thumb may be gleaned from reported decisions:

(a) where the machinery of the second agreement is substantially similar to that of the first then the second agreement is invariably to the "like effect" as the first;[20]
(b) where the first agreement is formal and written and the alleged breach of the Court order is an oral arrangement the differences in form do not preclude a finding of contempt by the Court;[21]
(c) where the second agreement is in a form similar to the first but is in scope narrower it may still be of "like effect" to the first;[22]

[15] *Re: Associated Transformer Manufacturers Agreement No. 2* [1970] 1 WLR 1589, 1597C.
[16] See e.g. *Black Bolt and Nut Associations Agreement* LR 2 RP433, 446.
[17] *ibid.*
[18] *ibid.*, p. 1598C.
[19] [1981] ICR 421 (RPC) noted Korah (1980) 77 LS Gaz 961; and [1983] ICR 215 (CA) affirming judgment in RPC.
[20] See *Galvanised Tank Manufacturer Association Agreement* (1965) LR 5 RP 315 at p. 345.
[21] *Black Bolt and Nut Association's Agreement No. 2* (1961) LR 2 RP 433 (RPC); (1961) LR 3 RP 43; [1962] 1 WLR 75 (CA); *Associated Transformer Manufacturer's Agreement* [1970] 1 WLR 1589; [1970] LR 7 RP 202.
[22] *British Concrete Pipe Association* [1981] ICR 421 (RPC); affirmed by [1983] ICR 215 (CA); *Mileage Conference Group of the Tyre Manufacturers Conference Ltd Agreement* [1966] 1 WLR 1137; (1966) LR 6 RP 49.

(d) where the second agreement is in a completely different form to the first but achieves a similar commercial purpose and effect then the second agreement may still be of "like effect" to the first.[23]

4. *Interim Orders*[24]

5.8 Where the Director General has applied to the Court for an order in respect of a registered agreement he may also apply for an interim order in respect of specified restrictions at any time before the Court has made its order whether that time is before or after the making of a declaration by the Court.[25] For such an application to succeed the Director must prove on a balance of probabilities, "that the operation of the restrictions or information provisions, during the period likely to elapse before an order can be made ... is likely to cause material detriment to the public or a section of the public generally, or to a particular person who is not a party to the agreement".[26] The Director General must satisfy the Court in addition that the restrictions and information provisions in question "could not reasonably be expected to be shown to fall within" any of the gateways in sections 10 (goods) or 19 (services) RTPA 1976. Thus interim orders are a practical possibility in cases involving serious restrictions only. Where the restrictions are of equivocal public interest value then it cannot be said that the restrictions "could not reasonably be expected" to fall foul of the public interest. The interim order is exactly the same in nature as a final order made by the Court at the close of proceedings.[27] Such an order ceases to have effect upon the first to occur of the following events:

(a) the period specified by the Court for its duration elapses;
(b) an event occurs which according to the terms of the order triggers its termination;
(c) the Court declares that the restrictions or information provisions are not incompatible with the public interest; or
(d) the Court makes a declaration that all the restrictions and information provisions are contrary to the public interest and makes a final order giving effect to that declaration.[28]

5.9 Interim orders are rarely sought by the OFT though they were threatened in 1979 in connection with an agreement made between London Weekend Television (LWT) and the Football League granting to LWT the exclusive right to televise league matches for a three-year period commencing 1 July 1979. This agreement superseded agreements between the League, the BBC and other independent television companies. The OFT contended that this would have reduced consumer choice and overall coverage of television football. It informed the parties that it would seek an interim order against the agreement. In view of this the parties abandoned the agreement and entered a new one which included the BBC.

5.10 The first application to be made by the DGFT and granted by the RPC was in *DGFT* v *Institute of Independent Insurance Brokers* (the "IIB").[29] The case arose out of a recommendation by the IIB, a service supply association under section 16 RTPA, to its mem-

[23] *British Concrete Pipe Association, ibid.*
[24] See C. Bright, "Interim relief in UK competition law" [1992] ECLR 21.
[25] s. 3(1) RTPA 1976.
[26] s. 3(3)(c) RTPA 1976.
[27] s. 3(4) RTPA 1976.
[28] s. 3(6) RTPA 1976.
[29] [1991] ICR 822.

bers not to place motor insurance with General Accident Fire and Life Assurance Corporation. This boycott was in response to General Accident's agreement with Ford Motor Company under which purchasers of new Ford motor cars would, subject to certain conditions, receive a year's motor insurance from General Accident paid for by Ford. This meant that Ford car purchasers would deal direct with General Accident and thus not use insurance brokers represented by the IIB to obtain insurance for their new cars.

5.11 The IIB registered its memorandum and articles of association together with a copy of the resolution recommending a boycott on 9 November 1990, the DGFT applied for an interim order on 17 December 1990 and the RPC made an interim order on 21 December 1990[30] requiring the IIB's members not to give effect to the restriction arising out of the recommendation.

5.12 The RPC required three conditions to be satisfied before the order could be granted. First, the restriction specified in the DGFT's application must be one to which the RTPA applies. In this case, the IIB's recommendation took effect as an agreement between its members to comply with the recommendation and was thus caught by sections 16(3) and (4) RTPA 1976.[31]

5.13 The second condition was that the restriction could not reasonably be expected to be shown to fall within one of the gateways set out in paragraphs (a) to (h) of section 19(1). The RPC emphasised that the test was "a stringent one. It is *not* enough that the Court be satisfied that it is, on balance, improbable that the Respondents will be able so to persuade it. On the other hand the court is not required to accept any argument, however far-fetched, put forward on behalf of the respondents to the effect that they might conceivably be able to show that the restriction passed through one of the gateways."[32] The RPC did not find helpful any analogy with any test in the High Court, such as the striking out of a pleading or proceedings for summary judgment, and emphasised that the words of section 3(3)(b) must be given their clear meaning. The IIB sought, unsuccessfully, to rely on four gateways in paragraphs (a), (c), (d) and (h) of section 19(1); and these are analysed in paras. 5.23 and following.

5.14 The third condition was that the operation of the restriction during the period likely to elapse before an order could be made in respect of it under section 2(2) was likely to cause material detriment to the public or a section of the public generally or to a particular person not a party to the agreement. Only this third type of detriment was considered as it was clearly a boycott of General Accident. This condition was satisfied by evidence that General Accident risked losing £25 million worth of motor insurance premium income, plus unquantifiable renewal income and associated other insurance business. An argument that £25 million income was not material when compared with General Accident's total worldwide income of over £3,250 million was rejected. Material appears to be an objective rather than relative assessment.

5.15 Thus the RPC was satisfied that it should exercise its discretion under section 3(3) and grant an order. In so doing, it held it had discretion under section 9(3) Restrictive Practices Court Act 1976 and rule 7 Restrictive Trade Practice Rules 1976 to allow proceedings to be brought and an order to be made against nominated Respondents representing the members of the IIB, all of whom would have the same interest in the proceedings. An order was made in the usual terms of section 2(2) RTPA against the IIB's members from giving effect to the agreement in respect of the restriction and from making any

[30] Subsequent to this interim order, a final order was made on 5 December 1991 under s. 2 RTPA against the IIB, see DGFT Annual Report 1991, p. 39.

[31] See para. 1.110.

[32] [1991] ICR 822, 830.

other agreement to like effect. The RPC also held that as the DGFT was exercising a law enforcement function, it need not be required to give a cross-undertaking in damages in the absence of special circumstances.[33]

5. *Variations to the Agreement and Court Orders*

5.16 The Court has jurisdiction to make a declaration in respect of variations to agreements submitted after the references to it by the Director General.[34] Court orders do not come into effect for 21 days following the expiration of the period within which any party to the case may appeal the declaration.[35] During that 21-day period parties to the agreement or to the proceedings may submit a revised agreement or a draft thereof to the Court which may then declare on the compatibility of the revision or draft with the public interest. The details of the variation must be notified to the OFT under section 24(2) RTPA 1976 before the Court can approve them.[36] If the variation entails a new agreement particulars must be duly furnished for registration. The Court may, if an application is made to it within 21 days, suspend its declaration and order for a further six months.[37] By this procedure, parties to agreements declared to be against the public interest by the Court, may have them saved by revising them to fillet out the parts considered objectionable by the Court.

6. *Variations of the Court's Decision*

5.17 The Court may under section 4 RTPA 1976, upon application, discharge any previous declaration or order or substitute in its place a new declaration or order. Applications may be made by the Director General for the OFT or by any person who is (or was at the time of the previous court case) subject to or entitled to the benefit of the restrictions in question (i.e. the parties to the agreement or persons benefiting from the agreement). Before an application may be made to the Court for a variation, leave of the Court must first be obtained.[38] In order to obtain this permission to commence an application the Court must be satisfied under section 4(4) that there is "prima facie evidence of a material change in the relevant circumstances". In *Cement Makers' Federation Agreement No. 2*[39] the Director General sought to have the previous declaration of the Court which declared that a

[33] See *DGFT* v *Tobyward Ltd* [1989] 1 WLR 517, and *Kirklees MBC* v *Wickes Building Supplies Ltd* [1993] AC 227, the latter noted by Robertson at (1993) 109 LQR 27.

[34] s. 2(6) RTPA 1976.

[35] s. 25 Competition Act 1980. Where such an appeal is brought the declaration does not become effective until 21 days after the date on which the appeal has been finally determined or withdrawn. See e.g. *Association of British Travel Agents No. 2* [1985] ICR 122.

[36] s. 26(2) C.A. 1980.

[37] s. 26(4) C.A. 1980. The period may be further extended on two subsequent occasions for periods of three months each at the discretion of the Court. Under s. 26(5) an extension may be made in respect of some but not all of the restrictions and information provisions. A s. 26 order was made following the hearing of *Association of British Travel Agents* [1984] ICR 12.

[38] The procedure for obtaining leave is set out in a Practice Direction, 11 December 1986 (Restrictive Practices: Variation of Order) [1987] ICR 128. If the parties to an agreement seek leave and the DGFT consents, then the RPC may grant leave without the necessity of a hearing.

[39] [1974] ICR 445. The earlier case is reported at (1961) LR 2 RP 241; [1961] 1 WIR 581 (RPC). See also *Building Employers Confederation's Application* [1985] ICR 167; and *National Association of Scaffolding Contractors Agreement* (1969) (unreported) No. 644 Register of Restrictive Trade Practices, for a copy of the Court order. In *Mallaig and Northwest Fishermen's Association (No. 2)* (unreported) noted DGFT Annual Report (1975), pp. 90, 91 the Court allowed a variation of a previous Court order. In 1970 the Court condemned a restrictive agreement relating to the fishing and landing of herring and the minimum prices

price-fixing agreement operated by the Cement Maker's Federation was not contrary to the public interest, discharged. The application failed but, none the less, the Court accepted the Director General's argument that the phrase "prima facie evidence of a material change in the relevant circumstances" meant that he had to show that by reason of new facts there was a prima facie change in an essential part of the reasoning by which the Court had come to its previous conclusion. This section has no effect in respect of interim orders of the Court issued under section 3 RTPA 1976.

5.18 It is to be noted that section 4 is concerned only with the discharge of previous declarations of the Court and any orders made by the Court pursuant to that declaration. The section does not address the situation where parties to an agreement have given undertakings to the Court in lieu of the making of an order. In practice the failure of section 4 to address the situation is not problematic since, invariably, the Order of the Court which incorporates the undertakings will contain an express liberty to apply. In *Associated Transformer Manufacturers Agreement No. 2*[40] the ten manufacturers party to the original agreement applied to the Court for a declaration that a new agreement into which they proposed to enter was not an agreement to the like effect as the original agreement and that they could therefore, consistently with undertakings given to the Court, enter the new agreement. Alternatively, the manufacturers sought the leave of the Court to enter into the new agreement and to be released from their undertakings to the extent necessary to enable them to enter such new agreement. It is clear from the judgment of the Court that the manufacturers applied pursuant to a liberty to apply contained in the original order. The application was for declaratory relief alone. The Court confirmed that in any event it had jurisdiction to grant a declaratory judgment where no other relief was sought but stated that this was a discretion which was to be exercised cautiously and sparingly. In the circumstances the declarations sought were granted.

5.19 Under a Practice Direction of the President of the Restrictive Practices Court of 11 December 1986[41] the Court has simplified the procedure for obtaining variations by consent. The Practice Direction applies in circumstances where (a) a variation of a previous decision of the Court is sought which would not in itself restrict or discourage competition to any material degree, and (b) the Director General and any other party who appeared at the hearing of the previous proceedings consents to the variation. In such circumstances the application for leave together with the previous declaration or order of the Court may be lodged with the proper officer of the Court for consideration by the Court. The application for leave should be made by affidavit containing a statement of the material change in the relevant circumstances and a statement that the proposed variation would not in itself restrict or discourage competition and exhibiting the signed

cont.
thereof ((1970 LR 7 RP 178). Following accession to the EC, UK fishermen accepted Reg. 2142/70/EEC which provided for the establishment of a common organisation of the market in fishery products involving pricing and trading rules. The regulation envisaged that fishermen would form trade associations for promotion of their industries. Accordingly, the Scottish Fisheries Organisation (SFO) and the Aberdeen Fish Producers Organisation (AFPO) came into being and commenced, in accordance with EC rules, to organise minimum prices and production and marketing rules. The parties considered that these rules were to some extent "to the like effect" as rules prohibited by the 1970 Court order. They, accordingly, sought a release from the orders. They applied to the Court on the basis that the accession of the UK to the EC constituted a "material change in circumstances". The OFT accepted this argument and did not oppose the application. The Court released the parties from the previous order to the extent necessary to enable them to comply with EC rules.

40 [1970] 1 WLR 1589, 1592. The entire question of burden and standard of proof was considered in *Net Book Agreement* (Judgment of Ferris J, 20 December 1996), which set out the position under both the RTPA 1976 and the RPA 1976.

41 [1987] 1 WLR 45; [1987] ICR 128.

consent of the Director General to the variation and any other party who appeared at the hearing of the previous proceedings. The position is different in cases to which cases section 4(5) RTP 1976 applies. Pursuant to that section leave to make an application for the discharge of a declaration or order of the Court made before the commencement of the Restrictive Trade Practices Act 1968 (25 November 1968) may, if the Applicant proposes to rely upon section 10(1)(h)[42] be granted upon prima facie evidence of the relevance of that paragraph to the application.

5.20 Upon lodging the affidavit with the Court, the proper officer will put the application for leave before the Court. If satisfied that leave may be given and that the application under section 4(1) should be granted the Court may grant leave and cause the proceedings to be listed. The decision to grant leave will be given in open court without the parties or their representatives being required to attend. It is clear, however, that the parties may attend if they so wish. If, upon the evidence, and upon any other evidence required by the Court, the Court is not satisfied that it is proper for the matter to be dealt with in this way the application under section 4(1) will be listed for hearing in the normal way. The Practice Direction emphasises that wherever possible the parties and their advisers should ensure that sufficient information is provided to enable the Court to be satisfied as to the propriety of making an order without hearing the parties since the purpose of the Direction is to save time and costs.

C. Defending Restrictive Agreements before the Restrictive Practices Court

1. *Introduction*[43]

5.21 Very few disputed agreements are heard before the Restrictive Practices Court. Indeed, only a minute proportion of cases registered have proceeded to litigation despite section 1(2)(c) RTPA 1976 which impresses upon the Director General of Fair Trading the duty to take proceedings before the RPC in respect of registered agreements. In stark contrast to the small number of litigated cases, tens of thousands of agreements have been actually registered. In reality, the Court plays a strictly limited role in the appraisal and development of competition law policy. None the less, in terms of the structure of the RTPA 1976, the Court sits centre stage and accordingly it must be given due weight. A party deciding to go to full trial in order to defend an agreement will have to convince the Court, on a balance of probabilities, that the restrictions defended are of positive advantage to the public interest. To achieve this highly difficult task (very few agreements have been accepted by the RPC to be in the public interest) parties must: (a) satisfy the Court that the restrictions confer public interest advantages of the sort specified in the "gateways". These are factors laid out in sections 10 (for goods agreements) and 19 (for service agreements) RTPA 1976; *and* (b)

[42] This section provides that the restriction or information provision does not directly or indirectly restrict or discourage competition to any material degree in any relevant trade or industry and is not likely to do so.

[43] For general analysis of the Court, its procedure, and case law, see: Cunningham, *The Fair Trading Act 1973* (1974); Korah, *Competition Law of Britain and the Common Market* (1982); Merkin and Williams, *Competition Law: Antitrust Policy in the United Kingdom and the EEC* (1984); Whish, *Competition Law* (3rd edn. 1993); Stevens and Yamey, *The Restrictive Practices Court: A Study of the Judicial Process and Economic Policy* (1965); Swan, O'Brien, Maunder and Howe, *Competition in British Industry* (1974); Allen, *Monopoly and Restrictive Practices* (1968); Brock, *The Control Restrictive Practices from 1956* (1966); Liesner Committee, *Review of Restrictive Trade Practices Policy* (1979) Cmnd 7512, Annex D. Wilberforce, Campbell, Elles, *Restrictive Trade Practices and Monopolies*, 1956; (2nd edn. 1966 and supplement 1973).

satisfy the Court that the restrictions are not unreasonable having regard to the balance between the benefits they confer and any detriments that result therefrom.

5.22 The criteria in section 10 for goods and 19 for services RTPA 1976 are very similar. In this section they will generally be dealt with together. In determining whether it is worth defending a restriction before the Court, parties thereto should bear in mind the strict approach traditionally adopted by the Court; the very considerable expense involved in defending an agreement given the protracted nature of the hearing; and the senior managerial time required in preparation for and attending Court. Having stated the position somewhat pessimistically, in the most recently fully litigated case under the gateways, the Court somewhat against expectations upheld a mutual exclusive dealing arrangement whereby if a firm joined the Association of British Travel Agents (ABTA) as a tour operator member it was constrained only to deal with travel agent members and vice versa.[44] While ABTA's rules were struck down in other respects they were at least relieved to have this mutual exclusive dealing arrangement officially preserved. No doubt the OFT was concerned about the precedent value the case might have, though the case can easily be confined to its particular facts.[45] Thus, whilst defending agreements is certainly risky it is not a venture entirely forlorn of hope. It should be noted that inherent in sections 10 and 19 RTPA 1976 is a presumption that restrictions are against the public interest unless proven otherwise. It will hence never suffice merely to show that a restriction is neutral *vis-à-vis* the public interest since that will not be sufficient to rebut the negative presumption. Parties to restrictions must prove positive benefits. In the text below each "gateway" will be examined separately. In discussion reference will be made to the goods gateways in section 10 RTPA 1976. This does not affect the meaning of the services gateways in section 19 since that provision repeats, *mutatis mutandis*, the language of section 10 RTPA 1976.

2. *Sections 10(1)(a) and 19(1)(a): Protection of Public against Injury*

5.23 The first gateway (a)—goods version—reads:

> "that the restriction or information provision is reasonably necessary, having regard to the character of the goods to which it applies, to protect the public against injury (whether to persons or to premises) in connection with the consumption, installation or use of those goods."[46]

This gateway is concerned with the protection of persons or premises, not goods or services. Arguments must be structured accordingly. An agreement between suppliers to supply their goods in special packaging needed to protect the goods from damage could not therefore be justified under this gateway. The burden of proof is to show that the restriction is "reasonably necessary": it need not be shown, therefore, that the restriction is the sole or optimum means of protecting the persons or premises in question.

5.24 The scope for use of this gateway is very limited. This is partly because the government passes specific legislation to safeguard health and property from dangerous goods.[47] The gateway is, in any event, buttressed by sections 9(5) and 18(5) RTPA 1976 which, as

[44] See *Association of British Travel Agents Ltd* [1984] ICR 12.

[45] Though note there is no formal rule of precedent in cases before the RPC; each case turns on its own special facts.

[46] The gateway was introduced to implement para. 240(a) of the MMC *General Report on Collective Discrimination* (1955) Cmnd 9504.

[47] See Stevens and Yamey, *The Restrictive Practices Court* (1965), p. 57; Brock, *The Control of Restrictive Practices from 1956* (1966), p. 51.

noted in Chapter 1, exclude from control restrictions adopted on the basis of British Standards Institute safety standards. In no case to date has gateway (a) been successfully pleaded. The test for success is that laid down by Devlin J in *Chemists Federation No. 2*:[48] "whether a reasonable and prudent man who is concerned to protect the public against injury would enforce this restriction if he could. He would not do so unless he was satisfied, first, that the restriction afforded an adequate protection and, secondly, that the risk of injury was sufficiently great to warrant it."[49]

5.25 This was amplified by the Court in *DGFT* v *IIB*.[50] There, between June and October 1990 a major motor car manufacturer (Ford) and a major insurance company (General Accident) operated a scheme under which most purchasers of Ford Fiesta Escort and Orion motor cars were provided by the insurance company with a year's free motor insurance, the manufacturers paying the premiums. On 1 October 1990 the IIB, an association of independent sole traders, firms and corporations registered under the Insurance Brokers (Registration) Act 1977, threatened the insurance company with trade sanctions unless it undertook not to repeat such a scheme in 1991. The IIB furnished to the OFT particulars of the threatened trade sanctions which included a resolution of the IIB's intention to recommend to its members a boycott of any insurer engaging in practices likely to destabilise the United Kingdom insurance market and refusing to undertake to desist. On 4 December 1990 the IIB wrote a letter to some 12,000 insurance brokers and intermediaries informing them that General Accident had declined to discuss discontinuing the scheme and recommended that all brokers and intermediaries should cease placing insurance business with the insurance company for a period of six months beginning from 1 January 1991 and every effort be made to re-broke existing businesses with other insurers unless the best interest of a particular client dictated otherwise. The DGFT, on 17 December 1990, sought interim measures pursuant to section 3 RTPA 1976. The IIB sought to defend the application for interim measures, *inter alia*, upon the basis that the recommendation fell within the scope of section 19(1)(a) RTPA 1976. The IIB submitted that the boycott of General Accident was reasonably necessary having regard to the character of the services to which it applied (namely the services of insurance brokers) to protect the public against injury in connection with the use of motor cars. The IIB's case, shortly stated, was as follows:

> "The effect of the boycott would be to deter General Accident and other insurance companies from doing direct business without applying normal underwriting criteria; because, under a scheme such as that operated by General Accident and Ford, policies were issued to purchasers of motor cars at a uniform rate of premium, young and inexperienced drivers buying high performance cars and drivers with bad records could thereby obtain insurance more cheaply than they otherwise could; the publicly thereby lost the protection of the normal loading of premiums in the insurance market as a result of which such drivers are charged 'premiums at prohibitive rates'. Because General Accident refused to discuss that matter with the IIB, and because no public authority had taken an interest in it, the boycott was ... an appropriate means of safeguarding that protection for the public."[51]

5.26 The Court stated that in determining whether a restriction was reasonably necessary to protect the public against insurance the Court:

[48] (1958) LR 1 RP 75.
[49] *ibid.*, at p.106.
[50] [1991] ICR 823, 831.
[51] *ibid.*, p. 831C, D.

> "must consider the magnitude of the risk of injury to the public that the restriction is said to be reasonably necessary to prevent, the effectiveness of the restriction in preventing it, and the extent to which the restriction itself is commensurate with those factors."[52]

The Court, having considered those three matters, was satisfied that there we no reasonable prospect of the IIB being able to persuade the Court that the boycott could be justified on this ground. In other words the Court was satisfied that the boycott could not reasonably be expected to be shown to pass through gateway (a). The test propounded by the Court may be said to involve an element of proportionality. Thus, a boycott of a motor insurer which supplied insurance to purchasers of new Ford motor cars at a uniform rate, thus not penalising through high premiums young and inexperienced drivers or drivers with bad driving records, even assuming that argument to be capable to be made out on the facts of full trial, would be a disproportionately excessive response to the objective of protecting the public.

5.27 It is quite clear from decided cases that the gateway cannot be used as a justification for restricting retail outlets. Thus an agreement limiting supplies through retail outlets employing qualified pharmacists is unacceptable since the Court takes the view that it is for the government and not private trade associations to take such regulatory decisions. Nor will it be justifiable, on grounds of person and premises protection, to restrict outlets for tyre sales on the basis of skill and expertise of retailers.[53]

3. *Section 10(1)(b) and 19(1)(b): Restrictions Confer Public Benefits and Advantages*

5.28 This gateway—goods version—reads:

> "that the removal of the restriction or information provision would deny to the public as purchasers, consumers or users of any goods other specific and substantial benefits or advantages enjoyed or likely to be enjoyed by them as such, whether by virtue of the restriction or information provision itself or of any arrangements or operations resulting therefrom."[54]

Gateway (b), in view of its generality, is the most important of the gateways and it is pleaded in many cases. Parties to the agreement must prove specific *and* substantial benefits to purchasers consumers and users. The Court has been inconsistent in its interpretation of the words "specific" and "substantial".[55] Indeed, the Court has expressly refrained from attempting "strictly quantitative or proportional assessment" of the word "substantial".[56] It is clearly a case for argument in every case. A similar conclusion applies to the word "specific". In the cases the Court has variously described specific benefits as being "definable and of special character" or as being "explicit and definable".[57] Thus parties would not succeed in proving a "specific" benefit for example if they merely expounded general fears about price wars, or the threat of external competition or about unidentified consequences for quality of product or service. Parties must establish causation between the re-

[52] *ibid.*, p. 831F.

[53] See *Tyre Trade Register Agreement* (1963) LR 3 RP 404; and *Motor Vehicle Distribution Scheme Agreement* (1961) LR 2 RP 173.

[54] The provision apparently derives from the MMC *General Report on Collective Discrimination, op. cit.*, at para. 240(c).

[55] Brock, *op. cit.*, at p. 52; Korah, *op. cit.*, at pp. 162, 163.

[56] See *Net Books Agreement (No. 1)* (1962) LR 3 RP 246 at p. 309.

[57] *See Permanent Magnet Association's Agreement No. 1* (1962) LR 3 RP 119 at p. 164; and *Net Book Agreement No. 1* (1962) LR 3 RP 246 at p. 310, respectively.

strictions and the benefits elaborated upon to the Court. Thus these benefits, to use the statutory language, must be enjoyed "by virtue of the restriction itself" or of "any arrangements or operations resulting" from the restriction. The phrase "arrangements or operations resulting" has received consideration from the Court. In *Permanent Magnet Association's Agreement (No. 1)*[58] the Court's conclusions lead to the following proposition. If X and Y operate a restrictive agreement and by virtue of, but collateral to, that agreement they are able to make significant joint research and development advances, then the RPC may hold that the benefits of the R&D exist by virtue of the restrictive price agreement. The question asked by the Court is *not* whether the joint and beneficial R&D could theoretically exist in the absence of the restrictive agreement but whether the R&D would continue in anything like its present form and efficacy.[59] The Court will essentially ask whether the benefits are the "natural and probable consequences" of the continuance of the restrictions.[60] Causation may be difficult to establish where the benefits alleged to result from the restrictions in dispute may arguably derive from an alternative source. Thus, in *Finance Houses Association Ltd Agreement*[61] a hire purchase code advocating the systematic use of reasonable deposits was considered unnecessary to achieve benefits where it was clear that experience taught traders to ensure that reasonable deposits were taken and that there was danger in requiring overly low deposits or no deposit at all. Parties must clearly demonstrate that the restrictions lead to positive benefits. There must be a significant element of gain involved. It is not adequate merely to prove no detriment; if a restriction is neutral in its effects then the presumption against it is not overcome. Equally, parties must show more than that the restriction is merely "reasonable and fair".[62]

5.29 Where goods agreements are concerned the restrictions in question must benefit "the public" as purchasers, consumers or users of any goods. It suffices that any of the three classes of beneficiary gain; it is unnecessary to prove benefit to all three, though, of course, the more the merrier. It does not suffice to show benefit to a small sub-category or percentage proportion of purchasers or consumers or users. It seems likely, however, that the Court will at least entertain benefit that flows to a majority of a class.[63] Although the converse is not wholly unarguable[64] it seems most likely that the parties to the agreement must be excluded from consideration when assessing benefits; the parties in this case do not count as the public. Where services are concerned section 19(1)(b) RTPA 1976 is slightly different from section 10(1)(b): this is due in part to an amendment to section 19(1)(b) introduced by section 28 Competition Act 1980. The relevant part of the amended version thus reads (new words are italicised): "That the removal of the restriction or information provision would deny to the public as users of any service, or as *vendors,* purchasers, consumers or users of any goods or *other property* in relation to which any services are supplied, other specific and substantial benefits." It is notable that the interests of vendors of goods has been added to the ranks of those interested in services agreements. Moreover the words "or other property" recognise that some providers of ser-

[58] *ibid.* See *Association of British Travel Agents* [1984] ICR 12 at p. 46D: "If [the restrictions] were to be removed, the compulsive force of this sanction would decline and the benefits of the safeguard would be lost."

[59] *ibid.*, at p. 168.

[60] *ibid.*

[61] (1965) LR 5 RP 366; [1965] 1 WLR 1419. See also *Birmingham Association of Building Trades Employers' Agreement* (1963) LR 4 RP 54; *Mallaig and North West Fishermen's Agreement* (1970) LR 7 RP 178.

[62] See *Blanket Manufacturers Agreement* (1959) LR 1 RP 208 at p. 255 (RPC); (1959) LR 1 RP 271 (CA).

[63] See *Black Bolt and Nut Association's Agreement* (1960) LR 2 RP 50 (RPC accepted that if two-thirds of the class were benefited this would suffice).

[64] See *National Sulphuric Acid Association's Agreement* (1963) LR 4 RP 169; *British Iron and Steel Federation and National Federation of Scrap Iron, etc.* (1964) LR 4 RP 299. In both cases the question was left unanswered. See also *British Waste Paper Association's Agreement* (1963) LR 4 RP 29.

vices carry out their activities in relation to various forms of intangible property, for example, copyright, leases or securities. These examples are "goods" within the meaning of section 43(1) RTPA 1976. Over 30 cases have been pleaded solely or in part upon the basis of this gateway. About ten have succeeded to some degree or other. From these cases may be gleaned some indications of judicial policy. Though, almost all the cases are of some considerable vintage and it cannot be automatically assumed that the Court would today adopt a similar position.[65] The following are factors for consideration.

(1) Price stability

5.30 Does the restriction keeps prices stable? The very early case of *Yarn Spinners' Agreement*[66] strongly suggests that the maintenance of price stability *per se* is not, as a rule, considered a benefit. This presumption has invariably been followed in other cases,[67] though, it is not inconceivable that price stability might be accepted. In *British Bottle Association's Agreement* it was thus stated: "On the evidence in the present case, we do not find any special circumstances which warrant the conclusion that price stabilisation confers a particular benefit sufficiently great to outweigh the loss of a free market."[68]

(2) Quality

5.31 To date the Court has not accepted that price wars are against the public interest because they encourage traders who seek to compete to reduce costs by lowering quality.[69] Quality is generally accepted as one of the inherent variables in an open market.[70] Indeed, the addition of newer, cheaper and lower quality goods or services on to a market where old varieties remain adds to consumer choice.

(3) Investment

5.32 The argument that expected lower profits brought about by abrogation of a restrictive agreement would lead to a decline in investment, research and development and general expansion has not been accepted by the Court.[71] Even if one can prove that the restrictions sustains research and development one must prove further that absence of the restriction would deprive the public to a *substantial* extent of the benefits of the research and development.[72]

(4) Level of stocks

5.33 In some cases the Court has accepted that there will be a risk attached to the holding of reasonable stocks inherent in fluctuating, non-controlled prices.[73] However, such recognition of the existence of the problem is unlikely to prevail over the presumption that levels of stocks will not fall to inadequate levels if a price-fixing agreement is abrogated.[74]

[65] Virtually all the cases have received devastating criticism. See especially Stevens and Yamey, *op. cit.*, note 47.
[66] (1959) LR 1 RP 118 at p. 189.
[67] See e.g. *Wholesale and Retail Bakers of Scotland Association's Agreement* (1959) LR 1 RP 347 at p. 376; and *Federation of Carpet Manufacturers* (1960) LR 1 RP 472 at p. 541.
[68] [1961] 1 WLR 760 at p. 789; (1961) LR 2 RP 345.
[69] See *British Bottle Association's Agreement ibid.*; *Re Linoleum Manufacturers' Association* [1961] 1 WLR 986; (1961) LR 2 RP 395.
[70] See MMC *Report on the Process of Calico Printing* (1954) HCP 140.
[71] See *British Heavy Steelmakers Agreement* (1964) LR 5 RP 33.
[72] See e.g. *Re Associated Transformer Manufacturers Agreement (No. 1)* [1961] 1 WLR 660; (1961) LR 2 RP 295.
[73] See *British Bottle Association's Agreement, ibid.*; and *Re Linoleum Manufacturer's Association, ibid.*
[74] See *Net Book Agreement (No. 1)* [1962] 1 WLR 1347 (1962) LR 3 RP 246.

(5) Abrogation of restriction likely to lead to mergers

5.34 The Court has not been very impressed with arguments to the effect that in the absence of close cooperation firms will substitute cooperation for merger and that correspondingly market concentration levels will suffer.[75] Such arguments might carry greater weight today given that empirical research on industries examined by the Court has suggested that parties to condemned restrictive agreement have often merged as an alternative means of ensuring legal cooperation.[76]

(6) Advice

5.35 The argument that abrogation of a restriction would lead to less advice for consumers was rejected in *Locked Coil Ropemakers' Association's Agreement.*[77]

(7) Keeps prices down

5.36 Arguments suggesting that restrictions curb the upward tendency of prices have found favour. This argument is particularly relevant in the case of joint purchasing groups where collective economic power can be used to obtain quantity discounts from major suppliers.[78] In decided cases, fixed minimum prices have been accepted as leading to lower prices on the basis that the minimum price is a reasonable one and that if the party traded below that level profit margins would be seriously hurt, with a knock on effect on investment, research and development, maintenance of capacity, etc.[79] Further, where the price fixed is set at a level that is significantly lower than that which would prevail in unrestricted circumstances, then a price restriction might succeed.[80]

(8) Restrictions necessary for consumer protection

5.37 In *ABTA's Agreement*[81] a system of enforced guarantee funds, reserve funds, insurance and financial scrutiny was accepted as necessary to protect the one million plus annual consumers of holidays who could fall victim to disasters brought about by the collapse of travel agents.

[75] See *Yarn Spinners Agreement* [1959] 1 WLR 154; (1959) LR 1 RP 118; *British Bottle Association's Agreement, ibid.*

[76] See Heath, "Restrictive practices and after" (1961) 29 *The Manchester School* 173–202; Swann, O'Brien, Maunder and Howe, *Competition in British Industry* (1974), pp. 172–178: "One of the most noticeable features of many of the industries studied in detail has been the decline in the number of firms producing particular products. Not all of this decline was due to mergers (other factors were at work such as the dropping of lines of production and total cessation of trading) but mergers were undeniably a major factor" (*ibid.*, at p. 172).

[77] (1965) LR 5 RP 146.

[78] See *National Sulphuric Acid Association* [1963] 1 WLR 848; (1963) LR 4 RP 169. The agreement was, following amendments, exempted from Art. 85(1) by means of Art. 85(3) EC by the Commission in 1980, [1980] 3 CMLR 429 and renewed OJ 1989 L190/22.

[79] See *Glazed and Floor Tile Home Trade Association's Agreement* (1964) LR 4 RP 239; *Distant Water Vessels Development Scheme* [1967] 1 WLR 203; (1966) LR 6 RP 242; *Standard Metal Window Group's Agreement* [1962] 1 WLR 1020; (1962) LR 3 RP 198. For classic statements on the dangers of overlow prices in common law restraint cases see *Commonwealth of Australia* v *Adelaide Steamship Co* [1913] AC 781 at p. 809 *per* Lord Parker: "It can never ... be of real benefit to the consumers of coal that colliery proprietors should carry on their business at a loss, or that any profit they make should depend on the miners' wages being reduced to a minimum. Where these conditions prevail, the less remunerative collieries will be closed down, there will be great loss of capital, miners will be thrown out of employment, less coal will be produced, and prices will consequently rise until it becomes possible to reopen the closed collieries or open other seams. The consumers of coal will lose in the long run if the colliery proprietors do not make fair profits or the miners do not receive fair wages. There is in this respect a solidarity of interest between all members of the public." See also *Hare* v *LNW Ry* (1 861) 2 J and H 80 *per* Page Wood VC.

[80] See *Cement Makers Federation Agreement* [1961] 1 WLR 581; (1961) LR 2 RP 241.

[81] [1984] ICR 12 at p. 48. See also *Building Employers' Confederation's Application* [1985] ICR 167.

(9) Obviates necessity of "shopping around"

5.38 In the famous decision in *Black Bolt and Nut Association's Agreement*[82] the Court accepted that fixed prices enabled parties to supply each other with varieties of the product not produced by the other. This enabled purchasers to obtain all of their requirements from one supplier thus saving "shopping time" which was very expensive and time consuming where there were in excess of 3,000 standardised varieties of nuts and bolts on the market. The "shopping" argument, however, has been rejected in other cases.[83]

(10) Maintenance of retail outlets

5.39 The ready availability of a service or good is of benefit to the consumer. A restriction requiring retailers to employ over a specified number of staff or possess a certain minimum display space may be construed as an attempt to exclude smaller traders. Conversely, resale price maintenance for "net books" prevents larger stores undercutting smaller booksellers thereby squeezing them from the market.[84]

(11) General attitude of the Court

5.40 It should be clear to parties to agreements that no hard and fast rule applies to possible justifications under gateway (b); all will turn upon the economic background to each case. Nor does it necessarily follow that a decision arrived at in (say) 1963 will indicate the philosophy of the Court many years later. The Court in the most recent case law has adopted a strict approach to the gateways. In *ABTA's Agreement*, the Court stated: "we can see no justification in going outside the ambit of the provisions themselves, except (and then with caution) to obtain guidance from other decisions of the Court involving the application of the same provisions to different facts. In giving weight to the various factors and in making the value judgments and balancing assessments required under the section, the Court must keep the onus of proof and the deeming provision well in mind."[85] In the same case the Court indicated that not only should restrictions be scrutinised separately but that they would also be examined collectively against the "total backcloth of the circumstances of the case".[86]

(12) Check list of benefits and advantages

5.41 In summary to gateway (b) a check list of possible benefits or advantages in certain common agreement types may be drawn up. This list is for guidance only; it is not exhaustive. It should be clear that ultimately whether a restriction is advantageous depends upon surrounding economic circumstances.

(a) Joint manufacture or provision of goods and services

- Standardisation of product/service enables cost savings to be realised and the pub lic to select between competing brands more effectively;
- Specialisation of product/service leads to greater research and development and ultimately improved quality.

82 [1960] 1 WLR 884; (1960) LR 2 RP 50.

83 See *Wholesale Confectioners' Alliance Agreement (No. 1)* (1960) LR 2 RP 135; *Glazed and Floor Tile Home Trade Association's Agreement* (1964) LR 4 RP 239.

84 See *Net Book Agreement (No. 1)* [1962] 1 WLR 1347; (1962) LR 3 RP 246, discussed at paras. 8.211–8.212. The DGFT announced on 15 August 1994 that the Net Book Agreement would be referred back to the RPC, pursuant to section 4(3) RTPA 1976, to see if it still justified exemption. The RPC held on 13 March 1997 that it no longer did.

85 [1984] ICR 12 at p. 23.

86 *ibid.*, at p. 24.

- Improvement in production techniques or plant and machinery and facilitated modes of provision of service (e.g. improved information retrieval, automatic cash dispensers, etc.) leads to a better product/service.
- More efficient utilisation of peripheral techniques and by-products may result.
- More efficient distribution of work helps ensure a more appropriate utilisation of capacity.

(b) Joint selling

- Transport economies of scale may be passed on to the consumer.
- Unification of selling/marketing departments and staff and joint advertising again enables cost savings to be made.
- Greater capacity and more capable infrastructure for export purposes may result.
- Distribution costs will be lower with fewer middlemen.

(c) Joint purchasing

- Cheaper credit and bulk/quantity discounts which can be passed on to consumers.
- There is greater security of supply for purchasers and in turn their customers.
- Unification of buying departments and staff enabling cost savings to be made and passed on.
- There is greater opportunity for comparison and selection facilitating more efficient purchasing practices and better service to the consumer.
- Standardisation of materials will enable more efficiency.

(d) Exchange of information

- Opportunity for exchanges of data and opinion on market data improves participants' knowledge of the market and enhances their efficiency.
- Exchange of data on costings does not enable parties to predict each others' prices but permits cost comparisons to be made and allows firms to pinpoint relative weaknesses and strengths in their own structures.
- Joint collection and dissemination of trade statistics increases market awareness.
- Joint promotion of scientific and technical research is enabled.

4. Sections 10(1)(c) and 19(1)(c): Defensive Measures and Self-Protection Cartels

5.42 Sections 10(1)(c) (goods) and 19(1)(c) (services) RTPA 1976 represent the third gateway. This allows for arguments on the basis that the restrictions are necessary to counteract the monopoly power of another person. This gateway reads:

> "that the restriction or information provision is reasonably necessary to counteract measures taken by any one person not party to the agreement with a view to preventing or restricting competition in or in relation to the trade or business in which the persons party thereto are engaged."[87]

This gateway must be read conjunctively with section 10(2)(b) and 19(2)(b) which read: "references to any one person include references to any two or more persons being in-

[87] This gateway derives form the MMC General Report on *Collective Discrimination, op. cit.*, at para. 240(d) which states: "Where the arrangement is a necessary means of enabling smaller concerns to compete effectively with a very large concern in that trade which is itself resorting to restrictive practices." Such cartels are known on the continent as *syndicats de défense industrielle* or *schutzkartelle*. For an American example, see, *Lorrain Journal* v *US* (1951) 342 US 143.

terconnected bodies corporate or individuals carrying on business in partnership with each other". For the meaning of "interconnected bodies corporate" see section 43(1) RTPA 1976; for discussion see paras. 1.39–1.42. The gateway has only been judicially analysed in an interim order case, *DGFT* v *IIB*,[88] though it has been pleaded in argument in other cases.[89] The reasons for its lack of uptake are that: (a) gateway (d) substantially overlaps it and is wider in ambit and therefore easier to establish; and (b) the OFT may wield extensive powers against dominant concerns acting anti-competitively such that those subject to such anti-competitive conduct are more likely to complain to the OFT rather than combine in a defensive cartel. To pass through gateway (c) the agreement in question cannot be in response to a non-abusive monopoly competitor; the monopoly concern must be taking measures designed at preventing or restricting competition. It follows that the existence of dominance is not justification *per se* for a cartel of remaining firms. This reveals another difficulty inherent in gateway (c). The parties to the agreement must prove, as a precondition of their own success, abusive behaviour by another (though there is no requirement that they prove the monopolist's behaviour was successful in restraining competition). One need only ponder for a second the lengths the OFT and MMC go to in order to investigate and establish monopolistic abuse to envisage the difficulties surrounding gateway (c). A monopolist's low prices might simply reflect efficiency based upon a proper appreciation of demand rather than predation; where and when efficiency shades into aggression is very difficult to determine.

5.43 In *DGFT* v *IIB*, the Court stated that IIB's boycott of the motor insurer General Accident would have to be "reasonably necessary to counteract measures taken by General Accident with a view to preventing or restricting competition in or in relation to the business of insurance brokers".[90] IIB's argument was based on the supposition that by dealing direct with purchasers of Ford motor cars, General Accident would reduce the overall market for insurance brokers and was thus attempting to squeeze motor insurance brokers out of the market. The Court dismissed this as "pure speculation", there being no evidence that this was General Accident's intent nor the likely effect of its conduct. Moreover, given its 10 per cent market share and third place in terms of UK market share, General Accident was not dominant and thus it was "implausible" that it could be taking these measures with a view to preventing or restricting competition by insurance brokers. It simply did not have the market power to enable it to do so.

5.44 In the light of this, the following might be suitable gateway (c) cases:

- Firms purchase in a joint buying group in order to combine purchasing muscle and force better terms from a dominant supplier. It must be shown, however, that the supplier was abusing his power for example by overpricing its goods.
- Where a trade association (which is therefore "one person") takes restrictive measures or recommends restrictive action to its members (for example the operation of a stop list or black book or some other boycotting device). A trade union registered as such would not count as "one person".[91]
- X, a vertically integrated manufacturer of widgets, is also dominant in the supply of the raw materials needed for widget production. X supplies the raw materials to competitors on discriminatory terms and in this manner influences the widget mar-

[88] [1991] ICR 822.
[89] See *National Sulphuric Acid Association's Agreement* [1963] 1 WLR 848; (1963) LR 4 RP 169 though is was not discussed by the Court who permitted the agreement to subsist on the basis of gateways (d) and (g) and later, gateways (b) and (g).
[90] [1991] ICR 822, 831.
[91] See, Wilberforce, Campbell and Elles, *Restrictive Trade Practices and Monopolies* (1956), pp. 395, 396.

ket to its advantage. An analogous case was found by the MMC to exist in their resort on man-made cellulosic fibres in respect of the behaviour of Courtaulds.[92] Presumably rival widget manufacturers (or competitors of Courtaulds who were being discriminated *against*) could have formed a defence cartel.

– X, Y and Z are very large purchasers who act upon a recognition of their interdependence. X occasionally performs acts designed to encourage the interdependence between the three firms. Suppliers join together in a joint selling agency on the basis of the behaviour of X who is seeking to cement the interdependence of the purchasers.[93]
– X is a foreign, dominant supplier of an important raw material. Purchasers join in a buying pool to combine their purchasing power and wield it against the anti-competitive conduct of X. There is no reason why X should be a person situate in the UK.[94]

5. Sections 10(1)(d) and 19 (1)(d): Countervailing Power Cartels or Agreements[95]

5.45 Gateway (d) reads (for goods):

> "that the restriction or information provision is reasonably necessary to enable the persons party to the agreement to negotiate fair terms for the supply of goods to, or the acquisition of goods from, any one person not party thereto who controls a preponderant part of the trade or business of acquiring or supplying such goods, or for the supply of goods to any person not party to the agreement and not carrying on such a trade or business who, either alone or in combination with any other such person, controls a preponderant part of the market for such goods."

The notion of "countervailing power" has been defined to describe the scenario whereby: "private economic power is held in check by the countervailing power of those who are subject to it. The first begets the second ... The fact that the seller enjoys a measure of monopoly power, and is reaping a measure of monopoly return as a result means that there is an inducement to those firms from whom he buys or those to whom he sells to develop the power with which they can defend themselves against exploitation."[96] Gateway (d) recognises the validity of countervailing power. The overlap with gateway (c)

[92] MMC Report, *Supply of Man Made Cellulosic Fibres* HC No. 130 (April, 1968). It was argued in *National Sulphuric Acid* (*op. cit.*) that the gateway operated only against a monopolist operating at a different level of trade though there is no reason why this should necessarily be so. In the UK a monopolist need only control 25 per cent of the market under the Fair Trading Act 1973.

[93] Though an attempt by X to induce concerted behaviour would almost certainly give rise to either a registrable agreement or an anti-competitive practice. In both cases the OFT could intervene.

[94] This was the case in *National Sulphuric Acid* where the monopolist was the American giant SULEXCO. That case however was finally decided under other gateways. See for a recent EC parallel Case C-250/92 *Gottrup Klim* [1994] ECR I-5641, 5687, para. 32.

[95] The theory of "countervailing power" is well established. Its leading exponent is J.K. Galbraith, *American Capitalism* (1970).

[96] *ibid.*, at p. 125. See also MMC Report, *Supply of Metal Containers* HC No. 6 (July 1970) at p. 312: "the bargaining power of customers is an important factor; and this, in turn, depends on, amongst other things, the customer's ability to make his own cans and competition from other independent can makers. Metal Box itself agrees that it makes great efforts to persuade customers not to make their own cans." In MMC Report, *Supply and Exports of Cigarette Filter Rods* HC No. 35 (July 1969) the dominance in the market of the producer of cigarette filter rods (83 per cent of total UK production) could not be abused because the customers, the cigarette companies, were powerful enough to manufacture the rods themselves should the supplier prove unsatisfactory. See also, MMC Report, *Supply of Flat Glass* HC No. 83 (February 1968). According to the MMC Report, *Supply of Chemical Fertilisers* HC 128 (1959–60), p. 19, a departmental committee of the Ministry of Munitions set up in 1917 recommended the formation of a comprehensive association of acid producers to cooperate in solving post-war supply difficulties. The National Sulphuric Acid Association was accordingly formed in 1919.

will be immediately appreciated: both gateways concern the protection of the parties to the agreement from outside economic power. This gateway has proven complex in practice. Five cases have sought passage through it,[97] only one successfully. The gateway essentially covers two situations: (a) where the restriction is reasonably necessary to enable the persons party to the agreement to negotiate fair terms for the supply of goods to, or the acquisition of goods from, any one person not party thereto who controls a preponderant part of the trade or business of acquiring such goods; and (b), where the restriction is reasonably necessary to enable the persons party to the agreement to negotiate fair terms for the supply of goods to any person not party to the agreement and not carrying on such a trade or business of acquiring or supplying such goods who, either alone or in combination with any other such person, controls a preponderant part of the market for such goods.

5.46 Before examining the two varieties of situation envisaged in gateway (d) it is necessary to consider some of the problems of language in the provision. The agreement in question must respond to a person or cartel which "controls a preponderant part" of the trade or business or market. A number of points may be made of this phrase. First, it is necessary to define the market. A supplier might be preponderant in the supply of mushrooms but will certainly not be so in the market for the supply of vegetables; a purchaser may be preponderant in that it acquires 68 per cent of a specific type of steel wire supplied but is certainly not preponderant in the general market for the steel wire. In *Locked Coil Ropemakers' Association's Agreement*[98] the parties to the challenged agreement asserted that the National Coal Board (NCB) was a preponderant buyer of class 1 mining ropes since they accounted for over 80 per cent of purchases. The question was whether class 1 mining rope was the relevant market or whether other stranded wire rope generally was the relevant market. The test, stated the Court, was whether any division or fragmentation was "commercially sensible". Whether a division is commercially sensible will turn on differences between the products. This will entail an examination of *inter alia* the: size, appearance, method of production and use of the product; the nature of machinery and equipment used, the nature and concentration level of sellers market; and the nature and concentration level of buyers market. In *Locked Coil Ropemakers* the parties argued that the price restrictions they operated for class 1 mining ropes were necessary. They contended the same, however, for other classes of mining rope since, they argued, if restrictions were removed on the other classes of rope the NCB would switch their purchases to these. The Court (employing additional evidence) construed this assertion to imply that the same machinery could produce different classes of rope and that the ropes were largely substitutable for each other. Accordingly, it was not "commercially sensible" to isolate class 1 mining ropes from other classes of mining rope. Secondly, it is necessary to define the appropriate territorial market of the preponderant firm. A supplier of a product might be preponderant among UK firms but might not be so when compared with other worldwide suppliers who could supply the UK market with ease and at prices acceptable to UK purchasers. In deciding the extent of control foreign markets must be considered.[99] Thirdly, it has been intimated by the Court of Appeal (in the unsatisfactory context, however, for purposes of proper legal argument of an application for an interim injunction) that for gateway (d) to apply the preponderant party must deal *direct* with the parties to the agreement.[100] If correct, a preponderant supplier could

[97] It was also pleaded in *DGFT* v *IIB* [1991] ICR 822, an interim order case.

[98] [1965] 1 WLR 121; (1964) LR 5 RP 146.

[99] See *Associated Transformer Manufacturers' Agreement* [1970] 1 WLR 1589; (1970) LR 7 RP 202; *National Sulphuric Acid Association's Agreement* [1963] 1 WLR 848; (1963) LR 4 RP 169.

[100] *Daily Mirror Newspapers Ltd* v *Gardner* [1968] 2 WLR 1239 (CA).

organise to trade via an agent or other intermediary and thereby negate the justification for purchasers to set up a joint buying agreement. However, it is not certain what effect the argument that, *de facto*, the purchasers would (regardless of the intermediaries) have to negotiate with the supplier would have on this proposition. If you negotiate direct with the preponderant party do you by definition deal directly with it?[101] Fourthly, the word "controls" implies present tense. However, in deciding whether a restriction is "reasonably necessary" the Court will look also to the likely future situation; it would not be "reasonably necessary" for parties to form a cartel if the power of the preponderant party was a temporary phenomenon. Fifthly, in terms of market share percentages there is no threshold for preponderance. In *National Sulphuric Acid Association* the Court stated: "while the relative size of the part is clearly important, we do not accept that respondents have necessarily to show that it exceeds 50 per cent. It is a question to be decided in the light of all relevant circumstances."[102] Sixthly, the reference to a person acting "in combination with any other such person" has been considered to "connote at least some degree of co-operation between the persons concerned".[103] It was insufficient to argue that one company could be in combination with other companies simply through their presence on a market at the same level of supply.

5.47 The word "negotiate" deserves brief mention. The Court has given it a very wide meaning. It does not simply connote face to face meetings or bundles of correspondence; it even includes, for example, suppliers putting in tenders at uneconomic prices.[104] The phrase "reasonably necessary" appears in a number of gateways. It has already been alluded to above in connection with the word "control". It appears to be true, from the cases, that while a countervailing restrictive agreement may be "reasonably necessary" to negotiate fair terms from a preponderant party which is not abusing its power,[105] it will none the less be easier to prove reasonable necessity where the preponderant party is acting unfairly.[106]

5.48 Finally, on terminology— "fair terms". The Court has been equivocal in its approach to the phrase. A number of tests exist which are apparently treated as alternatives. Thus "fair terms" are definable as terms upon which an efficient producer can make and sell his goods at a reasonable profit to a preponderant purchaser.[107] An alternative test describes "fair" not in relation to one efficient party's reasonable costs but more widely in relation to general market circumstances. Thus, "fair terms"—again in the context of a preponderant buyer—would be terms that would prevail if there were other buyers in the market who would negotiate with the supplier in order that the latter obtained reasonable profits and the former a reasonable purchase price.[108] The two formulations are not contradictory. In a recession an efficient supplier might reasonably be forced to cut his prices

[101] See *Water-Tube Boilermakers' Agreement* [1959] 1 WLR 1118; (1959) LR 1 RP 285.

[102] (1963) LR 4 RP 169 at p. 227. See also *Water-Tube Boilermakers' Agreement* [1959] LR 1 RP 285 at p. 339; *National Federation of Retail Newsagents (No. 3)* (1969) LR 7 RP 27 at p. 74. Market shares that have been held to connote preponderance have been: 100 per cent in *Water-Tube Boilermakers, ibid.*; 75 per cent in *Associated Transformers, ibid.*; 49 per cent in *National Sulphuric Acid, ibid.*, However, 38 per cent was inadequate in *Locked Rope Coilmakers op. cit.*, n. 78; and 41 per cent in *National Federation of Retail Newsagents (No. 3), ibid.*, was inadequate. On these figures the definition of monopoly in s. 6 of the Fair Trading Act 1973 which is 25 per cent of the market apparently does not equate to "preponderance" in gateway (d). In *DGFT* v *IIB* [1991] ICR 822, 832, 833 the RPC held that General Accident, with a 10 per cent market share, could not be said to hold a "preponderant part of the market".

[103] *DGFT* v *IIB* [1991] ICR 822, 834.

[104] See *Water-Tube Boilermakers' Agreement* [1959] 1 WLR 1118; (1959) LR 1 RP 285 at pp. 340, 341.

[105] *ibid.*

[106] See e.g. *Associated Transformer Manufacturers' Agreement (No. 1)* [1961] 1 WLR 660; (1961) LR 2 RP 295 at p. 342. For commentary see Cunningham, *op. cit.*, at pp. 333, 334.

[107] See *Water-Tube Boilermakers' Agreement* [1959] 1 WLR 1118; (1959) LR 1 RP 285.

[108] See *Associated Transformer Manufacturers' Agreement (No. 1)* (1961) 1 WLR 660; (1961) LR 2 RP 295.

to earn only marginal profits which, under the circumstances, would be counted as "fair". Likewise, it might not be possible to find out what the supplier's costs really are to determine whether or not his prices are reasonable. This might, for example, be because the supplier is a foreign company. In such a case the second test is easier to apply, i.e. what are fair terms by comparison to other actual or potential suppliers? This was the case in National Sulphuric Acid where the preponderant supplier was SULEXCO a giant American export cartel. The Court stated: "A suitable initial approach, in the present case, is to apply the test: Are the prices which the buyers would have had to pay, in the absence of the restriction, likely to be substantially higher than the prices which they would have had to pay in market conditions which are similar, except that there is no one supplier controlling a preponderant part of the trade or business."[109]

5.49 In summary "fair terms" in the preponderant buyer case may imply:

(a) sellers earning "fair" profits;
(b) the attainment of equality of treatment as between buyers;
(c) the prevention of unfair profits being earned by the preponderant buyer; and
(d) the attainment of a selling price that would prevail in the absence of the preponderant buyer.[110]

5.50 Where preponderant seller cases are at stake the converse implications apply. Finally, attention will be returned to the two varieties of countervailing power agreement envisaged by the terms of gateway (d). The first variety of agreement is where the parties combine to counter the power of a single person who controls a preponderant part of either the "trade" of acquiring or selling those goods or the "business" of supplying those goods (i.e. from their production or manufacture). The countervailing agreement here is not set against another agreement that would be registrable and hence subject to control under the RTPA 1976. The preponderant party though may be prone to investigation as a monopoly under the Fair Trading Act 1973 or its practices may be reviewable under the Competition Act 1980. However, it has *not* been held by the Court that the preponderant party must abuse its power before a gateway (d) case arises. Hence a countervailing power agreement blessed under gateway (d) may be simply a means of artificially creating a more equitable supply/purchase balance of bargaining power, it being accepted that free market forces have failed to achieve this balance. The second variety of agreement envisages an agreement set against a preponderant purchaser or group of purchasers who together are preponderant. In this variety of case the preponderant concern(s) are not involved in the trade or business that the parties to the countervailing agreement are. This fact differentiates the case from first variety of case. For example: turkey farmers in a region agree to a maximum sale price for their turkeys; together the farmers are preponderant purchasers of seed. This agreement is blessed under gateway (b) or is given clearance by the OFT under section 21 (2) RTPA 1976. Because the farmers accept lower profits they cannot pay suppliers of poultry feed high prices. The feed suppliers enter a joint selling agreement to negotiate fairer (higher) prices from the turkey farmers. Neither farmers nor feed suppliers are in the same market though farmers together control a preponderant part of the feed supply market.

[109] [1963] 1 WLR 848; (1963) LR 4 RP 169 at p. 228. This test was applied in *Locked Coil Ropemakers' Association's Agreement* [1965] 1 WLR 121; (1964) LR 5 RP 146.

[110] See Stevens and Yamey *The Restrictive Practices Court: A Study of the Judicial Process and Economic Policy* (1965), p. 58.

6. Sections 10(1)(e) and 19(1)(e): Serious and Adverse Effect on Unemployment in an Area

5.51 This gateway—for goods—reads:

> "that, having regard to the conditions actually obtaining or reasonably foreseen at the time of the application, the removal of the restriction or information provision would be likely to have a serious and persistent adverse effect on the general level of unemployment in an area, or in areas taken together, in which a substantial proportion of the trade or industry to which the agreement relates is situated."

It will be appreciated that the gateway relates to the general level of unemployment in an area, not to unemployment levels in the specific trade or industry in question. One must, therefore, effectively prove that abrogation of the restriction would be likely to create unemployment in the specific trade or industry and that displaced workers would be unlikely to be redeployed in the area. The sole agreement to pass through this gateway was in *Yarn Spinners Agreement*.[111] In that case it had been almost impossible to estimate the amount of unemployment in the relevant Lancashire areas as at the date of the hearing, although rough estimates were made of 4 per cent (there was full employment elsewhere). In the absence of the price restrictions it was estimated that unemployment would rise to about 6 per cent. The Court accepted therefore that gateway (e) was satisfied. The case was lost, however, on other grounds. The gateway was not passed through in *British Jute Trade Federal Council's Agreements*.[112] The jute industry was centred in Dundee, an area of high unemployment. The industry and locality was protected by the Jute Controller—an official—who regulated the influx of cheap imports. The parties argued that their agreements were necessary to support the activities of the Jute Controller. The Court rejected this argument holding that the Jute Controller could operate effectively without the agreements. To succeed under this gateway the unemployment must be both serious *and* persistent. Moreover, it must be proven that a substantial proportion of the trade or industry to which the agreement relates is situate in the areas in issue. This suggests that the gateway may be pertinent to those industries which are for historical or other reasons localised: shipbuilding; mining; automobile industry; textiles, etc. The Liesner Committee in their *Review of Restrictive Trade Practices Policy* in 1979[113] commented on the economics problems of this gateway:

> "As to the wording of the gateway from an economic stand point a restriction may well lead to higher employment in a limited area or for a short period, but result in lower employment in the industry affected over a wider geographical area or a longer time span. Moreover, account should properly be taken of the indirect effect which a change in employment in one industry has on employment in the service and other industries. It is hard to quantify these various influences and even more difficult to weigh up their relative importance as additional jobs may be more important in one area than in another or at different moments in time. However, to the extent that an agreement may be said to have a harmful effect on employment elsewhere (for example, by its effects on suppliers, purchasers or competitors), this would be a detriment which could in principle be considered in the tailpiece. It is admittedly not possible to argue wider employment benefits of a restriction under this gateway, but it appears that such benefits would normally be associated with other advantages like reduced costs which could be argued under gateway (b)."

[111] See *Yarn Spinners' Agreement* [1959] 1 WLR 154; [1959] LR 1 RP 118.
[112] (1964) LR 4 RP 399.
[113] Cmnd 7512, Annex D, para. 7, at p. 111.

7. *Section 10(1)(f) and 19(1)(f): Exports and the Balance of Payments*

5.52 Gateway (f)—goods version—reads:

> "That having regard to the conditions actually obtaining or reasonably foreseen at the time of the application, the removal of the restriction or information provision would be likely to cause a reduction in the volume or earnings of the export business which is substantial either in relation to the whole export business of the United Kingdom or in relation to the whole business (including export business) of the said trade or industry."

5.53 This gateway assists export boosters, not import preventers. The clause must be seen in the light of jurisprudence on export agreements under Article 85 EC. The RPC might (under Article 5 EC) bear in mind Article 85 EC and modify its interpretation of gateway (f) accordingly where exports to the EC are concerned. It should be noted that agreements *solely* concerned with exports are outside the scope of the RTPA 1976 and hence not registrable, though they are notifiable to the OFT.[114] No sanctions flow from non-notification.

The parties must prove that abrogation of their agreement would cause a "substantial" decline or reduction in export trade. This decline or reduction may be quantified in terms of "volume" or "earnings". Thus factors such as quantity or value would be relevant to "volume". "Earnings" is less clear: factors such as gross foreign exchange receipts would appear to be relevant.[115] The Court has also stated that "earnings" means "turnover".[116] There is little clear judicial guidance on the meaning of "substantial". In *Water-Tube Boiler Makers* the Court stated that the loss of one overseas contract could represent a substantial reduction in exports. Thus, loss of the sale of a major engineering contract in the Middle East could entail loss of vast revenues, the solitary nature of the contract being irrelevant. The gateway itself provides two tests: (a) substantial by reference to the whole export business of the UK; and (b) substantial by comparison to the whole business (domestic and foreign) of the trade or industry in question. These two tests are somewhat idiosyncratic. A reduction of, export earnings satisfying (a) (i.e. substantial by reference to the whole UK export business) would have to be of astronomical proportions. By contrast a reduction of export earnings satisfying (b) (i.e. substantial by comparison to the business of the trade in question) could be relatively small. Indeed, for a small industry only a comparatively small decline would quickly be countable as substantial. None the less gateway (f) treats the two tests as alternatives. This effectively means that test (a) is otiose.

5.54 The gateway is, in practical terms, of little relevance. Only one case has ever successfully passed through it, though it has been pleaded in seven reported cases. In the one successful case, *Water-Tube Boilermakers*, parties agreed to hold a preliminary meeting every time an export inquiry was received. There would be a detailed exchange of information at the meeting of technical and commercial issues relating to the inquiry. A member of the association would be selected for the order though weight was accorded to the customer's preference. The aim of the agreement was to ensure that the order came to the UK. The Court accepted that removal of the restriction was likely to result in a decline in foreign orders. In all of the other cases arguments under gateway (f) have failed. Thus the Court has generally rejected the argument that abrogation of a price restriction would result in an overall decline in quality and a corresponding fall-off in for-

114 s. 25 RTPA 1976 and Sch. 3 paras. 6 and 9 (agreements as to goods or services with overseas operation).
115 *Water-Tube Boilermakers' Agreement* [1959] 1 WLR 1118; (1959) LR 1 RP 285 criticised by Cunningham, *op. cit.*, at p. 346, and see comments by Korah, *op. cit.*, at p. 173.
116 *Associated Transformer Manufacturers' Agreement* (1961) LR 2 RP 295; [1961] 1 WLR 660.

eign orders.[117] Nor has it accepted the argument that termination of a price restriction in the domestic market would lead to a decline in technical collaboration which would have the result of a loss of exports. The Court in such cases points out that if technical collaboration is perceived as beneficial it will not fall with the restriction.[118] Generally, the Court rejects the argument that abrogation of a domestic restriction will harm exports where the restriction in question is primarily focused upon the home market.[119] The difference with *Water-Tube Boilermakers* was that the domestic restrictions were an integral element in securing foreign orders and not, as in other cases, simply an ancillary support to the search for such orders. At base the Court has not been convinced of the causative link between domestic restraint and foreign order.[120]

8. Sections 10(1)(g) and 19(1)(g): Restriction Required to Support other Acceptable Restriction

5.55 Gateway (g)—goods provision—reads:

> "that the restriction or information provision is reasonably required for purposes connected with the maintenance of any other restriction accepted or information provision made by the parties, whether under the agreement or under any other agreement between them, being a restriction or information provision which is found by the Court not to be contrary to the public interest upon grounds other than those specified in this paragraph, or has been so found in previous proceedings before the Court."

The gateway is useful to obtain a blessing for minor or ancillary restrictions which are necessary to the operation of a restriction which has been accepted by the Court. The nexus linking ancillary restriction and main, already accepted restriction, is one of reasonable requirement. Thus it need not be shown that the main restriction is inoperative without the supporting restriction; it suffices to show that the ancillary restriction improves the operation of the main restriction. Thus, in *Cement Makers Federation Agreement*[121] a price restriction had been accepted under gateway (b). The issue now was whether an ancillary restriction could attach itself to the main restriction and pass through gateway (g). The ancillary restriction was to the effect that if orders for cement were made a substantial period of time in advance, they had to be concluded at the price prevailing on the day of dispatch. This restriction was accepted on the basis that, in its absence, cement users would make advance orders at fixed prices and reap a cost advantage when the cement was delivered at a future date due to the effects of inflation on cement prices. The Liesner Committee commented on this gateway: "Although it has been pleaded successfully on seven

117 See *Water-Tube Boilermakers' Agreement* (1959) LR 1 RP 285; [1959] 1 WLR 118. In this case the Court felt unable to accurately quantify the extent of the loss in earnings. It did agree that abrogation of the restriction would lead to a sharp cut in prices. Furthermore, since the size of individual boilers was increasing a loss of a single export contract could amount to a substantial reduction in earnings from exports for the industry.

118 *Linoleum Manufacturers' Association's Agreement* (1961) LR 2 RP 395 at pp. 428 and 431.

119 See *Federation of British Carpet Manufacturers' Agreement* [1960] 1 WLR 356; (1959) LR 1 RP 472.

120 See *Associated Transformer Manufacturers' Agreement* [1961] 1 WLR 660; (1961) LR 2 RP 295; *Locked Coil Ropemakers Association Agreement* [1965] 1 WLR 121; (1964) LR 5 RP 146; See also *Linoleum Manufacturers' Association's Agreement* [1961] 1 WLR 986; (1961) LR 2 RP 395; *Permanent Magnet Association's Agreement* [1962] 1 WLR 781; (1962) LR 3 RP 119; *Net Book Agreement* [1962] 1 WLR 1347; (1962) LR 3 RP 246.

121 [1961] 1 WLR 581; (1961) LR 2 RP 241. See also for examples of successful passage through gateway (g): *Black Bolt and Nut Association's Agreement No. 1* [1960] 1 WLR 884; (1960) LR 2 RP 50; *National Sulphuric Acid Association's Agreement* [1963] 1 WLR 848; (1963) LR 4 RP 169; *Permanent Magnet Association's Agreement* [1962] 1 WLR 781; (1962) LR 3 RP 119; *British Iron and Steel Federation's Agreement* (1964) LR 4 RP 299.

occasions it has not given much difficulty partly because so few restrictions have got through the main gateways."[122]

9. *Sections 10(1)(h) and 19(1)(h): De Minimis, Minimal Effect upon Competition*

5.56 Gateway (h)—goods provision—reads:

> "that the restriction or information provision does not directly or indirectly restrict or discourage competition to any material degree in any relevant trade or industry and is not likely to do so."

This gateway was designed specifically for information agreements and was introduced by the RTPA 1968 for that purpose though, it has never to date been used for information agreements. The first case under this gateway was *Scottish Daily Newspapers (No. 2)*.[123] Publishers agreed not to publish newspapers pending the end of an unofficial strike. This agreement was registrable. The Court condoned it under gateway (h) on the basis that it was intended as a means of ending the strike and restoring competition between the publishers. Given its transitory nature the Court accepted that it would have no effect on competition. This gateway did not succeed in *DGFT* v *IIB*[124] where a boycott was proposed for an initial period of six months. This was regarded as more than transitory, especially as it could be renewed. Gateway (h) uses the words "any relevant trade or industry". Presumably a restrictive agreement in the market for apples which has little effect upon that market but which has an appreciable effect in the market for pears would not be condoned under gateway (h). It will be noted that the gateway uses the indefinite article "any" relevant market and not the definite article "the" relevant market. Thus since pears are a substitute product for apples the pear market is presumably a relevant market. From an economic common sense point of view, it is unlikely, given the strict approach of the Court and the presumption against restrictions that the statue seems to imply, that a restriction, innocuous in the parties' own market, but harmful in another market would be acceptable. The words "trade or industry" are used frequently throughout the gateways. Trade may be taken to mean buying and reselling; industry may be taken to mean manufacture and supply. In the services context the words mean essentially the same with appropriate modifications. It should be noted further that the parties must prove a negative effect, i.e. that *no* "material" restrictions on competition derive from the agreement in question. The Liesner Committee noted one possible use of this gateway: "However, one possible application would be to challenge before the Court the Director General of Fair Trading's refusal to make a section 21 (2) representation to the Secretary of State, or the latter's refusal to discharge the Director General of Fair Trading from taking an insignificant agreement before the Court."[125]

10. *The Balancing Tailpiece*

5.57 In both sections 10 and 19 RTPA 1976 there exists what has become known as the "balancing tailpiece". The goods version reads:

122 Liesner Committee, *op. cit.* at Annex D at p.112.

123 1972) LR 7 RP 401. See also *Building Employers Confederation's Application* [1985] ICR 167 at pp. 171, 172.

124 [1991] ICR 822, an interim order case. The Court also rejected an argument that the vagueness of the gateway meant that a court at the interim stage could not say there was no reasonable expectation of the IIB succeeding at full trial.

125 Liesner Committee, *op. cit.*, at p. 112.

> "and is further satisfied (in any such case) that the restriction or information provision is not unreasonable having regard to the balance between those circumstances and any detriment to the public or to persons not parties to the agreement (being purchasers, consumers or users of goods produced or sold by such parties, or persons engaged or seeking to become engaged in the trade or business of selling such goods or of producing or selling similar goods) resulting or likely to result from the operation of the restriction or the information provision."

The words "purchasers", "consumers" and "users" include persons purchasing, consuming or using for the purpose, or in the course, of trade or business or for public purposes. References to any one person includes reference to any two or more persons being interconnected bodies corporate or individuals carrying on business in partnership with each other.[126] When the case concerns services the balancing tailpiece is slightly different; the elaboration of who is meant by the "public" or "persons not parties to the agreement" includes: "users of services supplied by such parties, or persons engaged or seeking to become engaged in any business of supplying such services or of making available or supplying similar services, or being vendors, purchasers, consumers or users of goods or other property in relation to which any such services or similar services are supplied".[127] The relevance of differences between the goods and services version is discussed below.

5.58 Under the "tailpiece" the Court must perform two tasks: (i) determine whether any detriments to the public or to non-parties exist; and (ii), if such detriments exist determine whether they are outweighed by the benefits which the Court has found to exist under the gateways. The Director General, through his Counsel, must assert the existence of detriments. These detriments must "result or be likely to result from the" restrictions.[128] Though it is clear that the onus of proof lies also with the parties to attempt to prove that the benefits from the restrictions outweigh the detriments following therefrom.[129]

(1) "The public": meaning

5.59 As stated above the Court must balance the benefits of the restriction against the detriments to the "public or to persons not party to the agreement". For this balancing process the Court must have a clear perception of which vested interests are included within the concept of public. For instance the phrase "the public" could include: consumers; purchasers; users; competitors or potential competitors to the parties; the parties themselves; and, suppliers of different goods (e.g. raw materials or components) to the parties. The concept of the public is, however, not this wide. In discussion of gateway (b) (goods) it was noted that the term "the public" used there was qualified by the wording following it: "as purchasers, consumers or users".[130] If this also applies in the tailpiece detriments experienced by either the parties themselves or suppliers *to* the parties are to be discounted in the balancing process. While this would be right and proper in the case of the parties themselves it is not so in the case of suppliers to the parties: detriments inherent in restrictions can certainly prejudice suppliers. The important question thus arises: are the interest of suppliers to the parties to be taken into account when balancing the pros and cons of restrictions in agreements? Whether the term "the public" does include the interests of suppliers to the parties is unclear from the wording of the tailpiece. This is because it is unclear whether the qualifying words in brackets in both sections 10 and 19

[126] s. 10(2) RTPA 1976.

[127] s. 19(2) RTPA 1976.

[128] See *Association of British Travel Agents* [1984] ICR 12 at p. 46F.

[129] See *Black Bolt and Nut Association's Agreement* [1960] 1 WLR 884; (1960) LR 2 RP 50.

[130] The same qualification to the concept of "the public" appears in the Resale Prices Act 1976.

apply to the word "public" or only to the phrase "persons not party to the agreement". There is no judicial analysis of this potentially important question though certain cases hint in an unsatisfactory fashion at one solution or the other. In *British Iron and Steel Federation's Agreement*[131] it was held that the interests of scrap creators were relevant to the balancing process. The scrap creators were *suppliers* to the parties to the restrictive agreement and would not, therefore, have fallen within the categories of persons described in the brackets (i.e. purchasers, consumers, users, competitors or potential competitors). *A fortiori*, scrap dealers must have been counted as part of "the public" which, therefore, may be assumed to include suppliers to the parties. This is, it is submitted, correct and sound in terms of policy. Thus the concept of "the public" for tailpiece purpose includes any vested interest adjudged by the Court to be worthy of consideration. The phrase "persons not party to the agreement" is construed more narrowly by reference to the words in brackets.[132]

5.60 This conclusion is partly supported and partly contradicted by an amendment to section 19 RTPA 1976 (services) introduced by section 28 Competition Act 1980. This section seeks to add "vendors" of services to the categories of persons whose interests are to be taken into account in the tailpiece. Thus since a supplier of services to parties to a restrictive agreement is a "vendor" of services such a person's interests are relevant to the balancing process.[133] Thus, parties to an agreement may plead before the Court that suppliers to them and other vendors of services may receive benefits as a result of their agreement. A number of important points must however be raised. First, why was not a similar amendment made to section 10 for goods? Does this failure to amend section 10 imply that the drafters of the 1980 Competition Act considered that the interests of suppliers to the parties and other vendors of goods were irrelevant to the tailpiece process? Alternatively in the light of case law (e.g. *British Iron and Steel Federation* case) on section 10, did the drafters of the 1980 Act consider that section 10 *already* embraced the interests of suppliers to the parties and other vendors of goods? Given the analysis of the tailpiece above the latter in-

[131] (1964) LR 4 RP 299 noted Yamey (1963) 26 MLR 185.

[132] Cunningham, *The Fair Trading Act 1973* (1974) appears to think otherwise, at pp. 354, 355. Korah, *Competition Law of Britain and the Common Market* (1982), in a more considered discussion, suggests that the opposite view holds true, at pp. 178, 179. Another case which supports the view that the interests of suppliers are relevant is *Yarn Spinners Agreement* [1959] 1 WLR 154; (1959) LR 1 RP 118 where the Court took into account the waste of national resources entailed by the preservation of excess capacity. This factor obviously falls outside of the bracketed, sectorial interests and assumes that such factors are relevant to "the public". Korah, *op. cit.*, at p. 178 states, in general fashion: "On the other hand it is very doubtful whether the Court should attempt to consider what the effect of increasing prices in one industry will be on the economy as a whole, as the Court attempted to do in *Yarn Spinners* (1959). The waste of resources in that industry was the relatively small number of strong young men who might have migrated to other regions to take jobs, the old men and married women (most of whom would have left the labour market), and the mills themselves—which did not seem at that time to have any other use, though they have since been used to breed broiler chickens. The value of these 'wasted resources' to the economy in their 'next best use' does not seem very great." As an excursus, doubts as to the appropriateness of the Court as an assessor of micro- and macroeconomic policy were expressed by Lord Kilmuir, the Lord Chancellor, during the second reading of the RTPA Bill in 1956: "A difficulty is felt that under the Bill the Government are placing on the Court a task which will take judges outside the ordinary field of judicial activity and involve them in applying economic and value judgements in which they are not trained. I am most anxious to make it clear that I have given careful consideration to this point and I have come to the conclusion that the questions at issue are not inappropriate for judicial determination within the framework laid in down in the Bill." (HL Deb 26 June 1956, col. 18). Finally it is pertinent to note that one case does imply the narrow construction of "the public": *Water-Tube Boilermakers' Agreement* (1959) LR 1 RP 285. The decision in *ABTA* [1984] ICR 12 at p. 46E is equivocal on this point.

[133] s. 28 Competition Act 1980 also adds "vendors" to s. 19(1)(b) RTPA 1976 (services) where "the public" is equated to users, vendors, purchasers, consumers or users of any goods or other property.

terpretation is in policy terms, it is submitted, the better one. Section 28 Competition Act 1980 equates the phrase "the public" with the categories of interests indicated within the brackets. The section states of section 19 RTPA 1976 that it "provides amongst other things that there is a presumption that a restriction or information provision is against the public interest unless the Court is satisfied the removal of it would deny benefits to the public as purchasers, consumers or users of any goods." It is strongly submitted that this equation of "the public" with the bracketed categories of person is not to be taken seriously. This is simply an instance of careless drafting. The words seek to summarise an important part of the tailpiece but in so doing fail to mention the important phrase "or to persons not parties to the agreement". This phrase, as a quick glance at the precise wording of section 19 will reveal, is inserted between the phrase "the public" and the bracketed interests. In the text above it has been suggested that the bracketed interests qualify the phrase "or to persons not parties to the agreement" and *not* "the public". It is thus very unhelpful and confusing for the draftsman to ignore these important words in the summary given in section 28 Competition Act 1980. Accordingly, little weight should be attached to the equation between "the public" and the bracketed interests.

(2) The tailpiece and "detriment"

5.61 The tailpiece, in practice, does not appear to be an undue obstacle to surmount where the Court has already accepted that the restriction passes through the gateways. The only case in which restrictions which passed through gateways were found to falter at the tailpiece hurdle was *Yarn Spinners Agreement* where gateway (e) on unemployment was passed through. However, the Court condemned the price fixing agreement on the basis that it would result in: slight increases in the price of cotton goods; a decline in export orders; and a squandering of national resources due to the maintenance of excess capacity. In all other cases success under the gateways has involved continued success with the tailpiece even though the Court has accepted that detriments do flow from the restrictions. In such cases the following have been held to amount to detriments:

(a) abolition of the availability of cheaper varieties or grades of the product;[134]
(b) the existence of higher prices for a minority of purchasers in the context of reasonable prices for the majority of purchasers;[135]
(c) the existence of "delivered" prices;[136]
(d) temporary withdrawal of product from a market due to exceptional circumstances;[137]
(e) creation of an obstacle to new forms, and innovative means of supply, of services;[138]
(f) creation of entry barriers.[139]

In all of these cases, however, the detriments have been considered to have been outweighed by the advantages.

5.62 Where the Court has found detriments but has accepted that the counterbalancing advantages are more important it has, on one recent occasion, made suggestions as to how the detriments could be abated or reduced without prejudice to the beneficial aspects of the restrictions. In *ABTA's Agreement* the Court suggested improvements to various trade association procedures and further suggested the "guiding principle" that in the exercise of

134 See *Blanket Manufacturers' Agreement* [1959] 1 WLR 442; (1959) LR 1 RP 208; *Glazed and Floor Tile Home Trade Association's Agreement* (1964) LR 4 RP 239.
135 See *Permanent Magnet Association's Agreement* [1962] 1 WLR 781; (1962) LR 3 RP 119.
136 See *Standard Metal Window Group's Agreement* [1962] 1 WLR 1020; (1962) LR 3 RP 198.
137 See *Scottish Daily Newspaper Society's Agreement No. 1* (1971) LR 7 RP 379.
138 See *Association of British Travel Agents* [1984] ICR 12 at p. 47.
139 *ibid.*

its powers over tour operator and travel agency services ABTA should "at all times regard the interest of the consumer as the paramount consideration".[140]

(3) Whether one unacceptable restriction negates an otherwise acceptable standard form contract

5.63 One serious problem that was solved by the Court in the *ABTA Agreement* case was the distinction between restriction and restrictions in standard form contracts (SFCs). The OFT had hitherto construed the law as being that restrictions expressed in SFCs had to be viewed collectively as a single restriction rather than a catalogue of separate restrictions. If this was so then if the Court found one restriction in a SFC, or a selection of restrictions out of a greater number, to be against the public interest then *all* the restrictions fell. This concerned the OFT which was worried that this would leave a serious vacuum in the structural framework of how trade was conducted in the market in question; if all the restrictions in a commonly used SFC were suddenly held to be unlawful this would cause great confusion for businessmen who had hitherto relied upon the SFC. The OFT was concerned at the "hammer to crack a nut" nature of this approach. The existence of one or two black clauses in a SFC does not necessarily render an otherwise acceptable SFC detrimental, harmful and positively against the public interest. The problem apparently lay in section 8(2)(a) and (b) (goods), and, 16(3)(a) and (b) (services) RTPA 1976. These provide effectively that where a trade association recommends to its members use of a SFC then the constitutional documents of the association are deemed to contain clauses providing that members are bound to comply with the SFC. Following a statement in *British Bottle Association's Agreements* the OFT was led to believe that the Court viewed restrictions in SFC's conjunctively, as a single restriction, on the basis of the singular nature of the deemed restriction in the trade association constitution requiring members to abide by the SFC.[141] However, it is clear following the *ABTA* case that a more flexible approach is being taken by the Court. There the Court analysed all of the restrictions separately against the setting of the gateways. It then held that certain restrictions were unlawful. With these restrictions out of consideration it proceeded to weigh in the scales of the balancing tailpiece those restrictions which had passed through the gateways. In effect certain restrictions of an unacceptable nature were excluded from the balancing tailpiece. This, of course, meant that there were fewer detriments placed in the scales and, accordingly, less to be set against the positive aspects of the restrictions. The basic approach of the Court is thus an individualised one, examining restrictions separately. However, the Court in *ABTA* also made it clear that it would additionally examine the restrictions in relation to each other and the "total backcloth of the circumstances of the case".

11. Variations to Agreements Approved by the Restrictive Practices Court: Minor Variations Orders

5.64 Where the RPC approves an order it may do so within defined terms and parties will subsequently be bound to execute their agreements according to defined limits. However, it may well be the case that in the light of experience of the operation of the agree-

140 *ibid.*, at p. 47G.

141 [1961] 1 WLR 760; (1961) LR 2 RP 345. The Court, at the end of its judgment, chose to examine a clause in a standard form contract which sought to exempt absolutely liability for third party claims. The Court examined the circumstances of this clause and commented "We would only say this: we should have had no hesitation whatever in declaring this restriction to be against the public interest, even if all the other restrictions had been in the public interest." Whilst there is a degree of ambivalence about this statement it appears to imply that had one clause in the SFC been struck down then all other clauses and restrictions held in the public interest would likewise have fallen ([1961] 1 WLR 760 at p. 792); (1961) L.R. 2 RP 345 at p. 392).

ment or of fluctuations in economic and commercial circumstances, the parties will seek to vary their agreement. Prima facie variations will have to be furnished, registered and referred to the RPC. The OFT would have no jurisdiction to condone the variations, given that they relate to agreements containing significant restrictions, albeit that the restrictions have been accepted as in the public interest by the RPC. This conclusion is of course most unsatisfactory. The variation might be innocuous or *per se* trivial yet can only come into force following an appearance in Court. This problem has been avoided by the RPC in recent cases. In *Building Employers Confederation's Application*[142] the RPC held that a rule whereby members of the Confederation were required to offer to customers a building guarantee insurance scheme when offering building services was in the public interest and passed through the gateways. Customers had the option of hiring the builders' services with or without ancillary insurance. The Court issued an order approving the scheme and included in the order a provision allowing "such variations (if any) as the Director shall in writing approve". The RPC added that the OFT (on behalf of the Director) could only approve restrictions which were *not* significant, i.e. they could use their powers under section 21(2) RTPA 1976. Presumably, though, it is not stated expressly in the judgment and the form of the actual Court order seems to indicate otherwise, the OFT must obtain the consent of the Secretary of State to variations in accordance with the normal section 21(2) procedure (see paras. 4.121-4.125). Where variations are significant they must be approved by the RPC. Though the legislation does not expressly provide for the OFT to approve variations the RPC has stated that the power is implicit within section 4(1) RTPA 1976 which permits the RPC to discharge or vary previous Court orders.

D. Restraining Orders under section 35(3) RTPA 1976: Proceeding Commenced by the Director General Against Unregistered Agreements

5.65 With respect to unregistered agreements under section 35(3) the Director General may apply to the Court for an order restraining all or any of the persons listed in section 35(4) from, "giving effect to, or enforcing or purporting to enforce—(a) the agreement in respect of any restrictions or information provisions; (b) other agreements in contravention of [section 35(1)]". Proceedings of this nature are common when contrasted with other types of proceeding. The OFT does not go the Court in respect of every unregistered agreement; the policy is to seek an order only in respect of those agreements which the OFT consider will recur without such an order or in respect of which it is considered the parties acted covertly or in respect of an agreement which had serious anti-competitive effects.[143] An order of the Court may be made against persons mentioned in section 35(4):

[142] [1985] ICR 167 at pp. 172, 173. See also *National Association of Scaffolding Contractors* (1969) (unreported) No. 644 Register of Restrictive Trade Practices where a similar order was made.

[143] e.g. action brought by OFT against Atlantic Steam Navigation (Townsend Thoresen) and Sealink in connection with prices quoted and charged for passenger carriage during 1982 on two Scotland to Northern Ireland lines. The agreement was discovered by the OFT following complaints about parallel prices (*British Business*, 21 January 1984, p. 81). See also Report of Registrar of Restrictive Trading Agreements 1969 (1970) Cmnd 4303, p. 2. See DGFT Annual Report 1979 at pp. 46 and 104–106, where it is noted that during 1979, s. 35(3) orders were made against parties forbidding them from giving effect to 172 agreements concerning the supply of ready made concrete or road surfacing materials. In 1985 the OFT referred to the RPC 153 further agreements relating to road surfacing materials: DGFT Annual Report 1985, p. 25.

"(a) any person party to the agreement who carries on business within the United Kingdom; (b) a trade association or a service supply association of which any such person is a member; or (c) any person acting on behalf of any such association."

Parties rarely contest such actions since no public interest arguments may be raised;[144] parties are sometimes represented in Court in order for Counsel to apologise to the Court for the non-furnishing it being hoped by this to persuade the Court of the repentant mood of the parties and placate the OFT. The one practical reason for being represented in Court is to persuade the Court as to the type of remedy or order to be made. In this respect a number of options exist:

(a) The Court may accept undertakings from the parties as an alternative to the Court granting an injunction. An undertaking has the same effect as an injunction and breach thereof is a serious contempt of Court.[145] Though, undertakings offered to the Court in lieu of an injunction will not necessarily be accepted by the Court.[146]
(b) Injunctive orders may be made against the agreement in question.
(c) Injunctive orders may be made against both the agreement in question *and* any future unregistered agreement. Whether or not the Court will order such a wide injunction depends on a number of factors:
(i) whether the parties were aware of the duty to register;
(ii) whether the parties were aware that their agreement in particular was subject to registration;
(iii) whether the parties had taken steps to discover whether their agreement was registrable;[147]
(iv) the duration of the agreement prior to discovery by the OFT;[148]
(v) the seriousness of the agreement in terms of its anti-competitive consequences.[149]

5.66 These criteria to be taken into account in deciding whether to grant an order under section 35(3) have been most recently considered by the Court in *Re Distribution of Newspapers*.[150] In that case, two newspaper wholesalers had entered into a "rationalisation agreement" whereby each withdrew from an area allocated to the other. The existence of the agreement only came to the OFT's attention through an article in the trade press. There was doubt as to whether this agreement was registrable. The OFT took the view that it was, although both the OFT and the MMC[151] had some years previously held the op-

[144] See *Agreements Relating to the Supply of Bread* [1977] ICR 946 at p. 950g: "it really is not any answer to say that the restrictions contained in a particular agreement are not very onerous, or to say that the duration of the agreement is not a very long one, or to say that there is only one agreement; because the failure complained of is the failure to register; and that, as it seems to us, is the salient point of this application".

[145] See *Mileage Conference Group of the Tyre Manufacturers' Conference's Agreement* [1966] 1 WLR 1137; (1966) LR 6 RP 49; *Milburn* v *Newton Colliery Ltd* (1908) 52 SJ 317; *Northern Counties Securities Ltd* v *Jackson and Steeple* [1974] 1 WLR 1133 at p. 1143.

[146] See *Aluminium Manufacturers' Agreement* (1968) LR 6 RP 510.

[147] *Agreements Relating to the Supply of Bread* [1977] ICR 946 at p. 951F.

[148] *Flushing Cistern Makers' Agreement* [1973] ICR 654 at p. 661. See also *Aluminium Manufacturers' Agreement* (1968) LR 6 RP 510; *Electrical Installations at the Exeter Hospital Agreement* (1970) LR 7 RP 102.

[149] *ibid.*, at p. 661E: "Something is seriously wrong if Mr. Powell and other Chairmen of Shires Ltd can permit the company to operate a restrictive price ring of the kind disclosed by the documents over a period of a dozen years after the Act of 1956 came into operation." And later (at p. 661F): "This constitutes a grave and persistent dereliction of the duty of responsible company officers so to direct and manage the company's affairs as to comply with the restrictive practices legislation"—*per* Cumming-Bruce J.

[150] *Re Agreement relating to the Wholesale Distribution of Newspapers, Magazines and Periodicals* [1994] ICR 200.

[151] MMC Report, *Wholesaling of Newspapers and Periodicals*, Cmnd 7214, 1978.

posite view about such rationalisation agreements. The wholesalers sought to resist registration and there was considerable correspondence between them and the OFT. Finally particulars of the agreement were furnished and registered, through registrability was still challenged. The OFT then sought a section 35(3) order against the wholesalers. Although the agreement in question had by now been determined, the OFT wished to ensure that future rationalisation agreements were furnished for registration upon a fail-safe basis.[152] The OFT thus sought an injunction against the wholesalers entering into any other agreement in contravention of section 35(1). One of the wholesalers, W.H. Smith Ltd, admitted through Counsel on the first day of the hearing before the Court that the agreement was registrable. However, it argued against the imposition of an injunctive order in such wide terms. The Court held that an injunctive order against any future unregistered agreement was appropriate. It stated that "[t]he crux is, in our view, that, on its own evidence, WH Smith Ltd has shown itself to be so managed that an agreement that ought admittedly to have been registered under the Act of 1976 was, through insufficient attention being given to the company's obligations under the Act, not registered ... [T]he imposition of that burden on WH Smith Ltd is appropriate in view of the laxity of its management that this case has revealed."[153]

5.67 In view of the change in the OFT's view about registrability of rationalisation agreements, it may be doubted whether such criticism was truly merited. W.H. Smith had taken appropriate legal advice in their dealings with the OFT, though doubt was expressed by the Court as to whether it was this rather than neglect which left the agreement unregistered. The Court also stressed that once the OFT had made its change of view know, the agreement ought to have been furnished. But the OFT's interpretation cannot be determinative of the duty to furnish particulars which is ultimately a matter for the Court in interpreting the Act. Showing that all reasonable steps had been taken to ensure compliance with the Act is clearly an important factor to be taken into account in determining the scope of an injunction, but it was not in that case, in the Court's view, decisive. Rather the Court seemed to consider that a failure to agree with the OFT's interpretation was evidence of a lack of readiness to comply with the Act and thus justified a more stringent injunction to ensure compliance for the future through the threat of contempt proceedings.

5.68 If the Court decides to make an injunctive order and include prohibitions against both the agreement in question and any future unregistered agreements then the parties must take great care. The prohibition against future agreements extends to *all* agreements, whether similar or not to the first agreement. Thus, if X and Y are brought to Court for price fixing and a wide order is made then the entering into of even an innocuous registrable agreement entails the parties in a serious contempt of Court if the agreement is not registered (see next section for details). An important case on this is *Diazo Copying Materials.*[154] In 1978 HTL was enjoined under section 35(3)(a) and (b) (i.e. a wide order) following disclosure of an unregistered price fixing agreement. In 1983 the Director General sought leave to issue writs of sequestration of the property and assets of HTL for alleged contempt of Court. It was contended that HTL had entered a subsequent, registrable agreement. Fortunately for HTL the Court held that the clause in question was exempted from registration by section 9(3) RTPA 1976.

152 See paras. 4.43–4.46.
153 [1994] ICR 200, 216–217.
154 [1984] ICR 429 (RPC).

E. Proceedings for Contempt of Court Against Parties to Agreements who Breach Court Orders[155]

1. *Legal Context*

5.69 Failure to comply with an undertaking given to the Court or an injunction or other order involves the wrongdoer in a contempt of Court. Over the years the Court has adopted a strict approach to defendants accused of contempt of court. Thus in *Galvanised Tank Manufacturers' Association Agreement* the Court stated:

> "We wish to give warning to others who have been made subject to injunctions in respect of condemned price-fixing agreements. It is abundantly apparent from all that has emerged in the course of this motion that those who, having been placed under an injunction or having given an undertaking such as here, thereafter exchange information of their intentions such as prices, or partake in discussions, formal or informal, with their competitors on such matters, may be in real peril of finding themselves in the position in which these companies now are: that is of having passed easily and quickly from that which may be legitimate into actions which constitute a grave contempt."[156]

5.70 The gravity of contempt is reflected in the level of fines imposed upon the companies. The Restrictive Practices Court has an unlimited jurisdiction to impose fines. In *Re Agreements relating to the Supply of Ready Mixed Concrete*[157] fines totalling £8,375,000 were imposed upon eight companies and groups of companies, with the three most serious transgressors being fined £3,850,000, £2,250,000 and £1,500,000. This marked a quantum leap from the previous highest fine in the RPC, which adjusted for inflation to the date of this award had only been approximately £250,000.[158]

5.71 In *British Concrete Pipes Association Agreement*[159] the Court stated that:

> "We think it right to record at this point in this judgment that the Court has been troubled by the lack of action hitherto taken against individuals, such as directors of companies, where their companies have committed contempt. We appreciate that there may well be difficulties in taking action, such as proceedings for aiding and abetting or for committal, against directors as well as proceedings for contempt against their companies. Separate representation may be necessary and the co-operation of directors with the Director General in unearthing agreements or arrangements made in breach of undertakings given to the Court or which should have been registered under the provisions of the Act is often of great value and should not be lightly jeopardised. But we desire, nevertheless, to draw attention to the warning on this topic of possible proceedings against individuals which would not necessarily be solely financial, given by this Court in ... *Galvanised Tank* ..."[160]

5.72 There is, in this dictum, a thinly disguised threat that gaol sentences may be contemplated as appropriate punishment for defaulting company directors and managers. Any doubt that imprisonment may be an appropriate punishment for individuals who deliberately flout court

155 See Korah, "Contempt of the Restrictive Practices Court" (1980) LS Gaz 961; *Cunningham, op. cit.*, at pp. 362–373.

156 (1965) LR 5 RP 315 at p. 345.

157 [1996] 15 Tr.LR 78.

158 *Re Galvanised Tank Manufacturers' Association's Agreements* (1965) LR 5 RP 315.

159 [1982] ICR 182. See also, *National Daily and Sunday Newspapers Proprietors' Agreement* [1986] 1 CR 44 at p. 51.

160 *ibid.*, at pp. 194, 195. See OFT Press Release (21 February 1985), and DGFT Annual Report 1985, p. 62. Somerville Nails Ltd were fined £100,000 for contempt. The company breached an undertaking given to the RPC and sought to fix prices and discounts.

orders or undertakings was removed by the Court in *Re Agreements relating to the Supply of Ready Mixed Concrete*. It stated that "we ... give this clear warning to those in industry ... [i]f individuals are ever again brought before this court for such blatant disregard of court orders on anything like such a scale, they should expect to go to prison for a significant period".[161] A company's liability for contempt on behalf of its directors, managers and employees is dealt with at paras. 5.76–5.85.

2. Conduct that is Forbidden: Meaning of "Giving Effect to, or Enforcing or Purporting to Enforce"

5.73 In both sections 2(2) and 35(3) RTPA 1976 on restraining orders against registered agreements declared contrary to the public interest and unregistered agreements that are void and unenforceable as a result of failure to register respectively, the words "giving effect to, or enforcing or purporting to enforce" appear. These words will form the active part of any injunctive order or undertaking; they describe actions or categories of conduct that the parties are prohibited from doing. An understanding of their implications is thus important. In *Diazo Copying Materials*[162] questions as to their meanings were raised. Two theories were proposed: (a) that for the defendant to have given effect to or enforced or purported to enforce an agreement in breach of the order it would have to be proven beyond reasonable doubt that the restriction caused the defendant not to do what he otherwise would have done;[163] and (b) that for the defendant to have given effect to, or enforced or purported to enforce an agreement in breach of a Court order it would have to be proven "that the existence of the restriction played a part in determining [the] traders conduct".[164]

5.74 The difference between (a) and (b) is one of degree. Under (a) the Director General must establish that the restriction was the dominant or even exclusive factor in determining the defendants conduct. Under (b) the Director General, in order to establish contempt, need only show that the restriction "played a part" in influencing the defendants conduct. Clearly, the burden of proof is more onerous on the Director General in (a) than it is in respect of (b). Unfortunately, in *Diazo Copying Materials*, Warner J refrained from deciding which burden of proof was the correct one, though a tentative preference appears to have been given to (b).[165] This is probably correct. As was critically pointed out by Counsel for the Director in respect of alternative (a):

> "Where a trader is restrained by an order of the Court from giving effect to a restriction requiring him not to do that which, as a matter of commercial policy, he has no wish to do ... it cannot be incumbent on the Director General in such a case, before he can prove a breach of the order, to prove that the trader's conduct would have been different in the absence of the restriction. It must be enough for him to show that the existence of the restriction played a part in determining that conduct. Here it was enough that, on at least two occasions, Mr Musto had rejected export enquiries expressly on the ground that HTL did not have "the export rights."[166]

161 [1996] 15 Tr LR 78. The individuals aiding and abetting the contempt in that case were fined, prison not being considered appropriate due to the fact that several other individuals who were also involved had not been brought before the Court, and in view of the period of time which had elapsed between the contempts and the court proceedings.

162 [1984] ICR 429.

163 For use of the phrase "beyond reasonable doubt" see *Re Bramblevale Ltd* [1970] Ch 128.

164 [1984] ICR 429 at p. 444.

165 *ibid.*, at pp. 444, 445.

166 *ibid.*, at p. 444 *per* Warner J recounting the argument of counsel.

Moreover, both sections 2(2) and 35(3) base liability upon the defendant "purporting to enforce" an agreement. The word "purporting" implies that a defendant can be in contempt for endeavouring but failing to enforce an agreement, i.e. non-enforcement can represent breach of an order. Thus, so long as the defendant reveals by his conduct an intention to enforce the agreement it would seem that he may be liable for contempt. In such a case the defendants actual conduct was not affected by the restriction. This conclusion is clearly more consonant with alternative (b) than it is with alternative (a).

3. General Nature of Contempt Actions[167]

5.75 The Restrictive Practices Court is, by virtue of section 9(3) of the Restrictive Practices Court Act 1976, a superior Court of record and it is vested with all of the powers of the High Court. Accordingly, it can punish contempts committed in its face *and* outside of the Court. Disobedience to the judgment or order of a Court or breach of an undertaking given to a Court is a civil contempt. It is not a criminal offence but none the less is punishable by a fine or imprisonment under the inherent jurisdiction of the Court. Alternatively an injunction may be made against the contemnor (the defendant in a contempt action). An additional remedy which is exclusive to civil contempt is a writ of sequestration under which the contemnor's property is placed temporarily in the hands of the sequestrators who manage the property and receive rents and profits from it until such time as the contempt is purged. The OFT has shown itself ready to pursue such drastic steps. In *Diazo Copying Materials*[168] the defendant had been involved in an unregistered agreement which, when unearthed by the OFT, was referred to the Court under section 35(3) RTPA 1976. The Court issued an order restraining the company from giving effect to or enforcing or purporting to enforce any other unregistered agreements. Subsequently, the OFT discovered what appeared to be an unregistered agreement being operated. Accordingly, it issued a Notice of Motion in 1983 applying to the Court for: (a) a writ or writs of sequestration of the property and assets of the defendant company for its failure to comply with the order; (b) any other order as might seem just to the Court by way of punishment of the company; and (c) costs.[169] The action failed since it was ultimately decided that the unregistered agreement alleged to be the breach of the court order was in fact excluded from the duty to furnish particulars. None the less, the moral of the case is clear. Imprisonment of a director or other officer is a real possibility.[170] It is ordered where the Court considers it necessary in order to ensure compliance with the order.[171] Deliberate flouting of a Court order, however, is likely to entail the risk of imprisonment.[172] According to *Black Bolt and Nut Association's Agreement (No. 2)*[173] where the

[167] See generally Borrie and Lowe, *Law of Contempt* (3rd edn. 1996) and for the powers of the RPC in contempt cases *ibid.* at pp. 506, 638. See also Miller, *Contempt of Court* (2nd edn. 1989).

[168] [1984] ICR 429.

[169] See generally RSC Ord. 45, r.5. Costs may be awarded on a standard basis: *AG* v *Walthamstow UDC* (1895) 11 TLR 533; *Stancomb* v *Trowbridge* [1910] 2 Ch 190. This may be sufficient punishment for minor breaches of an order: *GCT Management* v *Laurie Marsh Group Ltd* [1973] RPC 432.

[170] See e.g. *Danchevsky* v *Danchevsky* [1975] Fam 17 (CA) which involved matrimonial proceedings. The Court of Appeal held that imprisonment of the contemnor was inappropriate since there was available a reasonable alternative means of securing obedience to the Court order.

[171] *Newspaper Proprietors Association and National Federation of Retail Newsagents* (1961) LR 2 RP 453 at p. 499; *Garage Equipment Association's Agreement* (1964) LR 4 RP 491 at p. 505.

[172] *Newspaper Proprietors' Association and National Federation of Retail Newsagents* (1961) LR 2 RP 453 at pp. 499, 500; *Mileage Conference Group of the Tyre Manufacturers' Conference Agreement* (1966) LR 6 RP 49 at p. 114.

[173] (1961) LR 2 RP 433 at p. 444, applied in *National Daily and Sunday Newspapers Proprietors Agreement* [1986] ICR 44 at p. 49. For the Court's jurisdiction to give a reasoned judgment in an unopposed case,

original Court hearing was unopposed and hence no reasoned judgment delivered then the "like effect" test of contempt (see paras. 5.5-5.7) will probably be inapplicable. Defendants are entitled to know with precision, clarity and particularity what it is they may not do. Where the original order arises in uncontested proceedings and is not very specifically formulated then Defendants are entitled to receive the benefit of the doubt.

4. *Companies' Liability for Contempt: Liability for Acts of Directors, Managers and Employees*

5.76 The *Ready Mixed Concrete* litigation has addressed the question of whether a company, subject to an order or injunction of the RPC, could be held to be vicariously liable in contempt as a consequence of an employee entering into another agreement "to like effect". The House of Lords in *DGFT* v *Pioneer Concrete (UK) Ltd (Ready Mixed Concrete No. 2)*[174] (the *Pioneer Concrete* case) held that a company could be so liable, overturning the Court of Appeal both in this[175] and an earlier case arising out of the same agreements involving different parties, *DGFT* v *Smiths Concrete Ltd (Ready Mixed Concrete No. 1)*[176] (the *Smiths Concrete* case), provided that the employee was acting "in the course of his employment".

5.77 The background to the litigation was that ready mixed concrete had been the subject of investigations by the DGFT on a number of occasions. Several companies, including Pioneer Concrete (UK) Ltd (Pioneer), Ready Mixed Concrete (Thames Valley) Ltd (RMC Thames), Hartigan Ready Mixed Ltd (Hartigan) and Smiths Concrete Ltd (Smiths) were brought before the Restrictive Practices Court (RPC) in March 1979. Each was restrained by order from giving effect to the specific agreements uncovered during that investigation and "from giving effect to or enforcing or purporting to enforce (whether by itself or by its servants or agents or otherwise) any other agreements in contravention of section 35(1) of the [Restrictive Trade Practices] Act of 1976". A subsequent investigation led to the RPC finding that employees of these four companies had entered into a market sharing and price fixing cartel for ready mixed concrete in the Bicester, Kidlington and Thame areas of Oxfordshire.[177] Three of the companies accepted that they were in contempt of court and that their employees concerned had aided and abetted this contempt. Smiths denied that it was in contempt, but the RPC held that it was in contempt and all four companies were fined amounts later described by Lord Templeman in *Pioneer Concrete* as "derisory".[178] Two employees concerned were fined for aiding and abetting the contempt.[179] Smiths successfully appealed against the finding of contempt against it.[180] The Court of Appeal quashed the finding of contempt on the basis that since Smiths had forbidden its employees to enter into agreements which would contra-

cont.
see *Re Agreements relating to the supply of freight forwarding services between the UK and Australasia* [1997] *The Times*, 24 January.

174 [1994] 3 WLR 1249.

175 [1994] ICR 57.

176 [1992] 1 QB 213.

177 *Smiths Concrete* [1991] ICR 52.

178 [1994] 3 WLR at 1253. Smiths was fined £25,000, RMC Thames and Pioneer £20,000 each and Hartigan £16,000.

179 The two employees were fined £1,200 and £1,000 for aiding and abetting these contempts, but the fines were stated to be reduced to take into account their additional liability for legal costs. Liability for aiding and abetting is discussed below.

180 [1992] QB 213; see Robertson, "Enforcement of the UK Restrictive Trade Practices Act: judicial limitations and legislative proposals" [1992] ECLR 82.

vene the RPC's 1979 injunction and had taken reasonable steps to enforce compliance, it could not be said to be a party to the new cartel agreement and, moreover, since it was not liable in contempt, its employee could not be liable for aiding and abetting contempt. The DGFT was refused leave to appeal to the House of Lords in November 1991.[181] As a consequence of this successful appeal by Smiths, two of the other three companies, Pioneer and RMC Thames, obtained leave to appeal out of time against the RPC's orders against them. They successfully argued before the Court of Appeal that the whole basis on which they had been advised by counsel to plead guilty to contempt had now been altered by that Court's ruling in *Smiths Concrete* and that therefore the findings of contempt should be quashed.[182] This time the DGFT was given leave to appeal by the House of Lords in November 1993.

5.78 The House of Lords held that the Court of Appeal's decision in *Smiths Concrete*, which had to be followed by that Court in the present case, should be overruled. The House of Lords' ruling contained two reasoned speeches, by Lord Templeman and Lord Nolan, both of which were concurred in by the remaining three members of the House of Lords. Both of their Lordships dealt with the question whether the Respondents, Pioneer and RMC Thames, were parties to agreements entered into by their employees, but only Lord Nolan went on to consider the law of contempt in detail.

5.79 Lord Templeman took the view that "an employee who acts for the company within the scope of his employment is the company. Directors may give instructions, top management may exhort, middle-management may question and workers may listen attentively. But if a worker makes a defective product or a lower manager accepts or rejects an order, he is the company."[183] On this basis, the employees entering into the cartel in question were committing their companies to that cartel and thus causing a breach of the court orders binding their companies.

5.80 Lord Nolan took the same view of the role of an employee in committing his company to an agreement, but took care to stress that this was for the purposes of the RTPA 1976: "[t]he Act is not concerned with what the employer says but with what the employee does in entering into business transactions in the course of his employment. The plain purpose of section 35(3) is to deter the implementation of agreements or arrangements by which the public interest is harmed, and the subsection can only achieve that purpose if it is applied to the actions of individuals within the business organisation who make and give effect to the relevant agreement or arrangement on its behalf".[184]

5.81 The second question for Lord Nolan was, having established that a company is party to an agreement contrary to an injunction issued by the RPC, whether the company thereby was in contempt of court. Lord Templeman appears to have assumed that this was the case without the need for further discussion, but Lord Nolan correctly, it is submitted, appreciated the need to consider what and whose *mens rea* was necessary for a finding of contempt against a company.

5.82 Approving a judgment of Warrington J in *Stancomb* v *Trowbridge UDC*,[185] as approved by Lord Wilberforce in *Heatons Transport (St Helens) Ltd* v *Transport and General Workers Union*,[186] Lord Nolan held that since "liability for contempt does not require any direct intention on the part of the employer to disobey the order, there [was] nothing to pre-

181 [1991] 1 WLR 1294.
182 [1994] ICR 57.
183 [1994] 3 WLR 1249 at 1255.
184 [1994] 3 WLR 1249 at 1264.
185 [1910] 2 Ch 190.
186 [1973] AC 15.

vent an employing company from being found to have disobeyed an order 'by' its servant as a result of a deliberate act by the servant on its behalf'.[187] Thus only conduct by an employee which was not deliberate in the sense of being, in Lord Wilberforce's words, casual or accidental and unintentional would escape the imposition of liability for contempt.

5.83 Accordingly, Lord Nolan reached the same conclusion as Lord Templeman that the respondents were correctly found to be in contempt of court and that the RPC's original order in *Smiths Concrete* should be allowed to stand.

5.84 The law relating to contempt in respect of orders made under the RTPA was thus restored to the state in which it was generally considered to be prior to the Court of Appeal's decision in *Smiths Concrete.* Companies which have been made subject to the court orders by, or which have given undertakings to, the RPC will have to continue to take all reasonable steps to ensure employees do not take action which would transgress the terms of those orders or undertakings. The consequence of the ruling in *Pioneer Concrete* is that if a company does take such reasonable steps, but an employee acting in the course of his employment commits the company to an agreement in breach of such order or undertaking, then the company is still in contempt of court and may be fined. Competition compliance schemes thus need to be all the more effective if fines are to be avoided, since a company will not be able to escape liability for contempt by showing it had taken reasonable steps to ensure its employees did not enter into the same agreement or one to like effect.[188]

5.85 If a company is found to be in contempt through the actions of a director, manager or employee, that person is liable for aiding and abetting that contempt.[189] However, a person cannot be liable for contempt without some form of active involvement. As stated above, contempt will not have been committed where the conduct is casual or accidental and unintentional. In *DGFT* v *Buckland*[190] Anthony Lincoln J held in a preliminary motion on a point of law before the RPC that a director of a company is not liable for contempt committed by the company, simply by virtue of occupying the position of director. The directors facing contempt proceedings in that case had not, on the pleadings, been personally involved in the activities said to constitute a breach and though aware of the previous injunctions and undertakings to the RPC, had not been directors at the time they were given.

5. *Factors for Presentation to the Court: Mitigation*

5.86 In contempt proceedings the remedy decided upon by the Court will very largely depend upon the mitigating circumstances pleaded on the defendant's behalf. It is not possible to catalogue exhaustively the points that may be pleaded. However, a few of the arguments that have been recited to the Court in the past may be briefly rehearsed here:

(a) that the parties took and acted upon legal advice whether from solicitors or from counsel. The Court may accept this as grounds for mitigation.[191]

[187] [1994] 3 WLR at 1269–1270.

[188] The final outcome of the litigation before the RPC in *Re Agreements relating to the Supply of Ready Mixed Concrete*, [1996] 15 Tr LR 78, was that fines totalling £8,375,000 were imposed for contempt upon eight companies and groups of companies.

[189] *DGFT* v *Smiths Concrete Ltd* [1992] ICR 229, 249.

[190] [1990] 1 All ER 545. The outcome of the proceedings against the directors' companies is reported in *Ready Mixed Concrete (Thames Valley) Ltd* v *DGFT* [1994] ICR 57.

[191] See *Mileage Conference Group of the Tyre Manufacturers Conference Agreement* (1966) LR 6 RP 49 at pp. 106 and 114. But cf. *Newspaper Proprietors' Association and National Federation of Retail Newsagents* (1961) LR 2 RP 453 at pp. 499, 500 where Diplock J held that the taking of legal advice would not be accepted as mitigation.

(b) that the infringement of the Court order was "not an act of wilful defiance". The Court has accepted as a mitigating factor that the contempt was committed by a subordinate member of the company in ignorance of express instructions to the contrary by his superior who mistakenly considered the subordinate to be aware of the strictures of the Court order.[192]

(c) that the contemnor is sincerely apologetic; humble apologies alone make little impression on the Court who appear to view such repentance in terms of "crocodile tears".[193] Cooperation with the OFT and RPC in an investigation into the contempt will count in the contemnor's favour.[194]

(d) that the company genuinely took steps to avoid the contempt by institution of a monitoring system. The Court has accepted that if a contemnor seeks legal advice as to how to avoid breaching the order and acts upon that advice by instituting an administrative monitoring and compliance system in his company then there may be grounds for mitigation. Indeed, it may well be that the use of a monitoring system prevents contempt being committed in the first place, as discussed in para 5.84 above. However, in *British Concrete Pipe* the Court still fined Redland Pipes £100,000 for contempt despite its having taken legal advice and having set up a monitoring system. The basis for the fine was apparently that the Company should not have allowed an administrative breakdown in control to occur.[195] In *Re Agreements relating to the Supply of Ready Mixed Concrete*[196] the RPC accepted as mitigation those compliance systems which went beyond distribution to advice on paper. Two companies received lower fines for having gone beyond setting up what the Court called "paper systems ... [t]hat is memoranda from head office and restrictive trade practices information from legal departments". The Court criticised the use of paper systems, even though "[i]n some cases they were expressed clearly and even contained references to participation in arrangements constituting misconduct in addition to the powers of the court. Unfortunately, many were written in relatively formal legal language, unlikely to deliver a clear message to the average salesman. Most such systems involved passing the documents down the chain of management or personnel and thus were only as strong as the weakest link, which in some cases was the general manager of the operating company who was himself involved [in the cartel] and continued to be so. Another serious criticism is that they were not proactive systems. There were ... no seminars, personal interviews or confrontations. Indeed ... [there was] little, if anything, by way of checks or direct investigations to see if the paperwork had even been received or understood let alone acted upon". For compliance to be in mitigation, it must take careful heed of these observations about the need to be proactive.

(e) that the company infringed the order through necessity as a result of dire economic difficulties caused by the state of the market. The Court rejected this in *British Concrete Pipes*.[197]

[192] *British Concrete Pipe Association* [1982] ICR 183 at pp. 195, 196. Though generally it is no answer to say that the act was not contumacious in the sense that there was no direct intention to disobey, only those acts which are casual or accidental or unintentional will be excluded from constituting a breach. *See Heatons Transport* v *TGWU* [1973] AC 15 approving *per* Warrington J in *Stancomb* v *Trowbridge* (above). See further, *British Concrete Pipe Association* (the BSC case) [1983] ICR 215 at pp. 219, 220.

[193] But see *Garage Equipment Association's Agreement* (1964) LR 4 RP 491 at p. 504.

[194] *DGFT* v *Smiths Concrete Ltd (Ready Mixed Concrete No. 1)* [1991] ICR 52, 70.

[195] *British Concrete Pipe Association* [1981] ICR 183 at p. 195 see also *DGFT* v *Smiths Concrete Ltd (Ready Mixed Concrete No. 1)* [1991] ICR 52, 70.

[196] [1996] 15 Tr LR 78.

[197] *ibid.*, at p. 197.

(f) that the managers of the company were unaware of the infringements and took rapid curative measures to end the infringements once they were discovered. One of the parties to the contempt in *British Concrete Pipe* apparently got a reduction in fine on this basis from £100,000 (being the sum another large party was fined) to £75,000.[198]

(g) that there was a long duration in time between the order and the entering of the agreements held to be in breach of that order. Length of time might be relevant but in *British Concrete Pipes* the parties were admonished for not setting up an adequate monitoring system to ensure long-term compliance.[199]

(h) that the contemnor is a small company with very limited financial resources. The Court certainly considered this relevant in *British Concrete Pipe* fining certain small concerns only £5,000 whereas larger firms were fined up to £100,000, and the RPC indicated it would have taken a similar action in *Smiths Concrete.* The RPC took into account the position of each corporate contemnor in its overall group when deciding upon the level of fines in *Re Agreements relating to the Supply of Ready Mixed Concrete* in 1995.[200]

(i) that the contempt was committed by a low-ranking employee. The Court might in such cases condemn the failure by senior managers, who should have known better, to institute a proper system of compliance. If it turns out that the breach was attributable to a small number of "rogue" employees this will usually be significant mitigation.

(j) the area affected and the market share under the unlawful agreement were not large. The fact that the agreement was unsuccessful in having little practical effect is not usually considered as carrying much weight.[201]

(k) the costs of complying with the investigation. "Very heavy" costs of £100,000 arising out of the OFT's investigation were taken into account in *Smiths Concrete.*[202] Legal costs were also considered relevant in reducing individual defendants liability for fines.[203] Huge costs of up to £5 million plus were taken into account in the 1995 *Ready Mixed Concrete* proceedings.

(l) in circumstances where contempt proceedings are not instituted against a potential defendant on the basis that the person concerned had assisted with the investigation and in return is to be granted what is effectively an amnesty,[204] the RPC has indicated that it will take that fact into account in sentencing others who are *not* granted immunity.[205]

6. Monitoring Systems: Avoiding Contempt

5.87 The Court has stressed the importance of a proper corporate, administrative systems designed to ensure continued compliance with a Court order. This it has done, bearing in mind that compliance is a long-term process:

[198] *ibid.*, at p. 194 see also *DGFT* v *Smiths Concrete Ltd (Ready Mixed Concrete No. 1)* [1991] ICR 52, 70.
[199] *ibid.*, at p. 197, 198.
[200] *DGFT* v *Smiths Concrete Ltd (Ready Mixed Concrete No. 1)* [1991] ICR 52, 71.
[201] *DGFT* v *Smiths Concrete Ltd (Ready Mixed Concrete No. 1)* [1991] 52, 70.
[202] *DGFT* v *Smiths Concrete Ltd (Ready Mixed Concrete No. 1)* [1991] 52, 70.
[203] *DGFT* v *Smiths Concrete Ltd (Ready Mixed Concrete No. 1)* [1991] 52, 72.
[204] A course to be adopted in the RPC's view only if "without the assistance of the immunised witness, there is a real possibility that proceedings will fail or cannot reasonable be instituted": *DGFT* v *Smiths Concrete Ltd (Ready Mixed Concrete No. 1)* [1991] ICR 52, 73.
[205] *DGFT* v *Smiths Concrete Ltd (Ready Mixed Concrete No. 1)* [1991] 52, 73.

"Not only would memories become dim with the passage of time but, to anyone who paused to think, the staff changes and possible reconstruction of companies likely to occur with the passing of the years made it essential for a system to be adopted so that the important limits to the freedom of the companies to enter into restrictive agreements with their competitors as well as the undertaking given to the Court should be continuously borne in mind and not forgotten and ignored. The directors and upper echelons of executives of the companies must have had well in mind a number of statutory obligations that had to be observed, such as the Factory Act and statutory provisions relating to quarrying, as well as the common law duties owed by an employer to his employee. Obligations under the Restrictive Trade Practices Acts should, perhaps, by reason of their comparative novelty, have been more actively borne in mind and observed by management and how much more so when the respondent companies had each of them been proceeded against in this Court and had given solemn undertakings not to enter into fresh arrangements to the like effect as those declared contrary to the public interest and void in respect of the restrictions they imposed."[206]

5.88 In order to minimise the risk of contempt proceedings the following points might be relevant:

(a) Persons subject to an order might request detailed legal advice on precisely what is entailed by the order. Those giving advice should bear in mind (and advise accordingly) the broad concept of "arrangement". The pursual of an informal, oral arrangement between the parties is as much a contempt as is pursual of a formal, written agreement where that second arrangement achieves similar commercial and economic goals as the first agreement subject to the Court order.
(b) Vulnerable parties should, following such legal advice, prepare circulars and memoranda setting out in non-technical language categories of conduct to be avoided, e.g. discussions with rivals over prices or discount levels, discussions with rivals over selling areas, exchanges of price lists with other competitors, meetings with personnel from other competitors, etc.
(c) These circulars and memoranda should be distributed to all directors and officers of the company who know the substance of the undertakings given to the Court or order made against it and who might be in a position whereby their conduct could bring the employer into contempt.[207]
(d) Distribution should also be made to third parties who know of the order and who might be responsible for assisting or advising the persons bound to infringe the order, company accountants and relevant trade associations are prime examples.[208]

[206] *British Concrete Pipe Association* [1989] ICR 183 at p. 194. See also, *National Daily and Sunday Newspapers Proprietors Agreement* [1986] ICR 44 at p. 51.

[207] See RSC Ord. 45, r. 5(1) which provides that writs of sequestration made in respect of contempt procedures against companies may be made against "any director *or other officer*". Those in charge at the time of the order thus stand in grave risk. The situation is unclear in so far as those directors or managers are concerned once they have ceased to be directors or managers of that company. The same query applies to their replacements though in their case when they become aware of the Court order and fail to take steps to ensure compliance with it there seems to be a strong case to suggest that they are at risk.

[208] e.g. *National Daily and Sunday Newspapers Proprietors' Agreement* [1986] ICR 44 at p. 51. Third parties may be liable for aiding and abetting another to breach an order. In *British Concrete Pipe Agreement* [1982] ICR 182 at pp. 198, 199, Mocatta J stated: "There is no doubt that if the appropriate evidence is available against a person as to his aiding and abetting a party who has given an undertaking to this Court to act in breach of that undertaking, the Court has jurisdiction to require contempt proceedings to be taken against such persons." For cases on point see *Elliot* v *Klinger* [1967] 1 WLR 1165; *Seaward* v *Paterson* [1897] 1 Ch 545. To be liable a third party would actively have to be a part of any breach *and* be aware of the Court order and its substance.

(e) Copies of the circulars and memoranda should periodically (frequently) be redistributed as a reminder to those involved.
(f) A system must be put in place whereby all recipients of such document must acknowledge that they have read and understood their contents. Preferably, this exercise should be carried out annually, perhaps as part of a yearly appraisal or similar review.
(g) A thorough review of all current marketing practices and existing contractual arrangements should be undertaken to ensure that no registrable agreements are being operated without senior management being aware of their existence, all unregistered agreements discovered should be terminated immediately and details furnished to the OFT.[209]
(h) A competent person should be placed in charge of "contempt auditing", to ensure that infringements are not taking place. This person should organise seminars and have the power to conduct personal interviews both to emphasise the importance of compliance and to be able to satisfy himself that compliance is in fact occurring.
(i) Trade associations might circulate to all members, details of all undertakings given and injunctions made by members since the inception of the legislation which first came into force in 1957. The association might accompany these circulars with warnings as to the dangers of assisting those who breach the Court order.
(j) Where a company is taken over by or takes over another company the new parent or subsidiary should be made cognisant of the obligations imposed by the Court order (see para 5.89 below).
(k) All new senior management who join the company should likewise be made aware of the Court order.

7. *Contempt and Mergers, Take-Overs and Transference of Obligations*

5.89 In the first contempt case brought against the British Concrete Pipe Association, the Court requested that the Director General commence proceedings against British Steel who had not been made defendants in the first case.[210] During 1969 the Iron and Steel Act which provided for the transfer of property from private steel companies, came into being pursuant to the Steel Companies (Vesting) Order 1970. This vested all the "property, rights, liabilities and obligations" of scheduled companies in the British Steel Corporation. Accordingly, Stanton and Staveley Ltd (SS) became, part of the Corporation. SS had given an undertaking to the Court in 1965, the RPC held, and the decision was affirmed by the Court of Appeal, that the duties and responsibilities arising for SS out of the Court order were transferred to the British Steel Corporation. Accordingly, the British Steel Corporation were responsible for infringements of the order made by SS. They were fined £50,000 for this contempt. The case is a salutary warning to companies who are taking over, or have been taken over by other companies. Sir John Donaldson MR in the Court of Appeal stated, in respect of the vesting:

> "The sixth point is that under this legislation construed as the Director General would have it construed and the court below has construed it, it would be possible for the corporation to be in breach of the undertaking inadvertently. That no doubt is right. Where the corporation is taking over a whole host of companies, they may not—they ought to, but they may not—be aware of what undertakings have been given. There cannot be all that num-

[209] See *Flushing Cistern Makers' Ltd's Agreement* [1973] ICR 654 at p. 659.
[210] [1981] ICR 421 (RPC); [1983] ICR 215 (CA).

> ber of undertakings given by steel companies to the Court, but it is just possible that the corporation might now know about them. If they did not know about an undertaking, that would go to penalty and no doubt full effect would be given to any such excuse."[211]

The importance of an offeror company or new parent taking proper inventory of undertakings and other obligations to the Court owed by the acquired concern is thus clear.

F. Actions Commenced by Parties or the Director General for a Declaration as to the Registrability of an Agreement

5.90 Under section 26 RTPA 1976 the RPC has power to declare that an agreement is not one to which the Act applies. This procedure may be useful where the parties are in need of a declaration in a test case on the application of the law or where a dispute as to registrability arises between the parties and the OFT. The section envisages a number of possibilities.

1. *Rectification of Register*

5.91 Section 26(1) reads: "The Court may, on the application of any person aggrieved, order the register to be rectified by the variation or removal of particulars included in the register in respect of any agreement."The aggrieved party must apply to the Court, the application will be for either total removal of the agreement from the register, or, variation of the register.[212] The category of persons entitled to apply is seemingly wider than that specified under section 26(2). Any "person aggrieved" may apply. An "aggrieved" person might include persons other than parties to the agreement or the Director General. It might include a competitor to the parties, or a supplier to or customer of the parties. They might be "aggrieved" because they consider that the scope and extent of the particulars registered does not match what they consider to represent the true situation. They might want the particulars varied by addition of new parties or by reference to new aspects of the agreement not referred to in the particulars.

2. *Declaration of Registrability*

5.92 Section 26(2) RTPA 1976 reads:

> "The Court may, on the application of—(a) any person party to an agreement; or (b) the Director, in respect of an agreement of which particulars have been furnished to him under this Act; declare whether or not the agreement is one to which this Act applies, and if so whether or not it is subject to registration under this Act."

[211] [1983] ICR 215 at p. 220. Interesting problems arose in that case because of the fact that the transfer of control was by statute. The Court of Appeal left it as an open question whether it would be contempt of court by the acquiring company where the acquired company was in breach of its undertaking on the day the statutory transfer took place: "you might have had an automatic contempt of court by operation of law" (*ibid.*, at p. 220C *per* Sir John Donaldson MR).

[212] See e.g. *Royal Institution of Chartered Surveyors* v *Director General of Fair Trading* (1981) (unreported) noted [1981] Com LR 112. This case concerned certain preliminary matters. The case was fully litigated in 1984. See [1985] ICR 330.

This provision is of some significance. Its obvious function is to allow either the OFT or the parties themselves to seek guidance on complex legal questions of registrability. In one notable case a very large property group brought such an action as a test case to determine whether leases and restrictive covenants contained therein were ever registrable.[213] The question arose as a result of the Restrictive Trade Practices (Services) Order 1976 which subjected service agreements to registration. The applicants owned and managed a large number of properties in the UK. Mr Justice Mocatta commented in judgment:

> "If, as a result of the statutory instrument I have mentioned, leases are brought under the control of the 1956 Act, this would clearly be a very serious matter for the applicants may well have current hundred if not thousands of leases and the result of the order would be that each of these would have to be examined in order to make certain whether or not there was an obligation under the ... Act ... to register ..."[214]

In the event the applicants brought the action as nominees of the British Property Owners Association. The applicant agreed to an abridgment of normal procedure with the OFT in order to expedite the proceedings since time was of the essence. The final legal date for registration was the 22 June 1976; the notice of application was issued on the 10 June 1976; the hearing of arguments occurred on the 16, 17 and 18 June. It will be appreciated that failure to register in time would have rendered restrictions in the agreement null and void under section 35(1) RTPA 1976. Thus, to expedite proceedings the OFT agreed that the hearing of the case should be treated as a final hearing and that the only evidence before the Court would be by way of the affidavits filed on behalf of the Applicants. The second importance of section 26(2) is that parties to agreements may escape obligations under those agreements by seeking a declaration of the registrability of that agreement. If successful in the application the agreement will be null and void and attempts to enforce it unlawful. This tactic has been used in a number of important cases and is examined below.

5.93 The Court also has power pursuant to section 26(2) to declare whether an agreement is a "non-notifiable agreement".[215] Where a party to an agreement makes an application for a declaration under section 26(2) the Director General shall not enter or file particulars of the agreement in the register during the time during which the proceedings and any appeal therein are pending. However, that provision, in effect staying the hand of the Director General, has no application where:

(a) the only question in relation to which the declaration is sought is whether or not the agreement is non-notifiable; and
(b) the Director General considers that any restrictions or information provisions by virtue of which the Act applies are of such significance as to call for investigation by the Court.[216]

3. Extension of Time for Furnishing of Particulars Pending section 26 Proceedings

5.94 Time for furnishing particulars may be extended in certain circumstances where the procedures laid down under section 26 have been invoked. Where the conditions referred

[213] *Ravenseft Properties* v *Director General of Fair Trading* [1977] 1 All ER 47.
[214] *ibid.*, at p. 49.
[215] Inserted by the Deregulation and Contracting Out Act 1994, s. 10(4) Sch. 3, paras. 1, 5.
[216] s. 26(3A).

to in section 26(3B) are satisfied the time for furnishing of particulars "shall be extended by a time equal to the time during which the proceedings and any appeal therein are pending and such further time, if any, as the Court may direct.[217] The (cumulative) conditions for the extension of time are as follows:

(a) a party to an agreement must have made an application for a declaration under section 26(2);
(b) the question in relation to which the declaration is sought must be relevant to the existence of a duty to furnish particulars of the agreement pursuant to section 25 RTPA 1976; and
(c) the application must have been made before the expiry of the time within which particulars of the agreement are ordinarily required to be furnished if the duty to furnish particulars under that section applies.

4. *Notice of Application under section 26*

5.95 The Notice of Application to the Court pursuant to section 26 is required to be served, in accordance with rules of Court, upon the Director General in the case of an application by a person other than the Director. Where the Applicant is the Director, the Notice of Application must be served on the parties to the agreement or such of them as may be prescribed or determined by or under the rules. Any person upon whom notice is so served shall be entitled to appear and to be heard upon the application. It is to be observed that in the case of an application by the Director General there is no provision for service upon persons other than parties to the agreement. In particulars there is no provision for the Notice of Application to be served upon a "person aggrieved" pursuant to section 26(1).

G. Action by Parties to an Agreement for a Declaration that the Agreement is Registrable: Using the Consequences of Failure to Furnish Particulars

5.96 Failure to furnish particulars of an agreement in due time, according to section 35(1) RTPA 1976, renders the agreement void in respect of all restrictions accepted or information provisions made thereunder and it becomes unlawful for any party to the agreement who carries on business in the UK to give effect to, or enforce or purport to enforce, the agreement in respect of any such restrictions or information provisions. However, innocuous agreements are not infrequently continued in ignorance of the duty to furnish. In a number of cases parties to agreements have sought declarations that their agreements are registrable notwithstanding a failure to furnish. A declaration to that effect entails the restrictions becoming null and void. This enables the party to escape what they now consider onerous obligations under the contract. Alternatively, in an agreement between X and Y whereby X sues Y for breach of contract, Y may plead in defence that particulars of the agreement have not been furnished in due time and restrictive clauses therein are null and void. An example of this strategic use of the RTPA 1976 as a defence is *Topliss*

[217] Inserted by the Deregulation and Contracting Out Act 1984, s. 10(4) Sch. 3, paras. 1, 5.

Showers Ltd v *Gessey*.[218] The facts may be summarised as follows. Prior to 1976 G Ltd and T Ltd were jointly owned and managed. Following share sales in 1976 and 1977 the two companies fell to separate ownership. However, G remained as a manufacturer of Mark IV valves and T remained as the marketers of the valves produced by G. Following a dispute between G and T it became clear that a complete parting of the ways was inevitable. According, G incorporated X Ltd to market the valves for it. In early 1979 a Tomlin Order was made between the solicitors to the parties in order to settle the proceedings which had been commenced by T against G.[219] Under the terms of this settlement the following, *inter alia*, were agreed upon: (i) G would sell Mark IV valves only to T until 31 July 1979; (ii) G would sell the valves to T until 31 December 1979 if such valves were available; (iii) G would not supply such valves to anybody other than T and X between 1 August and 31 December 1979; (iv) G would sell the valves to T at prices fixed by the parties; (v) G would supply X with the valves at prices which were not less than those charged to T; (vi) X would not sell or offer for sale the valves at prices less than the published price of T and would not offer discounts which were more favourable than those offered by T; (vii) G would not stockpile the valves. The terms of this settlement were not registered with the OFT. None the less, had they been it is almost certain that they would have been given dispensation under the section 21(2) RTPA 1976 procedure (discussed at paras. 4.96–4.114). The settlement was between two small companies and was of a very transient nature. The agreement was in reality between two companies who were by the settlement easing their way to full competition with each other. Subsequent to this settlement T commenced an action against G and X claiming damages and injunctive relief for alleged breaches of the Settlement. G and X denied these allegations and, in the alternative, argued that even were the allegations true the settlement was not registered and hence the relevant restrictions were void and unenforceable. Neill J held that, irrespective of any finding on breach, the settlement was registrable and the consequences in section 35 applicable. He added however: "I reach this conclusion without enthusiasm because it seems to me to be a very technical and artificial defence in the circumstances of the case where the relevant restrictions were accepted for such very short periods."[220]

5.97 The defence of non-registration has been raised in other cases. There are a number of cases in which vendors of estate agency businesses escaped being bound by registrable non-competition restrictions as a consequence of failure to register by the purchaser.[221] In another context, in *Academy Sound and Vision* v *WEA Records*[222] an agreement was signed between an assignor of copyright in certain master recordings and the plaintiff assignee. Under this agreement the assignor had a limited period of three months in which to commercially dispose of his stock of records made from the master recording. After the three-month period had expired the plaintiff had the exclusive right of sale. The plaintiffs brought an action against the assignor alleging that the latter continued to sell records even after the three-month period. The assignor denied breaching the agreement and, alternatively, claimed that the agreement was void and unenforceable for want of registration. The argument, however, failed on the ground that the agreement was excluded from the RTPA

[218] [1982] ICR 501 (QBD) noted, Whish (1983) BLR. 102.
[219] On Tomlin orders, see *Supreme Court Practice* (1997) Vol. 2 para. 4616.
[220] [1982] ICR 501 at p. 518.
[221] *Donald Storrie Estate Agency Ltd* v *Adams* [1989] SLT 305; *Sterling Financial Services Ltd* v *Johnston* [1990] SLT 111; *Snushalls Team Ltd* v *Marcus*, judgment of 21 March 1990, unreported, noted by Tulley, *Law Society's Gazette* 22 August 1990.
[222] [1983] ICR 586.

1976 by virtue of paragraph 5A of Schedule 3 to the RTPA 1976 which excludes from registration agreements in respect of the assignment in, *inter alia*, master recordings.[223] The tactic of pleading the illegality of one's own agreement is not uncommon and occurs also at common law in the tort of restraint of trade, and in respect of Article 85 EC.[224]

H. Private Actions for Damages: Failure to Register Agreements, Resale Price Maintenance, Breach of Competition Act Ministerial Orders

1. *Legal Context*

5.98 Section 35(1) RTPA 1976 reads:

> "If particulars of an agreement which is subject to registration under this Act are not duly furnished within the time required by section 24 above, or within such further times as the Director may, upon application made within that time, allow—
> (a) the agreement is void in respect of all restrictions accepted or information provisions made thereunder; and
> (b) it is unlawful for any person party to the agreement who carries on business within the United Kingdom to give effect to, or enforce or purport to enforce, the agreement in respect of any such restrictions or information provisions."

Section 35(2) RTPA 1976 creates private law consequences for continuing the operation of an unregistered agreement. "No criminal proceedings lie against any person on account of a contravention of subsection (1)(b) above; but the obligation to comply with that paragraph is a duty owed to any person who may be affected by a contravention of it and any breach of that duty is actionable accordingly subject to the defences and other incidents applying to actions for breach of statutory duty."

5.99 A similar cause of action is provided for under section 25(2) Resale Prices Act 1976 against persons unlawfully imposing individual or collective resale price maintenance. In relevant proceedings reliance may be placed upon findings of fact and law made in proceedings before the RPC brought by the Director General under section 35(3) RTPA 1976.[225] The damages would be to compensate persons for any loss suffered as a consequence of the operation of an unregistered agreement. Thus, for illustration, a local authority could sue a ring of collusive tenderers of building materials for the difference in price between the uncompetitive, fixed price and the free market price that would have

[223] *ibid.*, at pp. 593, 594. See for other cases on the defence of non-registration *Vernon* v *Universal Pulp, Containers* [1980] FSR 179; *Fisher* v *Director General of Fair Trading* [1982] ICR 71; *Unit Marketing* v *Christenson* (1984) (unreported) non-competition arrangement concluded as part of a sale of customer lists void and unenforceable for non-registration. However void clauses did not affect the existence of a debt created by remainder of the sale agreement. The case shows that the plea of non-registration invalidates only those clauses which constituted registrable restrictions. This approach was adopted by Mackinnon J in *Smshalls Team Ltd* v *Marcus*, judgment of 21 March 1990, unreported, noted by Tulley, *Law Society's Gazette* 22 August 1990, p. 23.

[224] See e.g. *Joseph Evans* v *Heathcote* [1918] 1 KB 418 (price fixing and profit pooling agreement held to be in restraint of trade and thus void and unenforceable); and, for an unsuccessful example *Alec Lobb (Garages) Ltd* v *Total Oil (Great Britain) Ltd* [1985] 1 WLR 173 (CA) (garage owners sought to escape exclusive purchasing tie in a solus agreement entered with Total Oil who had given substantial financial aid and assistance to garage owners. Court of Appeal held tie to be valid and reasonable and not in restraint of trade).

[225] s. 35(7) RTPA 1976.

prevailed in the absence of the collusion. To date no formal proceedings have ever been taken to full trial under this section. The problem is apparently one of assessing the correct quantum of damages. In a consultative document issued by the Department of Trade in 1980 the following comment was made: "The sanction of civil damages alone reduces the deterrent since civil litigation is known to be time consuming, expensive and uncertain. It can often be difficult to assess damages (what would the price have been in the absence of collusion), and the purchaser may not wish to exacerbate relations with a long standing supplier with whom he may well wish to continue to deal."[226]

5.100 If the RTPA 1976 does not apply no private damages action can lie under section 35, though a complaint to the OFT under the Competition Act 1980 is feasible.

2. *Negotiated Settlements*

5.101 These difficulties have, however, resulted in actions under section 35(2) being settled out of Court. In the early 1970s certain area health authorities recovered damages from electrical and mechanical contractors who were alleged to have colluded to fix tenders and prices. In 1978 the Post Office negotiated a settlement of £9 million from parties to an unregistered agreement among cable manufacturers. This latter instance was the climax of a series of proceedings brought by the OFT against manufacturers of telephone cables. Prior to 1952 suppliers of insulated electric wires and cables operated a collusive tendering scheme with regard to orders from purchasers including the Post Office. When the scheme was discovered during an early MMC investigation the suppliers agreed to terminate it.[227] In 1974 the MMC was asked to undertake a new investigation of the supply of insulated electrical wires and cables.[228] During the investigation they unearthed a collusive tendering scheme that had been operated since 1965 and which had concerned sales to the Post Office of approximately £400–500 million.[229] As a result of this discovery, the OFT referred the agreement to the RPC, along with another collusive tendering agreement concerning the supply of switchboard and other internal telephone cables to the Post Office. With respect to the first scheme the suppliers collectively controlled almost all of the market, with regard to the second agreement the parties were not the only suppliers. The OFT successfully proceeded under section 35(3) RTPA 1976.[230] The RPC ordered that each of the companies concerned should be restrained from giving effect to the agreements or any other agreement contravening section 35(1) RTPA 1976. Following this hearing the parties gave undertakings to the Post Office to supply on a competitive

[226] *Collusive Tendering: A Consultative Document*, Department of Trade (30 July 1980), para. 11.

[227] MMC *Report on the Supply of Insulated Electric Wires and Cables* (1952) Cmnd 209 esp. at pp. 43, 44, paras. 150, 151.

[228] Reference made in July 1974, Report not made until 1979, MMC *Report into Supply of Electric Wires and Cables* (1979) H.C. 243, See *The Times* (7 March 1975) "Monopolies Panel study"; *The Times* (15 March 1975), "Cable suppliers register agreements", *Accountancy Age* (14 March 1975); *Financial Times* (27 March 1975) "Cartels: what Britain approves Europe may reject".

[229] See No. 3850 Register of Restrictive Trade Practices, *Agreement between BICC Ltd, Pirelli General Cable Works Ltd, Standard Telephone and Cables Ltd*, and *Telephone Cables Ltd*. Another agreement existed between these parties (No. 3852 Register of Restrictive Trade Practices) relating to the supply and installation of cable to users other than the Post Office. The aim of this agreement was to fix selling prices at above the level of sales to the Post Office and to operate a preferred tenderer scheme. In practice this agreement had little effect on the parties' behaviour.

[230] See No. 3851 Register of Restrictive Trade Practices, *Agreement between AEI Cables, Pirelli General Cables Works, Standard Telephone and Cables*, and *Telephone Cables Ltd*. See also DGFT Report 1975 at p. 91 for details of the case. The case was heard under s. 7(1)(3)(a) and (b) RTPA 1968 which equate to s. 35(1), (2) and (3) RTPA 1976. See *Financial Times* (21 November 1975) "Cable agreement too restrictive, says PO"; *The Guardian* (22 November 1975) "Post office calls for cable profits"; *The Times* (21 November 1975) "Court ban on cable makers' price rings".

basis in future and in March 1977 the RPC agreed on an application by the parties for the proceedings to be stood over indefinitely on the basis that the agreements were no longer in operation. The Post Office then decided to commence legal action for damages against the suppliers. A major difficulty for the Post Office was the lack of information upon which they could assess the supplier's profits. In the face of resistance by the suppliers to the Post Office's requests to inspect their books, the latter placed an embargo on future placement of orders with these firms. The embargo lasted almost one year until the suppliers succumbed to the request. The Post Office and their accountants examined the supplier's books for evidence of overcharging. Upon the evidence unearthed, the Post Office, after performing some detailed calculations, negotiated a settlement under which the Post Office was reimbursed by way of a £9 million rebate on the price paid for the supply and installation of telephone cable during the period concerned. Subsequently the Post Office retained the right to inspect the supplier's books to ensure that all bids were based upon competitive tendering.[231] The strength of the Post Office's case will have been much enhanced by the proceedings before the Court, since, as noted earlier, facts disclosed therein may be relied upon in the civil suit.

5.102 A further case is that of the *North Eastern Fuel Oil* cartel.[232] Domestic fuel oil suppliers had started a price fixing cartel, only to be caught by a keenly price conscious customer noticing prices becoming the same in a previously competitive market. The customer reported the matter to the OFT, which was to uncover the cartel; undertakings were given to the RPC by the participants. The customer then initiated an action for damages based upon a breach of statutory duty to furnish particulars. The claim was settled out of court, and the customer reimbursed costs for making the claim.

5.103 It will be noted that in claiming damages the plaintiff is subject to the usual constraints. He must make a reasonable attempt to mitigate his damage and ensure that his damages are not due to his own negligence or other failings. The usual defences for breach of statutory duty exist for the defendant.[233]

3. *Quantifying Damages*

5.104 Quantifying the damages suffered is very difficult in cases of illegal price fixing. The logical way to commence viewing this question is to calculate a competitively set market price for the goods as at the date(s) and place(s) of delivery and to determine the difference (if any) between that price and the price actually charged.[234] Not all cases, however, will concern supply—purchase relationships. Thus, X might seek damages from trade association T in respect of a boycott of X organised by T and its members. In such a case X's profits may well suffer, how is he to assess damages? X might be able to compute damages by refer-

231 See Post Office Press Releases (January 7 1976) *Cable Contracts*; (June 12 1978) *Cable Companies Agree to Pay Back £9m.*

232 DGFT's Annual Report, 1991, p. 39. The story of the detection of the cartel is told by Walker-Smith [1991] ECLR 71 "Collusion: its detection and investigation".

233 See Winfield and Jolowicz, *Tort* (14th edn. 1994), Chapter 7; Halsbury's *Laws of England* (4th edn.), Vol. 45, paras. 1279–1300. Clerk and Lindsell on Torts (17th edn. 1995), paras. 11.29 *et seq.*

234 See *Elbinger Actien Gesellschaft* v *Armstrong* (1874) LR 9 QB 473 at p. 476: "It is, no doubt, quite settled that, on a contract to supply goods of a particular sort which at the time of the breach can be obtained in the market, the measure of the damages is the difference between the contract price and the market price at the time of the breach. Where from the nature of the article, there is no market in which it can be obtained, this rule is not applicable; but it would be very unjust if, in such cases, the damages would be nominal." See also, *Bridge* v *Wain* 1 Stark 504; *Borries* v *Hutchinson* 18 CB (NS) 445 at p. 465. See further *Chitty on Contracts* (27th edn. 1994), Vol. 2, pp. 1255–1257, para. 41–275; See also, s. 51 Sale of Goods Act 1979; *McGregor on Damages* (15th edn. 1988), pp. 482–492, paras. 741–755 and on the concept of "market value" at pp. 482–483, paras. 741–743.

ence to the difference between his profit levels before and after commencement of the boycott; this would enable some degree of comparison to be made between profits earned in a competitive environment and those earned under restricted conditions. If, to change the example, T organised a boycott of X, who was *preparing* to commence trade but who had *not yet* entered the market, then, how would damages be assessed? T and its members are setting up a substantial entry barrier; X will not yet have earned any profits to be used as a benchmark for comparison. In such cases X's damages will be speculative. In sale of goods cases the price that could have been obtained on resale by the buyer is generally irrelevant.[235] This is understandable in competition law cases on the basis that if the buyer pays an inflated price and then resells at a normal profit margin, the price he sells at will also be a supra-competitive inflated price and not reflective of market value. Where the market price and actual price have *de facto* been the same, Courts have awarded nominal damages.[236] If there is no prevailing market price by which to contrast the actual price or no near-equivalent product to base a comparison on, then the question is more difficult.[237] This might be the case where the parties to the agreement control all of the market and there is no market outside of those parties, for example, where the victim purchaser is a statutory monopoly so that the only supplies are to that purchaser. This indeed was essentially the case in the Post Office dispute. There are two possible solutions to this problem. First, the plaintiff can make an estimate of the defendant's costs, add a reasonable profit margin and use the resulting price as the benchmark against which to measure the actual price. However, this method implies that the plaintiff is in a position to assess the defendant's costs, which in practice is rarely the case, though such evidence might be obtainable upon discovery. Such an approach, however, might prove a starting point for negotiations or for discussions as to damages in Court. The second solution is to simply request the Court to assess damages with the assistance of expert evidence. In a classic decision in international trade law—*Kwei Tek Chao* v *British Trade's and Shippers Ltd*[238] Devlin J, when requested by the plaintiffs to assess damages where no market existed for the purposes of comparison, created what was effectively a notional market value to work with;[239] difficulties of quantification were not permitted to hinder proper recovery.[240]

4. Breach of an Order made Under the Competition Act 1980

5.105 The Secretary of State has power under the Competition Act 1980 to issue statutory orders against firms who, following an adverse MMC report, steadfastly refuse to give suitable undertakings in negotiations with the OFT. The powers of the Secretary of State

[235] See e.g. *Cox* v *Walker* (1835), 6 A and E 523n, noted in McGregor, *op. cit.*, at p. 451, para. 633.

[236] e.g. *Erie County Natural Gas and Fuel Co Ltd* v *Carroll* [1911] AC 105 at pp. 117, 118 (PC); *Charter* v *Sullivan* [1957] 2 QB 117.

[237] Chitty, *op. cit.*, at p. 1262, para. 41–279. In the USA plaintiffs generally seek guidance from prices in the nearest substitute or comparable market. See, e.g. *Ohio Valley Electric* v *General Electric* (1965) Trade Cas (CCH), para. 71, 458. See also Timberlake, *Federal Treble Damage Anti-trust Acts* (1965); Parker, "Measuring damages in federal treble damage actions" (1972) 17 *The Antitrust Bulletin* 497–517; Kuhiman and Johnson, "Estimating damages on highway construction contracts" (1984) 29 *The Antitrust Bulletin* 719–738.

[238] [1954] 2 QB 459 (QBD).

[239] *ibid.*, at pp. 498, 499.

[240] *Elbinger Actien Gesellschaft* v *Armstrong* (1874) LR 9 QB 473 at p. 476. In Germany an interesting approach to determining damages has occurred. In one case involving over 2,000 building firms engaged in collusive tendering the Federal Cartel Office (FCO) imposed fines in excess of DM35 million. The fines were calculated by reference to extra profits that were presumed to have been made by the firms. Thus the FCO assumed that the excess profits amounted to 2 per cent of the turnover subject to the prohibited agreements (Hermann and Jones, *Fair Trading in Europe* (1977), pp. 167, 168).

are the same as those granted by the Fair Trading Act 1973 in respect of monopoly and merger cases. Accordingly, the consequences of breach of an order are the same. Section 93(1) Fair Trading Act 1973 provides that breach of an order is *not* a criminal offence. Section 93(2) reads:

> "Nothing in the preceding subsection shall limit any right of any person to bring civil proceedings in respect of any contravention or apprehended contravention of such an order, and (without prejudice to the generality of the preceding words) compliance with any such order shall be enforceable by civil proceedings by the Crown for an injunction or interdict or for any other appropriate relief."

This wording is ambiguous. Does it create a right of action or is it merely intended to confirm that existing rights are unaffected to the extent that such rights exist, if at all? Assuming a right exists it does not apparently extend to breaches of formal undertakings given to the government.[241] *Locus standi* is not covered by section 93 though presumably any person or firm or trade association who can prove damage may bring an action. The Act is silent as to the nature of the cause of action or the remedies available though by analogy to section 35(2) RTPA 1976 and section 25(3) Resale Prices Act 1976, the action is probably for breach of a statutory duty. Private parties could seek injunctive relief to prevent contemplated breaches by those subject to an order.

I. Criminal Law Proceedings for Conspiracy to Defraud

5.106 It seems almost certain that certain types of agreement may be prosecuted as common law conspiracies to defraud by the Director of Public Prosecutions. In practice the only agreements fitting this description will be certain collusive tendering agreements.

J. Enforcement of section 36 Notices: section 37—Court's Power to Order Examination on Oath

5.107 Where the Director General has given notice to any person under section 36 (as to which paras. 4.66–4.72) the Director General may apply to the Court for an order that the person to whom the notice has been given attend the Court and be examined on oath concerning the matters in respect of which the Director General has given notice to him pursuant to section 36.[242] Where the Director General's application is granted the Court may require the person examined to produce any such particulars, documents or information in his possession or control as may be specified in the section 36 notice.

5.108 Where the notice has been given to a body corporate an order granting the application of the Director General for examination on oath may be made for the attendance and examination of any director, manager, secretary or other officer of the body corporate, or, of any person who is employed by the body corporate and appears to the Court

[241] *Fogg* v *Esso Petroleum* (6 April 1990 *per* Marman J, unreported). It would appear to be the case that shareholders of either the infringing company or of companies connected thereto do not have an action against the controllers of the infringing company for a remedy for unfair prejudice: *ICI, Re Carrington Viyella plc* (3 February 1973) (unreported) (Ch D) judgment printed [1983] 1 BCC 98, 951. See also *Mid Kent Utilities plc* v *General Holdings plc* [1996] 3 All ER 132.

[242] s. 37(1).

to be likely to have particular knowledge of any of the matters in respect of which the notice was given.[243] The powers of the Director General in relation to a body corporate apply equally in relation to a trade association or a service supply association which is not incorporated.[244]

5.109 In this regard "manager" means a person with responsibility for the affairs of the company as a whole and does not include a branch manager who, also, is not an "officer".[245] The Director General shall take part in the examination and may be represented by a Solicitor or Counsel. The person examined shall answer all such questions as the Court may put or allow to be put to him, but may at his own cost employ a Solicitor with or without Counsel, who shall be at liberty to put to him such questions as the Court may deem just for the purpose of enabling him to explain or qualify any answer given by him. Notes of the examination shall be taken down in writing and shall be read over to or by, and signed by, the person examined and may thereafter be used in evidence against him.[246] Nothing in section 37 is to be taken as compelling the disclosure by a barrister, advocate or solicitor of any privileged communication made by or to him in that capacity, or the production by him of any document containing such communication.[247]

K. Offences in Connection with Registration under section 36

5.110 A person failing without reasonable excuse to comply with a notice duly given to him pursuant to section 36 is guilty of an offence and liable on summary conviction to a fine.[248] What is a reasonable excuse is largely a question of fact.[249] Ignorance of the statutory provisions provides no reasonable excuse,[250] nor does a mistaken view of the effect of those provisions.[251] It is open to question whether reliance upon the advice of an expert can amount to a reasonable excuse.[252] Once evidence of a reasonable excuse emerges it is for the prosecution to eliminate the existence of that defence to the satisfaction of the Court.[253] If a person who furnishes or is required to furnish any particulars, document or information under the Act: makes any statement, or furnishes any document which he knows to be false in a material particular; or recklessly makes any statement or furnishes any document which is false in a material particular; or wilfully alters, suppresses or destroys any document which he is required to furnish as aforesaid, he is guilty of an offence under this section. To the extent that knowledge is a requirement of an offence under section 38(2) it must be proved by the prosecution. Knowledge includes the state of mind of a person who shuts his eyes to the obvious.[254] Moreover, there is authority for concluding

243 s. 37(3).
244 s. 37(5).
245 *Registrar of Restrictive Trading Agreements* v *W.H. Smith and Son Ltd* [1969] 1 WLR 1460; [1969] 3 All ER 1065 (CA).
246 s. 37(2).
247 s. 37(6).
248 s. 38(1).
249 cf. *Leck* v *Epsom RDC* [1922] 1 KB 383.
250 cf. *Aldridge* v *Warwickshire Coal Co Ltd* (1925) 133 LP 439 CA.
251 *R* v *Philip Reid* [1973] 1 WLR 1283 (CA).
252 See in this regard *Saddleworth UDC* v *Aggregate and Sand Ltd* (1970) 69 LGR 103.
253 See *R* v *Clarke* [1969] 2 All ER 1008; [1969] 1 WLR 1109 (CA).
254 See e.g. *James and Son Ltd* v *Smee* [1955] 1 QB 78, 91 *per* Parker J and *Westminster City Council* v *Croyalgrange Ltd* [1986] 1 WLR 674 (HL).

that where a person deliberately omits to make enquiries the result of which he might not care to have, this constitutes knowledge of the facts in question.[255] Mere neglect to ascertain what might have been found out by making reasonable enquiries is not tantamount to knowledge.[256] Where section 38(2) requires falsity a statement may be false on account of what it omits even though it is literally true.[257] Whether or not the person making the false statement gains all advantages as a result therefrom is irrelevant.[258] "Material particular" in section 38(2)(a) and (b) includes the situation whereby a particular renders another statement more credible.[259]

5.111 A person guilty of an offence under section 38(2) is liable not only to imprisonment but also to a fine.[260] If any default in respect of which a person is convicted of an offence under section 38(1) continues after the conviction that person is guilty under section 38(4) of a further offence and is liable to be punished for that additional infringement.[261] For the purposes of section 38(4) a default in respect of furnishing of any particulars, documents or information shall be deemed to continue until the particulars, documents or information have been furnished. Where an offence committed by a body corporate is proved to have been committed with the consent or connivance of, or to be attributable to any neglect on the part of, any director, manager, secretary or other similar officer of the body corporate or any person who was purporting to act in any such capacity, he as well as the body corporate is guilty of that offence and liable to be proceeded against and punished accordingly.[262] For the purposes of section 38 "director" in relation to a body corporate established by or under any enactment for the purpose of carrying on under national ownership any industry or part of an industry or undertaking, being a body corporate whose affairs are managed by its members, means a member of that body corporate.[263]

No proceedings for any offence under section 38 shall be instituted in England and Wales except by or with the consent of the DPP or the Director General; and in Northern Ireland except by or with the consent of the Attorney General for Northern Ireland or the Director General.[264]

L. Stays of Proceedings of the RPC: Inter-relationship of UK and EC Competition Law

5.112 It is often the case that the OFT and the European Commission will be considering the same agreement or practice. In such circumstances it is possible that the DG will refer an agreement to the RPC while, concurrently, the European Commission will be investi-

[255] See e.g. *Knox* v *Boyd* (1941) JC 82, 86; *Westminster City Council* v *Croyalgrange Ltd* (*ibid*.); *Mallen* v *Allon* [1964] 1 QB 385, 394.

[256] See e.g. *Taylor's Central Garages (Exeter) Ltd* v *Roper* (1951) 115 JP 445 *per* Devlin J and *London Computator Ltd* v *Seymour* (1994) 2 All ER 11.

[257] See *R* v *Lord Kylsant* [1932] 1 KB 442; *R* v *Bishirgan* [1936] 1 All ER 586; *Curtis* v *Chemical Cleaning and Dyeing Company Ltd* [1951] 1 WLR 399; *Barrass* v *Reeve* [1980] 3 All ER 705, [1981] 1 WLR 408.

[258] See e.g. *Jones* v *Meatyard* [1939] 1 All ER 140; *Stevens and Steeds Ltd and Evans* v *King* [1943] 1 All ER 314; *Clear* v *Smith* [1981] 1 WLR 399; *Barrass* v *Reeve* [1980] 3 All ER 705, [1981] 1 WLR 408.

[259] See e.g. *R* v *Tyson* (1887) LR 1 CCR 107 as to whether evidence should be adduced to show why a piece of information was a material particular, see *R* v *Mallett* [1978] 1 WLR 820 (CA).

[260] s. 38(3).

[261] s. 38(4).

[262] s. 38(6).

[263] s. 38(7).

[264] s. 39, see also s. 39(2)–(6) for provisions relating to the venue of any trial and the limitation period within which any information relating to an offence must be laid.

gating a complaint in relation to the same agreement, considering an application for negative clearance or alternatively exemption pursuant to a notification. From the perspective of the parties to the agreement it is obviously undesirable to be defending the agreement in two jurisdictions at the same time. Accordingly, the issue arises whether the RPC should stay its proceedings pending the deliberations of the Commission. Guidance can be given as to the considerations affecting the decision of the RPC whether to grant a stay. It is appropriate to consider a number of issues. First, the jurisdiction of the RPC to grant a stay. Secondly, the nature of the discretion to be exercised by the RPC in determining an application for a stay. Thirdly, the factors and criteria which the RPC will take into consideration in deciding whether or not to grant a stay.

1. Jurisdiction

5.113 The RPC has concluded that it has jurisdiction to grant a stay.[265] There are three bases the Court has referred to notwithstanding that there is no express provision in the RTPA 1976 which gives the Court power to stay proceedings before it.

5.114 First, rule 70 of the Restrictive Practices Court Rules 1976 provides in effect that the Court has power to regulate its own procedure. There are no express provisions precluding a power to order a stay. None the less, the Court has taken the view that it is empowered to order a stay as part of the regulation of its own procedure. Further, the Court has observed that pursuant to Rule 22 of the Restrictive Practice Court Rules the Court pursues the general object of securing the just expeditious and economical disposal of proceedings before it which object is achieved in appropriate circumstances by granting a stay.

5.115 Secondly, as a superior court of record[266] the Court has an inherent jurisdiction to prevent abuse of its process. Abuse of process is a wide concept and is capable of covering a case in which what is sought to be done is not conducive to the achievement of a just result.[267] The power includes the power to stay.

5.116 Thirdly, even if a power to say could not otherwise be extracted from the statutory sources, European Community law would require that such a power be assumed by the Court if such were necessary to avoid a conflict between national and Community law.[268] It follows from the general principles of Community law that if any rule of national law prevents the Court from granting a stay so as to give effect to the duty of the national court to avoid a conflict between Community and national law, that rule must be set aside.[269]

5.117 Ferris J has thus stated:

> "I take the view that there is no rule preventing the stay being granted by the Court and that, on the contrary, the Restrictive Practices Court Rules and the inherent jurisdiction of the Court to provide the ability to avoid conflict with Community law by ordering a stay. It is not therefore necessary to look to a further source for the requisite jurisdiction."[270]

[265] See *DGFT* v *Publishers' Association* 21 August 1996 (unreported); *British Sugar plc* v *DGFT* 21 August 1996 (unreported).

[266] See s. 1(1) Restrictive Practices Court Act 1976.

[267] cf. *Metropolitan Bank* v *Pooley* (1988) 10 App. C. 210, 221 cited by Ferris J in *DGFG* v *Publishers' Association* (21 August 1996, transcript p. 15D).

[268] cf. Case 14/68 *Walt Wilhelm* v *Bundeskartellamt* [1969] ECR 1 at pp. 14, 15: "where, during national proceedings, it appears possible that the decision to be taken by the Commission at the culmination of a procedure still in progress concerning the same agreement may conflict with the effects of the decision of the national authorities, it is for the latter to take the appropriate measures."

[269] See e.g. *R* v *Secretary of State for Transport ex parte Factortame Ltd (No. 2)* [1991] 1 AC 603.

[270] *DGFT* v *Publishers' Association (ibid.)* transcript p. 16C. The power to stay probably arise also from s. 3 RTPA 1976 pursuant to which the Court has the power to "decline or postpone" the exercise of

2. *Nature of the Discretion*

5.118 In *DGFT* v *Publishers' Association* the Court concluded that the jurisdiction to stay proceedings should be exercised cautiously and with due regard to preserving a balance between, on the one hand, refusing to allow a properly constituted application to be brought to a hearing before the Court and, on the other hand, inflicting an injustice on one of the parties by requiring it to conduct concurrently two sets of proceedings in relation to the same subject matter in circumstances where the outcome of one of these sets of proceedings may have an important, or even decisive, bearing outcome upon the other.[271] The Court stated further that it should stay properly constituted proceedings which were within its jurisdiction only if "substantial grounds" were shown.[272]

3. *Factors Affecting Discretion*

5.119 The facts which the Court is likely to take into account are many and varied. There is no definitive or exhaustive list which may be posited. However, the Court has given an indication of the facts and matters which will weigh in any discretion.

5.120 First, the Court will take into account the nature of the proceedings before the European Commission. In particular the Court will consider whether or not there is a prospect of negative clearance or exemption being granted pursuant to Article 85(3). Exemption will not usually be a prospect if the Commission is seised of a complaint in relation to past conduct not covered by any notification though negative clearance might be available. It is, of course, possible that even in relation to past conduct the parties to the agreement, decision or concerted practice in question will be able to invoke Article 4 of Regulation 17/62/EEC and thereby, on even a tardy notification, empower the Commission to grant retroactive exemption. If the proceedings before the Commission entail an application for exemption then the Court will need to consider what the likely outcome of the application will be. The Court will take into account case law of the Commission, Court of First Instance and Court of Justice as well as documents produced by the Commission in relation to the case (e.g. statements of objections, draft decisions, etc.). The Court will also consider the scope and terms of any exemption that is likely to be granted and whether it would dispose of the issues arising under the RTPA 1976 or any of them.

5.121 Secondly, the Court will consider the time which will elapse before the Commission grants its decision. In this regard the Director General may put evidence before the Court to the effect that the Director has contacted the Commission and elicited an indication of the relevant time-frame for the adoption of a decision. In the absence of such an indication it would be open to the Restrictive Practices Court itself, to contact the Commission in order to obtain an indication of likely time scale. The Court will also take into account whether the Commission is acting with urgency, the amount of time already elapsed, and whether appeals from any Commission decision are likely.

5.122 Thirdly, the Court will take into consideration that the compatibility of UK and EC competition law may be better reconciled at a substantive hearing. This is a considera-

cont.
jurisdiction under ss. 1 and 2 RTPA 1976 insofar as the Court considers right having regard to directly applicable Community provisions which would include Regulation 17/62/EEC. The regulation governs the Commission's jurisdiction in relation to complaints, notifications and other modes of investigation by the Commission in respect of the vast majority of agreements, decisions and practices.

271 *DGFT* v *Publishers' Association* (*ibid.*) transcript p. 17B.

272 *ibid.*, p. 25D.

tion which would apply, in particular, to applications for stays of proceedings before the Court which are at an early stage.

5.123 Fourthly, the Court will take into consideration the undesirability of a defendant being required to defend two sets of proceedings concurrently. The Court will also take into consideration the fact that costs might be saved if the defendant fights only upon one front at a time. However, in this regard, given that the issues before the Commission and before the Court are, to a significant degree, likely to be similar there may be substantial economies of scale which will be obtained by the parties to the agreement and, in such circumstances, the Court may consider that any savings made by being embroiled in one set of proceedings at a time will not be material.

5.124 Fifthly, the Court will take into account that competition policy is applied for the protection of the public interest and that a stay will delay the progress of a procedure designed to ascertain the public interest.

5.125 Sixthly, the Court will consider whether, on the facts of the particular case, national proceedings have, or may have, an impact upon the deliberations of the Commission. This will particularly be the case if the issue the Restrictive Practices Courts has to decide is whether or not any restriction is indispensable in the public interest. In such a case there may be an overlap, and even a substantial overlap, between the fact finding of the Court and the fact finding to be undertaken by the Commission in deciding whether or not the restrictions are indispensable for the purposes of applying Article 85(3). The role of the national court will therefore have a bearing upon the decision to be taken by the Commission. It has been argued that the Commission, an implementation of the general principle of sound administration, is bound to have regard to the findings of fact of the Restrictive Practices Court. The Court of Justice has, in effect, confirmed this argument in *Publishers' Association* v *Commission*.[273] The Restrictive Practices Court has pointed out that there is a certain lack of logic in that Court staying proceedings and thus declining to reach a conclusion upon a question which the Commission will inevitably have to form a view upon.

4. Examples

5.126 In the two cases, to date, brought by parties to agreements to stay proceedings before the Court pending a decision of the Commission, the application have been rejected.

5.127 In *British Sugar plc* v *Director General of Fair Trading*[274] British Sugar plc applied for orders staying proceedings brought by the DGFT under the Act in relation to an alleged agreement relating to the supply of sugar in the United Kingdom. The facts of the case may be summarised as follows. In the 1980s the two major suppliers of sugar in the United Kingdom were British Sugar plc (BS) and Tate and Lyle Industries Ltd (TLF). On 15 April 1991 TLF furnished a memorandum to the DGFT setting out a summary of arrangements involving BS and TLF commencing sometime after 20 June 1986 which were ended in July 1990. Paragraph 4 of the memorandum described that BS had announced at a meeting on 20 June 1986 that a price war then current in the United Kingdom sugar market and which had resulted from BS's then commercial policy, would cease. The memorandum recorded that in the context of an on-going investigation by the European Commission into the price practices of BS, that company was concerned to ensure that there was no further possibility of the company engaging in a form of pricing policy which would give rise to a complaint to the Commission or to the Director General of Fair Trading

273 Case C-360/92P *Publishers' Association* v *Commission* [1995] ECR II-23 at paras. 40–44 of the judgment.
274 21 August 1996, unreported.

of predatory pricing or other abuses of its dominant position. The memorandum then stated:

> "Both TLF and BS believe that as a consequence of the unilateral decision taken by BS to end the price war:
> (a) Retail market shares would tend to remain to around the level that the parties believed existed at the time of the making of the announcement by BS; and further to that end,
> (b) BS would not price aggressively with the result that BS would not price aggressively although they would nevertheless still be a band of tolerance in relation to their respective market shares."

The DGFT concluded that the memorandum revealed the existence of an agreement particulars of which had not been furnished in due time under the Act. Accordingly, on 6 June 1991 the OFT informed the parties that the DG had decided to refer the agreement to the Court with a view to obtaining orders under sections 1 and 2, and also to seek orders under section 2 and 35 RTPA 1976.

5.128 After the DGFT had commenced proceedings BS and TLF indicated that the proceedings would not be opposed and that appropriate undertakings would be given in lieu of the injunctions envisaged by sections 2 and 35 RTPA 1976. Shortly thereafter BS altered its position and asked for a postponement in the commencement of proceedings. In the event proceedings were not commenced until 7 July 1994 when two separate sets of proceedings were instituted by the DGFT, namely a reference under section 1 and an application under section 35(3). The reason for the change of heart on the part of BS was that the European Commission had initiated a second investigation into the commercial activities of BS and other suppliers of sugar within the European Community. On 4 May 1992 the Commission had served upon BS Statement of Objections alleging infringements of Articles 85 and 86. The ground covered by the Statement of Objectives was wider than that covered by the memorandum, particulars of which had been furnished to the DGFT, BS took the view that its defence to the Statement of Objection would be prejudiced if it were to accept that it had been a party to an agreement registrable under the RTPA 1976 but particulars of which had not been furnished in due time. BS also took the view that its position before the Commission would be weakened if it were to make admissions and given undertakings for the purpose of enabling the proceedings to commence by the DGFT to be dealt with upon an unopposed basis. In these circumstances BS applied to the Court under section 26 RTPA 1976 seeking an order that the register be rectified by removal of all particulars registered in respect of the agreements in question and for a declaration that the agreement is not an agreement to which the RTPA 1976 applied. Further, there were applications seek a stay of, not only British Sugar's own proceedings under section 26, but also the proceedings commenced by the DGFT under sections 1 and 35 RTPA 1976. The Court refused British Sugar's applications. The factors which lead the Court to reject the applications are as follows.

5.129 First, Community competition law presents no absolute bar to the application of national competition law. The respective tasks of the Restrictive Practices Court and of the Commission are different. The Court is concerned on the applications under sections 35 and 26 with the technical and mechanical question whether the memorandum placed upon the register by the DGFT disclosed the acceptance by two or more parties of restrictions falling within section 6(1) RTPA 1976. The Commission, on the other hand, is concerned with a much broader and wider ranging examination of the commercial relationship and activities of suppliers of sugar with a view to determining whether they have the economic effects referred to in Articles 85 and 86 EC. Secondly, if the Commission were persuaded by BS, or other parties, that its Statement of Obligations was unfounded this would not dictate the result of any proceedings brought before the Court. The proceedings before the Commission were unlikely on the facts to have any material impact upon the applications before the Court. Any stay would therefore only result in delay. Thirdly, the time which would elapse before the decision to the Commission was unknown but appeared to be substantial. The OFT had enquired of the Commission as to the likely time scale. This evidence was admitted before the Court to establish this fact. Fourthly, because of the public interest element in matters relating to competition law a stay should not be lightly granted for it could prevent others being made which Parliament had envisaged as being appropriate in the public interest. Fifthly, while it would be convenient to BS not to have to fight on two fronts at once and while BS would also save some costs by not having to do so, it was none the less the case that a considerable part of the ground which would have to be covered if the proceedings before the Court continued without a stay would also be ground which was being covered by BS in dealing with the Statement of Objection. The Court was of the view that the additional cost of having to continue with the proceedings would not therefore be very great. Sixthly, TLF was a respondent to the Director General's application under sections 1 and 35 jointly with British Sugar and would be affected by a stay of proceedings. TLF had indicated that it did not oppose a stay if the Court thought fit to grant one. Seventhly, the Court took into account the change of position on the part of BS who had, initially, been content to concur in the forwarding to the OFT of the memorandum which was subsequently placed upon the register. Later, BS changed its position and sought to contend that the memorandum was defective in, as of the date of the application to stay, an unspecified way. The Court observed:

> "It is ... of prime importance that the registered particulars are accurate. It appears ... that where, as here, a party has furnished particulars which are subsequently, albeit only as an alternative case, said to be inaccurate, a burden lies upon the party to deploy its case to that effect with diligence and due despatch. To seek a stay of proceedings is not consistent with the discharge of this obligation."

In weighing up the various particulars referred to above, the Court concluded that points 1–4 and 7 above pointed heavily against a stay. The Court accepted that the fifth ground (the interest of BS and the possible saving of costs) militated in favour of a stay but had limited weight. The position, on the facts, of the other respondents to the proceedings commenced by the Director General (the sixth ground above) was neutral.

5.130 In *DGFT* v *Publishers' Association*[275] the Court likewise decline to grant the Publishers' Association's application for stay of proceedings commenced by the DGFT. The proceedings in that case arose under section 4 RTPA 1976. Pursuant to this provision the Court is empowered to discharge any previous declaration of the Court in respect of any restriction or information provision and any order made by the Court in pursuance of that declaration and substitute such other declaration and make such order in pursuance of that declaration as appears to the Court to be appropriate at the time of the hearing of the application. Applications under section 4 are made by the Director or by any person who is or was at the time of the previous determination of the Court subject to or entitled to the benefit of the restriction or information provision in question. In order to make such an application the leave of the Court is required under section 4(4) RTPA 1976. The Court will not grant leave except upon prima facie evidence of a material change in the relevant circumstances. The Court had by a judgment in 1957 concluded that the Net Book Agreement was not contrary to the public interest.[276] The Net Book Agreement was an agreement concluded between members of the Publishers' Association.

[275] 21 August 1996, unreported.

[276] *Re Net Book Agreement 1957* (1962) LR3 RP 246. This exemption was subsequently revoked by the RPC in its judgment on 13 March 1997.

Subsequently, the same result was arrived at in respect of restrictions contained in a similar agreement made between certain publishers who were not members of the Publishers' Association.[277] Upon the DGFT applying for leave under section 4(4) RTPA 1976, the Publishers' Association applied to stay the proceedings pending the outcome of the deliberations of the European Commission upon the application for exemption of the Net Book Agreement under Article 85(3).

5.131 By a decision of 12 December 1988[278] the Commission adopted a decision concluding that the Net Book Agreement constituted an infringement of Article 85(1) to the extent that the agreement covered the book trade between the Member States. The Commission refused the Publishers' Association's application for an exemption. The Association was required, by the decision, to take all steps necessary to bring the infringement to an end. The Publishers' Association successfully obtained interim measures suspending the Commission's decision pending an appeal to the Court of First Instance. Upon the appeal, the Court rejected the application for annulment.[279] The Association appealed to the Court of Justice.[280] The Court of Justice set aside the judgment of the CFI. It proceeded to examine the decision of the Commission and, while it left standing that part of the decision which determined that the agreement infringed Article 85(1), the Court of Justice set aside the remainder of the decisions. The Court noted that the Commission had not apparently taken account of the facts as found by the RPC. The net effect was that the Commission was required once again to consider the Publishers' Association's application for an exemption pursuant to Article 85(3). It was in these circumstances that the Association sought to stay the proceedings before the Restrictive Practices Court pending the decision of the Court upon the application for an exemption. As noted above, the Court rejected the application. The grounds for rejecting the application were not dissimilar to those which led to the rejection of British Sugar's application described above. A summary of the grounds were as follows.

5.132 First, the Court was unable, pending the decision, accurately to appraise its impact upon the application before the RPC. this militated against the stay. Secondly, there was uncertainty as to the time which would elapse before the Commission adopted its decision. This militated against a stay. Thirdly, the protection of the public interest indicated that the national proceedings should continue. This militated against a stay. Fourthly, it could not be said with complete certainty that the outcome of the application to the Commission would determine the fate of the Net Book Agreement. The argument that the agreement should not be condemned under national law at a time when it could still be approved under Community law was an argument which could more easily be evaluated at the time of the hearing of the substantive application before the RPC than at the time of the application for stay. Fifthly, there was likely to be an initial saving of costs to the Publishers' Association if a stay was granted. However, for a number of reasons the savings were likely to be limited. Sixthly, the proceedings before the RPC were likely to have a special impact upon the deliberations of the Commission. This fact in particular, was decisive against the stay. The Publishers' Association invited the Court to request the Commission to express a view whether it would be assisted by the Court reaching the conclusion on the pending applications. The invitation was rejected. It did not come clearly within the terms of the Commission's Notice on cooperation between Na-

277 See *Re Net Book Agreement 1957 No. 2 (1964)*LR4 RP 484.

278 OJ 1989 L22/12.

279 Case T-66/89 *Publishers' Association* v *Commission* [1992] ECR II-1995.

280 Case C-360/92 *Publishers' Association* v *Commission* [1995] ECR II-23.

tional Courts and the Commission in the application of Articles 85 and 86. In any event, the Court was of the view that it should make up its own mind.

M. Judicial Review of the Director General of Fair Trading, the MMC and the Secretary of State

1. *Legal Context of Action for Judicial Review*

5.133 Considerable discretionary powers are exercised by the DGFT, the MMC and the Secretary of State. Decisions made by these agencies are subject to judicial review by the Courts at the instance of an affected person. Redress is by way of the process of judicial review under Order 53 RSC and section 31 Supreme Court Act 1981. The latter lays down basic procedures whilst the former elaborates upon the detail. Actions for judicial review may be based upon, *inter alia*, the following grounds.

5.134 (i) That the rules of natural justice have been breached thereby invalidating any decision adopted pursuant to the breach. Two aspects of natural justice are pertinent here. First, if a person deciding a case has a personal interest in the outcome that decision may be invalidated.[281] Secondly, if a person or firm or association that may be deleteriously affected by a decision is not given a chance to state their side of the case either orally or by written submissions, then the decision taken in breach of the right of hearing might be invalidated. In practice the OFT in their working procedures goes to considerable lengths to enable all interested parties to make their views known.

5.135 (ii) That the decision taken is *ultra vires* being one that the agency in question has no authority to take. The exercise of certain statutory powers may also be subject to the *ultra vires* doctrine. Thus, for instance, the power to issue notices under section 36 RTPA 1976 is circumscribed by the language of the section. An exercise of the power not falling within the statutory compass would be reviewable as *ultra vires*. Such might also be the case where the person making the decision takes into account an improper consideration. For example, if the Secretary of State granted dispensation from proceedings before the RPC for a registrable agreement upon the basis that his brother's company was a party to the agreement, such a decision could be invalidated upon the basis that it was made taking into account an improper consideration.

5.136 (iii) That the person or agency deciding a case has to follow certain objective criteria or conditions laid down by statute and that these criteria or conditions have been ignored or that they have not been fulfilled. This ground of review will rarely be relevant in the competition context since most of the criteria laid down in the legislation entail a significant degree of subjective discretion. For instance in section

[281] See MMC Report into the merger between Charter Consolidated-Anderson Strathclyde (1982) Cmnd 8771, and *R* v *Secretary of State for Trade ex parte Anderson Strathclyde* [1983] 2 All ER 233 at p. 237. The Minister possessed a shareholding in the offeror company to a take-over bid. The MMC concluded against the take-over and the Minister, because of his personal interest in the decision, delegated responsibility for it to a junior minister. The junior minister did not follow the MMC's conclusions and permitted the take-over to proceed. For an analysis of the controversy over this case see Green, "Crisis in the Monopolies and Mergers Commission: *Anderson Strathclyde* and other recent developments" (1983) BLR 303.

29 RTPA 1976 (on exemption from registration for agreements important to the national economy) criteria are laid down in section 29(2)(a)–(e) that, if met, qualify an agreement for exemption. However, irrespective of any discretion contained in the criteria themselves, section 29(1) is prefaced with the words: "If it appears to the Secretary of State ... that the conditions set out in subsection (2) below are complied with". The width of the discretion thus conferred renders the criteria in section 29(2)(a)–(e) difficult to subject to the process of judicial review. Similar discretion exists in respect of section 21(2) RTPA 1976 (dispensation from reference to the RPC). But however subjectively phrased, discretion is always subject to the requirement that it be exercised reasonably and so the High Court may intervene to determine the boundaries beyond which an exercise of discretion may not go.[282]

2. Informal Investigations into Firm's Behaviour

5.137 The OFT undertakes many informal investigations each year into corporate conduct primarily following a complaint by a third party. Depending upon the conclusions reached the OFT might take action, *inter alia*, under either the RTPA 1976 or the Competition Act 1980. However, this informal process has no statutory basis and is intended solely to put the OFT into a position whereby they can decide how best to exercise its discretionary powers, if they are to be exercised at all. An analogous situation must exist in relation to Department of Trade Inspectors which might be appointed to conduct investigations into the affairs of certain companies.[283] The investigations of these inspectors are not judicial; they are not even quasi-judicial. The inspectors simply investigate and report.[284] The inspectors have been held by the Court of Appeal to be "masters of their own procedure"[285] subject only to a duty to act fairly and to give everyone whom they intend to criticise in their report an opportunity to answer what is alleged against them.[286] The OFT is presumably under a legal duty to act fairly entailing giving those with a proper interest a right to make their views known.[287] In this respect the OFT does take steps to guarantee these minimum standards of fairness. A similar conclusion may be arrived in respect of the informal procedure, followed by the OFT, in investigating registered agreements for an assessment of whether restrictions contained in the agreement are of an insignificant enough nature to warrant an application to the Secretary of State under section 21(2) RTPA 1976. Again, the OFT takes pains to ensure that all parties to such informal inquiries are treated fairly.

[282] *R* v *MMC ex parte South Yorkshire Transport Ltd* [1993] 1 All ER 289, noted by Robertson [1993] ECLR 217.

[283] See Gower, *Principles of Modern Company Law* (5th edn. 1992), pp. 673–686.

[284] *Re Pergamon Press Ltd* [1970] 3 WLR 792 at p. 797 *per* Lord Denning MR, decision approved in *Paul Wallis Furnell* v *Whangarei High Schools Board* [1973] 2 WLR 93 (PC).

[285] *ibid.*, at p. 798.

[286] *ibid.* See also *Maxwell* v *Department of Trade and Industry* [1974] QB 523 (CA); *Norwest Holst* v *Secretary of State for Trade* [1978] Ch 201 (CA).

[287] This is apparently the opinion of the Director General himself: "It has been suggested during the debates that I ... might act unreasonably in conducting an investigation, might dream up something in my bath that there was no ground for—and the company goes for investigation. Well, if I act in a grossly unreasonable way it can be challenged in the Courts. And my office would lose its credibility if it kept coming up with reports which showed that the investigation was not worthwhile or, alternatively, I was repeatedly slapped down by the Monopolies Commission" (*Sunday Times*, 6 April 1980, "Facing up to fair trade").

3. Decisions to Investigate Anti-Competitive Practices by the Director General

5.138 The decision to undertake a formal investigation into the possible existence of an anti-competitive practice by the OFT is a discretionary decision under section 3(1) Competition Act 1980. This for all practical purposes renders the decision to investigate free from review by the Courts. The Act provides no criteria whatsoever for regulating when and in which circumstances an investigation may occur. Similarly, a complainant who wishes to force the OFT to commence an investigation will probably have no joy since the Act lays down no criteria against which a refusal to investigate may be measured. However patently unreasonable decisions to investigate may well be subject to review for irrationality.

4. The Conduct of Formal Investigations

Following the decision of the House of Lords in *Hoffman-La Roche* v *Secretary of State for Trade and Industry*[288] it is clear that the conduct of investigations by the MMC is subject to the rules and requirements of natural justice. Moreover, that infringement of these requirements renders the report of the MMC, or any operative part thereof, voidable at the discretion of the Court. However, until such time as an MMC Report is avoided by a Court, the Secretary of State may proceed to enforce its findings in normal fashion. Where an MMC report is struck down by a Court then any order issued by the Secretary of State is susceptible to the same fate.[289] The Fair Trading Act 1973 sets out procedural rules and standards and, provided these are complied with, few opportunities for challenge will arise. None the less, simply because they are complied with does *not* necessarily imply absolutely compatibility with the rules of natural justice.

5.140 The OFT, in the conduct of investigations into anti-competitive practices will also be subject to the rules of natural justice, albeit that the Act is silent on all rules of procedure for this investigation. In practice the OFT follows exacting rules to ensure fairness. It is aware that in many instances it stands between a complainant and a complained-off and is expected to act as advocate, jury and judge. Accordingly, all sides to a case are given ample opportunity to present their case. The report of the Director General following an investigation is subject to judicial review in the same way as is the report of the MMC. If a Court were to strike down the conclusions of the OFT in a report signed by the Director General this, it is submitted, would have no bearing upon a subsequent hearing and decision of the MMC. The MMC operate by way of complete re-investigation of whether the conduct is anti-competitive and assesses for itself the public interest. There is, accordingly, no necessary point of correlation between the two procedures.

5. Decisions of the Secretary of State

5.141 The Secretary of State decides upon the action to be taken following an MMC report. He is *not* bound to follow the conclusions of the MMC though he must actively take their recommendations into account.[290] In respect of decisions made under section 21(2) RTPA 1976, the Secretary enjoys a discretion whether or not to grant an application made

[288] [1974] 2 All ER 1128.
[289] *ibid.*, at p. 1153 *per* Lord Cross and at p. 1159 *per* Lord Diplock.
[290] *R* v *Secretary of State for Trade ex parte Anderson Strathclyde* [1983] 2 All ER 233 at p. 242; *Lonrho plc* v *Secretary of State for Trade and Industry* [1989] 2 All ER 609, 617–621.

by the OFT seeking dispensation from the RPC for a registered agreement. This discretion is exercisable when it appears to the Secretary of State that restrictions in an agreement are not significant. Even where the Secretary finds that restrictions are insignificant section 21(2) still gives him a discretion to refuse dispensation. Accordingly, unless it can be proven that the decision of the Secretary of State took into account improper considerations judicial review of the decision appears a forlorn hope.[291]

6. The Attitude of the Courts towards Judicial Review in Competition Cases

5.142 There have been a number of judicial review applications in respect of the conduct of MMC investigations under the Fair Trading Act 1973. The majority have arisen from merger situations,[292] but there have also been cases arising from the conduct of monopoly investigations.[293] One case has been heard arising out of a reference to the MMC under the Competition Act 1980.[294]

5.143 In general the Courts have espoused a robust, public policy based view of judicial review. In *R* v *Monopolies and Mergers Commission, ex parte Argyll Group PLC*,[295] the Masters of the Rolls strongly intimated that the Courts, in exercising their discretion, should bear in mind the requirements of "good public administration". This, it was held is concerned with: (a) the substance of a decision rather than its form; (b) the benefits of rapid decision making; (c) a proper consideration of the public interest; (d) a proper consideration of the legitimate interests of individual citizens however rich and powerful and whether natural or juridical but always remembering the purpose of the administrative process concerned; and (e) the desirability of decisiveness and finality unless there are compelling reasons to the contrary. The effect of this judgment appears to be that judicial review, at least in the context of competition policy, will be less amenable to cases of technical default and more amenable to cases of maladministration appraised by standards which allows the authorities a margin of error.[296]

5.144 Indeed, the Courts have never allowed judicial review of the MMC on the basis of a breach of natural justice. Thus in *R* v *MMC ex parte Elders IXL Ltd*,[297] the MMC was allowed to adopt a procedure which it considered best suited its need to discharge its statutory function, even though it created a perceived detriment to one of the parties whose merger plans were being investigated. Similarly in *R* v *MMC ex parte Matthew Brown plc*,[298]

291 Failure to grant s. 21(2) dispensation may be indirectly challenged before the RPC by reference to ss. 10(1)(h) (goods) or 19(1)(h) (services) see Liesner Committee, *op. cit.*, at p. 112.

292 *R* v *MMC ex parte Argyll Group plc* [1986] 2 All ER 257; *R* v *MMC ex parte Elders IXL Ltd* [1987] 1 All ER 451; *R* v *MMC ex Matthew Brown plc* [1987] 1 All ER 463; *R* v *MMC ex parte Air Europe Ltd* 1988] BCC 182; *R* v *MMC ex parte south Yorkshire Transport Ltd* [1993] 1 All ER 289; *R* v *MMC ex p Stagecoach Holdings plc* [1996] *The Times*, 23 July. See also *Lonrho plc* v *DGFT*, Divisional Court, 11 November 1988, unreported, in which a challenge to the DGFT's duty to make recommendations to the Secretary of State in a merger situation was turned down, and *Lonrho plc* v *Secretary of State for Trade and Industry* [1989] 2 All ER 609, in which the House of Lords refused judicial review of the Secretary of State's decision not to make a merger reference.

293 *R* v *MMC ex parte Visa International Service Association* [1991] CCLR (Consumer Credit Law Reports) 13; *R* v *MMC ex parte Ecando Systems Ltd*, Court of Appeal, unreported 12 November 1992; *R* v *MMC ex parte National House Building Council* [1994] The Times, 25 January. See also, under the Monopolies and Restrictive Practices (Inquiry and Control) Act 1948, *Hoffmann-La Roche* v *Secretary of State for Trade and Industry* [1974] 2 All ER 1128.

294 *R* v *DGFT ex parte Southdown Motor Services* (1993) 12 Tr LR 90.

295 [1986] 2 All ER 257 at p. 266.

296 In the case the Court held that the Chairman of the Commission had exceeded his powers but not in a way which equated to maladministration. See at pp. 265e, 269 e–h.

297 [1987] 1 All ER 451

298 [1987] 1 All ER 463

non-disclosure of evidence to a target company put to the MMC by the would-be acquiring company was held not to constitute such manifest unfairness as to make the report liable to judicial review. In *R* v *MMC ex parte Air Europe Ltd*[299] Lloyd LJ commented on this reluctance to make the MMC disclose all evidence to all parties as deriving from the need to allow the MMC to conduct their investigation in the time allotted by the Secretary of State. As monopoly investigations are given rather more time than merger references, typically nine or ten months compared to three, then it may be that the courts would be more willing in a monopoly investigation to impose a duty to disclose all relevant evidence to the parties for comment and to regard a failure to do so as a breach of natural justice.

5.145 There have been a number of challenges on the basis of the MMC misdirecting itself on a point of law, but ultimately none of these has been successful either.[300] In *R* v *MMC ex parte Visa International Service*,[301] Hodgson J stated that a MMC Report "must not be read as if it were a statute or a judgment ... it should be read in a generous not a restrictive way and the court should be slow to disable the MMC from recommending action considered in the public interest or to prevent the Secretary of State from acting thereon unless any perceived errors of law are both material and substantial". In *R* v *MMC ex parte South Yorkshire Transport Ltd*,[302] Lord Mustill stated that the statutory definition of a "substantial part" of the United Kingdom in determining whether a merger situation qualified for investigation under section 64(3) Fair Trading Act 1973 was one for that of the MMC to assess. The Court was only entitled to substitute its own opinion "if the decision is so aberrant that it cannot be classed as rational" and in that case the conclusion arrived at "was well within the permissible field of judgment".[303] Therefore it seems that the courts are reluctant to substitute their judgment for the MMC on points of interpretation of the relevant legislation except in the clearest cases.

299 [1988] 4 BCC 182, 187.

300 See Hornsby, "Judicial review of decisions of the UK competition authorities: is the applicant bound to fail?" [1993] ECLR 183.

301 *R* v *MMC ex parte Visa International Service Association* [1990] CCLR 72, 86.

302 [1993] 1 All ER 289, noted by Robertson [1993] ECLR 217. Lord Mustill gave the sole reasoned judgment with which the rest of their Lordships agreed, overturning judgments to the contrary by the Court of Appeal (Nourse LJ diss), [1992] 1 All ER 257 (see Robertson [1992] ECLR 180) and Otton J in the High Court.

303 [1993] 1 All ER 289, 298.

6 Agreements and Trade Association Practices Caught by European Competition Law

A. Introduction

6.1 In this chapter commercial agreements and trade association practices which fall within the EC competition rules are discussed. The chapter follows the pattern given below:

Section B.	Forms of joint conduct caught by Article 85 EC.
Section C.	Proving an effect on trade between the Member States.
Section D.	The object or effect of an agreement.
Section E.	"Preventing, restricting or distorting competition".
Section F.	Article 85(2): restrictions automatically void.
Section G.	Agreements exempted under Article 85(3). Detailed analysis of Article 85(3) is left until Chapter 7.
Section H.	Article 86 EC: abuse of a dominant position.
Section I.	Overlap between EC and UK law.
Section J.	Notification to the European Commission. This Section weighs the advantages and disadvantages of notifying the existence and details of an agreement to the Commission.
Section K.	Form A/B; the method of notification.
Section L.	Form C; complaints by third parties.

B. Forms of Joint Conduct Caught by Article 85 EC[1]

6.2 Article 85(1) is drafted so as to catch *all* forms of inter-firm consensus or arrangement, however informal. It also includes all forms of trade association recommendation. It is,

[1] For an analysis of the wide ambit of Art. 85(1), see Bellamy and Child, *Common Market Law of Competition*, 4th edn. 1993, 1st supp 1997 Chapter 2 Whish; *Competition Law* (3rd edn.), Chapter 7; Butterworths, *Competition Law*, Chapter 1.

in effect, impossible to draft an agreement or devise an arrangement so as to exclude Article 85(1) EC. The following categories of inter-firm arrangement fall within Article 85 EC. The enumeration below is non-exhaustive. The meaning of certain other key words in Article 85 EC is also given.

1. "Agreements between undertakings"

6.3 The concept of an "agreement" is extraordinarily wide. An agreement can be between any number of parties above one. Not all of the parties need accept restrictions, it being sufficient if only one party accepts restrictions (unlike the RTPA 1976). The agreement need not be formal, it can be simply an informal understanding between firms.[2] Likewise "gentlemen's agreements", "breakfast agreements" and "honour only agreements" are equally caught within Article 85 EC.[3] If X agrees with Y that he will unilaterally refrain from selling in Y's primary marketing area or will refrain from undercutting Y then this is an "agreement", albeit that Y is passive and gives nothing to X in return for these promises.[4] Agreements between trade associations are agreements caught by Article 85.[5] Likewise, private understandings, perhaps developed informally at association meetings, are "agreements" for Article 85 purposes.[6] A series of connected agreements may be treated as a single agreement if the connecting feature suggests an overall or master design.[7] The constitutional documents of an association may amount to an agreement.[8]

6.4 The name given to an agreement is immaterial. Indeed, attempts to describe sets of trading rules formally as "Fair Trading Rules" may be viewed as suspicious by the Commission.[9]

6.5 It matters not whether an agreement is between parties at the same or at different levels of distribution. Thus, price fixing agreements between rival manufacturers are caught, as are exclusive distribution systems involving agreements between suppliers and dealers.[10] Nor does it matter that an agreement is no longer in existence and has been aban-

[2] e.g. *National Panasonic (UK) Ltd* [1983] 1 CMLR 497. Agreement consisted of internal memoranda, a telex message and some correspondence.

[3] e.g. *Quinine Cartel* [1969] CMLR D41; [1970] ECR 661.

[4] e.g. *Franco-Japanese Ball-Bearings Agreement* [1975] 1 CMLR D 8.

[5] e.g. *NAVEWA-ANSEAU* [1982] 2 CMLR 193; Case 67/63 *Sorema* v *High Authority* [1964] ECR 151 (under the European Coal and Steel Treaty); Case 71/74 *Frubo* v *Commission* [1975] ECR 563; [1975] 2 CMLR 123; *Central Heating* [1972] CMLR D130. Mutual or reciprocal exclusive dealing agreements whereby the members of one association agree only to trade with the members of another trade association (thereby putting a premium on association membership) are also agreements subject to Art. 85 EC.

[6] e.g. *SSI* [1982] 3 CMLR 702 at p. 741, para. 106: "An understanding between associations of undertakings may constitute an agreement within the meaning of Art. 85(1) even if its terms have not been set down in a written document signed by the parties."

[7] In *Polypropylene Cartel* [1988] 7 CMLR 347 the Commission construed the plan to regulate prices in the polypropylene market as an "overall framework agreement which was manifested in a series of more detailed sub-agreements worked out from time to time". The conclusion that there was one continuing agreement was not altered by the fact that some producers were not present at every meeting. See for an example in the national courts the observations of the Master of the Rolls about certain arrangements at Lloyd's, the insurance market: *Society of Lloyd's* v *Clementson* (1995) CLC 117 esp. at 131 C, D.

[8] *SOCEMAS* [1968] CMLR D28. Though similar documents have also been described as a "decision"—*ASPA* [1970] CMLR D25.

[9] *European Glass Manufacturers* [1974] 2 CMIR D50; *IFTRA Rules for Producers of Virgin Aluminium* [1975] 2 CMLR D20.

[10] e.g. Cases 56 and 58/64 *Consten and Grundig* v *Commission* [1966] ECR 299; [1966] CMLR 418. There are literally thousands of agreements between parties at different distributional levels which have been reviewed by the Commission under Art. 85 EC. Indeed approximately 20–30 per cent of the Commission's case load has in the past concerned distribution schemes.

doned if it continues to produce effects.[11] The fact that an existing agreement upon which breach of Article 85 is founded was entered prior to the coming into force of the Treaty of Rome is immaterial.[12] Nor does it matter that one party only consented to the agreement after strong pressure to accept a deal that was against its own economic interest.[13]

6.6 A conveyance of property or other transfer constitutes an agreement. In *Sirena* the assignment of a trade mark was held to constitute an agreement.[14] The same rule applies in the UK.[15]

6.7 Agreements between members of the same group of companies are prima facie not agreements under Article 85(1) EC. Thus an agreement between a parent and subsidiary is not within Article 85 EC. Nor is an agreement between subsidiaries of the same parent company within Article 85 EC. This important proviso to Article 85 is discussed fully below.

6.8 Where an agreement is held not to exist, there can nevertheless be a concerted practice caught by Article 85(1) EC. Thus in practice should there be insufficient evidence of a concerted practice, there may be sufficient evidence of a concerted practice nevertheless.

6.9 Article 85 catches "agreements between undertakings". What is an "undertaking"? The notion of "undertaking" is very wide and includes almost all types of economic enterprise, firm or company, etc.[16] Article 85 assumes an undertaking to be capable of concluding agreements. An undertaking can attack decisions of the Commission under Article 173 EC (judicial review of binding decisions). Constituents of an undertaking (plants, branch offices, works divisions, etc.) are not undertakings in their own right. Public or nationalised companies are undertakings in the same way as are private undertakings.[17] Thus a

[11] e.g. *IFTRA rules for Producers of Virgin Aluminium* [1975] 2 CMLR D20. See also Case 40/70 *Sirena* v *Eda* [1971] CMLR 260 where the assignment of a trade mark in 1937 was held to constitute an agreement for the purposes of Art. 85 when the Treaty of Rome became operative some twenty years later; Case 51/75 *EMI* v *CBS* [1976] ECR 811; Case T-7/89 *Hercules* [1991] ECR II–1711, para. 257; Case 243/89 *Bison* [1985] ECR 2015 [1985] 3 CMLR 800.

[12] See *Sirena* (*ibid.*).

[13] *Fisher/Quaker Oats-Toyco* OJ 1988 L 49/19, [1989] 4 CMLR 513; *Gosme/Martell-DMP* OJ 1991 L185/23.

[14] *ibid.*, see C-9/93 *Ideal Standard* [1994] ECR I-2789 [1994] 3 CMLR 857. The assignment of intellectual property rights is discussed at para. 13.42.

[15] See *Ravenseft* v *Director General of Fair Trading* [1977] 1 All ER 47 (QBD). Though for other reasons it is considered to fall outside of the RTPA 1976, see paras. 2.201–2.210.

[16] In Case C-41/90 *Höfner* v *Macrotron* [1991] ECR I-1979, para. 21, the ECJ stated: "in the context of competition law, the concept of an undertaking encompasses every entity engaged in an economic activity, regardless of the legal status of the entity and the way in which it is financed". This has included agricultural co-operatives: *Meldoc* OJ 1986 L 348/50, [1989] 4 CMLR 853 (see B. Jacobi and P.L. Vesterdorf, "Co-operative societies and the Community rules on competition" (1993) 18 ELRev 271), but not public social security schemes, Joined Cases C-159 and 160/91 *Poucet* v *Calmurac* [1993] ECR I-637. See also C-244/94 *Federation Française des Sociétés d'assurance et OCS* v *Ministère de L'agriculture et de la pêche* [1995] ECR I-4022. Hirst J in the Commercial Court accepted in *Irish Aerospace* v *European Organisation for the Safety of Air Navigation (Eurocontrol)* [1994] ECC 97 that an international organisation set up under Treaty to provide air navigation services was not an undertaking, since it was regulatory, not commercial, in nature notwithstanding it levied charges for its services. In *Society of Lloyd's* v *Clementson* [1994] ECC 481, Saville J held that the Society of Lloyd's was not an undertaking for the purposes of Art. 85. This was overturned on appeal [1995] CLC 117. The Court of Appeal accepted that underwriters and Lloyd's. Names were also "undertakings" and held that it was arguable that Lloyd's was also. In any case since a Name was an undertaking, Lloyd's was an association of undertakings. The legal form of an undertaking is irrelevant—*GEMA I* [1971] CMLR D35.

[17] This has long been orthodox Commission thinking. See Commission answers to WQ No. 48, OJ 1963 2234; and, WQ No.149 OJ 1968 C 109/5. See also WQ 1152/82 OJ 1982 C 339/15 where the Commission stated: "The Commission has already indicated on a number of occasions that not only nationalized firms, as regards their own conduct, but also the Member States, as regards their conduct towards such firms, are entirely subject to the provisions of the EC Treaty, including those concerning

state monopoly or association is an undertaking. A local authority may also be an undertaking.[18] The legal form of an undertaking is irrelevant.[19] Thus it makes no difference that the undertaking is incorporated or unincorporated, nor does it matter that the undertaking is non-profit making.[20] Natural persons can be undertakings. In *Re UNITEL*[21] an artiste was held to be an undertaking. Article 85 EC applies, for example, to sports and theatrical agents and their clients. Thus in *1990 World Cup tickets*,[22] FIFA, the world governing body of football, the Italian Football Association and the Italian World Cup organising committee were held to be undertakings for the purpose of Article 85(1) EC.[23]

6.10 An enterprise will be active in business and commerce. This means that the undertaking will be involved in the production, manufacture, wholesale, retailing or other exchange of goods or services. The legal form of the commercial activity is not relevant: it is the very fact of commercial activity which transforms a person conducting an activity into an undertaking for the purposes of Article 85. In essence the word "undertaking" is a functional one. The degree or extent of economic activity should be more than *de minimis*. Thus, a person who holds a single antiques market for charity does not it is submitted thereby become transformed into an "undertaking". However, if such were organised on a regular basis the element of continuity might lead to the conclusion that the organisers were "undertakings" for Article 85 purposes. That the concept of "undertaking" may be a question of degree is shown by the fact that a shareholder in a company is not, *per se*, an undertaking but may become one if the degree of involvement extends beyond mere administration of the shareholding into administration of the company.[24]

6.11 A foreign, semi-statutory company the staff of which are governmentally appointed and which has as its main task the export of its goods may be an undertaking where it is involved in commercial activity.[25]

6.12 The involvement of government in the creation of an agreement does not result in the disengagement of Article 85(1). However, where government is involved it is necessary to consider whether the degree of involvement renders any subsequent harmonised conduct between competing undertaking not the object or effect of an agreement, concerted practice or decision of an association undertakings, as required by Article 85(1). Articles 85 and 86 are concerned only with the conduct of "undertaking" and not with laws or regulations adopted by Member States. However, it is settled law that those articles, read in conjunction with Articles 5 and 3(g) of the Treaty, require Member States not to introduce or maintain in force measures, even of a legislative or regulatory nature,

cont.
freedom of competition. As far as Community law is concerned, the position of nationalized firms is therefore no different from that of private firms."

18 Case 26/75 *General Motors* v *Commission* [1975] ECR 1367— private company given statutory monopoly right in respect of a service to be provided to car importers. However, see *AROW* v *BNIC* [1982] 2 CMLR 240 at pp. 254, 255: a government Commissioner who notifies to a trade association under statutory authority a minimum price for the sale of its members goods is *not* an undertaking under Art. 85(1) EC.

19 *GEMA I* [1971] CMLR D35.

20 See e.g. *GVL* [1982] 1 CMLR Z21. A non-profit making performing rights society was held to be an undertaking under Art. 86 EC on abuse of a dominant position. The Society did take a small percentage of the royalties it collected to defray its administrative overheads.

21 [1978] 3 CMLR 306.

22 OJ 1992 L 136/31.

23 In Germany the cartel rules have been applied to boxers (see BKA 3 May 1961; BB, 1961, 657).

24 See, e.g. *Reuter/BASF* [1976] 2 CMLR D44; and *AOIP* v *Beyrard* [1976] 1 CMLR D14. In Case 170/83 *Hydrotherm* v *Andreoli* [1985] 3 CMLR 224 the European Court held that a man and two companies he controlled constituted one undertaking.

25 *Cafeteros de Columbia* [1983] 1 CMLR 703.

which may render ineffective the competition laws applicable to undertakings.[26] Further, Articles 3(g), 5 and 85 are infringed where a Member State requires or favours the adoption of agreements, decisions concerted practices contrary to Article 85 or reinforces their effects or where it deprives its own rules of the character of legislation by delegating to private economic operators responsibility for taking decisions affecting the economic sphere.[27] The distinction between a measure of central government and an agreement, concerted practice or decision of an association or undertakings has arisen particularly in relation to the rules of Member States providing mandatory tariffs applicable to contracts for provision of carriage. In this respect the Court of Justice has held that the competition rules do not preclude such rules *provided* that the persons setting the tariffs in question are not representatives of the commercial sectors affected by the tariffs, are responsible for fixing the tariffs independently and upon the basis of consideration relating to the public interest and provided that the public authorities, by retaining overall control of the tariff-setting system, do not relinquish their powers to fix tariffs. In deciding whether Article 85 applies the following (inter-related) questions (of fact) will need to be asked:

(a) Independence: are the persons allocated responsibility for fixing the rates or terms and conditions of trade empowered to act independently of the companies being regulated or are they bound or materially influenced by orders or instructions emanating from the sectors affected by their decisions? If the answer is the latter this would point in favour of the tariffs or trading terms being the object or effect of an agreement as opposed to the regulatory or legislative measure of government.
(b) Public interest: are the decision makers required to take account of the broader public interest or are they influenced or their decisions affected by the interests of one or more of the economic sectors concerned? If the answer is the latter this, again, suggests that the tariffs or terms or conditions are set by industry and are the object of the effect of an agreement etc.
(c) Representation: are the decision makers representative of all the commercial sectors affected by the decision or are they representative of only a part of the economic sectors affected or are they independent of the industry? A close relationship to the industry affected suggests that the tariff or terms and conditions are the object or effect of an agreement.
(d) Appointment: does the appointment of the persons taking the relevant decisions stem from a public authority or, alternatively, from the industry concerned? If the deci-

[26] See e.g. Case 267/85 *Van Eycke* [1988] ECR 4769, para. 60: Case C185/91 *Reiff* [1993] ECR I-5801, para. 14; Case-C153/93 *Delta Schiffahrts* [1994] ECR I-2517, para. 14; Case 13/77 *GB-Innon-BM* [1977] ECR 2115, para. 31 (in relation to Art. 86); in the *Society of Lloyd's* v *Clementson* [1995] CLC 117 at pp. 127, 128 the Court of Appeal was concerned to decide whether the Central Fund operated by Lloyd's was capable of falling within Art. 85(1). The Master of the Rolls stated: "the Court of Justice has more than once pointed out, and it cannot be doubted, that Article 85 of the EC Treaty concerns only the conduct of companies is not directed at legislative or regulatory measures emanating from the Member States ... If, therefore, it appeared that the adoption or terms of the Central Fund Byelaw were required of Lloyd's by the express or implied terms of national legislation, that would enable the Court to rule that the relevant decision (if it was such) fell outside the scope of Article 85. But Lloyd's were unable to point to any national legislation which required that the Central Fund should be established in the way or on the terms it was. It was Lloyd's which adopted the Central Fund Byelaw and Lloyd's which operated the Central Fund. If the Secretary of State had any relevant reserve power, it is not suggested that he exercise them" (*ibid.*, 127 C, D).

[27] *Van Eyke* (*ibid.*), para. 16; *Reiff* (*ibid.*), para. 14; *Delta Schiffahrts* (*ibid.*), para. 14; Case C-96/94 *Centro Servizi Spediporto Srl.* [1995] ECR I–2883, para. 21.

sion makers are appointed by industry this, again, indicates the existence of an agreement as opposed to a legislative or regulatory measure.[28]

(e) Delegation of authority: does the public authority delegate its power to take the relevant decision to private economic operators? In this regard the national court will need to consider, upon the basis of the relevant legislation, what powers and duties are conferred upon the public authority, whether the persons delegated the responsibility for fixing prices are subject to control by the public authority and, whether, in the final analysis the public authority reserves residual powers to fix the tariffs itself.

2. *"Decisions by Associations of Undertakings"*

6.13 As with other phrases in Article 85 a wide interpretation is accorded here. An association of undertakings usually refers to a trade association but can equally refer to some other organisation which is not labelled an association as such. Thus organisations can be derived from memorandum and articles of association (as with the usual trade association) or from deeds of partnership or charters, etc. A "decision" implies some binding effect. However, under Article 85(1) EC the word is construed more widely. Thus, where a trade association issues to members non-binding recommendations which as a rule are complied with then the Commission treat the recommendations as decisions under Article 85(1) EC.[29] It would thus be true to say that any exhortation, encouragement, recommendation or other statement whether made orally or in writing may be a decision if it either is accepted by the members or is intended to be accepted by the members. The "recommendation" need not even be direct, it could simply be in the veiled form of a circular to members which states that: "the association staff have undertaken research into costs and have discovered that on average members are paying 2.3 per cent more for ingredients than they were 6 weeks ago". If members responded by raising prices 2.3 per cent the circular might well be construed as a decision. Compliance by members with recommendations, exhortations etc. will amount to a concerted practice between the members and probably in full-scale agreement.

6.14 The decision need not necessarily be made by the association. An individual who has authority to act on behalf of the association, for example, its chief executive, may make a decision which is subject to Article 85. An association may be fined in its own right for breach of the rules.

6.15 A decision laying down minimum prices taken by a governmental authority is not a decision under Article 85(1), though a decision laying down minimum prices taken by a private association is within the article. An association decision remains within Article 85 EC even though a governmental authority may subsequently extend the ambit of the decision beyond the trade association's membership to other undertakings.[30]

3. *Whether a Group of Companies is a Single Undertaking*

6.16 Considerable debate has occurred as to whether a group of companies is to be considered as a single or a multipartite entity.[31] The Court has laid down the general framework for analysis as follows:

[28] Though, the fact that the persons appointed are appointed by the state does not necessarily exclude the application of Art. 85: see e.g. Case 123/83 *BNIC* v *Clair* [1985] ECR 391.

[29] e.g. Cases 96–102, 104–105, 108 and 110/82 *IAZ International Belgium SA and Others* v *Commission* [1984] 3 CMLR 276 at para. 20 of the judgments; Case 71/74 *FRUBO* [1975] ECR 580 (ECJ) (for Commission decision see [1974] 2 CMLR D89); *Vereeniging Van Cementhandelaren* [1973] CMLR D16.

[30] *AROW* v *BNIC* [1983] 2 CMLR 240; see also *Society of Lloyd's* v *Clementson* [1995] CLC 117, 127, 128.

[31] G. Assant, "Anti-trust intracorporate conspiracies: a comparative study of French, EEC and American laws" [1990] ECLR 45.

> "Article 85 does not apply to agreements or concerted practices between undertakings belonging to the same group in the form of parent company and subsidiary, if the undertakings form an economic unit within which the subsidiary does not have real autonomy in determining its line of conduct on the market and if the agreements or practices have the aim of establishing an internal distribution of tasks between the undertakings."[32]

It is thus clear that the Court and Commission will treat as a single entity, a group where the component subsidiaries have no real independence and form an integral part with the parent. The simple fact that the subsidiaries are, in law, separate legal persons from the parent is immaterial.[33] This contrasts with the UK legal position whereby a parent is considered to be a separate legal entity altogether from its subsidiary.[34] The fact that a corporate group may be considered a single entity has two very important consequences.

6.17 First, the behaviour of a subsidiary may be attributed to its parent so that the latter incurs liability also under competition rules for the conduct of the former. In *Dyestuffs* the European Court stated:

> "The fact that a subsidiary has separate legal personality is not sufficient to exclude the possibility of imputing its conduct to the parent company. Such may be the case in particular where the subsidiary, although having separate legal personality, does not decide independently upon its own conduct on the market, but carries out, in all material respects, the instructions given to it by the parent company ... In view of the unity of the group thus formed, the actions of the subsidiaries may in certain circumstances be attributed to the parent company."[35]

Thus a foreign *parent* company may be subject to EC law if its subsidiaries or agencies that are dependent on it are found to be in breach of that law.[36] However, there is no automatic presumption that a parent is liable for the acts of its subsidiaries.[37] It is accepted that a subsidiary may diverge from a pursuance of its parents wishes.[38]

6.18 Secondly, Article 85(1) does not apply to relationships between parent and subsidiaries if the relationship is close enough for the undertakings to be treated as a single economic unit. In such a case there can be no "agreement" between the undertakings.

6.19 For Article 85(1) to be precluded the subsidiary should not enjoy "real autonomy in determining its course of action in the market.[39] Article 85 is also precluded where the subsidiary "has no real freedom to determine its course of action on the mar-

[32] Case 16/74 *Centrafarm BV and de Peijper* v *Winthrop BV* [1974] 2 CMLR 480; [1974] ECR 1183 at para. 32 of judgment.

[33] See e.g. T-102/92 *Viho Europe BV* v *Commission* [1995] ECR II-17.

[34] See *Salomon* v *Salomon* [1897] AC 22 and see also s. 736 Companies Act 1985. See Mann (1973) 22 ICLQ 35 at p. 48 for commentary on this aspect. See also s. 43(2) RTPA 1976 which states that for purposes of identifying whether two or more persons have entered into an agreement "any two or more interconnected bodies corporate, or any two or more individuals carrying on business in partnership with each other, shall be treated as a single person."

[35] Case 48/69 [1972] CMLR 577; [1972] ECR 619 at paras. 132–135 of the judgment. See also Case 107/82 *AEG Telefunken* v *Commission* [1984] 3 CMLR 325, (1983) ECR 3151 at para. 50. See also *Peroxygen Cartel* [1985] 1 CMLR 481 at para. 49—the present owner of an undertaking which infringes Art. 85 before the present owner acquires control is none the less responsible for the subsidiary if, after it obtains control, it adopts the policies and objectives of the subsidiary.

[36] See e.g. *Cafeteros de Colombia* [1983] 1 CMLR 703; *Johnson and Johnson* [1981] 2 CMLR 287.

[37] But cf. *Moet et Chandon (London) Ltd* [1982] 2 CMLR 166 where the Commission held the parent responsible for the behaviour of its subsidiaries and fined the parent accordingly.

[38] See e.g. Cases 32 and 36 82/78 *BMW Belgium* v *Commission* [1980] 1 CMLR 370; [1979] ECR 2435 at para. 24 of the judgment: "the bond of economic dependence existing between a parent company and a subsidiary does not preclude a divergence in conduct or even a divergence of interests between the two companies".

[39] Case 48/69 *ICI* v *Commission* [1972] ECR 619, para. 134; Case T-102/92 *Viho* v *Commission* [1995] ECR II-17, 34, para. 47.

ket".[40] Article 85 refers only to relations between economic entities "which are capable of competing with one another and does not cover agreements and concerted practices between undertakings belonging to the same group in the undertakings form an economic unit".[41]

6.20 If a parent wholly owns a subsidiary, may appoint the members of its board, may direct its marketing behaviour and ensure compliance with its directions, then it is a single entity with the parent.[42] A lesser degree of control over a subsidiary than that mentioned above may still lead to the conclusion that parent and subsidiary are as one. The parent need not own all of the shares of the subsidiary; control over a company may of course be exercised with only 51 per cent of its shareholding or less.[43] Indeed with some companies *de facto* control may exist with *under* 50 per cent. In each case it will be a question of fact.[44]

6.21 The view of the Court of Justice is that Article 85 EC is excluded where the subsidiary lacks economic independence. The test is hence one of degree of economic freedom. In *Viho*[45] the Court of First Instance was concerned with the position of Parker Pen which owned 100 per cent of the capital of its subsidiaries established in Germany, France, Belgium and the Netherlands. The sales and marketing activities of the subsidiaries were directed by an area team which was appointed by the parent company and which controlled, in particular, sales targets, gross margins, sales costs, cash flow and stocks. The area team also laid down the range of products to be sold, monitored advertising and issued directives concerning prices and discounts. The Court concluded that the Commission had correctly classified the Parker group as a single economic unit within which the subsidiaries did not enjoy real autonomy in determining their course of action in the market. The Court stated: "where, as in the case, the subsidiary, although having a separate legal personality, does not freely determine its conduct on the market but carries out the instructions given to it directly or indirectly by the parent company by which it is wholly controlled, Article 85(1) does not apply to the relationship between the subsidiary and the parent company with which it forms an economic unit".[46] Thus it would appear that the extent of the ownership of the capital of the subsidiary and the extent to which the parent has, on a day to day basis, governed the direction in which the subsidiary would act upon the market, will be the central factors determining whether or not a

[40] Case 66/86 *Ahmed Saeed Flugreisen* [1989] ECR 803, para. 35.

[41] *Viho* (*ibid.*), p. II-34, para. 47; Joined Cases T-68/89, T-77,89 and T-78/89 *SIV and Others* v *Commission* [1992] ECR II-1403, para. 357.

[42] See *Christiani and Nielsen* [1969] CMLR D36; *Kodak* [1970] CMLR D19; Case 6/72 *Continental Can* [1973] ECR 215; *Beguelin* v *Import Export and Marbach* [1972] CMLR 81; [1971] ECR 949. See also Art. 4 of Reg. 83/83/EC OJ 1983 L 173/1.

[43] *Zoja/ICI* [1973] CMLR D50 (Commission decision).

[44] But cf. *Langenscheidt/Hachette* [1982] 1 CMLR 181 an agreement between an undertaking and its 50 per cent owned joint venture company was an agreement within Art. 85(1) EC; See also *Remington Rand Trade Mark* Bull EC 3/69 Nos. 40, 41; *Scott Paper* OJ 1968 C 110/2; *Gosme/Martell* [1992] 5 CMLR 154. In Case T-141/89 *Tréfileurope* v *Commission*, judgment of Court of First Instance of 6 April 1995, the CFI rejected a submission that a 25 per cent shareholding was enough to constitute an economic entity between the shareholder and the company in which it held those shares, since two other shareholders had larger shareholdings. That is not to say that a 25 per cent shareholding could never be proof of an economic entity: the key question is whether the subsidiary has real freedom to determine its conduct on the market.

[45] *ibid.*

[46] *ibid.*, para. 51, p. II-35. See generally for other relevant cases: *Kodak* [1976] CMLR D19; Case 52/69 *Geigy* [1972] ECR 787 case 6/72 *Continental Can* [1973] ECR 215, 242; Case 15/74 *Centrafarm* v *Sterling* [1974] ECR 1147, 1168; *Zoja/ICI* [1973] CMLR D50.

subsidiary constitutes a single undertaking with its parent. Ultimately, the issue is to be one of fact and degree.[47]

6.22 The fact that a parent and subsidiary, or indeed members of the same group of companies, may be treated as a single undertaking may have the consequence that the Group may act, as between themselves, in a manner which would be prohibited were the separate companies to constitute separate "undertakings". In *Viho*[48] the Court of First Instance was concerned with the policy of Parker Pen which had adopted a policy of prohibiting subsidiaries from supplying Parker products through customers established in Member States other than that of the subsidiary. The Court stated:

> "While, admittedly, it cannot be excluded that the distribution policy applied by Parker, which consists of prohibiting its subsidiaries from supplying Parker products to customers established in Member States other than that of the subsidiary, may contribute to preserving and partitioning the various national markets and, in so doing, thwart one of the fundamental objectives to be achieved by the Common Market, it nevertheless follows ... that such a policy, followed by an economic unit such as the Parker group within which the subsidiaries do not enjoy any freedom to determine their conduct in the market, does not call within the scope of Article 85(1) of the Treaty."[49]

The Court recognised that this may leave a "gap in the system of regulation laid down by the Treaty".

4. *Concerted Practices*

6.23 A concerted practice is an extraordinarily wide concept; it catches everything that the other criteria in Article 85 EC exclude.[50] However, it is not without its own limitation. A "concerted practice" has two elements: (a) concert; and (b), a practice. Both elements must exist before Article 85(1) applies.[51]

[47] Among the factors revealed by past case law are the following: (a) the permanence of the control exercised by the parent company will be relevant. If control is only temporary then the subsidiary may be said to retain independence (*Zoja/ICI* [1973] CMLR D50). The fortuitous existence of majority control of a general meeting would be temporary control and probably inadequate to exclude Art. 85. In Case T-141/89 *Tréfileurope* v *Commission* (6 April 1995 CFI) the Court rejected a submission that a 25 per cent shareholding was enough to constitute an economic entity between the shareholder and the company in which it held that the shares, since two other shareholders possessed larger shareholdings; (b) if the parent can appoint majority of the subsidiaries board this should indicate control (Joined Cases 40/48–50, 54/56, 111, 113, 114/73 *Suiker Unie* [1975] ECR 1163, 1196; [1976] 1 CMLR 295); (c) if the parent can direct the way in which the subsidiary invests its money this may indicate control; (d) if the parent can use for its own benefit the assets of the subsidiary this should indicate control. See also for an analysis of "control" in the context of concentrations: Commission Notice on the notion of a concentration of 31 December 1994 (OJ 1994 C 385/5).

[48] Case T-102/92 [1995] ECR II-17.

[49] *ibid.*, para. 52, pp. 35, 36.

[50] See *Re Dyestuffs* [1969] CMLR D23; on appeal, *ICI* v *Commission* (Case 48/69) [1972] ECR 619; [1972] CMLR 557 at p. 622: "If Article 85 distinguishes the concept of 'concerted practice' from that of 'agreements between enterprises' or 'decisions by associations of enterprises', this is done with the object of bringing under the prohibitions of this Article a form of co-ordination between enterprises which, without going so far as to amount to an agreement properly so called, knowingly substitutes a practical co-operation between them for the risks of competition. By its very nature, then, the concerted practice does not combine all the elements of an agreement, but may, inter alia, result from a coordination which becomes apparent from the behaviour of the participants." This definition is very similar to the definition of "arrangement" in s. 43 RTPA 1976 discussed at paras. 1.7–1.35.

[51] Cases 40–48, 50, 54–56, 111, 113, 114/73 *European Sugar Cartel* [1976] 1 CMLR 295; [1975] ECR 1663 at pp.1993 and 2035.

(1) Meaning of "concert"

6.24 Very loose forms of consensus amount to concerted practices. This has been defined by the Court of Justice in *European Sugar Cartel*[52] as covering "any direct or indirect contact between such operators, the object of effect whereof is either to influence the conduct on the market of an actual or potential competitor or to disclose to such a competitor the course of conduct which they themselves have decided to adopt or contemplate adopting on the market". There is no need to prove a legally binding transaction; even a vague "gentlemen's agreement" or "breakfast agreement" is not a necessity. The Commission look for some consensus or meeting of minds between the parties. The Commission have stressed that in determining whether there is a concerted practice, "[t]here are many forms and degrees of collusion and it does not require the making of a formal agreement. An infringement of Article 85 may well exist where the parties have not even spelled out an agreement in terms, but each infers commitment from the other on the basis of conduct".[53] Thus, if X sees his rival Y in a bar and says to him, "costs are escalating I shall have to raise prices by 3 per cent at the beginning of next month", then, if Y responds by pushing his prices up 3 per cent, a concerted practice might have arisen. The statement of X will have been the catalyst which triggers off a consensus with Y, i.e. that both should raise prices with effect from the beginning of next month. An interesting question is whether a supplier responding to complaints of its dealers amounts to an agreement or concerted practice. In *Dunlop Slazenger International*[54] the Court of First Instance upheld the Commission's finding that complaints made by Dunlop's exclusive distributors in the Benelux about products being exported into their territories by Newitt, one of Dunlop's UK distributors, established that the export ban imposed by Dunlop on Newitt was not a unilateral act, but was the result of a concerted practice between Dunlop and its exclusive distributors.[55]

(2) Parallel conduct and concerted practices

6.25 Mere parallel action however is not a concerted practice.[56] If, in the above example, X had unilaterally raised prices by 3 per cent and Y, without any prompting from X, followed suit then there would be no concerted practice between X and Y. They have taken parallel commercial decisions without communicating in any way. It follows that if firms, as a consequence of observing the behaviour of rivals, follow the price leader, then they have not entered a concerted practice. What is known as "conscious parallelism" is not caught by Article 85 EC. It is natural, economically speaking, in oligopolistic markets where a few large firms dominate, for participants in the market to observe and monitor each other, to calculate and predict each other's future behaviour, and to adjust and adapt to meet the expected conduct of rival firms. For this natural market occurrence to be considered a "concerted practice" there must be some form of inter-firm communication which acts to cement the mutual interdependence which has arisen naturally. The form of this communication is immaterial. There is little the Commission can do about

52 [1975] ECR 1663; [1976] 1 CMLR 295.

53 *ICI/Solvay (Soda Ash)* [1994] 4 CMLR 454, para 55.

54 T-43/92 *Dunlop Slazenger International* v *Commission* [1994] ECR II-441. But contrast T-41/96 *Bayer* [1996] ECR II-383.

55 This can be contrasted with the caution displayed by the US Supreme Court towards interpreting dealer complaints as evidence of a concerted practice in *Monsanto* v *Spray-Rite* 465 US 752 (1984).

56 See e.g. the various dyestuffs judgments of the European Court: Case 49/69 *BASF* [1972] ECR 713; Case 51/69 *Bayer* [1972] ECR 745; Case 52/69 *Geigy* [1972] ECR 787; Case 54/69 *Francolor* [1972] ECR 851; Case 55/69 *Cassella* [1972] ECR 887; Case 56/69 *Hoechst* [1972] ECR 927; Case 57/69 *ACNA* [1972] ECR 933.

parallel behaviour arising naturally, though, they adopt a very strict approach to any attempts by firms to foster parallelism artificially. In *Dyestuffs* the Court of Justice stated:

> "Although a parallelism of behaviour cannot by itself be identified with a concerted practice, it is nevertheless liable to constitute a strong indication of such a practice when it leads to conditions of the market, having regard to the nature of the products, the importance of the enterprises and the volume of the said market. Such is the case especially where the parallel behaviour is such as to permit the parties to seek price equilibrium at a different level from that which would have resulted from competition, and to crystallise the status quo to the detriment of effective freedom of movement of the products in the Common Market and free choice by consumers of their suppliers."[57]

6.26 Firms in oligopolistic markets where conscious parallelism is either exists or is a possibility must thus take stringent compliance measure to ensure that a concerted practice does not arise. Middle management must know clearly how they may and may not respond to rivals. The Commission, it should not be overlooked, may impose very severe fines on companies breaching competition rules. The problem is that natural marketing behaviour may appear as if it derived from a concerted practice. Thus, firms may harmonise prices through matching each others' price moves or because they forgo marketing or selling in each other's primary marketing areas. In the absence of any inter-firm communication such behaviour is lawful.

(3) Proving concerted behaviour

6.27 How do the Commission prove concert? As the quote from *Dyestuffs* above shows they need not establish the very existence of inter-firm communication. It suffices to show that the surrounding economic circumstances point the way to the existence of some communication. These surrounding circumstances must be viewed collectively and the characteristics of the market taken into account.[58] The following may be pointers to the existence of a concerted practice:

- unilateral declarations of policy by a company (whether made privately to a rival or publicly via the media is immaterial); the important point is that a "message" has been broadcast;
- that the time period between a declaration of intent as to future policy and the implementation of that policy is long enough to enable competitors to consider their positions and respond;
- that the behaviour of the parties is unnatural when compared to the expected patterns of behaviour in the market. Where after five years of intense price competition a sudden uniformity of price develops, then the Commission may suspect the existence of concert. If, for example, a rigid market sharing exists in a situation where competition could be expected then an inference of concert will be taken and ar-

[57] [1972] CMLR 557 at p. 622, para. 66. The definition was essentially confirmed in *European Sugar Industry* above, n. 43 at paras. 173 and 174 of the judgment. The Court of Justice affirmed the position it adopted in *Dyestuffs and Sugar: Zuchner* v *Bayerische Vereinsbank* (Case 172/80) [1982] 1 CMLR 313; [1981] ECR 2021. For the Commission's practical application of these principles see *Hasselblad* [1982] 2 CMLR 233 at paras. 42–51 of the decision; *SSI* [1982] 3 CMLR 702 at paras. 123–130; *Rolled Zinc* [1983] 2 CMLR 285 at paras. BI and II.

[58] *ICI* v *Commission* (Case 48/69) [1972] ECR 619 at p. 659; *BP Kemi-DDSF* [1979] 3 CMLR 684. *CRAM* v *Commission* (Cases 29 and 30/83) [1985] 1 CMLR 688 at para. 10 of the judgment. Cases C-89/85 etc. *Ahlstrom Oy* v *Commission (Wood Pulp)* [1993] ECR I-1307, [1993] 4 CMLR 407. See also *Fourteenth Commission Competition Report* (1984) pp. 57, 58.

guments that the market sharing is the direct consequence of heavy transport and freight costs may be rejected.[59]

6.28 Cases involving allegations that a concerted practice exists will thus turn upon the existence or otherwise of cogent evidence pointing towards something other than conscious parallelism. In *Wood Pulp*[60] the Commission found that producers of wood pulp had engaged in a concerted practice to fix prices in the Community. The Commission found parallel conduct upon the market between 1975 and 1981. However, no evidence of explicit agreements to fix prices was detected by the Commission. The decision was premised upon two factors. First, the existence of exchanges of information between the parties which had created an artificial price transparency. Secondly, an economic analysis of the market demonstrating that it was not oligopolistic in nature so that conscious parellelism was not to be expected. The economic analysis suggested that the market was competitive, there being many sellers producing a different product in circumstances where the producers faced different cost structures and were located in different parts of the world. The economic evidence suggested inferentially that in the absence of collusion producers would sell at different prices. The Commission concluded that the only explanation for the harmonised pricing was therefore the existence of a concerted practice. On appeal, the Court of Justice substantially annulled the decision. The Court held that the fact that the producers announced price rises to users in advance upon a quarterly basis did not by itself involve an infringement of Article 85(1). The Court held that making information available to third parties did not eradicate the producer's uncertainty as to what other producers would do.[61] Moreover, there were alternative explanations for the system of price announcements and the parallelism of prices could be explained by factors other than the mere existence of a concerted practice.[62] The judgment demonstrates that there is a heavy burden upon the Commission to prove the existence of concerted practice by tangible evidence and, in particular, if it is to rely upon economic analysis alone, to preclude the possibility that any reasonable alternative explanation for the parallelism of conduct exists. It remains true to say that a concerted practice may *still* be inferred from an economic analysis of the market demonstrating that the only possible reasonable explanation for harmonised prices is a concerted practice since were concentration not to exist prices and other terms and conditions would be different.[63]

6.29 Once a concerted practice has been established the Commission is legally entitled to assume that it continues in existence until such time as it is demonstrated to have been ended by the parties.[64] This presumption of continuance is very relevant when the question of extent of fines is being considered by the Commission.

[59] e.g. Cases 100–103/80 *Musique Diffusion Française SA* v *Commission (Pioneer)* [1983] 3 CMLR 221; see also *Fertiliser* Bull EC 1/77 No. 2 119.

[60] Commission decision OJ L85/1; [1985] 3 CMLR 474; on appeal, Cases C-89/85 etc. *A Ahlstrom Oy* v *Commission* [1993] ECR I-1307 [1993] 4 CMLR 407. See A. Jones [1993] ECLR 272; G. van Gerven and E. Navarro Varona, "The *Wood Pulp* case and the future of concerted practices" (1994) 31 CMLRev 575. See also L.M.P. Antunes, "Agreements and concerted practices under EEC competition law: is the distinction still relevant?" (1991) 11 YEL 57.

[61] *ibid.*, paras. 59–65.

[62] *ibid.*, paras. 66–127.

[63] See also Joined Cases 29, 30/83 CRAM and *Rheinzinc GmbH* v *Commission* [1984] ECR 1679, [1985] 1 CMLR 688; Joined Cases T-68/89 etc. *SIV* v *Commission* [1992] ECR II-1403 [1992] 5 CMLR 302; Case 172/80 *Zuchner* v *Bayerische Verinsbank AG* [1981] ECR 2021, [1982] 1 CMLR 313; *Zinc Producer Group* OJ 1984 L220/27, [1985] 2 CMLR 108, *Peroxygen Products* OJ 1985 L35/1, [1985] 1 CMLR 481.

[64] *Hasselblad GB* v *Commission* (Case 86/82) [1984] 1 CMLR 559 *per* Advocate General Slynn.

5. Public Bodies, Quangos and Article 90

(1) Public and private distinction

6.30 Public and nationalised companies and other commercial organisations backed by government cause problems in antitrust law. Article 85 is essentially a private law provision which is unsuitable for the regulation of governmental behaviour. Other public law provisions of the Treaty of Rome are, however, tailor-made to deal with public interference in the market, e.g. Articles 30 and 34 EC on quantitative restrictions on imports and exports and measures having equivalent effect. These provisions prohibit government behaviour which directly or indirectly, actually or potentially inhibits or hinders trade between the Member States so that all non-tariff barriers to trade are caught.[65]

6.31 Article 90 EC is addressed to Member States, not to undertakings and it elaborates upon the general obligations imposed upon Member States to support and further the objections of the Treaty by Article 5 EC. Article 90, in effect, provides a *modus operandi* for enforcement of the obligation contained in Article 5. It provides that all rules enacted by Member States should be compatible with the rules contained in the Treaty and in particular the competition rules. Article 90(1) EC provides:

> "In the case of public undertakings and undertakings to which Member States grant special or exclusive rights, Member States shall neither enact nor maintain in force any measure contrary to the rules contained in this Treaty, in particular to those rules provided for in Article 7 and Articles 85–94."

Member States may be liable pursuant to Article 90(1) in relation to all rules provided for the Treaty and not just the competition rules.[66]

6.32 Article 90(2) is addressed to undertakings entrusted with the operation of services of general economic interest or having the character of revenue producing monopolies. It provides a qualified immunity for such undertakings from the rules contained in the EC treaty and in particular the competition rules. The provision applies to private undertakings if they had been entrusted with the operator of services of general economic interest by virtue of an act of public authority.[67] Immunity from the provisions of the Treaty only arises where the application of such rules may obstruct the performance of particular tasks assigned to the undertaking in question. However, the immunity is itself qualified insofar as the immunity is disapplied if the development of trade is effected to an extent which would be contrary to the interests of the Community. Article 90(2) provides in full:

> "Undertakings entrusted with the operation of services of general economic interest or having the character of a revenue producing monopoly shall be subject to the rules contained in this Treaty, in particular to the rules on competition, insofar as the application of such rules does not obstruct the performance, in law or in fact, of the particular tasks assigned to them. The development of trade must not be affected to such an extent as would be contrary to the interests of the Community."[68]

[65] See *Procureur Du Roi* v *Dassonville* (Case 8/74) [1974] 2 CMLR 436, [1974] ECR 837 at p. 852 which defines a measure having equivalent effect to a quantitative restriction in these extraordinarily wide terms. See Oliver, *Free Movement of Goods in the European Community* (3rd edn, 1995).

[66] See e.g. Commission Decision 85/276/EEC *Greek Insurers* OJ 1985 L152/25.

[67] See e.g. Case 127/73 *BRT* v *SABAM* [1974] ECR 313; [1974] CMLR 238, 284.

[68] The language of Art. 90(2) is complex. See generally *Murphy, Butterworths Competition Law Encyclopedia*, division IX, Chapter 1; Bright, "Article 90 economic policy and the duties of Member States" (1993) ECLR 263; Commission's *Twentieth Report on Competition Policy*, paras. 53, 355–60; Edward and Hoskins, "Article 90: deregulation, EC law" (1995) 32 CMLRev 157.

6.33 Pursuant to Article 90(3) the Commission is required to "ensure the application and the provisions of this Article and shall, where necessary, address appropriate directives or decisions to Member States". An example of the exercise of the power contained in Article 90(3) is in the decision of 28 June 1995 *Zaventem*.[69] British Midland complained to the Commission on 8 February 1993 in respect of the system of discounts on landing fees at Brussels National Airport (Zaventem). The Complaint considered that the system of stepped discounts, which increased in line with an airline's volume of traffic, favoured carriers with a high volume of traffic at Zaventem and thereby placed smaller carriers competing with such carriers at a disadvantage. Moreover, it was complained that there was no objective justification for the grant of such discounts since the services which an arriving or departing aircraft required were the same, however many times they were supplied. Article 1 of a Royal Decree of 22 December 1989 authorised the Airways Authority to charge the fees laid down therein for the use of Zaventem. Article 2 of the decree fixed landing fees at a certain amount per tonne according to whether or not the aircraft carried only cargo. Paragraph 2 of the Article established the system of discounts complained of by British Midlands. In 1991 and 1992 only three airlines qualified for the reductions. The Commission concluded that the Airways Authority was a public undertaking within the meaning of Article 90(1). Further, it decided that the decree constituted a state measure within the meaning of Article 90(1). In that context it proceeded to analyse the effect of the decree upon the market place. The Commission concluded that the Airways Authority held a dominant position in the market in services linked to access to airport infrastructures for which a fee was payable (i.e. the exploitation and maintenance of runways, taxiways and aprons and approach guidance). The Commission held that the system of discounts on landing fees established by the Decree of December 1989 had the effect of applying dissimilar conditions to airlines for equivalent transactions linked to landing and take-off services thereby placing some of them at a competitive disadvantage. The Commission rejected the alleged objective justifications raised by the Airways Authority to justify the discounts. The Commission noted that the Belgian authorities had not invoked the derogation provided for in Article 90(2). In any event the Commission considered that in the case in issue application of the competition rules did not obstruct the specific purpose of the Airways Authority which was to construct, develop, maintain and exploit Zaventem. Nor would application of the competition rules obstruct any specific public service function assigned to an airline. The Commission therefore concluded that the state measure referred to infringed Article 90(1) read in conjunction with Article 86. In accordance with Article 90(3) the Commission addressed a decision to the Kingdom of Belgium. Pursuant to the decision the system of discounts on landing fees introduced by Decree was held to be a measure incompatible with Article 90(1) in conjunction with Article 86 and the Belgian government was required to bring the infringement to an end and to inform the Commission of the measures taken to achieve that objective within two months of the notification of the Decision.

(2) Areas of overlap

6.34 However, the general application of these principles may be noted here. Nationalised companies are subject to Articles 85 and 86 EC.[70] However, where a privately incorporated body is, *de facto*, simply an extension of government then it seems to fall outside of Articles 85 and 86 and becomes subject to the public law provisions of the Treaty of Rome.

[69] Commission Decision 95/364 EC OJ 1995 L 216/8 (under appeal).

[70] See para. 6.09.

Thus, in *Buy Irish Campaign: Commission* v *Ireland*[71] the Irish government incorporated a body called the Irish Goods Council (IGC) which was to advertise and promote Irish goods at the expense of imports. The IGC thus sought to incite consumers to discriminate against foreign products. Despite the fact of its private status the IGC was viewed as an arm of government and the Irish government was held by the Court of Justice to have infringed Article 30 EC. Similarly in *Van Luipen* the Court of Justice was required to rule on the compatibility with Article 34 EC of a national rule requiring that exporters belong to a trade association as a precondition of being allowed to export their goods. The Court stated, of this compulsory affiliation rule:

> "It is contrary to the freedom of commercial transactions for national legislation to make the exportation of the product in question conditional on the exporters being affiliated to a public body or a body approved by an official authority."[72]

6.35 Both cases noted above concerned actions against Governments yet the conduct complained of in each could have been perpetrated by purely private bodies. Could Article 85 apply in such cases? The policy of the Commission on this is now fairly clear. Following the *Buy Irish* case a number of parliamentary questions were asked of the Commission. One such question noted that Marks and Spencers, British Airways and Debenhams were jointly intending to urge British families to "Buy British". The Commission responded: "So long as a campaign of the kind described ... is conducted entirely by industry, independently of the State, it does not contravene Community rules on the free movement of goods (Articles 30 to 36 of the EC Treaty)."[73] In a later parliamentary question on substantially the same issue the Commission added that, "where a buy national campaign grew out of an agreement between undertakings, a decision by an association of undertakings or a concerted practice then the competition rules in Articles 85 or 86 might apply".[74]

6.36 Whether Articles 85 or 86 apply will, in the final analysis, depend upon the degree of governmental involvement. In some cases on Article 85 a surprisingly high degree of government involvement has existed yet Article 85 has still been held to apply. Thus in *AROW* v *BNIC*[75] a statutory backed national cognac industry trade association called *Bureau National Interprofessionel du Cognac* (BNIC) was held to contravene Article 85 because of certain resale price maintenance schemes operated by it. Article 85 applied despite the association being under the direct supervision of a government commissioner and despite the board of BNIC being appointed by the government. In their decision the Commission stressed some of the private elements in BNIC's make-up and rather played down the public control elements. It thus seems that where an organisation is a mix of public and private ingredients then Article 85 EC may apply. Where the organisation is dominated by government then Article 85 is excluded and public provisions, in particular, Article 90 EC or Articles 30 and 34 EC, may apply. Where the Commission wish to

[71] Case 249/81 [1983] 2 CMLR 104; [1982] ECR 4005.

[72] Case 29/82 [1983] 2 CMLR 681 at p. 692, para. 9. See also Case 94/79 *Vriend* [1980] 3 CMLR 473; [1980] ECR 327.

[73] WQ No. 1081/82, OJ 1982 C 331/11 (22 August 1982).

[74] WQ No. 2097/82, OJ 1982 C 219/1 (1 February 1983). It is known that in 1982/3 the CBI were considering a "Buy British Campaign".

[75] [1982] 2 CMLR 240. The Commission fined BNIC 160,000 ECU. The desire to punish BNIC meant that the Commission had to use Arts. 85 and 86 and treat BNIC as a private body since the Commission may not fine Member States and their agencies under Arts. 30–36 EC. They may only refer governments to the Court for a declaration that the Member State has failed to fulfil an obligation under the Treaty (see Art. 169 EC for this procedure). See for the view of the Court to this question: Case 123/83 *BNIC* v *Guy Clair* [1985] 2 CMLR 430 noted Hendry, (1986) ELRev 150.

impose a fine they must rely upon Articles 85 or 86, they have no competence under other provisions to impose pecuniary sanctions.

6.37 If government does not compel conduct contrary to Articles 85 or 86, a business may only escape liability if it comes within Article 90(2). This provides an exemption for a business which is either a revenue producing monopoly or operating services of general economic interest, but only in so far as necessary to perform the tasks assigned to it. While revenue producing monopolies are relatively easy to identify, the same cannot be said for businesses "entrusted with the operation of services of general economic interest". Each case depends on its facts, but it can be said that neither the Commission nor the Court of Justice has applied this principle liberally. It has, however, been found to exist in the provision by a public undertaking of a national postal service[76] and in the provision by a private undertaking of non-commercially viable air transport services.[77] Hence, while Article 90 is potentially a far-reaching provision of the Treaty as far as governmental competence to grant or maintain special or exclusive rights is concerned, its principal importance for business is restricted to where a service of general economic interest is being provided.

C. Proving an Effect on Trade Between the Member States

6.38 Article 85 applies where an agreement "may affect trade between Member States". These words are jurisdictional and designed to distinguish the application of national from Community law.[78] An agreement not affecting inter-state trade is of no interest to the Community but may well be of interest to the authorities (e.g. the OFT) in the Member State where the parties are situate. Despite their apparent simplicity these words have given rise to a considerable volume of case law. The constituents of the phrase will be considered separately. It is sometimes said that the Commission and Courts readily assume an effect upon trade. Whether or not it was true in the past it is certainly not true now. The Commission, partly to avoid being swamped by over-work, are careful to examine the inter-state effects of an agreement before assuming jurisdiction. National Courts tend to view the requirement of an affect upon trade as a substantive requirement of proof requiring hard evidence to be adduced.[79]

1. *"May affect": Meaning*

6.39 The Commission does not have to establish an existing effect on trade between the Member States, it is adequate to establish only that it "may" have such an effect. The Court has stated that: "it must be possible to foresee with a sufficient degree of probability on

[76] C-320/91 *Corbeau* [1993] ECR I-2533, [1995] 4 CMLR 621.
[77] 66/86 *Ahmed Saeed* [1989] ECR 803, [1990] 4 CMLR 102.
[78] See Case 56 and 58/64 *Consten and Grundig* v *Commission* [1966] CMLR 418; [1966] ECR 299 at pp. 322 and 389; Case 22/78 *Hugin* v *Commission* [1979] 2 CMLR 345; [1979] ECR 1869 at para. 17 of the judgment. See also Case 71/74 *Frubo* v *Commission* [1975] 2 CMLR 123 [1975] ECR 563 at para. 38 of the judgment; Case 56/65 *La Technique Minière* v *Maschinenbau Ulm GmbH* [1966] CMLR 357; [1966] ECR 235.
[79] Although it is often regarded as an easily satisfied requirement, in proceedings in the English courts it is necessary to adduce evidence of an effect: *Panayiotou (t/a George Michael)* v *Sony Music Entertainment (UK) Ltd* [1994] ECC 395.

the basis of a set of objective factors of law or of fact that the agreement may have an influence, direct or indirect, actual or potential, on the pattern of trade between Member States".[80] Trade is affected when the restrictions in the agreement cause the pattern of trade to change. There will be an effect on trade if: the level of trade decreases; the level of trade increases;[81] the places where business is set up are altered; the direction and movement of trade changes albeit that the volume of trade remains static or insulating the common market from trade from outside EC. Agreements involving undertakings who are situate in near-proximity to a border will find that they have a greater capacity to affect inter-state trade than do undertakings more centrally located. An agreement concerning a raw material or semi-completed product in respect of which there is no or only *de minimis* trade between Member States, may none the less affect trade because down-stream products which include the product the subject of the agreement in question themselves are subject to inter-state trade.[82] The Commission's policy is that trade should flow along naturally developed routes which derive from the free play of market forces. A restrictive agreement which affects these forces is subject to review under Article 85.

The following are examples of agreements which may affect inter-state trade.

(1) Price equalisation in joint selling agency

6.40 Agency pays its participants the same price whether its goods are exported elsewhere in the EC or are sold on the domestic market. This would affect trade because it reduces the incentive on individual members to export individually since the export price they receive through the joint selling agency will be greater than they could obtain by their own efforts.[83]

(2) Aggregated rebate schemes

6.41 Schemes whereby customers are given rebates depending upon their total purchases from the group discourages customers from purchasing from suppliers elsewhere in the EC who are not aligned to the group.[84]

(3) Joint purchasing agencies

6.42 Agency purchases on behalf of its members. It requires members to take a certain percentage of their purchases through the agency. To the extent that members are committed they are excluded from purchasing from other suppliers in the EC.[85]

80 *Consten and Grundig* v *Commission* (above); See also Case 61/80 *Stremsel-Kleurselfabriek* v *Commission* [1982] 1 CMLR 240; [1981] ECR 851 at para. 14 of judgment which repeats the *Consten and Grundig* formulation. The fact that the Court speaks in terms of probability presumably derives from the French text of the Treaty of Rome which uses the phrase "susceptibles d'affecter" instead of "may". See also *Vacuum Interupters* [1977] 1 CMLR D67; *TAA* OJ 1994 L376/1; Case C-41/90 *Hofner* v *Macrotou* [1991] ECR I-1979; Case T-65/89 *BPB Industries* [1993] ECR II-385; *Scottish Nuclear* OJ 1991 L178/31.

81 For example, in proceedings under Art. 86 EC *Napier Brown/British Sugar* OJ 1988 L284/41, [1990] 4 CMLR 196, the effect of the abuse was artificially to increase trade between Member States, since the refusal of supplies to Napier Brown by British Sugar in the UK meant it had to import from elsewhere in the EC.

82 *Commercial Solvents* [1974] ECR 223; *Soda-Ash/Solvay* OJ 1991 L152/21.

83 *Re Comptoir Francais de L'Azote* [1968] CMLR D57; *Comptoir Belge de L'Azote (Cobelaz)* [1968] CMLR D68; *Cimbel* [1973] CMLR D167; *Fine Papers* [1972] CMLR D94.

84 e.g. *German Ceramic Tiles* [1971] CMLR D6; *Gas Water Heaters* [1973] CMLR D231; Case 73/74 *Groupement des Fabricants de Papier Peints de Belgique* v *Commission* [1976] 1 CMLR 589; [1975] ECR 1491.

85 e.g. *National Sulphuric Acid* [1980] 3 CMLR 429.

(4) Distribution agreement prohibiting dealer from selling outside of his defined territory

6.43 Such clauses always affect trade between the states since the dealers ability to sell elsewhere in the Community is curtailed.[86] Distribution agreement whereby dealers are prohibited from selling to customers who are situate in another Member State affect trade because the freedom of the customer to purchase in the Community is limited as is the freedom of the dealer to sell.

(5) Agreements between undertakings in the same Member State

6.44 Agreements between undertakings affect inter-state trade if they regulate sales in such a manner as to influence trade coming into or out of their state.[87] Thus an agreement between X, Y and Z in the UK to maintain identical export prices affects the price of those goods abroad. An agreement between X, Y and Z not to supply foreign wholesalers where UK wholesalers exist affects the trade of foreign wholesalers.[88] An agreement not to sell directly to consumers abroad obviously affects trade.[89] An agreement between a supplier in the UK and a number of exclusive dealers in the UK may affect inter-state trade if foreign suppliers are hindered in obtaining effective dealers to distribute their goods for them. This will be the case if efficient dealers are scarce and the UK supplier has tied them up in his distribution network and contractually precluded them from selling another supplier's goods.[90] An agreement which covers the entirety of a Member State has by its very nature the effect of reinforcing the compartmentalisation of markets upon a national basis thereby hindering the economic interpenetration sought by the Treaty.

(6) Exclusive intellectual property licences

6.45 An exclusive patent licence can affect inter-state trade since no one other than the licensee can produce the patented product and this may reduce export potential. This analysis holds equally good for other types of intellectual property licences, which are discussed in Chapter 13.

(7) Trade fairs

6.46 A trade association organises trade fairs for the advertising of its members products; members may not show at fairs other than those organised by the association. This affects trade because the ability of members to advertise abroad through foreign trade fairs may be prejudiced.[91]

2. "Trade": Meaning

6.47 "Trade" includes virtually all forms of commercial exchange and the term is to be construed widely. Products covered by the ECSC Treaty (i.e. coal and steel) are subject to

[86] e.g. Case 19/77 *Miller International Schallplatten GmbH* v *Commission* [1978] 2 CMLR 334; [1978] ECR 131 at para. 7 of the judgment. An export ban to a non-EC state may affect inter-state trade if without the restriction there is a reasonable probability that the goods would be re-imported. See decisions of Commission in: *SABA* [1976] 1 CMLR D61; *Junghans* [1977] 1 CMLR D82; *Campari* [1978] 2 CMLR 397. The effect might particularly occur where the export ban is to EFTA countries which enjoy free trade rights with the EC under the EEA.

[87] e.g. *Junghans* [1977] 1 CMLR D82. Case 42/84 *Remia and Nutricia* v *Commission* [1985] ECR 2545, [1987] 1 CMLR 7, at para. 22. See also *Roofing Felt* [1991] 4 CMLR 130; *Meldoc* OJ 1986 L348/50, [1989] 4 CMLR 853.

[88] *ibid.*

[89] *Deutsche Philips* [1973] CMLR D241.

[90] e.g. Case 23/67 *Brasserie de Haecht SA* v *Wilkin (No. 1)* [1968] CMLR 26; [1967] ECR 407; C-234/89 *Delimitis* v *Henningeer Brau* [1991] ECR I-935.

[91] See paras. 11.163–11.172.

their own special rules on competition. Indeed, Article 232(1) EC expressly provides that its provisions do not affect the ECSC Treaty.[92] Article 232(2) EC provides the same for the Euratom Treaty. Regulation 141 EC exempts transport from the *procedural* provisions of Regulation 17/62. Regulation 141 provides for procedures for regulating air transport. It does not preclude Articles 85 and 86 EC.[93]

6.48 In *Olympic Airways* the Commission confirmed that competition rules applied to air transport and moreover that handling services at airports are not within the scope of Regulation 141 and therefore fall to be examined in accordance with normal rules and procedure.[94] Regulation 1017/68/EEC[95] applies Articles 85 and 86 to rail, road and inland waterways. Regulations have now been adopted applying competition policy to maritime transport[96] and to international air transport.[97] With regard to agriculture Article 42 EC applies the competition rules to the production of and trade in agricultural goods in so far as the Council of Ministers has made specific provision. Regulation 26 disapplies Article 85(1) from agreements which are a part of a national market organisation or which are necessary to the attainment of the goals of the CAP as laid out in Article 39 EC. Where Community rules do allow some freedom, competition must be allowed to operate and the Commission have applied competition rules to various products.[98]

3. "Between Member States": Meaning

6.49 The relevant geographical territories are those comprising the European Economic Community. The ambit of these rules may also extend to territories belonging to Member States which have been expressly incorporated by declaration or protocol or other EC legislation. The rules may also apply by virtue of agreement between the Community and third countries.

4. De Minimis: Insignificant Agreements

6.50 An agreement is not within Article 85 if its effect on inter-state trade is insignificant. An appreciable affect on both trade *and* upon competition must be established before Article 85 is engaged.[99] One must examine how the market would have developed in the ab-

[92] See Case C-128/92 *Banks* v *BCC* [1994] ECR I-1268.

[93] See Joined Cases 209-213/84 *Ministère Public* v *Lucas Asjes (Nouvelles Frontières)* [1986] ECR 1425, [1986] 3 CMLR 173. Reg. 141 EEC is at OJ 1962 124/2751.

[94] OJ 1985 L46/51.

[95] OJ 1968 2141/65.

[96] Reg. 4056/86, OJ 1986 L378/4. See also the Liner Shipping Consortia Exemption, Reg. 479/92, OJ 1992 L55/3 and Reg. 870/95, OJ 1995 L89/7.

[97] Reg. 3975/87, OJ 1987 L374/1, as amended by Reg. 1284/91, OJ 1991 L122/2 and 2410/92, OJ 1992 L240/18; the procedural regulation is Reg. 4261/88, OJ 1988 L376/10. Two block exemptions are in force: Reg. 3652/93 OJ 1993 L333/0 on computerised reservation systems for air transport services and Reg. 1617/93 on joint planning and coordination of schedules, joint operations, consultations on passenger and cargo tariffs on scheduled air services and slot allocation at airports, OJ 1993 L155/18. Reg. 82/91, OJ 1991 L10/7, on ground handling services this expired on 31 December 1992 and has not been replaced. In addition there have been two rounds of air transport liberalisation measures, the most recent being set out in three regulations: 2407/92 OJ 1992 L240/1 on licensing of air carriers, 2408/92 OJ 1992 L240/8 on access to routes, and 2409/92 OJ 1992 L240/15 on fares and rates.

[98] See generally Kerse, *Antitrust Procedure* (3rd edn. 1994), pp. 26–27. See for examples of relevant cases, Case 83/78 *Pigs Marketing Board (Northern Ireland)* v *Redmond* [1979] 1 CMLR 177; [1978] ECR 2347; *Mushrooms* [1975] 1 CMLR D83; *Cauliflowers* [1978] CMLR D66; *Maize Seed* [1978] 3 CMLR 434; *Rennet* [1980] 2 CMLR 402; *European Sugar Cartel* [1973] CMLR D65 Commission decision; see *Second Competition Report* (1973), paras. 58 and 65. See *Butterworths Competition Law*, Vol. 3, s. IX (Agriculture).

[99] See Case 5/69 *Volk* v *Vervaecke* [1969] CMLR 273; [1969] ECR 295.

sence of the: restrictive agreement. If the agreement has *any* material influence, whether advantageous or harmful, then an effect has occurred. The balancing of advantages and disadvantages takes place under Article 85(3).[100]

(1) Examples

6.51 Market share is important, a market share of only 0.6 per cent may be assumed to be insignificant even where the distribution agreement in question contains clauses that would normally be challenged (e.g. absolute territorial protection).[101] In *SOCEMAS* a purchasing association with only 10 per cent of the market was found not to have a significant effect on the suppliers market position.[102] However, the Commission has found that where market shares of 8.7 per cent and 5.9 per cent were proven a perceptible effect on trade could occur.[103] A Commission notice on minor agreements refers to a 5 per cent market share coupled to a maximum turnover level (see below). The Court of First Instance has held that Article 85(1) EC should be applied whenever it is evident that the sales of at least one of the parties to an anti-competitive agreement constitute a "not inconsiderable" proportion of the relevant market.[104]

6.52 Other than market share such factors as extraordinarily high customs or other charges may swamp the perceptible effects of an agreement.[105] Equally the cost of freight and carriage to distant markets may render the influence of the parties negligible in an overall context.[106] Though freight is a factor the Commission treat with a degree of caution.[107]

(2) Commission Notice on minor agreements[108]

6.53 This Notice is not legally binding, it is simply an indication of Commission thinking. If in doubt as to its applicability parties may always notify their agreements. Parties properly relying on the notice whose agreement is subsequently challenged by the Commission will be protected from fines. The notice applies a quantitative test of market share and turnover. The notice suggests that agreements fall outside of Article 85(1) if:

> "— the goods or services which are the subject of the agreement ... together with the participating undertakings' other goods or services which are considered by users to be equivalent in view of their characteristics, price and intended use, do not represent more than 5% of the total market for such goods or services in the area of the common market affected by the agreement and

[100] See e.g. *Machines Outils* [1968] CMLR D23; *Dunlop/Pirelli* OJ 1969 L323/21 and, OJ 1986 C114/2, *SAFCO* [1972] CMLR D83—parties argued that agreement served to open up and increase penetration of a market.

[101] See Case 5/69 *Voelk* v *Vervaecke* [1969] CMLR 273; [1969] ECR 295. See also Case 1/71 *Société anonyme Cadillon* v *Hoss* [1971] CMLR 420; [1971] ECR 351.

[102] [1968] CMLR D28. In Case 3 19/82 *Société de Vente de Ciments et Betons De L'est SA* v *Kerpen and Kerpen* [1985] 1 CMLR 511 the Court held that where the quantity of goods in question represented more than 10 per cent of French exports to Germany of those goods *de minimis* could not be claimed as a defence.

[103] *White Lead* [1979] 1 CMLR 464 (Commission decision). See also *AEG Telefunken* v *Commission* (Case 107/82) [1984] 3 CMLR 325, [1983] ECR 3151 at para. 58—5 per cent of the relevant market is not insignificant.

[104] T-22/92 *Parker Pen Ltd* v *Commission* [1994] ECR II-549.

[105] *Grossfillex-Fillistorf* [1964] CMLR 237.

[106] *Raymond/Nagoya* [1972] CMLR D45; *AEG/Rieckermann* [1968] CMLR D78.

[107] See *European Sugar Agreement* [1973] CMLR D65 (Commission decision).

[108] See OJ 1986 C231/2. Previous versions of the Notice were issued on 27 May 1970, OJ 1970 C64/1 and on 29 December 1977, OJ 1977 C313/3. The Commission subsequently raised the turnover threshold to ECU 300M, 1994 OJ C368/20, 23 December 1994. The Commission issued proposals in January 1997 that the turnover threshold should be removed and that for vertical agreements the market share threshold should be increased to 10 per cent, retaining 5 per cent for horizontal agreements; OJ 1997 C29/3.

> — the aggregate annual turnover of the participating undertakings does not exceed 300 million ECU."

It should be stressed that both tests have to be satisfied. Agreements involving firms with larger turnovers *or* larger market shares do not come within the terms of the Notice.

6.54 In deciding upon who is a "participant" all subsidiaries and other undertakings which a primary participant directly or indirectly controls are to be considered.

6.55 The calculation of market share may be difficult since that depends upon a definition of the "market" which entails analysis of the product and the geographical markets. The test for product market is one of consumer preference, i.e. which products are considered to be equivalent by the consumer by reference to the qualities, use or price of the goods or services. Defining a market and hence market share is never straightforward. The Commission tend to define market share narrowly. For example, spare parts for a firm's products often may constitute a separate market in their own right in which that firm has a monopoly.[109] Hence reliance on the Notice is often a matter of making a judgment about market share, in circumstances where one cannot be completely sure that the Commission would take a similar view. The Commission state in the Notice that fines will not be levied in circumstances where firms wrongly assess turnover or market share, unless that is due to negligence. In calculating the exchange rate or the unit of account (ECU), parties may take advantage of the European Currency Unit conversion service which operates by a telex with an automatic answering device which gives the conversion rates in a number of currencies. The service is available from 3.30 pm until 1.00 pm the following day. Users of this service should do as follows: (a) call telex number Brussels 23789; (b) give their own telex code; (c) type the code "CCCC" which puts the automatic system into operation resulting in the transmission of the conversion rates of the European Currency Unit; (d) the transmission should not be interrupted until the end of the message, which is marked by the code "ffff."

5. Agreements between non-EC Parties

6.56 Agreements between non-EC parties fall within Article 85(1) if the agreement restrains trade between the Member States. In *Wood Pulp*,[110] the Commission imposed fines on 43 non-EC companies (but no EC companies) who produced bleached sulphate pulp for an unlawful pricing system. The Commission stated:

> "Article 85 of the EC Treaty applies to restrictive practices which may affect trade between member-states even if the undertakings and associations which are parties to the restrictive practices are established or have their headquarters outside the community, and even if the restrictive practices in question also affect markets outside the EC".

In applying Article 85 to the parties, the Commission noted particularly: (a) that many of the parties had subsidiaries, branches or agencies within the Community; (b) that all the parties were exporting directly to or doing business within the Community; (c) that the restrictive contract clauses complained of were all applied in contracts with EC buyers; (d) that the shipments in question amounted to about two-thirds of total shipments to the EC and some 60 per cent of EC consumption. In effect the fact that parties had

[109] 22/78 *Hugin* v *Commission* [1979] ECR 1869, [1979] 2 CMLR 345.
[110] [1985] 3 CMLR 474 at para. 79.

headquarters outside the EC was overshadowed by the strong effect of the restrictive agreements on the EC market.

6.57 The Court of Justice, on appeal in *Wood Pulp*[111] from the Commission's decision on the issue of whether non-EC parties could be subject to the jurisdiction of Article 85 EC, held that an agreement entered into by non-EC parties would be caught by Article 85 if "implemented" within the EC.[112]

6. Agreements Affecting the European Economic Area (EEA)[113]

6.58 If an agreement affects Liechtenstein, Norway and/or Iceland, consideration has to be given as to whether the EC or the EEA competition rules apply. Substantively, little is likely to turn on this question, since the competition provisions of the EEA agreement largely mirror those in the EC Treaty.[114] The EEA incorporates the principal EC block exemptions.[115] Thus substantive compliance with EC competition law is likely to ensure substantive compliance with EEA competition law.

6.59 Procedurally, however, it may be important to determine whether the EEA or the EC has jurisdiction if an exemption is to be sought for an agreement, or if a complaint is to be made about an abuse of a dominant position. This is because, just as the EC Commission supervises the EC's competition rules, so does the EFTA Surveillance Authority[116] supervise the EEA competition rules. However, it does so very much as a junior partner to the EC Commission.

6.60 The EEA competition articles apply to agreements or practices which may affect trade between EFTA states. Jurisdiction is allocated between the EC Commission and the EFTA

[111] 89, 104, 114, 116–117, 125-129/85 *Wood Pulp* [1988] ECR 5193; [1988] 4 CMLR 901; see Lange and Sandage (1989) 26 CMLRev 137 The *Wood Pulp* decision. The appellants were largely successful on appeal from the substance of the decision in Cases C-89/85 etc. *Ahlstrom Oy* v *Commission (Wood Pulp)* [1993] 4 CMLR 407; see A Jones [1993] ECLR 272.

[112] 89, 104, 114, 116–117, 125-129/85 *Wood Pulp* [1988] ECR 5193; [1988] 4 CMLR 901, para 16. For comment, see D.G.F. Lange and J.B. Sandage, "The *Wood Pulp* decision and its implications for the scope of EC competition law" (1989) 26 CMLRev 137; W. van Gerven, "EC jurisdiction in antitrust matters: the *Wood Pulp* Judgment" [1989] *Fordham Corp L Inst* 451; P.M. Roth, "Reasonable extraterritoriality: correcting the 'balance of interest'" (1992) 41 ICLQ 245.

[113] The European Economic Area Agreement, OJ 1994 L1/3, was signed on 2 May 1992 by the then 12 EC states and the then 7 EFTA states, Austria, Finland, Iceland, Liechtenstein, Norway, Sweden and Switzerland. Three EFTA states joined the EC with effect from 1 January 1995 (Austria, Finland and Sweden). Switzerland refused to ratify following a vote against membership in a referendum on 6 December 1992. The EEA thus entered into effect on 1 January 1994 but only with effect to Iceland and Norway. Liechtenstein delayed ratification, while it reconciled membership with its customs union with Switzerland, and so the EEA only came into effect for it on 1 May 1995. It was given effect in the UK by the European Economic Area Act 1993. On the EEA see S. Norberg, K. Hökborg, M. Johansson, D. Eliasson and L. Dedichen *EEA Law* (1993). On the EEA's application to competition rules and provisions on free movement of goods, see T. Blanchet, R. Piipponen and M. Westman-Clément, *The Agreement on the European Economic Area (EEA)* (1994).

[114] Arts. 53 and 54 EEA are equivalent to Arts. 85 and 86 EC respectively, Art. 59 EEA to Art. 90 EC, while Art. 57 EEA applies the EC Merger Control Regulation 4064/89 to undertakings in EFTA states.

[115] Annex XIV, which covers exclusive distribution (Reg. 1983/83), exclusive purchasing (1984/83), motor vehicle distribution (1475/95), patent licences (2349/84), know-how licences (556/89), franchising (4087/88), specialisation agreements (417/85), R&D agreements (418/85) together with transport (1017/68, omitting the transitional provisions of Art. 6) and maritime transport (4056/86). It also applies the provisions of the various administrative and guidance notices issued by the Commission, such as those relating to commercial agents, OJ 1962 L39/3921, and agreements of minor importance, OJ 1986 C231/2.

[116] It is located at Rue Marie-Thérèse 1-3, B-1040 Brussels, Belgium, telephone 00-322-226-6811.

Surveillance Authority.[117] Subject to the proviso below, the EFTA Surveillance Authority only has jurisdiction to examine restrictive agreements or concerted practices if only trade between EFTA states is affected or if the turnover of the undertakings concerned in the EFTA states is at least one-third of the total turnover of those undertakings in the whole EEA. Similarly, it may only examine an abuse of a dominant position if the dominant position exists only in the EFTA states or if the dominant undertaking derives at least one third of its EEA wide turnover from the EFTA states.

6.61 The proviso to these tests is that the EC Commission can examine any agreement or abuse of a dominant position instead of the Surveillance Authority which appreciably affects trade between EC Member States. Therefore, unless the agreement only affects trade between EFTA states or the dominant position only exists in EFTA states, the EC Commission has the right to examine or investigate instead of the EFTA Surveillance Authority. Notification to either is done on the same Form.[118]

7. *Agreements Affecting States which have Signed Europe Agreements*

6.62 Europe Agreements have been entered into by the EC with a number of Central and Eastern European states[119] which have begun the process of transformation to market economies. It is envisaged that other such states will also sign up with the EC in this way. These agreements state that, subject to transitional provisions restrictive agreements and abuses of dominant positions which distort trade between the EC and each state are prohibited, as is the operation of state monopolies in an anti-competitive manner. They set up a dispute mechanism for dealing with breaches of these rules. While the agreements operate intergovernmentally and do not directly affect those entering into agreements, it should be appreciated that in such states laws will have to be enacted, to the extent that they are not already in existence, to give effect to the international obligations undertaken under the Europe Agreements.

D. The "Object or Effect" of an Agreement

6.63 Article 85 prohibits agreements which have "as their object or effect the prevention, restriction or distortion of competition within the Common Market". It is important to appreciate that an agreement need not actually restrain competition for Article 85 to apply; an agreement which merely has a restrictive objective is enough irrespective of the agreements capacity to attain that object. Article 85 may apply to an agreement that has been formally abandoned by the parties but whose effects "linger" on.[120] In assessing an agreement the Commission will consider:

117 Art. 56 EEA.

118 OJ 1994 L377/28.

119 Hungary OJ 1993 L 347/1; Poland OJ 1993 L348/1; Czech Republic OJ 1994 L360/1; Slovakia OJ 1994 L359/1; Bulgaria OJ 1994 L358/2; Rumania OJ 1994 L357/1. Each was preceded by an interim agreement. See P.J. Slot and A. McDonnell, "Procedure and enforcement in EC and US competition law" (1993), Chapter 29; A. Haagsma, "The competition rules of the EEA and the Europe agreements: lawyer's paradise or user's safe harbour?" Co-operation agreements are also been entered into with other states such as Slovenia, Albania, Russia, the Ukraine and the Baltic States. Europe Agreements are being negotiated with the Baltic States. See Kennedy and Webb, "The limits of integration: Eastern Europe and the European Communities" (1993) 30 CMLRev 1095.

120 See e.g. Case 51/75 *EMI Records Ltd* v *CBS UK Ltd* [1976] 2 CMLR 235; [1976] ECR 811 at para. 30 of the judgment.

- what the object of the agreement is by objective reference to its terms and taking into consideration the economic context of the agreement; and/or,
- if no anti-competitive object is ascertainable whether the agreement as a matter of fact perceptibly restricts competition. This is determined by reference to the competition that would exist in the absence of the restriction taking account of the economic context.[121] In examining effect the Commission will consider other participants in the market, other suppliers to and customers of the parties and, of course, consumers.

1. *Approach of Commission*

6.64 The Commission must adopt a pragmatic but objective view of an agreement assessing among other things: the size of the parties, their market share, the nature of the agreement, the economic context, the nature of the product, the relationship of the agreement in question to other similar agreements adopted by those parties or even by other parties, etc. With this data the Commission can make an appraisal of the object and effect of an agreement.[122]

6.65 When considering the object of an agreement the Commission need not take into consideration the value of ancillary objects or goals. Thus the Court has held that an agreement infringed Article 85 even though it had the ancillary objective of safeguarding public health and minimising the cost of conformity checks.[123] Arguments of this nature, while not relevant to the economic analysis in Article 85(1) may be relevant in the analysis under Article 85(3).

6.66 Psychology plays a significant role in competition. Thus, an agreement with a restrictive objective but not proven mal-effects may be caught.[124] The Court has spoken of a "visual and psychological climate" which stifles competition.[125] The more power to exercise a restriction can lead to parties adjusting and altering their conduct away from the norm.[126] If X and Y agree not to sell in each other's primary marketing area but do not take steps to implement the agreement, they might none the less restrict competition between them because they might refrain from intensifying their sales in each other's area for fear of retaliation and an ensuing price war. The mere existence of the agreement may be a psychological cause for the maintenance of a status quo. Again, with regard to attitude the Commission when considering the object of an agreement do not view the mental state of the parties as conclusive. If the Commission decide that an agreement between X and Y could not, given the economic context, possibly harm competition then they might not apply Article 85 to it even though they might be aware of the parties intentions to restrict competition.

6.67 A disregard for mental state applies with regard to proving the restrictive effect of an agreement. An agreement can fortuitously and unintentionally restrict competition, the parties may not even be aware they have restricted competition, yet the effect is undeniable and Article 85 may apply. However, there are some indications that effects that are

[121] See e.g. Case 99/79 *Lancôme* v *Etos* [1981] 2 CMLR 164; [1980] ECR 2511 at para. 24 of the judgment.

[122] See e.g. Case 47/76 *De Norre* v *Concordia* [1977] 1 CMLR 378; [1977] ECR 65 where the Court employed this broad analytical approach in respect of requirements contracts in tied house agreements.

[123] See e.g. *NAVEWA-ANSEAU* [1982] 2 CMLR 193.

[124] For example, the Commission stated in *PVC Cartel* [1990] 4 CMLR 345 that, in the case of a price fixing and market sharing cartel that it is not strictly necessary, given its manifestly anti-competitive object, for an adverse effect upon competition to be demonstrated.

[125] See Case 19/77 *Miller Schallplatten* v *Commission* [1978] 2 CMLR 334; [1978] ECR 131 at p. 148.

[126] *FEDETAB* [1978] 3 CMLR 524 (Commission decision) where the Commission contended that the *threat* of some disadvantage was likely to result in significant effects.

wholly unforeseeable and remote are to be excluded from consideration. The test of foresight is objective, i.e. what would an outsider foresee, and not subjective, i.e. what would the parties foresee.[127] Thus: X and Y enter a joint R & D venture in the UK and in order to purchase a required input commodity that is not always readily available, they agree to pay high prices to their suppliers. An Italian producer complains that he is going out of business because he cannot obtain supplies of input commodities at reasonable prices due to the "inflationary" willingness of the UK producers to pay higher prices. This has, he claims, pushed the general price of the input commodity up. Such a consequence might be viewed as unforeseeable and the restrictive effect excluded by the Commission from their considerations. Cases affected by this principle however are very rare in practice. Indeed, it is uncertain whether unforeseeability of effect is relevant to anything other than the decision whether or not to fine and/or the level of fine.

E. "Prevention, Restriction or Distortion of Competition"

1. *Prevent, Restrict, Distort*

6.68 These terms describe the object or effect of an agreement the relevant part of Article 85 reads: "which have as their object or effect the prevention, restriction or distortion of competition within the Common Market". The meaning of prevention of competition is obvious: if X prohibits his exclusive dealer Y from selling outside of his contract territory then Y is prevented from competing outside of that area; if X and Y in the UK agree not to supply any wholesaler in France other than at a mutually agreed price then price competition is prevented between X and Y. Likewise the word restriction is clear: if X and Y agree not to increase their marketing efforts in each other's primary marketing area then competition between them is restricted. The meaning of "distortion" is less clear. Distort does not imply the elimination, or even the lessening of competition. It implies, rather, the rechannelling or redirecting of competition from the channels or directions it would have taken in unrestricted circumstances. If a trade association requires its members to impose a surcharge on the price of lower quality goods then customers might switch their purchases away from the lower quality goods to higher quality products. This would distort competition between lower and higher quality goods.[128] It does not necessarily mean that the volume of trade (the consumer demand) would decrease.

6.69 In practical terms the three terms ensure that an agreement which has either a negative, positive or distortive impact on the market is subject to Article 85. The volume of competition may hence be reduced, increased or merely forced to change direction.

2. *"Competition": Notion of "Workable Competition"*

6.70 The Treaty of Rome does not define "competition", which is perhaps surprising given that it is at the very heart of the economic principles underlying the EC.[129] However, it

[127] See *Pabst and Richarz—BNIA* [1976] 2 CMLR D63.

[128] See e.g. *GISA* [1973] CMLR D125; See also *German Ceramic Tiles* [1971] CMLR D6.

[129] Some assistance may be derived from Art. 3(g) EC which specifies as one of the Community's activities "a system ensuring that competition in the internal market is not distorted". Also relevant is Art. 3a which commits the Community to adopting an economic policy "conducted in accordance with the principle of an open market economy with free competition".

is not surprising when one considers that the concept of "competition" is the subject of enormous economic debate and that a precise definition is therefore impossible. The Commission, in common with all competition law authorities, operate with a concept of "workable competition". This notion is to be distinguished from "perfect competition" and "monopoly". Perfect competition describes a market where there are an adequate number of firms so that no individual can affect the overall market price, where there are no significant entry barriers, and where all traders have perfect knowledge of the marketplace. Monopoly describes the market of one firm who may act in terms of pricing and other decisions without reference to any competitive pressures. Neither "perfect competition" nor "monopoly" is feasible as a workable model of competition; both are extremes which rarely exist in practice. "Workable competition" is the economist's compromise; it lays down an object which may reasonably be sought by a competition authority and preaches a relatively pragmatic approach to the evaluation of agreements. The most important tenets of "workable competition" are:

(a) that access to markets is not *unduly* hindered by artificial entry barriers;
(b) that changes in supply and demand may be *reasonably* reflected in the prices of the relevant goods and services;
(c) that production and output should not be *artificially* restrained so as to negate their link with demand;
(d) that freedom of action is not *unreasonably* or disproportionately curtailed;
(e) that the choice of suppliers, purchasers and consumers remains reasonably unrestricted.

6.71 These limited objectives do not aim to achieve perfect competition in markets; they seek only to ensure that undertakings compete with each and do not attain economic power through uncompetitive devices. Each case will depend upon its facts and upon an analysis of the market. One very important point is that Article 85 catches agreements between undertakings and does not attach only to agreements between competitors. A supplier and his exclusive dealer are not direct competitors yet their agreement may be subject to Article 85. Such an agreement though not between rivals may affect competition in the supplier's market (if other suppliers cannot obtain suitable dealers due to exclusivity requirements) and competition in the dealer's market (if rival dealers cannot obtain supplies from a supplier who is contractually bound to supply one dealer only in an area).

3. Unworthy Competition

6.72 Article 85 does not extend to *all* forms of competition. There is no breach of Article 85 if competition that is unworthy of protection is restricted. The Commission judge whether the competition in question is worthy of protection not the parties. So that if X, Y and Z draft an agreement entitled "Fair Trade Rules" and in the agreement proceed to restrict competition between them, the Commission will not refrain from intervening.[130] Sometimes the boundary line between fair and unfair competition is unclear. Thus, it may be a defence to a charge of exchanging price information with a competitor, that one of the parties only exchanged the data in order to verify or disprove the claim of a customer that the other supplier was offering better terms. Thus, an exchange of price information might conceivably be justified if absolutely necessary to overcome the problem of "buyers' tales".[131] The

[130] e.g. *IFTRA rules for Producers of Virgin Aluminium* [1975] 2 CMLR D20. IFTRA stood for International Fair Trade Practices Rules Administration. See also *European Glass Manufacturers* [1974] 2 CMLR D50.
[131] See paras. 9.34–9.35 on information agreements for details.

fair/unfair boundary is unclear where rivals seek to undercut each other to such an extent that they sell at below cost in order to squeeze the other from the market. Discounting is an integral component of competition but when dominant suppliers sell at below cost with the systematic aim of destroying a rival the Commission may view this as unfair predatory pricing.[132] Conversely, selling below cost is not always unfair where it is designed as a competitive device to "shake up" a foreign market or to get a toe hold in a new market.[133] Indeed, below cost selling by a non-dominant undertaking is not caught by Article 85 at all.

6.73 In arguing with the Commission that an agreement seeks only to restrain and prevent unfair competition, the burden of proof is upon the parties. It seems that they must establish that there are serious doubts about the fairness or legality of the competition. In practice this is a high burden to overcome and only in very exceptional circumstances is the Commission likely to be other than sceptical. If an explanation *is* (exceptionally) accepted this might go only to justification under Article 85(3) and not negative clearance under Article 85(2).[134]

F. Article 85(2): Restrictions Automatically Void

6.74 Article 85(2) states: "Any agreements or decisions prohibited pursuant to this Article shall be automatically void." Restrictions rendered void under Article 85(2) are without legal effect and no consequences flow in civil law from their breach. Further, they may not be enforced against a third party.[135] Article 85(2) has prospective *and* retroactive effect.[136] Essentially the effects sought by the parties from the inclusion of the restrictions in the agreement do not materialise. There are two qualifications to be noted.

1. *Severance of Restrictions*

6.75 The nullity envisaged in Article 85(2) does not automatically embrace the whole agreement. Only such clauses as infringe Article 85(1) are automatically void.[137] A whole agreement becomes void only if the offending clauses cannot be separated from the contract.[138] In examining an agreement or decision the Commission must determine whether the restrictions are severable. This is done by considering objectively all of the surrounding circumstances of the case. The Commission does not consider the subjective views of the parties. This process is essential when the Commission considers the remedy to be applied: is the whole agreement void or are only the offending clauses void? If the clauses are severable then the Commission must confine its decision to the void clauses only.

132 *ECS–AKZO* OJ 1985 L374/1 upheld by the Court of Justice in C-62/86 *AKZO* v *Commission* [1993] 5 CMLR 215.

133 *IFTRA rules for Producers of Virgin Aluminium* [1975] 2 CMLR D20 at paras. 21–23.

134 See *Sirdar/Phildar* [1975] 1 CMLR D93; *Penneys* [1978] 2 CMLR 100.

135 See Case 22/71 *Beguelin Import* v *G.L. Import Export* [1972] CMLR 81; [1971] ECR 949 at p. 962.

136 See Case 48/72 *Brasserie de Haecht SA* v *Wilkin (No. 2)* [1973] CMLR 287; [1973] ECR 77 at para. 27 of judgment.

137 See Case 58/64 *Consten and Grundig* v *Commission* [1966] CMLR 418; [1966] ECR 299 at p. 392; Case 319/82 *Société de Vente de Ciments et Betons De L'est SA* v *Kerpen and Kerpen* [1985] 1 CMLR 511.

138 See Case 56/65 *La Technique Minière* v *Maschinenbau Ulm GmbH* [1966] CMLR 357; [1966] ECR 235 at p. 250: "The automatic nullity in question applies only to those elements of the agreement which are subject to the prohibition or to the agreement as a whole if those elements do not appear severable from the agreement itself. Consequently, all other contractual provisions which are not affected by the prohibition, since they do not involve the application of the Treaty, fall outside the Community law."

If an agreement is being disputed before the national court the test of severance is a question of national *not* Community law. In the UK the Court will first, extract the offending clauses and secondly, examine the residue to assess whether it, "could be said to fail for lack of consideration or any other ground, or whether the contract could be so changed in its character as not to be the sort of contract that the parties intended to enter into at all."[139]

6.76 Thus, an agreement can fail because the consideration for the contract is contained in a void and unenforceable clause. Alternatively, the agreement can fail because, without the void clauses the parties would not have entered the agreement at all, or the agreement in a farm materially similar to that which was originally concluded.

6.77 It is clear that a restrictive clause can be held to be partially void: X wishes to sell his business to Y and includes in the contract of sale, a clause whereby X will not enter into a competing business with Y for a period of 12 years after the sale. The Commission treat the non-competition clause as unduly restrictive and decide that a lesser period of 4 years is adequate to ensure the transfer to Y of the full commercial value of the business. In this case the non-competition clause has been modified by the Commission's decision and not struck down outright.[140]

2. *"Old" and Accession Agreements: "Provisional Validity"*

6.78 The Court has held that a national court may not apply Article 85(2) to "old" agreements.[141] An "old" agreement is one that was already in existence at 13 March 1962, this being the date when the enforcement machinery under Regulation 17/62/EEC for Article 85 and 86 came into existence.[142] These "old" agreements are "safe" until the Commission takes a decision in respect of them, so long as they were notified to the Commission in due time or are exempt from the need to notify.[143] "Safe" in this regard means that, pending a Commission decision, such agreements are valid and enforceable. A Commission decision that an agreement infringes Article 85(1) and is not exempt under Article 85(3) nullifies the provisional validity and brings Article 85(2) into play.

6.79 Accession agreements are treated in the same way. An "accession agreement" is one which falls within Article 85(1) due to the accession to the EC of the Member State(s) in which the parties are situate and in which the agreement operates. Thus for the UK, Eire and Denmark the accession date was 1 January 1973; for Greece, 1 January 1981; for Spain and Portugal, 1 January 1986 and for Austria, Finland and Sweden, 1 January 1995.

6.80 One very important proviso to the above must be made. In *Lancôme*[144] the Court of Justice limited the provisional validity granted to notified "old" agreements. The Court held that once the Commission had informed parties that it was unlikely to exempt their agreement provisional validity would end. Traditionally, validity is withdrawn by a formal decision condemning the agreement. However, now it seems that an informal letter from a senior Commission official achieves the same effect.

139 *Chemidus Wavin Ltd* v *Société pour la Transformation et L'Exploitation des Resines Industrielles SA* [1977] FSR 181; [1978] 3 CMLR 514 at p. 519 per Buckley LJ. (Court of Appeal). For an example and a confirmation of the test see *Alec Lobb (Garages)* v *Total Oil (Great Britain)* [1985] 1 WLR 173 at p.192 *per* Waller LJ (CA). See also *Inntrepeneur Estates Ltd* v *Mason* [1993] 2 CMLR 293, 311; and *Marchant and Elliot* v *Higgins* (CA 21 December 1995 *per* Legatt CJ in relation to the Standard Agency Agreement employed in the Lloyd's Insurance market).

140 See e.g. *Nutricia/Zuid Hollandse Conservenfabriek* [1984] 2 CMLR 165 (Commission decision).

141 See Case 48/72 *Brasserie de Haecht SA* v *Wilkin No. 2* [1973] ECR 77; [1973] CMLR 287; Case 59/77 *Etablissements A de Bloos* v *Bouyer* [1978] 1 CMLR 511; [1977] ECR 2539.

142 See Reg. 17/62/EEC OJ sp. ed. 1959–62, 87.

143 *ibid*., Art. 4(2) for exempt agreements.

144 Case 99/79 *Lancôme* v *Etos* [1981] 2 CMLR 164; [1980] ECR 2511.

6.81 The Court further made it clear in *Lancôme* that the attachment of provisional validity to old agreements was justified by reference to the exclusive power of the Commission to issue formal exemptions. Once it became clear that the Commission did not intend to issue a formal decision or take further action on an agreement and that they were "closing the file", then the Court saw no reason to prolong the life of the provisional validity. The decision has caused some disquiet to businessmen who seek to negotiate a result with the Commission in respect of an agreement. When they finally achieve consensus on the necessary amendments and objectionable clauses are removed, the Commission may send them a "comfort letter" informing them that the file has been closed and giving the reasons. Having thus danced to the Commission's tune the provisional validity of their agreement is removed. The Court has provided some solace only in that it has indicated that national courts should take the Commission's view that the agreement is not now in breach of Article 85 into account. National courts are not, however, bound by comfort letters. Some legal advisers view *Lancôme* as imposing a penalty on notification and negotiation.

3. "New" Agreements

6.82 The category of "old" agreements (above) is, excepting accession agreements, limited. The vast majority of cases to which EC rules apply have been entered into since the coming into force of the enforcement machinery in 1962. These agreements may be termed "new" agreements. Such agreements do *not* enjoy provisional validity merely because they have been notified to the Commission. If parties desire to enter restrictive agreements they do so at their own risk. The Court has thus stated:

> "Whilst the principle of legal certainty requires that, in applying the prohibitions of Article 85, the sometimes considerable delays by the Commission in exercising its powers should be taken into account, this cannot, however, absolve the [national] court from the obligation of deciding on the claims of interested parties who invoke the automatic nullity. In such a case it devolves on the Court to judge ... whether there is cause to suspend proceedings in order to allow the parties to obtain the Commission's standpoint, unless it establishes either that the agreement does not have any perceptible effect on competition or trade between Member States or that there is no doubt that the agreement is incompatible with Article 85."[145]

6.83 One may ask what the value of notifying an agreement to the Commission is if this does not give any form of legal protection. The answer is that notification is an important factor in the Commission's decision to fine an undertaking. Notification in most cases means that if the Commission ultimately arrive at an adverse decision they will not fine the parties. This is not an absolute rule and parties who notify a price fixing agreement in the hope that it will take two years for the Commission to issue a negative decision in which time the cartel would have achieved its restrictive objective might yet be fined. In such a flagrant case a swift Commission response may be expected. The pros and cons of notification are discussed below at paras. 6.120–6.145.

4. The Consequences of Article 85(2) in National Courts: "Euro-defences"

6.84 The fact that parts of a restrictive agreement are void under Article 85(2) has been used in the UK courts as a defence by parties who, when sued for breach of contract, counter by

[145] Case 48/72 *Brasserie de Haecht SA* v *Wilkin No. 2* [1973] CMLR 287; [1973] ECR 77.

asserting the nullity of the contract in question. Using EC law in this fashion has become known as pleading a "Euro-defence". Actions of this type usually arise in one of two ways. First, in intellectual property cases where a proprietor seeks an injunction to prevent licensees[146] and other persons[147] from infringing rights, it is now commonplace for the defendant to claim that the agreement or part of it is caught by Article 85(1) and void under Article 85(2) and/or that in enforcing the right in question the Plaintiff is seeking to enforce or implement an anterior illegal agreement. The UK courts look rigorously at Euro-defences, perceiving them as generally unmeritorious.[148] However it is accepted that they may have substantive merit even though they may be viewed as somewhat unmeritorious. Consequently, following the line laid down by the House of Lords in *American Cyanamid* v *Ethicon*[149] on the use of discretion in interlocutory injunction proceedings, courts have often been content to leave Euro-defences until full trial of the issues rather than examine them at the interim stage. Secondly, Euro-defences have been in issue in cases where the plaintiff has applied to the court under RSC Order 18 rule 19 or the inherent jurisdiction to have a defence struck out on the grounds that it is unarguable and without any foundation. Courts do not, without more ado, adopt the view that a Euro-defence is at least arguable and should not be peremptorily struck out.[150] Courts examine cases with care and many judges are nowadays sufficiently familiar with EC competition law to feel confident about forming a clear view of the merits at an early stage.

G. Agreements Exempted under Article 85(3)

6.85 Article 85(3) lays down criteria which, if satisfied by an agreement caught by Article 85(1), can lead to an exemption being granted to parties to a restrictive agreement by the Commission. The provision lays down detailed criteria and it is by reference to these that parties must base their arguments when negotiating with the Commission. Article 85(3) is examined at paras. 7.70–7.92 and discussion of the provision will be delayed until then. It is pertinent, however, to note at this stage that certain types of restrictive agreement are deemed to obtain exemption automatically if their terms conform to rules laid down in certain regulations. The principal regulations in question concern: exclusive dealing agreements; exclusive purchasing agreements; selective distribution in the motor industry; specialisation agreements; technology transfer agreements; and, research and development

[146] See e.g. *Dymond* v *Britton* [1976] FSR 330 where the Court felt unable (regretfully) to grant summary judgment to the plaintiff patentee due to the existence of a Euro-defence by the defendant licensee which was at least an arguable defence if no stronger. See also *Chemidus Wavin* v *Société pour la Transformation et l'Exploitation des Resines* [1977] FSR 181; [1978] 3 CMLR 514 where a French licensee refused to pay royalties on sale. In defence of an action by the patentee for recovery of these payments the licensee pleaded the Euro-defence that the minimum royalty payments clause in the licence was contrary to Art. 85(1) EC and hence was void under Art. 85(2) EC. The Court of Appeal rejected this assertion. With respect to a non-competition clause in the licence, the Court accepted that it could be within Art. 85(1) but refused to strike down the agreement on that account alone. Rather, they severed the offending clause from the remainder of the agreement. Judgment was given to the patentee.

[147] e.g. *British Leyland* v *TI Silencers* [1981] FSR 213; *Dow Chemical* v *Spense Bryson* (1981) (unreported).

[148] See, e.g. *British Leyland* v *Armstrong Patents* [1983] FSR 50; *Hoover* v *George Hulme* [1982] FSR 565; *Netlon* v *Bridport Gurundy* [1979] FSR 530; *IBM* v *Phoenix International (Computers) Ltd*, Ferris J, unreported judgment of 30 July 1993.

[149] [1975] AC 396.

[150] *British Leyland* v *TI Silencers* [1981] FSR 213; *Lansing and Bagnall* v *Buccaneer Lift Parts* [1984] 1 CMLR 224; *Pitney Bowes* v *Francotyp-Postalia* [1989] 3 CMLR 466; *Digital Equipment Corp* v *LCE Computer Maintenance Ltd*, Mervyn Davies J, unreported judgment of 22 May 1992.

agreements. There are many block exemptions in existence which deal with specific sectors of industry (e.g. insurance, marine transport, air transport, motor vehicles, etc.).

6.86 A regulation granting automatic exemption in this fashion is termed a "block exemption" and simply indicates that certain types of agreement obtain exemption *en bloc*.

6.87 Typically a block exemption permits certain clauses as not being restrictive of competition in a "whitelist" (ie the clauses are not caught by Article 85(1) at all), exempts in a "greylist" other clauses which while caught by Article 85(1) merit exemption under Article 85(3), and finally "blacklists" clauses which are caught by Article 85(1) and which cannot justify automatic block exemption under Article 85(3). Such blacklisted clauses may, in come cases, be exempted if an individual application for exemption is made. While the Commission might seem to have the power under the enabling regulation for block exemptions, Regulation 19/65,[151] to blacklist clauses not caught by Article 85(1), since the purpose of block exemptions is to apply Article 85(3), it can be argued that Regulation 19/65 does not have the *vires* to enable control of clauses not actually caught by Article 85(1). Therefore, it would be possible to challenge blacklisting of a clause if in fact it could be shown that the clause in question was not in fact caught by Article 85(1), notwithstanding the wording of the block exemption. Parties to an agreement fitting within the rules laid down in a block exemption need *not* notify their agreement to the Commission though they may do so if unsure of its compatibility with the block exemption. The Commission reserves the power to remove the benefit of a block exemption from any agreement, should it consider in the particular circumstances either the conditions for the application of Article 85(3) are not met, or that the agreement itself could constitute an abuse contrary to Article 86. The Court of First Instance confirmed the Commission's power to do the latter in *Tetra Pak No. 1 (BTG Licence)*.[152] The question then arises as to the effect upon the validity of the agreement of the removal of the block exemption for the whole of the agreement. The Commission seem to have assumed in *Tetra Pak No. 1 (BTG Licence)*[153] that the removal of the block exemption could only apply prospectively, though the Commission's decision in *Decca Navigator System*[154] could be interpreted as meaning that the agreement was to be treated as never having been exempt. It is submitted that the former view is to be preferred, being more consistent with the principle under EC law of legal certainty. The block exemptions are discussed in depth in later chapters.

H. Article 86 EC: Abuse of a Dominant Position

1. *Definition*

6.88 The vast majority of cases dealt with by the Commission fall under Article 85. However, some are dealt with under Article 86. This reads:

> "Any abuse by one or more undertakings of a dominant position within the Common Market or in a substantial part of it shall be prohibited as incompatible with the Common Market in so far as it may affect trade between Member States. Such abuse may, in particular, consist in:

[151] Art. 2, Reg. 19/65: "The [block exemption] regulation shall define the categories of agreements to which it applies and shall specify in particular: (a) the restrictions or clauses which must not be contained in the agreement; (b) the clauses which must be contained in the agreements, or the other conditions which must be satisfied."

[152] T-51/89 *Tetra Pak (I)* [1990] ECR II-309 [1991] 4 CMLR 334.

[153] OJ 1988 L 272/27.

[154] OJ 1989 L 43/27, para. 127.

(a) directly or indirectly imposing unfair purchase or selling prices or unfair trading conditions;
(b) limiting production, markets or technical development to the prejudice of consumers;
(c) applying dissimilar conditions to equivalent transactions with other trading parties, thereby placing them at a competitive disadvantage;
(d) making the conclusion of contracts subject to acceptance by the other parties of supplementary obligations which, by their nature or according to commercial usage, have no connection with the subject of such contracts."

6.89 Article 86 is aimed at the unilateral behaviour of economically dominant undertakings who employ their dominance in an abusive manner. In a contractual sense this might be because a dominant supplier forces unfair terms and conditions upon a weaker customer who has little or no bargaining power. Article 86 may also be employed against two or more dominant suppliers who collectively exploit their economic power. The provision speaks of, "Any abuse by one or more undertakings" and it has been held that this means that Article 86 may apply to undertakings jointly or collectively holding a dominant position.[155] Statutory monopolists are bound by Article 86.[156]

2. Article 86 EC: Difference between Dominance and Abuse

6.90 The mere possession of dominance is not prohibited, it is only the abuse of dominance that is forbidden. Article 86 enumerates examples of such abuse in subparagraphs (a)–(d). This list is not exhaustive.

3. Meaning of "Dominance"

6.91 Dominance usually manifests itself as an ability to act independently on the market without having to consider competitive pressures:

> "The dominant position referred to in this Article relates to a position of economic strength enjoyed by an undertaking which enables it to prevent effective competition being maintained on the relevant market by affording it the power to behave to an appreciable extent independently of its competitors, its customers and ultimately of consumers."[157]

In determining whether or not a large, ostensibly powerful undertaking is legally "dominant" the Commission may examine a number of factors.

(1) Market share

6.92 A firm with a very high market share may be presumed to be dominant.[158] Thus, the possessor of 80 per cent of a market is almost certainly dominant. The Court of Justice has stated that a 50 per cent market share, save in exceptional circumstances, is evidence of dominance.[159] However, if company X has 50 per cent of the market it might still be subject to intense competition from two competitors Y and Z with 18 per cent and 23

[155] The concept of joint or collective dominance is examined in detail at paras. 6.110–6.113 below. The terms "joint" and "collective" are completely interchangeable and both are used in practice.
[156] e.g. Case 41/83 *British Telecommunications* [1985] 2 CMLR 368.
[157] Case 27/76 *United Brands* v *Commission* [1978] 1 CMLR 429; [1978] ECR 207 at paras. 65 and 66 of the judgment. For examples, see Case 322/81 *Michelin* [1983] ECR 3461 [1985] 1 CMLR 282; *GVL* [1982] 1 CMLR 221; *British Telecommunications* [1983] 1 CMLR 457 (Commission Decision); Case 41/83 [1985] ECR I-873 [1985] 2 CMLR 368 (ECJ).
[158] Case 85/76 *Hoffman-La Roche* v *Commission* [1979] 3 CMLR 211; [1979] ECR 461.
[159] C-62/86 *AKZO* v *Commission* [1991] ECR I-3359 [1993] 5 CMLR 215, para 60.

per cent of the market, respectively. Any abuse by X, for instance by excessively high pricing, will simply lead to Y and Z taking up X's dissatisfied customers. Conversely if X held only 40 per cent of the market and the next largest competitor held only 2 per cent (i.e. the market had one giant and a plethora of small firms) it is highly likely that X would be dominant. "Dominance" is not necessarily synonymous with success. A dominant undertaking may have bad years when it makes a loss. This fact does not mean that the undertaking is not dominant though if the undertaking in question continued to do badly this might be evidence that there were competitive pressures on it in the form of other firms and this might imply a limitation to its dominance. Indeed the analysis of a firm's market share must be coupled to a simultaneous analysis of the degree of external competition. A large undertaking's ability to exploit its economic power will depend largely upon the disciplining effect of the residual firms.

(2) Entry barriers

6.93 The existence of entry barriers may operate to cushion the dominant undertaking from potential competitors who might enter the market to challenge that undertaking's superiority and steal away its market share. The strength of an entry barrier and its' effectiveness as an obstacle to new firms will of course vary according to circumstances. Indeed economic theorists vary greatly in the importance they attach to different types of entry barrier. Entry barriers might derive from the undertaking's own behaviour. For example, an undertaking owns a major part of the market for an input product into its own manufacturing process and restricts access of rivals to this product.[160] Alternatively entry barriers might also derive from governmental restrictions on entry to the market;[161] prohibitively high R&D costs; prohibitively high plant costs; costs of raw materials[162] etc.

(3) Exit barriers

6.94 The existence of exit barriers can operate as entry barriers if potential competitors realise that once in the market they will be effectively barred from exit because of (say) the general lack of a market for excess plant and equipment. If a firm wishes to take a risk it is less likely to do so in a market where failure involves abandoning expensive plant and machinery. Exit barriers encountered by customers can create entry barriers to the supplier's market. An undertaking which purchases a mainframe computer incurs a very heavy capital investment. Having made the decision to buy and allocated the necessary resources the purchaser is most unlikely to abandon the computer for a rival manufac-

[160] e.g. Case 6 and 7/73 *ICI and Commercial Solvents* v *Commission* [1974] CMLR 309; [1974] ECR 223 where Commercial Solvents enjoyed what was virtually a world monopoly in the manufacture and sale of a chemical needed in the manufacture of an anti-tuberculosis drug. Commercial Solvents was also active in the market for this drug. Its power over the input product gave it very significant economic power over the drug. The existence of such power over an input product could thus be exploited to exclude competitors in the product made from that input. See also *Napier Brown/British Sugar* [1990] 4 CMLR 196.

[161] e.g. Case 26/75 *General Motors* v *Commission* [1976] 1 CMLR 95; [1975] ECR 1367 where a statutorily granted monopoly to issue conformity licences on imported vehicles meant that the possessor of the statutory right was protected from competition by the statutory monopoly which operated as an absolute entry barrier. See also *Derek Merson* v *British Leyland* [1984] 3 CMLR 92 at p. 98, para. 25. See also, for a brief overview of the relevance of entry barriers, Korah, *EC Competition Law and Practice* (5th edn. 1994), pp. 11–15; see for detailed analysis, Gyselen and Kyriazis, "Article 86 EC: the monopoly power measurement issue revisited" (1986) ELRev 134 at p.138 *et seq.*

[162] *Napier Brown/British Sugar* [1990] 4 CMLR 196.

turer's computer. The extent of the investment creates a financial disincentive to purchase a rival product. Having taken one manufacturer's mainframe the buyer is likely to take that producer's accessories albeit that rival manufacturers might produce plug compatible accessories. The purchaser becomes economically tied to a manufacturer and the resultant exit barrier for the buyer from that manufacturer's product creates a substantial entry barrier to rival suppliers who are effectively foreclosed from that customer.

(4) Expansion barriers

6.95 If supplier X has an extensive network of exclusive dealers across the EC and because X has already incorporated all of the best dealers into his network there is a shortage of effective dealers to distribute new or other suppliers' goods, then not only is this an entry barrier for prospective suppliers but it can be an expansion barrier to existing firms who may wish to expand output but are concerned that they will not be able to achieve effective and rigorous market penetration through further dealership representation. X might feel secure in his dominant position because most of the most effective dealers are tied up in his network and contractually prohibited from holding other suppliers products.

(5) Degree of vertical integration

6.96 If X is alleged to be a dominant manufacturer it might be relevant that he owns his own resources for making the product and that he owns his own distribution and retail outlets, i.e. there is full integration from production of raw materials to sale of the finished product to the consumer. This gives X an advantage over less integrated manufacturers who may be subject to greater uncertainties in the markets for raw materials and in the efficiency of a distribution and transport system.[163]

(6) Technical knowledge coupled to R&D capacity

6.97 The degree of technical knowledge enjoyed by an undertaking might be a function of an undertaking's financial capacity to conduct extensive R&D. In high-technology markets where a premium is placed upon creativity, the ability to maintain a position at the forefront of technology will be central in sustaining dominance.

(7) Marketing and advertising capacity

6.98 The success of an undertaking's advertising in creating consumer preferences may be relevant in cementing dominance. A dominant concern may enjoy greater advertising revenues to devote to creating consumer loyalty. In *United Brands* the dominant undertaking was able to persuade consumers to pay between 30 per cent and 40 per cent more for bananas branded with the "Chiquita" mark than for unbranded bananas although the price difference appeared not to have been objectively justified.[164]

[163] e.g. Case 27/76 *United Brands* v *Commission* [1978] 1 CMLR 429; [1978] ECR 207. In Case 322/81 *Michelin* [1985] 1 CMLR 282 at paras. 55–58, the Court of Justice commented upon the potential advantages an undertaking might enjoy as a result of being within a group of companies operating throughout Europe and even the world. In particular the Court stressed the advantages of enhanced R&D and distribution mechanisms, that membership of a group could entail. See also *Napier Brown/British Sugar* [1990] 4 CMLR 196, in which the Commission commented that as British Sugar had a well-developed integrated production system, it made "it difficult for a new producer, which produces only on one level of production, to operate".

[164] *United Brands* (above).

(8) Other political factors and time

6.99 In *BP* v *Commission*[165] the existence of the 1973 oil crisis engendered by the OPEC boycott of western states gave the oil companies temporary political and economic significance out of all proportion to their everyday market power. This factor alone was enough to give BP "dominance" on the Dutch market for the currency of the crisis despite the fact that BP held only 10 per cent of the EC market for the relevant product. The case shows, *inter alia*, that dominance can be temporary.

6.100 The list above is by no means conclusive of possible indicia of market power. An analysis of the investigated undertaking's price policies over time might yield useful pointers, for example: that the firm was repeatedly able to sustain profit margins during periods of economic downturn; that the firm's market share has remained steady over periods of time when it might have been expected to have come under pressure; that the firm was repeatedly successful in repulsing competitors.

4. The Importance of Defining the Geographical Market

6.101 In determining dominance a central question is market definition. The nub of this enquiry is whether the undertaking in question is: a small fish in a big pond, a big fish in a small pond, or even, a big fish in a big pond. A nationalised telecommunications operator might be dominant in one Member State but would not be dominant in the overall EC telecommunications market where it competes with other nationalised and privatised authorities.[166] Accordingly, delineation of market area is an important function undertaken in an Article 86 case. Transport costs may be important in deciding this question: X might sell in northern Member States but not in southern Member States because, given the bulky nature of the product, the freight costs are too great to render southern sales profitable. The geographical market need *not* be the whole of the EC. Article 86 speaks of abuse, "within the Common Market or in a substantial part of it", The meaning of "substantial part" has caused some debate in cases before the Court of Justice. In *BRT* v *SABAM* the Advocate General stated: "What is essential is the quantitative assessment of the market in relation to the whole of the market, that is to say, its relative economic importance. For this purpose one must consider above all the density of the population, the level of its resources and the extent of its purchasing power."[167] On this basis, Belgium has been accepted by the Advocate General and Court to be a substantial part of the Common Market. Likewise Southern Germany has been held to be a "substantial part".[168] The opinion has been expressed that "substantial part" should not be analysed narrowly but should be seen as a *de minimis* requirement, i.e. all but the smallest areas are substantial parts of the EC. In *BP* v *Commission*, Advocate General Warner thus stated:

> "There is ... a danger in focusing attention exclusively on percentages. The opposite of 'substantial' is 'negligible' and what may seem negligible when looked at in terms of a per-

[165] Case 77/77 *BP* v *Commission* [1978] 3 CMLR 174; [1978] ECR 1513. See Case 322/81 *Michelin* [1985] 1 CMLR 282 at para. 59, temporary lack of profitability in a company does not necessarily negate the fact of an undertaking's dominance.

[166] See *British Telecommunications* [1983] 1 CMLR 457 at para. 26 of the decision: "British Telecommunications has a statutory monopoly, under the Telecommunications Act 1981, for the running of telecommunication systems throughout the United Kingdom and the Isle of Man. British Telecommunications therefore holds a dominant position in the United Kingdom, which constitutes a substantial part of the Common Market, for the provision of telex and telephone systems."

[167] Case 127/73 *BRT* v *SABAM* [1974] 2 CMLR 238; [1974] ECR 313 at p. 324.

[168] Cases 40–48, 50, 56, 111, 113 and 114/73 *European Sugar Cartel (Suiker Unie)* [1976] 1 CMLR 295; [1975] ECR 1663.

centage may seem otherwise when looked at in absolute terms. The population of Luxembourg is, I believe, about 0.23 per cent of the whole Community. I would, however, shrink from saying that one who had a monopoly or near monopoly of the Luxembourg market for a particular product was exempt from the application of Article 86."[169]

On this basis the Commission may define a market in narrow geographical terms thereby swelling the economic importance of the undertaking whose behaviour is challenged. One caveat to this is that in *BP* v *Commission* the Court held that BP—the defendants—were not in breach of Article 86 EC so did not confirm or disapprove of the views of the Advocate General. However, the tenor of their analysis is that they were not materially in disagreement.

6.102 In construing the word "substantial part", the distinction between an area or location and an activity should be borne in mind. Advocate General Warner in *Pigs and Bacon Commission* v *McCarren*[170] adopted the position that a specific flow or current of trade, for example the export of Irish bacon to the UK, did not comprise a "part" of the Common Market within the meaning of Article 86. In *Felixstowe Docks and Railways Board* v *British Transport Docks Board*[171] the High Court denied that the Humberside ports comprised a "substantial part" of the Common Market. On the other hand, a specific location can, through its economic importance, constitute a substantial part. The port of Holyhead, being the shortest direct link by sea from the UK to Ireland, was held to be a substantial part by the Commission in an interim measures case.[172]

5. The Importance of Defining the Product Market

6.103 Similar problems of identification exist when considering product market. X might be dominant in the supply of music cassettes but may be subject to competition from producers of records and compact discs. The product market may thus be wider than just music cassettes. Y might be dominant in the supply of peaches but peaches may be in competition with other soft fruit or even all fruit. The greater the degree of competition from other similar or competing products the less the opportunity for an undertaking to exploit its power over a single product. If Y pushed the price of peaches up too high then consumers would simply switch to alternative fruits. In defining the relevant product market, the Commission focuses on product interchangeability both from the demand side of the market and from the supply side. When defining the scope of a market, the Commission considers short-term rather than long-term substitutability. In *Tetra Pak II*[173] the Commission stated that the reason for this was that "over a long period, during which technological progress may occur and consumer habits evolve, structures will change and the very boundaries between the various markets shift. A short period corresponds

[169] Case 77/77 *BP* v *Commission* [1978] 3 CMLR 174; [1978] ECR 1513 at p.1521. But cf. *Cutsforth* v *Mansfield Inns Ltd* [1986] 1 CLMR 1 at p. Il, para. 34 Sir Neil Lawson held that the north of England was not a substantial part of the common market when taken as a whole. This finding must be open to question. For the definition of substantial part of the United Kingdom under Fair Trading Act 1973, see *R* v *MMC ex parte South Yorkshire Transport* [1993] 1 All ER 289, noted by Robertson [1993] ECLR 217.

[170] Case 177/78 [1979] 3 CMLR 389; [1979] ECR 2161.

[171] [1976] 2 CMLR 665.

[172] *Sealink/BandI* [1992] 5 CMLR 255. See also *ICG/Morlaix Chamber of Commerce* Commission Press Release 15 May 1995, IP/95/492, in which interim measures were ordered by the Commission pursuant to Art. 86 EC, requiring the operators of Roscoff in Brittany to grant access to an Irish ferry operator. In *Felixstowe Docks and Railways Board* v *British Transport Docks Board* [1976] 2 CMLR 665, the High Court held that the Humberside ports did not constitute a substantial part.

[173] [1992] 4 CMLR 551.

more to the economic operative time during which a given company exercises its power on the market".

(1) Demand-side substitutability

6.104 The test of demand substitutability is essentially a matter of consumer preference. One examines which products are sufficiently similar in terms of price, quality and intended use to be regarded by *users* or *consumers* as reasonable substitutes for each other. There is no precise test for determining what is a sufficient degree of demand side interchangeability; it is a matter of fact and degree. *United Brands*[174] is the classic example of a case in which the physical characteristics of a product were important. In considering whether other fruits were interchangeable with bananas so as to form part of the same product market, the Court of Justice agreed with the Commission that bananas, like other fruits, could be eaten as part of a meal or as a dessert, but said that a banana has characteristics which set it aside in a market of its own, namely "appearance, taste, softness, seedlessness, easy handling ...". In determining demand side substitutability, it is also relevant to look the use of a product. For example, in *Tetra Pak II*[175] aseptic cartons were held by the Commission to be in a different market to non-aseptic cartons, one of the reasons being that the latter could not be used for long-life milk. Tetra Pak had argued that the relevant market included all ways of packaging liquid food products, such as glass, plastic and tins for milk, fruit juices or mineral water. The Commission rejected this definition on two grounds. First, cartons cannot technically be used for some foods, such as fizzy drinks. Secondly, other containers compete only in the long term, when a food seller is installing the original or replacement system for packaging the liquid.

6.105 Products may not be interchangeable because of differences in their price. A good example is the luxury perfume market. There is evidence that consumers do not regard cheap perfumes as interchangeable with luxury perfumes, as the higher cost of the latter is an essential part of their luxury brand image vital to the customer. The price of a product is relevant for another reason. One way of establishing interchangeability is to measure the cross-elasticity of demand. Thus, where a 5 per cent increase in the price of one product causes a significant switch by customers to another, this suggests those products are within the same market. It is clear that the Court of Justice is prepared to take into account cross-elasticities of demand,[176] but it is equally clear that there are problems with the test and that it is inappropriate to use it as the sole criterion.[177]

(2) Supply-side substitutability

6.106 It is necessary to consider the degree of ease with which a producer of similar products which are not demand substitutable could switch to producing the product in question. In *Continental Can* v *Commission*[178] the Court of Justice criticised the Commission's approach to market definition saying that it should have made it clear why it considered that producers of other types of containers would not be able to adapt their production to compete with Continental Can. In *Tetra Pak II*[179] the Commission, in defining the relevant product markets, took into account the fact that producers of milk packaging ma-

174 Case 27/76 *United Brands* v *Commission* [1973] ECR 215.

175 [1992] 4 CMLR 551.

176 Case 6/72 *Continental Can* v *Commission* [1973] ECR 215; Case 27/76 *United Brands* v *Commission* [1978] ECR 207.

177 Among the problems in using it is that the choice of product for which the change in demand is measured will affect the outcome, and further that reliable data may not exist upon which to base the test.

178 Case 6/72 [1973] ECR 215.

179 [1992] 4 CMLR 551.

chines could not readily adapt their production to make aseptic packaging machines and cartons.

6.107 One problem with the concept of supply-side substitutability is that it is difficult to distinguish it from the question of entry barriers, which is relevant not to market definition but to the issue of how much market power an undertaking possesses. If there are no factors preventing a firm from switching production this shows that there are no barriers to entry. Thus there is a danger of conflating the issue of market definition with supply side substitutability and assessing power on a defined market by reference to entry barriers.

6. *The Concept of "Abuse"*

6.108 The existence of dominance in an undertaking attracts no legal consequences. It is *abuse* of that dominance which results in application of Article 86. The question the Commission will ask itself, according to the Court of Justice, is whether the dominant undertaking, "has made use of the opportunities arising out of its dominant position in such a way as to reap trading benefits which it would not have reaped if there had been normal and sufficiently effective competition".[180] In another case the Court added that abuse of dominance "has the effect of hindering the maintenance of the degree of competition still existing in the market or the growth of that competition".[181] An abuse may even consist of denying a third party access to an "essential facility", i.e. one which it is necessary for that party to use in order to be able to compete with the dominant undertaking.[182] It is not intended to elaborate at length upon "abuse" here. In subsequent chapters the application of Article 86 to specific practices and commercial agreements is examined at length.

6.109 One point to note is that an abuse is only within Article 86 if it affects trade between Member States. As with Article 85, the requirement of an effect on trade between Member States is designed to differentiate the application of Community and national law. A practice that affects only the national market is for national authorities to challenge; it is only where trade between Member States is affected that Article 86 applies.[183] Though, whereas with Article 85 it is the agreement which must affect trade, in the case of Article 86 it is the abuse which must exert the requisite effect on trade.

6.110 Article 86 EC, as already noted, refers to an abuse "by one or more undertakings". This was initially interpreted as referring to undertakings forming part of the same economic entity,[184] but the Commission and both Courts have since held that the phrase is of wider significance.[185] Thus undertakings which are legally independent may now be found to oc-

[180] Case 27/76 *United Brands* v *Commission* [1978] 1 CMLR 429; [1978] ECR 207 at para. 249 of the judgment.

[181] Case 85/76 *Hoffman-La Roche and Co AG* v *Commission* [1979] 3 CMLR 211; [1979] ECR 461 at para. 91 of the judgment.

[182] *Sealink/B&I* [1992] 5 CMLR 255; Draft Notice on the application of the EC competition rules to cross-border credit transfer systems OJ 1994 C 322/7, para 6.

[183] See generally, Vogelenzang, "Abuse of a dominant position in Article 86: the problem of causality and some applications" (1976) 13 CMLRev 61; Siragusa, "The application of Article 86 to the pricing policy of dominant companies: discriminatory and unfair prices" (1979) 16 CMLRev 179; Korah, "Interpretation and application of Article 86 of the Treaty of Rome: abuse of a dominant position within the Common Market" (1978) 53 *Notre Dame Lawyer* 768. Baden-Fuller, "Article 86 EC: economic analysis of the existence of a dominant position" (1979) ELRev 423; Gyselen and Kyriazis, "Article 86 EC: the monopoly power measurement issue revisited" (1986) ELRev 134.

[184] e.g. *Continental Can* OJ 1972 L7/25.

[185] For the Court of First Instance's acceptance of the collective dominance theory, see Joined Cases T-68, 77 and 78/89 *Societa Italiano Vetro SpA* v *Commission* (*Italian Flat Glass*) [1992] 5 CMLR 302. The Court of Justice has since accepted this in C-393/92. *Almelo* [1994] ECR I-1477, stating at para. 41 that "the

cupy a "joint" or "collective" dominant position on the market and their behaviour controlled under Article 86. Joint dominance is a relatively new development in the interpretation of Article 86. Many questions still remain as to its applicability and scope.[186] The main question is precisely what degree of connection is required between undertakings in order for their position on the market to be assessed collectively rather than individually. The Commission has stated[187] that there were two essential features of joint dominance: (i) that a small number of enterprises account for most of the turnover in the market in question without a single enterprise being dominant, and (ii) that there is a high degree of interdependence among the decisions of the undertakings. In *Italian Flat Glass*,[188] the Court of First Instance held that "there is nothing, in principle, to prevent two or more economic entities from being, on a specific market, united by such economic links that, by virtue of that fact, together they hold a dominant position *vis-à-vis* the other operators on the same market". The Court then gave as an example a situation "where two or more independent undertakings jointly have, through agreements or licences, a technological lead affording them the power to behave to an appreciable extent independently of their competitors, their customers and ultimately of their consumers". In *Almelo*[189] the Court of Justice held that in order for a collective dominant position to exist the undertakings in the Group must be linked in such a way that they adopt the same conduct upon the market.[190] In *Centro Servizi Spediporto* [191] the Court of Justice repeated the definition given in *Almelo*. The Court held that national legislation which provided for the fixing of road-haulage tariffs by the public authorities could not be regarded as placing economic agents in a collective dominant position characterised by the absence of competition between them simply because those agents, in complying with the tariffs, eradicated price competition. A necessary condition, therefore, of joint dominance is the existence of "economic links" between the undertakings. Since a wide variety of links exist in practice between businesses, this phrase merits further examination.

(1) Links due to the oligopolistic nature of the market

6.111 Since it is unlikely that parallel action in the absence of concertation could be condemned under Article 85, an important question is whether Article 86 can be used to control oligopolistic markets. Is the interdependence between undertakings which is often seen in an oligopolistic market sufficient on its own to satisfy the requirement of an economic link? The Commission decision in *Italian Flat Glass*[192] found that three glass producers enjoyed a collectively dominant position on the market as well as forming a concerted practice contrary to Article 85(1). It did so largely on the basis of the structure of the market. The Commission held that the producers' collective dominant position derived from the fact that their combined market share was very high, that they were able to pursue a commercial policy that was not dependent on market trends and the conditions

cont.
undertakings in the group must be linked in such a way that they adopt the same conduct on the market". The ECJ, disappointingly, failed then to elaborate on what those "links" might be, stating in the following paragraph that it was in that case a matter for the national court to consider. For an analysis of the case law prior to these judgments, see M. Schödermeier, "Collective dominance revisited: an analysis of the EC Commission's new concepts of oligopoly control" [1990] ECLR 28.

186 See R. Whish and B. Sufrin, "Oligopolistic markets and EC competition law" (1992) 12 YEL 59.

187 *Sixteenth Report on Competition Policy*.

188 T-68, 77 and 78/89 *Societa Italiano Vetro SpA* v *Commission* [1992] ECR II-1403 [1992] 5 CMLR 302.

189 Case C-393/92 *Alemlo* [1994] ECR I-1477, 1519, 1520.

190 In this regard citing Case 30/87 *Bodson* [1988] ECR 2479, para. 22.

191 Case C-96/94 *Centro Servizi Spediporto Sri* [1995] ECR I-2883.

192 OJ 1992 L 134/1.

of competition and that they presented themselves on the market as a single economic entity. The Court of First Instance overturned this decision,[193] and indicated that collective dominance could not arise from the structure of the market. The Court stressed that collectively dominant undertakings need be united by economic links, but only gave examples of how this could occur, not a conclusive definition. The examples given were of technological leads enjoyed through agreements or licences. Thus if there are technology sharing agreements or licences, then that would come within the Court's concept of what was necessary to establish collective dominance. But it is perfectly open to argument that other economic links suffice, and maybe it is not completely out of the question still to argue that links through oligopolistic interdependence are sufficient, as the Commission itself had held in its decision. The test described by the Court of Justice in *Almelo* and *Centro Servizi Spediporto* is seemingly wider than that set out by the CFI in *Italian Flat Glass.*

(2) Links though share-holdings

6.112 If undertakings are linked so closely that they are considered to be a single economic entity, it is settled that their position on the market is to be assessed collectively. What, however, if the link through share holdings falls short of the parent subsidiary relationship? In *French West African Shipowners' Committee*[194] the Commission decided that the market position of the members of the ship owners' committee had to be assessed collectively. One of the reasons given for this was that the members were connected to varying degrees through shareholdings.

(3) An agreement between undertakings

6.113 In *Italian Flat Glass*[195] the Court of First Instance stated that for the "purposes of establishing an infringement of Article 86 of the Treaty, it is not sufficient ... to 'recycle' the facts constituting an infringement of Article 85, deducing from them the finding that the parties to an agreement or to an unlawful practice jointly hold a substantial share of the market, that by virtue of the fact alone they hold a collective dominant position, and that their behaviour constitutes an abuse of that collective dominant position". Thus, the mere existence of an agreement between the parties, even if that agreement is anti-competitive does not, *per se*, constitute a sufficient link for the purpose of joint dominance. This does not mean, however, that an *agreement* cannot operate to establish requisite economic links since if this were the case the CFI could not have held that agreements leading to technology sharing could not give rise to joint dominance. In *Gøttrup Klim*[196] the Court of Justice accepted that a purchasing co-operative, comprising many different individual undertakings as members, could itself enjoy a dominant position and in arriving at this conclusion the Court was not concerned with the notion of joint or collective dominance.

I. Overlap Between EC and UK Law

6.114 A number of practical points may be made with respect to the boundaries between EC and UK law.

[193] T-68, 77 and 78/89 *Societa Italiano Vetro SpA* v *Commission* [1992] ECR II-1403 [1992] 5 CMLR 302.
[194] OJ 1989 L33/44.
[195] T-68, 77 and 78/89 *Societa Italiano Vetro SpA* v *Commission* [1992] ECR II-1403 [1992] 5 CMLR 302.
[196] Case C-250/92 [1994] ECR I-5641, 5690, 5691.

1. *"May affect trade between Member States": Overlapping Jurisdiction*

6.115 The words "may affect trade between Member States" have already been examined in the context of Article 85 and 86 (see above). In essence the words differentiate those parochial agreements that are the province of the national authorities from those agreements in which the Community also has an interest. Nevertheless there are many agreements which the OFT deal with under the RTPA 1976 that are large enough to be of interest to the Commission. An agreement entered into by UK parties alone can still affect inter-state trade even if the agreement is expressed to apply to the UK alone. This is because such an agreement may hinder exporters abroad from selling in the UK. A good example of such cases may be found under section 29 RTPA 1976 which empowers the Secretary of State to exempt from registration under the RTPA 1976 agreements of substantial importance to the national economy. The section is administered by the Department of Trade and Industry (DTI) in London who advise the Secretary of State. An agreement of substantial importance to the national economy will invariably have repercussions on the EC market. Section 29 agreements are usually dealt with by the DTI as high priority matters and a decision granting exemption may arise in only a few weeks. Negotiations with the Commission can last months or even years. Consequently the DTI will grant a section 29 exemption even though no positive blessing has as yet been received from Brussels.[197]

6.116 Where a clash between EC law and UK law occurs, for example, with the EC granting an exemption under Article 85(3) and the UK authorities seeking to strike down an agreement, EC law should take precedence.[198] The OFT is sensitive to the potential for conflict which, in practice, rarely arises. It is even less likely in future now that the new class of non-notifiable agreements has been created, removing the obligation to furnish particulars to the OFT under the RTPA 1976 agreements covered by an EC block exemption.[199] However, provision exists under the RTPA 1976 for resolution of the conflict. Section 21(1)(a) RTPA 1976 empowers the Director General to refrain from taking proceedings before the Restrictive Practices Court in so far as he considers it appropriate to so refrain having regard to directly applicable EC legislation. Where an English court (as opposed to the OFT) is examining an agreement under Article 85(1), it has no authority to apply the exemption criteria in Article 85(3). That is the exclusive prerogative of the Commission. The national court may, however, suspend or stay proceedings in order to allow the parties to obtain the Commission's opinion.[200] If a formal decision is issued by the Commission exempting an agreement under Article 85(3), then the national court is bound by the doctrine of the supremacy of Community law to respect the exemption. The Commission have issued a Notice summarising its interpretation of these principles,[201] which is discussed at paras. 7.3–7.8. The English courts have shown themselves reluctant in practice to seek the opinion of the Commission. Where the view of the Commission has been evident from documents, such as correspondence, the English courts are willing to take note of the opinion but have not to date accepted that the view binds. Where there

[197] This "don't wait" approach would appear to be in line with the thinking of the European Court. See Case 48/72 *Brasserie de Haecht* v *Wilkins II* [1973] ECR 77 at p. 87 para. 11 of the judgment.

[198] See Case 14/68 *Walt Wilhelm* v *Bundeskartellamt* [1969] CMLR 100; [1969] ECR 1.

[199] Restrictive Trade Practices (Non-notifiable Agreements) (EC Block Exemptions) Order 1996, S.I. 1996 No. 349, discussed at paras. 2.250 and following.

[200] See *Brasserie de Haecht* v *Wilkins II*, above; C-234/89 *Delimitis* [1991] ECR I-935, para. 52.

[201] Notice on Co-operation between National Courts and the Commission in applying Arts. 85 and 86 of the EEC Treaty, 1993 OJ C39/6. Paras. 17–32 deal with the application of Arts. 85 and 86 by national courts. Paras. 33–42 outline the ways in which the Commission envisages it may help national courts in the application of competition laws.

is genuine doubt about the legal principles to be applied the courts are more likely to refer the issues arising under Article 177 EC to the Court of Justice. The national court must take cognisance of the Commission's view or opinion when deciding whether to stay proceedings. Where the Commission has actually taken a decision prohibiting an agreement, or imposing a fine the position may be different.

6.117 The position of a decision of the Commission which has been affirmed by both the Court of First Instance and the Court of Justice, before the national courts was considered in *Iberian UK Ltd* v *BPB Industries plc and British Gypsum Ltd.*[202] In that case the Plaintiff sought to rely on a decision of the Commission finding an infringement of Article 85 on the part of the Defendant which decision had been affirmed by both appeal courts in Luxembourg. A number of preliminary issues were ordered to be tried namely: whether the findings of fact set out in the decision, the judgment of the CFI, the opinion of the Advocate General and the judgment of the Court of Justice were admissible in the national proceedings; whether the decision, the judgment of the CFI, the opinion of the Advocate General and the judgment of the Court of Justice were conclusive as to those facts in the proceedings; whether the conclusions as to the interpretation and/or applicability of Article 86 of the EC Treaty set out in the decision, the judgment of the CFI, the opinion of the Advocate General and the judgment of the Court of Justice were admissible in the proceedings; and whether those conclusions were conclusive of such issues in the proceedings. The judge considered first whether the proceedings before the Commission, the CFI and the Court of Justice in relation to competition cases were of such a nature as to fit within the doctrine of issue estoppel. Notwithstanding the similarities between the case before the national court and the Community Institutions the judge held that there was no issue estoppel. The judge then went on to consider a broader approach namely that even if the facts did not fall squarely within the doctrine of issue estoppel whether they were such as to invite the application of the general public policy principles underlying *res judicata*. In this regard the judge considered that the central question to be asked was as follows:

> "In all of the circumstances of this case should the complainant and investigatee be allowed to open up and dispute in these proceedings the final conclusions of fact or law reached in competition proceedings in Brussels and Luxembourg? If the answer to that is in the negative, it does not matter whether it is categorised as a part of the law of res judicata— i.e. that the complainant and investigatee are bound by those conclusions—or as part of the law of the abuse of process—i.e. that any attempt by either of them to challenge the conclusions is improper. In either case the same public policy considerations are at work."[203]

6.118 The judge then proceeded to consider the nature of the complaint before the Commission, the special characteristics of European competition proceedings and in particular the duty of the national court to avoid a risk of conflict with decisions or likely decisions of the Commission. He then concluded that the Courts should take all reasonable steps to avoid or reduce the risk of arriving at a conclusion which was at variance with the decision of the Commission or judgments on appeal therefrom and that except in the clearest cases of breach or non-breach, it would be a proper exercise of discretion to stay national proceedings to await the outcome of the European proceedings. Having come to the conclusion, that it would be wrong to permit the Defendant to re-litigate the same point that it had lost in Europe, the Judge considered also whether the Defendants were bound by the Commission decision upon the legal basis that a decision, pursuant to Article 189 EC, binds the addressee and it was therefore not open to them to assert that

[202] [1996] 2 CMLR 601, Laddie J.
[203] [1996] 2 CMLR 601, 619.

those decisions or their underlying reasons were wrong in any national court. The judge concluded that it would be an abuse of process to allow the Defendants to mount a collateral attack on the Commission decision in proceedings against any party before any national court. It follows from the above that, prima facie, Commission decisions and all proceedings subsequent of that decision on appeal, are admissible and conclusive, at least to the extent that an undertaking has been found guilty of an infringement by the Commission and that decision has been upheld on appeal.

2. *The Direct Effect of Article 85 and 86 EC: Eurochallenges*

6.119 Article 85 and 86 EC have direct effect, i.e. they may be pleaded as sword or shield by private parties before national courts.[204] Actions based upon breach of directly effective EC law are becoming increasingly common with parties also settling out of court on the basis of Articles 85 and 86.

J. Notification to the European Commission

6.120 Under the RTPA 1976 parties entering restrictive agreements *must* furnish details of their agreements to the OFT for registration. No equivalent duty exists in EC law though there are strong incentives to notify an agreement to the Commission. Some of the practical issues are discussed below.[205]

1. *Form of Notification*

6.121 Agreements are notified to the Commission on Form A/B. Details of this form and its contents are given in ensuing sections.

2. *Types of Notification*

6.122 The main purpose of notifying an agreement to the Commission is to obtain a "negative clearance" (a ruling that the agreement is not within Article 85(1)) or to obtain an exemption under Article 85(3) on the basis that although the agreement is caught by Article 85(1) it satisfies the criteria for exemption in Article 85(3) EC. Form A/B is used for both types of notification. "Notification" is a loose term describing the furnishing of copies of the agreement and of certain other information to the Commission.

(1) Notification to obtain a negative clearance

6.123 Under Regulation 17/62/EEC the Commission has power to, "certify that, on the basis of the facts in its possession, there are no grounds under Article 85(1) or Article 86 of the Treaty for action on its part in respect of an agreement, decision or practice".[206] This certification that Article 85 or 86 is inapplicable is the negative clearance. A decision of

[204] See Case 127/73 *BRT* v *SABAM* [1974] 2 CMLR 258; [1974] ECR 51.

[205] For a more detailed account of procedure in EC competition law cases see Kerse, *EC Antitrust Procedure* (3rd edn. 1994). This comprehensive text examines EC competition procedure in an exhaustive and readable fashion. Businessmen seeking a nuts and bolts account of EC competition law procedure may refer to this work for guidance.

[206] Reg. 17/62/EEC, OJ Spec. edn, 1959–62, p. 87, Art. 2.

the Commission granting this clearance will state why there are no grounds for Article 85 or 86 to apply. Form A/B must be used where negative clearance is sought for an agreement to which Article 85 might apply.[207] Form A/B need not be used for cases possibly falling under Article 86, though use of Form A/B making changes as appropriate is often viewed as a useful method of notification in Article 86 cases.[208] In any event applications for negative clearance in respect of Article 86 must contain a full exposition of the relevant facts including an account of the practices in question and of the markets in' question. Parties should be liberal in furnishing data; the Commission decide to grant negative clearance on the basis of facts in their possession and these largely depend on the information given by the parties. Facts should be accurate. Fines may be imposed for intentionally or negligently furnishing erroneous or misleading data.[209]

6.124 In negative clearance cases where the Commission intend to grant a favourable decision they will publish in the Official Journal a summary of the relevant application and will invite interested third parties to submit their comments. A time period of not less than a month is given for these comments to be made. This publication is required to safeguard the confidentially legitimate business secrets of the parties. Often in the notice the Commission expressly state that they intend to adopt a favourable attitude to the application.

(2) Notification to obtain an exemption

6.125 Parties may notify their agreement on the basis that although it falls within Article 85(1) it may be suitable for exemption under Article 85(3). This procedure is not the same as an application for negative clearance. In that case the application is to establish the non-applicability of competition rules; in the case of an application for an exemption the parties may accept that Article 85(1) applies to their agreement but contend that it is suitable for exemption under Article 85(3). A decision granting exemption cannot be made by the Commission unless the agreement has been notified by the parties.[210] The fact that an agreement obtains exemption under Article 85(3) does not necessarily exclude the possibility of Article 86 applying though, in practice, this is unlikely since the Commission cannot grant exemption if the agreement eliminates an excessive amount of competition and if such competition is eliminated exemption would not normally be granted so that Article 86 would not become an issue.[211] Parties need not apply for an exemption if they can fit their agreement within the terms of a block exemption. These are regulations which lay down criteria which if met by an agreement entitle the parties to assume that exemption under Article 85(3) applies to their agreement. The fact that an agreement enjoys the benefit of the block exemption does not preclude the application of Article 86 to a party to the agreement.[212] Moreover, parties to agreements need not notify their agreement if it is of a type specified in Article 4(2) of Regulation 17/62/EEC. This exempts certain specified agreements from notification.

These categories of exempt agreements are discussed below.

[207] Reg. 27/62/EC, OJ 1962, 35/1118, Art. 4(1) (concerning the form of notifications).
[208] *ibid.*, Art. 4(4).
[209] Reg.17/62/EEC Art. 15(1)(a).
[210] *ibid.*, Art. 4(1), see Case 126/80 *Salonia* v *Poidomani* [1982] 1 CMLR 64; [1981] ECR 1563 at paras. 28–31 of the judgment.
[211] Case 27/76 *United Brands* v *Commission* [1978] 1 CMLR 429; [1978] ECR 207 at paras. 291, 292 of the judgment; Case 85/76 *Hoffman-La Roche and Co. AG* v *Commission* [1979] 3 CMLR 211; [1979] ECR 461 at para. 116.
[212] T-51/89 *Tetra Pak (I)* [1990] ECR II-309 [1991] 4 CMLR 334.

3. *Why Notify: Main Practical Benefits*

(1) Exemption under Article 85(3)

6.126 Exemption under Article 85(3) is unobtainable unless an agreement has been notified.

(2) Protection in national courts

6.127 National courts must respect an exemption granted under Article 85(3) and such a cartel may be enforced before national courts without fear of the other side pleading a Euro-defence, i.e. that they are not bound by the agreement because it is caught by Article 85(1) and hence void under Article 85(2) EC. The national court, if it believes the decision to be incorrect, may refer the question of the validity of the decision to the Court of Justice under Article 177EC and in very exceptional cases is empowered to suspend, on an interim basis pending the ruling on invalidity, the decisions or a part of it. However, save in these exceptional circumstances a national court may not take a decision which notes a conflict with that of the Commission. An agreement that has not been notified is not secure from Article 85(2), a national court can not grant exemption under Article 85(3) and may thus be forced to strike down an agreement under Article 85(2) even though the national court considers the agreement to be capable of exemption. However, the court may decide to suspend the hearing to enable the parties to obtain the Commission's opinion though it is not bound to adopt this course of action. A court which stays its proceedings in order to permit the parties, or some of them, to notify the Commission may still permit part of the proceedings to continue. For example, if an agreement is notified after many years of operation a Commission decision granting exemptions would only be from the date of the notification and would not be retroactive (save exceptionally under Article 4 of Regulation 17/62/EEC) and, accordingly, would not protect the parties from damages claims arising prior to notification.

(3) Negative clearance

6.128 Notification enables the parties to seek a Commission negative clearance decision that their agreement is not within Article 85 or 86 EC. Such a decision does not bind a national court though a court should endeavour to avoid a conflict with the Commission.

(4) Fines

6.129 Under Article 15(5) of Regulation 17/62/EEC fines may not be imposed on parties to agreements notified to the Commission in respect of conduct operative from the date of the notification to the date of a decision in respect of Article 85(3). Immunity from fine does not exist for the period prior to notification nor does it apply to any activity not strictly defined in the notification documents. A mere application for negative clearance, however, affords no immunity from fines. Most parties couple their application for negative clearance with one for Article 85(3) exemption in order to get around this difficulty. Joint applications are envisaged in form A/B.

6.130 Under Article 15(6) of Regulation 17/62 the Commission may by decision withdraw immunity from fines from a notified agreement. The Commission has used Article 15(6) where it has informed the undertaking concerned that after preliminary examination it is of the opinion that Article 85(1) applies and that application of Article 85(3) is not justified, as a means whereby the Commission can express its view upon the exemptibility of a notified agreement rapidly. The procedure under Article 15(6) is relatively short since it does not require consultation by the Commission of the Advisory Committee. In *Dutch Cranes*[213] the FNK, an association of firms that hire out mobile cranes, contained provisions in its statutes reserving membership to companies established in the Netherlands and also requiring members to acquire additional cranes only from other members and to charge reasonable hiring prices. The hiring of extra cranes from other crane-hirers occurred on a large scale in the sector. On 13 January 1992 11 main hire companies complained to the Commission that the FNK in conjunction with a foundation known as the SCK (which had as its object the guaranteeing of the quality and competence of affiliated firms which for the most part comprised firms which were members of FNK) restricted competition by excluding non-member firms from the mobile crane-hire trade by fixing prices. FNK and SCK subsequently notified their statutes and rules. The complainants, at the same time as lodging a complaint, commenced proceedings before the national courts. These proceedings led ultimately to the suspension of the hire ban until the Commission had the opportunity to adopt a decision on the matter. The Commission concluded that since the application of Article 85(3) seemed plainly to be excluded, the immunity from fines should be withdrawn pursuant to Article 15(6) in respect of the notified hire ban.

(5) Establishing credibility with the Commission

6.131 If parties notify their agreement to the Commission they have the advantage of having demonstrated openness and good faith. As such they are more likely to have their version of the facts and assessment of the market accepted. If it becomes clear that parties have only notified because they have heard that the Commission are "on to them" or that a rival or customer has complained to the Commission, the latter may be unlikely to accept at face value the parties' version of events when it is notified.

(6) Old agreements

6.132 In the case of an "old" agreement duly notified to the Commission provisional validity exists, see paras. 6.78–6.81. Moreover, the Commission may under Article 7 of Regulation 17/62/EC, validate an old agreement that has been modified to fit within Article 85(3). This provision provides an incentive for old cartels and agreements not qualifying for exemption to modify to obtain exemption. If they modify, the Commission *may* grant exemption with retroactive effect, i.e. for the period during which they were not notified.[214] As time marches on this provision has decreasing relevance as "old" agreements become scarcer.[215] A Commission decision under this provision does not prejudice the interests of third parties or affect pending legal actions.[216]

(7) Accession agreements

6.133 It is believed that the same principles as apply to old agreements apply to accession agreements, i.e. agreements which become subject to competition rules as a result of accession of a state to the EC.[217]

[213] OJ 1994 L117/30, 13 April 1994.

[214] There is no right to require the Commission to grant retroactive exemption: e.g. *ASPA* [1970] CMLR D25; *SUPEXIE* [1971] CMLR D1; *CEMATAX* [1973] CMLR D135; *Davidson Rubber* [1972] CMLR D52; *Fine Paper* [1972] CMLR D94.

[215] See, e.g. *CEMATAX* [1973] CMLR D135; *Davidson Rubber* [1972] CMLR D52.

[216] *Isbecque* [1965] CMLR 242.

[217] See Commission's *Third Report on Competition Policy* (1973), para. 5(a).

4. *Agreements Exempt from Notification under Article 4(2) of Regulation 17/62/EEC*

6.134 Article 4(2) of Regulation 17/62/EEC exempts from the need to notify four categories of agreement because they are considered only minimally disruptive of competition. An agreement exempt is only free from the duty to notify, it is *not* free from the prohibition in Article 85(1). To obtain exemption under Article 85(3) parties must still notify the agreement. Though, of course if the agreement fits within a block exemption it need not be notified and Article 85(3) exemption may be assumed. One may ask what benefit Article 4 of Regulation 17/62/EEC confers. One answer is immunity from fine; Article 4 covers types of agreement generally considered to be innocuous. Non-notification is hence not viewed as serious. Should the Commission subsequently decide that the agreement is restrictive it may refrain from imposing fines, though the European Court has held that even where an agreement satisfies Article 4(2) the Commission may impose fines in respect of unnotified agreements.[218] The Commission did in fact impose fines in *Belgian Roofing Felt*[219] in respect of unnotified agreements exempt from notification by virtue of Article 4(2). The parties may, if they wish, notify the agreement to the Commission who will probably deal with the matter by means of a comfort letter. The second answer is that if an agreement is notified it may be given retroactive exemption i.e. to the date the agreement was entered into and not only from the date of the notification. Four categories of agreement fall within Article 4(2). These may essentially be summarised as:

(i) purely domestic agreements;
(ii) certain restrictions on price accepted by only one party;
(iii) certain intellectual property agreements; and
(iv) certain small scale joint ventures.

(1) Purely domestic agreements

6.135 Article 4(2)(1) exempts from notification agreements, decisions and concerted practices where:

> "enterprises of only one Member State take part and the agreements, decisions or practices relate neither to imports nor to exports between Member States."

The test here is legal domicile of the undertaking and not the location of management even though the latter is the nerve centre of the company. The Court has held that an agreement which operates locally in a Member State does not relate to imports or exports even though the contract goods are imported. Thus if X in the UK is an importer of German radios and appoints Y to be his local dealer in a small area of the UK, then the agreement is exempt from notification since it has only local operation; it is immaterial that the product is imported.[220] However, this might not be the case if the agree-

[218] Joined Cases 240–242, 261, 262, 268, 269/82 *Stichting Sigarettenindustrie* v *Commission* [1985] ECR 3831, [1987] 3 CMLR 661.

[219] [1991] 4 CMLR 130.

[220] See Case 63/75 *Fonderies Roubaix-Wattrelos* v *Fonderies A. Roux* [1976] 1 CMLR 538; [1976] ECR 111 at paras. 6–8 of the judgment. But cf. WQ No. 440/70, OJ 1971 C 29/9—Commission of opinion that an agreement should be notified where it differentiates between products made and sold in the domestic state and products imported from or exported to other Member States.

ment attempts appreciably to restrict parallel imports, on whatever scale.[221] Indeed, any attempt to protect a national market from imports will fall outside Article 4(2).[222]

6.136 The exemption and benefit of Article 4(2) may not be obtained simply by a foreign parent delegating the negotiation and conclusion of contracts in a Member State to local agents or subsidiaries there. Thus, if X, a large UK parent, instructs its subsidiary Y in France to enter a series of local agreements then Article 4(2) affords no sanctuary. The agreements will be treated as if it were entered by X and not Y.[223] Article 4(2)(1) has been useful in the past in respect of patent licences between two undertakings in Member States. To be exempt the licence must not contain any export restrictions or other disincentives.[224] Where in doubt parties may well decide to notify their agreement as a precautionary measure. Indeed Form A/B makes special provision for parties to express the fact that notification is viewed by them as a precautionary measure (see paras. 6.146–6.148 below).

(2) Certain restrictions on price accepted by only one party

6.137 Article 4(2)(2)(a) exempts from notification agreements etc. where:

> "not more than two undertakings are party thereto, and the agreements only restrict the freedom of one party to the contract in determining the prices or conditions of business upon which the goods which he has obtained from the other party to the contract may be resold ..."

Vertical fixing of resale prices and terms and conditions of trade are exempt from notification. It should be noted that resale price maintenance is regulated in the UK by the Resale Prices Act 1976. Indeed, the Commission and Court are hostile to vertical resale price control and the article has thus marginal significance. Under Article 4(2)(2)(a) only agreements setting resale prices and terms concerning goods which one party purchases from the other are excepted from notification. This exception does not apply to services though there is no logical reason for the distinction. To be exempt the agreement must relate to the fixing of resale prices or conditions exclusively. If additional restrictions exist in the agreement, e.g. non-competition clauses, restrictions of customer clauses, restrictions on market in which goods may be sold clauses, then no exemption lies.

6.138 The agreement must be between *two* persons only and the restrictions accepted by one party only.[225] It matters not that the parties are incorporated and domiciled in different Member States. Under this article a single supplier may impose identical restrictions on all its customers (dealers) and the article applies. Thus, if supplier X enters ten different agreements with wholesalers which fix resale prices, this system comprises simply ten separate agreements of two parties. One does not view the agreements collectively.[226]

[221] 96-102, 104-105, 108 and 110/82 *IAZ International Belgium* v *Commission* [1983] ECR 3369, [1984] 3 CMLR 276, para 35.

[222] See Commission decisions in *Meldoc* [1989] 4 CMLR 853 and *Belgian Roofing Felt* [1991] 4 CMLR 130.

[223] See e.g. *BP Kemi–DDSF* [1979] 3 CMLR 684.

[224] e.g. *Vaessen–Moris* [1979] 1 CMLR 511.

[225] See e.g. Cases 209–215 and 218/78 *FEDETAB* v *Commission* [1981] 3 CMLR 134; [1980] ECR 3125 at paras. 54–56 of the judgment.

[226] See Case 1/70 *Parfums Marcel Rochas* v *Bitsch* [1971] CMLR 104; [1970] ECR 515 at p. 524. More generally an export ban imposed by a supplier on a purchaser is not a "condition of business" for the purposes of Art. 4(2)(2)—*Moet et Chandon Ltd* [1982] 2 CMLR 166 at para. 15 of the decision.

(3) Certain intellectual property agreements

6.139 Article 4(2)(2)(b) has two elements to it. It ponders that agreements are exempt from notification where:

> "not more than two undertakings are party thereto, and the agreements only impose restrictions on the exercise of the rights of the assignee or user of industrial property rights— in particular patents, utility models, designs or trade marks—or of the person entitled under a contract to the assignment, or grant, or the right to use a method of manufacture or knowledge relating to the use and to the application of industrial processes."

This section applies to: patents, utility models, designs, trade marks, and other intellectual property rights, for example, copyright[227] and know-how. It is generally considered that this exemption has very limited application.

6.140 Article 4(2)(2)(b) first element only applies to exempt restrictions on the exercise of the "rights" of the intellectual property. The following terms and restrictions applicable to a licensor (party granting the licence) would *not* fall within the sanctuary of the article since that provision applies only to the use of the intellectual property by a licensee or assignee:[228]

- restriction on licensor not to grant any other licence, i.e. licensor grants licensee an exclusive licence;
- restriction on licensor not to grant additional licences to third parties without original licensee's consent;
- obligation on licensor to protect licensee's territory;
- restriction on licensor requiring him to refrain from producing or selling competing products (i.e. non-competition clauses);
- restriction on licensor requiring him to refrain from undercutting licensee's price or requiring him to sell at a fixed price.

6.141 Article 4(2)(2)(b) second element only exempts from notification restraints upon the licensee's or assignee's behaviour (i.e. not the original holder of the right). The only restrictions benefiting are those which relate exclusively to the rights of the licensee, user or assignee to "use a method of manufacture or knowledge relating to the use and to the application of industrial processes". This also is a narrow exemption. The following have been held not to be exempt:

- no-challenge clauses;[229]
- exclusive purchasing requirement on licensee with respect to products not covered by the patent;
- obligation on licensee to calculate royalties by reference to selling price of completed product produced in accordance with a patent;
- obligation on licensee to affix notices about the licence on the finished product;[230]
- obligation on licensee to acknowledge trade marks not relevant to the licence.

It is generally advised that no great reliance should be placed on this exemption. The Commission have taken a narrow view of it.[231] Reference to Commission decisions on the licensing and assignment of intellectual property rights should be made and to the block exemption on technology transfer agreements discussed in Chapter 13.[232]

[227] See 193/83 *Windsurfing* [1986] ECR 611, [1986] 3 CMLR 489.
[228] *ibid.*
[229] *ibid.*
[230] *ibid.* See also *Toltecs/Dorcet* [1983] 1 CMLR 421 at p. 426.
[231] See e.g. *Burroughs/Delplanque* [1972] CMLR D67; *AOIP/Beyrard* [1976] 1 CMLR D14.
[232] See at paras. 13.18–13.124.

(4) Certain joint ventures: standards and types

6.142 Under Article 4(3)(a) certain joint ventures are exempt from notification. These include agreements which have as their *sole* object: "the development or uniform application of standards or types."[233] The word "standards" usually refers to parts of specific products whereas "types" applies to whole products or aggregates of products. This distinction is not absolute, the European DIN (industrial) standards include not only parts but also whole products. The distinction in practice may be discarded since agreements relating to specific product parts and to whole products may be exempt; though only agreements relating to development or application may be exempt. Thus, an agreement between X and Y to charge a certain price for products of a certain standard is not exempt. The subject matter of the agreement is irrelevant, it can relate to shape, colour, size, form, design, technical levels, components, etc. The number and domicile of the participants to the agreement is also irrelevant.

6.143 The following comments apply also to paras. 6.144 and 6.145. To be exempt the agreement must have the *sole* object specified in the Article. This is a serious limiting factor; the existence of any other objective in an agreement negates application of the exemption. Both R&D and specialisation agreements have specific block exemptions devoted to them thus rendering the Article 4 exemption somewhat redundant. Both block exemptions are discussed in Chapter 12 on joint ventures and co-operation to which reference may be made. In terms of overlap between these "sole object" provisions, an agreement between X and Y which has specialisation and R&D features exempt under the respective parts of the article will *not* be free from notification since the article only exempts an agreement which has as its main object one of the objects laid down in Article 4(3)(a)–(c).

(5) Certain joint ventures: research and development

6.144 Agreements having as their *sole* object, "joint research and development" are exempt from notification under Article 4(3)(b). The agreement must thus not incorporate any restrictions on production or sale or general distribution since these do not relate solely to the R&D. The number of participants and their domicile is irrelevant.

(6) Certain joint ventures: specialisation agreements

6.145 Certain specialisation agreements are exempt from notification under Article 4(3)(c) of Regulation 17/62/EEC. To earn exemption the agreement must satisfy certain quantitative criteria. The article excludes agreements having as their sole object:

> "Specialisation in the manufacture of products, including agreements necessary for the achievement thereof;
> – where the products which are the object of specialisation do not, in a substantial part of the Common Market, represent more than 15 per cent of the volume of business done in identical products or those considered by the consumers to be similar by reason of their characteristics, price and use, and
> – where the total annual turnover of the participating undertakings does not exceed 200 million units of account."

Specialisation agreements and the block exemption—Regulation 417/85/EEC—are discussed at paras. 12.199–12.223 on joint ventures and co-operation to which reference may be made. The exemption in the article applies where the agreement concerns specialisation

[233] A similar exemption exists in UK law for goods and services. See ss. 9(5) and 18(5) RTPA 1976 discussed in at paras. 1.96–1.98.

alone. The existence of any other restrictions unrelated to specialisation renders the exemption inapplicable. The Article only applies to products; no exemption exists for services. Agreements "necessary" for the achievement of the specialisation agreements are exempt from notification, e.g. repair and after-sales service agreements and other collateral guarantees. The number and domicile of participants is irrelevant.

K. Form A/B: Method of Notification

1. *Relevance of Form A/B*

6.146 Use of Form A/B is considered an obligatory condition of a proper notification by the European Court who justify their strict line on the necessity of easing the administrative burden of the Commission.[234] If X and Y notify on Form A/B a restrictive agreement, for example, a standard form contract, and then at a later date amend the standard form contract in a material fashion, the new amended standard form contract must also be notified on Form A/B. Parties must not assume that they can obtain Article 85(3) exemption for an amendment simply by sending a copy of the amended agreement to the Commission.[235] Furthermore, even if the Commission, when discussing an amendment with the parties, employ in correspondence the reference number assigned to the original agreement, this does not imply that the Commission will consider the amendment in conjunction with the original agreement. Use of reference numbers is simply an administrative convenience.[236] However, the Court of Justice has held that formal notification on Form A/B to seek an extension of an existing exemption, where the amended version does not differ in principle from the originally notified agreement, is not required.[237] The distinction between notification of new terms and conditions required to be on form A/B and notification of a mere amendment not required on form A/B is too subtle to be left to chance. If at all in doubt about variations and amendments parties should notify the changes on Form A/B.

2. *Contents of Form A/B*

6.147 Form A/B[238] must be completed in conjunction with any additional information required by the Commission.

[234] Case 209–215, 218/78 *FEDETAB and others* v *Commission* [1981] 3 CMLR 134; [1980] ECR 3125 at para. 63 of the judgment: "The use of that form is therefore mandatory and is an essential prior condition for the validity of the notification. It takes account, for the purpose of laying down detailed rules for the application of Art. 85(3), of the need, expressed in Art. 87(2)(b) of the Treaty, to ensure effective supervision and to simplify administration to the greatest possible extent."

[235] e.g. Case 30/78 *Distillers* v *Commission* [1980] 3 CMLR 121; [1980] ECR 2229 at paras. 23, 24 of the judgment, but cf. for a slightly more relaxed view Case 106/79 *VBBB* v *Eldi Records* [1980] 3 CMLR 719; [1980] ECR 1137 where the Court held that where an agreement had been appended to Form A/B which had been fully completed but which was not 100 per cent perfect in its accuracy, this would be counted as proper notification. On this basis, the case can be distinguished from *Distillers* where the amendment, which was of a substantial nature, was not notified on Form A/B.

[236] *ibid.*

[237] See Case 73/74 *Papiers Peints de Belgique* [1974] 2 CMLR D102 on appeal to the Court of Justice [1976] 1 CMLR 589; [1975] ECR 1491.

[238] Form A/B is set out in Reg. 3385/94, OJ 1994 L 377/28, which replaces the original Form A/B provided for by Reg. 27/62, as amended from time to time.

The information required on a Form A/B is summarised below, but this should not be taken as indicating that completion of a Form A/B is an administrative formality. On the contrary, it requires the compilation of a significant amount of information both about the parties to the agreement and the markets in which they operate. Full completion will normally require substantial investment of time and resources, and is not to be undertaken lightly.

The information required falls into the following categories:

(a) identity of an information about the parties submitting the notification;
(b) information on whether any formal submission has been made to any other competition authority;
(c) full details of the agreement being notified, together with a short non-confidential summary for publication in the Official Journal, as part of the Commission's procedure for inviting the views of third parties;
(d) information about the relevant market. More substantial information is required in respect of structural joint ventures seeking accelerated clearance, an option discussed at paras. 12.68–12.71;
(e) statement of reasons for applying for negative clearance and/or exemption; most Form A/Bs are submitted requesting both in the alternative. In practice, a comfort letter rather than a decision will be issued, stating either that the agreement appears to merit clearance or an exemption;
(f) declaration by or on behalf of all notifying parties, stating awareness of liability for fines of up to 5,000 ECUs for intentionally or negligently supplying incorrect or misleading information.

6.148 The form A/B is submitted in one original version, together with 16 copies and three copies of the notifying parties' previous three years annual report and accounts. The Commission also now require three copies of the most recent in-house or external long-term market study or planning document analysing the relevant market and three copies of any internal analysis of the notified agreement. No doubt parties notifying will take this into account in drawing up the terms of reference for any such documents, since failure to appreciate that such documents will be required for the Commission may lead to statements being included which do not reflect the notifying parties' case to best advantage. Indeed, there is a need for certain "political correctness" to be observed in drawing up such documents.

3. *Provisional Immunity from Fines*

6.149 Parties should ensure the accuracy of the details they notify. The Commission may impose financial penalties for the intentional or negligent notification to them of incorrect or misleading information.[239] Once notified an agreement enjoys provisional immunity from fines pending a Commission decision. However, this protection only applies to agreements which fall within the limits of the activity described in the notification.[240] The immunity may however be lifted by decisions under Article 15(6).

[239] Art. 15(1)(a) Reg. 17/62/EEC.
[240] OJ 1989 C26/6.

L. Complaints by Third Parties: Form C

6.150 The making of a complaint is a valid and legitimate aspect of commercial practice. The Commission have developed a form—Form C—for use by complainants. Use of Form C (unlike Form A/B) is non-obligatory; a complaint may be made by simple letter or in any other form. A complaint may even be made anonymously, though in such cases the Commission feel under no obligation to follow up the complaint, although of course they may well do so. Complaints may be made in respect of Articles 85 or 86 EC. Complaints may also be made in respect of a failure by a Member State to comply with Community law and a separate form has been issued which can be used for this purpose.[241] If a complaint is submitted, it is best to follow the form of Form C in order to ensure that the appropriate information is provided.

1. Form of Complaint

(1) Details of complaints

6.151 Complainants should provide identification material which is similar to that needed in Form A/B. Details of the alleged infringement should be given setting out the facts which make up the alleged infringement. The Commission further require information on the extent to which trade between Member States may be affected.

(2) Existence of legitimate interest

6.152 To submit a complaint a legitimate interest must be established. This is not a difficult requirement. Indeed, if a person with only a purely theoretical interest in a case were to submit a complaint and it had clear validity then the Commission would most likely respond. A complainant may be a natural person, a company, an association, a trade union, or a consumer association.[242] A legitimate interest exists if the complainant will or might suffer prejudice from the complained of parties' conduct. Thus, customers, rivals, suppliers, etc. are covered. Even parties to an agreement itself may complain.[243] A complaint under Form C may only be made in respect of the competition rules in Articles 85 or 86 EC. In respect of other matters, e.g. agriculture, complaints would be made to relevant directorates of the Commission other than that responsible for competition.[244]

(3) Evidence

6.153 The Commission requires information concerning persons able to testify to the facts set out in the complaint and concerning persons affected by the alleged breach. A complainant should send all relevant documentary evidence, for example, texts of agreements, minutes

241 See e.g. Case 113/73 *Unione Nazionale Consumatori* [1976] 1 CMLR 295; [1973] ECR 1465 at pp, 1468, 1469. See also *Distillers* [1978] 1 CMLR 400 (distributor whose exports were curtailed by an export ban); *Johnson and Johnson* [1981] 2 CMLR 287 (importer suffering consequences of an export ban from the producers market); *Dutch Bicycles* [1978] 2 CMLR 194 (trade association member complaining of punishment by association) *Continental Can* [1972] CMLR D11 (target company threatened with take-over); Case 26/76 *Metro–SB—Grossmarkie* v *Commission* [1978] 2 CMLR 1; [1977] ECR 1875 (wholesaler); *Michelin* [1982] 1 CMLR 643 (wholesaler against his supplier's discount practices) *GVL* [1982] 1 CMLR 221 (pop group refused services of royalty collecting association); *British Telecommunications* [1983] 1 CMLR 457 (message transmitting company hindered by restrictive policy of nationalised industry).

242 *FRUBO* [1974] 2 CMLR D89.

243 Using the form published at OJ 1989 C26/6.

244 See WQ No. 1012/80, OJ 1980 C316/12.

of negotiations and meetings, terms of transactions, business documents and circulars. Any pertinent statistics may be submitted, e.g. in respect of, price trends, terms of transactions, terms of supply or sale, etc. Any technical data pertaining to production or sale, etc. are of value to the Commission. The complainant might also name experts able to supply this information. The Commission will be interested in all approaches made and all steps taken prior to the complaint with a view to terminating the infringement. Thus results of proceedings commenced before national authorities or complaints thereto should be furnished. Copies of Form C may be obtained from the Commission's Information Offices in each Member State and also outside the EC. In London forms may be obtained from: 8 Storey's Gate, London SW1P 3AT. Tel: (0171) 222 8122. There are also offices in Belfast, Cardiff and Edinburgh.

(4) Time

6.154 The processing of a case can span three months to three years and more. Where a complainant can establish the need for rapid Commission action the process may be expedited.[245] There exists the possibility for the Commission to take a decision ordering interim measures. Complainants should indicate in the complaint whether they wish the Commission to consider this option.

(5) Refusal by Commission to follow up a complaint

6.155 The Commission's resources do not enable it to investigate every complaint. However, it is under a duty to consider every complaint, in order that it may assess whether it would be appropriate to open an investigation. In making that assessment, it has stated in a Notice that it will reserve investigations for those cases which have "particular political, economic or legal significance for the Community".[246] The *Automec II*[247] judgment of the Court of First Instance, which laid the foundations for the Notice established that in cases where adequate remedies and protection exist before national courts the Commission may prioritise its workload. The ruling gives some guidance as to assessing the Community interest. It mentioned the importance of the alleged infringement to the Community and whether it would be possible to establish an infringement. In the case, the dispute was essentially contractual and already in the national court, so there seemed no reason why the competition law aspects should not also be considered by the national court.

6.156 It is therefore important to address the issue of the Community interest when making a complaint. Factors that may weigh with the Commission, beyond any particular political, economic or legal considerations special to the case, are the difficulty in obtaining evidence to prove an infringement under national evidentiary rules and the difficulty in enforcing a judgment obtained in the court of one Member State throughout the Community.

6.157 The Commission may also refuse to pursue a complaint where there appear to be "insufficient grounds" for initiating the procedure for establishing the existence of a breach of the rules.[248] Where the Commission reject the complaint they must inform the com-

[245] 210/81 *Demo-Studio Schmidt* [1983] ECR, [1984] 1 CMLR 63.

[246] Notice on Co-operation between national courts and the Commission in applying Arts. 85 and 86 of the EEC Treaty, 1993 OJ C39/6, para. 14. The Court of First Instance's decision in Case T-24/90 *Automec II* [1992] 5 CMLR 431 approved the Commission's practice of giving different degrees of priority to competition complaints. See further paras. 7.3–7.8. See also the Commission's draft "Notice on Cooperation between National Competition Authorities and the Commission in handling cases falling within the scope of Articles 85 or 86 of the EC Treaty", OJ 1996 C 262/5, esp. para II/2.

[247] Case T-24/90 *Automec II* [1992] ECR II-2223 [1992] 5 CMLR 431.

[248] Art. 6 of Reg. 99/63/EEC.

plainant of their reasons and allow the latter to submit any further comments in writing.[249] If the complainant submits fresh facts, the file may of course be reopened.[250] Commission practice at the end of the procedure is to notify the complainant by a formal letter. Such a letter is an" act" of an institution of the Community and hence may be made the subject to judicial review proceedings before the Court under Article 173 EC, i.e. the complainant may appeal to the Court.[251]

6.158 It has not yet been definitively established whether a complainant has a right to demand a decision from the Commission on the matter irrespective of whether the latter's *practice* is to issue a letter which may be the basis of an appeal to the Court. It has been cogently argued that since the Court has expressed concern for the legitimate rights of a complainant these cannot be effectively safeguarded if the latter is not *entitled* to a decision or other "act" of the Commission.[252]

(6) Absolute privilege for documents submitted in a complaint: confidentiality

6.159 It has been established by the Court of Appeal in the UK that documents submitted to the Commission in the course of a complaint are protected by absolute privilege from use in defamation proceedings (e.g. brought by the party complained of). The Court has held that the public interest demands a level of protection for complaint documents, otherwise the Commission would be in the dilemma of either not being able to use such evidence at all because it would be unable to disclose it to the complained of undertaking, or using and disclosing it and suffering the consequences of complainants refusing to give evidence to the commission for fear of reprisals.[253] Complainants may submit their views to the Com mission in confidence. They should make sure the Commission is aware of the need for this though they are not obliged to justify their request. The Commission treats confidential complaints that they wish to follow up as "own initiative complaints".[254] Confidential complaints and supporting documents will not be made available to the complained of party. Indeed Article 214 EC imposes a duty of non-disclosure of information covered by the obligation of "professional secrecy, in particular information about undertakings,

[249] This letter is not challengeable under Art. 173 EC, T-64/89 *Automec I* [1990] ECR II-367. This is because it is only an intermediate stage in the proceedings, giving the opportunity for the complainant to submit further observations. The complainant may *require* the Commission to provide it with a reasoned refusal and to give it a time period in which to submit its comments: see Art.175 EC. This grants a right of action to any natural or legal person who wishes to complain that a Community institution has failed to address to it any act other than an opinion or recommendation. There are certain procedural steps that must be gone through first however. These are mentioned in Art. 175(2). See T-28/90 *Asia Motor France I* [1992] ECRII-2285 [1992] 5 CMLR 431.

[250] See Case 125/78 *GEMA* v *Commission* [1980] 2 CMLR 177; [1979] ECR 3173 at para. 17 of the judgment.

[251] See Case 210/81 *Firma Demo–Studio Schmidt* v *Commission* [1984] 1 CMLR 63, Commission did not dispute that its letter was an "act" within the meaning of Art. 173 EC. See also Case 26/76 *Metro–SB–Grossmarkte* v *Commission* [1978] 2 CMLR 1; [1977] ECR 1875 where the European Court stated that it was in the best interests of the satisfactory administration of justice and the proper application of competition rules that a person whose complaint has been rejected should be able to have that refusal reviewed before the Court. See also Case T-24/90 *Automec v Commission (No. II)* [1992] 5 CMLR 431.

[252] In Case 146/80 *Armstrong Patents* v *Commission* withdrawn from the Court by the complainant, the Commission pleaded that a complainant had *no* right to a decision. Following *Demo-Studio Schmidt* v *Commission* (above) this position is perhaps difficult to sustain. See Kerse, *Antitrust Procedure in the EC* (3rd edn. 1994), pp. 81–83.

[253] See *Hasselblad (GB) Ltd* v *Orbinson* [1984] 3 CMLR 679 (CA) at para. 8 of the judgment. See also, *Hasselblad (GB) Ltd* v *Hodes* [1985] 3 CMLR 664.

[254] See *Twelfth Commission Competition Report* (1982), p. 40, para. 3.5, n. 2 and related text.

their business relations or their cost components". Failure by the Commission to respect professional secrecy in principle renders the authority liable in damages to an aggrieved plaintiff under Article 215 EC. In *Adams* v *Commission*[255] the Commission accidentally disclosed the identity of a complainant with the result that the complainant was prosecuted and convicted in Switzerland for economic espionage under Article 273 of the Swiss Penal Code. The complainant sued the Commission for damages and succeeded. The Court held that the duty in Article 214 covers voluntary complainants who request the Commission to treat the complaint as confidential. However, they reduced the complainant's damages by half for contributory negligence on the basis that the complainant failed to notify the Commission of the fact that his identity could be discerned from coded markings on the documents submitted, and, by the complainant's failure to request the Commission to keep him informed of progress in the case. A number of points arise from the case: (a) complainants should, where secrecy is desired, expressly request confidentiality in their communications with the Commission; (b) complainants should expressly request that they be kept fully informed of developments; (c) the Commission should be expressly notified of any documents which could possibly reveal the complainant's identity, e.g. department codes, typists initials, etc. Where the Commission does not know the identity of the person providing information, it will only show those documents to the business under investigation after first assessing the risk of the person being identified and weighing that up against the value of the documents to the investigation. Should the Commission infringe the duty of professional secrecy a complainant has five years in which to bring an action under Article 215 against the Commission.[256]

6.160 From the *Adams* case it appears that the limitation period runs from the date when the plaintiff became aware of the events giving rise to the cause of action. It is probably also true that time also runs from the date the plaintiff ought to have became aware of the events giving rise to the action.

6.161 Finally, it is advisable, in a complaint, to separate the confidential parts of a complaint from the non-confidential parts. This will enable the Commission, where necessary, to show the non-confidential part to the other interested parties.

[255] Case 145/83 [1985] ECR 3539. See also Case 53/85 *AKZO* v *Commission* [1986] ECR 1965, [1987] 1 CMLR 231. See generally on Art. 215 EC: Hartley, *The Foundations of European Community Law* (3rd edn. 1994), pp. 467–498.

[256] Art. 43 of the Protocol of the statute of the Court of Justice of the EC: "Proceedings against the community in matters arising from non-contractual liability shall be barred after a period of five years from the occurrence of the event giving rise thereto" (first sentence only). In Case 145/83 *Adams* v *Commission* [1985] 2 ECR 3539 the Court construed Art. 43 liberally holding that an applicant was not time barred where that applicant only belatedly became aware of the event giving rise to the existence of the cause of action and thus could not have had reasonable time in which to submit his application under Art. 215 EC within the limitation period.

7 General Enforcement and Negotiations with the European Commission

A. Introduction

7.1 In this chapter the subject of enforcement is considered. It includes an overview of Commission procedure. Article 85(3), the basis of formal and informal negotiations with the Commission, is also discussed. The prospect of remedies before the national courts is considered including actions for damages.[1] In this chapter the following will be discussed:

Section B. Survey of Commission procedure—starting with the initiation of formal proceedings and ending with the possible appeal of a formal decision to the Court of First Instance and ultimately to the Court of Justice.

Section C. The legal basis of formal negotiations—in this Section Article 85(3), the exemption formula, is discussed. Consideration is given to the factors the Commission take into account in determining exemption.

Section D. Formal enforcement in national courts—private parties may sue other parties before national courts for damages or injunctive relief. The relevant causes of action and remedies are discussed.

[1] Kerse, *Antitrust Procedure in the EC* (3rd edn. 1994); See also P.J. Slot and McDonnell (eds.), *Procedure and Enforcement in EC and US Competition Law* (Sweet and Maxwell, 1993) (especially L. Gyselen, Chapter 10 "The Commission's fining policy in competition cases—'Questo è il catalogo'"; J.H.J. Bourgeois, Chapter 13, "Undertakings in EC competition law"; N. Green, Chapter 17, "Evidence and proof in EC competition cases"; D. Vaughan, Chapter 20, "Access to the file and confidentiality"; L. Gyselen, Chapter 27, "Publication policy of the Commission with regard to comfort letters"); Van Bael, "The antitrust settlement practice of the EC Commission" (1986) 23 CMLRev 61; O. Due, "Le respect des droits de la defense dans le droit administratif communautaire" [1987] *Cahiers De Droit* 383; Joshua, "Proof in contested competition cases: a comparison with the rules of evidence in Common Law" (1987) 12 ELRev 315; J. Faull, "The enforcement of competition policy in the European Community: a mature system" [1991] Fordham Corp L Inst 139; Shaw, "Competition complaints: a comprehensive system of remedies?" (1993) 18 ELRev 427; B. Vesterdorf, "Complaints concerning infringements of competition law within the context of European Community law" (1994) 31 CMLRev 77.

Section E. Overlap between EC and national proceedings—problems may arise when the same subject matter gives rise to parallel or overlapping cases in the EC Courts or Commission on the one hand and the UK Courts or competition authorities on the other.

Section F. Negotiating informal settlements with the Commission—guidance is given as to the procedure and practice surrounding informal negotiations with the Commission.

Section G. The opposition procedure—consideration is given to the accelerated procedures for notification and clearance of certain types of agreement set out under certain block exemptions.

B. Survey of Commission Procedure

1. Initiation of Procedure by Commission

7.2 The Commission usually initiates proceedings following a notification by parties or as a result of a complaint.[2] It may also act upon its own initiative as a result of research into specific sectors of the market, the monitoring of trade journals and questions asked in the European Parliament. The Commission's workload comprises about 60 per cent notified agreements, 25 per cent complaints and 15 per cent own-initiative proceedings.[3] The Commission discusses matters with national authorities. The Commission also has the power to conduct general inquiries into any sector of the economy where it appears that competition in the common market is being restricted or distorted.[4] This power could be developed into a means for the Commission to investigate markets in the way that the UK Monopolies and Mergers Commission does under the Fair Trading Act 1973. The Commission has not to date used this power in this manner.

7.3 The Commission is not obliged to initiate a procedure every time it receives a complaint, even where there is good cause to believe that there is an infringement of the competition rules. Due to being seriously under-resourced as well as to the principle of subsidiarity, the Commission has been encouraging more of the enforcement of the competition rules to take place in the national courts. To this end, it has published a Notice on Cooperation between National Courts and the Commission in Applying Articles 85 and 86 of the EC Treaty.[5] Apart from setting out practical advice for national courts, the Notice also states that the Commission intends henceforth to concentrate on notifications, complaints and own-initiative proceedings "having particular political, economic or legal significance for the Community".[6] This statement of practice was given legal force in the *Automec (No. 2)*[7] judgment where the Court of First Instance, dismissing an action challenging the Commission's decision not to initiate a procedure, affirmed the Commission's right to prioritise cases in order to concentrate on major cases and the development of policy in cases where an adequate remedy exists before the national court.

[2] See Kerse, *op. cit.*, at pp. 74–79. A complaint cannot form the basis for a libel action in English law, as held by the Court of Appeal in *Hasselblad Ltd* v *Orbinson* [1985] QB 475 (May LJ dissenting).

[3] *Twenty-third Report on Competition Policy* (1993), para. 208.

[4] Art. 12, Reg. 17/62. This has been done in respect of the European beer market.

[5] OJ [1993] C39/6.

[6] See, in particular, paras. 13–16 of the Notice.

[7] Case T-24/90 *Automec* v *Commission (No. 2)* [1992] ECR II-2223 [1992] 5 CMLR 431.

7.4 The position of complainants, in particular the extent to which they can force the Commission to consider complaints and initiate a procedure, is discussed below (see paras. 7.155–7.163). It is necessary, at this point, to set out the factors which may indicate whether the Commission will initiate an investigation, or whether it will refuse to do so, leaving the applicant to seek a remedy in the national court. There are pros and cons to each method of proceeding.[8] However, a would-be complainant to the Commission will need to be reasonably sure that the Commission will not apply the principle in *Automec (No. 2)* and reject his complaint, as this could lead to much unnecessary expense and delay. The CFI's judgment in *Automec (No. 2)* seeks to analyse the grounds on which the Commission may refuse to conduct an investigation. The main points arising out of the judgment are set out below:

(a) The Commission is not obliged to investigate every complaint.
(b) If the Commission issues a decision refusing to conduct an investigation, this decision will be susceptible to review by the CFI.[9]
(c) The Commission is entitled to define priorities in dealing with complaints and in determining the degree of priority to be applied to the examination of alleged infringements is justified in referring to the "Community interest" of a case. However, the Community interest cannot be evaluated in an abstract manner. The Commission is required to set forth the legal and factual considerations which prompts it to conclude that there is an insufficient Community interest. It should take into account *inter alia* the impact of the alleged infringement on the functioning of the Common Market, the probability of being able to establish its existence and the extent of the necessary investigative measures.[10] The relevance of these last two considerations is ambiguous. It is unclear whether the Court is saying that, if an investigation is likely to be particularly burdensome, the Commission would be justified in not following it up, or, whether it means that the Commission *should* deal with complex disputes which are referred to it. The latter interpretation seems the more likely given that the Court in *Automec* viewed its task as determining whether, "in referring the complainant enterprise to the national court, the Commission misconstrued the extent of the protection which the national court can provide to safeguard the rights derived by the applicant from Article 85(1)".[11]

7.5 In upholding the Commission's determination in the *Automec* case that there was no sufficient Community interest in pursuing the investigation of the matter, the CFI stated that the following considerations were significant:

– The applicant had already referred a related dispute to the Italian courts: "Reasons pertaining to saving unnecessary proceedings and the proper administration of jus-

[8] For a discussion of the pros and cons of each, see Whish, "The enforcement of EC competition law in the domestic courts of Member States" [1994] ECLR 60; Van Bael, "The role of the national courts" [1994] ECLR 3; A.J. Riley, "More radicalism, please: the Notice on Co-Operation between National Courts and the Commission in applying Articles 85 and 86 of the EEC Treaty" [1993] ECLR 91; J. Goh, "Enforcing EC competition law in member states" [1993] ECLR 114; M.B. Hutchings and M. Levitt, "Concurrent jurisdiction" [1994] ECLR 119; Editorial, "The Commission's Notice on Cooperation between National Courts and the Commission in applying Articles 85 and 86 EEC" (1993) 3 CMLRev 681.

[9] Subject, of course, to the conditions of Art. 173 of the Treaty being satisfied. If, however, the Commission does not issue a formal decision rejecting a complaint, but merely fails to follow it up, matters are more complex. For an analysis of the rights of complainants see paras. 7.155–7.163.

[10] See para. 86 of the Court's judgment.

[11] Para. 89 of the Court's judgment. This latter interpretation seems to be confirmed by the Court's judgment in T-114/92 *Bureau Européen des Medias de l'Industrie Musicale (BEMIM)* v *Commission* [1995] ECR II-147.

tice militate in favour of examination of the matter by the court already dealing with associated questions."[12]

- The complaint mainly turned on the applicability of a block exemption which was a matter which could be determined by a national court sufficiently easily, especially as the whole purpose of block exemptions was to minimise the intervention of the Commission in the enforcement of Article 85(1).[13]
- The applicant produced nothing to indicate that Italian law provided no legal remedy which would enable the Italian court to safeguard its rights in a satisfactory manner.[14]

7.6 The Court of First Instance has given further guidance on the meaning of "Community interest" in *BEMIM* v *Commission*.[15] The case involved a challenge by an association representing French discothèque owners to the Commission's rejection of its complaint against SACEM, the French copyright collecting society for musical works. The Commission did so, *inter alia*, because "the centre of gravity of the alleged infringement is in France; its effects in the other Member States can be only very limited; consequently this case is not of particular importance to the functioning of the Common Market; the Community interest does not therefore require the Commission to deal with these complaints but requires that they be referred to the French national courts and administrative authorities". Indeed, the substance of the complaint was before a number of French courts as well as the *Conseil de la Concurrence* at the same time as the complaint was before the Commission. The Court of First Instance considered that where the effects of infringements alleged in the complaint were essentially confined to the territory of one Member State and where proceedings had been brought before the courts and competent authorities of that Member State by the complainant, the Commission was entitled to terminate the investigation, provided that the rights of the complainant could be adequately safeguarded, in particular by the national courts.

7.7 The Court then went on to elaborate on what were adequate safeguards. It stated that an argument that national courts were unable to handle issues of law raised by cases under Articles 85 and 86 could not be accepted, since the Article 177 EC preliminary reference procedure existed to advise courts in such cases. However, the rights of a complainant would not be sufficiently protected by a national court if that court were not reasonably able, in view of the complexity of the case, to gather factual information necessary in order to assess whether an infringement had been committed. The Court rejected, however, the complainant's argument that French courts were unable to gather such information.

7.8 To sum up, the Court's judgment in *Automec* establishes that the protection of the rights of the individual derived from Articles 85 and 86 is fundamental to the Court's supervision of the Commission's exercise of discretion in establishing priorities; if national courts cannot effectively protect the Community rights of individuals, then the Commission is not entitled to devolve its duties. This may seem odd as EC law proceeds on the assumption that national courts are *required* to protect directly effective Community law rights and provide effective remedies against infringements of those rights.[16] However, while the Commission retains the exclusive right to apply Article 85(3) it is often difficult for national

[12] Para. 88.
[13] Para. 95.
[14] Para. 94.
[15] Case T-114/92 *Bureau Européen des Medias de l'Industrie Musicale (BEMIM)* v *Commission* [1995] ECR II-147.
[16] Under Art. 5 EC.

courts to reach a final conclusion. Even where this is not an issue, national courts, in general, have less potent investigatory powers and less experience than the Commission in dealing with such disputes. Collating evidence may be particularly problematic where it is located within more than one country. In such circumstances difficult questions of jurisdiction may also arise. By requiring the Commission to ascertain that national courts are able to properly protect individual rights, the Court of First Instance is implicitly acknowledging these problems.[17] Thus, even if a dispute raises no particularly novel or important issue of law or policy, an applicant is probably safe in choosing the Commission as an avenue for redress if it is clear that its resolution will be sufficiently complex to cause difficult problems for national courts.[18] The position is different in respect of the ECSC competition rules (Articles 4, 60, 65 and 66(7) ECSC) where the Commission has exclusive jurisdiction and no proceedings may be taken before national courts in the absence of a Commission decision. Thus, the Commission cannot reject a complaint on the basis that an adequate remedy exists before the national courts.

2. *Procedure Following a Complaint*

7.9 The Commission procedure following the making of a complaint has been set out by the Court of First Instance[19] as comprising three stages:

> "During the first stage, following the submission of the complaint, the Commission collects the information on the basis of which it decides what action it will take on the complaint. That stage may include an informal exchange of views between the Commission and the complainant with a view to clarifying the factual and legal issues with which the complaint is concerned and to allowing the complainant an opportunity to expand on his allegations in the light of any initial reaction from the Commission. During the second stage, the Commission may indicate, in a notification to the complainant, the reasons why it does not propose to pursue the complaint, in which case it must offer the complainant the opportunity to submit any further comments within a time limit which it fixes. In the third stage of the procedure, the Commission takes cognisance of the observations submitted by the complainant. Although Article 6 of Regulation 99 does not explicitly provide for the possibility, this stage may end with a final decision."

3. *Investigation and Discovery*

7.10 The Commission has wide ranging powers of investigation to support its fact-finding functions. Refusal by the parties to comply with these investigations can result in fines being imposed. An investigation may commence with a simple request for information; it may, however, entail inspectors "turning up" on the doorstep armed with a search mandate. These options are discussed below.

4. *Requests for Information*

7.11 Requests for information are covered by Article 11 of Regulation 17/62/EEC. This empowers the Commission to obtain "necessary" information from the governments and

[17] These issues are elaborated on below, see paras. 7.93–7.116.
[18] More specific problems in applying the Notice on Cooperation are dealt with at paras. 7.112–7.116.
[19] T-37/92 *BEUC* [1994] ECR II-285, para. 29; see also T-64/89 *Automec I* [1990] ECR II-367, paras. 45–47. See R. Forster, "Taking on the Commission: procedural possibilities for an applicant following submission of a complaint" [1993] ECLR 257.

competent authorities of the Member States (e.g. the OFT in the UK or the Bundeskartellamt in Germany), from undertakings, and from trade associations.[20] Requests are made in writing and are sent by registered post to the firm(s) concerned with an advice of receipt. In urgent cases requests may be made by telex or fax. The request is constituted by all of the document sent to the firm pursuant to Article 11 and not simply the various questions seeking answers. A request sent by the Commission will state the legal basis of the request, its purpose and also the penalties for supplying incorrect information.[21] There is apparently no duty on those "requested" to supply the information, no drastic consequence attached to outright refusal to disclose.[22] Failure to comply will, however, lead to the Commission issuing a *formal* decision requiring disclosure and fixing an appropriate time limit within which compliance must occur if fines are to be avoided. Community law does include a privilege against self-incrimination. In *Orkem*,[23] the Court of Justice held that observance of the rights of the defence, as a fundamental principle of Community law, did, however, prevent the Commission under a request for information issued pursuant to Article 11(5) from compelling an undertaking to provide it with answers which might involve an admission of an infringement which it is incumbent upon the Commission to prove.[24] Parties may appeal against this formal decision to the Court of First Instance under Article 173(2) EC. A copy of this decision is sent to the relevant authority in Member States where the undertaking is situated. This is the OFT in the UK. The national authorities may also receive copies of replies to Article 11(3) requests and 11(5) decisions, but may not make use of such information to launch inquiries under either EC or national law. However, if a national authority is alerted to a competition infringement as a result it is not required to turn a blind eye and may initiate its own requests for information in accordance with its national laws.[25]

7.12 In practical terms refusal to comply or only part compliance with a request may give that undertaking breathing space. It will take time for Commission officials to obtain a formal decision from the Commission requiring disclosure of information and, subsequent to that, it will take more time to obtain a formal decision imposing fines.[26] The maximum fine that can be imposed is 5,000 ECUs.[27] The Commission may also impose periodic fines which apply for every day of non-compliance. These may range from 50 to 1,000 ECUs per day. Fines will not be imposed until parties have had an opportunity to explain themselves. It is advisable to comply with Commission requests. If it has to issue formal deci-

[20] The notion of "necessary" information is to be construed widely: see Case 31/59 *Acciateria di Brescia* v *High Authority* [1960] ECR 71; *Re UNITEL* [1978] 3 CMLR 306; Case T-39/90R *SEP* v *Commission* [1991] ECR II-1497 [1992] 5 CMLR 27, paras. 25–32. The Court of First Instance stressed in this last case that the information is necessary if it "can be legitimately considered to be related to the presumed infringement"; on this test only unrelated information fails to be subject to disclosure.

[21] See Kerse, *op. cit.*, at pp. 97–109 for a searching analysis of this subject.

[22] Art. 11(4) of Reg. 17/62/EEC, however, states that undertakings "shall" supply the information requested. But see Commission answer to WQ No. 677/79 OJ 1979 C 310/30 where the latter acknowledge that undertakings are not legally obliged to furnish information unless a formal decision of the Commission has been obtained.

[23] Case 374/87 *Orkem* v *Commission* [1989] ECR 3283.

[24] The same privilege does not apply in national proceedings for breach of the competition rules. In such as situation, national law on self-incrimination applies and the Commission may not take advantage of any information it learns as a result of such national proceedings to initiate proceedings or as evidence of an infringement: C-60/92 *Otto* v *Postbank* [1993] ECR I-5683.

[25] Case C-67 91 *Direccion General de Defensa de la Compentencia* v *Association Espanola de Banca Privada* [1992] ECR I-4785.

[26] For discussion of this two-stage procedure see *per* Advocate General Warner in Case 17/74 *Transocean Marine Paint Association* v *Commission* [1974] 2 CMLR 459 at pp. 471, 472, [1974] ECR 1063 at pp. 1089, 1090.

[27] See Arts. 15 and 16 of Reg. 17/62/EEC.

sions and impose fines it will naturally be less well disposed to the parties when it comes to deal with the substance of the agreement or practice later. It might also ask itself why the parties were so reluctant to furnish information and may draw adverse conclusions. Indeed, the Commission might be induced into undertaking a surprise on the spot investigation if it feels that information is being or might be concealed from it. If parties experience genuine difficulties in collecting data then such as has been collected should be transmitted to the Commission along with an accompanying letter explaining the reasons for the partial compliance and promising disclosure of the remainder of the information as soon as it becomes available. Time periods given for disclosure by the Commission are generally quite short, often under a month. Additional periods of time may be requested by the parties in order to facilitate compliance. It is often advised that if parties are in doubt about the accuracy of information to be disclosed they should delay its notification and verify its accuracy as soon as possible. There is a clear danger in notifying inaccurate data that the Commission will construe it as "incorrect" and impose fines on the parties.[28] If the Commission requests information on market share, for example, it will be essential to ensure that the person responsible for complying with the request has defined the market correctly. If the Commission, for example, requests a figure for volume of ex-works deliveries but the firm possesses only figures for sales, the firm should contact the Commission and ask whether these figures would represent acceptable substitutes. If figures were given for the UK alone the undertakings in question could appear significantly more powerful than if figures were given for the whole of the EC. In practice the Commission has to issue very few decisions in order to enforce its requests.[29] The Commission must respect the confidentiality of information supplied.[30] None the less, it is probably wise to mark especially strategic documents as being secret or to enclose them in a separate file. Confidentiality is no excuse for non-disclosure.[31]

7.13 Article 11(4) lists the persons responsible for supplying information: head of the firm or his representative, or, in the case of companies their lawyers. In practice this usually means the heads of departments possessing the data required (e.g. accountants, sales managers, in-house lawyers, independent law firms). Information is supplied to the Commission in the name of the firm.

5. On the Spot Inspections

7.14 The Commission has the power to send inspectors into commercial premises: "(a) to examine the books and other business records; (b) to take copies of or extracts from the books and business records; (c) to ask for oral explanations on the spot; (d) to enter any premises,

[28] See Arts. 15 and 16 of Reg. 17/62/EEC. Under Art. 15(1)(b) of Reg. 17/62/EEC which empowers the imposition of fines for the furnishing of incorrect data, "incorrect" has been defined as: "any statement ... which gives a distorted picture of the true facts asked for, and which departs significantly from reality on major points. Where a statement is thus false or so incomplete that the reply taken in its entirety is likely to mislead the Commission about the true facts, it constitutes incorrect information within the meaning of Article 15(1)(b)": *Telos* [1982] 1 CMLR 267 at para. 21 of the decision. See also *National Panasonic Belgium* [1982] 2 CMLR 410; *Comptoir Commercial d'importation* [1982] 1 CMLR 440.

[29] See Korah, *Narrow or Misleading Replies to Requests for Information* (1982) 2 BLR 69.

[30] See, e.g. *Re UNITEL* [1978] 3 CMLR 306; *Misal* [1973] CMLR D37; *Fire Insurance (D)* [1982] 2 CMLR 159; *Deutsche Castrol* [1983] 3 CMLR 165. See also C. Lavoie, "The investigative powers of the Commission with respect to business secrets under Community competition rules" (1992) 17 ELRev 20; J.M. Joshua, "Balancing the public interests: confidentiality, trade secrets and disclosure of evidence in EC competition procedure" [1994] ECLR 68.

[31] See Case 31/59 *Acciaieria de Brescia* v *High Authority* [1960] ECR 71 at p. 82; *CSV* OJ 1976 1192/ 27. See also *FNICF* [1983] 1 CMLR 575; Case T-39/90R *SEP* v *Commission* [1992] 5 CMLR 27, para. 60.

land and means of transport of undertakings."[32] "Business records" means *inter alia*, memos, correspondence, financial documents (balance sheets, invoices, etc.), photographs, films, slides, tapes, cassettes, minutes, computer programmes, microfilms. The phrase effectively means all forms of information storage. Officials may exercise these powers only upon presentation of a written authority or decision specifying the subject matter and purpose of the investigation and the penalties for incomplete production of documents. In practice the Commission officials identify themselves by presentation of their staff cards. To assist the undertakings, the Commission attaches to the authorisation or decision, an explanatory memorandum outlining the scope and limits of the Commission's powers and the rights of the undertaking.[33] If requested the Commission officials will explain to a firm what the object of the investigation is, as well as procedural matters and questions of confidentiality. Such explanations are informal and do not in any way modify, or enlarge upon, the basic authority to carry out an investigation. The Commission must give prior warning to the relevant authorities in the Member State concerned of their investigation and those authorities may assist the Commission with the investigation. The OFT in the UK regularly attend at investigations. Alternatively, the Commission may request a national authority, the OFT in the UK, to carry out an investigation on its behalf.[34] The Commission has only recently begun to exercise this power, but it is anticipated that more use of it will be made in future.[35] The Commission may come with an authorisation but frequently it arrives already armed with a formal decision. There is no requirement that the Commission start with an authorisation and only then proceed to a formal decision as there is with regard to requests for information.[36] The Commission tends to use a formal decision where it suspects than an investigation might be obstructed or where there are a number of parallel investigations being launched at the same time. As with requests for information, an obstructive attitude on the part of the investigated undertaking may lead the Commission to draw certain adverse conclusions. With regard to the summoning of legal assistance the Commission state the following in the explanatory memorandum to both an authorisation and a decision: "The undertaking may consult a legal adviser during the investigation. However, the presence of a lawyer is not a legal condition for the validity of the investigation, nor must it unduly delay or impede it. Any delay pending a lawyer's arrival must be kept to the strict minimum to ensure that the business records will remain in the place and state they were in when the Commission officials arrived. The officials' acceptance of delay is also conditional upon their not being hindered from entering into and remaining in occupation of offices of their choice. If the undertaking has an in-house legal service Commission officials are instructed not to delay the investigation by awaiting the arrival of an external legal adviser."

[32] Art. 14(1) Reg. 17/62/EC. See generally Kerse, *op. cit.*, n. 1 at pp. 120–129; *Eleventh Commission Competition Report* (1981), pp. 28–30, paras. 17–21; *Twelfth Commission Competition Report* (1982), pp. 39, 40, paras. 33, 33. See, e.g. *Fides* [1979] 1 CMLR 650 on the spot investigation of a trust company appointed by parties to a price-fixing agreement to organise and operate the cartel. The trust company claimed it was not obliged to submit to investigation because it was not involved in the production or marketing of the relevant product. The Commission rejected this view on the basis that the services provided by the company were directly concerned with the circumstances of the case.

[33] See *Twelfth Commission Competition Report* (1982), p. 39, para. 32. The text of the. explanatory memorandum may be found in the *Thirteenth Commission Competition Report* (1983) at pp. 270–272 (annex).

[34] Art. 13(2) Reg. 17/62.

[35] The first OFT investigation under this procedure was carried out in 1992. See DGFT's Annual Report 1992, pp. 35–36. See A.M.C. Inglese, "EC competition law procedure: role of the competent authority" [1993] ECLR 197. See Case 136/79 *National Panasonic* v *Commission* [1980] 3 CMLR 169; [1980] ECR 2033.

[36] Cases 46/87 and 227/88 *Hoechst* v *Commission* [1989] ECR 2859, [1991] 4 CMLR 410.

7.15 The Commission does not have a general power of search.[37] If an undertaking obstructs access to documentation, it is for the competent national authority to provide all necessary assistance in obtaining access.[38] In the UK, the OFT will have lawyers on standby during an investigation to seek a High Court injunction to order compliance or face contempt of court proceedings.[39] In practice an Order of the High Court can be obtained in a matter of hours upon the *ex parte* application of counsel for the Treasury Solicitor. The Order will, post haste, be faxed to the undertaking under investigation. The Order is in nature not dissimilar to an *Anton Piller* save that it is intended to enforce Community law, not national law.

7.16 The Commission may ask oral questions on the spot. If personnel of the undertaking decide to answer, their explanations may be minuted and a copy given to the undertaking. The duty to answer questions is limited. The Commission's view appears to be that it can require oral answers to specific concrete questions arising out of the books and business records. Apparently, it accepts that it has no right to demand answers to questions requiring careful consideration and perhaps the gathering of information.[40]

7.17 Undertakings usually grant the Commission the use of a photocopier. If this is not granted the Commission officials may copy out longhand the text of any relevant document they consider necessary, thus involving them in a longer stay at the premises. The Commission will pay for use of a photocopier. It may be wise for an officer of the undertaking to perform the photocopying, thus enabling extra copies to be made for use of legal advisers and to keep a proper record of all documents taken. The destruction of documents will, if discovered, lead to fines.[41] The conspicuous absence of specific documents in a series, for example a potentially key letter in a sequence of correspondence between rivals, invokes the suspicions of the Commission. Suppression of documents is not advisable.

7.18 Correspondence between an independent legal adviser (*not* an in-house lawyer), qualified to practice in the EC[42] and the undertaking in question is privileged and need not be disclosed.[43] This was the judgment of the Court of Justice in *AM&S Europe* v *Commission*.[44] The Commission has interpreted this judgment to mean that: "the protection of the principle of confidentiality implies, in respect of the condition concerning the rights of defence, that it must cover all written communications exchanged after the initiation of the administrative procedure which may lead to a decision on the application of Articles 85 and 86 of the Treaty or to a decision imposing a pecuniary sanction on the undertaking, and that it must also be possible to extend it to earlier written communica-

37 Cases 46/87 and 227/88 *Hoechst* v *Commission* [1989] ECR 2859, [1991] 4 CMLR 410.

38 Art. 14(6) Reg. 17/62/EEC.

39 An injunction was sought and granted on the same day in *Ukwal* [1993] 5 CMLR 632.

40 *ibid.* See Kerse *op. cit.*, at pp. 81–84.

41 See *Business Records of Vereinigung Deutscher Frieform Schmieden* [1978] 1 CMLR D63. In *Pioneer* [1980] 1 CMLR 457 the Commission considered the failure to take minutes an aggravating factor when considering fines.

42 Though in practice the Commission extends privilege to communications between client and non-EC qualified lawyers.

43 See *Twelfth Commission Competition Report* (1982), p. 54, para. 52. An "independent" lawyer according to the Commission is one subject to "the rules of professional ethics and discipline which are laid down and enforced in the general interest by institutions endowed with the requisite powers for that purpose". This is related to the position of a lawyer as a collaborator in the administration of justice. There is some doubt as to the scope of this privilege, see: Faull (1983) 8 ELRev 411; Forrester (1983) 20 CMLRev 75; Joshua (1983) 8 ELRev 15; Boyd (1982) 7 ELRev 493; Ghandi (1982) 7 ELRev 308.

44 Case 155/79 [1982] 2 CMLR 264; [1982] ECR 1575. See for Commission interpretation, *Twelfth Commission Competition Report* (1982), pp. 52–55.

tions which have a relationship to the subject matter of that procedure" [and][45] "that in the initial stages of any dispute it is for the Commission to decide whether a document is protected by legal privilege. Where an undertaking refuses, on the ground that it is entitled to protection of the confidentiality of information, to produce, among the business records demanded by the Commission, written communications between itself and its lawyer, it must provide the Commission's authorised agents with the relevant material of such a nature as to demonstrate that the communications fulfil the conditions for being granted legal protection, although it is not bound to reveal their content."[46]

7.19 The Commission may order disclosure by a formal decision. This may be challenged by the parties before the Court of First Instance.[47] Failure to submit to an investigation begun by formal decision, though not by authorisation, is punishable by fines, as is failure (either intentional or negligent) once an investigation of either type is under way to submit complete information.[48]

6. *Statement of Objections*

7.20 Where, following fact-finding, the Commission considers it necessary to pursue the case, a formal procedure is opened. There is some doubt as to what legally constitutes the opening of a formal procedure.[49] In practice, the Commissioner responsible for competition signs a form declaring proceedings open. In due course the undertakings and competent authorities in the Member States concerned are notified. The Commission will then issue a statement of objections and this will be served on the undertakings concerned. Service of the statement of objections may be at the same time as the giving of notice of the opening of a formal procedure.[50] A statement of objections is not issued in every case. In the majority of cases the Commission proceed more informally by negotiating with the parties to achieve modifications of the agreement which will enable the Commission to conclude the negotiations on an informal basis. This informal procedure is examined at paras. 7.127–7.141. The statement of objections will include the basic facts as perceived by the Commission, the reasons for the applicability of Article 85 or 86, and the grounds for refusing exemption under Article 85(3) EC where applicable. This is not a legally binding document and may *not* be challenged before the Court of First Instance.[51] The document is not usually very long but can, in exceptional cases, run to hundreds of pages.[52]

[45] *Twelfth Commission Competition Report* (1982) at p. 53, para. 52.
[46] *ibid.*, at p. 54 para. 53.
[47] *ibid.*, and see also at p. 39, para. 33. See, *Asphaltoid-Keller* OJ 1971 1161/32.
[48] Art. 15(1)(c) Reg. 17/62. Daily fines of up to ECU 1,000 for continuing failure to submit to a decision to investigate are provided for under Art. 16(1)(d).
[49] In Case 60/81 *IBM* v *Commission* [1981] 3 CMLR 635, [1981] ECR 2639 the Court held that the initiation of a procedure was *not* a decision subject to judicial review under Art. 173 EC. It held that it was simply a procedural step adopted prior to a formal decision on the case.
[50] Cases 48, 49, 5 1–57/69 *ICI* v *Commission* [1972] CMR 557; [1072] ECR 619.
[51] Case 60/81 *IBM* v *Commission* [1981] 3 CMLR 635, [1981] ECR 2639 at para. 21 of the judgment. The Court explained its reasoning as follows: "A statement of objections does not compel the undertaking concerned to alter or reconsider its marketing practices and it does not have the effect of depriving it of the protection hitherto available to it against the application of a fine, as is the case when the Commission informs an undertaking, pursuant to Art. 15(6) of Reg. No. 17, of the results of the preliminary examination of an agreement which has been notified by the undertaking. Whilst a statement of objections may have the effect of showing the undertaking in question it is incurring a moral risk of being fined by the Commission, that is merely a consequence of fact, and not a legal consequence which the statement of objections is intended to produce" (para. 19 of the judgment).
[52] As is believed to have been the case in the *IBM* case (above). The IBM response however included a request for further details of the Commission's complaint which ran to over 100 pages and the actual IBM reply is reputed to have been in the order of 7,000 pages.

7.21 Supplementary statements of objections may be served at a later date. If the Commission wishes to rely on specific documents, it must supply those for comments together with the statement of objections.[53]

7. *The Parties' Written Reply: Access to Commission file*

7.22 Parties to proceedings have a right to reply.[54] The Court of First Instance has stated that the "procedure for access to the file in competition cases is intended to allow the addressees of a statement of objections to examine evidence in the Commission's files so that they are in a position effectively to express their views on the conclusions reached by the Commission in its Statement of Objections on the basis of that evidence".[55] This involves responding to the statement of objections and presenting their own position. In making submissions, the parties may have a right of access to certain Commission documents.[56] Parties are informed of the contents of the Commission's file by means of annex to the statement of objections (or to the letter rejecting a complaint). This lists all of the documents in the file and indicates documents or parts thereof to which parties may have access. Copies of all documents to be disclosed to the undertakings involved are sent with the statement of objections.[57] Requests for additional documents should be addressed to the Hearing Officer and should be sufficiently reasoned in order to enable him to carry out his role as an arbiter of what disclosure should take place.[58] The following documents will *not* be made available to the parties:

(a) documents or parts thereof containing other undertakings' business secrets;
(b) internal Commission documents, such as notes, drafts or other working papers;
(c) any other confidential information such as documents enabling complainants to be identified where they wish to remain anonymous, and information disclosed to the Commission subject to an obligation of confidentiality.[59]

7.23 Having laid down these rules, the Court of First Instance has ruled that the Commission is under a duty to disclose all other documents on the file.[60] In particular, the Commission considers that is under a duty to disclose documents favourable to the undertakings being investigated, known as exculpatory documents.[61]

53 Case T-11/89 *Shell* v *Commission* [1992] ECR II-757, para. 55.
54 See Art. 19(1) Reg. 17/62/EC, Kerse, *op. cit.*, at pp. 152–161.
55 Cases T-10-12 and 15/92 *Cimenteries* v *Commission* [1992] ECR II-2667, [1993] 4 CMLR 243, para. 38. The Commission has now issued a "Notice on the Internal Rules of Procedure for processing requests for access to the file in cases pursuant to Articles 85 and 86 of the EC Treaty, Articles 65 and 66 of the ECSC Treaty and Council Regulation (EEC) No. 4064/89", OJ 1997 C23/3.
56 This practice has been adopted by the Commission in preference to inviting undertakings to inspect documents at the Commission: see *Twenty-third Report on Competition Policy* (1993), para. 201.
57 *ibid.*, para. 205(ii).
58 Cases 56 and 58/64 *Consten and Grundig* v *Commission* [1966] CMLR 418; [1966] ECR 299 at para. 5 of the judgment: "[the parties] must be informed of the facts upon which these complaints are based. It is not necessary, however, that the entire contents of the file should be communicated to them." In Case 85/76 *Hoffman-La Roche* v *Commission* [1979] 3 CMLR 211; [1979] ECR 461 at para. 11 of the judgment the Court was a little more elaborate: "the undertaking concerned must have been afforded the opportunity during the administrative procedure to make known their views on the truth and relevance of the facts and circumstances alleged and on the documents used by the Commission to support its claim that there has been an infringement of Article 86 of the Treaty".
59 See *Twelfth Commission Competition Report* (1983), pp. 40, 41, paras. 34, 35. See Case 53/65 *AKZO* v *Commission* [1986] ECR 1965; [1987] ECMLR 231.
60 Case T-7/89 *Hercules* v *Commission* [1991] II-1711 [1992] 4 CMLR 84.
61 See *Twenty-Third Report on Competition Policy* (1993), para. 202.

7.24 Where an undertaking makes a justified request to consult non-accessible documents the Commission may make a non-confidential summary of the contents available. It is for the Hearing Officer to decide what should be divulged.[62] Of course, where several undertakings are the subject of the same investigation, they may agree to waive confidentiality *vis-à-vis* each other, provided that in obtaining confidential information about each other they do not use that to act in contravention of Article 85(1).[63] The Commission has no right to decide which documents or classes of document are to be disclosed upon grounds of relevance since it is for the undertaking and its advisers to decide what is relevant to the defence, not the Commission. Material failure to grant access by the Commission may result in annulment of the decision upon an application under Article 173 EC for judicial review.

7.25 Following the judgment of the Court in *ICI* v *Commission*[64] the Commission has developed internal guidelines on access to documents on the Commission's file. The broad principles which will be applied by the Commission are as follows:

(i) The Defence is entitled in principle to the clearest possible picture of the documents on file and of the documents upon which the Commission's objections are based. In principle a common file is to be established for each case and not a file for each Defendant. The file will contain access to exculpatory and "smoking gun" documents.

(ii) The Commission accepts that it is not for its officials to decide what is and what is not relevant to the Defence.

(iii) The documents which may be excluded from the file fall into two categories, namely business secrets and international documents of the Commission (examples of the latter include advice from legal service, documents emanating from other services within the Commission and most correspondence passing between the Commission and Member States).

(iv) In exceptional cases the Commission may use documents constituting business secrets if there is a strong public interest in so doing. In such a case these business secrets will be put on file and the Defendants will be given access thereto. The Commission accepts that it cannot develop a case against the Defendant based upon information constituting a business secret not included on the file. The definition of business secrets is unclear. Proprietary technology or know-how constitutes a business secret. Reports which may be purchased do not constitute business secrets. The Commission is likely to evaluate claims for business secrecy with much greater care in the future. Disputes as to whether a document constitutes a business secret or not may be determined by the Hearing Officer on appeal. The Commission consider that if the Hearing Officer decides that the document is not a business secret and that it may therefore be put on the file that decision may be subject to judicial review before the Court but if the Hearing Officer decides not to give access that decision is not subject to appeal.

(v) The Commission will seek to adopt a sophisticated document identification system to facilitate the task of defence lawyers in identifying documents which are excluded from the file.

[62] *ibid.*, para. 205(v).

[63] *PVC* [1990] 4 CMLR 345; see Chapter 9 for the application of Article 85 EC to information sharing agreements.

[64] Case T-36/91 [1995] ECR II-1851.

7.26 The statement of objections will specify a time period for submission of a defence. Deadlines for replies to statements of objections have been "standardised" by the Commission, which has summarised the position thus:[65]

> "In cases of average importance, a general period of two months will be granted, and for complicated cases, a period of three months. An extra two weeks will automatically be allowed when these general periods fall at Christmas or Easter, and an extra one month will be granted automatically where the periods include all or part of the month of August ... unlike practice followed in the past, these fairly long periods will not normally be extended. [However, in] expedited procedures, for example where interim measures are being considered ... only the minimum period of two weeks provided for in Article 11 of Regulation 99/63 will therefore be granted and without any extension."

It is for the Hearing Officer to decide whether a deadline is too short.[66]

7.27 A challenge to a refusal to grant access by the Commission can only be made as part of a challenge to a later reviewable act; a refusal to grant access is not itself an independently reviewable act; a refusal to grant access is not itself an *independently* reviewable act, being only a preparatory act.[67] In the general the period will never be less than two weeks and may well be very considerably longer. Usually, however, a period of about six to eight weeks is given.[68] The time limit is extendable, though the longer the original period allotted by the Commission the less likely it is that an extension will be granted.[69] Parties should be wary about admitting facts or issues in these written proceedings.

7.28 Submissions in reply should carry the proviso that the contents of the reply including any admissions made therein are without prejudice to anything the parties may wish to argue before the Court at a later date. It appears that an admission at this stage forecloses the opportunity of raising the issue in a hearing before the Court.[70]

8. Oral Hearings

7.29 Article 19 of Regulation 17/62/EEC requires the Commission to permit the parties an opportunity to make oral representations before the Commission arrives at a formal decision.[71] For this purpose the Commission conduct a hearing presided over by a Hearing Officer.[72] This officer is appointed to ensure that the rights of the defence are respected not only during the oral hearing itself but also in the stages preceding the hearing. The Hearing Officer is separate from the Commission officials conducting the case. The officer is fully responsible for conduct of the hearing. In 1982 the Commission stated:

65 *op. cit.*, note 61 para. 207.

66 *ibid.*, para. 205(I).

67 Cases T-10-12 and 15/92 *Cimenteries* v *Commission* [1992] ECR II-2667, [1993] 4 CMLR 243. However, once a challengeable act has been adopted, it may then have found a successful challenge to that act, as in Case T-36/91 *ICI* v *Commission* [1995] ECR II-1851.

68 See Art. 2(4) Reg. 99/63/EC. See Case 19/70 *Almini* v *Commission* [1971] ECR 623—where the Commission failed to fix a time a sufficient time period to enable the parties to properly exercise their rights must be assumed. See also Cases 6, 7/73 *ICI* v *Commission* [1974] 1 CMLR 309; [1974] ECR 223—Advocate General Warner described the two-week period set for such a complex case as "patently unreasonable".

69 See Ferry, "Procedures and powers of the EC Commission in anti-trust cases" [1979] EIPR 126 at p. 129.

70 See Case 30/78 *Distillers* v *Commission* [1980] 3 CMLR 121 [1978] ECR 2229.

71 See also Hearing Reg. 99/63/EC OJ sp. edn. 1963–64, p. 47. This lays down procedural rules governing the hearing.

72 The Commission has summarised its view of the role of the Hearing Officer in *Twenty-third Report on Competition Policy* (1993), paras. 203–206. See also H. Johannes, "The role of the hearing officer" [1989] *Fordham Corp L Inst* 347; Kerse [1994] ECLR 40 "Procedures in EC competition cases: the oral hearing".

> "Administratively, the Hearing Officer belongs to the Directorate General for Competition. To ensure his independence in the performance of his duties, he has the right of direct access to the Member of the Commission with special responsibility for Competition policy; if he considers it appropriate he may refer to the Member his comments on the draft decision. In order to make sure that the Commission, when taking a decision on a draft decision on an individual case, is fully informed of all relevant factors, the Member of the Commission with special responsibility for competition policy may also submit to it the Hearing Officer's opinion."[73]

7.30 The Hearing Officer organises preparations for the hearing, fixing the date, time and place. He may warn undertakings of questions and issues of special relevance to the hearing. To this end pre-hearing meetings may be organised with the parties and even with the relevant Commission department. Statements of submissions from those who are to speak on behalf of the undertakings may be requested. During the hearing the Hearing Officer controls the admissibility of new documents, witnesses who may corroborate the facts relied on, and, whether to hear all interested parties together or separately (e.g. complainant may wish confidentiality). The Hearing Officer's Report need not be disclosed to the Commission,[74] to the parties[75] or to the Advisory Committee.[76]

7.31 The hearing date is usually set for a few weeks after the end of the period allotted to the written reply and takes place in Brussels. It is difficult to persuade the Commission to change this date, given that the latter has to arrange for translation services and rooms to be available in advance. In practice, the Commission rely most heavily on the written proceedings. The hearing is of short duration, usually one day only. Often it is divided so that parties may submit comments in the morning and other interested parties, including the Member States and complainants, may make submissions in the afternoon. A complainant may only hear such evidence as is not confidential. Parties must, therefore, be prepared to split their submissions into confidential and otherwise.[77] As implied above the hearing is open not just to the parties but also to Member States, to complainants and to anyone else with a "sufficient interest."[78]

7.32 In the *IBM Settlement*[79] case the hearing held in February 1982 lasted one week. IBM presented the evidence of 20 witnesses (17 in person, 3 by written deposition) who represented not only IBM but also competitors and computer-user associations. Moreover, a string of American and European academics, economists and other experts intervened. One US government official also attended as observer.[80] Following the hearing, the Commission sent IBM a statement of proposed remedies, and following informal negotiations, a second hearing took place in June 1983. The *IBM Settlement* case is one of the most extensive ever undertaken by the Commission, albeit that it ended in a negotiated result rather than a formal decision. Minutes will be taken of proceedings at the oral hearing and the undertakings have a chance to read and approve their contents as a true record.

[73] *Twelfth Commission Competition Report* (1982), pp. 41, 42, paras. 36, 37. The terms of reference of the Hearing Officer are set out by Commission Decision 94/810 of 12 December 1994, OJ L330/67. This is a useful document to refer to for any parties involved in oral hearings.

[74] Case T-7/89 *Hercules* v *Commission* [1992] 4 CMLR 84, para. 303

[75] Case 212/87 *ICI* v *Commission* [1987] 2 CMLR 500.

[76] Case T-7/89 *Hercules* v *Commission* [1992] 4 CMLR 84, para. 303.

[77] For a detailed account of proceedings before the Hearing Officer parties should see Kerse, *op. cit.*, at pp. 161–70. The functioning of the post of Hearing Officer was reviewed by the Commission in its *Eighteenth Report on Competition Policy* (1988), para. 44, concluding that it had proved its worth in practice, particularly through being able to supply advance notice of matters to be discussed at a hearing and thus enabling the discussion to be focused.

[78] See Art. 5 of Reg. 99/63/EEC and Art. 19(2) of Reg. 17/62/EEC.

[79] The results of the settlement are reported at [1984] 3 CMLR 147.

[80] But cf. Commission answer to WQ No. 292/82 OJ 1982 C174/20.

This enables the Commission and the Advisory Committee (see below) to have an accurate record of proceedings. In multi-partite cartel cases hearings do often take a number of days to complete.

9. The Advisory Committee on Restrictive Trade Practices and Monopolies

7.33 The Advisory Committee comprises officials represented by each Member State who are competent in antitrust law.[81] The Committee is influential and is consulted by the Commission prior to the taking by it of: (a) decisions establishing infringements under Articles 85 or 86; (b) decisions giving negative clearance; (c) decisions renewing, amending or revoking an exemption under Article 85(3); (d) decisions imposing fines or periodical penalties. While it normally receives minutes of an oral hearing, failure to do so is not a breach of an essential procedural requirement if the Committee would not be materially misled.[82] The Advisory Committee advises further on: investigations by the Commission into specific sectors of the economy (sector inquiries); draft block exemptions; application of the opposition procedure under the block exemptions; other procedural questions. The opinion of the Advisory Committee is secret;[83] the parties have no opportunity to view it. Nor indeed is the opinion usually disclosed in Court proceedings before the Court of Justice. The existence of this secret opinion has been widely criticised.[84] Since the equivalent opinions in cases under the Merger Control Regulation may now be published in the Official Journal,[85] it is difficult to see the justification for continued non-publication of opinions under Regulation 17/62.

10. Decisions of the Commission[86]

7.34 The Commission takes very few decisions per annum, perhaps a dozen at most. By contrast a large number of informal settlements are arrived at. These are considered below. Given the relative unimportance of formal decisions relative to the negotiation process, only a brief survey of the complex law governing their issue will be given here.

(1) Interim measures decisions

7.35 The Commission may issue interim orders where requested by a party making a complaint. This is not frequently done; on average there is less than one order made each year. These measures are akin to interlocutory injunctions in English law. However, by comparison they are much slower to obtain and the applying party is not obliged to give a cross undertaking in damages. The power to take interim measures derives impliedly from Regulation 17/62/EEC[87] but can only be exercised upon proof of certain very strict criteria.

[81] See Kerse, *op. cit.*, note 1 at pp. 183–188.

[82] Case T-69/89 *RTE* v *Commission* [1991] 4 CMLR 596.

[83] It is annexed to the Commission's draft decision.

[84] See *per* Advocate General Warner in Case 30/78 *Distillers* v *Commission* [1980] 3 CMLR 121; [1978] ECR 2229, Van Bael, "EC antitrust enforcement and adjudication as seen by defence counsel" (1979) 7 *Revue Suisse du Droit International de la Concurrence* 1; UNICE Memorandum, "EC procedures in competition cases" (21 February 1981).

[85] Art. 19(7), Reg. 4064/89.

[86] Kerse, *op. cit.*, Chapter 6.

[87] See Art. 3(1) Reg. 17/62/EEC. The power was confirmed by the Court in Case 792/79R *Camera Care* v *Commission* [1980] 1 CMLR 334; [1980] ECR 119. The power to take interim measures under the ECSC Treaty was confirmed some years earlier in Cases 109 and 114/75 *National Carbonising Co* v *Commission* [1975] 2 CMLR 457; [1977] ECR 381. See Ferry, "Interim relief under the Rome Treaty: the European Commission's powers" [1980] EIPR 330; Temple Lang, "The powers of the Commission to order interim measures in competition cases" (1981) CMLRev 49.

The Court has stressed that interim measures must be indispensable to the effective exercise of the Commission's functions; limited to urgent cases; temporary and conservatory. In essence the measure must be necessary to avoid serious and irreparable damage to a complainant.[88] It is only necessary to show a prima facie breach of Articles 85 or 86 EC, not that it be "clear and flagrant".[89] The Court has held that the Commission cannot require of a party by an interim order, something that they could not require in a final decision. Thus the Commission cannot compel a supplier to manufacture a product and supply it where a refusal to supply that product is not in breach of Articles 85 or 86 and hence could not be made the subject of a final decision.[90]

7.36 In terms of time taken to obtain relief the current minimum would be in the region of eight to ten weeks,[91] If both complainant and complained of are situate in the UK an application to the national court for an interlocutory injunction may be a more rapid means of securing relief (though not necessarily a cheaper one) Moreover, an *ex parte* injunction cannot be obtained from the Commission, due to the need to initiate proceedings and issue a Statement of Objections.[92] However, the threat of interim measures and the associated Commission investigation may persuade the infringing party to settle.[93] In *Re Hilti*[94] the Commission accepted an undertaking in "good faith" from a firm alleged to be abusing its dominant position as an alternative to the imposition of an interim decision. The seeking of appropriate undertakings is currently considered an acceptable and more expeditions procedure to adopt in such cases.[95]

[88] See Commission comment on *ECS/AKZO* [1983] 3 CMLR 694 at *Thirteenth Commission Competition Report* (1983) at p. 95 para. 151. In case T-44/90 *La Cinq* v *Commission* [1992] ECR II-1 [1992] 4 CMLR 449, the Court of First Instance held that the Commission should only look at whether the Commission's final decision could remedy the harm complained of, not whether it might be remediable through national courts. Thus the non-availability of damages as a remedy to the Commission is relevant in assessing whether a decision should be taken, irrespective of the availability of damages to a national court.

[89] Case T-44/90 *La Cinq* v *Commission* [1992] ECR II-1 [1992] 4 CMLR 449. Similarly in T-23/90 *Peugeot* v *Commission* [1991] ECR II-653, [1993] 5 CMLR 540, the Court of First Instance held that it was not necessary for the Commission to determine definitively whether an agreement came within block exemption before taking interim measures (*in casu*, Reg. 123/85 on motor vehicle selective distribution).

[90] See Cases 228, 229/82 *Ford-Werke* v *Commission* [1984] ECR 1129 [1984] CMLR 649 noted, Hendry (1984) ELRev 344. However in T-23/90 *Peugeot* v *Commission* [1991] ECR II-653 [1993] 5 CMLR 540, the Court of First Instance did allow an interim measures decision to require the supply of cars of Peugeot to a parallel importer at levels pre-existing the conduct complained of. It seems that the difference between *Ford* and *Peugeot* is that in the latter case, a final decision condemning the conduct in question, termination of sales to agents for car purchasers in other EU states, would not have placed any positive obligation on Peugeot to continue sales, whereas in *Ford* the order being sought would have dictated to Ford to whom to sell.

[91] *ECS/AKZO* [1983] 3 CMLR 694: 13 May 1983 request to Commission for interim measure; 8 June 1983 statement of objections sent; 23 June oral proceedings; 4 July Advisory Committee; 29 July decision of Commission issued. A period of approximately 10 weeks thus elapsed between request for an interim measure and actual decision. Furthermore, the Commission received the first complaint in June 1982 so would have been in possession of some (or most) of the facts prior to the actual request for interim relief. Where the request is made contemporaneously with the initial complaint the Commission may have to devote more time to fact collection. Compare with the unusually protracted timetable in the decision in *Peugeot/Ecosystem* [1990] 4 CMLR 449, analysed in detail in *Butterworths' Competition Law Encyclopaedia* Section X, paras. 800–810, which took over ten months from initial complaint to the interim measures decision being issued.

[92] Contrast with the speed with which *ex parte* injunctions can be granted in English law: see *Ukwal* [1993] 5 CMLR 632, above where an *ex parte* injunction was granted immediately upon application to the High Court.

[93] See *Sea Containers Ltd/Stena Sealink* 1994 OJ L15/8, where the Commission issued a decision rejecting an application for interim measures because, *inter alia*, a suitable offer of access to the port of Holyhead had been made.

[94] [1985] 3 CMLR 619 at para. 6. See also, *Ford Motor Company Ltd, Fifteenth Commission Competition Report* (1985); DGFT Annual Report 1985, p. 29.

[95] See e.g. *Napier Brown/British Sugar* [1986] 3 CMLR 594; *Irish Distillers* [1988] 4 CMLR 840.

(2) Provisional decisions

7.37 Under Article 15(6) of Regulation 17/62/EEC the Commission may inform parties who have notified their agreements on Form A/B and hence have obtained provisional validity that they consider the agreement to infringe Article 85(1) and be inappropriate for exemption under Article 85(3). Having so informed the parties, provisional validity ends and with it the immunity from fines disappears.[96] In appraising the parties of this situation the Commission is issuing a decision. Provisional decisions have been relatively rare. Although such a decision may be used as an alternative to interim measures.[97] With growing awareness of EC law, this must be balanced against the consideration that it is less likely an agreement will be notified containing terms contrary to Article 85(3).[98]

(3) Final decisions

7.38 The Commission has wide ranging powers when issuing decisions. A decision may grant an exemption for an agreement, with or without conditions. Alternatively, a decision may prohibit conduct (a cease and desist decision) or it may declare conduct to be in breach of the law where the conduct in question is already terminated and a cease and desist order hence inappropriate.[99] The Court of Justice has held that the burden of proof for a breach of Article 85 is that there must be "sufficiently precise and coherent proof".[100] There is some suggestion that this is higher than the normal civil balance of probabilities test applied in civil law, and may even amount to a criminal burden of proof.[101] It is uncertain whether the Commission has power to prospectively forbid an agreement which has not been made.[102] Though, following a Commission warning, parties who subsequently enter an agreement risk heavy fines. The Commission may include in a decision matters not expressly covered in the statement of objections.[103] If the Commission wishes so to do, and the matters are material, the Commission must give the undertaking sufficient time for comment upon those matters.[104]

7.39 The Commission may make positive as well as negative orders in a decision. This is done by ordering the parties to take specific action to cure a breach. Therefore a resumption of supply has been ordered in the case of a refusal to supply contrary to Article 86 EC.[105] Going

[96] Cases 8–11/66 *Cimenteries* v *Commission* [1967] CMLR 77; [1967] ECR 75. See also Case 10/69 *Portelange* v *Smith Corona Marchant International* [1974] CMLR 397; [1969] ECR 309; *Sirdar/Phildar* [1975] 1 CMLR D93; *Bronbemaling/Heidemaatschappij* [1975] 2 CMLR D67 cf. note (1979) ELRev pp. 413, 414.

[97] Cases 228, 229/82 *Ford-Werke* v *Commission* [1984] CMLR 649 at paras. 17–24. See also for Commission appreciation of this potential, *Fourteenth Commission Competition Report* (1984) at pp. 95, 96 paras. 122–124.

[98] For a recent example of a provisional decision, see *Vichy* OJ 1991 L75/57, upheld on appeal Case T-19/91 *Vichy* v *Commission* [1992] ECR II-415.

[99] Art. 3 Reg. 17/62/EEC. See for example *Roofing Felt* [1991] 4 CMLR 130.

[100] 29-30/83 *Cie Royale Asturienne des Mines and Rheinzing* v *Commission* [1984] ECR 1679, 1702, [1985] 1 CMLR 688, 711.

[101] N. Green, "Evidence and proof in EC competition cases", pp. 138–43 in P.J. Slot and A. McDonnell (eds.), *Procedure and Enforcement in EC and US Competition Law* (Sweet and Maxwell, 1993).

[102] The Commission takes the view that it does. It may order termination of an agreement and order an undertaking not to enter into any agreement "having an equivalent effect" as in the decisions in *Hilti* [1988] 4 CMLR 489 and *Tetra Pak II* [1992] 4 CMLR 551, the former being upheld on appeal, though not specifically addressing this issue, before the Court of First Instance in Case T-30/89 *Hilti* [1991] ECR II-1439 [1992] 4 CMLR 16 and by ECJ in Case C-53/92 P, [1994] ECR I-667.

[103] See Case 41, 44, 45/69 *ACF Chemiefarma* v *Commission* [1970] ECR 661 at paras. 91–93 of the judgment; Cases 209–215, 218/78 *FEDETAB* v *Commission* [1981] 3 CMLR 134; [1980] ECR 3125 at para. 68 of the judgment.

[104] 107/82 *AEG-Telefunken* v *Commission* [1993] ECR 3151, [1984] ECR 3 CMLR 325, para. 27; Case T-11/89 *Shell* v *Commission* [1992] ECR II-757, para. 55.

[105] e.g. Case 67/73 *ICI and Commercial Solvents* v *Commission* [1974] 1 CMLR 309; [1974] ECR 223; Cases 56 and 58/64 *Consten and Grundig* v *Commission* [1966] CMLR 418; [1966] ECR 299.

further, the Commission ordered the grant of a licence of intellectual property rights in *Magill TV Guide*.[106] The Court of First Instance and the Court of Justice sanctioned this on appeal on the basis that the infringement of Article 86 EC involved in refusing to license copyright protected television programming listings justified the imposition of specific measures,[107] as these were the only ways possible of bringing the infringement to an end. This is to be contrasted with *Automec II*, where the Commission had ordered that an operator of a selective distribution system for BMW cars in Italy include the complainant in that system. The Court of First Instance held that the Commission had strayed beyond merely ordering the termination of an infringement: "it is not for the Commission to impose upon the parties its own choice among the different potential courses of action which all conform to the Treaty".[108]

7.40 While the Commission may refrain from taking a final decision if the infringement has been terminated,[109] it will not so refrain if there are proceedings in national courts for which a decision would be relevant.[110] In practice, although a formal mechanism exists for recommending termination of an infringement,[111] the normal method is for proceedings to be settled informally.

(4) "Short form" exemptions

7.41 A frequent complaint about Commission procedure stems from the fact that if parties wish the Commission to adopt a formal decision, for example granting exemption or confirming negative clearance, then delays of many months and even years may elapse from notification to actual decision. However, if parties wish to conclude a case upon an informal basis with the Commission then, although the process is much expedited, an informal "comfort letter" from the Commission provides less legal certainty and security than does a formal decision. In an attempt to overcome these difficulties the Commission, in 1985, announced the use of a short form exemption. Under this procedure the Commission publish details of a notified agreement in the Official Journal, await comments from interested third parties, and then issue a decision that is considerably shorter in its factual economic and legal analysis than decisions are accustomed to be. By this abbreviated procedure it was hoped to speed up the decision-making process. A number of problems arise from this procedure. How will the Commission reconcile the addressee and affected third parties' legal rights to know the reasoning behind a decision with the need to expedite decision making? As noted above the short form decision will contain a much shortened substantive content. How will the Court view such decisions when set against the unequivocal obligation in Article 190 EC imposed on the Commission to give reasons for its decisions. In practical terms these problems may not arise. First, when the Commission give the details of the agreement in the Official Journal they invite comments from interested parties. A person who considered his legitimate interests harmed by the agreement could, at that stage, complain to the Commission. Where the Commission were aware of objections they could deal with the case by full decision rather than by short form decision. An examination of the first and so far the only short form decision issued by the Commission—*BP–Kellogg*[112]—reveals that the Commission will have very little addi-

[106] *Magill TV Guide* [1989] 4 CMLR 757.
[107] Case T-69/89 *RTE* v *Commission* [1991] ECR II-485 [1991] 4 CMLR 586, paras. 97–8, upheld on appeal by the ECJ in Joined Cases C-241 and 242/91P *RTE and ITP* v *Commission* [1995] ECR I-743 [1995] 4 CMLR 718.
[108] Case T-24/90 *Automec* v *Commission* [1992] 4 CMLR 431, para. 52.
[109] e.g. *Napier Brown/British Sugar* OJ 1988 L284/41.
[110] *Florimex* [1989] 4 CMLR 500.
[111] Art. 3(3) Reg. 17/62/EEC.
[112] OJ 1985 L 369/4.

tional work to do other than to summarise the contents of the agreement and the submissions of the parties; the analytical portion of the decision is a mere four short paragraphs. The reason for the effective abandonment, at least for the time being, of the short form exemption appears to be that the Commission is concentrating its resources on dealing with the more complex issues raising points of wider significance. Seen in this light, a short form exemption involves more work than a comfort letter, and despite the increased advantage to the addressee, there is no corresponding benefit to the Commission. In practice the procedure has not been invoked since its experimental early days.

(5) Form of decisions: summary

7.42 Decisions must be reasoned. The Commission must set out in a clear and relevant fashion the principles of law and fact upon which it bases its findings.[113]

7.43 Decisions may confer negative clearance, i.e. that on the facts before it the Commission can find no grounds for the application of Articles 85 or 86 EC. However, decisions conferring negative clearance do not bind the national court, though the latter will no doubt take notice of them but, if new facts emerge, the national court is perfectly entitled to apply Article 85(1) and grant appropriate remedies against the parties. A decision granting negative clearance does not prevent future action by the Commission should circumstances change.[114] A decision may grant an exemption under Article 85(3) or renew, amend or revoke such a decision. Decisions of this type will be of fixed duration and will often attach conditions to their operation.[115] A decision may be appealed against to the Court of First Instance under Article 173 EC (see below).

11. Fines, Penalties

7.44 Article 15 provides for fines to be imposed in a number of situations. Fines of between 100 and 5,000 ECUs may be imposed where undertakings or associations,[116] intentionally or negligently:

(a) supply incorrect or misleading information in notifying an agreement and/or applying for negative clearance;
(b) supply incorrect or incomplete information in response to a request for information made by the Commission;
(c) fail to supply information within the time limit fixed by a decision demanding information;[117]
(d) disclose documents in an incomplete form during an on the spot investigation; or
(e) refuse to submit to an on the spot investigation ordered by a formal decision.

7.45 Under Article 15(2) fines of between 1,000 and 1,000,000 ECUs or a sum in excess of that but not exceeding 10 per cent of the turnover in the preceding business year of the

[113] Art. 190 EC. See Case 24/62 *Germany* v *Commission* [1963] CMLR 347 at p. 367; [1963] ECR 63 at p. 69: "In imposing upon the Commission the obligation to state reasons for its decisions, Article 190 is not taking mere formal considerations into account, but seeks to give an opportunity to the parties defending their rights, to the Court of exercising its supervisory function and the Member States and all interested nationals of ascertaining the circumstances in which the Commission has applied the Treaty."

[114] The principle of *res judicata* has no application though the doctrine of legitimate expectations should apply.

[115] Conditional exemptions are contemplated by Art. 8(1) Reg. 17/62/EEC. See, e.g. *International Energy Agency* [1984] 2 CMLR 186 noted, Green (1984) ELRev 449.

[116] Individuals (not being undertakings in their own right) are not liable to fines.

[117] See, for example, *AKZO Chemicals BV*, OJ 1994 L294/31, where the maximum fine of 5,000 ECUs was imposed for negligent failure to allow inspectors access to a director's office.

relevant undertaking, may be imposed for intentional or negligent infringements of Articles 85(1) or 86 EC. Fines of identical gravity may be imposed in respect of breaches of conditions imposed in decisions granting exemption under Article 85(3). The limitation period is five years from the date of the last infringement,[118] though this is interrupted by action of the Commission for the purpose of preliminary investigation. However, the imposition of a fine will be definitively time-barred if ten years has elapsed from the date of the cessation of the infringement without the imposition of a fine by the Commission.[119]

7.46 The power to impose fines of up to 10 per cent of the "turnover in the preceding year" is an effective sanction. Though the sanction has only been regularly imposed since 1969 it is today a standard part of the Commission's machinery.[120] The phrase "turnover in the preceding business year" refers to turnover of all products for the whole world. It is *not* turnover for the relevant products in the EC or even turnover of all products in the EC. The justification for the wide formulation is based simply upon the ability of an undertaking to pay a fine. The Court has stated that the upper limits mentioned in Article 15(2) exist "to prevent fines from being disproportionate in relation to the size of the undertaking".[121] Article 16(1) of Regulation 17/62/EEC provides for periodic penalties of between 50 to 1,000 ECUs per day. These may be imposed to compel an undertaking to:

(a) terminate an infringement forthwith;
(b) refrain from any act prohibited by a decision made in relation to an Article 85(3) exemption;
(c) supply complete and accurate information demanded by a decision; and
(d) submit to an on the spot investigation ordered by a decision.

7.47 Fines under Article 15 and penalties under Article 16 are not mutually exclusive, as they perform complementary functions. A fine is a punishment for past behaviour as well as deterring future non-compliance;[122] a penalty payment is a sanction to ensure future compliance. Fines are expressed in ECUs (European Currency Units)[123] and will also be expressed in local currencies. For rough purposes only an ECU equals approximately 70p (UK). This figure should of course be verified by reference to prevalent exchange rates.[124]

7.48 In fixing fines the Commission must (under Article 15(2) of Regulation 17/62/ EC) have regard to both, "the gravity and to the duration of the infringement". Although the Commission is not under a duty to set out the criteria according to which it plans to impose a fine, the Court of First Instance has stated that it is desirable for the Commission to indicate the method of calculation to the undertaking being fined.[125]

7.49 The Commission has adopted a noticeably tougher approach to fining commencing with its decision in *Tetra Pak II*,[126] in which one undertaking was fined ECU75 million (approximately £50 million) for breach of Article 86 EC. Large cartels have been heavily fined as well. The *Cartonboard* cartel, involving 19 undertakings, was fined a total of ECU132 million,[127] while the *Cement* cartel saw fines totalling ECU248 million imposed

[118] Council Reg. 2988/74, OJ 1974 L319/1, Art. 1.
[119] Council Reg. 2988/74, OJ 1974 L319/1, Art. 2.
[120] See *Thirteenth Commission Competition Report* (1983), pp. 56–58, paras. 62–66.
[121] Cases 100–103.80 *Musique Diffusion Française SA* v *Commission (Pioneer)* [1983] ECR 1825, [1983] 3 CMLR 221 at para. 109 of the judgment. See also *Johnson and Johnson* [1981] 2 CMLR 287.
[122] 100-103/80 *Musique Diffusion Française* v *Commission* [1983] ECR 1825, [1983] 3 CMLR 221, para. 105.
[123] The ECU is the unit of account referred to in Reg. 17/62/EEC.
[124] For determining precise rates see para. 6.55.
[125] Case T-148/89 *Tréfilunion* v *Commission* [1995] ECR II-1063.
[126] [1992] 4 CMLR 551.
[127] OJ 1994 L243/1.

on 48 undertakings across the EC.[128] The starting point is that undertakings breaching Articles 85 and 86 EC cannot be allowed to profit from their own wrong, that they must be punished and the fines must also have a deterrent effect.[129]

7.50 In *Cartonboard* the Commission summarised the factors it had taken into account in imposing large fines thus:[130]

> "In determining the general level of fines in the present case the Commission has taken into account the following considerations:
> —the collusion on pricing and market sharing are by their very nature serious restrictions on competition,
> —the cartel covered virtually the whole territory of the Community,
> —the Community market for cartonboard is an important industrial sector worth some ECU 2,500 million each year,
> —the undertakings participating in the infringement account for virtually the whole of the market,
> —the cartel was operated in the form of a system of regular institutionalised meetings which set out to regulate in explicit detail the market for cartonboard in the Community,
> —elaborate steps were taken to conceal the true nature and extent of the collusion (absence of any official minutes or documentation for the [meetings]; discouraging the taking of notes; stage managing the timing and order in which price increases were announced so as to be able to claim that they were 'following', etc),
> —the cartel was largely successful in achieving its objectives."

7.51 In assessing the fine to be imposed on each undertaking, the Commission in addition to the above takes account of:

> "—the role played by each undertaking in the collusive arrangements,
> —any substantial differences in the duration of their respective participation in the cartel, if such is the case,
> —their respective importance in the industry (size, product range, market share, group turnover and turnover in cartonboard),
> —any mitigating factors including the degree of cooperation with the Commission after the investigation and the extent to which any such cooperation may have materially contributed to facilitating or expediting the conclusion of the present proceedings.
> In so far as there is any good reason to accept that one or another undertaking may have participated for a substantially lesser period than did the others ... this is reflected in the amount of the fine imposed upon it. The Commission will also take into account any substantial change in the nature or intensity of the role played in the cartel by particular producers. It is not, however, intended in calculating each fine to employ some precise mathematical formula reflecting the exact number of days, months or years for which that producer adhered to the cartel."

7.52 The following are relevant factors to be taken into account in making an assessment of the likelihood and extent of fines.[131]

(1) Nature of the infringement

7.53 If the infringement concerns a practice known to be habitually challenged under Articles 85 or 86 by the Commission (for example price discrimination, refusal to supply, loyalty rebates, price-fixing, market sharing, export bans) then a large fine may be imposed. Con-

[128] OJ 1994 L343/1.
[129] *Twenty-first Report on Competition Policy* (1991), para. 139.
[130] OJ 1994 L243/1, paras. 168–169.
[131] See Kerse, *Antitrust Procedure* (3rd edn. 1994), pp. 251–276; P.J. Slot and A. McDonnell (eds.), *Procedure and Enforcement in EC and US Competition Law* (Sweet and Maxwell, 1993); L. Gyselen, "The Commission's fining policy in competition cases: 'Questo è il catalogo'".

versely, if the practice is one that the Commission has not examined before, or if the market is unusual for some reason, the Commission may refrain from imposing fines on account of the novelty of the case.[132] But where it is known by the undertakings concerned that competition rules could apply to their sector, then there is no mitigating circumstance by which fines may be reduced or not imposed.[133] In cases involving a degree of novelty where an informal settlement has taken place and the parties are thus made fully aware of the Commission's position then a subsequent breach of an undertaking given in good faith to the Commission as part of the settlement may well result in a formal decision and the imposition of a fine.[134]

(2) Knowledge of the parties

7.54 The Commission will consider the extent to which the parties were aware or should have been aware of the breach.[135] Fines may, it will be recalled, be imposed for intentional or negligent infringements. Negligence includes not removing offending provisions by oversight.[136] Nor is ignorance of the law a defence.[137] Failure to follow legal advice is an aggravating factor.[138] Part of the reason for not imposing fines in respect of novel cases (see above) is that the parties were probably infringing the law innocently rather than intentionally or negligently.

(3) Conduct of parties

7.55 The Commission may consider whether the parties operated their agreement in a covert and secret manner or whether they openly notified it to the Commission. In *Cast Iron and Steel Rolls*[139] the parties operated a "warning mechanism" which was activated in the event of a sudden inspection or visitation from the authorities. In such an event a "neutral" telex would be sent to other parties which read: "Re IRMA, attention Mr []. The figures from a German company for the next market survey are wrong. They will therefore be distributed at a later date." The end of panic telex would state: "Re IRMA, attention Mr []. We have now received the correct figures from the German Company. You will receive

132 In *Italian Flat Glass* [1990] 4 CMLR 535, no fines were imposed for abuse of a collective dominant position contrary to Art. 86 EC as this was the first time the Commission had applied this concept in practice. The decision was later annulled by the Court of First Instance on evidentiary grounds, Cases T-68, 77 and 78/89 *Italian Flat Glass* [1992] 5 CMLR 302. See also *Distribution of Package Tours* during the 1990 World Cup OJ 1992 L326/31.

133 *French-West African Shipowners' Committees* OJ 1992 L134/1, para. 74.

134 See for an example of a "good faith undertaking" the *IBM Settlement* [1984] 3 CMLR 147 at p. 152. IBM gave to the Commission an undertaking which commences as follows: "IBM undertakes in good faith". The Commission reason that infringement of this undertaking will constitute by IBM's own admission "bad faith". A very heavy fine commensurate with IBM's world strength would probably follow. See also, *Re Hilti* [1985] 3 CMLR 619, where a dominant firm gave good faith undertaking not to tie products together. However, the Commission found in its final decision, [1989] 4 CMLR 677, this act of good faith contradicted by several factors, including prior knowledge that breach was being committed and so a considerable fine was payable, this being upheld by the Court of First Instance, Case T-30/89 *Hilti* [1991] ECR II-1439 [1992] 4 CMLR 16, and by the Court of Justice in C-53/92, [1994] ECR I-667.

135 See Case 322/81 *Michelin* v *Commission* [1985] ECR 3461 [1985] 1 CMLR 282 at para. 107 of the judgment—Michelin deemed to be aware of previous decisions of the Commission and judgments of the Court and therefore could not argue that they did not have knowledge of the likely attitude of the Commission. See also in *Hilti* [1989] 4 CMLR 677, where the undertaking was aware from legal advice that it faced potential conflict with the competition rules, but did not change its practices.

136 C-277/87 *Sandoz* v *Commission* [1990] ECR 45.

137 19/77 *Miller* v *Commission* [1978] ECR 131, [1978] 2 CMLR 334.

138 *London European Airways/Sabena* OJ 1988 L317/47.

139 [1984] 1 CMLR 694 at paras. 20–22, 55 and 64 of the decision. See also *Peroxygen Cartel* [1985] 1 CMLR 481 at para. 54 of the decision; and *Polypropylene* 1988 4 CMLR 347 para. 108.

the market survey in a few days. Thank you for your comprehension." The implication drawn from this alarm system by the Commission is obvious. The Commission concluded: "The alarm system ... and the code system ... make it clear that the parties were fully aware that their conduct constituted infringements of Community legislation." In *ECS–AKZO*[140] the Commission imposed a fine of ECU10 million on AKZO for predatory pricing. A number of factors underpinned this very substantial punishment. Two are of especial interest. First, AKZO continued its policy of conscious, sustained aggression against ECS after both a High Court injunction issued in London, and, an interim decision of the Commission. Secondly, AKZO had given a totally misleading version of the events to the High Court. These factors, considered the Commission, aggravated the severity of the offence. The Court of Justice, however, reduced the fine on AKZO for three reasons.[141] First, some aspects of the infringement relating to pricing raised novel issues for which there was no previously settled competition law. Secondly, the infringement had only had a limited effect on the parties' market shares. Thirdly, there had not in fact been an infringement of the actual terms of the interim measures decision by AKZO.

(4) Nature of the product and its relevance to consumers

7.56 The Commission consider the importance of a product to the consumer. An agreement fixing prices for an important product (commonly used foodstuffs, motor vehicles, alcohols) may attract larger fines than an agreement concerning specialist consumer luxuries.[142]

(5) Economic context

7.57 The Commission may consider the political and economic context of the market. Thus, where an agreement occurs in the context of a declining market and international moves are in operation to restructure and rationalise the industry, the Commission might refrain from imposing heavy fines where this would impose additional financial strain on the resources of the undertakings in question.[143] In *PVC Cartel*,[144] the Commission regarded it as a mitigating rather than aggravating factor that the parties had been fined previously for operating a polypropylene cartel.[145] This may be a tacit acknowledgment that that particular part of the chemicals industry appeared to be so cartelised that there was in practice little actual competition to restrict. Normally repeated conduct is an aggravating factor.[146] However, an agreement between parties which hinders competition and stifles development in a market considered by the Commission to be of strategic or technological relevance will be considered a serious breach.[147]

(6) Number and size of undertakings

7.58 Where the combined market share of the parties is high this will be an indication of the gravity of the agreement for the market. A price fixing agreement between X, Y and Z

[140] OJ 1985 1374/1 at p. 25 para. 97.

[141] C-62/86 *AKZO* v *Commission* [1991] ECR I-3359, [1993] 5 CMLR 215, paras. 161–164.

[142] See e.g. *Theal/Watts* [1977] 1 CMLR D44 (record cleaning devices). For a contrast see *Polypropylene*, *ibid.*, n. 136.

[143] *Cast Iron and Steel Rolls* [1984] 1 CMLR 694 at paras. 72–76 of the decision.

[144] *PVC Cartel* OJ 1989 L74/1. The judgments of the Court of First Instance, Joined Cases T-79, 84–86, 91–92, 97, 96, 102 and 104/89 *BASF* v *Commission* [1992] 4 CMLR 357 and, on further appeal, the Court of Justice, Case 137/92 P [1994] ECR I-2555, do not affect this point, as they both decided to quash the decision on procedural grounds. The decision was subsequently readopted: OJ 1994 L239/14.

[145] *Polypropylene Cartel* [1988] 4 CMLR 347.

[146] Case T-7/89 *Hercules* v *Commission* [1992] 4 CMLR 84, para. 348.

[147] See, e.g. *Siemens-Fanuc*, OJ 1985 1376/29 at paras. 34, 35.

who together control 63 per cent of a market will have significantly more restrictive consequences than a similar agreement between A, B and C who, combined, control only 12 per cent of the market.[148]

(7) Extent of participation

7.59 Parties may be involved to a greater or lesser degree in a cartel. This will be considered as an important factor when determining the level of fines to be imposed.[149] In *Roofing Felt*[150] certain manufacturers who were not part of the main price-fixing cartel nevertheless agreed with members to join in a policy of restricting discounts. The Commission condemned their participation but declined to impose fines because, although "the non-members had been eager to give the impression of going along with the plans ... they had not real intention of abiding by the agreements. In any case the duration of the infringements established against the non-members was limited".[151] In *BPB Industries/British Gypsum*[152] the Court of First Instance upheld the Commission's decision to impose fines both on BPB, the parent company, and on British Gypsum, its wholly owned subsidiary. The Court observed that the conduct of a subsidiary may be attributed to the parent company where the parent company does not decide independently upon its own conduct but carries out, all material respects, the instructions given to it by the parent company. A wholly owned subsidiary, in principle, necessarily follows the policy laid down by the parent company.

7.60 Where an association of undertakings has been involved in an infringement, the fine may be calculated by reference to the turnover of the constituent undertakings, even though imposed on the association.[153]

(8) The state of national law

7.61 The Commission recognise that an undertaking may, by complying with national law, be forced into an infringement of Community law. While the latter takes precedence over the former, the Commission may appreciate that an undertaking's breach of Article 85 or 86 is, to an extent, involuntary. Compliance with national law, however, is *not* a defence to breach of Community law.[154]

(9) Profits made by the undertakings

7.62 The Commission bear in mind the relationship between cartel profits and level of fines. The latter must have a deterrent value and hence may be related to the level of profits earned as a result of the cartel.[155] The Commission has stated[156] that "Wherever the Commission can ascertain the level of this ill-gotten gain, even if it cannot do so precisely, the calcula-

148 e.g. *Floral* [1980] 2 CMLR 285. In Cases 100–103/80 *Musique Diffusion Française SA* v *Commission (Pioneer)* [1983] 3 CMLR 221 at para. 120 of the judgment the Court stressed that in assessing fines the Commission may consider, "the volume and value of the goods in respect of which the infringement was committed and the size and economic power of the undertaking and, consequently, the influence which the undertaking was able to exert on the market"—thus the Court apparently link size of parties to restrictive effect.

149 The Commission must, in imposing fines, respect the equitable notion of non-discrimination between firms in comparable situations; see answer to WQ No. 2296/85, OJ 1986.

150 OJ 1986 L232/15.

151 OJ 1986 L232/15 para. 111. See also *Cewal* OJ 1993 L34/20.

152 T-65/89 *BPB Industries* v *Commission* [1993] ECR II-389.

153 Joined Cases T-39 and 40/92 *Europay* [1994] ECR II-49, para. 139.

154 See e.g. Case 73/74 *Groupements des Fabricants de Papiers Peints de Belgique* v *Commission* [1976] 1 CMLR 589, [1975] ECR 1491. Though, the involvement of government may be a factor in mitigation of fine—*AROW* v *BNIC* [1983] 2 CMLR 240 at p. 260 para. 77.

155 See e.g. *Kawasaki* [1979] 1 CMLR 448. Or to operating losses sustained during currency of the cartel, horizontal cartels often arise in depressed markets, see *Polypropylene, ibid.*, n. 139.

tion of the fine may have this as its starting point. When appropriate, that amount could then be increased or decreased in the light of the other circumstances of the case, including the need to introduce an element of deterrence or penalty". In *Eurocheque*[157] a practice contrary to Article 85(1) was held to have led to financial gain of ECU5 million, and led to a fine of the same amount.

(10) Ability to pay

7.63 The Commission consider the defendants capacity to pay a fine. Thus, in *Cast Iron and Steel Rolls*[158] a relevant factor was the depressed financial position of the parties and their need to preserve capital to assist in restructuring. In *Cewal*,[159] one of the members of the shipping conference which was held to have infringed Articles 85 and 86 was held by the Commission not to have gained any advantage from the practices established by Cewal "as is shown by its serious financial difficulties at the present time" and it was decided that no fines should be imposed upon it "which would further weaken its position". It is also possible to argue that inability to pay because of other fines for competition infringements should preclude the imposition of a fine. In *LdPE*[160] the Commission, in fixing the amount of the fines imposed on a price fixing cartel, took into account the fact that the majority of undertakings involved had already been the subject of substantial fines for their participation in another cartel relating to a different product.

(11) Duration of infringements

7.64 In assessing the fine the Commission obviously consider the duration of the breach. In practice duration will play a part in assessing gravity.[161]

(12) Mitigation, good faith undertakings and Commission practice

7.65 In terms of mitigation the Commission may consider, *inter alia*: the extent to which parties relied upon legal advice; the extent to which the parties relied upon a non-binding notice issued by the Commission; the extent to which the parties were open in their dealings with the Commission; and to the extent to which they voluntarily abandoned their cartel. The Commission will also pay great weight to whether a party was a "whistle blower" who divulged details of a cartel to the Commission and who co-operated fully with the Commission thereafter in the course of an investigation. It is possible that immunity from fines could be the price paid to the whistle blower. In *Wood Pulp*[162] the Commission imposed significant fines on 43 non-EC companies who fixed prices for bleached sulphate pulp. However, the Commission, in the decision, made a point of indicating that they had "substantially" reduced the fines on those who had "co-operated" with the Commission and who had given detailed written "good faith" undertakings about their future conduct in respect of prices and the exchange of information. It is an undecided point whether breach of the undertaking entitles the Commission to reimpose

[156] *Twenty-first Report on Competition Policy* (1991), para. 139.

[157] OJ 1992 L95/50. However, this was subsequently reduced on appeal as the Court of First Instance found that elements of the infringement were not properly substantiated by the evidence adduced by the Commission: Joined Cases T-39 and 40/92 *Europay* [1994] ECR II-49. See also *Cewal* OJ 1993 L34/20.

[158] See above n. 143.

[159] *Cewal* OJ 1993 L34/20.

[160] OJ 1989 L74/21, [1990] 4 CMLR 382. The decision was subsequently quashed on procedural grounds. Cases T-80, 81, 83, 87, 88, 90, 93, 95, 97, 99, 101, 103, 105, 107 and 112/89 *BASF* v *Commission* [1995] ECR II-729.

[161] Thus in *Polypropylene* [1988] 4 CMLR 347, the Commission found that the cartel had been operating for about six years; this was considered to be of long duration and so the fines imposed were heavy.

[162] [1985] 3 CMLR 474.

fines of a level that would have been applied in the absence of the undertaking or indeed at an enhanced level reflecting censure of the undertakings "bad faith".

7.66 The Commission has identified three broad types of situations in which companies' may be able informally to negotiate reduced fines, going beyond the normal scope of a defence. First, if the company co-operates fully with the Commission and on its own initiative provides significant information about he unlawful behaviour in question, which the Commission had not previously obtained. Cooperation that goes further and actively helps in the dismantling of a cartel may be rewarded with a higher level of rebate of the fine that otherwise would be made. In *Cartonboard*,[163] a fine on one undertaking was reduced by two-thirds on this basis. Second, if the company takes measures in addition to those it is in any case obliged take, to make the market more competitive, such as divestiture or offers to license technology. Thirdly, a company might provide generous compensation for those injured by its conduct, at least to the level of the losses incurred.[164] Offering to institute a compliance programme,[165] on the other hand, is not a reason for a reduction in fine, as a company is advised to have one in place in any event. Even if institution of a compliance programme is taken into account in mitigation,[166] once in place, further breaches of the competition rules may then be seen as intentional, and thus aggravate liability to fines.

7.67 It may also be a mitigating factor if one of the parties only entered into the agreement as a result of strong pressure. In *Fisher Price/Quaker Oats–Toyco*[167] Fisher Price refused to supply Toyco if it did not comply with an export ban. The Commission fined Fisher Price but did not fine Toyco as it "agreed to stop supplies ... only after having been put under strong pressure by an ultimatum from Quaker Oats/Fisher Price". Current Commission practice is to impose fines of up to about 8 or 9 per cent of total turnover for especially serious infringements (e.g. long-term horizontal price fixing). The Commission do not calculate fines by any mathematical formulae but, as suggested above, work by reference to a host of factors which include the duty to punish individual infringements.

12. Appeals to the Court of First Instance

7.68 Parties may appeal a Commission decision to the Court of First Instance under Article 173 EC. This reads:

> "(1) The Court of Justice shall review the legality of acts adopted jointly by the European Parliament and the Council, of acts of the Council, of the Commission and of the European Central Bank, other than recommendations or opinions, and of acts of the European Parliament intended to produce legal effects vis-à-vis third parties.
>
> (2) It shall for this purpose have jurisdiction in actions brought by a Member State, the Council or the Commission on grounds of lack of competence, infringement of an essential procedural requirement, infringement of this Treaty or of any rule of law relating to its application, or misuse of powers.

[163] OJ 1994 L243/1, para. 171.

[164] In *Rover Group*, the Commission decided not to initiate a formal investigation into price fixing practices between Rover and its car dealers because senior management voluntarily notified the Commission of what had taken place and agreed to contribute £1 million to projects designed to benefit UK car purchasers: see *Twenty-third Report on Competition Policy* (1993), para. 228.

[165] D.H. Marks, "Setting up an antitrust compliance programme" [1988] ECLR 88.

[166] *Hilti* [1988] 4 CMLR 489.

[167] OJ 1988 L49/19, [1989] 4 CMLR 513.

(3) The Court shall have jurisdiction under the same conditions in actions brought by the European Parliament and the European Central Bank for the purpose of protecting their prerogatives.

(4) Any natural or legal person may, under the same conditions, institute proceedings against a decision addressed to that person or against a decision which, although in the form of a regulation or a decision addressed to another person, is of direct and individual concern to the former.

(5) The proceedings provided for in this Article shall be instituted within two months of the publication of the measure, or of its notification to the plaintiff, or, in the absence thereof, of the day on which it came to the knowledge of the latter, as the case may be."

7.69 Although Article 173 EC refers in terms to the Court of Justice, appeals against competition decisions brought by natural or legal persons are heard by the Court of First Instance.[168] Appeal from decisions of the Court of First Instance lies on points of law to the Court of Justice.[169] The addressee of a decision may appeal to the Court of First Instance whether fines are imposed or not.[170] Third parties (for example, the complainant or other competitors, suppliers or customers of the addressee) may also apply to the Court of First Instance to have the decision reviewed if they can prove that it is of "direct and individual concern" to them (see the wording of Article 173, para. 4, above). A person who makes a complaint has a right under Article 173 to seek review of the decision.[171] It has been argued that any person who might suffer direct loss or injury as a consequence of the decision or "act" in question should have the right to use Article 173. Thus, if the Commission issue a decision exempting X, Y and Z under Article 85(3) and rivals of X, Y and Z see this as a threat to their legitimate interests they should be entitled to challenge the exemption on the basis of Article 173.[172] The grounds of review are those set out in Article 173, paragraph 2.[173] Though to establish *locus* such rivals should, ordinarily, have participated in the review procedure, as complainants, leading up to the decision. The Court also enjoys unlimited competence to review fines imposed by the Commission.[174]

[168] Jurisdiction was transferred from the Court of Justice by Council decision 88/591 EEC dated 24 October 1988, OJ 1988 L319/1, corrected version OJ 1989 C215/1, [1989] 3 CMLR 458. The jurisdiction of the Court of First Instance was extended by a Council decision of 8 June 1993, OJ 1993 L144/21. See generally on the Court of First Instance, T. Millett, *The Court of First Instance of the European Communities* (1990).

[169] See K.P.E. Lasok, *The European Court of Justice* (2nd edn. 1994) generally for practice and procedure before the Court of Justice and in particular Chapter 15 on appeals from the Court of First Instance.

[170] Art. 173 allows review of "acts"; this is wider than just a formal decision. See Case 22/70 *Commission* v *Council (ERTA)* [1971] CMLR 335; [1971] ECR 263 at paras. 38–42 of the judgment. "Decision" is widely construed, see, e.g. Case 792/79R *Camera Care* v *Commission* [1980] 1 CMLR 33; [1980] ECR 119—Advocate General Warner thought refusal by Commission, in a letter, to take an interim measure was a decision.

[171] Case 26/76 *Metro SB Grossmarkte* v *Commission* [1978] 2 CMLR 1; [1977] ECR 1875 at para. 13 of the judgment. Noted, Dinnage, (1979) 4 ELRev 15; Temple Lang (1978) ELRev 177.

[172] 75/84 *Metro* v *Commission (II)* [1986] ECR 3021, [1987] 1 CMLR 118, para. 20. In Case T-37/92 *Bureau Européen des unions des Consommateurs and National Consumer Council* v *Commission* [1994] ECR II-285, a consumers' organisation was held to have sufficient standing to mount a successful Art. 173(4) challenge. See generally Kerse, *op. cit.*, at pp. 327–328.

[173] See Kerse, *op. cit.*, note 1 at pp. 325–342; Hartley, *The Foundations of European Community Law* (3rd edn. 1994), Chapter 15 and generally Chapters 11–16; Usher, "Exercise by the European Court of its jurisdiction to annul competition decisions" (1980) ELRev 287.

[174] Art. 172 EC. See also Art. 17 of Reg. 17/62/EEC. "The Court shall have unlimited jurisdiction within the meaning of Article 172 of the Treaty to review decisions whereby the Commission has fixed a fine or periodic penalty payment; it may cancel, reduce or increase the fine or periodic penalty imposed."

C. The Legal Basis of Formal Negotiations: Article 85(3)

7.70 Parties may negotiate with the Commission in respect of amendments to agreements which will enable the latter to grant an exemption under Article 85(3). Only the Commission may grant an exemption. Neither the Court in Luxembourg nor national courts may do so. Negotiations may also arise on how parties may bring their agreement within the terms of relevant block exemption. Such discussions will only be feasible where the parties have notified their agreement in proper manner. Where the parties have operated a clandestine cartel the Commission may be unsympathetic to moves, following discovery of the agreement, by the parties to initiate exemption discussions. The criteria for Article 85(3) exemption are given below. The application of these principles to specific types of agreement and trade association practice is discussed in the later chapters. There is no type of agreement that in theory cannot benefit from Article 85(3).[175] However, many exemptions are subject to conditions and obligations imposed upon the parties, and each exemption is granted only for a specified period of time in accordance with Article 8 of Regulation 17/62/EEC.

1. *Article 85(3): Text*

7.71 Article 85(3) states:

> "The provisions of paragraph 1 may, however, be declared inapplicable in the case of: any agreement or category of agreements between undertakings; any decision or category of decisions by associations of undertakings; any concerted practice or category of concerted practices; which contributes to improving the production or distribution of goods or to promoting technical or economic progress, while allowing consumers a fair share of the resulting benefit, and which does not: (a) impose on the undertakings concerned restrictions which are not indispensable to the attainment of these objectives; (b) afford such undertakings the possibility of eliminating competition in respect of a substantial part of the products in question."

7.72 Article 85(3) thus contains four elements all of which must be satisfied: two positive elements which parties must seek to establish their agreements exhibit; and two negative elements which parties must seek to establish their agreements are devoid of.[176] The positive elements are:

- contributing either (i) to improving the production of goods; or (ii) to improving the distribution of goods; or (iii) to promoting technical progress; or (iv) to promoting economic progress; and
- allowing consumers a fair share of the resulting benefit.

The two negative elements are:

[175] See Commission answer to WQ No. 675/76 OJ 1977 C50/16.

[176] Case T-66/89 *Publishers' Association* v *Commission (II)* [1992] ECR II-1995 [1992] 5 CMLR 120, para. 69. However, the Court of First Instance's decision was overturned on appeal by the Court of Justice because of the failure by the Commission and the Court of First Instance properly to consider the applicants' submissions under Art. 85(3) in C-360/92P, *Publishers' Association* v *Commission* [1995] ECR I-23. Joined cases T-528, 542, 543 and 546/93. See also *Metropole Télévision* v *Commission* [1996] 5 CMLR 386, in which the Court of First Instance stressed, at para. 93 of its judgment, that all four conditions for exemption had to be satisfied and that the Commission was under a duty to consider these carefully and impartially. The Court annulled the Commission's decision to grant exemption to Eurovision's sports broadcasting arrangements, OJ 1993 L 179/23, because the Commission had taken undue account of Art. 90(2) in taking its decision under Art. 85(3).

- imposing restrictions which are not indispensable; and
- affording the possibility of eliminating competition in respect of a substantial part of the relevant products.

7.73 Although not expressly stated in Article 85(3) a fifth element exists, namely that the positive elements outweigh any negative elements, i.e. that the advantages of the agreement outweigh the disadvantages. A possible sixth element is whether Article 85(3) leaves a residual discretion to the Commission to refuse to grant exemption to an agreement which prima facie satisfies all of the requirements of that provision. Advocate General Slynn in *Ford Werke* v *Commission* suggested tentatively that a residual discretion does exist and cited as authority the non-mandatory implication of the phrase: "The provisions of paragraph 1 may, however, be declared inapplicable" in the opening to Article 85(3) EC. The Advocate General commented:

> "If such a discretion does exist then it should normally be exercised in favour of granting an exemption if the four conditions are satisfied. If, however, some overriding principle of the Community (e.g. maintaining the unity of the Common Market) is violated despite the fact that the four conditions are satisfied, then, prima facie it seems to me that a discretion remains as to whether exemption should be granted."[177]

7.74 The Court in the *Ford* case did not comment on the issue. A situation in which exemption could be refused is where the agreement might meet the requirements of Article 85(3) but would facilitate the abuse of a dominant position contrary to Article 86 EC. Thus in *Tetra Pak (BTG licence)*,[178] the Commission indicated that it would remove the benefit of a block exemption from an agreement, the enforcement of which would lead to an abuse of a dominant position.

Many agreements, as notified, are unsuitable for Article 85(3) treatment. Parties wishing to gain acceptance of their agreement must be willing to change it and should notify their willingness to modify to the Commission. Of course an agreement can only be varied by consent by the parties. If one party is unwilling to vary the agreement then the Commission cannot compel amendment. In such circumstances the Commission would be compelled to reject the agreement as drafted. It may well be that the Commission do not proceed to a formal decision, following discussions and amendments but conclude an informal settlement. This procedure is discussed below. In practice, the formal Article 85(3) procedure is cumbersome and of limited use. Only a very small handful of cases each year (perhaps five or six) pass through this gateway to exemption. Almost all agreements are informally settled, as the figures in para. 7.126 illustrate.

2. *First Positive Requirement*

7.75 "[C]ontributes to improving the production or distribution of goods or to promoting technical or economic progress". To determine whether improvements exist the Commission objectively compares the situation that exists with that which would exist in the absence of the agreement, decision, concerted practice, etc. Given that this entails a comparison of the actual with the hypothetical, the analysis cannot be absolutely precise. Accordingly,

[177] Case 25-26 *Ford* v *Commission* [1985] ECR 2725 at p. 2734 [1985] 3 CMLR 528 at p. 538.

[178] [1988] 4 CMLR 881; upheld on appeal in Case T-51/89 *Tetra Pak (I)* [1990] ECR II–309 [1991] 4 CMLR 334. Although the case involves a block rather than individual exemption, the principle would seem to be the same. However, it is unlikely to happen more than rarely, since the possibility of an abuse would probably lead to the final requirement of Art. 85(3) not being satisfied in most situations.

the Commission must be satisfied with a reasonable probability of improvements. The starting point for the Commission is that free market forces ensure improvements more effectively than restrictive agreements.[179] Thus, the Commission set out to determine whether the agreement in question *de facto* improves upon free market forces. The subjective assertions of the parties themselves will, therefore, be immaterial.[180] Moreover, if the agreement only improves the economic interests of the parties then the Commission will not apply Article 85(3).[181] (See second positive requirement below.) The following factors *inter alia* may be relevant to parties arguing in favour of improvements under Article 85(3).

(1) Reduction of costs

7.76 Agreements which enable costs to be reduced and which, accordingly, allow the benefits of reduced costs to be passed on to consumers by way of lower prices are smiled upon by the Commission. The benefits of cost saving or the more efficient use of capacity are manifold. The Commission thus, for example, look for increased output, lower tooling costs, lower raw materials costs, more rapid amortisation of investments, improved quality, increased diversity, reduced marketing and advertising expenses, etc. Parties must prove that the improvement is substantial, i.e. that it is not superficial. The Commission may look for a "before and after" analysis of costs.[182]

(2) Expansion of outlook and improvement in distribution

7.77 The Commission looks for what they term "broadening the offers". This simply means expanding outlook and economic activities. An agreement might lead to increased diversity of product, new R&D potential, increases in the number of suppliers to serve a market, expansion of points of sale, improvement and updating of procedures and services, improvements in transport and distribution.

(3) Increased market penetration and new markets

7.78 The Commission might be impressed with proof that new markets will be opened up. Thus, a joint venture between X and Y to create a new product might be accepted on the basis that it creates a new market, particularly if it involves the transfer of technology from a non-Community undertaking to a Community undertaking.[183]

(4) Improved transparency

7.79 The model of the perfect market envisages perfect knowledge by all traders of market conditions, of prices and terms and conditions of sale. However, the Commission may be cautious about allowing transparency improving agreements, since if X has more knowledge about the pricing policy of Y, X will be better armed to follow Y's price moves. Transparency can substitute the risks of competition for the concerted behaviour of greater knowledge, especially in oligopolistic markets. Transparency will be viewed more sympathetically in highly atomistic, dispersed markets.[184]

[179] *Bayer/Gist Brocades* [1976] 1 CMLR D98; *Gerofabriek* [1977] 1 CMLR D35.

[180] Cases 56 and 58/64 *Consten and Grundig* v *Commission* [1966] CMLR 418; [1966] ECR 299 at p. 396.

[181] *Consten and Grundig* v *Commission* (above); *German Floor Tiles Manufacturers Association* [1971] CMLR D6; *Central Heating* [1972] CMLR D130.

[182] e.g. *Prym-Beka* [1973] CMLR D250; *EMO* OJ 1979 111/16 (17 January 1979) (calculation need not be very precise, generalisations which are as accurate as may reasonably be expected appear to be satisfactory).

[183] See for example *KSB/Lowara/Goulds/ITT* OJ 1991 L 19/25, [1992] 5 CMLR 55; *Olivetti/Canon* OJ 1988 L 52/51, [1989] 4 CMLR 940; *Optical Fibres* OJ 1986 L 236/30; *Eirpage* OJ 1991 L 306/22, [1993] 4 CMLR 64.

[184] See e.g. *UK Agricultural Tractor Registration Exchange* [1993] 4 CMLR 358. See generally Chapter 9 below. See also *International Energy Agency* [1984] 2 CMLR 186 where the Commission exempted an information

(5) Employment

7.80 The Commission has not laid down in any detail its views on preservation of employment or job creation. Such factors do not directly impinge on the competitive situation. The question has however been focused upon with respect to so-called "crisis cartels" designed to reduce structural overcapacity in declining industries. The Commission has condoned, under Article 85(3), these rationalisation agreements where they satisfy a number of criteria. The Commission has stated in this regard: "production can be considered to be improved if the reductions in capacity are likely in the long run to increase profitability and restore competitiveness, and if the co-ordination of closures helps to mitigate, spread and stagger their impact on employment".[185] Employment and social condition thus have at least some part to play.[186] From a more positive perspective, the Commission regards the creation of new employment in the developing parts of the EC has a relevant factor. In approving the *Ford/VW* joint venture to build a multi-purpose motor vehicle in a new factory set up on Setubal, Portugal, creating up to 15,000 new jobs, the Commission noted that the joint venture "contributes to the promotion of harmonious development of the Community and the reduction of regional disparities which is one of basic aims of the Treaty".[187] It stressed that this would not be sufficient in its own right to gain exemption, but it was nevertheless an element the Commission would take into account. The Court has indirectly approved this approach, stating that stabilising the provision of employment is an objective to which reference may be had under Article 85(3), since it improves the general conditions of production.[188]

(6) Specific agreement types

7.81 With respect to exclusive dealing agreements, the Commission look for improvements in distribution, enhanced penetration of foreign markets, improved after-sales services, adequate stocking of spare parts, continuous supply, and the overcoming of legal and linguistic problems associated with foreign markets. With selective distribution systems, the Commission looks for expert dealers able to market effectively the suppliers products, with

cont.
system operated by the major oil companies within the framework of the International Energy Agency (IEA). The IEA is a sub-body of the OECD and operates an emergency oil sharing scheme for periods of crisis supply. The involvement of the oil majors, being the principal carriers of bulk oil in the world, is essential to the scheme. It is they that will, in an emergency, undertake the redistribution and allocation of supplies. Accordingly, exemption under Art. 85(3) was a political necessity. The fact that the IEA scheme involved exchanges of data between the firms concerned and resultant increased transparency was essentially viewed as a necessary evil. See for commentary, Green (1984) ELRev 449. The Commission indicated their intention to renew the exemption in an Art. 19(3) Notice, OJ 1993 C300/8, [1994] 4 CMLR 506.

185 See *Twelfth Commission Competition Report* (1982), pp. 44, 45, para. 39. See *Stichting Baksteen (Dutch Bricks)* OJ 1994 L131/15; see also *Twenty-third Report on Competition Policy* (1993), para. 89 and OJ 1993 C34/11. Crisis cartels are considered at paras. 12.234 and following.

186 See WQ No. 2182/83, OJ 1984 C158/16 concerning control of restructuring by multinationals. The Commission was asked whether it was concerned that corporate restructuring could take place without due regard to employment. The Commission commented that the Vredeling Proposal on disclosure of information to employees (OJ 1983 C217/3, 12 August 1983) would help in this matter. Generally, they considered that employment and social consequences were of importance: "The Commission wishes restructuring plans to be carried out with full account being taken of the social consequences of the decisions envisaged and it hopes that it will be possible to create new jobs in regions particularly severely affected by the crisis." It would be inconsistent with this policy for unemployment not to be relevant to Art. 85(3).

187 *Ford/VW* [1993] 5 CMLR 617, para. 36.

188 Case 26/76 *Metro* v *Commission* [1977] ECR 1875, para. 43, cited with approval in Case 42/84 *Remia and Nutricia* v *Commission* [1987] 1 CMLR 1, para. 42. See also 136/86 *BNIC* v *Aubert* [1987] ECR 4789, para. 21, where employment was mentioned as a factor which might be relevant under Art. 85(3), though not 85(1).

adequate demonstration, storage and general advertising space. With regard to specialisation agreements, the Commission looks primarily for an improvement in production by the parties and improved quality of product. With regard to licensing agreements the Commission adopt a clause by clause approach. In particular, they have exempted restrictions on the licensor not to grant any more exclusive licences thereby encouraging the licensee to concentrate his efforts and either improve market penetration or open up new market possibilities. The same philosophy may also justify restrictions on the licensee actively selling outside of his contract territory. As for the disadvantages that the Commission will look for and which may ruin chances under Article 85(3) there are certain pointers. Any agreement tending to separate off national markets will be frowned upon. Thus, export bans, prohibitions on selling to customers outside of national bounds, no-dumping clauses whereby parties in different Member States agree not to sell below the price of the market leader in another Member State, etc., will almost never be accepted. A similarly strict attitude is taken to agreements which exclude competitors or erect artificial entry barriers. New firms improve and contribute to the promotion of technical and economic progress; anything imposing barriers to entry will thus be incompatible with Article 85(3) exemption. Certain practices may be assumed to be unacceptable. Thus, price fixing, market sharing, export bans and exchanges of price lists are examples of habitually unlawful practices albeit that in EC law no notion of *per se* illegality exists as it does in the USA.[189]

3. *Second Positive Requirement*

7.82 "[W]hile allowing consumers a fair share of the resulting benefit". "Consumers" is construed widely and means all purchasers of the products or services concerned. Thus a wholesaler may be a "consumer" of a supplier-manufacturer; a retailer may be a "consumer" of a wholesaler. The High Street shopper is of course the ultimate "consumer".[190] The word "benefit" is likewise construed widely and means any advantage which is likely to result from the agreement.[191]

(1) "Equitable participation in the resulting profit"[192]

7.83 The primary advantage the consumer benefits from is lower prices.[193] This may be manifest as maintained prices in spite of increased costs.[194] In deciding whether the cost advantages will be passed on to consumers, the Commission examine the state of the market. If the market is competitive they might conclude that sufficient incentive exists to ensure that cost savings and other economies are passed on. The existence of some competitive pressure on the parties thus tends to satisfy the Commission. Such pressures may derive from direct rivals to the parties or from powerful purchasers who can exert pressure on suppliers thereby ensuring that the latter supply on favourable terms. Potential competition, i.e. competition from undertakings willing and able to enter the market should the existing par-

[189] See for example *Roofing Felt* [1991] 4 CMLR 130; *Welded Steel Mesh* [1991] 4 CMLR 13.

[190] See WQ No. 307/84, OJ 1984 C243/2. The Commission stated: "Also, it must be remembered that the term 'consumer' in this context refers not only to end-users, but includes trader purchasers, which may require a different type of approach."

[191] *ibid.*: "the decisions in which Article 85(3) has been applied show a wide range of different benefits which the agreements in question brought about: lower prices, a more extensive offer of products, greater stability in terms of quantities supplied and prices, better information and orientation for consumers, efficient after-sales service, faster delivery."

[192] See *KEWA* [1976] 2 CMLR D15; *United Processors GmbH* (URG Cartel) [1976] 2 CMLR D1—the actual phrase used by the Commission.

[193] e.g. *Cematax* [1973] CMLR D135.

[194] *FNCFOJ* 1971 L134/6. See also *Vacuum Interrupters* [1977] 1 CMLR D67.

ticipants fail to satisfy the consumer, may be another relevant factor. However hypothetical competition will rarely be as effective a disciplining force as actual competition. Where the supplier distributes via exclusive dealers, the fact that the supplier's dealers are subject to competition from other dealers might convince the Commission that profits will be passed on down the chain of distribution. Where the Commission finds no evidence of competitive pressures they are far more sceptical of arguments suggesting that economies have been passed on; their experience teaches them that in the absence of an effective competitive incentive benefits are rarely passed on.[195]

(2) Other benefits to the consumer

7.84 "Benefit" may materialise in a number of forms: increased output to satisfy demand; improved customer services, guarantees and after-sales services; regularity of supply, wider range of products; increased stocks; greater market transparency through more accurate and informative advertising; technical improvements in products and services etc. In some circumstances it is clear that so-called benefits are in reality unacceptable. Thus, a cartel in which the parties improve average product quality by eliminating lower quality products or services and rediverting resources to the production of higher quality products or services may be unacceptable because of the reduction in choice entailed. Low quality cheaper products or services may form an integral part of consumer choice. A short-term benefit may not be sufficient if there is detriment in the longer term. Thus in *Eurosport*,[196] the creation of a new satellite sports channel creating additional choice in the short term was considered to be likely to prevent the creation of other competitive sports channels and thus would restrict choice in the longer term. It was thus held not to constitute a benefit to consumers.

(3) "Fair share"

7.85 Benefits conferred must be adequate; it is not enough for the parties to throw the scraps to the consumer and keep the lion's share for themselves. So far as is practicable the consumer must obtain a fair share of *all* the benefits perceived to flow from the agreement. Thus, if an agreement confers cost savings and higher quality produce or services, the consumer must obtain the higher quality product or service at a reasonable price which reflects the cost savings. Another relevant consideration is whether the advantages enjoyed by the consumer outweigh, or are outweighed by, disadvantages flowing from restrictions in the agreement. This consideration is discussed below.

4. First Negative Requirement: Indispensability

7.86 The agreement must not, "(a) impose on the undertakings concerned restrictions which are not indispensable to the attainment of these objectives."

As with the other elements of Article 85(3) whether a restriction is indispensable to the attainment of the "positive" requirements (the benefits) is objectively decided, the subjective expressions and exhortations of the parties are immaterial. Parties must thus always ask themselves whether they really need all of the restrictions. If the Commission, on examining an agreement, decides that it contains superfluous (dispensable) restrictions then an immediate rejection of an application for an exemption may follow. It is often easier to prove dispensability than it is to prove the existence of positive benefits (above). Parties may

195 *SNPE-LEL* [1978] 2 CMLR 758; *Gerofabriek* [1977] 1 CMLR D35.
196 [1992] 5 CMLR 273.

of course modify their agreements. Parties sometimes contend that a restriction is indispensable because they would not have concluded the agreement without it. This particular test of indispensability is not acceptable to the Commission, it is linked to the subjective views of the parties and is not an objective test of necessity or indispensability.[197] A more reliable test in the eyes of the Commission is whether a reasonable, hypothetical businessman would have entered the agreement without the restriction. To apply this test the Commission will look to see whether the restriction in question is central or peripheral to the substance of the agreement. A restriction in a joint venture agreement between X and Y requiring both parties not to compete with the joint venture company may be essential to that agreement to make it work. A second restriction on X and Y not to compete with each other for 12 years following termination of the joint venture is most unlikely to be central to that agreement. An objective businessman may not consider it worth entering the agreement without the first restriction; he may still enter the agreement without the second. Certain restrictions are generally considered indispensable to the materialisation of certain benefits. Thus exclusivity clauses in exclusive dealing agreements (dealer purchases only from single supplier) may be indispensable in achieving effective distribution of the supplier's goods.[198] Exclusive licences of intellectual property rights may be necessary to provide the incentive for the licensee to exploit the rights effectively. Restrictions on inter-party competition may be necessary in a specialisation agreement to enable the parties to devote their research and development efforts to the respective products and accelerate advancement thereby.

7.87 Neither is the view of a national court determinative of the question, as the Court of First Instance held in *Publishers' Association* v *Commission*.[199] Despite the fact that the UK's Restrictive Practices Court upheld resale price maintenance for books in the UK under the Net Book Agreements as being a necessary restriction in the public interest, the Commission and the Court of First Instance held that from the perspective of trade in the Common Market, it deprived customers of choice and was not indispensable. However, on further appeal to the Court of Justice the Court of First Instance's ruling and the Commission's decision were quashed because both had ignored the argument that the Net Book Agreements produced beneficial effects meriting exemption on the Irish as well as the UK market.[200] It is perhaps pertinent to add that clauses not caught by Article 85(1) may be as superfluous, burdensome and illogical as national laws allow. Not being within Article 85(1) there is no need to establish that they are indispensable under Article 85(3).

5. *Second Negative Requirement: Elimination of Competition*

7.88 The agreement must not, "(b) afford such undertakings the possibility of eliminating competition in respect of a substantial part of the products in question."

As with the first negative requirement, this is an absolute barrier to exemption. An agreement can prove technologically radical and of manifest benefit to consumers, yet fail at either of these two negative hurdles. In assessing this requirement the Commission must define

[197] See *Consten and Grundig* [1964] CMLR 489 (Commission decision).

[198] See para. 8 of the preamble to Commission Reg. 1983/83/EEC, OJ 1982 C172/3; [1982] 2 CMLR 642: "The other restrictions on competition allowed under this Regulation in addition to the exclusive supply obligation produce a clear division of functions between the parties and compel the exclusive distributor to concentrate his sales efforts on the contract goods and the contract territory; they are, where they are agreed only for the duration of the agreement, generally necessary in order to attain the improvement in the distribution of goods sought through exclusive distribution." Note that the Commission use the word "necessary" instead of indispensable, the two words appear to be interchangeable.

[199] Case T-66/89, [1992] 5 CMLR 120.

[200] C-360/92P *Publishers' Association* v *Commission* [1995] ECR I-23.

the product market and focus upon the market share of the parties to the agreement. The following indications and exemptions appear to be relevant:

(a) Parties together control 100 per cent of market: competition no longer possible, exemption not grantable other than in exceptional circumstances.[201]
(b) Parties together control 80 per cent of market: most unlikely that effective competition could survive after the agreement has come into operation, exemption very unlikely.[202]
(c) Parties together control 60 per cent of market: effective competition outside of agreement will be under severe strain from agreement, exemption unlikely.
(d) Parties together control 50 per cent of market: exemption feasible yet still unlikely but will depend on external factors such as the vigour of residual competition.
(e) Parties together control 30 per cent of market: effective competition can probably thrive outside of the agreement. If parties to the agreement are thereby enabled to compete with larger existing firms then the agreement may even enhance competition.[203]
(f) Parties together control approximately 10–20 per cent of market: exemption probable.[204]
(g) Parties together control 0–10 per cent of market: unless remainder of market populated by a plethora of very small firms agreement most unlikely to affect competition adversely. Even if agreement makes parties the largest group in the market competition outside is probably still likely to be effective, exemption is therefore very probable.

7.89 Factors other than market share may be relevant. The existence of intense competition on the world market may justify even an agreement between major oligopolists within the EC or even between an EC and a non-EC undertaking.[205] The Commission seems to accept that agreements may be valid, even where they effectively preclude competition altogether on the market, if on expiry of the agreement competition will be restored in a more healthy form. Thus a controlled reduction of capacity agreement (rationalisa-

[201] See *United Reprocessors GmbH (The URG Cartel)* [1976] 2 CMLR D1, three major reprocessors of nuclear fuels combined in a joint R&D recovery and marketing cartel—the URG cartel. This provided, *inter alia*, for price fixing, investment co-ordination, allocation of orders, control of licences, exchange of know-how. There was no effective competition in Western Europe outside of the parties. Although the exemption under Art. 85(3) is silent on the matter it is understood that the agreement obtained exemption because of the political need for the EC to have a corporation that could compete on the world market with intense American competition. There were apparently also Community energy policy considerations in play. See for commentary, Green (1983) ELRev 58.

[202] See for example Cases 209–215 and 218/78 *Van Landewyck* v *Commission* [1980] ECR 3125, [1981] 3 CMLR 134.

[203] For example ten firms combine in an agreement controlling 30 per cent of the market. Together they compete with A who controls 17 per cent of the market, B who controls 25 per cent of the market, and, C who controls 28 per cent of the market. The sudden arrival of the new agreement can disturb the status quo between A, B and C and engender competition which hitherto had been eliminated between the oligopolists A, B and C.

[204] e.g. *BMW* [1975] 1 CMLR D44. See Reg. 418/85/EC, OJ 1985 153/5 para. 8 of preamble and Art. 3—for the 20 per cent market share test for R&D joint ventures.

[205] See *United Reprocessors GmbH (URG Cartel)* [1976] 2 CMLR noted above. See also *Olivetti/Canon* OJ 1988 L52/51, para. 58, for a joint venture setting up OCI between two major competitors on the world market. In *Fiat/Hitachi* OJ 1993 L20/10, para. 26, concerning a "structural" cooperative joint venture, the Commission discussed "substantial elimination of competition" in the terms of the creation of dominant position, in terms strikingly reminiscent of one of the criteria under Art. 2(2), Reg. 4064/89 (the Merger Control Regulation).

tion scheme or "crisis cartel")[206] between firms in declining markets may be justified on the basis that once restructuring has occurred a healthier competitive climate may prevail.[207] Finally, an agreement between X, Y and Z who, between them, control 75 per cent of production may not eliminate competition if their purchasers (customers) are large and capable enough of commencing own production should X, Y and Z act anti-competitively.[208]

6. *Positive Elements Outweigh Negative Elements*

7.90 It is implicit in Article 85(3) that when the Commission evaluate an agreement it will balance pros and cons. To gain exemption pros must outweigh cons. Before a decision rejecting exemption is given, parties will have been given a fair idea of how the Commission weigh individual factors in the balance from the statement of objections and from any informal discussions. Accordingly, parties must be prepared to attempt to redress the balance in their favour by eliminating or modifying clauses or by suggesting other changes to their agreements and practices.

7. *Conditional Exemption*

7.91 The Commission may impose conditions on or attach obligations to exemptions.[209] The imposition of conditions and/or obligations enables the Commission to feel more confident about granting exemptions. Parties must, therefore, accept a price to be paid for an exemption over and above any modifications they may have to make to their agreements in order to render them suitable for exemption. The difference between a condition and an obligation is that breach of a condition automatically removes the benefit of the exemption, whereas it is for the Commission to decide what action to take should an obligation be broken. It may amend or revoke the exemption,[210] or it may simply fine the undertakings involved.[211] Whether a condition or an obligation is imposed, it seems that it must both be relevant to competition and must not be disproportionate.[212] Conditions that may be imposed include requirements on parties to an agreement to refrain from disclosing competitive information to each other, such as price or marketing information.[213] The following types of obligation are often imposed: notification conditions whereby parties must report back to the Commission any consultations with government, minutes of board meeting, copies of know-how and other intellectual property licences, details of prices charged or paid, all amendments to existing agreements, etc. The exemption must be granted for a specific period.[214] In practice, the usual period is five to ten years.[215]

[206] See paras. 12.234 and following.
[207] See *Twelfth Commission Competition Report* (1982), pp. 43–45, paras. 38–41. See also *Bayer/BP* [1989] 4 CMLR 24, paras. 39–41; *Enichem/ICI* [1989] 4 CMLR 54, paras. 47–8.
[208] e.g. see Case 6/72 *Europemballage and Continental Can* v *Commission* [1973] CMLR 199; [1973] ECR 215. Former purchasers of a dominant manufacturer of metal containers commenced own-production. For example, Nestles produced cream cans, Shell produced oil cans.
[209] Art. 8(1) Reg. 17/62/EEC.
[210] Art. 8(3)(b), Reg. 17/62.
[211] Art. 15(2)(b), Reg. 17/62.
[212] Case 17/74 *Transocean Marine Paint Association* [1974] ECR 1063, [1974] 2 CMLR 459, *per* Warner AG. There has not yet been a Court ruling on this point.
[213] *Optical Fibres* OJ 1986 L236/30; *Ford/VW* [1993] 5 CMLR 617.
[214] Art. 8(1), Reg. 17/62.
[215] Occasionally longer periods, even up to 15 years as in *Optical Fibres* OJ 1986 L236/30 and 20 years as in *Delta Chemie/DDD* [1989] 4 CMLR 535, have been granted but these are the exception.

8. *Involvement of Third Parties*

7.92 The granting of an exemption to X and Y might distress Z who is a rival of X and Y. Z might submit its comments to the Commission in confidence at any time. The Commission will publish the main facts of a proposed exemption in the Official Journal of the European Communities (the OJ) and will invite interested parties to comment within not less than one month prior to the making of the formal exemption decision.[216] The views of such third parties will be taken into account and the substance of any relevant comments (though not the identity of the party making the comments) may well be included in the decision with Commission commentary on those comments. As noted above third parties may challenge an exemption if it materially affects them before the Court.

D. Enforcement in National Courts[217]

7.93 Articles 85 and 86 EC are directly effective.[218] That is, they may be pleaded by private parties against other private parties before national courts. Parties with a legitimate grievance need not complain to the Commission, they may take matters into their own hands and sue the parties causing them damage in the national courts. The threat of a damages claim or an injunctive order may be a powerful bargaining counter for use by an aggrieved party. Moreover, it is only at the national level that compensatory damages may be obtained; such are not available to private parties at the Community level. Actions for damages based on Articles 85 and 86 are increasingly common in the United Kingdom courts. At any one time a (conservative) guestimate is that there are between 50–75 actions proceedings through the Courts. Apparently, the same increase in litigation has not been experienced in other Member States.

1. *Causes of Action*

7.94 A cause of action is a legal justification for bringing a court case. In UK law there are four possible causes of action relevant to Articles 85 and 86 EC: (i) breach of statutory duty; (ii) causing loss by unlawful means; (iii) conspiracy; and (iv) the so-called "new torts". The relevance of this categorisation is that the different causes of action available in English law have different rules relating to the class of persons who may sue, the degree of

[216] See Art. 19(3) Reg. 17/62/EC. See also OJ 1983 C295/6 (2 November 1983). Notice from the Commission on procedures concerning notifications pursuant to Art. 4 of Council Reg. 17/62. Commented on by the Commission in answer to WQ No. 307/84, OJ 1984 C243/2,3.

[217] See generally on this topic: Green, "The Treaty of Rome, national courts and English common law: the enforcement of European competition law after *Milk Marketing Board*" (1984) *Rabels Zeitschrift* 509; Kerse, *op. cit.*, note 1 at pp. 369–380; Rew, "Actions for damages by third parties under English law for breach of Article 85 of the EC Treaty" (1971) 8 CMLRev 462; Picanol, "Remedies in national law for breach of Articles 85 and 86 of the EC Treaty: a review" (1983) 2 LIEI 1; Jacobs; "Damages for breach of Article 86 EC" (1983) ELRev 353. N. Green and A. Barav, "Damages in national courts for breach of Community law" (1986) 6 YEL 55; Steiner, "How to make the action suit the case: domestic remedies for breach of EEC law" (1987) 12 ELRev 102; M. Hoskins, "Garden cottage revisited: the availability of damages in the national courts for breaches of EEC competition rules" [1992] ECLR 257; Whish, "Enforcement of EC competition law in the domestic courts of member states" (1994) 5 ELRev 3; Brealey and Hoskins, "Remedies in EC law: law and practice in the English and EC courts" (1994), pp. 62–72.

[218] Case 127/73 *BRT* v *SABAM* [1974] 2 CMLR 238; [1974] ECR 313.

culpability required, the type of causation necessary and the remoteness of damage for which damages are recoverable. In practice litigants generally plead that Articles 85 and 86 are directly effective and confer rights which must be protected. Often it is averaged that those articles may be enforced as breach of statutory duties. However, in recent years the somewhat sterile debate as to how to categorise breaches of Articles 85 and 86 has abated and the Courts do not look to clothe what is a Community cause of action in a domestic mantle. None the less the various principal options are considered below.

(1) Breach of statutory duty[219]

7.95 Where a statute imposes a prohibition and a person breaches that prohibition thereby causing damage to another person, then that other person may, in some circumstances, sue the wrongdoer for damages regardless of the fact that the statute does not expressly provide him with a remedy. Articles 85 and 86 EC impose prohibition on parties. Article 85 forbids restrictive agreements; Article 86 forbids abuses of a dominant position. Neither article allows private citizens to recover damages in action brought at the Community level. If the Commission imposes a fine the money received goes into the Community purse; neither the Commission nor the Court may award damages to an aggrieved party. It has now been established by the House of Lords that breaches of Article 85 and 86 give rise to an action for breach of a statutory duty.[220] Aggrieved parties may go to court to collect damages and/or[221] obtain injunctions preventing other parties from breaching the competition law or from continuing with a breach of the competition laws. It is clear that national remedies may be more effective than complaining to the Commission. Indeed, it appears to be unnecessary to establish the conditions generally considered necessary to prove the existence of the right to sue for damages in a breach of statutory duty case where the duty breached derives from Article 86 EC. The House of Lords in the leading case of *Garden Cottage Foods* v *Milk Marketing Board*[222] seemed to *assume* that the conditions were fulfilled in the case of Article 86 EC. Other courts have sought to follow this approach with respect to other directly effective provisions of the Treaty of Rome.[223]

[219] See, *Winfield and Jolowicz on Tort* (14th edn. 1994), Chapter 7 for an excellent, succinct account of the conditions that must be satisfied before the tort exists. See also *Clerk and Lindsell on Torts* (17th edn. 1995), Chapter 11.

[220] *Garden Cottage Foods* v *Milk Marketing Board* [1983] 3 WLR 143 (HL) majority judgment given by Lord Diplock, dissenting judgment by Lord Wilberforce. See also Neil J in *An Bord Bainne Cooperative* v *Milk Marketing* Board [1984] 1 CMLR 519, 528; Parker LJ in *Bourgoin* v *Ministry of Agriculture, Fisheries and Food* [1986] 1 QB 716; Morritt J in *Plessey* v *GEC* [1990] ECC 384, 393–394. Similar conclusions have been derived in foreign courts. See *BMW cars* in Germany, BGH (23 October 1979)—Case KZR 21/78, English version of the judgment at (1980) 3 ECC 213. See also *URS* v *NV Scheld Sleepvaartbedrijf* [1965] CMLR 25 1 (Holland)—damages available for breach of Art. 85 EC.

[221] Plaintiffs may sue for damages; if they are suing for an injunction they may also obtain damages. See s. 50 Supreme Court Act 1981. In Joined Cases C-46/93 and C-48/93 *Brasserie du Pecheur SA* and *Ex parte Factortame Ltd* [1996] ECR I-1029 the ECJ held that in principle damages were available for breach of any directly effective right: see para. 22.

[222] [1983] 2 WLR 143 at p. 152.

[223] See *Bourgoin* v *Ministry of Agriculture, Fisheries and Food* [1985] 3 All ER 585 [1985] 1 CMLR 528, Mann J applied the tort of breach of statutory duty to Art. 30 EC in a case where the government was being sued for £19 million damages in respect of an illegal import ban of French turkeys. However on appeal the Court of Appeal ([1985] 3 All ER 603) in a majority decision (Nourse and Parker LJs) held that Art. 30 EC was *not* actionable on the basis of breach of statutory duty but *was* actionable on the basis of misfeasance in public office. However Oliver LJ in a powerful dissent held that Art. 30 EC was actionable also as a breach of statutory duty and the *Garden Cottage Foods* judgment was not distinguishable. In *R* v *Attorney General ex parte Imperial Chemical Industries PLC* [1985] 1 CMLR 588 Woolf J had to consider whether 134 and Sch. 18 of the Finance Act 1982 constituted state aids within the meaning of Art. 92 EC. If they were state aids then the UK government would have breached Art. 93(3) EC which imposes a duty on governments to notify new aids to the European Commission prior to implementing them. ICI claimed that the sections of

7.96 A problem arises when both parties can be said to be in breach of a statutory duty. Since Article 85 imposes a duty on all parties to an agreement, it can be argued that each of them is in breach of that duty when the agreement is caught by Article 85(1). If an aggrieved party to that agreement wishes to argue that it has suffered loss as a result of the operation of the agreement, it faces the problem that by virtue of being a party to that agreement, it too is in breach of statutory duty. Arguably the *in pari delicto* defence would apply to preclude a party recovering damages, at least in cases of genuine equal fault. The weaker or innocent party should be allowed to bring an action for damages. To hold otherwise would deprive all but third parties of the possibility of bringing private actions for breach of Article 85(1), when it is very often the parties to the agreement who have most incentive to sue. This in turn would deprive EC law of its effectiveness in this area, contrary both to the policy of both the Treaty and the Commission.[224]

(2) Causing loss by unlawful means

7.97 There would appear to be a cause of action in English law based upon the following: "If one person, without just cause or excuse, deliberately interferes with the trade or business of another, and does so by unlawful means, that is, by an act which he is not at liberty to commit, then he is acting unlawfully. He is liable in damages, and, in a proper case, an injunction can be granted against him."[225] The tort may be committed even though the unlawful means, by themselves, do not confer private rights. The tort will have limited value in terms of EC competition law. To prove the tort the plaintiff must establish: (a) that the defendant used unlawful means; and (b) that the defendant deliberately interfered with the trade of the plaintiff.[226] It has been accepted that a defendant who breaches his statutory duty employs unlawful means.[227] Thus, in the cases of breaches of Articles 85 and 86 the unlawful means requirement is not hard to satisfy. It is, however, very difficult to prove that the defendant deliberately focused his unlawful behaviour on the plaintiff. If X and Y agree to supply their goods at the same fixed price and customer A decides to purchase goods of the type produced by X and Y, then those latter two parties can hardly be said to have deliberately sought to interfere specifically with A's trade.[228] The case may differ if Z a dominant supplier operates a predatory pricing regime to force a small new-

cont.
the Finance Act above gave tax relief to their competitors, Woolf J held that the sections of the Act did not amount to state aids. However, he did state: "If I had come to the conclusion that Article 93(3) had been infringed in a manner which gave ICI rights under the directly applicable final sentence, I would have had no doubt that ICI had *locus standi*. ICI would then have a cause of action as Lord Diplock makes clear in his speech in *Garden Cottage Foods Ltd* v *The Milk Marketing Board*" (*ibid.*, at p. 608).

224 Notice on Co-operation between national courts and the Commission in applying Arts. 85 and 86 of the EEC Treaty 1993 OJ C39/6. See also the opinion of Advocate General van Gerven in Case C-128/92 *HJ Banks* v *British Coal* [1994] ECR I-1209 [1994] 5 CMLR 30. In US antitrust, a defendant has an "equal involvement" defence if it can prove that "the plaintiff bears at least substantially equal responsibility for an anti-competitive restriction by creating, approving, maintaining, continually and actively supporting, relying upon, or otherwise utilising and implementing, that restriction to his or her benefit", US Court of Appeals, First Circuit, *Sullivan* v *Tagliabue*, judgment of 16 September 1994, (1994) 67 ATRR 331.

225 *per* Lord Denning MR in *Acrow (Automation) Ltd* v *Rex Chainbelt* [1971] 3 All ER 1175 at p. 1181 approving the judgment in, *Torquay Hotel Co Ltd* v *Cousins* [1969] 1 All ER 522 at p. 530. S

226 See generally *Winfield and Jolowicz on Tort* (14th edn. 1994), p. 546; Heydon, *Economic Torts* (1978).

227 *Lonhro Ltd* v *Shell Petroleum Co Ltd (No. 2)* [1982] 3 WLR 33 (HL).

228 It is not sufficient that X and Y might foresee that due to their price fixing all purchasers, including A, will suffer interference with their trade in the form of higher pricing. Foreseeability of the harm is not enough: *Lonhro Ltd* v *Shell Petroleum Co Ltd (No. 2)* above. In that case Shell could foresee that if it illegally continued to supply Rhodesia (as it then was) with oil during the currency of the UK government ban on trade with that country (following its UDI in 1965) then the state of emergency would continue for a prolonged period and Lonhro's commercial interests in Rhodesia would be further harmed. However, Shell through its unlawful behaviour (breach of the government ban on trade) did not

comer to the market into bankruptcy. In such a case the requisite degree of deliberateness of harm to a specific person exists. Although the position is not unequivocal, it may be that deliberateness may be satisfied by express foreseeability of the consequences.

(3) Conspiracy

7.98 A cause of action exists for civil conspiracy in either of two cases:[229] (a) if two or more persons act together with the predominant intention of causing injury to another, whether or not the means used are lawful; or, (b) if two or more persons act together with the intention of causing injury to another by use of unlawful means, whether or not their predominant purpose is to further or protect their own interests. This tort is apt to grant a cause of action to those injured by the operation of a cartel. It is not necessary that the unlawful means, in variant (b), would not *per se* give rise to a cause of action.

(4) The "new torts"

7.99 In *Application des Gaz* v *Falks Veritas Ltd*[230] Lord Denning commented of Articles 85 and 86 EC: "So we reach this important conclusion: Articles 85 and 86 are part of our law. They create new torts or wrongs. Their names are 'undue restriction of competition within the Common Market'; and 'abuse of a dominant position within the Common Market'. Any infringement of those articles can be dealt with by our English Courts. It is for our Courts to find the facts, to apply the law and to use the remedies which we have available." However, despite the inventiveness of Lord Denning other judges have been critical of this new tort.[231] Indeed the House of Lords in *Garden Cottage Foods* v *Milk Marketing Board* implied that it was superfluous and unnecessary.[232] In view of the availability of the tort of breach of statutory duty the view that the "new torts" are unnecessary is probably valid, as a matter of English law.[233]

2. *Remedies*

7.100 The principal remedies sought by the plaintiff will be: (a) damages; and/or (b) an injunction; (c) a declaration that an agreement or practice is or is not within Articles 85 or 86 EC or the terms of a block exemption. The fact that there is a machinery designed to enforce competition law operative at the Community level (i.e. under Regulation 17/62/EEC) is irrelevant when considering remedies at the national level.[234]

cont.
deliberately seek to harm Lonhro. In *Lonrho* v *Fayed* [1990] 2 QB 479, Dillon LJ stated that a plaintiff must show "that the unlawful act was in some sense directed against the plaintiff or intended to harm the plaintiff", but not that the predominant purpose was to harm the plaintiff.

229 *Lonrho* v *Fayed* [1992] 1 AC 448.

230 [1974] Ch. 381 at p. 396 (CA), repeated by Lord Denning in *Garden Cottage Foods* in the Court of Appeal [1982] 3 WLR 514 at p. 516. The new tort theory was apparently accepted by Parker J in the High Court of that case (unreported at p. 3 of the solicitors' agreed note of judgment).

231 See *Valor International* v *Application de Gaz SA and EPI Leisure* [1978] 3 All ER 585; [1978] 3 CMLR 87 at p. 100, para. 43 *per* Lord Justice Roskill; *Bourgoin* v *Ministry of Agriculture Fisheries and Food* [1985] 1 CMLR 528 *per* Mann J.

232 See [1983] 3 WLR 143 at pp. 152, 153 *per* Lord Diplock who was very critical of the new tort theory.

233 Advocate General van Gerven argued in his opinion in C-128/92 *H.J. Banks* v *British Coal* [1994] ECR I-1209 [1994] 5 CMLR 30, paras. 36–54, that it should be for the Court of Justice to develop uniform rules for the recovery of damages in competition cases, given that such rules now exist for the recovery of damages for breach of Community law in some circumstances by states following C-6 and 9/90 *Francovich* [1991] ECR I-5357, [1991] 2 CMLR 66, and advanced his proposals for such rules. The Court of Justice decided the case on other grounds.

234 *Garden Cottage Foods* v *Milk Marketing Board* [1983] 3 WLR 143(HL). See the judgment of the European

7.101 The plaintiff will normally be a company or individual suffering harm as a result of the particular anti-competitive practice. In the case of a company, a further question arises as to whether a shareholder may sue for the fall in value of its shares as a consequence or harm suffered by that company, following a breach of Articles 85 or 86 as an exception to the rule in *Foss* v *Harbottle*.[235] The justification for such an exception would be the directly effective nature of the remedy sought under the Treaty, the plaintiff shareholder arguing that the principle of an effective remedy for a breach of EC law should give rise to a remedy even in circumstances where national law would do so. The Irish Supreme Court in *O'Neill* v *Ryan*[236] stated that it would not allow such an action, on the ground that the damage done was to the company and therefore the company was the proper plaintiff. A shareholder's remedy, if any, lay against the company to require it to enforce its rights for breach of Articles 85 and 86. In *Intergraph Corporation* v *Solid Systems et ors*[237] Ferris J declined formally to strike out a claim by shareholders on a counterclaim for breach of Articles 85 and 86 however he made clear that he accepted the Plaintiffs submission that the shareholders had no cause of action applying *inter alia Prudential Assurance* v *Newman Industries (No. 2)*[238] and *O'Neill* v *Ryan*. He suggested that it might be an issue for reference to the Court of Justice.

(1) Damages

7.102 It is now established that an action for damages will lie for breach of Articles 85 and 86 EC.[239] Where the Court grants an injunction, for example to prevent a dominant concern from refusing to supply customers, an aggrieved party may claim damages in addition. Damages may also be claimed against the Member State under the *Francovich* principle.[240]

7.103 A question then arises as to the appropriate standard of proof to be adopted by an English court in hearing a claim for damages. Though it might be thought that the ordinary civil standard should be applied,[241] the High Court in *Shearson Lehman Hutton* v *McLaine Watson*[242] took the view that a higher, though not criminal, standard of proof should be adopted. Webster J proposed that a plaintiff should be able to prove its case on

cont.
Court in Case 28/67 *Firma Molkerei-Zentrale Westfalen-Lippe GmbH* v *Hauptzollamt Paderborn* [1968] ECR 145 at p. 153 where the Court differentiates between the philosophy of Community enforcement by the Commission and national enforcement by private citizens. The former seeks Community objectives the latter seeks private objectives. The two levels of enforcement are hence complementary and *not* mutually exclusive. This meets the concern of Lord Wilberforce (dissenting) in *Milk Marketing Board, ibid.* at p. 159 E–F that to grant national remedies entails an unwarranted enlargement of Community remedies.

235 (1843) 2 Hare 461.

236 [1993] ILR 557.

237 [1995] ECC 53.

238 [1982] Ch 204. See also *Ex parte Else* [1993] 2 WLR 70 *per* Legatt LJ in particular.

239 *Garden Cottage Foods* v *Milk Marketing Board* [1983] 3 WLR 143 (HL). See also *Argyll* v *Distillers* [1986] 1 CMLR 764 (Outer House, Court of Sessions) and, *Cadbury Ireland* v *Kerry Co-Operative Creameries* [1982] ILRM 77 (High Court, Ireland).

240 Cases C-6 and C-9/90 *Francovich and Bonifaci* v *Italy* [1993] 2 CMLR 66; see Craig (1993) 109 LQR *Francovich*: "Remedies and the scope of damages liability"; also noted by Ross (1993) 56 MLR 55 and by Steiner (1993) 18 ELRev 3. See the opinion of Lord Goff in *Kirklees BC* v *Wickes building Supplies* [1992] 2 CMLR 765, noted by Robertson (1993) 109 LQR 27, that damages would be available against the UK for the consequences of Sunday Trading legislation if that were in breach of Article 30 EC. This casts doubt on the Court of Appeal's decision in *Bourgoin* v *Minster of Agriculture, Food and Fisheries* [1985] 3 All ER 585.

241 As held by the High Court of Ireland in *Masterfoods Ltd t/a Mars Ireland* v *HB Ice Cream Ltd* [1992] 3 CMLR 830.

242 [1989] 3 CMLR 429.

"a high degree of probability" rather than the normal balance of probabilities.[243] The justification for this was that a finding of infringement could lead to the possibility of Commission fines. It is to be doubted whether this is a compelling justification for raising the standard of proof in English court proceedings. The Commission is bound by EC law on the standard of proof.[244] The finding of infringement in a UK court does not bind the Commission. The Commission has indicated that in some circumstances it would regard the existence of national proceedings as a reason for not commencing its own investigation.[245] As a finding of infringement in a national court does not lead to the imposition of fines by the Commission, there is no need for the English courts to take this into account in fixing the standard of proof, which should, it is submitted, remain at the same level as in other civil cases. To do otherwise is to run the risk of offending the principle of the effectiveness of EC law.

(2) Injunctive relief

7.104 Irrespective of any damages claim a plaintiff may seek an end to the practice or agreement which threatens the business of the plaintiff. A plaintiff may request either an interlocutory injunction (a temporary or interim injunction pending full trial) or a perpetual injunction. An interlocutory injunction will be ordered where the Court is satisfied of a number of conditions:[246] (a) that there is a "triable issue" to be determined as between the parties;[247] (b) that damages would be an inadequate remedy for the plaintiff as a substitute to an injunction; (c) if damages would be inadequate for the plaintiff, whether damages would be adequate compensation for the defendant if, at full trial, the plaintiff failed and the question of compensating the defendant for the burden of the injunction arose; (d) if damages would suit neither plaintiff nor defendant the Court considers whether the "balance of convenience" lies with the plaintiff or defendant;[248] (e) finally, all things being equal

[243] Approved, *obiter*, by Aldous J, *Chiron Corp* v *Organon Teknika* [1992] 3 CMLR 813, 817.

[244] See para 7.38.

[245] See Commission's *Fifteenth Report on Competition Policy* (1985), point 38; *Sixteenth Report on Competition Policy* (1986), point 41; *Aluminium* [1987] 3 CMLR 813, para. 18.2; *Building and Construction Industry in the Netherlands* [1992] OJ L92/1; Notice on Cooperation between National Courts and the Commission in applying Arts. 85 and 86 of the EEC Treaty 1993 OJ C39/6. For an example of parallel proceedings where the Commission continued an EC-wide investigation notwithstanding national litigation, see the *Ice Cream Distribution* saga, see *Schöller*, Decision 93/405/EEC, 1993 OJ L183/1, 26 July 1993; [1994] 4 CMLR 51; *Langnese-Iglo*, Decision 93/406/EEC, 1993 OJ L183/19, 26 July 1993; [1994] 4 CMLR 83. On this investigation, see Robertson and Williams, "An ice cream war: the law and economics of freezer exclusivity I" [1995] ECLR 7.

[246] See *American Cyanamid* v *Ethicon* [1975] AC 396 HL and the consideration of that case by Lord Diplock in *Garden Cottage Foods* v *Milk Marketing Board* [1983] 3 WLR 143 (HL). See also *Cutsforth* v *Mansfield Inns* [1986] 1 CMLR; *Holleran and Evans* v *Thwaites plc* [1989] 2 CMLR 917 and *James Budgett* v *British Sugar Corporation* (unreported) noted Korah (1979) ELRev 417. The British Sugar Corporation (BSC) refused to accept orders from a large sugar merchant for the supply of its named, regular customers contrary to Art. 86 EC. An interlocutory injunction was granted (*ex parte*) on Friday 16 February and was discharged the following Tuesday by the Court following an undertaking being given by BSC on similar terms pending full trial. Breach of an undertaking given to a Court is contempt of court. The parties later settled their dispute so the case was not heard on its merits. There are several cases in which interlocutory injunctions have been refused, apart from *Garden Cottage Foods: Argyll* v *Distillers* [1986] 1 CMLR 764 (a Scottish case decided in the Outer House of the Court of Session); *Plessey* v *GEC/Siemens* [1990] ECC 384; *Megaphone* v *British Telecom* 28 February 1989 (unreported); *Lewis* v *Interflora* [1990] ECC 178; *Macarthy* v *Unichem* 24 November 1989 (unreported); *Leyland DAF* v *Automotive Products* [1994] ECC 289.

[247] It is *not* necessary for the defendant to go so far as to prove a prima facie case, the burden of proof is less onerous. See *American Cyanamid* v *Ethicon* (above). See *Argyll* v *Distillers* [1986] 1 CMLR 764.

[248] The Court may consider all relevant considerations when assessing the balance of convenience including the degree of disturbance the granting of interlocutory relief would cause to the defendants business. This factor was considered by Parker J in the High Court in *Garden Cottage Foods* v *Milk Marketing Board*

the Court will probably order that the status quo (taken at the date of the writ) be preserved pending trial. This may well entail granting an interlocutory injunction in order to freeze the situation. The grant of an interlocutory order entails the plaintiff giving a cross undertaking in damages to the defendant.

7.105 In cases where the facts are not complex (rare in competition cases) or where the parties agree to the interlocutory hearing being treated as a final hearing courts may determine applications for injunctive relief by reference to whether a *prima facie* case has been made out (i.e. on merits). However in most competition cases the factors above will apply.[249]

7.106 In *Plessey* v *GEC/Siemens*[250] Morritt J refused to grant an interim injunction restraining a takeover on the ground that it would effectively bring it to an end the proposed merger. As this matter was being notified to the Commission for approval under Articles 85 and 86, it was held that it was not suitable to grant what would effectively be summary judgment by an English court.[251] The decision of the High Court in granting or refusing interlocutory relief will only be overturned on appeal in exceptional cases.[252]

7.107 Injunctive relief may however be an appropriate remedy in many situations. In *ECS–AKZO* (6 December 1979, unreported) ECS successfully obtained an *ex parte* interim injunction under Article 86 EC against AKZO who planned to embark upon a campaign of predatory and discriminatory pricing designed to coerce ECS into "behaving" (i.e. not competing). Indeed, AKZO threatened to force ECS out of business if it refused to toe the line. The High Court ordered AKZO to refrain from lowering its prices. The action was subsequently settled with AKZO undertaking to refrain from predatory and discriminatory pricing. The firm subsequently infringed this undertaking and eventually the Commission adopted an interim and ultimately a final decision against AKZO.

7.108 Injunctions coupled to declarations will be relevant in cases where the defendant does an act which, it is claimed, is exempt under a block exemption but which the aggrieved plaintiff claims is not within the block exemption and is caught by Article 85(1) EC. In such cases the plaintiff will seek a declaration as to the non-applicability of the block exemption and an injunction to restrain the conduct in breach of Article 85(1).[253]

cont.
(unreported) at p. 4 of agreed solicitors note: "I reject the application for interlocutory relief on two principal grounds which may overlap each other, which come within the balance of convenience. The position is as follows. If no relief is granted the Plaintiff is still able to purchase butter albeit less profitably from four appointed distributors and others. It would therefore appear that a remedy of damages would be available in due course. If relief though is granted the defendants will have to disrupt their business and the business of their distributors. It appears to me therefore that this is a sufficient ground for rejecting this application." The application was also rejected on the grounds that the wording of the injunction as suggested by counsel was not sufficiently precise to enable the defendants to know how to behave without breaching the injunction. As a proviso: Only where the judge is unable to make up his mind about where the balance of convenience lies may he make an assessment of the relative strengths of each parties case from the affidavits. This proviso has been criticised. See Winfield and Jolowicz, *op. cit.*, at p. 679, and *Fellows* v *Fisher* [1976] QB 122 at p. 138 *per* Browne LJ.

249 See *Garret* v *Waters* [1976] 3 All ER 417; *Office Overload* v *Gunn* [1977] FSR 39; *NWL* v *Woods* [1979] 1 WLR 1294.

250 [1990] ECC 384.

251 See *Argyll* v *Distillers* [1986] 1 CMLR 764, 769, for similar reasons motivating the Scottish Outer House of the Court of Session refusing to grant an interim interdict during a take-over battle.

252 *Garden Cottage Foods* v *Milk Marketing Board* [1983] 3 WLR 143 at p. 146 B–E (HL) affirming *Hadmor Productions* v *Hamilton* [1983] 1 AC 191 (HL). The only reasons for which an appellate Court may apparently overturn a trial courts ruling are: (a) trial judge misunderstood law or evidence before him; (b) trial judge based his ruling on an inference of facts which subsequently proved to be incorrect; (c) existence of a change of circumstance which, were the trial judge to become aware of, he would vary his order; (d) trial judge acted wholly unreasonably.

253 *Cutsforth* v *Mansfield Inns* [1986] 1 CMLR 1. See also *Holleran and Evans* v *Thwaites* [1989] 2 CMLR 917.

7.109 The jurisdiction of the Court to grant a perpetual injunction against anti-competitive conduct is discretionary, albeit that the power will be exercised in accordance with case law. Injunctions are rarely appropriate if damages will suffice. If the plaintiff is in any way responsible for the anti-competitive conduct (e.g. he is an ex-party to an agreement caught by Article 85(1)) the Court may refuse the remedy.[254] Proceedings seeking an injunction must be brought without undue delay.[255] No final injunction has yet been ordered in such a case by an English court.

7.110 Perpetual injunctions may be *prohibitory* or *mandatory*. A prohibitory injunction restrains the doing, continuance or repetition of the unlawful act. Thus a prohibitory injunction may prohibit the parties to an agreement from fixing prices; it may prohibit a dominant supplier from discriminating in price between customers; it may prohibit a trade association from recommending unreasonable standard terms and conditions for use by members. A mandatory injunction requires the defendant to undo some wrongful act, for example, an order requiring a dominant supplier to re-supply a customer who has been unlawfully refused supplies in breach of Article 86 EC.[256] Most injunctions are of the prohibitory form. Where a party has been successful in obtaining an injunction the Court may order damages in addition to or in lieu of the injunction.[257]

(3) Declaratory relief

7.111 Declarations will be useful where the application or otherwise of a block exemption is at stake. Thus X and Y might enter an exclusive dealing agreement under which X is the supplier and Y the dealer. Y might seek to be released from his contractual obligations so pleads the incompatibility of the agreement with Article 85(1) EC as a means of escaping the contract. If X can prove that the agreement falls within Regulation 1983/83/EEC on block exemption for exclusive distribution then a national court can declare the block exemption applicable and the agreement subsisting. Alternatively, X and Y might have entered a joint venture to promote R&D; Z, however might consider its economic interests threatened by the joint venture so sue X and Y on the basis of breach of Article 85(1). If X and Y can establish the applicability of Regulation 418/85/EEC on block exemption for R&D joint ventures, then the national court may declare its relevance and Z's action will almost certainly be dismissed. Declarations are also used by parties seeking to establish that an agreement to which they are party is unlawful and not binding upon them.

(4) Stay of proceedings

7.112 A stay of proceedings in the UK court may be appropriate where the dispute is being investigated by the EC Commission. While the Commission's Notice on Co-operation between

[254] This is usually termed the "clean hands rule": *Measures Bros Ltd* v *Measures* [1910] 2 Ch 248 (CA). See also the equivalent equitable principle of *ex turpi causa non oritur actio* discussed at para. 7.96.

[255] This requirement in applications for judicial review is expressly set out by RSC Order 53 rule 4(1), stating that leave must be sought promptly, but since an injunctive relief is discretionary, delay is a factor that is taken into account in the exercise of that discretion in any type of case. An application for leave to bring judicial review proceedings for breach of Art. 86 was refused on this ground in *R* v *Minster for Agriculture, Fisheries and Food ex parte Dairy Trade Federation Ltd*, Dyson J, 26 September 1994, unreported, noted by Fiona Smith (1995) 20 ELRev 214. Leave was also refused because it was considered that a complaint to the Commission would be the appropriate remedy for the applicant.

[256] e.g. *James Budgett* v *British Sugar Corporation* (unreported) noted above note 246.

[257] s. 50 Supreme Court Act 1981: "Where the Court of Appeal or the High Court has jurisdiction to entertain an application for an injunction or specific performance, it may award damages in addition to or in substitute for, an injunction or specific performance." s. 50 simply repeats the effect of s. 2 of the Chancery Amendment Act 1858 (Lord Cairns' Act). See for examples, *Leeds Industrial Co-operative Society* v *Slack* [1924] AC 851; *Johnson* v *Agnew* [1979] 1 All ER 883 (HL) (damages in lieu of specific performance); and *Kennaway* v *Thompson* [1980] 3 WLR 361 (CA) (damages in lieu of an injunction).

National Courts and the Commission in Applying Articles 85 and 86 of the EEC Treaty[258] endeavours to ensure that EC competition proceedings are allocated appropriately and in accordance with the principle of subsidiarity between the Commission and national courts, inevitably there will be situations in which a complaint has been made but where EC competition law is also being pleaded in national proceedings arising out of the same circumstances.

7.113 In such a situation, it has been stated that there are "two cardinal principles: 1. The party invoking the powers of the court in protection of its legal rights should not be denied access to the court. 2. A Defendant should not be required to argue its case simultaneously in two jurisdictions".[259]

7.114 The reconciliation of these two principles is governed by Community law and in particular by the ruling of the Court of Justice in *Delimitis*.[260] In that case the Court emphasised that it was the duty of national courts to avoid a risk of conflict with the Commission.[261] In *MTV Europe* v *BMG Records (UK) Ltd and Ors*.[262] The Court of Appeal affirmed the judgment of Evans Lombe J in a case in which concurrent proceedings were pending before the Chancery Division and before the European Commission. The judge as first instance considered the merits of the Plaintiffs' statement of claim and complaint and considered that, at least on a provisional view, they appeared strong. The judge, however, was mindful of the duty of the Court to avoid a risk of conflict between the proceedings of the Commission and any likely decision arrived at by the national court and concluded that it could not be said with total certainty that the Plaintiffs would succeed before the Commission. In those circumstances he considered it necessary to grant a stay. First, he granted a stay for six months while the Defendants were preparing for and attending an oral hearing before the Commission. Thereafter the case was to proceed according to rule until the point arrived at which the case would be set down for trial. At that point the Plaintiffs were required to give an undertaking (and presumably) in the absence of an undertaking the Court would have ruled to the same effect) that they would not set down the case for trial pending the determination of the issues by the Commission. The Defendants, notwithstanding that a stay of sorts had been obtained, appealed.

7.115 The Appeal Court affirmed the judgment of the High Court. The Master of the Rolls, in the leading judgment, set out the relevant case law and stated:

> "There is, in my Judgment, nothing which suggests that in a case where the answer is not clear in favour of the Plaintiff or the Defendant, the national court *must* at once stay the proceedings pending a decision by the Commission. The Court's concern is to avoid inconsistent decisions. There is no ground for seeking to prohibit the preparation of an action for trial so long as it does not lead to a decision in advance of a decision by the Commission."

Lord Justice Millett stated:

> "It is incumbent on a national court to avoid the risk of reaching a decision which conflicts with the ruling, or future ruling, of a Community institution. To that end it may grant an immediate stay of proceedings before it, or take whatever other measures are open to it under

[258] OJ 1993 C39/6, [1993] 4 CMLR 12.

[259] *Per* Sir Godfray Le Quesne QC sitting as a deputy judge of the Queen's Bench Division in *ICS* v *Institute of Personnel Management* case (1993), unreported, cited by Evans-Lombe J in *MTV Europe* v *BMG Records (UK) Ltd* [1995] ECC 216.

[260] Case C-234/89 *Delimitis* v *Henninger Brau AG* [1991] ECR I-935.

[261] See also Case C-250/92 *Gottrup-Klim* [1994] ECR I-5641 at p. 5693, paras. 57–60, to the same effect as the rule in *Delimitis*.

[262] [1997] Eu LR 100, Court of Appeal (Sir Thomas Bingham, Lord Justice Millett and Lord Justice Schiemann). The ruling of the High Court is at [1995] ECC 216.

> the national rules of procedure. In the present case, the Judge recognised the risk that premature judgment in the action might conflict with a later ruling of the Commission. He decided that it was sufficient to direct that the action should not be set down until one month after the Commission had published it decision. I am unable to comprehend why it should be thought that he had no jurisdiction to make such an order."

Lord Justice Schiemann agreed with both of the judgments of the Master of the Rolls and Lord Justice Millett.[263]

7.116 On the other hand, stays have not been granted by of proceedings under the RTPA 1976 where Commission proceedings were underway, where the decision of the Restrictive Practices Court was either relevant factor for the Commission to take into account in its proceedings[264] or where the RTPA case involved much more limit questions than those before the Commission which were not directly relevant to the Commission's investigation.[265]

E. Overlap between EC and National Proceedings[266]

7.117 EC proceedings may overlap and potentially conflict with national proceedings (and vice versa) both in terms of procedure and with respect to the remedies which may be ordered. The Commission's Notice on Co-operation between National Courts and the Commission in Applying Articles 85 and 86 of the EEC Treaty[267] has already been discussed at paras. 7.3–7.8, with respect to the Commission's powers and duties of investigation. The Notice seeks to, *inter alia*, identify the respecti ve fields of competence of the Commission and national courts and to explain how the Commission attempts to assist national courts. However, whatever its aim, the Notice does not deal with all the problems which may arise in practice, which may be divided into two broad categories: those arising in relation to use of evidence and those which concern remedies. These will be dealt with in turn after considering first the general principles applicable in this area.

263 For other cases on stay see *British Leyland Motor Corporation* v *Wyatt Interpart* [1979] FSR 583, [1980] FSR 18, Graham J stayed proceedings on the basis that the Defendant made an appropriate complaint to the Commission and prosecuted that complaint diligently. In *ICI* v *Institute of Personnel Management* (1993) (unreported) Sir Godray le Quesne QC, sitting as a deputy judge of the Queen's Bench Division, was prepared to grant a stay to the Defendant despite a submission that such a stay could be open ended. The Plaintiffs had sought an interlocutory injunction before the High Court. The application was refused. Immediately thereafter they complained to the Commission and sought interim relief. The Defendants thereafter applied to stay the proceedings pending a determination of the Plaintiffs' application for interim relief and a decision of the Commission on whether they would accept the Complaint or leave it to be resolved before the national court. In the event, the decision of the Commission deciding not to pursue the Complaint and to leave it to be resolved before the national court took approximately 18 months. See also *DTI* v *British Aerospace* [1991] 1 CMLR 165 in which Ognall J stayed proceedings for the recovery of state aid deemed by the EC Commission to have been illegal pending the outcome of an appeal to the Court of Justice. In *IBM* v *Phoenix International (Computers) Ltd* (unreported, 30 July 1993) Ferris J granted a stay of a counterclaim which alleged infringements of Arts. 85 and 86 and in respect of which complaint had been made to the European Commission. The Commission dismissed the complaint for interim measures: see *Twenty-second Report on Competition Policy* (1992), p. 427. However, Ferris J did not stay the Plaintiff's claim in the case, which related to trade mark infringement and which was not an issue over which the Commission, in the view of the judge, had jurisdiction.

264 *Re Net Book Agreement 1957: DGFT* v *Publishers' Association*, 9 August 1995, unreported judgment of Ferris J; see paras 5.130–5.132.

265 *Re an Agreement relating to the Supply of Sugar: British Sugar plc* v *DGFT*, 9 August 1995, unreported judgment of Ferris J; see paras 5.127–5.129.

266 See Kerse, *op. cit.*, note 1, Chapter 10.

267 OJ 1993 C39/6, [1993] 4 CMLR 12.

1. General Principles

7.118 Commission and national procedures may conflict in a number of ways. A national competition investigation or competition litigation in a national court may take place at the same time as a matter is being investigated by the Commission. If only EC law is in issue, then it is clear that although national courts and the Commission possess concurrent powers to apply Articles 85(1) and 86, only the Commission may decide whether to grant an exemption under Article 85(3).[268] If a national court is dealing with a case raising issues about the application of Articles 85 or 86, it may seek advice from the Commission.[269] This advice may be of a procedural nature, to determine whether a case is currently before the Commission and if it is what the Commission's timetable for dealing with it is likely to be. The Commission states that it "will endeavour to give priority to cases which are the subject of national proceedings ... in particular when the outcome of a civil dispute depends upon them". In such a case, the party concerned may seek to stay proceedings pending the Commission taking action. The Commission states that its views of points of law may also be sought, but in the light of the Article 177 EC preliminary ruling reference procedure, its view cannot be definitive. Given the adversarial approach of common law litigation, it is unlikely that a UK court would seek the Commission's views on points of law[270] and is more likely to refer a contentious point of law to the Court of Justice under Article 177 EC.[271]

7.119 On the other hand national authorities may only conduct an investigation utilising Articles 85(1) or 86 if authorised to do so under national law. None of the UK competition authorities have been so authorised and may thus only apply domestic UK competition law.[271a]

7.120 If the national proceedings raise the same or similar issues under national competition law to those being investigated by the Commission, then the Commission's view is that "the simultaneous application of national competition law is compatible with the application of Community law, provided it does not impair the effectiveness and uniformity of Community competition rules and the measures taken to enforce them".[272] Therefore national courts cannot require action to be taken under national competition laws which would be contrary to EC competition law. However, this principle is not easy to translate into practice, since it is not clear what constitutes a conflict between EC and national law. This is discussed below in relation to overlapping remedies.

[268] C-234/89 *Delimitis* v *Henninger Bräu* [1991] ECR I-935, [1992] 5 CMLR 210, para. 44.

[269] Notice on Co-operation between National Courts and the Commission in Applying Arts. 85 and 86 of the EEC Treaty, OJ 1993 C39/6, paras. 37–39.

[270] In *Hasselblad* v *Orbinson Ltd* [1985] QB 475, the Court of Appeal invited the Commission to address it as a "European amicus" on the role of the Commission in investigating competition complaints. The question at issue in the litigation was whether a complaint made to the Commission could form the basis for a libel action under English law. The Court of Appeal held (May LJ dissenting) that it could not on the ground that it would be against the public interest thus to restrict complaints.

[271] For Art. 177 references, see D. Anderson, *References to the European Court* (1995).

[271a] The EC Competition Law (Arts. 88 and 89) Enforcement Regulations 1996, S.I. 1996 No. 2199, authorises the Secretary of State, as advised by the DGFT and MMC, to rule on the applicability of Arts. 85 and 86, but only in those areas where the Commission does not have power to do so under regulations made pursuant to Article 87 of the EC Treaty. This means, in practice, air transport services between Member States and countries outside the EC, and international maritime tramp vessel services.

[272] Notice on Co-operation between National Courts and the Commission in Applying Articles 85 and 86 of the EEC Treaty, OJ 1993 C39/6, para. 12. A submission that the Director General of Telecommunications was acting in breach of this principle was rejected by the Divisional Court in *R* v *Director General of Telecommunications ex p British Telecommunications plc*, 20 December 1996.

2. *Overlapping Remedies*

7.121 Overlap in the area of damages may occur when one dispute has generated parallel proceedings. Fines levied by the Commission should be taken into account by national authorities in imposing fines, to avoid the imposition of a double punitive sanction.[273] Whether the Commission should take into account fines or damages awarded in national proceedings in assessing fines under Regulation 17 has not yet arisen as an issue, but it is submitted that the principle of no double punitive sanctions would apply as a general principle of EC law. Whether a national court should take into account a Commission fine in assessing damages in a case has not been decided. Since damages are to compensate and fines are to punish, it is submitted that the two should not offset each other. Fines could only offset exemplary damages.

7.122 A Commission order, either final or interim, cannot be overturned within the territory of one Member State.[274] Equally the fact that a national investigation finds a practice as not being contrary to the public interest does not prevent the Commission from finding that practice contrary to Articles 85 or 86 EC. Thus in *Ice Cream*[275] the MMC found that the practice of freezer exclusivity did not operate against the public interest, whereas the Commission found with respect to the analogous situation in the Irish market that it did operate contrary to Articles 85(1) and 86 EC.[276]

7.123 National competition laws may apply to prohibit conduct to which Articles 85 and 86 are not applicable.[277] In the case of conduct exemption by the Commission under Article 85(3) or under a block exemption, it would seem that the uniform application of EC law would be prejudiced by the application of a stricter national prohibition. However, there is no authority on this point and commentators remain divided.[278] The UK government seems to have taken the approach that national laws can impose stricter rules, thus explaining why it was necessary to issue a Statutory Instrument under the RTPA 1976 exempting block exempt agreements from notification under the RTPA 1976.

3. *Evidential Overlap*

7.124 Evidential overlap concerns the possibility of using documents obtained during proceedings before national courts for the purpose of complaining to the Commission. Under English law, documents obtained by discovery shall not be used by a solicitor for any purpose other than the conduct of the client's case.[279] However, in *Apple Corp* v *Apple Computer*[280] the High Court was prepared to release a party to the litigation from this undertaking in order to inform the Commission of a suspected breach of Article 85. However, the Court of Justice subsequently ruled in *Otto* v *Postbank*[281] that the Commission may not use information which it discovers arising out of such a dispute either as grounds itself for initiating

[273] Case 14/68 *Walt Wilhelm* v *Bundeskartellamt* [1969] ECR 1 [1969] CMLR 100, para. 11.
[274] 45/85 *Veerband der Sachversicherer* v *Commission* [1987] ECR 405 [1988] 4 CMLR 264, paras. 17–24.
[275] *Ice Cream: A Report on the Supply in the UK of Ice Cream for Immediate Consumption*, Cm 2524 (1994).
[276] Commission Press Releases IP/95/229, 10 March 1995, and IP/97/147.
[277] Case 253/7 and 1-3/79 *Procureur de la République* v *Giry and Guerlain SA* [1980] ECR 2327 [1981] 2 CMLR 99.
[278] See Kerse, *op. cit.*, note 1, pp. 385–388, who states at p. 387 that "it would appear that the position as regards the status and effects of Community exemptions is uncertain. It is undecided whether all, some or none need necessarily be respected by national law and, if so, to what extent."
[279] *Harman* v *Home Office* [1983] 1 AC 280. Breach of this implied undertaking to the court is punishable as a contempt of court.
[280] [1992] 1 CMLR 969.
[281] Case C-60/92 *Otto BV* v *Postbank BV* [1993] ECR I-5683. For the Commission's comment on this case, see *Twenty-third Report on Competition Policy* (1993), para. 351.

an investigation or for establishing proof of an infringement which could lead to the imposition of penalties. That case concerned a Dutch rule of evidence compelling witnesses to answer, unless such evidence might expose the witness to criminal proceedings. It therefore seems to be the case that the Commission can only rely upon such evidence as it can acquire directly using its own procedures. It may not rely upon evidence supplied to it which it could not directly acquire itself.

7.125 However, the same is not the case for a national authority which acquires evidence of an infringement of national competition law as a result of being notified under Regulation 17 of Commission proceedings. In those circumstances, the Court of Justice ruled in *Spanish Banks*[282] that although the national authority cannot use that evidence, it is not required to turn a blind eye to it and can use it in order to launch its own investigations. As regards a private party, it can use knowledge it acquires as a result of a Commission investigation in order to bring an action in the English courts under EC or national law, provided evidence it relies upon satisfies the English rules of evidence. For example, the consequence of the Commission investigation into British Leyland's refusal to supply certificates of conformity was that an action for damages was brought before the High court by the injured party.[283]

F. Negotiating Informal Settlements with the Commission

1. *Relevant Statistics*

7.126 Very few notified agreements reach a formal decision. Conversely, hundreds of agreements each year are settled informally between the parties and the Commission. The statistics on the next page give an indication of this pattern.[284]

	Decisions	*Comfort letters*	*Informally settled*
1989	15	46	382
1990	15	158	710
1991	13	146	676
1992	20	176	553
1993	12	na	na
Average	13	132	580

2. *Commencement of Negotiations: Procedure*

7.127 Parties invariably request the Commission to consider settling notified cases on an informal basis. It is important to consider at what stage of proceedings this request should be made or even if it should be made at all. If parties to an important agreement seek to obtain a formal decision from the Commission, clearly they will make no request and the Commission will (in theory) proceed to a formal decision. Invariably, however, parties are con-

282 Case C-83/91 *Dirección General de Defensa de la Competencia* v *Asociación Española de Banca Privada* [1992] ECR I 4785.

283 *Merson* v *Rover Group* (1992), judgment of 22 May 1992, unreported in which the High Court refused summary judgment under Order 14. The case was settled before an appeal to the Court of Appeal could be heard. The Commission decision, 84/379, is reported at OJ 1984 L207/11, [1984] 3 CMLR 92, and the Commission's decision was upheld in 226/84 *British Leyland plc* v *Commission* [1986] ECR 3263, [1987] 1 CMLR 185.

284 Information obtained from Commission *Competition Reports* for years 1989–93. The figure for decisions includes all decisions, not just those relating to notified agreements.

tent to negotiate a compromise without the Commission opening the formal procedure and preparing a statement of objections. This may be the case with relatively common and straightforward types of agreement (e.g. patent licences or exclusive dealing agreements) where the Commission is sure of its ground.

7.128 Traditionally the Commission have dealt with negotiation by means of what have become known as "comfort letters"—letters addressed to parties stating that the Commission intends to close the file on a case without issuing a formal decision. It has also adopted the practice of settling cases by accepting an undertaking in good faith from the parties that they will not proceed with the complained of conduct. Such undertakings may be a necessary precursor to the Commission issuing a comfort letter. Both of these procedures are examined below.

7.129 In more complex cases or in cases involving more serious restrictions, the Commission may well issue a formal statement of objections. In such cases an oral hearing might also occur enabling the parties to present their views orally to the Commission. The institution and continuation of the formal procedure does not preclude an informal settlement. Indeed, it can facilitate a settlement since, with the issuance of the formal statement of objections, the parties will be better informed concerning Commission thinking and hence better placed to respond.

7.130 Parties may submit memoranda of proposed alterations to their agreements at any time and the Commission will give its response on the adequacy of the suggestions. Negotiations may continue in this form over many months and even years. If the Commission consider that the parties in making submissions are, in reality, stalling for time, they are more likely to proceed formally to a prohibitive decision.

7.131 In the famous *IBM Settlement* case[285] the Commission used the formal process of a bargaining counter to expedite IBM's negotiating response and to encourage an effective settlement. In an answer given to a Written Question in the Parliament the Commissioner responsible for Competition stated: "At a hearing in June 1983, IBM made known its views on the action it would be required to take in the event of a decision under Article 86 of the EEC Treaty. It subsequently asked the Commission to terminate the proceedings without taking a formal decision. The only pressure to which IBM was subject stemmed from the fact that the formal proceedings were conducted in parallel with the informal discussions."[286] It is understood that the Commission and IBM met in a sequence of meetings during 1983 and 1984 in order to work out a settlement and that the Commission informed IBM that in the absence of an agreed settlement by a specified date in mid-1984, the Commission would issue the formal decision that they had already drafted. The actual settlement was arrived at following an eleventh hour meeting with the Commission.

7.132 In the *Microsoft Settlement*,[287] the party under investigation invited the European Commission to conduct its investigation in cooperation with the US Department of Justice,

[285] Details of the settlement are published at [1984] 3 CMLR 147; and Bull EC 10/84, Annex 4, p. 96. It is unusual for the entire undertaking to be published in this manner, though the Commission does issue Press Releases on points of particular significance. These Press Releases are noted in the daily publication *Agence Europe* and in the Commission's monthly *Bulletin of the EC* and quarterly *Competition Policy Newsletter* (CPN), as well as being available on the RAPID database. See bibliography for details of Internet availability of Commission documents.

[286] See WQ 457/84 and WQ 695/84, OJ 1984 C 344/2 (24 December 1984) at p. 3.

[287] Commission Press Release IP/94/653, (1994) 1 CPN, Issue 2, p. 17. the settlement between Microsoft and the European Commission was made in a settlement dated 15 July 1994. The US investigation is reported at (1994) 67 ATRR106 and was due to be settled by a consent decree. However, somewhat unexpectedly, the judge refused assent to the terms of the consent decree on the basis that its scope was too narrow and

Antitrust Division, and thus pre-empted the issue of a Statement of Objections. As business and competition law both become increasingly international in nature, such procedural cooperation may become more attractive. Indeed, it may be suggested that for an undertaking under investigation, it may be tactically possible to reach a situation in which one competition authority may be played off against another, leading to a settlement which represents only the lowest common denominator of obligations which might be required in a settlement.[288]

7.133 Some general guidance may be given about the practicalities of presenting a case before the Commission. Negotiation before the Commission is not like commercial negotiation, where the parties may expect to compromise mid-way. The Commission sees itself as having to do whatever is necessary, but no more, to ensure the proper application of EC law. Negotiations can only concern modifications of agreements or of conduct, not plea bargaining about past conduct. Written submissions should be succinct, as they may well require translation. Figures should be presented to back up arguments. Economic and econometric arguments should be advanced on the basis of qualified advice. Evidence should be annexed to the submissions.

3. Settlement Procedure: Good Faith Undertakings and Suspension of Proceedings

7.134 In the *IBM Settlement* case the Commission settled with IBM on the basis of an undertaking given by the latter in good faith to the Commission. The Commission, agreed to suspend proceedings against IBM and in a letter from the Commissioner responsible for competition to the general counsel of IBM it was stated:

> "Furthermore, you may be assured that the Commission will not seek to reactivate the suspended proceedings so long as IBM's implementation succeeds in giving substantial satisfaction. You will appreciate nevertheless that the suspension of a particular proceeding cannot preclude the Commission, as a public authority, from terminating this suspension or from initiating a new proceedings in respect of IBM's conduct. Should the Commission reactivate the suspended proceeding it will rely exclusively on Articles 85 and 86 of the Treaty, and not upon your undertaking, in this or any other proceeding.

You will readily acknowledge that the effect and implementation of IBM's undertaking must be kept under constant review by my services. Apart from other action, I have instructed my services to call a meeting annually to take stock of the implementation of your undertaking and its effects. If need be, adjustments will then be discussed. The essential purpose of your undertaking is to provide necessary interface information and we shall welcome close cooperation with you to carry this out. The way in which this is done will be important and the spirit of the undertaking should prevail over the letter of particular examples or particular phrasing."[289]

Although the case is now of some vintage it remains informative as an example. A number of points may be made about this case which indicate Commission policy:

cont.
did not constitute an effective antitrust remedy, as required by the Tunney Act. That decision was overturned on appeal and the consent decree was entered on 21 August 1995, (1995) 69 ATRR 268. For comment on the *Microsoft Settlement*, see the report of the Symposium at (1995) 60 AB 257.

288 This may be the suspicion which led the US judge in *Microsoft* initially to refuse assent to the consent decree.

289 See Bull EC 10/84, Annex 4, p. 103; [1984] 3 CMLR 147 at p. 151 noted Faull (1986) ELRev 91. See also *Re Hilti* [1985] 3 CMLR 619 (good faith undertaking given in lieu of interim decision); *Ford Motor Company Ltd* Bull EC 1/86 p. 26—Ford's gave undertaking that they would offer licences to competitors in the UK for the manufacture and sale of body parts. As a result of the undertaking interim proceedings were suspended.

(1) Undertakings are not decisions

7.135 An undertaking does not constitute a formal decision; it may be expressed to have no legal consequences at all. To this extent it would not fit within the definition of a decision laid down by the Court of Justice.

(2) Undertakings suspend proceedings

7.136 An undertaking of the IBM type is merely a suspension of proceedings; it is not a termination of proceedings.

(3) Undertakings have no legal effect

7.137 An undertaking of the IBM type has no legal effects as between the Commission and the parties. The IBM undertaking was expressed to be "without prejudice". Article 19 of that undertaking provides that the undertaking and all related documents (correspondence, memoranda and discussions between parties and Commission) were not to be used in any way by the Commission or IBM. Moreover, Article 19 continued, "it is fundamental to this undertaking that it shall not be enforceable by any other natural or legal person or any additional authority or agency".

A formal, published undertaking given by a party to the Commission cannot bind or require a national court to take no notice of it. The admissibility of such evidence before a national court presumably depends upon national rules of evidence, e.g. on the value (if any) of documents stated to be without "without prejudice". Further, the undertaking and related documents are public documents, they are not confidential or private documents.

(4) Good faith undertakings

7.138 Undertakings may be given in "good faith". Any breach of a "good faith" undertaking may be construed, by the Commission, as bad faith. In arriving at a formal decision following reactivation of formal proceedings bad faith breach of an undertaking may be relevant in deciding upon fines. The Commission may also consider an undertaking in semi-contract terms, i.e. IBM or the party concerned will modify its behaviour and the Commission, for its part, will suspend formal proceedings, although, it is notable that the Commission, as evidenced by the letter quoted from above, may agree not to rely on the undertaking if formal proceedings are reactivated. It is unclear whether this applies to the substance of any subsequent decision only or whether it includes fining policy also.

(5) Monitoring

7.139 Undertakings may involve monitoring by the Commission. The Commission, in the *IBM* case, required IBM to keep it informed of such data as the former deemed necessary to effectively monitor the undertaking.[290] The Commission expect IBM's competitors to assist in the monitoring by making complaints where appropriate.[291]

[290] *Twenty-third Report on Competition Policy* (1993), Annex III, para. 15 states that since the inception of IBM's undertaking until the end of 1993, there have been 189 requests from 23 competitors containing 1,487 individual questions. Seven of these companies have signed and received information from IBM under technical disclosure agreements.

[291] See Commission answer to WQ 457/84 and WQ 695/84, OJ 1984 C344/2 (24 December 1984) at p. 3, para. 3 of answer; Commission answer to WQ No. 1269/84, OJ 1985 C 65/25 at p. 26(3); and, Commission answer to WQ No. 1990/85, OJ 1986 C123/12. It is apparent from the judgment of Ferris J in *IBM* v *Phoenix International (Computers) Ltd* (1993), unreported judgment of 30 July 1993 that a complaint to the Commission was made by Phoenix in relation to IBM's failure to maintain IBM machines which had been modified by Phoenix. The High Court litigation involved an action by IBM to restrain Phoenix's use of the IBM trade mark. A Euro-defence that IBM was abusing its dominant position by its

(6) Periodic adjustments

7.140 Undertakings may be subject to periodic adjustments. This will occur in the light of monitoring and supervision by the Commission.

(7) Duration

7.141 The undertaking may be of limited duration. The Microsoft undertaking has a duration of six and a half years running from 15 July 1994. The IBM undertaking operated until 1 January 1989 (it was signed on 1 August 1984), remaining in force thereafter until one year after IBM give notice to the Commission of their intention no longer to comply with the undertaking. Alternatively, it lapses if at any time the Commission issue a formal decision against IBM.

4. *Settlement Procedure: Comfort Letters*[292]

(1) Content of comfort letters

7.142 The *IBM* and *Microsoft* cases discussed above were novel both as to substance and procedure, the final meetings involved a number of EC Commissioners as well as the Director General and other senior officials from DG IV. In more normal circumstances parties to agreements or trade association officials will discuss their cases with ordinary officials from DG IV. When agreement is reached a letter will be sent to the parties signed by a senior Commission official or a Director in DG IV. This letter—the "comfort letter" —states that the Commission intends to close the file on the case; usually but not always a reason is given. The information provided in a comfort letter varies from case to case.[293] It may, for example state: that the agreement falls within a block exemption;[294] that in view of the changes made by the parties the Commission do not intend to take further action; that the agreement does not fall within Article 85(1). The letter might reserve the right of the Commission to reconsider the position in the light of further developments.[295] It might also provide for supervision of the future behaviour of the parties.

(2) Publication procedure

7.143 Before issuing a comfort letter to conclude a case the Commission have developed a procedure for allowing interested third parties to intervene. In 1982 and 1983 the Commission published two notices. The first notice concerned comfort letters as a means of closing cases where the parties apply for negative clearance.[296] The second notice concerned comfort letters as a means of closing cases where the parties seek exemption under Article 85(3) EC.[297] The procedure for both is fairly similar. In brief the Commission

cont.
failure to maintain hardware worked upon by Phoenix was struck out as disclosing no nexus with IBM's case that Phoenix was breaching its trade mark rights.

[292] See D. Stevens, "The 'comfort letter': old problems, new developments" [1994] ECLR 81.

[293] See Temple-Lang, "Community antitrust law: compliance and enforcement" (1981) 18 CMLRev 335 at p. 355 for examples of the contents of comfort letters.

[294] e.g. *AEG-Telefunken* [1982] 2 CMLR 386 (Commission decision): Commission notified parties that on facts before it, the distribution agreement as notified fell within the block exemption then applying to distribution agreements (Reg. 67/67/EC). See also, *Eighth Commission Competition Report* (1978), para. 78.

[295] As was the case with the comfort letter issued to Schöller stating the Commission's view that its impulse ice cream distribution agreements would fall within the exclusive purchasing block exemption. The text of the comfort letter is set out in Case T-9/93 *Schöller* v *Commission*, [1995] ECR II-1611, para. 1.

[296] See Notice from the Commission on procedures concerning notifications pursuant to Art. 2 of Council Reg. 17/62, OJ 1982 C343/4; [1984] 1 CMLR 38.

[297] Notice from the Commission on procedures pursuant to notification pursuant to Art. 4 of Council Reg. 17/62, OJ 1983 C295/6; [1984] 1 CMLR 128.

will publish, in the Official Journal of the European Communities, the essential ingredients of the agreement. This can run to three or four pages. The Commission will state that it intends to close the file on the case in question and it will then invite third parties to comment usually within a one-month period. Having received comments the Commission will then send a provisional letter. According to the Notice: "Such letters will not have the status of Decisions and will therefore not be capable of appeal to the Court of Justice. They will state that the Directorate General for Competition, in agreement with the undertakings concerned, does not consider it necessary to pursue the formal procedure through to the adoption of a Decision under Article 85(3)." The Notice on negative clearance is, *mutatis mutandis*, the same. The only difference is that the Commission stated that in respect of exemption comfort letters, a list of the cases dealt with in this manner, following publication of their details, would be appended to the annual Commission Competition Report. The practice now is to refer to cases in which this procedure has been used in the Report.[298] In respect of negative clearance comfort letters, third parties would be notified of the sending of the letter by means of a notice published at a later date in the Official Journal simply noting the existence of the comfort letter.[299] These procedures have now been used on a number of occasions.[300] However, the Commission does not issue these notices in respect of every comfort letter sent out. Indeed, it would appear to be a relatively rarely used procedure.

(3) Legal effect of publication procedure

7.144 There is one question that should be asked in respect of these procedures. Both notices justify the procedures by reference to Article 19(3) of Regulation 17/62/EEC; the question is how? Article 19(3) reads: "Where the Commission *intends to give* negative clearance pursuant to Article 2 or *take* a decision in application of Article 85(3) of the Treaty, it shall publish a summary of the relevant application or notification and invite all interested third parties to submit their observations within a time limit which it shall fix being not less than one month. Publication shall have regard to the legitimate interest of undertakings in the protection of their business secrets" [emphasis added].

7.145 Article 19(3) envisages the positive taking of a decision—see the words in italics; when the Commission issues a comfort letter it has no positive intention of taking a decision. Indeed the converse applies with the comfort letter acting as a substitute for a decision. Article 19(3) cannot strictly be authority for the comfort letter publication procedure. The nearest that one can realistically come is to say that the Commission has in the interests of natural justice and due process initiated a procedure analogous to that outlined in Article 19(3). However, it is most unlikely that the Court would look unfavourably on this procedure in light of the concern expressed by the Court for procedural fairness and of the general calls for greater transparency made by various bodies, including the European Parliament.[301]

[298] See, for example, Annex III, *Twenty-third Report on Competition Policy* (1993).

[299] *Twelfth Commission Competition Report* (1982), p. 38, para. 30. See also Commission Answers to WQ No. 815/82, OJ 1982 C259/26 (4 October 1982); and WQ No. 874/82, OJ 1982 C287 (4 November 1982).

[300] See e.g. *Europages* OJ 1982 C343/5; [1984] 1 CMLR 38; *Rovin* OJ 1983 C295/7; [1984] 1 CMLR 87; *BPCL/ICI* OJ 1984 C20/9 [1984] 1 CMLR 257; *Kathon Biocide* OJ 1984 C59.

[301] See the criticism made by the Parliament in its Resolution on the Commission's *Tenth Competition Report* OJ 1982 C 11/78 at para. 42 where they called, "for more information to be provided in the Annual Reports and in other publications, on the principles and criteria guiding the Commission in reaching its informal settlements, in order to provide more guidance for affected undertakings." See also para. 43 of the resolution where the Parliament call for the publication of the internal rules of procedure of the Commission for the investigation and adjudication of suspected infringements. In the Resolution of the

5. The Legal Value of Comfort Letters

7.146 Comfort letters are not formal decisions issued pursuant to Regulation 17/62/EEC. They are simply administrative letters which are based upon the facts as known to the Commission.[302] They cannot be relied upon by the addressee as against third parties nor do they prevent national courts, seised of a case under Articles 85 or 86, from arriving at a different assessment of the agreements concerned in the light of the information available to them. Nevertheless, while comfort letters do not bind national courts, the opinion they express constitutes a matter which national courts may take into account. Thus, a comfort letter is no safeguard against a national court declaring the agreement void under Article 85(2).[303] Indeed, only the Commission may grant an exemption under Article 85(3).[304] The Commission has suggested in its Notice on Cooperation between National Courts and the Commission in applying Articles 85 and 86 of the EEC Treaty[305] that a national court should take account of a comfort letter in determining whether it is likely that an exemption would be granted. If not, then the court may proceed to apply Articles 85(1) and 85(2), but if it is likely, then the court should suspend proceedings pending the Commission's decision, inviting, if necessary, the Commission reopen proceedings.[306] The practice of the English courts is to admit the expressions of opinion of the Commission and comfort letters into proceedings as persuasive and relevant in determining whether there is a risk that the national court will take a decision in conflict with that of the Commission and, if so, whether it should grant a stay of proceedings.

7.147 While clearly not formal decisions in the Regulation 17/62/EC sense, comfort letters do exert a legal effect.[307] It is, accordingly, perhaps arguable that a comfort letter is a reviewable act under Article 173(4) EC.[308] The Court of First Instance, under that provision, may review decisions addressed to natural or legal persons. It may also review: (a) decisions addressed to third parties which are of direct and individual concern to the plaintiff;

cont.
Parliament on the *Twelfth Commission Competition Report* (*Thirteenth Commission Competition Report*, Annex 1, p. 237 at p. 240, para. 35) the Parliament acknowledges the attempts of the Commission to improve the status of comfort letters by the publication procedure. See more generally the Commission's comments on"transparency" in the application of the competition rules in its *Twenty-first Report on Competition Policy* (1991), paras. 66–68, *Twenty-second Report on Competition Policy* (1992), paras. 115–119 and *Twenty-third Report on Competition Policy* (1993), paras. 182–188.

302 In *Inntrepreneur Estates Ltd* v *Mason* [1993] 2 CMLR 293, M. Barnes QC sitting as a Deputy Judge of the High Court in the Queen's Bench division, held that a letter indicating the Commission's intention to issue an Art. 19(3) Reg. 17/62 Notice as a preliminary to proceeding to the grant of an exemption could
cont.
not be regarded as comfort letter, since a comfort letter was an alternative means to an exemption of disposing of a matter. The Deputy Judge commented on the uncertainties facing a national court when faced with a comfort letter, at pp. 306–307, in the view of its uncertain exact legal status.

303 See Commission answer to WQ No. 1508/81, OJ 1982 C85/6 where the Commission stress that comfort letters have limited legal effect. See, for a searching analysis of this area, Korah, "Comfort letters: reflections on the perfume cases" (1981) ELRev 14.

304 C-234/89 *Delimitis* [1991] ECR I-935, para. 44.

305 1993 OJ C 39/6.

306 The published draft of this Notice would have gone further by suggesting that an agreement caught by Art. 85(1) but the subject of a comfort letter stating its compatibility with Art. 85(3) should be enforceable. This suggestion was dropped from the Notice, probably because it would have been inconsistent with *Delimitis*.

307 For the leading judgments of the Court on comfort letters see the following cases, known collectively as the *Perfumes* cases: Case 33/79 *Anne Marty* v *Estée Lauder* [1981] CMLR 143; [1980] ECR 2481; Case 99/79 *Lancome* v *Etos* [1981] 2 CMLR 164, [1980] ECR 2511; Cases 253/78 and 1–3/79 *Procureur de la Republique* v *Guerlain, Rochas-Lanvin, Nina Ricci* [1981] 2 CMLR 99, [1980] ECR 2327; Case 31/80 *L'Oreal* v *PVBA* [1981] 2 CMLR 235; [1980] ECR 3775.

308 See Korah, *op. cit.*, at n. 303 pp. 30–33.

and (b) decisions which are in the form of a regulation but which are also of direct and individual concern to the plaintiff. In this context the Court of Justice has widely construed the word "decision". In *IBM* v *Commission*[309] the Court stated: "any measure the legal effects of which are binding on, and capable of affecting the interests of, the applicant by bringing about a distinct change in his legal position is an act or decision which may be the object of an action under Article 173 for a declaration that it is void. However, the form in which such acts or decisions are cast is, in principle, immaterial as regards the question whether they are open to challenge under that article."

7.148 A number of points arise. First, so called "old agreements" which enjoy provisional validity once notified *lose* that validity by a comfort letter. This brings about a serious change in the parties position and there appears to be a case for saying that such a comfort letter constitutes an act or even a decision which may be appealed.[310] If a comfort letter is a decision then, under Article 190 EC it must be properly reasoned. For the vast majority of cases, i.e. the "new" cases there is more doubt. A comfort letter does affect the parties rights; it effectively deters the Commission from considering the possibility of an exemption under Article 85(3) EC. Thus, an agreement which might have benefited from the exemption is now bereft of formal exemption and vulnerable before a national court.[311] On this basis it is arguable (though not as strongly as with "old" agreements) that comfort letters are reviewable acts or decisions. If this is so they must be reasoned.

7.149 Some support for this proposition may be gained from the Court of First Instance's decision in *Nefarma*.[312] In deciding that a letter from the Competition Commissioner stating that an agreement would be unlikely to benefit from Article 85(3) exemption was not an act subject to review under Article 173 EC, the Court stressed that this was because the competition investigation was still being carried out when the letter was written. The Court did not examine what would have been the case had the letter terminated the Commission's investigations, but it is possible to interpret the judgment as meaning that a letter producing effects comparable to those of an exemption could be reviewable.[313]

7.150 In practice, much of the above will be immaterial. The Commission has stated that it will only issue a comfort letter if the parties are content for it to close the procedure in this manner.[314] Hence, if for practical reasons of certainty, parties prefer the Commission to proceed to formal decision the Commission will respect this wish. It seems that very few parties do so desire and almost inevitably parties are happy to receive a comfort letter.

6. Can the Commission be Compelled to Settle? Article 175

(1) Article 175: failure to act

7.151 Articles 175(1)–(3) EC read:

[309] Case 60/81 [1981] 3 CMLR 635; [1981] 1 ECR 2639 at para. 9 of the judgment. Court held the statement of objections was not an act subject to judicial review. See also Case 69/69 *Alcan* v *Commission* [1970] CMLR 337, [1970] ECR 385 at p. 393; Case 125/78 *GEMA* v *Commission* [1980] CMLR 177; [1979] ECR 3173 *per* Advocate General Capotorti.

[310] Korah, *op. cit.*, n. 303 at pp. 30–33.

[311] But cf. Commission answer to WQ No. 1508/81, OJ 1982 C85.6—Commission indicated that the new publication procedure would "upgrade" the value of the comfort letter and thereby help avoid national Court judgments at variance with them, a view effectively reiterated in its Notice on Cooperation between national Courts and the Commission in Applying Arts. 85 and 86 of the EEC Treaty, OJ 1993 C39/6, para. 25.

[312] Case T-113/89 *Nefarma* v *Commission* [1990] ECR II-797.

[313] *ibid.*, paras. 86–87.

[314] See *Thirteenth Commission Competition Report* (1983), p. 61, para. 62.

"(1) Should the European Parliament, the Council or the Commission, in infringement of this Treaty, fail to act, the Member States and the other institutions of the Community may bring an action before the Court of Justice to have the infringement established.
(2) The action shall be admissible only if the institution concerned has first been called upon to act. If, within two months of being so called upon, the institution concerned has not defined its position, the action may be brought within a further period of two months.
(3) Any natural or legal person may, under the conditions laid down in the preceding paragraphs, complain to the Court of Justice that an institution of the Community has failed to address to that person any act other than a recommendation or an opinion".[315]

7.152 A private party may under Article 175(3) call upon the Commission to act. If the Commission fail to respond within two months of being called upon the private party may bring a direct action before the Court within two months of the end of the earlier two-month period within which the Commission should have responded. It should be stressed at the outset that action under Article 175 will be barred the moment the Commission, within the two-month time period allotted to them, "define their position". The meaning of a definition of position is nowhere defined. However, it is understood to imply a clear and definite statement by the Commission either accepting the request wholly or in part or rejecting the request. If the Commission define its position two courses of action are open to the private party. It may proceed under Article 175 by arguing that the Commission's response was inadequate as a definition of position and hence that the Commission has failed to respond. Alternatively, or in addition, it may challenge the Commission's letter of response rejecting the applicant's request as a reviewable act under Article 173(4) EC.

7.153 In considering the first option, one must bear in mind the inherent limitations of Article 175 EC. Although that provision has been described by the Court of Justice as prescribing the "same method of recourse"[316] as Article 173 EC, it does not necessarily follow that a private party under Article 175(3) EC can only request the Commission to adopt an act that the private party could have legally sought judicial review of under Article 173(4) EC. The Court of Justice stated in *Comitology* that "[t]here is no necessary link between the action for annulment and the action for failure to act".[317] The Court of First Instance confirmed in *Automec II*[318] that the Commission has a discretion when to investigate a complaint. If the Commission does not respond to a complaint, then it may be compelled to respond under Article 175[319] by way of a letter under Article 6, Regulation 99/63. Whether this applies beyond complainants to parties to an agreement seeking a settlement is unclear. The Advocate General in *Automec II* and *Asia Motor France I*[320] considered that Article 175 could be seen as a general remedy to enable an undertaking being complained against or the complainer to "prod" the Commission into activity. However, he recognised that it might also be the case that the Commission could only be compelled to issue a letter under Article 6, Regulation 99/63. While recognising that this latter interpretation was theoretically less attractive, he did not find it necessary to express a definite opinion. If his former suggestion is followed, then given that only the Commission may apply Article 85(3), it seems that the parties to an agreement could insist upon a decision under Article

315 Art. 175(4) omitted.
316 Case 15/70 *Chevalley* v *Commission* [1970] ECR 975, para. 6.
317 Case 302/87 *Parliament* v *Council (Comitology)* [1988] ECR 5615, para. 16.
318 Case T-24/90 *Automec* v *Commission (No. 2)* [1992] ECR II-2223 [1992] 5 CMLR 431.
319 Case T-28/90 *Asia Motor France* v *Commission (No. 1)* [1992] ECR II-2285 [1992] 5 CMLR 431.
320 The cases cited in notes 318 and 319 *supra* are not joined, but the Advocate General, David Edward, gave a single opinion for both cases.

85(3) and thus *a fortiori* a settlement. The Court did not find it necessary to choose between these alternative theories either because a final decision had been reached by the Commission before the Court's judgment and so the point was rendered moot. It seems clear that a private party cannot use Article 175 EC to compel the Commission to issue a general regulation. However, since it is possible for a private party in exceptional circumstances to challenge a regulation under Article 173(4) EC,[321] it may not be completely out of the question for a private party to use Article 175 in this way.

7.154 The second option, that of challenging the Commission's letter of response will involve demonstrating that the letter is "a measure definitively laying down the position of the Commission ... on the conclusion of that procedure, and not a provisional measure intended to pave the way for the final decision".[322] It would seem that a refusal to settle could be construed as a final disposal of the case by the Commission and hence be reviewable, but is more likely to occur as an interim stage to the Commission finally issuing a decision or comfort letter, in which case it would not be reviewable. In practical terms a private party should write to the Commission requesting that the latter adopt a specific course of action.[323] It is considered wise to state expressly that this letter constitutes a call for action under Article 175 EC.[324] This notifies the Commission of their obligation to reply within the two-month period. However, the Commission cannot be compelled to issue a letter under Article6, Regulation 99/63 or a decision within this two-month period where it is still investigating. In such a case, there has been no failure to act reviewable by Article 175 EC, as the Commission is still acting.[325]

(2) What can a private party request?

7.155 (a) Decisions addressed to applicant: a private party can almost certainly use Article 175 to compel the Commission to adopt a formal decision under Regulation 17 with respect to its own position, e.g. granting or refusing exemption or negative clearance. This is because only the Commission has the power to grant exemptions and so can be compelled to exercise this power.[326] Granting negative clearance or refusing exemption are the corollaries of this. The Commission has stated in its Notice on Cooperation between National Courts and the Commission in Applying Articles 85 and 86 of the EEC Treaty[327] that it will, provided a national court suspends its hearing, grant an exemption decision.

7.156 (b) Adoption of a comfort letter with regard to the applicant: it is unlikely that an applicant can require the Commission to issue a comfort letter to it. A comfort letter is intrinsically different from a decision. The latter may be negative (prohibitory) or positive (permissive); the former is only positive. A party requesting a decision seeks clarification of an equivocal position, a party requesting a comfort letter seeks a positive exercise of discretion by the Commission in the applicant's favour, i.e. it seeks to tie the hands of the Commission when the applicant's behaviour may not justify an exercise of discretion in its favour.

321 Case C-309/89 *Codorniu* v *Council* [1994] ECR I–1853, noted by Usher (1994) 19 ELRev 636, in which the Court of Justice quashed, at the suit of a Spanish producer, that part of a Regulation on names for wines which purported to reserve the term *crémant* for French and Luxembourg producers.

322 Case 60/81 *IBM* v *Commission* [1981] ECR 2639, para. 10.

323 This is not a mandatory precondition of an Art. 173(4) challenge to a subsequent letter or other act: Case T-2/92 *Rendo* v *Commission (II)* unpublished order of 23 March 1993.

324 See, for example, Case T-28/90 *Asia Motor France (No. 1)* [1992] ECR II-2285 [1992] 5 CMLR 431, para. 28.

325 Case T-74/92 *Ladbroke Racing (Deutschland) GmbH* v *Commission*, [1995] ECR II-115.

326 See Case T-24/90 *Automec* v *Commission (No. 2)* [1992] ECR II-2223 [1992] 5 CMLR 431, para. 75.

327 OJ 1993 C39/6, para. 30.

7.157 (c) Adoption of a comfort letter with regard to the applicant where the applicant complies with a statement of objections issued by the Commission: the Court has held that for the Commission to ignore a draft agreement submitted by the parties as a possible basis for a negotiated settlement would represent a breach of the requirement of good administration.[328] Two situations may be distinguished here. There can surely be no obligation on the Commission to settle proceedings with parties who have misconducted themselves over a period of time simply because those parties co-operate with the Commission and modify or terminate their behaviour when caught "red handed". The Commission may proceed to a formal prohibitory decision which also imposes pecuniary penalties. Conversely, the requirements of good administration *might* indicate that if parties notify their agreement prior to its being put into effect and subsequently modify the agreement so as to comply wholly with Commission objections, then a duty to settle arises. This proposition has not yet been tested before the Court.

7.158 (d) Adoption of an Article 6 Regulation 99/63 letter: if a party has called upon the Commission to investigate under Article 175 EC, the Commission is under a duty to respond either by issuing a reasoned decision or by issuing a letter under Article 6, Regulation 99/63, giving its provisional response.[329] This letter cannot be challenged under Article 173 EC, being provisional in nature.[330]

7.159 (e) Adoption of a decision with regard to a third party which is of direct and individual concern to the applicant: in *Bethell* v *Commission*[331] Lord Bethell, MEP, brought proceedings under Articles 173 and 175 against the Commission for a declaration that the latter's refusal to issue a decision against the airlines for their alleged price fixing was unlawful. The action failed because the Court held that Lord Bethell had no *locus standi* to bring the action. Prima facie a private party cannot compel the Commission to issue a decision to a third party.[332] However, the Court appears to have hinted that an applicant *may* challenge the Commission's failure to adopt a decision to a third party where that decision would be of *direct and individual concern* to him had it been issued.[333]

[328] Cases 96–102, 104, 105, 108, 110/82 *IAZ International Belgium* v *Commission* [1984] 2 CMLR 276 at para. 15.

[329] Case T-28/90 *Asia Motor France (No. 1)* [1992] ECR II-2285 [1992] 5 CMLR 431, para. 29. See also T-74/92 *Ladbroke Racing (Deutschland) GmbH* v *Commission* [1995] ECR II-115.

[330] Case T-64/89 *Automec (No. 1)* [1990] ECR II-367.

[331] Case 246/81 [1982] 3 CMLR 300; [1982] ECR 2277 noted, Hartley, (1982) ELRev 391.

[332] See also Case T-24/90 *Automec* v *Commission (No.2)* [1992] ECR II-2223 [1992] 5 CMLR 431.

[333] Case 246/81 *Bethell* v *Commission* [1982] ECR 2277, [1982] 3 CMLR 300, at para. 13 of the judgment. Advocate-General Slynn adopted the narrower view that the *only* decisions an applicant could challenge were those that could have been addressed to him personally and not those addressable to a third party which were of direct and individual concern to him. This narrower view is based on the Danish, French, Irish, German and English texts of Art. 175 which speak only of decisions addressed to the applicant. However, the Dutch and Italian texts are wider and refer to decisions of the Commission "with respect to him:" a decision addressed to a third party of direct and individual concern to the applicant (who might have been the original complainant) is arguably one with respect to him. In *Bethell* the Court spoke of Commission's failure under Article 175 in terms of failure "to adopt in relation to him a measure which he was legally entitled to claim." This has been widely construed (e.g. Hartley *ibid.*) as indicating judicial acceptance of the wider view of Art. 175. This view has been expressly supported by Advocate-General Lamothe in Case 15/71 *Mackprang* v *Commission* [1971] ECR 797 at pp. 807, 808. The Court in that case was silent on the point. Conversely, in Case 125/78 *GEMA* v *Commission* [1980] 2 CMLR 177; [1979] ECR 3173 the Court decided that a complainant could *not* compel the Commission to adopt a decision on the existence of an alleged breach of Art. 85 or 86 by other persons. It is arguable that post *Bethel* the Court adopts a more lenient view than that propounded in *GEMA*.

7.160 It will be appreciated that under Article 173(4) an individual may seek judicial review of a decision addressed to him or of one addressed to another person which is of direct and individual concern to him. The Court of First Instance in *Ladbroke Racing (Deutschland) GmbH* v *Commission*[334] held that the complainant could challenge the Commission's failure to investigate a complaint under Article 86 EC, even though the Commission was dealing with the matter under Article 85 EC. It stressed that although it was for the Commission to determine the degree of importance to be given to a complaint in the light of the Community interest, the decision to deal with the complaint under Article 85 rather than Article 86 should have been explained to the complainant.

7.161 Applicants may request Commission action with respect to the above matters. Should the Commission define its position by rejecting the applicant's request, that refusal may be construed as a negative decision and *per se* challenged under Article 173(4).[335] It should be noted that under Article 173(4) there may be other things that a private party can challenge, e.g. a settlement between the Commission and a third party which the private party considers is of direct and individual concern to him. These matters are noted below.

7. *Can Third Parties Challenge a Settlement?*

7.162 An informal settlement between the Commission and the parties involving closure of the file and notification thereof to the parties by a comfort letter may give rise to grave concern by a third party or a complainant who considers this unsatisfactory. Where the Commission adopts a formal decision granting an exemption or negative clearance, this may be challenged under Article 173(4) by any person who can prove that the decision, although not addressed to him, is none the less of "direct and individual concern" to him. It is established that an actual complainant has *locus standi* to bring an action under this provision and this apparently extends to any other person who also has a legitimate interest to bring a complaint.[336] Comfort letters or other forms of informal settlement may be challenged by third parties meeting the *locus standi* requirements of Article 173(4) EC since "those letters have the content and effect of a decision, inasmuch as they close the investigation, contain an assessment of the agreements in question and prevent the applicants from requiring the reopening of the investigation unless they put forward new evidence".[337] A complainant may also seek judicial review under Article 173(4) EC of a letter addressed to that complainant by the Commission informing the complainant that the Commission has found no evidence of breach of the complained of party and are accordingly "closing the file",[338] or while maintaining "a close watch on developments in this market" are not proposing to pursue an investigation.[339]

[334] Case T-74/92 [1995] ECR II-115.

[335] See generally, Hartley, *The Foundations of European Community Law* (3rd edn. 1994), Chapter 13; Schermers, *Judicial Protection in the European Communities* (3rd edn. 1983), pp. 213–25; Kerse, *op. cit.*, note 1 at pp. 234–240.

[336] See Case 26/76 *Metro* v *Commission* [1978] 2 CMLR 1; [1977] ECR 1875; Case 210/81 *Demo-Studio Schmidt* v *Commission (Revox)* [1984] 1 CMLR 63 [1983] ECR 3045. See also, Dinnage, "Locus Standi and *cont.*
Article 173 EC: the effect of Metro SB Grossemarkte v. Commission" (1979) ELRev 15; Temple Lang, "The position of third parties in EC competition cases (1978) 3 ELRev 177. Greaves, "*Locus Standi* under Art. 173 EC when seeking annulment of a Regulation" (1986) ELRev 119 (on the position of complainants especially in dumping cases).

[337] Cases 42 and 156/84 *BAT and Reynolds* v *Commission* [1987[ECR 4487, para. 12.

[338] Case 10/81 *Demo Studio Schmidt* v *Commission* [1984] 1 CMLR 63; 298/83 *CICCE* v *Commission* [1985] ECR 1105 [1986] 1 CMLR 486.

[339] Case C-39/93P *Syndicat Français de l'Express International (SFEI)* v *Commission* [1994] ECR I-2681, overruling the Court of First Instance in Case T-36/92 *SFEI* v *Commission* [1992] ECR II-2479.

7.163 Although the Commission has no enforceable duty to investigate a complaint under *Automec II*, once it has decided to investigate, the Court of First Instance held in *Asia Motor France II*[340] it must do so "with the care, seriousness and diligence required to be able to assess, in full knowledge of the facts, the factual and legal considerations submitted by the complainants for its assessment". Therefore failure to take proper reasoned account of material submitted by the a complainant will be a ground for review under Article 173(4) EC.

8. Lobbying

7.164 It is worth noting that parties may employ lobbyists in competition cases if they feel this will assist their cause.[341] The Commission does not verify or in any way validate the credentials of those acting for parties to proceedings before the Commission. None the less, the Commission adopt a generally cautious stance to lobbying tactics.[342] It is understood that in the *IBM Settlement* case[343] IBM persuaded certain high level American politicians to make their presence known to the Commission. Indeed, the Commission entered into lengthy discussions with the US Department of Justice over the case though the latter was not necessarily against the Commission's action, given that it had hitherto failed in a mammoth antitrust suit against IBM.

9. Division of Labour in DG IV: The Competition Directorate

7.165 The Directorate General for Competition—DG IV—comprises some 400 persons under the control of a Director General. DG IV is broken down into seven directorates.[344] A covers general competition policy and coordination, including coordination between the other four directorates, C, D, E and F which are broken down into divisions dealing with different sectors of industry. So when dealing with the Commission, it is useful to know which directorate will be dealing with a case.[345] Normally a member of directorate A together with a member of one of the other directorates as appropriate, will be assigned to a case.

7.166 In larger[346] cases a team of four or five persons may combine. In complex negotiations with major multinationals an even larger team may operate which may include senior personnel and even Commissioners in exceptional cases.

340 Case T-7/92 *Asia Motor France* v *Commission (No. 2)* [1993] ECRII-669 [1994] 4 CMLR 30, para. 36.

341 For a case study on the impact of lobbying, see A.M. Mclaughlin, G. Jordan and W.A. Maloney, "Corporate lobbying in the European Community" (1993) 31 JCMS 191.

342 Commission answer to WQ 306/84, OJ 1984 C 225/20. This has, however, been criticised by Van Bael, "Comment on the EC Commission's antitrust settlement practice: the short-circuiting of Regulation 17" (1985) *Swiss Review of International Competition Law* 67 at p. 71. See WQ 497/84, OJ 1984 C243/20 (12 September 1984) where MEP Mr Anthony Simpson defined lobbying, in a parliamentary question to the Commission, as: "the term 'lobbying' may be taken to mean: persons in a position of influence, hired for the purpose, addressing or soliciting members of the Commission outside the framework of established administrative procedures in order to obtain, in an adversary proceedings, an outcome different from that which would normally issue from the usual and foreseeable application of existing competition policy to a set of facts before the Commission".

343 [1984] 3 CMLR 147.

344 Including Directorate B, the Mergers Task Force and Directorate G for State Aids, not covered in this summary.

345 For an up to date list of DG IV officials, see the first copy of volume 4 of the CMLR each year for a list of officials. The Commission's *Competition Policy Newsletter* (CPN) updates this list. For the most recent list at time of writing, see (1997) 3 CPN, issue 1, p. 32.

346 As in the *IBM* case *ibid.*

G. The Opposition Procedure

1. *Legal Framework*[347]

7.167 The Commission has issued block exemptions for patent[348] and know-how[349] licensing agreements now amalgamated into a single technology transfer regulation,[350] R&D[351] and specialisation[352] agreements and franchise[353] agreements.[354] These block exemptions contain lists of permissible (white) clauses and non-permissible (black) clauses. Agreements satisfying the criteria as laid out in the block exemptions need not be notified. Where agreements contain restrictions or exceed thresholds that are not expressly permitted but are not expressly prohibited, the block exemption may be extended to cover the agreement. Details of the process of extension are given below.

2. *Details of Opposition Procedure: How to Apply*

7.168 The rules apply only to patent and know-how licensing agreements and technology transfer agreements, R&D and specialisation agreements and franchise agreements. Under the procedure the block exemption accorded by the various Regulations covering those agreement types is extended to include agreements duly notified to the Commission. The exemption covers these agreements six months from the date the notification is received by the Commission provided the latter raises no objections in the interim.[355] Notification must be on Form A/B. Thus a considerable amount of information must be supplied to the Commission. To so benefit an agreement must *not* contain any of the "black" prohibited clauses described in the various regulations. This expedited procedure only operates where parties make *express reference* to the article of the block exemption covering the relevant type of agreement which refers to the opposition procedure. This reference must occur in *either* the notification or an accompanying communication. Thus the opposition procedure operates only where the parties apply for it to operate. The Commission may not activate the procedure if the notification is incomplete and not in accordance with the facts. The procedure may apply to agreements notified prior to entry into force of the relevant Regulation provided parties submit a communication to the Commission expressly referring to the Article of the relevant block exemption covering the opposition procedure and to the notification.

3. *When will Opposition be Raised?*

7.169 The Commission may oppose the exemption at any time during the six-month period. The Commission *must* oppose the exemption if it receives a request so to do from a Mem-

[347] For detailed analysis including discussion of whether the procedure is *ultra vires* see Venit, "The Commission's opposition procedure" (1985) CMLRev 163.

[348] Reg. 2349/84, see paras. 13.125–13.223.

[349] Reg. 556/89, see paras. 13.224–13.324.

[350] Commission Reg. 240/96/EC OJ 1996 L31/2, 9 February 1996; see paras. 13.18–13.124.

[351] Reg. 418/85, see paras. 12.123–12.184.

[352] Reg. 417/85, see paras. 12.202–12.223.

[353] Reg. 4087/88, see paras. 10.270–10.315.

[354] There are also block exemptions for land, maritime and air transport which include equivalent opposition procedures.

[355] Where the notification is made by registered post the period of six months runs from the date shown on the postmark of the place of posting. Under Reg. 240/96 for technology transfer agreements, the period is 4rather than 6 months (see Art. 4(1), Reg. 240/96.

ber State within three months of the transmission to the Member State of the notification (or of the communication where related to a notification made prior to commencement of the regulation). Member States, however, may only justify opposition on considerations relating to competition policy. The Regulations give no guidance on whether parties may view objections made by Member States. Presumably there is no right of inspection, though given the greater degree of access to Commission files tolerated by the Commission a request to see any opposition raised might be considered. The Commission may withdraw their opposition at any time. Where the opposition was first raised at the request of a Member State and this is maintained, withdrawal of opposition may only occur following consultation with the Advisory Committee on Restrictive Practices and Dominant Positions. Thus, Member States retain an input into any Commission decision to withdraw opposition. The Commission, is however, not bound by the opinion of the Advisory Committee. Commission opposition may further be withdrawn where either the parties establish that the conditions of Article 85(3) are satisfied, or, the parties amend the agreement so as to satisfy Article 85(3). Where such is the case exemption applies from the date of notification or the date of amendment respectively. Where the Commission oppose exemption and this is maintained, the usual procedure envisaged by Regulation 17/62/EEC applies. The Commission will notify the parties of any opposition by letter.

4. *Commission Response*

7.170 The Commission issues comfort letters at the end of the opposition period which state that an exemption could be obtained if the formal procedure were continued with. They expect recipients generally to be satisfied with this comfort letter, despite the legal questions hanging over the precise status of comfort letters. In practice parties will almost certainly be satisfied with a comfort letter.

7.171 The Commission has more or less standard letters for use by the Directors of DG IV who are responsible for the class or category of product subject to the opposition procedure. The letters vary in content. A number of examples are as follows:

(a) The letter might indicate that some of the clauses in the notified agreement fall within a blacklist and hence the regulation cannot apply. Such a letter will probably add that the parties should fillet out the offending black clauses. Further, the letter will probably provide that unless the parties respond within X weeks to inform the Commission that the agreement has been amended then the Commission will treat the notification as a request for exemption under Article 85(3).

(b) Where parties omit to refer to the specific "opposition procedure" provision in the regulation the Commission may send out a standard letter providing that there are clauses in the agreement that are not covered by the whitelist but that the Commission is closing its file on the case subject to a future right to reopen the file should circumstances change. In cases such as these parties may consider re-notifying (or request the Commission whether they can modify their earlier notification) under the relevant provision in order to attain the greater degree of legal certainty that the opposition procedure may confer.

(c) The Commission may, in appropriate cases, provide that clauses that are in neither the white- or blacklists (so called "grey" clauses) are too serious to be acceptable, and that the notification is being treated as an application for exemption under Article 85(3). This letter would only, of course, be sent where, as in example (b), the parties had omitted to expressly refer to the opposition procedure provision in the relevant regulation.

(d) The Commission may send a letter providing that the agreement or licence, etc., as notified falls within the block exemption, that the exemption appears to the Commission to have applied from a specified date, and, that the Commission will take no further action and will close the file.

(e) The Commission may provide in a letter that no opposition has been raised to an agreement and that the agreement hence falls into the category of block exempt agreements subject always of course to the power in the regulation to withdraw exemption in appropriate cases.

The examples above do not, by any means, exhaust the possibilities. Clearly, there will be additional Commission letters opposing exemption or withdrawing opposition.

5. The Opposition Procedure in Practice

7.172 There have not been many applications to use the opposition procedure, and of those, only a small proportion have been allowed (either with or without amendments to the notified agreement), as the table below shows for the period 1990– 93.[356]

Block exemptions	*Applications under opposition procedure*	*Applications granted*
Specialisation & R&D	8	2
Patent & know-how	11	4
Franchising	10	1
Total	29	7

7.173 Applications have failed not just because the clauses taking the agreement outside the block exemption were unacceptable, but also, more frequently, because the criteria for use of the opposition procedure were not met. This came about either because a blacklisted clause was included, because the information supplied was incomplete, because the agreements in question were not in fact caught by Article 85(1) EC due to lack of effect on competition or inter-state trade, or because the block exemption did in fact apply.

[356] Information taken from Commission *Reports on Competition Policy* for those years.

Part II

Commercial Agreements and Trade Association Practices

8 Pricing Practices and Restrictions

A. Introduction

8.1 In this chapter the following pricing practices, restrictions and related issues are examined:

Section B.	Legal framework: relevant statutory provisions in the UK and EC.
Section C.	Pricing fixing *simpliciter*: approach of Commission and OFT to different types of price fixing.
Section D.	Discount schemes: analysis of discounts with particular reference to aggregated rebate schemes, loyalty rebates, turnover rebates, and other overrider rebates, etc.
Section E.	Price discrimination: when differential discounts and prices are legal or otherwise.
Section F.	Predatory pricing: price cutting designed to exclude or injure competitors.
Section G.	Excessive pricing: exploitation by dominant undertakings or monopolies.
Section H.	Resale price maintenance: vertical control prices.
Section I.	Equalisation of receipts schemes: "profit pooling" schemes.
Section J.	Delivered pricing (base or parity point pricing): methods of incorporating freight costs into price.
Section K.	Cost calculation models: trade association assistance to members in the calculation of costs in an efficient manner.
Section L.	Renegotiation and variation (cost escalation) clauses: standard form contracts incorporating unfair or unreasonable clauses concerning cost escalation.
Section M.	Collusive tendering: the sharing out of bids in response to invitations to tender. Analysis and guidance on how to detect collusion.

B. Legal Framework

1. *EC Law*

8.2 Article 85(1) EC prohibits agreements or arrangements which *inter alia* "directly or indirectly fix prices or selling prices or any other trading conditions". Price fixing agreements whereby parties agree on a set price to charge stand virtually no chance of being exempted from the prohibition in Article 85(1). It makes no difference whether the agreement relates to goods or services.[1] Nor does it matter whether the agreement is conducted by individual[2] firms *inter se* or under the aegis of a trade association.[3] Moreover, as with other forms of restrictive agreement, it makes no difference (other than factually in respect of evidence) whether the agreement is written down or simply agreed orally between the parties. Many price agreements are operated via trade associations and in this context it is important to note that recommendations to members made by the association and described as non-binding are invariably caught within Article 85(1). This surprises many trade association officials who argue that so long as their advice to the membership is not binding they cannot be accused of fostering agreement between the members. The view of the European Commission is that "recommendations" invariably result in "uniform and coordinated conduct"[4] leading to restrictions on competition. The European Court has condemned recommended prices on the basis that they enable competitors to foresee with a reasonable degree of certainty what the price policy of their rivals will be.[5] Parties cannot escape Article 85(1) EC by arguing that the agree-

[1] For Commission involvement in insurance services, see, e.g. *Industrial Fire Insurance* [1982] 2 CMLR 159. An association of property insurers recommended standard premiums for its members to use in fire and consequential loss insurance. The Commission condemned the agreement on the basis that it was equivalent to a decision by a trade association to fix prices. See also *Insurance* Bull EC 5/69, p. 34: companies established in four Member States had, through their respective trade associations, agreed on the increased rates of premiums to be charged when a company in one state took over a contract already made by an insurance company in another state. Furthermore, when a contract was taken over in this manner there followed a detailed exchange of information on otherwise confidential information. Following Commission intervention the agreement was dropped. In *Nuovo-Cegam* [1984] 2 CMLR 484 about 15 Italian direct insurers linked by a reinsurance treaty with firms based outside Italy operated a trade association (Nuovo-Cegam) whose constitutional rules infringed Art. 85(1) EC. The association drew up risk premium tariffs with rates based on common accident statistics which thus excluded loading elements for such items as administrative costs, taxes and profits. Following Commission objections certain aspects of the agreement were modified. Members would subsequently use these tariffs as a basis for independently determining commercial premiums actually charged to policy holders. Each direct insurer thus sets prices independently. This fact represented a significant change from the practice operating prior to Commission intervention whereby the association's tariff was expressed in terms of commercial premiums. This change enabled the Commission to exempt the agreement under Art. 85(3) for a 10-year period subject to notification conditions. See also *Protection and Indemnity Clubs* OJ 1985 L376/2.

[2] See, e.g. Case 48, 51–57/69 *ICI* v *Commission* [1972] ECR 619; *Cartel in Quinine* [1969] CMLR D41.

[3] See e.g. *Members of the Genuine Vegetable Parchment Association* [1978] 1 CMLR 534 (international association of paper producers); VCH [1973] CMLR D16 (Dutch association of cement traders—Commission decision) *GISA* [1973] CMLR D125 (Dutch association of wholesalers of plumbing equipment); *The Agreement of Stichting Sigarretten Industrie* [1982] 3 CMLR 702; *Woollen Fabrics* (*UIB*) *Twelfth Report on Competition Policy* (1982), para. 71 (Italian association of woollen fabric producers). The same rules apply to professional bodies as to trade associations; CNSD, *Twenty-third Report on Competition Policy* (1993), para. 219, condemning price tariffs fixed by an Italian customs agents' body. In *Colegi Oficial de Agentes de la Propriedad Industrial (COAPI)* OJ 1995 L122/37, an agreement for minimum fees between Spanish patent agents was held to be contrary to Art. 85(1), and ordered to be terminated, though no fine was imposed.

[4] See *VCH* [1973] CMLR D16 at p. D28, para. 47 (Commission).

[5] e.g. Case 8/72 *Vereeniging Van Cementhandelaren* [1973] CMLR 7; [1972] ECR 977.

ment was not effectively operated and that there were departures from it. Article 85(1) EC is concerned with the effect of an agreement and not the loyalty of the parties to it.[6] Likewise the Commission view as equivalent to price fixing schemes designed to foster price parallelism by *indirect* means. Thus the Commission have condemned an agreement between a large number of non-EC suppliers trading on the EC market who quoted prices in a single world currency (US dollars) so as to facilitate price transparency and, ultimately, uniformity.[7]

8.3 The operation of price agreements prohibited by Article 85(1) and not susceptible to exemption under Article 85(3)EC may be vulnerable to fines ranging from between 1 and10 per cent of total turnover on all goods and services in the previous year imposed by the Commission. Price fixing invariably attracts heavy fines.[8]

2. UK

8.4 Unlike EC law, which applies a sweeping ban on restrictive agreements, the UK legislation is complex and obscure. Section 6 RTPA enumerates the agreements which are to be subject to the procedure of the Act. Section 6(1)(a) and (b) cover price agreements. Section 6(1)(a) provides that Act applies to agreements "in respect of": "the price to be charged, quoted or paid for goods supplied offered or acquired, or for the application of any process of manufacture to goods." Section 6(1)(b) applies the Act to agreements "in respect of": "the prices to be recommended or suggested as the prices to be charged or quoted in respect of the resale of goods supplied."

8.5 Section 6(1)(a) and (b) is not all-embracing. It excludes from the Act certain types of price agreement. These may apparently be carried on without the need to register:

(a) Agreements whereby the parties notify each other of the prices they *have* charged, quoted or paid for goods. It would seem that an agreement between X and Y whereby the latter will—only minutes *after* concluding a transaction— communication the price details to the former is not caught by the Act despite its obvious anti-competitive potential. This exception from the Act flows from the use of the future tense (i.e. "to be") in Section 6(1)(a) and (b). The draftsman omitted to include the additional words "or which have been charged, quoted or paid", etc.

(b) The limited ambit of the words "to be" means also that another variety of price agreement is excluded from the RTPA 1976. An agreement concerning the price of the product concluded *after* the transaction is concluded is exempt. Thus, a trade association rule forbidding members to renegotiate the contract price in the light of fluctuating market prices for the commodity involved has been held by the Court of Appeal to be outside the scope of the Act.[9]

[6] *ibid.*, at para. 21 (ECJ).

[7] *Wood Pulp* [1985] 3 CMLR 474. The Court of Justice in annulling the Commission's decision, through not this specific aspect, in Joined Cases C-89, 104, 114, 116, 117 and 125-129/85 *Ahlstrom Oy and Others* v *Commission (Wood Pulp)* [1993] ECR I-1307, [1993] 4 CMLR 407. found that the introduction of pricing in US dollars was welcomed by purchasers who found it meant that they could ensure that they were not paying more than their competitors: see para. 79 of the judgment.

[8] e.g. in the *Cement Cartel* 1994 OJ L343/1, fines totalling ECU248 million (approximately £200 million were imposed). The Commission takes a "strict approach" to "hard core cartels": see *Twenty-fourth Report on Competition Policy* (1994), para. 130.

[9] See *Blanket Manufacturer's Agreement* (1959) LR 1 RP 208; [1959] 1 WLR 442 (RPC); (1959) LR 1 RP 271; [1959] 1 WLR 1148 (CA). The Court of Appeal held that a trade association agreement where under members could only renegotiate contract prices with customers in the light of variations in world wool market prices with the consent of a committee of the association, was *not* within s. 6(1)(a) RTPA 1976.

8.6 With regard to these exceptions three provisos should be noted. First, by virtue of Restrictive Trade Practices (Information Agreements) Order 1969 S.I. 1969 No. 1842, particulars of agreements whereby parties agree to notify each other of prices charged are now required to be furnished thus partially plugging the gap created by exception (a) above. For detailed analysis of this Order see paras. 9.18–9.26. Secondly, simply because an agreement does not fall within the grasp of the UK law it cannot be assumed it will escape EC law. Article 85(1) catches agreements between parties situated in one Member State if the agreement, none the less, exerts an effect upon trade between Member States: "An agreement extending over the whole of a territory of a member state by its very nature has the effect of reinforcing the compartmentalisation of markets on a national basis, thereby holding up the economic interpenetration which the Treaty is designed to bring about and protecting domestic production."[10] Thirdly, pricing practices excluded from the ambit of the RTPA 1976 may fall within the Competition Act 1980 which controls anti-competitive practices. Agreements caught by the RTPA 1976 are expressly excluded from the enforcement procedure under the 1980 Act but clearly practices excluded from the RTPA 1976 may be caught by the CA 1980.[11] The 1980 Act is primarily focused upon restrictive practices by individual undertakings not acting in concert. However, a firm seised of a dominant or otherwise strong market position which employed that economic power to refuse to (say) renegotiate contract prices, once concluded, despite fluctuations in contract commodity prices, might fall within the Act; such a company could afford to act in this manner if it was confident there were few alternative supply sources for the purchaser to switch to.

8.7 Section 6(1)(b) RTPA 1976 brings under the control of the Act agreements whereby suppliers agree *inter se* that they will each recommend specific prices. This also applies to a trade association that recommends its members to adopt a fixed profit margin in sales to customers. While resale price maintenance is generally outlawed, it is legal for *individual* firms to recommend prices to dealers provided no steps (for instance boycott or blacklisting of the dealer) are taken to enforce the price. *Agreements* between suppliers to "recommend" prices, however, are considered potentially restrictive of competition and are hence subject to control. It is uncertain whether section 6(1)(b) covers the situation whereby X and Y merely agree to recommend prices without specifying the level of the price to each other. Section 6 (1)(b) seems to require that the agreement be as to the actual price as well as to the fact of recommendation. However, the decision of the Court in *Re Motor Vehicle Distribution Scheme Agreement*[12] may be viewed as implying that an agreement as to recommending prices rather than as to the level of price to be recommended would be registrable. In that case the Motor Trade Association introduced a written scheme which included a clause requiring members to prescribe the retail price of their products and the discounts that could be allowed. Later the scheme was amended to require each member to publish his resale prices. This was duly declared by the Court to be a restriction within section 6(1)(b). Whether the earlier less coercive agreement was equally caught is unclear. The Court has held, in a case under section 6(1)(c), that an obligation in an agreement not to do something *in casu* not to publish any daily newspapers for a period, was a registrable restriction.[13] By analogy, it is arguable that an agreement not to recom-

[10] e.g. Case 8/72 *Vereeniging Van Cementhandelaren* v *Commission* [1973] CMLR 7 [1972] ECR 977 at para. 29, concerning a trade association of Dutch cement dealers which recommended to its members the price of cement in Holland. Art. 85(1) applied regardless of the fact that no equivalent recommendation applied to exports.

[11] s. 2(2) Competition Act 1980. For details of Competition Act 1980 see Chapter 3.

[12] (1961) LR 2 RP 173.

[13] *Scottish Daily Newspaper Society's Agreement (No. 1)* (1971) LR 7 RP 379.

mend a resale price is a restriction as to the prices to be recommended. Might the converse be true that an agreement simply to recommend prices is a registrable restriction as to the price to be recommended?[14]

8.8 Finally, a number of points concerning the language of section 6(1)(a) and (b). First, "price" includes a charge of any description.[15] Secondly, a restriction concerning any element of price at all is a restriction "in respect of" price within the meaning of section 6. Hence a price agreement relating to a service to be performed on goods is a registrable agreement.[16] Thirdly, "supply" includes, *inter alia*, lease or hire transactions.[17]

8.9 With regard to services, section 11(2)(a) RTPA 1976 provides that agreements concerning "the charges to be made, quoted or paid for designated services supplied, offered or obtained", may be called up for registration. Thus, an agreement between X and Y that they will quote identical prices to customers or that they will charge prices which stay within a specified price band will be registrable. Similarly, an agreement between A and B that they will not pay more than a specific price for services they require is also registrable. The restrictive agreements noted in section 11 are only registrable, however, to the extent that they are specifically called up for registration by statutory instrument. Such restrictions have been called up for registration by the Services Order of 1976 (S.I. 1976 No. 98 discussed at paras 1.67–1.71) and are hence registrable in the normal way. However, there is no equivalent to section 6(1)(b) in section 11. Thus an agreement between X and Y over the prices to be *recommended* or *suggested* as the prices to be charged or quoted in respect of the resale of the services provided is *not* registrable. The reasons for this lacuna is that section 6(1)(b) RTPA 1976 was only added to the legislation as an afterthought by section 95 FTA 1973 which itself was a consequence of various specific recommendations relating to goods agreements made by the MMC in their general report on Recommended Resale Prices (1968-69 HC 100). However, the lacuna means that those providers whose services may be resold (e.g. insurance, travel agents) enjoy a leeway not enjoyed by counterparts in goods industries.

8.10 Where trade associations are concerned recommendations to members are expressly covered by sections 8 (goods) and 16 (services) RTPA 1976. These provisions are examined at paras. 1.108–1.112.

3. Mere Stipulations as to Price: The Overlap of sections 6 and 11 and sections 9 and 18 RTPA

8.11 Doubt exists as to whether the stipulation as to price in a simple contract of sale amounts to a restriction within the meaning of section 6 RTPA. In *Registrar of Restrictive Trading Agreements* v *Schweppes Ltd (No. 2)*,[18] it was suggested that the reason why an agreement whereby one party agrees to sell some goods to another party at a specified price does not constitute a restriction within the meaning of the Act is because of the disregarding provision in section 9(3). This implies that were it not for the said disregarding provision such a price stipulation would constitute a restriction within the meaning of the Act. It is submitted that this analysis is incorrect[19] since obligations, whether as to price or otherwise, contained in an agreement between seller and purchaser which simply define the

[14] But cf. Cunningham, Fair Trading Act 1973 (1974), p. 242, paras. 14–21.

[15] See s. 43(1) RTPA 1976.

[16] See *Scottish Master Monumental Sculptors' Association's Agreement* (1965) LR 5 RP 437 (RPC). Agreement relating to the price of lettering services on tombstones.

[17] See s. 43(1) RTPA 1976.

[18] (1971) LR 7 RP 336, 375 F–G, [1971] 1 WLR 1148, 1172.

[19] Although it was accepted in *Re Cadbury Schweppes Ltd Agreement* [1975] 1 WLR 1018, 1031.

parties' obligations to each other should not be held to be restrictions.[20] A number of reasons lead to this conclusion. First, it is true that once supplier X has agreed to sell his products at a fixed price to purchaser Y, X may not sell the self-same products to another purchaser and/or may not sell the same products to Y at a different price. X is ostensibly restricted as to the persons to whom goods may be supplied and as to the price at which he may supply goods. However, those "restrictions" arise from the mere fact of the agreement and it is open to both parties to vary such terms should they see fit. Section 6 refers to "restrictions ... accepted ... in respect of ... the following matters ... (a) the prices to be charged". The language of section 6 suggests that a restriction arises because the price to be charged is restricted. Stipulating the actual price to be charged is not *per se* a restriction on that price. There must be some additional ingredient, i.e. the restriction in respect of the price to be charged. The following is *not* a restriction: "I will sell my car to you for £5,000." The following *is* a restriction: "I agree with you that I will not sell my car to X for less than £5,500." The first example merely reflects the price being stipulated. The second example reflects the price being restricted. Secondly, and in any event, X retains the freedom to supply any goods to Y at any different price and any goods to any third party. Nothing in the agreement between X and Y prevents that freedom on the part of X.

8.12 Conversely, if a stipulation as to price (or indeed any other term) constitutes *per se* a restriction, then it may still be a disregardable restriction within the meaning of section 9(3) RTPA, in so far as it applies to goods. That provision provides that in determining whether an agreement for the supply of goods or for the application of any process of manufacture to goods is an agreement to which the Act applies "no account shall be taken of any term which relates exclusively to the goods supplied, or to which the process is applied, in pursuance of the agreement". For section 9(3) to apply, the "term" which is subject to analysis must relate exclusively to the goods supplied. The meaning of the word "exclusively" is unclear. If X agrees to supply goods to Y located in Birmingham at a fixed price, this is a term relating to the goods in question but it is also a term relating to the location at which the goods may be supplied. It could be said that the term relates not only to the goods but *also* to the place of supply and therefore the term does not relate "exclusively" to the goods. A "term" which does relate exclusively to the goods could, for example, be as follows: "The purchaser shall not modify the goods without the consent of the supplier". Such a clause relates to the physical integrity of the goods themselves and not to any ancillary fact or matter. A detailed analysis of the scope and effect of section 9 is set out at paras. 1.75–1.86.

8.13 Even in circumstances where it is unclear whether section 9(3) applies so as to, prima facie, enable a term to be disregarded, account must be taken of section 9(4). This *disapplies* section 9(3) where "any such restrictions ... are accepted ... as between two or more persons by whom, or two or more persons to or for whom, goods are to be supplies, or the process applied, in pursuance of the agreement". Section 9(4) is designed to prevent section 9(3) operating as an escape route for naked horizontal cartels. For example, if X, Y and Z all agree as to the price at which they will supply goods, this restriction may, arguably, be disregardable under section 9(3) since the restriction relates exclusively to the goods supplied. Section 9(4) would preclude reliance as section 9(3) in these circumstances. However, section 9(4) could also apply in the vertical context of a distribution agreement. The factual situation identified in section 9(4) is characterised by restrictions accepted by two or more persons by whom, to or from whom "goods are to be supplied, or the process applied, in pursuance of the agreement". If in the context of a distribution

[20] See *Chitty on Contracts* (27th edn. 1994), paras. 40–054, 40–055, pp. 968, 969.

agreement, the supplier accepts a positive obligation to supply goods to the dealer and the dealer accepts, for example, a best endeavours clause to supply the same goods to customers or alternatively accepts performance targets and obligations, then both supplier and dealer are supplying goods "in pursuance of the agreement". Accordingly, section 9(4) could apply so as to prevent the application of section 9(3) to a price stipulation in the distribution agreement. If this analysis were correct, then the strict interpretation of the case law referred to above would apply and a price stipulation in a contract for the supply of goods would constitute a restriction within the meaning of the Act. However, this would not, in the authors' view, be within the purpose of section 9(4) which was to ensure that the Act applied to horizontal agreements. There is no authoritative guidance on this point.

8.14 Sections 18(2) and (3) affect the operation of section 11 in relation to services in the same way as sections 9(3) and (4) affect the operation of section 6 for goods. The language of sections 18(2) and (3) is very similar to that of sections 9(3) and (4).

C. Price Fixing *Simpliciter*

1. EC Law

8.15 Price fixing agreements whereby parties agree upon a specific price system for their activities may take a number of forms. There is but little chance that any will pass Article 85(1) EC unscathed. The problem facing the businessman often lies in recognising that his type of price agreement is susceptible to legal challenge. The following is a, non-exhaustive, enumeration of varieties of price-fixing agreement together with a brief assessment of economic effect and legal validity.

(1) Maximum prices

8.16 Agreements not to exceed specified maximum prices are unlawful. Ostensibly a ceiling price aids the consumer. However, where the adoption of prices is set at such a level that, given the transport costs involved for getting the goods to the market, only domestic or local suppliers can afford to meet or undercut the maximum price, then competition is harmed. Such agreements operate to isolate markets preserving them for domestic sales.[21]

8.17 Agreements not to exceed specified maximum commissions or margins would normally be treated in the same way.[22] Article 85(1) may also be infringed by agreeing on "target" prices to be achieved.[23] Price "recommendations" as to the prices to be charged or price increases to be sought[24] may also infringe Article 85(1).

(2) Minimum prices

8.18 Agreements between parties to sell above a floor price are unlawful. Although price differences may occur above the agreed price attempts by parties to improve their market share by dramatically lowering their prices thereby risking starting a price war are pre-

[21] See *European Glass Manufacturers* [1974] 2 CMLR D50.

[22] Exemption was granted for an agreement to fix maximum commission charges in *Eurocheques* [1984] 3 CMLR 434; see para. 8.34.

[23] *Welded Steel Mesh* OJ 1989 L 260/1, [1991] 4 CMLR 13. It was no defence that the prices actually achieved were often below the aimed-for prices as they were "certainly in excess of those that could have been achieved on the market under normal competitive conditions".

[24] Case 45/85 *VdS* v *Commission* [1987] ECR 405.

vented. The consumer may well be paying a supra-competitive price.[25] In *Polypropylene Cartel*[26] the Commission imposed heavy fines on 15 polypropylene producers who had taken part in a series of meetings in which they set a "floor-price" to avoid a substantial drop in price levels.

(3) Adherence to price lists

8.19 Agreements whereby parties agree to bind themselves to published price lists are considered to be serious infringements of the competition rules. In *IFTRA Rules for Producers of Virgin Aluminum*,[27] the parties claimed that departures from published price lists led to a "falsification of competition". The Commission dismissed this argument reiterating its view that such behaviour constituted a serious restriction on competition. In *Roofing Felt*[28] the Commission condemned an agreement adopting a price list covering virtually all the types of roofing felt sold by the members of a cartel. In the course of proceedings, it was argued that alignment of prices was a consequence of Belgian price control legislation. This argument was rejected by the Commission. Although the legislation allowed trade associations to lodge applications collectively on behalf of members, firms were free to apply individually. Even when a collective application had been made, approval was given for a maximum increase, which did not necessarily have to be applied in full. Thus there remained opportunities for competition. This case may be contrasted with the Commission's decision granting exemption in *Concordato Incendio*.[29] This concerned an association of fire insurance companies recommending, but not requiring, the imposition of a common insurance tariff. The recommendation was granted exemption under Article 85(3). In granting exemption, the Commission stressed particularly the fact that "the existence of standard conditions makes it easier for consumers to compare the prices offered by various firms and come to a decision in full knowledge of the facts. In effect, the consumers, due to the existence of the premium tariff and standard conditions, can compare and choose not simply in relation to the commercial premium which is being requested of them but also the extent of the coverage and all other services, which an insurance company is supposed to provide".

(4) Bargain and introductory prices

8.20 Agreements not to sell at introductory or bargain price are unlawful because they hinder the parties' efforts to increase market share through temporary, attractive prices. They may also deter firms from introducing new product lines which could disturb the status quo between existing products by increasing the consumer's choice since the inability to set tempting introductory prices to gain custom is a hindrance to entry of that market.[30]

(5) Disruptive and dumping level prices

8.21 Agreements not to make shock or disruptive offers in another Member State or marketing territory are equally caught under Article 85(1) EC. Where occasional loss-leader or

25 See *VCH* [1973] CMLR D16 (Commission); Case 8/72 [1972] ECR 977; [1973] CMLR 7 ECJ.
26 [1988] 4 CMLR 3467; appeal dismissed in Case T-1/89 *Rhône-Poulenc* v *Commission* [1991] ECR II-869.
27 [1975] 2 CMLR D20.
28 OJ 1986 L232/15, [1991] 4 CMLR 130. Appeal dismissed in Case 246/86 *Belasco* v *Commission* [1989] ECR 2117.
29 OJ 1990 L15/25, [1991] 4 CMLR 199.
30 See *VCH* [1973] CMLR D16 (Commission); Case 8/72 [1972] ECR 977; [1973] CMLR 2 (ECJ). In *Roofing Felt* the Commission also condemned an agreement to limit discounts to customers. The fact that certain members were able to give discounts higher than the limits set in the agreement was not held to prove that the agreements did not exist or were not applied.

cheap but above cost prices are quoted in another's territory they can seriously disrupt that market in the extreme, destroying that trader's business. Aggressive pricing of this nature in a competitive market exerts a healthy downward pressure on prices. It makes no difference whether the aggressor's motives are related to a desire to increase his market share or are retaliatory. Curbs on predatory producing do exist under Article 86 EEC. Though an agreement between non-dominant undertakings collectively to sell at disruptive or dumped levels in another territory or to the customers of a competitor would fall within Article 85(1).[31]

8.22 In *IFTRA Rules for Producers of Virgin Aluminum* the parties were ingenious in dealing with shock pricing, they categorised pejoratively such prices as "dumping level prices", i.e. prices sold abroad at levels below those set for domestic sales. They, accordingly, agreed not to "dump" in each other's territory. This prohibition was buttressed by reference to Article VI of the GATT which covers "dumping". The Commission rejected this argument upon the basis that the practice of dumping is no longer recognised *within* the EC market: "A low-price sale from one Member State to another is not more subject to such rules than such a sale from one zone to another within the same Member State. It is clear that the sole object and effect of the IFTRA rules relating to 'dumping', as far as sales from one Member State to another are concerned, is to prevent the type of unconventional competitive offer which is no longer prevented by any Community legal provision."[32] A dominant firm, may not predate, by below-cost pricing, on smaller undertakings so as to squeeze them from the markets thereby securing further their economic dominance.

(6) Price leader agreements

8.23 Agreements whereby one party becomes the "price leader" whose price others will observe and adhere to are unlawful. Such agreements "eliminate the possibility of unforeseen or unforeseeable reactions by competitors, thus removing a large element of the risk normally attaching to any individual action in the market".[33] As with other forms of price restriction price leader agreements tend towards an isolation of markets and supra-competitive prices.

8.24 In *Polypropylene Cartel*[34] the condemned price fixing agreement included a system of "account leadership" whereby one producer was designated "account leader" in respect of a particular customer and would "guide, discuss and organise price moves". Other producers who had regular dealings with the customer were known as "contenders" and would co-operate with the account leader in quoting prices to the customer in question. To protect the account leader and contenders, any other producers approach by the customer were to quote prices higher than the desired target.

(7) Meeting external prices

8.25 This is similar to (6) above, agreements not to undercut a rival's prices in his primary marketing territory. Whereas in (6) one price—the price leader's—will prevail across the market, here, a number of prices will prevail with each exporter finding out the price prevailing in the export territory and refraining from undercutting it. In *Re European*

[31] See e.g. *ECS/AKZO* [1983] 3 CMLR 694.

[32] *IFTRA Rules for Producers of Virgin Aluminium* [1975] 2 CMLR D20 at p. D32, para. 22 (cf. also at paras. 19–26). See also *Zinc Producer Group* [1985] 2 CMLR 108 at para. 73, price fixing cannot be justified on the grounds that harmonised prices are needed to counter dumping from states with centrally planned economies.

[33] *European Glass Manufacturers* [1974] 2 CMLR D51 at p. D71, para. 43; *Zinc Producer Group* (*ibid.*).

[34] Commission decision [1988] 4 CMLR 347; appeal dismissed in Case T-1/89 *Rhône-Poulenc* v *Commission* [1991] ECR II-867.

Glass Manufacturers the Commission condemned such an agreement on the basis that "such provisions thus tend to prevent competitive behaviour, such as the practice of the most efficient and viable undertaking offering lower prices than those of its competitors, or applying special prices and discounts to achieve penetration of the market."[35]

(8) Meeting external aggregate prices

8.26 The same prohibition as in (6) and (7) above applies where the agreement is to meet and not undercut the aggregated market price for the export territory. The aggregation of price is usually performed by a trade association and then disseminated to parties though this may be performed by a price leader or other organisations. Such a practice has been categorised by the Commission as an "especially serious restriction of competition, since its result is to prevent the economic integration of the Common Market and to deny the consumer all of its benefits in respect of the product in question".[36]

(9) Enforced profit margins and price rises

8.27 Agreements whereby parties set a common profit margin or agree simultaneously a percentage price increase are unlawful despite the fact that the agreement does not involve parties selling at uniform levels. The obligation is only to raise one's price—whatever that might be—by a fixed percentage. Freedom to choose an appropriate profit market or select an appropriate moment for a price increase are important elements of price competition. Agreements of this nature tend to prevent fluctuations in market share and hence encourage ossification of the market.[37]

(10) Prohibition of "deceptively" low prices

8.28 It would appear probable that a code of ethics or set of rules discouraging "deceptive" bids or prices would infringe Article 85 EC. In August 1984 the US Department of Justice, in a business review letter addressed to the consulting Engineers Council of Metropolitan Washington, stated that they could not guarantee approval of a code of ethics which rendered it unethical for a council member to submit a deceptively low bid. Deception was defined generally in terms of an engineer using superior knowledge and experience to deceive a client by proposing to do less than was objectively required by the client in order to be able to charge a low fee. In their letter to the council, the Department of Justice stated that "the adoption of the proposal is likely to be perceived ... as a signal to maintain or increase the price level of their bids or to refrain from vigorous competitive bidding". In essence the authorities viewed the proposal as a means of discouraging price rivalry. The authorities' conclusions on this were partly based on their finding of no evidence of a problem of deceptive bidding. There is nothing unusual about this case to suggest that a similar approach would not be adopted by the Commission.

2. *Defences: EC Law*

8.29 Various excuses and justification have been advanced by parties to price agreements. Often these are raised in the hope of ameliorating a fine rather than in the hope of earning exemption under Article 85(3). They are, none the less, interesting as an indication of Commission policy.

[35] *ibid.*, note 33 at p. D68, para. 35.
[36] *IFTRA Rules for Producers of Virgin Aluminium* [1975] 2 CMLR D20 at p. D36, para. 45.
[37] *VCH* [1973] CMLR D16 (Commission); Case 8/72 [1972] ECR 977; [1973] CMLR 7 (ECJ).

8.30 (a) It is impermissible to introduce price controls for agricultural produce in the absence of a common organisation of the market.[38]

8.31 (b) Agreements preventing or deterring "dumping level prices" on the grounds that the agreement is necessary to prevent the destruction of domestic industry are unacceptable.[39] Thus, in *LdPE*[40] the Commission condemned a price-fixing cartel and held it to be no defence that there was over-capacity in the industry. In particular, the Commission rejected the arguments of one of the participants that any agreements were prompted by a desire on the part of the industry to prevent unprofitable price-cutting saying that "if competitive conditions in a particular product area ... are such that it is difficult for producers to operate profitably, the remedy does not lie in collusion by the producers to raise price levels".[41]

8.32 (c) The existence of governmentally imposed minimum or maximum price controls does not legitimate the operation of ancillary private restrictions.[42] In any event governmentally imposed controls may themselves be unlawful under Articles 30 or 34 EC which prohibit measures having equivalent effect to quantitative restrictions.[43]

8.33 (d) The labelling of restrictive clauses as "fair trade rules" or equivalent does not preclude antitrust intervention; if anything it encourages it. The authorities are interested in object and effect, not appearances.[44]

8.34 (e) It may be possible to obtain exemption for a price fixing agreement in exceptional circumstances. In *Eurocheques*[45] exemption was granted for a restriction on payee banks participating in the Eurocheque payment system (whereby bank customers holding

[38] See e.g. *Import of Seeds for Forage Plants into France* Bull EC 3/76, para. 2109. The governments of four Member States complained about levies imposed on imported herbage seeds into France. The *Union interprofessionel des Semences Fourragéres* (UISF), its five member-trade associations and five other French trade associations representing producers, breeders distributors and importers of herbage seed charged levies on imports of the main varieties of herbage seed into France. The levies broadly corresponded to the price differential between the high domestic price and the substantially cheaper prices elsewhere in the Community. The agreement set up a scheme of minimum guaranteed prices for breeders, threshold prices for imports of each variety and a range of levies in amounts varying according to variety. Imports from other Member States and in particular Denmark were significantly hindered. The Commission requested UISF to terminate the agreement before the start of the next sowing season and to repay all of the levies unlawfully collected.

[39] *Belgian Agreement on Industrial Timber* Bull EC 10/75 para. 2104, *Fifth Report on Competition Policy* (1975), para. 37. The agreements in question affected Belgium and the border areas of other timber-producing Member States. Under the agreement parties agreed: (i) not to purchase timber at above the maximum price fixed by the association for each production area; (ii) not to grant loyalty rebates; (iii) not to draw up lists of suppliers; (iv) to exchange data on purchasing policy; and (v) to employ a standard form contract. The parties claimed that the agreements were necessary to prevent disruptions on the industrial timber market from adversely affecting the performance of contracts between growers and users. The agreement—so it was claimed—was also necessary to prevent harmful speculation on the market to the detriment of Belgian users which included board producers, joiners, printers, publishing houses, etc.; were the industries to suffer from such market vicissitudes they might develop into targets for foreign take-over bids. The Commission condemned the agreements replying that where serious economic difficulties were envisaged it was not for private parties to take curative action but for public authorities and/or the Commission to adopt appropriate measures.

[40] OJ 1989 L74/21 [1990] 4 CMLR 382.

[41] See also *Scottish Salmon Board* OJ 1992 L246/37 where the Commission considered that the difficulties faced by the industry at the time could not excuse a price fixing agreement.

[42] See e.g. *Cimbel* [1973] CMLR D167.

[43] See e.g. Case 65/75 *Tasca* [1976] ECR 291; Case 88-90/75 *Sadam* [1976] ECR 323; *Inno-ATAB* (Case 13/77) [1977] ECR 2115; Case 82/77 *Van Tiggele* [1978] ECR 25; Case 5/79 *Buys* [1979] ECR 3203; Case 16-20 *Danis* [1979] ECR 3327.

[44] e.g. in the *IFTRA Rules for Producers of Virgin Aluminium* case "IFTRA" stood for International Fair Trade Rules Association.

[45] [1984] 3 CMLR 434.

Eurocheque cards could cash cheques free from charge[46] at banks in other Member States in the local currency) charging drawee banks more than a maximum commission for providing the service of cashing cheques. This was held to be an indispensable restriction as the alternative would have involved the 15,000 participating banks in concluding individual bilateral agreements over the rates of commission to be charged. Moreover the Eurocheque system was designed to encourage cross-border trade and movement of capital by allowing individual account holders the ability to use their accounts outside their own member state without making special arrangements such as ordering travellers' cheques. The Eurocheque scheme also faced significant competition from other forms of payment which could also be used across borders such as cash machine and credit cards.

3. The Oligopoly Defence (Parallel Conduct or Conscious Parallelism): EC Law

8.35 In *ICI* v *Commission* (*Dyestuffs*)[47] the European Court accepted the principle that identical pricing patterns amongst competitors may be explicable by natural market forces rather than collusion. This statement simply reflects accepted economic wisdom on "oligopoly" whereby it is natural in a market of only a few undertakings where the products produced are similar for traders to be sensitive to each others' prices. In *Dyestuffs* the Court stated that parallel pricing might be "natural" where:

(a) there were only a few competitors controlling the market;
(b) the products were homogeneous or readily interchangeable, at least in the eyes of the purchaser; and
(c) the pricing structure of the market was such that competitors would be almost immediately sensitive to price changes effected by competitors.

8.36 The Court of Justice's decision in *Wood pulp*,[48] largely overturning the Commission's findings of concerted practices,[49] showed other circumstances in which parallel pricing could take place without concertation in response to market conditions. The Commission had found that parallel pricing was taking place in the European wood pulp market, both in announced prices and in actual transaction prices, after discounts had been negotiated with purchasers. It concluded that the only national explanation for such parallel pricing was an underlying concerted practice. The Court commissioned experts to examine the Commission's findings and came to the conclusion that there were other rational economic explanations for this phenomenon that did not depend on concertation. These explanations were:

(i) The market was characterised by long term relationships between purchasers and buyers, both recognising the cyclical nature of the demand for wood pulp and so having a common interest in ensuring continuity of supply. Hence the system of announcing prices in advance, so that purchasers could plan their costs, while having a system whereby the actual transaction cost could be at a price negotiated below that, to re-

[46] The breach of this principle by French banks was held to contravene Art. 85(1) without exemption in the Commission's decision in *Eurocheque: Helsinki Agreement* OJ 1992 L95/90.

[47] [1969] CMLR D23 (Commission); Case 48, 49, 51-57/69 *ICI* v *Commission* [1972] ECR 619; [1972] CMLR 557.

[48] Joined Cases C-89, 194, 114, 116, 117 and 125–129 *Ahlstrom and Others* v *Commission* (*Wood Pulp*) [1995] ECR I-1307, [1993] 4 CMLR 407.

[49] *Wood Pulp* [1985] 3 CMLR 474.

spond to more recent changes in the market. The system of announcing price increases in advance did not in itself remove each supplier's uncertainty about the level of pricing to be adopted by its competitors.

(ii) There were fewer buyers than suppliers, who also bought through traders and agents, as well as from each other. This meant that when a supplier quoted a price, it quickly became known to all buyers, each of whom was astute to ensure that it did not pay more than its competitor. Indeed, this concern led purchasers to welcome the move to all pricing being in US dollars to aid comparison of prices. Thus similarity of both announced and transaction prices as well as in the timing of price announcements resulted from the transparency in the market created by the buying practices of purchasers.

(iii) These factors were strengthened by the way in which the market had developed into a group of oligopolies-oligopsonies, as each producer developed particular blends of woodpulps for particular buyers. Hence, although there were 40 producers of wood pulp alleged to have taken part in the cartel, in practice the market was further segmented, thus leading to a situation where in reality there were only a few undertakings operating within each market segment. At that point, the oligopoly defence seems more plausible. The converse of this is that the 40 producers only represented 60 per cent of the Community market. The Court regarded it as implausible that a cartel could survive while 40 per cent of the market was open to free competition and therefore could have offered purchasers lower prices.

8.37 Drawing on *Dyestuffs* and *Wood pulp*, it is possible to identify factors (in addition to those already listed) which should be taken into account in determining the legitimacy of parallel pricing. Among these are included:

(a) Costs: do the parties bear similar production costs since "conscious parallelism" is more likely where costs are relatively uniform to all producers? However, even where products costs vary (e.g. one producer may be integrated with a supplier of necessary raw materials thereby reducing costs) competitors might none the less feel the need to match each others' prices. A, B and C might all charge £X per unit although because of variable costs A and B might earn 12 per cent profit whereas C, who is integrated with to his suppliers, might earn 17 per cent profit.

(b) Level of use of capacity: where capacity is underemployed and the level of stocks is high one would expect vigorous competition by firms anxious to unload capacity. Where the expected rivalry does not translate into price competition suspicions may be roused. Though, such parallel pricing might be accounted for by fears, independently entertained by traders, of a ruinous price war engendered by an unexpected lowering oil prices.

(c) The age of the market: old, mature, probably contracting, markets are populated by firms who are experienced in each others' ways, probably content with their market share and often reluctant to break the status quo through maverick pricing. The chances of parallel pricing occurring naturally are thus high. The converse may reasonably be expected from new, immature and expanding markets.

(d) The elasticity of global demand: fixed demand by customers for an industry's products and the inability of those customers to change to rival supplier's products may deter price uniformity without concerted action by suppliers. Thus if a product has a long amortisation period and requires substantial investment by purchasers this may preclude further sales to a buyer for a number of years. Profitable tacit collusion is best facilitated where orders are small, frequent and regular. Thus where the converse applies tacit collusion is made improbable.

8.38 In essence, traders arguing that parallel pricing is the consequence of natural market circumstances will have to prove the existence of those circumstances to the Commission or Court.[50] There is a danger that the authorities will view parallel pricing as prima facie evidence of collusion, accordingly, traders will find it necessary to "prove the market" by adducing empirical and/or expert evidence[51] and supporting economic theories.[52] The test applied by the authorities is whether the pricing conduct actually prevailing could be expected in natural circumstances. They will, thus, seek extrinsic evidence to determine how natural the prices are. The following are considered as indicators of collusion:

(a) the announcement of price moves prior to implementation including a sufficient interim time between announcement and implementation to allow the announcing undertaking to judge rivals' reactions.[53]
(b) The informal exchange of information on commercial matters of pricing usually deemed secret (stocks, production, orders, etc.).[54]
(c) The level of prevailing prices. If, given the costs and setting involved, profit margins of only 10 per cent could be expected whereas margins greatly in excess are earned the authorities might consider that such profits could only result from collusion.[55]
(d) The separation and isolation of markets where this is not explicable by high freight rates.[56]
(d) Export prices coinciding with local prices on the foreign market might suggest an agreement to respect home markets,[57] as does any other systematic adaptation to foreign prices, though clearly exports must, to a degree, be sensitive to foreign prices.
(e) The addition of surcharges for export contracts where the increment is unrelated to provable costs or risks may suggest collusion.[58]

[50] For analysis of these factors, see Wathelet, "Pratiques concertées et comportements parallèles en oligopole" (1975) *Revue trimestrielle de droit européen* 664; Joliet, "La notion de pratique concertée et l'assêt ICI dans une perspective comparative" (1974) *Cahiers de droit européen* 254; Schere and Ross, *Industrial Market Structure and Economic Performance* (1990), Chapters 6–8.

[51] Cases 48, 49, 51-57/69 *ICI* v *Commission* [1972] ECR 619 at p. 659. In Joined Cases C-89, 104, 114, 116, 117 and 125-129 *Ahlstrom and Others* v *Commission* (*Wood Pulp*), the Court itself commissioned two studies by experts, which seem to have been regarded by it as decisive.

[52] Though, the authorities may be suspicious of some economic or empirical theories. See European Sugar Industry [1973] CMLR D65. Economic theory that manufacturers are "normally" only interested in selling to distributors or dealers was rejected; manufacturers often sell to other competitors. See also Joined Cases C-89, 104, 114, 116, 117 and 125-129 *Ahlstrom and Others* v *Commission* (*Wood Pulp*) [1993] ECR I-1307, [1993] 4 CMLR 407.

[53] See Cases 48, 49, 51-57/69 *ICI* v *Commission* [1972] ECR 619 at pp. 661, 662; *Tar Colours* [1969] CMLR D23.

[54] The Commission has cited the classic economic article by Stigler, "The kinky oligopoly demand curve and rigid prices" (1947) *Journal of Political Economics* Vol. 45, p. 431, as authority. In *Zinc Producer Group* [1985] 2 CMLR 108 pp. 128, 129, para. 75, the Commission examined the zinc market. It noted that certain long-standing price agreements had been terminated in 1977 with the consequence that a vacuum existed, there being no natural leader to act independently in the knowledge that others would follow. The Commission citing Stigler stated: "The situation prevailing in this case seems to have been more characteristic of that which could give rise to what is known in economic theory as 'barometric price leadership'. This does not remove from undertakings the ability to 'determine independently the policy which (they intend) to adopt on the Common market.' Under such circumstances parallel pricing behaviour in an oligopoly producing homogeneous goods will not be in itself sufficient evidence of a concerted practice. However, sufficient evidence may result from parallel pricing in combination with other indications, such as contacts between undertakings on desirable price changes prior to price changes, or the exchange of information which reinforces contacts of this kind."

[55] cf. *B.P. Kemi-DDSF* [1979] 3 CMLR 684.

[56] cf. *Pioneer* OJ 1980 L 60/21, 34.

[57] cf. *IFTRA Rules for Producers of Virgin Aluminum* [1975] 2 CMLR D20 at p. D36.

[58] cf. *European Sugar Industry* [1973] CMLR 65.

(f) The existence of interlocking directorates which act as channels for the reciprocal flow of confidential data and provide opportunities for concerted action.[59]

4. UK Law

8.39 The law as decided by the Restrictive Practices Court (RPC) has, with a few much criticised exceptions, invariably condemned price agreements. The OFT adopts a similarly strict approach. Indeed, the OFT invariably refers unregistered price fixing agreements to the RPC for an injunctive order to be made against the parties. The OFT has referred many hundreds of such cases. Invariably the action is undefended. Breach of a court order is contempt of court. This section highlights the types of price agreement struck down by the Court and invariably attacked by the OFT.

(1) Minimum and fixed prices

(a) Minimum prices

8.40 While the Court has accepted that minimum prices are not as objectionable as fixed prices since they do permit some degree of flexibility, it has, none the less, struck down almost all those appearing before it.[60] This injunction applies even where the effect of the price restriction is apparently negligible as where it is equated with costs and operates as a "stop loss" price[61] or, where the price of the commodity in question is only remotely connected to the price of the finished product. Moreover, the argument made in *Yarn Spinners* that abrogation of a minimum price agreement could lead to ruination of the industry has been held by the Court to be irrelevant.[62] It should be recalled, however, that the Court decisions on this issue are in most cases 20–40 years old and the RPC today might be more willing to take a sympathetic attitude to truly recession hit industries such as that in *Yarn Spinners*. Though the current thinking is that recession struck industries burdened with serious excess capacity should consider restructuring agreements rather than price fixing.

(b) Fixed prices

8.41 Fixed price agreements are presumptively more serious restrictions on competition and will invariably be condemned by the authorities.[63] The only fixed price agreements escaping

[59] See e.g. *BIS-SCR* Bull EC 11/76, para. 2119. A US export cartel sanctioned under the US Webb-Pomerene Act was condemned by the Commission for collusion in *Wood Pulp*, this finding being upheld by the Court in Joined Cases C-89, 104, 114, 116, 117 and 125–129 *Ahlstrom and Others* v *Commission (Wood Pulp)* [1995] ECR I-1307, [1993] 4 CMLR 407 paras. 128–47.

[60] e.g. *Federation of Wholesale and Multiple Bakers (Great Britain and Northern Ireland) Agreement* (1959) LR 1 RP 387; [1960] 1 WLR 393 (RPC). See also *Wholesale and Retail Bakers of Scotland Association's Agreement* (1959) LR 1 RP 347; [1959] 1 WLR 1094 (RPC); *Associated Transformers Manufacturers' Agreement* (1961) LR 2 RP 295; [1961] 1 WLR 660 (RPC); *Linoleum Manufacturers' Association's Agreement* (1961) LR 2 RP 395; [1961] 1 WLR 781 (RPC); *British Bottle Association's Agreement* (1961) LR 2 RP 345; [1961] 1 WLR 760 (RPC); No. 3167 Register of Restrictive Trade Practices, *Plastic Pressure Pipes* (1974) agreements not to sell at prices below those of the market leader.

[61] e.g. *Blanket Manufacturers' Agreement* (1959) LR 1 RP 208; [1959] 1 WLR 442 (RPC); *Federation of Wholesale and Multiple Bakers' (Great Britain and Northern Ireland) Agreement* (1959) LR 1 RP 387; [1960] 1 WLR 393 (RPC).

[62] *Yarn Spinners' Agreement* (1959) LR 1 RP 118; [1959] 1 WLR 154 (RPC). See also *British Jute Trade Federal Council's Agreement* (1964) LR 4 RP 399 which involved a price fixing agreement in similarly depressed market circumstances and elicited an equally unsympathetic response from the Court.

[63] e.g. *Federation of British Carpet Manufacturers* (1959) LR 1 RP 472; [1960] 1 WLR 356 (RPC); *Phenol Producers Agreement* (1960) LR 2 RP 1 [1960] 1 WLR 464 (RPC); *British Heavy Steel Makers Agreement*

have exhibited exceptional market circumstances as well as reasonable prices and methods of computation. For details see paras 8.44–8.51. An illustration revealing the consistently hard line approach of the OFT and Restrictive Practices Court concerned 26 sellers of household coal, anthracite and phurnacite in south-west Wales.[64] These sellers abided by prices fixed by their trade association and circulated on a price list. In 1978 the Price Commission discovered the agreement and notified the OFT who commenced proceedings before the Restrictive Practices Court despite the fact that the parties terminated the agreement while claiming that the prices had never been binding. This latter claim was clearly open to dispute given that summaries of minutes of meetings of the Association among documents registered on the Restrictive Practices Register reveal that the association went to great lengths to agree on price levels with members and to impose pressure to conform on price cutters.[65] Special pleading for fixed price agreements invariably falls on deaf ears. In *British Paper and Board Makers' Association*[66] the parties argued that the price-fixing agreement was to guarantee a standard annual price at which waste paper (an important raw materials in the paper and board industry) was to be purchased from local authorities. This guarantee gave local authorities the security they required if it was to be economical for them to collect waste paper for sale. The Restrictive Practices Court replied that the price fixing agreement was not necessary in order that adequate price guarantees be accorded to local authorities.

(2) Attitude of the OFT

8.42 Businessmen cannot expect a sympathetic response from the OFT to attempts to fix prices.[67] Nor should professionals.[68] Where trade association practices are moving into controversial waters, the OFT will often require the association and members to give written un-

cont.
(1964) LR 5 RP 33 (maximum fixed price); *British Paper and Board Makers' Association's Agreement* (1963) LR 4 RP 29; *Wire Rope* (1965) LR 5 RP 146; [1965] 1 WLR 121 (RPC).

64 No. 4550 Register of Restrictive Trade Practices, *South West Wales Coal*. See also Nos. 3731, 3732 Register of Restrictive Trade Practices, *Plastic Pressure Pipes* (1974) concerning agreed percentage increases to published list prices less quantity discounts the parties notified to each other. The RPC held the agreement to be against the public interest. The parties did not defend the agreement.

65 The documents on file No. 4550 (*ibid.*) record that at three meetings of the association set over a period of years the following events occurred: 8 May 1971: "There was a complaint against a Merchant undercutting the price of coal in another Merchant's area. This was discussed and finally agreed that the Chairman contacts Mr A Hughes on the matter". 23 March 1977: "Unable to come to an agreement as to prices". 13 April 1977: "Milford Haven Merchants threaten to walk out of Association on prices issue."

66 (1963) LR 4 RP 29.

67 The OFT regularly challenge price-fixing agreements and require the parties to determine agreements between them. Often the parties are referred to the RPC for an injunctive order to be made prohibiting continuance with the agreement. For examples on the Register of Restrictive Trade Practices, see: No. S. 120 *London Tugowners' Association* recommended tariff and standard terms and conditions (1976); No. S. 331, Agreement between Cory *Ship Towage Ltd and C J King and Sons (Tugs) Ltd* concerning verbal consultation and agreement on prices to be charged for ship towage services-agreement (1981); No. S. 100 *Southampton Isle of Wight and South of England Royal Mail Steam Packet Company Ltd and Alexandra Towing Company Ltd* concerning an oral agreement over tariffs to users of tug and tender services in the Port of Southampton and the sharing of any new business in the port secured by either party; *British Reinforcement Manufacturers' Association* DGFT Annual Report 1982, p. 98. Association gave an undertaking to the RPC binding upon each of the Members not to enforce the following restrictions or make any agreement to like effect: (i) not to import reinforcing steel from countries outside the EEC; (ii) not to sell their products below agreed floor prices and to abide by the Association's rebate scheme; and (iii) not to limit their deliveries by reference to a formula governing individual market shares. Price fixing agreements seem to have been particularly prevalent in the construction industry. The DGFT Annual Reports and press releases show continuing investigations against companies involved in the supply of ready-mixed concrete, cement, steel roofing purlins and thermal insulation materials to the construction industry; freight forwardings; and double glazing materials.

68 For example, the MMC in *Private Medical Services* (Cm 2452, 1994) condemned price guidelines issued for consultants' services by the British Medical Association as they operated in practice as a price-fixing tariff.

dertakings that prices will not be fixed. Thus in one case concerning the *Scots Timothy Seed Growers' Association*, the Association was required to sign a document, which was placed on the register undertaking that their recommendations to members were not binding.[69] Further they gave undertakings that no recommendations would be made as to:

(i) the price at which an approved merchant could sell seeds to customers;
(ii) the price the consumer would pay to his supplier for sowing seeds;
(iii) restrictions on the movement of seeds within the UK or for exportation;
(iv) varieties of "Timothy" seed which fell outside the quality standards set out in the associations rules; and
(v) the restrictions to be imposed upon merchant members in buying seeds from sources other than the Association.

8.43 As with EC law, it matters not that the restriction relates to services. The OFT prohibited the *Motor School Association of Great Britain* from recommending "reasonable fees" to driving instructors for them to charge pupils. Undertakings, in triplicate, were required from the Association to this effect.[70] Evidence, however, of a more pragmatic approach by the OFT may be found in their handling of the recommendations of the *National Association of Drinks Manufacturers Ltd*[71] on the amount of deposit given on soda syphons. The Association made it abundantly clear to its membership that the recommendation was not binding. The OFT apparently treated the case on the basis that since the deposit was refundable and a higher deposit would increase the incentive on consumers to return the bottles which, in turn, would prevent cost increases and therefore price increases (fewer bottles would have to be produced), a permissive response was appropriate.

(3) Factors relevant in the negotiation or defence of price restrictions

8.44 From cases decided before the RPC a number of factors have arisen which might, if present in the circumstances of a price agreement, render it more acceptable. Though it should be stressed these factors derive from cases heard in the late 1950s and early 1960s which have been much criticised for being too lenient on price fixing.[72]

(a) Reasonableness of prices

8.45 This has been treated by the Court almost as a *sine qua non* to the acceptance of a price restriction. To establish that a price is "reasonable" it appears to be usually necessary with detailed accountancy evidence to prove that the price covers overheads and allows only a small margin of profit.[73] This definition, however, is not universal.[74] Prices that are fixed by reference to the maximum the market will bear have never been viewed as reasonable and will inevitably lead to the condemnation of the agreement.[75]

[69] No. 3018 Register of Restrictive Trade Practices. See also from the Register: No. 3162 *National Association of Agricultural Contractors* (guide prices unacceptable to OFT); No. 3763 *Egg Producers' Association* (recommended minimum prices for ex-farm sales of ungraded first quality eggs unacceptable to OFT).

[70] No. S. 112 Register for Restrictive Trade Practices (1977). A copy of the *MSA Journal* for October 1977 is contained on the file which records that the Association: "are permitted to respond to requests on any subject and remain free to reply to letters from members as best we can, but no longer can we circulate general information on the question of tuition fees."

[71] No. 577 Register of Restrictive Trade Practices.

[72] See in particular Stevens and Yamey, *The Restrictive Practices Court* (1965) for penetrating criticisms of decisions of the RPC in this area.

[73] See *Water-Tube Boilermakers' Agreement* (1959) LR 1 RP 285 at p. 334.

[74] See *Associated Transformer Manufacturers' Agreement* (1961) LR 2 RP 295 at p. 344.

[75] See e.g. *Federation of British Carpet Manufacturers' Agreement* (1959) LR 1 RP 472 at p. 534; *British Bottle Association's Agreement* (1961) LR 2 RP 345 at p. 365.

(b) Use of a proper cost calculation model

8.46 Businessmen employing a proper costing formula which can establish costs and profit margins stand a better chance of proving the reasonableness of their prices. In *Permanent Magnets* the Court thus commented: "The figures produced for this reference can, however, be taken as reliable and, no doubt many members of the association will have learnt much as the result of their production and analysis."[76] However, the Court has been critical where businessmen use "informed guesswork" to compute the appropriate price.[77] In *Carpets* the Court described prices so determined as "arbitrary".[78] Similarly, prices based upon average industry costs have been condemned. In *Yarn Spinners* the minimum price was described as: "an artificial price calculated on a hypothetical average cost. It does not represent the cost actually incurred by an individual mill and every mill will therefore be above or below it by a small or large margin".[79] Average costs were only acceptable in cases such as *Black Bolt and Nuts* where the parties produced thousands of similar cost, similar type products such that individual costings were impossible.[80] None the less *overall* costings and profit figures were available revealing no great spread of costs and reasonable profits. Where, because of the unusual nature of an industry, accurate analysis of prices and costs is impossible the Court has used a negative approach. Thus in *Phenol*[81] it concluded that the prices were unreasonable upon the basis that: (i) the price was almost certainly above that which would prevail in unrestricted conditions;[82] (ii) the price was unrelated to production costs; (iii) the price was computed by reference only to market capacity; and (iv), the price fixing scheme was rigid and not susceptible to variation.[83]

(c) Agreement keeps prices down

8.47 In a number of cases the fact that the agreement actually led to reduced prices found favour with the Restrictive Practices Court. Thus in *Glazed and Floor Tiles*[84] the parties fixed the prices for standardised and unstandardised varieties of tile with the latter being upward of 25 per cent more expensive than standardised types. This discriminated in favour of the standardised products boosting their sales. Abrogation of the agreement would have removed the element of discrimination which was necessary to encourage the standardisation process. Standardisation uniformly resulted in economies of scale and hence ultimately lower prices. In *Cement Makers' Federation Agreement*[85] a discriminatory multiple base point pricing scheme[86] gave the parties sufficient security to enable them to accept a lower return on capital than they would otherwise have done. This led to substantially lower prices. In *Distant Water Vessels*[87] a minimum reserve price at fish auctions

[76] *Permanent Magnet Association's Agreement* (1962) LR 3 RP 119 at p. 174.

[77] The Court expects detailed accountancy evidence to be adduced if attempts are even to be made to seek to justify harmonised prices.

[78] *Federation of British Carpet Manufacturers' Agreement* (1959) LR 1 RP 472 at p. 534.

[79] *Yarn Spinners' Agreement* (1959) LR 2 RP 241 at p. 279.

[80] *Black Bolt and Nut Association's Agreement* (1960) LR 2 RP 50 at p. 61. See also for similar Court reaction, *British Bottle Association's Agreement* (1961) LR 2 RP 345 at p. 365.

[81] *Phenol Producers' Agreements* (1960) LR 2 RP 1. Phenol is one of a number of products derived from the refining of crude tar acids; the apportioning of costs, therefore, between the different chemicals produced during the refining process was inevitably arbitrary. Furthermore, the raw material itself was not purchased on the open market and thus had no set price.

[82] A conclusion made by either the Court or the OFT that the price would be lower in unrestricted conditions may sometimes be questionable at least where the restriction is already long-lived as in *Black Bolt and Nut* where the agreement had existed for 27 years before arriving before the Court.

[83] (1960) LR 2 RP 1 at p. 41.

[84] *Glazed and Floor Time Home Trade Association's Agreement* (1964) LR 4 RP 239 (RPC).

[85] *Cement Makers' Federation Agreement* (1961) LR 2 RP 241; [1961] 1 WLR 581 (RPC).

[86] For analysis see paras 8.226–8.237 below.

[87] *Distant Water Vessels Development Scheme* (1966) LR 6 RP 242; [1967] 1 WLR 203.

preventing ruinous returns on capital forcing fishermen out of the market. Fewer vessels would have meant smaller overall catches, demand exceeding supply and rising prices. To establish that price restrictions reduce prices rather than raise them parties to agreement will have to furnish convincing statistical and empirical evidence.

(d) Agreement enhances international competition

8.48 Agreements which enable the parties jointly to meet external competition more effectively thereby maintaining international competitive forces may succeed. It would necessarily have to be proven that in the absence of agreement the domestic firms would not be able to compete and that the market would fall prey to foreign companies.[88] In this context "foreign" means, for all practical purposes, non-EC, since an agreement enabling UK firms to compete better with EU rivals would, in most cases, be prohibited under Article 85(1).

(e) Agreement saves purchasers "shopping time"

8.49 In *Black Bolt and Nut*[89] the price fixing agreement coupled to the inter-firm arrangement to supply by each other with varieties of the product not produced by the purchaser meant that a purchaser could satisfy his requirements from one supplier thereby saving significant administrative costs. This "shopping around" argument, however, has been rejected in all the other cases in which it has been pleaded.[90] It succeeded in *Black Bolt and Nut* because there were in excess of 3,000 varieties of the product available and purchasers orders were invariably complex.

(f) Agreement improves the quality of R&D

8.50 Where a price agreement actually makes possible patent pooling and/or the exchange of technical data thereby improving industry standards of innovation the agreement might prove acceptable.[91]

(4) Factors rejected as negotiating elements

8.51 Various factors have been rejected as proper defences to price restrictions. These will be briefly noted: (a) loss of price stability—stability is not considered a virtue since it may mean stability as a supra-competitive level;[92] (b) reduction in levels of investment—the argument that lower prices means lower profits means lower reinvestment and less incentive for outsiders to invest in the industry, though perhaps feasible in extreme cases, has never been accepted in cases presented to the Restrictive Practices Court;[93] (c) reduction to inadequate level of stocks—the nexus between drastic reductions in stocks and abrogation of a price agreement has never yet been accepted in a straight horizontal price scheme;[94] (d) increase in degree of concentration in the market—the Court has never been

[88] See e.g. *Permanent Magnet Association's Agreement* (1962) LR 3 RP 119; [1962] 1 WLR 781 (RPC).

[89] *Black Bolt and Nut Association's Agreement* (1960) LR 2 RP 50; [1960] 1 WLR 884 (RPC).

[90] See e.g. *Glazed and Floor Tile Home Trade Association Agreement* (1964) LR 4 RP 239 (RPC); *Wholesale Confectioners' Alliance's Agreement* (1962) LR 3 RP 119; [1962] 1 WLR 781 (RPC).

[91] See e.g. *Permanent Magnet Association's Agreement* (1962) LR 3 RP 119; [1962] 1 WLR 781 (RPC).

[92] See e.g. *Wholesale and Retail Bakers of Scotland Association's Agreement* (1959) LR 1 RP 347 at p. 376; *Federation of British Carpet Manufacturers* (1960) LR 1 RP 472 at p. 541; *Linoleum Manufacturers' Association's Agreement* (1961) LR 2 RP 395 at p. 426.

[93] See e.g. *British Heavy Steelmakers' Agreement* (1964) LR 5 RP 33.

[94] See e.g. *British Bottle Association's Agreement* (1961) LR 2 RP 345; *Linoleum Manufacturers' Association Agreement* (1961) LR 2 RP 395; But cf. in respect of vertically imposed price restraints *Net Book Agreement (No. 1)* (1962) LR 2 RP 246; [1962] 1 WLR 1347 (RPC) see section H for details.

sympathetic to arguments that a price agreement has kept firms in existence and hence prevented the emergence of oligopolistic (or even monopolistic) conditions.[95]

D. Discount Schemes

1. *EC Law*

8.52 In general terms there is nothing to stop a non-dominant undertaking from applying whatever prices and terms and conditions it pleases *provided* that it takes its pricing decisions *unilaterally*. If discriminatory or arbitrary pricing decisions are taken as a result of agreements between competitors or agreements between (say) a supplier and a distributor in relation to prices to be charged third parties (such as a potential parallel exporter), then Article 85(1) will engage to regulate the pricing policy. Equally, if a company is dominant or has monopoly power than the fact that the pricing policy is determined unilaterally will provide no defence against the application of competition rules. This section is concerned with discounts applied pursuant to agreement, concerted practice or decisions of trade associations and by dominant undertakings so far as EC law is concerned. Discounts by providing the customer with a reduction on the list, normal or quoted price are central to a competitive pricing policy. There are two main antitrust problems related to discounts. The first is discrimination whereby supplier X gives purchaser A a 15 per cent reduction on the list price but makes B pay the full list price. By its pricing action, X is affecting the competitive position between A and B to the latter's detriment. Secondly, where suppliers agree on a discounts policy the opportunity for individual suppliers to act competitively and award larger discounts is negated. Moreover, the opportunity for a purchaser to win greater discounts through more effective bargaining disappears. It is essentially with the second problem that this section is concerned. The first problem is dealt with at paras. 8.93–8.108.

(1) Legal context

8.53 Agreements whereby parties supply or purchase according to uniform prices and discounts require little discussion for their incompatibility with Article 85(1) EC to be established.[96] The same prohibition applies to agreements to adhere strictly to price lists and refrain from discounting. In *Rover Group* a scheme whereby Rover's dealers were denied additional payments if they exceeded a maximum level of discount to purchasers of certain models of Rover cars was acknowledged by the Rover Group to constitute price fixing contrary to Article 85(1).[97] Thus in *Re Gista*[98] members of a trade association of plumbing installation

[95] See e.g. *Yarn Spinners' Agreement* (1959) LR 1 RP 118; *British Bottle Association's Agreement* (1961) LR 2 RP 345.

[96] See e.g. *Gisa* [1973] CMLR D125; *Italian Flat Glass: Community* v *Fabbrica Pisana* [1982] 3 CMLR 366; *Cimbel* [1973] CMLR D16; *The Agreement of Stichting Sigarettenindustrie* [1982] 2 CMLR 702 (Commission) affirmed by the ECJ (Cases 240-242, 262, 262, 268, 269/82); *SSI* v *Commission* [1985] ECR 3831; [1987] 3 CMLR 661; see also, Case 260/82 *NSO* v *Commission* [1985] ECR 3801; [1988] 4 CMLR 755.

[97] *Twenty-third Report on Competition Policy* (1993), para. 228. No action was taken by the Commission because Rover management had owned up to the scheme, ended it and disclosed the infringement to the EC and UK competition authorities. Rover also reimbursed dealers the withheld additional payments and agreed to make payments totalling £1 million to schemes designed to be of benefit to car purchasers within the UK. Similarly, prohibitions of non-standard discounts were condemned by the Court of Justice in Case 311/85 *VVR* v *Sociale Dienst* [1987] ECR 3801; [1989] 4 CMLR 213.

[98] [1973] CMLR D125.

equipment were forbidden from discounting. The trade association rigorously enforced the rule by requiring members: to supply all invoices to its secretariat for checking; to allow it immediate access to offices and warehouses; and to pay fines for covert discounting. In their decision condemning the agreement the Commission stated that it deprived parties of the freedom to "determine their own prices and conditions of sale and to attract orders for the articles in question to the detriment of their competitors by quoting lower prices, bigger discounts and better conditions of sale".[99] In *Roofing Felt*[100] the Commission condemned an agreement between roofing felt manufacturers which established a price list and then limited the discounts which members could offer. The fact that certain members were able to give discounts higher than the limits set in the agreement was not held to prove that the agreements did not exist or were not applied. The ability to set prices to one's competitors' detriment is a central element of price competition. Similar prohibitions apply to schemes whereby groups of suppliers grant rebates only to "approved" purchasers.[101]

(2) Aggregated rebate cartels: mechanisms

8.54 The simple fixing of discounts presents few problems of either identification or legality. Businessmen are generally aware that fixed discount agreements are usually prohibited. Aggregated rebate cartels, however, are of greater complexity. A description of the mechanism of these schemes is as follows. An aggregated rebate is a discount calculated at rates which vary according to either the total value or the total quantity or the individual customer's purchases from members of the group (usually the trade association). The characteristic features of such schemes are, first, an aggregation of the customer's qualifying purchases, and secondly, an ascending ladder or scale of rebates such that the more the customer buys from the group (irrespective of how much he purchases from individual suppliers within the group) the greater his rebate. Three main varieties of method for computing the quantum of rebate may be identified:

(a) By total purchases from group during a given period. There is thus an incentive for the purchaser to continue buying from the group in order to increase his rebate.
(b) By subdividing total purchases into rebate layers. Thus if a purchaser places £100,000 worth of orders with the group over a time period he might be given a rebate of 1 per cent on the first £30,000, a rebate of 2 per cent on the next £30,000, a rebate of 3 per cent on the next £30,000 and so on. The benefit to the purchaser under this discount scheme may not be so pronounced as it is under (a) above.
(c) By granting a rebate for orders over a fixed threshold. For example rebate of 1.5 per cent given on annual orders exceeding £150,000. For the purchaser this is the least attractive scheme since if his projected orders do not exceed the threshold there is no incentive to purchase exclusively from the group.

8.55 Various methods of payment of rebate may also be identified:

(a) As a lump sum payable at the end of the year, though, payment may be at shorter intervals.
(b) As a lump sum with payment delayed until the end of the following year and perhaps dependent upon continued loyalty to the group.
(c) As a discount from current purchases calculated either by reference to total purchases in the preceding period, or, by reference to estimated sales for the current period with

[99] *ibid.*, at p. D133.
[100] OJ 1986 L232/15 [1991] 4 CMLR 130.
[101] *Cimbel* [1973] CMLR D16.

evidence of such sales deriving from the previous period and discrepancies found to exist at the end of the period being rectified by lump sum payments. This is the simplest payment method involving no cash collections and transfers. It benefits the purchaser who pays in the first instance the final price.

8.56 Payments are usually made to purchasers according to calculations made by accountants for the group. The discount is paid for by the suppliers in proportion to the amount each has sold to the purchaser. Often the trade association makes itself responsible for collecting the sums from the suppliers and paying the purchaser, although, alternatively the trade association simply makes the calculation and notifies the suppliers of the amounts they owe various purchasers.

(3) Legal objections to aggregated rebates

8.57 Industry views such schemes simply as methods of granting justifiable quantity rebates to high purchasing customers. However, these arrangements invariably presuppose the existence of price control and accordingly are viewed with great suspicion by antitrust authorities. Companies operating such schemes argue that they ameliorate the anti-competitive effects of price fixing since they permit variable prices to be charged and do not harm outside suppliers who can always match or beat the group's level of discounts. Moreover, if the group consists of large suppliers dealing with large purchasers and outsiders are smaller companies dealing with smaller purchasers then those outsiders will not be affected since buyers placing only small volume orders would not, in any event, qualify for rebates and will not therefore be influenced by financial incentives to remain loyal to the group.[102] In favour of such schemes it has also been argued that they keep smaller firms in business, since if discounts were related to orders placed with individuals rather than the group, purchasers would obviously deal with large suppliers carrying large stocks and this could lead to smaller firms being squeezed from the market. Furthermore, because a purchaser need not take exclusively from one supplier, flexibility is introduced to the market; it permits purchasers to buy from sources at locations closest to home without harming his discount. For example, a building contractor operating nationally can reduce transport costs by purchasing materials near the site location rather than carrying materials with him. The same applies to the transportation of materials which are not heavy but are bulky or fragile. Suppliers likewise benefit since they can afford to specialise without needing to carry huge stocks, moreover, they can refused orders without fearing that the customer will suffer loss.

8.58 These arguments, though genuine, are generally considered to be outweighed by the disadvantages. These are:

(a) Suppliers cannot grant individually negotiated discounts but must abide by a commonly agreed rate.[103]

(b) Aggregated discounts are not determined objectively having no bearing to the relationship (measured in turnover) between a purchaser and supplier. In *Re German Ceramic Tiles*[104] the Commission objected to such a scheme on the basis that it was "independent of the economic relations in fact operating between a given pro-

[102] Though it does harm smaller outside firms who are expanding and will in time be capable of supplying larger purchasers. Unless they join the group such suppliers may have those selling options foreclosed to them and as such the scheme may operate as an expansion barrier.

[103] See e.g. *Gas Water Heaters* [1973] CMLR D231.

[104] [1971] CMLR D6.

ducers and a given purchaser".[105] Such schemes take no account of the fact that one supplier might provide better services to purchasers than another. In *Re Gas Water Heaters*[106] the Commission thus commented that such schemes deprive undertakings "of the possibility of determining all their conditions of sale in accordance with their own judgment and according to the services which the buyers do in fact give, quite apart from the category in which they are classed by the agreement". In essence aggregated rebates damage the prospects of durable supplier–purchaser relations.

(c) Discounting is an essential ingredient of competition in oligopolistic markets predominated by only a few suppliers. It is often *only* through secretly negotiated individual rebates that price competition exists at all.[107]

(d) Aggregated rebates do not serve the same purpose as individual discounts. In the latter case individual economies of scale may be passed on. However, in the former case this will not necessarily hold true since the rebate does not reflect scale economies enjoyed by a particular supplier.

(e) Aggregated rebates have been condemned in EC law on the basis that they encourage purchasers to focus orders on the group to the obvious detriment of outsiders. This point was viewed as central by the European Court of Justice in *Groupement des Fabricants de Papiers Peints de Belgique* v *Commission*[108] where the Court stated that such schemes "have the effect of concentrating orders with members of the [group] with the result that the customer who has already covered part of his requirements from members of the [group] is encouraged to buy his entire requirements from those members in order to obtain the highest possible rebate".[109] In *German Ceramic Tiles*[110] this meant that purchasers concentrated on purchasing only from domestic German suppliers to the disadvantage of foreign suppliers seeking penetration of that market. In this sense aggregated rebates can prevent market integration.[111] Where year to year loyalty is also rewarded by extra discounts the incentive to buy from outside of the group further diminishes. In *Coca Cola*[112] such rebates were required by the Commission to be calculated only every three months in order to reduce this incentive to an acceptable level.[113]

(4) Collective price discrimination by discounts

8.59 A concerted attempt to favour one category of customer at the expense of another by means of discriminatory discounts where no objective reasons exist to justify the differentiation will infringe Article 85(1). Thus, if members of a trade association grant 15 per cent discounts to P^1 but charge P^2 strictly according to a price list with the aim of harming P^2 relative to P^1 then a breach of Article 85 might have occurred. Differentiation, by means of variable discount, between purchasers is justified if it is closely related to quantities purchased thereby enabling the supplier to realise scale economies which may be shared (in the form of the discount) with the customer. It should be noted, in this re-

105 *ibid.*, at p. D13.
106 [1973] CMLR D231.
107 See e.g. *German Ceramic Tiles* [1971] CMLR D6.
108 Case 73/74 [1975] ECR 1491; [1976] 1 CMLR 589.
109 *ibid.*, at p. 1514, para. 28. See also *per* Advocate General Trabucchi at p. 1522.
110 [1971] CMLR D6.
111 See Case 73/74 *Groupement des Fabricants de Papiers Peints de Belgique* v *Commission* [1976] ECR 1491 at p. 1523 *per* Advocate-General Trabucchi.
112 *Nineteenth Report on Competition Policy* (1989), para. 50.
113 See further paras. 10.221–10.222.

spect, that Article 85(1)(d) expressly prohibits agreements which: "apply dissimilar conditions to equivalent transactions with other trading parties, thereby placing them at a competitive disadvantage".

(5) Collective predatory pricing

8.60 A collective attempt to drive competitors out of the market by concerted predatory pricing will infringe Article 85(1). In *Roofing Felt*[114] the Commission condemned concerted action aimed at discouraging other manufacturers from pursuing a price-cutting policy and at taking customers away from them. Similarly in *Meldoc*[115] the Commission condemned an agreement between milk producers in the Netherlands to charge low prices to selective customers in the Netherlands in order to make it worth their while not to import cheaper Belgian milk. The losses were shared between the members. This was followed by a "dumping" campaign on the Belgian market. There was evidence that it was a joint campaign and that the margin of loss on the "dumped" milk was considerable. The fact that there was no evidence that the costs of the operation were shared did not, in the Commission's view, "lessen the seriousness of the operation".

8.61 In *Cewal*[116] the Commission considered the issue in further detail drawing a distinction between predatory pricing carried out by a dominant firm and a low-pricing campaign carried out by several undertakings pursuant to an agreement to drive out a competitor. In the former case, in order to establish an infringement of Article 86, it is necessary to apply the criteria established by the ECJ based on production costs. In the latter case, however, "the multilateral and intentional character demonstrates the abusive nature of conduct that consists in establishing a concerted exceptional price with the aim of removing a competitor". The case involved a shipping conference the parties to which decided to offer low rates on those ships which were facing competition from competitors.[117] The Commission held that the members of the conference were in a collective dominant position and that by charging low prices were abusing that position. It is arguable that this approach is unsustainable; if the Commission chooses to proceed against a group of undertakings under Article 86 rather than alleging a price fixing cartel under Article 85 then there is no reason why the test for predatory pricing should be less stringent than that normally applied under Article 86.

(6) Justifiable discounts

8.62 Discounts are justifiable where attributable to savings made by the supplier on a transaction. These savings may be based on quantities supplied, promotion costs, transport, invoicing and handling of goods, etc. In essence quantity rebates are perfectly legal. If purchaser X buys in bulk and hence saves supplier Y money then it would be unfair on X for Y not to pass on some of the scale economies to him by way of discount.[118] Suppliers, in granting discounts, may be accused of discriminating in favour of that purchaser by a rival purchaser who is denied such advantageous terms. Suppliers may justify their

114 [1991] 4 CMLR 130.

115 OJ 1986 L348/50 [1989] 4 CMLR 853.

116 OJ 1993 L34/20. The Commission's decision was upheld on appeal by the Court of First Instance in Joined Cases T-24–26 and 28/93 *Compagnie Maritime Belge Transports SA* v *Commission*, judgment of 8 October 1996.

117 Known as "fighting ships".

118 For examples of rebate schemes approved by the Commission, see the notice of intention to approve British Gypsum's schemes: *Super Stockist* [1993] 4 CMLR 143; *Buying Societies Plasterboard Rebate Scheme* [1993] 4 CMLR 145; *The Efficiency Rebate Scheme* [1993] 4 CMLR 147; *Accessories and Do-it-yourself Promotion Scheme* [1993] 4 CMLR 149.

discounts by reference to detailed costings. Where these are unavailable the Commission accepts cost justifications based upon such statistics and data as the supplier can muster.[119]

(7) Non-justifiable discounts: dominant undertakings and Article 86 EC

8.63 Where the discount is found to be unrelated to scale economies or other commercial justifications then a dominant supplier might be liable to a charge of discriminatory or exclusionary practices.

(a) Fidelity or loyalty discounts

8.64 Discounts given to purchasers who take all or a given percentage of their requirement from the supplier may have the effect of excluding small rival suppliers from customers. The discount operates as an incentive for the purchaser to increase his purchases from the dominant supplier to the exclusion of rival suppliers. Purchasers become linked to suppliers and rival suppliers are denied sales opportunities. Where the supplier holds a dominant position the discount almost certainty infringes Article 86 EC.[120] In *BPB Industries/British Gypsum*[121] the CFI affirmed the abusive nature of loyalty rebates. The fact that the promotional payments represented a response to requests from customers was held not to justify the inclusion of exclusivity clauses.

(b) Target discounts

8.65 Where a dominant supplier sets a series of targets based upon purchases from the supplier which, if met by the buyer, entitle him to a discount or increased discount Article 86 might be infringed. In *Michelin* the supplier instituted a system of discounts conditional upon the attainment of sales targets. As a buyer exceeded the threshold for each target his discount increased. The system was operated in an informal manner so that dealers were unaware of the consequences of attaining their targets or failing to do so. The European Court commented that the system was designed to impose pressure on Michelin purchasers to remain loyal to Michelin. The Court concluded:

> "All those factors were instrumental in creating for dealers a situation in which they were under considerable pressure, especially towards the end of a year, to attain Michelin NV's sales targets if they did not wish to run the risk of losses which its competitors could not easily make good by means of the discounts which they themselves were able to offer. Its network of commercial representatives enabled Michelin NV to remind dealers of this situation at any time so as to induce them to place orders with it.
>
> Such a situation is calculated to prevent dealers from being able to select freely at any time in the light of the market situation the most favourable of the offers made by the various competitors and to change supplier without suffering any appreciable economic disadvantage. It thus limits the dealer's choice of supplier and makes access to the market more difficult for competitors. Neither the wish to sell more nor the wish to spread production more evenly can justify such a restriction of the customer's freedom of choice and independence. The position of dependence in which dealers find themselves and which is created by the discount system in question is not therefore based on any countervailing advantage which may be economically justified."[122]

[119] See Case 85/76 *Hoffman-La Roche* v *Commission* [1979] 3 CMLR 211; [1979] ECR 461; *Sugar Cartel* (*Suiker Unie*) (Joined Cases 40-48, 50, 56, 111, 113, 141/73) [1976] 1 CMLR 295; [1975] ECR 1663; Case 322/81 *Michelin* [1985] 1 CMLR 283 at para. 71 of the judgment.

[120] Case 322/81 *Michelin* [1985] 1 CMLR 282; *Cewal, Cowac and Ukwal* OJ 1993 L34/20, paras. 84–91; Case T-65/89 *BPB Industries* v *Commission* [1993] ECR II-389. See also *Napier Brown* (*British Sugar*) [1990] 4 CMLR 196.

[121] Case T-65/89 *BPB Industries* v *Commission* [1993] ECR II-389.

[122] *ibid.*, at p. 333, paras. 84, 85.

8.66 In *Coca Cola*[123] the Commission required Coca Cola not to set distributors' sales targets for periods exceeding three months. Also condemned were rebates linked to targets for purchases in the previous year and rebates based on the customer purchasing a total amount of both Coca Cola and other soft drinks produced by Coca Cola.

8.67 The European Commission has had cause to consider in a discussion document the operation of fidelity and loyalty discounts and target discounts in the context of frequent flier programmes in the internal aviation market.[124] Frequent flier programmes are generally of two types. First, a passenger may earn a free flight ticket after having effected a set number of flights with the airline offering the scheme. Secondly, the traveller participating in the scheme receives "bonus points" of "miles" for each flight taken where the number of such points is either related to the distance travelled or to the geographical zone in which the destination is situated. In its discussion document the Commission considered the judgments of the ECJ in *Hoffman-La Roche*[125] and *Michelin*.[126] According to the Court, in order to determine whether a rebate system amounts to an abuse under Article 86, it has to be "investigated whether, in providing an advantage not based on any economic service justifying it, the discount tends to remove or restrict the buyer's freedom to choose his sources of supply, to bar competitors from access to the market ... or to strengthen the dominant position by distorting competition". In *Michelin* the Court judged as abusive a target rebate scheme observing that, towards the end of the reference period set for the attainment of the target, the purchaser was under considerable pressure to reach the target or lose the rebate, thus discouraging him from choosing freely at all times between the offers made by different suppliers. Applying these principles to frequent flier programmes (FFP), the Commission noted that it appeared that a scheme would infringe Article 86 when it was designed as a fidelity rebate based on an explicit or implicit condition that the passenger would obtain all or most of its supplies from the airline operating the scheme or where it was designed as a target rebate, i.e. a certain number of flights or a certain mileage was to be effected within a specific reference period. However, given the wide scope of application of FFPs and the fact that they normally entail an open invitation to all passengers to become members independent of their individual demand of air transport services, the Commission concluded that it was highly unlikely for an FFP to be operated as a fidelity rebate. This could, however, be the case for specific forms of corporate discounts offered by airlines to individual companies. In addition the principles outlined by the Court regarding target rebates do not prevent FFPs being designed so that no award was made unless a certain minimum distance was flown or with cut-off dates after which accumulated points were lost, provided that these cut-off dates were "rolling", i.e. linked in each case to the date on which the points are awarded. Accordingly, programmes where points were accumulated over a continuously changing period are more likely to be lawful than programmes which put special pressure on passengers at the end of (for example) a calendar year.[127]

(c) Optional discounts and "English clauses"

8.68 A dominant supplier who requires purchasers to notify it when a rival supplier offers more favourable terms coupled to an option exercisable at the instance of the dominant sup-

[123] *Nineteenth Report on Competition Policy* (1989), para. 50.

[124] "Frequent flier programmes in the internal aviation market" (1992), European discussion document.

[125] Case 85/76 *Hoffman-La Roche* v *Commission* [1979] ECR 461, [1979] 3 CMLR 211.

[126] Case 322/81 *Michelin* v *Commission* [1983] ECR 3461, [1985] 1 CMLR 282.

[127] See also *Soda-Ash–Solvay* OJ 1991 L152/21; *Cewal* OJ 1993 L34/20.

plier to match the rival's offer or allow the buyer to accept supplies from the rival, infringes Article 86. Such clauses have a number of interrelated anti-competitive effects. First, they tie customers to the dominant supplier; secondly, they interfere with competition between the dominant supplier and other suppliers; thirdly, they enable the dominant supplier to learn of its rivals prices and terms and conditions of sale; fourthly, they enable the dominant supplier to determine whether his rivals should win an order or not; and fifthly, the rebate made to the purchaser will not be based on economically justifiable grounds and will invariably involve discrimination as between buyers.[128] An "English clause" can refer to an option granted by a supplier to a purchaser who has accepted a purchasing obligation *vis-à-vis* the supplier, allowing the purchaser to take from rival suppliers if the main supplier is unable to match the rival's price or supply in sufficient quantities. This is clearly different from the clause described above in which the option rests with the supplier not the buyer. "English clauses" when properly used are a means of reducing the anti-competitive effects of exclusive purchasing agreements and used properly may be welcomed by the Commission.[129]

(d) Unreasonably large discounts

8.69 An undertaking in a dominant position may abuse that position contrary to Article 86 by granting large discounts to certain customers, which are not justified by objective reasons, in an attempt to drive out or weaken a competitor. Thus in *Tetra Pak II*[130] the Commission held that Tetra Pak had infringed Article 86 by granting "large discounts determined not by the size of the order but by the desire to eliminate competitors from certain markets ... It is all the more serious in cases where those discounts are so large that the sale makes a loss." This last sentence indicates that granting large discounts may constitute an abuse even where the prices charged are not predatory. The Court of First Instance upheld the Commission's finding,[131] applying predatory pricing text laid down in *AKZO*.[132]

(e) Non-price, cost-saving assistance

8.70 Suppliers do not always discriminate overtly between customers by granting differential discounts; they may discriminate indirectly by affording certain favoured buyers non-price related assistance, thus saving those buyers' costs. This could be an abuse contrary to Article 86 EC,[133] alternatively, the agreements for the provision of such assistance could be caught by Article 85(1) EC.[134]

128 Case 85/76 *Hoffman-La Roche* v *Commission* [1979] 3 CMLR 211; [1979] ECR 461.
129 Such clauses may be exempted under Article 1, Reg. 1984/83/EEC OJ 1983 L 173/5 on block exemption for exclusive purchasing agreements. See Commission explanatory notice OJ 1983 C 355/7 at para. 35.
130 [1992] 4 CMLR 551.
131 Case T-83/91 *Tetra-Pak* v *Commission (No. 2)* [1994] ECR II-755.
132 Case C-62/86 *AKZO* v *Commission* [1991] ECR I-3359.
133 In Case T-65/89 *BPB Industries* [1993] ECR II-389, the Court upheld the Commission's condemnation under Art. 86 of assistance given to buyers favoured because of exclusive purchases from BPB in priority of supply over non-exclusive purchasers in event of shortage of stock, even though the delay in supplying non-exclusive buyers did not exceed one day.
134 The provisions of a free ice cream freezer in return for exclusively stocking the supplier's ice cream was condemned by the European Commission as contrary to Art. 85(1) in the Art. 19(3) Notice in respect of *Van Den Bergh Foods Ltd*, OJ 1995 C211/4; exemption would only be merited if the freezer was charged for separately and did not provide a price incentive to accept exclusivity.

(8) Non-justifiable removal of discount

8.71 Just as some discounts may be unjustifiable, so the refusal to give some discounts may also be unjustifiable. In *Gosme/Martell*[135] an agreement between the producer and supplier of a brand of cognac which included provisions aimed at eliminating discounts granted to the distributor in the event of export of the cognac outside of that distributor's territory was held to be contrary to Article 85(1) as its object and effect was to protect a higher price level in the country of destination.

8.72 A similar conclusion was reached by the Commission in *Dunlop Slazenger*[136] where it was found that discounts granted to a UK wholesaler of Dunlop Slazenger's balls were reduced in pursuance to Dunlop Slazenger's agreements with its exclusive distributors after the wholesaler started supplying those products outside the UK into other Community states in which Dunlop had appointed exclusive distributors. Dunlop Slazenger sought to justify this on the ground that exclusive distributors outside the UK had to bear costs which were not incurred by UK wholesalers. The Commission rejected this argument by disputing that such costs (e.g. advertising and promotion, administrative and sales staff) were special to exclusive distributors as compared to wholesalers; the level of such costs would be determined primarily by a firm's turnover. To the extent that there were any specific costs, it was argued that these would be counterbalanced by specific benefits such as being broadly associated with the brand by way of being known as the exclusive distributor. Additionally, the Commission found that Dunlop Slazenger was not able to justify the particular reduction in discount by reference to any particular quantifiable costs: rather it was evident that the discount had been reduced by an amount calculated to remove any economic incentive for parallel exporting into other Member States.

8.73 Both these decisions were taken under Article 85(1) as the decisions were implemented as part of exclusive distribution agreements. The same reasoning would apply under Article 86 to condemn a dominant firm taking such pricing decisions unilaterally. Thus it is important for alterations in the level of discounts to be determined by reference to objective and ascertainable factors relating to increased costs, for example. The Commission has accepted that a manufacturer may discriminate in terms of the discounts it offers in favour of particular dealers who accept ancillary obligations owed to the manufacturer. In the *Eighteenth Report on Competition Policy*[137] the Commission stated: "On the other hand, there is no general obligation on a manufacturer under Community competition law to contract with another party, irrespective of the latter's place of residence. There may be valid business considerations for not supplying a particular dealer. Furthermore, the manufacturer may decide not to offer certain discounts because the party in question is not expected to provide the corresponding services, such as for example, stocking or sales promotion."

2. *UK Law*

(1) Aggregated rebates

8.74 The description of mechanisms and the discussions of surrounding arguments and conclusions set out above in respect of EC law apply with regard to the UK. The problem of collective discounting was recognised and discussed by the Monopolies and Merg-

[135] 1991 OJ L185/23.

[136] *Newitt/Dunlop Slazenger International and Others* OJ 1992 L131/32, substantially upheld by the Court of First Instance in T-43/92 *Dunlop Slazenger* v *Commission* [1994] ECR II-441.

[137] *Eighteenth Report on Competition Policy* (1988) para. 21.

ers Commission in a seminal report of 1955, *Collective Discrimination: A Report on Exclusive Dealing, Collective Boycotts, Aggregated Rebates and Other Discriminatory Trade Practices.*[138] The Report concluded that all of the types of practice referred operated against the public interest. However, it did state that in exceptional cases the practices might be justifiable. The Report was partly responsible for the cartel legislation which was subsequently enacted.[139] With respect to aggregated rebate schemes the MMC stated: "Aggregated rebates accentuate the more dangerous features of common prices and this effect generally outweighs any advantage which such rebates have in assisting the smaller manufacturers operating within the common price system."[140] However, "an aggregated rebate might in certain exceptional circumstances be an essential feature of a common price system which might itself be found to be in the public interest."[141] The judgment of the RPC in *Re Cement Makers Federation Agreement*[142] sums up the attitude of the RPC:

> "It has not been seriously argued by the federation that there is any economic justification for a rebate calculated on the total tonnage purchased by an individual purchaser or merchant from all manufacturers. There may well be economic justification for charging a lower price for large orders from a single manufacturer, and in an industry such as the cement industry, where considerable economies in cost may be obtained by working to capacity, there may also be economic justification for charging a lower price to a purchaser who places large orders for cement with a single works during the course of the year, but the effect of a rebate granted irrespective of whether orders are placed for cement with one works or forty-nine different works is to create a privileged class of purchaser and under the method of fixing price adopted by the federation and based upon the overall profits of the industry, any reduction in price to this privileged class must be at the expense of the majority of purchasers who are not entitled to the rebate."[143]

Furthermore the system has,

> "the positive disadvantage of discouraging purchasers from buying cement from non-members of the federation, thus making it more difficult for a member to resign from the federation or for a new manufacturer to enter the industry without joining the federation."[144]

8.75 Under UK law the only realistic way of legitimising such a scheme is apparently as a necessary support or adjunct to a price agreement deemed to be in the public interest. However, the two are not necessarily connected since in the *Cement* case the price agreement was upheld whereas the aggregated rebate scheme was struck down. As a general rule discounts will be acceptable where they are individually negotiated and only to the extent that the reduction in price, "corresponds broadly to savings in cost of production, delivery, or sale due to the size, regularity, or nature of the order".[145]

(2) Other discounts subject to the RTPA 1976

8.76 Agreements, perhaps in the form of standard form contracts recommended by trade associations, which advocate concerted behaviour on discounts are registrable under sec-

[138] Cmnd 9604 (1955)
[139] The Restrictive Trade Practices Act 1956, now consolidated in the RTPA 1976.
[140] *ibid.*, at para. 213. In the Monopolies and Mergers Commission Report on the *Supply of Metal Containers* (1970) HCP 6 the MMC condemned aggregated rebates on the basis that they did not equate to scale economies and led to entry barriers.
[141] *ibid.*
[142] (1961) LR 2 RP 241; [1961] 1 WLR 581.
[143] [1961] 1 WLR 581 at p. 604.
[144] *ibid.*, at p. 605.
[145] *ibid.*

tion 6(1)(a) and/or (b) and/or (c) RTPA 1976.[146] Where the agreement seeks to prevent all discounts, limit the extent of discounts, regulate the purchaser who may be given discounts, etc, then the chances of section 21(2) dispensation are remote.[147]

(3) Discounts and the Competition Act 1980: types of discount

8.77 Generally problems with discounts arise in the context of dominant concerns and companies with market power.[148] Accordingly, the OFT is most likely to review discounts under the CA 1980.[149] The list below describes some of the discount systems which may give rise to concern under the Act.

(a) Favourable terms for delivered quantities

8.78 These take the form of discounts based upon large delivery quantities being granted to favoured customers who only purchase small quantities, i.e. the discount is not justified by scale economies on delivery.

(b) Retrospective discounts or rebates

8.79 These discounts which are often called "overrider" discounts may be accorded a purchaser at the end of the year (or other discount reference period) for the fulfilment of certain conditions by the latter. The conditions are usually in the form of the achievement of predetermined sales targets. Alternatively there may be a series of ascending targets attracting ascending rates of discount. Such systems have been condemned by the Court of Justice in the *Michelin* case described above. The MMC have concluded that overriders are likely to be anti-competitive where they are operated by a supplier with significant economic power.[150]

[146] e.g. *British Reinforced Manufacturers Association* (unreported) noted DGFT Annual Report 1982, p. 98; *Aluminium Ingots* DGFT Annual Report 1984, p. 34; *National Daily and Sunday Newspapers* DGFT Annual Report 1985, p. 62.

[147] See e.g. No. S.311 Register of Restrictive Trade Practices, Agreement between *AA and Mercantile Credit* as to preferential interest rates on loans for members of the AA. Certain restrictive terms had to be removed before s. 21(2) treatment could be applied (1978); No. 3749 Register of Restrictive Trade Practices, *National Association of Musical Instrument Industry* (1975); No. S. 1735 Register of Restrictive Trade Practices *Scarborough and District Driving Instructors Association* (1985) s. 21(2) dispensation was granted only after a clause providing that discounts and special offers for driving lessons would not be below an agreed minimum level was deleted from the Association rules. *Sharman Newspapers and Peterborough Estate Agents' Association* DGFT Annual Report (1983), p. 33—Sharman Newspapers gave discounts to members of the Estate Agents Association as *quid pro quo* for those members agreeing not to place advertisements for domestic property in any journal unless it was also placed in a Sharman paper. Clearly the agreement created considerable entry and expansion barriers to rival advertising mediums who would have difficulty in tempting the estate agents to advertise with them. The OFT referred the agreement to the RPC for prohibitive orders; No. S. 1373 Register of Restrictive Trade Practices (1985) *Association of Average Adjusters*. The association in its rules categorised as a breach of the standards of fair dealing and integrity the conduct of members who allowed to any person any abatement or discount from a fee. The association explained that this restriction was necessary: "the prohibition of discounting is to ensure that an underwriter is not called upon to reimburse an assured in respect of the adjuster's charges for an amount in excess of that which has been paid to the adjuster by the assured." The OFT were unconvinced and the discounting clause had to be deleted before section 21(2) treatment could be accorded to the agreement.

[148] MMC General Report into *Discounts to Retailers* (1980–81) HC 311. See for related Ministerial statement to parliament HCDeb (1980-81) Vol. 4, No. 102, col. 269–71 (13 May 1981) reprinted DGFT Annual Report (1982), pp. 117, 118. See also OECD Report on Buying Power, *The Exercise of Market Power by Dominant Buyers* (1981).

[149] See *ibid.*, at p. 60, paras. 8.23–8.25.

[150] A variety of such discounts were condemned by the MMC in *The Supply of Matches and Disposable Lighters*, Case 1854 (1992) at paras. 7.45–7.50.

8.80 However, the tone of the MMC is not always critical of such rebate systems.[151] In their General Report on discounts the MMC concluded that discounts, the rates of which were related to the volume of the customers' purchases or the size of his accounts, were of equivocal effect. No generalised conclusions could be derived. In particular the MMC made a number of points which may be relevant in predicting OFT policy under the CA 1980.

(i) Where the discounts increase as the volume of purchases increases so that there exists an incentive to keep with a single supplier, then a barrier exits to rival suppliers wishing to sell to a customer. Often, this tying effect (of customer to single supplier) is temporary, typically three months to a year. At the end of the relevant period each buyer can without loss switch to another supplier. However this ability to compete with a supplier at the end of the accounting period will be lessened if there is a follow over effect from one accounting period to the next, e.g. discounts are 10 per cent in the first year but 12 per cent in the next year *if* the customer obtained the maximum discount in the year just past, i.e. incentives exist for the buyers to stay with one supplier from one accounting period to the next.

(ii) Overriding is unlikely to be a problem in trades where purchasers (wholesalers or retailer) need to supply their customer with a wide range of different brands. In such markets purchasers will necessarily take from many suppliers.

(iii) Overriders may be anti-competitive where applied across the whole range of a supplier's goods.[152] These discounts are given by reference to total purchasers of *all* goods and not by reference to total purchases of specific types of goods. The incentive here is for the buyer to keep taking a *range* of goods from the supplier.

(iv) Overriders may constitute a barrier to entry to new suppliers. Thus, if a purchaser is tied by the discount incentive to remain with a single supplier opportunities for rival suppliers to compete are reduced.

(v) The MMC concluded: "It appears to us that all discounts, the rates of which are related in some way to the volume of the customer's purchases or the size of his account, may have the effect of encouraging the customer to concentrate his purchases, and to this extent they may be said to have some 'tying' effect. Even a scale of delivered quantity discounts may have this effect. Overriders and other discounts conditional on the buyers specific performance may in certain circumstances have anti-competitive effects, especially when accorded y dominant suppliers, but in general overriders according to large retail buyers are to be regarded as part and parcel of competitive selling terms. They do not, in our view, cause these buyers to concentrate their purchases to a significantly greater extent that other types of discounts related to the volume of their purchases. The preferential terms which large buyers are in general able to obtain compared with small buyers appear to us

[151] e.g. MMC Report into *Frozen Foodstuffs* (1976) HC 674 MMC criticised retrospective discounts because they encouraged retailers to concentrate their purchases on a single supplier and this created entry and expansion barriers for other suppliers; in MMC Report into *Cat and Dog Foods* (1977) HC 447 similar objections were made to retrospective discounts. The MMC were also critical because the discounts were unrelated to costs. However, they concluded that the quantity of the discount (on average 0.7 per cent of gross sales) was insignificant. Compare this with the view of the European Court in *Michelin* (Case 322/81) [1985] 1 CMLR 282 at pp. 332, 333, paras. 80, 81, discounts of between 0.2–0.4 per cent were *not* insignificant when operative over a 12-month period. In MMC Report into *Ice Cream* (1979) Cmnd 7632 the MMC recommended that retrospective discounts were not anti-competitive but that they should be limited to 12 months in duration and that there should be no follow-over of the discount reference period from one annual supply contract to the next.

[152] See e.g. MMC Report into *Frozen Foodstuffs* (1976) HC 674.

to be of greater economic significance in the context of our reference than the particular form which a volume-related discount may take."[153]

8.81 In sum, the MMC has not adopted a particularly robust view towards volume related discounts. The OFT may well be conditioned in its thinking by this report.[154] Subsequent investigations by the MMC have revealed a continued pragmatic approach to discount schemes. If complainants wish to challenge such discounts and they can prove some effect on trade between the Member States of the EC, then a complaint to the Commission may prove more worthwhile or the issuance of a writ. An effect on inter-state trade may occur if foreign suppliers or importers or vendors of goods produced elsewhere in the EC are hindered, by the discount policies of major UK suppliers, in their attempts to sell their goods to the UK.

(c) Discounts for membership to suppliers' network

8.82 Many suppliers supply to authorised and non-authorised dealers. As an inducement to belong to the suppliers' network discounts over and above those according to non-authorised dealers may be granted to authorised dealers. The OFT was critical of such a system in *Still Service Ltd*[155] where the manufacturer gave additional discounts to dealers appointed by them as distributors of Still original equipment. The OFT noted that the discounts were not related to size of order or to the manufacturers production or distribution costs. It concluded that the discounts were anti-competitive, in particular it stated that they gave appointed dealers an unfair cost advantage over those not appointed and moreover they could act as an entry barrier to those dealers considering entry to the market.[156] In September 1982 to avoid a reference to the MMC the Company gave undertakings to the OFT by which, *inter alia*, it undertook not to grant any discounts which had the effect of discriminating between customers. The undertaking did allow the company to grant justifiable discounts reflecting cost economies in the suppliers production or distribution system.[157]

8.83 A novel form of membership discount was condemned by the MMC in its report on *UniChem Ltd*[158] made following a reference by the DGFT under the Competition Act 1980. UniChem was an industrial and provident society supplying pharmaceuticals to retail outlets, who were members of UniChem. Its shares were unquoted and untraded and so did not reflect the true value of the company. UniChem was in the process of conversion into a plc prior to its flotation on the stock market. As part of this scheme, it allocated shares in itself to customers based on purchases. These shares were expected to increase in value on flotation. Given the low margins (2 per cent) operating in this industry, this was a form of non-price competition, not based on improving the quality of goods or services supplied, the opportunity for which only arose because of UniChem's flotation, and which could not be reacted to by its competitors. Taking advantage of this one off opportunity to increase its market share (which it did, from 30 to 35 per cent) was held by the MMC to be an anti-competitive practice likely to operate against the public interest.[159]

153 MMC General Report into *Discounts to Retailers* (1980–81) HC 311 at p. 41, para. 6.35.

154 See DGFT Annual Report (1984), p. 36. See OFT Report, *Competition and Retailing* (a study to update information in the 1981 report of the Monopolies and Mergers Commission, *Discounts to Retailers*) (June 1985) where the OFT generally affirm the conclusions of the MMC.

155 22 July 1982, OFT investigation under the CA 1980.

156 *ibid.*, at p. 23, para. 7.16.

157 DGFT Annual Report (1982), pp. 83, 84 for text of undertaking.

158 Cm 691 (1989).

159 This share scheme was subsequently prohibited by the UniChem Ltd (Allotment of Shares) Order 1989 (S.I. 1989 No. 1061).

(d) Differential credit terms

8.84 Discrimination based upon differential credit terms is rare. However, many suppliers do not apply their credit terms strictly so that certain powerful customers may enjoy better credit terms than others. Anti-competitive discrimination can arise in such circumstances. The MMC has condemned lack of price transparency by dominant suppliers on a number of occasions.[160]

(e) Non-price, cost-saving assistance[161]

8.85 Suppliers need not necessarily discriminate overtly between customers by granting differential discounts; they may discriminate indirectly by affording certain favoured buyers non-price related advantages. Thus, for example, suppliers might provide: shelf filling, labelling and/or price marking services; technical training for staff; special delivery services; warehouse or shop equipment; goods in special containers to customer's requirement, etc. Such assistance by the supplier obviously saves the buyer money and as such can influence his costings when selling price is being determined. If the supplier enjoys dominance discrimination between buyers of this sort can affect their competitive position *inter se.*[162]

8.86 In its report into *Ice Cream,*[163] the MMC investigated the practice of freezer exclusivity, whereby the dominant suppliers of impulse ice cream provided retail outlets with free freezers *only* to be used for those suppliers' products. The MMC found that since the savings to the customer in having a free freezer were reflected in a higher price charged for ice cream supplied, this did not in practice exclude other suppliers from the impulse ice cream market and was not therefore against the public interest. Conversely, it can be presumed that if the costs of this support to customers were not offset by higher prices, this would have been condemned by the MMC.[164]

(f) Advantages not involving reduced price

8.87 Where the supplier provides financial support that is related to supply price the effect can be to reduce the buyer's costs thereby enabling him to resell the goods more cheaply. Thus, for example, suppliers might provide: advertising help; promotion fees; free guarantee services; payment for special displays, etc.[165]

(g) Advertising discounts

8.88 If a dominant suppliers accords discounts where the buyer agrees to set aside all or a specific percentage of his advertising space to the suppliers goods, the discount may be anti-competitive where rival suppliers goods are being excluded from advertising space.[166]

[160] *Postal Franking Machines* Cmnd 9747 (1986); *Steel Wire Fencing* Cm 79 (1987); *Gas* Cm 500 (1988), *Electric Contracting at Exhibition Halls in London* Cm 995 (1990).

[161] MMC General Report into *Discounts to Retailers, op. cit.*, at p. 14, paras. 4.18–4.20.

[162] *ibid.*, at p. 15, para. 4.24.

[163] Cm 2524, March 1994.

[164] Robertson and Williams argue in "An ice cream war: the law and economics of freezer exclusivity I" [1995] ECLR 7, that even if there were no price discrimination, the supply of free freezers nevertheless operates as an exclusionary practice, and that the MMC ought to have condemned it as contrary to the public interest. See also the Art. 19(3) Notice in respect of *Van Den Bergh Foods Ltd*, OJ 1995 C211/4.

[165] MMC General Report into *Discounts to Retailers, op. cit.*, at p. 15, para. 4.23.

[166] See, e.g. MMC Report into *Frozen Foodstuffs* (1976) HC 674 where MMC critical of discounts given to suppliers who agreed to devote a set percentage of cabinet space to Birds Eye products. But see *Ice Cream*, Cm 2524, March 1994.

(4) Discounts and payment of an agent's commission

8.89 The OFT has sought to combat price discrimination through discounts in the context of payment for agency services. An important and early step in OFT policy development derives from its investigation into *Yellow Pages Advertising*.[167] British Telecommunications (BT) owns Yellow Pages Directories (YP). For a number of years BT had granted a 10 per cent discount to advertising agents who placed adverts in YP. By this discount BT hoped to encourage agents to place a higher percentage of their advertising revenue with YP. The discount proved ineffective as an incentive and in early 1981 BT suddenly withdrew the discount. Advertising agents complained to the OFT alleging that the withdrawal of the discount was anti-competitive, since it meant that agents had to raise prices to their customers. The OFT, following an investigation into this and other matters, concluded that BT's sudden withdrawal of the discount was not anti-competitive though they accepted that it had exerted a "disruptive" effect upon the market. The OFT pointed out that the discount had been discriminatory since firms and others who sought to place adverts direct in YP without the intermediary services of an agent did not receive the discount. Moreover, the OFT objected to the discount system since it had led to an artificial method of payment of agents' fees. Agents would be given their commission by the media based upon the value of advertisements booked through the agency. The commission varied between 10 and 15 per cent. The OFT's comments upon this are important for any principal/agent relationship. The OFT were critical of the system whereby the principal (the advertiser) avoided paying the agent's commission because it was taken in the form of a discount from the media. The OFT raised two main objections:

(i) First, the system obscured the working of the market for agency services in a manner that is not possible if the client pays directly for the services provided to it.
(ii) Secondly, the system may be discriminatory if different commission rates or terms are obtained by different agencies from the same supplier of advertising space.

8.90 An illustration of this is seen in the MMC Report into *Foreign Package Holidays*.[168] In that case, tour operators (principals) and travel agents (agents) operated upon the basis that the agents received a 10 per cent commission on all sales of holidays calculated by reference to the list price. The operators sought to prevent the agents from offering pecuniary and other discounts to customers. The MMC were critical of this conduct and concluded that it was against the public interest. However, they accepted that operators could fix prices at which the agents should be free to offer inducements to customers where were financed out of the agents' commission. Thus the MMC indirectly supported the view that principals should not interfere in the way that agents spend their commission.

(5) Attitude of the OFT and MMC: generally

8.91 Prima facie discounts should be related to costs. However, the MMC has accepted on a number of occasions that suppliers will not be acting anti-competitively by giving non-cost related discounts where they are granted to a powerful buyer who can exert its own "muscle power". Moreover, it has also stressed, as has the OFT under the CA 1980, that discounts must have some *appreciable* effect to be anti-competitive, i.e. a *de minimis* rule applies.[169] On this point, however, it is worth noting the dictum of the Court of Justice

[167] *British Telecommunications (Pricing Policy for the Placing of Advertisements in Yellow Pages Directories)* (10 October 1984) OFT investigation under the CA 1980. See also DGFT Annual Report 1979, p. 44.
[168] Cmnd 9879, 1983.
[169] See MMC Report on *Sheffield Newspapers*, investigation under the CA 1980 (1983) Cmnd 8664. *Sheffield Newspapers* (SN) granted annual discounts of 5 per cent to estate agents on the condition that they should

in *Michelin* when confronted with the argument that the rebate gradations in question in that case were too small to be significant:

> "In this regard it must first be stated that the variation of 0.2 to 0.4 per cent as established during the procedure before the court, in the discounts based upon the attainment of the sales target is indeed slight. Nevertheless the effects of the discount under discussion can by no means be assessed solely on the basis of the percentage variation in the discounts linked to the targets. The discount system in question was based on an annual reference period. However, any system under which discounts are granted according to the quantities sold during a relatively long reference period has the inherent effect, at the end of the period, of increased pressure on the buyer to reach the purchase figure needed to obtain the discount or to avoid suffering the expected loss for the entire period. In this case the variation in the rate of discount over a year as a result of one lost order, even a small one, affected the dealer's margins of profit on the whole year's sales of Michelin heavy-vehicle tyres. In such circumstances, even quite slight variations might put dealers under appreciable pressure."[170]

Thus small rebates, depending of course on the market context, may have an appreciable effect where they operate over a long reference period.

8.92 In the final analysis it will probably be the exclusionary effect of a discount, i.e. whether it excludes rivals, which will be the determining factor.[171] Indeed, given the inherent problems encountered by competition authorities in proving anti-competitive discrimination it is unlikely that anything other than the clearest cases of discrimination by discount will be actively pursued. On the problems of proof connected with discriminatory discounts the OFT has observed:

> "The MMC report contained an analysis of the value of special terms negotiated by manufacturers with their largest retail customers compared with other customers. It noted that the data could not provide an unqualified measure of the extent of price differentiation let alone price discrimination. For example, if a trade price list does not fully reflect cost savings generated by large orders special terms negotiated in respect of such orders would be partly cost-related and therefore not wholly overstate the degree of discrimination. Also, companies applied their own methods, which may not be comparable with each other, for calculating the value of special terms. Further, it should be noted that special terms include allowances granted by manufacturers for which they may receive compensating benefits in which case such terms would not be discriminatory."[172]

E. Price Discrimination[173]

8.93 Price discrimination is often achieved by means of the grant of differential (discriminatory) discounts. In this section the practice of charging different customers different prices will

cont.
advertise in the *Property Telegraph* for at least 48 weeks out of 52. The MMC stated that the test for whether the discount was anti-competitive was whether it prevented advertiser estate agents from placing adverts in rival medias (at p. 70, para. 7.62). It concluded that, in the circumstances, a 5 per cent discount over one year was inadequate to persuade estate agents to place all of their adverts with *Property Telegraph*. Accordingly, no anti-competitive effect was found to exist.

170 Case 322/81 *Michelin* v *Commission* [1983 ECR 3461, [1985] 1 CMLR 282 at paras. 80, 81 of the judgment.

171 See *Sheffield Newspapers*, above.

172 para. 406 of its 1985 in-house study—*Competition and Retailing* (a study to up-date information in the 1981 report on the Monopolies and Mergers Commission *Discounts to Retailers*).

173 See Howe, "Policies towards market power and price discrimination in the EEC and the UK" in George and Joll (eds.) *Competition Policy in the UK and EEC* (1975) at p. 151. A broad study of the law primarily

be discussed. The discrimination here is hence similar to that in Section D above. Price discrimination may loosely be defined as the failure to charge like customers like prices based upon the true cost of supply. If supplier X charges 10 units per item to A and 8 units per item to B then X has influenced the competitive position between A and B to the former's detriment. Some dominant firms may employ price discrimination in a geographical way. Supplier X charges 10 units in the UK, 12 units in France and 14 units in Germany, the differential being designed to exploit the maximum price the market in each area will yield. The price charged in each country is not related to cost but, rather, to a profit maximising objective. On the plus side economists recognise some beneficial aspects to price discrimination. A public transport authority that grants concessionary rates to old age pensioners, youths and the unemployed might create a demand for the transport service that would not exist in the absence of the discrimination and simultaneously serve social purposes.

1. EC Law

(1) Price discrimination by dominant firms

8.94 The European Court has adopted a strict approach to price discrimination. It has held that substantial price differentials are strong evidence of discrimination in the absence of objective justification.[174] Moreover, that price discrimination is almost always an infringement of Article 86 EC where the undertaking holds a dominant position.[175] The defence argument that discrimination was forced upon the undertaking by the muscle of a dominant purchaser is generally rejected.[176] Indeed, if on the facts, a dominant purchaser did exist the supplier would not be dominant because it could not act without regard to the interests of its customer(s). By definition the (dominant) customer would be able to act independently of its suppliers.

8.95 The European Courts, and the Commission, lay great store by the need to avoid artificial divisions of the single market. Practices which reinforce national boundaries are hence viewed as particularly serious. A supplier who, having instituted artificial differential pricing in different Member States, seeks to enforce those differentials runs the risk of large fines. In *United Brands*[177] the supplier imposed price differentials for supplies of bananas. To prevent entrepreneurs buying bananas in cheap territories and transporting them to expensive areas and there undercutting the prevailing price level, the supplier contractually prohibited cross-supplies of green bananas between dealers in different Member States. The "green-banana" clause prevented cheap (unripe) bananas being sold in

cont.
as developed by the MMC. See, for a review of the varieties of form price discrimination may take, Machlup, "Characteristics and types of price discrimination" in *NBER Business Concentration and Price Policy* (Princeton University Press, 1955); Perott, "Pricing Policy and Community Rules on Competition and Free Movement of Goods" in *Yearbook of European Law* (1982), p. 207; Bishop, "Price discrimination and Hoffman La Roche" (1981) 15 JWTL 305; and, "Price discrimination under Article 86 of the EEC treaty: a comment on the UBC case" (1982) 31 ICLQ 36.

174 See e.g. Case 78/70 *Deutsche Grammophon* v *Metro* [1971] CMLR 631; [1971] ECR 487 at p. 501; Case 40/70 *Sirena* v *Eda* [1971] CMLR 260; [1971] ECR 351. See also *HOV SVZ/MCN* Commission decision of 29 March 1994 OJ 1994 L104/34.

175 Case 27/76 *United Brands* v *Commission* [1978] 1 CMLR 429; [1978] ECR 207; *AKZO* [1993] 5 CMLR 215, the Commission decision being at [1983] 3 CMLR 694 at para. 30 (interim decision); OJ 1985 L374/1 (final decision).

176 See, e.g. *Brinkhof* v *NS and DB* [1970] CMLR 264 Dutch district Court even suggested that acceptance of such pressures might be a prohibited concerted practice with the customer. Though in such a case a fine might not be imposed.

177 Above at note 175.

expensive areas; bananas cannot be transported in a ripe state. By this clause the supplier sought to maintain the differentials. The Court held this practice to be an abuse of a dominant position.

8.96 As a general proposition prices should be related to cost. Thus differentials should be justified by reference to scale economies and other savings enjoyed by the supplier simply because a dominant undertaking differentiate prices on a state by state basis is not necessarily unlawful. It should be an objective justification that a lower margin (and hence a lower price) was all that could be obtained in certain national markets. Provided no steps are taken to preclude or deter parallel trade such differentials are not abusive. However, in *Tetra Pak II*[178] the Commission held that Tetra Pak had infringed Article 86 by charging prices for its cartons which varied considerably from one Member State to another. The Commission found that the price differences could not be explained in economic terms particularly since "raw materials— the prices for which are determined on a world scale—account for more than 70 per cent of the cost of cartons" and that transport costs werenegligible. The Commission also held that Tetra Pak guilty of price discrimination regarding the sale of its machines: "the major price differences for Tetra Pak machines observed between the Member States are not the result of objective economic factors. Even more than in the case of cartons, the transport costs of machines are quire negligible in relation to the market value of the product ... these price differences can be explained only by the system of national market compartmentalization made possible by Tetra Pak's dominant position." The Court of Justice of First Instance upheld the Commission's findings, no objective justification having been advanced by Tetra Pak for the differences in prices.[179]

8.97 Discrimination may occur through the application of a single price to customers who are different and justify different treatment. The most common example of this is found in base point or delivered price systems. These are discussed at paras. 8.226–8.237.

8.98 A dominant undertaking which adopts price discrimination in a very selective manner with an intent to exclude a rival by offering very favourable terms to the rival's customers but not offering equally favourable terms to normal customers almost certainly infringes Article 86. Indeed the offering of excessively low prices to certain categories of customer, coupled to an exclusionary design, comes perilously close to predatory pricing as the *AKZO* case examined below at paras. 8.120–8.127 on predatory pricing demonstrates. Such behaviour is likely to attract heavy financial penalties from the Commission.

8.99 It is also possible that firms in a joint dominant position may abuse that position contrary to Article 86 by engaging in price discrimination. In *NALOO*[180] the Commission upheld in part a complaint lodged by a trade association of small mines. The complaints alleged, *inter alia*, that its purchasers—the electricity generators in the UK—had discriminated against its members in favour of British Coal Corporation (BCC) as to the price paid for coal purchased. The complaint arose in the context of new contracts for the supply of steam coal to power stations in England and Wales which came into operation between BCC and National Power (NP) and PowerGen (PG) on 1 April 1990 under

178 [1992] 4 CMLR 552.

179 Case T-83/91 *Tetra Pak* v *Commission (No. 2)* [1994] ECR II-755 upheld on appeal by the ECJ in Case C-333/94, judgment of 14 November 1996. See also the Commission Decision in *HOV SCZ/MCN (Deutsche Bahn)* OJ 1994 L104/34, where the charging of higher prices for rail transport to and from Dutch and Belgian ports than those for German ports was found not to be objectively justified. The Commission therefore condemned it as an abuse; see also the Commission's *Twenty-fourth Report on Competition Policy* (1994), para. 210.

180 Commission Decision 23 May 1991 [1993] 4 CMLR 615, appealed to CFI, T-57/91 *NALOO* v *Commission*, judgment of 24 September 1996.

which the latter agreed to buy over 90 per cent of their coal requirements from BCC at a particular price. The prices and terms subsequently offered to the small mines by the electricity companies were significantly less favourable than those offered to BCC. The Commission held that NP and PG were the only purchasers of coal for electricity generation and were, therefore, jointly dominant as buyers of this coal. The differences between the terms offered to the small mines and those offered to BCC in accordance with the new contracts constituted an unlawful discrimination contrary to Article 86.

(2) Price discrimination and Article 85

8.100 Price discrimination is invariably a function of dominance. Companies not in a dominant position are free to discriminate at will provided such is the result of unilateral decision making. However, where rivals agree as to prices then discrimination may result from the agreement. In *Meldoc*[181] the Commission condemned an agreement between milk producers in the Netherlands to charge low prices to selective customers in the Netherlands in order to make it worth their while not to import cheaper Belgian milk. The losses were shared between the members. Thus, a trade association whose members adopt base point or delivered pricing may infringe Article 85. Similarly, an agreement whereby competitors agree *not* to give discounts discriminates against purchasers who deserve discounts, e.g. because they buy in bulk, or collect the goods ex-works rather than have them delivered, etc. Where members of a trade association seek to maintain joint control of a market by selective rebates to customers which have the effect of excluding new customers, an unlawful agreement contrary to Article 85 might arise.[182]

(3) Product differentiation and price discrimination

8.101 If price discrimination is carried out geographically, with different prices in different Member States, it would be economically rational in most circumstances for goods to be traded across borders to take advantage of these differences. However, it may be that the producer of such goods exploits differences in trade names or in the composition of the goods to ensure that what is marketed in one state may not be allowed onto the market in another state. This may be due to the consumers' lack of familiarity with different brand names or to differing national rules on composition. The Commission has indicated that undertakings which take advantage of this and deliberately exploit product differentiation to maintain price differentials may be regarded as in breach of the competition provisions of the Treaty. This has been applied in the case of a non-dominant distribution network,[183] but the principles would be equally applicable to a dominant undertaking's policy.

2. *UK Law*

(1) Price discrimination and the MMC

8.102 The MMC has only condemned price discrimination where practised by concerns with market.[184] It has objected where the practice has been used, or has had the effect, of cre-

[181] OJ 1986 L348/50 [1989] 4 CMLR 853.

[182] e.g. *Union de Remorquage et de Sauvetage* v *Schelde Sleepvaarbedriff* [1965] CMLR 251 (Commercial Court, Antwerp).

[183] *Zera Montedison/Hinkens Stähler, Twenty-third Report on Competition Policy* (1993), para. 242.

[184] See e.g. MMC Report on *Asbestos* (1972–73) HC 3 discrimination not objectionable since supplier held insufficient market power; but cf. MMC Report on *Man Made Cellulosic Fibre* (1968) HC 130 where the MMC rejected justifications from a near monopoly firm for its discriminatory pricing. See also MMC Report on *Electrical Equipment for Vehicles* (1963) HC 21 at paras. 990 *et seq.*

ating entry and expansion barriers to other suppliers. Thus, if X, a dominant concern, charges discriminatory low prices to customer Y as a specific inducement to keep Y "sweet" and prevent rival suppliers selling to him then the practice has an exclusionary effect and is anti-competitive.

8.103 In an investigation of British Gas's pricing policy,[185] discrimination on prices for gas based on how easily a customer could switch fuels was condemned. It rejected British Gas's argument that this was merely responding to the competitive pressure brought to bear upon it by its customers, as this ignored the fact that it was a dominant supplier, able to charge those who were unable to switch fuels easily what were in effect arbitrary prices. British Gas was also indulging in exclusionary tactics, selectively discounting to seek to prevent new entrants to the gas supply market. The MMC's recommendation was to encourage greater price transparency through publication of prices by British Gas, together with measures to encourage new entrants into the gas supply market.

8.104 Similar tactics adopted by dominant supplier Rentokil in *Pest Control Services*,[186] which was the only national supplier of such services, were found to be against the public interest by the MMC. However, as in *Gas* it could only recommend price transparency through Rentokil fully itemising its quotations and bills to customers to enable customers to look for cheaper local suppliers, while hope that a competing national service would develop to provide competition.

8.105 Conversely, a refusal to discriminate may also be condemned if it prevents different costs being reflected. In *Credit Card Services*,[187] the MMC disapproved of the refusal of credit card companies Visa and Mastercard to allow traders to charge customers different prices for using those credit cards to pay. This refusal meant that effectively non-credit card users were required to subsidise those who chose to pay by credit card.[188]

8.106 In *Reprographic Equipment*, the MMC found that price discrimination was not anti-competitive.[189] Rank Xerox dominated the copier market. It discriminated in charges for rental of the machines by increasing the charge with the number of copies taken from the machine. The rate of increase in charges was not related to the increase in use of the machine by the customer, nor was it related to the increased cost of supply and servicing that would occur with greater use. Thus, more intensive users paid proportionally more per sheet than did less intensive users. However, this discrimination was considered justifiable. The MMC accepted that it was necessary for intensive users to subsidise less intensive users on the basis that if the latter were forced to pay the full cost the charge would have been prohibitive and use of the machines would have been discouraged.

8.107 One of the most comprehensive statement of principle made by the MMC on discriminatory pricing is as follows:

> "The prices to individual buyers should be related to the cost of supplying them and to the value of the business to the supplier. Since distribution costs vary with the quantities delivered the most appropriate method, and the one most conducive to efficient distribution, is a suitable scale of discounts related to the size or value of individual consignments. We would, however, see no objection in the circumstances of this industry to terms which also, if a manufacturer so wished, give some recognition to the size of the whole order (covering more than one consignment) or to the value of the total business which a buyer places with him.

[185] MMC Report in *Gas* Cm 500 (1988).
[186] MMC Report, Cm 302 (1988).
[187] Cm 718, (1989).
[188] After a period of consultation, the Secretary of State acted on the MMC's recommendation rule by the Credit Cards (Price Discrimination) Order 1990 (S.I. 1990 No. 2159).
[189] MMC Report on the *Supply of Indirect Electrostatic Reprographic Equipment* (1976) HC 47.

> We would also see no objection to the provision of different scales of discounts for wholesalers, retailers and other buyers if the manufacturers considered it desirable to give wholesalers and retailers some extra reward in recognition of their part in selling and distributing. We can see no reason, however, for any differentiation in treatment between one class of user buyer and another which is not related to the cost or value of the business to the supplier."[190]

(2) Price discrimination and the OFT

8.108 In *British Railways Board (Facilities for Car Hire and Advertising of Self-drive Vehicle Hire at Railway Stations)*[191] the OFT investigated BR's policy of allowing one car-hire firm an exclusive right to provide services at BR stations. The selected firm—Godfrey Davis (Car Hire) Ltd—set prices according to a costing calculated on all of the stations. The firm stated that if they had been forced to price their services by reference to costs at each individual station, then approximately 50 per cent of the stations would have been unprofitable. Thus, by charging a price related to overall cost and not individual cost the car hire firm discriminated against customers at profitable stations who subsidised customers at unprofitable stations.[192] The OFT apparently did not object to this pricing system.[193] The OFT adopts a similarly pragmatic line to that of the MMC.

F. Predatory Pricing

1. *Legal and Economic Context*

8.109 Predatory pricing is usually defined in terms of a dominant firm selling below cost. It is prohibited because of the concern that the dominant company sacrifices present revenues with the purpose of driving rivals from the market and then recouping its losses through higher profits earned later in the absence of competition. Equally, predatory below cost pricing may be used to deter potential entrants from the market. Below cost selling by non-dominant companies is not anti-competitive save in circumstances where below cost or otherwise very low prices are the result of an agreement, concerted practice or trade association decision or recommendation. The cost level is generally viewed as an important element in analysis because it is assumed that there can be few economic explanations for selling at a loss other than a predatory design on competitors. However, a price above cost can in principle exert similar predatory or exclusionary effects and competition authorities generally accept that in exceptional circumstances an above cost but excessively low price may be anti-competitive if a predatory intention on the part of the undertaking concerned can be proven. In cases of above cost pricing, the issue is complicated by the difficulty of differentiating a predatory price from a highly competitive price. Many complaints alleging predatory pricing turn our to be no more than very competitive pricing which the complainant is unable to match. Indeed, an ongoing concern of the

[190] MMC Report on the *Supply of Electric Lamps* (1968) HC 4 at para. 81.

[191] 18 May 1983. See also the informal investigation into *Scottish Milk Marketing Board* DGFT Annual Report (1982), p. 103.

[192] *ibid.*, at p. 30 para. 7.2 (the complainant to the OFT in this case was not a customer alleging price discrimination but a rival car hire firm denied access to BR stations).

[193] *ibid.*, at pp. 37, 38, at paras. 8.14–8.17. The main concern of the OFT was with the entry barrier caused by BR's exclusive grant of rights to Godfrey Davis. It concluded that the exclusive grant had an insignificant effect upon competition.

competition authorities generally is that challenges to low prices may chill aggressive competitive pricing strategies and stifle innovative price schemes.

2. *Examples of Justifiable Below Cost Prices*

8.110 Not every price charged or quoted by a dominant undertaking that is below cost is necessarily predatory though there seems to be a strong prima facie presumption that it is predatory. The following are examples of below cost prices that may be justifiable.

(1) Introductory offers to build demand

8.111 A firm entering a new market sells below cost for a relatively short period of time to build demand especially in the case of a new product or service (see discussion of the *SUNL* case, at para. 8.130).

(2) Sale of old stock

8.112 A firm that is changing its product design or is ending production of a particular model may wish to unload residual stock quickly so as to clear the stores for the new lines. Such a firm may decide that it is worth selling at below cost in order to offload the stock in the shortest amount of time. This may be the case in respect of products with a short life span where the off-loading of old stock will not create an obstacle to the marketing of its newer replacement.

(3) The pricing of individual products or services in the context of an overall product or service

8.113 Firms may determine price according to the cost of producing the whole product with the result that individual constituents of the overall product may be imprecisely costed. This problem arises, for example, in the pricing of air fares for particular route segments when examined in the context of a carriers total route system. The problem is particularly relevant in respect of the "hub and spoke" networks that air carriers operate. "Hub and spoke" networks allow carriers to augment the loads they carry with passengers who start or end their journey at a point other than the origin or destination cities of a particular non-stop flight. An *ex post facto* evaluation of the fares measured against the costs incurred on a particular route segment or "spoke" might reveal that the portion of the overall network was being priced below cost. A small carrier operating only on that route segment would need to cover all of its costs from revenue derived from that route and might conclude that its large rival was engaged in predatory pricing. The "hub and spoke" carriers, however, would dispute that its overall network was profitable and its intentions were aimed at profit maximisation not predation.[194]

(4) Very low marginal costs

8.114 The "hub and spoke" example above demonstrates one of the problems inherent in viewing cost as a sole indicator of liability. Another issue, factually related to the "hub and spoke" example, stems from the exceptionally low marginal costs that sometimes arise in industries whose products and services are perishable. Marginal costs in the transportation industry are for this reason very low. Once a trailer or boxcar or airplane is set to

[194] See Business Review letter US Department of Justice Antitrust Division (20 December 1984) *British Airways*; see also Seiden, "Predatory pricing in the transportation industry: one man's discount is another man's war", paper to the Public Utility section of the American Bar Association (14 March 1985, Washington).

depart for its destination the marginal cost of adding freight or extra passengers is very low. To carriers with an incentive to fill capacity it is economical to offer reduced fares. Hence, the low fares offered by airlines based on the time or date of departure, or the early or late purchase of the ticket or the limited number of available seats may also be explicable by reference to low marginal costs.

(5) Below cost pricing by firms lacking market power

8.115 Since it is generally presumed that dominant firms sell below cost in order to exclude competitors and thereafter reap dividends in the form of supra-competitive monopoly profits, it follows that a non-dominant firm who can never maximise its price advantage cannot be acting anti-competitively if it sells below cost. There will always be effective competition to prevent the price cutter from reaping monopoly profits. However, in *Tetra Pak II*[195] the Commission decided that Tetra Pak had engaged in predatory pricing in Italy in relation to non-aseptic cartons, which had been sold below average variable cost over a period of seven years, even though the Commission found that Tetra Pak was not dominant in the market for non-aseptic cartons. However, Tetra Pak was found to be dominant in the market for aseptic cartons and the Commission concluded that this position enabled the company to engage in predatory pricing in the neighbouring market for non-aseptic cartons. Given that one rationale for predatory pricing is the intention on the part of the predatory undertaking to increase prices upon "eviction" from the market of the rival that it is targeting, it is difficult to see how this could be achieved in the absence of dominant market power in the non-aseptic carton market.[196] However, since the Court of First Instance in *Tetra Pak (No. 2)* has found that recoupment is not a necessary part of the test for predatory pricing under Article 86,[197] it was not receptive to such an argument and upheld the Commission's finding.

3. Methods of Calculated Cost

8.116 Since a critical component of predation is the identification of cost, it is obviously important to have a widely accepted definition. The *AKZO* decision discussed below under EC law provides valuable guidance as to the positions of the European Courts and the Commission. American law, where the issue has been widely considered, is informative and a brief summary of US law is given below. A number of measures of cost may be identified:

(a) Average total cost (ATC): ATC is the sum of fixed costs and total variable costs, divided by output. Fixed costs represent the sum of all costs which do not vary with output; total variable costs represent the sum of all costs which do vary with changes in output.[198]

(b) Average variable cost (AVC): AVC is the sum of all variable costs divided by output. Variable costs are those which change with output. AVC is generally viewed as a workable substitute for short run marginal costs (SRMC). SRMC represents the increment to total cost that results from producing an additional unit of output where some outputs or production are variable and others are fixed. SRMC is an

195 [1992] 4 CMLR 551.

196 The decision is criticised by V. Korah, "The paucity of economic analysis in the EEC decisions on competition—*Tetra Pak II*" [1993] CLP 148.

197 Case T-83/91 *Tetra Pak* v *Commission (No. 2)* [1994] ECR II-755, para. 150. Appeal dismissed on this point by the Court of Justice in its judgment of 14 November 1996, Case C-333/94 P.

198 For discussion of how American courts determine which costs are fixed and which are variable see *William Inglis and Sons Baking Co* v *ITT Continental Baking Co* 668 F.2d 1014 at pp. 1036–1038 (9th Cir. 1981).

economic concept that cannot effectively be derived by conventional accounting methods. American courts have accepted AVC as an acceptable evidentiary proxy for SRMC.

(c) Fully distributed cost (FDC): FDC is an accounting concept focusing on the historical costs reflected in the books of the company. FDC requires an allocation of the firm's total costs to the firm's various product lines. Ostensibly tempting, FDC has received almost universal criticism in American courts as inherently arbitrary and lacking a proper economic basis.[199]

8.117 Bearing these measures of cost in mind, the legal position prevailing in American antitrust may now be considered. The most widely accepted test is known as the Areeda–Turner test.[200] This establishes conclusive presumptions that prices are either lawful or predatory and unlawful depending on the relationship between those prices and certain measures of the firm's costs. Under this test, a price at or above ATC should be conclusively deemed lawful irrespective of the motives of the firm setting that price. The logic behind the presumption is that a firm pricing at or above ATC covers its total costs with total revenues. Such a price squeezes out *only* less efficient rivals who are unable to produce equivalent goods or services at as low (efficient) a cost as the dominant firm. Essentially, competition by efficiency of costs is competition by merit. More controversial, though none the less attracting a fairly wide measure of support, is the contention that a price at or above reasonably anticipated SRMC or its evidential proxy AVC should *also* be conclusively presumed lawful. The Areeda–Turner theory recognises that *more* efficient producers might be squeezed out by such pricing because they have less staying power than the dominant firm. None the less, pricing as low as marginal cost is considered desirable because it produces the competitive and socially optimal result in the short run. Pricing below SRMC or AVC is presumed predatory and anti-competitive.

8.118 The Areeda–Turner test is the most widely accepted legal test of predation in American law. However, recently a less black and white test has been adopted by the Ninth Circuit Court. This test is known as the *Inglis–Transamerica* test.[201] According to this test, the idea that courts should distinguish lawful from unlawful pricing solely by reference to cost/price analysis has been rejected. Instead, to establish predatory pricing a plaintiff must prove that the defendant's price could eliminate or discipline competitors and thereby enable the defendant to reap, in the long term, the benefits of monopoly power. This test is based on the specific economic effect of the defendant's prices. However, it does not discard cost/price

[199] See e.g. *Southern Pacific Communications* v *AT&T* 740 F.2d 980 (D.C. Cir. 1984); *Northeastern Telephone Co* v *AT&T* 651 F.2d 76 at pp. 89, 90 (2d Cir. 1981); *Aeronautical Radio Inc* v *FCC* 642 F.2d 1221 at pp. 1236-1247 (D.C. Cir. 1980); *MCI Communications* v *AT&T* 740 F.2d 1081 at pp. 1116-1118 (7th Cir. 1983).

[200] Areeda and Turner, "Predatory pricing and related practices under section 2 of the Sherman Act 1898" *Harvard Law Review* 697 (1975). See for analysis and other views Bork, *The Antitrust Paradox* (1978), pp. 144–160; Posner, *Antitrust Law: An Economic Perspective* (1978), pp. 189–196; Baumol, "Quasi-permanence of price reductions: a policy for prevention of predatory pricing" 89 *Yale L.J.* 1 (1979); Scherer, "Predatory pricing and the Sherman Act: a comment" 289 *Harvard Law Review* 869 (1977). See further *Hanson* v *Shell Oil* 541 F.2d 1352 (9th Cir. 1976); *Janich Bros.* v *IBM* 613 F.2d 727 (9th Cir. 1979).

[201] See *Transamerica Computer Co* v *IBM* 698 F.2d 1377 (9th Cir.); and, *William Inglis and Sons Baking Co* v *ITT Continental Baking Co* 668 F.2d 1014 in particular at pp. 1032-1036 (9th Cir. 1981). But cf. *Barry Wright Corp* v *ITT Grinnel Corp* 724 F.2d 227 at pp. 233–236 (1st Cir. 1983) which rejected the *Transamerica* test and held that prices above both AVC and ATC are conclusively presumed lawful even if they are not profit maximising. For the most recent comprehensive survey of US case law, see Areeda and Turner's *Antitrust Law*, (as updated by Areeda and Hovenkamp's annual supplements) para. 711.

analysis altogether. Cost/price analysis determines the burden of proofs. First, if the plaintiff proves that the defendant's prices were below AVC or SRMC then prima facie it has established predatory pricing and the defendant can only rebut the presumption with a justification not based on the destructive or exclusionary effect of the prices. Secondly, if the plaintiff proves that the defendant's prices were below ATC but above AVC, then the plaintiff bears the legal burden or proving that the defendant's pricing was predatory in the sense used above. Finally, if the plaintiff cannot prove that the defendant's prices were below ATC, then the plaintiff must prove by clear and convincing evidence that the defendant's pricing was predatory in the sense used above. The *Inglis–Transamerica* test recognises that, in exceptional circumstances, an above cost price may be predatory.

8.119 In terms of the balance between the two tests in American law it is probably true that the Areeda–Turner test holds sway[202] though the *Inglis–Transamerica* test may be useful in cases where the defendant wishes to raise direct evidence of economic justification for the below cost pricing. The *Inglis–Transamerica* test is hence more pragmatic than the Areeda-Turner test where the illegal/legal divide appears more black and white and less conducive to arguments about justification. The Court of Justice in *AKZO* (discussed below) has adopted a test nearer to the *Inglis–Transamerica* test, though not so clearly articulated in terms of presumptions.

4. EC Law

(1) Legal context

8.120 Complaints of predatory pricing are relatively uncommon in EC law. The leading decision is that in *AKZO*[203] where the Court upheld the Commission's imposition of a fine on AKZO for its predatory behaviour in respect of a small rival, ECS. This decision is analysed at length below.[204] The facts may be recited briefly. ECS manufactured organic peroxide benzoyl, a product utilised in flour milling and as a catalyst in other chemical processes, for example the manufacture of polymers. ECS traditionally used organic peroxide benzoyl as part of its flour milling processes as an additive. It subsequently decided to expand output and commence marketing the chemical to customers in the wider polymer industry. This expansion brought ECS into direct rivalry with AKZO, the major EC producer. AKZO, in an attempt to eliminate ECS as a competitor, first threatened and then implemented deep price cuts in the sales of the product to customers in the commercial baking sector. This had the effect of inducing the customers of ECS to switch to AKZO for supplies. In 1979 ECS successfully sought an *ex parte* injunction against AKZO

202 See *Brooke* v *Brown & Williamson* 113 S Ct 2578 (1993).

203 Case C-62/86 *AKZO Chemie BV* v *Commission* [1991] ECR I-335a; [1993] 5 CMLR 215. See also, Yamey (1972) 15 *Journal of Law and Economics* 129. Professor Yamey was instructed as an expert witness for AKZO. Apparently he gave a view during oral evidence on the concept of predation which contradicted the view he expressed in the leading article noted above. The Commission were clearly sceptical of his evidence on this basis (paras. 78, 79 or the decision). Moral: ensure that expert witnesses have not written leading articles in the past which contradict current testimony. See [1983] 3 CMLR 694 (for the interim decision) and [1986] 3 CMLR 213 (for the Commission's final decision).

204 See L.M.H. Martinez, "Predatory pricing literature under European competition law: the *AKZO* case" LIEL 1993/2, 95. See also *Macron/Angus* [1987] 3 CMLR 715 where, following a complaint by Macron Fire Protection Ltd, the Commission investigated the behaviour of Angus Fire Armour Ltd, which held about 70 per cent of the UK fire hose market. Macron alleged Angus had abused its dominant position by adopting pricing policies designed to limit or exclude Macron as a competitor in that market. The Commission considered this policy was potentially abusive and Angus undertook to comply in future with the competition rules in the Treaty, in particular, by avoiding unfair pricing. Macron, having received an *ex gratia* payment from Angus, formally withdrew its complaint, and the file was closed without a decision.

in the High Court in London restraining the latter from reducing its selling prices. The case was subsequently settled with AKZO giving an undertaking not to reduce its normal selling price with the intention of eliminating ECS as a rival. AKZO also paid the legal costs of ECS. Despite these proceedings AKZO was alleged to have continued its predatory campaign against ECS. Accordingly, following a complaint by ECS to the Commission, the latter adopted an interim decision against AKZO prohibiting it from selling at a price which failed to incorporate a substantial profit margin. AKZO subsequently failed to comply with the decision and this resulted in the final Commission decision which imposed a (then) very heavy fine of ECU10 million. The Court substantially upheld the Commission's decision, though, it reduced the fine to ECU7.5 million.

A number of very important conclusions may be drawn from both the judgment of the Court and the Commission's decision. These are examined below.

(a) The test for predatory pricing[205]

8.121 The Commission was presented by AKZO with a test of predatory pricing which bore many resemblances to the Areeda_Turner formula (above). Although the Commission rejected the precise arguments put forward by AKZO, the decision issued by the Commission and upheld by the Court expounded a test of predatory pricing which certainly involves a detailed cost/price analysis. In the final outcome whether a price is predatory or not will depend not only upon cost/price analysis but also upon other factors such as exclusionary effect, actual predatory intent, and the perceptions of victims and others of the dominant concern's behaviour. The Court adopted this approach of the Commission, albeit in a somewhat simplified fashion. It seemed more concerned than the Commission to apply clear cut rules for determining predatory pricing while, at the same time, acknowledging that predatory pricing might require proof of intent where the price in question was above a certain measure of cost. The assessment given below employs an analytical structure based upon cost/price analysis, but taking into account other factors. The relevance of other factors is demonstrated by the Commission's decision in *Napier Brown–British Sugar.*[206] The pricing policy of British Sugar regarding its sales of retail sugar since Napier Brown's entry onto the retail sugar market was held to be abusive. The Commission first of all took a cost-based analysis approach comparing the price British Sugar charged for raw materials and that which it charged for the derived product and concluded that the difference was insufficient to reflect British Sugar's own costs of transformation. This application of a cost/price analysis was controversial since the Commission did not compare the price charged for the derived product with the *cost* of the raw material but, rather, with the *price charged for the raw product to competitors.* As British Sugar was found to be in a dominant position it is conceivable that the price it charged competitors for the raw product was excessive with the result that the price charged for the derived product need not necessarily be predatory. The Commission then went on to hold that this constituted an abuse given that "the intention or natural and foreseeable consequences of the maintenance of this pricing policy by British Sugar would be the removal of Napier Brown from the British retail sugar market". As to the presumptions to be applied at different measures of cost the analysis of the AKZO decision is informative.

8.122 *(i) Price below average variable cost (AVC)* The Commission in AKZO held that while the quoting of a price below AVC was not conclusively abusive when made by a dominant

[205] See at paras. 72–87 of the decision.
[206] [1990] 4 CMLR 196.

concern, it would almost certainly be presumptively so unless the dominant concern justified its behaviour on objective economic grounds which were wholly unrelated to a predatory design. The examples given in the introduction above may represent instances of justifiable below price selling. The Court on appeal held[207] that

> "Prices below average variable costs (i.e. those that vary in light of quantities produced) through which an undertaking tries to eliminate a competitors must be considered to be abusive, a dominant undertaking has indeed no interest to practise such prices other than to eliminate competitors in order to increase its prices by benefiting from its monopoly position, since each sale entails a loss, namely the total of the fixed costs (i.e. those that remain constant whichever the quantities manufactured), and at least part of the variable costs relating to the unit produced."

Thus a bright line is established whereby prices below AVC are held to be predatory without proof of any other matter.

8.123 *(ii) Price above AVC but below average total costs (ATC)* In *AKZO*, AKZO predicated its defence upon the argument that a price above AVC (as the accepted proxy for marginal cost) was legal since it was economically justified. The argument ran as follows. Only less efficient firms will be harmed by pricing above AVC. Further (presumably as an alternative) that a price cut would not be abusive where it was profit maximising in the short term for the leading firm even if at the same time it would inevitably damage the business of a smaller (equally efficient) rival. Emphasis was hence to be placed upon the conception of the leading firm of its own short-term best interests rather than upon the intention of the firm with regard to competitors. The Commission rejected both these contentions and in particular the idea that the test of abuse turned upon a mechanical application of a *per se* test based upon marginal or variable cost which adopted as its basis a static and short-term perception of efficiency. In answering AKZO's arguments the Commission mentioned five factors. First, Article 3(f) of the Treaty which lays down broad objectives for competition rules embraces wider macroeconomic and microeconomic criteria than efficiency alone. Secondly, AKZO's formulation ignores the longer-term strategic exclusionary considerations which underlie sustained price cutting. Thirdly, the AKZO formula overlooks (conveniently) the fact that such behaviour may involve price discrimination which itself may infringe Article 86 EEC apart from any consideration of predation. Thus AKZO's policy discriminated between customers of the product as between those benefiting from AKZO's low prices (i.e. the customers of ECS) and those not so benefiting. Fourthly, the AKZO argument that only less efficient competitors suffer was incorrect: "it is not only the 'less efficient' firms which will be harmed if a dominant firm sells below its total cost but above variable cost. If prices are taken to a level where a business does not cover its total costs, smaller but possibly more efficient firms will eventually be eliminated and the larger firm with the greater economic resources—including the possibly of cross-subsidisation—will survive".[208] Fifthly with regard to the (alternative) "profit maximising" argument the Commission stated that the additional objection lay that "it would excuse almost any behaviour, no matter how destructive of competition, if it served the dominant producer's short-term interests".[209] The Court adopted this approach but only referring specifically to predatory intent:[210] "Prices below

[207] [1991] ECR I-3359; [1993] 5 CMLR 215, paras. 71 and 77 of the decision.
[208] para. 78 of the decision.
[209] [1991] ECR I-3359; [1993] 3 CMLR 215, para. 72.
[210] *ibid.*, paras. 73 and 79 of the decision.

the average total costs which include fixed and variable costs, but in excess of the average of variable costs must be considered to be abusive when they are fixed in the context of a plan which has for its purpose to eliminate a competitor. These prices can indeed exclude from the market companies which may be as efficient as the dominant undertaking but which by reason of their lower financial capacity are incapable of resisting this competition." However, the Court did not rule out application of other factors beyond intent in establishing abuse, since it emphasised that these criteria were the criteria relevant to the facts of the case presently before it.[211]

8.124 *(iii) Price at ATC or above* Obviously, a firm who genuinely covers its total costs and thereby earns a profit will be less susceptible to a successful charge of predation than a dominant firm whose pricing is set at sub-ATC levels. None the less, the Commission considers that there may exist situations where an above-ATC level will prove predatory. The Commission thus made the pertinent comments in AKZO:

> "The dominant firm has an interest in achieving its aim at the lowest cost to itself (thus in the present case AKZO concentrated its price cuts on the flour additives market which was extremely important to ECS but of relatively minor significance to AKZO in the context of its overall organic peroxides business). The important element is the rival's assessment of the aggressor's determination to frustrate its expectations, for example as a rate of growth or attainable profit margins, rather than whether or not the dominant firm covers its own costs. There can thus be an anti-competitive object in price-cutting whether or not the aggressor sets its price above or below its own costs (in one or other meaning of the term),"[212]

The point is thus made that a dominant firm's decision to set prices at or near ATC may represent a red warning light to the rival that the dominant firm has the financial strength (whether derived from the ability to cross-subsidise or otherwise) to sustain a price war over a period of time long enough to effectively eliminate it. This perception by the "victim" may itself exert a disciplining force on competition. It may equally constitute an entry barrier to potential rivals who are scared away by the evident threat of confrontation or an expansion barrier to existing firms who will refrain from expanding output and posing a threat to the dominant undertaking. The Court did not discuss this in the AKZO other than leaving the issue open by implication.

8.125 *(iv) Recoupment* It is a feature of US law that in order to demonstrate predation, it is necessary to prove that the predator would be able to recoup the expense of predation after elimination of the would-be competitor.[213] This is because any other strategy is irrational: the costs of predation are not recouped, so it is irrational to predate. The *AKZO* judgment makes no mention of recoupment, and the Court of First Instance, upholding the Commission's findings of predation in *Tetra Pak (No. 2)* held that there was no recoupment requirement to establishing predation under the *AKZO* test.[214]

(b) The meaning of variable and fixed costs

8.126 Given the importance of cost/price analysis firms will need to have guidance upon which ingredients of cost are to be allocated as fixed and which as variable. This distinction is

[211] *ibid.*, para. 94.
[212] *ibid*, para 79 of the Commission decision.
[213] See *Matsushita* v *Zenith* 475 US 574 (1986), *Brooke* v *Brown & Williamson* 113 S Ct 2578 (1993).
[214] Case T-83/91 *Tetra Pak* v *Commission (No. 2)* [1994] ECR II-755, para. 150. This was confirmed on further appeal to the Court of Justice, Case C-333/94 P *Tetra Pak* v *Commission (No. 2)*, judgment of 14 November 1996.

critical in determining AVC and ATC (see the definition above of these concepts). The *AKZO* decision demonstrates clearly the strict approach of the Commission to the allocation of costs as between fixed and variable. AKZO argued that it had maintained its price levels at above AVC. However the Commission, on an analysis of AKZO's costings, concluded that the firm had adopted an inaccurate and artificial definition of variable costs with which to work. The Commission accordingly readjusted AKZO's definition of variable cost *adding* in to the formula cost components for labour, repair and maintenance. Having added these ingredients the Commission concluded that AKZO had, in some instances, been selling at as much as 50 per cent below AVC. It is important to understand which cost components the Commission view as fixed and which they view as variable. In the view of the Commission fixed costs (i.e. those which remain constant in spite of changes in output) included: management overheads, depreciation, interest and property taxes. This list is in line with the Areeda–Turner enumeration which excludes from variable cost only: capital cost (interest on debt, etc) attributable to investment inland, plant and equipment; property and other taxes unaffected by output; and, depreciation on plant attributable to obsolescence. The Commission viewed variable costs (i.e. those which vary with changes in output) as including: materials, energy, direct labour, supervision, repair and maintenance, and royalties. The Court accepted this with the exception of labour, which it found on the facts not to have varied with output and thus to have been a fixed cost. It stressed that categorisation of these items as fixed or variable depended on examining the facts of each case, not on a precise legal definition.[215] It is worth noting that the Commission and the Court accept the definitions of total cost and average cost employed in US law, i.e. total cost is the sum of fixed and variable costs; average costs is total cost divided by output; and marginal cost is the addition to cost resulting from the production of an additional unit of output.

(c) Conclusions

8.127 The *AKZO* case answers many questions. It does not, however, provide great legal security for dominant concerns seeking a predictable legal basis upon which to predicate pricing decisions. There are two main sources of problems. First, identification of whether a cost is fixed or variable. Allocating specific costs to production is inexact in all but the most simple firm. Secondly, evidence of intent to predate when prices are set between AVC and ATC is not always going to be easy to adduce or interpret. The Commission will seek documentary evidence but may attempt to establish intent from an analysis of the surrounding circumstances. Thus the inherent problem of this area, distinguishing competitive from predatory intent, remains at the centre of the legal test for predation. These problems are illustrated by the decision in *Tetra Pak II*.[216] It was alleged that Tetra Pak had engaged in predatory pricing of its non-aseptic cartons in Italy and of its machines in the UK and Italy. With regard to the sale of machines, the Commission analysed Tetra Pak's accounts over a four-year period and found that "machine operations were loss-making in a not insignificant number of cases". Given the variations seen from year to the next, however, the Commission drew conclusions from the statistics only in relation to the UK where "machine operations were consistently and increasingly loss-making over a period of at least 4 years". According to Tetra Pak's own estimates they did not cover even direct variable costs for three of the four years. Even though these sales largely took place on the non-aseptic market where Tetra Pak's virtual monopoly on the aseptic markets which enabled it to wage a price war on the

[215] [1991] ECR I-3359, at para 94.
[216] [1992] 4 CMLR 551.

neighbouring and associated non-aseptic market.[217] However, the Commission also considered the allegations relating to predatory pricing of cartons. It found that "Rex" non-aseptic cartons were being sold in Italy below average direct variable cost with the intention of eliminating a competitor. The Commission concluded that this confirmed "that Tetra Pak's conduct was opposed to any economic rationality other than as part of an eviction strategy". The Commission's findings were upheld by the Court of First Instance, which found that the necessary intent for sales below average total cost was to be inferred from "the duration, the continuity and the scale ... of the losses made."[218]

(2) Other predatory practices

8.128 It is not just pricing *per se* which can be predatory. In *Cewal*,[219] a shipping conference (i.e. a cartel of shipping companies) was held to have abused its dominant position (held jointly by its members) by adopting the practice of "fighting ships" in an effort to undermine competition on shipping routes. The fighting ships tactic involved scheduling ships to run at the same time as a competitor's ship, offering cheaper rates and subsidising the cost of doing so from its other services.[220]

(3) Mergers and the incipient predation theory

8.129 A question which has in the past caused some concern for American antitrust authorities is whether a prospective merger between two competing firms may be anti-competitive because the resulting company will be able to price at predatorily low prices. The "incipient predation" theory resulted in a prospective merger in the US between two beef packers being prohibited by injunction at the behest of a rival beef packing firm.[221] The American Department of Justice has viewed such actions with extreme scepticism especially where the plaintiff stands to suffer from aggressive price competition. However, the Department accepted that the "incipient predation" theory could be feasible where the plaintiff can establish that the merger will produce a market structure in which predation is economically credible. Moreover, the plaintiff would probably have to prove that predation was more than a hypothetical possibility. In the EC such a merger might be vulnerable to investigation under the EC Merger Control Regulation.[222]

217 See Korah's criticism of this part of the decision in "The paucity of economic analysis in the EEC decisions on competition: *Tetra Pak II*" 1993 CLP 148 at pp. 179–80. Korah argues that, in view of the tying-in by Tetra Pak of the sale of cartons to machines, there was no need to recoup the loss made on the sale of the machines since every such sale brought with it high profits from the sale of cartons. "The conduct makes commercial sense without expectations of raising prices later to recoup, so should not be treated as predatory."

218 Case T-83/91 *Tetra Pak* v *Commission (No. 2)* [1994] ECR II-755, para. 190.

219 *Cewal, Cowac and Ukwal* OJ 1993 L34/20.

220 *ibid.*, paras. 73–83.

221 *Montfort of Colorado* v *Cargil Inc* 761 F.2d 570 (10th Cir. 1985). See also *Christian Schmidt Brewing* v *Heileman Brewing* 753 F.2d 1354 (6th Cir. 1985): H Ltd agreed to purchase the shares of P Ltd. However, in order to avoid antitrust difficulties H also agreed to divest itself of the shares of S & P Ltd. CSB Ltd and SB Ltd successfully sought a declaration and injunctive relief against the proposed merger between H Ltd and P Ltd. The Court state: "The merger would eliminate competition between Heileman and Pabst, and allow the combined firm to target its competitive efforts on other smaller brewers such as Schmidt." The Commission might proceed against predatory mergers under the rule in Case 6/72 *Continental Can* v *Commission* [1973] MCLR 199; [1972] ECR 215. In Case 6-7/73 *Commercial Solvents* v *Commission* [1974] 1 CMLR 309; [1974] ECR 223 the Commission and European Court concluded that the defendant abused its dominant position by refusing to supply a smaller company. The Commission were apparently influenced by the fact that the dominant concern had previously failed to take over the smaller company. The bid was construed as an attempt to take over and then eliminate the small rival: ([1973] CMLR D50 at pp. D54, D56, D57, D60). The European Court appeared to take the same view: [1974] ECR 223 at p. 253.

222 Council Reg. 4064/89/EEC.

5. UK[223]

(1) OFT attitude

8.130 The OFT receives a number of complaints each year concerning predatory pricing.[224] The majority of these cases prove unfounded and the low prices complained of turn out to be evidence of competitiveness rather than anti-competitiveness. The approach of the OFT under the CA 1980 was indicated in the early investigation in *Scottish and Universal Newspapers Ltd* (*SUNL*). This case arose from the conflict between free and paid-for newspapers. During 1982 the OFT investigated the response of SUNL to the issue of a free newspaper by a rival publishing house in the Hamilton and Motherwell District and adjacent areas of the old county of Lanark in Scotland. SUNL sought to prevent the issue of the rival paper or destroy its feasibility if it were printed. To achieve this it issued its own competing free newspaper, the *Lanarkshire World*, within a week of the launch of the rival's new paper. Moreover, it gave away large amounts of free advertising space over an unreasonable period initially with the condition that the advertiser should not take advertising space in another free paper in the region. Furthermore, it priced a high percentage of its advertising space at below the marginal cost of its production and distribution. The OFT concluded that the conduct of SUNL was designed to frustrate the viable establishment of a competitor and, in the longer term, to protect its own profitability.[225] To avoid a reference to the MMC, SUNL gave undertakings to the OFT, *inter alia*, not to supply or offer to supply advertising space to any person at a charge "which does not equal or exceed that part of the marginal cost of producing and distributing the [*Lanarkshire World*] attributable to that advertising space".[226]

8.131 A succession of investigations into the supply of local bus services after deregulation under the Transport Act 1985 has given the OFT and MMC the chance to reiterate this approach to predatory pricing.[227]

8.132 *Highland Scottish Omnibuses* may be taken as an illustrative example. Highland Scottish, at that time publicly owned, responded to the entry of a workers cooperative owned bus company—ITL—on to the market in Inverness by drastically increasing its service mileage and reducing its fares. ITL went into liquidation, only to be replaced by another company, Alexanders, which also subsequently folded in the fact of Highland Scottish's tac-

223 See generally on predatory behaviour OFT Research Paper 5 (by G. Myers) "Predatory behaviour in UK competition policy" (1994).

224 The OFT Competition Act 1980 reports dealing with predation are: *Becton Dickinson Ltd* (1988), *West Yorkshire Road Car Company Ltd* (1989), *Highland Scottish Omnibuses Ltd* (1989), *South Yorkshire Transport Ltd* (1989), *Kingston upon Hull City Transport Ltd* (1990), *Southdown Motor Service* (1992), *Thamesway Ltd* (1993) and *Fife Scottish Omnibuses Ltd* (1994). Since deregulation in 1985, the OFT has received over 250 complaints of predation in the bus industry.

225 11 January 1983 at p. 42, para. 8.28.

226 DGFT Annual Report (1983), p. 86. The OFT in *Grey-Green Coaches*, intervened to prevent commuter coach services from offering free travel to users (see para. 81 Department of Transport Response to 2nd Report of HC Transport Committee (July 1985) Cmnd 9561), and DGFT Annual Report 1985, p. 64.

227 The MMC Report into *The Supply of Bus Services in the North East of England* Cm 2933 (1994) condemned a series of predatory practices in Darlington, South Shields and North Durham and made some more general observations about the damages of consolidation in the bus industry. See Everton [1993] ECLR 6 for a discussion of the following OFT reports: *West Yorkshire Road Car* (1989), *Highland Scottish Omnibus* (1989), *South Yorkshire Transport* (1989), *Kingston-upon-Hull City Transport* (1990) and *Southdown Motor Services* (1992). Of these, two were referred for further investigation by the MMC: *Highland Scottish Omnibus* Cm 1129 (1990) and *Southdown Motor Services* Cm 2248 (1993), the latter reference having to be amended as a consequence of *R v DGFT ex parte Southdown Motor Services*, *The Times*, 18 January 1993. The OFT also carried out a full investigation into alleged predatory pricing in *Becton Dickinson UK Ltd*, 15 June 1988.

tics. Finally, a subsidiary of the economically stronger Stagecoach group entered in Alexanders' place and Highland Scottish, having incurred losses to that point in removing ITL and Alexanders from the market, decided to end its policy and returned to more normal market practice, accepting the existence of a competitor in Inverness. The MMC and DGFT both condemned Highland Scottish's actions, though due to its change in policy and its impending privatisation no further remedial action was ordered. What is particularly worthy of note is the concern of the MMC to take action against predation in order to ensure that new entrants were not deterred, recognising that the threat of predation dents entrepreneurial confidence.

8.133 The OFT and MMC have thus confirmed that their objections to predation are based: (a) on the exclusionary effect of the practice; (b) on the design of the predator to secure its long-term dominance; and (c) on the need to ensure that new entrants are not deterred by the threat of predation. These conclusions generally reflect the best policy of the MMC.[228] In one the MMC was critical of the below cost pricing for domestic electrical goods of the London Electricity Board who, primarily through inefficiency rather than predatory design, sustained the low price through cross-subsidisation from profits earned in electricity supply.[229] Conversely, the OFT rejected a complaint by Dixons[230] who alleged that the regional electricity companies maintained loss-making retail activities by cross-subsidisation from electricity supply and distribution activities. The OFT concluded that although there was evidence that the retail activities were loss-making, no company was significant enough to command market power and therefore such loss-making activities were not a cause of concern. In so far as there was distortion of competition it was insignificant. The OFT stated that the losses did not enable the electricity companies to charge higher prices for the supply of electricity. Furthermore, it concluded that consumers' interests were not harmed by low retail prices.

As with EC law an excessively low (but not necessarily below cost) price designed to damage a rival may be anti-competitive.

8.134 In summary, the OFT looks at the following categories of evidence when investigating allegations of predatory pricing:

(a) whether the market, its structure and characteristics are such as to make predation a sensible and viable business policy;
(b) whether the alleged predatory company incurs losses arising out of the course of conduct;
(c) what the intentions of the alleged predatory company are including evidence of its conduct and behaviour in other markets.[231]

8.135 The OFT in its investigation into *Southdown Motor Services Ltd*,[232] stated as follows:

> "Predatory behaviour involves the deliberate acceptance of losses by setting prices below the costs. There is, however, considerable controversy about the relevant definition of costs

[228] See e.g. Report on *Annual Waste* (1985) Cmnd. 9470 para. 9.34; MMC Report on *Supply of Certain Industrial and Medical Gases* (1956) HC 13; MMC Report on *Supply and Export of Matches and Supply of Match-Making Machinery* (1953) HC 161—extensive price cutting to frustrate incipient competition condemned by MMC.

[229] *London Electricity Board* OFT Investigation under the CA 1980 (29 April 1982) at pp. 53–56, paras. 7.10–7.19. For MMC Report see (3 March 1983) Cmnd 8812.

[230] OFT Press Release, 11 November 1993.

[231] See OFT investigation under the Competition Act 1980 into Thamesway (August 1993); DGFT Annual Report 1993, p. 36; DGFT Annual Report 1994, p. 46.

[232] *Southdown Motor Services Ltd* (the registration and operation of services 262 and 242 in Bognor Regis), 15 July 1992, investigation under section 3 of the Competition Act.

to be used. My office's views have been developed in reports of previous Competition Act investigations. I believe that pricing below short-run variable costs—that is the costs association in the short term with producing an extra unit of output—is indisputably predatory as revenue would be insufficient to cover out-of-pocket running expenses. However, I also believe that pricing above short-run variable costs may be predatory, if, for example, prices are maintained below those necessary to contribute fully to overheads and the minimum return necessary to remunerate investment. Other competitors in the industry which are just as efficient may then be forced out of business. Since the making of losses in this sense cannot be said unambiguously to be predatory and may reflect other factors such as temporary excess capacity, I do however also need to consider any evidence on the motives and intentions of the firm."

8.136 In assessing an allegation of predatory pricing the OFT undertaken detailed analysis of the costs of the alleged predator. In *Southdown Motor Services Ltd*[233] the OFT obtained detailed costings from the company concerned and categorised these as short-run-variable costs (staff costs, fuel, tyres and lubricates); semi-variable costs (depreciation charges, cleaning and maintenance); and fixed overheads. The OFT then examined the extent to which revenues from the services in question made a contribution to each of the categories of costs concerned.[234] Further, the OFT examined evidence of predatory intent on the part of Southdown and concluded that such evidence corroborated the conclusions drawn from the analysis of Southdown's costs. In addition to evidence of cost and intent the OFT also examined the effect of Southdown's behaviour on competition. In particular, it examined the cost structure of Easy Rider—a competitor of Southdown—and concluded that its services were more efficient in the sense that its costs per mile and costs per hour were lower, than those of Southdown. Furthermore, the OFT compared the revenue per mile of Southdown and Easy Rider and concluded from the fact that Easy Rider earned higher revenues per mile, that it was meeting customer needs better than Southdown. To the OFT, the net result of this assessment was that if Southdown succeeded in its predatory conduct the outcome would be a less efficient and less popular service. It concluded:

"The Competition Act defines an anti-competitive practice as a course of conduct which has or is intended to have or is likely to have the effect of restricting, distorting or preventing competition. Competitors may be eliminated by the very workings of competition if they are less efficient. But for a more efficient competitor to be eliminated by predation clearly prevents competition from that firm and thereby restricts competition in the market in question. The very act of subsidising uneconomic activities distorts competition. A practice which deters potential competitors by the threat of overwhelming retaliation is a prevention of competition, and the feasibility of predation depends upon the likely success of deterring entry. Successful predation therefore implies a course of conduct which prevents, restricts and distorts competition in the market. Southdown's actions were intended to have the effect of forcing Easy Rider's withdrawal from the market. Accordingly, I conclude that Southdown's behaviour was anti-competitive under the terms of the Act."[235]

8.137 The OFT observed that the predatory conduct of Southdown was successful in forcing the exit of Easy Rider from the market. It noted further that the removal of this competitor could serve as a deterrent to bus operators seeking to enter the market in Bognor Regis and in other areas where Southdown was dominant. Notwithstanding the exit of

233 *ibid.*
234 *ibid.*, see paras. 2.20–2.27, pp. 13–15, and, Tab. 2.2 (p. 14) and Tab. 4.2 and 4.4 (pp. 24 and 25).
235 *ibid.*, see paras. 2.31, 2.32, p. 16.

Easy Rider from the market the OFT therefore decided that a reference to the MMC was justified under the Act. The MMC confirmed the OFT's condemnation of these predatory practices in *Southdown Motor Services*.[236]

8.138 It may be that a distinction can be drawn between predatory behaviour, which involves the acceptance of short term losses by the predator, and other anti-competitive behaviour falling short of predation *per se*. It seems that the term "predation" may be considered by the OFT as only appropriate for pricing which involves the acceptance of loss. Other pricing strategies may be anti-competitive (for example, the exclusionary pricing practices referred to above in the SUNL case), but are not to be regarded as predatory because they do not involve actual loss-making activities.[237] However, this distinction seems to break down because it is possible to consider that break-even pricing may be predatory, since it is pricing carried on which will not give the normal rate of return on capital, and therefore the only rational explanation or motive (if it is not a reflection of cut-throat competitive conditions in a market) is an exclusionary one.

(2) Whether introductory discounts are predatory

8.139 In the *SUNL* case (above) the OFT commented:

> "When a new product is launched, it will tend initially to be at a disadvantage in the market because it is unknown and commands no consumer loyalty. It is therefore normal practice to make introductory offers in order to encourage potential customers to test and assess the product and to enable the producer to assess the product's market appeal. Such offers are not in themselves necessarily anti-competitive. They may, however, become so if they are made on such a scale, or over such a period of time, as to lead to the conclusion that their primary intention is to eliminate competition rather than establish the new product on the market."[238]

(3) Determining costs

8.140 If predation means selling below costs the central question concerning the meaning of cost rises again. In the SUNL case the OFT focused upon the marginal cost of producing and distributing the product in question. It defined marginal cost in the undertaking SUNL gave as, "an amount equal to the same proportion of the marginal cost of producing and distributing the [*Lanarkshire World*] as that advertising space bears to the total advertising space supplied in the [*Lanarkshire World*] to persons other than SUNL".[239] This suggests that UK law will treat sub-AVC pricing as anti-competitive. In *Highland Scottish Omnibuses*, it was clear that prices were being set below ATC with predatory intent leading to losses being incurred. It seems that the investigations of both the OFT and MMC look at preda-

236 Cm 2248, 1993.

237 This is argued by G Myers in paras. 2.3–2.5 OFT Research Paper 5 *Predatory Behaviour in UK Competition Policy* (1994).

238 OFT investigation into *Scottish Universal Newspaper Ltd* (11 January 1983), p. 39, para. 8.16.

239 DGFT Annual Report (1983), p. 86. In *Foreign Package Holidays* (Cmnd 4879, 1986) the MMC considered the position of a new entrant to a market who competed with existing companies by cross-subsidisation from profits earned elsewhere in its business to the new line of business (*ibid.*, paras. 6.13 and 10.16. The MMC did not express a fixed view on cross-subsidisation in this context. It is probable that cross-subsidisation is anti-competitive only where an undertaking with market power exploits one market in order to expand or reinforce its market power in another. It would seem unlikely that where X subsidises a policy of discounting by cross-subsidisation, this is anti-competitive in the absence of market power on the part of the company concerned. See also *Grey-Green Coaches*. OFT Report 1985, p. 654 (the provision of loss leading free services as a deterrent to new entry).

tory intent as well as the issue of costs. Neither the OFT nor the MMC has given clear guidance on whether a price below ATC is anti-competitive. The OFT in *SUNL* made it clear that some below cost prices may be pro-competitive (e.g. introductory offers). As suggested above the European Commission's view in *AKZO* may well be informative. Conversely, it may be possible to argue that discounting to prices at or only slightly above marginal cost may be regarded as predatory and against the public interest. The MMC Report into *Concrete Roofing Tiles*[240] condemned selective deep discounting to marginal cost prices for which the only explanation appeared to be the appearance of a new entrant upon the market, and which operated as a barrier to entry to that market.

8.141 In negotiating with the OFT, parties alleged to be acting in a predatory manner, may need to determine a precise breakdown of costs. This will necessarily entail the use of accountancy assistance. During 1984 British Airways (BA) filed for approval with the UK and US regulatory authorities, a discount fare lowering the applicable price of a round-trip ticket between London and New York to US$378 from US$597, a reduction of 35 per cent on BA's previous winter apex fare. The UK authority, the Civil Aviation Authority, rejected the fare on the basis that, while they considered the fare economic, it considered that in the US a different view might be adopted and a charge of predation raised. There was concern that a small UK airline, Virgin Atlantic, might carry out its threat to challenge the fare in a private treble damages antitrust suit before the US courts. BA, accordingly, requested the US Department of Justice to issue to it a business review letter stating whether it had any intention to proceed against BA for predation. BA provided the Department of Justice with detailed costings of:

(a) flying operation:
   – fuel and oil,
   – cabin and flight crew variables,
   – route facility charges;
(b) maintenance (including flight equipment);
(c) rentals: flight equipment;
(d) passenger in-flight expense:
   – catering variables,
   – passenger service charges/security levies,
   – load insurance/Airline operating certificate;
(e) aircraft servicing;
(f) traffic servicing.

8.142 In a business review letter by the Department of Justice to BA the former stated:

> "Moreover, it is questionable whether, except under the most extreme circumstances, the antitrust laws may appropriately be used to interfere with the unilateral business judgment of an air carrier that a proposed fare reduction will be profitable in the short-run. First, it is extremely difficult to allocate costs and revenues to particular routes, flights, or fare types. Thus, there are any number of valid accounting assumptions that might be made in concluding that a unilateral fare reduction was profit-maximising in the short-run. For example, fare levels that might appear to be below cost on a particular route segment might well cover cost when examined in the context of the carrier's total route system. Second, even if one limits the analysis to a particular route segment, marginal cost in the schedule airline industry may be extremely low. Once a flight is scheduled to depart, the marginal cost for additional passengers may properly be viewed as quite low. Given a strong incen-

[240] 18 November 1981, HCP (1981–1982) 12.

tive to fill empty seats, airlines often have found it makes economic cense to reduce the fare applicable to particular market segments. In recent years, airlines have offered reduced fares based, *inter alia*, on time of day, day of week, season, advance or late purchase by the passenger or a limited number of seats allocated per plane. Thus it is doubtful that even drastic unilateral fare reductions by an airline can be proven predatory merely by reference to the fare level."[241]

"Cost" is not a precise concept, it will be a matter for debate in each case and parties who are complained of will almost certainly need accountancy assistance to determine a cost model to present to the OFT.

G. Excessive Pricing[242]

8.143 Excessive pricing is a problem related to market dominance. If a small firm overprices its goods consumers will simply go elsewhere. If a dominant firm overprices its goods consumers may have little choice but to pay the supra-competitive price. Excessive pricing practices are the mirror image of predatory pricing practices. Similar problems of computing cost may occur since excessive prices may be viewed in terms of a cost—price differential. However, measuring differentials is not a perfect test of effectiveness. A high differential may be justified by a firm's efficient costs and not by profit maximisation. For example: X has costs of four units; Y has costs of five units; and, Z has costs of six units. The market price is set at seven units. X in selling at four units is making 75 per cent profit but that is not necessarily excessive since the market price of seven units still provides a reasonable return for X's rivals. The single criticism is that X not be passing on some of the financial rewards of his efficiency to customers.

8.144 Excessive pricing cases are, however, rare. A firm which charges wildly in excess of costs and thereby maximises profits will be vulnerable to potential competition from new entrants who recognise the possibility of high profits. Thus, to that extent excessive pricing is only likely to be a temporary phenomena. Conversely, if the dominant firm is protected from potential entrants by high entry barriers then it is a more serious problem.[243]

1. *EC Law*

(1) Meaning of excessive pricing

8.145 The Court of Justice has, on a number of occasions, decried excessive pricing. In *Sirena v Eda*[244] the Court stated,

241 See Business Review letter—US Department of Justice Antitrust Division (20 December 1984) *British Airways*.

242 See for analysis Perott, "Pricing policy and Community rules on competition and free movement of goods", in *Yearbook of European Law* (1982) at pp. 211–20. See also, Schwarz in Van Damme, *Regulating the Behaviour of Monopolies and Dominant Undertakings in Community Law* (1977) at pp. 381 *et seq.* For briefer commentary see Wyatt and Dashwood, *European Community Law* (1993), pp. 459–60.

243 See e.g. Case 26/75 *General Motors Continental* [1976] 1 CMLR 95; [1975] *Derek Merson* v *British Leyland* [1984] 3 CMLR 92—both General Motors and British Leyland enjoyed sole authorisation to perform tasks connected with the importation of vehicles. Both companies thus enjoyed protection from potential entrants and were hence free to abuse their monopoly power over prices.

244 Case 40/70 [1971] CMLR 260, [1971] ECR 69 at p. 85. See also Case 24/67 *Parke, Davis* v *Probel* [1968] CMLR 47; [1968] ECR 55 at p. 72. Court held that for a plaintiff to sue for infringement of its patents as

"Although the price level of a product may not, of itself, necessarily suffice to disclose the abuse of a dominant position ... it may, however, if unjustified by any objective criteria and if it is particularly high, be a determining factor."

8.146 The Court in that case did not elucidate on when high prices were justified, what objective factors would suffice, or, what was meant by excessively high prices. In *General Motors Continental*[245] the Court hinted that excessively high meant a price which was "excessive in relation to the economic value of the service provided". In *United Brands*[246] the Court stated that it would be an abuse to set a price which "has no reasonable relation to the economic value" of the product or service. In *Ahmed Saeed*[247] the Court answered questions referred by the German courts regarding the tariffs charged by an air carrier in a dominant position to other air carriers operating on the same route. The Court held that an abuse may exist where "such imposed tariffs must be regarded as unfair conditions of transport with regard to competitors or with regard to passengers. Such unfair conditions may be due ... to the rate of tariffs imposed being excessively high". The Court went on to say that interpretative criteria for assessing whether the rate employed is excessive may be inferred from Directive 87/601 which lays down criteria to be followed by the aeronautical authorities for approving tariffs. In particular, "tariffs must be reasonably related to the long-term fully allocated costs of the carrier, while taking into account the needs of consumers, the need for a satisfactory return on capital, the competitive market situation, including the fares of other air carriers operating on the route, and the need to prevent dumping.

8.147 The same problems as arise in connection with predation arise here, i.e. in defining cost. Defining costs is exceptionally difficult. For example, at what rate should plant be depreciated, to what extent is investment in new plant or in R&D attributable, what rate of inflation is to be incorporated, etc? It is clear that "excessive" is not a term of art and that a less precise definition of cost will suffice than for predation where notions of cost are more central to liability.

(2) Criteria for recognising excessive prices

8.148 The Commission and Court, in the relatively few decided cases, have given some guidelines.

(a) Miscalculation of cost components

8.149 In *General Motors Continental* the company included in the fee for performing vehicle conformity inspections, a component based upon the non-recurring cost of obtaining *general* approval of the vehicle model. However, the company based this cost component on type approval for General Motors American models. The actual cost of obtaining type approval for the European vehicles in question was much less. Accordingly, the company included an unjustified element in its fees. In *Hachette*[248] the Commission was critical of the company Hachette which was dominant on the French market for the distribution of newspapers, periodicals and books. Hachette included French VAT in its price to wholesalers in Belgium although it was always refunded the French VAT on exports from France. The Commission stated that this cost component was unjustified and hence unfair. Where a cost com-

cont.
a means of preventing parallel imports was not *per se* an abuse under Article 86. However, they did accept that, "the sale price of the protected product may be regarded as a factor to be taken into account in determining the possible existence of an abuse."

245 Case 26/75 [1976] 1 CMLR 95, [1975] ECR 1367 at pp. 1378, 1379.

246 Case 27/76 [1978] 1 CMLR 429, [1978] ECR 207 at p. 301.

247 66/86 [1989] ECR 803.

248 *Hachette et Nouvelles Messageries de la Presse Parisienne* [1979] 2 CMLR 78.

mission stated that this cost component was unjustified and hence unfair. Where a cost component is unwarranted, e.g. because it is based on miscalculation or a cost that is not borne, a breach of Article 86 seems automatic.

(b) Existence of differentials between national markets

8.150 The Court has held that differentials between Member States may be abusive if unjustified and particularly marked.[249] Thus, where transport or other freight related costs do not justify differences on various markets there may be an implication that on some markets at least excessive prices are being charged.[250]

(c) Existence of differentials between rival suppliers

8.151 Where other suppliers with comparable goods or services are charging considerably less then there will be an implication of abusive pricing. However, potential for abuse will only arise where a purchaser has no choice but to take from a particular supplier. In *General Motors Continental* other manufacturing agents charged about half that charged by General Motors Continental (GMC). However, purchasers could not switch from GMC to other suppliers since once they had made the decision to purchase an Opel car they could *only*, by virtue of Belgian law, obtain vehicle conformity inspections from GMC, i.e having elected to buy Opel they were tied to GMC who enjoyed a statutory monopoly. In *Bodson*, the Court of Justice held that the "fairness" of prices charged by undertakers operating a local monopoly concession could be established by a comparison with prices in those areas in which no such concessions were granted.[251]

(d) Prices bear no relation to costs

8.152 The factors in (a)–(c) above may only be evidence indicating that a price is excessive in relation to assumed costs. Such tests are useful where cost analysis is impossible or unhelpful. Where cost analysis is feasible it should be possible to determine whether a price is excessive. However, it may not always be necessary to know *precise* costings. In *British Leyland*[252] the Commission fined the company for charging £150 for the provision of type approval numbers for certain imported vehicles. They sought to justify the price upon the basis of increased overheads. However, the Commission, without seeking to assess accurately British Leyland's overheads made the assumption that the defendant's overheads could not possibly be so large as to warrant a price of £150. Thus where there is proof in logic though not in fact of an excessive cost–price differential, a presumption of abuse might lie.

In *CICCE*[253] the Court of Justice indirectly considered whether dominant licensees paying low royalty rates in copyright licences granted to them were infringing Article 86. The Commission considered that the fees paid would be "unfair" depending upon a test of the relationship between the cost of production and the economic value of the service provided. The Commission rejected an argument that an abuse could be established by showing that the buyer allocated only a very small portion of its budget to the purchase of the copyright article in question (films) and/or that the average licence fee was low.[254] Advocate

249 Case 78/80 *Deutsche Gramophon* v *Metro* [1971] CMLR 631, [1971] ECR 487.

250 e.g. Case 27/76 *United Brands* v *Commission* [1978] 1 CMLR 429, [1978] ECR 207. See also Case 395/87 *Ministère Public* v *Tournier* [1991] 4 CMLR 248, 290, para. 43; Case 110/88 *Lucazeau* v *SACEM* [1991] 4 CMLR 248, 295, para. 33. The French Competition Council held, in an advisory opinion, that SACEM (the French performance rights royalty collection agency) was abusing a dominant position under Art. 86 EC by charging a licence fee of up to 15 times that charged in other Member States (1994) 7 WIPR 180.

251 Case 30/87 *Bodson* v *Pompes Funèbres* [1989] 4 CMLR 984, 1018, para. 31.

252 [1984] 3 CMLR 92 at p. 99, para. 28.

253 298/83 *CICCE* v *Commission* [1985] ECR 1105.

254 *ibid.*, paras. 22 and 23.

General Lenz stated that, in the case of heterogeneous products, such as films, which vary in value as a result of age, success history, expected rating and audience age, etc, no general presumption as to the test to be applied could arise.

(e) Price does not enable customer to make a profit

8.153 In *NALOO*[255] British Coal Corporation (BCC) was alleged to have infringed Article 66(7) ECSC (the equivalent of Article 86 EC). BCC was the owner under statute of all the unworked coal existing in the UK. It also held statutory powers to grant licences to third parties to extract such coal. NALOO, a trade association of small open-cast mining companies, complained to the Commission that BCC was abusing a dominant position contrary to Article 66(7) ECSC in, *inter alia*, imposing an excessive royalty requirement upon them. The Commission, in its Decision stated that the "level of royalty cannot be considered in isolation. The relationship between the price received for the coal and the costs, including the royalty, of producing that coal must be such as to enable efficient companies to make a profit and must not impose a significant competitive disadvantage on them."[256] On the facts of the case, however, the Commission decided that the royalty was not sufficiently high to be unlawful a least after BCC had substantially reduced the royalty and backdated the reduction so as to provide a measure of compensation to the licensee.[257]

(f) The evolution of prices over time

8.154 If a dominant undertaking commences selling at £5 per unit but over a period of two years increases the price to £17 per unit then, in the absence of any objective justification for the increase such as an escalation in costs, the logical assumption is that the later price is excessive. While it is possible that the initial price was set at an uninformed and inadequate level, it is not an unreasonable assumption to make that the later prices are excessive. In such circumstances the calculation whereby £5 is multiplied by inflation will probably not result in £17. In *BL* v *Commission*[258] the Court of Justice appeared to adopt this approach to the determination of excessive prices under Article 86. The Court recorded the price history of the service in question and noted a 600 per cent increase in prices over the period. The Court rejected the possibility that such an increase was explicable by virtue of cost increases and concluded that the highest prices, at least, were abusive. This approach enables a Court or the Commission to decide whether at any point excessive prices have been charged; it does not enable a proper conclusion to be arrived at about the extent or quantum of the excess profit earned since such a conclusion would require the authority to pinpoint in time when the price first became excessive.

(g) Existence of differentials between different products and/or services of the same supplier

8.155 In *BL* v *Commission* the Court of Justice pointed out[259] that at one time, prior to Commission intervention, there existed a six fold difference in prices between essentially identical services (*in casu*, the provision of certificates of conformity for right-hand and left-hand drive vehicles respectively). The Court concluded, with minimal analysis of the cost bases of the respective services, that the differential was unjustified and the higher price must be excessive.

255 *National Association of Licensed Opencast Operators (NALOO)* [1993] 4 CMLR 615; appealed to CFI, Case T-57/91 *NALOO* v *Commission*, judgment of 24 September 1996.
256 *National Association of Licensed Opencast Operators (NALOO)* [1993] 4 CMLR 615, 627, para. 72.
257 NALOO's appeal dismissed in Case T-57/91 *NALOO* v *Commission*; judgment of 24 September 1996.
258 Case 226/84 *BL* v *Commission* [1986] ECR 3263; [1987] 1 CMLR 185.
259 *ibid.*, para. 28.

(3) Proving excessive prices: evidence

8.156 Some guidance upon the evidence needed to establish excessive pricing may be gleaned from the Commission's decision in *Olympic Airways*[260] which concerned the Commission's attempt to obtain information from the airline about its pricing policy for handling services at Greek airports. Following a complaint from the Association des Compagnes Ariennes de la Communaut, that handling charges imposed by Olympic had increased by nearly 50 per cent in one year, the Commission requested information from Olympic about the charges. In the face of a lack of cooperation from the airline the Commission adopted a decision under Article 11(5) of Regulation 17/62/EEC compelling disclosure and threatening fines should Olympic fail to comply with the decision. For current purposes the demand made by the Commission are informative as to the type of evidence the Commission viewed as potentially of probative value. The text of the demand is set out verbatim below though it will be appreciated that demands 1 and 3 are related to the existence of dominance and not excessive pricing as such:

> "1 Indicate the number of airports which are used by commercial airlines in Greece.
>
> 2 In how many of these does Olympic Airways alone provide handling services?
>
> 3 Is it open to any other airline to provide handling services at any Greek airport for itself and any other airline? If not, are the obstacles legal or economic. If legal, provide the text of the laws in question.
>
> 4 For the years 1982 and 1983 indicate the fixed and variable costs of providing handling services at Athens airport and at other Greek airports.
>
> 5 What provisions is made, if any, for deducting the proportion of total costs attributable to providing handling services to Olympic Airways' own airplanes?
>
> 6 Pricelist 'A' showing Basic Charges for Passenger Aircraft, effective from 1 April 1984, shows charges in basic handling services for heavier aircraft averaging 50 per cent above the 1983 price. Have costs incurred in providing these services increased by a similar amount? What other reasons are there for these increases?
>
> 7 On the other hand, handling services for small and light aircraft show increases for the period from 1 April 1984 by an average of 35 per cent. Can you explain why the average increase for smaller and lighter average aircraft is so much lower than that for heavier aircraft?
>
> 8 Can you explain why the proposed 50 per cent increase is applied with effect from 1 January 1984 for some airlines and for others from 1 April 1984?"

The demands above are mostly self-explanatory. Number 5 is interesting since it demonstrates that the Commission was sensitive to the possibility of a dominant concern charging other operators a price which included an element relating to the dominant undertakings own use of the service it provided, i.e. rivals were possibly being forced to subsidise the dominant concern.

2. UK Law

(1) Accounting method

8.157 Excessive pricing is subject to the CA 1980 and the FTA 1973. The MMC has regularly undertaken analysis of a company's profits.[261] The test usually adopted is rate of return

[260] OJ 1985 L 46/51. See also Commission answer to Working Question no. 320/85, OJ 1985 C 310/1.

[261] See Liesner Committee Report, *A Review of Monopolies and Mergers Policy* (1978) Cmnd 7198, p. 21, para. 3.42 which indicates that some of the MMC's problems with appraising prices have been accountancy problems: "MMC reports demonstrate that monopoly pricing or profits do occur in a few industries. It is true that in only eight of the 32 reports in the period since 1959 did the MMC find unambiguous evidence of unreasonable prices and profits ... The difficulty of assessing reasonable profits must, however, be borne in mind while some of the remaining cases were found to be characterised by inefficiency and higher costs than could be expected with keener competition."

on capital. The MMC compare the profits of the investigated company with comparable companies. Statistics for the comparison may derive from tables compiled by the DTI which incorporate data for approximately 3,000 plus companies. There appears to be no firm rule as to how profits are to be calculated. In some cases the historic cost of the purchase of building plant and equipment minus an amount for depreciation has been used. In other cases the MMC has operated upon a replacement cost basis[262] and tends to prefer this latter test which enables it to take into account the replacement costs of assets as at the time of the investigation. Where technology is rapidly advancing, replacement costs may be high and hence replacement cost analysis tends to result in lower profit conclusions than historical cost analysis.

(2) Indications of policy

8.158 It is not easy to predict in a given case how either the MMC or OFT will view profit margins. Where barriers to entry are low the MMC has accepted that the liberty of a dominant firm to overprice its goods or services may be curtailed by the potential threat of new entry.[263] Conversely, where entry barriers are high the MMC has adopted a stricter analysis of the cost price relationship. In such cases it has also considered whether the cost structure of the company concerned is efficient. For example, in *White Salt*[264] the MMC investigated the duopolistic position of British Salt and ICI in the white salt market. The MMC concluded, *inter alia*, that British Salt had the more efficient cost basis but pointed out that British Salt was the market follower, not the market and price leader. The MMC were critical of the fact that ICI which was less efficient in relative terms set the price at which salt was sold. The MMC stated that British Salt should have taken the initiative on price and forced ICI to reassess its cost structure. The MMC considered that the situation was partly attributable to the high entry barriers to the market. In other cases the MMC has rejected firms' assertions that high profits were needed to enable a firm to undertake the investment in new products necessary if the firm was to be able to diversify away from declining products.[265]

8.159 The MMC does not generally complain of profit margins under 20 per cent. In its now old report into *Chlordiazepoxide and Diazepam* it was highly critical of profits of over 70 per cent.[266] In *Industrial and Medical Gases*, they criticised profits of only 25 per cent where earned by a dominant concern supplying a low risk, stable demand.[267] Conversely, in *Cigarette Filter Rods*[268] a 40 per cent margin was considered acceptable where it was perceived as a reward for the high efficiency of the manufacturer. In *Soluble Coffee*,[269] Nestlé's profitability, although producing returns on capital of over 100 per cent, was not re-

262 See e.g. MMC report on the *Supply and Processing of Colour Film* (1966) HC 1; MMC Report on the *Supply of Contraceptive Sheaths* (1975) HC 135 at paras. 170 and 196. New entry attracted by demand expansion in the condom market led to the MMC to recommend removing price controls on the dominant condom supplier, LRC Products Ltd, in *Contraceptive Sheaths*, Cm 2529, March 1994. The company had been subjected to profit controls in 1972 replaced by price controls in 1982, as a result of previous MMC investigations into this market.

263 e.g. MMC Report on the *Supply of Cat and Dog Food* (1977) HC 447. Where entry costs are high the MMC has been more stringent, see MMC Report on the *Supply of Chlordiazepoxide and Diazepam* (1973) HC 197—entry costs into the drug manufacturing market are high. A 70 per cent profit margin was however concluded to be excessive after initial marketing stages. See the Liesner Committee Report, *A Review of Monopolies and Mergers Policy* (1978) Cmnd 7198 at p. 21, para. 3.43 and at p. 74, para. 10—where it is suggested that MMC Reports show that excessive pricing is usually accompanied by the existence of entry barriers.

264 Cmnd 9778, June 1986.

265 MMC Report on *Supply of Contraceptive Sheaths* (1975) HC 135.

266 (1973) HC 197.

267 (1956) HC 13.

268 (1969) HC 335.

269 MMC Report on *The Supply of Soluble Coffee* (1991) Cm 1459.

garded as being against the public interest, having regard to its efficiency and the competitiveness of the market. More recently, in *Matches and Disposable Lighters*,[270] a 25 per cent margin was condemned as excessive, even though it was at least partly attributable to efficiency gains following a merger creating a dominant business, as there was also evidence that anti-competitive rebates and full-line forcing tactics had been adopted with exclusionary effect.

8.160 The MMC has accepted that high initial prices may be justifiable to overcome marketing and planning costs.[271] However, once these have been offset the justification disappears.[272]

8.161 The experience in regulating privatised industries has led to an increased emphasis on the possibility of using price capping without direct limits on profits as a means of reducing prices while promoting efficiency in markets where there was little prospect of opening up new competition.[273] This has already been used in *White Salt*,[274] where the MMC recommended a price cap on the more efficient of the duopolists in this market, leading the less efficient duopolist to have no choice but to improve efficiency or lose market share. Barriers to entry in this market were high, caused by large economies of scale and declining demand.

8.162 Alternatively, the MMC has been prepared to wait for new entrants attracted by the high prices to introduce competitive pressure to drive prices down, where there are no high barriers to entry. This was the MMC's justification for not recommending price controls in *Tampons*,[275] where barriers to entry to a duopolistic market were found not to be insuperable (one barrier, that on advertising on TV, was in the process of being removed by the television advertising body) and there was evidence of new entry. It was considered that all price controls might be in the short-term interests of consumers, but that over the long term this would deter investment, innovation and new entry and would fossilise the market into its present structure.[276]

8.163 In *Opium Derivatives*,[277] a combination of these approaches was recommended by the MMC: short term price controls on the monopoly supplier, combined with a removal in the medium term of barriers to entry arising out of government licensing restrictions.[278] Concern about apparently excessively high CD prices in the UK led to an MMC investigation. Its Report into *The Supply of Recorded Music*[279] found that differences between parties in the UK and the USA were largely explained by different sales taxes, the remaining differences mirrored the general price differential between the UK and the USA on manufactured goods and in any event, prices in the UK were lower than in many other

[270] MMC Report on *The Supply of Matches and Disposable Lighters* (1992) Cm 1854.
[271] MMC Report on the *Supply of Credit Card Franchising Services* (1982) Cmnd 8034.
[272] MMC Report on *Supply of Chlordiazepoxide and Diazepam* (1973) HC 197.
[273] *Per* Sir Bryan Carsberg, former DGFT, Eleventh Annual Antitrust Conference, Robinson College, Cambridge, 11 September 1992.
[274] Cmnd 9778 (1986). The cap was subsequently revised downwards, see DGFT Annual Report 1992, p. 27.
[275] Cmnd 9705 (1986).
[276] However, concern about the pricing policy of the leading supplier of tampons, Tambrands Ltd (which enjoys about 60 per cent of the UK market), which apparently gave additional discounts in return for full-line stocking, led to it being referred to the MMC in June 1995, but the MMC found in its report, *Tambrands Ltd* (Cm3168, 1996), that in view of the countervailing purchasing power of the retailers, those practices were not against the public interest.
[277] Cm 630 (1989).
[278] In the event the government stated it would act in the short term to remove entry barriers thus obviating the need for price controls: DTI Press Notice dated 20 April 1989.
[279] Cm 2599, 1994.

industrialised countries. Accordingly, it did not make any adverse public interest findings in relation to prices.

(3) Remedies: monitoring of price by OFT

8.164 The MMC usually, in an adverse report, recommends price monitoring by the OFT. In *Contraceptive Sheaths*, following a number of years of having its prices and profits monitored by the OFT, the dominant concern, LRC, complained that the price controls were hindering its ability to undertake R&D. Accordingly, a second reference was made to the MMC who, in like tone to the first reference, considered that the firm was still dominant on the market and that the need for control remained. It recommended that the firm should not be permitted to increase prices at a rate greater than 1.5 percentage points less than any percentage rise in a special index constructed to reflect the dominant concerns production costs.[280] The price controls were released in 1994 following a third MMC investigation,[281] as there had been a number of new entrants, the market was expanding and there was countervailing purchasing power from the NHS. LRC was required to give an undertaking not to require wholesalers or retailers to accept exclusivity.[282]

8.165 In *Chlordiazepoxide and Diazepam* the MMC suggested that the price of certain drugs, namely valium and librium, be reduced by 25 per cent and 40 per cent respectively. This extreme remedy included an element of restitution to the National Health Service who had been the main UK buyer.[283]

8.166 Control of proofs cannot always be achieved by supervision of prices. If X reduces prices by 10 per cent this might serve only to stimulate demand and ultimately profits. Indeed the prospects of competing with lower prices might deter potential competitors from entering the market. Conversely, over-zealous price regulation might harm X's ability to perform R&D and diversify. To counter these problems, the OFT takes costs and profit levels, as well as prices, into account in determining their policy. The MMC and OFT, in this respect, are different to the European Commission who is loathe to act the part of day to day regulator.[284] Regulation is not always successful. In *White Salt*, a price cap had to be revised downwards in the light of evidence that the original cap had not performed its function of requiring greater efficiency from the less efficient of the duopolists.[285]

H. Resale Price Maintenance

8.167 In the UK and in the EC resale price maintenance (rpm) is prima facie frowned upon. First, if all dealers or purchasers of a product have to resell according to specified price dictates then the incentive for the efficient dealer goes unrewarded; he may not cut price and ultimately the overall level of retail prices remains supra-competitively high. Secondly, since the fixed resale price may be set so as to sustain the least efficient dealer, an inefficient price network may be kept in operation, thus discount warehouses and retailers may be hindered in their expansion. Thirdly, although it may be true that where price competition is negated, non-price competition (services, promotion, advertising, etc.) thrives, the ef-

[280] See DGFT Annual Reports 1982 at pp. 71, 72 and 1983 at pp. 79, 80.
[281] MMC Report on *The Supply of Contraceptive Sheaths* (1994) Cm 2529.
[282] DGFT Annual Report 1994, p. 36.
[283] (1975) HC 135.
[284] *Fifth Report on Competition Policy* (1975) at para. 3.
[285] DGFT Annual Report 1992, p. 27.

fect is to force the buyer to accept the higher level of services. Given the choice, many consumers might prefer lower prices and fewer pre-or post-sales services. Fourthly, in terms of consumer benefits, price competition is generally perceived as a more vigorous form of competition than non-price competition.

8.168 The main arguments in favour of rpm have developed in the context of what has become known as the "free rider" question. In short where a manufacturer of a luxury or technically complex products supplies dealers with that product the manufacturer will be concerned to ensure that the goods are sold under proper conditions. Indeed, the manufacturer's reputation (which may be closely allied to a trademark) may depend upon the proper distribution of the goods. Accordingly, the manufacturer may impose stocking, advertising and pre-and post-sales servicing obligations on the dealer. The "free rider" problem arises where a discount or "no-frills retailer" sells the same goods at a price below that of the main dealer in the area. Customers may exploit the services and qualified staff at the main dealer but actually purchase from the cheap retailer. The effect is that the main dealer is paying the promotion costs of the cheap retailer; the latter takes a "free-ride" on the services provided by the former. Where free-riding occurs, the incentive for the main dealer to continue a high level of services diminishes and if service are cut back then the goods may be sold under inadequate conditions. Ultimately, the manufacturer's reputation is harmed. One way to overcome free riding is to impose rpm since in such circumstances customers will always take from retailers providing high levels of services. While the free-rider argument certainly has some economic validity in exceptional cases it has generally been rejected as a justification for rpm. The alternative justification for rpm (which has been advanced principally in respect of books and medicaments) is that by enabling a retailer to earn high profit margins on certain lines the retailer is able to stock other lines which would not otherwise be economical to stock. In effect the resale price maintained product facilitates cross subsidisation of other products. It is thus argued that rpm increases consumer choice.

1. *EC Law*

(1) Legal context[286]

8.169 Attempts by suppliers to enforce rpm will fall foul of Article 85[287] or Article 86 where a supplier is dominant. Where rpm is introduced by a supplier in conjunction with the dealer there may exist a concerted practice between all the dealers to comply with the scheme. If the consensus between the dealers is more formal or is buttressed by meetings then the vulnerability to Article 85 increases since an agreement to maintain prices invariably arises. The Commission however usually concentrates upon the manufacturer–dealer agreement rather than any agreement or concerted practice between the dealers *inter se*.

8.170 The Commission does not differentiate between manufacturers' recommendations as to retail price and actual rpm where the effect of the recommendation is to flatten dealer prices into uniformity. If dealers are entitled to fix own prices but must obtain the manufacturer's permission to deviate from them, or if a dealer must give prior notice to the

[286] See Gammelgaard, *Resale Price Maintenance (European Productivity Agency of the Organisation for European Economic Co-operation*, Paris, 1958) cited with approval by Advocate General Verloren Van Themaat in Cases 43 and 63/83 *VBVB & VBBB* v *Commission* [1985] 1 CMLR 27 at p. 46 note 7.

[287] e.g. *Deutsche Philips* [1973] CMLR D241; *Gerofabriek* [1977] 1 CMLR D35. See also *per* Advocate General Verloren Van Themaat in Cases 43 and 63/82 *VBVB & VBBB* v *Commission* [1985] 1 CMLR 27 at p. 51 where the Advocate-General quotes Commission policy: "the Commission has made it clear from the beginning that it was an avowed opponent of any price agreement relating to the price for the ultimate consumer, whether in the form of a direct agreement or of a resale price imposed on distributors."

manufacturer of any deviation from the latter's recommended price, this will be viewed as indirect pressure on the dealer to adhere to the recommended price.[288] However, the Court has held that franchisors may recommend resale prices to franchises without infringing Article 85(1) *provided* that no agreement or concerted practice exists, either between the franchisor and franchisees or between the franchisees *inter se*, effectively to apply the recommended prices. Similar principles apply to other forms of distribution, in particular selective distribution.

(2) Types of rpm

8.171 In *VBVB and VBBB* v *Commission*[289] Advocate General Verloren van Themaat outlined three broad varieties of rpm scheme:

(a) Individual resale price maintenance: individual producers or several individual producers make agreements with every dealer or intermediate trade link as to the resale price of an article.
(b) Collective, individual resale price maintenance: this entails a collective obligation for all producers in a given sector individually to impose rpm on their dealers.
(c) Collective resale price maintenance: rpm is effected collectively, e.g. through all producers and dealers being bound to each other to uphold resale price maintenance. Usually, rather than achieving this via multilateral agreement, the parties organise a joint secretariat or trade association as an enforcement machinery.[290]

(3) Where confined to one Member State

8.172 Resale price maintenance schemes executed by parties in one Member State only may none the less infringe Article 85(1). The European Court has stated:

> "An agreement extending over the whole territory of a Member State by its very nature has the effect of reinforcing the compartmentalisation of markets on a national basis, thereby holding up the economic inter penetration which the Treaty is designed to bring about and protecting domestic production."[291]

8.173 However, not every national rpm scheme is unlawful.[292] In *VBVB and VBBB* v *Commission*[293] the Advocate-General stated in respect of a national collective system of rpm that no every such rpm system would satisfy the test described above. First, rpm schemes usually protect retailers not producers, "producers remain free under such a system to determine their own sale prices, consumer prices and trade margins". Secondly, it was not necessarily the case that national collective rpm which did not affect imported or exported goods resulted in a reinforcement of national compartmentalisation: "In the absence of incidental restrictions on competition such as collective rules on exclusive distributorship, producers from other countries remain entirely free to export to the country in question with or without resale price

288 e.g. *Hennessy-Henkel* [1981] 1 CMLR 601; *Camera Care/Hasselblad* [1982] 2 CMLR 233—manufacturer threatened to withdraw credit from dealers deviating from a recommended price band.
289 Case 43 and 63/82 [1984] ECR 19 at pp 74–75 [1985] 1 CMLR 27 at pp. 46, 47.
290 e.g. Cases 209-15 and 218/78 *AROW* v *BNIC* [1983] 2 CMLR 240; *FEDETAB* [1981] 3 CMLR 134 [1980] ECR 3125.
291 Case 8/72 *Vereeniging Van Cementhandelaren* [1973] CMLR 7, [1972] ECR 977.
292 See e.g. *Papier Peints* [1974] 2 CMLR D102—where Commission relying on principle in *Cementhandelaren* proceeded against the Belgian wallpaper industry for attempts at collective resale price maintenance. On appeal (Case 73/74 [1976] 1 CMLR 589; [1975] ECR 1491) the Court reaffirmed their dictum in *Cementhandelaren* but quashed the Commission's decision on the basis that they had not adequately established an effect on trade between the Member States.
293 Case 43 and 63/82 [1984] ECR 19 at pp 76–77 [1985] 1 CMLR 27 at pp. 49, 50.

maintenance and trade, including retail trade, from the country in question remains completely free as respects dealing in such imported products with or without resale price maintenance." The second point was considered the more important of the two.

8.174 In considering national schemes the decision of the Commission in *Deutsche Philips*[294] warrants mention. In that case Deutsche Philips enforced individual rpm in Germany on domestic products only. However, retailers were prohibited from selling Deutsche Philips's products to customers in other Member States at prices lower than those fixed in West Germany. Furthermore, Deutsche Philips required dealers to apply rpm to the goods irrespective of where the goods had been purchased. The scheme was thus designed to prevent reimportation and hence safeguard the purely domestic price levels. The Commission objected to the scheme: "This re-import price fixing thus prevented the German retailer from entering into competition with other German retailers as regards price when reselling reimported goods in Germany." The Commission added that a scheme, "cannot be justified by the fact that it serves to protect the price fixing which is legally permitted in Germany by preventing the sale of imported goods below the prices fixed in Germany."

8.175 In response to a written question from the European Parliament[295] regarding the price maintenance on books in Germany, Sir Leon Brittan, answering on behalf of the Commission, repeated the Commission's position in *Net Book Agreements (UK)*, namely, that "collective, horizontal price-fixing agreements in respect of books may contravene Article 85(1) ... if they affect trade between Member States" and went on to say that the Commission was currently examining whether price-fixing systems in other Member States appreciably restrict competition and affect inter-state trade.

8.176 The Commission may intervene in national schemes irrespective of the effect such intervention has on the national scheme, for example, by rendering its operation more difficult or even impossible.[296] If the Commission does intervene in a national scheme, it must take into account any beneficial effects that scheme may have on other Member States' markets in assessing whether an exemption is merited under Article 85(3). It was the failure of the Commission to have considered the argument that the UK Net Book Agreement had beneficial effects in the Republic of Ireland which led to the Court of Justice, overturning the Court of First Instance, to quash the Commission's decision that the Net Book Agreement contravened Article 85(1) and did not qualify for an exemption under Article 85(3).[297]

(4) National consensus immaterial to Commission policy

8.177 The fact that national laws might tolerate forms of rpm does not mean that EC law must follow the consensus:

> "national legislative or judicial practices, even on the supposition that they are common to all the Member States, cannot prevail in the application of the competition rules set out in the treaty. The same reasoning applies with even greater force in relation to practices of private undertakings, even where they are tolerated or approved by the authorities of a Member State."[298]

[294] [1973] CMLR D241 at consideration 7(c).

[295] Written Question no. 2151/88.

[296] *per* Advocate General Verloren Van Themaat in *VBVB and VBBB, op. cit.*, n. 287, pp. 59–61.

[297] C-360/92P *Publishers' Association* v *Commission* [1995] ECR I-23; the Court of First Instance's decision is reported under the same name Case T-66/89; [1992] ECR II-1995; [1992] 5 CMLR 120 and the Commission's decision is at OJ 1989 L 22/12; [1989] 4 CMLR 825.

[298] *VBVB op. cit.*, n. 287 at pp. 92, 93, para. 40 (ECJ). Thus because some of the Member States tolerate resale price maintenance for books this does not mean that the same should apply in EC law. See also *Application of the Verband Der Sachversicherer eV* [1985] 3 CMLR 246 at para. 28—the Commission stated

(5) Resale price maintenance not justified as a cure for loss-leader tactics

8.178 The European Court has rejected the argument that rpm is a valid cure for loss-leading. This practice entails the fixing of very low sale prices for goods in order to attract customers. Supporters of rpm to curb loss leading advance three main justifications. The product is probably being subsidised by excessive prices on other goods. Further, it is alleged to harm the manufacturer's reputation since consumers may equate low price with low quality. Finally, it may lead to a disruptive price war:

> "The fact that a system of resale price maintenance may have the incidental effect of preventing unfair competition of the kind described ... is not, however, a sufficient reason for failing to apply Article 85(1) to a whole sector of the market ... It is open to undertakings which may have suffered injury as a result of unfair competition to have recourse to legislation on trade practices such as exists in one form of another in all the Member States, which provides remedies against abuses such as those mentioned by the applicants. On the other hand, the fact that such abuses exist cannot in any circumstances justify an infringement of the Community rules on competition."[299]

8.179 Suppliers withholding supplies from loss-leading dealers are justified in so doing in the UK under section 13 Resale Prices Act 1976. However, UK suppliers, in relying on section 13, should enure that their conduct does not affect inter-state trade so as to engage EC rules.

(6) Resale price maintenance: when exemptible under Article 85(3)

8.180 It appears to be the case that rpm may be exemptible under Article 85(3) in exceptional cases where price competition is relatively unimportant to the consumer and where non-price rivalry is central. Where price competition is important exemption is highly unlikely. In *Metro* v *Commission*[300] a third party contested a Commission decision approving, under Article 85(3), an rpm scheme. The Court affirmed the Commission's competence to approve rpm. Resale price maintenance was acceptable in markets for products where marketing and pre-and post-sales services were relatively more important than price. In these markets rpm was permissible if it facilitated competition between dealers in services. The rpm thus cemented a switch in intra-brand competition from price to services. Where intra-brand rivalry remained high (i.e. rivalry between different brands) then competition from other manufacturers would enure that prices remained competitive.

8.181 In *Eurocheques*,[301] the Commission gave an exemption for a price fixing agreement between banks operating the Eurocheque system, whereby banks agreed to charge a standard commission to customers for encashment and to each other for clearing. The exemption was justified both by the cost and complexity of the clearing scheme for such cheques without uniform commissions, the Commission noting that the alternative would be bilateral negotiations between the 15,000 banks party to the scheme, and by its overall goal of single market integration by improving payment facilities throughout the Common Market. More-

cont.
that simply because national authorities condone a practice (*in casu* a recommendation by an association of property insurers to abide by a set percentage increase in fire risk premiums) the application of Article 85 is unaffected. The Commission added somewhat cryptically that they would none the less seek to avoid frustrating the policy decisions of national authorities without good reason.

299 *VBVB op. cit.*, n. 287 at p. 92, para. 37.

300 Case 26/76 [1978] 2 CMLR 1, [1977] ECR 1875. See also Case 56/77 *Agence Europeene d'Interims* v *Commission* [1978] ECR 2215—in recruiting temporary staff via an agency European Commission not bound to accept lowest tender made by an agency since price was not the essential competitive element; the quality of the agency and the social duty to pay higher salaries to better qualified employees were more imported factors. See for a difference conclusion *Pharmaceutische Handelsconventie* [1978] 1 CMLR 509 price considered essential ingredient in competition for particular drugs.

301 [1985] 3 CMLR 434.

over, there remained substantial competition from other payment methods capable of use across borders, such as travellers cheques and credit cards.

8.182 Indeed, in the *Net Book Agreement*[302] case, the Court of Justice did not rule out the possibility that the Commission might grant exemption for rpm in books under Article 85(3) for the same reasons as had led the Restrictive Practices Court to condone the agreement. It was the failure of the Commission to acknowledge that this was even a possibility which led to the Commission's decision being quashed.

8.183 The relative importance of price and non-price factors in competition is not the only question of relevance. The useful life span of a product coupled to the need for rapid marketing may be another. This argument has been raised in respect of newspapers as a result of the nature of the very limited period during which they are saleable and not yet outdated. At the end of the period (which varies according to the nature of the product in question) newspapers and journals are of almost no value. Furthermore, newspapers and periodicals are heterogeneous products for which there is little or no elasticity of demand, each paper or journal having well-established readerships. By the very nature of the product market, substantial numbers of the product have to be produced to meet potential demand. Frequently, retailers are left with unsold copies which are invariably returned to the publisher who either refrains from charging for them or who credits the retailer with their price on return. Both publisher and retailer incur costs in the transmission of these unsold copies. The natural corollary of this is that so it is contended the publisher should be allowed to fix both the quantities he distributes and the prices he sells at. A clear need for a permanent and stable demand based upon the calculation of likely demand levels accordingly exists and the arguments for Article 85(3) exemption appear feasible.[303]

8.184 The Court of Justice in *Pronuptia* has accepted that franchisors may recommend resale prices to franchisees and, provided the element of recommendation does not trespass into coercion, such recommendations will not fall within Article 85(1) (no question therefore of exemption arising). However, in *ARG/Unipart*[304] the Commission held, in the context of an exclusive distribution agreement, that the obligation on Unipart to transmit to authorised dealers ARG's non-binding recommendation of retail prices for certain parts influenced "the purchasing and sale policies of ARG's dealers and the consumers, and thereby restricts Unipart's freedom to establish its own commercial and pricing structures". The obligation was, therefore, contrary to Article 85(1) but was granted exemption under Article 85(3).

2. *UK Law*[305]

(1) OFT practice

8.185 Resale price maintenance in the UK is governed by the Resale Price Act 1976 (RPA 1976, hereafter). This Act has been singularly successful in eliminating rpm. The OFT, however, receives a significant number of complaints each year (between 20 and 30 on average) often from dealers who consider that the refusal of their supplier to maintain nor-

[302] C-360/92P *Publishers' Association* v *Commission* [1995] ECR I–23.

[303] cf. Case 243/83 *Binon* v *Agence et Messageries de la Presse* [1985] 3 CMLR 800. See, Commission answer to Written Question no. 2056/85, OJ 1986 C130/37, and *Fifteenth Report on Competition Policy* (1985).

[304] OJ 1988 L45/34; [1988] 4 CMLR 513.

[305] See generally Cunningham, *The Fair Trading Act 1973* (1974), Chapter 17; Korah, *Competition Law of Britain and the Common Market* (1982), Chapter 8 and for even older commentaries: Summerfield and Stanbrook, *The Resale Prices Act* (1964); Macdonald, *Resale Price Maintenance* (1964); Pickering, *Resale Price Maintenance in Practice* (1966); Yamey, *Resale Price Maintenance* (1966).

mal trading with them was due to price cutting on their behalf. On investigation the OFT usually discover that about 15 per cent of all complaints warrant action.[306] The OFT often deals with violations of the Act by seeking an undertaking from the infringing party, which cures the violation. However, more usually cases are dealt with by the OFT suggesting to a supplier that they amend the wording of sales or promotional documents so as to avoid misinterpretation by dealers or the public.

(2) Collective resale price maintenance[307]

8.186 The following points may be noted:

(a) Supplier cartels: it is unlawful (though not a criminal offence) for two or more suppliers carrying on business in the United Kingdom as good suppliers to make or perform any agreement under which they agree:
   (i) to refuse supplies to a dealer who is reselling, or has resold, goods in breach of the suppliers price conditions;
   (ii) to refuse supplier to dealers who deviate from suppliers price conditions other than on discriminatory terms;
   (iii) to supply to other suppliers (e.g. wholesalers) who agree to supply dealers on the same basis as the two situations above.[308]

   Moreover it is unlawful for two or more suppliers to agree to recover or seek to enforce penalties from defaulting dealers.[309]

(b) Dealer cartels: it is unlawful for dealers to agree to withhold orders for supplies from suppliers who continue to supply price cutters.[310]

(c) Trade associations: the prohibitions on suppliers and dealers above apply equally to trade associations.[311]

(d) Registrability under the RTPA: where an association, for example, a joint purchasing agency, recommends or suggests to members selling prices for special promotions or "own-brands" this is registrable under section 6(1)(b) RTPA 1976.

(3) Individual resale price maintenance: void terms under section 9

8.187 Any term of condition in a contract between a supplier and a dealer which provides for *minimum* rpm is void.[312] The same applies to a contract between a supplier and a wholesaler requiring the latter to incorporate rpm clauses in contracts with dealers. It is essential to note that section 9 applies only to *minimum* prices. It remains legal for supplies to fix *maximum* prices and/or to *recommend* resale prices.[313] Though any pressure imposed on dealers to comply with a recommendation is unlawful.

[306] This action is usually advice to the supplier to amend publicity literature. In other cases informal undertakings are accepted from suppliers.

[307] "Price" in this context includes a charge of any description (s. 8(1)). Moreover price conditions include conditions: (i) as to the amount of discount allowed on resale of the goods; and (ii) as to prices to be paid on the resale of goods for other goods taken by way of exchange (s. 6).

[308] s. 1(1)(a)–(c) RPA 1976.

[309] s. 1(2) RPA 1976.

[310] s. 2 RPA 1976.

[311] s. 4 RTPA 1976.

[312] s. 9 RPA 1976.

[313] Though, if a supplier fixes a "maximum price" which in reality is used, and is intended to be used as a price for dealers to adhere to and not undercut, this will probably be treated as a minimum price contrary to s. 9. See *Wholesale and Multiple Bakers' Federation Agreement* (1959) LR 1 RP 387. RPC treated maximum price as a fixed price where parties adhered to it.

8.188 It is unlawful for a supplier or trade association or other person representing a supplier to: include a term that is void in a contract; require, as a condition of supplying a dealer, the inclusion of any clause which seeks rpm; or, notify to dealers (or publish) a price in relation to any good which is to be understood as a minimum price for resale.[314]

8.189 The prohibitions above extend to patented goods.[315] However, it is clear that a price clause in a patent licence requiring the licensee to maintain a certain price is *not* subject to the Act.[316] The patent holder *is* prohibited however from granting a restricted sales licence to purchasers who have obtained the goods directly or indirectly through the patent holder or through the licensee and thereby maintain rpm. This would be relevant for technically complex consumer goods which may incorporate parts which are patented, e.g. cars, stereos, radios, dishwashers, etc.

(4) Unlawful withholding of supplies to dealers who cut price

8.190 It is unlawful to "withhold supplies" to price cutting dealers on the basis that: (a) the dealer has undercut the supplier's stipulated price; (b) the dealer has supplied contract goods to a third party who has undercut the suppliers stipulated price; (c) the dealer is likely if the goods are supplied to him to undercut the suppliers stipulated price; (d) the dealer is likely if the goods are supplied to him to supply those goods to a third party who would be likely to undercut the supplier's stipulated price.[317] Where these prohibitions apply to a supplier, it is equally unlawful for that supplier to organise for any other supplier to refuse to supply the dealers.[318] An agreement between suppliers to this effect is, in any event, prohibited by section 1 of the Act. Furthermore, the second supplier would likewise be prohibited from refusing to supply in the same way as is the first supplier.

8.191 Section 12 RPA 1976 explains the meaning of "withhold supplies". A supplier is to be treated as "withholding supplies" from a dealer: (a) if he refuses to meet the dealer's orders; (b) if he refuses to supply a dealer other than at prices or on terms or conditions as to credit and discounts, etc. which are significantly less favourable than those at or on which he normally supplies such goods to other similar dealers; (c) he supplies the dealer but he significantly discriminates against the dealer when compared to other such dealers in terms of times or methods of delivery or other matters arising from performance of the contract.

8.192 In practice it may prove difficult for a dealer to prove that a supplier has significantly discriminated against him. First, the term "significantly" used in section 12 appears to exclude discrimination against a price cutter which is of a minimal nature, it will be a question of fact in each case whether the discrimination is "significant" or not. Secondly, dealers can only complain of discrimination that differentiates him from other comparable dealers. Section 12(1) speaks of "other dealers carrying on business in similar cir-

314 s. 9(2) RPA 1976.

315 s. 10 RPA 1976.

316 s. 10(3) RPA 1976. There are a number of reasons for this. First sales by a licensee are not *resales*, they are *new* sales; secondly, the licensing of intellectual property is not apparently the supply of goods or services— *Ravenseft* v *Director General of Fair Trading* [1977] 1 All ER 47, DGFT Annual Report (1976), p. 36 (see also the view taken by Aldous J in the Patents Court under Article 86 EC in *Chiron Corporation* v *Organon Teknika Ltd* [1992] 3 CMLR 813); thirdly, such a price clause would be exempt under Sch. 3(5) RTPA 1976 exempting patent licences (where not in a patent pool) from the RTPA 1976.

317 s. 11(1) RPA 1976. "Resale price" in respect of a sale by description is defined in s. 11(2) and means: any price published or notified to dealers as a minimum price or as a recommended minimum price; and, any price prescribed for that purpose by a contract between the dealer and supplier. For an example of OFT intervention against a firm refusing to supply price cutters, see, *Apple Computer UK Ltd—Assurance* DGFT Annual Report (1984), p. 107.

318 s. 11(3) RPA 1976.

cumstances". How does one determine whether dealers are in similar circumstances? Does "circumstances" refer to geographical location, volume of turnover, profit margins, willingness to provide pre-and post-sales services, advertising space and stockholding capacity, etc?[319] It would seem that suppliers may be able to justify discriminating against a price-cutter on the grounds that the dealer was not in similar circumstances to another dealer. The test here is an objective one, i.e. *not* whether the supplier personally considers dealers to be in similar circumstances, but, whether a hypothetical reasonable supplier would so consider them to be.

(5) Lawful withholding of supplies to dealers who cut price

8.193 Suppliers may refuse to supply price cutters if, in addition to the price cutting there are additional grounds which standing alone would have led the supplier to withhold supplies.[320] On the precise wording of the statute the test is subjective, i.e. did the supplier actually have reasons other than the price cutting of the dealer to withhold supplies? There is nothing in the Act which states explicitly that these reasons must be objective or reasonable. The point is not free from doubt. The *Black and Decker* case referred to above suggests that the Act may incorporate objective tests, not subjective tests. However, unreasonable grounds may operate to throw substantial doubt upon the genuineness of the supplier's assertion that the ground was the predominant reason for withholding supplies. It appears, therefore, that a supplier may refuse supplies to a multiple retailer or discounter who is providing inadequate pre-and post-sales services to protect the manufacturer's reputation. Though, such a refusal to supply may be anti-competitive under the CA 1980 and the OFT may accordingly assess the economic effect of any refusal to supply irrespective of the RPA 1976.[321] Indeed, the Act embodies a presumption that a withholding of supplies is unlawful where: (a) up until the time the supplier withheld supplies the supplier was doing business with the dealer or with other similar dealers; *and* (b) the dealer, to the supplier's knowledge, had within the previous six months cut prices or supplied another dealer who had cut prices. Note that this is only a presumption, it may be rebutted by the supplier showing that there was another reasons for the withholding of supplies.[322] It is clear that the presumption will operate in most cases. The presumption does *not* operate where the proof that supplies were withheld consists only of evidence of requirements imposed by the supplier in respect of the time or form of payment for goods supplied.[323]

(6) Resale price maintenance lawful to prevent loss-leading

8.194 As noted above the Court of Justice has refused to allow rpm as a cure for loss-leading. The opposite applies in the UK. Section 13 RPA 1976 states that it is not unlawful for a supplier to withhold supplies (or to organise for another supplier to withhold supplies) from a dealer where the supplier has "reasonable cause" to believe that within the past 12 months the dealer (or any other dealer who is supplied by the dealer) has been using the contract goods as loss-leaders.

[319] See Korah, *op. cit.*, at note 305 at p. 187 for examples of problems related to this wording.

[320] s. 12(2) RPA 1976. See e.g. *Comet Radiovision* v *Farrell-Tandberg* (1971) LR 7 RP 168—RPC granted interlocutory injunction against supplier who withheld supplies from dealer who advertised that he sold at "cut prices". RPC said to withhold supplies in this situation was the same as withholding supplies from a dealer who was likely to cut prices. In *Oxford Printing Co Ltd* v *Letraset Ltd* (1970) LR 7 RP 94 RPC refused an interlocutory injunction against a supplier who had withheld supplies, not because dealer cut prices, but because the dealer advertised to customers to use a competitor's product.

[321] See e.g. OFT investigations under the CA 1980 into: *Raleigh Industries* (27 February 1981); *Arthur Sanderson* (27 August 1981); *Still Services* (22 July 1982).

[322] s. 12(3) RPA 1976.

[323] *ibid.*

8.195 A loss-leader sale is defined in section 12(2) as a sale "not for the purpose of making a profit on the sale of those goods, but for the purpose of attracting to the establishment at which the goods are sold customers likely to purchase other goods or otherwise for the purpose of advertising the business of the dealer."[324] Though the point is not absolutely clear it seems that a loss-leader sale is not necessarily a sale below cost, it can be a sale incorporating a significantly smaller mark-up than that envisaged by the supplier recommended price.[325]

8.196 In *Black and Decker*,[326] the MMC refused to accept Black and Decker's argument that retailers supplying at low margins (*in casu*, below 12.5 per cent) were automatically selling as loss leaders. The MMC analysed the section at some length before concluding that whatever it meant, it required determinations of loss leading to be done on an individual case by case basis, not on general assumptions.[327]

8.197 The test here is objective; it is not whether the supplier believes that the dealer was loss-leading, it is whether that supplier has reasonable grounds for believing that the dealer loss-led the goods either: (a) to attract customers who might purchase other goods; and/or (b) generally to advertise the dealer's business.

8.198 In *JJB (Sports) Ltd* v *Milbro sports Ltd*[328] a dealer sought an interlocutory injunction to restrain the supplier from wrongfully withholding supplies. The Court accepted the supplier's defence that the refusal to supply was in response to the dealer's loss-leading. The Court noted that the plaintiff's statement of claim was premised entirely upon the allegedly past unlawful withholding of supplies and did not refer to threatened refusals to supply in the future. A plaintiff seeking relief should request a Court order to deal with both past infringement and any future refusals to supply. Both should be covered by the statement of claim.

8.199 What is less clear is whether a supplier may seek an injunction to restrain a distributor from loss leading. Although the RPA only envisages the remedy of withholding supplies, it may be that supplies are readily available through other distribution channels. In such a case it would seem that an injunction for breach of a statutory duty should be available to prevent conduct which the RPA recognises is unfair competition.[329]

8.200 Under section 13(3) RPA 1976 the following are *not* loss-leaders: (a) genuine seasonal or clearance sales of goods not purchased for such purposes; (b) sales made with the consent of the manufacturer; and (c) sales of goods made to the design of a supplier, or to the order and bearing the trade mark of a supplier, made with the consent of that supplier. None of these exceptions is without difficulty; (a) in particular has given rise to serious problems in those sectors of the retail economy where "seasonal" or "clearance" sales seem to be endemic and almost never ending.

(7) Supplier practices outside the scope of the Act[330]

8.201 A number of practices though perhaps economically undesirable have been generally accepted as falling outside of the RPA 1976. However, such practices may be reviewed under

[324] s. 13 RPA 1976.
[325] See *JJB (Sports) Ltd* v *Milbro Sports Ltd* [1975] ICR 73 at p. 75A.
[326] Cm 805, 1989.
[327] Cm 805, 1989, at paras. 6.60–6.76; the MMC concluded that the problems of interpreting section 13 were "indicative of the ambiguity of the section, which does not appear to us to be drafted in such a way which adequately defines loss leading."
[328] *supra* note 325.
[329] In *Black and Decker*, the MMC noted that there had only been one action brought by a supplier for an interlocutory injunction, which failed at the interlocutory stage and did not proceed to full trial.
[330] See Liesner Committee *Review of Restrictive Trade Practices Policy* (1979) Cmnd 7512, pp. 51–3, paras. 5.59–5.65.

the CA 1980 if they amount to a course of conduct, i.e. have a repetitive or non-isolated nature.

8.202 (a) Credit control—"minimum advertised prices": the practice turns upon the supplier practice of providing credit to dealers to finance their stocks. Suppliers warn dealers that if they undercut an advertised price or if they advertise at below the supplier's recommended price then the supplier will have to reconsider the creditworthiness of the particular dealer. The low price charged by the dealer will give insufficient profit to make the dealer viable and obviously suppliers must protect against bad debts. The OFT has received complaints of supplier behaviour of this nature, especially in respect of expensive camera equipment, but has been unable to provide a remedy. Suppliers can justify this behaviour under section 12(2) RPA 1976 on the ground not that the dealer shaved prices but that the dealer was not creditworthy. It will be recalled that withholding supplies under section 12(2) is legal where the motive is not related to the price cutting of the dealer.

8.203 (b) Guarantees: many suppliers give guarantees to the ultimate consumer of their goods but provide that the guarantee is only operative if the goods are sold at the recommended retail price. This is not a condition imposed on the dealer so is not embraced by the Act. It does affect the dealer in that if he undercuts the supplier's recommended price he cannot transfer the guarantee to the customer. Clearly, there exists in this an incentive for the dealer to maintain the price and pass over the guarantee since this affords the dealer greater security against contractual responsibility for defective goods and may be an important selling point for the customer. Often though the guarantee is more valuable to dealer than customer.

8.204 (c) "Dealer noise"—complaints by dealers: if a major dealer threatens to change his supplier unless that supplier refuses to deal with a small dealer who is causing trouble by pricing cutting, then the supplier may be able to justify withholding supplies from the smaller dealer on the basis that failure will entail the loss of a more important customer. The greater the volume of "dealer noise" the more compelling becomes this argument. Where dealers, in concert, agree to pressurise a supplier this is unlawful under section 2 RPA 1976.[331]

8.205 (d) Product reputation: suppliers who employ selective distribution techniques may decline to supply price cutters on the basis that this will affect the reputation of the goods albeit that the supplier does not otherwise object to his goods being cut priced. Suppliers might content that if a dealer were to cut prices and commence a price war then other dealers would also have to cut prices; this would necessarily mean that pre-and post-sales services would have to be cut back and this in turn could mean that the goods were sold under conditions harmful to the supplier's reputation.[332]

[331] In the USA it has been held that the existence of dealer complaints coupled to a subsequent refusal to supply by a supplier to a price-cutting dealer does not, in the absence of additional evidence, amount to a combination or conspiracy to fix resale prices under the Sherman Act, s. 1—*Monsanto Co* v *Spray-Rite Service Corp* 104 S. Ct. 1464 (1984). Monsanto however lost on the facts and was required to pay US$10,500,000. The Supreme Court stated that there must exist, in addition to evidence only of buyer noise *and* a refusal to deal, "direct or circumstantial evidence that reasonably tends to prove that a manufacturer and others had a conscious commitment to a common scheme designed to achieve an unlawful objective". The Supreme Court stressed the need to find an agreement between supplier and distributor to charge a certain level of prices in *Business Electronic* v *Sharp* 99 L Ed 2d 808 (1988).

[332] But the CA 1980 applies, see *Raleigh Industries* (27 February 1981) which seems to doubt whether the OFT and MMC will accept this argument.

8.206 (e) Advertising: the MMC found in *Specialised Advertising Services*[333] that a policy of advertising goods in magazines without quoting prices distorted competition because it reduced the supply of pricing information to consumers. It thus lessened the likelihood of price competition and so contributed towards the maintenance of the manufacturers' recommended level of retail prices for the outdoor equipment in question.[334]

8.207 It should finally be stressed that refusals to deal based upon these considerations though outside the scope of the RPA 1976 may be subject to the CA 1980 (and of course Article 85 EC). None the less, under the Act they are not automatically unlawful and, in any event, will only encounter legal problems when (and if) the OFT decides to investigate. Dealers refused supplies in the above ways may of course complain to the OFT under the RPA 1976; explanations given by a supplier may not be genuine.

(8) Obtaining exemption via the Restrictive Practices Court

8.208 For all practical purpose the right accorded by the Act to suppliers or their trade associations to apply to the RPC for exemption for their rpm schemes is an irrelevance. Two cases have, it is admitted, succeeded by this method to obtain exemption. However both cases have received criticism and all other attempts have failed.

8.209 The RPC may exempt goods where satisfied that loss of RPM would entail one or more of five mal-consequences outlined in the Act. These are:

(a) substantial decline in the quality or variety of goods available on the market;
(b) a substantial decline in the numbers of retail outlets;
(c) long-term increases in prices;
(d) danger to health as a result of misuse by the consuming public; and
(e) the cessation or substantial reduction in necessary post-sales services to the consuming public.

Moreover, the Court must be satisfied that the detriment from RPM is *less* than the detriment from loss of rpm.

8.210 Originally over 500 rpm schemes were registered pending a hearing before the RPC. Only four reached the Court. *Confectionery Suppliers*[335] and *Footwear Suppliers*[336] failed. *Medicaments* succeed despite opposition from the government.[337] The Net Book Agreement succeeded with the assent of the government.[338]

8.211 The essence of the argument that succeeded before the RPC in the *Net Book Agreement* is as follows. The maintenance of stocking levels is very important in book selling since demand is not primarily related to price changes. Stocks can only be maintained if the risk involved in purchasing books (i.e. due to unpredictable buyer tastes) is minimised. A system of rpm gives sellers a degree of financial security sufficient to enable them to buy books in for stocks. If prices fell, stock levels would also fall and the less popular, minority taste, titles would have to be deleted from sellers' buying lists. Furthermore, with

333 Cm 280 (1988).
334 This recommendation was enforced by the Restriction on Conduct (Specialist Advertising Services) Order 1988 (S.I. 1988 No. 1017).
335 *Chocolate and Sugar Confectionery Reference* (1967) LR 6 RP 338.
336 *Footwear Reference* (1968) LR 6 RP 398.
337 *Medicaments Reference* (1970) LR 7 RP 267. The case has now been referred back to the RPC by the DGFT under section 4(3) of the RTPA 1976.
338 *Net Book Agreement* (1962) LR 3 RP 246, [1962] 1 WLR 1347 noted Yamey (1963) 26 MLR 691, criticised passim in, Stevens and Yamey, *The Restrictive Practices Court* (1965); and Turner, *Competition and the Law* (1966). See also, Hornsby, "Public and private resale price maintenance systems in the publishing sector: the need for equal treatment in European law" (1985) ELRev 381.

fewer books being purchased, publisher production runs would have to be reduced thereby losing scale economies. Ultimately prices would rise. The *Net Book Agreement* has now collapsed as a result of industry pressure.

8.212 The Net Book Agreement exemption has now been revoked by the RPC in proceedings pursuant to section 4 RTPA 1976 and section 17 RPA.[339] In the meantime, it has been considered by the Commission as contravening Article 85(1) but not meriting an exemption.[340] However, although this finding was upheld by the Court of First Instance,[341] the decision was subsequently quashed by the Court of Justice[342] on the ground that it failed to consider whether the arguments which were successful before the RPC justified the grant of an exemption because of their beneficial effects on both UK and Irish markets.

8.213 As time progresses it will presumably be increasingly difficult to justify exemption before the Court. First, the Court will have at its disposal statistical and economic evidence over a long period of time about the effects of no rpm on the market so that mere hypothesis about what the market will be like without rpm will not suffice; secondly, given that the legislation is now long-standing[343] it might be asked why suddenly there should evolve a pressing need for rpm. Conceivably the issue might arise in respect of a new product or technological development.

8.214 Where a supplier has been allowed to enforce rpm he may employ section 26 RPA 1976. This entitles the supplier to apply to the Court for an injunction restraining any dealer who is *not* a party to the contract with the supplier but who obtains the goods with notice of the rpm condition from selling the goods in breach of the condition.[344] Section 26 only applies to dealers who are to resell the goods, it does not apply to consumers. The section further applies to any other resale price condition that is lawfully a maximum price condition.[345]

It will be appreciated that section 26 is a statutory circumvention to the ordinary contract rule of privity whereby a supplier cannot enforce contractual terms against persons not party to the contract.

(9) Enforcement by the OFT: assurances

8.215 Section 25(2) entitles the Crown to commence proceedings for an injunction or other relief against a party breaching the Act.[346] Section 23(3) gives a remedy to a private party

339 Judgment of RPC of 13 March 1997. Those proceedings were being prosecuted despite its abandonment, in order that the exemption for the *Net Book Agreement* be ended to prevent any further agreement taking advantage of the exemption. The *Net Book Agreement* was abandoned on 28 September 1995 by the publishers following the decision by major publishers Penguin, HarperCollins and Random House to withdraw. However, individual publishers remain free to set net prices until the formal termination of the exemptions under the RTPA and RPA.

340 OJ 1989 L22/12, [1989] 4 CMLR 825.

341 Case T-66/89 *Publishers' Association* v *Commission* [1992] ECR II-1995, [1992] 5 CMLR 120.

342 Case C-360/92P *Publishers' Association* v *Commission* [1995] ECR I-23.

343 The RPA 1976 was a consolidation of earlier legislation, i.e. Monopolies and Restrictive Practices (Inquiry and Control) Act 1948 which subjected rpm to investigation by the MMC. Early MMC reports were critical, e.g. MMC Report on *Supply of Electrical Equipment for Mechanically Propelled Land Vehicles* (1963) HC 21.

344 See *Goodyear Tyres* v *Lancashire Batters* (1957) LR 1 RP 22; *County Laboratories* v *Mindel* (1957) LR 1 RP 1; *Mackintosh* v *Bakers Bargain Stores (Seaford) Ltd* (1965) LR 5 RP 305, (1965) 1 WLR 1182 (sale by liquidator not a resale, liquidator does not acquire title, purchaser from liquidator may be bound) and in the context of the *Net Book Agreement, Chatto and Windus* v *Pentos*, unreported, 13 October 1990.

345 On whether the provision of non-price benefits may be prohibited see *Gallagher* v *Supersave Supermarkets* (1964) LR 5 RP 89; *Beechams Foods* v *North Supplies* (1959) LR 1 RP 262.

346 See e.g. *Director General of Fair Trading* v *Hotpoint* DGFT Annual Report 1979, p. 47—proceedings settled on basis of an undertaking given by the defendant, Hotpoint Ltd, to supply their electrical appliances to Comet Radiovision Services Ltd on terms not significantly less favourable than those normally applied

who has been harmed by breach of the Act to sue the infringer for damages by way of the tort of breach of a statutory duty. In practice both such remedies are all but irrelevant. In reality complaints are made by aggrieved parties to the OFT who investigate and if (in the rare event) the complaint proves justified, pressurise the infringing party into compliance. Usually, suppliers are encouraged to recommence supplies to a price cutting dealer. Where the OFT is unconvinced of the willingness to comply of the supplier it will seek an informal assurance from that party that the Act will, in future, be complied with. These assurances generally obtain up to four negative elements and two positive elements:

(a) Negative elements.[347] The OFT, depending on circumstances, seek undertaking from the parties whereby they will not:

"notify to dealers or otherwise publish of or in relation to any goods a price stated or calculated to be understood as the minimum price which may be charged on the resale of those goods in the United Kingdom";

"require as a condition of supplying goods to any dealer the inclusion of a term or condition or the giving or an undertaking establishing or providing for the establishment of a minimum rice to be charged on the resale of those goods";

"withhold supplies from a dealer on the grounds that the dealer has sold or is likely to sell the goods at less than minimum prices";

– "discriminate in any way against a dealer for the reason that such dealer sells, advertises or displays for sale its goods at prices below any price which it may communicate to a dealer in relation to the sale, advertisement or display for sale of its goods."

(b) Positive requirements: frequently the OFT includes the following clauses in an undertaking to be given by a supplier.

"with a view to ensuring that the relevant provisions of the Resale Prices Act 1976 are understood and observed throughout the Company's operation in the United Kingdom, it will bring the provisions of this assurance to the attention of all its employees concerned with the marketing, promotion or sale of its goods";[348]

"the Company shall circulate to all its dealers a statement conveying the substance of this assurance and advising them that they are free to sell, advertise and display for sale its goods at whatever price they may choose to do so".[349]

cont.
by Hotpoint to dealers carrying on business in similar circumstances to Comet. The court order also contained agreements and undertakings by Hotpoint and Comet with regard to a range-stocking agreement between them. In addition Hotpoint gave an informal, out of court undertaking to the OFT to comply with the Act.

347 For examples of negative assurance cases see DGFT Annual Report 1990, p. 110. See also previous annual reports for similar undertakings given under the Resale Prices Act 1976. Since the 1991 Report, the OFT has departed from previous practice by not reprinting the text of undertakings, which remain published by press releases and can be obtained from the OFT's Press Office and are available on the Internet (see bibliography for details).

348 e.g. *Shulton (Great Britain) Ltd* DGFT Annual Report 1980, pp. 116, 117, clause 4 of the undertaking; and *Revlon International Corporate* DGFT Annual Report 1980, p. 117, clause 4 of the undertaking.

349 e.g. *Lanvin Perfumes Ltd* DGFT Annual Report 1980, p. 117, clause 1 of the undertaking *Aqualisa Products Ltd* DGFT Annual Report 1985, p. 63; *BSA Guns Ltd* DGFT Annual Report 1985 63, 64. The OFT may also require suppliers to obtain confirmation in writing from dealers that they are aware that the suppliers policy has changed. In *Ault and Wiborg Paints Ltd*, DGFT Annual Report 1981, p. 113 the supplier gave an assurance to the OFT on the following lines: "we have already advised those of our distributors presently holding agreements that the relevant clauses have been deleted and have asked for their confirmation of such deletion in writing". Clearly, some of the undertakings given to the OFT may involve suppliers in obtaining their dealers approval to the amendment to existing contracts though it should be recalled that clauses providing for rpm are automatically void under s. 9(1) RPA 1976.

I. Equalisation of Receipts Schemes (Profit Pooling)

8.216 Equalisation schemes of profit pooling systems as they are sometimes termed, exert only an indirect effect upon prices but are none the less caught within competition rules. The essentials of an equalisation scheme were evident in *Cimbel*.[350] The parties sold cement on both the domestic (Belgium) and export markets. Given transport costs for such a heavy, low value per unit, product export profits were lower than domestic profits. The equalisation scheme sought to reduce the financial penalty suffered by exporters *vis-à-vis* domestic sellers. The trade association in question—Cimbel—collected the receipts of all transactions and made the necessary calculations to arrive at a fictitious average price for domestic sales and exports combined. Suppliers then compensated those suppliers whose lower than average profits were due to a concentrating of effort on export sales. The amount paid would be by reference to the fictitious average price. The parties claimed that this enabled them to increase competition on foreign markets (in the absence of the agreement exports on existing scales would be impossible). Further, that the scheme enabled them to employ maximum capacity thereby realising scale economies. An important feature of the scheme was that prices on the domestic market were fixed at supra-competitive levels.

1. *EC Law*

(1) Nature of scheme

8.217 In *Cimbel* (see para. 8.216) the Commission objected to an equalisation scheme on the following grounds:

(a) It operated as a private aid scheme to exporters giving them an artificial advantage on the export market. Manufacturers in other Member States were hence competing not only with the exporter but, *de facto*, with all domestic producers in that country also.

(b) The scheme allowed producers in the scheme to undeservedly offload surplus capacity on export markets irrespective of the efficiency or ability of each individual exporter.

(c) The scheme was financed by excessive receipts obtained on the domestic market. Without the equalisation of receipts and compulsory prices these receipts would necessarily have been lower.[351]

8.218 The Commission also views such schemes unfavourably for the "smothering" effect they have on prices. Thus invariably loss leader selling or sales prices below a certain minimum are excluded from the equalisation process thereby discouraging the maverick quotations which characterise competitive pricing.[352] It is still an unlawful restraint on competition if the equalisation of profits is confined to transactions with non-Member States.[353]

350 [1973] CMLR D167. See also *Milk Production Fund* [1985] 3 CMLR 101 where association members paid a levy to support promotion and advertising on export market. All members contributed irrespective of whether they were exporters. The Commission objected on the basis that such aided exporters benefited as against unaided exporters elsewhere. They might also have objected on the basis that non-exporter members of the association subsidised exporter members.

351 *ibid.* at p. 184, 185, para. 37.

352 *Fine Papers* [1972] CMLR D94.

353 *Cimbel* [1973] CMLR D167.

(2) The defence of economic necessity

8.219 In *Cimbel* the parties argued that the scheme protected the industry from economic ruin. Investment costs for cement works were three or four times the annual turnover and hence, to preserve outlets during periods of intense competition, cement producers had to sell at prices which guaranteed a profit otherwise they would be forced to gradually consume the substance of their business (i.e. investment costs would exceed return and eat away at reserves). The Commission refused to accept that the cartel was necessary to continued existence. It noted that it had not led to improvements in production or distribution such as would compensate for the restrictive effects of the cartel. However, it did imply that in appropriate circumstance a defence of economic necessity might be feasible: "The purely potential danger of ruinous competition, regarded as a theoretical and uncertain future event, cannot justify at present the elimination of competition between the parties with regard to price."[354] Arguably this implies that price restrictions might be justified where an acute recession actually threatens.

The Commission are prepared to exempt schemes to assist industries in long term structural decline, the so-called "crisis cartels", but only where such measures involve permanent reduction of capacity.[355] These are discussed at paras. 12.234 and following.

2. *UK Law*

(1) Whether registrable

8.220 It is clear that profit pooling is registrable under either section 6(1)(d) RTPA 1976 as concerning restrictions on the quantities to be supplied, or, under section 6(4) RTPA 1976 which expressly provides that schemes with mechanisms such as are used in profit pooling concern restrictions in respect of the quantities of goods to be produced or supplied. In *Linoleum Manufacturers' Association Agreement*[356] Ungoed-Thomas J thus explained that the right of a party to a scheme to receive payment:

> "depends upon the relationship of the quantities of goods supplied to him to the total quantities of goods supplied by all members. For each member there is a break-even point, namely a point at which he is neither paid nor pays. If he supplies a quantity of linoleum exceeding that proportion of the total linoleum supplied by all members which determines his break-even point, then and then only is he obliged to pay."

(2) Assessment

8.221 There are three situations requiring examination under UK law: (i) where the parties to the equalisation agreement are all situate in the UK but the aim of the agreement is to boost export sales to the EC; (ii) as above but where the aim of the agreement is to boost export sales to non-EC states; (iii) where the parties are all situate in the UK and equalisation is in respect of receipts earned on the domestic market only. These options will be considered in turn.

8.222 First, where the parties are all situate in the UK but use the scheme to boost EC sales this will fall foul of Article 85(1) EC. A parallel case was *Cimbel* where although the price fixing agreement was only in response of the Belgian market the anti-competitive effects were felt elsewhere in the EC. A decision of the Commission prohibiting such an agreement or imposing a fine in respect of it will not prevent similar prohibitive or punitive action being taken at national level. Enforcement at the national level would be in response

354 *ibid.* at p. D196, para. 49.
355 See the Commission's *Twenty-third Report on Competition Policy* (1993), paras. 82–89.
356 (1963) LR 4 RP 156; [1963] 1 WLR 897 at p. 903. See also at p. 904.

to anti-competitive consequences felt on the home market, whereas Community enforcement responds to anti-competitive consequence on trade between Member States. It should be noted, however, that national law cannot exempt such an agreement if it has been prohibited under Community law since Community law always take precedence.[357] Accordingly, this type of equalisation scheme stands little or no change of success.

8.223 Secondly, where national firms party to an equalisation scheme export outside the EC. In *Agreement of Papeteries Bollore SA and Branstein Freres SA*[358] an equalisation scheme operated by undertakings in one Member State with the aim of supporting non-EC exports was still prohibited under Article 85(1). The reasons for this are unclear. However, in explaining the Commission's strict approach it may be relevant that the scheme was only one of a bundle of other restrictions objected to by the Commission which had to be terminated before the overall export agreement could receive exemption under Article 85(3) EC. It is arguable that an equalisation scheme operating independently of other restrictions which boosts non-EC exports might be legitimate under EC law and hence potentially legitimate under UK law. No harmful effect upon intra-Community trade would occur where imports from other EC state are not hindered. Indeed, a price fixing agreement in the UK (as a constituent part of the equalisation scheme) resulting in supra-competitive prices might encourage domestic importer and foreign EC exporters to market foreign products in the UK and undercut the high domestic price. However, in view of the current EC approach caution should be exercised. Even were EC exemption to be available the fact that equalisation schemes invariably entail domestic price fixing would suggest that a strict approach would prevail in the UK. It might be argued in this context that an equalisation scheme boosting non-EC exports would fall under section 10(1)(f) RTPA 1976—the export gateway. This gives as a ground for exempting restrictions,

> "That, having regard to the conditions actually obtained or reasonably foreseen at the time of the application, the removal of the restriction would be likely to cause a reduction in the volume of earnings of the export business which is substantial either in relation to the whole export business in the United Kingdom or in relation to the whole business (including export business) of the said trade or industry."

8.224 While case law on this section need not be repeated it is pertinent to note that of seven cases pleaded on this section only one has succeeded.[359] Moreover, no case has ever employed this provision as possible justification for an equalisation scheme. The main stumbling block in the failed cases has always been in persuading the Restrictive Practices Court that the export advantages outweigh the domestic price-fixing. Moreover, to stand a chance under this provision the domestic fixed price would have to be "reasonable" whereas in the EC cases the domestic fixed price has always been supra-competitive, indeed it must be high in order to be able to compensate for low export earnings. Equalisation schemes, though affecting exports, are *not* pure export agreements which are free from antitrust restraints under UK

[357] See Case 14/68 *Wilheim* v *Bundeskartellamt* [1969] CMLR 100; [1969] ECR 1; "One and the same agreement may, in principle, be the object of two sets of parallel proceedings, one before the Community authorities under Article 85 of the EC Treaty, the other before the national authorities in application of internal law ... However ... such parallel application of the national system should only be allowed in so far as it does not impinge upon the uniform application, throughout the Common Market, of the Community rules on restrictive business agreements and of the full effect of the acts decreed in application of those rules ... Conflicts between the community rule and the national rules on competition should be resolved by the application of the principle of the primacy of the Community rule."

[358] [1972] CMLR D94. cf. also *Central Stikstof Verkoopkantor* [1979] 1 CMLR 11 at p. 35, para. 74 for an analogous situation commented upon by the Commission.

[359] i.e. *Water-Tube Boilermakers' Agreement* (1959) LR 1 RP 285; [1959] 1 WLR 1118 (RPC).

law.[360] Equalisation agreements are more properly viewed as domestic agreements with export consequences.

8.225 Thirdly, a purely national scheme involving no element of export aid would stand minimal chance of success since it would effectively be a method of smothering price competition. If a firm's earnings will be harmed rather than enhanced by an expansion of sales (i.e. there will be no compensating increase in profits from increased volume of trade) then the incentive to derogate from a common price is reduced. In the *Linoleum* case noted above members of the association paid a levy to a central pool calculated upon the basis of average manufacturing cost multiplied by the quantity sold to specified types of customer divided by two. The agreement provided that the pool proceeds would be distributed between the parties in pre-determined, fixed proportions. However, the only sum payable to a member was the difference between his levy and his share of the pool. Thus, if his levy exceeded his pool share he had to pay the different to the pool; if his levy was less than this pool share he was paid the difference by the pool. Whether a member's levy exceeded or fell below his share of the pool depended upon the relationship between the quantities or products sold by him to the total quantities of relevant products supplied by all the members. Such a scheme is inappropriate to section 21(2) treatment; it stands but minimal change of success before the RPC. Such agreements tend to lead to fixed prices and stable market shares.

J. Delivered Pricing (Base or Parity Point Pricing)

1. *Economic Framework*

(1) Nature of problem

8.226 These systems have caused problems for antitrust authorities with certain forms of the system unlawful and others almost certainly legitimate. The major problem lies in identifying legitimate schemes and differentiating them from unlawful schemes. In industry these schemes are known variously as: delivered price systems; base point pricing; multiple base point pricing; parity point pricing; freight equalisation systems; Franco-zone pricing systems; and, spatial pricing systems. Whatever the title of the system its basic function is to determine how freight costs are absorbed into ultimate price. A number of freight pricing methods exist. One—so-called "postage stamp" pricing—involves sellers charging a uniform delivered price to every buyer irrespective of distance (and hence true transport costs) from the production source. Alternatively, buyers in particular zones perhaps delineated by state may be charged identical freight costs. In each case the producer absorbs higher freight costs on shipment to distant customers than on shipments to customers nearer its plant. The producer therefore discriminates in favour of distant customers and against local customers. Postage stamp pricing is used more commonly for commodities whose value is high relative to transport costs. In the legally ideal world however—which does apply in the case of some bulky, low value commodities—a system of uniform ex-mill pricing is adopted: producers announced a mill price with purchasers bearing their own freight costs. If delivery by the producer is preferred only those freight charges actually incurred are added to the price. This is the "ideal" system because it involves no geographical price discrimination since purchase price relates directly to freight

[360] See Sch. 3, paras. 6 and 9 RTPA 1976.

costs whilst the seller receives a uniform mill net price after outward freight charges have been covered.[361]

8.227 To demonstrate some of the problems two examples based upon a hypothetical multiple base-point system are noted below. Under this system each major production centre becomes a basing point and producers located on that point effectively charge realistic prices. Firms who are distant from the base point may, however, find it convenient to quote delivered prices incorporating freight cost calculated from the base point rather than from their own works. Though, firms on or around a base point might invade an area served by another base point centre of production and compete in that market by absorbing their own freight costs.

Example 1. A base point centre of production if at X. A supplier is located at point Y which is 400 miles due south of X. A purchaser is located at point Z which is 400 miles due north of X. If the supplier wants to sell to the purchaser he will charge freight *only* from base point X to point Z (i.e. for only 400 miles rather than for 800 miles). In other words the purchaser pays freight *as if* the supplier were located at base point X. In this way the supplier can compete with the other suppliers actually located at X.

Example 2. As above, but the purchaser is located only 20 miles away from the supplier at point Y. However, he is still charged freight costs *as if* the supplier were located at base point X. The supplier, in this case earns extra profits based upon freight costs that have not been incurred, these profits are described as "phantom freight costs" profits.

(2) Competition law analysis and objections

8.228 Base point pricing has, in the USA at least, often been equated with collusion.[362] This is theoretically incorrect as the European Commission has recognised: "The question that arises in the scrutiny of individual cases is whether parallel conduct by several firms in the same industry is based on overt or covert collusion between them or inspired by a dominant firm's strategy."[363] Thus, if a smaller supplier away from a major production centre feels that he *has* to base his freight costs on that major centre in order to be able to compete, this is simply a response to a competitive situation and not evidence of agreement. Indeed, if a small firm charged only small freight costs to a customer close by to him thereby undercutting the large suppliers at the centre, the latter could retaliate by loss-leader pricing to the small firms customers until that small firm was put out of business or otherwise disciplined. Though retaliatory behaviour of this nature from a dominant concern will almost certainly represent an abuse of dominance under Article 86 EC or a practice reviewable under the CA 1980. Accordingly, the earning of "phantom freight costs" profits is not conclusive evidence of violation. Moreover such profits might arguably be viewed as a *quid pro quo* or compensation for freight costs absorbed by the supplier in supplies made long distance.[364]

[361] For detailed economic analysis see Scherer and Ross, *Industrial Market Structure and Economic Performance* (3rd edn. 1990), pp. 502–508.

[362] See, e.g. *Fort Howard Paper Company* v *FTC* 156 F.2d. 899 (7 Cir. 1946); *US* v *National Lead Company* 332 US 319 (1947); *United States Maltsters' Association* v *FTC* 152 F.2d. 161 (7 Cir. 1945); *Milk and Ice Cream Can Institute* 333 US 683 (1948). For analysis of these cases, see Neale and Goyder, *The Antitrust Laws of the USA* (3rd edn. 1980) at pp. 53–57.

[363] See Commission Reply to Written Question no. 1002/77, OJ 1978 C113/8 at p. 9.

[364] Though caution should be used in this defence point. Base point pricing encourages supplier to sell close to home in relying on order to reduce freight costs, hence it is not unlikely that a substantial majority of a smaller suppliers trade will be to purchases close to him. Thus, on *most* sales he may earn "phantom freight costs" profits.

8.229 Base point pricing may be objectionable because of the following economic consequences:

(a) It tends to underpin price agreements aimed at maintaining a geographical structure of delivered prices fixed to maximise the supplier group's profits.
(b) Delivered prices penalise and discriminate against buyers close to production centres and subsidise those further away. This distorts the competitive relationship between customers punishing firms who have located close to production centres who in reality deserve a price advantage.
(c) Systems employing a single or only a very few base points harm consumers located at centres of production which have not been selected as base points. Furthermore such a system can affect regional development by leading to the geographical concentration of buyers around the dominant base points.
(d) Customers cannot buy ex-works or ex-warehouse or make their own transport arrangements. The system thus unjustifiably ties sale of the product to use of the supplier's distribution network even though the purchaser may be able to provide his own more efficient and economical transport.
(e) Producers using the system refraining from using their location as an argument in their favour when seeking new customers. This distorts competition between suppliers. Compliance with a delivered price published by a majority of firms in a given trade is a rigidity which can seriously disrupt competition.
(f) Where reference areas coincide with the borders of the Member State of the EC then the system can harm the unity of the market by creating and supporting differential price zones.[365]

8.230 Base point pricing should not infringe Article 85(1) where it represents the policy of a supplier decided upon and applied *unilaterally*. In such cases no agreement or concerted practice exists to engage Article 85(1). Where adapted as policy through consensus with others (whether competitors or even the suppliers customers or some of them) Article 85(1) may be engaged. Where adopted as a policy by a dominant undertaking it is capable of representing an abuse of unfair or discriminatory pricing or even tying contrary to Article 86 EC.

2. EC Law

8.231 The Commission has stated:

> "For obvious reasons, what is known as the base point system, by removing all uncertainty as to the manner of calculating delivered prices, makes for perfect price transparency. The fact that competing firms systematically align their prices on the base prices plus the freight by the traditional supplier to the relevant area or country could sell point to a price-fixing agreement."[366]

8.232 However, the Commission has rejected the argument advanced by some that base point pricing is *always* unlawful. As explained earlier, there should be nothing wrong for a smaller supplier located away from a base point who adopts that base point for freight charge purposes in order to prevent predation or retaliation by large suppliers located on the point.

[365] See Working Question no. 1002/77, OJ 1978 C113/8 by MEP Mr Glinne and Commission answer, OJ 1978 C113/9. See also *Sixth Report on Competition Policy* (1976), paras. 48–50.

[366] *ibid.*

The fact that the smaller supplier may earn "phantom freight cost" profits is not conclusive of anything. The question arises how is a genuine situation distinguished from a collusive one. The Commission has not given guidance on this other than to state that antitrust problems are exacerbated where the commodity is of low unit value.[367] From American cases which have examined the problem the following features have emerged as indications of collusion:

(a) existence of a central trade association disseminating freight charges for adoption by suppliers to various zones;
(b) disciplinary action by a trade association (boycotts; warning letters; fines, etc.) against suppliers not adhering to the published freight costs;
(c) loss leader or otherwise predatory pricing by large firms against small firms who do not adhere to published freight costs (surrender on the part of the smaller firm may result in an agreement or concerted practice arising. It is no defence to Article 85(1) that the agreements was entered unwillingly or that one party was coerced into entering it. Such facts may be relevant but only to fines);
(d) opposition to carriage by transportation means other than those approved by a trade association and disciplinary reactions to those using different transport means.[368]

8.233 An overview of case in the EC suggests a strict approach. Thus in *European Glass Manufacturers*[369] the Commission stated:

> "This system ... has the object of nullifying any competitive advantage which a producer ... might gain from the proximity to his customers. It favours distant customers at the expense of those who are near; as the price is identical for both, the nearer customer pays for costs of delivery higher than those actually incurred by the seller, while the distant customer benefits from a discount on the actual freight costs. The system being of exclusive application, the sale of the products is automatically tied to the user accepting their delivery to his location, a supplementary obligation which has no necessary connection with the sale of the goods, since users of glass containers most often have their own means of transport."[370]

Consequently, competition between producers *inter se* and purchasers *inter se* was distorted.

8.234 Where joint selling agencies have also employed joint distribution networks whereby a number of firms use a single distribution scheme thereby incurring identical freight costs the Commission, again, has been critical.[371] Such a common freight network might be justified only if the joint selling agency itself gained exemption under Article 85(3) EC. The Commission has accepted that a nexus between joint agency and joint distribution may exist. Thus in *Central Stiktof Verkoopkantor* the Commission commented that a freight equalisation system operated by fertiliser producers was "in fact merely a logical consequence of the joint sale of their products."[372]

[367] cf. *ibid. per* Mr Glinne MEP who was sceptical of the competitiveness of geographical price systems in "a market structure characterized by a standard product with a low value per unit of weight, no elasticity of demand and an oligopolistic market supply situation." He continued later: "Does the Commission agree that as long as such geographical price systems continue, the prohibition of other concerted practices is often likely to be ineffective? Is there not a danger that they will seriously undermine the unity of the Common Market?" The gist of the Commission reply was that whilst most systems were in danger from Arts. 85 and 86 EC some systems developed naturally in the market and were hence legal.

[368] See *FTC* v *Cement Institute* 333 US 683 (1948).

[369] [1974] 2 CMLR D50.

[370] *ibid.* at pp. D72, 73, para. 48. See also *Comptoir Belge De L'azote (Cobelaz) Agreement* [1968] CMLR D68 at pp. D75, D76, para. 16.

[371] See e.g. *Central Stikstof Verkoopkantor* [1979] 1 CMLR 11 at p. 42, para. 191; *Floral Dungemittel Verkaufsgesellschaft* [1980] 2 CMLR 285 at pp. 291, 292, paras. 27–30.

[372] *ibid.*

It is worth reiterating that suppliers who adopt base points away from their plant may be acting lawfully if they can prove that this is simply a response to market circumstances and not evidence of collusion.

8.235 There is nothing to prevent *individual* firms from operating delivered pricing systems so long as there is sufficient competition to ensure that, despite the equalising effect on the freight component, prices remain competitive and reasonable and alternative supply sources exist. An individual firm in a dominant position employing such a system might be susceptible to challenge under Article 86 EC from purchasers close by who could claim that the dominant concern was price discriminating against them *vis-à-vis* more distant customers. Dominant suppliers, who pressurise smaller suppliers in the area to use them as a base point will probably be infringing Article 86 EC. This conclusion is almost a certainty where the dominant concern employs predatory pricing or other tactics against the smaller supplier. Where a dominant firm does employ base point pricing it might be well advised to give customers the option of arranging their own deliveries.

3. UK Law

8.236 An agreement or arrangement to adopt base point pricing is registrable. Such agreements are generally inappropriate to section 21(2) treatment.

The economic arguments discussed above would apply equally within the framework of United Kingdom law. In Cement Makers' Federation Agreement,[373] however, a multiple base point pricing system operated by a trade association was accepted by the RPC. The scheme is interesting since it did make provision for increasing freight costs to be taken into account in the final selling price. The Federation fixed cement prices: these had as their basis a "base price". This was the price to be paid within a five-mile radius of the works or group of works (the basing point) where the cement was manufactured. Concentric circles of radii increasing by successive five miles delimited zones within which the price was increased by specific amounts as cement was delivered further away from the works. The price increases progressively diminished the further away cement was delivered, thus there was a subsidy granted to distant customers. The price structure encouraged suppliers to sell close to home and to locate as near as possible to demand. The element of discrimination inherent in many systems was less pronounced here since the subsidy granted to distant customers was only a partial one; freight costs were staggered but not averaged. Hence local customers could gain a cost advantage over distant rivals. The judgment of the RPC also reveals that the market was dominated by a market leader who supplied most of the distant customers thus (somewhat philanthropically) bearing most of the subsidy costs itself. Furthermore, the Court seems to have considered that if a price war broke out the other firms would have little chance against the market leader. The Court thus highlighted a number of features which they considered made the system a reasonable one: the industry had operated on a modest profit margin and there were strong indications that the average rate of profit on capital employed was appreciably lower than that prevalent elsewhere in industry; the industry had operated efficiently expanding capacity in proper relationship to increases in demand and changes in geographical demand; the fixed prices were reasonable, giving firms a return on capital of under 10 per cent. In the risky free (unrestricted) market it was considered that firms

[373] (1961) LR 2 RP 241; [1961] 1 WLR 581 (RPC). The RPC subsequently reaffirmed their acceptance of the cement cartel: [1974] ICR 445. The Cement cartel was abandoned by the parties to the agreement in February 1987; see DGFT Annual Report 1987, p. 31.

would require a minimum of 15 per cent return on investment. Consequently, the Restrictive Practices Court accepted that the multiple base point pricing system gave the parties the security they required to fix prices at a low-level.

8.237 As with other cases that have successfully passed through the Restrictive Practices Court exceptional facts and market circumstances prevailed. None the less, the case demonstrates that a moderated system coupled to very reasonable prices may exceptionally be legal. Where the practice has been examined by the Monopolies and Mergers Commission it has invariably been condemned and the lesson to learn from this is that jointly operated and agreed systems are unlikely to receive official blessing.[374] Agreements to operate base point pricing will not be suitable for section 21(2) treatment.

K. Cost Calculation Models

1. *Nature of Model*

8.238 Many firms set prices inefficiently through ignorance of their cost structure. Hence a relatively common practice of trade associations is the dissemination of statistical and economic data relating to the construction of cost calculation models. The process of "educating" members as to the proper method of price calculation can be broken down into at least six stages. It should be stressed that not all stages necessarily reflect legal behaviour.

(i) Stage one: the association provides standard forms specifying, for example, cost components to be taken into account in total cost analysis. This helps eliminate "guesswork" prices.

(ii) Stage two: the association informs members of the correct method of calculating costs. Thus guidance for example on determining charges for raw materials, depreciation and distribution of overheads might be circulated. This further assists members in undertaking accurate cost analysis.

(iii) Stage three: the association publishes the aggregate cost for some or all components of production throughout the manufacturing process. The disseminated data will relate not to actual costs but to a set of costs for the fictitious average firm.

(iv) Stage four: the association openly recommends a universal "efficient" profit margin. This does not imply price-fixing since low cost producers may still underprice high cost producers. The profit margin may be determined by such factors as comparative margins in other analogous industries, minimum amount of profit required to give an adequate return on investment, etc.

[374] See e.g. Monopolies and Mergers Commission Reports into: *Plasterboard* (1974) HC 94 where the conduct against the public interest was BPB's system of uniform delivered prices. The MMC recommended that a "zonal system" be introduced within which the delivered price for each type and load of plasterboard would be based on the total cost of production plus average freight costs to that zone; *Building Bricks* (1976) HC 474 where the MMC responded to a delivered pricing system by recommending that transport costs should be specific to the customer. In both cases the MMC was concerned that the system discriminated unjustifiably between customers and in both cases appropriate undertakings had to be given to the OFT. The undertakings to this effect were released following the MMC's subsequent Report into *Plasterboard* Cm 1224 (1990), DTI Press Release, 2 October 1990, as new entrants to the market had exposed BPB to effective competition and the restrictions on prices to be charged by BPB from different plants were now operating anti-competitively. This shows a greater faith in the markets to operate, as at the time of release of these undertakings, BPB still held some 65 per cent of the UK market, and it seems doubtful that a resumption of its earlier non-cost related pricing policies would be acceptable under Art. 86 EC, whatever the position under UK law.

(v) Stage five: the association (as an alternative to stage four) introduces an allowance for profit into the figures for average cost that are disseminated to members. Effectively the average cost that now exists represents a recommended selling price. Whereas the aggregated cost data described in stage three might be useful to members in assessing critically their cost structures, the incorporation of a profit margin tends to suggest an attempt to harmonise prices. Indeed, where covert price fixing is aimed at under the cover of a campaign to "educate members" the association will probably not recommend a profit margin in stage four. Where the use of a stage four profit margin is advocated openly it is unlikely that collusion is intended. Where a profit margin is artificially incorporated into the notion of average cost a conclusion of collusion is not unreasonable. However open behaviour such as that in stage four may be viewed as too blatant to underpin collusion.

(vi) Stage six: the association enforces adherence to the "average cost" (stage five) by editorial commentaries in trade journals, resolutions passed at association meetings and conferences, lectures and seminars on "accountancy" and direct correspondence between association secretariat and members. Of course for the unsophisticated association fines, expulsions, boycotts and blacklistings might be a more immediate means of ensuring adherence.

8.239 Not all industries require this form of assistance; many firms employ their own accountants and view their cost calculation systems as trade secrets. Knowledge of own costs has been made more common by tax laws requiring more detailed accounting and by negotiations for public or other large contracts which must be based on accurate cost information. Though cost calculation modelling does exist some industries have turned to operating ratio reports as means of comparing and analysing industry costs (see paras. 9.52–9.53).

8.240 Whatever form the cost model takes trade associations should bear in mind the following caveats: (a) so far as is possible data used in compiling the model should be accurate and premised upon actual and current information, accordingly artificial, "inflationary" items should not be added so as to bolster the cost increments; (b) trade associations should not issue memoranda, recommendations, advice, etc., to members concerning the use of the model since this may be interpreted as a method of encouraging price conformity. Nor should there be close monitoring of members' use of the model or penalties for non-use. There is, however, nothing untoward in the trade association disseminating basic explanations to members of how the model has been constructed; (c) where possible the association should publish the background data upon which the model is based in anonymous aggregated form, this minimises any hint of secrecy and collusion.

2. EC Law

(1) Under Article 85(1) EC

8.241 In *Community* v *Bundesverband Deutscher Stahlhandel*[375] (a case decided under Article 65(1) ECSC but of relevant to Article 85(1) EC) an association of steel stockholders with over 1,100 members representing virtually the entire German industry disseminated cost calculation models. It claimed that members' costs were largely comprised of fixed overheads which in each case had to be related to contract weight before a price could be calculated. The pricing process was accordingly very complex and only major firms had the

[375] [1980] 3 CMLR 193.

resources to perform the mathematics accurately. Other, smaller firms were prone to error and, consequently, loss through miscalculation. The Commission rejected this view of the situation noting that the disseminated models went beyond mere "education" since they gave exact values which acted as recommendations of price. This encouraged price parallelism: "Model calculations of this type have the effect of recommendations. They encourage the user companies to work from the figures contained in the models, or at least to keep close to them, when calculating their costs and thus indirectly their selling prices."[376]

8.242 As regards the inclusion of average data in the model (which incorporated a profit margin) the Commission stated:

> "The inclusion of such data in model calculations leads many users to rely on fictitious quantities when calculating their operating costs rather than working from their actual costs and thereby to arrive at misleading figures."[377]

The view of the Commission is thus that models which, through the inclusion of exact values (whether expressed as straight figures or in the form of percentage surcharges) for individual cost components based upon industry averages tend to encourage parallelism of pricing by users of the model, infringe competition rules. This has been confirmed in other cases.[378] It is noteworthy that in the *Bundesverband* decision, the association disseminated data on cost components usually computed individually whereas it declined so to do for components the members could satisfactorily analyse themselves (e.g. freight costs and constant cost headings).

(2) Legitimate models

8.243 In *Bundesverband* the Commission stated:

> "There is an alternative means of catering for firms interest in having a realistic analysis of costing comparisons and inter firm comparisons. It would be sufficient simply to compare the highest and the lowest cost actually observed for each cost component, or to take a selection of the data submitted and offer them as examples; the latter method must not, however, amount in practice to disguised publication of a scatter diagram. There would be no objection to relating the figures thus published to classes of firms classified by size."

and also,

> "A price information system is unobjectionable for the purposes of anti-trust law and does not amount to a concerted pricing practice only where at the very least it does not enable an individual party to the system to identify the competitive behaviour of the other parties. If a trade association intends to play a role in that field, it has in principle to restrict itself in reporting on general price trends on the relevant product markets in a period of time without disclosing the course of price conduct which individual firms have decided to adopt or contemplate adopting."[379]

The major objection to cost models is that they have a tendency to encourage price parallelism between users thus switching the focus of competition from selling price to lev-

[376] *ibid.* at p. 204, para. 54. See also *P&I Clubs* OJ 1985 L376/2 at paras. 12(d), 17, 28,. 29, 37—the Commission, due to exceptional market circumstances, accepted a cost calculation system which embraced a significant degree of cost uniformity.

[377] *ibid.*, at p. 205 para. 55.

[378] See e.g. *European Glass Manufacturers* [1974] 2 CMLR D50 at p. 64, paras. 19, 20; *IFTRA Rules for Producers of Virgin Aluminium* [1975] 2 CMLR D20 at pp. D35, D36, para. 43.

[379] [1980] 3 CMLR 193 at p. 205, para. 56, and, p. 209, para. 69 respectively.

els of discount off selling price. Discount competition is viewed as second best to direct price competition.

8.244 In the light of the above the following conclusions may be drawn:

(a) Progress to stage two is legal does not fall within Article 85(1).
(b) Progress to stage three falls within Article 85(1) but may be exemptible under Article 85(3) EC in exceptional cases where industry costs are neither easy to determine nor relatively fixed so that members may experience considerable difficulties in arriving at accurate costings without assistance.[380]
(c) Associations may be well advised to publish the background statistical and economic data upon which they rely to justify the "reasonableness" of the costings provided such data is not confidential. Data that is disseminated should be in aggregated form which does not enable individual firms to be identified within the statistics. See Chapter 9 on information dissemination for details.
(d) Trade association should be wary of proceeding to stage four since this might suggest a desire to harmonise prices. Stage four action might be allowed where the nature of the market makes accurate estimation of required profit margins very difficult to determine. Trade associations should do nothing to enforce directly or indirectly the recommended margin if, in exceptional cases, the Commission allow such action.
(e) Wherever publication of data (stages three and four) may *encourage* price parallelism it will almost certainly be unsuited to exemption.
(f) Progress past stage four is almost certainly illegal without exception.

8.245 In 1968 the Commission issued a Communication concerning agreements, decisions and concerted practices in the field of co-operation between enterprises.[381] This is a non-binding instrument and caution is advisable when consulting it since the Commission is not bound to adhere to it. The Communication states: "Calculation models contained specific rates of calculation must be regarded as recommendations that may lead to restraints of competition.[382] *A fortiori*, joint schemes devoid of specific rates of calculation, are legal. The Communication applies only to agreements which have as their "sole" object, the joint preparation of cost models. Where the model is one of a number of restrictions the Communication does not apply. In any event the communication adds little to more recent Commission analysis.

[380] e.g. in *Nuovocegam* [1984] 2 CMLR 484 the Commission granted Art. 85(3) exemption to an agreement whereby a central trade association in the market for engineering insurance collected statistical data on claims experience from its members. The Association used the data to draw up a common tariff of basic premiums for various type of risk. Members agreed to abide by this basic premium though they were entirely free to add margins for expenses, commission and profit. Art. 85(3) exemption was granted for the following reasons: (i) the engineering insurance market in Italy was characterised by weak demand and relatively limited supply; (ii) to do business an insurer needed highly specialised resources and considerable technical skill and knowledge. The trade association provided specialist expertise (statistical data, risk studies, prevention techniques, etc.) and hence improved the production and distribution of insurance services and promoted technical and economic progress; (iii) consumers benefited since the work of the association helped enlarge the capacity of the industry thereby widening the choice available to consumers and led to the offering of a more technically advanced product on competitive terms. It should be understood that firms remained free to set their own final prices, the trade association tariff was only a bare price to which other components had to be added.

[381] OJ 1968 C75/7 [1968] CMLR D5.

[382] *ibid.*, Art. II(1)(4).

3. *UK Law*

8.246 The position under UK law is obscure. The Restrictive Practices Court has examined cost models at depth in relationship to questions of whether fixed prices were reasonable, holding in almost every case that proper calculation models were necessary if parties were to persuade the Court of the reasonableness of their prices (see Chapter 8). However, the Court has never actually examined the model itself to determine whether, *per se*, it was against the public interest. None the less, it can be reasonably assumed that similar conclusions to those reached under EC law would apply. Indeed, if, as EC law appears to do, calculation models containing specific values are viewed as recommendations as to price, then they would fall within section 6(1)(b) RTPA 1976 and hence particulars would need to be furnished to the OFT.

8.247 An argument which, it is submitted, might be feasible is that cost calculation models disseminated by trade associations are species of information agreement relating to cost. Information agreements are subject to registration only if the Secretary of State, by statutory instrument, has made an order calling them for registration.[383] To date only information agreements relating to prices charged have been made the subject of an order.[384] If cost models can be seen as information agreements relating to cost then, arguably, they need not be registered. This argument should be treated with caution since in EC law at least information agreements and cost models have always been treated as different species of agreement. The latter is a mechanism for encouraging costing conformity whereas an information agreement pertains to inter-firm flows of date.

8.248 Whether or not a cost model is registrable will depend largely upon the nature of the data disseminated. If only cost guidance data (stages one and to above) are included in the model then probably the model escapes registration. If, however, the model incorporates profit margins then it comes perilously close to constituting recommended prices which are registrable under Section 6(1)(b) RTPA 1976. Where the model includes stage three elements only (i.e. aggregated cost data) then the issue is less clear though the argument based upon cost information agreements appears feasible.

L. Renegotiation and Variation (Cost Escalation) Clauses

1. *Nature of Problem*

8.249 Contractual clauses providing for an alteration in price even after the contract has been concluded are fairly common. These clauses often provide for a renegotiation of the price with resort to arbitration in the event of dispute or for automatic price variation at the sellers discretion with the customer having an option to terminate the contract at that stage or continue on the varied terms. Such clauses are necessary in industries where input costs to the production of the product in question are prone to fluctuation usually because of variations in raw materials prices on the national or international market. Though, variations in fuel costs, for illustration, may likewise impact upon production or transport costs. Another important variable are wage costs where seasonable advances may be greater than expected. Sometimes *force majeure* factors beyond the control of either party may cause costs increases.

383 See s. 7(1) RTPA 1976.

384 Restrictive Trade Practices (Information Agreements) Order 1969, S.I. 1969 No. 1842.

8.250 Clauses of this nature are only likely to cause competition problems in two main contexts. First, where they are imposed by trade associations on members for use in dealings with customers, or alternatively where the association recommends members to use the clause in contracts with customers. Secondly, where the clause is imposed by a dominant undertaking on its trading partners in which case it may be abusive, unfair and anti-competitive.

(1) Legal problems: different types of contract clauses

8.251 The following situations might give rise to competition problems:

(a) Sanctity of contract clauses: agreements by trade association members never to renegotiate contracts once concluded destroy an element of price competition, i.e. the willingness of individual suppliers to renegotiate the contract price and reduce it in the event of reduction in input costs, thereby permitting some of the economies to be passed on to the customer.

(b) Escalation clauses: an agreement to incorporate a clause in contracts with customers which provides for increase in the contract price to cover increases in costs may have anti-competitive effects. Such a clause might mean that the supplier retains a normal profit margin despite cost increases; it will not necessarily mean that the customer benefits from a reduction in the supplier's costs since the price variation is only activated by cost increases and not cost decreases. This clause transfers the risks inherent in the supplier's production process to the customer. Such a clause usually reflects unequal bargaining power between the parties.

(c) Selective renegotiation clauses: suppliers agree to renegotiate prices in the event of cost fluctuations with certain purchasers only. These purchasers might be favoured because of their loyalty to the suppliers group. The effect can be discriminatory distorting the competitive position between competing customers *inter se*.

(d) Risk transfer clauses: if the supplier can renegotiate the contract price to take account of increases in costs due to the failure of his production or distribution functions, then the customer is essentially insuring the supplier against the latter's bade management. Again, such a clause, might reflect an unequal bargaining situation with the supplier exploiting his superiority.

(e) Withdrawal clauses: a clause not providing for renegotiation but allowing the supplier to withdraw from the contract in the event of an escalation of costs where an equivalent clause permitting customer withdrawal if supplier costs decrease is not included may be anti-competitive. The clause is made worse if there is no provision for the customer to be compensated for the abrupt withdrawal.

(f) Procedural limitation clauses: a clause providing for reasonable variation or renegotiation which also provides for procedural conditions making it hard for the customer to benefit from the process may be anti-competitive, e.g. a clause which requires the customer to decide within 12 hours whether he will elect to terminate or continue the contract. The normal "decision" period is approximately seven days which is sufficient time for the customer to be able to reassess the value of the contract at the higher price to him. A period such as this is necessary given that the customer might need to recontact his own customers (presuming he is not the ultimate consumer) in order to renegotiate prices with them.

(g) Supplier option clauses: where a purchaser is tied, probably by an exclusive purchase or requirements contract, to a supplier, other suppliers might tempt that purchaser with very low offers. A clause requiring the purchaser to notify the main supplier of such an offer, which also allows the main supplier to then choose whether to allow the rival supplier to succeed (i.e. the main supplier releases the purchaser from the exclusive purchasing or requirement clause) or whether the main supplier will himself meet the rivals price, may be anti-competitive where the main supplier is dominant. Where the clause arises in a non-dominant context, for example, exclusive purchasing, it can serve to mitigate the restrictive effect of the purchasing obligation.

2. EC Law

8.252 The issue of such clauses has not been prominent in decided cases. None the less, such clauses are common throughout European industry and commerce. An agreement by the members of a trade association to rely upon the sanctity of the contract and never to renegotiate prices would fall under Article 85(1)(a) which prohibits anti-competitive agreements fixing directly or indirectly trading conditions. Likewise, an agreement by suppliers to use these clauses only selectively with customers would be subject to Article 85(1)(d) EC which prohibits anti-competitive agreements applying dissimilar conditions to equivalent transactions. It is not, however, necessary that a clause should be expressly covered by the provisions of Article 85(1)(a)–(e) since the clauses specified in the Article are non-exhaustive.

8.253 The adoption of such clauses by an individual supplier in this dealings with customers may fall under Article 86 EC if the supplier, or the party imposing the terms, is in a dominant position. Article 86 EC covers abuse of price and business terms interchangeably. Unfair or unreasonable variation clauses may both be examples of abuse.[385] Whether a clause is unfair is determined by weighing the competing interests of those concerned, which includes third parties.[386] Conditions and terms designed to expand a party's dominance are viewed especially critically.[387] A clause allowing withdrawal by one party would almost certainly be abusive if imposed by a dominant concern unless there were some objective reason to justify the apparent unfairness.[388] Supplier option clauses (described above) have been held to breach Article 86 EC if imposed on customers by dominant suppliers.[389]

3. UK Law

8.254 The OFT adopts the position that renegotiation clauses are legitimate if: (a) they are freely negotiated between the parties; and (b) their terms are fair and reasonable. Free negotiation is prima facie presumed where the parties are of roughly equal bargaining strength such as would be the case if the clause was negotiated by trade association representing both the supply and purchase sides of the contract. Where parity of bargaining power prevails this also means that the terms will be prima facie deemed to be reasonable; *laissez faire* and *caveat emptor* combined may reasonably prevail in such situations. Where inequality of bargaining power exists, perhaps because only one side is represented by a trade association or is a dominant concern, then the term of the provision will be more closely examined. The following fairly typical clauses have been given dispensation under section 21(2) RTPA 1976.

[385] Case 155/73 *Italy* v *Sacchi* [1974] 2 CMLR 177; [1974] ECR 409 at p. 431.
[386] Case 127/73 *BRT* v *SABAM* [1974] 2 CMLR 238 (ECJ); [1974] ECR 313 at p. 317.
[387] *Gema* [1971] CMLR D35 (Commission).
[388] *ibid.*
[389] See e.g. Case 85/76 *Hoffman-La Roche* v *Commission* (*Vitamins*) [1979] 3 CMLR 211; [1979] ECR 1869. For analysis of the objections to this clause see para 8.68.

8.255 Formulae employed to adjust the contract price are often considered as desirable since they give the customer an idea of the extra money he has to pay. Where the formulae are based upon indices of labour and materials costs published by Government departments, the OFT generally adopts the view that they are acceptable. Where cost adjustments arise because of severe and frequent fluctuations in raw materials' prices the formulae may be based on cash sums rather than percentages of the contract price. These cash sums may be suitable for section 21(2) treatment though the OFT scrutinise them more closely than formulae expressed in percentages.

(1) Acceptable clause types and section 21(2): Examples

(a) Force majeure clause

8.256 The example is typical of clauses incorporated in contracts in the paper and board industry:[390]

> "In the event of increases in costs of production of [product] caused by the act of God, hostilities, threat of war, riot, strike or lock out, the seller shall notify the buyer of such increase in the cost in respect of any unfulfilled portion of the contract and the buyer shall have the option of agreeing to pay the extra cost or cancelling the remainder of the contract. Any such notification shall be sent in writing and unless the buyer within seven working days of receiving the sellers notification of increased cost shall by notice in writing to the seller refuse to pay such increased cost the buyer shall be deemed to have elected to accept the remainder of the contract and it shall be executed accordingly."

(b) Cost variation clause

8.257 The example is typical of many clauses found to be acceptable by the OFT:[391]

> "In the event of a variation of costs necessarily and properly incurred by the seller after the acceptance of an order but before the date which it is necessary to proceed with manufacture in order to meet the delivery requirements of the order, the price shall be increased or decreased within the limits of such variation, subject to reasonable notice being given by either the seller or buyer in respect of orders or balances of orders outstanding. The buyer shall have the option to cancel order or balances of orders outstanding by notice in writing to the seller within seven days of receiving the seller's notification of an increase in price. Any quotation should also be subject to variation in like manner unless specifically stated otherwise."

(c) Selective cost variation clause

8.258 The example is from the agreement negotiated between the British Wool Confederation and the Worsted Spinners Federation. The clause was the result of an agreement between the associations that members should not be required to use the clause but that it should be available as an option:[392]

> "It is mutually agreed between the parties to this contract that the contract price(s) shall be firm in respect of goods delivered within a period of four months after the date of contract. Thereafter the contract price of goods delivered may be adjusted to take account of subsequent in-

[390] e.g. No. 1283 Register of Restrictive Trade Agreement between *British Paper and Board Industry Federation, National Association of Paper Merchants, British Paper Bag Federation* and the *British Paper Box Ltd.*

[391] *ibid.* A clause in a standard form contract providing that there will be no variations between the price quoted by a supplier when a booking was made and the price actually charged the client, may be suitable for s. 21(2) treatment. See e.g. No. 39 Register of Restrictive Trade Practices, *National Association of Holiday Centres* (1979).

[392] No. 3827 Register of Restrictive Trade Practices, Agreement between the Members of the *British Wool Confederation and the Worsted Spinners' Federation* (1980). See also No. 1147 Register of Restrictive Trade Practices, Agreement between the *CEGB and the Thermal Insulators Contractors' Association* (1981).

creases in combing charges, plus a further 10 per cent of any such increase to cover topmaking costs. Provided however, that no adjustment shall be made in the contract price in respect of goods delivered within three weeks of the date of any increase in combing charges. The British Wool Confederation, after consultation with the Worsted Spinners' Federation Ltd, will from time to time, but not more frequently than at intervals of three months, issue a list of combing charge variations and any price adjustments to be made under this clause shall be related to such variations."

(d) Wage cost increase variation clause

8.259 The example was employed by the Worsted Spinners Federation based upon figures calculated by the Federation accountants. The substantive part of the clause is as follows:[393]

> "If after the date of this contract, any new wage advance shall be agreed between The Confederation of British Wool Textiles Ltd and the NAUTT the price of all yarn not delivered within one calendar month after the effective date of each and every such new wage advance, or of any cost of living advance, shall be increased as follows."

The clause continued to provide that for each 1 per cent of wage advance yarn prices would increase by *X* pence/kilo depending upon quality of yarn.

(2) Clauses not subject to registration

8.260 The only case before the Restrictive Practices Court held that an agreement between members of a trade association not to *renegotiate* contract prices after conclusion of the contract was not an agreement relating to price "to be" charged or in respect of terms and conditions "to be" applied. The Court of Appeal in *Blanket Manufacturers Agreement*[394] held that section 6 RTPA 1976 "is looking to a point of time when the contract is about to be entered into and is not contemplating the case where the contract had already been made".[395] The Restrictive Practices Court had held however that the clause though "highly beneficial to the members of the association, was not for the benefit of the general public or the wholesalers or retailers dealing with members of the Association and was therefore contrary to the public interest".[396]

8.261 The extent of *Blankets* is uncertainty. It only exempts from registration clauses which do *not* relate to prices or terms and conditions "to be" charged or applied. Presumably a clause which envisages possible price renegotiation in the future concerns a price "to be" charged or a term or condition "to be" applied. Hence most renegotiation clauses will be subject to the Act.

The OFT could investigate "sanctity of contract" and other clauses outside the scope of the RTPA 1976 under section 2(1) CA 1980 where they were imposed by a company with market power.[397]

(3) Clauses subject to Unfair Contract Terms Act 1977 (UCTA 1977)

8.262 Two clauses at least noted in the list above ((d) and (f)) might be subject to the "reasonableness" test in the UCTA 1977. Risk transfer clauses may be viewed as attempts by a

393 No. 1569 Register of Restrictive Trade Practices, Agreement amongst members of *Worsted Spinners' Federation* (1981).
394 [1959] LR 1 RP 208; [1959] 1 WLR 442 (RPC); (1959) LR 1 RP 271; [1959] 1 WLR 1148 (CA).
395 [1959] 1 WLR 1148 at p. 1153.
396 [1959] 1 WLR 442 at p. 455.
397 See Chapter 3 for details of the CA 1980 procedure.

supplier to exclude of limit loss clauses by his own negligence since the loss caused is borne by the customer. If this analysis is correct they may be subject to the reasonableness test by virtue of section 2(2) UCTA 1977 which regulates contract clauses excluding liability for loss or damage caused by negligence. Procedural limitation clauses may fall subject to the test of reasonableness by virtue of section 13(1) UCTA 1976 which regulates clauses "making the liability or its enforcement subject to restrictive or onerous conditions".

8.263 The test of reasonableness includes such factors as: relative bargaining power; whether the customer received an inducement to accept the clause; whether the customer was aware of the clause; whether liability is excluded only in certain cases. In effect the criteria generally under the section 21(2) procedure. The role of the UCTA 1977 is more closely examined at paras. 11.16–11.22.

8.264 Where such clauses are included in contracts with consumers account will also have to be taken of the requirements of the Unfair Terms in Consumer Contracts Regulations 1994[398] considered at paras. 11.23–11.25.

M. Collusive Tendering

8.265 Contracts for the supply of services or the purchase of commodities are often preceded by a tendering procedure whereby prospective clients or buyers invite interested firms to submit tenders for the supply of the goods or services in question.[399] Given the growth of public procurement rules for the public sector and for certain utilities the opportunity for collusive tendering remains substantial. An invitation to tender may be public or private to specific firms. Invariably, the winning bid is the best priced one, though ancillary criteria of a technical or quality related nature may be specified. The tender procedure is used commonly for services required, for which detailed specifications are already fixed, or for commodities lacking a relatively stable market price. In these situations tenderers have a wide latitude to adapt their price estimates to meet the specified requirements.

8.266 Tenders are favoured methods of allocating work since they represent an objective and uniform means of assessing services or commodities supplied by competing firms. Moreover, since the process reflects somewhat an auction, the winning bid should mirror a truly competitive price. The method is used by governments wishing to sell of or lease state-owned natural resources or surplus capacity. Public authorities also employ the procedure in respect of constructional work (build installations, construct physical plant, etc.) and in respect of the procurement of large job lots of standardised products. Tender procedures are also commonly used in respect of: non-scheduled transport; printing and publishing; and machine manufacture, etc. Public procurement rules make certain types of contract needs automatically subject to tendering processes.

1. Legal and Economic Framework

(1) Legal problems: collusive tendering

8.267 Tenderers find it advantageous collectively to share out contracts between them and fix the price at which bids are made. This represents a very serious problem for many authorities who

[398] S.I. 1994 No. 3159, implementing Directive 93/13/EEC of 5 April 1993 on unfair terms in consumer contracts OJ 1993 L95/29.

[399] For detailed analysis of the practice see OECD *Report of the Committee of Experts on Restrictive Business Practices, Collusive Tendering* (1980).

place their trust in tender procedures to result in competitively priced bids and who often, accordingly, renounce their right to negotiate prices with the tenderers. Since collusive tendering leads to high, supra-competitive prices, the public purse in effect supports the tenderers profit margins where the buyer is a public authority.[400]

8.268 In tenders for contracts for highly complex or technical services or goods, the tenderer often knows more than the client or purchaser. The inclusion of very precise or restrictive technical specifications in the invitation has the effect of limiting the field of potential tenderers.[401] In America, in such market circumstances, it has been found to be an offence for bidders to collude with state specifications officers to prescribe requirements particulars to those bidders.[402]

8.269 Collusive tendering is often found during periods of recession when companies agree to share out contracts as an alternative to competition whereby parties undercut each other to a ruinous extent in their attempts to obtain work. The orderly sharing out of work has the advantage of keeping prices high and thereby helping companies maintain capacity.[403]

8.270 Collusive tendering may be organised by a central agency or trade association. Parties are required to notify the association of the contracts they propose to bid for, sending in also copies of the bid. The association then disseminates the data to rival bidders. More often managers in rival companies meet covertly to exchange information on jobs and prices and then to allocate contracts. Many different mechanisms exist to facilitate the cartel. The following are commonly used examples.

(a) Cover bids

8.271 Whereby parties take it in turn to win a contract by submitting the lowest bid. This requires a pre-examination of tenders by the association or the parties themselves to ensure that the designated parties' bid is in fact the lowest and that the calculations contained in the bid are correct. The fact that a number of bids are made by firms not intended to succeed misleads the client/purchaser into believing that the bids are competitive.

(b) "Give and take bids"

8.272 Which have been common in the construction industry and provide that a contractor who is uninterested in a tender inquires as to the quotation made by his competitors, he then "takes" that price and exceeds it. Conversely, one who is interested in a bid "gives" a price to competitors who agree to cover it.[404]

Collusive tendering is subject to control in both the EC and the UK and given its clandestine (semi-fraudulent) nature is never acceptable. Given the almost *per se* illegality of price fixing agreements, it is believed that collusive tendering has become more common as a surrogate.

[400] See OECD Report *op. cit.*, at p. 10 where it is noted that in the UK public contracts amounted to about 13 per cent of GNP. An average figure for developed nations would be in the region of 10 per cent.

[401] See *Whittan* v *Paddock Pool Builders* 424 F.2d 25, 30 (1st Cir. 1970) cert. denied 400 US 850 (1970).

[402] OECD Report *op. cit.*, at pp. 12–16. Collusive tendering is most common in industries where there are a large number of medium-sized enterprises and where strong price competition prevails. It is rare in a concentrated and oligopolistic markets since price competition may not in any event be prevalent and the collusion would be difficult to keep secret.

[403] Specifications designed to favour national over EC suppliers infringe the free movement of goods provisions of the Treaty of Rome: see Case 45/87 *Commission* v *Ireland (Dundalk Council)* [1988] ECR 4929.

[404] *ibid.*, at pp. 16–23. See *Jones* v *North* (1875) LR 19 Eq. 426 (trade association selected approved supplier and ordered others to refrain from bidding).

(2) Detecting collusive tendering[405]

8.273 The main problem with the practice lies in its detection. Authorities or companies who put work out to tender clearly desire competitive bidding. How can they detect when bids submitted to them are rigged? The OFT has published guides for purchasers generally as well as specifically for local authorities,[406] in which guidance is given in determining when conditions are ripe for collusive tendering. The factors to look out for and the questions to ask are:[407]

(a) Does the industry or product have characteristics which make it easier to organise, police and sustain a cartel? For example, are there few sellers, homogeneous products with little scope for competition in quality, service or delivery? Do suppliers have similar costs of production and distribution? Can the market be easily monitored?
(b) Are there any transient factors making a cartel attractive, such as declining demand?
(c) What explanations are there for price movements? Have there been moves to more uniform prices? Is there any regular pattern of price changes?
(d) How are price changes announced? Is there any similarity in wording or timing? Does the wording give any indication of collusion (e.g. the industry has decided that prices should move to more reasonable levels)?
(e) Do suppliers meet regularly to discuss their industry? Are there are identifiable consequences of such meetings?

8.274 Obviously these factors can also be found in ordinarily competitive markets. They can only give an indication of whether it is plausible for collusive tendering to be taking place. The next step is to look more closely at the tenders themselves. The following criteria may be useful in detecting the practice and drive from an analysis of prices and detailed costings ((a)–(g) below) and from evidence of collusion found in the formal record of the opening of sealed bids ((h)–(k) below).

(a) Some of the bidders have quoted prices so high that it is reasonable to assume they had no serious intention of winning the contract.
(b) Since most schemes operate upon some form of a rota with firms taking it in turns to win a bid, a comparison of the bids of firm X in successive tenders submitted by X might reveal a suspicious discrepancy between the average bid made and the exceptional winning bid.
(c) Detailed costings might be inconsistent with the firm's accounting data. It is usual for firms awarded the contract to calculate each unit price in its estimates by applying a fixed global coefficient to the cost of labour or supplies to cover costs of supervision, operating expenditure, overheads and profits. Comparison between the supposedly "global" coefficients used by the winning firm and: (i) other losing firms; and (ii) the same firm on another occasion when it lost, might reveal a discrepancy suggesting that the "global coefficient", far from being fixed, varies according to whether the firm is expected to win or not.

405 These are based upon the successful criteria developed for use by the French Department of Internal Trade and Prices. See generally, for US experience, Coate, "Techniques for protecting against collusion in sealed bid markets" (1985) 30 The Antitrust Bulletin 897.

406 Both entitled *Cartels: Detection and Remedies*. For an example of the detection of such a cartel, see the ground maintenance price fixing agreement detected by vigilant purchaser, the Property Services Agency, which became aware of tendering patterns pointing to the existence of a possible cartel and at that point involved the OFT. The eleven ground maintenance contractors were required to give undertakings to the RPC in May 1995 not to enforce the agreement or any other similar agreements contained restrictions to like effect, [1995] ECLR R-161.

407 This list is based on the two OFT guides.

(d) The costings of tenderers other than the designated firm might reflect the latter's price structure. Generally, group prices are calculated by reference to the designated firm's prices. Since that firm is unaware of competitor's accounting systems he will do no more than ensure that unit prices in detailed costings of cover bids are higher than his own. Thus global prices will be higher. Thus if the designated bidder traditionally allows himself a large margin on labour costs but only a small one on supplies, the same characteristic may appear in other parties' costings.

(e) Comparison of the global price of the designated tenderer and the second lowest bid will usually show a significant disparity, whereas the price difference between the second bidder and the rest may be small. This arises because the designated tenderer seeks to ensure that his is *clearly* the lowest bid and that he is protected from his own mathematical errors losing him the contract.

(f) Where a genuine outsider also bids, a comparison of his and the other losing bids will reveal anomalies, coincidences amongst the insiders, simultaneous omissions and errors, etc. and the existence of special "balancing" items used in "rigging" prices.

(g) The tender from the designated firm often shows features suggesting it is expected to win. Thus, for example, in a contract for the replacement of pipes, the precise length of the new piping will be known, whereas the amount of earth to be removed would not. A confident contractor could submit precise costing for items with exact specifications and propose cheaper alternatives where the authorities have overestimated. This induces confidence in the contractor by the authority. However, where the authority has underestimated items, the contractor does not notify the authority but simply quotes a very high price. When the contract is won and the work commenced the contractor is in a strong position to have these estimates adjusted upwards, thereby maximising his profits on them.

(h) Often, for practical reasons, designated bidders are located in the area of the work suggesting that the parties are sensitive to each other's wishes.

(i) Frequently, only the designated firm conducts a serious study of the project. Others will not waste time on futile bids.

(j) Often, only the designated bidder is present when tenders are opened. Alternatively, when a call for tenders is declared inconclusive because price limits have been exceeded, the authorities may call for tendering firms to attend discussions; only the designated firm shows up.

(k) Unexpected coincidences, for example, two firms tendering at almost identical levels might occur suggesting that the price level is a floor-price below which firms have agreed not to tender.[408]

2. *EC Law*

8.275 Collusive tendering falls under Article 85(1) EC and has almost no chance of exemption under Article 85(3) EC. The real problem, therefore, lies in those suffering from the practice being able to detect it. In the sugar industry the Commission discovered, on in-

[408] See Department of Trade Consultative Document: Collusive Tendering (30 July 1980) para. 6. "Tenderers might agree not to submit tenders below a certain price, or to add an amount or proportion to the price they would otherwise propose. There are however difficulties with these approaches. If more than one tender is received at the same price—the 'floor price'—collusion will immediately be expected. The other approach—the 'surcharge' approach—requires an excessive amount of mutual trust among the tenderers, since they will be strongly tempted to adjust their initial price downwards, taking account of the agreed surcharge, in order to secure the contract."

vestigation, that enterprises holding large surpluses had concerted their bids in response to invitations to tender for refunds for exports of sugar to third countries. The practice artificially influenced the volume of sugar being exported between Member States and was condemned, accordingly, under Article 85(1) EC.[409]

8.276 In *Dutch Building and Construction Cartel* [410] the Commission found that 28 associations, including more than 4,000 construction undertakings in the Netherlands, had participated in a system of co-ordinated tenders. These associations had set up an organisation called the SPO which had enacted uniform price-regulating rules which were binding on all its members. The rules of SPO held felt to have as their object or effect the restriction or distortion of competition, since they:

(a) provided for exchanges of information prior to tendering procedures;
(b) provided for concerted action in price tenders and fixed selling prices and other trading conditions in respect of construction contracts;
(c) shared between members the demand side of the market.

The Commission held that, even if they had been notified, the agreements would not have been granted exemption under Article 85(3).

8.277 Even though collusive tendering is more common in a purely national context, the decision shows that this will not prevent the finding of an effect on intra-Community trade. The practices were held to effect inter-state trade since they acted as an obstacle to building and construction firms wishing to tender for contracts in the Netherlands.

3. *UK Law*

(1) Prevalence

8.278 Collusive tendering is not uncommon in the UK. Even in 1979 a government committee expressed concern at the growth of this practice:

> "Collusive tendering is clearly a registrable agreement under the present legislation. However, it is obvious that a form of collusion which is designed to eliminate competition when such competition is precisely the object of the tendering procedure is almost certain not to pass through any of the gateways of the legislation. Since the parties will wish to conceal their collusion, they have no reason to register their agreement. Because of the growing evidence of evasion of the law in respect of collusive tendering and because of the fraudulent nature of the practice we recommend that more stringent action should be taken against this particular practice."[411]

No such stricter action has however been taken. Hence, again, the problem is mainly of detection for which guidelines have been given above.

[409] See Cases 40–48, 50, 54–56, 111, 113, 114/74 *Sugar Cartel* [1976] 1 CMLR 295 ECR 1663 (ECJ). See also *Cast Iron and Steel Rolls* [1984] 1 CMLR 694.

[410] OJ 1992 L92/1. An appeal was dismissed in Case T-29/92 *Vereniging van Samenwerkende Prijsregelende Organisaties in de Bouwnijverheid (SPO)* v *Commission* [1993] ECR II-1.

[411] The Liesner Committee, *A Review of Restrictive Trade Practices Policy* (1979) Cmnd 7512, p. 50, para. 5.52. The practice is indeed common: (i) following an investigation into firms concerned with electrical installations or mechanical services in building projects between 1963–69 over 70 different collusive tendering agreements were discovered and condemned. The agreements related to work on sub-contracts in major public and private sector works. (ii) At the beginning of 1975 it was disclosed that, in the preceding 10 years, the supply of telephone cables to the Post Office had been subject to collusion. The 4 suppliers of external telephone cable (who controlled almost all of this market) allocated quotas to the various contractors and adjusted prices to ensure the designated distribution of work. (See DGFT Annual Report (1975) at p. 91.) (iii) In 1978 the Restrictive Practices Court condemned over 60 collusive tendering arrangements made in the cement industry covering almost the whole country. For a selection of the *Cement* cases agreements themselves, see No. 4218, 4246, 4221, 4223, 4257, 4305 Register of Restrictive Trading Practices. For an

(2) Under the RTPA 1976

8.279 The OFT will virtually never consider collusive tendering appropriate for section 21(2) treatment.[412] Indeed, when discovered, the parties are always referred to the RPC for prohibitive orders to be made against them.[413] Breach of court order is contempt of court for which gaol and/or fines may be imposed. The OFT has dealt with a number of cases upon this basis involving: ready-made concrete and road surfacing materials; milk; electrical and mechanical services; building projects; and telephone cables.

It almost goes without saying that collusive tendering arrangements are registrable.[414]

(3) Private remedies in tort: section 35(2) RTPA 1976

8.280 Private parties who have suffered damage as a result of collusive tendering may sue the parties to the tendering agreement for damages under section 35(2) RTPA 1976, which permits private actions on the basis of breach of a statutory duty to be proceeded with against parties to unregistered agreements. However, at least seven cases are known to have been settled out of court upon the basis of this provision. One of the cases involved a settlement of £9 million. Details and analysis of these cases and the related problems may be found at paras. 5.98–5.104.

(4) Criminal sanctions

8.281 In 1980 the DTI was considering whether to render collusive tendering a criminal offence under statute.[415] However, in 1982 it was decided that such a step was unnecessary[416]

cont.
interesting sequel to these cases, see *British Concrete Pipe Agreement* [1982] ICR 182 (RPC). (iv) In recent years in the USA the enforcement policy of the Department of Justice Antitrust Division has been focused upon price fixing, market sharing and collusive tendering. The latter practice has been found to be very widespread. Between 1980–85 the Antitrust Division filed 418 criminal cases against 1,002 defendants (527 companies and 475 individuals). These cases resulted in total fines exceeding US$100 million US (US$95 million for companies, $5 million for individuals). In addition 200 corporate officials were gaoled for average periods of 119 days. The total period of gaol for these persons was 65 years, see Boch, "Antitrust compliance programs and litigation: myth and reality", paper to 18th New England Antitrust Conference, Harvard University Law School (2 November 1984).

412 But cf. No. 3592 Register of Restrictive Trade Practices, Agreement between members of *Builders Conference* (1977). Parties notified information regarding invitations to tender, tenders submitted and contracts awarded, to the Secretariat of the conference who disseminated the information to members who signified an interest in the same work. The information disseminated included details of tender prices though these were *not* communicated either to the Secretariat or to the other members until *after* the closing date for submission of tenders. The OFT granted dispensation from reference to the RPC rather surprisingly. They apparently accepted that the conference could not be abused and was a useful data dissemination organisation.

413 See e.g. Register of Restrictive Trade Practices Nos.: 3579 *Tendering Agreement at Craigmount School* (1974); 3588 *Mechanical Services at Corby Town Centre Phase I* (1974); 3612 *Mechanical Services at Herdamflat Hospital* (1974); 3613 *Mechanical Services at Littlewoods Store Croydon* (1974); 3628 *Mechanical Services at Hindley Pool* (1974); 3654 *Mechanical Services at Tolworth Hospital* (1974); 3665 *Mechanical Services at Broughton Secondary School* (1974); 3706 *Mechanical Services at Shrewsbury Telephone Exchange* (1974) see also No. 3733 Register of Restrictive Trade Practices *Plastic Pressure Pipes* (1974).

414 See e.g. *Birmingham Association of Building Trades Employers' Agreement* (1963) LR 4 RP 54 where a narrow view was taken. However a wider view of registrability subsequently became the norm. See *Exeter Hospital Electrical Contractors' Agreement* (1970) LR 7 RP 102, [1970] 1 WLR 1391; *Telephone Apparatus Manufacturers' Application* (1962) LR 3 RP 98 and on appeal at p. 462.

415 Department of Trade and Consultative Document *op. cit.*, at n. 408 at pp. 5–9, paras. 15–31. The statute would apparently have been along the lines of the Auctions (Bidding Agreements) Act 1927 as amended in 1969.

416 HC Deb. Vol. 34, No. 37, col. 641 (23 December 1982).

given that the criminal offence of conspiracy to defraud already embraced collusive tendering.[417]

(5) Breach of contract (non-collusion clauses)

8.282 Some more prudent companies incorporate anti-collusion clauses in contracts with winning tenders under which the tenderer signs a declaration of non-collusion. Moreover, clauses permitting the client to rescind the contract totally upon proof of collusion are sensible and demand liquidated damages based on a reasonable pre-estimate of loss.[418]

[417] See *Scott* v *Metropolitan Police Commr.* [1975] AC 819 at p. 1039 *per* Viscount Dilhorne: "It is clearly the law that an agreement by two or more by dishonesty to deprive a person of something which is his or to which he is or would be or might be entitled and an agreement by two or more by dishonesty to injure some proprietary right of his, suffices to constitute the offence of conspiracy to defraud." See further *Welham* v *DPP* [1961] AC 103: "A person is also defrauded if he is deceived into acting contrary to his public duty"—it is surely a local authority's public duty not to squander rate payers money on excessive tenders. If a plaintiff is induced by fraud into taking an economic risk which he would not have otherwise taken but for the deception then the offence will have taken place: *Allsop* [1976] Crim LR 738 (CA); *Hamilton* (1845) 1 Cox cc 244; *Carpenter* (1911) 22 Cox 168.

[418] See Department of Trade Consultative Document, *op. cit.*, at n. 408 at p. 4, para. 13.

9 The Exchange and Dissemination of Information

A. Introduction

1. Introduction

9.1 An information agreement may be described as an arrangement whereby companies exchange between themselves information concerning, inter alia, production costs, selling prices, market demand, creditworthiness of customers, stock levels etc. Such agreements are common in business where they are used to improve their own and the market's efficiency.[1] Conversely, such agreements may simply be mechanisms to facilitate a price fixing or market sharing agreement.[2] For example, the exchange of data on prices to be charged (e.g. by exchanging price lists before their publication) is a common method of organising a price fixing agreement. Some information agreements are operated innocently but, none the less, have an anti-competitive effect because of prevailing market circumstances. It is, accordingly, very important for businessmen and their advisers to be able to differentiate the competitive from the anti-competitive agreement. In this chapter the following will be examined:

Section B. Legal framework: the system of control in the EC and UK.
Section C. Price information.

[1] See H. Niemeyer, "Market information systems" [1993] ECLR 151.

[2] See e.g. *Zinc Producer Group* [1985] 2 CMLR 108 para. 19; in *Wood Pulp* [1985] 3 CMLR 474 the Commission fined 40 producers of market woodpulp located in the USA, Canada, Sweden, Finland, Norway, Portugal and Spain. The infringements of Art. 85 comprised detailed exchanges of information designed to stabilise prices. The Court of Justice rejected this interpretation in Joined Cases C-89/85, 104, 114, 116, 117 and 125-129/85 *Ahlstrom and Others* v *Commission (Wood Pulp)* [1993] ECR I-1307, [1993] 4 CMLR 407, holding that most of the exchanges of information occurred because of the particularly transparent nature of the market in question.

Section D. Detecting anti-competitive price exchanges: EC and UK: some guidelines on how to detect exchange of price data cartels.
Section E. Information about contract terms and conditions: EC and UK.
Section F. Exchange of general market data: common trade association practices are considered, e.g. inter-firm comparisons; business ratio pyramids; global industry data, etc.
Section G. Refusal to disclose information: when the refusal by a dominant firm to provide information may be anti-competitive.
Section H. Negotiations leading to an agreement between competitors: when pre-contractual negotiations might be caught by Article 85(1)?
Section I. Specimen compliance scheme: rules summarising the relevant principles.

2. Economic Background: Rules of Thumb

9.2 Exchanges of information are of ambiguous value to the market. Some exchanges enhance competition; others stifle it. Much depends upon the nature of the data exchanged and the economic context of the market. If three oligopolistic firms holding markets shares of, for example, 26 per cent, 17 per cent and 30 per cent exchange price data and this leads them to price their goods uniformly then the market suffers, cartel-like price rigidity has evolved from an exchange of price data. Conversely, if a number of small firms exchange data on various market criteria relating to their respective cost structures this may enable them to respond in a more educated and hence efficient manner to larger competitors. As a general rule the more concentrated the market the less likely the chances of an official sympathetic response. Where statistical and other data is being disseminated a number of rules of thumb may be used. The four central rules are that exchanged dated should be: historical; anonymous; aggregated; and, compiled independently.

(i) Data should be past

9.3 Data that refers to past market conditions, transactions, etc. cannot easily be used by parties to determine accurately the future conduct of rivals. Competition authorities take the view that it is uncertainty as to rivals future intentions which fosters competitive behaviour.

(ii) Data should be anonymous

9.4 Information should, when disseminated, not refer to individual participants; it should not be possible to identify a rival's "vital statistics" from disseminated information. Though individualised data is acceptable when it is disseminated back, in the processed form, only to the party supplying the raw data.

(iii) Data should be aggregated

9.5 Information should be in summary, composite form. Again, this prevents accurate figures being given which may be attributed to specific firms.

(iv) Data should be independently compiled

9.6 Responsibility for compilation and dissemination of data should be entrusted to an independent person, to ensure that the businesses concerned do not have someone in their organisation possessing data transgressing the foregoing general principles. There is a general level of scepticism (which may or may not be justified) about the efficacy of Chinese Walls as a device for preventing leakage of confidential information.

B. Legal Framework

1. EC Law

9.7 Information agreements relating to goods and/or services can be caught by Article 85(1) although not expressly listed in the examples of restrictive practices in Article 85(1) (a)–(e). Below is set out a summary of the main factors the Commission take into account when assessing information exchange agreements. The Commission approach has been endorsed by the CFI. The essential elements of the approach may be summarised as follows. First, a rule of reason approach applies to the analysis of exchanges of information with the degree of concentration on the market in question and the nature of the information being exchanged being central to the assessment.[3] Secondly, the Commission have broadly categorised exchanges of assessment into three groupings, namely exchanges directly concerning price, exchanges not directly concerning price but which underpin other anti-competitive arrangements, and exchanges of non-price data *not* underpinning other anti-competition arrangements. The first two categories may be analysed as having both an anti-competitive object and effect whereas the third category will generally be assessed by reference to effect alone it being accepted that there is no anti-competitive object.[4] Thirdly the first two categories of exchange will invariably be treated less sympathetically than the third category. In particular price exchanges and exchanges supporting other restrictive arrangements will generally require exemption under Article 85(3) whereas exchanges in the third category will, in appropriate market conditions, be capable of falling out with Article 85(1) altogether and thereby be able to obtain negative clearance if it is applied for. Fourthly, there is now sufficient case law and guidance for the Commission to justify fining companies for seriously restrictive exchanges of information.

(1) Market structure

9.8 The Commission attach considerable relevance to market analysis as is evidenced by their 1968 Communication Concerning Agreements, Decisions and Concerted Practices in the Field of Co-operation between Enterprises. In this non-binding expression of opinion it is stated that the exchange of certain types of information[5] falls outside Article 85(1) where it is used by parties to determine their market strategy freely. However, where the data is used to coordinate the participants' behaviour, "a restraint of competition may occur in particular on an oligopolistic market for homogeneous products". Thus, the Commission will examine the structure of the market within which the information exchange operates and the more concentrated it is, the more likely the Commission is to hold that competition is being restricted in some way.[6] In *UK Agricultural Tractor Registration Exchange*[7] the Commission condemned an information exchange agree-

[3] e.g. Case T-34/92 *Fiatagri* [1994] ECR II 905 at paras. 85 and 91 in particular.

[4] *Fiatagri (ibid.)* para. 91 and the analysis at para. 79 *et seq.*

[5] Notably, exchanges of opinion and experience, joint market research, execution of joint comparative studies of enterprises or industries, joint preparations of statistics and cost models.

[6] See also *Seventh Report on Competition Policy* (1977), pp. 18– 21, points 5–8: "In assessing information agreements the Commission pays close attention to the structure of the relevant market. The tendency for firms to fall in line with the behaviour of their competitors is particularly strong in oligopolistic markets. The improved knowledge of market conditions aimed at by information agreements strengthens the connection between the undertakings, in that they are enabled to react very efficiently to one another's actions, and thus lessens the intensity of competition."

[7] OJ [1992] L68/19, [1993] 4 CMLR 358, appeal dismissed by the Court of First Instance in T-34/92 *Fiatagri and Ford New Holland* v *Commission* [1994] ECR II-905 and T-35/92 *John Deere* v *Commission* [1994] ECR II-957.

ment, giving considerable weight to the fact that the UK tractor market was oligopolistic. In particular, the agreement covered eight suppliers comprising 88 per cent of the UK market, with the four largest firms holding an 80 per cent market share. The Commission emphasised[8] that "market transparency between suppliers in a highly concentrated market... is likely to destroy what hidden competition there remains between the suppliers in that market on account of the risk and ease of exposure of independent competitive action". The Commission also took note of the fact that entry barriers were high and that there was an absence of significant imports. The Commission published a Press Release after this decision in which it said that the same result would not necessarily arise in the car market which was more competitive.[9] The Court of First Instance has made clear that on a truly competitive market transparency between traders is in principle likely to lead to the intensification of competition between suppliers since the fact that such a trader takes into account the information made available to him in order to adjust his conduct is not likely, having regard to the atomised nature of the supply to reduce or remove for the other traders any uncertainty about the foreseeable nature of its competitors conduct. Conversely, in a concentrated market the exchange of information on a regular and frequent basis of information concerning the operation of the market has the effect of periodically revealing to all the competitors the market positions and strengths of the various individual competitors.[10]

(2) Subject matter of the information exchanged

9.9 The Commission regards the exchange of particularly sensitive information as contrary to Article 85(1) regardless of market structure. It has objected very strongly to exchanges about prices[11] but has also condemned information exchanges relating to a variety of other matters including production and investment plans,[12] conditions of sale and terms of business[13] and customers.[14] The rest of this chapter describes in detail the approach taken by the Commission in relation to the exchange of all these various types of information.

(3) Level of detail of the information

9.10 As a general proposition, the Commission is far more concerned about information which identifies undertakings individually than about aggregate data.[15] The reason for this is that data about individual firms enables competitors to predict what their future conduct will be and adjust their own behaviour accordingly, thus distorting competition. However, in *UK Agricultural Tractor Registration Exchange*[16] the Commission objected to even the exchange of aggregate industry data to the extent that, in respect of specific geographic areas, product breakdowns or time periods, the reports contained less than ten tractor units for any such specific category. The Commission considered that "below this minimum

[8] At para. 37; see further paras. 37–43.
[9] Commission Press Release IP(92)148 of 4 March 1992.
[10] *Fiatagri (ibid.)* para. 91.
[11] See below.
[12] e.g. *Re Cimbel* OJ [1972] L303/24; *Zinc Producer Group* OJ [1984] L220/27.
[13] e.g. *Re VNP and COBELPA* OJ [1977] L240/10.
[14] *Sixth Report on Competition Policy* (1976), para. 135.
[15] See Commission statements in *Re VNP and COBELPA* OJ [1977] L240/10. See also, *EWIS* (*Eighteenth Report on Competition Policy*) where the Commission took the view that there were no grounds for actions under Art. 85(1) in respect of an information exchange scheme whereby paper and board manufacturers sent statistical data to a central information service which then distributed the information to members in the form of aggregated figures or weighted averages.
[16] OJ 1992 L68/19, [1993] 4 CMLR 358.

number of total sales there is a high risk that even aggregate data will allow, directly or indirectly, the identification of the exact sales volume of individual competitors". In addition, the Commission held that the fact that a government department made available to the industry registration data identifying the sales of individual companies, and therefore that the data was in the public domain did not in the circumstances of the case prevent the application of Article 85(1) to the conduct in question.[17]

(4) Timing of the information

9.11 If information relates to the future behaviour of firms then it will most probably be caught by Article 85(1). However if it is truly historic *and* is of no or no significant value in predicting future behaviour it will, generally, not be caught by Article 85(1). The difficulty arises in assessing whether information relating to past behaviour could be a guide to future conduct. This question can not be answered in isolation; the issues of market structure and whether the information is individual or aggregate are of much relevance. In *UK Agricultural Tractor Registration Exchange*[18] the Commission held that, in a market where demand is stable or declining, forecasts of competitors' future actions can largely be determined on the basis of past transactions. "The more accurate and the more recent the information ... the more impact this information has on the future behaviour of the firms in the market." However, the Commission accepted that, from a certain point in time, market information relating to past transactions becomes truly historic and no longer has any impact on future behaviour.[19] It will be a question of fact in each case as to the point in time at which historical data has no significant future predictive value.

(5) Mode of exchanging information

9.12 The fact that information has been exchanged through the medium of trade associations has not tended to affect the Commission's assessment.[20] The making available of information otherwise freely available in official statistics, etc. is clearly legitimate, e.g. the notification *inter se* of patent applications or trade mark registrations. However, where through an agreement, firms obtain non-official, commercially valuable data which they could have obtained individually only at far greater expense and effort (e.g. through their own distribution network of dealers etc.) the Commission will view the agreement suspiciously. In *Re VNP and COBELPA*[21] they stated that such a system "artificially alters the conditions of competition and establishes between competitors a system of solidarity and mutual influence".[22] Agreements to which only one side of the market (i.e. suppliers and not customers) are party, cannot be justified on the basis that they "perfect" the market i.e. they render the market transparent, since in perfect markets data is available to buyers *and* sellers.

[17] On the contrary, the Commission stated that the public authority may, in certain circumstances, also be laying itself open to the allegations of an infringement of Arts. 5, 85 and 3(g).

[18] OJ 1992 L68/19, [1993] 4 CMLR 358.

[19] e.g. the Commission considered that an annual exchange of one-year-old sales figures of individual competitors in the UK, sales according to region and land use, and sales with a breakdown by model could be accepted as "commercial data with no appreciable distorting effect on competition between the manufacturers or between the dealers operating on the UK market".

[20] See, for example, *Re Italian Cast Glass* OJ [1982] L383/19, [1982] 2 CMLR 61; and *UK Agricultural Tractor Registration Exchange* OJ [1992] L68/19.

[21] [1977] 2 CMLR D28.

[22] *ibid.* at pp. D36, 37, para. 30. See also *Wood Pulp* [1985] 3 CMLR 474 at p. 502, para. 85.

(6) The possibility of exemption pursuant to Article 85(3)

9.13 If an information agreement is held to be caught by Article 85(1) there is a possibility that it will gain exemption under Article 85(3).[23] In *UK Agricultural Tractor Registration Exchange*[24] the Commission held that the requirement of indispensability had not been met as, in the Commission's opinion, own company data and aggregate industry data were sufficient to operate in the agricultural tractor market. An example of the Commission granting exemption in respect of an agreement to exchange information is provided by its decision in *International Energy Programme*.[25] A programme was drawn up between 21 states to establish co-operation in the event of disruptions in the supply of oil. Participating companies were required to supply important and sensitive information in the event of such a disruption. The Commission granted an exemption as it considered that the benefit of maintaining constant supplies of oil outweighed the loss of competition occasioned by the exchange of information. In principle there is no reason why exchanges of information, even in concentrated markets, should not warrant exemption. The difficulties lie in the fact that to render such an agreement suitable to exemption the Commission would probably require changes to many schemes which in net effect would make the scheme of dubious or strictly limited value to the participants.

2. UK Law

9.14 United Kingdom law is very complex; only certain species of informational exchange need be registered. In brief the possible forms of agreement potentially subject to registration are those listed in sections 7 (goods) and 12 (services) RTPA 1976. From those listed *only* those made the subject of a calling up order by the Secretary of State need be registered.[26] Thus, agreements are only registrable if so designated by Statutory Instrument. This section examines those agreements enumerated in sections 7 and 12 RTPA 1976 which *might* be called up for registration and those agreements which *have already* been called up.

(1) Sections 7 and 12 RTPA 1976: forms of agreement for calling up

9.15 Attention will be concentrated upon section 7 since section 12 (services) repeats, *mutatis mutandis*, its terms and no calling up order has yet been made in respect of it. Section 7(1) RTPA 1976 defines "information agreement" as:

> "an agreement between two or more persons carrying on within the United Kingdom any such business as is described in section 6(1) [RTPA 1976] ... whether with or without other parties, being an agreement under which provision is made for or in relation to the furnishing by two or more parties to each other or to other persons (whether parties or not) of information in respect of any of the following matters."

[23] See Commission statements to this effect in *Re VNP and COBELPA* OJ [1977] L240/10.

[24] OJ 1992 L68/19, [1993] 4 CMLR 358.

[25] OJ 1983 L376/30, [1984] 2 CMLR 186. This ten-year exemption was subsequently renewed for a further ten years: *International Energy Agency* OJ 1994 L68/35.

[26] Under s. 7(5) RTPA 1976 the Secretary of State must, before laying before Parliament the draft of an Order under s. 7(1) RTPA 1976, publish in such manner as he thinks fit an appropriate notice describing the classes of information agreement to which the proposed Order would apply and specifying a period, which may not be less than 28 days, within which representation concerning the proposal may be made to the Secretary of State. These representations must be "taken into consideration" S.I. 1969 No. 1842 was made on 18 December 1969 and came into force on 1 February 1970.

These "matters" are listed in section 7(1)(a)–(h) and may be summarised as follows: (a) prices charged, quoted or paid or to be charged, quoted or paid; (b) prices to be recommended as resale prices; (c) the terms and conditions on which goods are supplied; (d) the quantities and descriptions of goods to be produced; (e) the cost of production or supply; (f) production methods; (g) supplier and customer details; (h) location of suppliers and customers. Section 12(1)(a) and (b) defines service information agreements in essentially the same terms as section 7(1) for goods. Section 12(2)(a)-(f) on services provides that calling up orders may be made in respect of information agreements concerning: (a) charges made, quoted or paid or to be made, quoted or paid for designated services offered or obtained; (b) terms and conditions of supply for services supplied or obtained or to be sup. plied or obtained; (c) extent or scale (if any) on which services are supplied or obtained or are to be supplied or obtained; (d) form or manner of services supplied or obtained or to be supplied or obtained; (e) cost incurred in making available, supplying or obtaining services; (f) customers or suppliers or locations thereof of services supplied or obtained or are to be supplied or obtained.

(2) Interpretation of sections 7 and 12 RTPA 1976

9.16 Sections 7(1) and 12(1) cover agreements between, for example, X and Y to furnish Z with information; they need not simply be between X and Y to supply each other with information. Thus section 7 also applies to an agreement between parties to supply a central body or trade association, i.e. the recipient of data need not be a party to the agreement. The phrase "under which provision is made" causes difficulties in interpretation. It implies that an agreement, to be registrable, must be of a relatively formal, premeditated nature.

9.17 The agreement must make provision for the exchange of information: X rings up Y and says "I shall be raising my prices 2 per cent on Friday", Y replies "so shall I be" they then both put the telephone down. If on Friday both X and Y raise prices by 2 per cent there may not be a registrable exchange of information agreement concerning prices. There is certainly no agreement which makes "provision" for the exchange. It is of course possible that there is an "arrangement" to fix price levels registrable under sections 6 or 11 RTPA 1976. Irrespective of the provisions of section 6, these words in section 7 seem to exclude from registration informal, irregular telephone call exchanges of information. If such conduct is outside the scope of the RTPA it might constitute "anti-competitive" conduct under the Competition Act 1980 (see Chapter 3). The phrase "for or in relation" used in section 7(1) and 12(1)(b) is very wide. An agreement between X and Y to exchange price data, for illustration, is an agreement under which provision is made "for" the exchange of information. If X and Y subsequently hire Z (perhaps an accountancy firm or computer programming partnership of firm of marketing consultants) to assist in collation and analysis of the data this presumably is an agreement "in relation to" the furnishing by two or more parties (i.e. X and Y) to each other of data listed in section 7(1) or 12(2)(a)-(f) RTPA 1976. Likewise, if Z merely gave passive advice on how X and Y should analyse their data this would be an agreement in relation to the agreement between X and Y. The relationship between Z and X/Y need not be written to be caught by the Act; nor indeed need it be contractual. Section 43(1) RTPA 1976 defines agreement very widely to embrace all forms of consensus.[27] In almost all matters listed in sec-

[27] See s. 43(1) RTPA 1976 under which "agreement" includes an "arrangement" whether or not it is intended to be legally binding. The term "arrangement" has been construed to include all informal agreements between parties intended to be acted upon. See *British Basic Slag Ltd's Application* (1963) LR 4 RP 116 at pp. 154, 155 *per* Diplock LJ (CA). See further paras. 1.7–1.42

tion 7(1) and 12(2) information provisions relating to past or future transactions are embraced. Both sections invariably use the past (quoted, charged, etc.) and future (to be quoted, charged, etc.) tenses. The *sole* exception is section 9(1)(b) which relates to exchanges of information concerning "the price to be recommended or suggested as the prices to be charged or quoted in respect of the resale of goods supplied". Data exchanges of prices already recommended (i.e. past tense) may not therefore be called up and consequently need not be registered.

(3) S.I. 1969 No. 1842: Information agreements concerning goods which must be registered

9.18 The only calling up order to date concerns goods.[28] It may be reiterated that only those information agreements covered by this order need be registered: S.I. 1969 No. 1842 Article 3(2)(a) and (b) covers agreements concerning:

> "(a) the prices charged or quoted or to be charged or quoted otherwise than to any of the parties to the relevant agreement for goods which have been or are to be supplied or offered or for the application of any process of manufacture to goods; (b) the terms or conditions on or subject to which goods have been or are to be supplied otherwise than to any such party or any such process has been or is to be applied to goods otherwise than for any such party."

9.19 Under Article 3(2)(a) (prices), both pre-notification agreements whereby X and Y inform each other of price *to be* charged in prospective transactions and post-notification agreements whereby X and Y notify each other *after* conclusion of the transaction with the customer must be registered. Agreements for exchange of prices actually charged or merely quoted are not differentiated between. In these days of instantaneous communication an agreement whereby X and Y inform each other of prices quoted or charged during the transaction (i.e. simultaneous notification) is a possibility; are such agreements registrable? The answer is almost certainly yes since there will inevitably be a time lag—even if of only minutes or seconds or fractions thereof—between charge or quotation and notification hence making the agreement "post-notification". The Order excludes agreements concerning prices paid or offered, i.e. buyers agreements. Hence buyers may exchange price data without having to register their agreement. Though the Order would appear to catch an agreement between buyers as to prices quoted to them.

9.20 Under Article 3(2)(b) (terms and conditions), no definition is given of a "term or condition" but presumably it means those provisions which impliedly or expressly, orally or in writing, are contained in the contract of supply. Included would, *inter alia*, be: price quantities, descriptions, packaging and advertising obligations, periods allowed for payment, method of payment and credit facilities, discounts and rebates, freight handling, carriage costs, insurance liability clauses, exclusion and limitation clauses, renegotiation and escalation clause, date and place of delivery, checking, etc. As with Article 3(1)(a) buyers agreements are excluded. Again agreements concerning terms and conditions which *have been* or are *to be* applied are included. The same question concerning instantaneous notification applies and the same answer may be suggested. One question which arises is whether information concerning "terms or conditions" extends beyond the scope of those provisions contained in the contract of supply. For example, firms within a particular industry may wish to exchange information regarding the creditworthiness of customers. In the context of such "credit circles", the parties may say to each other: "cus-

[28] Ordinary agreements relating to services *are* subject to registration however under S.I. 1976 No. 98 Restrictive Trade Practices (Services) Order 1976.

tomer X was on harsh terms" or "customer Y was on preferential terms". It is likely that exchanges of information of this general type would fall within the scope of the Order and would be registrable on the basis that they still represent exchanges of information "which relate"[29] to terms and conditions. In addition, the OFT might consider that such exchanges of information are within the mischief of the Order. Where companies are broadly aware of the terms and conditions upon which competitors supply goods, exchanges of information of this more general type could be deciphered by rivals in such a way that rivals could make accurate predictions as to the terms and conditions applied by competitors. It appears, however, that it *would* be permissible for members of a credit circle to inform each other that they have refused to supply a particular customer since this reveals nothing about the terms and conditions in the contracts that supplier uses with its customers. The same applies, in principle, to the information that a certain customer is *X* days overdue with his payment or is a "bad debt". However, if a member of the circle includes in his contracts of supply a definition of "bad debt" then the exchange of information relating to which customers were bad debts would be impermissible since it would relate to the terms or conditions of the supply contracts; the circle would have to arrive at an independent definition of that phrase in order that discussions fell outside the terms of the Order.

9.21 The RPC has held that not every contract clause constitutes a term or condition.[30] Various elements of a supply contract may, therefore, fall outside Article 3(2) of the Order. Thus, exchanging information as to a new customer to be supplied or a customer to be resupplied would fall outside the Order as the identity of a contracting party would not be held to be a term or condition on or subject to which goods are supplied.

9.22 S.I. 1969 No. 1842 is absurdly complex in its drafting. The following is a summary of those information schemes otherwise caught by Article 3(2)(a) and (b) but which are expressly excluded by the Schedule to the Order:

(a) Agreements relating to exports which are not generally registrable in any event under Schedule 3 paragraph 6 RTPA 1976. However, UK export agreements to the EC fall within Article 85(1) as do agreements to non-EC states if they none the less affect trade within the EC (e.g. because of re-importation).
(b) Agreements relating to information furnished to a government department or other specific authority listed in Part II of the Schedule. The most important of the many bodies referred to are: any government department; any committee established by any such department; The Monopolies and Mergers Commission; any royal commission. This list is not exhaustive, various other industrial and agricultural trade bodies are also referred to.
(c) Agreements whereby parties agree separately and directly to furnish a non-trading body (e.g. a trade association) with information which relates only to itself and where information based upon that furnished is returned only to that party.
(d) Agreements whereby parties agree separately and directly to furnish information to a specified authority at the written request of that authority (e.g. government department or other body listed in Part II of the Schedule) in a form that prevents

[29] See s. 3(1): "It is directed that the provisions of Part 1 of the Act of 1956 ... shall apply in relation to the following class of information agreements ... which relate to any of the matters specified in paragraph (2) of this Article, whether or not they relate to any other matters."

[30] See e.g. *British Waste Paper Association's Agreement* [1963] 1 WLR 540, 547 (CA): restriction as to nomenclature is not a restriction as to terms and conditions; *Re Blanket Manufacturers' Agreement* [1959] 1 WLR 42 affirmed by CA [1959] 1 WLR 1148: clause forbidding members to break contracts or vary the terms without the consent or a third party was held not to be a restriction as to terms and conditions.

the information being identifiable as relating to any particular party, though of course the party furnishing the data may recognise it.

(e) Agreements relating to the furnishing of information already published or to be made public.[31]

(f) Agreements relating to the furnishing of data as an incidental matter in agreements already excluded from registration under sections 7 and 8 RTPA 1956 (covered now, in shortened and consolidated form, in section 9 RTPA 1976 relating to provisions in agreements to be excluded from the purview of the Act; see paras. 1.74–1.100).

(g) Agreements entered into by an agricultural marketing board of a kind referred to in section 45 Agriculture (Miscellaneous Provisions) Act 1968.

(4) The requirement of two parties: whether unilateral disseminations are caught

9.23 An information agreement is defined in section 7 RTPA 1976 as being between "two or more persons carrying on within the United Kingdom ... business." Hence, where only one person furnishes information the Act is excluded. However, a practice where a single firm X regularly informs Y of his price intentions could fall under section 2(1) CA 1980. Under section 2(1) CA 1980 such a practice could constitute a "course of conduct which ... has or is intended to have or is likely to have the effect of restricting, distorting or preventing competition". The phrase "course of conduct" excludes "one-offs". Hence would a single, unilateral dissemination by X to his major rival Y be a "course of conduct"? A narrow view would be that an isolated instance is beyond the scope of the Act: an alternative analysis postulates that if Y responds to X's communication and a pattern of concerted behaviour arises then the single dissemination by X coupled to the behaviour of X in subsequently acting may be a "course of conduct". The activity in question would in this case be confined to X's actions alone.

9.24 If a single dissemination by X enabled Y to align his prices and thereafter act in conscious parallelism with X, this might comprise a "complex monopoly" under sections 6–11 FTA 1973 entitling the OFT to refer X and Y to the MMC for analysis. A "complex monopoly" exists where a number of firms together control 25 per cent or more of the market whether that market be for the whole of the United Kingdom or only a part thereof. Although, as noted above certain buyers' agreements are excluded from S.I. 1969 No. 1842 they are not excluded from either section 2(1) CA 1980 or the monopoly provisions of the FTA 1973.

(5) The goods/services distinction

9.25 It is worth recalling that only information agreements concerning *goods* need be registered and then only those described in S.I. 1969 No. 1842. Parties may proceed with *services* information agreement without needing to furnish particulars of them. However, care should be taken that the information agreement is not simply part and parcel of an ordinary agreement which fixes prices, shares markets or imposes quotas, etc. If this is the case the OFT might treat such agreements as an ordinary registrable agreement or arrangement.

(6) Summary: types of agreement that are registrable

9.26 In the UK only information agreements concerning goods need be registered. Conceivably, the conduct of a party to an information agreement concerning services may be in-

[31] Para. (c) of the Schedule gives as an example: "the furnishing of particulars of prices charged for goods at any market or other place at which such goods are regularly offered for sale by a substantial number of sellers".

vestigated by the OFT under the CA 1980. There is, however, no published investigation on such practices to date. Within the category of goods information agreements only those agreements which concern matters mentioned in S.I. 1969 No. 1842 need be furnished. i.e. information concerning prices and terms or conditions. Other types of information exchange are not registrable.[32]

C. Price Information Exchange Agreements

9.27 The exchange of price information is rarely acceptable to the OFT or the European Commission especially where the parties inhabit oligopolistic markets. In the past parties have argued that "open pricing"—a term first coined by Chicago lawyer A.J. Eddy in a treatise entitled *The New Competition*,[33] beneficial to the market. Eddy described the practice as pricing "that is open and above board, that is known to both competitors and customers, that is marked wherever possible in plain figures on every article produced, that is accurately printed in every price list issued—a price about which there is no secrecy, no evasions, no preferences. In contract work it means that every bid made and every modification thereof shall be known to every competitor for the order." Such a rationale has never been accepted in America[34] where it was engendered, nor in Britain or the EC where it has not infrequently been rehearsed.[35] The objections are: first, rarely if ever do information agreements make their data available to their customers; and secondly information agreements in oligopolistic markets can be anti rather than pro-competitive. The exception to this general rejection of "open pricing" has been transport. Thus, in relation to international maritime services carried out by shipping liner conferences. Regulation 4056/86/EEC[36] confers by Article 3 thereof, block exemption upon international maritime price fixing by liner conferences. An essential element of tariff fixing is, of necessity, tariff consultation. However, under the Regulation it is or conditions of exemption that shipowners and shippers consult over the tariff and that all tariffs are published. In this section with respect to EC law "price information" is construed widely to include all elements and constituents of price: profit margins, discounts and rebates (whether published or hidden), freight costs and other handling charges, labour, materials and other inputs which directly affect overall price. It also includes the dates of changes of any components of price. This is wider than the narrow definition given in section 43(1) RTPA 1976 which defines price for purposes of UK law as including "a charge of any description". Though section 43(1) is inclusive not exclusive of the meaning of "price".

[32] For an example of an information agreement condemned by the Commission but not caught by S.I. 1969 No. 1842 see the Commission's decision in *UK Agricultural Tractor Registration Exchange* OJ 1992 L68/19, [1993] 4 CMLR 358.

[33] Eddy, *The New Competition* (New York, 1912).

[34] See e.g. *American Column and Lumber Co* v *US* 257 US 377 (1921); *US* v *American Linseed Oil Co* 262 US 371 (1923); *Sugar Institute Inc* v *US* 297 US 553 (1936); but cf. for cases where "open pricing" was upheld: *Maple Flooring Manufacturers* v *US* 268 US 563 (1925); *Cement Manufacturers' Protective Association et al.* v *US* 268 US 588 (1925); *Tag Manufacturers' Institute* v *FTC* 174 F. 2d 452 (1949).

[35] See e.g. *Dutch sporting cartridges, Third Report on Competition Policy* (1973), point 55; *Dutch Agreement in the Record Industry, Fourth Report on Competition Policy* (1974), point 76; OFITOMEP, Bull EC 12/1976 No. 2127; *VVVF* [1970] CMLR D.1; *Non-Ferrous Semi-Manufacturers, FifthReport on Competition Policy* (1975), point 39; *Ships Cables, Fifth Report on Competition Policy* (1975), points 40, 41.

[36] See OJ 1986 L378/4.

1. EC Law

9.28 The following are examples of informational exchanges that may infringe Article 85(1) EC. "Pre-notification agreements" refers to the exchange of information about conduct before that conduct takes place. "Post-notification agreements" are exchanges of information about transactions after they have occurred.

(1) Pre-notification agreements

9.29 Pre-notification agreements are usually operated by trade associations who collect, collate and disseminate the data. In *IFTRA Rules for Producers of Virgin Aluminium*[37] the Commission condemned a pre-notification agreement on the basis that it gave "the parties the means to know each other's costs, and, particularly in view of the structure of the relevant market, [enabled] them to predict each other's price policy with greater certainty, whereby price competition [would] be diminished or eliminated".[38] A more comprehensive condemnation was given by the Commission in *European Glass Manufacturers*[39] to a pre-notification scheme of discounts from list prices:

> "It is contrary to the provisions of Article 85(1) of the EC Treaty for a producer to communicate to his competitors the essential elements of his price policy such as price lists, the discounts and terms of trade he applies, the rates and date of any change to them and the special exceptions he grants to specific customers. An undertaking which informs its competitors of such elements of its price policy will only do so when certain that, in accordance with the agreement entered into with such competitors in pursuance of the [agreement], they will pursue a similar price policy for deliveries to the market where the undertaking is a price leader. By such means it is sought to eliminate the possibility of unforeseen or unforeseeable reactions by competitors, thus removing a large element of the risk normally attaching to any individual action in the market."[40]

As a rule pre-notifications of pricing data agreements will infringe Article 85(1). In this context it should be noted that slightly different rules apply for steel and coal under the European Coal and Steel Community Treaty (ECSC).[41] Article 60(2) ECSC obliges steel producers to publish price lists which are available to seller *and* buyers alike. However, in other respects Article 65(1) ECSC largely mirrors Article 85 EC.

(2) Post-notification agreements

9.30 In practice the Commission refuses to differentiate between pre-and post-notification on the basis that subtle use of post-notification agreements can still give sellers the chance to predict accurately each other's pricing policy.[42] For an agreement to be innocuous the time-lag between transaction with customer and notification with competitor would have

[37] [1975] 2 CMLR D20. See also *OFITOMEP* Bull EC 12/76 No. 2127.
[38] [1975] 2 CMLR D20 at p. D36, para. 43.
[39] [1974] 2 CMLR D50.
[40] *ibid.*, at p. D71, para. 43.
[41] Note also that different rules also apply to the airline sector. There is a block exemption (Commission Reg. No. 84/91, OJ 1991 No. L10, 15 January 1991, p. 14) which authorises air carriers to hold tariff consultations under certain conditions. However, if these conditions are not met, then the information exchange will fall to be considered under the general principles outlined above. This was demonstrated in *British Midland* v *Aer Lingus* (OJ 1992 L96/34) where the Commission held that Aer Lingus had infringed Art. 85(1) by exchanging information on airline costs and tariff objectives. The airline's conduct did not benefit from the block exemption as the Commission considered that consultations had exceeded the lawful purpose of facilitating interlining.
[42] *ibid.*, at p. D71, para. 42(ii); *Community* v *Associated Lead Manufacturers Ltd* [1979] 1 CMLR 464 at p. 472, paras. 24 *et seq.*

to be long enough to nullify the predictive value of the data to the competitor. Such a period may well have to be counted in months. The period would also have to be long enough to avoid the rival having a chance to undercut the person notifying. Such undercutting might be the design in a market sharing agreement where parties are designated specific quotas: where X has filled his quota of sales but Y has not, notification of a price quoted to a customer but notified to Y before the sale is formally entered will allow Y to "steal away" that customer by undercutting X. In this manner the pre-agreed quotas may be honoured. In *Flat Glass*[43] the Commission imposed fines of between ECU765,000 and ECU1,450,000 (approximately £460,000–870,000) on glass manufacturers who exchanged sales figures as a means of monitoring each other's market share and thereby maintaining the status quo:

> "The exchange of sales figures by the competitors served not only to keep them better informed of the general state of the market but also to allow them to monitor closely the sales of their main rivals so that they could react more effectively if this proved necessary. The exchanges thus helped the parties to ensure they maintained their relative positions within the planned fluctuation margin, for not only were the data which were exchanged very detailed, but the exchanges were frequent (quarterly) and they were the subject of discussions on interpretation and calculation methods."

Thus a three monthly exchange was too short a period to "sanitise" the exchange of sales data.

9.31 The Commission condemned a relatively unsophisticated information exchange agreement in *Fatty Acids*[44] where the three largest producers of fatty acids with a combined market share of 60 per cent in a declining market exchanged information about their historical sales to establish their relative market shares, and then exchanged sales details quarterly. The purpose of the agreement seems to have been to enable a reduction of capacity by all three to take place without losing market share, and hence the information seems to have been exchanged as part of what was effectively a quota fixing agreement.[45] The Commission fined each of the participants ECU50,000.

9.32 The *UK Agricultural Tractor Registration Exchange* demonstrates the first example of a Commission decision condemning a pure information exchange agreement, not involving any overt or covert direct forms of quota fixing. Tractor registration documents were sent by the parties to the exchange agreement to a central co-ordinator. Figures on tractor sales were available to members fully broken down by model, retailer geographical area and over any time period down to daily. The result was to create complete transparency among the tractor suppliers and their dealers to whom this information was also sup-

[43] OJ 1984 L212/13 at pp. 19, 20, para. 45. See at para. 47 for the Commission's assessment of the effect on trade between the Member States. In *Nuovo Cegam* [1984] 2 CMLR 484 the Commission granted an Art. 85(3) exemption to an association of engineering insurers which collected statistical data on claims experiences from members. This data was used to draw up a common tariff of basic premiums for various types of risk which the members agreed to apply. Members retained freedom to add to the basic premium margins for expenses, commission and profit, etc. The agreement clearly had the effect of harmonising prices. However, the agreement was exempted under Art. 85(3) on the basis that the market in Italy for this type of insurance operated inefficiently, and was characterised by weak demand and relatively limited supply. To do business the insurer required highly specialised resources and knowledge. The Commission stated, in respect of Art. 85(3) that the agreement by enhancing the efficiency of members improved the production and distribution of insurance services and promoted technical and economic progress. Consumers could be said to have obtained a fair share of the resulting benefit since the promotion work of the association helped to enlarge the capacity of the industry and could lead to a technically more advanced service on terms competing with those of other operators in the market (*ibid.* at p. 493 paras. 19, 20). See the Commission comment on this case *Fourteenth Report on Competition Policy* (1984) at p. 68, para. 76.

[44] [1988] 4 CMLR 445.

[45] [1988] 4 CMLR 445, para. 39.

plied. The agreement covered eight suppliers comprising 88 per cent of the UK market. Given that this was a concentrated market, with the four largest firms holding a 80 per cent market share, the Commission prohibited this agreement though without imposing fines.[46]

The Commission invariably view post-notification price agreements as either hiding collusion or likely to foster conscious parallelism.

(3) Exchange to enforce resale price maintenance: customer boycotts

9.33 Such exchanges will be invariably unlawful: competitors exchange customer lists; competitors learn, through absence from the list, that customer A is no longer being supplied by supplier X. This indicates that A has been departing from the stipulated resale price and X's refusal to deal must be supported by other competitors. In this manner the data exchange initiates a boycott of A and an enforcement/disciplining system for resale price maintenance.

(4) Price verification schemes

9.34 The "buyers' tales" problem—dealer A receives a quotation of £100 per unit from Supplier X; he loses nothing by misrepresenting to supplier Y that X has quoted him £90 per unit and that a matching or undercutting quote would secure Y the order. If X and Y exchange price data they can test the veracity of A's claims and ultimately eradicate "buyers' tales" from the market. No formal decision has been issued by the Commission but a similar approach might well be adopted to that of American law. The problem is not uncommon in the EC.[47] American law has derived primarily in the context of price-discrimination cases. The cases adopt variations on the following scenario. Supplier Y quotes US$100 per unit in formal transactions; dealer A induces him to quote US$89 per unit in order to better a fictitious quotation from Supplier X. Other dealers learn of the US$89 quotation to A but when quoted $100 per unit by Y complain that he is discriminating in price between his customers.[48]

9.35 The legal problem is whether an agreement between suppliers to verify each others prices is a legal method of countering buyers' tales (which force them to quote unprofitably) and allegations of price discrimination. It is generally considered a justification for price discrimination that the low quotation was made in order to meet a rival's low bid.[49] In USA the following conclusions would appear to prevail. (a) Where there is a clash between price fixing law and price discrimination law, the vitality of price fixing laws must be maintained even at the expense of price-discrimination laws. Price fixing is a more serious and widespread practice.[50] (b) The evidentiary burden of a "meeting competition" defence to a price-

[46] Appeals were dismissed by the Court of First Instance in T-34/92 *Fiatagri and Ford New Holland* v *Commission* [1994] ECR II-905 and T-35/92 *John Deere* v *Commission* [1994] ECR II-957.

[47] See e.g. *OFITOMEP* Bull EC 12/76 No. 2127; *European Glass Manufacturers' Agreement* [1974] 2 CMLR D50 at p. D71 para. 41(ii) last sentence.

[48] See e.g. *LCL Theatres Inc* v *Columbia Pictures Industries Inc* 421 F. Supp. 1090 (N.D. Tex 1976) modified 566 F. 2d. 494 (5th Cir. 1978) where the false quotation was considered to be fraudulent.

[49] In America the "meeting competition defense" is statutorily enshrined in s. 2(b) Robinson-Patman Act 1936. This provision allows suppliers to defend against allegations of price discrimination "by showing that his lower price or the furnishing of services or facilities to any purchaser or purchasers was made in good faith to meet an equally low price of a competitor or the services or facilities furnished by a competitor".

[50] See e.g. *US* v *US Gypsum Co* 346 F.2d. 115 (1977); affirmed 438 US 422 (1978); *Automatic Canteen Co* v *FTC* 346 US 61, 73 S.Ct. 1017 (1953) affirmed in *Great Atlantic and Pacific Tea Co* v *FTC* 99 S.Ct. 925 (1979). A number of older cases, however, suggest that the burden of proof for the "meeting competition" defence required suppliers to show *conclusive* evidence of misrepresentation by the customer to

discrimination allegation may be satisfied by less than a regular exchange between rivals of prices quoted. The defence may be proven by the low quoting supplier simply demonstrating that the purchaser had quoted an artificial price to him and that he believed it. Alternatively, suppliers can organise a trade association to disseminate anonymous ranges of prices quoted, *perhaps* broken down by area. To gain exemption for a trade association scheme under Article 85(3) EC suppliers would have to satisfy the Commission that the practice of buyers tales was common, that customers were complaining and that suppliers were suffering financially as a result. It might well be only the truly exceptional case that earns an exemption. Perhaps where the customer was in a dominant or otherwise powerful position,[51] effectively abusing a monopolistic (or oligopolistic) position.

(5) Anti-dumping complaints

9.36 The Commission has informally expressed concern that trade associations which have ostensibly been collecting price data for the compilation of an anti-dumping complaint have, in reality, used the dumping complaint as a smokescreen for a price cartel. "Dumping" occurs where undertakings in a non-EC state sell in the EC at prices below those prevailing on their own domestic market. Under Article 5 of Council Regulation 2423/88/EEC[52] trade associations may submit complaints to their national authorities or to the Commission. The complaint shall "contain sufficient evidence of the existence of dumping or subsidisation and the injury resulting therefrom". A proper complaint would necessarily involve close co-operation between trade association and members with respect to prices, costs, market shares, sales trends, etc. Genuine complainants should ensure that the dossier they submit cannot be used to foster collusion; this would probably involve screening procedures being adopted by the association.

(6) Price revision undertakings in anti-dumping proceedings

9.37 In the course of dumping proceedings it remains open to the offending non-EC exporters to file a written document with the Commission expressing a willingness to raise prices on goods to be exported to the EC.[53] In excess of half of the dumping proceedings opened by the Commission are settled in this manner. Theoretically the exporter unilaterally indicates a willingness to give price undertakings. In practice the Commission must ensure that all of the exporter's increases are uniform and that the European producers will not unfairly exploit the undertakings by undercutting the exporter's raised prices. The achievement of an acceptable *modus operandi* necessitates a certain amount of negotiation about price between local industry and exporters to the EC with the Com-

cont.
justify agreement by means of price verification. For examples of such cases which have apparently been overtaken by the cases above, see, *Cement Manufacturers' Protective Association* v *US* 268 US 588 (1925); *Wall Products Co* v *National Gypsum Co* 326 F. Supp. 295 (N.D. Col. 1971) and the petroleum cases in which major oil corporations conferred with rivals during a price war to verify its rivals prices before granting temporary price concessions to its own local retailers, *Webster* v *Sinclair Refining Co* 388 F. Supp. 248 (S.D. Ala. 1971); *Belliston* v *Texaco* 455 F. 2d. 175 (10th Cir.) cert. denied 408 US 928, 925 S. Ct. 2494 (1972); *Gray* v *Shell Oil* 469 F. 2d. 742 (9th Cir. 1972) cert. denied 412 US 932, 93 S.Ct. 2773.

51 For American cases supporting this conclusion see e.g. *US* v *US Gypsum Co* 346 F. 2d. 115 (1977) affirmed 438 US 422 (1978); *Great Atlantic and Pacific Tea Co* v *FTC* 99 S. Ct. 925 (1979). These overrule earlier cases demanding a higher burden of proof, i.e. that the supplier had grounds which would lead a "reasonable and prudent person to believe that the granting of a lower price would in fact meet the equally low prices of a competitor". *FTC* v *AE Staley* 324 US 746 at pp. 759, 760. See also *Viviano Macaroni Co* v *FTC* 411 F. 2d. 255 at pp. 259, 260 (3rd Cir. 1969).

52 OJ 1988 L209/1 on protection against dumped or subsidised imports from countries not members of the European Economic Community. See for analysis, Van Bael and Bellis, *EC Anti-Dumping and other Trade Restriction Laws* (2nd edn. 1990).

53 Art. 10 Reg. 2423/88.

mission as intermediary. It is conceivable that under the cloak of respectable negotiations producers could employ the opportunity to agree clandestinely on price levels. There is little doubt that such an agreement would infringe Article 85(1) EC and given the clandestine nature of the agreement the Commission might see fit to visit such underhand behaviour with heavy fines. There is no case to date on the point.

(7) Warning mechanisms

9.38 Informational exchanges employed to warn confederates in a price fixing agreement that the Commission or some other authority has discovered their agreement or is investigating their premises will be viewed as proof of anti-competitive intent. In EC law it may be viewed as an aggravating factor and encourage the imposition of a fine. In one case parties agreed that in the event of an official visit a telex would be sent to competitors. The "alarm" was: "Re IRMA. Attention Mr [] The figures from a German Company for the next market survey are wrong. They will therefore be distributed at a later date." The "alarm over" telex would state: "Re IRMA. Attention Mr[] We have now received the correct figures from the German company. You will receive the market survey in a few days. Thank you for your comprehension." The Commission commented: "The alarm system ... [makes] it clear that the parties were fully aware that their conduct constituted infringements of Community competition legislation."[54]

2. UK Law

(1) Pre- and post-notification agreements

9.39 Both pre- and post-notification agreements must be registered under S.I. 1969 No. 1842 Article 3(2)(a). The Restrictive Practices Court has been invariably strict with such agreements which are usually adjuncts to more formal price agreements,[55] though, in very exceptional cases such information agreements have been permitted to co-exist with a price fixing agreement found to be in the public interest and hence legal.[56] However, a considerable body of criticism has been levelled at these cases and it is by no means certain that the current Court would be equally liberal.[57] Certainly in everyday negotiations the OFT bases its judgment on the stricter line of cases. This will be particularly so in concentrated markets. An analysis of the Restrictive Practices Register reveals that most information agreements specifying price would be unsuitable for section 21(2) RTPA 1976 representations since they are generally: (a) specific in identifying the supplier and customer involved; and (b) specific in identifying the prices actually involved in the transaction.[58]

[54] *IRMA* OJ 1983 1317/1 at p. 13, para. 54.

[55] See e.g. *Glazed and Floor Home Trade Association's Agreement* (1964) LP 4 Rp 239 where the Court upheld the price-fixing agreement but condemned the exchange of information; *Mileage Conference Group of the Tyre Manufacturers Conference Ltd Agreement* (1966) LR 6 RP 49; [1966] 1 WLR 1137; *Galvanised Tank Manufacturers' Association's Agreement* (1965) LR 5 RP 315; [1965] 1 WLR 1074 where the Court condemned a post-notification agreement employing a two day time-lag; *Crane Makers' Association Agreement* (1965) LR 5 RP 264; [1965] 1 WLR 542; No. 3732 Register of Restrictive Trade Practices, *Plastic Pressure Pipes* (1974) parties notified each other of changes in published price lists thereby enabling the parties to harmonise their prices. The RPC held the agreement to be against the public interest, the parties did not defend the agreement.

[56] See e.g. *Standard Metal Window Group Agreement* (1962) LR 3 RP 198; [1962] 1 WLR 1020; *Permanent Magnet Association's Agreement* (1962) LR 3 RP 119; [1962] 1 WLR 781.

[57] See e.g. Stevens and Yamey, *The Restrictive Practices Court* (1965), pp. 211–18; Hunter, *Competition and the Law* (1966), p. 126; O'Brien and Swann, *Information Agreements Competition and Efficiency* (1968), pp. 144–147.

[58] See e.g. the following cases on the Register of Restrictive Trade Practices: No. 838, *Midland Hosiery, Dyers and Finishers' Association* involving notification of price lists to the trade association and notification of changes thereto not before notification to customer but before application of modification; No. 729,

To even stand a chance of being accepted, an information agreement should be anonymous and its data aggregated so that individual firms and transactions cannot be identified. Even where this is done the chances of success are slim. Thus, for price agreements to be acceptable parties would have to adduce evidence to the OFT of: a competitive market with no oligopolist tendencies amongst participants; positive benefits to the market being conferred by the agreement; use of aggregated data presented in anonymous form. Only then could restrictions be said to be not "significant" thereby enabling section 21 (2) dispensation to be sought.

9.40 An example of a case actually satisfying these criteria is *Banbury Marketing Services*[59] which concerned mushrooms. The market for mushrooms is characterised by a large number of growers varying enormously in size. The product is fungible, it has a very short post-harvesting life and must be marketed within 48 hours. The short-lived nature of the product, the often small size of the producers and the unpredictable nature of demand rendered the operation of the market somewhat inefficient. The exchange of information concerned was designed to "perfect" the market by providing the six participants with improved information of prevailing price levels in the market centres around the UK and of the level of demand experienced at those centres. Under the system a number of wholesalers in all the various markets were contacted daily and data (some rather anecdotal) on: quantities received, quality, price levels, strength of demand and likely supply levels for the following day, was obtained. The participants would then telex or phone in to a centre in Banbury their expected daily despatches to the various markets by grade. This supply data would then be summarised and the results disseminated to the participants with comments on apparent over- or under-loading on individual markets. Each participant was then free to reassess the situation and reallocate supplies. A number of points are worth stressing: (a) the parties did not fix prices they merely exchanged data on existing price levels and demand patterns in different locations; (b) all data was disseminated in summary form; (c) no data concerning parties business or prices was disclosed to other parties; (d) the collation centre did not recommend parties to undertake specific courses of action—parties retained total freedom to choose how they acted upon the data; (e) the agreement may reasonably be expected to have served the consumer by improving the continuity of supply to markets and by reducing the risk of wild price fluctuations. The OFT undertook an analysis of the market. It apparently accepted the view that collusion was difficult where the product was not homogeneous (mushrooms come in different grades though clearly a degree of substitutability exists) and speed of marketing was essential. The strength of competition to the parties was also a significant factor.

cont.
Linoleum Manufacturers Agreement, exchange of data on general terms of payment, cash discounts, dating of invoices, carriage and delivery charges, other services costs; No. 390, *Pin and Allied Trade Association Agreement,* exchange of detailed price data; No. 2904, *Association of Master Plumbers and Domestic Engineers (London),* voluntary exchange of price lists for plumbing materials—such an agreement would have little impact upon prices if labour costs were not also exchanged. See also OECD *Report on Information Agreements* (1967), p. 21, *Linen Sewing Thread Manufacturers' Association Agreement*—a term of the agreement stated: "In the event of any sales being affected by a participating member at prices lower than his current list prices particulars of such sales shall be furnished by the member concerned to the secretaries immediately after each sale is made." See for examples of agreements where the data was aggregated and anonymous No. 2693, *Cheshire Cheese Makers*; No. 4336, *Banbury Marketing Services (Mushrooms)*—para. 5(b) and (c) of a Memorandum submitted to the OFT provided: "No information whatsoever relating to an individual participant's operations is released by Banbury to other participants. All figures are dealt with in summary form. Each participant while agreeing to co-operate in smoothing the distribution of product between market reserves the absolute right to operate according to the best interests of his own business and within its constraints." Section 21(2) dispensation was given to this case.

[59] No. 4336 Register of Restrictive Trade Practices.

(2) Price fixing surrogates

9.41 Price fixing agreements unearthed by the OFT are often referred to the Restrictive Practices Court for a formal prohibitive order despite the fact that the parties have abandoned the agreement and do not defend themselves before the Court. Firms subject to a court order (see paras. 5.5–5.7) may not enter agreements to the "like effect". They may *not*, therefore, enter price information agreements as surrogates for price fixing agreements. In this respect the Court has stated:

> "We wish to give warning ... It is abundantly apparent ... that those who, having been placed under an injunction or having given an undertaking ... thereafter exchange information of their intentions on matters such as prices, or partake in discussions, formal or informal, with their competitors on such matters, may be in real peril of ... having passed easily and quickly from that which may be legitimate into actions which constitute a grave contempt."[60]

(3) Exchanges to enforce resale price maintenance

9.42 As with EC law an exchange of data designed to enforce resale price maintenance can expect no sympathy from the OFT. Section 11 of the Resale Prices Act 1976 prohibits the withholding of supplies to dealers who undercut supplier's stipulated prices. Agreements to collectively refuse to deal are, *a fortiori*, anti-competitive and will be condemned by the OFT. Moreover, collective action of this variety will probably amount to the common law tort of unlawful means conspiracy or unlawful interference with trade. A person suffering thereunder may sue for damages and/or an injunction. The unlawful means is the infringement of the Resale Prices Act and/or the RTPA 1976.[61]

(4) Price verification schemes

9.43 Similar conclusions to those derived from EC law may be assumed to apply.[62] An economically powerful or dominant buyer who employs misrepresentation as a tactic might be subject to investigation under the CA 1980.

(5) Anti-dumping complaints

9.44 As noted in respect of EC law complaints may be made to national authorities for transmission to the Commission. A sham complaint which hides a price fixing or market sharing, etc. agreement would be treated as a registrable agreement and assessed as such. The agreement would almost certainly *not* benefit from the exemptions from registration granted by Part I of the Schedule to S.I. 1969 No. 1842, para. 2(a) and (b)(ii) to information agreements for furnishing specified authorities with information since it is not: (a) submitted by the parties "separately and directly to the specified authority"; and/or (b) submitted to the authorities "at the written request of the authority"; and/or (c) submitted in a form which "prevents any information being identified except by the party to whom the information relates".

(6) Warning mechanisms

9.45 See the commentary in respect of EC law above. Similar conclusions should apply in the UK though of course the OFT has no power to fine.

[60] *Galvanised Tank Manufacturers' Agreement* (1965) LR 5 RP 315 at pp. 344, 345.

[61] See *Daily Mirror Newspapers* v *Gardner* [1968] 2 WLR 1239; [1968] 2 QB 762; [1968] 2 All ER 163 (CA); *Brekkes Ltd* v *Cattel* [1972] 1 Ch 105 at p. 122 *per* Pennycuick VC; (1972) LR 7 RP 150.

[62] Such cases are not unknown in UK law see No. 390 Register of Restrictive Trade Practices, *Pinn and Allied Trades Association Agreement*. Item 18 of the rules states: "To the intent that members shall not be misrepresented or misled by purchasers Members shall send to the secretary their current prices ... and shall where possible notify the secretary immediately of any changes therein."

D. Detecting Anti-Competitive Price Exchanges: EC and UK

9.46 The following factors may be used to detect exchanges of price data.[63] It will be appreciated that the factors below are similar to those often used to detect straight price fixing agreements. Clearly,.this is because price data agreements may be closely related to price fixing agreements.

(a) Is there an agreement to abide by published price lists? An affirmative answer suggests collusion over price.

(b) Are details of price offers exchanged between the parties even though actual sales may not be made at the offered price? This helps ensure uniformity.

(c) Are individual buyers and sellers identified in the exchanged or disseminated data? Where anonymity is not the rule parties who breach the agreement, e.g. by not abiding by a rival's notified price, may easily be detected and pressure to comply exerted by other parties or a central trade association.

(d) Is disseminated data made available to buyers or their trade associations? The Commission has frequently complained of one-sided agreements where disseminated data is reserved for suppliers only.

(e) Are competitors books open to inspection by each other? An affirmative answer suggests collusion.

(f) Is there a delay between conclusion of a transaction and notification to competitors or the trade association? The shorter the time-gap the greater the implication that the data is intended for price coordinating purposes.

(g) Is information on prices to be charged notified to the trade association, i.e. before it is notified to the customer? Pre-notification suggests a concerted attempt to harmonise prices.

(h) To what extent do buyers find that on placing an order, quotations of the price by the seller may be delayed for a few days? Where delays exist this might be because the seller must confirm his prices with competitors.

(i) To what extent do buyers find that prices quoted to them vary very little between sellers? Where competition should be fierce such uniformity suggests collusion.

E. Contract Terms and Conditions: EC and UK

9.47 Contractual terms and conditions are important ingredients of competition especially in oligopolistic markets or other markets where prices tend naturally to be uniform. There, the only competition remaining in existence may focus upon terms and conditions of supply. Exchanges of information on supply terms and conditions are registrable in the UK[64]

[63] These are similar to the factors which were traditionally employed by the US Department of Justice. See Kaysen and Turner, *Antitrust Policy* (Harvard University Press, 1959), p. 120.

[64] Under S.I. 1969 No. 1842, Art. 3(2)(b). See e.g. No. 3755 Register of Restrictive Trade Practices *Independent Marketing Services*.

and, of course, are subject to Article 85(1) EC where they affect trade between the Member States. Such agreements where they tend to lead to the standardisation of contractual terms and conditions may be significantly anti-competitive. In this section terms and conditions include any aspect of the supply contract which purchasers view as important, i.e. to what extent would a customer choose supplier X over supplier Y because the former's contract terms are preferable despite the fact that X and Y quote a similar price. Examples of such terms/conditions would include: quantities, descriptions, packaging and advertising, periods allowed for payment, methods of payment and credit facilities, discounts and rebates, freight handling and carriage costs and insurance, liability clauses, exclusion and limitation clauses, renegotiation and escalation clauses, date and place of delivery, checking and return of defective items, etc.

9.48 In examining an exchange of such data the authorities will:

- consider how important the clause is to customers;
- consider the extent to which competition in that industry is price related or whether terms and conditions of supply are very important;
- consider the degree of concentration in the market; the more oligopolistic in characteristics the market the less sympathetic the approach;
- pay attention to the desires of customers (many trade associations have negotiated standard form contracts with customers' trade associations. In such cases the authorities will recognise that customers may well be able to take care of themselves);
- examine whether exchanged data is in anonymous and aggregated form.

9.49 It is not intended to examine every type of contract term or condition since the rules above cover the official approach to such data, It may, however, be noted that the exchange of data on contract terms and conditions which have a direct bearing upon price will rarely be acceptable.[65] Thus exchanges of discount and rebate terms should be avoided. Similarly exchanges on common credit terms are of dubious legality: if X and Y through natural market-forces charge uniform prices but X allows customers six months to pay and Y only two months then X's real price undercuts that of Y; a customer of X can offset the six months' interest he earns on the purchase amount against the purchase price.[66] This section may be concluded by a general statement of Commission policy:

> "the organised exchange of individual data from individual firms, such as figures on quantities produced and sold, prices and terms for discounts, higher and lower rates, credit notes and general terms of sale, delivery and payment, will generally be regarded by the Commission as practices which have as their object or effect the restriction or distortion of competition within the common market, and which are therefore prohibited."[67]

9.50 A reasonably strict approach may likewise be expected from the OFT so that section 21 (2) dispensation will rarely be appropriate. (See Chapter 11 for general analysis of terms and conditions.)

[65] See e.g. *VNP and COBELPA* [1977] 2 CMLR D28 at p. D36, para. 29; *Groupement Belge des Fabricants de Papier Peints* [1974] CMLR D102.

[66] See *Seventh Report on Competition Policy* (1977), para. 7(1). In America credit standardisation has been held to violate the Sherman Act. See *Plymouth Dealers' Association of Northern California* v *US* 279 F. 2d 128 9th Cir. (1960) an agreement that no member would give credit and all would demand cash-down payment violated the Sherman antitrust law. See also *Swift and Co* v *US* 196 US 375 (1905).

[67] See *Seventh Report on Competition Policy* (1977), point 7(1), para. 2.

F. General Market Data

9.51 Firms have a legitimate interest in seeking to improve efficiency by the increase of relevant knowledge. Where efficiency is enhanced and lower costings and other benefits are passed on to the consumer, Article 85(3) might be satisfied. If the agreement is registrable the OFT might be prepared to obtain section 21(2) dispensation for the parties. In this section the data disseminated and exchanged pertains to the general market rather than to the contract specifically. Included in this very important category are: cost analysis, turnover analysis,[68] technical product data, cost of entry and exit data, investment data, advertising information, process and time, demand data, stocks and inventories, etc. Exchanges of such data among small and medium-sized firms in competitive, unconcentrated markets helps to improve competitiveness and efficiency. Conversely, the same exchange in concentrated markets with homogeneous products can encourage conscious parallelism and lead to the downfall of competition. The nature of the market will thus largely determine the legal position. Pre-notification will play a large part of other types of agreement prohibited under Article 85, such as collusive tendering,[69] quota fixing and straightforward price fixing.[70]

1. *EC Law*

(1) Inter-firm comparisons

9.52 Trade associations of buyers and sellers often collect, collate and disseminate market data to members.[71] The form of the dissemination is all important in competition law. Data should be *historic, aggregated and anonymous*, and should be independently compiled and disseminated. This prevents any member being able to identify specific statistics relating to individual competitors in the data. Where such identification is possible the data may allow competitors to predict rivals' behaviour and may no longer be viewed as simply of educational value. A common form of dissemination is the inter-firm comparison whereby for each function (turnover, demand, costs, etc.) the association disseminates data upon the average and the first and third quartiles. This data allows members to assess their own performance: they may compare the figures for their own firm against those of the industry as a whole. For an example consider that the fuel costs of X are £5,000 per annum. The data disseminated to him by his trade association gives three figures which are based upon data given to it by 100 firms. To compute the quartile figures, the association will

[68] e.g. the exchange of turnover data could dispel supplier X's fears that he is losing market share because the data reveals that global turnover is down; or it could reveal that supplier X is losing ground to rivals and that he must redouble his efforts.

[69] For an example of information dissemination as part of a full blown 30-firm cartel, see *Dutch Building and Construction Cartel* OJ 1992 L92/1, where information about possible alternative bids from outside the cartel was used to enable the cartel to respond to the potential competition: paras. 98–9. An appeal against this decision was dismissed in T-29/92 *Vereniging van Samenwerkende Prijsregelende Organisaties in de Bouwnijverheid (SPO)* v *Commission* [1995] ECR II-289.

[70] See for example, a series of Commission decisions arising out of investigations in the petrochemicals industry: *Polypropylene* [1988] 4 CMLR 347, upheld by the Court of First Instance in Joined Cases T-1-4 and 6-15/89 *Rhône Poulenc* v *Commission* [1991] ECR II-867; *PVC* [1990] 4 CMLR 345, decision annulled in C-147/92P *Commission* v *BASF* [1994] ECR I-2555 (on appeal from Joined Cases T-79, 84-86, 89, 91-92, 94, 96, 98, 102 and 104/89 *BASF* v *Commission* [1992] ECR II-315); *LdPE* [1990] 4 CMLR 382. In Joined Cases C-89, 104, 114, 116, 117 and 125-129/85 *Ahlstrom and Others* v *Commission (Wood Pulp)*, [1993] ECR I-1307, [1993] 4 CMLR 407, the Court of Justice upheld the Commission's finding that exchange of pricing information through a trade association was concerted practice to fix prices.

[71] See D.S. Evans, "Trade associations and the exchange of price and non-price information" [1989] *Fordham Corp L Inst* 709.

collate the data furnished to it and list the firms in order of expenditure on fuel, or, even in order or expenditure on fuel relative to size (since a firm's fuel efficiency can only realistically be seen as a function of expenditure against size). Having ranked the firms it disseminates only the quartiles, not the complete list:

1st Quartile	£3,800 (i.e. the average figure for the first 50 firms)
Median	£5,500 (i.e. the average figure for all 100 firms)
3rd Quartile	£7,600 (i.e. the average figure for firms 51–100)

X learns that his fuel costs are better than average but not as good as a number of other firms. In the ranked list of 100 firms, X would probably be approximately 45th. More elaborate systems may employ business ratio pyramids whereby the comparison consists of the drawing up of a pyramid of ratios (see the diagram opposite). Each firm is given its figures in respect of the ratio thus allowing it to assess its performance *vis-à-vis* rivals. First and third quartile figures may be given. The system satisfies the requirements of aggregation and anonymity. The dissemination should *not* be accompanied by analysis or commentary or backed up by trade association meetings to discuss the results.[72] Firms should be allowed to draw their own conclusions. In America businessmen are advised to walk out of association meetings where clear attempts are being made to foster concerted behaviour. Disassociation in public from such activities is considered to be a method of avoiding the heavy penal sanctions of American law—a similar approach is now generally considered desirable in the EC where fines can be very heavy on individual firms. Indeed, some legal counsel already advocate the strategic walking out of "dangerous" trade association meetings. Trade associations whose members are economically powerful must expect close Commission supervision. The time period between disseminations should be reasonable: three-monthly publications for example provide less scope for collusion or conscious parallelism than bi-weekly issues. Though in *Flat Glass*[73] the Commission considered three monthly exchanges far too frequent. Parties were fined very heavily for exchanging sales data which facilitated market sharing. In *Agricultural Tractor Registration Exchange*[74] the Commission was only prepared to sanction annual exchanges of historical data.

9.53 Moreover, dissemination of inter-firm comparisons might set the parameters within which firms in that industry could disclose information bilaterally and so build up a picture of the figures of other firms through a process of elimination. Thus what would have been an acceptable information exchange in *Polypropylene* was rendered unacceptable by the conduct of the firms receiving that information in using it to compile and check individual figures for firms.[75]

9.54 The Commission Notice on Co-operation Agreements permits the joint carrying out of comparative studies of enterprises and industries but gives the familiar caveat that if it leads to concerted or consciously parallel behaviour it may violate Article 85(1) EC. Moreover, that this might especially be the case in oligopolistic markets.[76] The Commission has condemned disseminations of costing, and production date where it has been indi-

[72] An example of dubious behaviour would be where at a trade association meeting members are exhorted of the wisdom of adopting the median figure for labour. They might be instructed that this is the "most intelligent means of costing". See also *Verband der Sachversicherer eV* [1985] 3 CMLR 246 at p. 263 Annex 3, letter—the pooling of statistics data is not generally objectionable but may be so, *even in unconcentrated markets*, where a central trade association issues recommendations to members concerning the proper way to respond to disseminated data.

[73] OJ 1984 L212/13, [1985] CMLR 350

[74] OJ 1992 L68/19, [1993].

[75] *Polypropylene* [1988] 4 CMLR 347, para. 66.

[76] See JO 1968 C75/3; [1968] CMLR D5, para. 1(c).

vidualised (i.e. not aggregated or anonymous) and confined only to sellers in concentrated markets.[77]

(2) Non-comparative global-industry data

9.55 Data relating to the whole industry raises many problems. The list below may be used as a guide to the Commission's response to various common data types.

9.56 *(a) Investment data*

Pre-notification of investments to competitors has been objected to by the Commission. Thus an agreement whereby X notifies Y of his intention to increase capacity[78] or whereby A consults with B leading to the joint reduction in investment as a means of reducing capacity and thereby keeping prices stable[79] or whereby X consults with Y over the extent of the increase or whereby X asks Y's permission to expand capacity,[80] will infringe Article 85(1) EC. A similar prohibition applies to the construction of new plant in another EC state.[81] However, in certain circumstances investment agreements are acceptable. Thus, where an agreement is needed to prevent the establishment of capacities exceeding the load limit of the market, exemption under Article 85(3) might be available. This is particularly true for investments where input costs are very high but demand fixed or at least relatively static.[82] The mere exchange of investment data in such market conditions would, *a fortiori*, be legitimate.[83] Likewise the simple discussion of market outlook and production capacity is legal provided the discussion does not lead to recommendations on investment.

9.57 *(b) Product specifications*

The exchange of product data may of course lead to an improved quality product. However, if it leads to product standardisation which reduces consumer choice and provides a more uniform cost basis for suppliers to coordinate prices upon then it will almost certainty breach Article 85(1) EC. In America the standardisation of the quantity of a scarce and expensive ingredient in a product has been held to infringe the antitrust laws.[84] None the less, the Commission has exempted trade associations undertaking research and dissemination of results into how products may best meet statutory health requirements.[85]

77 *Community* v *Associated Lead Manufacturers* [1979] 1 CMLR 464 at pp. 471, 472, paras. 21–27; *Community* v *Genuine Vegetable Parchment Association* [1978] 1 CMLR 536 at pp. 547, 548, paras. 62–70; *VNP and COBELPA* [1977] 2 CMLR D28 at pp. D35, 36, paras. 25–28; *The IFTRA Rules for Producers of Virgin Aluminium* [1975] 2 CMLR D20 at pp. D35, 36, para. 43.

78 *Cimbel* [1973] CMLR D167.

79 *Zinc* OJ 1984 L22027 at p. 33, para. 36. See also at para. 68.

80 *Cimbel* [1973] CMLR D.167. See WQ No. 192/72 JO 1972 C138/38 by MEP Mr Vredeling on "limitations des exportations d'acier et de produit sidérurgiques de la Communauté à destination des Etats Unis."

81 See Commission Communication on Co-operation Agreements which expresses strong reservations over the exchange of investment data: JO 1968 C 75/3; [1968] CMLR D.5, para. 1.

82 See *United Reprocessors* [1976] 2 CMLR D1 where the three nuclear fuel reprocessors in the EC formed a joint venture and undertook detailed data exchanges including investment exchanges. The Commission stated (at p. D10, para. 44): "In the absence of an agreement to co-ordinate investments it is to be feared that certain states would rapidly take an incoherent series of decisions to finance from their national budget plants which would be either too small or in advance of market requirements, thus preventing any plant in the Common Market from quickly reaching its optimum load factor. This would certainly harm the Community's interests for the processing industry would then get structured on the basis of national rather than Community requirements."

83 See *Second Report on Competition Policy* (1972), para. 18. But an exchange of data which provides the basis for inter-firm compromise so that a firm might modify its projected plant size to a level beneath that needed to avail itself of optimal scale economies would almost certainly infringe Art. 85(1) EC.

84 See *National Macaroni Manufacturing Association* v *FTC* 345 F. 2d 421 (7th Cir. 1965).

85 See, e.g. *SOCEMAS* [1968] 4 CMLR 28; and *Department Stores* [1979] 3 CMLR 637.

9.58 *(c) Costs of entry data*

The exchange of such data should rarely cause problems. Potential entrants may obtain such data from official statistics or existing companies annual reports or from their own commissioned market reports. A trade association that deliberately misleads potential entrants about entry costs as a device to keep them out might be in breach of Article 85(1) EC. No formal decision has been made in this respect.

9.59 *(d) Demand*

Evidence of demand derived from comparisons of output against orders or shipments, inventory levels, extent of unfilled orders or idle capacity, etc. may be exchanged legitimately. This will not be legal if the exchange is intended to prevent firms from making competitive efforts to achieve a greater market share.[86]

9.60 *(e) Supply sources*

Trade associations which discover and disseminate to members data on best sources of supply, new products and best buys but leave purchasing decisions up to members do not infringe Article 85(1).[87]

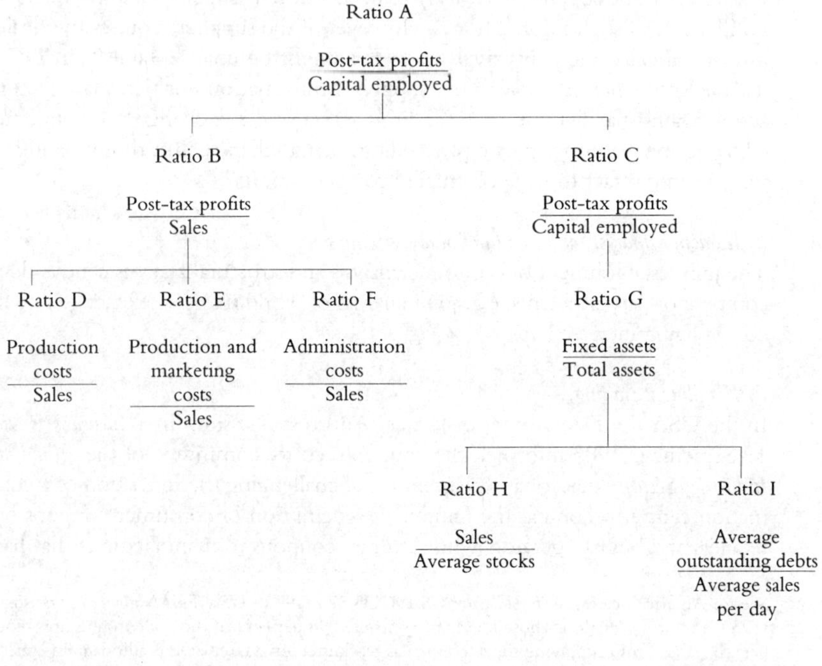

[86] *Potash I* [1973] CMLR D219. But exchanges may be legal, even by oligopolists, in exceptional cases see *International Energy Agency* [1984] 2 CMLR 186, noted, Green (1984) ELRev. 449. See now *International Energy Agency* OJ 1994 L68/35.

[87] e.g. *Socemas* [1968] 4 CMLR 28; *Department Stores* [1979] 3 CMLR 637.

9.61 *(f) Process*

Informational exchange on R&D methods and results is examined at paras. 12.114 and following. Brief mention should be made of pre-notification of new inventions/models agreements. If the period between notification and commencement of first marketing is long enough to enable competitors to adjust their marketing policies or even their product lines an infringement of Article 85(1) EC might result. Such agreements curb the competitive advantage an inventor would have by unannounced introduction of a new product.

9.62 *(g) Credit information*

Credit information creates many problems in practice. Standardisation of contractual credit terms is usually viewed as analogous to price fixing; dissemination of credit data designed to foster standardisation will accordingly be viewed strictly. Any attempt by firms to use the exchange of credit data as a means of enforcing a blacklist or stoplist will be unlawful and probably punishable by a fine.[88]

9.63 *(h) Vertically imposed obligations, i.e. supplier-dealer*

The Commission has permitted suppliers to require their dealers (wholesalers and/or retailers) to notify them of general business conditions, sales trends, stocks, etc.[89] It does not matter if the supplier *incidentally* learns about rival suppliers and products through the notification of such information.[90] However, if the supplier requires the dealer to notify him specifically about his rivals trade this might be unacceptable.[91] In *UK Agricultural Tractor Registration Exchange*[92] the supply of information enabled manufacturers to take action against parallel importers, and this aspect of the exchange was condemned as a facilitating mechanism separate proceedings being taken against those manufacturers who were found in fact to have obstructed parallel imports.[93]

9.64 *(i) Economic analysis and structural analysis centres*

The joint establishment of economic analysis and structural analysis centres does not cause competition law problems, e.g. joint analysis of world markets, exchange rate fluctuations, cost of living increases, etc.[94]

9.65 *(j) Fraudulent trading.*

In the USA the Department of Justice (Antitrust Division) in a *Business Review* letter of 19 September 1985 informed the coupon security committee of the *American Society for Industrial Security* that it had no intention of challenging the formation of a coupon information centre to combat the fraudulent redemption of consumer coupons by unethical retailers and bogus operators who returned coupons to manufacturers that had not been

[88] See for American cases, *Swift and Co* v *US* 196 US 375 (1905); *US* v *First National Pictures Inc* 282 US 44 (1930) a trade association whose members controlled 98 per cent of the trade in question required members to refrain from supplying films to cinemas blacklisted on a circulated credit data list was held to be in violation of the Sherman Act; *US* v *Alexander and Reid Co.* 280 F. 924 (SDNY 1922) a stop list was considered a serious breach of antitrust law, the case gives an interesting account of the type of market conditions which lead to such practices.

[89] See, e.g. *BMW* [1975] 1 CMLR D44. See further paras. 11.66–11.74.

[90] *ibid.*

[91] See Case 85/76 *Hoffman-La Roche* v *Commission* [1979] ECR 211, [1978] 3 CMLR 211; Dominant supplier in breach of Art. 86 EC for requiring purchasers to notify it of rival supply bids. Hoffman-La Roche retained option to meet or undercut the rival bid.

[92] OJ 1992 L68/19, [1993] 4 CMLR 358.

[93] *Ford Agricultural* OJ 1993 L20/1.

[94] See Commission *Communication on Co-operation Agreements*, *op. cit.*, n. 50 at para. 1.

submitted to them by consumers. The information centre collected and collated data of alleged frauds and notified the information to the scheme's subscribers and to law enforcement agencies. The disseminated data did *not* concern the sales activities of members nor were there facilities for inter-firm discussions. The Department of justice stated in their letter: "Coupon fraud raises costs to manufacturers and thereby can result in increased costs to consumers. Detection of fraud therefore can promote efficient competition among firms and thereby result in lower prices to consumers." Given that the disseminated data was not price related it may be reasonably presumed that the Commission would have treated the scheme in a similar fashion.

2. *UK Law*

9.66 Article 3(2)(b) of S.I. 1969 No. 1842 requires information agreements specifying terms/conditions to be registered. Excluded from the order, however, are information agreements concerning general market data. Where parties conclude such an agreement but which also covers either price or terms/conditions particulars must be furnished unless all registrable provisions are deleted. The dividing line between terms/conditions and general market data may sometimes by very fine. The OFT does assess provisions which it considers may be defined as price or terms/conditions agreements or which affect price or contractual terms and conditions.[95] The analysis of such provisions and the problems they raise follows the EC line and reference to commentary thereon may be made. Special reference may be made of credit data. Use of credit lists to operate a stop list will be illegal and will almost certainly be a common law tort of causing loss by unlawful interference with trade. The OFT discourages credit reporting by trade associations. First, since such schemes can be legally problematic it is best to leave them to the professional credit reporting companies which exist. Secondly, where a customer has been listed on a credit list as having been convicted of a criminal offence and credit is denied to him, the listing might not take account of the Rehabilitation of Offenders Act 1974. This provides that convictions for offences in respect of which the offender has received a sentence not exceeding 30 months' imprisonment and where a specified time varying from five to ten years (depending on sentence) has elapsed since the conviction, shall be treated as spent, i.e. never having taken place. Section 4(3)(b) of that Act provides that a spent conviction shall not be a proper ground for "dismissing or excluding a person from any office, profession, occupation or employment, or for prejudicing him in any way in any occupation or employment". Thus, a trade association may not justify blacklisting a person with a spent conviction. Thirdly, given that credit reports often list persons with criminal records and that errors may be made in the listing, it is defamatory to impute a crime to someone by erroneously incorporating their name on the list.[96]

G. Refusal to Disclose Information

9.67 Firms are, as a general rule, under no obligation to disclose confidential data relating to their technology or business methods. Indeed, much of this chapter operates upon the premise that

[95] See e.g. No. 3283 Register of Restrictive Trade Practices, Agreement between members of the *Lighting Industry Federation* to notify to each other the intention to market new developments. See also, No. 3686 Register of Restrictive Trade Practices *Land Mark Cash and Carry* (1977) discussed at para 12.111.

[96] In respect of defaming a person by inclusion on a blacklist because of a spent decision, see the defences available in s. 8 Rehabilitation of Offenders Act 1974.

such disseminations may be unlawful. However, it is becoming clear that certain firms in a dominant economic position may have an obligation not to withhold information from competitors where those competitors have become economically and commercially reliant upon the past dissemination of that data. There may well be a legal distinction to be drawn between "blowing hot and then cold", on the one hand, and never having blown hot at all, on the other. In the latter case rivals never evolve in reliance upon a dissemination so may hardly complain about a refusal to disclose. However, a refusal to disclose information which enables a dominant firm to extend its dominance into a neighbouring market may well be condemned under Article 86 EC as an illegitimate extension of a monopoly,[97] rather than simply only condemned if it constituted a discriminatory licensing practice.

9.68 The question of whether there is a right to demand the supply of information is relevant to the wider issue of whether there is a right of refusal for dominant firms to license intellectual property (IP) rights. As well as the obligations imposed by Article 86 EC, there are provisions in the relevant IP legislation providing for compulsory licensing as well as definitions of what acts do not constitute infringement of IP rights. These are discussed in Chapter 13.

1. EC Law

(1) Case law: *IBM Settlement*

9.69 The failure to disseminate information question arose in the *IBM Settlement*[98] case. The Commission considered that IBM was in a dominant position in the market for mainframe computers. IBM was naturally also very powerful in the market for compatible accessories to its computers. Other manufacturers also produced equipment that could be attached to the IBM computers. However, to be able to manufacture this equipment effectively rivals need to know details of the interfaces of IBM machines. An interface may be defined as the logical and physical interconnection point between a computer and other machines. Interface data thus allows machines to "speak to each other". Traditionally IBM disclosed such data. However, when, as a matter of commercial strategy, it decided to refrain from disclosure, manufacturers of compatible equipment complained to the Commission. Following protracted and complex negotiations the Commission settled with IBM and hence a formal decision holding that IBM had abused its dominant position was not issued. Under the terms of the settlement IBM agreed to make available information on the interfaces to hardware products four months prior to date of announcement of the product concerned. IBM was not required to disclose unique interfaces which could reveal product design. Indeed, IBM did not have an open-ended duty to disclose interface data, those applying to IBM for data were required to enter an "information disclosure agreement" the terms of which may be summarised as follows:

(a) requester must represent and upon request provide satisfactory evidence that it is established and doing business in the EC; and, that it is a company which develops and manufactures products of a relevant type for which it asks interface information;
(b) limitations are imposed on disclosure to third parties which include restrictions on disclosure to third parties prior to general availability other than confidential dis-

[97] See the *Magill TV Guide* Cases T-69, 70 and 76 *RTE, BBC and ITP* v *Commission* [1991] ECR II-485, [1991] 4 CMLR 586 *et seq.*; upheld on appeal by the Court of Justice on different grounds in C-241-242P/91P *RTE and ITP* v *Commission* [1995] ECR I-743, [1995] 4 CMLR 718; see Robertson (1992) 108 LQR 39 and (1995) 111 LQR 588.

[98] [1984] 3 CMLR 147.

closure to employees or subcontractors (the latter may be required to sign the same agreement);

(c) any competing undertaking seeking interface data from IBM must be prepared to disclose corresponding data to IBM on the same terms;

(d) fees and royalties based upon usage will be payable on: external licences, IBM's normal licences, established copyright program licences, and, licences for other proprietory information protected by any legally enforceable right;

(e) patent rights are not waived;

(f) restrictions on usage and copying of source-codes will be imposed;

(g) parties requesting data from IBM will be required to pay reasonable costs for reproduction and dissemination of information;

(h) the agreement will also provide for penalties for breach of the agreement or of any IBM patent or copyright.[99] Since this undertaking was given to the end of 1993, IBM had received 189 requests for information from 23 competitors containing 1,487 individual questions. Seven of these companies signed and received information under technical information disclosure agreements.[100]

9.70 It should now also be noted that legal constraints are imposed under the Software Directive to require software owners to allow access to their software to enable interoperable systems to be developed.[101] This applies irrespective of whether the software owner is dominant.

(2) General principles

9.71 The withholding of proprietory information may be anti-competitive where the possessor of the information is dominant; where the possessor has in the past disclosed such data; and where rivals or other firms have evolved in reliance on that data or where the data constitutes an essential raw material or facility for the production of downstream or secondary products. The leading authority upon this issue is *RTP and ITP* v *Commission (Magill TV Guide)*.[102] In that case the Court of Justice stated at paragraph 54–56 inclusive:

> "54. The Appellants' refusal to provide basic information by relying on national copyright provisions thus prevented the appearance of a new product, a comprehensive weekly guide to television programmes, which the Appellants did not offer and for which there was a potential consumer demand. Such refusal constitutes an abuse under heading (b) of the second paragraph of Article 86 of the Treaty.
> 55. Second, there was no justification for such refusal either in the activity of television broadcasting or in that of publishing television magazines.
> 56. Thirdly, and finally, as the Court of First Instance also held, the Appellants, by their conduct, reserved to themselves the secondary market of weekly television guides by excluding all competition on that market (see the judgment in Joined Cases 6/73 and 7/73 *Commercial Solvents* v *Commission* [1974] ECR 223, para. 25) since they denied access to the basic information which is the raw material indispensable for the compilation of such a guide."

9.72 The Court of Justice emphasised that the information in question, notwithstanding that it was protected by copyright, was to be categorised as an "indispensable raw material".[103]

[99] *ibid.*, at pp. 160, 161.

[100] *Twenty-third Report on Competition Policy* (1993), Annex IIIA, para. 15.

[101] Council Directive of 14 May 1991 on the legal protection of computer programs, OJ 1991 L122/42. 91/250/EEC. This Directive was implemented into UK law by the Copyright (Computer Programs) Regulations 1992 (S.I. 1992 No. 3233).

[102] Joined Cases C-241/91P and C-242/91P [1995] ECR I-743.

[103] *ibid.*, para. 53.

The Court laid down, in effect, two circumstances in which refusal to supply such information by a dominant undertaking would constitute abuse contrary to Article 86. First (as set out in paragraphs 54 and 55 of the judgment) where the refusal to provide the basic information prevented the appearance of a new product which the dominant undertaking did not offer and for which there was a potential consumer demand and where there was no justification for such a refusal on the part of the dominant undertaking. Secondly (as set out in paragraph 56 of the judgment) where the dominant undertaking reserved to itself a secondary market by excluding all competition on that market through the denial of access to the basic information which is the raw material indispensable for the production of the secondary product. It would appear that this latter category of abuse is triggered by conditions precedent differing from those set out in paragraphs 54 and 55 of the judgment. Thus, there is no need for the secondary product to be "new", nor that it should be a product the dominant undertaking did not, itself, offer. In fact, it would appear that the abuse described by the Court of Justice in paragraph 56 of the Judgment is broader than that set out in paragraphs 54 and 55.

9.73 The Commission never issued a formal decision in the *IBM Settlement* case so that the detailed reasoning behind its position is not available for analysis. However, it is arguable that there is a significant difference between firms which blow hot and cold, i.e. disclose then cease to disclose, and firms which have never disclosed. Another important factor may be the extent to which firms in the market have become technologically interdependent with the dominant firm. In the IBM case, rival manufacturers were dependent upon IBM interface data because it enabled them to manufacture compatible accessories more efficiently. Thus, the extent to which the dominant firm has made past disclosures, the extent to which rivals have relied upon these disseminations, and, the degree of technological interdependence may all be relevant factors in such cases. In all cases the extent to which substitutes for the information are available would also appear to be relevant. There is another side to this issue which warrants some attention although the Commission refused to accept it in the IBM case. It is possible to view the case in terms of an investment/reward ratio. IBM invest a vast amount each year in R&D, indeed this has been a major factor in their success. Rival companies who evolved in reliance on IBM interface data were to an extent enjoying the fruits of IBM's labour and investment, they were "free-riding" on IBM. When IBM decided as a matter of commercial policy to withhold data in the future it was arguably simply taking steps to protect the investments it had already made and prevent competitors from free-riding on its efforts. A company that due to intensive R&D possesses secret know-how and intellectual property rights has a legal right to exploit its know-how and intellectual property in a manner which maximises its profits and enables it to recoup its investment costs. On this basis IBM may be said to have been acting in a logical economic fashion. As noted above this view was not accepted by the Commission. Their perception of the relationship between IBM and its competitors was not so much one of parasitic free-riding but was one of smaller companies being forced to adapt themselves to a larger, dominant concern in order to remain even minimally competitive. To a degree speculation about the implications of the *IBM Settlement* case has become of limited value following the ruling in *RTE and ITP* v *Commission* (*ibid.*). In the light of that ruling and with the benefit of hindsight IBM may be rationalised as a case where the company was felt, by the Commission, to be acting excessively or disproportionately since any problem over free-riding could have been resolved by making the free-rider pay a licence fee. Indeed, in *RTE and ITP* the remedy of compulsory licence was specifically endorsed by the Court.

2. UK Law

9.74 The OFT could investigate a refusal to supply information by an economically powerful firm under the CA 1980. Guidance may be found in two cases involving the refusal to grant copyright licences, In *Ford Motor Company (Licensing for the Manufacturer or Sale of Replacement Body Parts)*[104] the OFT stated:

> "Copyright confers on one person (the owner of the right) the exclusive right to control the supply of a particular good (a good made to the registered design of the owner or copies from work in respect of which he owns the artistic copyright) and to prevent all unauthorised persons from supplying that particular good to the market. To the extent that this right is exercised competition in the supply of the good in question is restricted. Prevention of other persons from supplying a particular good is, however, unlikely to amount to an anti-competitive practice in markets where there are substitutes for the good or where substitutes may be freely developed by others.
>
> The effects on competition thus arising from the exercise of copyright depend on the market in which the particular good is supplied. Where there are reasonable substitutes for the particular good or alternative designs or developments can be made, the exclusive rights of supply do not confer monopoly rights in the market and the exercise of copyright is unlikely to have an anti-competitive effect."[105]

9.75 Upon this basis, the refusal to license information may be anti-competitive where the information is not reasonably attainable from other sources which is likely where the possessor of the information enjoys a dominant position. In the Ford case the failure to license was in respect of the drawings or designs for body parts for Ford vehicles. It is pertinent to note that Ford traditionally accepted that other producers were manufacturing Ford spare parts. It was the sudden change of policy and the subsequent attempt to prevent this production that was the cause of complaint. In *BBC and ITP*[106] the OFT concluded that the failure on the part of the BBC and ITP to license copyrighted forward programme planning information was anti-competitive even though there was no prior history of dissemination. The OFT considered that the failure to license created entry and expansion barriers for magazines and journals which could carry forward programmes and which therefore could have actively competed with the *Radio Times* and the *TV Times*. The MMC agreed that the failure was anti-competitive yet declined to find that the failure was contrary to the public interest. The MMC seems to have been persuaded by the *de minimis* argument, that the failure did not have a significant competitive effect on the market. Further, that it was not possible to prove that the market would be improved by increased disseminations. The value of this case as a pointer to policy is limited by the fact that the MMC was equally split over the final conclusion and it was the fact that the chairman sided with the status quo which was, therefore, legally decisive. The anti-BBC and ITP members considered that the market should be the determinant of whether extra information was necessary. On balance the economic interests of the possessor/creator of the information were considered more important than those of consumers and other market participants. It will be noted that this case goes beyond *Ford* (and the *IBM Settlement*) in that, in this case, there was no significant history of prior dissemination. It might well be, however, that the case may be confined to its special facts. The particular

[104] 21 March 1984, OFT Report; for MMC Report see Cmnd 9437 (1985).

[105] OFT Report *ibid.*, at pp. 37, 38, paras. 8.4 and 8.5.

[106] *British Broadcasting Corporation and Independent Television Publications Ltd (The Publication of Programme Information)* (13 December 1984), OFT Report; for MMC Report see (September 1985) Cmnd 9614.

problem over programme listings is now settled by compulsory licensing provisions introduced by the Broadcasting Act 1990.[107]

9.76 The Director General of Fair Trading has investigated competition issues arising out of the dissemination of information in the context of his obligation to report to the Secretary of State for Trade and Industry pursuant to the Financial Services Act 1986 the results of his reviews of the rules of the International Stock Exchange (ISC). These reports express clearly the principles the OFT will apply to the dissemination or licensing of information by dominant undertakings. The DGFT has undertaken a number of reviews. In his general review into the International Stock Exchange in April 1988 the DGFT stated as follows.

9.77 On that occasion the DGFT was unable to conclude that the ISC rules in question gave rise to any significant effect on competition. However, he decided to keep the matter under review. In April 1990 the DGFT published a report entitled *Trade Publication and Price Transparency on the International Stock Exchange.* In that case the DGFT investigated, *inter alia,* the issue of the delay in the dissemination of information concerning reported trades to the market at large. In particular the Exchange sought to introduce a 24-hour delay in the publication of the details of large trades in so-called "Alpha stocks". Of this rule the DGFT stated as follows:

> "1.8. The delay in trade publication denies the market, for 24 hours, information which is relevant to the valuation of a security. In 1989 deals over £100,000 in Alpha stocks accounted for £217 bn of turnover–some 78.5% of all Alpha stock trading at around 55% of all equity turnover. The delay, therefore, affects a very large part of Exchange business and withholds a significant amount of information from the market. This loss of transparency diminishes pricing efficiency and increases uncertainty. The resulting increase in risk is likely to be reflected in wider buy—sell spreads and hence higher dealing costs which may in turn have an adverse effect on trading volume. Far from improving liquidity, delayed publication may, therefore, actually harm liquidity.
>
> 1.9. The delay in large trade publication also creates an information asymmetry. While in a period of over capacity I cannot predict the precise timing or sequence of events I am clear that it will have a number of adverse effects.
> - It leads to cross-subsidy between those involved in large transactions and those involved in transactions in smaller sizes.
> - A market maker undertaking a large trade will have a competitive advantage over rivals. The advantage accrues mainly to those which dominate the market and large deals. Over time smaller firms and recent entrants are likely to find it more difficult to compete. This may distort the decisions of firms to enter or exit from the market.
>
> 1.10. In my view these effects mean that rule 372.1, which provides for a delay to the publication of large trade details, is likely to have to a significant extent the effect of restricting and distorting competition.
>
> 1.11. The delay in trade publication has two other potential effects on competition.
> - It gives market makers a new privilege denied to broker/dealers. This may alter the balance between the two in favour of the market makers.
> - It may lead to distortions in the London Traded Options Market and the London International Financial Futures Exchange."

9.78 In his report of June 1990 *The International Stock Exchange: Dissemination of Company News* the DGFT considered the Exchange's arrangement for regulating the distribution of information provided by companies about themselves. This report was a partial fulfilment of the commitment made by the DGFT in the April 1988 report referred to above to

[107] The matter remains a live issue in EC law, as seen by the Court of Justice's decision in Joined Cases C-241 and 242/91P *RTE and ITP* v *Commission* [1995] ECR I-743 [1995] 4 CMLR 718.

review the information vending arrangements made by the Exchange. In this report the DGFT noted that during the 1980s there had arisen a demand for company news, both in real-time for those dealing in shares and in historic-time for the later retrieval of information for research and analysis. The DGFT also noted that during the same period there was a rapid development in the services provided by commercial information vendors. It was observed that the Exchange held about 75 per cent or more of the real-time market for such information. This position of dominance was attributable to the Exchange's position as the sole source of domestic company news. The DGFT stated as follows:

> "1.5. The Exchange has argued that the sole source approach is necessary to prevent the disorderly or improper release of company news. I am not convinced that a sole, rather than a multi-source dissemination of such news is necessary, even with the Exchange's competing market maker trading system. I am concerned that a sole source approach gives that source a dominant position which is capable of abuse.
>
> 1.6 In judging whether the Exchange's current arrangements and those which it proposed for the future are, or are likely to be, significantly anti-competitive I have considered six criteria. These are that there should be:
> - a clear separation of regulatory and commercial roles;
> - equality of treatment for all commercial information vendors;
> - no unnecessary restrictions on the re-use of company news;
> - no class subsidy between regulatory and commercial roles;
> - arrangements to contain the cost of regulatory services; and
> - an allocation of costs recovery which is in line with the benefits received.
>
> 1.7. I have concluded that the Exchange's present arrangements meet none of these criteria. The Exchange gives its commercial information vending services privileged early access to information it has acquired for regulatory reasons, thereby disadvantaging its commercial competitors. It also fails to identify clearly what is a regulatory and what is a commercial income and expenditure, limiting the pressure to contain costs and charges through the forces of competition and, potentially, allowing the cross-subsidy of commercial services by the charges imposed for regulatory functions."

9.79 These investigations on the part of the DGFT demonstrate that information *per se* can constitute a relevant service of economic importance; that the possessor or such information can hold a dominant position in the market for such information; and that such possessors should ensure that the rules and practices they adopt for the dissemination of such information are reasonable and proportionate. In short, the rules must be non-discriminatory provide for maximum transparency and the charges levied for the provision of such information should be reasonable and related to cost. These principles are of particular relevance to organisers of markets, such as the Exchange.

H. Negotiations Leading to an Agreement Between Competitors

1. EC law

9.80 It is an observable fact that most pre-contractual negotiations are not notified to the Commission. However, it does not follow from this that such negotiations are necessarily exempt from the competition rules. In particular, where the negotiations involve the exchange of otherwise confidential information, the Commission may well take the view that they are caught by Article 85(1). Indeed, the Commission on at least one occasion has adopted this attitude in relation to multipartite discussions leading up to a rationalisation agreement. Article 85(1) requires there to be an agreement or concerted practice. When parties agree to negotiate a deal, then it is often implicit in that agreement that information will be exchanged. For the purposes of Article 85(1) there does not appear to be anything to differentiate an agreement to exchange information for the purpose of negotiating a further agreement (e.g. a joint venture) from an agreement the sole purpose of which is the exchange of information (as in *UK Agricultural Tractor Registration Exchange*).[108] The motivation behind the disclosure of the information may be different, but the application of Article 85(1) is not dependent on the intention of the parties;[109] it is only necessary that the object or effect of the behaviour is to distort competition.

9.81 It may theoretically, therefore, be advisable for firms exchanging information in this sort of context to inform the Commission. Obviously, the need for this depends on the type of information which is being exchanged as well as the market in question. For example, if the information which is disclosed consists of a trade secret, the firm which has disclosed it would be able to take steps to prevent it being used for any purpose other than that for which it was disclosed. The Commission would be much more concerned about the exchange of other market data, such as prices, market share, quantities produced and prices and terms of discounts. The characteristics of the market in question are also significant. The Commission has pointed out[110] that, in an oligopolistic market, the exchange of sensitive information, which is not readily available elsewhere, could destroy what little competition remains between firms. In contrast, the availability of such data in the context of a competitive market could operate to increase transparency and enhance competition.

9.82 There are obvious practical problems with notifying pre-contractual negotiations to the Commission, the first being that it simply flies in the fact of commercial reality. No business is conducted in a vacuum; all transactions involve some form of discussion, however formal or informal, with other parties; it would be absurd to expect firms to notify all such contact to the Commission. Even if the duty to notify is confined to firms on an oligopolistic market who expect to exchange confidential information (this being the type of situation most likely to be caught by Article 85(1)) there are still substantial problems. It may not be clear (given difficulties in satisfactorily defining markets) whether a particular market is oligopolistic or not. Even in a clear-cut case there is the question of when and what the parties should notify. Notification must take place before an agreement comes into effect; discussions could arise at any time and without any advance warning.[111] Even if they are pre-planned, it is often not clear exactly what and how much information will be disclosed until the parties are seated around the negotiating table. It is difficult, then, to see what the notification should consist of.

9.83 The reason the Commission is moving towards applying Article 85(1) in this novel way probably derives from the gap in the Commission's powers when it comes to making oligopolistic markets more competitive (contrast the investigative powers of the MMC). This was also the drive behind the development of the concept of

[108] *UK Agricultural Tractor Registration Exchange* OJ 1992 L68/19.

[109] e.g. Case C-277/87 *Sandoz* v *Commission* [1990] ECR I-45; Case C-279/87 *Tipp-Ex* v *Commission* [1990] ECR I-261.

[110] *op. cit.*, note 108.

[111] In which case the maxim *carpe diem* should apply.

joint dominance in the context of Article 86. Given, however, that the consistent application of Article 85(1) to pre-contractual negotiations is clearly impractical, the question remains of how firms in such a situation should proceed. If, understandably, a firm is unwilling to notify, one way of helping to secure its position vis-à-vis the Commission would be to ensure there is evidence (e.g. in correspondence) making clear that any exchange of information takes place solely for the purpose of concluding a subsequent agreement. If the subsequent agreement falls outside Article 85(1) then there is authority for the proposition that anything which is essential to the agreement, itself falls outside Article 85(1). For example, in the context of franchise agreements, the Court of Justice held in Pronuptia[112] that ancillary restraints necessary for the operation of the franchise system fell outside Article 85(1). What happens, though, where the negotiations fail to lead to an agreement, or the agreement falls apart or, even, where an agreement is reached but the information which has been exchanged went beyond what was necessary for the conclusion of the agreement? Theoretically, the Commission could hold that the parties involved entered into an agreement to exchange information which is caught by Article 85(1). As the parties have not notified there would be no possibility of exemption under Article 85(3) and the firms could be fined. However, it is submitted that this would be a very heavy-handed approach for the Commission to take. It could be argued that exchanges of information are a necessary element in the contracting process, and that the contracting process itself does not invariably lead to the successful conclusion of contracts. Indeed, in many industries negotiations of potential contracts outnumber those actually concluded. Competition law should not be applied to regulate the ordinary process of negotiation, unless there is evidence that negotiations are a sham, concealing an exchange of information with no intent on either side to proceed to a contract should negotiations prove successful. This may well be a difficult line for the Commission to draw, but the consequences of holding that pre-contractual negotiations are potential information exchange agreements would be to placed an unnecessary fetter on ordinary commercial transactions as well as to inundate an already over-worked bureaucracy with yet more notifications.

2. *UK law*

9.84 Pre-contractual negotiations are unlikely to involve the acceptance of restrictions and so would be likely to fall outside the RTPA itself. However, pre-contractual negotiations might conceivably qualify as registrable information agreements under the terms of S.I. 1969 No. 1842, if they could be said to constitute a separate agreement or arrangement in their own right. This will involve a consideration of similar factors to those involved in deciding whether pre-contractual negotiations can constitute an agreement or concerted practice under Article 85(1) EC as discussed above.

9.85 The terms of the Order are limited to information as to prices and terms and conditions. Information as to other matters can be exchanged without being caught by the Order, though might fall within section 2(1) Competition Act 1980.

112 Case 161/85 *Pronuptia de Paris gmbH* v *Pronuptia de Paris Irmgard Schillgalis* [1986] ECR 353, [1986] 1 CMLR 414.

I. Specimen Compliance Scheme

9.86 A number of trade associations and international federations of trade associations employ competition law compliance schemes. The following is an example of various schemes that have been used in Europe by various trade associations. Often such rules are formalised by incorporation into constitutional documents or ratified by a governing board. Where a compliance scheme is drafted in respect of an agreement which has national application only, then the exceptions allowed under S.I. 1969 No. 1842 will have to be taken into account more specifically. If the agreement in any way has the potential to affect inter-state trade then the dictates of EC law should prevail in addition to UK law. The system below is based upon EC considerations.

Rule 1. Members of the Secretariat's staff should not reveal the exact or approximate data on any company, and should not disclose the relative position of any company as shown by data submitted to the Secretariat. The Secretariat should be independent of any of the companies involved.

Rule 2. No person, except those members of the staff specifically assigned for this purpose, should be permitted access to the data submitted by individual companies for inclusion in statistical reports.

Rule 3. Statistical summaries or totals for particular items on statistical summaries should not be released if it is probable that the data of any particular company would be disclosed through such a release. In particular, this should be deemed to preclude the release of any summary, or of any particular item on any summary where: (a) there are less than four companies participating; or (b) there are four or more companies reporting and the figure from one company is more than 60 per cent of the total.[113]

Rule 4. No data on prices, charges, discounts and rebates, or invoices should be disseminated.

Rule 5. No comments, analysis, observations, or recommendations regarding the results of the programme should be made. Each company should make its own analysis of the statistics.

Rule 6. Participation in the statistical programme should be open to all Western European producers.

Rule 7. Participation in the statistical programme by members should be entirely voluntary. Any members may decline to participate and, equally, no member may be refused the right to participate.

Rule 8. Each individual company report of statistical data should be destroyed upon incorporation of the data into a statistical report and upon determination of the Secretary General that retention of the report is no longer necessary to ensure the accuracy of the statistics.

Rule 9. Each sponsor of a statistical activity should have the responsibility for determining the distribution of summaries, subject to the following: (a) one copy of each summary should be sent to each company whose data is reflected in the report. (b) one copy of each summary should be retained on

[113] The figures given in this paragraph should not be taken as absolutes. Analysis of the commercial setting will be necessary to determine correct cut-off figures which take into account the degree of market concentration. Clearly the aim of this rule is to prevent data disseminations being used to foster conscious parallelism.

file in the Secretariat where it should only be made available to interested persons if the concerned sector groups deem it desirable.

Rule 10. Company's submission should be under code number and, only if requested, under company's name.

9.87 In *Wood Pulp*[114] the Commission has indirectly given some guidance as to its policy on compliance schemes. In its decision the Commission imposed fines on 11 American, 6 Canadian, 11 Swedish, 12 Finnish, 1 Norwegian, 1 Portuguese and 1 Spanish, company (but no EC companies). However, fines were substantially reduced in respect of companies who co-operated and signed formal undertakings regulating their future pricing conduct.[115] Companies undertook to eschew all publicity for pulp prices and not to disclose information to any person or entity who was not:

- an agent or other person or entity within the company's sales and distribution system;
- an actual (or potential) customer;
- a final institution with a legitimate interest in the company's prices;
- a supplier to the company under an arrangement requiring the supplier to obtain data as to the company's pulp prices;
- an accountant or other consultant who provides services for the company and who has a legitimate interest in the company's prices;
- any other person with a legitimate interest in the company's prices and as to which dissemination of the data does not have anti-competitive consequences.

9.88 It is important to note that the Commission do not prohibit: First, a company's right to answer inquiries from the press or financial or securities analysts about economic conditions and general price levels in the relevant markets, though such information should not include details of prices charged to named EC customers; secondly a company's right to conduct discussions of price and market conditions either internally or with an affiliated entity in which it holds an ownership interest of 50 per cent or more or which is owned 50 per cent or more by a common parent; and thirdly, a company's compliance with applicable laws and regulations and generally accepted accounting principles. With respect to the second point above it is notable that the Commission makes no mention of price and market discussions with entities in which the company owns less than 50 per cent of the shares but none the less has a controlling interest. Provided such companies form part of the same "undertaking" as the disseminator there should be no difficulty under Article 85(1).

[114] [1985] 3 CMLR 474 at pp. 526, 527.

[115] Although the decision was largely annulled by the Court of Justice (5th Chamber) in Joined Cases C-89, 104, 114, 116, 117 and 125-129/85 *Ahlstrom and Others* v *Commission I* [1993] ECR I-1307, [1993] 4 CMLR 407, the principle of obtaining undertakings of future compliance in return for a reduction in damages was not rejected by the Court: see paras. 178–185.

10 Distribution

A. Introduction

10.1 In this chapter the following matters will be discussed:

Section B.	Exclusive distribution agreements in general.
Section C.	The block exemption for exclusive distribution in EC law: Regulation 1983/83/EEC.
Section D.	The negotiation of exclusive distribution agreements falling outside the block exemption in EC law.
Section E.	Exclusive dealing in UK law.
Section F.	Exclusive purchasing agreements in general.
Section G.	The block exemption for exclusive purchasing in EC law: Regulation 1984/83/EEC.
Section H.	The negotiation of exclusive purchasing agreements falling outside the block exemption in EC law.
Section I.	Exclusive purchasing in UK law.
Section J.	Commercial agents.
Section K.	Franchise agreements.
Section L.	Selective distribution.
Section M.	Dealers refused supplies: complaints and remedies.

B. Exclusive Distribution Agreements in General

10.2 This section examines exclusive distribution agreements whereby a supplier agrees to appoint a dealer as the sole or exclusive distributor of his goods within a defined area. Usually, the dealer agrees to hold only the supplier's brand of goods to the exclusion of competing brands.

10.3 The term "exclusive" is normally used to mean an agreement whereby the supplier is also prevented from selling the goods into the dealer's territory, whereas a "sole distributorship is one in which the supplier reserves the right to sell into the dealer's territory.

1. General Considerations

(1) Attitude of OFT and EC Commission

10.4 In both jurisdictions, exclusive distribution is recognised as a beneficial contractual relationship and statutory exemptions are provided for agreements satisfying certain criteria. In the UK exemption is afforded by Schedule 3, para. 2 RTPA 1976. In the EC exemption is afforded by Regulation 1983/83/EEC discussed in depth below. Neither exemption is absolute. Agreements not falling within the exemptions may be given individual clearance from the relevant authorities. In the UK parties must negotiate with the OFT generally on the basis of section 21(2) RTPA 1976; in the EC parties must negotiate with the Commission upon the basis of Article 85(3).

10.5 It is relevant to note that in the UK agreements exempt under Schedule 3, para. 2 RTPA 1976 are none the less subject to the Competition Act 1980.

(2) Economic arguments in favour of exclusive distribution agreements

10.6 Paragraphs 5 to 7 of the preamble to Regulation 1983/83/EEC (see below) lay out what the Commission consider are the benefits of exclusive distribution. Their view, which is summarised here, is reflective also of that of the OFT. First, exclusive distribution agreements lead to a general improvement in distribution because: the supplier may concentrate his sales activities; he need not maintain numerous business relations with a larger number of dealers; he is accordingly able more easily to overcome distributional problems in international trade deriving from linguistic, legal and other differences. Secondly, exclusive distribution facilitates the promotion of sales and leads to intensive marketing, continuity of supplies and the rationalisation of distribution. As a result competition between different brands of products is heightened. Thirdly, exclusive distribution whereby a distributor assumes responsibility for sales promotion, customer services and the carrying of stocks is often the only way in which a new manufacturer can penetrate a market. Fourthly, exclusive distribution, by intensifying inter-brand competition and encouraging efficient distribution is of benefit to consumers who enjoy a wider choice of goods at competitive prices sold at outlets which are conveniently located.

(3) Economic arguments against exclusive distribution

10.7 Exclusive distribution blunts intra-brand competition, i.e. rivalry between dealers supplying the *same* brand. Economically, this might cause no problem if inter-brand competition is effective, i.e. rivalry between dealers supplying *different* brands of a product. Where inter-brand competition is weak the OFT and Commission will be concerned that dealers will not be subject to effective competitive pressures and will not serve the consumer well. The degree of inter-brand competition will always be important. This in turn depends mainly upon how entry opportunities are affected.

10.8 "Entry opportunities" will be harmfully affected if a significant percentage of the available dealers in a geographical market are tied up in agreements with suppliers which prevent them from holding a new supplier's brand of product. Where a large percentage of the appropriate dealers are "foreclosed" from new firms in this manner then prospects for effective inter-brand competition are reduced. Firms desiring to enter the market are prevented or hindered by the scarcity of good dealers to distribute their goods for them.

10.9 Where exclusive distribution exists in a market where inter-brand competition is low and entry barriers are high as a result of "foreclosure", then consumers are at risk. Dealers enjoy economic power in their territories which they may exploit by overpricing the goods or by not providing the sort of service to customers that could be expected from dealers in a truly competitive market.

10.10 Some commentators have criticised the Commission for being unduly hard on agreements in distribution systems which are subject to strong inter-brand competitive forces. It is complained that clauses that might be unacceptable in systems subject to weak competition have little or no opportunity to operate anti-competitively where competition is strong. Such critics contend that the Commission should concentrate in their analysis, more on economic effect than on contractual form. The Commission published a Green Paper in January 1997 seeking views on the development of EC law and policy in this area in which some of these criticisms were acknowledged. This may indicate the future trend for EC law.

C. The Block Exemption for Exclusive Distribution in EC Law

10.11 Exclusive dealing or distributorship agreements which comply with the terms of Regulation 1983/83/EEC discussed below need not be notified to the Commission. Agreements complying therewith are deemed to be legally acceptable under Article 85(3). If for some reason the Commission decide that block exemption is inappropriate for a particular agreement they will then have to issue a formal decision withdrawing exemption. To date this has never occurred.[1] Consequently, there are great advantages in drafting an agreement so as to comply with the Regulation. Failure to comply with the Regulation means that the agreement must be notified to the Commission if it is to be exempted. Parties who are unsure about the application of the Regulation to their agreement may, if they so wish, notify it to the Commission who will advise them accordingly.

10.12 For quick reference, an outline of the Regulation and the analysis of it in this section is given below.

(1) Introduction: interpretation. Main points on how to interpret the Regulation.
(2) Article 1: basic provision. Detailed analysis of meaning of Article 1. This provision describes the main permissible restriction on the supplier.
(3) Article 2 (1): additional permissible restriction on supplier.
(4) Article 2(2) and (3): permissible restrictions on the dealer. Examination of restrictions dealer may be required to accept.
(5) Article 3: non-exempt restrictions: agreements between competing manufacturers. Detailed analysis of Article 3(a) which denies exemption to mutual exclusive dealing between competing manufacturers, and Article 3(b) which provides a limited exception for non-reciprocal agreements where one party is a small or medium-sized undertaking.
(6) Article 3(c): other non-exempt restrictions: where no alternative source of supply exists. Analysis of Article 3(c) which denies automatic exemption where users of the relevant goods have no alternative sources of supply to the exclusive dealer.

[1] The Commission has taken such a course of action under the patent licensing block exemption. See Case T-51/89 *Tetra Pak (I)* [1990] ECR II-309, [1991] 4 CMLR 334.

(7) Article 3(d): other non-exempt restrictions: analysis of Article 3(d) which denies automatic exemption to agreements seeking to hinder parallel imports.
(8) Article 6: withdrawal of exemption from automatically exempt agreements. Analysis of the power of the Commission to issue a formal decision to withdraw exemption.
(9) Transitional periods: time limits for compliance.
(10) Excluded agreements: beer and petrol supply.

1. *Introduction: Interpretation*[2]

10.13 Each year literally thousands of exclusive distributorship agreements are drafted so as to fit within the terms of the block exemption. The current block exemption is contained in Regulation 1983/83/EEC[3] and if an agreement complies with its strictures it need not be notified and exemption under Article 85(3) may be assumed. Though, as is implicit in the recitals to the Regulation, the measure operates on the basis that not every exclusive distribution agreement falls within Article 85(1) but that in so far as an agreement is caught, it may benefit from exemption. There are clearly many advantages to be obtained from drafting an agreement so as to comply with Regulation 1983/83/EEC. It should be stressed that agreements falling outside of the Regulation must be individually notified to the Commission if they are to earn exemption under Article 85(3) or are to be settled informally by comfort letter. It is important to understand that, even if all the express terms of an exclusive distributorship agreement comply with the block exemption, the Commission and Court may hold that there are implied terms or a surrounding commercial policy which cause the agreement to lose the benefit of Regulation 1983/83. For example, in *Dunlop Slazenger International* v *Commission*[4] the distributorship agreements contained no mention of conferring absolute territorial protection on Dunlop Slazenger's (DSI's) exclusive distributors on the Continent. However, the CFI concluded that the distribution agreements contained an unwritten term to this end and that, in accordance with this, DSI's sales agreements with its resellers and distributors contained a condition of sale, also unwritten, prohibiting them generally from exporting its products to the territories of each of its exclusive distributors. Two factors led the Court to this conclusion. The first was that DSI had taken measures to prevent Newitt, one of its UK dealers, exporting its products; the second was that its exclusive distributors complained to DSI that their absolute territorial protection was being threatened by imports.

10.14 In this section the terms of the Regulation will be examined clause by clause. Reference shall be made throughout to a Commission Notice which lays down the Commission's policy in interpreting the Regulation.[5] This notice is not a legally binding document but, in practical terms, may be relied upon to afford an accurate guide to Commission

[2] See Korah and Rothnie, *Exclusive Distribution and the EEC Competition Rules* (2nd edn. 1992); Joanna Goyder, *EC Distribution Law* (1992); Taylor and Marks in *Butterworth's Competition Law* (looseleaf), Division IV.

[3] Commission Reg. 1983/83/EC of 22 June 1983 on the application of Art. 85(3) of the Treaty to categories of exclusive distribution agreements, OJ 1983 L173/1. See for minor amendments to the wording and grammar Corrigenda OJ 1983 L281/24. The only substantial difference is in relation to Art. 5(3).

[4] Case T-43/92 *Dunlop Slazenger International Ltd* v *Commission* [1994] ECR II-441.

[5] Commission explanatory notice concerning Commission Regs. 1983/83/EEC and 1984/83/EEC of 22 June 1983 on the application of Art. 85(3) of the Treaty to categories of exclusive distribution and exclusive purchasing agreements: OJ 1983 C355/7.

thinking and will be persuasive authority in proceedings before national courts.[6] When using this notice as an interpretative guide the caveat expressed by the Commission in its introduction may be considered:

> "This notice sets out the main considerations which will determine the Commission's view of whether or not an exclusive distribution or purchasing agreement is covered by the block exemption. The notice is without prejudice to the jurisdiction of national Courts to apply the Regulation, although it may well be of persuasive authority in proceedings before such Courts. Nor does the notice necessarily indicate the interpretation which might be given to the provisions by the Court of Justice."[7]

10.15 Further, on interpretation of the Regulation it is always relevant to refer to the preamble as a means of guidance. The Commission give an explanation of policy in the preamble and this also is a valuable tool of construction.[8] Finally, it must be remembered that block exemptions are to be construed narrowly since they are derogations from the basic prohibition in Article 85(1).[9]

10.16 An exclusive distribution agreement need only comply with the strictures of the block exemption if it falls within Article 85(1). The Court of Justice in *Delimitis*,[10] in a case concerning the supply of beer through a tied estate network, laid down certain criteria which had to be met if an agreement was both to affect trade between Member States and restrict, distort, or prevent competition to an appreciable degree and thereby to trigger the application of Article 85(1). The Court identified five stages to the relevant analysis.

10.17 (i) Identification of relevant product markets: it is necessary to define the product market since it is only in respect of a particular product market that trade can be affected between Member States or competition prevented, restricted or distorted.

10.18 (ii) Identification of relevant geographical market: it is necessary to identify the geographical market since it is only within that defined area that competition can be distorted. In *Delimitis* the Court stated:

> "the relevant market is delimited from a geographical point of view. It should be noted that most beer supply agreements are still entered into at a national level. It follows that, in applying the Community competition rules, account is to be taken of the national market for beer distribution in premises for the sale and consumption of drinks."[11]

6 In other contexts the Court of Justice has stressed that such notices are "important" as guides to interpretation. See Case 149/73 *Witt* v *Hauptzollamt Hamburg Ertcus* [1973] ECR 1587 at p. 1593 in respect of the explanatory notes issued by the Commission on the Common Customs Tariff. Though that is a Council Regulation and not a Commission Regulation, though whether that is a useful distinction is questionable. See for example of reference being made to the Notice by a national court, *Cutsforth* v *Mansfield Inns* [1986] 1 CMLR 1. Korah and Rothnie, *op. cit.*, note 2 above, pp. 65–7, doubt whether these guidelines should be taken as being authoritative. In Case C-226/94 *Grand Garage Albeigeois* and Case C-309/94 *Nissan France SA* [1996] 4 CMLR 78 the Court emphasises that a Commission notice can clarify but not alter the scale of a Regulation, *ibid.*, p. 795, para. 21, and, p. 809, para. 22.

7 Commission Notice (above n.4) at para. 3.

8 *ibid.*, at para. 2. See also *Fonderies Roubaix* v *Fonderies Roux* (Case 63/75) [1976] 1 CMLR 538; [1976] ECR 111; Case 47/76 *De Norre* v *NV Brouwerij Concordia* [1977] 1 CMLR 378, [1977] ECR 65. In both cases the Court of Justice construed Reg. 67/67/EC (the predecessor was 1983/83) by reference to the preamble thereby leading them to ignore the literal meaning of the Regulation.

9 See e.g. Case C-70/93 *Bayerische Motorenwerke AG* v *Ald Auto Leasing D GmbH* [1996] 4 CMLR 478, para. 78; and Case C-266/93 *Bundeskartellamt* v *Volkswagen AG* [1994] 4 CMLR 478, para. 33.

10 Case C-234/89 [1991] ECR I-935.

11 *ibid.*, para. 18, p. I-985.

10.19 (iii) Identification of networks of similar agreements: the Court stated that networks of exclusive purchasing agreements operated by competing suppliers could create an obstacle to penetration of the market by third party suppliers of competing products. However, the existence of networks is not *per se* enough to result in the application of Article 85(1) to an individual agreement. In *Delimitis* the Court stated:

> "The existence of a bundle of similar contracts, even if it has a considerable effect on the opportunities for gaining access to the market, is not, however, sufficient in itself to support a finding that the relevant market is inaccessible, in as much as it if only one factor, amongst others, pertaining to the economic and legal context in which an agreement must be appraised ... the other factors to be taken into account are, in the first instance, those also relating to opportunities for access".[12]

10.20 (iv) Identification of impediments to access as noted above; it is insufficient simply to establish that a network of similar agreements exists, it must also be determined whether the networks in question constitute an impediment to access to the market and the geographical area in question. In conducting this particular analysis the Court in *Delimitis* identified the following factors relevant to the beer supply market many of which are more generally relevant in and applicable to other product markets: the legal rules and agreements upon acquisition of companies and the establishment of outlet (e.g. licensing rules and merger control rules); the minimum number of outlets necessary for the economic operation and distribution system; the existence of beer wholesalers not tied to producers; the number and size of producers on the market; the degree of saturation upon the relevant market and in this regard the trend in beer sales and the resale trade would indicate the relevant demand; customer fidelity to existing brands. It follows from the above that even if a particular market is characterised by a high incidence of networks this does not by, that fact alone, mean that an individual exclusive purchasing or dealing agreement operated by one of the larger players will fall within Article 85(1).

10.21 (v) Contribution of individual agreement to impediment to access; furthermore, even if (and only if)[13] the cumulative effect of the network of similar agreements does create an impediment to access, the next issue to be determined is whether the individual network in question makes "an appreciable contribution"[14] to the foreclosure effect in the geographical market in question. In order to assess the extent of the contribution of an individual agreement to the "cumulative sealing-off effect"[15] the market position of the contracting parties must be taken into consideration. It must be demonstrated by reference to the market share held by the supplier and by reference to the market share held by the supplier and by reference to the number of outlets tied to it that such an "appreciable contribution" exists.[16]

[12] *ibid.*, para. 20.
[13] *ibid.*, para. 23.
[14] *ibid.*, para. 24.
[15] *ibid.*, para. 25.
[16] *ibid.*, para. 25. See also the judgment of the Court of First Instance in Case T-7/93 *Langnese-Iglo GmbH* v *Commission* [1995] ECR II-1533 in particular at paras. 94 *et seq.* where the CFI confirmed and applied the criteria laid down by the Court of Justice in *Delimitis*. The CFI also relied upon the ruling of the Court of Justice in Case 23/67 *Brasserie de Haecht* [1967] ECR 525 which, itself, was cited with approval in *Delimitis*.

2. *Article 1: Basic Provision*

10.22 Article 1 of the Regulation reads:

> "Pursuant to Article 85(3) of the Treaty and subject to the provisions of this Regulation, it is hereby declared that Article 85(1) of the Treaty shall not apply to agreements to which only two undertakings are party and whereby one party agrees with the other to supply certain goods for resale within the whole or a defined area of the common market only to that other."[17]

Since this is the core of Regulation 1983/83/EEC its wording will be examined in detail.

(1) "For resale"

10.23 The dealer must acquire the goods for resale to others. If a dealer acquires goods or raw materials for processing and transformation into other goods then there is no resale. The same applies to the purchase of components which are combined with other components into a different product.[18] The Commission requires that the essential "economic identity" of the product as supplied remains when it is resold. However, this "economic identity" is not destroyed simply because the dealer separates out and repackages the goods prior to resale.

10.24 Obviously many dealers do perform acts in connection with the contract goods.[19] Simply because a certain amount of alteration or reprocessing occurs does not necessarily mean that exemption is lost. It is a question of degree in each case.[20] Thus, where the dealer performs extra operations to improve the quality, durability, appearance, or taste then the Commission will ask how much value has been added to the goods: a slight addition might not alter the economic identity of the goods; a larger addition will alter the economic identity. Trade usage will be relevant in determining the dividing line.[21]

(2) "Goods"

10.25 The Regulation excludes services; only goods agreements benefit.[22] However, the provision of after-sales services by a dealer in respect of goods is within the scope of the exemption. To remain exempt, however, the charge for the after sales services must not exceed the price of the goods. It thus follows that the after-sales services may be of some value provided the value of the goods is greater.[23] The Commission considers that the hir-

[17] See at paras. 8–16 and 27–29 of the explanatory notice.

[18] Though if a dealer sells components as spare parts he will be reselling them albeit that most of the components may be used in the production of a main product by the dealer.

[19] e.g. fizzy drinks dealer who adds gas and water to an essence supplied by the supplier; pharmacist who encapsulates and packs drugs for sale.

[20] See *Campari* [1978] 2 CMLR 397, Campari Milano granted trade mark licences to its dealers who also purchased a secret concoction of herbs to which licensees (the dealers) added local wines in accordance with a specified recipe. Exemption was given by analogy to Reg. 67/67/EC, the predecessor to Reg. 1983/83/EEC. For Campari this was a cheaper and safer method of distribution than transporting heavy glass bottles. Campari subsequently changed its policy to manufacturing locally through wholly owned subsidiaries or appointing exclusive distributors — see Commission's *Eighteenth Report on Competition Policy* (1989), para. 69.

[21] In the explanatory notice (para. 10) the Commission note that it applies "the same principles to agreements under which the reseller is supplied with a concentrated extract for a drink which he has to dilute with water, pure alcohol or another liquid and to bottle before reselling." If supplier X required supplier Y to add champagne to his essence then the addition would greatly increase the value of the finished product; if Y simply had to add cheap, local white wine then a much smaller increase would occur. See the *Campari* case—the addition of wine (which is not inherently cheap) appears not to disturb the exemption.

[22] See e.g. *Distribution of Package Tours during the 1990 World Cup* OJ 1992 L326/31.

[23] If a dealer sells moderately priced goods and provides expensive after-sales services and incorporates the price of the after sales services into that for the goods then the Commission would probably undertake their own analysis of the relative costs for purposes of comparison. See para. II of the explanatory notice.

ing or leasing out of goods for consideration comes closer to a sale than a service, though if related service charges exceed the hire or lease price then the hire or lease will almost certainly be considered as the provision of services.

(3) "Only two undertakings are party"

10.26 Only bilateral agreements are covered, i.e. one supplier and one dealer. The meaning of "undertaking" has been discussed at paras 6.9-6.22. Thus several undertakings forming one economic unit count as a single undertaking. Thus in *Hydrotherm* v *Compact*[24] the Court of Justice held that an agreement between, on the one hand, an Italian entrepreneur and two companies he controlled, and on the other hand, a German dealer, was an agreement between two undertakings only. Although Article 1 of the Regulation makes no express reference to the point, the Commission accept that a supplier may delegate the performance of his contractual obligations to a connected or independent undertaking whom he has entrusted with the distribution of his goods. Thus a dealer may have to purchase from a representative of the supplier.[25] The involvement of these other parties must be confined to the performance of distribution functions (e.g. carriage, freight forwarding, etc.).[26] The fact that only two parties may be exempt means that an agreement between suppliers A and B to share out the supply to dealer X in equal proportions would not be exempt: the agreement. would be between three parties. Likewise an agreement between a supplier's trade association and a dealer's trade association is an agreement between all supplier members and all dealer members and is thus not between two parties only.[27]

10.27 According to paragraph 14 of the explanatory notice the supplier may enter into a series of bilateral exclusive dealing agreements with various dealers and retain the exemption for the agreements.

(4) The exclusive supply obligation: the main restriction

10.28 The main exempt restriction allows the supplier to agree to supply only the contract dealer within the whole or a defined area of the common market, i.e. the supplier will not appoint another dealer in the contract territory. Thus, if X supplies exclusively to three dealers in a territory under different contracts and refuses to supply any other dealers the contracts are not exempt exclusive dealing agreements. The Commission contend that exclusivity is necessary to ensure that the economic benefits of exclusive dealing do materialise.

10.29 A supplier who thus merely controls the number of dealers he appoints rather than appointing a single exclusive dealer must notify his agreement to obtain exemption under Article 85(3) EC.[28] Alternatively, if this is set up observing the rules on selective distribution discussed at paras. 10.348–10.393, the agreements will fall outside Article 85(1) EC and will therefore not require notification.

[24] Case 170/83 [1984] ECR 2999 [1985] 3 CMLR 224.

[25] para. 15 of the explanatory notice. The possibility of delegation of responsibility by the supplier is expressly recognised in respect of exclusive purchasing under Reg. 1984/83/EEC. See Arts. 1, 6 and 10 thereof.

[26] A clause requiring the parties to ensure that connected undertakings discharge their duties properly will be exempt—para. 16 of the explanatory notice.

[27] See Case 126/80 *Salonia* v *Poidomani* [1982] 1 CMLR 64. See also *VDH Thirteenth Report on Competition Policy* (1983), p. 80 at para. 110. A German trade association held exclusive import rights in respect of Finnish wood, only members could import the wood. Following Commission intervention VDH issued a circular to its members making it clear that contracts between foreign suppliers and their agents should no longer include a clause restricting import transactions to certain purchasers. See also for a similar decision *IMA Statut* OJ 1980 L318 (26 November 1980) noted in *Tenth Report on Competition Policy* (1980), paras. 106, 107.

[28] See e.g. *Junghans GmbH* [1977] 1 CMLR D82 at para. 32 of the decision—Reg. 67/67/EEC (the predecessor to Reg. 1983/83/EEC) held not to apply where supplier appointed three dealers in a territory, but Commission granted exemption by analogy to the Regulation.

10.30 It would appear to be the case that if X manufactures and supplies glass and appoints: A as exclusive dealer for glass use in greenhouses and horticulture; B as exclusive dealer for glass used in factories; and C as exclusive dealer for glass used in domestic settings, then exemption should lie since the agreements may arguably relate to different products. It is certainly arguable that horticultural glass, industrial glass and domestic glass are different products when their usage is considered. A, B and C would enjoy exclusive rights of resale in that they would not be competing with each other. If a supplier considers that his products are *de facto* different (e.g. the different types of glass require different production methods and have different properties) so that they have very limited interchangeability of usage, then non-notification may be justified on the basis that they are indeed different products.[29] If there is doubt over this and suppliers prefer certainty they should consider notifying the Commission.

10.31 One very important point to note is that the Commission apparently take the view that while a supplier can grant exclusivity to a dealer he may still retain the freedom to supply unsolicited orders. Thus, a supplier may agree not to *actively* sell to customers (who may be end users or other dealers) but he need not agree to refuse to supply unsolicited orders. Where a supplier does supply unsolicited orders he may agree not to supply them in the exclusive dealer's territory; it does not matter that a customer from outside may then parallel import them into the exclusive dealer's territory and compete with that dealer. In its explanatory notice the Commission states:

> "The exclusive supply obligation does not prevent the supplier from providing the contract goods to other resellers who afterwards sell them in the exclusive distributor's territory. It makes no difference whether the other dealers concerned are established inside or outside the territory. The supplier is not in breach of his obligation to the exclusive distributor provided that he supplies the resellers who wish to sell the contract goods in the territory only at their request and that the goods are handed over outside the territory. It does not matter whether the reseller takes delivery of the goods himself or through an intermediary, such as a freight forwarder. However, supplies of this nature are only permissible if the reseller and not the supplier pays the transport costs of the goods into the contract territory."[30]

10.32 Thus the supplier can sell to other dealers where: (a) orders are unsolicited; (b) the goods are handed over outside of the exclusive dealers territory; and (c) the customer (i.e. the reseller) pays the costs of transporting the goods into the exclusive dealers territory from outside. Surprisingly, given the permissive nature of the above, the Commission have *required* a supplier to modify his dealership agreements so as to permit him to meet unsolicited orders as a condition of granting the supplier a comfort letter and discontinuing their investigation.[31] Does this imply that the Commission require that suppliers must retain freedom to supply unsolicited orders? The language of the Regulation and the explanatory notice issued by the Commission require the supplier to meet unsolicited orders at the price prevailing in the supplier's own territory.[32] Presumably, if a supplier has no sales and marketing capacity of its own (e.g. is purely a manufacturer) then there would

[29] See para. 19 of Explanatory Notice where Commission accept that different varieties of the same generic may constitute different product markets.

[30] para. 27 of the explanatory notice. This has been strongly criticised. See Korah and Rothnie, *op. cit.*, at pp. 92–97, Joanna Goyder, *op. cit.*, at pp. 63–64.

[31] *La Maison de Bibliothèque* [1984] 1 CMLR 261.

[32] If the supplier (French) had increased the price to the unsolicited customer (in Belgium) in the *La Maison de Bibliothèque* case above, as a means of discouraging him and thereby increasing the incentive for him to go back to his nearest dealer that would have been unacceptable. Though, a dealer is not bound to sell to customers at the price and on the same terms as the supplier provides goods to the dealer—see *Wooden Racing Kayaks, Twelfth Competition Report* (1982), pp. 68, 69, paras. 79, 80.

be no obligation to supply unsolicited orders. This view receives implicit support from the Commission's decision in *Tipp-Ex*[33] which states that there is no general right to be supplied by a manufacturer. A manufacturer may decide not to supply a dealer established in the territory of an exclusive distributor "for business reasons", provided other sources of supply are open to that dealer in the common market.

10.33 The Commission elaborated on this ruling in the *Eighteenth Report on Competition Policy*[34] stating that the manufacturer need not offer a dealer the same price discounts as it does to its exclusive distributor because the dealer is not offering the same services, such as stocking or sales promotion, as the exclusive distributor does. But there is a warning that if a manufacturer refuses to supply on the ground that the destination of the goods is another member state, such a policy would be regarded as indicative of an agreement or concerted practice to protect exclusive distributors against "bona fide [sic] parallel imports". The Commission threatens a thorough investigation in such circumstances.

(5) "Within the whole or a defined area of the Common Market"

10.34 Commission experience has suggested that an agreement covering the whole of the EC can be economically appropriate. The Court of Justice has confirmed that this is so.[35] Agreements may be drafted so as to cover the whole of the EC or only a part thereof.[36] A point of interest is whether an agreement between X and Y whereby Y is the exclusive dealer for certain EC states and certain other non-EC states is exempt? Under the old Regulation 67/67/EEC (now replaced by Regulation 1983/83/EEC) the Commission and Court took the view that provided the possibility of parallel imports remained, i.e. there were no restraints on cross frontier trading, the exemption applied.[37] The same should apply under Regulation 1983/83/EEC.

10.35 An agreement between an EC supplier and a dealer whose territory lay outside of the EC might fall within Article 85(1) EC where the agreement exerts economic effects within the Community. If the Commission construes the factual situation in the same way as they would an analogous technology transfer agreement then the block exemption should apply. At least the Commission consider that the Technology Transfer Block Exemption (Regulation 240/96EC, discussed at paras. 13.18–13.124) applies where the licence covers non-EC states but has effects within the Community (see para. 7 of the preamble to the Regulation). If the Commission adopt a contrary view individual exemption should be forthcoming. Such an agreement should benefit consumers because of increased productivity by the supplier within the Community which may result in scale economies which may be passed on to consumers.

(6) "Agreements"

10.36 Article 9 of the Regulation provides that the Regulation applies to concerted practices of the type defined in Article 1. Thus, as the Commission explain in paragraph 26 of the explanatory notice, this enables "arrangements which are operated by undertakings but are not the subject of a legally-binding agreement" to be exempt. To be exempt, however, the concerted practice must be in effect on the terms of the Regulation.

33 [1989] 4 CMLR 425; upheld on appeal by the Court of Justice Case 279/87 *Tipp-Ex GmbH* v *Commission* [1990] ECR I-261.

34 Commission's *Eighteenth Report on Competition Policy* (1989) para. 21.

35 See Case 47/76 *De Norre* v *NV Brouwerij Concordia* [1977] 1 CMLR 378; [1977] ECR 65.

36 See *Europair International and Duro-Dyne Corp* [1975] 1 CMLR D62 (Commission decision) this case was under the old Reg. 67/67/EC which only exempted agreements for a "defined area" of the EC which, according to the decision, was an area less than the whole of the EC.

37 *Compact-Hydrotherm* [1981] 3 CMLR 670; Case 170/83 *Hydrotherm* v *Compact* [1985] 3 CMLR 224.

(7) "Only to that other"

10.37 The duty on the supplier to supply only to the contract dealer thus permits restrictions on "skip deliveries", i.e. supplies made by the supplier to a level of trade below that of the dealer, e.g. by the supplier to a retailer where the contract dealer is a wholesaler. The supplier may thus be bound to his distributional function. A similar clause imposed upon the dealer is not however exempt; no exemption exists under Article 2 (permissible restrictions on dealer, see paras. 10.41–10.57) which embraces prohibitions on "skip-deliveries". Though, the Commission adopts a pragmatic view of such clauses and individual exemption may be obtained. They accept that confining a firm to its specified distributional function may enhance the effectiveness of a distribution system.

3. Article 2(1): Additional Permissible Restriction on Supplier

10.38 Article 2(1) allows an obligation on the supplier "not to supply the contract goods to users in the contract territory". In the light of the analysis of Article 1 above this may have to be read to mean that the supplier may agree not to *actively* supply users in the contract territory, i.e. he must retain the right to supply unsolicited orders. Though the wording of Articles 1 and 2 do not expressly indicate that a supplier *must* always effect a supply. Where an unsolicited order is made the supplier must satisfy it outside of the exclusive dealer's territory.[38] Thus, a UK supplier may supply a customer from Belgium in the United Kingdom though the customer would have to pay the freight costs back to Belgium. Exemption is not lost in such a case even though the customer will export the goods to Belgium and sell them there in competition with the resident exclusive dealer. A supplier may refuse to supply an unsolicited order if the supplier and the dealer are situate in the same area, e.g. a supplier in the UK and an exclusive dealer for the whole of the UK. In such cases, in any event, it may be that the supplier does not maintain any sales capacity and concentrates solely on production.

10.39 The restriction on the supplier need not be absolute, clauses allowing the supply of certain specified (e.g. specialised) customers may be incorporated. Further, a compensation clause by which the supplier pays, for example, a sum per sale to the dealer, is permissible. However, these direct sales by the supplier can only be to end-users or consumers, they may not be to other dealers in the area. If the supplies are to other dealers then the block exemption does not apply and the agreement should be notified. The preamble explains this in terms of the need to maintain a clear "division of functions" between the parties thereby compelling the dealer to concentrate his sales efforts on the contract territory and the contract goods and in so doing ensuring the realisation of the distributional advantages sought by the regulation.[39] The regulation thus allows suppliers to consider how best to supply large or specialised users by reference to the relative costs and capacities of the supplier and the dealer. What if a supplier appoints an exclusive dealer, but reserves the exclusive right to serve certain specified customers itself? In such a case, the block exemption still applies provided the dealer also remains free to supply those customers. While the Notice permits the supplier to be able to supply certain customers,[40]

[38] See *La Maison de Bibliothèque* [1984] 1 CMLR 261.

[39] See para. 8 of the preamble to Reg. 1983/83/EEC. Thus the Commission's decision in *BP Kemi* [1979] 3 CMLR 684 is unlikely now to be followed—supplier reserved right to supply large users; the Commission decided that the exemption in Reg. 67/67 only applied where a very clear division of functions existed between supplier and dealer.

[40] Thus para. 17 of the explanatory notice states: "If they agree on further obligations restrictive of competition, the agreement as a whole is no longer covered by the block exemption and requires individual exemption. For example, an agreement will exceed the bounds of the Regulation if the parties relinquish the possibility of independently determining their prices or conditions of business or undertake to refrain, or

it prohibits restrictions on the dealer from supplying certain categories of customer.[41] While the relationship between these two provisions remains unclear, it seems better to permit a supplier the right to serve specified customers without making it exclusive.

10.40 It appears to be unlikely that any other restrictions on the supplier may be incorporated without exemption being lost. The Regulation operates on the basis that *any* customer restriction attracts the operation of Article 85(1) and requires exemption. Since the Regulation is exhaustive of the customer restrictions which may be imposed the inclusion of any further restriction disapplies the block exemption. However, the Court adopts more of a pragmatic view and has held that not all restrictions on conduct necessary injure competition. Given the current state of the law it should however be assumed for practical purposes that additional restrictions on the supplier entail the necessity to notify. Though it would appear that advertising obligations on the supplier (e.g. supplier will expend 10 per cent of his annual turnover on advertising) are not within Article 85(1) on a *de minimis* basis (see below under Article 2(3)(c)) and hence may be imposed on the supplier without losing block exemption.

4. *Article 2(2) and (3): Permissible Restrictions on the Dealer*

10.41 Article 2(2) and (3) focus on permissible dealer restrictions and emphasises the need to avoid customer restrictions. The Regulation is clear that only certain restrictions are exempt. In paragraph 8 of the preamble it is thus stated: "further restrictive obligations and in particular those which limit the exclusive distributor's choice of customers or his freedom to determine his prices and conditions of sale cannot be exempted under this Regulation. 'Thus, no other dealer restrictions other than those specified are allowed and in particular restrictions on the dealer's freedom over choice of customers, prices and conditions of sale are outside the exemption.[42] The restrictions allowed in Article 2 may last only for the duration of the agreement, no longer.[43] Article 2(2) and (3) contain a number of parts.

(1) Article 2(2)(a): non-manufacture or distribution

10.42 This provision permits the supplier to restrict the dealer from manufacturing or distributing goods which compete with the contract goods. For a discussion of the notion of "competing goods" see analysis under Article 3(a) and (b) below.[44]

(2) Article 2(2)(b): exclusive purchase

10.43 This provision permits an obligation on the dealer to purchase the contract goods exclusively from the supplier. Under this Regulation exemption lies if there is an exclusive supply obligation (i.e. Article 1) *and* an exclusive purchase obligation (i.e. Article 2(2)(b)). If an agreement *only* has an exclusive purchase obligation, Regulation 1983/83/EEC is irrelevant but block exemption may be obtained if the agreement satisfies Regulation 1984/83/EEC on exclusive purchasing. This provision goes wider than the restriction which may be imposed on a franchisee under the franchising block exemption[45] or which

cont.
even prevent, cross-border trade, which the Regulations expressly state must not be impeded. Among other clauses which in general are not permissible under the Regulations are those which impede the reseller in his free choice of customers."

41 para. 30 of the explanatory notice.

42 para. 29 of the explanatory notice.

43 para. 8 of the preamble and para. 18 of the explanatory notice.

44 Note that under the equivalent provision of the RTPA, Sch. 3(2), a restriction on manufacture is not exempted: see para. 2.145.

45 Reg. 4087/88; see paras. 10.270–10.315.

may be imposed on a distributor under the Commission's rulings on selective distribution,[46] where a franchisee or distributor must remain free to acquire from other franchisees or distributors in the same network.

(3) Article 2(2)(c): active marketing outside exclusive area

10.44 This provision permits clauses entailing, "the obligation to refrain, outside the contract territory and in relation to the contract goods, from seeking customers, from establishing any branch and from maintaining any distribution depot." The provision relies upon the distinction between passive and active marketing. A dealer may not go hunting sales outside of his territory but he must retain the right to satisfy unsolicited orders. If further restrictions on the dealers right to "sell away" exist they must be given individual Commission blessing. Thus, in *Campari*,[47] an exceptional case, the Commission exempted a pure exclusivity clause, i.e. no sales whatsoever outside of territory, on the basis that it was needed to ensure that the licensee of a trade mark took adequate steps to invest and improve its distribution system.

10.45 The "exemptibility" of monitoring clauses, e.g. a clause requiring the dealer within 14 days after the end of each month to supply to the other party a statement of any exports or sales outside of his territory, is uncertain. It is arguable that this clause serves only to check that the dealer fulfils his obligations under the main exempt clause and hence should also be exempt. However, it is also arguable that such a clause could be viewed as a mechanism whereby the supplier imposes informal pressure on the dealer to prevent him selling outside his territory. The Commission apparently adopts the view that so long as the monitoring clause is employed genuinely it is legitimate.[48]

10.46 It appears to be open as to whether a supplier can be required to impose the same ban on active sales on other distributors.[49] It is thought that generally Commission officials would not object to such a clause. Should a distributor insist on such a clause, it seems that the wisest course would be to notify in the hope of a comfort letter.

10.47 Apparently an exclusive dealer may be prohibited from satisfying orders from outside the EC.[50] This was so under the old Regulation 67/67/EEC and the wording of the provision in Article 2(2)(c) of Regulation 1983/83/EEC is exactly the same as the old provision. The Commission consider that the higher prices dealers will charge to cover freight, customs, additional profits, etc. make reimport very unlikely and hence inter-Member State trade even more improbable. Such a clause is not expressly exempted under the Regulation; it might be wise to seek informal Commission clearance by way of a comfort letter. Such a prohibition would not however be acceptable to the Commission where it concerned States, which have a free trade agreement with the EC since reimportation is more likely than where the ban is to states having no trade agreement with the EC.

10.48 If the supplier seeks to impose the advertising and active marketing ban on dealers *below* the level of the exclusive dealer (i.e. on sub-dealers of the exclusive dealer) then individual exemption must be sought. An obligation on a dealer to impose the same terms on

[46] See paras. 10.349–10.393.

[47] [1978] 2 CMLR 397.

[48] *BMW* [1975] 1 CMLR D44; *SABA* [1976] CMLR D61, para. 37 *SABA No. 2* [1984] 1 CMLR 676 at p. 685 paras. 40, 41. But cf. *Stoves and Heaters* [1975] 2 CMLR D1 at p. D39, para. 39.

[49] Korah and Rothnie, *op. cit.*, at pp. 107–108, would not regard such a clause as restriction of competition and therefore not falling within the block exemption. This view may be supported to an extent by the patent and know-how licensing block exemptions and technology transfer regulation (see Chapter 13 below) which do not regard most favoured licensee clauses as restrictive of competition, though a most favoured licensee clause does not of itself require that the same terms be imposed on all licensees.

[50] *Kodak* [1970] CMLR D19; *Omega* [1970] CMLR D49.

his sub-dealers is a restriction on the terms and conditions on which the dealer may resell the goods. Exemption is given if the ban results in sub-dealers concentrating their efforts on meeting demand in the territory and thereby bringing about sought after distributional advantages.[51]

(4) Article 2(3)(a): complete ranges of goods

10.49 This allows the supplier to require the dealer to purchase complete ranges of goods or minimum quantities of goods. Although drafted in the alternative both requirements may be (and commonly are) imposed simultaneously.[52] It appears probable that a complete range of goods means the same as it does under Article 2(3)(a) of Regulation 1984/83/EEC on exclusive purchasing (discussed below). If that is so then a complete range of goods means a complete range of goods which are by their nature or commercial usage connected to each other. Thus, the tying of uncomplimentary and unconnected goods together might entail loss of exemption.

(5) Article 2(3)(b): trade mark and packaging[53]

10.50 This allows the suppliers to require the dealer to "sell the contract goods under trade marks, or packed and presented as specified by the other party". This restriction causes no antitrust problems. Indeed it might be illegal (viz., tort of unfair competition and/or passing off) for the dealer to remove the trade mark, design or packaging.[54] The dealer may be obliged to display the trade mark variously on stationery, in correspondence related to the goods, in brochures, leaflets, price lists, and in general advertising. He may also be required to affix the trade mark prominently in the business premises.[55] Further, the dealer may be restricted in his use of the mark, e.g. in combination with the dealer's own trade mark or design. The supplier's right (and also his capacity) to regulate use of a trade mark by a dealer will also stem from relevant national intellectual property law. However, in some cases restrictions on repackaging may be considered anti-competitive. Thus, in *Bayer Dental*[56] Bayer's General conditions of Sale and Delivery required its dental product packages to be resold in unopened form. Another of the conditions was that the products must not be sold outside Germany. The Commission held that both these requirements were caught by Article 85(1). The ban on repackaging was held to be anti-competitive because it left out of account "forms of repackaging which do not affect the original state of the dental preparations. The provision is apt to awaken in the minds of resellers so much doubt as to their actual rights that they will refrain from reselling packaged products. In doing so the prohibition pursues the object of restricting competition." Bayer's statements that, in practice, it tolerates all forms of repackaging which did not alter the original state of its products was held to be irrelevant since it was the *object* of the prohibition which was important. However, this provision cannot be used to argue that a

[51] *BMW* [1975] 1 CMLR D44.

[52] *ibid.* But note that under Reg. 1984/83/EEC on exclusive purchasing, the requirement that the dealer accept minimum quantities of goods is limited only to those goods that are subject to the exclusive purchasing requirement.

[53] See generally, Baden Fuller, "Economic issues relating to property rights in trade marks: export bans, differential pricing, restrictions on resale and repackaging" (1981) ELRev 162.

[54] The obligation to sell in the suppliers packaging is not a restriction within Art. 85(1): *Dupont de Nemours* [1973] CMLR D226, p. D228; *BMW* above at para. 32 of the decision but cf. *Hoechst BECham Pharma* Bull EC 7–8/76 at para. 2122; Case 170/83 *Hydrotherm* v *Compact* [1985] 3 CMLR 224 (certain grants of trade mark rights do not threaten the exemption).

[55] See the German case, *Rose Marie Reid OLG* Stuttgart (23 January 1976) W/W/E OLG 1674 at p. 1678.

[56] OJ [1990] L351/46.

franchise agreement is exempt under this provision:[57] reference will have to be made to the block exemption on franchise agreements.[58]

(6) Article 2(3)(c): measures for promotion of sales

10.51 The supplier may require the dealer to:

> "take measures for promotion of sales, in particular:
> to advertise,
> to maintain a sales network or stock of goods,
> to provide customer and guarantee services,
> to employ staff having specialized or technical training."

It is fundamental in every distribution contract that the dealer shall use "best endeavours" to promote the supplier's goods; often an express clause to this effect is included in the contract. It is sometimes questioned whether general promotional obligations are restrictions at all under Article 85(1). The Commission adopts the view that technically they are capable of falling within Article 85(1) but that they usually do not have an appreciable effect on competition so fall out of Article 85(1) on the basis of *de minimis*, i.e. negligible effect.[59] If a promotion clause specifies a required turnover level or requires a dealer to take a specified quantity at specified times then an appreciable restriction might arise.[60] Though even this should be exempt under the Regulation since in the preamble it is stated that it is a matter for free negotiation between supplier and dealer as to the desirability of incorporating promotion clauses.[61]

10.52 The enumeration in Article 2(3) is non-exhaustive. Thus other promotion clauses not mentioned may be incorporated. A duty on the dealer to report back sales data should be exempt. Such a clause permits the supplier to monitor sales trends and adjust his marketing policies accordingly.

10.53 As regards advertising the supplier may require the dealer to undertake a specified minimum amount of advertising or include a specified content in his advertising. Moreover, the dealer may be prohibited from advertising in trade fairs, etc. without the supplier's permission, though it might be that such permission should not be unreasonably withheld.[62] However, it is unlikely that exemption exists if the dealer is required to undertake advertising in excess of that needed to draw attention to the supplier's goods in an effective manner.[63]

10.54 As regards a "sales network", the supplier may regulate such factors as the qualifications and activities of the dealer's staff and the number of visits made per month to customers. Presumably reporting obligations on the dealer to keep the supplier informed are also covered. The supplier may regulate the stocks of the dealer as regards minimum quantities of certain types, etc.[64] Where the reseller is to set up a distribution network the reseller may, according to paragraph 20 of the explanatory notice, be prohibited from supplying

[57] Case 161/84 *Pronuptia* [1986] ECR 353; [1986] 1 CMLR 414, at para. 33, where the Court of Justice held that a franchise agreement was different in nature to a distribution agreement and so not exempt under Reg. 67/67.

[58] See paras. 10.270–10.315.

[59] e.g. *Krupps* OJ 1980 L120/26 at p. 28, para. 15 (Commission decision granting negative clearance).

[60] *ibid.*

[61] para. 6 of preamble.

[62] *BMW* [1975] 1 CMLR D44, paras. 30 and 31.

[63] *ibid.* at para. 31 of the Decision.

[64] *ibid.* at para. 30 of the Decision. See also *Krupps* OJ 1980 L120/26, p. 27, para. 14. Such a requirement is potentially a restriction under Art. 85(1) but usually will be given negative clearance on a *de minimis* basis, i.e. no appreciable effect on competition.

the contract goods to unsuitable sub-dealers. The Commission state that: "such clauses are unobjectionable if admission to the distribution network is based on objective criteria of a qualitative nature relating to the professional qualifications of the owner of the business or his staff or the suitability of his business premises, if the criteria are the same for all potential dealers, and if the criteria are actually applied in a non-discriminatory manner". This is an example of a clause which technology amounts to a customer restriction (i.e. can appoint only certain sub-dealers) but, none the less is, according to well established principles of selective distribution, outside Article 85(1). Where the reseller employs quantitative criteria in selecting sub-dealers the agreement is *not* block exempt and may need to be notified to the Commission. In *Ivoclar*[65] the reseller was prohibited from selling to both other dealers and other specialised firms capable of handling the goods (dental equipment). This fact, *inter alia*, meant that block exemption was unavailable. However, the Commission granted formal exemption on the basis that only authorised dealers could give the technical back-up services that the products demanded. Moreover, non-authorised dealers would not be able to carry adequate stocks because of inadequate sales volumes.

10.55 With respect to after sales service and guarantees the supplier may require the dealer to follow his guidelines. A common problem occurs where the supplier requires the dealer to use the supplier's spare parts in providing after sales service. This should be exempt provided the use of these spare parts are technically necessary to effect repairs or protect the quality of the product. Where such conditions are not met the Commission may well take the view that the supplier is trying to create a market in the spare parts that he would otherwise not enjoy. The Commission's view will probably be influenced by the nature of the spare parts market and by the extent to which independent suppliers of spare parts are excluded from the market by prohibitions on the dealer from accepting such alternative supplies.

10.56 Regulation 1983/83/EEC will not apply if the dealer is prevented from providing after sales or guarantee services to the supplier's goods which are brought into the dealer's territory by parallel imports, i.e. by someone other than the exclusive dealer. The Commission adopts a similar view if the dealer is required to give different (inferior) treatment to parallel imported goods.[66] Suppliers may not justify different treatment on technical or safety standards grounds,[67] at least not unless those grounds are demonstrable and compelling.

[65] OJ 1985 L369/1.

[66] See *Ford Garantie Deutschland, Thirteenth Competition Report* (1983), pp. 78, 79, para. 104–6. The Commission, in response to complaints by the European Bureau of Consumers' Unions, intervened to prevent what they suspected was a dealer cartel attempting to prevent parallel imports. The dealers had advertised in German newspapers saying: "We do not carry out guarantee work on new Ford cars reimported after being purchased elsewhere in the European Community." Following Commission pressure the dealers publicly retracted this statement. In *Constructa, Fourth Report on Competition Policy* (1974), paras. 109—Commission persuaded the supplier (a manufacturer) to organise after-sales service in such a way that it would be available throughout the common market regardless of country of purchase. See also *Seventh Report on Competition Policy* (1977), pp. 24–6, paras. 17–20 for general commentary on after sales services and competition law. See also, *Omega* [1970] CMLR D49; *BMW* [1975] 1 CMLR 44; *SABA* [1976] 1 CMLR D61 (all Commission decisions); and, Case 31/85 *ETA* v *DK Investment* [1985] ECR 3933.

[67] *Seventh Report on Competition Policy*, p. 25, para. 19: "In the electrical appliances industry the guarantee can be of particular importance. But difficulties have arisen because of different technical and safety standards in the Member States of the Community. Certain manufacturers have invoked these differences as grounds for refusing to grant a guarantee for parallel imports or use of their products in a Member State other than that to which they were originally imported. The Commission has not accepted the argument. It has concluded that these differences are not so great as to raise an insurmountable barrier to trade in the relevant goods and that the relevant exporters ought to be free to assess the business value of making any alterations that may be necessary." See also *AEG Telefunken, Fourth Report on Competition Policy* (1974), para. 106.

10.57 With respect to staffing the dealer may be required to employ staff having specialised skills which will guarantee that the goods in question are properly marketed and that the reputation of the supplier is thereby protected. A supplier may specify training programmes for dealers staff to be undertaken under either independent supervision or under the dealer's supervision.

(7) Other restrictions are non-permissible

10.58 Other than those restrictions allowed by Article 2 no others are allowed. It should be stressed that the supplier may *not* impose restrictions on: the customers the dealer may supply; the price the dealer charges at; or, the terms and conditions the dealer supplies on.[68] The Regulation is exhaustive of permissible restrictions. It is an exception to the basic prohibition in Article 85(1) and is to be construed narrowly. As regards customers it will be recalled that the supplier may reserve the right to supply specialised or large customers that he feels the dealer is unable to cope with. Compensation payments may be made in respect of these sales. However, the supplier may not expressly restrict the customers to whom the dealer may supply, e.g. dealer *cannot* supply specialist customers who will be served by the supplier. If such restrictions are imposed the parties will need to obtain the Commission's express approval. As regards prices, any attempt by the supplier to enforce resale price maintenance will be outside the exemption and most unlikely to obtain Article 85(3) exemption. The phrase "terms and conditions" covers a multitude of sins. It covers, for example, credit, payment periods, discounts, delivery, insurance, etc. The dealer must be given freedom to determine his own policy. Individual exemption from the Commission must be sought where restrictive clauses are included.

5. Article 3: Non-Exempt Restrictions: Agreements between Competing Manufacturers

10.59 Article 3(a) provides that no exemption is available where:

> "manufacturers of identical goods or of goods which are considered by users as equivalent in view of their characteristics, price and intended use enter into reciprocal exclusive distribution agreements between themselves in respect of such goods."

Article 3(b) provides an exception to this where, first, the agreement is non-reciprocal, and secondly one of the parties has an annual turnover of no more than ECU100 million. Both the basic rule and the exception are examined below.

(1) Basic rule: no exemption for mutual exclusive dealing

10.60 Reciprocal exclusive dealing between rival manufacturers may be exempted but this must be obtained via individual representation to the Commission. The reason lies in the concern that if two competitors entrust the distribution of their goods to each other, then each competitor will, in marketing the goods, devote greater effort to their own brand than to their rivals. Thus, a tendency towards market sharing may emerge. If X in the south entrusts distribution in the north to Y; and Y entrusts distribution in the south to X, then X's goods may be sold more effectively in the south and Y's goods more effectively in the north.[69] The block exemption does not apply where the two manufacturers

[68] para. 17 of the explanatory notice, and, para. 8 of the preamble to Reg. 83/83/EC. See, e.g. *Ivoclar* OJ 1985 1369/1 at para. 18 (though individual exemption may be obtained from the Commission).

[69] See para. 10 of the preamble, and paras. 21–3 of the explanatory notice. See e.g. *Siemens–Fanuc* OJ 1985 1376/29 at paras. 21–6. Fines of 1m ECU were imposed on both parties for entering a mutual exclusive

are producers of "identical" goods or of "equivalent" goods. The meaning of "equivalent" requires explanation. Equivalence is determined by a "consumer preference" test, i.e. would the user view the two manufacturers' goods as equivalent.[70] The test is essentially one of substitutability: are the goods interchangeable in view of their characteristics, price and intended use? Goods might have similar characteristics in that they are fungible, or combustible or edible, etc. Oranges and peaches are different products but have important similarities or characteristic. Similar goods, conversely, may not be equivalent because of price differentials. Thus, manufacturers of fish paste and caviar both produce fish products but it can hardly be said that the products are equivalent.

10.61 With respect to intended use X and Y might be fruit farmers but whereas X supplies only the confectionery trade, Y supplies only the specialist fruit wine trade and hence the intended use of the fruit might mean that the goods do not effectively compete (though they may be potential competitors). Alternatively, goods might not be "equivalent" because consumers/users are unaware of their substitutability albeit that objectively the products are interchangeable. For instance two very different chemicals may perform the same function but because users are unaware of the complementary characteristics of the chemicals they are not perceived as equivalent.

10.62 The Commission elaborated upon the consumer preference test in *Whisky and Gin*.[71] The Distillers company notified on behalf of subsidiaries over 20 non-reciprocal sole distributorship agreements concluded between those subsidiaries and companies in other Member States. In the majority of the agreements (category A cases) the dealer, or a member of the group of companies to which it belonged, was a producer of alcoholic spirits but not of whisky or gin. In the remaining cases the dealer or a member of the group to which the dealer belonged, did produce whisky or gin (category B cases). With respect to the category A cases the question was whether the dealers were competing manufacturers given that they or members of their group, produced alcoholic spirits. The Commission concluded that the dealers did *not* compete with the suppliers and hence the block exemption applied in normal fashion to the agreements. This decision suggests that the Commission will adopt a pragmatic view of the notion of competing products. The reasoning of the Commission is thus of importance. First, the Commission stated that the definition of the product market under Article 3(b) (and presumably *a fortiori* Article 3(a)) need not be the same as that used in other areas of Community law where different goals were to be achieved. Secondly, the Commission elaborated upon the test to be applied in analysing the market. The test is double-limbed. Limb one concentrates upon the consumer preference test. Limb two analyses the market to see whether there is any danger of market sharing between the partners, and/or, whether the dealer will use less than best endeavours to market the contract product because of perceived competition between the supplier's and dealer's products. Clearly both limbs are inter-related since if, under limb one, consumers would not view the products as substitutable, then presumably the dealer would not view the success of the contract product as a threat to sales of his own product. The

cont.
dealing agreement covering a large portion of the world market, which concerned a product of considerable technological relevance to the EC and which resulted in supra-normal prices.

70 See para. 21 of the explanatory notice: "In certain cases ... goods can form a separate market on the basis of their characteristics, their price or their intended use alone. This is true especially where consumer preferences have developed." See the interpretation of the consumer preference test in *Whisky and Gin* OJ 1985 1369/19 at p. 22 para. 18, the Commission state that: "in certain cases differences as to only one of those features can lead to the formation of separate product markets, especially where consumer preferences have developed."

71 OJ 1985 1369/19.

consumer preference limb is hence the central test to be applied. In applying this test the Commission considered a wide range of factors including the primary ingredients of gin and whisky as compared with other alcoholic beverages; the distillation or manufacturing processes; the typical flavour of the drinks; the intended use (aperitif, digestif, long-drink base, etc.). These latter two factors were particularly important in the consumer preference test. On the basis of this test the Commission concluded that whisky and gin formed discrete sub-markets in the wider market for alcoholic drinks. An important question that will be asked in cases of this nature will be: does the existence of *some* product interchangeability necessarily mean that the products are deemed to be competing and will hence lose block exemption? The answer is no, limited interchangeability does *not* threaten block exemption. It is obvious that whisky and gin *are*, to a degree, substitutes for aquavits, vodkas, brandy, etc. However, the Commission's test was simply whether a consumer looking for whisky or gin would "readily" buy a spirit from another category; the test was *not* whether the consumer would reject other drinks *altogether* in the event of unavailability of whisky or gin.

10.63 Thus, if parties supply products which by their characteristics, price and intended use are different then a mutual exclusive dealing arrangement may be exempt. In such a case the manufacturers will not be competitors. Arrangements such as these are not uncommon for example with respect to specialisation agreements. Producer X and Producer Y might have agreed to concentrate R&D and marketing on different types of complementary drug. They might also have agreed to cross-supply each other with their own brand of product. Such an agreement may well be exempt under Regulation 417/85/EEC[72] on block exemption for specialisation agreements.

10.64 In *Phillips/Fluke*,[73] the Commission allowed an agreement between two manufacturers of testing and measurement products for the reciprocal distribution of each other's range of products. Part of this range was considered to be equivalent by users, and hence Article 3(a) applied. But the rest of their respective ranges were complementary. As the purpose of the agreement was to enable each to break into the other's geographical market (Phillips's being in the EC and Fluke's in the USA), previous attempts to do so on their own having largely failed as their market shares in a highly competitive market were small, and as there was only a small degree of overlap in the otherwise complementary product ranges, the Commission was prepared to grant an exemption and dealt with the matter by granting a comfort letter.[74]

10.65 It is an open question whether there must be actual competition between the rival manufacturers in the "equivalent" goods for Articles 3(a) and (b) to apply. There is no reference in these provisions to such a requirement; its absence has led different authorities to reach directly opposite inferences.[75] It would be safer to assume that the issue of whether there is actual or potential competition between the rival manufacturers is not relevant. The test is limited to the express wording of Articles 3(a) and (b); if parties to an agreement come within that despite not being actual competitors, the only safe course is to apply of individual exemption in the hope of obtaining a comfort letter.

10.66 The commentary above applies irrespective of whether the parties to the agreement's are within or without the common market. See the *Cansulex–SNEAP* case referred to at

72 OJ 1985 L53/1.

73 [1990] 4 CMLR 166.

74 See Commission's *Nineteenth Report on Competition Policy* (1990) at para. 47.

75 Taylor and Marks, *Butterworth's Competition Law*, Division IV, para. 308 take the view that "it is not necessary for the manufacturers concerned to be in actual competition in the same geographical market". Korah and Rothnie, *Exclusive Distribution and the EEC Competition Rules* (2nd edn. 1992), p. 134, take the view that in the absence of actual competition, these provisions do not apply.

para. 10.70 for an example of this. Where one or both of the parties to the agreement is part of a group or is controlled by another party reference should be made to the commentary at paras. 10.73–10.76 on "connected undertakings".

(2) The exception: non-reciprocal agreements where one side is a small or medium sized undertaking

10.67 Article 3(b) permits a manufacturer to entrust distribution to a rival where: (a) the agreement is *not* reciprocal, i.e. only one party entrusts distribution to another; and (b) one party has a total annual turnover of less than ECU100 million, i.e. is a small or medium-sized undertaking in Community terms. It is recognised by this exception that certain manufacturers make ideal dealers for other rival manufacturers. Indeed, for a small manufacturer, X, an agreement with an existing large manufacturer, Y, whereby Y acts as dealer for X's goods may be one of the only means of penetrating a market. Y will use its own existing distribution network to market X's goods. The test to be used in calculating "total annual turnover" is given in Article 5 of the Regulation. The relevant calculation period is the last financial year. The turnover to be assessed is that of the relevant party *and* all connected undertakings (see below) and includes the turnover of *all* goods *and* services. In making this calculation a number of exclusions must be taken into account. These are: (a) all taxes and other duties paid by the relevant undertaking and all connected undertakings; (b) all turnover derived from dealings between the parties to the agreement; (c) all turnover derived from dealings between a party to the agreement and its connected undertakings; and (d) turnover derived from dealings between the connected undertakings.[76] It is helpful in comprehending the above to note the Commission's view:

> "Annual turnover is used as a measure of the economic strength of the undertakings involved. Therefore, the aggregate turnover from goods and services of all types, and not only from the contract goods, is to be taken. Turnover taxes and other turnover related levies are not included in turnover. Where a party belongs to a group of connected undertakings, the world wide turnover of the group, excluding intra-group sales ... is to be used."[77]

10.68 Where parties find that their agreement fits within the exemption they will not lose it simply because the smaller party has a turnover that for a period slightly exceeds the 100 million ECU threshold. Article 5(2) permits the exemption to remain "... where during any period of two consecutive financial years the total turnover referred to in Article 3(b) is exceeded by no more than 10 per cent." However, block exemption *will* be lost if, at the end of the second financial year, the total turnover over the preceding two years has been over ECU220 million. If block exemption is suddenly lost parties must either abandon the agreement or notify it rapidly.[78]

Obviously, if both parties fall below the ECU100 million ceiling exemption is automatic.

[76] Note that the wording of the second sentence of Art. 5(3) in the version of the Regulation at OJ 1983 L173/4 is incorrect. The Commission amended the second sentence to read: "For this purpose no account shall be taken of dealings between the party to the agreement and its connected undertakings or between its connected undertakings." See *Corrigenda* OJ 1983 L281/24.

[77] para. 22 of the explanatory notice.

[78] If the agreement suddenly becomes non-exempt it should either be rapidly abandoned (and contractual provision might be made to allow a short period of notice to cover this eventuality) or it should be notified to the Commission, Failure to notify means that the agreement has no provisional validity and the clauses which render it subject to Art. 85(1) (i.e. all the restrictions) will be void under Art. 85(2). Moreover, the agreement would be unenforceable in a national court. It might be wise therefore to impose contractual requirements on the other party to notify changes in turnover. Appropriate indemnities could also be included.

(3) Exemption under Article 85 (3)

10.69 Where an agreement is not automatically exempt what are the chances of individual exemption? Where the parties are powerful firms or are oligopolists the chances are very slim. The Commission has stated:

> "The Commission is not opposed to co-operation between competing manufacturers in the distribution of their products provided all the conditions of Article 85(3) are fulfilled. The Commission's experience has shown, however, that agreements of this type between large undertakings having strong market positions will normally not result in such improvements in distribution and benefits to consumers as to outweigh the disadvantages for competition which are involved."[79]

In particular the Commission pinpoint as an obstacle Article 85(3)(b) EC which provides that exemption is unavailable where the agreement affords the undertakings the possibility of eliminating competition in respect of a substantial part of the relevant product market.[80] The *Whisky and Gin* case discussed above demonstrates that the Commission may, where inter-brand competition is healthy, adopt a pragmatic view with regard to the more technical features of Article 3(b), concentrating upon economic effect rather than the precise degree of product substitutability. However, as the quote above demonstrates, in more concentrated markets where the disciplining effects of inter-brand competition are weakened, the Commission is likely to be stricter in its analysis and conclusions.

10.70 A case in point, which was settled by abandonment of the agreement by the parties following Commission intervention was *Cansulex—SNEAP*.[81] Cansulex, the world's leading sulphur exporter, proposed to transfer sole distribution rights for its products in Western Europe and North Africa to Société Nationale Elf Aquitaine Production (SNEAP) the largest sulphur producer in the EC. Prior to this proposal Cansulex marketed sulphur in the EC via an independent distributor which competed with SNEAP. The Commission refused to permit the proposal to materialise. The following factors were relevant to their refusal and are informative in respect of Commission policy in this field:

(a) The Community market in crude sulphur was characterised by very tight oligopolistic conditions in which the leading three suppliers controlled over two-thirds of the total sales. The Commission are wary of any form of agreement whereby oligopolists are strengthened. SNEAP and Cansulex were competitors and the agreement would have strengthened the rigid market structure.

(b) The structure of the sulphur market was deteriorating. SNEAP the largest EC producer had recently acquired Texas Gulf who possessed Arabian sulphur supplies which would in the imminent future be exported to the EC. Thus, the number of independent firms in the market was decreasing.

(c) The general political-economic climate suggested that Cansulex would become very much more important on the EC market. Uncertainty concerning the security of Polish supplies and increasing demand suggested a growing significance for the Canadian exporter. The Commission noted: "The proposed co-operation would have enabled SNEAP to control the sale of Canadian sulphur in Europe and not only

[79] See Commission answer to WQ No. 2178/83 OJ 1984 C200/7 at p. 8, para. 4.

[80] *ibid.*, at para. 3.

[81] Bull EC 2/82 para. 2.1.20; *Twelfth Report on Competition Policy* (1982), p. 69 para. 81 commented on by Commission at OJ 1983 C 200/8 in response to WQ No. 2178/83.

restrict existing competition but also prevent the keener competition expected in the future."[82]

(d) It is also noteworthy that it was the larger of the two parties (Cansulex) who sought to act as supplier and the smaller (SNEAP) who sought to act as dealer.

10.71 One justification for allowing such agreements is that they allow a small supplier to use a distribution network the scale of which it would otherwise have been unable to afford. Where the supplier is the world leader this justification can hardly apply. Though, in other circumstances large companies may legitimately be the supplier, e.g. where the large party supplies the smaller party with complementary goods to complete its range of goods. In *Sugar Beet*[83] Belgian sugar refiners agreed to give priority to Belgian sugar beet growers in obtaining their supplies. The Commission held that this was contrary to Article 85(1) and that, even if it had been notified, would not have been granted exemption pursuant to Article 85(3) as, even if the view was taken that it could contribute to improving Belgian beet production, "it must also be borne in mind that, since such benefits can be obtained only by means of restrictions imposed on other beet suppliers established outside Belgium, such other suppliers necessarily incur disadvantages in their production which exactly offset the advantages achieved in Belgium".

10.72 In *Whisky and Gin* (para. 10.62) the Commission *did* give individual exemption to a mutual exclusive dealing agreement. As noted above most, though not all of the agreements involved dealers who did not compete. However, some did compete. None the less, exemption was given on the basis that the nature of the market (very competitive) would discourage abuse of the agreements. Further that the agreements enabled the manufacturers to concentrate their sales on one dealer who was familiar with the economic/legal market context of the territory. This would intensify marketing efforts and improve the supply situation to consumers.

(4) Meaning of "connected undertakings"

10.73 The phrase "connected undertakings" is relevant to an understanding of the competing manufacture provisions in Article 3(a) and (b); it is also a phrase that occurs repeatedly in other block exemptions. Article 4 provides that no exemption applies where the contract goods in an exclusive dealing arrangement between competing manufacturers are manufactured by an undertaking connected with a party to the agreement. This provision is necessary to avoid circumvention of Article 3(a) and (b). A manufacturer X could incorporate a wholly owned subsidiary ABC Ltd to act as its main distributing arm. ABC Ltd would then enter an agreement with a manufacturer Y who would distribute the goods supplied to it by ABC Ltd but manufactured by X. The ABC Ltd/Y agreement would not be between competing manufacturers and could be dressed up to fall within the exemption in the Regulation. The economic reality is an agreement between X and Y which would not be exempt.

10.74 A connected undertaking is an undertaking which either, directly or indirectly, controls or is controlled by another Company. Control means: (a) ownership of more than half the capital or business assets; or (b) power to exercise more than half the voting

[82] *Twelfth Report on Competition Policy* (1982), p. 69, para. 81(4). The Commission stated also (at OJ 1983 C200/8 para. 2): "If the sole distribution agreement envisaged between the parties had been tolerated SNEAP would have been able to strengthen its position to an unacceptable degree by extending its control over the sales of a competitor with a considerable economic potential and an increasingly important role on the European market."

[83] [1991] 4 CMLR 629.

rights; or (c) power to appoint more than half the members of the supervisory board, board of directors or bodies legally representing the undertaking; or (d) the right to manage the affairs of the company.

10.75 If a company which controls an undertaking which itself controls a party to the actual agreement is a manufacturer then no exemption will lie. Thus in a modified version of the hypothetical example above where Z who controls X (a holding company) who controls ABC Ltd, is a manufacturer, the agreement between ABC Ltd and Y (a competing manufacturer to Z) is outside of the exemption. In reality it is an agreement between two rival manufacturers Z and Y. Article 4(2) prevents what are in effect competing manufacturer agreements being set up through non-manufacturing subsidiaries and holding companies.

10.76 Companies that parties to an agreement jointly control are treated as being connected with each of the parties to the agreement. Thus joint production companies are connected to the joint venture parents. Rival manufacturers cannot therefore incorporate joint venture companies to distribute their goods and obtain block exemption.[84]

6. Article 3(c): Other Non-Exempt Restrictions: Where no Alternative Source of Supply Exists

10.77 Article 3(c) provides that no exemption lies where, "users can obtain the contract goods in the contract territory only from the exclusive distributor and have no alternative source of supply outside the contract territory." The exemption thus only lasts whilst the possibility of parallel imports prevails, i.e. that there is an alternative supply of the contract goods available to users outside of the exclusive territory. If the exclusive dealer has as his territory the whole of the EC, then supplies must be available outside of the EC.[85] Availability implies that goods must actually be obtainable in adequate quantities and available at the ordinary price prevailing there. If goods are theoretically available but at materially discriminatory prices or on unreasonable terms and conditions, then their availability will be more theoretical than actual and the potential for the existence of alternative sources to act as a competitive force to the exclusive dealer will be minimal.[86] Thus, if X manufactures shoes, brand name "Hob Boots", in the UK and appoints Y his exclusive dealer for the whole of the EC (which is the only selling area for the shoes) then a user cannot obtain "Hob Boots" outside of the EC and he *must* purchase from Y. The absence of an alternative source of supply of Hob Boots means that Y is not subject to the additional competitive pressures of a parallel importer. Accordingly, no block exemption exists and individual exemption must be sought for the agreement. Where alternative supplies do exist but at prices and on terms and conditions which are less favourable than those offered by the dealer, then it is presumably a question of degree whether the differences in prices and terms and conditions are sufficiently different to render the availability of these alternative supplies a practical non-starter. Where the difference is a minor one then the block exemption should not be lost; where it is significant block exemption should not be assumed. Differences in prices, terms and conditions may be the result of a number of causes. If the differences are due to attempts by the contract parties to hinder the free move-

[84] Art. 4(3) of the Regulation.

[85] See *Europair-Durodyne* [1975] 1 CMLR D62 a case where alternative supplier *were* available. See para. 11 of the preamble to the Regulation.

[86] See at para. 31 of the explanatory notice. But cf. Korah, *op. cit.*, at n. 2 p. 23 who doubts whether the Commission interpretation as regards the cost of goods from elsewhere is legally justified by reference to the wording of the Regulation.

ment of the goods then block exemption almost certainly lapses immediately. If differences are due to natural market forces then a closer analysis of the cause is required. For example, if a purchaser is situated in London close to the authorised dealer and the alternative suppliers are available only in Athens, then, although the Athenian supplier might offer the goods for sale at identical prices and on identical terms to the authorised London dealer freight costs from Athens to London might mean that the Athenian source of supply is not an economic possibility and hence is not a competitive force to the London dealer. The situation might of course be different if the alternative supply source is located in Paris or Amsterdam.

10.78 Article 3(c) is really only a major problem where the dealer enjoys absolute territorial protection as where he is the *only* appointed distributor. The problem may be circumvented by allowing the supplier to represent an alternative source of supply. The supplier must be prepared to supply the goods on request to final users located in the contract territory.[87] The Regulation only speaks of "users" being able to obtain alternative supplies, not other dealers. In practice, it may well be substantial size firms that require the product as an input into their own production system who will seek the alternative supplies.

10.79 The alternative supplies will presumably consist of the identical brand to the product sold by the exclusive dealer. Indeed, Article 3(c) refers to the "contract goods".[88] Though, if the alternative is slightly different, for example because they use a different trade mark to suit linguistic differences[89] or because they have different components or ingredients to suit slightly different national tastes, a problem arises. In such cases whether the alternative supplies satisfy the requirements of the Regulation, i.e. whether they are a viable alternative to the exclusive dealers goods, will probably be a question of fact. Thus an identical product with a different trade mark will probably be adequate provided there is no consumer objection to that trade mark which will render those alternative goods inadequate or provided the differences in components or ingredients of the alternative goods are not such as to make them unsuitable for use in the territory of the exclusive dealer.[90] Where a supplier can foresee problems of this nature he may be advised to act as the alternative supplier and to supply unsolicited orders himself.

7. *Article 3(d): Other Non-Exempt Restrictions: Where Parties Attempt to Protect Exclusive Territory*

10.80 Article 3(d) excludes the exemption where either the supplier or the dealer hinder other dealers, users or other intermediaries obtaining the contract goods from other dealers inside the EC, or where no alternative sources of supply exist inside the EC from outside the EC.[91] The preamble explains this provision as follows:

[87] para. 31 of the explanatory notice.

[88] Although the phrase "contract goods" is not defined in Reg. 1983/83, in Art. 2(1) Reg. 1984/83 there is a reference to "contract goods or goods which compete with the contract goods", which implies that contract goods are the very goods supplied under the contract.

[89] e.g. a Danish sounding trade mark may confuse users in France; a German sounding trade mark name might confuse UK users. Indeed foreign sounding trade mark names might dissuade domestic purchasers.

[90] e.g. the alternative supplies have slight differences in construction in order to qualify for safety standards in that state. However, the changes mean that they are incompatible with safety or quality control standards in the exclusive dealers own territory.

[91] Thus, if alternative supplies are available within the common market it is only these supplies which must not be hindered. Alternative supplies from outside of the EC *may* be hindered without endangering the block exemption in such circumstances.

> "The parties cannot be allowed to abuse industrial property rights or other rights in order to create absolute territorial protection. This does not prejudice the relationship between competition law and industrial property rights, since the sole object here is to determine the conditions for exemption by category."[92]

10.81 The Commission has stressed in the explanatory notice that block exemption evaporates the moment that either party seeks to block parallel imports into the contract territory. Moreover, the Commission states:

> "Agreements in which the supplier undertakes with the exclusive distributor to prevent his other customers from supplying into the contract territory are ineligible for the block exemption from the outset. This is true even if the parties agree to prevent imports into the Community from third countries. In this case it is immaterial whether or not there are alternative sources of supply in the Community."[93]

10.82 The Commission note two examples of practices which if adopted lead to inapplicability of the exemption. These are:

(i) where one or both of the parties exercises industrial property rights so as to prevent dealers or users from obtaining outside, or from selling in, the contract territory properly marked or otherwise properly marketed contract goods; and
(ii) where one or both of the parties exercise other rights or take other measures so as to prevent dealers or users from obtaining outside, or from selling in, the contract territory contract goods.

10.83 Thus, the enforcement of a trade mark or patent with the improper objective of ensuring, or seeking to ensure, absolute territorial protection is not exempt. In *Hydrotherm* v *Compact*,[94] however, the Court held that the Regulation did *not* exclude from block exemption the case where an industrial property right, e.g. a trade mark, was granted in order simply to allow an otherwise exempt agreement to operate normally. They held further that the exemption applied where the right to use the intellectual property was assigned on terms which raised no doubt that the exclusive dealership was an "open right"(i.e. it did not hinder parallel imports). They continued that the prohibition in Article 3 would only apply:

> "if either the terms of the agreement itself or the actual conduct of the parties suggest that an industrial property right is being exercised abusively in order to create absolute territorial protection. The mere possibility of such use, arising from the fact that the parties have not adopted any express provisions in their agreement, is therefore not a sufficient reason for excluding an agreement from bloc exemption."

10.84 A supplier may assign a mark to dealers to enable them to challenge local infringements. However, the right may *not* be used to hinder parallel imports. Suppliers might consider drafting guidelines for dealers on the valid and invalid use of a mark.

10.85 It is clear that in some circumstances, however, suppliers may take measures to hinder exports by a dealer to another exclusive territory. Under Article 2(2)(c) the supplier may require the dealer to refrain from *actively* selling outside his contract territory (as distinct from just meeting unsolicited orders). Thus, where a dealer goes about actively

92 para. 11.
93 para. 33.
94 Case 170/83 [1984] ECR 2999 [1985] 3 CMLR 224. See, also Case 56 and 58/64 *Consten and Grundig* v *Commission* [1966] CMLR 418; [1966] ECR 299; Case 22/71 *Beguelin Import* v *Import-Export* [1972] CMLR 81, [1971] ECR 949 at p. 961; *Theal-Watts* [1977] CMLR D44; *Garoche* v *Striker Boats (Nederland)* [1974] 1 CMLR 469.

seeking customers outside of his territory then this would constitute a breach of contract justifying the supplier in terminating supplies and rescinding the contract. Provided the supplier acts within the confines of Article 2 he may control the extent to which his dealers supply goods into the territories of other dealers.

8. Article 6: Withdrawal of Exemption from Automatically Exempt Agreements

10.86 Under Article 6 the Commission may withdraw the exemption from an agreement that would otherwise be exempt. This it will do when it discovers an agreement to have anti-competitive consequences. Article 6 gives four examples of situations that might lead to loss of exemption. At the outset it should be stressed that the Commission rarely use this provision. No formal decision has ever been taken withdrawing exemption under this or its predecessor provision in Regulation 67/67/EEC. However, the Commission do use it as a bargaining counter in negotiations to persuade firms to amend and modify their agreements.[95] If the power was used it would require a formal Commission decision to withdraw the exemption. Such a decision must be reasoned and it is subject to judicial review by the Court of Justice under Article 173 EC.[96] Regulation 17/62/EEC (procedure in respect of competition cases) applies and, therefore, the Commission must respect the rights of the defence. They must accordingly issue a statement of objections and permit the parties scope to express their opinions. It is implicit that pending a formal decision an agreement retains its validity. It would be a breach of the principle of *securité juridique*—legal certainty—for a decision withdrawing exemption to operative retroactively.[97] Parties to an agreement threatened by a retroactive decision may appeal under Article 173 EC. As a further ground of appeal it is probably a breach of the principle of "protection de la confiance legitime"—protection of legitimate expectations.[98] Under this principle, Community measures or acts must not violate the legitimate expectations of those concerned unless justified by some overriding public policy consideration.[99] This ground of appeal may be based upon the explanatory notice which, in paragraph 24, expressly states that a formal decision will not have retroactive effect. If the Commission did issue a retroactive decision parties could argue the legitimacy of their agreement relying upon the public statement of the Commission in the explanatory notice.

The situations in which withdrawal of exemption may occur are as follows.

(1) Inter-brand competition weak, Article 6(a)

10.87 Where: "the contract goods are not subject, in the contract territory, to effective competition from identical goods or goods considered by users as equivalent in view of their characteristics, price and intended use." Thus, exemption may be withdrawn if interbrand

[95] Such use was made of the equivalent provision in the Patent block exemption in *Tetra Pak (No. 1)* [1990] 4 CMLR 47.

[96] In Case T-51/89 *Tetra Pak (I)* v *Commission (BTG Licence)* [1990] ECR II-309, [1991] 4 CMLR 334, an appeal against such a decision was heard as part of the appeal against a decision finding Tetra Pak in breach of Art. 86 EC.

[97] See Case 100/63 *Kalsbeek* v *Sociale Verzekeringsbank* [1964] CMLR 548; [1964] ECR 565 at p. 575—in the absence of an unequivocal provision stating otherwise legislation is presumed not to be retroactive. Art. 6 is silent on retroactivity so that the presumption would appear to apply. See also Case 70/72 *Commission* v *Germany* [1973] CMLR 741; [1973] ECR 813 at p. 844 *per* Advocate General Mayras; Case 7/76 *IRCA* [1976] ECR 1213 at p. 1237–9 *per* Advocate General Warner. Furthermore, the Court of Justice has held that retroactivity is unlawful unless a valid reason may be propounded justifying it: *Racke* [1979] 1 CMLR 552; [1979] ECR 69 at para. 20 of the judgment.

[98] See generally Usher, "The influence of national concepts on decisions of the Court of Justice" (1976) ELRev 359.

[99] See, e.g. *Denka* v *EVGF* [1975] 2 CMLR 28, [1975] ECR 421; Case 112/77 *Topfer* v *Commission* [1978] ECR 1019.

competition (i.e. competition between rival manufacturers goods) is weak. This might be the case where oligopolists each operate fairly tightly controlled distribution networks.

(2) Existence of barriers to entry, Article 6(b)

10.88 Where: "access by other suppliers to the different stages of distribution within the contract territory is made difficult to a significant degree". This covers the problem of points of sale foreclosure, i.e. effective dealers being tied into established distribution networks and restrained from carrying the goods of competing supplier. Where a high percentage of the available distributors are foreclosed from rival suppliers an obstacle to the entry of potential suppliers might arise. In other words, the existence of exclusive dealing networks may *per se* constitute an entry barrier. The problem may, in particular, arise where the supplier needs specialised dealers with specific skills in handling and marketing the suppliers goods. Such specialist dealers may not be available in large numbers.

(3) Hindrances to obtaining supplies outside of territory, Article 6(c)

10.89 Where: "for reasons other than those referred to in Article 3(c) and (d) it is not possible for intermediaries or users to obtain supplies of the contract goods from dealers outside the contact territory on the terms there customary." This is a "catch all" provision which operates in the unlikely event that an agreement which hinders parallel imports directly or indirectly should escape Article 3(c) and (d). A possible safeguard against use of this provision may be a clause in the contract whereby the dealer may be required to supply outside of their territories on prices and terms and conditions prevailing *within* their territories taking due account of carriage costs.

(4) Refusal to supply, Article 6(d)

10.90 Where the exclusive dealer: "1. Without any objectively justified reason refuses to supply in the contract territory categories of purchaser who cannot obtain contract goods elsewhere on suitable terms or applies to them differing prices or conditions of sale; 2. Sells the contract goods at excessively high prices" exemption may be withdrawn. This provision provides for withdrawal of exemption where a dealer, who enjoys significant albeit not absolute territorial protection, exploits the economic power his exclusive dealership affords him to the detriment of the consumer or other purchaser. It will be recalled that to justify Article 85(3) EC exemption consumers must obtain a fair share of the resulting benefit of an agreement. If the dealer refuses to supply a final user for no apparent reason, Article 85(3) can hardly be satisfied. If the dealer refuses to supply a customer because he suspects that customer to be a parallel importer who will transport the goods to another territory where they are more expensive and sell them there at a price which undercuts the resident exclusive dealer, then exemption may be withdrawn because the dealer is hindering parallel imports. Such a clause would also probably fail under the test in Article 6(c) above. As regards the second instance specified above, if the dealer prices the goods at an excessively high level, then the Commission may withdraw the exemption if there is no prospect of a parallel importer introducing the contract goods into that territory at a lower price to exert a procompetitive pressure and thereby force the exclusive dealer to reduce his prices.

9. Transitional Periods: Time Limits for Compliance[100]

10.91 Any agreement entered *after* 31 December 1983 must conform to the Regulation if it is to obtain exemption.

[100] Art. 7 of the Regulation.

Any agreement entered *before* 31 December 1983 and which is exempt under Regulation 67/67/EEC, the predecessor to Regulation 1983/83/EEC, is valid up until 31 December 1986. Thus, there was for this category of agreement, a three-year transitional period. After 31 December 1986 all such agreements must comply with Regulation 1983/83/EEC if they are to remain block exempt. Regulation 1983/83/EEC, is to be extended by two years from its original duration, and is to continue in force until 31 December 1999.

10. Excluded Agreements, Beer and Petrol Supply[101]

10.92 Agreements for the resale of drinks (principally beer) or for the resale of petroleum products in petrol stations are excluded from Regulation 1983/83/EEC. Such agreements are expressly covered in Articles 6 to 13 of Regulation 1984/83/EEC. These provisions are examined below

D. The Analysis of Exclusive Distribution Agreements Falling Outside the Block exemption in EC Law

10.93 Where an agreement is not exempt under Regulation 1983/83/EEC it must be notified individually to the Commission if exemption is desired. Parties may consider the points below as a means of assessing the likely attitude of the Commission.

1. Market Structure: Inter-Brand Competition

10.94 Where the supplier is the possessor of economic power then distortions of competition may derive from an exclusive dealing agreement. A supplier who grants a dealer an exclusive right to sell his goods in a widely defined area gives to that dealer a virtual monopoly over the sales of that brand of product. If inter-brand competition is weak (i.e. there are not many rival suppliers) then the exclusive dealer may enjoy considerable autonomy over prices and terms and conditions of trade which may work to the consumer's detriment. Analysis by the Commission will very much focus upon the extent of inter-brand competition. Where this is vigorous and healthy the effectiveness of intra-brand competition (competition between dealers stocking the *same* brand) is not quite so important.[102] For example, if Supplier X grants exclusive dealerships which confer upon the appointee a sole right to supply their national markets, then the Commission will examine the degree of market concentration in each national market and in the whole EC market as an integral part of assessing the effects upon competition. Where the Commission find very little inter-brand rivalry its attitude will be stricter than where there are other effective suppliers to exert competitive pressure on X and his dealers. Inter-brand competition, of course, will not be the sole criterion, it will, none the less be an important one.

[101] Art. 8 of the Regulation.

[102] See e.g. *Mitsui-Bridgestone, Fifteenth Report on Competition Policy* (1985)—agreement whereby supplier had less than 5 per cent of the market insignificant when viewed in the context of a rival supplier who enjoyed an 80 per cent market share. See also the opinion of Advocate General Verloren Van Themaat in *Pronuptia* (Case 161/84) [1986] ECR 353, [1986] 1 CMLR 414 who considered inter-brand competition of great importance in assessing the economic effect of clauses in a franchise agreement; see para. 10.265 for analysis. Though, the Court did not dwell upon the point and concentrated upon a more functional clause by clause analysis.

2. *Foreclosure*

10.95 The foreclosure problem is common to both exclusive dealing *and* purchasing agreements. When a dealer agrees with a supplier to purchase only that supplier's brand of goods for resale then that dealer has been foreclosed as an outlet for other suppliers. Foreclosure is not a problem so long as there exists sufficient dealers of appropriate qualifications to re-sell other suppliers goods. Where, however, the great majority of dealers are locked into a supplier's network and are prohibited from "dualling"— carrying dual brand lines of a product–then prospective manufacturers may experience considerable difficulty in obtaining proper representation or existing manufacturers may experience difficulty in expanding. The problem is exacerbated where a number of competing suppliers operate tight distribution networks. The absence of available dealerships thus operates as a substantial barrier to market entry and expansion. Whether or not dealers are foreclosed will depend upon various factors such as the nature of the product and the structure of the dealership market.[103] Thus, the Commission will consider:

> "the nature and quality, limited or otherwise, of the products covered by the agreement, the position and importance of the grantor and the concessionaire on the market for the products concerned, the isolated nature of the disputed agreement, or, alternatively, its position in a series of agreements, the severity of the clauses intended to protect the exclusive dealership or, alternatively the opportunities allowed for other commercial competitors in the same products by way of parallel exportation and importation."[104]

10.96 A non-technical, non-fungible product may be sold through a wide variety of commercial outlets: if a supplier is refused representation through one type of dealer he may seek representation with other types. Camping equipment may be sold through sports equipment shops, DIY shops, large supermarkets and specialist camping equipment dealers. If the specialists are foreclosed, then the product may be stocked by other non-specialist dealers. Thus, the nature of the product and the nature of the dealership required by the supplier must be considered. If a supplier is unable to find properly qualified representation he may be forced to set up his own distribution network. Very few suppliers have the capital to follow this course of action. Normally, use of dealers is the only means many manufacturers have of selling their goods.

3. *Parallel Imports: Export Bans*

10.97 It is a basic tenet of Commission policy that suppliers may not give to their dealers *absolute* territorial protection. Agreements which seek to prevent the export of goods by the dealer from his territory or which hinder the import of the suppliers goods into an exclusive dealers territory by a third party are always in violation of Article 85(1). EC competition law seeks, as a primary objective, the elimination of trade barriers to the free movement of goods within the EC. The underlying logic is to enable parallel importers to take advantage of price differentials between different states for the same or competing products and thus ensure a genuine single market, the goal of the Treaty of Rome.[105]

[103] See in particular the Court of Justice's discussion of this analysis as it applies to exclusive purchasing agreements in C-234/89 *Delimitis* v *Henninger Brau* [1991] ECR I-935, Case T-7/93 *Langnese-Iglo* v *Commission* [1995] ECR II-1533 (now under appeal as Case C-279/95 P to Court of Justice) and Case T-9/93 *Schöller Lebensmittel* v *Commission* [1995] ECR II-1611, see para. 10.144.

[104] Case 56/65 *Société Technique Minière* v *Maschinenbau Ulm* [1966] CMLR 357; [1966] ECR 235 at p. 250.

[105] Studies commissioned by the Commission indicate that this ideal situation remains some way distant. See, for example, the *Study on Consumer Prices* noted at Annex IVB, para. 37, *Twenty-third Annual Report on*

Artificial barriers, for instance absolute export prohibitions on dealers, erected in the context of distribution agreements are hence prime candidates for challenge by the Commission.[106] Export bans or bans on reimportation may however be legal where applicable to non-EC or EEA states only. None the less such bans may affect trade between the Member States so as to activate Article 85(1) EC if there is a possibility that the product might profitably be reimported to the EC market because, for example, prices on the export market are considerably lower than those on the EC market. Admittedly such cases may be unusual though where the export country is a party to a free trade agreement with the EC it should not be overlooked that the chances of reimport may be increased. Indeed most free trade agreements incorporate provisions analogous to Articles 85 and 86 EC.

10.98 The following less overt hindrances to parallel imports have been attacked by the Commission. It should be understood that the incorporation of any of the clauses below is likely to lead to a strict Commission approach probably involving the imposition of fines upon the supplier *and* the dealer. Indeed Commission policy is strongly in favour of punishing by fine dealers as well as suppliers who accept on contractual clauses which implement export bans.[107]

10.99 It is no defence to state that a restriction on parallel imports was never enforced in practice[108] nor that it was entered into without the company's authority.[109] However, if an ex-

cont.
Competition Policy (1993), reporting significant price differences across the EC as a whole in the consumer electronics market, though also a significant degree of convergence across the German, French and British markets for these products.

[106] See Cases 56, 58/64 *Consten and Grundig* v *Commission* [1966] CMLR 418; [1966] ECR 299; *Du Pont de Nemours Deutschland* [1973] CMLR D226; *Deutsche Philips GmbH* [1973] CMLR D241; *Junghans* [1977] 1 CMLR D82; *Theal-Watts* [1977] 1 CMLR D44; *Gerofabriek* [1977] 1 CMLR D35; *Distillers* [1978] 1 CMLR 400; *Teacher* [1978] 3 CMLR 290. For more recent examples see Polistil *and Arbois* [1984] 2 CMLR 594; *Eughucon* 5 *Thirteenth Report on Competition Policy* (1983) at pp. 79, 80, paras. 107–9; *John Deere* OJ 1985 L35/58 where a fine of ECU2 million was imposed upon the supplier (approx £1.2 million) for enforcing export prohibition clauses in distributorship agreements; *Application of the Federaci* on *Nacional de Cafeteros de Colombia* [1983] 1 CMLR 703.

[107] See e.g. *John Deere* OJ 1985 L35/58 at pp. 63, 64, paras. 35–42: "Dealers which accept contracts containing export bans are also guilty of an infringement and, in the agreements are not notified, they also are liable to fines. However, the contractual export bans in this case are contained in preprinted standard contracts; clearly, therefore, the dealers had not taken the initiative to have the bans included in their contracts and had largely ignored them. Moreover, this is the first such case in the agricultural machinery sector. The Commission feels it appropriate, therefore, not to impose a fine on the dealers in this case" (*ibid.*, at p. 64, para. 42). The supplier was fined ECU2 million. See also, *Sperry New Holland* OJ 1985 1376/21, following the *John Deere* case the Commission imposed a fine of ECU750,000 on a supplier of agricultural machinery who sought in conjunction with dealers to prevent parallel imports. Commenting on the case—(IP (85) 588)— the Commission have warned that in future dealers will incur fines for accepting and/or implementing contractual clauses containing export bans. Further, the Commission expect dealers to notify the Commission of such clauses. Despite the obvious problems of conflict of loyalty this arouses informing the Commission might be the only means of avoiding heavy fines.

[108] Case 277/87 *Sandoz* v *Commission* [1990] ECR 45, the Court of Justice held that an export ban included on invoices was an infringement of Art. 85(1) even though no steps were ever taken to enforce it in practice.In T-77/92 *Parker Pen* v *Commission* [1994] ECR II-549 the Court of First Instance held that the fact that a clause prohibiting exports has not been implemented by the distributor with which it had been agreed, does not prove it has had no effect because "its existence may create a visual and psychological effect which contributes to a partitioning of the market and, accordingly, the fact that a clause which is intended to restrict competition has not been implemented by the contracting parties is not sufficient to remove it from the prohibition in Article 85(1) of the Treaty".

[109] In *Viho/Parker Pen* 1992 OJ L233/27, Parker was fined ECU700,000 and its German distributor ECU400,000 in respect of an export ban included, according to Parker, solely on the initiative of a marketing director acting without proper authority, and only reluctantly complied with by the distributor. Appeals were dismissed in T-77/92 *Parker Pen* v *Commission* [1994] ECR II-549 and T-

port ban is clearly detrimental to a dealer's economic interests and it was agreed to only after strong pressure from the supplier, the Commission may refrain from imposing a fine upon the dealer for breach of Article 85(1).[110]

(1) Unfair competition

10.100 Article 85(1) prohibits threats made to third parties that the parties will invoke national law on unfair competition to prevent them importing into the territory of the contract dealer. Even where parallel imports are discouraged by national law such threats by the parties violate Article 85;[111] Community law is supreme over conflicting domestic law. Other measures taken to remove parallel imports will also be caught. A supplier may not buy up parallel imports to remove them from an exclusive dealer's market.[112]

(2) Concerted pricing practices

10.101 Concertation between suppliers and exclusive dealers aimed at charging higher prices to dealers in areas where the product is cheaper in order to discourage them from exporting will be treated by the Commission as an export ban contrary to Article 85(1). For example, in *Dunlop Slazenger International*[113] the Court of First Instance upheld the Commission's finding that DSI, in concert with its exclusive distributors for Belgium and the Netherlands, had taken pricing measures against Newitt and other dealers in the UK to make their exports to the markets of the other Member States uncompetitive.

(3) Compensatory payments

10.102 Where a supplier stops granting rebates or discounts to dealers who export, this may be treated as an export ban by the Commission depending on the nature of the discount which has been withdrawn. For example, in *Gosme/Martell-DMP*[114] Martell and its exclusive distributor for France, DMP, cooperated to discourage parallel exports by refusing to grant discounts to wholesalers, such as Gosme, where products sold to them by DMP were exported. The Commission found that this was, in substance, an agreement to ban exports contrary to Article 85(1) and that Gosme was a participant in the agreement. The withholding of "automatic" discounts deducted from the invoices was deemed contrary to Article 85(1) whereas the abolition of discounts granted as payment for specific promotional acts was held to be justified.

cont.
66/92 *Herlitz* v*Commission* [1994] ECR II-531, and by the ECJ in C-73/95 P *Viho Europe* v *Commission*, judgment of 24 October 1996.

[110] See *Fisher Price/Quaker Oats-Toyco* 1988 OJ L49/19, [1989] 4 CMLR 513, where the Commission did not fine Toyco for complying with Fisher Price's order not to export its goods from the UK to Ireland since Toyco complied only as a result of Fisher Price's threat to refuse to supply it if it did not comply.

[111] Case 22/71 *Beguelin Import* v *Import and Export Co* [1972] CMLR 81; [1971] ECR 949. See also *AEG Telefunken* Fourth Report on Competition Policy (1974) at para. 106—in principle, national technical safety standards and regulations in the Member State of destination do not justify export prohibitions. See for examples under Art. 86 EC: Case 26/75 *General Motors* v *Commission* [1976] 1 CMLR 95; [1975] ECR 1367—dominant undertaking abused its position by exploiting the statutory monopoly it enjoyed to supply conformity certificates and identity signs in respect of the import of Opel cars into Belgium; *French Mineral Water Companies* Bull EC 4/76 at para. 2111. For an analogous US decision, see *Bunch* v *Artec International Corp* 559 F. Supp. 961 at pp. 971–972 (SDNY 1983).

[112] *Konica* [1988] 4 CMLR 848; *Newitt/Dunlop Slazenger International* OJ 1992 L131/32 at para. 58.

[113] Case T-43/92 *Dunlop Slazenger International Ltd* v *Commission* [1994] ECR II-441.

[114] OJ [1991] L185/23.

10.103 Compensatory payments made by a dealer to another dealer where the former has exported outside of his territory into the territory of the latter may well be treated as equivalent to export bans.[115] The payer is thus penalised for undertaking parallel supply and his goods are made more expensive. Such a system tends to discourage parallel supplies. The rule against compensatory payments is not absolute. Such payments *may* be valid, however, if they form part of a scheme entered into by a number of suppliers who are seeking jointly to compete on the world market with much larger suppliers.[116] It is also justifiable for the dealer to be compensated for sales into his territory by the contract supplier.[117] Further, it is legitimate for one dealer to compensate another dealer for documented expenses and gratuitous after sales services performed by the dealer whose territory has been "breached".[118] Where the supplier appoints a second dealer in an area that had hitherto been reserved for a single dealer (perhaps because the dealer has inadequately exploited the territory in question), the Commission may treat a payment made by the new to the old dealer as compensation and recognition for the efforts the first dealer has made in penetrating the market, i.e. it justifiably prevents the second dealer from free-riding on the marketing efforts of the first dealer.[119] Such payments may be made in lump-sum form provided they are reflective of actual costs and do not seek to provide a cover for a compensation system which inhibits parallel supplies.

(4) Restriction on resale: "cross deliveries" and "skip deliveries"

10.104 There are a number of ways in which a supplier may seek to restrict a distributor's freedom of resale. An absolute restriction on resale will render the agreement different from a distribution agreement as the essence of such an agreement is that goods are supplied for resale.[120] Such a restriction may be caught by Article 85(1). In *Bayo-n-ox*,[121] restriction on resale of animal feedstuff additive was found to be imposed in order to stop buyers selling on to higher priced markets elsewhere in the Community rather than for any safety reason justifiable under Article 85(3), a classic example of dividing the single market.

10.105 A restriction on selling only to certain specified dealers further down the chain of distribution may not be caught by Article 85(1) provided that those dealers are chosen on objectively justifiable criteria.[122] This is summarised in guideline 20 of the Commission Notice on Regulations 1983/83 and 1984/83, which states such clauses are unobjectionable:

> "if admission to the distribution network is based on objective criteria of a qualitative nature relating to the professional qualifications of the owner of the business or his staff or the suitability of his business premises, if the criteria are the same for all potential dealers, and if the criteria are actually applied in a non-discriminatory manner."

[115] *Transocean Marine Paint I* [1967] CMLR D9; *Transocean Marine Paint II* [1974] 1 CMLR D11; *Rank-SOPELEM* [1975] 1 CMLR D72. The exemption for the Transocean Marine Paint Association was renewed again in 1988 for a further 11 years [1989] 4 CMLR 621 by which time the compensation provision had been dropped, but it is not clear if this was under pressure from the Commission.
[116] *Transocean Marine Paint I* (above).
[117] See Art. 2(1) of Reg. 1983/83/EEC OJ 1983 L173/1 and see para. 30 of explanatory notice to Reg. 1983/83/EEC, OJ 1983 C355/7, see p. 442 above.
[118] *Rank-SOPELEM* [1975] 1 CMLR D72.
[119] e.g. *Ivoclar* OJ 1985 1369/1 at para. 22a.
[120] See Art. 1 Reg. 1983/83.
[121] [1990] 4 CMLR 930.
[122] For a full discussion of what constitute objectively justifiable criteria, see paras. 10.348 and following on selective distribution agreements.

10.106 A restriction on selling to another dealer at the same level of distribution is often known as a cross-delivery ban. Cross-delivery bans are usually treated as obstacles to parallel imports. These are bans on a dealer selling to any other dealer (but not non-dealers) at the same level of distribution.[123] The contractual prohibition may extend to bans on cross-deliveries at all levels of distribution.[124] If the ban on cross-deliveries covers only non-dealers (e.g. wholesalers) and allows deliveries to other dealers this is still within Article 85(1) though limited bans of this nature do sometimes obtain exemption under Article 85(3).[125]

10.107 Where prohibitions on "skip deliveries" are concerned (ban on deliveries between general importer and consumer which jump or "skip" over intermediaries, e.g. wholesalers, retailers) the Commission adopts the view that such restrictions are exemptible especially when confined to parties in a single Member State. They confine each party to specific roles in the distribution chain and by enforcing the division of work between the parties seek to guarantee that the distribution system operates effectively.[126] A prohibition on wholesalers supplying private customers, i.e. skipping over retailers is *not* restrictive of competition. Indeed the Commission even consider such a ban pro-competitive on the basis that competition would be distorted if wholesalers whose costs are lower than retailers competed at the retail level.[127] "Reverse" or "back delivery" clauses which bans the dealer from supplying *up* the distributional chain, e.g. retailer to wholesaler, will rarely be tolerated. Such transactions are, by their very nature, abnormal so will only occur where there is good economic reason for them, for example, where it is profitable, due to steep price differentials, for a dealer in one Member State to supply a wholesaler in another. Such transactions are hence, in Commission terms beneficial to the elimination of price differences between Member States. Bans can probably not be justified, as can bans on skip deliveries, by reference to improvements in the distribution system.

(5) Restrictions on the provision of after sales services: guarantees

10.108 This causes problems where a supplier bans dealers from affording services to purchasers of his brand acquired outside of the dealers territory. Thus, if customer X purchases a Ford car in Belgium and, on bringing it back to the UK, discovers that Ford dealers in the UK refuse to provide after sales services or provide them only at discriminatory prices, this will operate as a disincentive to X and other prospective customers from purchasing outside the UK. The Commission requires manufacturers to require their dealers to include parallel imported goods in their customer services and guarantees.[128] Further, it is clear that a supplier who provides a guarantee only to the customers of its exclusive deal-

123 See e.g. *German Spectacle Frames* [1985] 1 CMLR 574 dealers allowed to sell solely to end consumers, i.e. not to other dealers who might parallel import the spectacle frames out of the country. The clause was reinforced by an export ban. The parties modified the clauses so as to comply with Commission objections; *FEDETAB* [1978] 3 CMLR 524 (Commission decision); *Omega* [1970] CMLR D49; *Sperry Rand, Fourth Report on Competition Policy* (1974), para. 104. Even cross-deliveries bans between parties in the *same* Member State may affect trade between the Member States and trigger the prohibition in Art. 85: *Deutsche Philips GmbH* [1973] CMLR D241; *BMW* [1975] 1 CMLR D44; *Gerofabriek* [1977] 1 CMLR D35.

124 e.g. wholesalers—SABA [1976] 1 CMLR D61; *Sperry Rand, Fourth Report on Competition Policy* (1974) at para. 107.

125 See e.g. *Omega* [1970] CMLR D49; BMW [1975] 1 CMLR D44; *SABA* [1976] 1 CMLR D61 (Commission decision).

126 *SABA* (above) and before the Court of Justice—Case 26/76 [1978] 2 CMLR 1; [1977] ECR 1875.

127 *Villeroy and Boch* OJ 1985 1376/15 [1988] 4 CMLR 461 at para. 36.

128 It was thus a condition of exemption for Grundig's selective distribution system, OJ 1994 L20/15, that its warranty terms provided that where a defective item was purchased in another Member State, a consumer could have it repaired in the Member State in which he lived. Grundig has indicated that it will be introducing a comprehensive Europe-wide warranty as a consequence, *Twenty-third Report on Competition Policy* (1993), para. 243.

ers places those dealers at a competitive advantage over parallel importers and, in so doing, infringes Article 85(1) EC.[129]

(6) Monitoring clauses

10.109 Clauses which require dealers to report back to the supplier details of sales and servicing including receipts, invoices, sales-slips, etc.. may be illegal if their purpose is to afford the supplier a means of discouraging the dealer from selling outside of his territory.[130] Thus, if supplier X marks his goods with serial numbers (e.g. 0–10,000 in France; 10,001–20,000 in Germany, etc.) he will be able to monitor the sales patterns of the goods. If a product numbered 11,500 is presented for servicing in France, X will know that it has been sold in France although it was distributed by a German dealer. X may then impose pressure on the German dealer to prevent him exporting to France. Such a system was condemned by the Commission under Article 85(1) in *Newitt/Dunlop Slazenger International.*[131] Monitoring systems designed, however, to enable the supplier to improve the efficiency of his network and which have no connection with the disciplining of maverick dealers are not restrictive of competition.

(6) Restrictions on the dealers freedom to advertise outside of his territory and to actively seek customers

10.110 These are generally exempted. Indeed, such a clause is permitted under Article 2(2)(c) of Regulation 1983/83/EEC (see above). Exemption will never lie, however, where an absolute ban on external sales is imposed; the legal restraint is only on *actively* seeking customers elsewhere. Thus, dealers must remain free to meet unsolicited demands (passive sales). In *ARG/Unipart*[132] the Commission exempted a restriction on Unipart in selecting independently the channels for distribution of spare car parts branded with both parties' marks.

(8) Restriction on resale recommended prices

10.111 A clause requiring a distributor to sell at a particular price will be caught by Article 85(1) and is highly unlikely to be exempted under Article 85(3).[133] This is the case even if national legislation permits resale price maintenance.[134] However, it will be legitimate to rec-

[129] Case 31/85 *ETA* v *DK Investment* [1985] ECR 3933 affirming Case 86/82 *Hasselblad* v *Commission* [1984] 1 CMLR 559; [1984] ECR 883. See further *Zanussi* [1979] 1 CMLR 81; *Moulinex and Bauknecht, Tenth Report on Competition Policy* (1980), pp. 82, 83, para. 121; *Matsusbiia Electrical Trading Company, Twelfth Report on Competition Policy* (1982), pp. 67, 68, paras. 77, 78; *Ford Garantie Deutschland, Thirteenth Report on Competition Policy* (1983), p. 78. *Sony, Seventeenth Report on Competition Policy*, para. 67. See generally *Sixteenth Report on Competition Policy*, para. 56. In *AKZO Coatings, Nineteenth Report on Competition Policy*, para. 45, a supplier of car paint undertook to provide after sales services to all users of its paint in the UK irrespective of place of purchase. The Commission also take a strict view of suppliers who hinder or prevent parallel imports of their own goods by refusing to grant certificates of conformity to the imports where that supplier has a statutory monopoly over the supply of such certificates— see *Derek Merson* v *British Leyland* [1984] 3 CMLR 92 (BL fined £208,000 for breach of Art. 86 EC). See also *Alfa Romeo Cars* [1985] 1 CMLR 481 where, for a similar breach the company was not fined and the case was settled informally.

[130] See *Ford Agricultural* 1993 OJ L20/1, *Twenty-second Report on Competition Policy*, para. 215.

[131] OJ 1992 L131/32.

[132] OJ 1988 L45/34; [1988] 4 CMLR 513.

[133] See paras. 8.169–8.184 for further details.

[134] See Commission decision in *Net Book Agreement* OJ 1989 L22/12, upheld by the Court of First Instance in Case T-66/89 *Publishers' Association* v *Commission* [1992] ECR II-1995. The Court of Justice overturning the Court of First Instance, quashed the decision on different grounds in C-360/92 *Publishers' Association* v *Commission* [1995] ECR I-23. The Net Book Agreement was abandoned on 28 September 1995.

ommend resale prices, provided that there is no underlying concerted practice to enforce such prices.[135]

10.112 Other restrictions on a distributor's ability to deal with goods supplied may be caught by Article 85(1). Although it has been said by the Court that Article 85(1) applies to any clause restricting use of goods supplied,[136] this cannot be applied in the context of a distribution agreement to all restrictions on a distributor, many of which are inherent in the purpose of a distribution network. In particular restrictions on resale to other dealers may be justified.[137] Although specifications relating to how products must be packaged and marked for resale are not usually caught by Article 85(1),[138] some restrictions may be caught if designed to prevent resale as part of a practice of division of the common market. Thus in *Bayer Dental*,[139] a condition of sale preventing the repackaging of dental products was held by the Commission to contravene Article 85(1) because it prevented a purchaser from repackaging and reselling. However, if goods are repackaged, the distributor may be required not to apply, change or delete the supplier's trade mark on the products.[140]

(9) Promotion obligations: stocks, full ranges, advertising

10.113 Restrictions requiring the distributor to hold minimum quantities of stocks of the products, to maintain a full range of the products and to advertise in accordance with the suppliers instructions are not normally caught by Article 85(1).[141] However, it is possible that such obligations could be set at such a level as to preclude a distributor from dealing in competing products: if that were the case, such *de facto* exclusively would be caught by Article 85(1).

(10) Non-competition covenants on distributor

10.114 A restriction on a distributor not to manufacture or distribute products which compete with the contract products will be caught by Article 85(1).[142] Provided that it lasts only for the duration of the distribution agreement, such a clause is likely to be exempted under Article 85(3) as it encourages the distributor to promote the contract products against other brands.[143] If, however, the effect of the exclusivity is such as to foreclose a market to competition to the detriment of consumers, exemption will not be granted.[144]

[135] Case 161/84 *Pronuptia de Paris* v *Schillgaliss* [1986] ECR 353, [1986] 1 CMLR 414, para. 25; this case related to a franchise agreement, for which see Section K below, but it seems that the same principle should apply to a distribution agreement.

[136] Case 319/82 *Société de Vente de Ciments* [1983] ECR 4173, [1985] 1 CMLR 511, para. 6.

[137] See paras. 10.104–10.107.

[138] See Art. 2(3)(b) Reg. 1983/83 and Commission Guideline 19; see further section C.4(5) above.

[139] 1990 OJ L351/46.

[140] *Omega Watches* [1970] CMLR D49, para. 5; *BMW* [1975] 1 CMLR D44, para. 32; but see Case 102/77 *Hoffmann-La Roche* v *Commission* [1978] ECR 1139, [1978] 3 CMLR 217, para. 14, which establishes that trade mark rights may not be validly exercised under Art. 36 EC to prevent repackaging if repackaging cannot adversely affect the nature of the product, the trade mark owner is given notice of the repackaging and the repackaged product states who has carried out the repackaging. See also Case 3/78 *Centrafarm* v *American Home Products* [1978] ECR 1823, [1979] 1 CMLR 326, paras. 11–22 which establishes that goods cannot be repackaged under another trade mark of the original trade mark owners different trade marks are applied to the same product marketed in different Member States, unless the trade mark owner used different marks with the purpose of dividing the common market.

[141] See Art. 2(3) Reg. 1983/83 and Commission Guideline 19; see further para. 10.49.

[142] See Art. 2(2)(a) Reg. 1983/83.

[143] *Goodyear Italiana* [1975] 1 CMLR D31, para. 15.

[144] *Brooke Bond Liebig* [1978] 1 CMLR 116, para. 26; in this case an exclusivity clause in an agreement between a spice producer holding a 39 per cent market share in Belgium and three supermarket chains holding a combined 28 per cent market share was not exempted under Art. 85(3).

10.115 Whereas under the original exclusive distribution block exemption, Regulation 67/67/EEC, a non-competition covenant for up to a year after termination of the agreement was exempted, Regulation 1983/83/EEC only exempts such a restriction for the duration of the agreement. It is unlikely that an exemption would be granted for a post-termination restrictive covenant unless it could be shown to be strictly necessary, for example to protect an intellectual property right or some other right or legitimate interest.[145]

(11) Exploiting legal obstacles to parallel imports

10.116 This may arise in the limited circumstances where traders require a licence in order to import a particular product, if the supplier and exclusive dealer make it more difficult for the licence to be acquired. In *Zera/Montedison*,[146] Montedison, the manufacturer of a chemical herbicide, and Stahler, the company's exclusive distributor in Germany, were held to have concerted to give Stahler absolute territorial protection by making it more difficult for parallel importers to obtain the requisite registration document. In order to sell a herbicide in the EC a registration is necessary in each Member State. A parallel importer would be able to bring the product in Germany provided it could convince customs that the product it is importing corresponds to the formula lodged by the manufacturer with the relevant agency. In order to prevent this happening, Montedison used a different formulation in manufacturing the product in Germany to that used elsewhere and instituted civil proceedings against Zera when it attempted to import the product into Germany. The Commission concluded that this amounted to a ban on parallel imports through product differentiation and held that the grant of absolute territorial protection was "an underlying premise of the exclusive distribution agreement". There was evidence to show that Stahler had taken an active part in the implementation of the agreement to prevent parallel imports, for example, it had discussed the product differentiation with Montedison and even taken part in the court proceedings against Zera. The above decision means that, if they choose to differentiate their products, manufacturers of chemicals and pharmaceuticals it must be objectively necessary to do so. Otherwise, if the Commission can show that the only explanation is to prevent parallel imports, then product differentiation may leave manufacturers open to an action under Article 85(1).

4. The "Free-rider" Problem: Protecting Promotional Investments[147]

10.117 Suppliers of luxury or technically complex goods face a problem if they wish to require dealers to take expensive promotional measures. Parallel importers bringing into the territory the suppliers brand of goods can rely on the contract dealers promotional measures to release him from the obligation to undertake his own promotion: customers may use the facilities available at the contract dealers showroom and, having done the mar-

145 Comparison may be made with Art. 3(1)(c) Reg. 4087/88, the franchising block exemption.

146 [1993] OJ L272/28. See *Twenty-third Report on Competition Policy* (1993), paras. 212 and 242.

147 The literature on the problem is voluminous. See Van Bael, "Heretical reflections on the basic dogma of EC antitrust: single market integration" (1980) *Revue Suisse de Droit International de la Concurrence* 39; Korah, "Goodbye, Red Label: condemnation of dual pricing by distillers" (1978) ELRev 62; Baden Fuller, "Economic issues relating to property rights in trade marks, export bans, differential pricing, restrictions on resale and repackaging" (1981) ELRev 162; Chard, "The economics of the application of Art. 85 to selective distribution systems" (1982) ELRev 83; Gyselen, "Vertical restraints in the distribution process: strength and weakness of the free rider rationale under EC competition law" (1984) CMLRev 647; Comanor, "Vertical price fixing, vertical market restrictions, and the new antitrust policy" (1985) 98 Harvard L Rev 983; Scherer and Ross, *Industrial Market Structure and Economic Performance* (3rd edn. 1991) pp. 550–555; Korah and Rothnie, *op. cit.*, pp. 15–22.

ket research, purchase from the parallel importer who can afford to undercut the dealer. Parallel importers thus take a "free ride" on the backs of the contract dealer. In this situation there is a theoretical conflict which the Commission has not yet fully come to terms with. The free-rider problem raises a possible justification for territorial restrictions and, as such, is of importance to those setting up or running distribution networks.

10.118 *View 1.* The parallel importer (the free-rider) undertakes a valuable service because he fosters the free circulation of the brand of goods thus contributing to market integration. Furthermore, he helps break down price differentials by moving goods from cheap areas into expensive areas undercutting the price there and contributing to the downward movement of prices.

10.119 *View II.* Parallel importers who free-ride are dangerous to integrational forces. By parasitically reaping where they have not sown free-riders reduce the incentive for contract dealers to maintain expensive advertising, display, demonstration, stocking, maintenance and repair facilities. This means that the suppliers goods are not marketed so efficiently and hence ultimately the goods are less competitive.

10.120 View I justifies a strict proscription of measures hindering parallel imports. View II justifies a more relaxed attitude towards some measures hindering parallel imports. What is the attitude of the Commission? It is clear that the Commission are sensitive to the free-rider problem and have on occasion allowed restrictions ostensibly upon its basis.[148] It is arguable upon the basis of these cases, that restrictions justified by reference to the free-rider problem will, in certain narrow and exceptional circumstances, be accepted by the Commission. Thus, where a new manufacturer or a small or medium-sized manufacturer seeks penetration of a market and requires dealers to take expensive promotional steps, then protection against parallel importers may be necessary if effective market penetration is to occur.[149] On this basis territorial restraints may be compatible with market integration theories. However, given the orthodox opposition to territorial restraints, parties relying upon the free rider argument must satisfy the Commission that free riding is a real problem and a serious obstacle to their penetration. Moreover, that any restriction on a dealer selling outside of his territory or supplying anyone likely to parallel import the goods to another dealer's territory, satisfies Article 85(3) EC. Given the opposition to territorial restraints this will be no easy task.[150] Whilst the Commission is unsympathetic to export bans they are more sympathetic to less extreme clauses. For example: clauses giving dealers areas of primary responsibility; clauses preventing the setting up of warehouses or retail outlets outside of the contract territory but which do not prohibit the satisfying of unsolicited orders;[151] compensation clauses providing for payment by the exporting dealer of certain types of compensatory sums to the dealer in whose territory he sells (see above).

[148] See *Transocean Marine Paint I* [1967] CMLR D9; *Rank— SOPELEM* [1975] 1 CMLR D72; *Campari* [1978] 2 CMLR 397; *Distillers*, notice pursuant to Art. 19(3) of Reg. 17/62/EC, OJ 1983 C 245/3.

[149] See for an analogous US case *Donald Rice Tire Co* v *Michelin Tire Corp* 483 F. Supp. 750 at p. 7.57 (D. Md. 1980) where the Court differentiated between a new manufacturer seeking penetration and an old manufacturer with a new product. The latter is not treated as a new entrant.

[150] Case 56, 58/64 *Consten and Grundig* v *Commission* [1966] CMLR 418; [1966] ECR 299 at p. 342: "although competition between producers is generally more noticeable than that between distributors of products of the same make, it does not thereby follow that an agreement tending to restrict the latter kind of competition should escape the prohibition of Article 85(1) merely because it might increase the former."

[151] See Art. 2(2)(c) of Reg. 1983/83/EEC.

E. Exclusive Dealing in UK Law[152]

1. Under the RTPA 1976

10.121 Most exclusive dealing agreements are excluded from the RTPA under Schedule 3(2) of that Act. Where services are concerned Schedule 3(7) is the analogous provision. An agreement so exempt *is* subject to the Competition Act 1980. Agreements caught by Article 85(1) EC and exempt under block exemption Regulation 1983/83/EEC are non-notifiable for the purposes of the RTPA, which therefore only applies to agreements falling outside the block exemption.[153]

10.122 It must be stressed that if an agreement is not drafted so as to benefit from either exemption it must be furnished to the OFT for registration on the Register of Restrictive Trade Practices. Failure to notify in due time means that the restrictions are void and unenforceable.[154] If a dispute between supplier and dealer arises the restrictions are unenforceable in Court and failure to register is a line of defence that either of the parties may raise.[155] Most agreements, if registered, will be suitable for dispensation under section 21(2) RTPA 1976 (for analysis see paras 4.96–4.114).[156] The OFT might require the parties to modify certain clauses though much will depend upon the OFT's assessment of the market. The following are a few pointers:

(a) If inter-brand competition is weak, i.e. the supplier has few real competitors, the OFT will take a stricter line with exclusive territories. They will be keen to ensure that competition within the brand remains keen and dealers of that brand can compete with each other. Accordingly, the OFT might consider whether the dealers exclusive territory is too widely drawn.

(b) Agreements between various dealers of the same brand must be registered under the RTPA. If dealers agree not to compete with each other or fix selling prices there will be very little chance of section 21(2) dispensation.

(c) If suppliers seek to enforce the price at which the dealer sells, this may be in breach of the Resale Prices Act 1976 and no section 21(2) dispensation will lie.

10.123 In assessing a registrable agreement the OFT will not take into account restrictions or terms which are disregardable under Section 9 or 18 RTPA 1976. Though, in furnishing details of the agreement these must be included in the bundle of documents delivered to the OFT.

152 In the common law of restraint of trade the courts have apparently taken the view that exclusive dealing agreements are perfectly reasonable and valid. See *North West Salt* v *Electrolytic Alkali Co* [1914] AC 461; *Boat Showrooms of London* v *Horne Bros* (1980) unreported; *Evans Marshall* v *Bertola* [1973] 1 ALL ER 992. However, exclusive purchasing agreement are in some cases subject to the law of restraint of trade, see, e.g. the solus cases: *Alec Lobb* v *Total Oil* [1985] 1 WLR 173; *Esso Petroleum* v *Harpers Garage (Stockport)* [1968] AC 269.

153 Restrictive Trade Practices (Non-notifiable Agreements) (EC Block Exemption) Order, S.I. 1996 No. 349, issued under section 27A RTPA 1976 (added by section 10 Deregulation and Contracting Out Act 1994).

154 s. 35(1) RTPA 1976.

155 s. 35(2) RTPA 1976. See paras. 5.96–5.97 for details of such cases.

156 See Nos 1727 Register of Restrictive Trade Practices *Debt Collection Services* (1985); No. 5028 Register of Restrictive Trade Practices, *Tamglass OY and Legibus Fortyfour limited*; No. 4890 Register of Restrictive Trade Practices, *Erskin Westayr (Engineering) Limited, Siemens A/S, and, Siemens Limited*; Nos. 4642, 4643, 4644, 4645 and 4886 Register of Restrictive Trade Practices, *Hisex Chickens*, whereby certain hatcheries are given exclusive rights in a defined area to a breed of chicken called Hisex; No. 4887 Register of Restrictive Trade Practice, *Bubble Gum Vending Machines* between three companies two of whom agree not to make retail sales of bubble-gum vending machines in the other's territory apart from the supplying of established customers there.

2. *Under the Resale Prices Act 1976*

10.124 Resale price maintenance is not condemned under the RTPA. Indeed, section 9(3) would allow it. RPM is generally precluded by the Resale Prices Act. However, stipulating a maximum resale price is not prohibited nor is recommending resale prices. Further a supplier can take action under the RPA against a distributor who is using the contract products as loss leaders.[157]

3. *Under the Competition Act 1980*

10.125 Agreements exempt from the RTPA 1976 may be reviewed under the Competition Act 1980 (CA 1980). The criteria for assessment here will not differ significantly from those under the RTPA 1976. However, when assessing the effect of an agreement under this Act, the OFT *will* consider the effects of restrictive clauses that would otherwise have been exempt under the RTPA. Most cases are dealt with informally by the OFT. For example, following initial investigation of a complaint, two suppliers of domestic water tanks abandoned their distribution policy of tying supplies of tanks to purchases of insulation and component parts for those tanks.[158] In another case in which satisfactory assurances were given avoiding the need for formal investigation, a supplier of ventilation equipment ceased requiring its distributors not to deal in competing products.[159] This latter case illustrates that action may be taken under the Competition Act against a restriction which, had it been incorporated in an agreement subject to Article 85(1), could have benefited from the block exemption contained in Regulation 1983/83/EEC.[160] Two cases involving exclusive concessions are of interest here.

10.126 In *British Railway Board*[161] (*Facilities for Car Hire and Advertising of Self-Drive Vehicle Hire at Railway Stations*) British Rail (BRB) granted an exclusive right to Godfrey Davis (Car Hire) Ltd (GD) to operate at British Rail stations. BRB sought to operate a "Rail-Drive Scheme" which coupled rail and road travel facilities together thereby easing the travel burden of passengers who, on arrival at a station, found themselves distant from their destination. GD provided car-hire services at a large number of stations, only about 50 per cent of these were profitable. This was an essential point. The parties argued to the OFT that the potential volume of rail-drive business was inadequate to support more than one national operator profitably. Moreover, they argued that if rival operators were allowed to establish facilities in competition with GD it was likely that they would concentrate on those stations with a relatively high demand for car hire. In such circumstances GD would not be able to maintain the rail-drive scheme since it would not earn sufficient from profitable stations to be able to cross-subsidise the unprofitable stations. Cross-subsidisation between stations was necessary if GD were to be able to provide and maintain services at unprofitable stations.

10.127 In its analysis the OFT, whilst recognising the economic logic of the parties' arguments, was concerned that the system as operated by BRB and GD affected the ability of other car-hirers (e.g. Hertz and Avis) to compete:

> "BRB has a monopoly of the facilities which can be offered to commercial undertakings at railway stations. It is therefore inevitable, given that exclusivity is necessary for BRB's Rail Drive Scheme in its present form, that the current operator should derive advantages

[157] See paras. 8.194–8.200.
[158] DGFT Annual Report 1989, p. 42.
[159] *Roof Units Group*, DGFT Annual Report 1991, p. 36.
[160] See para. 10.42.
[161] 18 May 1983.

over its competitors. In the view of the Office, the various advantages that [GD] obtains are such as to affect the ability of firms other than GD to compete in the relevant market. The arrangements between BRB and GD, which maintain exclusive rights in respect of the provision of self-drive car hire facilities at railway stations, are therefore, anti-competitive."[162]

10.128 However, despite this finding, the OFT concluded that the practice was insignificant in its impact upon competition. The value of the relevant market was assessed at £60 million; the value of trade diverted by the BRB-GD agreement was only £2 million, i.e. about 3–4 per cent of the total market. No reference was thus made to the MMC.

10.129 Before itemising the practical relevances of this case, another case, on similar facts, deserves mention. In *British Airports Authority*[163] (arrangements for the provision of chauffeur-driven car-hire services at Gatwick airport) the Authority granted an exclusive franchise to a single car-hire firm to provide facilities at Gatwick airport. In this case there were no compelling economic arguments such as existed in the British Railways Board case to justify the agreement. Accordingly, it was held to be anti-competitive and suitable for reference to the MMC.

The following important points derive from these cases.

(1) Arguments the OFT may not consider

10.130 The OFT accepts that exclusive dealing may have beneficial consequences. In *British Airports Authority* it listed these advantages:

> "(i) control of the quality and type of goods or services provided, particularly where corporate identity associated with the goods is important;
> (ii) increased operational efficiencies and improved resource allocation arising from, for example, predictability of supply and/or demand or benefits of sale."[164]

However, it continued:

> "It should be noted, however, that these effects, if present, are essentially questions of public interest, and do not bear directly on the question of whether the arrangement is anti-competitive."[165]

Thus, arguments about the economic benefits of an agreement are said to be public interest arguments for the MMC to assess. This cannot be an absolute rule. It must be open to parties to argue for example that the agreement, by enhancing a supplier's distributional system, enhances inter-brand competition and, *a fortiori*, intensifies competition.

(2) Importance of market analysis and inter-brand competition[165a]

10.131 In British Airports Authority the OFT stated:

[162] *ibid.*, at pp. 37, 38, para. 8.14.

[163] 22 February 1984.

[164] *ibid.*, at pp. 41, 42, para. 8.6. But see also, *British Railways Board* (18 May 1983) at p. 38, paras. 8.15, 8. 16 where the OFT appeared to take into account various economic arguments of this nature although they stated, somewhat obliquely, "The Office has not been able to measure the effects of these benefits. The Office considers, however, that they do not bear on the conclusion that there is an anti-competitive practice in terms of the Act."

[165] *ibid.*

[165a] See more generally on this topic OFT Research Paper No 12 on *Vertical Restraints* by Paul Dobson and Michael Waterson (November 1996).

> "Exclusive concessions or franchises are not necessarily anti-competitive. This will depend on the structure of the market in which the restriction on the ability to supply the particular good or service occurs, and a concession is unlikely to be anti-competitive if there is competition in the relevant market (for example if substitutes are available for the particular good or service). Where there is little or no competition in the market, an exclusive concession or franchise is likely to be anti-competitive. In these circumstances the terms and conditions under which the franchise is granted may nevertheless eliminate the effects that might arise from the lack of competition. For example competitive tendering at suitable intervals between parties able to supply the goods or services might eliminate the effects of lack of direct competition in the relevant market.
>
> Alternatively the concession agreement might include controls or conditions aimed at simulating the effect that might be predicted to arise from competition."[166]

10.132 Thus, tolerance by the OFT is likely only where inter-brand competition is strong. Where it is not parties must take special care to avoid anti-competitive effects.[167] The OFT and MMC are keen, for example, that dominant concerns with the capacity to grant exclusive rights should ensure that the contracts they grant are subject to periodic tendering. This is particularly the case in the context of the granting of concessions which of course are not the same as the granting of sole distribution rights. In the latter case it would be unrealistic to expect suppliers to have to renegotiate dealership arrangements every few years.

(3) *De minimis*

10.133 An agreement that, on the face of it, is anti-competitive may, when the market context is considered, turn out to be insignificant. In *British Railways Board* the OFT found that the exclusive right given to GD was anti-competitive. However, the total value of the agreement to GD was small when compared with the total value of the relevant market (about 3–4 per cent). Accordingly, there was no need to refer the agreement to the MMC.[168] The MMC is similarly predisposed to find that *de minimis* restrictions based upon exclusivity are not against the public interest by reason of their small scale.[169]

(4) The importance of market definition

10.134 Parties negotiating with the OFT must analyse with care the relevant market. The wider the market the less important becomes the investigated conduct. In *British Railways Board* it was the relatively wide definition of the relevant market which enabled the OFT to apply the *de minimis* rule and refrain from referring the agreement to the MMC.[170]

166 *ibid.*, at p. 42, para. 8.7. See also, *British Airports Authority* MMC investigation under section 11 Competition Act 1980 (Cmnd 9644, December 1985), pp. 109–111.

167 See e.g. *Book Clubs Exclusive Book Cub Rights*, DGFT Annual Report 1983 at p. 107. The OFT persuaded four major book clubs to voluntarily limit the extent to which they would obtain exclusive book club rights to any title. The OFT were worried that the acquisition of exclusive rights could have resulted in an undue concentration of the more popular and important titles. This would limit the range of books open to smaller book clubs and, moreover, the limited availability would create entry barriers to new firms.

168 18 May 1983 at p. 38, para. 8.17. *De minimis* is not apparently considered a public interest argument.

169 *ibid.*, at p. 37, para. 8.11.

170 See *Films* Cm 2673 (1994), where exclusive distribution of films for cinema performance was found to be anti-competitive, para. 2.25, but not sufficiently widespread to have anything other than a small impact from the perspective of the public interest, para. 2.141 and accordingly no recommendation was made. A similar approach was adopted in *Historical On-Line Database Services*, Cm 2554 (1994).

F. Exclusive Purchasing Agreements in General

10.135 This section examines exclusive purchasing agreements whereby a dealer agrees to purchase his total requirement of a particular product from one supplier. The dealer is *not* given an exclusive territory in which to operate. Also covered, though more briefly, are requirements clauses whereby the dealer agrees to purchase a fixed percentage of his requirements from a supplier.

1. *General Considerations*

(1) Attitude of OFT and EC Commission

10.136 In both jurisdictions exclusive purchasing is recognised as a beneficial contractual relationship and statutory exemptions are provided for agreements satisfying certain criteria. In the UK, exemption is afforded by Schedule 3(2) and (7) RTPA 1976 for goods and services agreements respectively. In EC law, exemption is found in Regulation 1984/83/EEC which applies Article 85(3) to certain categories of exclusive purchasing agreement. Agreements not falling within these exemptions may be given individual clearance by the relevant authorities. In the UK, agreements may obtain individual exemption from reference to the Restrictive Practices Court under section 21(2) RTPA 1976. In the EC the Commission may grant individual exemption under Article 85(3) EC or, more likely, issue a comfort letter stating that the Commission have no objections and are closing the file on the Agreement. It is relevant to note that an agreement exempt under Schedule 3(2) or (7) RTPA 1976 *is* subject to the Competition Act 1980.

(2) Economic arguments in favour of purchasing agreements

10.137 Exclusive purchasing agreements are recognised as having beneficial effects. These are described below.

Exclusive purchasing may lead to distributional improvements. Paragraph 5 of the preamble to Regulation 1984/83/EEC reads:

> "Whereas the exclusive purchasing agreements defined in this Regulation lead in general to an improvement in distribution; whereas they enable the supplier to plan the sales of his goods with greater precision and for a longer period and ensure that the reseller's requirements will be met on a regular basis for the duration of the agreement; whereas this allows the parties to limit the risks to them of variations in market conditions and to lower distribution costs."[171]

10.138 These distributional improvements should be felt by consumers who are able to obtain the contract goods more quickly and more easily. The benefits should be ensured by the intensification of competition that such agreements can lead to. First, the dealer is obliged to concentrate his sales efforts on one brand of goods thereby maximising their sales potential. This enhances competition between different brands of goods. Secondly, exclusive purchasing may be the only means by which a supplier might penetrate a market and compete with other manufacturers already present. Thus exclusive purchasing provides an avenue into a market and increases competition therein. Thirdly, suppliers often contribute to the cost of improving or expanding the distribution network which is, accordingly, rendered more effective.[172]

[171] OJ 1983 1173/5 (30 June 1983).

[172] See *Seventh Report on Competition Policy* (1977), pp. 21–4, paras. 9–16. For an American view see *Standard Oil Co of California* v *US* (1949) 337 US 293 at pp. 306, 307.

(3) Economic arguments against purchasing agreements

10.139 The principal problem in connection with purchasing agreements is "foreclosure". One of the likely effects on competition of exclusive buying requirements is that they may lead to a restriction of competition in that, if a supplier imposes exclusivity on any person, other suppliers and potential customers may be hindered or prevented from competing for that person's custom and part of the market may thus be closed to them. "Foreclosure" thus describes the market whereby appropriate dealers are, by virtue of being tied to specific suppliers, foreclosed from other suppliers who seek representation for their goods. The existence of whole networks of such agreements operated by a number of suppliers may prove an insurmountable barrier to entry to a new manufacturer trying to penetrate a market but who is unable to find suitable dealers. In such cases, it is only if the supplier can afford to set up his own retail network that he may penetrate the market. Few suppliers can afford such an expensive commitment.

A second problem is that purchasing agreements tend to encourage a rigid market structure. Not only do they hinder entry by other firms, they also hinder expansion by existing firms. If dealer X is tied to supplier Y for five years, the other existing suppliers are denied the chance of sales to X for the duration. During that period Y might become less efficient; rivals might become more efficient, yet such changes in efficiency are not reflected in sales to X who is locked-in to an inefficient supplier.

Prices are an ever-present problem. In the example given above Y might be overpriced by comparison to rivals. However, X must still purchase from Y because of the five-year exclusive purchasing tie. Consumers of X will thus suffer because they will not receive the benefits of the lower prices that would have been charged them were X free to switch his suppliers.

G. The Block Exemption for Exclusive Purchasing in EC Law

10.140 Some businessmen and indeed legal advisers have problems in legally differentiating an exclusive dealing from an exclusive purchasing agreement. The essential difference is as follows. In an exclusive dealing contract the dealer is given an exclusive territory in which he alone enjoys the contractual right to sell his supplier's brand of goods. In an exclusive purchasing agreement the dealer is *not* given an exclusive territory; the supplier may enter agreements with as many dealers in a territory as he sees fit. The nub of an exclusive purchasing agreement is that the dealer agrees to take supplies exclusively from a single supplier.

10.141 Exclusive purchasing does not figure largely in international commerce.[173] Where trade between Member States is concerned, it is much more usual to find exclusive distributorship agreements with the dealer possessing an exclusive territory. Where purchasing agreements do exist they tend to be between manufacturers or wholesalers and specific retailers. Such agreements are, it follows, often domestic in character with both parties deriving from the same Member State. However, the Court of Justice has indicated that exclusive purchasing agreements between parties in a single Member State can affect

[173] Since the enactment of Reg. 1984/83, there has only been one reference in the Commission's Annual Reports on Competition Policy to an agreement raising problems under the block exemption which did not relate to the specific issues arising out of either Title II beer-supply, Title III petrol-supply or improve ice cream distribution arrangements; see *Fifteenth Report on Competition Policy* for 1985, para. 19.

trade between the Member States so as to trigger the application of Article 85(1) EC.[174] However, the Court of Justice has stated, in the context of exclusive beer purchase contracts, that a realistic economic and legal analysis must be undertaken before it can be assessed whether an exclusive purchasing agreement is caught by Article 85(1).[175] Beer supply agreements are examined in detail below, but the *Delimitis* case has more general implications for assessing whether exclusive purchasing agreements are caught by Article 85(1) at all.

10.142 *Delimitis* arose out of a contractual dispute over outstanding sums owed by a tenant of licensed premises who in return for being able to rent the bar premises from the brewery had agreed to purchase from it minimum quantities of beer and other related products. The tenant pleaded the invalidity of the agreement under Article 85(2). In answering the questions under the Article 177 reference, the Court gave guidance on assessing whether an exclusive purchasing agreement was caught by Article 85(1). A detailed breakdown of the stages in the analysis are set out at paras. 10.16–10.21 above. Thus five stages are identified. Three of those stages focus on foreclosure created by networks of similar exclusive purchasing agreements in broad terms the analysis is as follows. Is the relevant market foreclosed to actual or potential competitors wishing to enter or increase market share? If the answer to that question is negative, the agreement cannot be caught by Article 85(1). If the answer is positive, a subsequent question is whether the agreement in question contributes significantly to that foreclosure. If it does, then Article 85(1) applies to that agreement. The first question involves an analysis of the relevant market structure. Various factors were identified by the Court in *Delimitis* as relevant to this analysis: does this particular agreement form part of a network of similar agreements having a foreclosing effect?[176] Are there other means for an actual or potential competitor to gain access to the market? The Court referred *inter alia* to the possibilities for setting up sales outlets, purchasing existing sales outlets or using existing wholesalers as a means of market entry.

10.143 The Court also indicated that an analysis is needed as a means of market entry to which extent do the patterns of consumption in the market suggest that there are possibilities for expansion? For example, a rapidly expanding market with many small producers should not pose foreclosure problems whereas a saturated market with only a few large producers to whom consumers show material fidelity would seem to foreclose the possibility of new competition.

10.144 The next question involves analysing the extent to which a particular agreement viewed together with other agreements entered into by that particular supplier contributes to the market foreclosure which must be found under the first question. If the effect of one brewery's agreements is insignificant, then Article 85(1) does not apply regardless of the result of the preceding analysis. There are two alternative ways in which the Court held that significance could be assessed: What position does the brewery hold on the relevant market?

[174] Case 23/67 *Brasserie de Haecht* v *Wilkin (No. 1)* [1978] CMLR 26, [1967] ECR 407; Case 47/76 *De Norre* v *Concordia* [1977] 1 CMLR 378, [1977] ECR 65. This view is confirmed by the Commission in para. 3 of the preamble to Reg. 84/83/EC, OJ 1983 1173/5. See now C-234/89 *Delimitis* v *Henninger Brau* [1991] ECR I-935, [1991] 4 CMLR 329 and applied by the Court of First Instance in T-7/93 *Langnese-Iglo* v *Commission* [1995] ECR II-1533 (now under appeal as Case C-279/95 P to Court of Justice) and T-9/93 *Schöller Lebensmittel* v *Commission* [1995] ECR II-1611; see Korah and Rothnie, *op. cit.*, pp. 159–169.

[175] Case C-234/89 *Delimitis* v *Henninger Brau* [1991] ECR I-935 [1991] 4 CMLR 329 see Korah and Rothnie, *op. cit.*, pp. 159–65; Lasok "Assessing the economic consequences of restrictive agreements: a comment on the *Delimitis* case" [1991] ECLR 194.

[176] Case 23/67 *Brasserie de Haecht* v *Wilkin (No. 1)* [1967] ECR 407; [1978] CMLR 26 identified this factor, but subsequently it has been taken as authority for the proposition that it was the only relevant factor, a misconception which cannot now survive *Delimitis*.

This depends not just on market share for the product but also on the proportion of sales outlets of that type on the relevant market tied to it. What is the duration of the agreement in question? If clearly disproportionately long compared to the market average, then it might have a foreclosing effect as a shorter agreement used by a brewery with larger market shares. The Court of First Instance applied the *Delimitis* test in *Langnese-Iglo* and *Schöller,*[177] disapproving the Commission's failure to use those tests in its decisions in those cases.[178]

1. *Introduction: Interpretation*

10.145 The points concerning interpretation made in respect of Regulation 1983/83/EEC on exclusive dealing above apply, *mutatis mutandis*, to Regulation 1984/83/EEC on exclusive purchasing agreements (see paras. 10.13–10.21).

2. *Article 1: Basic Provision*

10.146 Article 1 of the Regulation reads:

> "Pursuant to Article 85(3) of the Treaty, and subject to the conditions set out in Articles 2 to 5 of this Regulation, it is hereby declared that Article 85(1) of the Treaty shall not apply to agreements to which only two undertakings are party and whereby one party, the reseller, agrees with the other, the supplier, to purchase certain goods specified in the agreement for resale only from the supplier or from a connected undertaking or from another undertaking which the supplier has entrusted with the sale of his goods."

For commentary upon the meaning of: "for resale"; "goods"; "only two undertakings are party"; and, "agreement", see above in respect of Article 1 of Regulation 1983/83/EEC on exclusive dealing. In the discussion below certain other features of Article 1 of Regulation 1984/83/EEC are described.

(1) The exclusive purchasing obligation: the main restriction

10.147 The core of Article 1 permits an agreement involving two parties whereby: "one party, the reseller, agrees with the other, the supplier, to purchase certain goods specified in the agreement for resale only from the supplier or from a connected undertaking or from another undertaking which the supplier has entrusted with the sale of his goods". Thus: a dealer may agree to purchase only from one manufacturer; a wholesaler may agree only to purchase from one manufacturer; a dealer may agree only to purchase from one wholesaler; a dealer may agree with a manufacturer to purchase only from a specified wholesaler.[179]

[177] Case T-7/93 *Langnese-Iglo* v *Commission* [1995] ECR II-1533 (now under appeal as Case C-279/95 P to Court of Justice) and T-9/93 *Schöller Lebensmittel* v *Commission* [1995] ECR II-1611.

[178] *Schöller*, Decision 93/405/EEC, 1993 OJ L183/1, 26 July 1993; [1994] 4 CMLR 51; *Langnese-Iglo*, Decision 93/406/EEC, 1993 OJ L183/19, 26 July 1993; [1994] 4 CMLR 83. It was criticised for failing to apply the *Delimitis* test properly, see Korah [1994] ECLR 171 "Exclusive purchasing obligations: *Mars* v *Langnese and Schöller*". See generally on this topic Robertson and Williams, "An ice cream war: the law and economics of freezer exclusivity I" [1995] ECLR 7.

[179] This raises an interesting question of English contract law. An agreement between a dealer and manufacturer whereby the dealer purchases exclusively from an independent wholesaler will be unenforceable by the wholesaler who will have paid no consideration for the advantage of being the exclusive supplier. If the wholesaler is made a party to the agreement this will be a tripartite agreement whereas the block exemption only allows bipartite agreements. One possible but artificial solution is for the manufacturer to sign the agreements as agent for the wholesaler who will be the principal. This should give the principal the right to enforce the contract. Alternatively, the manufacturer may enforce the contract if the dealer purchases from someone other than the designated supplier thereby breaching the contract.

(2) Exclusive purchase: restriction must be total

10.148 To be exempt there must exist an *exclusive* purchase requirement. The Commission adopts the view that a partial requirement is not exempt.[180] Thus, if X agrees to purchase 80 per cent of his requirement from supplier Y and the remainder from other suppliers, such an agreement would require individual clearance. This might seem a strict approach to adopt. However, it is justified in the preamble to the Regulation on the basis that total exclusivity is necessary to ensure the distributional benefits the agreement may bring: "whereas the appointment of several resellers, who are bound to purchase exclusively from the manufacturer and who take over sales promotion, customer services and carrying of stock, is often the most effective way, and sometimes the only way, for the manufacturer to penetrate a market and compete with other manufacturers also present; whereas this is particularly so in the case of small and medium-sized undertakings ..."[181]

10.149 A less than absolute restriction is thus not exempt. A clause granting the dealer an end of year rebate (fidelity rebate) if he takes 100 per cent of his requirement from a specified supplier is not an absolute restriction, although it might result in a dealer taking all of his supplies from one undertaking. The clause does not *require* exclusivity. In such a case, it would be necessary to argue that the agreement as a whole did not fall within Article 85(1)[182] and therefore did not require either individual or block exemption.

(3) English clauses

10.150 However, the Commission do permit to be incorporated so-called "English clauses" which reserve to the dealer the right to obtain the contract goods (not competing goods) from other suppliers, should these sell at prices which are cheaper or our terms which are more favourable than the main supplier.[183] If the Commission accepts that such a clause is exempt they will presumably further accord exemption to a monitoring or verification clause whereby the dealer is required to notify the main supplier or provide him with copies of receipts, invoices, orders, etc. of purchases from other suppliers of the contract goods.[184]

(4) Release clauses

10.151 Release clauses permitting the dealer to purchase elsewhere should the supplier be "unable" to supply are, in the Commission's view, also exempt.[185] Precisely what is meant by "unable" is unclear. If the supplier is one month late in satisfying the dealer's requirement does this enable the dealer to look to alternative supplies? The answer should depend on the urgency with which the dealer needs supplies. If the supplier cannot meet the full extent of the dealer's needs then presumably this entitles the dealer to look elsewhere.

(5) Brand or denomination mark

10.152 The contract goods must be specified by brand or denomination in the agreement. The Commission consider that such precision is necessary for the agreement to accurately de-

180 para. 35 of the explanatory notice.

181 Though if a dealer must take 60 per cent of his supplies from a main supplier and 40 per cent from a supplier "connected" to the main supplier within the meaning of Art. 4 then exemption presumably remains. The two suppliers are treated as one economic unit.

182 para. 6 and see para. 35 of the explanatory notice.

183 See para. 10.226.

184 But cf. Case 85/76 *Hoffman-La Roche* v *Commission (Vitamins)* [1979] 3 CMLR 211; [1979] ECR 461.

185 Or the manufacturer if the agreement is between the dealer and the manufacturer and the agreement specifies another undertaking as the supplier.

fine the scope of the dealers exclusive purchasing obligation (in Article 1) and of the ban on dealing in competing products (in Article 2 discussed below). It will not be permissible to define contract goods by reference to some price list or other specification outside the actual contract which may then be subsequently amended by one of the parties:[186] the list of contract goods must be defined as at the time of contracting. A certain confusion has arisen as to the meaning of the phrase "brand or denomination", in particular in the context of beer supply agreements. There, it has become common, for brewers to specify in beer supply agreements the beers which are subject to the tie by reference to their type as opposed to their brand. It was supposed that by so doing the brewer was identifying the product subject to the purchasing obligation by reference to the "denomination" i.e. its generic name as required by Regulation 1984/83/EEC and the Commission Notice. However, the Commission has expressed certain (unresolved) reservations about the true meaning of these words. In particular the Commission has suggested that it may be appropriate for suppliers to specify the products the subject of the tie by their brand in order that the supplier may not vary and expand, unilaterally, the scope of the tie by adding or substituting various products within a generic tie but of a different brand. The correct meaning to be attributed to the words "brand or denomination" remains unclear. None the less, it is fair to say that the Brewers Society obtained clarification from the Commission in 1988 that reference to *type*, as opposed to brand, in leases containing beer supply ties, *was* appropriate and compatible with the block exemption.

3. Article 2(1): Permissible Restrictions on Supplier, Non-Competition Clauses

10.153 Article 2(1) permits the supplier to be restrained contractually from distributing the contract goods or goods which compete with the contract goods in the dealer's "principal sales area" and at the dealer's "level of distribution". "Principal sales area" means, according to the Commission, the geographical area covered by the dealers "normal business activity".[187] This is not a very precise test. Many dealers will have a reasonable idea of their catchment area but will probably not be able to define it with precision. It might be prudent to define what is the dealer's principal sales area in the contract. This would bind the supplier (not to sell within it) but would *not*, of course, bind the dealer (not to sell outside it). Any attempt by the supplier to prevent the dealer from selling outside the principal sales area will result in withdrawal of the exemption in Regulation 1984/83/EEC and bring into play Regulation 1983/83/EEC on exclusive dealing. Moreover, while the supplier may be prohibited from selling within the principal sales area, he cannot be prohibited from either appointing other dealers in the area, or supplying dealers outside the area who will import the goods into the area.[188]

10.154 "Level of distribution" in Article 2(1) relates to a permissible obligation on the supplier not to distribute the goods or competing goods at the dealer's level of distribution. The dealer may be a wholesaler or a retailer or even a rival manufacturer in certain narrow circumstances (see Article 3(b) noted below). If the dealer is a wholesaler and a retailer (e.g. the "cash and carry" or "open warehouse" type of sales point) then presumably the supplier may be refrained from selling at both those levels.[189]

186 para. 35 of the explanatory notice.

187 Case 234/89 *Delimitis* v *Henninger Brau* [1991] ECR I-935, [1991] 4 CMLR 329 at para. 36; this related to Title II on beer supply, but the principle is the same.

188 para. 37 of the explanatory notice. See, Korah and Rothnie, *op. cit.*, n. 2 at pp. 181–183 on the meaning of the word "distribute" in the light of the various language versions of the Regulation.

189 *ibid.*

4. *Article 2(2) and (3): Permissible Restrictions on the Dealer*

(1) Article 2(2): non-manufacture or distribution

10.155 Article 2(2) permits a restriction on the dealer from either manufacturing *or* distributing goods which compete with the contract goods. The Commission stressed that the contract goods should be clearly specified by brand or denomination in the agreement so as to clearly delimit the dealers obligations.[190] For a definition of goods which compete reference should be made to Article 3 which speaks of "goods which are considered by users as equivalent in view of their characteristics, price and intended use". This definition has been analysed in respect of Article 3 of Regulation 1983/83/EEC on exclusive dealing and readers should refer to the discussion on that provision above.

(2) Article 2(3)(a): complete ranges of goods

10.156 The supplier may require the dealer "to purchase complete ranges of goods". This is similar to Article 2(3)(a) of Regulation 1983/83/EEC on exclusive dealing. It is implicit here that a "range of goods" means a range of goods which are by their nature or commercial usage connected to each other. If they are not so connected, an agreement requiring a purchaser to take the goods exclusively from one supplier is *not* exempt. This is expressly stated in Article 3(c) (below).[191]

(3) Article 2(3)(b): minimum quantities of goods

10.157 The supplier may require the dealer to "purchase minimum quantities of goods which are subject to the exclusive purchasing obligation". Thus the dealer may be contractually required to take certain quantities of the goods. This may, depending upon the quantities, impose pressure on the dealer to promote those goods vigorously.

(4) Article 2(3)(c): trade marks and packaging

10.158 The wording of Article 2(3)(c) is exactly the same as under Article 2(3)(b) of Regulation 1983/83/EEC on exclusive dealing and reference thereto may be made for commentary.

(5) Article 2(3)(d): measures for promotion of sales

10.159 The wording of Article 2(3)(d) is exactly the same as under Article 2(3)(c) of Regulation 1983/83/EEC on exclusive dealing and reference thereto may be made for commentary.

(6) Other restrictions are not permissible

10.160 As with Regulation 1983/83/EEC on exclusive dealing no other restrictions are allowed other than those stated in the exclusive purchasing Regulation. Paragraph 8 of the preamble states:

> "Whereas this Regulation must define the obligations restricting competition which may be included in an exclusive purchasing agreement; whereas the other restrictions of competition allowed under this Regulation in addition to the exclusive purchasing obligation lead to a clear division of functions between the parties and compel the reseller to concentrate his sales efforts on the contract goods; whereas they are, where they are agreed only for the duration of the agreement, generally necessary in order to attain the improvement in the distribution of goods sought through exclusive purchasing; whereas further restrictive oblig-

[190] In some EC countries, for example Germany, there is statutory regulation of certain forms of commercial activity which prevents such dual functioning.

[191] para. 36 of the explanatory notice.

ations and in particular those which limit the reseller's choice of customers or his freedom to determine his prices and conditions of sale cannot be exempted under this Regulation."

10.161 It may be assumed that a restriction which is not expressly exempted but which is ancillary to, and in reality within the ambit of, another restriction which is expressly exempt, is exempt by analogy. Thus, for example (and assuming it is a restriction at all), it is expressly provided that the dealer may be required to take promotional measures. It should also be permissible to impose on the dealer notification or "reporting back" obligations which do no more than enable the supplier to monitor the effectiveness of the promotional measures. The exception to this, of course, is the exclusivity clause itself. An obligation on the dealer to take less than 100 per cent is *not* exempt under the block exemption although it is a lesser obligation than the 100 per cent requirement.

5. Article 3(a) and (b): Non-Exempt Restrictions: Competing Manufacturers' Agreements

10.162 Article 3(a) provides that no exemption exists for reciprocal exclusive purchasing agreements. Thus if manufacturer X agrees to purchase exclusively from rival manufacturer Y who, in turn, agrees to purchase exclusively from X, the agreement does not earn automatic exemption. Article 3(a) is, *mutatis mutandis*, the same as Article 3(a) of the exclusive dealing Regulation and reference thereto should be made for commentary.

10.163 Article 3(b) provides a limited exemption where one or both of the parties has a total annual turnover of no more than ECU100 million and the agreement is non-reciprocal. For discussion see text on Article 3(b) of the exclusive dealing Regulation. The same applies to the definition of "turnover" in Article 5 and the definition of "connected undertaking" in Article 4.[192]

6. Article 3(c): Non-Exempt Restrictions: Clauses Tying Together Unconnected Goods

10.164 No exemption lies where: "the exclusive purchasing obligation is agreed for more than one type of goods where these are neither by their nature nor according to commercial usage connected to each other."[193] This provision may be seen as a limitation on Article 2(3)(a) discussed above which permits the supplier to require the dealer to take complete ranges of goods.[194] No definition is given of "type of goods". However, the Commission considers three factors, at least, to be relevant. First, the existence of a *technical* relationship may be sought.[195] A technical relationship may exist between a machine, accessories to it and spare parts for it. For example: a stereo system may be linked to tuners and cassette decks of the same brand. It follows that products may be technically related even though alternative products may be used in conjunction with them. Thus, a Sony cassette deck may be used in conjunction with a Hitachi record player.[196] Secondly, the existence of a relationship based upon *commercial* grounds. A commercial nexus may exist

[192] This is confirmed by para. 38 first sentence of the explanatory notice.

[193] paras. 21–23 of the explanatory notice.

[194] This provision follows the pattern of Art. 85(1)(e) EC which prohibits agreements which: "make the conclusion of contracts subject to acceptance by the other parties of supplementary obligations which, by their nature or according to commercial usage, have no connection with the subject of such contracts."

[195] See para. 38 of the explanatory notice.

[196] The "technical relationship" exception has been accepted in US antitrust jurisprudence. See *US* v *Jerrold Electronics Corp* 187 F. Supp. 545 (E.D. Pa. 1960) affirmed *per curiam* (1961) 365 US 567 (television and

between several products used for the same purpose. Thus cassette tapes, records and compact discs are different products, but may be used for the same purpose. Thirdly, the existence of a relationship based upon *trade usage* may be sought. Such a link will be found between different goods that are customarily found together. In determining what is trade usage reference should be made to what is common amongst *all* relevant dealers at the contract dealers level of trade. What is common and usual for the contract dealer need not be common for other dealers. Precisely how common the trade usage must be is not specified. Would a tie-in that was common in a specified region (due to historical custom) but which was rare outside of that region be acceptable? If in doubt, parties should notify the Commission requesting the latter to declare, in a comfort letter, whether its agreement complies with the Regulation. It is understood that the Commission will endeavour to respond rapidly to such requests for guidance.[197] In determining what is common trade usage, note may also be taken of the prevailing situation in other forms of distribution, e.g. in franchise systems.

10.165 Exclusive purchasing agreements covering goods which do not "belong" together can only be exempted by an individual decision.[198]

7. *Article 3(d): Time Limits for Duration of Agreement*

10.166 Article 3(d) provides that no exemption exists where: "the agreement is concluded for an indefinite duration or for a period of more than five years". Where an agreement concerns beer or petroleum products different rules apply, see below. The Commission has stated that agreements which specify a fixed term but which are automatically renewable unless one of the parties gives notice to terminate are considered to have been concluded for an indefinite period,[199] a view which was upheld by the Court of First Instance in *Schöller*.[200] It should be noted that agreements incorporating five-year "break clauses" are exemptible, i.e. a clause providing that the contract shall be renegotiated every five years and that the dealer shall have the right to terminate and seek supplies elsewhere.[201]

8. *Article 14: Withdrawal of Exemption from Automatically Exempt Agreements*

10.167 Article 14 is similar to Article 6 of Regulation 1983/83/EEC on exclusive dealing. It empowers the Commission to withdraw by formal decision the exemption from an agree-

cont.
service and installation contract); *Dehydrating Process Co* v *A.O. Smith Corp.* 292 F. 2d. 653 (14 Cir. 1961) cert. denied, 368 US 931.

197 See para. 22 of the preamble to Reg. 84/83/EEC commented on by White, (1984) ELRev 356 at p. 365.

198 para. 38 of the explanatory notice.

199 *ibid.*, para. 39.

200 Case T-9/93 *Schöller Lebensmittel* v *Commission* [1995] ECR II-1611, paras. 122–124.

201 In *Schöller, Commission's Fifteenth Report on Competition Policy* (1985), para. 19, a standard form exclusive purchasing agreement for ice cream containing provision for it to be terminable on six months' notice after the expiry of an initial two year term and thereafter annually was regarded by the Commission as compatible with Art. 85 and therefore dealt with by way of comfort letter. The crucial extrinsic factors were that the average length of such contracts in practice was three years and only about 30 per cent of the market was foreclosed by contracts of this type entered into either by Scholler or its competitors. The Commission subsequently changed its mind and initiated proceedings against Schöller when presented with evidence by a complainant that the market was foreclosed to new entrants: see *Schöller*, Decision 93/405/EEC, 1993 OJ L183/1, 26 July 1993; [1994] 4 CMLR 51; See also *Langnese-Iglo*, Decision 93/406/EEC, 1993 OJ L183/19, 26 July 1993; [1994] 4 CMLR 83.

ment that is otherwise exempt.[202] The enumeration in Article 14(a)–(c) contains examples only; it is non-exhaustive.

10.168 Article 14(a) is similar to Article 6(a) of Regulation 1983/83/EEC. It allows the Commission to withdraw exemption where the contract goods are not subject "in a substantial part of the Common Market" to effective competitive from competing goods. The Commission is concerned that inter-brand competition should remain effective. The meaning of "in a substantial part of the Common Market" is unclear, although, the phrase only has relevance when the Commission decides to issue a formal decision so that there will be ample scope for parties to present their views on the meaning of the phrase.

10.169 Article 14(b) is similar to Article 6(b) of Regulation 1983/83/EEC, i.e. Commission may withdraw exemption where rival suppliers encounter significant problems of access to suitable dealers. Reference should be made to commentary on the foreclosure argument above. The problem is that the existence of whole networks of exclusive purchasing agreements makes it extra difficult for a new supplier to find and appoint well-qualified dealers, since those that exist may already be tied up in contractual arrangements with suppliers. There is some debate as to when foreclosure is objectionable. Clearly, the Commission may withdraw exemption if it discovers that existing suppliers are using exclusive purchase agreements as a device to keep out new firms. However, if the existence of widespread networks is due entirely to the efficiency of the suppliers already in the market, are those firms to be punished for their efficiency? The argument that any foreclosure effects are entirely due to the efficiency of existing firms may be made to the Commission should the latter threaten withdrawal of exemption.

10.170 Article 14(c)(1) provides for withdrawal of exemption where the supplier "without any objectively justified reason" refuses to supply categories of dealer who cannot obtain the contract brand of goods elsewhere on suitable terms, or can only obtain supplies on discriminatory terms. This provision has a counterpart in Article 6(d)(1) of Regulation 1983/83/EEC and reference thereto may be made for commentary. Article 14(c)(2) provides for withdrawal of exemption where the supplier discriminates more in terms of price or terms and conditions in sales against dealers tied by an exclusive purchase clause than he does when compared to dealers who operate at the same level of distribution as the tied dealers, i.e. the supplier discriminates against the dealer. Could a dealer complain that his supplier was selling to supermarkets cheaper than to him? Almost certainly not. Article 14(2) *permits* discrimination where it is "objectively justified": cheap supplies to a supermarket may well be justified upon the basis of scale economies.

10.171 Article 14 may *not* be used to withdraw block exemption from future agreements.[203]

9. Article 15: Transitional Periods: Time Limits for Compliance

10.172 Under Article 15(1) all agreements which were concluded and which entered into force before 1 January 1984 remained covered by the exemption in Regulation 67/67/EC (the predecessor Regulation) until 31 December 1986. From 1 January 1987 *all* agree-

[202] In the MMC's Report on *The Supply of Beer*, Cm 651 (1989), it was recognised that measures recommended under the fair Trading Act to remedy a complex monopoly situation operating against the public interest might conflict with the block exemption; it was considered that many of the anti-competitive features of the beer supply market in the UK identified in the report would justify the European Commission taking action under Art. 14, but in the event no action has been taken.

[203] Case 234/89 *Delimitis* v *Henninger Brau* [1991] ECR I-935, [1991] 4 CMLR 329; See Lasok "Assessing the economic consequences of restrictive agreements: a comment on the *Delimitis* case" [1991] ECLR 194.

ments seeking block exemption had to comply with the Regulation if automatic exemption was required.

Different rules apply to beer supply and petrol supply agreements.

10. Article 16: No Overlap with the Exclusive Dealing Regulation

10.173 Article 16 provides that Regulation 1984/83/EEC shall not apply where the supplier grants the dealer an exclusive territory and the dealer concludes an exclusive purchasing clause with the supplier. Such contracts are governed by the exclusive dealing Regulation 1983/83/EEC. Exclusive purchasing agreements do not have an exclusive territory.

11. Article 17: Mixed Agreements not Exempt

10.174 Regulation 1984/83/EEC divides into three parts. Part I concerns general agreements; Part II concerns beer supply agreements; Part III concerns petrol supply agreements. An exclusive purchase agreement whose subject matter spans more than one part is not exempt.

12. Exclusive Purchasing and Beer Supply Agreements: Tied Houses, Articles 6–9[204]

10.175 Two sectors of the economy raise particular problems—tied public houses and tied petrol filling stations. Accordingly, these have special rules governing them. Articles 6–9 of Regulation 1984/83/EEC cover beer supply (tied public house) agreements. If a beer supply agreement fits the criteria of the Regulation it need not be notified and it obtains block exemption. Agreements not within the Regulation and caught by Article 85(1) EC may obtain individual blessing from the Commission. Since the Court of Justice's decision in *Delimitis* v *Henninger Brau*,[205] it may be more possible to argue that an agreement falls outside Article 85(1). In order to clarify matters, the Commission has issued a notice setting out criteria on which exclusive beer supply contracts may be considered as of minor importance and thus not caught by Article 85(1).[206] This notice however is plainly adopted on a very cautious basis and many agreements not fitting within its ambit may none the less escape Article 85(1).

In the commentary below, the publican, whether he is a premises owner or tenant or whatever, is described as the "dealer". The explanatory notice goes into considerable depth on some aspects of the beer market. At times the notice appears to lay down rules which are not apparent from the regulation. It is as well to bear in mind that the notice is not binding though no doubt it will be very influential in Commission thinking, and possibly in the thinking of national courts.

[204] The tied public house question raised very considerable interest in the European Parliament. See WQ No. 2363/82, OJ 1983 C279/1; WQ No. 2187/82 OJ 1983 C266/2; WQ No. 2326/82, OJ 1983 C266/4; WQ No. 197/83, OJ 1983 C266/21; WQ No. 1720/84, OJ 198S C85/20. It has also been the subject of a considerable number of informal investigations into complaints by the Commission; see Commission's *Fifteenth Report on Competition Policy* (1985), para. 19; Commission's *Seventeenth Report on Competition Policy* (1987), para. 29; Commission's *Eighteenth Report on Competition Policy* (1988), para. 22. The Commission has indicated that it has not yet taken any steps to review the block exemption's application to tied house agreements, since the block exemption is not to expire until 31 December 1999: see answer to Written Question E-650/94, OJ 1994 C349/41. In the meantime, the OFT has conducted a review of beer prices to tied houses in the UK, but did not find them to be operating anti-competitively.

[205] Case T9/93 *Schöller* v *Commission* [1995] ECR II-1611, 1670, para. 162, 163.

[206] [1992] 4 CMLR 546; see paras. 10.167–10.174.

Finally, it should also be remembered that the provisions of Title IV Articles 14–19 apply to beer supply agreements covered under Title II.[207]

(1) Basic provision

10.176 Article: 6(1) reads:

> "Pursuant to Article 85(3) of the Treaty and subject to Articles 7 to 9 of this Regulation, it is hereby declared that Article 85(1) of the Treaty shall not apply to agreements to which only two undertakings are party and whereby one party, the reseller, agrees with the other, the supplier, in consideration for the according of special commercial or financial advantages, to purchase only from the supplier, an undertaking entrusted by the supplier with the distribution of his goods, certain beers, or certain beers and certain other drinks, specified in the agreement for resale in premises used for the sale and consumption of drinks and designated in the agreement."

10.177 In essence block exemption is given where the dealer, in return for financial or other commercial assistance, accepts an exclusive purchasing obligation.

The beers[208] and other drinks[209] must be specified by brand or denomination in the agreement.[210] The exclusive purchasing agreement can only be imposed on the dealer for drinks which the supplier specifies by brand or denomination at the time the contract takes effect and provided that they are supplied in the required quantities, at sufficiently regular intervals and at prices and on conditions allowing normal sales to the consumer. The Commission considers that an extension of the agreement to cover drinks not specified in the agreement will necessitate the entering of an additional agreement satisfying the terms of the Regulation. However, a change in the brand or denomination of a drink specified in the agreement does not affect the exemption.[211] Similarly, a supplier may conclude an agreement with a dealer with respect to a number of outlets controlled by the dealer. The names of the outlets must be specified in the agreement.

10.178 If the parties subsequently decide to add new premises to the agreement, the extension must be the subject of a new exempt agreement. However, presumably, if the parties decide simply to extend an existing premises or change its address no new agreement is needed. This is not a change materially influencing the scope of the agreement.[212] "Premises" means any premises used for the sale and consumption of drinks. This includes private clubs. However, exclusive purchasing agreements between suppliers and off-licences are governed by the ordinary rules on exclusive purchasing (Articles 1– 5).[213]

207 See sections G.8–11 above and G.12(6) below.

208 Beers includes non-alcoholic beers: *Twenty-first Report on Competition Policy* (1991), para. 115.

209 Other drinks includes the supply of drinks as concentrates or solids for rehydration: *Twenty-first Report on Competition Policy* (1991), para. 116.

210 In Case 234/89 *Delimitis* v *Henninger Brau* [1991] ECR I-935, [1991] 4 CMLR 329 the Court held at para. 36 that this specification could not be by reference to any document, such as a price list, which could be unilaterally changed from time to time by the supplier. In *Re Bass Tenancy Agreement* [1989] 4 CMLR 103, the Commission indicated that it would issue a comfort letter for a tenancy agreement in which beer types were specified and a price list incorporated setting out the specific brands or denominations of those beer types, but whereas the price list was subject to unilateral amendment as to brands or denominations to be supplied, the list of beer types was not. In interlocutory proceedings before the English High Court in *Holleran* v *Thwaites* [1989] 2 CMLR 917, it was held by Peter Gibson J at p. 926 that it was at least arguable that only listing beer *types* in an agreement did not comply with the requirements of the block exemption.

211 para. 40 of the explanatory notice.

212 *ibid.*, at para. 41.

213 *ibid.*, at para. 42.

10.179 "Special commercial or financial advantages" includes, *inter alia*: the grant of loan finance on favourable terms; obtaining for dealers loan finance on favourable terms; the provision of services; equipping dealers with a site or premises for conducting the business; the provision of equipment, fixtures and fittings; the undertaking of investments, e.g. with respect to improvements or extensions of the premises for the dealers benefit, etc.[214] These are only examples. The Commission define "special commercial or financial advantages" as "those going beyond what the [dealer] could normally expect under an agreement".[215] In any given case, the Commission point to the nature, extent and duration of the obligations undertaken by the parties as relevant. Trade usage will also be a very important factor. The rationale for these "special" advantages is as consideration for the tie, i.e. the exclusive purchasing obligation. Article 6 exempts agreements where the dealer contracts with a brewery in respect of specific types of beers and with a wholesaler in respect of beers of other types and/or other drinks. The two agreements may be combined into one document.[216] This extends the exemption to situations whereby the wholesaler is an agent of the supplier or whereby a dealer accredited by the supplier acts as a supplier to the dealer. It also exempts agreements whereby a subsidiary of the supplier acts as a supplier to the dealer. The Commission accepts further that a wholesaler can operate as the main supplier's agent to an extent by concluding the contract with the dealer on the main suppliers behalf as well as concluding a contract with the dealer on his own behalf. The wholesaler may undertake delivery of all the drinks and may also be validly required to make a financial contribution to the dealer.[217]

10.180 Can these various contracts concluded between the three parties be incorporated in a single agreement? Article 6 speaks only of agreements "to which only two undertakings are party". However, if the wholesaler is a subsidiary of or is otherwise "connected"(within the meaning of Article 4 of the Regulation) to the main supplier, then they may be viewed together as a single entity. The Commission seem to consider that the various agreements (dealer/main supplier and dealer/wholesaler) may be incorporated in a single document. If the main supplier and the wholesaler are not connected together then it is probably safest to conclude two separate contracts ensuring that both are exempt under the Regulation. If a question of the interpretation of Article 6 arose before a national court, the Commission's view as expounded in the explanatory notice, whilst persuasive, is not binding on the national court. Consequently, if in doubt compliance with Article 6 may be ensured by drafting two agreements, both of which contain only two parties. Article 6(2) of the Regulation extends Article 6(1) by providing that the latter provision also applies where the exclusive purchase requirement is imposed on the dealer in favour of the supplier "by another undertaking which is itself not a supplier".

10.181 This covers a number of situations. First, as noted above, the exemption extends to a wholesaler who contracts with a dealer on a main supplier's behalf. Secondly, where a supplier affords financial or other assistance to the owner of premises to help in equipping him as a public house or restaurant, etc. and in return the owner imposes on his *tenant* an exclusive purchase obligation in favour of the supplier, then Article 6(2) guarantees block exemption. Thirdly, as in the second example but with the owner imposing the obligation on a successor in title.[218]

214 para. 13 of the preamble.
215 para. 44 of the explanatory notice.
216 *ibid.*, at para. 45. The Commission uses the word "document" not agreement.
217 *Twenty-first Report on Competition Policy* (1991), paras. 117–118.
218 *ibid.*, at para. 45.

(2) Article 7: other permissible restrictions on dealer

10.182 Article 7 is expressed to be exhaustive of the restrictions that may be imposed on the dealer. The imposition of additional restrictions may necessitate the obtaining of individual exemption from the Commission. Though Article 9 does provide that, *inter alia*, Article 2(3) shall apply also. Article 2(3), it will be recalled, covers various additional obligations, for example, advertising and promotion requirements. Article 2(3) has an almost exact counterpart in Article 2(3) of Regulation 1983/83/EEC on exclusive dealing. Commentary on these provisions should suffice for purposes of Article 9 of the Regulation on beer supply agreements.

10.183 Article 7(1)(a) permits the dealer to be restrained from selling competing beers and other drinks which are of the "same type"[219] as those covered by the contract in the premises designated in the contract. The Commission states that this obligation applies only where the supplier is capable of meeting the demand anticipated by the dealer. This expression of Commission policy, though sensible, goes beyond the strict letter of Article 7(1)(a). Article 7(1)(b) entitles the dealer to sell beers of other types in draught form if the other party has tolerated this in the past. If this is not the case the dealer must establish that there is a "sufficient demand" from customers to warrant the sale of other draught beers. The demand will be deemed sufficient in the Commission's view "if it can be satisfied without a drop in sales of the beers specified in the exclusive purchasing agreement. It is definitely not sufficient if sales of the additional draught beer turn out to be so slow that there is a danger of its quality deteriorating. It is for the [dealer] to assess the potential demand of his customers for other types of beer; after all, he bears the risk if his forecasts are wrong."[220] Article 7(1)(b) also permits the supplier to require the dealer to sell competing beers supplied by other undertakings only in bottles, cans or other small packages. Thus speciality beers may be sold but not in a form directly competing with the main suppliers beers.[221]

10.184 Article 7(1)(c) permits the imposition of advertising restrictions on goods supplied by other undertakings within or outside the premises such that they may be advertised "only in proportion to the share of these goods in the total turnover realized in the premises". This enables competing products to be properly marketed in proportion to their importance to the dealer. Advertising for products which the dealer has just begun to sell may not be excluded or unduly impeded.[222] Article 7(2) states: "Beers or other drinks are of different types where they are clearly distinguishable by their composition, appearance or taste".[223] It will be noted that the test is not solely one of consumer preference (i.e. "appearance" to, or "taste" as appreciated by, the consumer). The test is also objective and supply side based in the sense that beers may be differentiated by "composition", i.e. chemical differences.

219 "[S]ame type" is defined in Art. 7(2) as corrected by *Corrigenda* OJ 1983 1281/24 (13 October 1983)) as: "Beers or other drinks are of different types where they are clearly distinguishable by their composition, appearance or taste."

220 para. 48 of the explanatory notice. If a pub is famed for its home-brewed beer or for the beer of a specialised local brewer then customers might consider the existence of these other draught beers as important. The dealer will be able to prove "sufficient demand" in such cases.

221 Pub goers in the UK will appreciate that speciality beers often have a dedicated band of followers. However, they will also appreciate that such beers are usually advertised from the rear or back counter of the bar whereas the main draught beers are sold and advertised from the front or main counter of the bar. A restriction in respect of the advertising of beers which requires the dealer to give preference to the main suppliers beers is exemptible under Art. 7(1)(c).

222 para. 49 of the explanatory notice.

223 *ibid.*, at para. 51. The Commission state, *inter alia*; "In doubtful cases, whether or not two beers are clearly distinguishable by their composition, appearance or taste depends on custom at the place where the public house is situated. The parties may, if they wish, jointly appoint an expert to decide the matter." The definition of beer in Art. 7 has given rise to some judicial mirth, see *Cutsforth* v *Mansfield Inns* [1986] 1 CMLR 1 at p. 9 para. 27 *per* Sir Neil Lawson.

(3) Article 9, application of Article 2(1): restriction on supplier

10.185 Article 9 provides that Article 2(1) applies. This latter provision is discussed at paras. 10.153–10.154 and reference thereto may be made for commentary.

(4) Article 8: situations where no exemption lies (including details of time periods)

10.186 Article 8 withdraws the exemption in a number of situations.

Article 8(1)(a): no exemption lies where the dealer is required to take goods or services other than drinks or services directly connected with the supply of drinks. According to paragraph 51 of the explanatory notice any action, by *whatever* means, by the supplier or person connected to or appointed by him, to pressurise the dealer into accepting unrelated goods or services involves immediate expiry of the exemption. The Commission apparently consider that proof of such pressure would amount to a defence to an action for breach of contract before a national court.

10.187 Article 8(1)(b): no exemption lies where the supplier restricts the freedom of the reseller to obtain from an undertaking of his choice goods or services for which neither an exclusive purchasing obligation nor a ban on dealing in competing products may be imposed. For example, in *Cutsforth* v *Mansfield Inns*[224] C had for some years supplied amusement and prize machines to public houses owned by NCB. In 1985 NCB were purchased by Mansfield Inns (MI) who, in a commercial shake up, sought to provide a new list of approved suppliers who could provide goods and services (including amusement and prize machines and back-up services) to the public houses now owned by them. Without any reasons being given C was excluded from the new list. C successfully sought an *ex parte* interim injunction preventing MI from disturbing the contractual relations between C and tenants and lessees of the public houses. At the inter-partes hearing in the High Court to determine whether the injunction should be continued C contended that the conduct of MI constituted an attempt by a supplier (MI) to restrict the freedom of the reseller (tenants and lessees) to obtain goods and services from an undertaking of their choice (c) and hence the effect of Article 8(1)(b) was to withdraw exemption thereby exposing the restrictions on exclusive purchasing in the tenancy agreement to Article 85 (1) EC. Sir Neil Lawson construed Article 8(1)(b) by reference to the Commission's explanatory notice noting that the Commission expressly referred to the policy of some breweries of restricting the access of resellers to approved suppliers of goods and services such as those relating to gaming machines. The judge continued to note that the Commission's explanatory notice allowed breweries a degree of control over the choice of suppliers where commercially justified by reference to objective criteria of a qualitative nature which were applied uniformly to suppliers of the equipment and without discrimination. In view of these guidelines the judge decided that there was a serious question to be tried and

[224] [1986] 1 CMLR 1. para. 52—the relevant provision in the case—provides for the Commission's policy on amusement machines: "The installation of amusement machines in tenanted public houses may by agreement be made subject to the owner's permission. The owner may refuse permission on the ground that this would impair the character of the premises or he may restrict the tenant to particular types of machines. However, the practice of some owners of tenanted public houses to allow the tenant to conclude contracts for the installation of such machines only with certain undertakings which the owner recommends is, as a rule, incompatible with this Regulation. Such private restrictions affecting the operations of undertakings installing amusement machines are not in breach of Community law, however, if the undertakings are selected on the basis of objective criteria of a qualitative nature that are the same for all potential providers of such equipment and are applied in a non-discriminatory manner. Such criteria may refer to the reliability of the undertaking and its staff and the quality of the services it provides. The supplier may not prevent a public house tenant from purchasing amusement machines rather than renting them."

that (applying the *American Cyanamid* principles for interlocutory injunctions) the injunction should be continued.[225]

10.188 Article 8(1)(c) and (d): no exemption exists where the agreement is concluded for either an indefinite duration or for a period of more than ten years and the agreement relates only to specified beers and other drinks. Where the agreement relates only to specified beers it may last for five years. These time periods do not affect the parties right to renew their agreement.

10.189 Article 8(1)(e): no exemption lies where the dealer is required by the supplier to impose the exclusive purchase tie on his successor in title for a longer period than the dealer would himself have remained tied to the supplier. Thus, restrictions may pass to successors in title but only for the residue of the unexpired time in the original dealer's agreement.

10.190 Article 8(2) covers the situation whereby the supplier leases the premises to the dealer or allows the dealer to occupy the premises upon some other ground.[226]

Article 8(2)(a) and (b): this states that the exclusive purchasing obligation and the ban on holding competing products may be imposed for the duration of the period in which the dealer operates in the premises. Thus, Article 8(1)(c) and (d) do not apply. However, under Article 8(2)(b) the agreement *must* provide for the dealer to have the right to obtain: first, non-beer drinks from other undertakings where these offer them on more favourable conditions than the main supplier does; and secondly, non-beer drinks of the "same type" as those specified under the agreement but which bear different trade marks from other suppliers where the supplier does not offer them.[227] The Commission state that Article 8(2)(b) must be construed in good faith by the parties, i.e. they must abide by the spirit and intent and not the strict letter of the provision.[228] Whether a third party actually does offer more favourable terms under the first category noted above depends primarily upon a comparison of prices. If a more favourable offer is made to the tenant/dealer the Commission states that:

> "he must inform the other party of his intentions without delay so that the other party has an opportunity of matching the terms offered by the third undertaking. If the other party refuses to do so or fails to let the tenant have his decision within a short period, the tenant is entitled to purchase the drinks from the other undertaking".[229]

[225] In *Re Bass Tenancy Agreement* [1989] 4 CMLR 103, the Commission indicated that requiring installation of amusement machines to be subject to the landlord brewer's written consent, even though this was not qualified by any requirement that consent was not to be unreasonably withheld, would be exempt under the block exemption.

[226] It is understood that the provision was the subject of heated argument between the National Union of Licensed Victuallers and the Brewers Society both of whom made repeated, detailed submissions to the Commission during the drafting of the Regulation. See *Carlsberg* OJ 1985, 1207/26 at pp. 30, 31 where the Commission note that in the UK nearly two-thirds of all sales of beer are sold via outlets *owned* by the brewery companies.

[227] See Commission answer to WQ No. 2187/82, OJ 1983 C266/2 at p. 3. The question asked, *inter alia*, the Commission to respond to the assertion "that where tenants are permitted to purchase from independent suppliers, the suppliers are normally required to pay the brewers royalties or other penalties thus increasing the price the ultimate consumer has to pay." The Commission responded, *inter alia*: "Furthermore, the right of the brewer to impose an exclusive tie for beer as well as for other drinks is subject to strict conditions: in the case of loan agreements, the duration of the tie may not exceed five years, the contracts must contain a so-called 'English clause' which enables the tenant to obtain the drinks, other than beer, normally covered by the exclusive purchasing obligation from third parties, if the brewer is not willing or able to supply these products at prices and conditions prevalent on the free market."

[228] para. 54 of the explanatory notice. Though, the duty to inform the main suppliers does *not* apply where the second category of case occurs (i.e. different trade marks)—para. 56 of the explanatory notice.

[229] *ibid.*, at para. 55. In *Re Bass Tenancy Agreement* [1989] 4 CMLR 103, a period of seven working days was indicated by the Commission to be compatible with Art. 85, though no formal decision was taken. It will

10.191 The Commission adds the important rider: "The Commission will ensure that exercise of the right to quote competing prices does not mean that brewers and wholesalers make it significantly harder thereby for other suppliers to have access to the market."[230] The tenant/dealer rights under Article 8(2) override any obligation to purchase minimum quantities imposed under Article 2(3)(b), (see above) to the extent that this is necessary to allow the tenant full exercise of those rights.[231]

(5) Agreements between competing manufacturers

10.192 The general rules in Article 3, 4 and 5 concerning competing manufacturers apply, *mutatis mutandis*, to beer supply agreements., Reference to commentary on those provisions above should therefore be made.[232] For the calculation of turnover, excise and similar duties may be excluded.[233]

(6) Article 15(2) and (3): transitional periods, time limits for compliance

10.193 Article 15(2) and (3) applies to both beer *and* petrol supply agreements. Article 15(2) provides that in the period 1 July 1983 to 31 December 1988, Article 85(1) did *not* apply to agreements which were in force either on 1 July 1983 or were entered into between 1 July 1983 and 31 December 1983. This non-application of Article 85(1) however was dependent on the agreement in question satisfying the conditions for exemption in Regulation 67/67/EEC (the predecessor to Regulation 1983/83/EEC). According to Article 15(3), agreements existing in force on 1 July 1983 and which expired after 31 December 1988 fell outside of Article 85(1) in the period from 1 January 1989 to the expiry of the agreement or 31 December 1999 (the expiry date of the regulation which was extended by two years from its original expiry date) whichever is the earliest. Thus for agreements entered before the date specified a long period of grace is conferred. However, Article 15(3) qualifies the period of grace by conditioning it upon the supplier releasing the reseller before 1 January 1989 from all obligations which are inconsistent with the provisions of Regulation 1984/83/EEC.

Paragraph 64 of the explanatory notice simplifies these somewhat complex provisions:

> "Under Article 15(2), all beer supply and service-station agreements which were concluded and entered into force before 1 January 1984 remain covered by the provisions of Regulation 67/67 until 31 December 1988. From 1 January 1989 they must comply with the provisions of Titles II and III of Regulation 1984/83. Under Article 15(3), in the case of agreements which were in force on 1 July 1983, the same principle applies except that the 10-year maximum duration for such agreements laid down in Article 8(1)(d) and Article 12(1)(c) may be exceeded."

cont.
be noted that the Commission have the power to withdraw exemption by formal decision under Art. 14(b). It is not known what the Commission's attitude will be towards excessive pricing of goods by the supplier as a quid pro quo for not being able to totally control the dealer's business. See for an example WQ 1720/84, OJ 1985 C85/20 (3 April 1985) where it is allegedF that Bass Holdings Ltd imposed surcharges on cases of spirits and wine which, in one instance, led to a sum of £365.50 per annum being added to rent. The MEP asking the question stated that this had been done to recover any losses due to the EC Regulation.

230 *ibid*. See e.g. Case 85/76 *Hoffman-La Roche* v *Commission* 3 CMLR 211; [1979] ECR 461.

231 para. 57 of the explanatory notice.

232 See paras. 6, 7 and 21–23 of the explanatory notice, although it should be borne in mind that this is only the Commission's view. Other commentators have argued that Art. 2(3)(b) overrides Art. 8(2), see Korah and Rothnie, *op. cit*., at p. 230.

233 *Twenty-first Report on Competition Policy* (1991), para. 119.

10.194 The Commission has accounted for the distinction between the three-year period of gracc for ordinary products and the longer periods for beer and petrol in the reply to European Parliament Written Question No. 264/83.[234] In that reply it noted that beer and supply agreements were traditionally of longer duration than for other agreements. It added:

> "With a view to the principle of fairness which exists in the legal systems of all the Member States, as well as in that of the Community, a broader transitional period is justified for such agreements of long duration, as compared to the three-year-period provided in Article 15(1) with respect to other branches of industry, where short-term agreements are the norm."

10.195 Finally on this matter, paragraph 66 of the explanatory notice provides that parties lose the benefit of the transitional provisions is they extend the scope of their agreement as regards persons, places or subject-matter, or incorporate into the agreement new restrictive clauses, such extensions create a *new* agreement which must accordingly comply with the regulation. The same result applies where the parties substantially change the nature or extent of their obligations to one another, for example, by revising the purchase price of goods supplied to the dealer or revising the rent for a public house or service station where such price or rent goes beyond mere adjustment to adapt to a changing economic and commercial environment. Thus changes imposed by the supplier purely to compensate him for amendments to the agreement would entail loss of the benefit of the transitional provisions since such changes are not firmly based in factors such as fluctuations in input costs to the supplier, etc.

(7) Agreements must not be extended during transitional period

10.196 According to paragraph 66 of the explanatory notice partners lose the benefits of the transitional provisions if they extend the scope of their agreements as regards persons, places or subject-matter or incorporate into it additional obligations restrictive of competition. The amended agreement will, in such a case, count as a new agreement, and will have to comply from that date with Regulation 1984/83/EEC. The same applies if the parties substantially change the nature or extent of the obligations to each other. A substantial change in this context includes a revision of purchase price of the goods supplied to the dealer or of the rent for the public house which goes beyond mere adjustment to the changing economic environment. Paragraph 66 applies to both beer supply *and* petrol supply agreements.

(8) *De minimis*: beer supply agreements of minor importance

10.197 Following its 1990 beer market review[235] and the *Delimitis* judgment, the Commission issued a Notice stating which beer supply contracts would be regarded as being of minor importance, hence outside Article 85(1) and so not requiring notification.[236] The Notice is cautious and it is clear that many agreements and networks exceeding the thresholds will fall outside Article 85(1).

10.198 A beer supply contract, whether it be a loan tie or property tie, will fall outside Article 85(1) if three conditions are met. First, the brewery's market share on the national market for the resale of beer in premises (i.e. pubs, hotels, restaurants) is not higher than 1 per cent. Second, the brewery's production must be not more than 200,000 hectolitres

[234] [1990] 4 CMLR 588; see Maitland-Walker "The EEC beer review: much ado about nothing" [1990] ECLR 131.

[235] OJ 1983 C266/25.

[236] [1992] 4 CMLR 546. For the position regarding agreements of minor importance generally, see paras, 6.50–6.55.

per year. Third, the duration of the contract must not, in the case or the exclusive supply of both beer and other drinks, exceed seven and a half years; if the contract is for the exclusive supply of beer only, the permitted duration is a maximum of fifteen years. These conditions will also apply if the contract is negotiated by a wholesaler, the assessment's being carried out in relation to the relevant brewery.

10.199 It is expressly stated that the Notice is without prejudice to the right of national legislation to provide such measures as appear necessary, in accordance with the Commission's policy on subsidiarity.

13. Exclusive Purchasing and Petroleum Supply Agreements: Tied Petrol Filling Stations[237]

10.200 The provisions of Article 10–13 on petrol supply stations follow closely those relating to beer supply agreements. Accordingly, the commentary below will concentrate on those provisions which are different.[238]

(1) Basic provision

10.201 Article 10(1) repeats the wording of Article 6(1) quoted in full above. The only difference is that Article 10(1) concerns "certain petroleum-based motor vehicle and other fuels specified in the agreement for resale in a service station" whereas Article 6(1) concerns "certain beers, or certain beer and certain other drinks, specified in the agreement for resale in premises used for the sale and consumption of drinks". Article 10 can cover either motor vehicle fuels alone, e.g. petrol, diesel, LPG or kerosene, or, motor vehicle fuels *and* other fuels, e.g. heating oil, bottled gas, paraffin, etc. However, all the fuels must be petroleum based. The fuels must be for use in motor-powered land or water vehicles or aircraft. The phrase "service station" is to be construed accordingly. It could, therefore, be a lake side filling station for motor boats or an air strip siting for the refuelling of aircraft. It is the product not the location that counts. The Regulation applies to petrol stations adjoining public roads *and* fuelling installations on private property not open to public traffic.[239]

10.202 Article 10 omits the wording of Article 6(2) however. Thus the situation whereby the exclusive purchasing obligation is imposed on the purchaser by someone who is not a supplier (such as a landlord leasing the property to the purchaser)[240] in favour of a supplier is not exempt under this Title.

(2) Article 11(a)–(d): permissible restrictions on the dealer

10.203 Article 11(a) is essentially the same as Article 7(1)(a) on beer and concerns a ban on the dealer supplying competing goods. Article 11(b) has no counterpart in Article 7. It entitles the supplier to impose an obligation on the dealer, "not to use lubricants or related petroleum-based products[241] within the service station designated in the agreement where the supplier or a connected undertaking has made available to the [dealer], or financed, a lubrication bay or other motor-vehicle lubrication equipment". The Commission takes

[237] See generally, Green, "European Community law and solus sites: the new regulation on exclusive purchasing" [1983] *Oil and Gas Law and Taxation Review* 74.

[238] Although petrol supply stations are often set up under exclusive purchasing arrangements, there are other legal forms which may be suitable, such as franchising agreements: see *Texaco Ltd, Twenty-third Report on Competition Policy*, para. 225.

[239] paras. 58–60 of the explanatory notice.

[240] For analogous examples under Title II, see para. 10.190.

[241] e.g. additives and brake fluids.

the view that such equipment should have a certain value and represent a significant investment, in order to justify this restriction.[242] The provision applies only to the *use* of lubricants and relates to the servicing and maintenance of motor vehicles. It does *not* affect the dealers freedom to purchase the products from other undertakings for *resale* in the service station.[243] Article 11(c) (on advertising) is exactly the same as Article 7(1)(c), reference to that provision should be made for commentary. Article 11(d) has no counterpart in Article 7. It permits the dealer to be required to "have equipment owned by the supplier or a connected undertaking serviced by the supplier or an undertaking designated by him". It should be noted that there is no equivalent to Article 8(2)(b), the English clause provision in relation to non-beer drinks on tenanted premises, and so there is no requirement that the purchaser be entitled to obtain any supplies of contract products even if offered on more favourable conditions.

(3) Article 13: application of Article 2(1): restriction on supplier

10.204 Article 9 provides that Article 2(1) applies. This latter provision is discussed above and reference thereto may be made for commentary.

(4) Article 12: situations where no exemption lies (including details of time periods)

10.205 Article 12 withdraws the exemption in a number of situations.

Article 12(1)(a) and (b): these are analogous to Article 8(1)(a) and (b) to which reference may be made. The provisions prohibit the application of the exclusive purchase tie to products other than motor-vehicle and other fuels. This prohibition does not apply to lubricants or related petroleum-based products (Article 11(b) above) or equipment owned or financed by the supplier (Article 11 (d) above).

10.206 Article 12(1)(c): this provides for time period. It allows exemption only for agreements that are for a period of no more than 10 years.[244] Contracts may be renewed by the parties. At the end of the 10-year period the dealer must have a real option not to renew. If longer ties are sought (and indeed they may well be justified by reference to the amount of the supplier's investment in the dealer) then individual exemption must be sought.

10.207 Article 12(1)(d): this concerns successors in title and the provision is analogous to Article 8(1)(e) and reference thereto may be made.

10.208 Article 12(2): this concerns exclusive purchasing where the supplier owns the service station or otherwise allows the dealer to occupy the premises. In such case the agreement lasts until the dealer no longer operates on the premises.[245]

---

242 *Twenty-first Report on Competition Policy* (1991), para. 120.

243 para. 61 of the explanatory notice. See, for example, *Spanish Service Stations*, *Twenty-third Report on Competition Policy*, para. 226.

244 See for example, *Spanish Service Stations*, *Twenty-third Report on Competition Policy*, para. 226.

245 *Quaere*: if a service station owner leases for 51 years the station to an oil company who then leases the premises back for 21 years, is the original owner who is now a sub-lessee in *occupation* because of the oil company (the supplier) or, is he in occupation in his own right? In *Alec Lobb (Garages) Ltd* v *Total Oil (Great Britain) Ltd* [1985] 1 WLR 173 (CA) noted, Green (1985) *Oil and Gas Law and Taxation Review* 277, the Court held, on facts similar to those above, that an agreement was not void for restraint of trade. The Court seemed to treat the original owner who became a lessee as if he were in occupation as the oil company's tenant. They pointed out that at the end of the agreement the oil company would enjoy a long residual tenancy and in reality the 21-year lease was analogous to a mortgage.

(5) Agreements between competing manufacturers

10.209 The general rules in Articles 3, 4 and 5 concerning competing manufactures apply, *mutatis mutandis*, to motor vehicle fuel supply agreements. Reference to commentary on those provisions above should therefore be made.

(6) Transitional periods: time limits for compliance

10.210 Motor vehicle fuel agreements must abide by precisely the same time constraints as beer supply agreements (see above). Finally, it should also be remembered that the provisions of Title IV Articles 14–19 apply to petrol supply agreements covered under title III.[246]

H. The Negotiation of Exclusive Purchasing Agreements Falling Outside the Block Exemption

10.211 Where an agreement is not exempt under Regulation 1984/83/EEC it may be notified individually to the Commission. Parties may consider the points below as a means of assessing the likely attitude of the Commission.[247]

1. Market Context

10.212 Is the market concentrated? The Commission will be more searching in their analysis under Article 85(3) if the market contains only six major firms with 80 per cent of the total sales between them than if it contains 30 firms none of whom possess more than 2 or 3 per cent of total sales each. The Commission has on occasion employed Article 86 EC on abuse of a dominant position against major companies:

> "An undertaking which is in a dominant position on a market and ties purchasers (even if it does so at their request) by an obligation or promise on their part to obtain all or most of their requirements exclusively from the said undertaking abuses its dominant position within the meaning of Article 86 of the Treaty whether the obligation in question is stipulated without further qualification or whether it is undertaken in consideration of the grant of a rebate."[248]

The imposition of exclusive purchasing by dominant suppliers will therefore only in the most exceptional case be permissible.

10.213 Imposition of exclusive purchasing where the market has only a few dominant suppliers will also be similarly impermissible. In *Schöller*[249] and *Langnese-Iglo*,[250] the Commission condemned exclusive purchasing agreements entered into by each of the two dominant suppliers of ice cream bars with retailers ("outlet exclusivity"), on the basis that this foreclosed entry to other potential competitors, most notably Mars.[251] The Commission also took the view that requiring that ice cream freezers supplied by the dominant supplier in

[246] See paras. 10.167–10.174.

[247] See J.D. Veltrop, "Tying and exclusive purchasing arrangements under EC competition law" (1994) 31 CMLRev 549.

[248] Case 85/76 *Hoffman-La Roche* v *Commission* [1979] 3 CMLR 211 at p. 289; [1979] ECR 461 at p. 539. See also *British Industrial Sand Limited, Sixth Report on Competition Policy* (1976) at paras. 122–125.

[249] 1993 OJ L183/1, [1994] 4 CMLR 51.

[250] 1993 OJ L183/19, [1994] 4 CMLR 83.

[251] The Court of First Instance upheld the Commission's Decisions in T-7/93 *Langnese-Iglo* v *Commission* [1995] ECR II-1533 (now under T-9/93 *Schöller Lebensmittel* v *Commission* [1995] ECR II-1611).

Ireland, Unilever, to be used exclusively for that supplier's products ("freezer exclusivity") could have the same effect as the outlet exclusivity, where it was neither likely that the cabinets would be replaced by the retailer's or another supplier's own nor commercially feasible for additional cabinets to be installed.[252]

10.214 The Court of Justice stated the principles underlying such a market analysis in *Delimitis*:[253] "account must be taken of the conditions under which competitive forces operate on the relevant market. In that connection, it is necessary to know not only the number and size of producers present on the market, but also the degree of saturation of that market and customer fidelity to existing brands, for it is generally more difficult to penetrate a saturated market in which customers are loyal to a small number of large producers than a market in full expansion in which a large number of small producers are operating without any strong brand names".

2. *Foreclosure*

10.215 In *Soda Ash* the Commission commented: "The Commission has established on numerous occasions that the simultaneous existence of such contracts may foreclose competition in respect of a substantial part of the market for the products in question on the various national markets."[254] Elsewhere the Commission has explained that the criteria for exemption under Article 85(3), "are not satisfied if the exclusive arrangements make it more difficult for other firms to sell on the market, and especially if they raise barriers to market entry. In such a case an application for exemption will usually fail, because the agreements will afford the parties the possibility of eliminating competition in respect of a substantial part of the products in question, and this is in direct conflict with Article 85(3)(b)."[255]

10.216 The Court of Justice emphasised in *Delimitis*[256] the importance of assessing whether the market was foreclosed to new entrants by exclusive purchasing agreements: "If an examination of all similar contracts entered into on the relevant market and the other factors relevant to the economic and legal context in which the contract must be examined shows that those agreements do not have the cumulative effect of denying access to that market to new national and foreign competitors, the individual agreements comprising the bundle of agreements cannot be held to restrict competition within the meaning of Article 85(1) of the Treaty." A more detailed analysis of the approach of the Court of Justice for foreclosure is set out at paras. 10.16–10.21.

10.217 Clearly, the extent or "network effect" of exclusive purchase agreements will be influential. The more widespread the clause the more cautious the Commission. As has been explained elsewhere the foreclosure effect will be a central part of Commission analysis. Of course, if there is a horizontal agreement to impose exclusive purchasing obligations

[252] *Van Den Bergh Foods Ltd* OJ 1995 C211/4. See also Commission Press Release IP/95/229. The Commission indicated that it was considering granting an exemption to Unilever to two conditions: first, that it give retailers the choice of buying their freezers free of any financial penalty for doing so and thus escaping the imposition freezer exclusivity, and, secondly, that it cease charging the same price for ice-cream, irrespective of whether a freezer was supplied free of charge, this practice discriminating against those not taking a freezer and having to invest in their own. See the Art. 19(3) Notice, OJ 1995. But see now Press Release IP/97/147.

[253] C-234/89 *Delimitis* v *Henninger Brau* [1991] ECR I-935, [1991] 4 CMLR 329, para. 22.

[254] *Soda Ash, Eleventh Report on Competition Policy* (1981), pp. 53, 54, paras. 73–76, noted also at [1983] FSR 61.

[255] *Seventh Report on Competition Policy* (1977), p. 24, para. 15. See also Commission answer to WQ No. 1049/82, OJ 1982 C312/16.

[256] C-234/89 *Delimitis* v *Henninger Brau* [1991] ECR I-935, [1991] 4 CMLR 329, para. 23.

on distributors then the network effect is likely to be substantial. Such agreements also operate as a device to share the market and will not qualify for exemption. For example, in *IJsselcentrale*[257] the Commission condemned an agreement between the four electricity generating companies in the Netherlands whereby the companies undertook not to export or import electricity and to impose the same import and export bans on their distributors in their supply agreements.

3. *Partial or Total Restraint*

10.218 An important question to ask is whether the clause require dealers to take all, most or merely a small part of his total requirements from the supplier? The higher the percentage of the obligation the greater the extent to which that dealer is foreclosed from rival suppliers who may wish to sell to it. If the dealer is a very important purchaser, e.g. he accounts for 30 per cent of *all* market purchases of the relevant product, a clause tying that dealer to a particular supplier will have a significantly anti-competitive effect on the suppliers market.[258]

10.219 The chance of exemption for a total (100 per cent) requirements clause must be stated to be slim where either party enjoys significant (albeit not dominant) market power. For example, in 1988 following a complaint, the Commission secured amendments to contracts between the Nutrasweet Company on the one hand and Coca-Cola and PepsiCo, on the other, for the supply of the sweetener Aspartame. Nutrasweet is the world's largest producer of Aspartame while Coca-Cola and PepsiCo are, respectively, the largest and second largest purchasers of the sweetener within the EC. The contracts were amended to remove clauses whereby the two companies agreed to buy all their requirements of Aspartame in the EC exclusively from Nutrasweet. Instead the two companies could purchase minimum fixed quantities of Aspartame from Nutrasweet for two years leaving them free to buy the remainder from other suppliers and, thus, avoiding market foreclosure.

10.220 None the less, where parties conclude an agreement which involves an *exclusive* purchasing requirement but which fails to earn block exemption because of some minor divergence from the terms of the Regulation, the Commission are unlikely to object to the exclusivity requirement simply because of the minor divergence. The attitude of the Commission is difficult to predict and much will depend on other market factors. With requirements of less than 100 per cent the chances of exemption obviously increase as the percentage decreases. There is inadequate case law to give indications as to exemptible percentages. In certain cases, the Commission will not allow suppliers to commit their purchasers to buying a fixed percentage of their requirements, whatever the percentage figure is fixed at. For example, the Commission required the world's major producers of industrial gases to amend clauses in their sales contracts for certain gases in order to remove any clauses which committed customers to obtaining all, or a fixed percentage of, their requirements from one supplier.[259]

[257] OJ [1991], L28/32, [1992] 5 CMLR 154..

[258] See *BP Kemi-DDSF* [1979] CMLR 684 at p. 699. See also *Billiton and Metal and Thermit Chemicals, Seventh Report on Competition Policy* (1977), pp. 104, 105, para. 131. Supplier was the largest EC producer of the product; the customer was the largest EC purchaser and took 50 per cent of the supplier's entire output. The significant market power of both parties encouraged the Commission to challenge the agreement (see *ibid.*, at pp. 23, 24 paras. 14, 15). The parties agreed following negotiations to modify their agreement so as to provide for supply on a normal commercial basis involving no restrictions. See also *Prym-Beka* [1973] CMLR D250.

[259] Commission Press Release IP (89) 428. However, in view of the safety arguments put forward by the producers, it was agreed that a supplier may have the exclusive right to fill (but not to supply) and to maintain gas storage tanks, on the understanding that if a customer wishes to have more than one supplier he must have more than one storage tank.

4. *Duration of the Agreement*

10.221 A further important question to ask is as to the duration of the agreement. The longer the duration the greater the length of time the tied up dealer is foreclosed from rival suppliers.[260] For example, the Court of Justice in *Delimitis*[261] stated, in the context of brewery tied house agreements, that "The contribution of the individual contracts entered into by a brewery to the sealing-off of that market also depends on the duration. If the duration is manifestly excessive in relation to the average duration of beer supply agreements generally entered into on the relevant market, the individual contracts falls under the prohibition under Article 85(1). A brewery with a relatively small market share which ties its sales outlets for many years may make as significant a contribution to a sealing off of the market as a brewery in a relatively strong market position which regularly releases sales outlets at shorter intervals". As a rule of thumb, the Commission seem to object to exclusive purchase obligations involving large firms extending for more than a couple of years.[262]

10.222 Longer periods may be justifiable if the supplier accords to the dealer significant commercial and/or financial assistance for example by way of low interest loans, improvement and extension grants, etc. It might be reasonable for a supplier who has invested heavily in a dealer to require that dealer to purchase exclusively from him over an extended period as a means of securing a return on his investment. Where such a case occurs the length of time permissible for the tie will depend not only upon the market context but upon the Commission's assessment of what the supplier fairly deserves in view of his financial commitment to the dealer.[263] Though in *Delimitis* the Commission is recorded as having contended that duration, at least in a beer supply agreement, was not critical. Indeed, in the beer market, long term (20 years) leases are common and have beer welcomed as giving the tenant a greater degree of business security.[264]

5. *Whether Tie Expressed as Fixed Volume or as a Proportion of Dealer's Total Requirements*

10.223 If the clause is expressed simply as a fixed volume, e.g. dealer X will purchase 100 tons of widgets from supplier Y, then the Commission usually refrain from viewing such agreements as falling within Article 85(1). Obviously, any ordinary fixed volume contract excludes rival suppliers to the extent of the purchase. However, that fact alone does not make the agreement anti-competitive.[265] Where a clause, conversely, is expressed as a proportion of the dealer's total requirements and is expressed in terms of time as well, rival suppliers are foreclosed not from a single contractual opportunity but from a portion of the dealer's needs. The Commission have explained the anti-competitive effect as follows:

260 *BP Kemi-DDSF* above at p. 699.

261 C-234/89 *Delimitis* v *Henninger Brau* [1991] ECR I-935, [1991] 4 CMLR 329, para. 26.

262 In *Soda Ash, Seventh Report on Competition Policy* (1977) at p. 54, para. 74 the parties, following negotiations with the Commission, agreed to reduce 5 years agreements to two years. In *Carlsberg* [1985] 1 CMLR 735 the Commission exempted an agreement for eleven years due to the peculiar structure of the UK beer market. The agreement which enabled Carlsberg to more effectively penetrate the UK market enhanced competition with existing firms seven of whom controlled over 80 per cent of the market.

263 e.g. see Commission Press Release IP(89) 428 regarding the amendment of sales contracts for industrial gases, where the Commission stated that, taking into account the high level of investment necessary to make supplies possible, tonnage contracts could be made for fifteen years.

264 Case 234/89 [1991] ECR I-935, 948.

265 See *BP Kemi-DDSF* above at p. 699: "It is true that when any agreement concerning the purchase of a given quantity of a product has been-concluded, other producers of the product in question are excluded to that extent (but no further) from covering the needs of the purchaser, but such producers are able to compete for each such contract before it is signed. This is the result of the normal role of competition which enables the purchaser to decide freely which of the offers is the most attractive when all factors are taken into account."

> "when a purchasing obligation of a longer duration is entered into, the relationship of supply is frozen and the role of offer and demand is eliminated to the disadvantage of inter alia new competitors who are thereby prevented from supplying this customer and old competitors who in the meantime may have become more competitive than the actual supplier."[266]

10.224 However, this is not to encourage the immediate redrafting of contracts from percentages to huge fixed volumes. There is little doubt but that if supplier X wishes to agree an exclusive purchase clause with dealer Y and they calculate together that over the next year Y will need 500 tons of widgets and then, instead of obliging Y to take 100 per cent of his requirements from X they draft a clause obliging Y to take 500 tons of widgets from X, the Commission will assess this on the basis that its *effect* is of an exclusive purchase clause.[267]

6. *Whether Agreement Designed to Allow Market Entry or Expansion*

10.225 Agreements between competing manufacturers may permit one of the parties to penetrate a market he would otherwise have been foreclosed from. X situate in France might need to use Y's distributional network as a channel for his own goods in the UK. In *Carlsberg*,[268] a producer and supplier of lager (Carlsberg) incorporated in Denmark wished to expand sales in response to increased demand in the United Kingdom. Carlsberg entered an agreement with Watney Mann and its parent Grand Metropolitan (GM) which entailed the latter acting as distributor of Carlsberg lager in the UK. Furthermore, they entered a production agreement whereby GM would produce Carlsberg lager under licence in the UK for the UK market. Carlsberg had 14 per cent of the UK lager market. The Commission accepted that a foreign supplier seeking penetration of the UK market would require the assistance of a UK brewer.[269] The Commission accordingly granted exemption for an 11-year period. This would enable Carlsberg to establish and secure production capacity in the UK.[270]

7. *The Inclusion of "English Clauses"*

10.226 In the Commission's view so called "English clauses" are of ambivalent value. Some advisers consider that such a clause will pacify the Commission and keep from them the antitrust bogey. This is not always so. An "English Clause" is a clause entitling a dealer to purchase goods from a rival supplier to the contract supplier where the rival supplier offers them on more favourable terms or the contract supplier is unable to supply or supply in time. The inclusion of a clause drafted along these lines would indeed alleviate many a restrictive agreement.[271] However, such clauses are often linked to other obligations: for example, to a notification clause whereby the dealer must inform the supplier of the

---

[266] *ibid.*

[267] See *British Industrial Sand Limited, Sixth Report on Competition Policy* (1976), paras. 122–125. In *Olivetti/Digital* OJ 1994 L309/24, the Commission held that the obligation on Olivetti to buy large volumes of its requirements from Digital was caught by Art. 85(1), but suitable for exemption under Art. 85(3) since it was part of a joint venture arrangement under which new technology would be more rapidly disseminated into the EC market.

[268] [1985] 1 CMLR 735.

[269] *ibid.*, at p. 740.

[270] *ibid.*, at pp. 749–751.

[271] *per* Advocate General Reischl in Case 85/76 *Hoffman-La Roche* v *Commission* [1979] 3 CMLR 211; [1979] ECR 461. See also Art. 8(2)(a) Reg. 1983/83/EEC, OJ 1983 1173/5 at p. 9 where the Commission recognise the utility of pure English clauses devoid of other limitations.

rival offer and afford the latter the option of meeting that offer or letting it go to the rival.[272] Alternatively, there are strict conditions imposed on acceptance of the rival offer which make its acceptance all but impossible.[273] In *Delimitis*, the Court of Justice considered that a clause allowing a dealer to purchase beer from other Member States would, if it gave a "real possibility" for undertakings in other states to supply that outlet, take an agreement outside Article 85(1). However, other contractual requirements might render such a clause meaning less, for example minimum purchase requirements.[274] Where the supplier is dominant these limitations invariably dissuade the Commission from a sympathetic view of "English Clauses" and turn them into a serious breach of Article 86 EC.[275] In principle a notification clause, such as that described above, enables the contract supplier to monitor his rivals pricing behaviour and enables the contract supplier to regulate the effectiveness of the rival's competitive bidding. Where the supplier is not dominant such clauses are more likely to be suitable for exemption provided the clause provides the supplier with a genuine alternative supply option.

8. Where Both Parties are in the Same Member State

10.227 Where both parties are in the same state there may still be an effect on trade between the Member States such as to trigger the application of Article 85. The Court of Justice's ruling in *Delimitis*[276] gives explicit guidance as to how this is assessed, and is discussed above. An illustration of this approach is practice is seen in *Castrol*[277] where the Commission had to investigate the economic effects of a purely national agreement. The Commission required the parties to submit to them the following data:

(a) the number of exclusive purchasing agreements concluded in the Member State concerned classifying the agreements according to their duration as follows: (a) over 15 years; (b) 10–15 years; (c) 15–10 years; and (d) 0–5 years;
(b) the total turnover of the supplier in the relevant products in the previous financial year;
(c) the share of the turnover in the relevant products, in value *and* percentage terms, which was attributable to business relations with firms obliged to purchase exclusively from the supplier;
(d) the estimated market share of the supplier in the Member State concerned.

[272] See *ibid.*, at [1979] 3 CMLR 211 at p. 294; [1979] ECR 461 at p. 545: "In fact the English clause under which Roche's customers are obliged to inform it of more favourable offers made by competitors together with the particulars above mentioned—so that it will be easy for Roche to identify the competitor—owing to its very nature, places at the disposal of [Roche] information about market conditions and also about the alternatives open to, and the actions of, its competitors which is of great value for the carrying out of its market strategy."

[273] *BP Kemi-DDSF* [1979] 3 CMLR 684—dealer could only accept rival offers if the quantity offered corresponded to the dealers total annual requirement, thus rendering impossible the acceptance of small volume purchases. Furthermore, dealers could only accept such offers from "serious" Western European suppliers.

[274] Case C-234/89 *Delimitis* v *Henninger Brau* [1991] ECR I-935, [1991] 4 CMLR 329, paras. 28–33.

[275] See e.g. Commission Press Release IP (89) 428.

[276] Case C-234/89 *Delimitis* v *Henninger Brau* [1991] ECR I-935, [1991] 4 CMLR 329. See also Case 23/67 *Brasserie de Haecht* v *Wilkin (No. 1)* [1968] CMLR 26.

[277] OJ 1983 L114/26 (29 April 1983).

I. Exclusive Purchasing in UK Law

10.228 Exclusive purchasing agreements are subject to control under both the RTPA 1976, as registrable agreements, and under the Competition Act 1980 (CA 1980). These two provisions are mutually exclusive. If the agreement falls within the RTPA 1976 it cannot be reviewed under the Competition Act 1980. If an agreement falls within the exemption for distribution agreements laid down in Schedule 3(2) RTPA 1976 and is hence excluded from that Act, it thus becomes subject to the CA 1980. As in EC law, there are additional provisions in the beer and petrol sectors. Agreements caught by Article 85(1) EC and exempt under block exemption Regulation 1984/83 are non-notifiable for the purposes of the RTPA, which therefore only applies to agreements falling outside the block exemption.[278]

1. *Under the RTPA 1976*

(1) Schedule 3(2) and (7): exemption from the Act

10.229 Most distribution agreements are exempt under Schedule 3(2) RTPA 1976 (goods). An equivalent exclusion for services is to be found in Schedule 3(7). The provision excludes from the Act bilateral agreements where neither party is a trade association and where the only restrictions imposed are:

> "(a) by the party supplying the goods, in respect of the supply of goods of the same description to other persons;
> (b) by the party acquiring the goods, in respect of the sale, or acquisition for sale, of other goods of the same description."

Exclusive purchasing agreements concern restrictions as in (b) above, i.e. restrictions on the dealer purchasing goods from anyone other than the contract supplier. A wide range of permutations of purchasing clauses are thus excluded. Many other commonly found restrictions are excluded by section 9(3) RTPA 1976: see paras. 1.75–1.86 for details.

10.230 It will be noted that exclusion from the Act only exists where the dealer *resells* the goods.[279] Where the dealer is restrained from own-production the agreement must be registered. In practice suppliers need not insist on such a clause since the dealer may legally be restrained from *selling* goods, including his own, other than the contract supplier's where those goods compete with the suppliers. It follows that the supplier may have to register the agreement if he imposes restrictions on the dealer in respect of the production and/or sale of goods which do not compete with the suppliers goods. However, such a clause should not represent an obstacle to section 21(2) dispensation given that such a clause may be necessary to ensure that the dealer employs best endeavours on the supplier's behalf. Such a clause forces the dealer to focus his attentions.

[278] Restrictive Trade Practices (Non-notifiable Agreements) (EC Block Exemptions) Order, S.I. 1996 No. 349, issued under s. 27A RTPA 1976 (added by section 10 Deregulation and Contracting Out Act 1994). See further paras. 2.250 and following.

[279] For the EC meaning of "resale" see Art. 1, Reg. 1984/83/EEC on block exemption for exclusive purchasing and the explanatory notice issued by the Commission at paras. 9 and 10, OJ 1983 C355/7 at p. 8. This is an important word and defines how much processing or reprocessing a dealer may do before the goods he purchases are transformed into a completely new product and sold anew.

10.231 The phrase "goods of the same description" is taken to imply goods of the same brand *and* goods of competing brands. (See note on meaning of these words in Chapter 2 section I.) The word "sale" is used in preference to the alternative word "supply". The latter word includes, according to section 43(1) RTPA 1976, lease or hire. However, since "sale" is used it cannot be assumed to be identical to "supply". "Sale" thus presumably excludes lease or hire. Though if EC law is used as a guide the word is given a wider meaning under the block exemption.[280]

10.232 An agreement involving a trade association is not excluded and particulars must be furnished. Such an agreement is deemed to include as parties all the members of the trade association and hence cannot be bilateral. Exclusive purchasing agreements have been given section 21(2) dispensation *inter alia* in the context of specialisation agreements. In *Croda-Manox*[281] Croda (c) and Manox (M) were manufacturers of paints and pastes. C agreed with M that C would stop production of "iron blue powder" and would transfer to M all existing know-how and stocks relating to that product. Under the agreement M stopped production of "lake red powder" and, likewise, transferred stocks and know-how to C. The agreement also provided that in future M would purchase its entire requirement of lake red from C and C would purchase its entire requirement of iron-blue from M. These exclusive purchase restrictions were coupled to so called "English clauses". Thus in Clause 2(d) of the transfer agreement of iron-blue from C to M the following clause appeared:

> "Croda undertakes to purchase its total requirements for iron-blue in the UK from Manox provided that Croda shall be released from this undertaking if Croda can demonstrate to Manox that equivalent material is available in comparable quantities on a continuing basis from a third party source at lower prices and Manox is unable to agree to supply at such lower prices or if Manox is unable for any reason to supply for a period of one month."

10.233 The agreement was registrable because it contained restrictions in addition to the purchasing requirements. For Schedule 3(2) to operate, the purchasing obligations must be the sole restrictions in the agreement. In this context there were restraints on both C and M manufacturing the products of which they have transferred stocks and know-how to the other party. Thus there was a clause requiring either party:

> "during the term of this agreement not to manufacture, sell or deal in the UK [the product] whether as principal or agent and in the event of breach of this undertaking to compensate [other party] for any loss of business up to a maximum compensation payment of £150,000 per annum."

This would be a restriction under section 6(1)(d) RTPA 1976 on "the quantities ... of goods to be supplied". None the less, section 21(2) dispensation was given following an analysis of the market by the OFT.

(2) Agreements not exempt

10.234 In practice, very few exclusive purchasing agreements become registrable. Most are drafted to fit within the exemption. Where they are registrable the attitude of the OFT will be similar to that of the EC Commission. The principal concern will lie with the degree to

[280] The word "sale" is implicitly given a wide meaning in Reg. 1984/83/EEC on block exemption for exclusive purchasing. Para. II of the Commission's explanatory notice states: "The hiring out of goods in return for payment comes closer, economically speaking, to a resale of goods than to provision of services. The Commission therefore regards exclusive agreements under which the purchasing party hires out or leases to others the goods supplied to him as covered by the Regulations."

[281] No. 5044 Register of Restrictive Trade Agreements (Agreement dated 1981).

which rival suppliers are foreclosed from the contract dealer. The OFT are concerned that networks of exclusive purchasing agreements may lead to reduced consumer choice as fewer suppliers enter the market and competitive pressures on existing suppliers are hence reduced.[282] Problems are only likely to arise where the parties enjoy significant economic power. The criteria for analysing such contracts may be assumed to be effectively the same as that under the Competition Act 1980.

2. Under the Competition Act 1980

10.235 The approach of the MMC and the OFT towards exclusive purchasing and partial requirements clauses incorporated in contracts where the parties enjoy significant economic power has generally been strict. They have demonstrated a marked concern with the problems of foreclosure. Thus in *Car Parts*[283] in 1982 the MMC in a Report under the FTA 1973 stated:

> "One of the likely effects on competition of exclusive buying requirements is that they may lead to a restriction on competition in that, if a supplier imposes exclusivity on any person, other suppliers and potential customers may be prevented from competing for that person's custom and part of the market may thus be closed to them."[284]

10.236 Exclusive purchasing tended to ossify the market structure:

> "In so far as components manufacturers are prevented by exclusive buying requirements from competing with one another and with car manufacturers and importers to supply part of the market, there is some limitation of the extent to which the most efficient component manufacturers can expand their business at the expense of the less efficient."[285]

10.237 There was, in addition, concern that exclusive purchasing could hinder price competition:

> "We do not suggest that there is no competitive limit to the prices that can be charged to or by franchised outlets, but we do believe that price competition is not fully effective, and that car manufacturers and importers have a substantial element of discretion in the determination of their prices. Since they are virtually the sole suppliers of replacement parts to their franchisees, we think it inherently likely that their prices are in many cases higher than they would be if there were other suppliers to that sector of the market."[286]

10.238 Where exclusive purchasing does not, however, foreclose the potential for rival suppliers to find and appoint suitable dealers, then it will be treated more sympathetically.[287] The OFT may seek the views of rival suppliers and other relevant third parties for their opinion on the availability of dealers. An important consideration will always be whether a product requires specialist dealers to handle it and how extensive the barriers to entry at the dealers level are. The question is: In the absence of other existing dealers can the supplier obtain effective representation without undue difficulty by persuading other resellers to commence stocking his goods? The answer will very much depend upon the nature of the product.

282 See for an analogous case *London Weekend Television Football League*, DGFT Annual Report 1979, p. 46.
283 *Car Parts*, HC 318 (February 1982).
284 *ibid.*, at para. 6.5.
285 *ibid.*, at para. 6.25.
286 *ibid.*, at para. 6.30. See also for back up to the MMC view that exclusive purchasing tends to lead to higher prices, *Prices, Costs and Margins in the Manufacture and Distribution of Car Parts* HC 220, October 1979, Report of the Price Commission, paras. 76 and 99 of summary.
287 See MMC *Report on Liquefied Petroleum Gas* HC 147 (1980–81).

10.239 Duration of agreement is also relevant: in *Petrol*[288] the MMC reluctantly accepted that where a supplier undertakes financial investment in a dealer then a longer term exclusive purchasing obligation may be justified than in cases where the supplier makes no investment in the dealer. The MMC stated that agreements in the petrol supply trade should normally be of no more than five years duration.[289] In other markets the MMC has considered two years to be a sufficient duration for a tie or requirements clause.[290]

10.240 Parties invariably plead improvements in distribution as a positive benefit flowing from exclusive purchasing or partial requirements agreements. The improvements are those described at the beginning of the text on exclusive purchasing above i.e. greater security of supply, economies of scale, improvement in dealers provision of services to customers, reduced costs, etc. The MMC will examine carefully any alleged benefits and whether they are outweighed by the perceived disadvantages. In general disadvantages appear to weigh most heavily. In one case the MMC stated in critical tone that the "system neither promoted efficiency in distribution or stimulated competition".[291] It admitted that the system increased the number of dealers but denied that this meant better service for consumers. The increase in dealerships was, it transpired, not justified by reference to demand. Consequently turnover was low and dealers, to compensate, demanded higher profit margins. Consumers hence did not reap any benefits from the over abundance of dealers.

3. Exclusive Purchasing Agreements and Beer Supply: Tied Houses

10.241 Following the MMC's Report on the Supply of Beer,[292] in which a monopoly situation under the Fair Trading Act 1973 was found to operate against the public interest, the government took steps to reduce the perceived foreclosure of the beer supply on licensed premises market.[293] Under the Loan Ties Order, operators of independent outlets who have borrowed from brewers are given the right to make early repayment. Provision is also made for transparency in pricing, the brewer being required to publish prices charged to tenants, other tied outlets and other purchasers. Moreover, a brewer may not refuse supplies to a reseller of beer, except on specified objective criteria relating to creditworthiness, return of containers and product quality assurance.

10.242 The Tied Estate Order required a brewer interested in more than 2,000 public houses either to cease brewing, to reduce that interest to under 2,000, or to notify tied houses to the OFT and release half their pubs over the 2,000 threshold from exclusive purchasing obligations. In the latter case, such a brewer must permit its tied premises subject to an exclusive purchasing obligation to sell a guest cask conditioned beer and cannot tie purchases of low or non alcohol beers or non-beer drinks. The European Commission has objected to the guest ale provisions of the order on the basis that it affords, in practice, a benefit to UK producers only and thereby infringes Article 30 EC.

288 *A Report on the Supply of Petrol to Retailers in the UK* (1965) Cmnd 264.

289 Petrol supply agreements are considered in more detail at para. 10.243.

290 e.g. *Report on the Supply of Metal Containers* HC 6 (July 1970). MMC objected to contracts of over two years duration under which the purchaser had to take specific quantities of cans from Metal Box, the dominant supplier. The purchasing clause was partial *not* exclusive in this case. But cf. *Alex Lobb* v *Total Oil* [1985] 1 WLR 173 very long-term purchasing obligation reasonable where offset by commercial advantages. Noted, Green (1985) *Oil and Gas Law and Taxation Review* 277.

291 MMC *Report on Wallpaper* (January 1964) HC 59 at para. 174.

292 *The Supply of Beer* Cm 651 (1989).

293 *The Supply of Beer (Loan Ties, Licensed Premises and Wholesale Prices)* Order 1989 (S.I. 1989 No. 2258); *The Supply of Beer (Tied Estate)* Order 1989 (S.I.1989 No. 2390).

4. *Exclusive Purchasing and Petroleum Supply Agreements: Tied Petrol Filling Stations*

10.243 The MMC has reported on petrol supply on a number of occasions, most recently in 1990.[294] In a 1965 report, recommendations were made as to the terms of petrol supply agreements, which led to petrol suppliers negotiating detailed undertakings with the Government.[295] Broadly, their effect is to limit petrol supply agreements to five years in duration, or if a loan is longer, to give a right to the retailer to pay back and terminate the tie after five years; to prevent ties of non-petroleum goods such as tyres, spare parts or accessories, and to impose limits on lengths of leases and rights of pre-emption. The 1990 Report showed that since the 1965 Report there had been a slight reduction in the level of concentration between the major suppliers of petrol; moreover there had been a number of new entrants to the UK market, demonstrating that current arrangements did not lead to foreclosure.

J. Commercial Agents

10.244 Commercial agents are considered, by both the OFT and the Commission, to fall outside of competition rules. A commercial agent is a person who for and on behalf of a principal either: (a) introduces a third party to the principal by soliciting orders from the third party; or (b), concludes contracts on behalf of the principal with the third party. Commercial agents are not independent of the principal (the manufacturer or supplier in the present context) but form an extended arm or quasi-employee of the principal. For this reason they are treated as a single economic entity with the principal.

1. *EC Law*[296]

10.245 It is clear that relations between principal and genuine commercial agent are not caught by Article 85(1). Commercial agency agreements need not be notified to the Commission although, in cases of doubt, parties may request a negative clearance. The Commission, however, will almost certainly seek to settle a case informally without issuing a formal negative clearance. It is clearly important to distinguish a commercial agent from an independent dealer or purchaser and, to this end, it is necessary to look at the Commission Notice on exclusive dealing contracts with commercial agents and recent Court and Commission decisions on the issue.[297]

[294] *The Supply of Petrol* Cm 972 (1990); see previously *Petrol* HCP (1964–65) 264; *Supply of Petrol by Wholesale* Cmnd 7433 (1978).

[295] The undertakings are set out in the MMC report on *The Supply of Petrol* Cm 972 (1990), Appendix 2.2, 328.

[296] B. Van Houtte, "Les contrats d'agence au regard de l'article 85 CEE" [1989] *Cahiers De Droit* 345; Agir pour Le compte D'autrui et Integration Dans Son entreprise; J. Maitland-Walker, "Proposal for a new Commission Notice on Agency Agreements" (1991) ECLR 215; M. Swanson and W. Brown, "Agency agreements: the Commission's new draft notice" [1991] ECLR 82.

[297] Note that a number of aspects of agency law have been harmonised by the Council Directive on Commercial Agents (86/653, OJ [1986] L382/17) which, *inter alia*, offers the agent protection in the form of severance payments and maximum permitted post-termination non-competition obligations. It was implemented in Great Britain by the Commercial Agents (Council Directive) Regulations 1993, S.I. 1993 No. 3053, as amended by the Commercial Agents (Council Directive) (Amendment) Regulations 1995, S.I. 1993 No. 3173, and in Northern Ireland by the Commercial Agents (Council Directive) (Northern Ireland) Regulations 1993, S.I. 1993 No. 483.

(1) Commission Notice on commercial agents

10.246 This Notice was published by the Commission in 1962 its purpose being to set out the criteria the Commission regarded as important in differentiating commercial agents from independent dealers and purchasers. However, it is now under review and an updated version is pending. Thus, although it provides some degree of guidance, it can no longer be regarded as an accurate reflection of the Commission's policy. A summary of it is set out below followed by a summary of the Commission's 1990 Preliminary Draft Notice. It should be noted, however, that even this Draft Notice is, itself, being (seemingly perpetually) revised and is, therefore, also of limited value.

10.247 *The 1962 Notice* The following criteria were considered to be important: Commercial agents do not assume any risk resulting from the transaction, although, they may accept the usual *del credere* obligations;[298] commercial agents do not conduct business on their own behalf; the title given to the representative is immaterial; commercial agents do not keep and are not required to keep as their own property a considerable stock of products covered by the contract; commercial agents do not organise maintain or ensure at their own expense a substantial service to customers free of charge; commercial agents do not determine prices or terms of business.

10.248 *The 1990 Preliminary Draft Notice* Unlike the 1962 Notice this Draft Notice does not point to the assumption of financial risk as being the decisive criterion. Instead, the Commission states that, in order to qualify as an agent, the representative must not assume the "primary responsibility" for the performance of the transaction by his principal, although the Commission recognises that the agent's remuneration may vary according to the outcome. Not all such agents will be outside Article 85(1). In order to qualify as an "integrated agent" and, thus, fall outside the competition rules, the Commission has taken the view that any outside interests the representative has must (i) be limited, and (ii) not interfere with the subject matter of the agency agreement. These two conditions are expanded upon as follows: (i) The business of the commercial agent under the agency agreement should account for at least one third of his activity; in the case of particularly large undertakings this share may be lower; (ii) outside interests will normally interfere with the subject matter of the agency agreement where they may conflict with the duty of loyalty of the commercial agent under that agreement. This will be the case, for example, where the commercial agent carries competing product ranges.

10.249 *The case law* In order to be sure that a representative will be considered an agent and not an independent trader, it is important to have regard to the case law on the matter. Recently the case law has indicated a shift away from the issue of risk allocation; it now seems that, irrespective of risk, an agent may in some circumstances be held to be sufficiently in-

[298] The *del credere* is a contractual promise by the agent to indemnify the principal should he suffer a loss as the result of the failure of a customer, introduced by the agent, to pay the purchase price. The *del credere* agent does not undertake to indemnify the principal in any event in which the transaction is not carried out, e.g. if a perfectly solvent purchaser refuses to accept the goods and therefore refuses to pay the price. Sometimes the principal increases the agent's commission in consideration for the latter's *del credere* liability. The standard *del credere* agency agreement issued by the Institute of Export contains the following clause: "(a) The Agent shall undertake *del credere* responsibility in respect of every sale by him of the company's goods. (b) In respect of all such sales the agent hereby agrees to indemnify and keep indemnified the company against all loss (or loss up to ... per cent) caused by the failure on the part of any purchaser to pay the whole or part of the purchase price where such failure arises out of the purchaser's insolvency or inability to pay. (c) The company agrees to pay the Agent *del credere* commission at the rate of ... per cent on the terms provided by paragraph ... hereof."

dependent of a principal to bring Article 85(1) in to play. It is necessary to look at the integration of the agent in practice. The relevant judgments of the ECJ and CFI and Commission decisions reveal that the following factors are important.

10.250 (a) It is necessary to look to the substance of the parties' relationship to determine whether a true agency situation exists. The label given to their relationship by the parties themselves is not a relevant consideration.[299]

10.251 (b) If the representative also carries on business on behalf of competitors of the principal then the representative is not an agent but an independent trader. For example, in *Vlaamse Reisbureaus*[300] the ECJ considered the relationship between travel agents and tour operators. The Court held that travel agents generally act for a large number of tour operators and could not, therefore, be considered as an integral part of an individual tour operator's undertaking. This approach was followed by the Commission in *Distribution of railway tickets by travel agents.*[301] The Commission held that travel agents selling railway tickets "cannot be treated as an auxiliary organ forming an integral part of a tour operator's undertaking" since "on the one hand, agents sell transport services, but also hotel, tourist, artistic and other services organised and supplied by a very large number of carriers, tour operators and other providers of services and, on the other, each ... railway company sells its services through a very large number of distributors, whether agents or other railway companies." This last sentence indicates that the number of representatives the principal deals with may also be a relevant factor. It is unclear what the position is if the representative is non-exclusive but that the other business it handles does not compete with that of the principal in question. In other words, there is no clear answer to the question whether the fact of conducting business in unrelated markets would make Article 85(1) applicable.

10.252 (c) If the representative buys a large stock of the principal's goods and then itself issues invoices to customers and receives payment, the Commission is unlikely to consider it to be an agent.[302]

10.253 (d) On occasion, the allocation of risk has proved to be the decisive factor, perhaps showing that there is still some vitality in the 1962 Commission Notice. In *ARG/Unipart,*[303] one aspect of the relationship was that Unipart would distribute ARG-branded parts for account of ARG and in return for a commission from ARG. The Commission held that, in this respect, "Unipart acts in the role of an agent bearing no entrepreneurial risk".[304] Another example is the Commission decision regarding *Distribution of Package Tours during the 1990 World Cup.*[305] The World Cup organising committee gave 90 Tour Italia the exclusive right to provide World Cup package tours. During the Commission proceedings some of the parties stated that the purpose of the contract was to entrust to the undertaking the function of carrying out a task on behalf of the organising committee which the organising committee was not in a position to perform. However, the Commission did not ac-

[299] See *Pitsburgh Corning Europe*, Commission Decision (72/403/EEC) OJ [1972] L272/35, [1973] CMLR D2.

[300] Case 311/85 *VZW Vereniging van Vlaamse Reisbureaus* v *VZW Sociale Dienst van de Plaatselijke en Gewestelijke Overheidsdiensten* [1987] ECR 3801, [1989] 4 CMLR 213.

[301] OJ [1992] L 366/47, on appeal Case T-14/93; *UIC* v *Commission*, [1995] ECR II-1503; see also *Suiker Unie* v *Commission* [1975] ECR 1663, [1976] 1 CMLR 295.

[302] See *Fisher Price/Quaker Oats-Toyco* OJ [1988] L49/19.

[303] OJ [1988] L45/34, [1988] 4 CMLR 513.

[304] The Commission specifically referred to the 1962 Commission Notice.

[305] OJ [1992] L326/31.

cept that 90 Tour Italia acted solely as an agent because it determined that it had accepted a high degree of commercial risk. This was because 90 Tour Italia had to acquire a considerable number of tickets for matches whose appeal to spectators was heavily dependent on the qualification of their team and, hence, unpredictable.

(2) Limitations upon the Notice

10.254 In certain exceptional cases Article 85(1) might apply to commercial agents.

First, if rival suppliers both appoint the same commercial agent then Article 85(1) will probably apply. A commercial agent cannot be an integral part of both suppliers and, if he is, then there is almost certainly a potentially notifiable agreement between the suppliers *inter se.*[306]

10.255 Secondly, if a representative has dual functions both as a commercial agent *and* as an independent trader then Article 85(1) will apply to the independent part of the representatives activities. It is not yet decided whether Article 85(1) applies to *all* of the representatives activities. It is probable that the commercial agency activities are still excluded from review. Thus, if X is commercial agent for Y's goods and is also exclusive dealer for Z (whose goods do not compete with Y's) then Article 85(1) should only apply to the agreement between X and Z. Though in such a situation it might be questioned whether X can be an integral part of Y's organisation.[307] In *ARG/Unipart*[308] Unipart was appointed exclusive distributor of ARG's own-branded parts. Unipart sold the parts in its own name but the Commission held that it was acting as an agent as it bore no entrepreneurial risk.

10.256 Thirdly, if the commercial agent is restrained from competing with the supplier after termination or expiration of the agreement Article 85(1) might apply.

2. UK Law

10.257 UK law may be dealt with briefly on this point. In all major respects it seems to follow the EC line. In *British Telecommunications*[309] (*Pricing Policy for the Placing of Advertisements in Yellow Pages Directories*), the OFT investigated under the Competition Act 1980 the practices of British Telecommunications (BT) concerned with the selling of advertising space in Yellow Pages directories, which they own. In 1981 BT appointed two sales contractors who were to be responsible, *inter alia*, for procuring advertising orders in Yellow Pages directories. A question arose as to the legal relationship between the contractors and BT. The OFT stated:

> "the sales contractors can be considered as an extension of BT's own resources for the preparation and publication of YP directories and therefore any competition between them would be a duplication of sales effort. The sales contractors can be distinguished from dealers or distributors who operate in other markets in that they do not buy or sell anything on their own behalf. Thus it is BT, through its sales contractors appointed by competitive tender, that supplies advertising space in YP directors."[310]

[306] See *Potash I* [1973] CMLR D219.

[307] If the goods of Y and Z are in competition with each other the Commission might have greater cause for concern since such an agreement would be very similar to that of rival suppliers appointing the same commercial agent. In such a case there could be scope for competition between Y and Z to be restricted. Indeed, there could be a covert agreement between Y and Z. In a genuine case Z would not make X his exclusive dealer because X would already be holding a competing product and X could not therefore take Z's goods subject to an exclusive purchasing obligation.

[308] OJ 1988 L45/34; [1988] 4 CMLR 513.

[309] 10 October 1984.

[310] *ibid.*, at p. 44, para. 7.4.

10.258 There is no reason to suppose that a similar conclusion would not apply under the RTPA 1976. Thus, if X appoints Y as his commercial agent to sell his goods in the North of England, and Z as his commercial agent to sell his goods in the South of England, then the agreements between X and Y, and, X and Z would not be registrable. For the RTPA to apply there must be at least two parties who either produce, supply or process goods, commercial agents perform none of these functions. Since agency, and its provision, is service, a clause whereby A engages as exclusive agent to P entails A accepting a restriction as to the persons to whom he will provide agency services. Equally, if P agrees only to use A as his agent P accepts a restriction as to the persons from whom services are to be required.

K. Franchise Agreements[311]

1. *Introduction*

10.259 Franchise systems have now become an accepted feature of European marketing. By 1990, for example, in Belgium, Denmark, France, Germany, Italy, the Netherlands and the UK, there were 1816 franchisors operating through 81,335 franchisees, with total sales exceeding US$41.2 billion.[312]

2. *EC Law*

(1) Characteristics of a franchise system

10.260 There is no accepted definition of what constitutes a franchise as a matter of law, though there is a definition for the purposes of the franchising block exemption.[313] Franchise systems are *sui generis* forms of distribution which link the identity of the franchisee to that of the franchisor. The following features characterise such systems:

(a) Ownership by the franchisor of a company name, trade name, trade mark, symbol, sign or initials whereby these names, marks, etc., are made available, in conjunction with know-how, to a franchisee who agrees to supply the franchisor's goods and/or services in accordance with specified business techniques notified to the franchisee. These techniques have been developed by the franchisor by research and by subsequent development and testing.

(b) The payment of some consideration by the franchisee to the franchisor in recognition of the services supplied by the franchisor in providing his name, format, technology and know-how.

(c) The franchise agreement is a closer relationship than conventional distribution and marketing arrangements entailing obligations accepted by franchisor and franchisee which would not exist in other distributional arrangements.

(d) The franchise agreement makes express provision in respect of: the method and conditions of payment of fees and royalties; the duration of the contract and the basis for renewal; the time and duration of notice periods; the right of the franchisor prior

311 See generally Adams and Prichard Jones *Franchising* (3rd edn. 1990); Abell (ed.) *European Franchising* (1991); Mendelsohn (ed.) *Franchising in Europe* (1992); J.H. Pratt *Franchising: Law and Practice* (looseleaf).

312 Source: Mendelsohn (ed.) *Franchising in Europe* (1992).

313 Art. 1(3), Reg. 4087/88/EEC.

to assignment by the franchisee; the territorial rights granted to the franchisee including options (if any) on adjoining territories; basis for distribution of the assets affected by the contract if terminated; distribution arrangements including transport and freight charges; terms of payment; services provided by the franchisor including, for example, marketing assistance, promotion, advertising, technology and know-how, managerial administrative and business advice, financial and fiscal advice, training etc.; obligations on the franchisee including to provide accounting and operating data, to accept training and to accept and apply inspection procedures.

10.261 In the leading case on the question, *Pronuptia*,[314] European Court described franchise systems in the following terms:

> "In a system of distribution franchises of that kind an undertaking which has established itself as a distributor on a given market and thus developed certain business methods grants independent traders, for a fee, the right to establish themselves in other markets using its business name and the business methods which have made it successful. Rather than a method of distribution, it is a way for an undertaking to derive financial benefit from its expertise without investing its own capital. Moreover, the system gives traders who do not have the necessary experience access to methods which they could not have learned without considerable effort and allows them to benefit from the reputation of the franchisor's business name. Franchise agreements for the distribution of goods differ in that regard from dealerships or contracts which incorporate approved retailers into a selective distribution scheme, which do not involve the use of a single business name, the application of uniform business methods or the payment of royalties in return for the benefits granted."

10.262 The integration of the franchisee into the franchisor's network is an integral part of the system. Indeed, the franchisee, once integrated, adopts the appearance of a subsidiary or division or branch of the franchisor. However, contrary to the case of a subsidiary division or branch, the franchisor does not have to carry any investment costs, nor does he perform market research in the territory of the franchisee's shop since, even in the event of inadequate sales, the franchisor bears no risks whatsoever as he is still entitled to the royalty, in the *Pronuptia* case 10 per cent of total turnover.

10.263 Franchise systems, as noted above, are *sui generis* forms of distribution which may not be legally equated with other distributional forms, for example, commercial agents, exclusive dealerships, brewery agreements (solus agreements), selective distribution systems, and, intellectual property licences. Though, principles relevant to an analysis of all these methods of distribution and marketing are of relevance to the analysis of franchises. Franchise systems are hybrids of all of these various other systems, a fact which led the European Court in *Pronuptia* to conclude that the compatibility of franchise systems with Article 85(1) will depend on the clauses actually incorporated into the contract, *and*, on the economic context in which they operate.

(2) When will franchise systems affect trade between the Member States so as to activate article 85(1) EC

10.264 Franchisors whose systems are confined to a single Member State do not necessarily escape Article 85(1) EC. Accordingly many national franchise systems may be caught by

[314] Case 161/84 *Pronuptia De Paris, GmbH* v *Pronuptia De Paris, Irmgard Schillgallis* [1986] ECR 353 [1986] 1 CMLR 414, at para. 15. For a copy of the actual agreement used by Pronuptia in dealings with its UK franchisees see No. 4578 Register of Restrictive Trade Practices; 30 franchise agreements in all were registered in the UK. See also the note by Korah, (1986) EIPR 99, and, Venit (1986) ELRev 2 13. See also, *Yves Rocher* [1986] 2 CMLR 95—copy of agreement: No. 4937 Register of Restrictive Trade Practices.

Article 85(1). Indeed where even a degree of uncertainty exists notification may be desirable given the potentially drastic consequences of non-notification. The main difficulty is that a disgruntled franchisee could seek to have the contract declared void by a national court as being in breach of Article 85(1) and a nullity under Article 85(2) and thereby avoid having to comply with the contract, for instance with respect to royalty payments. It will be appreciated that national courts have no jurisdiction to apply Article 85(3).[315] At this point it is important to appreciate that there are divergent approaches to assessing whether a franchise agreement is caught by Article 85(1). The Court of Justice in *Pronuptia* gave some indication that there will be many cases in which a franchise agreement will not be caught. On the other hand, the Commission in a number of decisions following that judgment[316] has taken a more restrictive approach to the application of Article 85(1), being more ready to exempt rather than grant negative clearance. This Commission thinking has informed the drafting of the block exemption, Regulation 4087/88. However, the Commission's views do not bind the courts, so it is important to assess whether an agreement is caught at all by Article 85(1) in the light of the Court's decision in *Pronuptia*.

10.265 The tenor of the opinion of the Advocate General in *Pronuptia* was that "vertical" restrictions in franchise agreements (i.e. those imposed as between franchisor and franchisee) were less significant, in competition terms, than the "horizontal" effect of franchise systems. By horizontal was meant the economic effects on third parties, namely, competitors, suppliers and purchasers. The Court was less forthcoming upon this question and concentrated upon a clause by clause analysis of the agreement before it. However, it did confirm that an analysis of the economic context was as important as an analysis of the actual clauses.[317] Unfortunately the Court failed to elaborate upon this point in the detailed reasoning. In the light of the opinion and the judgment a number of points may be made.

10.266 In assessing the economic impact on inter-state trade of a domestic network, franchisors will have to consider what has become known as the "network effect" and the "foreclosure" problem. These have already been considered above as part of the analysis of exclusive purchasing agreements. Basically, if a franchisor integrates into his network all or most of the available retailers and thereby creates an economic obstacle to rival suppliers being able to find and appoint representatives (whether as franchisees, exclusive dealers, commercial agents, etc.) of adequate quality and in adequate numbers then the existence of the "network" of franchisees has foreclosed the market to competitors. The entry or expansion barrier is exacerbated where a number of suppliers control networks (whether of franchisees or exclusive dealers, etc.) so that there exists a cumulative network effect which forecloses opportunities in the market.

10.267 The Court[318] stated also that clauses leading to a sharing of markets between the franchisor and the franchisee or between the franchisees *inter se* are liable to affect trade between the Member States even where the parties are confined to a single state to the extent that they hinder a franchisee from setting up abroad. This dictum seems to extend earlier statements of the Court on affecting trade between the Member States which focus upon the

315 An agreement containing an exclusivity clause which is backed by location clauses falls within Art. 85(1). If a national court holds these clauses void it might well be that the remainder of the agreement also fails, including royalty payment clauses. See, *Chemidus Wavin* v *TERI* [1977] 3 CMLR 514.

316 *Pronuptia* OJ 1987 L13/39, [1989] 4 CMLR 355; *Computerland* OJ 1987 L222/12, [1989] 4 CMLR 259; *Yves Rocher* OJ 1987 L8/49, [1988] 4 CMLR 592; *ServiceMaster* OJ 1988 L332/38, [1989] 4 CMLR 581; *Charles Jourdan* OJ 1989 L35/31, [1989] 4 CMLR 591.

317 Case 161/84 [1986] ECR 353; [1986] 1 CMLR 414, para. 27.

318 *ibid.*, para. 26.

effects of an agreement which restrict or distort the *pattern* of trade across national frontiers. Here the Court refers to trade being affected where a franchisee is hindered from *setting up* abroad. The statement demonstrates that a trader's ability to set up abroad is as important as his ability to export to or import from another Member State.

10.268 In *Pronuptia* Advocate General Verloren Van Themaat concluded that Article 85(1) EC applied to franchises in, *inter alia*, a number of situations:

(a) Where they are concluded between a franchisor, or its subsidiary, and one or more franchisees in one or more other Member States and through the subsidiaries or franchisees in one or more of those other Member States (or in a significant part of their territory) the franchisor has a substantial share of the market for the relevant product. The Advocate General considered that the place where the franchisor was situate need not be material since it was the network effect of the franchisees on a single market territory that exerted the economic impact.

(b) Where the agreements prevent or hinder, or are intended to prevent or hinder, parallel imports of the products covered by the agreement into the contract territory or exports of those products by the franchisee to other Member States. Thus export bans and other forms of market sharing between franchisees should be avoided if Article 85(1) is to be avoided. The European Court as noted above extended this view by holding that franchise clauses leading to a sharing of markets between the franchisor and franchisees or between franchisees *inter se* were likely to affect trade between Member States even where concluded between firms established within the same Member State to the extent that they prevented franchisees from setting up in another Member State.

(c) Where the agreements result in the setting of unreasonably high retail prices, i.e. prices that could not exist if effective competition existed, even allowing for superior product quality. Such supra-competitive prices might result in a number of contexts: where local or regional monopolies for the products are established by virtue of the contracts; where royalty provisions are such as to raise franchisee's costs to levels which necessitate financial burdens being passed on to customers; where the franchisor and franchisees were involved in concerted practices over selling prices; and where there was inadequate inter-brand competition to ensure that prices were competitive.

10.269 The Court did not expressly adopt the Advocate General's reasoning in this respect. Though, there is nothing in the Court's judgment which casts doubt upon the above analysis.

3. The Franchising Block Exemption: Regulation 4087/88/EEC

(1) Introduction: interpretation

10.270 The Commission enacted the franchising Block Exemption[319] having first gained experience of franchising agreements in its decisions in the *Pronuptia*, *Computerland*, *Yves Rocher* and *ServiceMaster* cases.[320] There is clearly much to be gained from drafting a franchise agreement so that it comes within the terms of the block exemption. If this is not done,

[319] OJ 1988 L359/46. See Korah, *Franchising and the EEC Competition Rules: Regulation 4087/88* (1989); Mendelsohn and Harris, *Franchising and the Block Exemption Regulation* (1991).

[320] *Pronuptia* OJ 1987 L13/39, [1989] 4 CMLR 355; *Computerland* OJ 1987 L222/12, [1989] 4 CMLR 259; *Yves Rocher* OJ 1987 L8/49, [1988] 4 CMLR 592; *ServiceMaster* OJ 1988 L332/38, [1989] 4 CMLR 581. There has been one subsequent decision, *Charles Jourdan* OJ 1989 L35/31, [1989] 4 CMLR 591, but this was in fact more or less contemporaneous with the enactment of the block exemption and so Reg. 4087/8 was not referred to in that decision.

then it will be necessary to see if any of the provisions of the agreement cause it to be caught by Article 85(1) and if so, application may need to be made for individual exemption.

(2) Article 1: basic provision

10.271 Article 1 of the Regulation is divided into three paragraphs. Article 1(1) of the Regulation reads:

> "Pursuant to Article 85(3) of the Treaty and subject to the provisions of this Regulation, it is hereby declared that Article 85(1) of the Treaty shall not apply to franchise agreements to which two undertakings are party, which include one or more of the restrictions listed in Article 2."

Article 1(2) goes on to extend the benefit of Article 1(1) to master franchise agreements where only two undertakings are party, providing that "[w]here applicable, the provisions of this Regulation concerning the relationship between franchisor and franchisee shall apply mutatis mutandis to the relationship between franchisor and master franchisee and between master franchisee and franchisee. Article 1(3) then goes on to give a number of definitions for the purposes of the Regulation, which will be discussed *infra.*

10.272 The interpretation of the phrase "to which two undertakings are party" has already been discussed,[321] reference is made to this. A master franchise agreement is defined in Article 1(3)(c) as an agreement whereby one undertaking, the franchisor, grants the other, the master franchisee, in exchange for direct or indirect financial consideration, the right to exploit a franchise for the purposes of concluding franchise agreements with third parties, the franchisees. In practice however, it is often the case that master franchise agreements are tripartite rather than bipartite. This arises from problems of privity under UK law of contract, and from problems relating to the ownership and possible sub-licensing of a trade mark owned by the franchisor.[322] Tripartite agreements would have to be notified for individual exemption as being agreements to which more than two undertakings are party, unless the master franchisor and master franchisee form one economic entity such as parent and subsidiary.

10.273 Both franchise and franchise agreement are defined. Article 1(3)(a) defines a franchise as "a package of industrial or intellectual property rights relating to trade marks, trade names, shop signs, utility models, designs, copyrights, know-how or patents, to be exploited for the resale of goods or the provision of services to end users." This definition therefore excludes from the block exemption an industrial or manufacturing franchise, where a licence is given to manufacture using particular intellectual property rights.[323] However, such an agreement might be brought within one of the intellectual property licensing block exemptions, discussed in Chapter 13. Much may depend on the importance of a trade mark in such a case; if it is more than ancillary to the industrial or manufacturing franchise, it may prevent the application of any block exemption.[324]

10.274 A franchise agreement is defined in Article 1(3)(b) as

> "an agreement whereby one undertaking, the franchisor, grants the other, the franchisee, in exchange for direct or indirect financial consideration, the right to exploit a franchise for

321 At paras. 10.26–10.27.

322 The problems surrounding sub-licensing of trade marks under the Trade Marks Act 1938 have now been eradicated by the Trade Marks Act 1994, which permits sub-licensing.

323 See Recital 4, Reg. 4087/88. It has been informally suggested that the Commission should enact a block exemption for industrial franchise agreements.

324 See *Moosehead* OJ 1990 L100/32, [1991] 4 CMLR 391; see para. 13.408.

> the purposes of marketing specified types of goods and/or services; it includes *at least* [emphasis added] obligations relating to:
> – the use of a common name or shop sign and a uniform presentation of contract premises and/or means of transport;
> – the communication by the franchisor to the franchisee of know-how;
> – the continuing provision by the franchiser to the franchisee of commercial or technical assistance during the life of the agreement."

The reference to "marketing" indicates that the block exemption covers franchises where goods or services are supplied other than by way of sale.[325] It is clear that the block exemption applies to franchises for the supply of goods and/or services. Article 1(3)(a) states that the exemption only applies where the goods or services are supplied to end users;[326] in other words only retail franchises are covered. Wholesale franchises would therefore have to be notified for individual exemption. There are three requirements noted above to be satisfied for an agreement to come within the definition of a franchise agreement. These requirements, despite the failure of text to clarify this, are cumulative, not alternatives.

10.275 A further series of definitions follows on from these definitions of "franchise" and franchise agreement. "Know-how" is defined in Article 1(3)(f) for the purposes of this block exemption as "a package of non-patented practical information, resulting from experience and testing by the franchisor, which is secret, substantial and identified". These latter three requirements are in turn defined.

10.276 Article 1(3)(g) states that "secret" means that the know-how, as a body or in the precise configuration and assembly of its components, is not generally known or easily accessible; it is not limited in the narrow sense that each individual component of the know-how should be totally unknown or unobtainable outside the franchisor's business. It seems that compilations of known information, where the compilation is not itself known (such as are typically found in a franchise manual), will be regarded as secret under this definition.

10.277 Article 1(3)(h) states that substantial "means that the know-how includes information which is of importance for the sale of goods or the provision of services to end users, and in particular for the presentation of goods for sale, the processing of goods in connection with provision of services, methods of dealing with customers, and administration and financial management; the know-how must be useful for the franchisee by being capable, at the date of conclusion of the agreement, of improving the competitive position of the franchisee, in particular by improving the franchisee's performance or helping it enter a new market." This threshold of substantiality does not seem set at a level which would cause genuine franchise agreements any problem; after all, why would a franchisee take a franchise if not to accomplish the objectives set out in this definition? Nevertheless, it might be wise to include a statement in the recitals to a franchise agreement where the franchisee acknowledges the importance at the date of the agreement of obtaining access to this know-how.

10.278 Finally, Article 1(3)(i) states that identified "means that the know-how must be described in a sufficiently comprehensive manner so as to make it possible to verify that it fulfils the criteria of secrecy and substantiality; the description of the know-how can either be set out in the franchise agreement or in a separate document or recorded in any other appropriate form." In franchises where know-how is set out in a manual, this will not prove a problem. Where know-how consists in oral teaching and demonstration (so-called "show-

[325] To be contrasted with Regs. 1983/83 and 1984/83, see paras. 10.23–10.24 and 10.146, which only cover cases where goods are supplied for resale.

[326] See also Recital 4, Reg. 4087/88.

how"), it would be necessary to record what was carried out, for example in agreed minutes of what was covered during such training.

10.279 The exemption granted under Article 1 is subject to three conditions set out in Article 4.

(3) Article 4: conditions for exemption

10.280 The exemption granted under Article 1 applies only if each of the three conditions set out in Article 4 are satisfied. Article 4(a) makes exemption subject to the condition that "the franchisee is free to obtain the goods that are the subject-matter of the franchise from other franchisees; where such goods are also distributed through another network of authorised distributors, the franchisee must be free to obtain the goods from the latter." This ties in with the whitelisted obligation under Article 3(1)(e) which entitles the franchisor to require the franchisee to supply only end users or other franchisees or distributors.[327] The purpose of this condition is to guarantee that competition is not eliminated for franchisee goods by enabling parallel imports via cross deliveries from other franchisees or distributors of the franchise goods.[328]

10.281 Article 4(b) states that were the franchisor obliges the franchisee to honour guarantees for the franchisor's goods, "that obligation shall apply in respect of other such goods supplied by any member of the franchised network or other distributors which give a similar guarantee, in the common market". This is also intended to remove what might otherwise be a barrier to parallel imports as a means of exposing the franchise goods to competition. Indeed, it is a common feature of the Commission's policy on distribution agreements generally that guarantees should be honoured throughout a distribution system on a Community-wide basis.[329]

10.282 Article 4(c) is imposed as a condition for reasons of consumer protection, although it is phrased in terms of the fair share of resulting benefit test set out in Article 85(3).[330] It requires that "the franchisee is obliged to indicate its status as an independent undertaking; this indication shall however not interfere with the common identity of the franchised network resulting in particular from the common name or shop sign and uniform appearance of the contract premises and/or means of transport." In practice, appropriate wording should be included on business stationery, in a sign on the franchise premises, and on any means of transport from which the franchise is conducted. However, it need not be included in such way as to detract from the common identity, so it is not necessary to go so far as to style a business, for example: "A Robertson Trading as Green's Commercial Agreements and Competition Law Ltd"; it would be sufficient to use that business name and then include a statement underneath to the effect that: "A Robertson is an independent business operating under franchise from Green's Commercial Agreements and Competition Law Ltd."

(4) Article 2: permissible restrictions of competition

10.283 Article 2 sets out what the Commission regard as restrictions of competition that would be caught by Article 85(1) and therefore require exemption. It may well be that the Commission are more strict in what is regarded as a restriction of competition than is warranted by the Court of Justice's decision in *Pronuptia*.[331] In particular, the Court indi-

327 See para. 10.296.
328 Recital 12, Reg. 4087/88.
329 See para. 10.56.
330 Recital 12.
331 See analysis at paras. 10.261–10.269.

cated[332] that territorial exclusivity granted to a franchisee is only restrictive of competition when it concerned a business name or symbol which was already well-known.

Article 2(a) exempts

> "an obligation of the franchisor, in a defined area of the common market, the contract territory, not to:
> – grant the right to exploit all or part of the franchise to third parties;
> – itself exploit the franchise or itself market the goods or services which are the subject-matter of the franchise under a similar formula;
> – itself supply the franchisor's goods to third parties.
> Franchisor's goods are further defined in Article 1(3)(d) as meaning "goods produced by the franchisor or according to its instructions, and/or bearing the franchisor's name or trade mark."

10.284 Article 2(a) therefore effectively allows a franchisee to be given exclusivity within its allotted territory, subject only to other franchisees, but not the franchisor, making unsolicited sales into its territory. This exclusivity can last for the duration of the agreement. Article 2(b) provides that a master franchisee can also be restricted from franchising outside its allotted territory, which is implicit in the very concept of master franchising.

10.285 Article 2(c) exempts an obligation on the franchisee to exploit the franchise only from the contract premises. "Contract premises" is further defined in Article 1(3)(e) as "premises used for the exploitation of the franchise or, when the franchise is exploited outside those premises, the base from which the franchisee operates the means of transport used for the exploitation of the franchise ([which is further defined as the] contract means of transport)."

10.286 Article 2(d) allows a restriction on active marketing by a franchisee outside its territory. It exempts "an obligation on the franchisee to refrain, outside the contract territory, from seeking customers for the goods or the services which are the subject-matter of the franchise." Although there is no mention of exemption for a restriction preventing establishing a branch or maintaining a depot outside the contract territory, in contrast to the exclusive distribution block exemption,[333] such a restriction is effectively exempted through the exemption for a restriction only to operate from the contract premises.[334]

10.287 Article 2(e) enables the franchisor to require the franchisee not to handle competing goods. It exempts "an obligation on the franchisee not to manufacture, sell or use in the course of the provision of services, goods competing with the franchisor's goods which are the subject-matter of the franchise; where the subject-matter of the franchise is the sale or use in the course of the provision of services both certain types of goods and spare parts or accessories therefor, that obligation may not be imposed in respect of these spare parts of accessories". The exemption of the restriction of the franchisee to using only the franchisor's goods, as defined in Article 1(3)(d),[335] is understandable. What is less clear is why there needed to be a proviso preventing the franchisor from requiring the franchisee from handling competing spare parts or accessories. While the Commission has taken steps to prevent the exercise of intellectual property rights in such a way as to extend a monopoly over goods protected by such rights to neighbouring markets, such as those for spare parts,[336] there does not seem to be a similar justification in the absence of either intellectual property rights or market power by the undertaking in question. The result is that analysis has to be made as to what are "goods",

332 [1986] ECR 353, [1986] 1 CMLR 414, at para. 24.
333 Art. 2(2)(c) Reg. 1983/83; see paras. 10.44–10.48.
334 Art. 2(c) Reg. 4087/88, *supra*.
335 "Franchisor's goods" is defined as meaning "Goods produced by the franchisor or according to its restrictions, and/or bearing the franchisor's name or trade mark." It therefore goes wider than simply goods manufactured by the franchisor.
336 See paras. 13.453–13.463.

and what are merely "spare parts" or "accessories". Items which might be regarded as spare parts or accessories could be included in the franchise agreement as "franchisor's goods", provided that the criteria in Article 1(3)(d), as expanded upon by Recital 9[337] are satisfied in respect of those goods, but this would not prevent a challenge to that classification being made on the ground that such goods were in truth only spare parts or accessories and did not form part of the essential subject-matter of the franchise. So, to take an example given by Korah[338] in a hamburger restaurant franchise, tomato ketchup might be regarded as a good to be supplied as part of the franchise, on the basis that (almost) all hamburgers have tomato ketchup added before serving, or it might be regarded as an accessory if it was provided separately for the customer to add to their meal.

10.288 Article 2(e) limits the extent of two of the provisions of the blacklist in Article 5, discussed below.[339]

(5) Article 3: permissible obligations—the whitelist

10.289 The Court in *Pronuptia* had identified several obligations in that agreement as not being restrictive of competition. Article 3 largely adopts the Court's approach in setting out a whitelist of obligations which are not caught by Article 85(1). The Court's approach was to identify two objectives for which obligations could be validly imposed. The first is the protection of intellectual property rights.[340] The second is the maintenance of the common identity and reputation of the franchise network.[341]

10.290 The drafting of the whitelist follows the Court's approach.[342] Article 3(1) covers obligations to meet these two objectives. Article 3(2) then goes on to cover obligations of the sort commonly encountered in franchise agreements which can be presumed not to infringe Article 85(1), but if for some reason they do, then Article 3(3) exempts them for the sake of certainty. Article 3(1) provides that the exemption applies "notwithstanding the presence of any of the following obligations on the franchisee, in so far as they are necessary to protect the franchisor's industrial or intellectual property rights or to maintain the common identity and reputation of the franchised network" and then goes on to list seven types of obligations. Before analysing those obligations, it must be stressed that these obligations cannot be looked at in isolation. Such obligations are only outside the scope of Article 85(1) in so far as they are necessary (as opposed to reasonable or desirable) to meet the objectives set out in the opening words of Article 3(1).

10.291 Article 3(1)(a) permits an obligation on the franchisee "to sell, or use in the course of the provision of services, exclusively goods matching minimum objective quality specifications laid down by the franchisor." This enables uniform standards throughout the franchise network. Article 3(1)(b) allows the franchisor to require the franchisee "to sell, or use in the course of the provision of services, goods which are manufactured only by the franchisor or by third parties designated by it, where it is impractical, owing to the nature of the goods which are the subject-matter of the franchise, to apply objective quality specifications." This limits the blacklisted restriction under Article 5(b) on a franchisee obtaining goods elsewhere of an equivalent quality to those offered by the franchisee.

337 Recital 9 states that the obligation not to supply competing goods "should only be accepted with respect to goods which form the essential subject-matter of the franchise. It should notably not relate to accesssories or spare parts for these goods." This limitation does not derive from the Court's judgment in *Pronuptia*; rather it appears to have derived from the Commission decisions cited in note 316 *supra*.

338 Korah, *op. cit.*, at p. 59.

339 Arts. 5(b) and 5(c); see para. 10.303.

340 Case 161/84 *Pronuptia* [1986] ECR 353, [1986] 1 CMLR 414, at para. 16.

341 Case 161/84 *Pronuptia* [1986] ECR 353, [1986] 1 CMLR 414, at para. 17.

342 See also Recital 11, Reg. 4087/88.

It is crucial to determine whether the franchisee goods are of a sort to which objective quality specifications cannot be applied. In *Pronuptia*, the Court held that fashion articles, *in casu* wedding apparel, were an example of such a good.[343]

10.292 However, Article 3(1)(b) does not limit the ambit of Article 5(c) which blacklists any restriction where "the franchisee is obliged to sell, or use in the process of providing services, goods manufactured by the franchisor or third parties designated by the franchisor and the franchiser refuses, for reasons other than protecting the franchisor's industrial or intellectual property rights, or maintaining the common identity and reputation of the franchised network, to designate as authorised manufacturers proposed by the franchisee." Therefore, even where objective quality standard standards cannot be applied, in order to take advantage of the block exemption, the franchisee must have the right to propose and have considered as alternative manufacturers to the existing suppliers, unless there are reasons relating to intellectual property rights or the common identity of the franchise network which would preclude this. A franchisor would be well advised to anticipate such suggestions and have procedures in place for dealing with any such proposal from a franchisee.[344]

10.293 An illustration of this principle is seen in the *Texaco*[345] service station franchise. The Commission confirmed the block exemption applied to a franchise package involving a service station and on-site shop. The Commission stated it was permissible to require the franchisee to stock certain brand name products in the shop and devote shelf space to those stocks, provided the franchisee was not required to purchase them from the franchisor. The franchisor had organised central purchasing of certain of those products, but it was to be left up to the franchisee to decide whether to purchase them elsewhere.

10.294 Article 3(1)(c) permits a franchisor to restrict a franchisee "not to engage, directly or indirectly, in any similar business in a territory were it would compete with a member of the franchised network, including the franchisor; the franchisee may be held to this obligation after termination of the agreement, for a reasonable period which may not exceed one year, in the territory where it has exploited the franchise." The post-termination restrictive covenant may therefore only operate in that particular franchisee's territory, so the franchisee can set up on competition with any other member of the franchise network apart from its successor in its territory. This limitation was not included in either the Court's judgment in *Pronuptia*[346] or in the subsequent Commission decision.[347] It was held in the Court's decision that a post-termination restrictive covenant could apply for "a reasonable period" in any area where the ex-franchisee may compete with a member of the franchise network, and the Commission cleared a post-termination restriction of a year's duration. If such a restriction is needed, then a solution would be to notify through the opposition procedure in Article 6 although there is no guarantee that opposition would not be raised.[348]

343 Case 161/84 *Pronuptia* [1986] ECR 353, [1986] 1 CMLR 414, at para. 21.

344 The Commission's *Twentieth Report on Competition Policy* notes at para. 48 that the failure to make provision for the nomination of alternative manufacturers was a reason for refusing exemption to a franchise agreement notified under the opposition procedure under Art. 6.

345 *Twenty-third Report on Competition Policy* (1993), para. 225.

346 Case 161/84 *Pronuptia* [1986] ECR 353, [1986] 1 CMLR 414, at para. 16.

347 *Pronuptia* OJ 1987 L13/39, [1989] 4 CMLR 355, at para. 25(I). The first decision in which this additional limitation was introduced is OJ 1987 L13/39, [1989] 4 CMLR 355, at para. 25(I). The first decision in which this additional limitation was introduced is *Yves Rocher* OJ 1987 L8/49, [1988] 4 CMLR 592, at para. 48.

348 See para. 10.308. In *Charles Jourdan* 1989 OJ L35/31, [1989] 4 CMLR 591, at para. 27, the Commission decided that a post-termination restrictive covenant would not have been exempted for two reasons: first, that the know-how involved, relating to the sale of quality shoes and accessories, was of a general commercial nature not justifying such protection, and second, that the franchisees were normally experienced retailers already carrying this type of business and therefore it would not be right to remove them from the market on the termination of the franchise.

10.295 Article 3(1)(d) allows a restriction on the franchisee "not to acquire financial interests in the capital of a competing undertaking, which would give the franchisee the power to influence the economic conduct of such undertaking." It should be noted that this needs to be justified by reference to the opening words of Article 3(1); it is not a general restriction that can be imposed regardless of objective, although it is common to restrict franchisees from being interested in the capital of competing undertakings, sometimes coupled with a proviso enabling the acquisition for investment purposes of a small shareholding in a publicly quoted competitor.[349]

10.296 Article 3(1)(e) enables the franchisor to require that the franchisee only "sell the goods which are the subject-matter of the franchise only to end users, to other franchisees and to resellers within other channels of distribution supplied by the manufacturer of these goods or with its consent." The use of the phrase "subject-matter of the franchise" would not seem to import the restriction in Article 2(e) excluding spare parts and accessories from that restriction; the same observation applies to Articles 3(1)(b) and 3(1)(f) where the same phrase is also used. Article 3(1)(f) makes provision for the franchisor to require the franchisee "to use its best endeavours to sell the goods or provide the services that are the subject-matter of the franchise only to end users, to other franchisees and to resellers within other channels of distribution supplied by the manufacturer of these goods or with its consent." This enables the franchise network's integrity to be maintained.[350]

10.297 Article 3(1)(g) permits on obligation on the franchisee "to pay to the franchisor a specified proportion of its revenue for advertising and itself carry out advertising for the nature of which it shall obtain the franchisor's approval."

10.298 Finally, it cannot be stressed too much that Articles 3(1)(a)–(g) are conditional on the opening words of Article 3(1). If obligations such as these are included in an agreement, it would be wise to draft recitals appropriately in order to forestall any argument that such obligations were not necessary to meet the specified objectives.

10.299 The second list of obligations in Article 3(2) can be dealt with more briefly. These obligations are not subject to any overall conditions within Article 3, though of course they may not go beyond the limits prescribed by the Article 5 blacklist. Article 3(2) is further backed up by Article 3(3) which provides that exemption applies even if any of the obligations for any particular reason are caught by Article 85(1). As Article 3(2) is self-explanatory, it will suffice to set it out in full here. It states that exemption will be given notwithstanding the following obligations on the franchisee:

[349] In *Computerland* OJ 1987 L222/12, [1989] 4 CMLR 259, the Commission cleared a clause allowing a franchisee to acquire financial interests in the capital of competing undertakings, although not to the extent that such participation would enable the franchisee to exercise control; no limit as to shareholding is specified in the decision. In *ServiceMaster* OJ 1988 L332/38, [1989] 4 CMLR 581, a restriction on the franchisees not to be engaged in a competing business subject to a proviso allowing the acquisition of up to 5 per cent of the shares of a publicly quoted company was cleared (at para. 10), on the basis that in this particular case, franchisees were generally small undertakings and so the prohibition on acquiring more than 5 per cent would not in practice hinder their development of their own activities. Some further guidance may be possible by considering the definition of control in the Merger Control Regulation: see Art. 3(3) Reg. 4064/89; see also Cook and Kerse, *EEC Merger Control* (1991), pp. 16–22.

[350] In Recital 12, the Commission observes that "[t]o guarantee that competition is not eliminated for as substantial part of the goods which are the subject of the franchise, it is necessary that parallel imports remain possible. Therefore, cross-deliveries between franchisees should always be possible. Furthermore, where a franchise network is combined with another distribution system, franchisees should be free to obtain supplies from authorised distributors."

"(a) not a disclose to third parties the know-how provided by the franchisor; the franchisee may be held to this obligation after termination of the agreement;[351]

(b) to communicate to the franchisor any experience gained in exploiting the franchise and to grant it, and other franchisees, a non-exclusive licence for the know-how resulting from that experience;

(c) to inform the franchisor of infringements of licensed industrial or intellectual property rights, to take legal action against infringers or to assess the franchisor in any legal actions against infringers;

(d) not to use know-how licensed by the franchisor for purposes other than the exploitation of the franchise; the franchisee may be held to this obligation after termination of the agreement;[352]

(e) to attend or to have its staff attend training courses arranged by the franchisor;

(f) to apply the commercial methods devised by the franchisor, including any subsequent modification thereof, and use the licensed industrial or intellectual property rights;

(g) to comply with the franchisor's standards for the equipment and presentation of the contract premises and/or means of transport;

(h) to allow the franchisor to carry out checks of the contract premises and/or means of transport, including the goods sold and the services provided, and the inventory and accounts of the franchisee;

(i) not without the franchisor's consent to change the location of the contract premises;

(j) not without the franchisor's consent to assign the rights and under the franchise agreement."

10.300 Articles 3(2)(h), (i) and (j) are qualified by Article 8(e) which enables the Commission to withdraw the benefit of the block exemption if the franchisor "uses its right to check the contract premises and means of transport, or refuses its agreement to requests by the franchisee to move the contract premises or assign its rights and obligations under the franchise agreement, for reasons other than protecting the franchisor's industrial or intellectual property rights, maintaining the common identity of the franchised network or verifying that the franchisee abides by its obligations under the agreement." So under Articles 3(2)(i) and (j), the franchisor's right to refuse consent is qualified by the possibility of the Commission exercising its rights under Article 8(e); accordingly, it might be as well in an agreement to draft such consent provisions as being on the basis that such consent will not be unreasonably withheld.

(6) Article 5: impermissible restriction—the blacklist

10.301 Seven types of restrictions are blacklisted. Inclusion of any of these will prevent the block exemption or the opposition procedure[353] from being applicable. Only individual application for exemption will be possible and even then it is unlikely, though not out of the question, that it will be forthcoming.

10.302 Article 5(a) prevents the block exemption from applying to horizontal agreements, i.e. where franchisor and franchisee are existing competitors. It states that there is no exemption where "undertakings producing goods or providing services which are identical or are considered by users as equivalent in view of their characteristics, price and in-

[351] This must apply only for so long as the know-how is secret and substantial, i.e. for as long as it can properly be called know-how within the definition of Art. 1(3)(f); any extension of his restriction beyond the time when the know-how as become generally known or easily accessible otherwise than through breach by the franchisee of its obligation of confidentiality will be blacklisted under Art. 5(d); see also Art. 2(1)(1) Reg. 240/96, Technology Transfer Agreements, for an equivalent provision; see para. 13.63.

[352] See previous note as to the limit on the duration of such an obligation.

[353] Art. 6, see s. (7) *infra*.

tended use, enter into franchise agreements in respect of such goods or services". It has been pointed out[354] that this definition of competitor is unduly limited, as it only looks at competition from the demand side. So it is possible that businesses which are not in fact competitors may nevertheless be caught by this more limited definition.

10.303 The provisions of Article 5(b), which "without prejudice to Article 2(e) and Article 3(1)(b)" blacklists a clause whereby "the franchisee is prevented from obtaining supplies of goods of a quality equivalent to those offered by the franchisor", have already been referred to *supra* in the discussions of those other provisions to which reference is made. The same applies to Article 5(c) which "without prejudice to Article 2(e)" refuses exemption to a clause under which "the franchisee is obliged to sell, or use in the process of providing services, goods manufactured by the franchisor or third parties designated by the franchisor and the franchisor refuses, for reasons other than protecting the franchisor's industrial or intellectual property rights, or maintain the common identity and reputation of the franchised network, to designate as authorised manufacturers third parties proposed by the franchisee".

10.304 Article 5(d) blacklists any extension of the obligation not to use licensed know-how "after termination of the agreement where the know-how has become generally known or easily accessible, other than by breach of an obligation by the franchisee." This correlates to the whitelisted obligation under Article 3(2)(a) discussed *supra*.

10.305 Any attempt to use the block exemption as a means of imposing resale price maintenance will be caught under Article 5(e), which applies to any case where "the franchisee is restricted by the franchisor, directly or indirectly, in the determination of sales prices for goods or services which are the subject matter of the franchise." However, it is permissible to include provisions as to recommended sales prices, since Article 5(e) is expressed to be "without prejudice to the possibility for the franchisor of recommending sales prices." The Commission has always taken the firmest line against resale price maintenance and is unlikely to exempt it if notified individually.[355] It should be noted that the wording of Article 5(e) blacklists the setting of both minimum and maximum resale prices. The Commission will also be concerned to check that obligations as to the use of approved advertising materials, which are not caught by Article 85(1), are not used by a means of determining the franchisee's pricing.[356] The same applies to the exercise of any rights the franchisor has reserved to inspect a franchisee's stock levels, accounts and balance sheets.[357]

10.306 A no-challenge clause is blacklisted under Article 5(f) which applies if "the franchisor prohibits the franchisee from challenging the validity of the industrial or intellectual property rights which form part of the franchise, without prejudice to the possibility for the franchisor of terminating the agreement in such a case".[358]

10.307 The final blacklisted provision aims to prevent market sharing. Article 5(g) applies where "franchisees are obliged not to supply within the common market the goods or services which are the subject-matter of the franchise to end users because of their place of residence." This is intended to enable end users to shop around franchise outlets, the corollary of allowing franchisees to parallel import.

354 Korah, *op. cit.*, at p. 82.

355 In the *Twentieth Report on Competition Policy*, the Commission notes at p. 47 that the opposition procedure under Art. 6 was held to be inapplicable to an agreement where the franchisor required the franchisee to accept the franchisor's prices.

356 *Computerland* OJ 1987 L222/12, [1989] 4 CMLR 259, at para. 23(vii).

357 *Yves Rocher* OJ 1987 L8/49, [1988] 4 CMLR 592, at para. 50.

358 However, no-challenge clauses are no longer blacklisted under the Technology Transfer Block Exemption, Reg. 240/96, Art. 4(2)(b).

(7) Articles 6 and 7: the opposition procedure

10.308 Unlike Regulations 1983/83 and 1984/83, Regulation 4087/88 incorporates an opposition procedure. Article 6(1) extends the exemption under Article 1 for agreements which fulfil the three conditions set out in Article 4, which do not contain any provisions blacklisted under Article 5, but which include restrictions not covered by Article 2 or 3(3). The opposition procedure enable such a agreements to be notified to the Commission in the way set out in Article 6 and the Commission can then give such agreements accelerated treatment. In essence, exemption automatically extends to the agreement if no opposition to it has been raised within a six-month period commencing from the date of notification.

(8) Article 8: withdrawal of exemption

10.309 The Commission may, in exceptional cases, withdraw the block exemption from a particular case by formal decision where it considers that an agreement has effects that are incompatible with Article 85(3). The following are examples of cases where exemption might be withdrawn, but the list is not exhaustive.

10.310 Article 8(a) sets out as an example the situation where "access to the relevant market or competition therein is significantly restricted by the cumulative effect of parallel networks of similar agreements established by competing manufacturers or distributors." This is the type of situation analysed by the Court of Justice in *Delimitis* and reference is made to the discussion of that case in the context of exclusive purchasing and distribution agreements.[359] The concern is that a particular market is foreclosed to potential new entrants due to the fact that potential distributors are tied through to existing franchisors.

10.311 Article 8(b) covers the case where "the goods or services which are the subject-matter of the franchise do not face, in a substantial part of the common market, effective competition from goods or services which are identical or considered by users as equivalent from the point of view of their characteristics, price and intended use." As noted with Article 5(a) above, this is a limited (some[360] would argue defective) definition of effective competition taking into account only the demand side and not supply side substitutability.

10.312 Article 8(c) relates to Article 5(g) on the blacklist. The Commission reserve the right to remove the benefit of the block exemption if "the parties or one of them, prevent end users, because of their place of residence, from obtaining, directly or through intermediaries, the goods or services which are the subject-matter of the franchise within the common market, or use differences in specifications concerning those goods or services in different Member States, to isolate markets". To the extent that it refers to both parties preventing end users obtaining goods or services on the ground of residence, it goes no further than repeating what is already blacklisted under Article 5(g). However, it goes further than Article 5(g) in two ways. First, it applies to unilateral action by one party only, whereas Article 5(g) applies where there is agreement. Secondly, it applies where differences in specifications are used to isolate national markets. This seems to be directed in particular at franchisors. A franchisor whose products do vary in specification in different Member States needs to be aware that if this proves an obstacle to parallel trade which would otherwise take place, for example, if there are price differentials which could be exploited, the Commission may well investigate under this Article, and will need convincing that objective justifications for different specifications exist, such as different national regulatory standards. As the single market moves to completion such arguments will be less likely to be successful.

[359] See paras. 10.16-10.21.
[360] i.e. Korah, *op. cit.*

10.313 Article 8(d) adds to the restriction on including resale price maintenance in an agreement contained in Article 5(e). It enables the Commission to withdraw the block exemption if "franchisees engage in concerted practices relating to the sales prices of the goods or services which are the subject matter of the franchise." A franchisor needs to be aware of the various mechanisms whereby franchisees could co-ordinate action in such a way. In particular, care should be taken in the organisation of "franchisee clubs"[361] to ensure that meetings of franchisees do not turn to discussing price-fixing *inter se*.

10.314 Finally, Article 8(e), which has already been discussed in the context of Articles 3(2)(h), (i) and (j)[362] reserves the Commission's right to refuse exemption if "the franchisor uses its right to check the contract premises and means of transport, or refuses its agreement to requests by the franchisee to move the contract premises or assign its rights and obligations under the franchise agreement, for reasons other than protecting the franchisor's industrial or intellectual property rights, maintaining the common identity and reputation of the franchised network or verifying that the franchisee abides by its obligations under the agreement".

(9) Duration of block exemption

10.315 The block exemption came into force on 1 February 1989 for a period of ten years and eleven months. It expires on 31 December 1999. Although no doubt the next block exemption will contain transitional provisions applicable to agreements exempted under this block exemption, it would be wise for a franchisor to include a clause enabling renegotiating in good faith should there be significant differences. This is particularly important in franchise agreements as these tend to be of longer duration than other distribution agreements covered in this chapter.

4. UK Law

10.316 Agreements caught by Article 85(1) EC and exempt under block exemption Regulation 4087/88 are non-notifiable for the purposes of the RTPA, which therefore only applies to agreements falling outside the block exemption.[363]

(1) Registrability under the RTPA 1976[364]

10.317 Franchise systems comprise many restrictions imposed on the franchisee by the franchisor. For example: territorial restrictions, price restrictions, method of sale restrictions,

361 See also paras. 10.346–10.347.

362 para. 10.300.

363 Restrictive Trade Practices (Non-notifiable Agreements) (EC Block Exemptions) Order, S.I. 1996 No. 349, issued under section 27A RTPA 1976 (added by section 10 Deregulation and Contracting Out Act 1994). See further para. 2.250 and following.

364 See generally M. Howe, "Franchising and restrictive practices law: the Office of Fair Trading view" [1988] ECLR 439. Many of the example clauses given in this section are drawn from cases registered with the OFT and given s. 21(2) dispensation. For examples of franchise agreements see: No. 4578 Register of Restrictive Trade Practices, Franchise between *Pronuptia and Youngs (Franchise) Ltd* and franchisees for the sale of bridal wear and accessories (1982); No. 4889 Register of Restrictive Trade Agreements, Franchise between Youngs Formal Wear and franchisees for Men's Formal Dress Wear (1982); No. 5149 Register of Restrictive Trade Agreements, Franchise relating to the supply of sandwiches and other allied food products under the trade name Dial-a-Sandwich (1983); No. 5325 Register of Restrictive Trade Agreements, Franchise concerning leather and imitation leather goods, travel bags, sports bags, suitcases, leather goods, accessories and ancillary goods (1983); Nos. 4103 and 4104 Register of Restrictive Trade Agreements, Concerning the operation of ice cream parlours (1981); No. 3262 Register of Restrictive Trade Practices, Franchise concerning wallpaper and paints (1974); Nos 1278 Register of Restrictive Trade Practices, Franchise Concerning Beauty Centres (1985).

premises restrictions. Conversely, the franchisor may accept restrictions. For example: on selling directly in a franchisee's territory; on advertising; on the provision of services. Many of these restrictions will ostensibly be caught by sections 6 and 11 RTPA 1976. These sections lay down the types of restrictive agreement that must be registered. However, many of these restrictions will also fall under exemptions provided in the Act. In particular, four sets of provisions will be relevant in exempting clauses in franchise agreements. These are summarised below for convenience:

(a) terms relating exclusively to the goods or services supplied may be disregarded when considering registrability—sections 9(3) (goods) and 18(2) (services) RTPA 1976;
(b) restrictions relating to staffing may be disregarded when considering registrability—sections 9(6) (goods) and 18(6) (services) RTPA 1976;
(c) restrictions on territory and on purchasing may be excluded under Schedule 3(2) (goods) and 3(7) (services) RTPA 1976; (d) restrictions on the franchisee's use of the franchisor's intellectual property (e.g. patents, registered designs, trade marks, copyright and know-how) may be exempt under Schedule 3 RTPA 1976 and under the general rules on licensing.

(2) Important points to note when considering registrability

10.318 The RTPA 1976 is of very considerable complexity. When construing a franchise agreement the following points should be borne in mind.

10.319 (a) Consider services and goods restrictions separately. Franchise systems may involve services *and* goods restrictions. The RTPA 1976 evaluates services and goods restrictions entirely separately. If an agreement contains some goods restraints and some services restraints the restraints are not added together when trying to determine whether two parties accept restrictions. For example, if the franchisor accepts restraints on the services he supplies and no other restraints and the franchisee accepts restraints on goods and no other restraints, then the agreement need not be registered. There will not be two persons accepting goods restrictions nor two persons accepting services restrictions. This might sound anomalous but it has none the less been accepted as a quirk of the Act by the government.[365]

10.320 (b) Establish that two parties accept registrable restrictions. If all of the restrictions are heaped upon the franchisee and none are accepted by the franchisor then there will not be two parties accepting restrictions and the Act does not apply. In deciding whether this is so all restrictions and terms exempted by sections 9 and 18 may be disregarded. Once those clauses have been ignored any clause exempted under Schedule 3 may be taken out of account. If, following this examination, restrictions are not accepted by two parties then the agreement is not registrable. When examining the contract for any Schedule 3 exempt restrictions it is important to note the proviso in (c) below.

10.321 (c) Schedule 3 exemptions are not cumulative. An agreement can only include restrictions exempt by one paragraph of Schedule 3. The wording of the Schedule 3 exemptions makes it clear that they only apply if in isolation from all other registrable restrictions (i.e. not counting sections 9 and 18 *disregardable* restrictions). Thus, for example Schedule 3(4) exempts from registration trade mark licences which impose restrictions on the licensees use of the mark. The actual provision also contains the fol-

[365] See Liesner Committee Report, *A Review of Restrictive Trade Practices Policy* (1979) Cmnd 7512 p. 39, para. 5.20.

lowing words which are to be found in all of the other exemption provisions "being an agreement under which *no such* restrictions as are described in section 6(1) above are accepted or *no such* information provisions as are described in section 7(1) above are made *other than* ...", restrictions on the use of the trade mark. Note that the words stressed indicate that no other restrictions other than the permitted restriction may be included in the agreement if exemption is to remain.[366] Thus a franchise containing trade mark licence restrictions and restrictions on the franchisor's right to supply other persons in the franchisee's territory would not be exempt albeit that both restrictions, if in isolation, would benefit from various provisions in Schedule 3.[367]

10.322 (d) Consider sections 9 and 18 restrictions first. Terms relating exclusively to the goods or services supplied may be "disregarded" under sections 9 and 18. Thus all restrictions so benefiting should be identified as the first task when considering registrability. Example clauses are given below.

(3) Clauses exempt: territorial restrictions

10.323 Territorial restrictions are exempt under Schedule 3(2) RTPA 1976.[368] However, for exemption to apply there must exist no other registrable restrictions in the franchise. In practice, few franchises rely upon territorial restrictions alone. Most will be combined with other restrictions. Indeed frequently territorial restrictions are of secondary importance when compared to clauses providing for the licensing of a trade mark and the communication of know-how. Where the territorial restrictions are linked to restrictions which relate exclusively to the goods or services supplied, then these latter restrictions may be exempt under sections 9(3) and 18(2) RTPA 1976 and the franchise agreement will remain unregistrable.

10.324 It is understood that the OFT regards the distinction between the grant of sole and exclusive rights to a franchisee as vital to the question of whether a restriction is accepted. A sole franchise is usually interpreted as meaning that no other franchisee shall be appointed for that territory, but that the franchisor may continue to trade in that area. In contrast, an exclusive franchisee enjoys protection from the competition from the franchisor as well as the sole right to operate a franchise in that territory. The OFT regards the grant of a sole right to a franchise as an obligation upon the franchisor not to grant rights to any person other than the franchisee in that area, and as such not a restriction of a type mentioned in sections 6 or 11 RTPA. It is submitted that this view is not correct. By granting a sole franchise, a franchisor restricts itself from appointing any other franchisee and therefore from supplying goods and/or services (depending on the nature of the franchise) to other potential franchisees. Such a restriction is clearly caught by section 6(1)(f) and/or 11(2)(e) RTPA. While a licence of intellectual property rights may not be caught as such,[369] a franchise agreement typically[370] contains provisions relating to the supply of goods and/or services to the franchisee.

10.325 It has been argued that a means of avoiding a registrable restriction is by the franchisor making it clear that it is not restricted from supplying the goods or services into the territory.[371] If this means that the only restriction upon the franchisor is not to license its intellectual property rights into the territory, then this may be sufficient to avoid

[366] See *Registrar of Restrictive Trading Agreements* v *Schweppes* (1971) LR 7 RP 336 at p. 375.
[367] Sch. 3(4) RTPA (trade marks) and Sch. 3(2) and (7) territorial restrictions, e.g. No. 5911 Register of Restrictive Trade Practices, *Second Hand Fashions* (1985)—s. 21 (2) dispensation given.
[368] See para. 2.143.
[369] See para. 13.327.
[370] Indeed necessarily in the case of one seeking block exemption under 4087/88, since services must be supplied as a condition of that block exemption under Art. 1(3)(b).
[371] J.H. Pratt, *Franchising: Law and Practice* (Sweet and Maxwell, looseleaf), para. 3.079.

the franchisor accepting a registrable restriction. Two comments may be made. First, such a solution may be commercially unrealistic, depending on how extensive the intellectual property rights are. Secondly, it depends upon a licence of intellectual property rights not being held to be the supply of a service, and as yet there is no judicial, as opposed to OFT, authority on this point.[372] In the absence of such authority, it would not be safe to depend upon the OFT's interpretation of restriction in this regard and so the grant of sole rights should be treated as the acceptance of a restriction by the franchisor.

(4) Clauses exempt: clauses relating exclusively to the goods or services supplied—sections 9(3) and 18(2) RTPA 1976

10.326 Sections 9(3) and 18(2) allow certain clauses to be disregarded when registration is being considered. The provisions exempt any restrictive "term which relates exclusively" to the goods or services supplied.[373] The following typical (mainly goods) clauses would appear to be exempt under these provisions.

(a) Recommended retail prices

10.327 "In respect of the relevant goods and accessories the franchisor shall procure that the recommended retail prices of all relevant goods and accessories will be such as to enable the franchisee to obtain an X% mark up on the prices invoiced to the franchisee." This clause since it relates exclusively to the goods should be within section 9(3). Though such a clause might be viewed as a restriction on the franchisors liberty to set recommended prices which would fall under section 6(1)(b) RTPA 1976. The relationship between sections 9(3) and 6(1)(b) RTPA 1976 is unclear. However the conflict is lessened as a result of the resale price act. Recommended retail prices are legal under the Resale Prices Act 1976.[374] In practice franchisees tend to adhere to such prices. Where they have territorial protection from competition from other franchisees of the same brand it rarely matters if they cut prices since such is very unlikely to start a price war with other franchisees. Care should be taken, if the franchise network extends into the EC, to ensure that the system of recommended prices does not breach Article 85 EC.

(b) Franchisor's sale price to franchisee

10.328 "The franchisor shall ensure that the relevant goods ordered by the franchisee from time to time are invoiced to the franchisee at the lowest prices and on the most favourable terms of the franchisor or other supplier as the case may be applicable from time to time and together with the benefit of the usual trade discount and cash discount." The price at which the franchisor supplies the franchisee is often the subject of a restriction. However, the restrictive term relates exclusively to the goods supplied and should benefit from section 9(3).

(c) Stocking requirement

10.329 "The franchisee shall use and maintain in stock at least one sample for display at all times in each of the shops of all the relevant goods shown in the franchisor's current year brochure from time to time issued by the franchisor for distribution to the public or shown on national advertising conducted by the franchisor." Many franchisors undertake national advertising on behalf of all the franchisees. This is the most logical way to conduct a broad advertising campaign. Accordingly, franchisees are required to hold samples of the goods in stock and on display. Such a clause thus relates exclusively to the goods supplied.

[372] See paras. 2.202–2.210.
[373] See paras. 1.75–1.86.
[374] s. 9(2) Resale Prices Act 1976.

(d) Ban on hiring out relevant goods

10.330 "The franchisee shall not hire out any of the relevant goods." Section 9(3) covers restrictions on the way in which goods are sold; thus a ban on the hiring out of goods would be exempt.

(e) Retail prices and franchisee obligation

10.331 "The franchisee will use its best endeavours (so far as is permissible by law) to sell the franchise goods at the retail prices recommended by the franchisor." Best endeavours clauses relating to the retail price of goods should fall within section 9(3). However, franchisors should not take measures to enforce recommended price either directly or indirectly. Such attempts would fall foul of the Resale Prices Act 1976.

(f) Insurance

10.332 "The franchisee will keep the relevant goods and all other articles in the shops insured to their full value against loss or damage by fire and other usual risks except theft with a reputable Insurance Company satisfactory to the franchisor." Again, the term relates exclusively to the goods supplied and section 9(3) applies.

(g) Warranties

10.333 "The franchisee will not give any warranty for or on behalf of the franchisor in respect of the relevant goods without the authority in writing of the franchisor." This term relates exclusively to the way in which the goods will be promoted, thus, the franchisee may not give warranties on behalf of the franchisor. Again, section 9(3) applies.

(h) Trade mark labels

10.334 "The franchisee may not remove from any relevant goods the trade mark X sewn in label or cardboard label affixed thereto." This restriction relates to the label exhibiting the trade mark, i.e. a physical part of the goods themselves. The clause thus relates to the goods and should be disregardable under section 9(3). Alternatively, the clause *may* be exempt under Schedule 3(4) (trade mark licences) as a restriction on the "description of goods bearing the mark" supplied, i.e. the franchisor is restrained from supplying the goods without the trade mark.

(i) Restrictions on services provided by franchisor to franchisee

10.335 "The franchisor shall at the franchisor's cost give to the franchisee continuing advice guidance and from time to time visit his principal place of business to analyse the franchisee's operating methods and techniques and advertising and furnish the franchisee with suggestions in writing for improvements thereof if any be required in the franchisor's discretion. The franchisee shall implement any such suggestions within twenty-one days of receipt thereof."

Typically franchisors provide extensive business guidance services to the franchisee. Terms which relate exclusively to these services should be exempt under section 18(2). The above clause restricts the franchisees absolute discretion as to business conduct (and hence might have been a registrable restriction under section 11(2)(d)) but apparently may be disregarded as relating exclusively to the service provided by the franchisor.[375]

[375] In many franchises, especially for luxury goods, it is expected that the franchisee will provide extensive pre and post sales services to the customer. The nature and manner of the provision of these services will often be laid down in detail by the franchisor. Restrictions of this nature on the franchisee should benefit from s. 18(2). For an example see Clause 5(d) No. 4578 Register of Restrictive Trade Practices, *Promptia and Youngs (Franchise) Ltd*, bridal wear; the franchisee shall, "strictly and continuously adhere to

(i) Stocks

10.336 "The franchisee agrees to use its best endeavours at all times throughout the currency of this agreement to maintain a stock of the whole range of the specified products available from time to time of a sufficient size in each such product to fulfil the normal and foreseeable requirements of the franchisee's business." A stocking clause which requires the franchisee to accept a range of products produced or supplied by the franchisor is a term which relates exclusively to the goods supplied and hence should benefit from section 9(3).

(5) Clauses exempt: staffing restrictions

10.337 Sections 9(6) and 18(6) RTPA 1976 allow to be disregarded when determining registrability a restriction, "which affects or otherwise relates to the workers to be employed or not employed by any person, or as to the remuneration, conditions of employment, hours of work or working conditions of such workers."[376] Franchisors not infrequently require the franchisee to employ staff who are specialised and/or experienced in the handling and presentation of the franchisors' types of goods. Such restrictions may be ignored when deciding upon registrability.

10.338 A very restrictive light, however, was cast upon this provision by the RPC in *Association of British Travel Agents*[377] where the Court held that staffing restrictions imposed by ABTA on members, although technically falling within section 18(6), were not exempt by that provision. The restrictions in question demanded, *inter alia,* that point of sale staff have at least three year's experience in the trade of travel agent, and that members employ at least two full-time staff to deal with the issue and arrangement of tickets. The Court stated that in isolation the staffing restrictions were covered by the strict wording of section 18(6). However, they stated that where the restrictions were members of a family of restrictions which, when viewed conjunctively, were against the public interest it would be "unthinkable" to assume that "Parliament intended the Court to leave intact a restriction which appears, in the light of that evidence, to be harmful to the public interest."[378] The Court thus refused to decide the issue by reference to the strict letter of sections 9(6) and 18(6) preferring rather to decide by reference to the overall effect of the restrictions. Such an approach may be questioned when the precise language of sections 9(6) and 18(6) are considered; it certainly does not ease the task of those seeking to predict the legality of staffing restrictions.

10.339 It is strongly suggested that where the staffing restrictions are imposed by the franchisor in order to protect the reputation of the product or service in question there should be few problems and sections 9(6) and 18(6) exemption should be assumed.

(6) Clauses exempt: intellectual property licences

10.340 Often the basis of a franchise will be in the licence by the franchisor to the franchisee of a trade mark. As has been stated before the OFT adopts the view that the licensing of patents, trade marks, copyright, etc., do not amount to restrictions within the RTPA 1976. It is considered that a licensee of such a right rather than being restricted actually gains rights

cont.
the franchisor's rules, regulations and standards as to methods, systems, operating procedures and programmes as specified in the Franchisor's standards of operation in the conduct of the Franchisee's business as the same may be published by the Franchisor from time to time."

376 e.g. No. 4937 Register of Restrictive Trade Practices *Yves Rocher* (1985).

377 [1984] ICR 12.

378 *ibid.*, at p. 51D.

since, prior to the licence, the licensee had no rights at all to use the patent, trade mark or copyright.[379] Hence, the OFT view limitations upon the use of intellectual property sympathetically and tend not to treat them as restrictions.

(7) Non-competition covenants

10.341 Non-competition covenants are by their nature likely to cause problems under competition law. First, under the RTPA, an agreement not to compete may render an agreement subject to registration. A particular problem is raised where the franchisee is a corporate entity. In such a case, it is normal for directors of that franchisee to give non-competition covenants as well, thereby rendering the agreement one where restrictions are accepted by two or more parties. Second, to be enforceable under the common law doctrine of restraint of trade, the covenant must not go further either geographically or in duration than is necessary to protect the franchisor's legitimate business interests[380] It is unclear whether the limitations imposed by the doctrine of restraint of trade apply even if the agreement has the benefit of the block exemption,[381] but these limitations will apply even if the agreement has complied with the RTPA. It may also be noted that there can also be non-competition restrictions placed on the franchisor not to compete under any trade name or business style with the franchise business in the franchise territory during the term of the franchise agreement. Such a restriction would be caught under the RTPA, but would likely be given clearance under section 21(2), discussed below.

(8) OFT attitude: dispensation under section 21(2)

10.342 The OFT rarely experiences problems with franchise agreements. It generally adopts a pragmatic view of franchise systems, accepting that the system is a package and that the franchisor will need to closely control the franchisee if a relatively uniform network of franchisees covering a wide geographical area is to be sustained.[382] Many restrictions may benefit from exemption under the provisions mentioned above. However, it should be added that views vary concerning the application of these provisions and there is scant judicial guidance to assist those concerned with questions of registrability. In granting section 21(2) dispensation, the OFT has given some guidance as to their attitude to some commonly caught clauses.[383]

(a) A restriction on the franchisee to engage in any other business without the franchisor's consent will normally not cause a problem since it is reasonable for the franchisor to expect the franchisee to devote his full personal attention to the business.

[379] See *Automatic Telephone and Electric Co Ltd* (1964) LR 5 RP 1; (1965) LR 5 RP 135 (CA); *Ravenseft Properties* v *Director General of Fair Trading* [1977] 1 All ER 47 (QBD); and see DGFT Annual Report 1976, p. 36.

[380] Whish, *Competition Law* (3rd edn. 1993), Chapter 2. In *Prontaprint plc* v *Landon Litho Ltd* [1987] FSR 315, an interlocutory injunction was granted by Whitford J enforcing a post-termination restriction not to engage in high speed printing and copying from premises within half a mile from the franchise premises for three years after the date of termination. It should be noted that that there was no argument about whether the duration of the restriction was reasonable: there are grounds for arguing that such a period would normally be excessive, and Art. 3(1)(c) Reg.s 4087/88 refers to a maximum of one year.

[381] See paras. 6.114-6.119 for a discussion of the interaction between Community and national laws; the Commission decisions on this aspect of franchise agreements have proceeded on the basis that national law may impose more strict limits than those contained in the block exemption: see *Computerland* OJ 1987 L222/12, [1989] 4 CMLR 259, at para. 22(iii).

[382] This conforms to the view in the USA, see, e.g. *Principle* v *McDonalds Corp.* 631 F. 2d. 303 (423 Cir. 1980).

[383] M. Howe, "Franchising and restrictive practices law: the Office of Fair Trading View" [1988] ECLR 439.

(b) It will be permissible to restrict the franchisee to supplying the franchise goods and/or services to within its territory, as it is reasonable to protect other franchisees or potentially franchisable territories.
(c) The OFT will take care to ensure that recommended prices do not restrict the right, however theoretical in practice, of the franchisee to charge lower prices.
(d) Post-termination covenants must also be carefully drafted to ensure they go no further than strictly necessary to protect the franchisor and other franchisees.[384]

10.343 Naturally the OFT does not give carte blanche to franchise networks and much will depend on the market context. If the franchisor has significant economic power and is subject to little inter-brand competition then the OFT may require alterations to the agreements to be made before section 21(2) dispensation is given. The OFT in such cases might be concerned that an economically powerful franchisor has tied up in his network many of the most effective franchisees foreclosing them as retail outlets to other potential suppliers of rival brands. Where this is a possibility the OFT might require amendment of clauses in franchise agreements requiring the franchisee to take all of his requirements from the franchisor. In *Boosey and Hawkes PLC Franchise Agreements*[385] the OFT persuaded Boosey and Hawkes PLC who produce, import and distribute musical instruments, to delete from franchise agreements with retailers a clause which was designed to prevent franchisees from obtaining foreign manufactured musical instruments, which were similar to those imported and distributed by Boosey and Hawkes, from any source other than that Company. Generally, however, the OFT views market conditions as the best guarantee of competition: "In a number of cases the franchised chain has a powerful brand name to promote but in none would entry appear difficult and in virtually all cases a significant number of competitors to the chain exists. Accordingly ... we have not been unduly concerned about the competition implications of this new and fast-developing format."[386]

(9) Avoiding registration

10.344 Below is a brief summary of the points to be borne in mind when drafting a franchise agreement that is non-registrable:

(a) An agreement which is within the EC block exemption 4087/88 is in any event non-notifiable under the RTPA.[387]
(b) The agreement may contain as many restrictions described in sections 9 and/or 18 RTPA 1976 as is desired. These restrictions are to be disregarded when registration is being considered.
(c) An agreement in which the franchisee accepts restrictions but the franchisor does not is not registrable: two parties must accept restrictions before the agreement becomes registrable. A problem clause here is one prohibiting the franchisor from selling direct in the franchisee's territory. Such clauses are prima facie exempt under Schedule 3(2) RTPA 1976. However, if the clause exists with any other registrable goods restriction, it is *not* exempt (Schedule 3 restrictions are *only* exempt if they sit in isolation from other registrable restrictions) and will be caught by sec-

384 See para. 10.341.
385 DGFT Annual Report (1983), p. 107. See also No. 3262 Register of Restrictive Trade Practices, *Franchise Concerning Wallpaper and Paint* (1974)—territorial restrictions removed before section 21(2) dispensation available.
386 Howe [1988] ECLR 439, 442.
387 Restrictive Trade Practices (Non-notifiable Agreements) Order, S.I. 1996 No. 349, issued under s. 27A RTPA 1976 (added by s. 10 Deregulation and Contracting Out Act 1994).

tion 6(1)(f) (goods) as a restriction on the persons or classes of person to whom goods are to be supplied. It may also be a restraint on the places in which goods may be supplied under the same provision (see section 11 (2)(e) for the services equivalent).

(d) Only one Schedule 3 exempt restriction should be included. It has already been noted that the Schedule 3 exempt clauses must exist in isolation. However, as a matter of practice the OFT treats restrictions on intellectual property rights as *not* restrictive. Thus parties may in the same agreement have exclusivity restraints exempt by Schedule 3(2) and trade mark licence restrictions exempt under general law, i.e. parties need not rely on the Schedule 3 exemptions for intellectual property licences. Even given this lenient view of intellectual property licences franchisors who seek absolute legal security may furnish agreements on a fail-safe basis.

(e) Restrictions on goods and services are to be treated separately. Thus, the franchisor might accept restrictions on the services he supplies to the franchisee, and, the franchisee might accept goods restrictions. Although both parties accept restrictions the agreement is non-registrable. There are not two parties accepting goods restrictions or two parties accepting services restrictions.

(10) Competition Act 1980

10.345 Agreements exempt from the RTPA 1976 are subject to the CA 1980, although it is unlikely that the OFT will concentrate its efforts under this procedure. When franchise related problems have emerged in MMC investigations the MMC has recognised that a franchise system requires restrictive clauses to bind it together and that, for example, tying clauses are part and parcel of the system.[388] None the less, should problems arise it is predictable that they will arise in connection with: tying; abuse of trade mark licences; exclusive purchase and supply obligations.[389] The attitude of the OFT will depend largely upon the degree of economic power wielded by the franchisor.

(11) Note on franchisee clubs

10.346 In many franchise systems the franchisor organises a franchise club thereby linking all franchisees together. These "clubs" may very easily turn into registrable agreements. If the franchisor encourages relations between the franchisee to such an extent that franchisees begin to standardise prices, terms, conditions etc. In *Pronuptia and Young (Franchises) Ltd Agreement*[390] a clause in the franchise agreement stated:

> "In the event of agreement by a majority of the Franchisor's franchisees within an area served by a regional advertising media that a regional advertising and publicity programme designed to promote the image and name of Pronuptia should be undertaken and further agreeing to the media to be employed and the amount to be expended the Franchisee specifically agrees to abide by the majority decision of any such agreement. *Any* decision

[388] See MMC General Report into *Full Line Forcing and Tie-in Sales* (1980–81) HC 212.

[389] See MMC *Report on the Supply of Ice Cream and Water Ices*, Cmnd 7632 (1979). The MMC were critical of the supplier's practice of requiring franchisees who operated mobile vans not to stock or sell any goods other than the brands specified in the franchise agreement, nor to be concerned in certain specified areas in any other mobile business in the relevant goods. The Secretary of State negotiated undertakings with the suppliers which removed exclusive purchase requirements, tying requirements and bans on supplying competing products. Given the highly concentrated nature of the market these practices were found to create entry barriers for new suppliers, create expansion barriers for existing suppliers, and, limit consumer choice. See the Parliamentary Statement of the Minister on the report at HC Deb (1981–82) Vol. 23, col. 105–108 reprinted in DGFT Annual Report (1982), pp. 73–76.

[390] No. 4578 Register of Restrictive Trading Practices 1982.

so made shall be subject to the consent of the Franchisor and the franchisee will comply with all directions made by the Franchisor in respect of such advertising and will contribute to the cost thereof in such proportions as the Franchisor's advertising Agents shall consider fair and reason able."

10.347 Where the franchisees are providing services, then an agreement as to advertising might well be registrable under section 11(2)(d), i.e. an agreement concerning the form and manner in which designated services are to be supplied. Though, the *Pronuptia* case, above, concerned goods, and agreements concerning advertising of goods are not registrable. There is no equivalent in section 6 RTPA 1976 to section 11(2)(d). Where a franchisee club agrees on advertising policy but (as in *Pronuptia*, above) advertising restrictions are imposed on franchisees solely in the context of the contract with the franchisee, then the restriction may be exempted under section 18(2) RTPA 1976 as a term relating exclusively to the service provided. Franchisee clubs should not be used as cloaks to hide attempts by franchisees to maintain and enforce standardised resale prices.

L. Selective Distribution[391]

1. *Introduction*

10.348 Many manufacturers, especially of luxury or technical goods, desire to regulate the retail outlets through which their goods are sold.[392] Usually, manufacturers employ technical criteria: ability to provide customer services; adequacy of facilities; staff with appropriate technical expertise and experience: etc., as the basis for selecting dealers. Prima facie there is no problem under competition law since a dealer has no right *per se* to be supplied by a particular supplier. Competition law intervenes, however, where such criteria are employed in the context of a distribution system which incorporates restrictions imposed on dealers as to the persons to whom they may re-sell (usually only end-users and other authorised dealers, i.e. excluding unauthorised dealers). In general two questions of misuse of selection criteria arise:

(i) Suppliers exclude qualified dealers from their networks in order to maintain high prices or exclude modern marketing methods.

[391] For literature on selective distribution see Chard, "The economics of the application of Article 85 to selective distribution systems" (1982) ELRev 83: Sharpe, "Refusals to supply" (1983) 99 LQR 96; *Thirteenth Report on Competition Policy* (1983), pp. 38–40, paras. 33–34. Ferry, "Selective distribution and other post-sales restrictions" (1981) 2 ECLR 209; Vajda, "Selective distribution in the European Community" (1979) JWTL 409. Gyselen, "Vertical restraints in the distribution process: strength and weakness of the free rider rationale under EEC competition law" (1984) 21 CMLRev 647; Temple Lang, "Selective distribution" (1985) 7 Fordham ILJ 323; Goebel, "Metro II's confirmation of the selective distribution rules: is this the end of the road?" (1987) 24 CMLRev 605. See also, generally, Joanna Goyder, *EC Distribution Law* (2nd edn. 1996), Chapter 5. M Schödermeier, "La distribution selective et les parfums: une nouvelle logique dans le raisonnement de la Commission?" [1993] *Cahiers de Droit* 649.

[392] In Germany, selective distribution is a particularly popular means of distribution due to a favourable legal regime which allows, *inter alia*, a supplier to obtain an injunction against a retailer not admitted to that supplier's selective distribution system from supplying its goods; see Weijer (ed), *Commercial Agency and Distribution Agreements* (1989), at pp. 198–202; C-376 *Metro* v *Cartier* [1994] ECR I-15, [1994] 5 CMLR 331, paras. 19–25.

(ii) Suppliers terminate the dealership of an existing dealer on the grounds that it is suspected of price-cutting or of exporting or importing the goods so as to take advantage of price differentials between different areas.

The European Commission, the OFT and the MMC have examined many cases on this issue. Complaints from dealers either refused admission to a manufacturer's network or expelled from such a network are common.

2. *EC Law*

10.349 Criteria for dealer selection can be both qualitative and quantitative. Qualitative criteria designed to ensure that dealers are technically capable of handling the supplier's goods and have adequate physical facilities include minimum requirements as to trained personnel, stocking, provision of after-sales services, etc. Quantitative criteria operate to limit the number of outlets in a given area by making use of such criteria as population and presumed income estimates. In cases on selective distribution the Commission has stated that,

> "selective distribution systems constitute as aspect of competition which accords with Article 85(1), provided that resellers are chosen on the basis of objective criteria of a qualitative nature relating to the technical qualifications of the reseller and his staff and the suitability of his trading premises and that such conditions are laid down uniformly for all potential resellers and are not applied in a discriminatory fashion (so-called 'qualitative selective distribution system'). With regard to the qualitative criteria, the Court [has] stated that it [is] necessary to consider whether the characteristics of the product in question necessitated a selective distribution system in order to preserve its quality and ensure its proper use and whether those objectives were not already satisfied by national rules governing admission to the resale trade or the conditions of sale of the product. Finally inquiry should be made as to whether the criteria laid down did not exceed the requirements of a selective distribution system based on qualitative requirements."[393]

10.350 In general criteria of an objective qualitative nature fall outside of Article 85(1); criteria of a quantitative nature usually fall within Article 85(1) but may obtain exemption under Article 85(3) in appropriate cases.

(1) General conditions to be met to avoid the application of Article 85(1)

10.351 The following are characteristics of a system outside Article 85(1):

(a) The product is of a type which necessitates selective distribution;
(b) criteria are objective;
(c) criteria are of a qualitative nature;
(d) qualitative criteria pertain to technical qualifications and/or the suitability of trading premises;
(e) the criteria are applied uniformly and without discrimination to all applicant dealers;
(f) the qualitative criteria actually adopted do not exceed the minimum necessary to operate the system effectively.

[393] *Grohe* OJ 1985 I 9/17 p. 20, para. 14 (23 January 1985). See also *Ideal-Standard* OJ 1985 120/38 at p. 41, para. 14 (24 January, 1985); *Metro* (Case 26/76) [1978] CMLR 1; [1977] ECR 1875; Case 31/80 *L'Oreal* [1981] 2 CMLR 235; [1980] ECR 3775; Case 126/80 *Salonia* [1981] ECR 1563; *SABA No. 2* [1984] 1 CMLR 676; Case 107/82 *AEG Telefunken* v *Commission* [1984] 3 CMLR 325, (1983) ECR 3151 at para. 35 of the judgment.

10.352 A manufacturer who sets the criteria at a very high standard may still avoid Article 85(1) provided the conditions above are met, although a supplier with a dominant position, who restricts outlets so as to restrain output thereby maintaining high demand which in turn sustains supra-competitive prices, might breach Article 86 EC on abuse of a dominant position. The first requirement, then, is that the product must be of a type which necessitates selective distribution. Neither the Commission not the ECJ have identified categories of such products; instead they have proceeded on a case-by-case basis. However, decisions do indicate that products will generally qualify if they are either technically complex or products the brand image of which is particularly important. Products for which a selective distribution system has been held to be appropriate include consumer electronic products such as televisions,[394] quality watches and clocks,[395] ceramic tableware[396] and perfumes and other cosmetics.[397] On the other hand, selective distribution systems have not been considered appropriate for mass produced watches,[398] plumbing products[399] and tobacco products.[400] The Commission has said that the eligibility of a product for a selective distribution system may change over time. This may occur, for example, where consumers become more sophisticated and less in need of advice from sales staff on how to use technical products.[401] The likelihood of this approach being applied in practice, however, must be queried; products such as televisions and hi-fis are familiar to the public yet the Court of Justice has confirmed that such products may continue to benefit from a selective system.[402]

10.353 Secondly, the criteria must be objective and of a qualitative nature. In addition they must be applied without discrimination to all applicant dealers. For examples of clauses which have been held to fulfil these conditions, see below.

10.354 Thirdly, the qualitative criteria must not exceed what is essential to meet the legitimate needs of the system as a whole. For example, in *Junghans*[403] the Commission complained that it was unnecessary to require the dealers to be trained clock and watch specialists since specialist staff could be found in non-specialist outlets which rendered them qualified to act as dealers.

10.355 Fourthly, selective criteria must not be discriminatory or arbitrary. Thus, for example, discount and department stores must be supplied where they meet the relevant criteria. The Commission also stresses that suppliers must not apply their criteria (however objective) in an arbitrary manner, e.g. by stalling for many months on the application of a suitably qualified dealer thereby deterring such firms and discriminating against them in relation to authorised dealers. In *Binon* v *Agence et Messageries de la Presse*[404] the Court of

394 Case 26/76 *Metro SB-Grossmarkte GmbH and Co KG* v *EC Commission* [1977] ECR 1875, [1978] 2 CMLR 1.

395 *Omega Watches* OJ [1970] L242/22, [1970] CMLR D 49.

396 *Villeroy and Boch* OJ [1985] L376/15, [1988] 4 CMLR 461.

397 *Yves Saint Laurent Parfums* OJ [1992] L12/24; *Parfums Givenchy system of selective distribution* OJ [1992] L236/11.

398 Case 31/85 *ETA Fabriques d'Ebauches SA* v *DK Investment* [1985] ECR 3933, [1986] 2 CMLR 674.

399 *Grohe* OJ [1985] L19/17, [1988] 4 CMLR 612; *Ideal-Standard's Distribution System* OJ [1985] L20/38, [1988] 4 CMLR 627. The Commission considered that it was "doubtful" whether plumbing fittings could be regarded as technically advanced products. Appeals against these decisions were later withdrawn.

400 Case 209-215/78 *Heintz Van Landewyck Sarl* v *EC Commission* [1980] ECR 3125, [1981] 3 CMLR 193. The ECJ observed that tobacco products were not highly technical goods and, therefore, traders did not have to be selected on the basis of qualitative criteria. The Court gave not consideration to issues of brand image.

401 See *dicta* of the Commission in *IBM Personal Computer* OJ [1984] L118/24, [1984] 2 CMLR 342 at para. 15.

402 e.g. Case 26/76 *Metro SB-Grossmarkte GmbH and Co KG* v *EC Commission* [1977] ECR 1875, [1978] 2 CMLR 1.

403 [1977] 1 CMLR D 82.

404 Case 243/83 [1985] ECR 2015, [1985] 3 CMLR 800; see also Case 107/82 *AEG Telefunken* v *Commission* [1983] ECR 3157 at paras. 40–43 and 67–76 of the judgment.

Justice held that a distribution agency which acted for most of the Belgian newspaper publishers as well as on its own behalf and which applied criteria of admission to a selective distribution scheme which were stricter for retailers who were not members of the distribution agency's own group of enterprises than for retailers who were members of the group, infringed Article 85(1). Some producers set up two-tier selective distribution systems. These involve the selection of both wholesalers and retailers. The Commission will be more likely to decide that a selective distribution system falls outside Article 85(1) where decisions concerning admittance to the network are not determined solely by the producer, but instead are left to or shared with wholesalers.

10.356 The Commission is also concerned to see that applications are dealt with swiftly; a producer may delay in processing applications as a device to limit the total number of dealers. However, only qualitative (and not quantitative) criteria fall outside Article 85(1). Thus in *Yves Saint Laurent Parfums*[405] the Commission required amendments to the admission procedure. In particular, the original procedure provided that dealers who wished to be admitted were placed on a waiting list. Each application was to be dealt with in the order in which it was entered onto the list but the decision to grant applications was taken only where the opening of a new account was justified in terms of the economic potential in the area in question. The terms were amended to include strict time limits within which the outlet of each applicant would be inspected and the provision of a reasoned response to the application which, if appropriate, would identify the work needed to be done at the premises to bring it up to the specified standard.

10.357 The fifth general condition is that the system must contain no contractual clauses caught by Article 85(1) or else the contract will be notifiable and exemption under Article 85(3) will have to be sought.

10.358 In addition, it may be that Article 85(1) would apply, notwithstanding that all of the above requirements are fulfilled, where the market is tied up with similar agreements. This point was made by the Court of Justice in *Metro* v *Commission (No. 2).*[406]

(2) Examples of selective distribution criteria not within Article 85(1)

10.359 Examples of clauses which have been held to fall outside Article 85(1) are given below. It should, however, be appreciated that whether an obligation avoids Article 85(1) may depend upon the product in question and upon market context. In particular, a condition which is held to be qualitative in relation to one product may be considered quantitative in relation to another if, given the nature of the product, it is not objectively necessary. Hence, not every clause listed below will escape Article 85(1) in every case.

10.360 (a) Dealers must possess a specialised department especially equipped to handle the product.[407]

10.361 (b) The location, name and fittings of the retail outlet must reflect the prestige of the brand name in question.[408] In *Yves Saint Laurent* the Commission commented that the "maintenance of a prestige brand image is, on the luxury cosmetics market, an essential factor in competition; no producer can maintain its position on the market without constant promotion activities. Clearly such promotion activities would

[405] OJ [1992] L12/24, [1993] 4 CMLR 120.

[406] Case 75/84 [1986] ECR 3021, [1987] 1 CMLR 118.

[407] See *Villeroy and Boch* OJ 1985 L376/15. The Commission granted negative clearance to a system in respect of the sale of ceramic tableware and ornaments.

[408] *Yves Saint Laurent Parfums* Commission Decision of 16 December 1991, [1992] OJ L12/24; *Parfums Givenchy* Commission Decision of 24 July 1992, OJ [1992] L236/11.

be thwarted if, at the retail stage, YSL products were marketed in such a manner that was liable to affect the way consumers perceived them. Thus, the criteria governing the location and aesthetic and functional qualities of the retail outlet constitute legitimate requirements by the producer, since they are aimed at providing the consumer with a setting that is in line with the luxurious and exclusive nature of the products."

10.362 (c) The retailer must stock and display a sufficiently wide and varied range of the product. In *Villeroy and Boch*[409] this condition was held not to restrict competition because (i) inter-brand rivalry was very high in the market; (ii) no sales targets were imposed upon dealers; (iii) dealers could hold competing stocks. However, in some cases, such stock-holding conditions have been held to be caught by Article 85(1).[410]

10.363 (d) Dealers must display the contract goods in an attractive manner and not in association with other products which might harm the supplier's brand image.[411] Other clauses relating to the size of the area set aside in an outlet for the manufacturer's goods and their proximity to other products have also been granted negative clearance by the Commission.[412] However, if the clause were to contain either contractual specifications as to the identity or number of brands sold alongside the suppliers products or minimum quantitative requirements regarding the allocation of the space set aside for the sale of the contract products, then it would be caught by Article 85(1) since its effect would be to limit the retailer's freedom to sell and promote competing brands.

10.364 (f) Dealers must offer after-sales services. In *Villeroy and Boch*[413] this requirement was held to be objectively necessary and, hence, qualitative, given the need to ensure continuity of supply to the customer. Dinner services and other ceramic products may include a large number of composite items; if these are broken and require replacement it is important that they can subsequently be purchased individually. In *IBM Personal Computer*[414] one of the clauses of the distribution agreement specified that dealers had to have facilities and staff able to service IBM personal computers.

10.365 (g) The producer retains the right to verify the qualifications of specialised dealers admitted to the network.[415]

10.366 (h) Sales staff must be properly trained. Again, whether this type of clause falls outside Article 85(1) is dependent on the nature of the product. For example, if a product is technically complex then the Commission will probably regard it as reasonable that there

[409] OJ 1985 L376/15; see also the Commission Decisions in *Krups* OJ [1980] L 120/26 and *Murat* OJ [1983] L 348/20, [1984] 1 CMLR 219.

[410] See paras. 10.383–10.384.

[411] *Villeroy and Boch* OJ 1985 L376/15.

[412] Thus, in *Yves Saint Laurent Parfums* Commission Decision of 16 December 1991, [1992] OJ L12/24, the distribution agreement contained a clause stating that "the area set aside for the sale of YSL products must not be disproportionate to the number of brands sold. In addition, it must allow the authorised retailer to provide, having regard to the other brands represented, a location reflecting the prestige of the YSL brand and allowing it to be identified by the consumer. The Commission held that this clause fell outside Art. 85(1) since shops could comply with it by having a specialised counter and thus department stores, etc., were not excluded. See also *Parfums Givenchy* Commission Decision of 24 July 1992, OJ [1992] L236/11.

[413] *Villeroy and Boch* OJ 1985 L376/15.

[414] [1984] 2 CMLR 342.

[415] Where the distribution system has two levels, the Commission will view the arrangement more favourably where the verification of the qualifications of the retailers is left to the wholesalers rather than the manufacturers para. 10.355.

should be trained staff available to demonstrate its use to customers. This was the case in *IBM Personal Computer*.[416] The Commission may also regard such requirements as reasonable where high quality, luxury goods are at issue. For example, in *Yves Saint Laurent Parfums*[417] the Commission held that a clause requiring retailers to employ staff with a professional qualification in perfumery fell outside Article 85(1). The Commission considered that "having specialised technical advice available in the retail outlet is a legitimate requirement in so far as the knowledge specifically required is necessary in order to help consumers select the products best suited to their tastes and requirements and to provide them with the best information on their use and preservation."

10.367 (i) Objectively justified technical criteria. An example is *D'Ieteren Motor Oils*[418] where, in the context of car dealer agreements, the Commission held that the supplier's recommendations to distributors to use only oils which were approved by Volkswagen was an objective criterion of a technical nature and, therefore, not caught by Article 85(1).

10.368 (j) Dealers must not supply non-approved dealers.[419] In some cases, however, the Commission has taken the view that such a clause is caught by Article 85(1).[420] Where such a clause is held to fall outside Article 85(1) it follows that obligations imposed on retailers which enable the supplier to check that supplies of products only come from authorised distributors will also fall outside Article 85(1) provided they go no further than is strictly necessary to ensure the cohesiveness of the distribution system.[421] In practice, this means, for example, that the supplier may only impose obligations to allow it to check a dealer's invoices if the supplier has concrete evidence that the dealer has been involved in selling to non-authorised parties.[422]

10.369 (k) Restrictions on warranties only being honoured if the product is sold through an authorised dealer are not contrary to Article 85(1). In *Metro* v *Cartier*[423] the Court of Justice explained that as it was legitimate to restrict suppliers to members of a selective distribution network, *a fortiori* it was legitimate to restrict warranties of those products to persons purchasing only from the authorised retailers within that distribution network. However, it will be necessary to ensure that a warranty for a product bought from an authorised retailer in one Member State can be honoured in other Member States. The Commission takes the view that otherwise cross-border sales transactions will be discouraged contrary to the aims of a single market.[424]

10.370 (l) Dealers must have appropriate demonstration and advertising display space and be willing to maintain display space for demonstration purposes.[425]

10.371 (m) Dealers must have a favourable banker's reference and credit rating.[426]

[416] [1984] 2 CMLR 342 noted by Green (1984) 2 *Journal of Computer Law and Practice* 70. The supply agreement further specified that dealers must, within the warranty period, provide services for *any* IBM machine irrespective of the place of sale or identity of the seller. See also, *Grundig's EC Distribution System* Commission Decision of 21 December 1993, [1994] OJ L20/15.

[417] *Yves Saint Laurent Parfums* Commission Decision of 16 December 1991, [1992] L236/11.

[418] OJ [1991] L20/42].

[419] *Grundig's EC Distribution System* Commission Decision of 21 December 1993, [1994] OJ L20/15. See also, *Metro SB-Großmarkte GmbH and Co KG* v *EC Commission* [1977] ECR 1875, [1978] 2 CMLR 1.

[420] See *Parfums Givenchy* Commission Decision of 24 July, 192, OJ [1992] L236/11.

[421] See *Yves Saint Laurent Parfums* Commission Decision of 16 December 1991, [1992] OJ L12/24.

[422] *ibid.*

[423] C-376/92 *Metro SB-Großmärkte GmbH* v *Cartier SA* [1994] ECR I-15, [1994] 5 CMLR 331.

[424] Grundig, *Twenty-third Report on Competition Policy*, para. 243.

[425] *IBM Personal Computer* [1984] 2 CMLR 342.

[426] *ibid.*

10.372 (n) Dealers must submit their advertisements (though not any price or conditions adverts) to the producer for approval.[427]

10.373 (o) Dealers must maintain records of customer names and addresses, serial numbers of purchases and dates of delivery for the purpose of repairs under warranty and make the records available to the producer in the event of any necessary safety changes.[428]

10.374 (p) Dealers must retain full records of deliveries to other approved dealers and supply them to the producer on request. Such a clause was held to fall outside Article 85(1) in *Grundig's EC Distribution System*;[429] however, the Commission stated that Grundig could only make such requests where there was evidence of products escaping the approved distribution channels. Furthermore, the inclusion of the clause was conditional upon Grundig agreeing to report annually to the Commission all cases where it has requested information. In the light of this, the Commission concluded that "there are no grounds for supposing that Grundig might use this clause in order to check resale prices and in particular to maintain different prices in different Member States."

10.375 (q) Dealers must not advertise in a manner likely to lead the consumer to believe that they are selling products without providing the quality of service that the supplier is seeking to establish, e.g. they may not advertise "cash-and-carry prices, self-service prices, or take-away prices."[430]

10.376 (r) Wholesalers must not supply private final customers. Where wholesalers sell to commercial private customers, a special declaration may be required to be signed, stating that the goods are to be used for business purposes and are "objectively justified".[431]

10.377 (s) Dealers prevented from selling the products by mail order. In *YSL Parfums*[432] the Commission held that this requirement was not an appreciable restriction of competition since, supplying the product under optimum conditions "presupposes direct contact between customers and sales staff"; in addition, the Commission viewed the requirement as "a necessary corollary to the criteria designed to ensure that the contract products are presented in as homogeneous a way as possible and that the producer can continuously supervise the qualitative level of its distribution network."

(3) Agreements falling within Article 85(1) seeking exemption under Article 85(3)

10.378 Agreements not falling outside of Article 85(1) may obtain exemption under Article 85(3). Clauses which will be caught by Article 85(1) include quantitative restrictions. These are restrictions which either directly or indirectly seek to impose numerical limits on the number of appointed dealers. Other restrictions which are generally caught by Article 85(1) include territorial restraints, restrictions on dealers' price margins, customer restrictions and turnover restrictions. In many cases such clauses are denied Article 85(3) exemption as the Commission views limitations on the number of dealers, for example, as harmful to consumer choice. In particular, a selective distribution system is unlikely to be granted exemption if it confers absolute territorial protection, or restricts parallel imports or attempts to control prices. However, in certain cases exemption has been granted (see below for examples).

[427] *ibid.*

[428] *ibid.*

[429] [1994] OJ L20/15.

[430] *ibid.*

[431] *ibid.*

[432] *Yves Saint Laurent Parfums* Commission Decision of 16 December 1991, [1992] OJ L12/24.

10.379 One of the requirements under Article 85(3) is that the agreement does not provide the parties with any scope for eliminating competition. The market share of the supplier will be relevant here as will the question of whether the market is ties up with many other similar agreements.[433] The Commission has also stated, with regard to the indispensability requirement of Article 85(3), that it "should be noted that indispensability does not mean that there must be no other feasible way of distributing the products, but that the restrictions of competition are necessary for the particular marketing strategy adopted by the manufacturer, which is judged to have the beneficial effects referred to in Article 85(3).

10.380 The most common argument raised in support of quantitative restrictions is the free-rider argument. Essentially, where a retailer is required to undertake expensive stocking, display and promotion services in connection with the sale of a product, there is a need for protection from sellers of the same brand of product who can, parasitically, "free-ride" on the promotional activities of the authorised dealers. Customers may exploit display and pre-sales services offered by an authorised dealer but then purchase from a cheaper non-authorised seller around the corner. If this trend continues, authorised dealers may be forced to discard promotional services in order to reduce price and remain competitive. In turn, the products will not receive the expert treatment they require and which is necessary to protect the manufacturer's reputation. Quantitative limits on dealer numbers protect dealers because the customer's ability to shop around is limited by the distance between dealers. This "free-rider" argument is easier to justify where technically complex goods are involved since they, by their nature, require specialist care.

10.381 A further argument in favour of quantitative limits is that they facilitate rational distribution and keep prices down. If manufacturers must supply advertising literature and supervise an unnecessarily large group of dealers, costs will increase which might have to be passed on; retailers whose turnovers were proportionately smaller as new dealers were admitted, might seek increased margins to compensate.

(4) Examples of clauses falling within Article 85(1) but gaining exemption under Article 85(3)

10.382 (a) Limitations on the number of dealers in a particular area. The Commission has long stated[434] that exemptions can be granted in respect of such clauses only in exceptional circumstances and then only where the technical or other nature of the product is such that there must be close cooperation between manufacturer and dealer which could not be secured under some other system. However, in three decisions the Commission has granted exemption in respect of systems involving territorial limitations on outlets.[435] The reasons given by the Commission for granting exemption were those explained above relating to 'free-riding' and rationalisation of costs.

10.383 (b) Retailers must keep adequate stocks of a representative selection of the whole range.[436]

[433] See, for example, *Grundig* Commission Decision of 21 December 1993, [1994] OJ L20/15 where the Commission renewed its grant of exemption to Grundig's selective distribution system, noting that (i) Grundig did not have a sufficiently large market share to eliminate competition between dealers, and (ii) many manufacturers distribute their products without selective distribution and, therefore, there was no significant danger that other forms of distribution (hypermarkets, etc.) would be excluded from distributing such products. See also *Twenty-third Report on Competition Policy*, para. 211.

[434] *Fifth Report on Competition Policy* (1975), points 12–13.

[435] See *Omega* [1970] CMLR D49, *BMW* [1975] 1 CMLR D44, *Ivoclar* OJ [1985] L369/1.

[436] *Grundig* Commission Decision of 21 December 1993, [1994] OJ L20/15.

10.384 (c) Wholesalers must carry and stock as far as possible the entire range.[437] The Commission usually regards such clauses as anti-competitive for two reasons. On the one hand, depending on the product, it may amount to a quantitative restriction as outlets may simply not have the space to comply with the requirement. Secondly, it restricts the ability of dealers to sell other products and contributes towards market foreclosure.

10.385 (d) Retailers must achieve a specified minimum annual purchase figure. This type of clause is usually[438] caught by Article 85(1). The Commission takes the view that it restricts both inter-brand and intra-brand competition since "it has the effect, on the one hand, of restricting access to the distribution network to resellers who are able to enter into such a commitment and, on the other, of obliging authorised retailers to devote a significant proportion of their activities to selling the contract products."[439] Exemption may be granted, however, as it was in *Yves Saint Laurent Parfums*[440] where the Commission stated that the obligation was a means of "ensuring, on the one hand, that the costs borne by the manufacturer will be covered by an adequate volume of business and, on the other, that the authorised retailer will contribute actively to enhancing the brand through customer service that is in line with the reputation of the contract products."

10.386 (e) The retail outlet must, within eighteen months of the date on which the distribution is concluded, carry a sufficient number of competing brands to reflect the image and reputation of the contract products. In *Givenchy*[441] the Commission stated that, although this clause did not in isolation restrict competition, it did have this effect when viewed alongside the clause requiring retailers to achieve a minimum annual purchases figure. This is because it could restrict the ability of authorised retailers go gain access to the selective distribution system as a result of the possible overlapping of the contractual obligations imposed by competing manufacturers. That such clauses are not always caught by Article 85(1) is demonstrated by *Compagnie des Cristalleries Baccarat*[442] where the Commission held that the requirement that other competing products be available at the point of sale fell outside Article 85(1).

10.387 (f) Dealers must cooperate in the manufacturer's advertising and cooperation activities. The Commission usually[443] considers that such clauses are caught by Article 85(1) since they result in the autonomy of authorised dealers to determine their own commercial policy being restricted. However, exemption will, generally, be granted as long as the constraints imposed by the requirement are not such as to prevent retailers from taking advantage of inter-brand competition.[444]

437 *ibid.*

438 But see *Compagnie des Cristalleries Baccarat* p. 76 of Commission's *Twenty-first Report on Competition Policy*. One of the requirements of Baccarat's selective distribution agreement was that, in order to continue selling Baccarat products, the distributor was required to have a minimum annual pre-tax turnover of an amount fixed at the manufacturer's discretion. Having received undertakings from Baccarat that this amount would be kept within the limits of a reasonable threshold determined notably by reference to the trend of the average turnover achieved by all of its distributors, the Commission concluded that the agreement was not caught by Art. 85(1).

439 *Yves Saint Laurent Parfums* Commission Decision of 16 December 1991, [1992] OJ L12/24.

440 *ibid.*

441 *Parfums Givenchy* Commission Decision of 24 July 1992, OJ [1992] L236/11.

442 See p. 76 of the Commission's *Twenty-first Report on Competition Policy*.

443 Note, however, that this requirement was considered qualitative and, therefore, fell outside Art. 85(1) in *Villeroy and Boch* OJ [1985] L376/15 and *Krups* OJ [1980] L120/26.

444 *Yves Saint Laurent Parfums* Commission Decision of 16 December 1991, [1992] OJ L12/24.

10.388 (g) Dealers must not supply to other non-authorised dealers. On occasion, the Commission has held that this type of clause falls outside Article 85(1).[445] In *Givenchy*[446] the Commission stated that this requirement restricted competition but, nevertheless, granted exemption, stating that it was "a necessary condition for ensuring the cohesiveness and tightness of the selective distribution system".

10.389 (h) Dealers on whose territory a new product has not yet been launched must refrain from engaging in active sale of it for one year as from the date on which the product was first launched in a Member State. The Commission stated in *Yves Saint Laurent Parfums*[447] that this constitutes a restriction of competition since it "has the effect of limiting authorised retailers' freedom of commercial initiative and of impeding cross-supplies between members of the distribution network". However, exemption was granted as the clause had the benefit of enabling the manufacturer to test a new product on a given market and to reserve the right, in the light of the results obtained on that market, to extend or stop the marketing of the product. However, it must be stressed that the Commission would not grant exemption to a clause which, not only prohibited active cross-border sales, but amounted to an export ban.[448]

(5) Examples of clauses which are not generally granted exemption pursuant to Article 85(3)

10.390 (a) Dealers must not supply other dealers within the Community. Restrictions on horizontal sales between distributors are thought to inhibit cross-border trade and rigidify the distribution system. The Commission's policy not to exempt such clauses is well-established and has received the approval of the ECJ. In 1990 Yves Saint Laurent amended clauses in its standard-form contracts to ensure freedom of cross supplies between members of its distribution network;[449] subsequently the Commission granted an individual exemption.[450] The fact that the prohibition on cross-supplies is not applied in practice does not affect the matter.[451]

10.391 (b) Dealers are prohibited from exporting to other EC countries.[452] The Commission has adopted a tough attitude towards export bans and is concerned to make sure that, even in the event of territorial exclusivity, the possibility of parallel imports remains. It is clear that exports bans are illegal even if they are not enforced; in addition, the Commission will refuse exemption to other, less overt, hindrances to parallel imports. This is examined earlier in this chapter.[453] In *Bayo-n-Ox*[454] the Commission considered an arrangement whereby Bayer, the German chemical firm, supplied goods at a discount to customers prepared to use the goods solely for their

[445] See para. 10.368.

[446] *Parfums Givenchy* Commission Decision of 24 July 1992, OJ [1992] L236/11.

[447] *Yves Saint Laurent Parfums* Commission Decision of 16 December 1991, [1992] OJ L12/24.

[448] See e.g. *Bayo-n-Ox* [1990] 4 CMLR 930; on appeal, Case C-195/91 P *Bayer* v *Commission* [1994] ECR I-5619.

[449] *Yves Saint Laurent Parfums SA* (Commission Notice) OJ [1990] C320/11, [1991] 4 CMLR 163. See also, *Compagnie des Cristalleries Baccarat*, p. 76, Commission's *Twenty-first Report on Competition Policy*.

[450] OJ [1992] L12/24, [1993] 4 CMLR 120.

[451] Case 86/82 *Hasselblad* v *Commission* [1984] ECR 883, [1984] 1 CMLR 559 para. 56.

[452] e.g. *Ford Werke* v *Commission* [1985] 3 CMLR 528. In *Chanel*, OJ 1994 C334/11, the Commission stated that it was only prepared to grant a comfort letter to a luxury watch distribution network on the basis that there was no export ban in the EC, EEA, Switzerland and all the countries which have concluded free trade agreements with the EC.

[453] See paras. 10.97-10.116.

[454] [1990] 4 CMLR 930; on appeal, Case C-195/91 P *Bayer* v *Commission* [1994] ECR I-5619.

own purposes. The Commission held that this was contrary to Article 85(1) as being tantamount to an export ban: "the own-use requirement ... has as its object and effect prevention of the resale of the product by such undertakings and hence also its export by them to other Member States. The very wording of the agreement makes it clear that such undertakings are to be ruled out as possible sources of supply for Bayo-n-Ox. The position of the other actual or potential suppliers is thus artificially reinforced and competition on the supply side restricted." The Commission rejected Bayer's claim that a contractual restriction on a group of resellers does not constitute a restriction of competition provided resellers are chosen on the basis of objective criteria of a qualitative nature, stating that, if a selective distribution system is to be unobjectionable from a competition point of view, it must include freedom to trade within the network of authorised firms.

10.392 (c) Fixing of selling prices: the Commission will generally not tolerate attempts by suppliers to set and enforce retail prices. Price rigidity is often inherent in selective distribution systems without supplier interference. This has been recognised by both the Commission and the European Court. In *AEG-Telefunken*[455] the Court noted that price rigidity was due to the fact that prices charged in specialist outlets tended to stay within a more narrow margin then they would have done had there been competition from non-specialist dealers. Further, they accepted that this price rigidity was counter-balanced by competition in the quality of services afforded customers. However, they added that the setting of minimum profit margins was unjustified where the effect was to exclude cheaper yet still specialist departments in new types of retail establishment which would provide equally extensive services in respect of goods. AEG Telefunken was fined for only appointing dealers who agreed to charge certain prices, for seeking to protect appointed dealers from further competition and for seeking directly and indirectly to dictate resale prices to dealers. It would seem from this judgment that price restrictions, if at all legal, will never be so where they are imposed and enforced so as to artificially sustain price levels and exclude new forms of marketing methods.

10.393 (d) Finally, in accordance with the requirements of Article 85(3), the Commission will not grant exemption to any restriction which is not indispensable to its objective. For example, in *Vichy*[456] the Commission refused exemption to a requirement that distributors of cosmetic products had to possess a diploma in pharmacy since, as in eight Member States that qualification was numerically limited, that was equivalent to a quantitative not qualitative restriction. It was held[457] to be disproportionate to require perfume retailers to hold such a qualification given the nature of the product involved.

(6) Selective distribution and motor vehicles

10.394 The Commission has adopted a special Regulation providing block exemption to certain selective distribution criteria for motor vehicle[458] distribution and servicing agree-

[455] Case 107/82 [1983] ECR 3757 at para. 42. But cf. Case 243/83 *Binon* v *Agence et Messageries de la Presse* [1985] ECR 2015, [1985] 3 CMLR 800. There are hints in this judgment that RPM might be exemptible under Art. 85(3) in the specialised context of newspaper distribution.

[456] OJ [1991] L75/57.

[457] At para. 18(c). This ruling was upheld by the CFI in T-19/91 *Vichy* v *Commission* [1992] ECR II-415.

[458] The term motor vehicle applies only to vehicles having three or more wheels. The Commission confirmed in its *Twenty-third Report on Competition Policy* (1993), para. 335, that the block exemption does not apply to motor cycle distribution agreements, for which the exclusive distribution block exemption or franchising block exemptions appear the most suitable means of applying a block exemption.

ments, Regulation 1475/95.[459] This new block exemption (replacing an earlier version) restricts the ability of motor car suppliers to place restrictions on dealers permitted by the earlier block exemption. For those requiring a detailed analysis of the language of this block exemption the Commission have published explanatory notes.[460] The block exemption recognises the need for specialist distribution particularly because vehicles are consumer durables that require expert maintenance and repair at periodic intervals. Moreover, the Commission recognise that close co-operation between manufacturers (or their importers) and a number of selected dealers and repairers guarantee the provision of specialised servicing for the product. Finally, the Commission has recognised that inter-brand competition may well be more relevant than intra-brand competition and that restrictions on competition between dealers and repairers may be tolerated.[461]

A brief summary of the main provisions of the Regulation appear below.

10.395 (a) Permissible restraints on the motor dealer: not to sell new vehicles of another manufacturer, except on separate sales premises, under separate management, in the form of a distinct legal entity and in a manner which avoids confusion between makes.[462]
Not actively to seek customers by personalised advertising outside his allotted territory.[463] This means that dealers may meet unsolicited orders from outside of their territory and may advertise for orders, provided this is done in a non-personalised manner.
Not to sub-contract distribution or servicing and repairs to other dealers or repairers without the permission of the manufacturer (or his importer).[464]
Not to sell new vehicles or replacement parts obtained from the manufacturer to dealers outside the distribution network.[465]

10.396 (b) Manufacturer restraints: manufacturers may restrict their freedom to appoint other dealers or to supply end-users direct in the allotted territory.[466]

10.397 (c) Restrictions imposed by the Regulation designed to protect competition and unrestricted freedom of consumers to purchase new cars *wherever* price and conditions are most favourable: consumers must be able to obtain servicing and repairs under the manufacturer's guarantee performed anywhere in the EC;[467] dealers

[459] OJ 1994 L145/25. This replaced the earlier block exemption on this topic, Reg. 123/85, OJ 1985 L115/1, with effect from 1 July 1995.

[460] The Explanatory Brochure is available from the Commission, and is published under the reference number IV/9509/95.

[461] See generally *Fourteenth Report on Competition Policy* (1984), pp. 42–44, in relation to Reg. 123/85.

[462] Art. 3(3), Reg. 1475/95. Under the previous block exemption the dealer could be restricted from dealing in competing makes under any circumstance.

[463] Art. 3(8), Reg. 1475/95.

[464] Art. 3(6), Reg. 1475/95.

[465] The Commission's Supplementary Notice of 18 December 1991, OJ 1991 C329/20, indicates that this restriction cannot be used to refuse to supply intermediaries or agents acting on behalf of and on the account of the final user of the vehicle. The Commission issued this Notice after issuing an interim measures decision against Peugeot, [1990] 4 CMLR 449, ordering it to cease preventing its Belgian and Luxembourg dealers supplying an intermediary, Eco System, which was purchasing cars for French customers. This decision was upheld by the Court of First Instance, T-23/90 *Peugeot* v *Commission* [1991] ECR II-653, [1993] 5 CMLR 540. See also Answer to WQ 1834/94, [1994] 5 CMLR 514, in which the Competition Commissioner confirmed that refusals to supply German private customers in Denmark would be contrary to the block exemption, even though the difference in prices between these two Member States is due to the very high tax imposed on car purchases in Denmark leading to lower pre-tax prices to compensate.

[466] Art. 1, Reg. 1475/95.

[467] Art. 3(10) Reg. 1475/95. The Commission stressed this requirement, in respect of which it has received many complaints from consumers about its non-fulfilment in practice, in its *Twenty-third Report on Competition Policy* (1993), para. 335.

must not become over-dependent on manufacturers. Agreements must specify at least one year's notice for termination and may require two years.[468] Consumers must be able to purchase new cars with the specifications they require at the place where they are to be registered from official dealers in other Member States who are willing to supply, if the manufacturer (or his importer) sells the model concerned via the official distribution network at both places. This prevents manufacturers and their importers from preventing or hindering the sales of right hand drive cars on the continent.

10.398 Breach of any of the above three situations may result in withdrawal of the block exemption, as will any of the other matters listed in Article 6 of the Regulation.

10.399 As regards the often acute price differentials existing between car prices in the Member States this is assumed to be a reflection of the particular play of market forces about which the Commission does not intend to take particular action.[469] However, the Commission has commented that very high differentials may be a sign of governmental or private restrictive measures. In extreme cases price differentials may lead the Commission to withdraw the block exemption. Moreover, the Commission has stated: "where European consumers wishing to buy a vehicle with the specifications of their own country in another Member State are confronted with supplementary charges which are not objectively justified, bringing the price of the vehicle above that which would result in normal competitive circumstances, a Commission proceeding to withdraw the exemption may follow."[470]

10.400 The block exemption applies retroactively to automobile dealership agreements existing prior to 1 July 1995 (date of coming into force of the Regulation), as well as to agreements concluded after that date. Agreements enjoying the benefit of Regulation 123/85 had until 30 September 1995 to be amended to comply with Regulation 1475/95.[471]

3. *UK Law*

(1) Selective distribution and the Competition Act 1980

10.401 Selective distribution is unlikely to involve the RTPA 1976. This is because restrictions are likely only to be accepted by one party, and even if the supplier also accepts restrictions, these are likely to be related only to the goods supplied, thus being disregarded under section 9(3) of the RTPA, or are otherwise within the terms of Schedule 3(2). Invariably OFT involvement is triggered by the complaint of a dealer who has either been refused supplies or whose dealership has been terminated by a supplier, In such cases the OFT treat the case as a possible anti-competitive practice by the manufacturer. The MMC in monopoly investigations has faced the problem on a number of occasions also. Both the OFT and MMC recognise the need for selective distribution and the need to confine supplies to specialist retailers. Thus the MMC has accepted for example that infant foods may be limited to chemists who have the expertise to proffer adequate advice to customers.[472]

468 Art. 5(2)(2), Reg. 1475 95.

469 The Commission has been conducting regular price surveys across the EC to monitor divergences in car prices and to discern the reasons, which it hopes will guide it in its revision of the block exemption: see *Twenty-third Report on Competition Policy* (1993), para. 335. See also Miller, "The price of a car in Europe: a glance at the future" [1992] ECLR 177.

470 *Fourteenth Report on Competition Policy* (1984) at p. 44, para. 40; *Fiat* Bull EC 5/84 at p. 38. See also Commission answer to WQ No. 2225/85, OJ 1986 C137/17.

471 Art. 13, Reg. 1475/95.

472 MMC Report on *Supply of Infant Milk Foods* (1976–77) HC 319. See also MMC *Report on the Wholesaling of Newspapers and Periodicals* (Cmnd 7214, 1978).

(2) Qualitative criteria

10.402 The first proper investigation under the CA 1980, *Raleigh*,[473] concerned selective distribution. The OFT and MMC analysis in this case has, however, received criticism.[474] Raleigh are bicycle manufacturers. Since 1972 when their market share was 67 per cent they had declined to a 40 per cent market share in 1980 owing to intensified domestic and import competition. The conduct complained of was Raleigh's refusal to supply multiple retail stores, since they preferred to supply only to specialist dealers who could provide specialist facilities for pre-sales inspection, advice, and spare parts. The OFT considered that the strength of Raleigh's brand image was of "critical importance" to the analysis. The enviable brand image of Raleigh meant that competition would be distorted if the multiples were refused supplies. The OFT concluded that the refusal to supply was anti-competitive and referred the case to the MMC.[475] This body considered the public interest arguments. It rejected Raleigh's proposition that public safety was improved by the nature of the appointed dealer. Conversely, the MMC accepted Raleigh's selection criteria based upon pre-sales services, display capacity, expertise of staff, stockholding, etc., i.e. ordinary qualitative criteria.[476] However, it added that dealers refused supplies should be given a reason for the refusal and that supplies should be made when the dealer satisfied the criteria. The MMC concluded by recommending that,

> "Raleigh should widen its distribution policy by selling to discount stores in certain circumstances. If Raleigh were to sell through discount stores which observed the same standards of pre-sale inspection and other technical service requirements as do comparable outlets (for example some department stores)already supplied by Raleigh, and if Raleigh were to supply bicycles to such discount stores under brand names other than Raleigh ... we believe that any risk of damage to Raleigh's reputation and brand image would be substantially eliminated."[477]

10.403 The value of Raleigh as a guide to OFT policy must be cautiously stated, particularly in the light of more recent reports by the MMC under the FTA 1973.[478] This was the first ever investigation under the CA 1980. It has been criticised for the OFT and MMC overstating the economic importance of Raleigh's market power.[479] None the less, it shows that strong brand owners must be careful about refusing to supply multiples who can provide adequate back up services. It further suggests that the OFT, like the EC Commission,[480] is concerned to ensure that new forms and methods of marketing are not hindered by brand owners refusing to supply. On the other hand, provided qualitative criteria are set, the OFT seems prepared not to dispute what criteria are appropriate, an approach also adopted by the MMC in *Fine Fragrances*.[481]

10.404 In *Sandersons*[482] the OFT accepted with few qualms a complex set of criteria based upon: creditworthiness, staff expertise, advertising capacity, stockholding, and, minimum purchase ability. There was coupled to these qualitative criteria an element of quantitative criteria (see below) which also passed muster.

[473] 27 February 1981 (OFT Report).
[474] Sharpe, "Refusal to supply" (1983) LQR 36 at pp. 57–63.
[475] MMC Report (1981–82) HC 67.
[476] *ibid.*, at para. 6.28.
[477] *ibid.*, at para. 6.29.
[478] In particular, *Fine Fragrances*, Cm 2380 (1993).
[479] Sharpe, *op. cit.*, at pp. 58, 59.
[480] *Thirteenth Report on Competition Policy* (1983), pp. 39, 40, para. 34.
[481] *Fine Fragrances*, Cm 2380 (1993).
[482] 27 August 1981 (OFT Report).

(3) Quantitative criteria

10.405 In *Sandersons* the OFT adopted a pragmatic view of quantitative criteria based on the number of outlets in an area. It declined to declare quantitative criteria inherently anti-competitive. In that case, the degree of competition from other brands was important. The stronger the level of inter-brand competition the less likely it was that anti-competitive effects would derive from the supplier regulating the number of outlets in an area:

> "It is necessary to look at the application by Sanderson of the geographical factors of its general assessment criterion—the number of other outlets in the area, the need for further outlets in the area to satisfy consumer demand, the suitability of the proposed outlet in relation to existing outlets, and the position and type of proposed outlet ... From the point of view of competition, refusal to supply on geographical grounds raises difficult issues. Some degree of geographical selectivity may be desirable from the supplier's point of view in order to reinforce the products brand image or when the costs of distribution to an unlimited number of outlets would be excessive. Selective distribution may, however, have anti-competitive effects, for example if the product is a dominant brand and the selected retailers are granted a territorial monopoly."[483]

10.406 Thus, the OFT accepts that quantitative limitations may be justified at least in two situations: (i) to protect the supplier's brand name; (ii) to ensure that the cost of servicing an outlet remains economical. With regard to the latter point Sandersons, as a rule, only supplied outlets who could purchase a minimum of £2,500 worth of goods per annum. This sum was considered the threshold below which the costs of supply were excessive in proportion to return. In the first MMC Report on *Newspapers and Periodicals Wholesaling* the MMC concluded that quantitative limitations were justified where they protected the profitability of authorised retailers who were therefore able to continue providing door-to-door delivery services.[484] Thus, as a third situation, restrictions designed to enable dealers to maintain services may be acceptable. However, in the second MMC Report into this area,[485] refusals to supply were condemned as anti-competitive and contrary to the public interest. The interest in protecting traditional newsagents and home delivery were insufficient. The proposed remedy was that other retailers be allowed to sell on, thus creating a parallel market at the retail level, rather than adding more burdens on to wholesalers to supply a wider range of outlets.

(4) Selective distribution and motor vehicles

10.407 The MMC subjected the pricing structure of the UK car market to close scrutiny in it report on the *Supply of New Motor Cars*.[486] It largely accepted the motor industry's contention that price differentials between the UK and other Member States were due to factors other than the selective distribution system being employed. The main underlying difference stems from different tax treatment for cars. The UK tax regime has traditionally favoured company fleet purchasers, thus the pricing structure favours bulk purchasing. Individual purchasers thus are less important to dealers and consequently there is less price competition for their customer. Most competition is on the basis of specification, not price. Differing tax treatment makes it less easy for true comparisons to be made on price between Member States. For example, in some Member States prices are low to counter the effect on the purchaser of high taxes. The outcome of the MMC report was to leave the UK's regulation of selective distribution of motor vehicles largely undisturbed.

483 *ibid.*, at p. 43 para. 6.22.

484 Cmnd 7214, June 1978.

485 *The Supply of National Newspapers*, Cm 2422 (1993). A call for a further inquiry in 1995 was rejected by the OFT.

486 Cm 1808 (1992); see Groves, Editorial, [1992] ECLR 97.

M. Dealers Refused Supplies: Complaints and Remedies

1. *Legal and Economic Context*

10.408 In this section attention focuses upon the position of a dealer who has either been refused supplies by a supplier or who has had his existing dealership terminated by a supplier. "Refusal to deal" cases may be considered in terms of the economic power of the supplier. If supplier X with 15 per cent of the market refuses to supply dealer Y then almost certainly no infringement has occurred. Y can go elsewhere for supplies or to other brands. X's refusal should not affect Y's economic health. In principle a non-dominant supplier may refuse to trade with another person and the motive is irrelevant provided it is a genuine unilateral decision or is not motivated by a desire to maintain resale prices. However, if X enjoys (say) 90 per cent of the relevant market a refusal to supply Y could force Y out of business since the chances of Y obtaining alternative supplies are remote.

10.409 Refusal to supply, therefore, may be perceived as a monopoly power problem. Accordingly, the following courses of action are available to a hypothetical dealer situate in the UK who is denied supplies:

(a) complain to the OFT under the CA 1980 alleging that the supplier has acted anti-competitively;
(b) commence action for an injunction and/or damages for breach of Article 86 EC before the national court, if it considered that the supplier enjoys a dominant position;[487]
(c) commence an action for an injunction and/or damages for breach of Article 85 EC before the national court, if it is considered that the refusal to supply is the result of a restrictive agreement or concerted practice between the supplier and other authorised dealers;[488]
(d) complain to the Commission alleging infringements of Article 85 and 86 EC on the basis of (b) and (c) above;
(e) commence an action for breach of statutory duty under section 25(3) Resale Prices Act 1976 alleging breach of sections 11 and 12 of that Act. Under these provisions damages may be awarded against a supplier who unlawfully withholds supplies from a dealer who fails to comply with the supplier's price stipulations.

[487] See e.g. *Garden Cottage Foods* v *Milk Marketing Board* [1983] 3 WLR 143 (HL) damages and/or injunction potentially available for breach of Art. 86 to dealer who was refused direct supplies from a monopoly supplier but who was permitted supplies from a designated wholesaler of the supplier. The Milk Marketing Board decided to rationalise its distribution network, accordingly refusing to supply 16 of its 20 dealers, informing them that henceforward the 16 should seek supplies from the 4 designated wholesalers. The case never reached trial on the merits and was eventually settled out of court for a relatively small sum. In *Leyland Daf Ltd* v *Automotive Products plc* [1994] ECC 289, Leyland Daf, then insolvent and in administrative receivership, failed to obtain an injunction under Art. 86 EC against its supplier of brakes and clutches to continue to supply without imposing a condition that the receivers discharge its pre-receivership debts. The Court of Appeal, affirming theHigh Court, held that the defendant was not in a dominant position, as Leyland Daf could, by providing the necessary specifications, contract with any competent engineer to provide these parts. In addition, even if it had been in a dominant position, refusal to supply would not have been an abuse because the plaintiff had not paid for previously supplied goods.

[488] See for a US example *Monsanto Co* v *Spray Rite Service Corp.* 104 S. Ct 1464 (1984). The unilateral refusal to deal by a supplier may be viewed, in EC law, as based on tacit collusion deriving from the contractual relationship between supplier and dealer: Case 107/82 *AEG Telefunken* v *Commission* [1983] ECR 3157. See, for US experiences with terminated franchises, Lockerby, "Franchise termination restrictions: a guide for practitioners and policy makers" (1985) 30 *The Antitrust Bulletin* 791.

2. Typical Situations of Refusal to Supply

10.410 Certain situations occur with seeming regularity. Some examples are briefly noted below. The detailed law concerning each type of case may be found elsewhere in the chapter.

(1) Dealer refuses to purchase exclusively from supplier

10.411 Suppliers may wish dealers to accept exclusive purchase obligations banning them from holding brands other than the supplier's. Where the supplier has economic power, exclusive purchasing can operate to exclude rival suppliers from the market since the best dealers will be contractually precluded from holding their goods. In such situations the dealer who wishes to hold rival brands may be refused supplies by the dominant supplier. Thus for example, in *Kango Wolf Power Tools*[489] the OFT received complaints from dealers of Kango "Task Force" power tools (in particular electro-pneumatic hammers) who indicated that the manufacturer was refusing supplies to dealers who refused to accept no dualling restrictions, i.e. restrictions on holding rival brands. The OFT encouraged Kango Wolf to change its policy so as to permit dualling. In consequence of this agreed solution the OFT did not proceed with formal proceedings under the CA 1980.

(2) Dealer refused supplies and/or dealership terminated because of refusal to maintain resale prices

10.412 Attempts by suppliers to enforce resale price maintenance are invariably illegal. Price cutting often comes to the supplier's notice through complaints from other dealers. Where dealers and supplier agree directly or indirectly to enforce resale prices, then an agreement subject to control will have evolved. A dealer denied supplies in this manner may complain to the authorities of the supplier's behaviour *per se* and of the dealer's and supplier's behaviour collectively. The former behaviour may be illegal under Article 86 EC or section 11 Resale Prices Act which renders it illegal for a supplier to withhold supplies from a dealer as a means of enforcing resale price control.[490] The latter behaviour may be: contrary to Article 85(1) EC; a registrable agreement under section 6 RTPA 1976 (with section 21(2) dispensation almost certainly unattainable);[491] and unlawful under section 2 Resale Prices Act 1976 as a concerted attempt to enforce resale prices.

(3) Dealer operates large department store or supermarket and is refused supplies, although he meets supplier's selective distribution criteria

10.413 In both the UK and the EC, the authorities have been critical of attempts by suppliers to hinder the growth of new retail methods. In *Raleigh*, the manufacturers refused supplies to multiple retailers justifying the refusal on the basis that to do so might lead eventually

[489] DGFT Annual Report 1984, p. 108.

[490] See e.g. *Apple Computer UK Limited Assurance* DGFT Annual Report 1984, p. 107. Apple Computers notified minimum prices to dealers and refused supplies to those who sold, advertised or displayed goods at prices below those communicated to them. The OFT obtained a written assurance from Apple along the following lines: (i) Apple would not seek to incorporate in contracts with dealers clauses establishing minimum prices for the resale of the goods; (ii) Apple will not notify prices to dealers understood to be minimum prices; (iii) Apple will not refuse to supply dealers or otherwise discriminate against dealers for the reason that the dealer sells, advertises or displays for sale the goods at prices below those recommended; (iv) Apple will circulate to its dealers a statement conveying the substance of the assurance and advising them of their freedom to set prices.

[491] See *Sanderson* (27 August 1981) OFT investigation under the Competition Act 1980 not the RTPA 1976. Dealers refused supplies complained to the OFT. The latter investigated but found that Sandersons refusal to supply certain dealers was not based upon considerations of resale price maintenance but upon the basis of justifiable qualitative (and some quantitative) criteria.

to a reduction in the number of bicycle dealers. They contended that to supply multiple retailers who were not specialist, who might not provide dealer services and who would almost certainly undercut the prevailing price level would place intolerable sales pressures on specialist dealers whose margins would be eroded. The OFT decided that Raleigh's conduct was anti-competitive and referred the case to the MMC who likewise condemned Raleigh's distribution policy. The MMC recommended that Raleigh be required to supply discount and multiple retail stores where such stores observed the same standards of pre-sale inspection and technical services as comparable specialist outlets.[492] Thus, Raleigh could not hinder the multiples from stocking their bicycles where the latter provided adequate services. The fact that their prices might prove too competitive for some specialist dealers was not accepted. The OFT, in its report stated:

> "The Group's argument that to supply the multiple retailers would lead to a reduction in the number of bicycle dealers is one that has been advanced in the past in defence of resale price maintenance in various retail trades. If, on any wide scale, it emerged that consumers preferred lower prices to the advantages of specialised service or presentation, it has to be accepted that the number of bicycle dealers would decline. This would only be a symptom of a more competitive and cost conscious market."[493]

10.414 On the other hand, the MMC, in an investigation into the distribution of luxury perfumes,[494] held that suppliers were permitted to choose qualitative criteria in keeping with the brand image of their products, which would rule out supplying bulk or discount outlets.

(4) Vertically integrated supplier of an important raw material refuses to supply a dealer because that dealer competes with the supplier's own dealers

10.415 Where the supplier enjoys economic power such a refusal to deal may be an abuse of a dominant position, it would be subject to the CA 1980 in the UK and even the monopoly provisions of the FTA 1973.[495] An example under Article 86 is found in the *Commercial Solvents*[496] case. CSC enjoyed a world monopoly over aminobutonol production, an input for certain drug manufacturing processes, in particular ethambutol production. Zoja obtained aminobutonol supplies from CSC via the latter's Italian subsidiary ICI. Subsequently Zoja was refused supplies by ICI. The European Court held the refusal to constitute an abuse of a dominant position designed to exclude Zoja from the market. They were unimpressed with the argument that ICI, having commenced production of ethambutol themselves used all excess production themselves and that there were no spare supplies of aminobutonol for Zoja. One important factor was that CSC had previously made an attempt to take over Zoja. The purpose of the (failed) attempt was presumed to be a desire to destroy Zoja as a competitor.

10.416 In the UK the OFT reported that the practice of Essex County Newspapers (ECN), in refusing to accept advertisements from estate agents since they competed with its own classified property advertising, was anti-competitive under the CA 1980. It stated:

> "The Office has estimated that ECN has a dominant position in the newspaper property advertising market in the Colchester area, accounting for over 80 per cent of the value of total newspaper property advertising ... The Office accept the argument put forward by es-

[492] MMC Report (1981–82) HC 67 at para. 6.29.
[493] OFT Report (27 February 1981) at pp. 30, 31, para. 7.21.
[494] *Fine Fragrances*, Cm 2380 (1993).
[495] See MMC General Report, *Refusal to Supply* (1970) Cmnd 4372, para. 33—dominance over an important raw material expressed to be a matter requiring scrutiny by authorities.
[496] Cases 6 and 7/73 [1974] 1 CMLR 309; [1974] ECR 223.

tate agents ... that the appearance of their advertising in ECN ... is highly important to their ability to gain new business and satisfy the requirements of their customers and that other media and forms of advertising are essentially complementary to rather than substitutes for advertising in these newspapers. The Office concludes that because of its position in the property advertising market, ECN has the power to affect the relative ability of different property agents to compete in the Colchester area house agency market by its decisions on whether or not to accept the advertisements of individual agents. The Office also concludes that ECN had no grounds for its contention either that advertisements from [estate agents] competed with its business in a way that advertisements from orthodox estate agents did not, or that the public needed to be protected from advertisements from these undertakings."[497]

(5) Refusal to supply spare parts

10.417 Manufacturers of products often enjoy a *de facto* monopoly in the supply of spare parts for their own products. Refusal to supply those spare parts to third parties for the purpose of repair or maintenance of those products can be contrary to both EC and UK law.

10.418 The Court of Justice confirmed in *Hugin*[498] that spare parts could constitute a separate market from the main product itself for the purposes of Article 86 EC, and that a dominant position in this market could be abused by a refusal to supply a third party repairer with those parts. The Court of Justice revisited the topic in the context of motor vehicle spare parts in two substantially identical cases decided in 1988, *Volvo*[499] and *Renault*.[500] In both cases national legislation granted industrial design copyright protection to car components, thus preventing other manufacturers from making compatible spare parts without a licence, which neither car maker was prepared to grant. The Court of Justice rejected an argument put forward in both cases that the refusal to grant licences was an abuse of the car makers' dominant positions. It did however acknowledge that the exercise of the intellectual property rights could be an abuse and gave three examples of such an abuse:

(i) where there was an arbitrary refusal to supply spare parts to an independent repairer;
(ii) where there was unfair pricing of spare parts: or,
(iii) where there was a refusal to continue to supply spare parts for a model of motor vehicle of which many were still in circulation.

10.419 It should be noted that none of these examples actually involve a duty to license use of the intellectual property rights in question; each relates to the use of products protected by intellectual property rights. Nevertheless, the cases make it clear that refusal to supply in such a situation can be attached as an abuse.[501] Cases have been brought in the national courts for injunctive remedies in similar situations involving the supply of repair and maintenance services for large bespoke copyright protected software programs, in situations in which the software suppliers have sought to withdraw such services.

10.420 Under UK law, the OFT may investigate a refusal to supply spare parts under the Competition Act 1980. Thus a manufacturer of autoclaves (medical sterilising equipment) undertook to the OFT to supply suitably qualified third party servicers with spare parts, thereby permitting the development of competition in the servicing sector, while two major suppliers of domestic water tanks abandoned a policy (under OFT pressure) of refusing to supply such tanks except as complete packages including insulation and other

497 *Essex County Newspaper Limited* OFT investigation (14 July 1983) at p. 39, para. 6.31.
498 Case 22/78 *Hugin* [1978] ECR 1513, [1978] 3 CMLR 282.
499 Case 238/87 *Volvo* v *Erik Veng (UK) Ltd* [1989] 4 CMLR 122, [1988] ECR 6211.
500 Case 53/87 *CICRA and Maxicar* v *Renault* [1990] 4 CMLR 265, [1988] ECR 6039.
501 The US Supreme Court has also taken the view that refusals to supply third party repair and maintenance service providers may constitute a breach of antitrust law, s. 2 Sherman Act, in *Eastman Kodak* v *Image Technical Services* 112 S Ct 2072 (1992).

components, a policy which would have restricted competition in the supply of those components.[502]

(6) Supplier refuses supplies because buyer uses fraud to obtain favourable terms from the supplier

10.421 Buyer (B) suspects that other dealers and retailers can purchase the goods from supplier (S) on more favourable terms that he can. B therefore sets up a shell company (X) to purchase the relevant goods from S. X represents to S that it intends to sell the goods in an area that S does not currently sell in. X obtains favourable terms but diverts the goods acquired to the use of B. S discovers the truth and terminates supplies to X and B. X and B sues on the basis of a restrictive agreement between S and its exclusive dealers to refuse to deal with B and X. S counterclaims for: fraud, breach of contract, interference with contractual relations, and breach of an implied covenant of good faith and fair dealing. In the United States this situation was decided in favour of the supplier. The fraud of the buyer coupled to the subsequent sale of the purchased goods in the exclusive dealer's territory was considered a legitimate business reason for the refusal to deal.[503] In terms of EC law Regulation 1983/83/EEC permits a supplier to refuse to supply persons other than the contract dealer in the contract dealers territory. Fraud by a purchaser who seeks to interfere with the contractual rights of supplier under an agreement that is exempt under the block exemption must surely be a valid reason for refusal to deal.

[502] DGFT Annual Report 1989, p. 42.
[503] *Landmark Development Corp* v *Chambers Corp* 752 F. 2d 369 (9th Cir. 1985).

11 Terms and Conditions of Trade

A. Introduction

11.1 In this chapter the following will be discussed:

Section B.	Legal framework: analysis of application of EC and UK laws to standard form contracts and unfair terms and conditions.
Section C.	Codes of Practice: self-regulation through Codes of Practice and Codes of Ethics.
Section D.	Exclusion, limitation of liability and other financial penalty clauses: exclusion and other similar clauses in standard form contracts; death and personal injury exclusion clauses, exclusion clauses, limitation of liability clauses, indemnity clauses, fixed liability clauses, surcharges on overdue accounts, non-exclusion clauses, liens and transfer of title clauses, redemption and early termination of contract clauses.
Section E.	Credit and other terms of payment: credit terms, credit control, credit scoring systems.
Section F.	Terms leading to market division: market sharing, quotas, geographical market sharing, mutual assistance clauses.
Section G.	Sale of assets agreements and non-competition clauses: non-competition clauses and covenants permitted in sale of assets and shares agreements.
Section H.	Premises and trading methods: restrictions imposed upon trade association members or dealers concerning the premises from which trade is conducted and general methods of trade.
Section I.	Staffing restrictions: restrictions in respect of employees their qualification and training.
Section J.	Advertising and trade fairs: advertising restrictions, methods of funding joint-advertising, trade fairs and restrictive rules governing such fairs.
Section K.	Standards, quality control and descriptions: attempts by trade association and firms to harmonise contract terminology and descriptions.

Section L. Customer and end-user restrictions: clauses imposing restrictions on customers to whom goods may be supplied and on uses or products once in the hands of customers, refusals to deal.

Section M. Tying clauses: clauses requiring customers to take supplemental goods or services in addition to a main product or service.

B. Legal Framework

1. EC Law: Collective Setting of Terms and Conditions

11.2 Article 85(1)(a) prohibits agreements, trade association decisions and concerted practices which, *inter alia*, directly or indirectly fix trading conditions. For some products price might not be the most important element of competition; the terms and conditions under which the goods or services are supplied may be equally, or even more, important to the purchaser. Agreements on the application of standard terms are therefore prime violations of Article 85(1) EC.[1] It makes no difference that parties do not agree on the full range of terms and conditions.[2] An agreement between the members of trade association X to supply on standard terms of credit may be as restrictive as an agreement to supply on a wider range of standard terms. Trade association standard form contracts which cover terms and conditions of trade and which are drafted for the use of members whose trade affects trade between the Member States might consider notifying their standard form agreements to the Commission. Where the standardisation of terms extends to matters the Commission considers important, then the possibility of exemption is remote. An important term is in principle any the consumer might consider relevant in making a selection between sellers. Thus clauses concerning credit, payment periods, discounts, warranties and guarantees, deliveries and transport etc. will often be important to competition. The need to impose "order" on a "chaotic" market is never accepted as a justification by the Commission.[3] Standard form contracts have not figured large in EC antitrust law at least when compared with other forms of commercial agreement (e.g. distribution and patent licensing agreements). Much of the case work on standard form contracts occurs at national level. Transnational trade associations are less likely to recommend standard form contracts than are domestic associations.

11.3 Not every set of standard terms and conditions applied across an industry engages Article 85(1). The Commission has, for example, granted negative clearance to the rules of most of the London terminal markets.[4]

11.4 The English courts have considered collective standardised terms and conditions in the context of agreements between on the one hand members and managing agents,

[1] *Cimbel* [1973] CMLR D167; *GISA* [1973] CMLR D125. See para. 2 of the Commission's Notice concerning Agreements, Decisions and Concerted Practices in the Field of Co-operation between Enterprises, OJ 1968, C75/3, [1968] CMLR D5, emphasising that the use of standard printed forms cannot be used to standardise the terms and conditions embodied in those forms. It is of course possible for standard terms and conditions to be exempted but only if notified. See e.g. for the position in relation to standard insurance policies: Regulation 3932/93/EC OJ 1992 L398/7; *TEKO* OJ 1990 L13/34; *Assurpol* OJ 1992 L37/16; *Concordats* OJ 1990 L15/25.

[2] *Belgian Industrial Timber* Bull EC 10/75, para. 2104; *Fifth Commission Competition Report* (1975), para. 37. Commission challenged agreement: fixing maximum purchase price; forbidding quantity rebates; regulating supplier lists; adopting a standard form contract; *Belgian Wallpaper* [1974] 2 CMLR D102—Commission decision; see for judgment of European Court Case 73/74 *Groupement des Fabricants de Papiers de Belgique* v *Commission* [1976] 1 CMLR 589; [1975] ECR 1491; *Tile Trade* [1975] 2 CMLR D1.

[3] *Belgian Industrial Timber, supra.*

[4] See for one example from many *London Sugar Futures Market* Case [1984] 1 CMLR 138. The individual cases are listed at note 162 below.

and on the other hand external names in the Lloyd's insurance market. In order for an external investor (a Name) to underwrite insurance business as Lloyd's the Name is required to sign a general undertaking pursuant to which the Name agrees to abide by the Byelaws of Lloyd's. Pursuant to certain Byelaws made in 1985 and 1988 Names were required to conclude standard agency agreements pursuant to which members and managing agents were appointed to conduct underwriting on the Names' behalf. One clause contained in the standard agency agreements was the "pay now sue later" clause. The effect of the clause was to require the Name to put the agent in funds whenever the agent requested funds and, in the event of a dispute between the Name and the agent the former was still required to put the agent in funds and was only entitled to commence proceedings against the agent after the agent had been duly put in funds. The term therefore precluded most defences including set-offs arising out of counterclaims. As a result of the now notorious underwriting crisis a significant number of underwriters were unable to meet liabilities to insured persons. Accordingly, Lloyd's stepped in and made payment out of its Central Fund to meet the underwriting liabilities of the Name to assured. Lloyd's thereafter sought repayment into the fund of the sums dispersed to meet underwriting debts on the Names' behalf, from the Name. These attempts to recover monies by Lloyd's were, for a considerable period of time, thwarted by litigation.[5] In order to circumvent the problem, Lloyd's instructed managing and members' agents to use powers under the standard agency agreement and in particular the "pay now sue later" clause to obtain monies from Names and thereby to avoid further depletions of the Central Fund. It was in this context that the Names sought to argue that the standard agency agreements and "pay now sue later" engaged the prohibition in Article 85(1). Since the relevant byelaw, and the individual agreements concluded thereunder, had not been notified to the EC Commission, it was contended that the byelaw and the agreements were void pursuant to Article 85(2). In particular, it was alleged that the "pay now sue later" clause was a discrete restriction of competition. The standard agency agreement adopted by Lloyd's had evolved over a number of years. Until the 1985 Byelaw, separate standard form agreements were required to be entered into between the Name and the Members' Agent and Managing Agent respectively. By virtue of the 1988 Byelaw, a single agency agreement embraced the Name, the Members' Agent and the Managing Agent. The agency agreements had been subject to scrutiny by a number of external critics who had pointed out that the "pay now sue later" clause could operate unfairly in certain circumstances. It appeared from the facts that the very process of negotiating and imposing standard terms and conditions upon the market entailed a curtailment of free market forces. In particular, it was possible to identify a number of alternative "pay" obligations which might have been included in agents' agreements. First, there was a "pay" obligation without any associated "sue later". Secondly, there was a "pay now sue later" obligation coupled to a right to arbitration to determine the right of the agent to be put in funds. Thirdly, there was pay now sue later in the form included in the standard agency agreement. Mr Justice Rix[6] held that the relevant byelaws, the standard agency agreements themselves, and the "pay now sue later" clauses did not infringe Article 85(1) since they did not restrict, distort or prevent competition. He concluded on the contrary that the standard agreement was essential to the market and was designed for the protection of Names. "Pay now sue later" was integral for the protection of policy holders and enabled Lloyd's to

[5] See e.g. *Society of Lloyd's* v *Clementson* [1995] 1 CMLR 693; [1995] CLC 117 (CA).

[6] *Marchant and Elliot Underwriting Limited* v *Higgins* [1996] 1 Lloyd's Rep. 313 affirmed on appeal (*Higgins* v *Marchant and Elliot Underwriting Limited* [1996] 2 Lloyd's Rep. 31.

compete more effectively in the international insurance market. Ultimately it was pro-competitive.[7]

11.5 Accordingly, even in relation to standard terms and conditions applicable across markets such as the Lloyd's insurance market a "rule of reason" approach applies such that the mere fact of standardisation does not, *per se*, activate Article 85(1). In each and every case it is necessary to consider the state of the market in the absence of the disputed terms and conditions and, further, to consider whether or not the standard terms and conditions in fact facilitate and enhance competition.

2. EC Law: Individual Setting of Terms and Conditions

11.6 The determination of terms and conditions by individual firms is subject to regulation where the firm enjoys a dominant position. A dominant concern acts abusively if it imposes unfair terms on its buyers or suppliers.[8] Whether a terms is unfair depends upon an economic and factual analysis of the interests of all those concerned. In assessing fairness the interests of third parties and the general public are relevant.[9] Thus, if a dominant supplier by imposing unfair terms on a dealer requires that customers of the dealer will pay more, or receive fewer after-sales services etc., then the interests of the general public may have been harmed. In *Hoffman-La Roche* v *Commission*[10] the defendant company required purchasers to notify it of any offers by rival suppliers and moreover to allow the defendant company the option of meeting the rival's price before the dealer was permitted to take from the rival. The European Court objected to this clause, *inter alia*, upon the basis that it permitted Hoffman-La Roche to control a rival supplier's ability to sell to customers of the dominant undertaking. The clause was thus unfair on third parties.

11.7 It is no defence that a practice is permitted by national law or even in the national laws of most Member States.[11] It is not necessary to show that the dominant undertaking coerced or forced the other party into accepting unfair terms. This is logical since a small buyer might simply agree to terms imposed by a giant supplier. The simple fact of capitulation does not necessarily imply contentment.

11.8 The Commission has no formal power to prescribe substitute terms and conditions; it may only prohibit abuse.[12] Informally, or during the course of formal proceedings, the Commission will often indicate what is acceptable or otherwise.

3. UK Law: Collective Setting of Terms and Conditions

(1) Registrability under the RTPA 1976

11.9 Standard terms and conditions are invariably organised under the aegis of a trade association. Under the RTPA 1976 trade association agreements are deemed to have been ac-

[7] *ibid.*, pp. 332 *et seq.* The judge was influenced by the approach of the Court of Justice in Case C-250/92 *Gottrup Klinn* [1994] ECR 5641.

[8] e.g. Case 155/73 *Sacchi* [1974] 2 CMLR 177; [1974] ECR 409 at p. 431.

[9] Case 127/73 *BRT* v *SABAM* [1974] 2 CMLR 238; ECR 313 at p. 317, see also *per* Advocate General Mayras: "An undertaking in a dominant position is prohibited from going beyond what is reasonable, and the measures which it chooses to attain its object must be the least restrictive possible." See further *GEMA I* [1974] CMLR D35.

[10] Case 85/76 [1979] 3 CMLR 211; [1979] ECR 461.

[11] Cases 40–48, 50, 54–56, 111, 113, 114/73 *European Sugar Cartel (Suker Unie)* [1976] 1 CMLR 295; [1975] ECR 1663 at p. 2016; Cases 43 and 63/82 *VBVB and VBBB* v *Commission* [1985] 1 CMLR 27 at pp. 92, 93 para. 40: "In that connection it must be observed that national legislative or judicial practices, even on the supposition that they are common to all the Member States, cannot prevail in the application of the competition rules set out in the Treaty. The same reasoning must apply with even greater force in relation to practices of private undertakings, even where they are tolerated or approved by the authorities of a Member State" (concerning resale price maintenance for books).

[12] See Reg. 17/62/EEC, Art. 3.

cepted by all the members.[13] Likewise, recommendations of trade associations, for example concerning the adoption of a standard form contract (SFC) in dealing with customers, are deemed to be complied with by members.[14] The effect of the Act is to require the registration of any trade association recommendation, or any agreement entered by an association which concerns a registrable matter.[15] Simply because members may not be bound to follow the recommendations does not exempt it from registration. The RTPA 1976 catches agreements whether relating to goods or services which concern the terms or conditions on or subject to which goods or designated services are to be supplied or acquired.[16]

11.10 In deciding whether a communication from an association is a registrable recommendation the Court must look at all the surrounding circumstances and the general effect of the whole document. Thus in *Association of British Travel Agents* (ABTA hereafter)[17] one issue was whether a clause in a standard agency agreement which stated "the agent shall use his best endeavours to persuade the customer to accept either the holiday insurance offered by the operator or some equivalent suitable insurance in order to ensure that the customer is adequately protected in the event of enforced cancellation, curtailment, medical and other expenses", was a registrable recommendation. The OFT contended that the clause was a recommendation when viewed in the context of intensive ABTA advertising designed to encourage members to promote use of the ABTA preferred insurance brand to customers. The RPC disagreed stating that the fact that ABTA had to use salesmanship and promotion techniques to extol the virtues of its favoured insurance indicated that the standard clause was not a recommendation to members who were free to use the insurance of their choice when advising customers. Not every communication from an association represents a recommendation; it is the effect of the communication that counts.

(2) General approach and section 21(2) RTPA 1976

11.11 Many of the cases encountered by the OFT concern standard terms and conditions recommended to members by trade and service supply associations.[18] Often the OFT welcomes standard form contracts (SFCs hereafter) as beneficial to both supplier and customer. This is particularly so where comparatively small firms which lack technical and legal expertise are concerned for otherwise contracts might be entered into which are unenforceable at law. The OFT has three broad rules for assessing SFCs.

11.12 (a) The terms should be fair and reasonable to all concerned. This includes not only the parties but also third parties and the general public. The OFT will often seek the views of interested third parties and their representative trade associations. Thus, for example, SFC's including clauses declared void under the Unfair Contract Terms Act 1977 are never suitable for section 21(2) dispensation. The same approach will be taken to unfair terms which are unenforceable against consumers under the Unfair Terms in Consumer Contracts Regulations, S.I. 1994 No. 3159. If a term is unfair if imposed in the context of relations between an individual supplier and customer, *a fortiori*, it will be unfair if imposed collectively to a group of suppliers.

13 ss. 8(1) (goods) and 16(3) (services) RTPA 1976.
14 ss. 8(2), (3) (goods) and 16(3), (4) (services) RTPA 1976.
15 See DGFT Annual Report (1979), p. 45.
16 ss. 6(1)(c) (goods) and 11(2)(b) (services) RTPA 1976.
17 *Association of British Travel Agents* [1984] ICR 12 at p. 37C–F.
18 See DGFT Annual Report 1980, pp. 51, 52; DTI and OFT, *Guidelines on the Operation of the Restrictive Trade Practices Act 1976* (September 1984), Annex C para. 4. See also OFT, *Restrictive Agreements: A Short Guide to the Law on Restrictive Trading Agreements* (1995), p. 6.

11.13 (b) The terms should not be likely to mislead users. Thus goods should not be described as "free gifts" if the purchased article is increased in price or decreased in quality as a result of the free give offer. Furthermore, the OFT often object to exclusion or limitation of liability clauses which are hidden amongst small print or whose meaning is obfuscated by unnecessarily complex language.

11.14 (c) The SFC must not unnecessarily exclude variations to meet special circumstances and requirements. If suppliers refuse to modify contracts to embrace a purchaser's special needs this will militate against section 21(2) dispensation. In general *mandatory* standard terms and conditions will not, for this reason, receive section 21(2) dispensation.

11.15 Essentially, the benefits to customers of having standard terms and conditions is balanced against the detriments to customers of not being able to negotiate individually with the supplier and thereby secure more favourable terms than those likely to result from the terms imposed upon them. The OFT examines SFCs on a clause by clause basis.

(3) Reasonable terms: Unfair Contract Terms Act 1977

11.16 In assessing the fairness or reasonableness of SFCs the OFT bears in mind the strictures of the Unfair Contract Terms Act 1977 (UCTA 1977 hereafter). Thus a contract clause that is either void or "unreasonable" according to that Act must by definition be significant for section 21(2) purposes. Accordingly, a SFC incorporating such terms will be inappropriate for dispensation from reference to the RPC. Trade associations may thus bear in mind the guidelines in the UCTA 1977 as to the meaning of reasonableness.[19] These may be summarised as following:

11.17 (a) Is there roughly equal bargaining strength as between the parties? Where a trade association recommends adoption of a SFC to members for use in dealings with individual customers inequality invariably exists since the customer faces a collective body of suppliers. Where supplier's and buyer's respective associations have jointly negotiated a SFC, then it is more likely that the terms will be deemed reasonable.[20]

11.18 (b) Does the customer have alternative sources of supply? If a customer accepts use of a SFC from a supplier whose trade association account for, say, only 35 per cent of all suppliers, this will suggest reasonableness. The customer could, had he objected to the SFC, have sought supplies from a supplier willing to negotiate individual terms. Conversely, if the SFC is used by 80 per cent of all suppliers then the availability of good or services on other terms is very limited. Similarly, if the purchaser may buy from the same supplier under alternative terms this might suggest a greater degree of reasonableness.[21] The alternative must of course represent a feasible choice.[22]

[19] Sch. 2(a)–(e) Unfair Contract Terms Act 1977.

[20] See, e.g. No. S. 161 Register of Restrictive Trade Practices, *British Tugowners Association Standard Terms and Conditions* (s. 21(2) dispensation given in 1984) for judicial utterances see *Photo Production Ltd* v *Securicor Transport Ltd* [1980] AC 827 (HL) presumption that where no inequality exists reasonableness is *prima facie* assumed. See also *Walker* v *Boyle* [1982] 1 All ER 634; *Green* v *Cade Bros. Farms* [1978] 1 Lloyd's Rep 602. See generally, *Chitty on Contracts* (27th edn. 1995) Chapter 14, s. 6, paras. 14.45 *et seq* and in particular para. 14.69 and cases cited in footnotes thereto.

[21] *Green* v *Cade Bros. Farms*, above—farmers purchased seed potatoes from supplier under agreement limiting the latter's liability to the cost of the seed should it prove defective and not consequential loss based upon lost-profits. However, the farmers could have purchased seed at a slightly higher price which was certified and thus less likely to be defective.

[22] See for an example *Peek* v *North Staffordshire Railway* (1863) 10 HLC 493; 11 ER 1109.

11.19 (c) Does the SFC offer any inducement or compensation to a buyer having to accept an onerous term? If the buyer obtains a price concession or some other favourable term as the quid pro quo for an onerous term, this might suggest reasonableness. Though, if the purchaser has no option but to accept the SFC and the inducement because alternative terms are unavailable then the simple fact of an inducement may be insufficient. The customer may prefer to do without the inducement in return for softened terms and conditions.

11.20 (d) To what extent was the customer aware of a term because, for example, it is customary in the trade, or, because it is based upon an earlier course of dealing between the parties? An onerous term of which the buyer was previously unaware is unlikely to be reasonable. A SFC should clearly state its terms; clauses which state that the purchaser may request in writing a copy of the supplier terms concerning credit and liability for defects should be avoided; if a clause is important to a consumer it should be clearly set out in the SFC. The OFT is always concerned to prevent buyers from being misled. Similarly, terms should not be obfuscated by legal jargon or other terminology likely to confuse non-specialist buyers.

11.21 (e) Insurance: the UCTA 1977 guidelines do not specifically refer to insurance. However, it has been recognised as of considerable relevance.[23] A SFC which shifts all of the risk on to the buyer may be reasonable where it has been earlier agreed that the buyer should obtain appropriate insurance thereby freeing the supplier from the obligation to insure and thereby enabling the supplier to keep his price down. In *British Tugowners Association Standard Towage Conditions*[24] the OFT gave section 21(2) dispensation to a SFC which excluded liability on the part of tugboat owners for almost all risks.[25] Thus, if in towing a large ship into port the ship collided with another ship or with a jetty owing to the negligence of the master, then the tugowner would *not* be liable. The prima facie unreasonableness of the SFC was ameliorated when the insurance position was considered. The protection and indemnity clubs ("P&I Clubs") are mutual assurance organisations which account for 90 per cent of the world's shipping insurance calculated by tonnage. As insurers for both tugowners and shipowners the P&I Clubs had been party to the drafting of the tugowner's SFC. The commercial basis of those terms was that hirers of towage services would arrange insurance with the P&I Clubs and the insurance imbalance would be compensated for in the price paid for towage services. Viewed in the overall context the exclusion clauses were reasonable.

11.22 It is pertinent to note that the OFT is not bound by UCTA. It simply uses that Act as a guide to the meaning of significance in section 21(2) RTPA 1976. Accordingly, it might use the criteria laid out in UCTA even where legally UCTA 1977 does not apply.[26]

23 Insurance in specifically included in s. 11(4)(b) UCTA 1977, but only for the purpose of assessing the reasonableness of a limitation of liability clause.

24 No. S. 161 Register of Restrictive Trade Practices (1984).

25 For example the SFC excludes liability for *inter alia*: (i) damage of any description done by or to the tug or tender, or done to the hirer's vessel, or done by or to any cargo or other thing on the hirer's vessel or being loaded thereon; (ii) loss of the tug or tender or the hirer's vessel or of any cargo or other thing on board or being loaded thereon; (iii) any claim by a person not a party to this agreement for loss or damage of any description whatsoever. These exclusions apply irrespective of whether the tugowner or his servant or agents at fault. Furthermore, the hirer, under the SFC, is obliged to indemnify the tugowner for any liability incurred by the latter. There exist additional exclusions covering such matters as loss or damage due to delay, or *force majeure* occurrences.

26 e.g. see the *Tugowners Association* case (above). Para. 2 of Sch. 1 of UCTA provides that *inter alia*, contracts of marine salvage or towage are excluded from the act.

(4) Fair terms: unfair terms in Consumer Contract Regulations 1994

11.23 The Unfair Terms in Consumer Contracts Regulations, S.I. 1994 No. 3159, came into effect on 1 July 1995, implementing an EC Directive.[27] They render unenforceable against a consumer any unfair term[28] in a contract if it has not been individually negotiated. Fairness is defined[29] as meaning "any term which contrary to the requirement of good faith[30] causes a significant imbalance in the parties' rights and obligations under the contract to the detriment of the consumer".

11.24 An illustrative list of clauses is set out in the Third Schedule to the Regulation. This applies to clauses which have as their object or effect the following:

(a) excluding or limiting the liability of a seller or supplier in the event of death or personal injury to a consumer caused by the act or omission of the seller or supplier;
(b) inappropriately excluding or limiting the legal rights of the consumer *vis-à-vis* the seller or supplier or another party in the event of total or partial non-performance or inadequate performance by the seller or supplier of any of the contractual obligations;
(c) making an agreement binding on the consumer whereas provision of the services by the seller or supplier is subject to a condition whose realisation depends on his own will alone;
(d) permitting the seller or supplier to retain sums paid by the consumer when the consumer decides not to conclude or perform the contract, without providing for the consumer to receive compensation of any equivalent amount from the seller or supplier where the latter is the party cancelling the contract;
(e) requiring any consumer who fails to fulfil his obligation to pay a disproportionately high sum in compensation;
(f) authorising the seller or supplier to dissolve the contract on a discretionary basis where the same facility is not granted to the consumer, or permitting the seller or supplier to retain sums paid for services not yet supplied by him where it is the seller or supplier himself who dissolves the contract;[31]
(g) enabling the seller or supplier to terminate a contract of indeterminate duration[32] without reasonable notice except where there are serious grounds for doing so;[33]
(h) automatically extending a contract of fixed duration where the consumer does not indicate otherwise, when the deadline fixed for the consumer to express this desire not to extend the contract is unreasonably early;

[27] Unfair Terms in Consumer Contracts Directive, OJ 1993 L95/29. 93/13/EC. See generally, "Six months on: unfair contracts at work", *Fair Trading*, No. 12, p. 14. See also OFT Briefing Document, "Unfair Standard Terms" (July 1995).

[28] Excluding terms defining the "main subject matter of the contract", Art. 3(2)(a), S.I. 1994 No. 3159. Nor may the fairness of the price be questioned: Art. 3(2)(b), S.I. 1994 No. 3159.

[29] Art. 4(1), S.I. 1994 No. 3159.

[30] To be defined having regard to Sch. 2, S.I. 1994 No. 3159.

[31] This paragraph does not apply to transactions in transferable securities, financial instruments and other products or services where the price is linked to fluctuations in stock exchange quotation or index or a financial market rate that the seller or supplier does not control, not does it apply to contracts for the purchase or sale of foreign currency, traveller's cheques or international money orders denominated in a foreign currency.

[32] cf. Art. 3(d), Reg. 1984/83.

[33] This provision is without hindrance to terms by which a supplier of financial services reserves the right to terminate unilaterally a contract of indeterminate duration without notice where there is a valid reason, provided that the supplier is required to inform the other parties immediately.

(i) irrevocably binding the consumer to terms with which he had no real opportunity of becoming acquainted before the conclusion of the contract;

(j)[34] enabling the seller or supplier to alter the terms of the contract unilaterally without a valid reason which is specified in the contract,[35] though a seller or supplier may reserve the right to alter unilaterally a contract of indeterminate duration, provided that he is required to inform the consumer with reasonable notice and the consumer is free to dissolve the contract;

(k) enabling the seller or supplier to alter unilaterally without a valid reason any characteristics of the product or service to be provided;

(l)[36] providing for the price of goods to be determined at the time of delivery or allowing a seller of goods or supplier of services to increase their price[37] without in both cases giving the consumer the corresponding right to cancel the contract if the final price is too high in relation to the price agreed when the contract was concluded;

(m) giving the seller or supplier the right to determine whether the goods or services supplied are in conformity with the contract, or giving him the exclusive right to interpret any term of the contract;

(n) limiting the seller's or supplier's obligation to respect commitments undertaken by his agents or making his commitments subject to compliance with a particular formality;

(o) obliging the consumer to fulfil all his obligations where the seller or supplier does not perform his;

(p) giving the seller or supplier the possibility of transferring his rights and obligations under the contract, where this may serve to reduce the guarantees for the consumer, without the consumer's agreement;

(q) excluding or hindering the consumer's right to take legal action or exercise any other legal remedy, particularly by requiring the consumer to take disputes exclusively to arbitration not covered by legal provisions, unduly restricting the evidence available to him or imposing upon him a burden of proof which, according to the applicable law, should lie with another party to the contract.

11.25 The Third Schedule's list of clauses includes many which would be caught under UCTA 1977, but some go beyond and it is in any case only illustrative. The overriding principle is that of good faith. Consequently, it would be prudent to ensure that all the provisions of SFCs comply not only with UCTA 1977 analysed above, but also do not contain any term specifically mentioned under the Third Schedule, unless it can be demonstrated that they are in good faith and fair in the particular circumstances of the SFC in question. The OFT has published a Briefing Document entitled "Unfair Standard Terms" (July 1995) which is an important guide to the approach the OFT might adopt to individual cases.

[34] This paragraph does not apply to transactions in transferable securities, financial instruments and other products or services where the price is linked to fluctuations in stock exchange quotations or indices or a financial market rate that the seller or supplier does not control, nor does it apply to contracts for the purchase or sale of foreign currency, traveller's cheques or international money orders denominated in a foreign currency.

[35] This does not hinder terms relating to alteration of interest rates in contracts entered into by suppliers of financial services.

[36] This paragraph does not apply to transactions in transferable securities, financial instruments and other products or services where the price is linked to fluctuations in stock exchange quotations or indices or a financial market rate that the seller or supplier does not control, nor does it apply to contracts for the purchase or sale of foreign currency, traveller's cheques or international money orders denominated in a foreign currency.

[37] This does not hinder lawful price indexation clauses provided the method by which prices vary is explicitly described.

(5) Approach of Restrictive Practices Court

11.26 SFCs recommended by trade associations to members were treated initially as *single* restrictions. This view was based upon the structure of the Act which treat recommendations as single restrictions. Sections 8 and 16 RTPA provide that an association recommendation is deemed to have been accepted by members. Consequently, if the RPC, on examination of a SFC, discovered a repugnant clause it could strike down the whole SFC as being a single restriction.[38] This approach is patently unrealistic; SFCs contain multifarious clauses and repugnant terms can be severed. The sudden abrogation of a SFC would leave a trading vacuum that would be unhelpful to both buyers and sellers. In *ABTA*[39] the RPC adopted a different approach held that restrictions in SFC's had to be assessed both individually and collectively. Thus, when it came to assess a SFC in the context of the "balancing tailpiece" (see paras. 5.61–5.62) the Court could balance the advantages and disadvantages of restrictions in isolation. Thus, whilst certain clauses may fall others might survive. This approach thus enables restrictions in SFCs to be viewed individually.[40]

4. UK Law: Individual Setting of Terms and Conditions

11.27 The OFT might investigate the imposition of onerous or restrictive terms and conditions under the CA 1980. In such cases the party imposing the terms will be investigated. The Act will apply if the supplier has significant market power. Thus a dominant purchaser may coerce its suppliers to grant it very favourable terms and conditions. More usually a powerful supplier imposes onerous or restrictive terms on purchasers. It is important to note that contract terms may be measured by dual standards. First, they may have restrictive economic consequences; secondly, they may be harsh and unfair. Though often the two strands are interlinked.

(1) Restrictive terms and conditions

11.28 Contract terms may have restrictive effects on two principal levels. First, at the level of the supplier. Secondly at the level of the buyer. An example of the first possibility would be a clause which required a purchaser to take two different products from the supplier, i.e. a tying clause. For example the powerful supplier of a new type of photocopier might require purchasers also to take copying paper. The supplier by its tying of photocopier to paper is created entry and expansion barriers to rival suppliers of paper for photocopiers. Thus the supplier is affecting competition at the supply levels.[41] Similarly, a supplier who requires buyers to take 80 per cent of their total requirements from them forecloses those customers to a substantial degree from rival suppliers. An example of the second type of restrictive effect would be where supplier X grants competing buyers Y and Z differential terms and conditions. Thus Y might enjoy more favourable terms. Since Y and Z are in competition X's discrimination distorts the competitive position between them.

[38] See *British Bottle Association's Agreement* (1961) LR 2 RP 345 [1961] 1 WLR 760 at p. 792.

[39] [1984] ICR 13 at pp. 23 and 24.

[40] It is believed that the OFT was considering appealing the judgment of the RPC to the Court of Appeal. However, it decided against this approach *inter alia* on the basis that while they might win on the substance at appeal the Court might reject the approach of the RPC to SFCs and this would have returned the Office to the earlier unsatisfactory position.

[41] In the US Supreme Court case of *Eastman Kodak* v *Image Technical Services* 112 S. Ct 2072 (1992), the supplier of sophisticated copying equipment tied in the supply of maintenance and spare parts; the Court held that this did lay it open to an antitrust suit under s. 1 Sherman Act 1890, notwithstanding that the market for the supply of this equipment was competitive.

(2) Harsh and unfair terms and conditions

11.29 Harsh and unfair terms may be imposed by a supplier who exploits superior bargaining power by requiring purchasers to accept clauses which benefit the dominant party only and which would not exist in circumstances of equal bargaining power. Thus, there might exist unreasonable exclusion clauses, or unreasonable credit and payment terms. Since the supplier does not discriminate between his buyers he does not influence their competitive position *inter se*. As has been noted above, the fairness or reasonableness of terms imposed collectively via SFCs has been a central feature of analysis.

(3) Fair terms and conditions may have restrictive effects

11.30 Simply because contractual term are fair and reasonable between parties does not mean that they are not restrictive or anti-competitive. If supplier X gives buyer Y discriminatory and favourable credit terms Y might be perfectly content whereas Z who competes with Y but who receives no equivalent benefit will suffer a competitive disadvantage even though the terms offered to Z, viewed in isolation, might not be intrinsically unfair. Contractual terms about which both parties are happy may yet be anti-competitive. This has been recognised by the MMC.[42]

C. Codes of Practice

11.31 Codes of Practice are common throughout British industry. A "code of practice" can imply a number of things. First, it can imply a guide for safeguarding and promoting the consumer's interests. Secondly, it can imply a set of rules used in industry self-regulation which do not necessarily have a bearing upon the consumer. Thirdly, it can be a disguise whereby parties collude beneath a respectable edifice. Competition authorities hence scrutinise Codes of Practice to ensure that they are not being abused. Authorities do not accept that honourable sounding names necessarily imply honourable conduct. Thus, in one case the European Commission stated of a set of rules entitled Fair Trade Practice Rules, "The mere labelling of an agreement between undertakings as rules against unfair competition does not suffice to remove the agreement from the ambit of Article 85(1) of the EEC Treaty."[43] In one classic American case a "Code of Ethics" was accepted as evidence of an illegal price-fixing agreement.[44] The code, adopted by an association of sugar refiners, the Sugar Institute, provided that: "All discrimination between customers should be abolished. To this end, sugar should be sold only upon price and terms publicly announced."[45] The Supreme Court accepted that this was evidence of a cartel to "sell only upon prices and terms openly announced."[46] In another case an association sought "to adopt and promulgate a Code of Ethics for the government of the members," and, "to establish and *maintain all such lawful trade customers and usages* for the protection of the members as the Institute may deem advisable."[47] Among these "customs and usages" existed an illegal base point pricing system.[48] In *British Sugar plc* v *DGFT*[49] the European Commission commenced an investigation into British Sugar plc (BS). Subsequently, BS

42 *Sheffield Newspapers* (1983), Cmnd 8664, at p. 56, para. 7.11.
43 *IFTRA Rules for Producers of Virgin Aluminium* [1975] 2 CMLR D20 at p. D30, para. 13.
44 *Sugar Institute* v *US* 297 US 553 (1936).
45 *ibid.*, at p. 579.
46 *ibid.*, at pp. 578, 579.
47 *FTC* v *Cement Institute* 333 US 683 (1948) reversing 157 F.2d 533.
48 157 F.2d 533 at p. 544. See 333 US 683 at pp. 716 and 719.
49 9 August 1995 (unreported).

furnished, out of time, a memorandum to the DGFT under the RTPA 1976 which recorded that in the context of the ongoing investigation by the European Commission, BS was concerned to ensure that there was no further possibility of the company engaging in pricing practices which would or could give rise to a complaint to the Commission. A memorandum stated that Tate and Lyle and BS believed that as a consequence of the unilateral decision taken by BS to end the price war retail market shares would tend to remain static and, to that end, BS would not price aggressively. Notwithstanding the ostensibly worthy motives enunciated in the memorandum, the DGFT concluded that the memorandum evidenced an arrangement, *inter alia*, as to prices and referred the same to the RPC demonstrating that fine words and motives, howsoever genuine, do not excuse an agreement from the scope of EC and UK competition law.

11.32 Not all codes are wolves in sheep's clothing. Many codes represent legitimate, "voluntary action to end abuses and to foster fair competitive opportunities in the public interest".[50]

1. EC Law

11.33 Many international organisations are involved in preparing Codes of Conduct for multinationals, including, amongst others, the United Nations (UN) the Organisation for European Co-operation and Development (OECD), the EC and even the World Council of Churches. To counter these regulatory moves many multinational federations and associations are evolving their own codes as an attempt to pre-empt superimposed alternatives. These codes are antitrust dynamite. They provide a cover for inter-firm consensus to develop. The Commission are well aware of the risk they connote and monitor their development with care. It is possible that in the future the Commission might order European firms to remain outside of international codes. There is a precedent for this in 1947 when the Federal Trade Commission in the US ordered firms not to belong to the International Electrical Association which had members from all over the world but which limited its operation to those areas of the world where antitrust laws were weakest, i.e. outside the USA and the EC.[51] Conversely, in exceptional cases, codes of practices which seek to impose collective price fixing upon an industry may be acceptable. The most striking example of this is the United Nations Convention on a Code of Conduct for Liner Conferences (the UNCTAD Code).[52] This Code seeks to impose rules to be applied by international liner shipping conferences for the carriage of goods by sea in international trade. The Code applies only to liner conferences which are defined in the Code as agreements between vessel operating carriers which operate under "uniform of common freight rates".[53] Accordingly, the Code only applies to groups of shipping lines who fix *inter se* as part of an overall international maritime transport service. By virtue of Council Regulation 954/79/EEC[54] the Council of Ministers permitted Member States to ratify the UNCTAD Code. However, certain reservations were required to be entered by ratifying Member States in order to ensure compliance with Community law. The recitals to the Council Regulation state that the Community was to adopt specific competition rules applicable to international maritime transport services. Council Regulation 4056/86/EEC[55] applies the competition rules to international maritime transport services.

[50] *Sugar Institute* v *US* 297 US 553 at p. 598 (1936) *per* Hughes CJ.
[51] See *The Economist*, "Power play by Congress" 31 January 1981.
[52] Geneva 1973 and 1974.
[53] Code, Chapter 1, Part One, Definitions.
[54] OJ 1979 L121/2, 17 May 1979.
[55] OJ 1986 L378/4, 31 December 1986.

The Regulation also introduced a block exemption, in Article 3, applicable to liner conferences. The definition of liner conferences in the Council Regulation is identical to that in the UNCTAD Code. The block exemption in Article 3 of the Regulation thus applies *only* to liner conferences within the meaning of the Code and, *a fortiori*, only to liner conferences which fix prices.

2. *UK Law*

11.34 The FTA 1973 imposes a duty on the Director General of Fair Trading to encourage trade associations "to prepare, and to disseminate to their members, codes of practice for guidance in safeguarding and promoting the interests of consumers".[56] Associations negotiate the substance of the code with the OFT and then register them. The OFT publishes leaflets explaining the Code to consumers. There are codes covering such trades as: electrical goods, cars, shoes, package holidays, launderers and dry cleaners, buying by post, funerals, photography, double glazing, furniture.[57] Once negotiated and registered these codes obtain section 21(2) dispensation. Many of the codes cover quite specific activities. Thus the *Society of Motor Manufacturers and Traders Code of Practice*[58] recommended to commercial vehicle manufacturers and operators specifications for the manufacture and fitting of fog lamps for articulated vehicles. The *Liverpool Provision Trade Association Ltd*[59] in 1984 issued a code relating to pre- and after-sales services provided for customers through dealers.

11.35 In negotiating codes, the OFT seeks to ensure that certain clauses are included relating to misleading and dishonest advertisements and descriptions, consumers rights concerning cancellation, adequacy of arbitration rights, deposits, exemption and limitation of liability and other unreasonable clauses, refunds, warranty transfers, compensation, guarantees, surcharges, performance times, information, spares, general display and testing facilities. Obviously, in negotiations the OFT is concerned to ensure that these clauses have no restrictive economic consequences. Indeed, the OFT must ensure that this is so before the code can legally benefit from section 21(2) treatment.

D. Exclusion, Limitation of Liability and Other Financial Penalty Clauses

11.36 Exclusion or liability limitation clauses are often methods of allocating risk in a contract. If X and Y agree that X will not be liable for supplying negligent goods, or for providing services in a negligent fashion, or for damage caused by his servants or agents, etc., then this may be in practice simply a means of contractually imposing an insurance burden on Y. Where X is relieved of the need to insure, his costs will be lower and cost savings may be passed on to Y in the price or fee charged. It is hence unrealistic to analyse exclusion clauses without considering the insurance consequences. The same applies to limitation of liability clauses. If X and Y agree that in the event of accident X shall be liable to a maximum as specified in the contract, then Y may, after a proper assessment of risk, take adequate insur-

[56] s. 124(3) FTA 1973. See DGFT Annual Report 1980, pp. 50, 51.

[57] See Woodroffe, "Government monitored codes of practice in the United Kingdom" (1984) *Journal of Consumer Policy* 171. See OFT, *Restrictive Practices: Provisions of the Restrictive Trade Practices Act 1976* (1990), p. 25.

[58] No. 1077 Register of Restrictive Trade Practices (1984).

[59] No. 588 Register of Restrictive Trade Practices (1984). No. 4994 Register of Restrictive Trade Practices (1983).

ance cover for damage exceeding the contract maximum. Likewise X may insure up to the contract maximum.

11.37 Similar principles apply to automatic liability clauses whereby in the event of breach or accident, X's liability will automatically be fixed at a specified sum. The contract might stipulate that in the event of breach X will pay Y £5,000. It matters not that Y's damages may be only £600 or alternatively as much as £20,000, subject of course to the overriding principle that any such clause must be a genuine pre-estimate of actual losses that would be incurred in case of breach else it will be an unenforceable penalty at common law.

1. *EC Law*

(1) Article 86 EC

11.38 Article 86(a) prohibits the imposition of "unfair trading terms" by dominant suppliers. When will exclusion or limitation clauses by "unfair"? There is a dearth of case law on the subject. Presumably it would be unfair where the dominant supplier shifts the risk to the purchaser but makes no compensating concessions in the form of lower prices. It might be argued that since the supplier is effectively charging the buyer for a cost component not borne by the supplier, then that is abuse. In a competitive market the supplier would be forced to pass over cost savings to purchasers. The Commission in *Eurofirma*[60] have categorised as an abuse of dominance the attempts by a dominant buyer to extract something for nothing. Thus, where Eurofirma, the largest EC buyer of railway rolling stock, required as a condition of contract that it be given, free of charge, unlimited use of all relevant patents, the Commission stated that this would represent an abuse of dominance. Might not a dominant supplier who charged for a cost component not borne also be extracting something for nothing and therefore abusing its position?

(2) Article 85 EC

11.39 Since exclusion and limitation clauses may have a bearing upon product or service price any attempts by parties collectively to determine exclusion and other analogous clauses may fall within Article 85(1). In appropriate factual cases a *de minimis* argument might apply to exclude Article 85(1). Where the clause exists as a result of negotiation of SFC's between both buyer and seller representatives or trade associations, then exemption may lie under Article 85(3). First, by clearly dividing insurance duties between seller and buyer the agreement might help parties avoid unnecessary double insurance, i.e. both sides paying insurance premiums to cover the same risks. Secondly, by firmly shifting risk to one side the possibility of expensive litigation to determine fault and, *a fortiori*, apportion insurance responsibility is avoided. Thirdly, where cost saving are made and are passed on then consumers may enjoy a fair share of the resulting benefits.

11.40 For examples of the type of clause that might give risk to problems, see the discussion below of UK law. Though it is not to be assumed that the Commission would treat such clauses in identical manner to the OFT.

[60] [1973] CMLR D217, *Third Commission Competition Report* (1973), paras. 68, 69. For cases where an undertaking abused its dominance by making a charge that was excessive in relation to cost (a variant on getting something for nothing), see para. 8.146.

2. *UK Law*

(1) Clauses imposed by individual firm: CA 1980

11.41 There are no cases to date where the OFT or MMC has investigated exclusion or other related clauses. As an example, an anti-competitive effect might arise where X, a dominant supplier, imposes upon buyer's terms and conditions whereby the obligation to insure rests with the dominant supplier.[61] A particular customer may prefer or need to obtain his own insurance (he may be able to obtain low premium rates or may have special needs) but is required to pay the suppliers usual price which includes an element of insurance. Such a customer may be forced to pay a double burden and, *vis- à-vis* competitors who rely exclusively upon the supplier's insurance, is placed at a competitive disadvantage. In such a case the refusal to negotiate individual terms with a supplier may be anti-competitive. Such a refusal might even be viewed as a form of tying practice whereby the buyer is bound to accept the supplier's insurance cover with his products or services.[62]

11.42 Buyers faced with exclusion or other clauses limiting or restricting the supplier's liability which they consider unreasonable may consider challenging the clause under the Unfair Contract Terms Act 1977. Consumers may resist unfair terms under the Unfair Terms in Consumer Contracts Regulations 1994.[63] Such actions of course are not competition law actions.

(2) Collectively imposed clauses: RTPA 1976

11.43 A recurrent feature of SFC's drafted by trade associations are clause provided for contractual liability for loss or damage. Each clause is examined on its merits and having regard to the general economic and legal context. Factors relevant to analysis are those discussed above in section B of this chapter, in particular the Unfair Contract terms Act 1977 (UCTA 1977) and the Unfair Terms in Consumer Contracts Regulations. The following are examples of commonly recurring clauses together with some relevant criteria for assessment.

(a) Liability for death or personal injury

11.44 A clause in a SFC (or indeed in an individual agreement) exempting one party from liability for death or personal injury arising out of that party's negligence is void and unlawful under statute.[64] Consequently, the OFT will not grant section 21(2) dispensation for a SFC including such a clause. The Tugowners Association in their 1974 towage conditions sought to exclude liability, "for any personal injury or loss of life howsoever, and wheresoever caused including personal injury or loss of life of the master and/or crew of and/or any person on board the tug or tender". Before section 21(2) dispensation could be granted in 1984 this clause had to be deleted from the SFC.[65]

[61] e.g. under a clause which imposes all risks on the supplier, a total exclusion clause benefiting the buyer might be an example. Ostensibly such a clause benefits the buyer. However, the party will pay for such benefits in the form of higher prices.

[62] The OFT seems to consider this to be anti-competitive when in a collectively imposed context, see DGFT Annual Report 1979, p. 45. See also *Building Societies Association* No. S. 15 Register of Restrictive Trade Practices (1984).

[63] S.I. 1994 No. 3159 implementing Council Directive 93/13/EC.

[64] s. 2(1) UCTA 1977.

[65] No. S. 161 Register of Restrictive Trade Practices, *British Tugowners Association Standard Terms and Conditions* (1984).

(b) Exclusion clauses

11.45 SFCs which provide for unqualified *acceptance* of liability are rare and generally impracticable. Where the more common converse applies, unqualified *exclusion* of liability, the OFT usually considers such exclusion as unreasonable, harmful to competition and inappropriate for dispensation under section 21(2). This is not an absolute rule. As stated above clauses providing for unqualified exclusion have been dealt with under section 21(2). Though, these have invariably been where the relevant SFC has been drafted by all sides of the industry jointly and where the exclusion clause operates to shift risk simply as a means of allocating insurance responsibilities.

11.46 Where a SFC is used by sellers in dealings with ultimate consumers it might follow that it is unreasonable to preclude liability at all since it is unreasonable to expect the man in the street to obtain specific insurance every time he makes a purchase from a shop.

11.47 In assessing exclusion clauses the OFT considers a number of factors. First, the relative bargaining power of the parties. Where a seller's trade association recommends use of a SFC to members in their dealings with customers and the latter are precluded from negotiating terms and conditions individually then the OFT will probably consider the exclusion unreasonable and incompatible with section 21(2) treatment. Where the buyers are not a homogeneous category so that the possibility for them to combine and thereby jointly negotiate fairer terms is remote, then again, the OFT is more critical. For example, the product might be ball bearings. The product is used by a wide range of different manufacturers/buyers. These buyers would not naturally meet under one trade association roof so that the possibility of a buyers' association arising is less probable. In any event, simply because a supplier trade association negotiates with, or obtains the acquiesence of a buyer association with respect to the use of a SFC, this is no automatic indication of reasonableness though it might encourage that conclusion. It is of course possible that there is gross inequality of bargaining power as between the associations. The sellers' association might represent 100 per cent of the sellers in the market whereas the buyer's association might account for only 20 per cent of the buyers. Relative bargaining power is hence not an absolute criterion.[66]

11.48 A second important factor is the undesirability of making a buyer or user pay for double insurance. If the SFC used by the seller provides for insurance by the seller (e.g. there is a clause whereby the seller accepts liability without limit) then the buyer must accept that clause; the cost of the seller's insurance premiums will have been included in the price. However, the buyer may well *already* have adequate insurance cover so has no need for additional cover provided by the seller. This is quite often the case with respect to carriage and storage services, for example. If the buyer is unable to negotiate a variation to the SFC, he will be forced to bear a double insurance burden. In such circumstances the OFT might consider the extent of the double burden and whether it is reasonable for sellers to alow negotiated variations to the SFC. The OFT might be unwilling to seek section 21(2) dispensation where a SFC does not offer several options as to acceptance of liability depending on the insurance required by the buyer and the charge to be made for the service.[67]

[66] As has been recognised by the Court of Appeal. See *Alec Lobb Ltd* v *Total Oil* [1985] 1 WLR 173 at pp. 181–183 *per* Dillon LJ, and at pp. 188, 189 *per* Dunn LJ.

[67] Support for this approach may be found in the decision on *Woodman* v *Phototrade Processing Ltd* (*The Times Business News*, 20 June 1981) X purchased film from ship which displayed a notice limiting liability to the replacement cost of the film. X's film was ruined during development and he claimed damages. The action succeeded and £53 damages were awarded for disappointment (the film was of a friend's wedding). The limitation clause was struck down as unreasonable under UCTA 1977 because the Court considered that the public should have been offered a choice—development of film under present arrangements at a low price or a more specialised service with better compensation at a higher price.

(c) Limitation of liability

11.49 Similar principles apply to clauses whereby one party (usually the supplier) contractually limits liability in the event of breach of contract or negligence to a specified sum. Such clauses may simply be means of allocating risk between the parties and hence insurance burdens. In practice, such clauses are more acceptable than absolute exclusion clauses.[68] Limitation clauses are often viewed as a compromise to absolute exclusion clauses since they may reflect a reasonable balance between the parties as to the risks each party should cover. In determining whether limitation clauses are reasonable reference may be made to section 11(4) UCTA 1977 which highlights two factors as relevant to the analysis: (a) the resources the party imposing the clause could be expected to have access to for the purposes of meeting the liability should it arise; and (b) the extent to which it was open for that party to cover himself by insurance.

(d) Indemnity clauses

11.50 A SFC incorporating a clause whereby the buyer is required to indemnify the seller may be unreasonable and inappropriate to section 21(2) treatment. Indemnity clauses are subject to the test of reasonableness in the UCTA 1977.[69] The OFT adopts a similar criteria of evaluation. Such clauses may come in various guises. The buyer may be contractually required to indemnify the seller in respect of the latter's liability for negligence or breach of contract. The seller's liability might arise in respect of the buyer directly or vicariously or in respect of a third party, e.g. a customer of the buyer. The RPC has taken a strict line with such clauses. In *British Bottle Association's Agreement*[70] the following was stated:

> "There is, however, one of the ancillary restrictions which we must briefly mention. It is contained in the conditions of sale of the association. It is headed 'Non-liability for Third Party Claims'. It provides, in effect, that a contractual clause is to be inserted in connection with all sales of glass bottles, whereby the purchaser agrees that the member shall not be liable for any claims for injury or damage sustained by the purchaser, his servants or agents, after the bottles have been delivered, and, further, that the purchaser shall indemnify the manufacturer against claims for loss, injury or damage sustained by a third party after delivery of the bottles. This means that the purchaser is left to bear the risk of any injury or damage resulting to the purchaser himself or to any third party as a result of the manufacturers having sold defective bottles even though the defect arises from the manufacturer's own negligence. It was explained on behalf of the association that this clause was introduced in order to ensure uniformity of conditions of sale, that it is the sort of matter which would reasonably be covered by insurance, that in fact the clause has never been used to defeat a claim by a purchaser, and that it was intended as a safeguard against unfounded claims. No purchaser who gave evidence and who was asked the question, was aware of the existence of this clause as a part of his contract for the purchase of bottles. We would only say this: we would have had no hesitation whatever in declaring this restriction to be against the public interest, even if all the other restrictions had been in the public interest."

11.51 Indemnity clauses may thus be generally unacceptable. They have the effect of making one party to the contract the other party's insurer. Why should a buyer be financially

[68] See *Ailsa Craig Fishing Co* v *Malvern Fishing Co* [1983] 1 All ER 101 at p. 105 *per* Lord Fraser; approved of in *George Mitchell (Chesterhall) Ltd* v *Finney Lock Seeds Ltd* [1983] 2 AC 803—under the UCTA 1977 limitation clauses are not to be judged by the same exacting standards that are to be applied to exclusion clauses.

[69] s. 4 UCTA 1977.

[70] (1961) LR 2 RP 345 [1961] 1 WLR 760 at p. 762, part of the reason for the highly critical tone may stem from the facts that: (i) purchasers were generally unaware of the clause; and (ii), it was not known to have been activated by the supplier and hence there was no justification for sustaining an outdated restrictive clause.

responsible for the seller's default? SFC's which contain clauses which simply make it clear that the party responsible for the liability shall indemnify the party who actually "pays up" will generally be suitable for section 21(2) treatment. Thus, if a retailer pays a consumer £500 compensation on a defective product, a clause requiring the manufacturer who produced the defective product to compensate the retailer may be acceptable. Where parties using a SFC operate in a trade or market which is subject to statutory regulations (e.g. health and safety regulations) then clauses requiring parties responsible for breaching their statutory duty to indemnify parties who were actually made liable for that breach may be reasonable. For example, if a subcontractor employs materials which breach safety regulations and accordingly is made liable for such breach then the main contractor who supplied the subcontractor with the offending materials may reasonably be required to indemnify the subcontractor.[71]

(e) Fixed liability and liquidated damages clauses

11.52 The OFT has experienced some difficulty with SFC's providing for liability to be predetermined in the event of breach of duty.[72] Such clauses are quite common in services contracts: frequently they are connected with contracts of bailment with the bailee made liable for a fixed sum on proof of negligence or breach of contract.[73] Thus if an employee of a bailee carriage and storage company crashes his lorry or turns off a cold storage plant or allows thieves to enter a warehouse then the bailee's liability is fixed. Usually the bailor imposes the SFC recommended for use by his trade association. The justification is that if the extent of liability is predetermined, parties may organise insurance accordingly. An objection to such a clause may be that a fixed sum is artificial and invariably unrepresentative of the true quantum of damage in a given case; the fixed sum may be greater than the damage actually incurred by the bailor. The relative bargaining power of bailee and bailor will be relevant. Also, the extent to which an accurate pre-estimate of loss may be made will be of significance; if the amount of loss suffered by the bailor can be reasonably accurately predetermined it may well be fair to set a contractual figure for that loss on proof of breach of duty.

11.53 In other contexts the OFT has objected to SFCs providing for fixed compensation fees to be paid to a provider of services in the event of cancellation by the user. The OFT does not object to cancellation fees but prefers the amount to be a matter for individual negotiation between provider of service and user. Where cancellation is a real risk, cancellation fees may be an important factor in a client's choice of which provider of service to hire. If all providers quote identical fees an important element of competition between the providers has been nullified.[74]

[71] e.g. No. 3550 Register of Restrictive Trade Practices, *Agreement between members of Spray Contracts Technical Committee* (concerning indemnity under the Asbestos Regulations 1969 BSS 3590/1963 and BSS CP 299/1968).

[72] At one time liability clauses were expressed in terms of so much per tonne entrusted to the bailee. Such clauses are rarer when inflation rates may render the rates per tonne unrealistic in quite short periods. The change to fixed sum liability clauses means that SFCs do not have to be varied quite so frequently.

[73] A bailee has been defined as follows: "Any person is to be considered as a bailee who otherwise than as a servant either receives possession of a thing from another or consents to receive or hold possession for another upon an undertaking with the other person either to keep and return or deliver to him the specific thing or to convey and apply the specific thing according to the directions antecedent or future of the other persons"—Pollock and Wright, *Possession* at p. 160.

[74] e.g. No. S. 892 Register of Restrictive Trade Practices, *Master Photographers' Association*. The Master Photographers Association SFC for use by photographers at weddings provided for a cancellation fee of "75 per cent of the then current price of the minimum order specified in the schedule". This was amended so as to allow the actual percentage to be freely negotiated between photographer and client.

11.54 The preferred OFT position is that damages should not be pre-set in SFCs and should be the subject of negotiation in each case. This might necessitate incorporation of a negotiation of damages procedure into a SFC or recourse to an independent arbitrator or assessor. However, the OFT appreciates that fixed liability clauses are often reasonable as means of avoiding lengthy negotiation or arbitration disputes and as means of apportioning risk and hence insurance

11.55 Fixed liability clauses which have effect as penalties, e.g. where the penalty is disproportionate to the loss,[75] will not be suitable for section 21(2) treatment. This is no more than the common law position which renders penalty clauses invalid and unenforceable.[76]

(f) Surcharges on overdue accounts

11.56 SFC's sometimes provide for surcharges on overdue accounts. Often rates of interest are specified. In such cases the OFT may require the party imposing the clause to justify the level of the interest rate by reference to losses or additional expenses borne by that party. Where the surcharge bears a reasonable relationship to the pre-estimate of loss such clauses are usually acceptable. Section 21(2) dispensation will not be accorded where a surcharge includes an element of penalty.

11.57 These surcharges should not be confused with discounts given by suppliers to buyers in respect of early payment of debts. Thus for example, many suppliers grant retailers a discount of (say) 2.5 per cent for payment within one month and an additional 2.5 per cent (i.e. 5 per cent) for payment within seven days.[77] Thus a buyer paying for goods after one month has to pay the list price; he is disadvantaged *vis-à-vis* early payers. It would be unrealistic to describe this as a penalty surcharge. Any buyer may obtain the discount by early payment and, furthermore, the discount is cost-justified by reference to savings earned by the supplier in being paid early.

(g) Non-exclusion clauses

11.58 Some trade association codes of practice recommend that members refrain from excluding their liability. Such clauses are generally suitable for section 21(2) treatment, although, it is possible that they exert a small effect on competition. Under normal circumstances suppliers might lawfully exclude liability, others might not. Thus, whether liability is excluded may be a factor in the customer's choice of supplier and hence an element of competition. However, the OFT usually considers that such clauses are not significant restrictions and are of benefit to consumers.[78]

(h) Liens, transfer of title

11.59 A SFC which contains clauses giving the user of the contract power over the other parties' goods may well be unreasonable, particularly where inequality of bargaining power

[75] This was the example given by Lord Halsbury LC in *Clydebank Engineering Co* v *Don Jose Ramos Isquierdo y Castaneda* [1905] AC 6 at p. 10.

[76] See *Dunlop Pneumatic Tyre Co* v *New Garage and Motor Co Ltd* [1915] AC 79 at pp. 87, 88 *per* Lord Dunedin. See generally, Treitel, *The Law of Contract* (9th edn. 1995) pp. 898–906.

[77] Though, if member of a trade association agree that they will all charge the same credit rates then this will be a registrable agreement under ss. 6(1)(c) or 11(2)(b) RTPA 1976. Almost certainly such an agreement will be unsuited to s. 21(2) treatment. See e.g. *Sharman Newspaper* Nos. S. 1161 and S. 1597 Register of Restrictive Trade Practices (1983) where the RPC condemned agreements whereby members of trade association agreed with the principal supplier on credit and discount rates to be accorded them. The rules in question provided that members would not obtain advertising services from the supplier of that service other than upon terms that an allowance of 10 per cent be made where payment is effected by last Friday of the month following invoice date.

[78] See e.g. No. S. 12 Register of Restrictive Trade Practices, *Association of British Launderers and Cleaners* (1977).

also exists. For example, the SFC may have clauses providing that the plant and materials of a contractor when on site become the property of the employer of the contractor. The SFC might give the employer rights over the property in the event of breach by the contractor of the contract or of any other legal duty causing damage to the employer or in the event of the liquidation of the contractor. Alternatively, where a SFC provides that the user of the SFC has a lien over the other parties' goods, again, this might prove unacceptable. A lien entitles a person who has done work for another to detain goods in his possession belonging to that other until the charges for the work has been paid. Thus, if an association whose members repair consumers goods, recommends a SFC for its members to use which contains clauses giving the members liens over those goods in situations which are unreasonable, e.g. where the consumer refuses to pay because the repairer has negligently lost the article in question, the OFT might object.

(i) Redemption and early termination of contract clauses

11.60 In contracts for the provision of services it is not uncommon to find clauses imposing a penalty where a customer prematurely ends the contract by early performance of his side of the bargain. Thus, many building societies impose redemption interest charges on borrowers who wish to redeem the amount due to them prior to the end of the period for which the loan was made. In 1982 the OFT informed the Building Societies Association (BSA) that, in the light of complaints it considered a clause on redemption interest in the BSA model rules to be significant and inappropriate to section 21(2) treatment.[79] The relevant clause stated: "Where however such a repayment is made in full or in part is made within 5 years after the date on which the advance was made, the Board may require him to pay in addition, if he has not given 3 month's notice in writing of the intended repayment, a sum not exceeding an amount equal to 3 month's interest at the rate applicable to the mortgage at the date of such repayment on the amount of principal so repaid." The BSA deleted the clause from the Model Rules and replaced it with the following clause: "How to meet the requirements of s. 4(1)(g) of the Building Societies Act 1962 is a matter for each Society to decide—paragraph (g) requires a Society's rules to set out among other things 'the conditions on which a borrower can redeem the amount due from him before the end of the period for which the advance was made.'"

11.61 While redemption, interest or analogous charges are not *per se* unreasonable (they may be compensation for the loss of fees earned by the service provider due to the early termination of the contract) the OFT is concerned that competition between providers of such services in the conditions they impose on early termination of contracts remains healthy.

E. Credit and Other Terms of Payment

11.62 Credit and other terms of payment are important factors in a customer's choice of supplier and are hence factors in competition between suppliers. Attempts by suppliers to harmonise credit and payment terms will generally be considered as unacceptable. Where a dominant or economically powerful supplier imposes unduly harsh payment and credit terms upon customers then that supplier may have abused its position. In this section discounts will *not* be discussed since these have already been examined in Chapter 8.

[79] No. S. 15 Register of Restrictive Trade Practices, *Building Societies Association* (1984) documents V 29 dated 25 November 1982 and V 33 dated 2 March 1983.

1. *EC Law*

11.63 The Commission and Court of Justice have both struck down attempts by parties jointly to fix credit and terms of payment.[80] This is especially so where the agreement is co-ordinated by a trade association and/or where the market is oligopolistic.

11.64 However, joint debt-collection associations comprising small and medium sized undertakings may legitimately undertake joint collection of outstanding debts. The association should only act upon the clear instructions of the creditor. Thus the association might apply different criteria when collecting debts on behalf of X than it will when acting on behalf of Y. The Commission has made it clear, however, in the Co-operation Notice it published in 1968,[81] that any attempts by an association to fix prices or terms and conditions of trade may infringe Article 85(1) EC. Thus, members of the association should avoid laying down uniform criteria for debt collection. If such uniformity is desired then the association would be advised to obtain clearance from the Commission.

11.65 The Notice also states that the creation of credit guarantee associations is outside of Article 85 since they do not affect the relationship between supply and demand. There is no reason why other forms of credit co-operation should not also fall outside of Article 85(1) EC, for example, investment trust or capital investment companies.

11.66 The exchange of data on the solvency of customers is also permissible.[82] Associations which collate such information should confine their activities to dissemination of data only: they should avoid recommending to members how they should interpret the information. Where such recommendations exist there may be a concerted practice between members as to the granting of credit facilities. Whereas most informational exchange systems should collect and collate data in anonymous, aggregated form, obviously individualised data is acceptable. Care must be taken by associations to maintain accurate records. Most Member States have rules on defamation which may render an association liable for wrongfully imputing a crime to a person (thereby implying that he is a bad credit risk). Furthermore, associations should not issue blacklists of customers which members should avoid supplying or giving credit to. Blacklists which entail collective boycotting or discrimination will represent serious infringements of Article 85(1) EC.[83]

2. *UK Law*

(1) Under the RTPA 1976

11.67 The OFT scrutinises closely trade association credit systems. It accepts that suppliers have a legitimate interest in controlling credit facilities. Bad debts increase costs and have an inflationary effect upon prices.[84]

[80] e.g. *FEDETAB* v *Commission* (Cases 209-215, 218/78) [1981] 3 CMLR 134, [1980] ECR 3125 at paras. 147–156 of the judgment. The setting by the manufacturer's trade association of a two-week period for payment of bills by customers was prohibited under Art. 85(1). It made no difference that the agreement was inspired by the need to counter strong market pressure to the contrary from powerful chains of supermarkets.

[81] Notice concerning Agreements, Decisions and Concerted Practices in the Field of Co-operation between Enterprises, JO 1968 C 75/3, [1968] CMLR D5.

[82] *ibid.* II (2)(b). For US cases adopting a similar position see *Swift and Co* v *US* (1905) 196 US 375 at p. 395; *Cement Manufacturers Protective Association* v *US* (1925) 268 US 588 at p. 604.

[83] Boycotts arranged via credit systems have been condemned as illegal in USA; *Swift and Co* v *US* (1905) 196 US 375; *US* v *Alexander & Reid* 280 Fed. 924 (SDNY 1922).

[84] See the dictum of the Court in *United States* v *Southern California Wholesale Grocers Association* 7 F.2d 944 (S.D. Cal. 1925) at p. 948: "Certainly it would be in the interest of economy in the general business of

11.68 Since credit terms are generally perceived as being an element of price, attempts by manufacturers to agree upon standard credit terms and conditions will be inappropriate for section 21(2) treatment and may be referred to the RPC for prohibitory orders to be issued.[85]

11.69 Credit control systems operated by trade associations may be suitable to section 21(2) treatment.[86] Such systems are most useful in markets in which sellers deal with a large number of small buyers in scattered localities and no central credit rating service is available. To be suitable for section 21(2) treatment credit systems should be: based upon objective criteria; scrupulously accurate; and, not used for anti-competitive purposes.

(a) Criteria should be objective

11.70 Associations must ensure that the criteria they adopt for determining how a person fits into a certain rating category (e.g. strong, satisfactory, weak, unsuitable for credit) are objective. Compliance with the Data Protection Act 1984 will also be necessary, if personal data is held on computer.[87] As a rule, the OFT accept criteria premised upon the financial soundness of the customer but reject subjective criteria based upon such factors as the association's estimation of the customer's competence or experience. Some ostensibly objective criteria may have anti-competitive consequences however. Thus the use of "red lining" criteria may bereft a system of section 21(2) dispensation. "Red lining" is the practice of refusing credit solely on the basis of where the applicant lives or operates from; in effect a no-credit line is drawn around what the association considers to be a high risk area for bad debts (e.g. inner city areas). "Red lining" may arbitrarily exclude good customers from obtaining credit and it may thereby place them at a competitive disadvantage *vis-à-vis* their competitors in "better" areas. Moreover, "red lining" might infringe legislation on racial and sex discrimination. Criteria incorporating such factors will almost certainly be "significant" in section 21(2) RTPA 1976 terms and inappropriate for dispensation from reference to the RPC.

11.71 Credit scoring is an objective method of credit analysis which is becoming increasingly popular.[88] It has been defined as "a mathematical method of assessing individual creditworthiness based upon a statistical analysis of a large sample of an equal number of accounts in which the payment history has been good, of accounts where there has been default, and of applications where credit was refused."[89] The methodology is used mostly in connection with individuals though it also has a commercial use. A well-designed credit scoring system may well be unobjectionable in competition terms. However, even well-

cont.
distribution, both as affecting the dealer and the customer, that loss suffered through the non-payment of retailers' accounts, whether due to dishonesty of the [debtor] or his financial irresponsibility, and which would necessarily become a part of the overhead cost of distribution, should be saved."

85 e.g. Nos. 3481, 2385 Register of Restrictive Trade Practices, *Agreements of the Sunday Newspaper Proprietors No. 2* (RPC 1972). The Association terminated a restriction in an agreement whereby the members agreed: "not to supply Daily newspapers on terms providing for credit to be given for newspapers returned for various reasons unless this is agreed by the members." The restriction terminated was similar to restrictions struck down by the RPC (for court order see No. 2385). See also No. S. 256 Register of Restrictive Trade Practices, *Access Credit Card Scheme* (1980), noted DGFT Annual Report 1980 p. 48.

86 e.g. No. 3669 Register of Restrictive Trade Practices, *Aberdeen Fish Salesmen's Association* (1974); No. 3089 Register of Restrictive Trade Practices, *Nottingham and District Wholesale Fruit and Potato Merchants* (1974).

87 For a comprehensive guide to the Data Protection Act 1984, see Chalton and Gaskill's *Encyclopaedia of Data Protection* (looseleaf).

88 For a discussion of credit scoring see OFT Consultative Document, *Credit Scoring* (1982).

89 *ibid.*, at p. 3, para. 3.2

designed systems may have unintended, exclusionary consequences. There will inevitably be some applicants for credit who fail to qualify because they have special characteristics which are not typical of the model used. To counter these cases, credit scoring systems should retain a degree of subjectivity or "overriding", i.e. the taking into account of factors or characteristics not included in the credit scoring system in order to accept or reject applicants who score less than the pass mark.[90]

(b) Criteria should be accurate

11.72 Credit rating systems may employ criteria based upon the honesty of the customer. Thus in *Aberdeen Fish Salesmen's Association*[91] the Association recommended to members that they refuse credit to any person convicted of theft or reset of fish (i.e. the practice of redisplaying for sale old fish). Associations employing such criteria must be extremely accurate. The wrongful listing of a person as a convicted criminal is defamatory and may lay the association bare to substantial damages claims. In this respect associations must consider the Rehabilitation of Offenders Act 1974 which provides that convictions for offences in respect of which the offender has received a sentence not exceeding 30 months' imprisonment and where a specified time varying from 5-10 years (depending on sentence) has elapsed since the conviction, shall be treated as spent, i.e. never having taken place. Associations who list as a convicted criminal a person whose sentence is spent may find that their incorrect listing renders them liable to the applicant (section 4(3)(b) of the Act).

(c) Systems must not be used for anti-competitive purposes

11.73 Credit systems should not operate as cloaks for the standardisation of members' terms and conditions. The OFT may be suspicious of a scheme where they consider that private credit rating services are available and adequate for the parties' purposes. Trade associations should restrict themselves to the mechanical analysis of credit data: they should avoid advising members on how to construe the data. Members should retain the freedom to supply credit to whomsoever they please irrespective of credit data supplied by the association.[92]

11.74 However, some degree of standardisation of terms may be justified where designed to protect privacy. In *Committee of Scottish Clearing Bankers (CSCB)*[93] the CSCB was concerned with the established custom whereby a banker gives an indication of the respectability and standing of customers if requested to do so by another banker. In the light of this the CSCB drew up a list of banks and similar institutions and agreed that enquiries received from parties on the agreed list could be replied to direct. The list was based on the Bank of England list financial institutions which are regarded as falling within the banking sector. Under the agreement status enquiries received from government departments would only be replied to with the consent of the customer concerned. This was not considered "significant" for section 21(2) purposes and was in the customer's interests. Standardisation of practice to secure privacy was no obstacle to dispensation under section 21(2) RTPA 1976.

[90] *ibid.*, at pp. 8–10, paras. 4.6–4.9.

[91] No. S. 3669 Register of Restrictive Trade Practices (1974).

[92] See *Newspaper Publishers Association*, DGFT Annual Report (1979), p. 44; *Newspaper Society, Periodical Publishers Association, Scottish Daily Newspaper Society, Independent Television Companies Association* DGFT Annual Report (1980), p. 48—media trade associations modified their credit rules so that in future they would recommend to members that credit be allowed to listed advertising agencies who satisfied specified financial criteria and who complied with the British Code of Advertising Practice.

[93] No. S. 636 Register of Restrictive Trade Practices (1983).

(2) Under the CA 1980

11.75 Where a dominant person discriminates between his customers as regards the credit terms he will grant them, and where no objective justification accounts for the discrimination, then the dominant party may be acting anti-competitively. Such discrimination can influence the competitive inter-relationship between those with whom the dominant party deals. The same applies to any other terms of payment. Such discrimination may be closely akin to price discrimination (examined at paras. 8.93–8.108).

F. Terms Leading to Market Division (Market Sharing)

11.76 It is axiomatic in competition law that market sharing is unacceptable. Division of market may be achieved via numerous techniques; in this section some of those used will be discussed. Market sharing has already been discussed in other chapters. For example, Chapter 8 gives examples of cases where price arrangements have been used as means of avoiding competition between parties in each other's primary marketing area, e.g. agreements not to undercut a competitor on his own patch. Chapter 9 gives examples of exchanges of information which may lead to market division. Chapter 10 examines the problem of market division in distribution networks.

1. EC Law

11.77 Market sharing almost always violates Article 85(1) EC which prohibits agreements, trade association decisions and concerted practices which: "(b) limit or control production, markets, technical development, or investment; (c) share markets or sources of supply."

(1) Quotas

11.78 Agreements whereby parties divide the market according to quotas almost always infringe Article 85(1).[94] The agreement still infringes Article 85 if it is not intended to be permanent as, for example, where it relates to a single transaction.[95] Though, it is acceptable where X and Y conclude an agreement for delivery of a fixed quantity of goods for X to arrange for the goods to be distributed through competitors to Y according to a set formula.[96] Where a quota scheme is prohibited it need hardly be stated that restrictions designed to facilitate the scheme are also unlawful. Thus equalisation of receipts schemes (discussed at paras. 8.216–8.225) are unlawful; exchange of data between competitors for instance in respect of quantities sold, customers, invoices, etc. will also be prohibited. The only types of scheme that may be allowed are rationalisation agreements between firms in "crisis" industries which are designed to reduce over-capacity in an orderly manner. These joint venture rationalisation agreements are examined at paras. 12.234 and following.

[94] e.g. *Italian Flat Glass*, OJ 1989 L33/44, [1990] 4 CMLR 535, on appeal T-68/89, etc. [1992] ECR II-1403, [1992] 5 CMLR 302; *Polypropylene* OJ 1986 L230/1, [1988] 4 CMLR 347. On appeal T-1-4/89–T-6-15/89 *Rhône Poulenc and Others* v *Commission* [1991] ECR II-867. *Zinc Producers Group* [1985] 2 CMLR 108; *Aluminium Imports from Eastern Europe* OJ 1985 L92/1 (30 March 1985); *Cimbel* [1973] CMLR D167; *GISA* [1973] CMLR D125; *Fine Paper* [1972] CMLR D94; *Italian Cast Glass* [1982] 2 CMLR 61; *ACF Chemiefarma* v *Commission (Quinine Cartel)* (Case 41/69) [1970] ECR 661, and for Commission decision [1969] CMLR D41.

[95] e.g. *Sugar Cartel* [1973] CMLR D65 (Commission decision). Market sharing is unlawful even if it only concerns defective goods or "seconds"—*European Glass Manufacturers* [1974] 2 CMLR D50.

[96] *Cementregeling Voor Nederland* [1973] CMLR D149.

(2) Geographical limitations and mutual assistance clauses

11.79 Parties who seek to divide markets by geographical territory infringe Article 85(1).[97] Usually division occurs along national boundaries. Such is anathema to all that the EC holds true.[98] Though it is equally unlawful where the agreements define territories that are unrelated to national borders. Market sharing may be achieved in numerous ways. Thus an agreement between X and Y not to license third parties in each other's territory is a breach of Article 85(1).[99] Agreements between X, Y and Z not to "disturb" the prevailing price in each party's primary marketing area are also unlawful; an agreement not to "dump" products in each other's main areas where the definition of dumping is any price lower than the market leader in that territory is also unlawful.[100]

11.80 Agreements which tend to encourage maintenance of the status quo during periods when fluctuations in market share might be expected will infringe Article 85(1). In *CRAM* v *Commission*[101] the Court of Justice examined mutual assistance clauses. These provide that the parties to the agreement shall supply each other in the even of serious technical or other disruptions resulting in significant loss of production. Such a clause is designed to prevent parties from benefiting from difficulties encountered by rivals and thus tends to maintain the status quo artificially. The clause entailed parties holding back supplies in order to meet competitors' calls for assistance should they arise. Both the Advocate General and the Court of Justice agreed with the Commission that such clauses were unlawful.[102]

11.81 Market sharing of territories outside of the EC are unaffected by EC rules unless they have some effect on the EC market, although such agreements may of course be caught by national or international laws prevailing elsewhere. Agreements not to sell into the EC market will be subject to EC law: they reduce the level of competitive activity by their non-participation.[103] Such an agreement only engages Article 85 if there is an effect upon trade between Member States. An agreement with a Chinese company not to sell into Europe only attracts Article 85(1) if, upon a realistic assessment of the facts, export to Europe is actually likely.

11.82 Market sharing by means of competitors allocating specific customers to each other will be unlawful, with the chances of exemption under Article 85(3) remote.[104]

11.83 Agreements whereby X and Y undertake to concentrate their efforts on different products (i.e. specialisation agreements) and hence share products between them may well be suitable for Article 85(3) exemption. See paras. 12.199–12.223 for details.

[97] *Preserved Mushrooms* [1975] 1 CMLR D83; *Deutsche Philips* [1973] CMLR D241; *WEA—Filipacci* [1973] CMLR D43; *Van Katwijk* [1970] CMLR D43; *Dutch Transport Underwriters* Bull EC 10/76, para. 2111; *Sand Pits* Bull EC 11/76, para. 2119; *Leopold-Kamei* Bull EC 11/75, para. 2122.

[98] e.g. Art. 3(c), (g) EC. But cf. *Transocean Marine Paint II* [1974] 1 CMLR D11 where market sharing between small and medium-sized undertakings enabled them to become more efficient and compete more effectively upon a concentrated world market. This was an exceptional case. The exemption was most recently renewed in 1988, see OJ 1988 L351/40; [1989] 4 CMLR 621.

[99] e.g. *SNPE-Leafield Engineering* [1978] 2 CMLR 758.

[100] e.g. *IFTRA Rules for Producers of Virgin Aluminium* [1975] 2 CMLR D20.

[101] Cases 29, 30/83 [1984] ECR 1679, [1985] 1 CMLR 688 for Commission decision see [1983] 2 CMLR 285.

[102] *ibid.*, at p. 704 *per* Advocate-General Mme Rozès and at p. 714, para. 35 *per* the Court.

[103] See e.g. opinion concerning the applicability of the Treaty of Rome to the Importation of Japanese products into the Community, JO 1972 C111/13. See also the Commission's response to WQ No. 299/72, JO 1972 C138/54. See also Case 86/75 *EMI* v *CBS Grammophon* [1976] 2 CMLR 235; [1976] ECR 871 at p. 908. Though it could be questioned whether such an agreement was implemented in the EC if carried out by non-EC businesses: Joined Cases 89, 104, 114, 116–117, 125–129/85 *Ahlstrom and Others* v *Commission (Wood Pulp: jurisdiction)* [1988] ECR 5193, [1988] 4 CMLR 901.

[104] e.g. *Prym-Beka* [1973] CMLR D250.

2. UK Law

(1) Under the RTPA 1976: Unacceptable agreements

11.84 Agreements between parties to divide markets whether geographically, by quota or by some other device are registrable and will not be suitable for section 21(2) treatment. Market sharing agreements between parties where the aggregate turnover in the United Kingdom of the parties and their respective groups does not exceed £20 million when the agree was entered into are non-notifiable and fall outside the Act unless the Director General specifically files particulars of such an agreement on the register and serves a notice upon the parties. See paras. 2.239–2.249. Agreements within the Act. They will, almost certainly, be referred to the RPC for a prohibitive order to be made against them wherever the OFT considers that the agreement has been operated in a clandestine fashion or has exerted serious, restrictive consequences.[105]

11.85 The RPC has generally adopted an unsympathetic stance to market sharing. Agreements not to market new products without the consent of other parties have been struck down.[106] Agreements not to poach on each other's primary selling areas are also unacceptable.[107] The RPC has also condemned an agreement between parties not to supply during a specified period of time products in such quantities as would "overload" the market.[108] In 1977 the *Publishers' Association*, as part of a review of its practices in the light of general competition law, revoked a clause in an agreement whereby publisher members would normally respect an 18-month to 2-year time gap between publication of hardback and softback books with the former being published first. Clearly this restriction was designed to reduce competition between soft and hardback books. Whilst the RPC was never required to hear the case because the parties abandoned the restriction it appears, prima facie, to have hampered consumer choice and artificially sustained a market in hardback books.[109]

(2) Under the RTPA 1976: acceptable agreements

11.86 It would appear to be established that quota schemes drafted in the form of positive selling or buying obligations are not registrable. Clauses obliging a party to supply to the other a specified amount of a product or obliging a party to purchase a specified amount of a

[105] See e.g. No. 2385 Register of Restrictive Trade Practices *Agreements of the Sunday Newspapers Proprietors No. 2* (RPC 1972). The RPC held to contravene the public interest a restriction in an agreement whereby proprietors of Sunday newspapers agreed, *inter alia*, not to supply Sunday newspapers to a particular person "unless he sells only within a particular area". The restriction would create market sharing as between newsagents. See also *Supply and Sale of Liquid Milk to Shops* DGFT Annual Reports (1983), p. 30 and (1984), p. 34 under the agreements parties: fixed prices and discounts to certain customers; fixed tendering levels for milk; restricted supply to certain customers; allocated milk round; and supplied milk to shops only in cartons or other non-returnable containers. *British Reinforcement Manufacturers' Association* DGFT Annual Report 1982, pp. 32 and 98—parties were the main UK producers of processed steel reinforced bars for concrete structures. Under the agreement parties undertook: not to import reinforcing steel from non-EC countries; not to sell below an agreed floor price; to abide by the Association's rebate scheme; and not to limit deliveries by reference to a formula governing individual market share.

[106] *Re Permanent Magnet Association's Agreement* (1962) LR 3 RP 119; [1962] 1 WLR 781.

[107] *Doncaster and Retford Co-operative Societies Agreement* (1960) LR 2 RP 105; See also *Betting Shops* DGFT Annual Report (1984), p. 32—parties to an agreement undertook to selectively close certain betting shops and, in other cases, not to compete with a specified distance of a closed betting shop. The OFT commenced proceedings before the RPC in respect of these agreements which were clearly designed to share markets between the parties.

[108] No. 1577 Register of Restrictive Trade Practices, *National Farmers' Union* (unreported, RPC 1971). This was condemned as a restriction under s. 6(1)(c) RTPA 1956 (now RTPA 1976).

[109] No. 7514 Register of Restrictive Trade Practices (1976). See No. 2385 Register of Restrictive Trade Practices, *Agreements of the Sunday Newspapers' Proprietors No. 2* (RPC 1972) struck down a restriction whereby newspaper proprietors agreed: "not to supply daily newspapers to the pubic before midnight without first giving notice to other members ... before 3 p.m."

product are terms that may be disregarded when determining registrability. This derives from section 9(3) RTPA[110] which provides:

> "In determining whether an agreement for the supply of goods ... is an agreement to which this Act applies by virtue of this Part, no account shall be taken of any term which relates exclusively to the goods supplied ... in pursuance of the agreement."

11.87 In *Cadbury Schweppes Ltd* v *Lyons*[111] CS agreed to purchase 43 per cent of its sales requirements of citrus concentrates from Lyons who was, in turn, required to supply CS with that amount in priority to other demands. CS and Lyons were both rival producers of concentrate but under the agreement CS was deterred from producing concentrates to the extent of the amount supplied to it by Lyons. CS has thus limited its output in favour of Lyons. The RPC held that the agreement was one whereby Lyons agreed to supply CS with goods and was hence within the exception.[112] This conclusion was reached despite acceptance by the Court of the avowedly restrictive purpose and effect of the agreement.[113] However, the Court stressed that in assessing the exemption no account was to be taken of the surrounding circumstances.[114]

11.88 Despite criticism of this case for opening up a loop-hole in the legislation the principle has been accepted subsequently by the RPC. In *Diazo Copying Materials*[115] the parties concluded a joint venture agreement for the design, manufacture and marketing of a highly specialised new kind of photocopying machine. Under the agreement HTL would manufacture the machine to the order of MSL. Further MSL would market the machine throughout the world exclusively, but would grant HTL a non-exclusive, non-assignable and non-divisible right to make retail sales and other disposals in the UK. The agreement thus operated a form of geographical market sharing between HTL and MSL. The RPC held that the agreement was for the supply of goods within the meaning of section 9(3) and that the restriction was on sale by HTL outside of the UK related exclusively to the goods supplied so was excluded by section 9(3) from consideration when considering registrability.[116]

11.89 Two other forms of potentially acceptable market sharing may be mentioned. First, specialisation agreements whereby the parties allocate to themselves different products upon which to concentrate development efforts. Secondly, rationalisation agreements whereby parties, by destroying capacity, reduce output in crisis industries.

(3) Competition Act 1980

11.90 Agreements outside the RTPA may be within the ambit of the CA 1980.[117] Thus, the Schweppes agreement being outside the scope of the RTPA could in theory fall for investigation under the CA 1980; likewise in respect of *Diazo Copying Materials*.

[110] The equivalent provision for services is s. 18(2) RTPA 1976. These provisions are examined in depth in paras. 1.75–1.86.

[111] [1975] ICR 240; [1975] 1 WLR 1018, noted Korah (1975) JBL 238, Cunningham, *The Fair Trading Act 1973* (Supplement 1978) at pp. 64–66.

[112] The statutory provision in question was s. 7(2) RTPA 1956, this became s. 9(3) RTPA 1976.

[113] [1975] 1 WLR 1018 at p. 1029.

[114] *ibid.*

[115] [1984] ICR 429 (Warner J (presiding) was a former Advocate General at the European Court of Justice).

[116] *ibid.*, at p. 437 approving the direction in *Registrar of Restrictive Trading Agreement* v *Schweppes (No. 2)* (1971) LR 7 RP 336 (one of the forerunners to the *Schweppes* case discussed above). The actual joint venture agreement does not appear to have exerted serious anti-competitive effects. Had it been registered it might have been suitable for exemption under s. 21(2) RTPA 1976. Though, there could have been an effect on inter-state trade so as to activate EC rules.

[117] In 1986 the OFT investigated an alleged "gentlemen's agreement" between the BBC and ITV companies in respect of the procurement of episodes of the soap opera *Dallas*. Under the agreement the

11.91 The CA 1980 might be suitable for attempts by an economically powerful supplier to foster parallelism and market sharing thereby (though this might also be a case for the monopoly provisions of the FTA 1973). If X consciously refrains from supplying into Y's primary marketing area in the hope that Y will refrain from breaching X's primary territory, then the conduct of X might be anti-competitive. If X's behaviour ultimately leads to an "arrangement" with Y, then the CA 1980 loses applicability and the RTPA 1976 takes over.[118]

G. Sale of Assets Agreements: Non-Competition Clauses

11.92 When a parent company sells a subsidiary to a rival as a means of exiting the market in which the subsidiary trade, there may well be included in the sale agreement a clause preventing the old parent from engaging in any rival business for a fixed period of time and within a fixed geographical area. Usually, such restrictions are immaterial to the old parent who has no intention of re-entering the market. For the purchaser such clauses are material in that they are guarantees that the full commercial value of the business has been properly transferred. The interest of competition authorities lies in ensuring that the old parent is not unduly restricted from possible re-entry to the market. Whilst re-entry might never actually occur there remains a valid interest in ensuring that it is at least a possibility. The restrictions which might be treated sympathetically are vendor restraints. Attempts to impose restrictions on purchasers would only very exceptionally be justifiable, if at all.

1. EC Law

(1) General framework under EC law

11.93 Transfers of businesses may be dealt with as mergers or "concentrations" under the Merger Control Regulation 4064/89, a full discussion of which is beyond the scope of this work.[119] Concentrations under EC law and restrictions ancillary to such a concentration are dealt with only by the Merger Control Regulation.[120] Provided the transfer of a business constitutes a "concentration" under the Merger Control Regulation, Article 85 cannot be applied. A "concentration" occurs when one person acquires control of another business, which can be through the acquisition of shares or assets.[121]

11.94 Therefore, a normal transfer of a business is dealt with under the Merger Control Regulation, not Article 85 EC. So is any ancillary restraint, such as a non-competition clause.[122]

cont.
acquisition of episodes would be negotiated by the channel or service actually screening the programme at the time without interference (competition) from the other party. The OFT concluded that a gentlemen's no-poaching agreement existed but decided that since the agreement did not exclude competition in the purchase of *new* programmes no reference to the MMC under the CA 1980 was necessary.

118 s. 2(2) Competition Act 1980.

119 OJ 1989 L395/1; reprinted amending errors OJ 1990 L257/14.

120 This being the view adopted by the Court of Appeal in *R v SS Trade & Industry ex parte Airlines of Britain* [1992] *The Times*, 10 December. There are arguments that there is a residual role for the application of Art. 86 EC to concentrations falling below the thresholds in the MCR, since it continues to be directly effective and is not dependent on implementing legislation for that effect.

121 Art. 3, Reg. 4064/89.

122 Recital 25, Reg. 4064/89.

The Commission has issued a Notice Regarding Restrictions Ancillary to Concentrations,[123] which states which restrictions will be regarded an ancillary. If a non-competition clause is considered to be more than merely ancillary and thus beyond the scope of the Merger Control Regulation, then it will be dealt with under Article 85 EC. In practice the Commission will regard as ancillary any non-competition clause which it would have permitted under Article 85. A clause which goes further than being ancillary would also not be permitted under Article 85 EC. Therefore, the case law which existed prior to the entry into force of the Merger Control Regulation[124] remains a reliable guide to what will be regarded as an acceptable ancillary restriction.

11.95 The mere transfer of a business does not *per se* restrain competition and is outside the ambit of Article 85 EC.[125] Contractual commitments given by vendors of assets or shares not to compete with the buyer for a set period of time and in a given geographical territory are regarded as legitimate means of ensuring the performance of the vendor's obligation to transfer the full commercial value of the business since the sale of a business involves the transfer not only of physical assets but also of commercial know-how and goodwill clientele.[126] These obligations are guarantors for the buyer that the value of the purchase will not be eroded by competition from the seller. In *Remia and Nutricia* v *Commission*,[127] the Court of Justice affirmed these principles reiterating that where vendor and buyer were competitors after the agreement a non-competition clause was necessary to ensure that the transfer was effective and did not fall within Article 85(1). Non-competition clauses may take different forms including restrictions on the amount of time during which the vendor is precluded from competing with the buyer; restrictions on the territory the vendor may recompete in; restrictions on disclosing information obtained during the running of the transferred business; restrictions on the scope of the activities the vendor may engage in; and restrictions on the solicitation or purchasers employees. Whether a restraint is no more than ancillary and necessary to the transfer is a question of fact in each case. The starting point will be an assessment of the interest transferred including its nature (plant, equipment, intellectual property rights, know-how, business documents, client and customer lists, etc.) and the consideration paid for the interest transferred. Also relevant will be whether the vendor and purchaser are direct actual or potential competitors before the transfer. The importance of these factors (value of assets and consideration) will affect the duration and scope (temporal and geographical) of the non-competition covenants which are ancillary and otherwise found to be reasonable. An agreement between competitors will be considered move rigorously than one between non-competition. If an agreement contains clauses which are not necessary then not only does Article 85(1) apply but, in most cases, the prospect of exemption under Article 85(3). In most cases therefore the Commission would require amendments or modifications to the agreement to be made as the price of negative clearance.

123 1990 C203/5.

124 21 September 1990.

125 *Nicholas-Vitapro* [1964] CMLR D505; *Reuter-BASF* [1976] 2 CMLR D44; *Nutricia* [1984] 2 CMLR 165; *Sedame-Precilec* Eleventh Commission Competition Report (1981), p. 64, pra. 95; *Tyler-Linde Eleventh Commission Competition Report* (1981), p. 65, para. 96; *Mercaniver-PPG* [1985] 3 CMLR 359. See Modrall, "Ancillary restrictions in the Commission's decisions under the Merger Regulation: non-competition clauses" [1995] 1 ECLR 40.

126 *ibid.* cf. also *BPCL-ICI* OJ 1984 L212/1 at p. 6, para. 26.4.

127 Case 42/84 [1985] ECR 2545 at paras. 18–20. The Court added that in determining whether Art. 85(1) applied the Commission had to undertake complex economic matters. Accordingly, the Court would limit its review to procedural matters (para. 34). The Court by refusing to "second guess" the economic analysis of the Commission has limited the scope of appeals from Commission decisions under Art. 173.

(2) Restrictions on time

11.96 The Commission's rule is that where the transfer of a business also involves the transfer of good-will and know-how, a period of approximately five years is usually acceptable.[128] However, when the sale involves only the transfer of goodwill a period of two years is acceptable.[129] The Commission's Notice states:

> "a period of 5 years has been recognised as appropriate when the transfer of the undertaking involves the goodwill and the know-how, and a period of two years when it includes only the goodwill. However, these are not absolute rules; they do not preclude a prohibition of longer duration in particular circumstances, where for example the parties can demonstrate that customer loyalty will persist for a period longer than two years or that the economic life cycle of the products concerned is longer than five years and should be taken into account".[130]

11.97 In *Reuter-BASF*[131] the Commission highlighted four factors as relevant to determining how long the non-competition covenant should last:

(a) The nature of the know-how transferred. If the know-how is very complex and the buyer needs a considerable amount of time to reach a point of maximum exploitation this suggests the need for a lengthy non-competition period;
(b) the opportunities for use of the know-how. If the opportunities for exploitation of the know-how are limited the buyer will require a longer period of protection from the vendor in order to reach a point of satisfactory return on the know-how;
(c) the extent of the buyer's knowledge: the time needed to maximise exploitation will depend to a degree upon the expertise of the buyer; and,
(d) whether the non-competition covenant relates to know-how existing at the date of transfer or new developments based upon or connected to the transferred know-how. A non-competition clause extending to new or further development can be of shorter duration.

11.98 In *Nutricia*[132] the Commission also took the view that the duration of a non-competition clause might depend upon an assessment of how long the buyer would need to consolidate its hold on its new customers. In *Fujitsu/AMD* the Commission took the view that a maximum period of eight years non-competition imposed on a party leaving a joint venture was necessary "in order to compensate for the very significant investment of financial and technological resources"[133] by the parties and therefore granted exemption. This does of course indicate that, in the view of the Commission, the agreement did not warrant negative clearance.

11.99 The Commission also apply these considerations to exclusive trade mark licences: X, in the USA, grants Y, in Germany, a 10-year exclusive trade mark licence. X then transfers his business in the USA to Z, another firm incorporated in the USA. The transfer is sub-

[128] See *Allied/VIL, Nineteenth Commission Competition Report* (1989), para. 41, a complaint that a five-year period was too long, was rejected on the basis that the acquiring company need time to take over the vendor's customers and develop the associated know-how and R&D facilities. Though a five-year covenant in *Hudson's Bay/Finnish Fur Sales, Nineteenth Commission Competition Report* (1980), para. 42, although initially outside Art. 85(1) would have been rendered contrary to Art. 85(1) by a subsequent sale of the business, as it would have had the effect of removing the covenantor as an active competitor from the market.

[129] *Thirteenth Commission Competition Report* (1983), p. 72, para. 88.

[130] Commission Notice Regarding Restrictions Ancillary to Concentrations, 1990 C203/5, para. IIIA2.

[131] [1976] 2 CMLR D44.

[132] [1984] 2 CMLR 165 at p. 173, para. 28.

[133] OJ 1994 L341/66, para. 35.

ject to existing licences. Z wishes to enter the EC market but is hindered by its inability to use the trade mark it purchased from X because of the subsisting licence held by Y. The Commission consider that the 10-year trade mark licence represents an unreasonable protection from competition and Y may no longer use the mark.[134]

(3) Restriction on geography

11.100 In respect of geographical extent the non-competition clause must not normally extend beyond those markets in which the seller was active before the sale or in which it may be regarded as a potential competitor on the basis of its relevant and demonstrable commercial activity.[135] The Commission Notice states:

> "The geographic scope of the non-competition clause must be limited to the area where the vendor had established the products or services before the transfer. it does not appear objectively necessary that the acquirer be protected from competition by the vendor in territories which the vendor had not previously penetrated."[136]

11.101 Thus, the buyer may prohibit the seller from re-acquiring his old customers in the areas where he operated prior to the transfer. Where the seller is a small businessman and only possesses facilities in one Member State, then a restriction on selling even in the entirety of the national territory may be over-broad if it prevents the seller from operating in hitherto unexplored areas. Thus, depending on the size of the seller, the territorial restriction may be less than the national territory.[137] Conversely, where the seller is a large corporation whose selling area embraced the whole of the EC the ban may be EC wide.[138]

(4) Restrictions on products and services

11.102 Finally, in the words of the Commission's Notice:

> "the non-competition clause must be limited to products and services which form the economic activity of the undertaking transferred. In particular, in the case of a partial transfer of assets, it does not appear that the acquirer needs to be protected from the competition of the vendor in the products or services which constitute the activities which the vendor retains after the transfer".[139]

If part of a business is sold, the remaining business may be free to compete with the products and services which have just been sold.

(5) Restrictions on the vendor

11.103 Restrictions protecting the vendor will not be normally be regarded as ancillary by the Commission,[140] and hence fall to be considered under Articles 85 or 86 EC. Thus, a covenant accepted by the purchaser limiting the ability to compete with the vendor in relation to the vendors other activities would breach Article 85(1).

134 *Tyler-Linde, Eleventh Commission Competition Report* (1981), p. 65 para. 96, no formal decision issued.
135 *Reuters-BASF* [1976] 2 CMLR D44.
136 Commission Notice Regarding Restrictions Ancillary to Concentrations, 1990 C203/5, para. IIIA3.
137 *Sedame-Precilec, Eleventh Commission Competition Report* (1981), p. 64 para. 95.
138 *Mecaniver-PPG* [1985] 3 CMLR 359 at para. 15.
139 Commission Notice Regarding Restrictions Ancillary to Concentrations, OJ 1990 C203/5, para. IIIA4.
140 Commission Notice Regarded Restrictions Ancillary to Concentrations, OJ 1990 C203/5, para. IIIA6.

(6) Restrictions on information

11.104 In *Reuter-BASF*[141] the Commission commented, in respect of a covenant on the seller not to disclose the know-how, that in view of the rapid development of the technology it was questionable whether the know-how was sufficiently valuable in economic terms to justify a long non-disclosure covenant. Five years was considered adequate in that case. The length of time non-disclosure may be enforced may depend on the rate of advancement of new technology: protection should presumably last only until the technology falls into the public domain at which point protection should no longer be necessary.

2. UK Law

(1) Under the RTPA 1976

11.105 A starting point is to determine whether two persons accept restrictions. Sale of assets agreements may be registrable where two parties accept restrictions. They are not registrable if only the buyer or the seller accepts restrictions since there will not be two persons accepting restrictions. Registrable agreements might arise if a parent company sells a subsidiary or business and covenants to the purchaser that it will not compete for a specific period of time and in a designated area. The subsidiary many covenant not to disclose confidential information about the former parent to the new purchaser (though this is probably not a registrable restriction), or it may covenant not to expand into areas the old parent is now concentrating on for a fixed period of time. In such a case two persons accept registrable restrictions. Another example might be where Director X and Director Y each sell their 50 per cent shareholding in XY Co to a purchaser and both covenant not to compete or have a financial interest (other than a purely disinterested investment) in a competing company for a fixed time period and in a designated area and not to disclose confidential data to competitors of the new owner. Again, two persons (X and Y) accept registrable restrictions in relation to the non-competition covenants. A restriction on taking a financial interest in another company is almost certainly not a restriction in respect of goods or services.

11.106 The OFT's experience prior to 1989 was that such agreements rarely contained significant restrictions. Indeed 630 such agreements received section 21(2) dispensation between 1980 and 1988.

11.107 As a consequence, specific Orders were enacted[142] to provide exemption from the Act which apply to goods and services agreements made on or after 30 June 1989. The purpose of the Orders is to exempt from registration the standard non-competition covenants taken on the change of ownership of a business, whether by share or assets transfer, or on the subscription for shares in a company. In the case of a transfer by shares, the transfer must be of more than 50 per cent of the nominal value of the issued share capital to one purchaser or to more than one purchaser if each of the purchasers is a member of the same group.[143] In the case of a transfer of a business, the vendor must transfer

[141] [1976] 2 CMLR D44 criticised by Korah (1977) JBL 76 cf. *Kabelmetal's Agreement* [1975] 2 CMLR D40 at p. D46. See Art. 2(1)(3) and 10(2) of Reg. 240/96, OJ 1996 L219/15 on technology transfer agreements which also use the "entering the public domain" test for lapse of secrecy of know-how.

[142] The Restrictive Trade practices (Sale and Purchase and Share Subscription Agreements) (Goods) Order 1989 (S.I. 1989 No. 1081) applies to goods agreements; the Restrictive Trade Practices (Services) (Amendment) Order 1989 (S.I. 1989 No. 1082) made equivalent amendments to the Restrictive Trade Practices (Services) Order 1976 (S.I. 1976 No. 98) which applies to services agreements by the addition of Arts. 5–9. Reference herein are to the Goods Order and apply *mutatis mutandis* to the Services Order.

[143] Art. 3(1)(b) Restrictive Trade Practices (Sale and Purchase and Share Subscription Agreements) (Goods) Order 1989 (S.I. 1989 No. 1081).

the whole of its interest in the business to a purchaser.[144] There are four main conditions to be satisfied for the Orders to apply.

11.108 First, the agreements must only contain those registrable restrictions specified in section 6(1)(c) to (f) of the RTPA.[145] Thus for example any registrable restriction pertaining to prices will be prevent the use of these exemptions.[146]

11.109 Secondly, the restrictions can only be accepted by vendors, their associated companies or by individuals, provided that none of those is also a body corporate or unincorporate (or in the same corporate group as such as body corporate or unincorporate) which is also a purchaser under the agreement.[147] The rationale behind this is to ensure that the only restrictions permitted are those placed on the vendor to protect what is being sold together with related restrictions in individual's service contracts, such as directors' restrictive covenants.

11.110 Thirdly, the restrictions can only limit the extent to which the person accepting the restriction may compete with the acquired enterprise, or be engaged in, interested in, disclose information to or otherwise assist any business which competes with the acquired enterprise.[148] This will not cover restrictions imposed on the enterprises to be acquired prior to completion. Thus typical restrictions placed on an enterprise between contract and completion, such as those requiring it only to continue to trade in the ordinary course of business, not to enter into any long term contracts or involving curbs on exceptional expenditure, may be registrable restrictions under section 6(1) RTPA, but are not exempt non-competition restrictions as they affect the continuing conduct of the enterprise prior to change of ownership. There is also an ambiguity in that it is not clear whether the business of the acquired enterprise is to be defined as being that at the date of acquisition or whether the non-competition provisions apply in respect of other business subsequently carried on by the transferee company. Given that the purpose of the exemption is to ensure that the vendor does not derogate from its grant it would seem that the former, more limited ambit is what the draftsman intended to cover.[149]

11.111 Finally, the permissible restrictions are limited in duration to the longer of either five years from the date of the agreement, or, for restrictions accepted by an individual under an employment or services supply contract with the acquired enterprise, the purchaser or a member of the same corporate group as the purchaser, a period from the date of the agreement until two years after the expiry or termination of the employment or services supply contract.[150]

11.112 If an agreement falls outside the terms of the Orders and is caught by the RTPA particulars will need to be furnished and it will require dispensation from the OFT in the usual way under section 21(2). In analysing these agreements the factors taken into account by the OFT are:

[144] Art. 3(1)(a) Restrictive Trade Practices (Sale and Purchase and Share Subscription Agreements) (Goods) Order 1989 (S.I. 1989 No. 1081).

[145] Arts. 3(1)(c) and (d) Restrictive Trade Practices (Sale and Purchase and Share Subscription Agreements (Goods) Order 1989 (S.I. 1989 No. 1081).

[146] For the OFT's attitude to pricing restrictions under the RTPA, see Chapter 8.

[147] Art. 3(2) Restrictive Trade Practices (Sale and Purchase and Share Subscription Agreements) (Goods) Order 1989 (S.I. 1989 No. 1081).

[148] Art. 4(1) Restrictive Trade Practices (Sale and Purchase and Share Subscription Agreements) (Goods) Order 1989 (S.I. 1989 No. 1081).

[149] A similar restrictive approach was taken by the Court of Appeal in the context of interpreting the ambit of a restrictive covenant in a contract of an employment contract statutorily transferred under the Transfer of Undertakings (Protection of Employment) Regulations 1989 (S.I. 1981 No. 1794) in *Morris Angel and Son Ltd* v *Hollande* [1993] IRLR 169.

[150] Art. 4(2) Restrictive Trade Practices (Sale and Purchase and Share Subscriptional Agreements) (Goods) Order 1989 (S.I. 1989 No. 1081).

(a) Whether the sale price contains an element for goodwill. Where it does it is reasonable to permit restrictions to be imposed by the buyer as a means of guaranteeing that the full commercial value of the purchase is protected.

(b) Whether the non-competition period of time is reasonable. Most agreements gaining section 21(2) dispensation have time periods of between two and five years (the same as with EC rules, see paras. 11.96–11.99).

(c) Whether the geographical location restriction is reasonable. This will depend upon the reach of the seller's activities prior to the sale. Restrictions covering the whole of the UK are not unreasonable in appropriate circumstances.[151]

(d) Whether there are unreasonable restrictions on the seller's capacity to use or disclose information: generally speaking restrictions on information should not extend beyond such time as the knowledge enters the public domain.[152] Though it will be only rarely that a confidentiality clause is registrable. See paras. 2.208–2.210 for discussion of restrictions on how-how.

11.113 Geographical restrictions will only be justifiable where they are factually and commercially linked to the sale of the assets in question. Where the nexus is tenuous then the OFT is unlikely to countenance geographical market sharing. In *Unit Marketing* v *Christenson* (1984, unreported) the plaintiff sold certain valuable "bookings" and customer lists to the defendants. As part of the agreement an informal arrangement was made about the areas in which the plaintiff and defendants would concentrate their sale efforts. The agreement was not furnished and in a dispute over the consideration to be paid for the bookings and customers lists, the question arose whether the agreement was void for want of furnishing. The Court held that the geographical restriction was, as a question of fact, unconnected to the consideration to be paid by the defendant. Accordingly, it was severable and did not taint the remainder of the agreement. Counterclaims for damages, however, based upon alleged breaches of the territorial restrictions were consequently bound to fail.

11.114 The case highlights the importance of registration furnishing particulars in cases not exempted under the orders. This is especially so given that sale of assets agreements incorporating geographical restrictions are invariably suitable for section 21(2) treatment. Further, it suggests that restrictions that, in commercial reality, are unconnected to the value of the sale may be severable. Indeed, for section 21(2) purposes unconnected restrictions may well have to be deleted; the justification for their acceptance is that they

[151] See No. 4983 Register of Restrictive Trade Practices, *Mills Marketing Services and Namasco Holdings*, restrictions on seller extended to whole of the UK for a period of five years (1982). See also No. 5087 Register of Restrictive Trade Practices, *Beaver Metals, Jacksons (Nuneaton) Ltd, Ian Fraser, James Jones* (1984) concerning the sale of Beaver by Jackson of scrap and other metals obtained in the course of business at premises leased from Beaver. This agreement was not a sale of assets but contained a restraint on the lessee provided that, "the lessee shall not at any time within two years of the determination of the term hereby created or any continuation or renewable thereof carry on or be in any way engaged, concerned or interested in the business of a scrap metal dealer within a radius of five miles of the demised premises". For another licensing agreement containing a geographical non-competition clause, see No. 5911 Register of Restrictive Trade Practices, *Second Hand Fashions* (1985)— licensor agreed not to sell within a two-mile radius of the premises used by the licensee.

[152] See e.g. No. S. 1437 Register of Restrictive Trade Practices, *Whitbread PLC, Integrated Leisure Ltd* and *L.R. Philby*, agreement concerning the management of a public house and discotheque. Agreement restricted manager, on leaving the employ of the Brewery Company, from competing for one year within a one-mile radius, from employing any person who has been employed by the Brewery during the agreement; and from disclosing any trade secret or confidential information which they acquired during the agreement until such time as the information became part of the public domain. Though, the registrability of this case did not depend upon the confidentiality clause.

are necessary to ensure full transfer of the value of the sale. Where the connection does not exist the justification for allowing such restrictions disappears.

(2) Under the Fair Trading Act 1973

11.115 The Secretary of State may refer to the MMC prospective mergers that he considers may conflict with the public interest. Simply because the agreement is registrable under the RTPA 1976 does not deny the MMC jurisdiction in merger cases. Hence powerful purchasers must consider this aspect of the law when considering the restrictions to be imposed upon sellers. Indeed, there is nothing to stop a monopoly reference being made concurrently, as in the *Gillette/Wilkinson Sword* merger[153] which was also investigated as part of the report on *Razors and Razor Blades.*[154]

(3) Under the doctrine of restraint of trade

11.116 Under the common law doctrine of restraint of trade,[155] a non-competition covenant is only enforceable to the extent that (a) it can be shown to protect a legitimate interest, (b) it is reasonable as between the parties and (c) it is not against the public interest. The courts' approach to making this assessment is much the same factors as the OFT's approach discussed above. However, obtaining dispensation under section 21(2) RTPA does not guarantee that a clause is not in restraint of trade. If a clause is found to be in restraint of trade, it is void and unenforceable. The offending portions of a clause in restraint of trade may be severed ("blue pencilled") and the remainder of the clause given effect to, but the courts are not prepared to rewrite a clause on a more limited basis in order to give it effect.[156]

H. Premises and Trading Methods

11.117 It is now recognised that restrictions upon the style in which, or forum from which, trade is pursued may be restrictive. The ability of traders to experiment with new methods of presentation or marketing is now viewed as a central element in competition. Restrictions upon the premises in which business is conducted, its size and geographical position, are carefully scrutinised, as are restrictions on trading method. Thus, if suppliers collectively or individually seek to prevent distribution of their goods through discount warehouses, cash and carry stores or multiple function retailers, serious distortions of competition might arise.[157]

153 *Sub nom Stora/Swedish Match/Gillette* Cm 1473 (1991).

154 Cm 1422 (1991).

155 See Heydon *The Restraint of Trade Doctrine* (1971); Wilkinson, *Restraint of Trade* (1991); and Mehigan and Griffiths, *Restraint of Trade and Business Secrets: Law and Practice* (3rd edn, 1996); *Chitty on Contracts* (27th edn. 1995), paras. 16-092 *et seq.*

156 *Marshall* v *V.M. Financial Management Ltd* [1995] 1 WLR 1461.

157 See e.g. MMC General Report on *Collective Discrimination* (1955) Cmnd 9504, p. 82, para. 234: "We have been impressed particularly by the effect of a binding and collective obligation in preventing manufacturers or distributors from experimenting and from trying out new or different ways of conducting their business. Such obligations crate an undue rigidity which may affect the numbers and kinds of concerns engaged in a trade, the trading methods adopted by those established in the trade and the level of prices both generally and to different classes of buyers." This view was confirmed subsequently by the Liesner Committee in their *Review of Restrictive Trade Practices Policy* (1979) Cmnd 7512, p. 18, para. 3.5. See also *Black and Decker* Cm 805 (1989), where measures ostensibly based on preventing loss-leading had the effect of insulating smaller hardware outlets from competition from large out of town outlets. For the EC view which is similar see, Case 107/82 *AEG-Telefunken* v *Commission* [1984] 3 CMLR 325; [1983] ECR 3151 at p. 3195, para. 37 of the judgment.

1. *EC Law*

11.118 Premises and trading methods restrictions appear most often in four contexts. First, in the criteria adopted by suppliers in selecting dealers. Secondly, in the obligations imposed by suppliers on dealers. Thirdly, in recommendations made by trade associations to members. Fourthly, where firms share physical facilities for warehousing or other purposes.

(1) Selection of dealers by suppliers

11.119 This subject has been examined at paras. 10.348–10.393 on selective distribution, to which reference may be made. A supplier is a non-dominant position who select dealers upon the basis of any criteria it pleases. In principle provided the decision to accept or reject a dealer is taken entirely unilaterally then Article 85(1) cannot be engaged.[158] It is otherwise if the suppliers (say) refuses to supply a cost-cutting discount chain as a result of communications (in the form of exhortations, complaints, demands for action, etc.) from other dealers and resellers of the supplier who object to the cost cutter. In such circumstances an agreement or concerted practice may arise pursuant to which new or lower-cost methods of distribution are excluded and competition between dealers *inter se* is restricted or distorted. In circumstances where a supplier wishes to adopt selective distribution and impose customer restrictions upon its dealers (obligation to sell only to end users and to other authorised resellers) then suppliers should select dealers on objective qualitative criteria and not subjective quantitative criteria. Moreover, those objective, qualitative criteria should pertain to technical qualifications and/or the suitability of trading premises. Without undertaking detailed analysis it is clear that a supplier may select dealers upon the basis of the suitability of their premises to the standard of marketing required for his goods. However, suppliers must not, through their criteria, exclude new forms of selling which satisfy the qualitative standards set up by the supplier who might adopt innovative methods which the supplier dislikes. In *AEG-Telefunken* v *Commission*[159] the Court of Justice stated:

> "Such a practice must be considered unlawful where the manufacturer, with a view to maintaining a high level of prices or to excluding certain modern channels or distribution, refuses to approve distributors who satisfy the qualitative criteria of the system."

11.120 Thus, a supplier who sets his criteria so as to avoid discount warehouses, department stores, multi-purpose retail outlets, etc., may infringe Article 85(1) EC. Criteria seeking this objective may for instance provide that authorised dealers must have floor space of only up to a certain amount, thereby excluding other outlets, such as discount warehouses, which will probably have a large floor space.

(2) Obligations imposed by suppliers on dealers

11.121 Suppliers may, within limits, employ premises and method of trading criteria to select appropriate dealers. Once admitted to a supplier's network, the latter may impose certain trading method restrictions upon the dealer. These are generally considered to be acceptable and designed to ensure adequate pre- and post-sales servicing and to protect the supplier's reputation. Indeed it is expressly lawful, under the block exemptions on exclusive dealing and purchasing (Regulations 1983/83 EEC and 1984/83/EEC), to require dealers to "take measures for promotion of sales" which include advertising, maintenance of sales net-

[158] See Case T-102/92 *Viho* [1995] ECR II-17 at para. 52, p. 35.
[159] *ibid.*, at para. 37 of the judgment.

works or stocks of goods, provision of customer and guarantee services. However, the caveat should be added that where these restrictions are designed to restrict competition by excluding new and innovative methods of trading, then the block exemption does not apply.[160]

(3) Recommendations made by trade associations to members and physical presence rules

11.122 Trade associations which seek to regulate the premises or methods of trading of members will violate Article 85(1). Thus, in *Stoves and Heaters*[161] the Commission condemned a Dutch trade association whose members were required, *inter alia*, to sell the products only on premises belonging to them. Membership of the association was limited to persons owning the retail outlet. Moreover, members were restricted in their ability to trade with non-members. The Commission objected largely on the basis that the rules created entry barriers to the market since new retailers had to purchase (rather than lease) premises as a pre-condition of membership to the association and membership of the association was critical to commercial viability (its members covered in excess of 90 per cent of the trade in certain heating appliances in Holland).

11.123 Trade associations which condition membership upon the adequacy of the trader's premises may violate Article 85 especially where membership of the association confers benefits which make membership a valuable commercial asset as in *Stoves and Heaters*, above. Thus, for example, an association might impose requirements of ownership, floor space, stock room capacity, display facilities, etc. The association might restrict membership to single line retailers and exclude multi-product line department stores. Where membership is at a premium, restrictive entry rules based upon premises or method of trading may operate as entry barriers to new firms particularly where compliance with the membership requirements involves expense.

11.124 In a series of cases involving the membership rules of various London futures markets the Commission, *inter alia*, have allowed a rule requiring that certain categories of member trade from an office in London established for that purpose. The physical presence rule is apparently justifiable in cases where the security and financial stability of members is essential to the efficiency and reputation of the market. In these cases, the physical presence rule was bundled up with a number of other rules designed to foster efficiency and reputation through security and financial stability of members. Clearly, international commodity markets of this nature rely heavily on the good name and standing of members.[162]

(4) Joint use of physical facilities (storage, warehousing, etc.)

11.125 The Commission has stated, in a non-binding notice, that the joint use of storage facilities of transport equipment does not infringe Article 85(1).[163] Such co-operation is con-

[160] Reg. 1983/83/EEC on block exemption for exclusive dealing, OJ 1983 L173/1 Art. 2(3); and Reg. 1984/83/EEC on block exemption for exclusive purchasing OJ 1983 L173/5, Art. 2(3). See Chapter 10 for details. See Commission Explanatory Memorandum to the block exemptions OJ 1983 C355/7 at para. 20: "Such clauses are unobjectionable if admission to the distribution network is based on objective criteria of a qualitative nature relating to the professional qualifications of the owner of the business or his staff or the suitability of his business premises, if the criteria are the same for all potential dealers, and if the criteria are actually applied in a non-discriminatory manner. Distribution systems which do not fulfil these conditions are not covered by the block exemption."

[161] [1975] 2 CMLR D1 at paras. 38 and 42.

[162] See *Coffee Terminal Market* OJ 1985 L369/31 *London Sugar Futures Market* OJ 1985 L369/25; *London Cocoa Terminal Market* OJ 1985 L369/28; *London Rubber Terminal Market* OJ 1985 L369/34.

[163] Notice concerning Agreements, Decisions and Concerted Practices in the Field of Co-operation between Enterprises, OJ 1968 C75/3; [1968] CMLR D5 at para. II(4). See, e.g. *Jernbranchen, Thirteenth Commission Competition Report* (1983), pp. 86, 87, para. 131.

fined to organisation and technical arrangements for the use of the facilities or equipment. The participating undertakings should, however, bear the utilisation costs themselves. Moreover, the agreement should not be used as a front for other agreements. Agreements between small- and medium-sized enterprises are intended as principal beneficiaries of this Commission Notice. If joint operations enable the companies to compete more effectively with larger companies it would be arguable that any restrictions which are necessary to the arrangement fall out with Article 85(1) altogether upon the basis of a "rule of reason" approach. Where large firms who can afford their own facilities co-operate the Commission may be more suspicious.

11.126 In conducting joint co-operation the operation rules must not be unnecessarily restrictive. Thus, for example, if X, Y and Z jointly own warehousing and storage facilities at an over-crowded port they must ensure that the rules for determining space allocation during peak periods and other times of excessive demand are fair as between the parties and do not artificially benefit one part to the other's competitive disadvantage.

11.127 There have been two cases in which the Commission has insisted that access to a port not be restricted by a dominant undertaking.[164] The same principles would apply if that port were operated by a joint venture. For example, in *Disma*[165] a joint venture set up to provide the infrastructure necessary for the supply of jet fuel at a new airport in Milan was required by the Commission to make those facilities available on a non-discriminatory basis to non-members of the joint venture.

2. *UK Law*

11.128 UK law may be assessed in the same way as EC law.

(1) Selection of dealers by suppliers

11.129 The OFT and MMC have adopted a position on selective distribution broadly similar to that of the Commission. Hence, suppliers may not exclude from their networks dealers who satisfy the qualitative criteria but who sell through discount warehouses or department stores, etc.[166] The principle is that selective distribution networks should not be used as entry or expansion barriers to dealers using innovative and modern channels of distribution.

(2) Obligations imposed by suppliers on dealers

11.130 Sections 6(1)(f) (goods) and 11(2)(e) (services) RTPA 1976 require the registration of agreements concerning "the areas or places in or from which, goods are to be supplied or ac-

[164] *Sea Containers/Sealink*, *Twenty-third Report on Competition Policy* (1993), para. 234 (in which the Commission stated that it was its view that a dominant firm could only satisfactorily provide non-discriminatory access if it separated out and ran separately those parts of its management which ran the port and those which operated its ferry service). In *Port of Rodby*, OJ 1994 L55/52, the Commission issued a decision under Art. 90(3) EC condemning a refusal by a state operated company to grant non-discriminatory access to port facilities as breach of Art. 90(1) read together with Art. 86. These cases, along with others in other areas of the economy highlighted in *Twenty-third Report on Competition Policy* (1993), para. 146, indicate that the principle of non-discriminatory access to essential facilities for third parties is assuming the status of a general principle of competition law for the purposes of Art. 85 EC as well as of Art. 86 EC.

[165] *Twenty-third Report on Competition Policy* (1993), paras. 80, 223–224.

[166] e.g. *Raleigh* OFT Report (27 February 1981) and MMC Report (1981–82) HC 67. In MMC Report on the *Supply in the UK for Retail Sale of Fine Fragrances*, Cm 2380, 1993, it was held that qualitative criteria could be applied which effectively ruled out distribution of luxury perfumes through ordinary supermarkets, provided that a supermarket which did meet those qualitative criteria could be admitted, since although this restricted competition, it was not against the public interest.

quired." It is submitted that restrictions on premises constitute restrictions on the places from which goods are to be supplied. "Places" can imply a geographical place (as in an area) or a physical place (as in a building). The latter interpretation seems reasonable given that the provision also expressly covers geographical area and hence "places" may be assumed to imply something else.[167] Thus, where a supplier requires a dealer to provide certain physical facilities, or a certain amount or type of display structure, etc., this may amount to a registrable agreement provided it entails goods or services. In *Agreements of the Sunday Newspapers Proprietors No. 2*[168] the RPC held to infringe the public interest a restriction in an agreement between proprietors of Sunday newspapers by which the proprietors agreed: "not to supply Sunday newspapers outside the London area by way of direct sale to the public except in or from private property." This restricted sales of goods from street stalls and protected the retail newsagents' Sunday trade. The restriction, by limiting sales to private premises restricted alternative methods of sale. Where services are concerned section 11(2)(d) (restrictions on the "form or manner" in which services are to be made available supplied or obtained might also be relevant. Though for the RTPA to apply both the supplier *and* dealer must accept registrable restrictions. Furthermore, they must both accept restrictions concerning services *or* goods. Thus, if a supplier accepted restrictions on the *goods* to be supplied and the dealer accepted premises restrictions relating to the *services* he provided in connection with goods, then the agreement would not be registrable.

(3) Recommendations made by trade associations to members

11.131 In *ABTA*[169] the RPC was required to examine a number of restrictions imposed by the association upon tour operator and travel agent members. These included the following:

(a) not to use premises for any purpose other than for organising and selling tours or holidays or other travel arrangements;
(b) not to carry on business as a travel agent at any premises unless a legal estate in those premises was vested in the member or spouse or in a parent company;
(c) not to carry on business as a travel agent in premises which did not meet the association's standards;
(d) not to carry on business as a travel agent from department stores or hotels in units which were totally isolated from other activities conducted thereat without the permission of the association.

11.132 Before the RPC, ABTA argued that these restrictions were in the public interest. They ensured adequate standards of accommodation were maintained so that the customer received a proper and efficient service. Further, adequacy of commercial accommodation was essential to the good name and reputation of ABTA. The RPC was unimpressed. Two main policy objections were raised against premises restraints. First, they created barriers to entry to new firms with new forms of competition and innovation which could benefit the public: "They impose a rigid structure on the industry which is not responsive to customer demand so that there is a danger that .. the industry will be come fossilized."[170] Secondly, premises restrictions deny the consumer choices between different qualities of services. The RPC made the important point that consumers may prefer lower

[167] This was apparently the presumption made by the RPC in *ABTA* [1984] ICR 12. It is understood that both the OFT and ABTA accepted that s. 11(2)(e) covered premises restrictions. See *Doncaster and Retford Co-operative Societies Agreement* (1960) LR 2 RP105 on "areas or place".

[168] No. 2385 Register of Restrictive Trade Practices (1972). The first case was in March 1966. See Nos. 2720, 2300 and 2003 Register of Restrictive Trade Practices for details of earlier agreements.

[169] [1984] ICR 12.

[170] *ibid.*, at p. 42G, H.

quality of services at cheaper prices rather than higher quality services at higher prices.[171] This point is of relevance also to trade association recommendations about product standardisation.

11.133 In view of this decision, trade association should be cautious about attempting to devise premises restrictions designed to control the supply of goods or provisions of services. Certainly rules requiring members to *own* premises, or rules preventing use of premises for multiple purposes will rarely be treated as insignificant so as to warrant section 21(2) treatment. Hence, they will have to be defended before the RPC if they are to be retained. Less extreme restraints for example concerning adequacy of fixtures and fittings may perhaps in appropriate cases be suitable for section 21(2) treatment. In any event restrictions should be clearly related to, and justified by, objective factors such as protection of consumer safety and health, or, protection of the product itself.

(4) Joint use of physical facilities (storage, warehousing etc.)

11.134 The joint use of physical facilities such as storage or warehousing is probably not registrable provided parties accept no restrictions as to the use of those facilities. If usage restrictions are imposed, e.g. as to percentage of total floor or shelf space allotted to each party for the sale of goods or provision of services, then there might be a restriction under section 11(2)(e) RTPA 1976, i.e. restriction on places in or from which services are to be made available. In principle there are no reasons why such an agreement should not normally benefit from section 21(2).

I. Staffing Restrictions

11.135 Restrictions upon qualifications and experience of staff may well be justified as necessary to protect the reputation of the supplier or to safeguard the consumer against misleading or technically unsound advice. Conversely, over-restrictive staffing requirements may impose entry barriers to new entrants and may stifle new and innovative methods of trading.

1. EC Law

11.136 Staffing restrictions usually appear in the context of the criteria used by suppliers to select dealers and in the actual contractual regulation of a dealer's business once he is appointed to the network. It is pertinent to clarify at this stage that an employee is *not* an "undertaking" under Article 85 or 86 EC. Hence agreements, however restrictive, concerning the employee–employer inter-relationship are outside of those provisions. This principle extends to the results of collective bargaining between employer and employee organisations.

(1) Selection of dealers by supplier

11.137 It is important to bear in mind that criteria adopted by suppliers seeking to appoint dealers on a non-selective distribution basis, do not fall within Article 85(1) *provided* the criteria are not formulated by reference to an agreement or concerted practice between the supplier and any third party. In principle any genuinely *unilateral* decision of a non-dominant supplier, howsoever discriminatory or arbitrary, is outwith Article 85(1).[172]

[171] *ibid.*, see also p. 41H and p. 42A–C.
[172] Case T-102/92 *Viho* [1995] ECR II 17, 35, para. 52.

11.138 With regard to selective distribution criteria, suppliers may set criteria as to the qualifications of staff without infringing Article 85.[173] Selective distribution criteria are reviewable under Article 85(1) because it is only if the selection criteria are qualitative and objective that the customer restrictions (dealer to sell to end users and other authorised dealers *only*) escape the ban in Article 85(1). Further, it is assumed that in the particular context of selective distribution the decisions as to admission to the network and the supplier are not properly analysed, unilateral decisions, but are taken in the context of the obligations owed by the supplier to other selective dealers and such "unilateral" decisions thus have a contractual context to them. Thus, a dealer refused supplies because his staff do not meet the supplier's objective standards almost certainly is without remedy. However, the supplier may have to accord supplies to a dealer whose staff *do* meet his objective criteria but who uses selling techniques that the supplier disapproves of. If the disapproved of techniques are innovative and modern then the Commission will construe a refusal to supply as a means of preventing new business techniques and as a barrier to entry.[174] It will not view the refusal as a justified attempt to maintain staff standards. Thus, if a supplier of plumbing fittings requires wholesalers to resell the fittings only to qualified plumbers this may represent an infringement of Article 85 EC. Ironmongers, DIY stores and department stores may be precluded from selling that supplier's fittings although they are perfectly well qualified to do so. In *Grohe*[175] the Commission stated:

> "Even assuming that there was a need for expert advice and guidance to be provided when selling plumbing fittings to final consumers, such a need would not mean that plumbing fittings could only be sold by plumbing contractors. It is not necessary to be a trained plumber to sell plumbing fittings. The advice and guidance at the point of sale can be provided by specially trained sales staff, and such staff can also be employed in other retail outlets. There is nothing to prevent retail outlets which do not offer plumbing contracting services from employing trained staff to sell plumbing equipment."

11.139 The Court of First Instance took a similar view in *Vichy*,[176] rejecting an argument that it was necessary to restrict the sale of beauty products to those outlets employing qualified pharmacists, on the basis, *inter alia* of the lack of need for qualified advice in the sale of cosmetics.

(2) Obligations imposed by suppliers on dealers

11.140 Suppliers may contractually require dealers to hire qualified staff or to have existing staff trained by the dealer or by the supplier.[177] Restrictions of this nature are exempt under the block exemptions on exclusive dealing and purchasing.[178] It is accepted that such restriction may be necessary in order to protect the suppliers reputation (inexperienced staff may incorrectly advise customers who become disenchanted).[179] Indeed, it is arguable that such obligations do not fall within Article 85(1) at all.

173 See para. 10.366.

174 Case 107/82 *AEG-Telefunken* v *Commission* [1984] 3 CMLR 325, [1985] ECR 3151 at p. 3195, para. 37 of the judgment.

175 OJ 1985 L19/17 at p. 22, para. 20. See also *Ideal-Standard* OJ 1985 L20/38.

176 Case T-19/91 *Vichy* v *Commission* [1992] ECR II-415, upholding the Commission's decision, OJ 1991 L75/57.

177 See e.g. *IBM Personal Computer* [1984] 2 CMLR 342 at p. 344, para. 6.

178 Reg. 1983/83/EEC on block exemption for exclusive dealing, OJ 1983 L173/1; Reg. 1984/83/EEC, OJ 1983 L173/5 on block exemption for exclusive purchasing.

179 *IBM Personal Computer* [1984] 2 CMLR 342 at p. 344, para. 4.

(3) Recommendations made by trade associations to members

11.141 An association which recommends standard criteria which members should apply when hiring staff may violate Article 85. This will occur where the recommended standards are of a level higher than that necessary to meet the "needs" of the goods or services provided. These "needs" may be determined by reference to the needs of the supplier in terms of reputation and the needs of the consumer in terms of adequate advice and assistance. The more complex the product or service the greater the need for specialist staff. If an association recommends unnecessarily high standards this might create entry barrier since the expense of hiring staff will rise so adding to the overall cost of entry. The effect will be exacerbated if association membership is considered a commercial necessity so than an incentive to comply with its recommendations exist. Whether a recommendation or rule infringes Article 85(1) at all depends on an analysis of all the surrounding facts.

11.142 Trade association recommendations that are as a rule complied with by members constitute "decisions" of association for purposes of Article 85(1) EC.[180]

2. UK Law

(1) Whether staffing restrictions registrable under RTPA 1976

11.143 Prima facie staffing restrictions are *exempt* from registration under sections 9(6) and 18(6) RTPA 1976. This reads:

> "In determining whether an agreement is an agreement to which this Act applies by virtue of this Part, no account shall be taken of any restriction or information provision which affects or otherwise relates to the works to be employed or not employed by any person, or as to the remuneration, conditions of employment, hours of work or working conditions."[181]

11.144 The exemption is drafted very widely, it excludes from the RTPA 1976 restrictions and information agreements which directly or indirectly concern: works to be employed; workers not to be employed; and, terms and conditions of employment. The first two of these categories are ostensibly wide enough to exempt association recommendations as to staff qualifications, and, recommendations not to employ staff with less than a minimum requirement of qualifications, and, requirements that staff be actually trained by a supplier or a dealer, etc.[182]

11.145 However, in *ABTA*[183] the RPC construed section 18(6) (the services exemption) very narrowly. First, the Court held that Parliament had not intended restrictions that were clearly against the public interest to be excluded from control.[184] Secondly, the Court stated that it had jurisdiction over such restrictions where they represented a "component of a cluster of restrictions all constituting a manner of traded."[185] From this it would appear that for a staffing restriction to be registrable it must: (a) be restrictive or against the public interest; and (b) form part of a cluster of restrictions which concern the manner of trading. The judgment of the RPC does not make it clear whether (a) and (b) are

[180] Cases 96–102, 104, 105, 108, 110/82 *IAZ International Belgium SA and Others* v *Commission* [1984] 3 CMLR 276 at para. 20 of the judgment.

[181] "Worker" is defined by those sections as "a person who has entered into or works under a contract with an employer whether the contract be by way of manual labour, clerical work, or otherwise, be express or implied, oral or in writing, and whether it be a contract of service or of apprenticeship or a contract personally to execute any work or labour."

[182] Though discrimination on sex and race grounds may infringe anti-discrimination laws on those issues.

[183] [1984] ICR 12, but cf. *ABTA No. 2* [1985] ICR 123 where the RPC pronounced on a revised set of rules submitted by the parties for approval.

[184] [1984] ICR 12 at p. 51D.

[185] *ibid.*, at p. 51E.

conjunctive or disjunctive conditions. After *ABTA* it is not safe to assume that staffing restrictions in trade association SFCs are excluded since such restraints (as in *ABTA*) are invariably part of a group of restrictions on members covering for example, premises, financial integrity, etc.

11.146 Finally, on this issue the correctness of the *ABTA* interpretation of section 18(6) must be questioned. The RPC, contrary to the whole philosophy of the Act, answered a question on the legal construction of a statutory provision by reference to the economic *effect* of the restriction in question, i.e. the staffing restriction is economically restrictive, *therefore* it was within the Act. However, it has always been viewed as axiomatic that whether a restriction was within the Act is decided by the *form* of the relevant clause and not its economic *effect*. *ABTA* is hence a radical departure form normal methods of construction of the Act. Furthermore, it conflicts with other decisions of the RPC on construction of the exemptions in section 9 and 18 which seem to deny that an effects-based approach applies to those provisions.[186]

(2) Types of registrable restriction: section 21(2)

11.147 If *ABTA* is to be accepted, then the OFT will scrutinise agreements for staffing restrictions: many may be dealt with under section 21(2). Parties might consider furnishing details of staff restrictions on a "fail safe" basis given that there is clearly scope for doubt as to the exemption in section 18(6) and, *a fortiori*, section 9(6). *ABTA* gives some indications as to the criteria for assessment, especially as regards trade association recommendations. First, the restrictions must not deny consumers the choice between lower quality services and cheaper goods, and higher quality services and dearer goods. Secondly, the restrictions must not raise traders' costs by imposing on them unnecessarily onerous requirements. Thirdly, the restrictions must not hinder entry to the market (this will be a consequence of the second factor). Fourthly, the restrictions must not hinder the development of technology and other forms of labour-saving inventiveness.

11.148 In *ABTA No. 2*[187] the RPC gave guidance as to the principles which should govern the legality of staffing restrictions. If an association is confident that its staffing provisions satisfy these criteria then they are entitled to rely upon the sanctuary of sections 9(6) and 18(6). If the provisions *do* come to be assessed by the OFT because they are registered then the following criteria might be relevant to section 21(2).

(a) Number of years and experience and training

11.149 Restrictions on the number of years *relevant* experience an employee must have had before being placed in a specified position (e.g. which requires dealing with and advising

[186] See, on s. 9(3), *Registrar of Restrictive Trading Agreements* v *Schweppes (No. 3)* [1975] ICR 240; [1975] 1 WLR 1018 at p. 1029; and *Diazo Copying Materials* [1984] ICR 429 at p. 437.

[187] [1985] ICR 123. A similar approach has been adopted by the US Department of Justice Antitrust Division. in *American Society of Travel Agents* (*Business Review Letter* 22 January 1986) the Division informed the Society (ASTA) that it had no intention of challenging the latter's proposed staff accreditation scheme. ASTA proposed to establish membership criteria that a travel school would have to meet in order to be admitted to membership. ASTA's proposed standards included:
(i) that certain subjects related to geography and computers be taught;
(ii) that instructors be subject to experience and continuing education requirements;
(iii) that 60 per cent of the students at a particular school pass the industry test/exam;
(iv) that schools enjoy at least a 50 per cent success rate in placing students in employment.
The relevance of the proposal is of course that it enhances a student's standing in the eyes of employers. AST guaranteed to the Antitrust Division that it would not make *any* efforts to make graduation from an accredited school a condition of employment by its members, not would it seek to discourage ordinary consumers and users of travel services from using services provided by sellers who are not from ASTA approved schools.

the public) may be acceptable if the requirement does not go beyond what is strictly necessary to meet the requirements of the consumer. Likewise, with training qualifications which require an employee to have obtained a requisite qualification. These may be acceptable where access to training courses is not unduly restricted and the course provides a clear yardstick for the assessment of competence. The standard of the qualification should be set at the minimum level which is necessary to enable the employee to become equipped with specialised skills appropriate to the job.

(b) Number of staff that should be employed

11.150 Requirements that a specific number of staff be hired may be restrictive if this discourages employers from using labour-saving technology in their offices. It will further be restrictive if it raises entry barriers to new firms who are forced to hire more staff than they might personally consider necessary or financially viable.

(c) Nature of employment

11.151 Requirements that no part-time employees be hired may be restrictive where, as in (b) above, this leads to obstacles to the introduction of new technology and/or entry barriers as a result of increased costs.

(d) Identity of employee

11.152 In some sale of assets agreements whereby X purchases the business of Y, there will be a clause preventing Y from setting up in competition to X for a specified number of years within a specified geographical area as discussed at para. 11.95 above. Moreover, there may be a clause prohibiting Y from hiring any or poaching any of the staff of X for the duration of the agreement. No poaching clauses of this type may be found in contracts given section 21(2) dispensation by the OFT.[188] They will also be subject to scrutiny under the common law doctrine of restraint of trade.

(3) Section 79, Fair Trading Act 1973: restrictive labour practices

11.153 Section 79 FTA 1973 institutes a machinery for allowing the MMC to investigate restrictive labour practices. These are defined in section 79(5) to mean restrictions or requirements which operate in relation to the employment of workers in any commercial setting or in relation to work done by any such workers. However, the restrictions must also be:

(a) such that they can be discontinued without breaching any statute or statutory instrument; *and*

(b) not necessary for, or in excess of anything required for, the efficient conduct of the relevant commercial activities.

11.154 Section 79(5) excludes restrictions or requirements relating exclusively to rates of remuneration. A practice whereby no worker may earn more than £X per hour would thus be excluded. But, is a practice whereby no worker may earn more than £X per week one relating to "rates" of remuneration? The intention of the Act would seem to be to exclude this also though some commentators consider otherwise.[189]

188 See, e.g. No. 4983 Register of Restrictive Trade Practices, *Mills Marketing Services, Namasco* (1982). See also No. S. 1437 Register of Restrictive Trade Practices, *Whitbread and Co plc, Integrated Leisure Ltd and L. R. Philby* (1984). In this agreement the covenantor who was to manage commercial premises of the company agreed not to poach employees of the company after the end of the management contract.

189 See Cunningham, *The Fair Trading Act 1973* (1974), pp. 192, 193 at para. 12.10.

11.155 The MMC may, upon a reference by the Secretary of State, consider: (i) whether the practice exists; (ii) whether it is a restrictive labour practice within the meaning of the Act; (iii) whether it can be expected to, or does, operate against the public interest; and (iv) what particular adverse effects the practice may be expected to, or does, exert.

11.156 Only one reference has been made under this provision, *Labour Practices in TV and Film Making*,[190] in which the MMC found a number of practices in those industries, such as the closed shop, agreements on staffing and job demarcation not to operate against the public interest.

J. Advertising and Trade Fairs

11.157 Trade association standard form contracts which seek to regulate advertising may be anticompetitive. Advertising is an integral part of competition. Hence agreements restricting the amount parties may spend, or the style or content of adverts may distort competition. Conversely, some advertising restrictions which seek to ensure that parties do not mislead the public or which seek other acceptable goals may be permitted despite restrictive effects. Furthermore, industry-wide advertisng may enhance competition where if facilitates more intensive marketing and thus stimulates rivalry between the advertised article and substitutes.

Suppliers may impose advertising restrictions upon dealer and distributors. These are generally not restrictive as they enhance the marketing or the suppliers' goods or services. Agreements between competitors as to advertising will, conversely, usually fall within Article 85(1).

1. EC Law

(1) Joint industry-wide advertising

11.158 Prima facie joint advertising of a generic nature is not contrary to Article 85 where it is designed to draw the buyer's attention to the products of an industry; as such it does not restrict competition between the participating enterprises.[191] However, industry wide or joint advertising is restrictive if it becomes a substitute for private initiatives or if it encourages advertising of prices to be charged thereby facilitating price harmonisation. In such a case competition may be restricted.[192] In some cases, however, the Commission has exempted under Article 85(3) advertising restrictions imposed by trade associations in respect of trades fairs (see below).

[190] Cm 666 (1989).

[191] Notice concerning Agreements, Decisions and Concerted Practices in the Field of Co-operation between Enterprises, JO 1968 C75/3 [1968] CMLR 5 para. 11 (7). For cases see *Eurogypsum* [1968] CMLR D1; *Wild-Leitz* [1972] CMLR D36; *ASBL* [1970] CMLR D31; *Parquet Flooring* WQ No. 386/85, OJ 1986 C119/1. A similar position is taken by the US Department of Justice Antitrust Division. In January 1984 they stated, in a business review letter to the *National LP-Gas Association* (NLGPA) that they would not object to the institution of a general fund to promote the use of propane as an automotive fuel through national advertising. The letter stated, *inter alia*, "Through a jointly funded advertising campaign, NLPGA hopes to increase sales of propane and propan-related equipment by increasing consumer awareness of propane as an alternative engine fuel. This may have the pro-competitive effect of stimulating competition with other forms of engine fuel and related equipment. Due to the expense of national advertising, it is unlikely that any one manufacturer or distributor could afford to advertise extensively enough to achieve this result" (Department of Justice Release, 6 January 1984).

[192] *Belgian Wallpaper* [1974] 2 CMLR D102; Case 246/86 *Belasco* v *Commission* [1989] ECR 2181, [1991] 4 CMLR 96.

11.159 Trade association rules regulating the manner or form of members advertising or the amount of money devoted to it may infringe Article 85. If an association requires members to refrain from advertising low quality products in favour of high quality products this distorts competition between different grades of product and hinders the consumers ability to make a proper choice between grades of product. An association which requires members to refrain from advertising a specific product because of recently discovered doubts concerning the health or safety consequences of that product may be exemptible under Article 85(3) but the trade association recommendation or rule may have to be notified to the Commission. The Commission has intimated that an agreement between parties to promote domestic products at the expense of foreign imports may infringe Article 85 or 86 EC.[193]

11.160 Thus, a "Buy British" campaign could conceivably violate competition rules. Though for an effect on trade between Member States to occur the campaign would presumably have to be of substantial proportions. A trade association that is controlled by the Government may be treated as a public undertaking. Government sponsored "buy national" campaigns which encourage consumers to discriminate against imports will infringe Article 30 EC which prohibits measures having equivalent effect to quantitative restrictions on trade (i.e. protectionist measures of a non-tariff nature).[194]

(2) Funding of joint advertising

11.161 Joint advertising may achieve results that parties individually would have been prevented from achieving through prohibitive costs. It thus enables the parties to market more intensively their product in competition with other brands or substitute products. Moreover, by collectively advertising, parties will pay their fair share of the overall costs and hence no one will benefit or "free-ride" on the advertising efforts of another. Formulae used in calculating each party's contribution to costs must be drawn up with care. Preferably the fees should be proportional to each parties' utilisation of the advertising. The Commission might object if an analysis of the fee structure revealed for example that large firms were subsidising smaller firms, or, where the fee is uniform irrespective of size, that small firms subsidised large firms. The latter is probably the more serious restriction on competition. It might be that a contribution based upon a specified percentage of the turnover on the advertised product is a reasonable means of assessment.

11.162 Where association members pay a levy which is devoted towards advertising and sales promotion of the member's goods, care must be taken to ensure that the enhanced advertising power gained through collective action is not used in a restrictive manner. Collective advertising may enable parties to reach consumers that individually they would have been prevented from reaching by virtue of a restricted advertising budget. In *Milk Production Fund*[195] the Commission pointed out, in respect of an advertising and pro-

[193] See Commission answers to WQ 1081/82, OJ 1982 C333/11; and WQ 2097/82, OJ 1983 C219/1. For an advertising case under Article 86 EEC, see Case 155/73 *Sacchi* [1974] 2 CMLR 177; [1974] ECR 409 at p. 430—TV station which discriminates in respect of advertising based on nationality of advertiser would abuse Art. 86. See also *Boat Equipment, Tenth Commission Competition Report* (1980), p. 82 paras. 119, 120.

[194] e.g. Case 249/81 *Commission* v *Ireland* (*Buy Irish Campaign*) [1983] 2 CMLR 104.

[195] [1985] 3 CMLR 101 at paras. 38, 39. See on funding the case of *NLPGA* above n. 191 (Department of Justice Release, 6 January 1984). The NLPGA was an industry-wide trade association which funded national advertising for propane. The Department of Justice in a business review letter stated: "Financing for the Fund is to be by voluntary contributions from participating NLPGA members and from consumers. Direct contributions to the Fund will be made by equipment manufacturers and distributors who will contribute one-tenth of 1 per cent of their annual gross sales, and propane tank manufacturers who will contribute 25 cents each unit sold. In addition, equipment distributors and tank manufacturers will each collect a one dollar voluntary contribution from purchasers of carburation units and propane tanks.

motion fund organised by an association and funded by a levy paid by members, that it artificially strengthened individual members' positions in that they benefited from advertising and promotion that individually they would be unable to afford. This distorted competition between members of the association and producers elsewhere. The savings members made by virtue of the scheme could be channelled into giving buyers on export markets more favourable terms and conditions; this again could lead to a distortion of competition between members and others. Of particular importance was the Commission statements that joint advertising, which was not brand orientated, which did not disparage other rival products, and, which did not commend a product on the basis of national origin, was prima facie acceptable. Thus generic advertising which merely stresses the special features of the product in question is unlikely to have an appreciable effect on competition. In this respect the Commission added that advertising which used a special characteristic of a particular kind of product as a selling point was acceptable even if those kinds of product were typically produced in the country of the advertisers. The case does show that joint advertising schemes may fall within Article 85(1). Further, that joint schemes should err on the side of generality rather than specificity in their content.

(3) Trade fairs

11.163 Trade fairs are commonplace in all Member States. They are often run by trade associations of the manufacturers of the relevant exhibited products. A number of restrictions may occur in the rules applicable to the exhibition. First, there may be restrictions on exhibitors participating, either directly or indirectly through representatives or advertising, in other similar exhibitions during a set period prior or subsequent to the exhibition or in other exhibitions not approved by the organising trade association. Secondly, there may be sanctions against persons infringing the first rule which take the form of expulsion from the current main exhibitions or the ensuing one, or the granting of a less favourable stand at the main show or the ensuing one.

11.164 Trade fair rules may gain Article 85(3) exemption.[196] The Commission have accepted that restrictions may have beneficial consequences. The exclusivity rules encourage traders to concentrate their exhibition activities on one event where almost all the relevant products or services are on show.[197] This is more economical, it intensifies competition between suppliers and enhances technical progress. It is more convenient for users and buyers who can see the whole range of products and services at one time without having to travel around. Thus, in *Sippa*[198] a restrictions on advertising only products shown at the exhibition was exempted, subject to the proviso that unsolicited enquiries about other

cont.
These contributions from consumers would b effectuated by adding one dollar to the cost of each carburation unit and propane tank sold and designating this charge on the invoice with the label 'Engine Power Promotional Fund'. A letter explaining that the contribution is voluntary is to accompany each invoice." The Department of Justice had no objections to this method of collection.

196 e.g. *Cecimo* [1969] CMLR D1; *Cematax* [1973] CMLR D135, exemption renewed OJ 1983 L140/27 (and notice under Art. 19(3) of Reg. 17/62, OJ 1983 C20/2); *UNIDI* [1975] 2 CMLR D51 exemption renewed [1985] 2 CMLR 38; EUMAPRINT Bull EC 1973, para. 2108; SMMT [1984] 1 CMLR 611; and *BPICA* [1983] 2 CMLR 40. See generally A. Brown, "Trade fairs and fair trade: the Commission's exemption policy" [1992] ECLR 66.

197 See *SMMT* [1984] 1 CMLR 611 and see also various earlier versions of the agreements in question which the Commission objected to: No. S. 1083 Register of Restrictive Trade Practices (1984) document V.5 (letter January 1985). Commission refused exemption until SMMT removed clause preventing members from exhibiting during years when there was no show planned.

198 OJ 1991 L60/19.

products could be answered, on the basis that this enabled the show to concentrate on promoting particular products. Moreover, trade fairs and exhibitions are generally only one form of advertising and the restrictions will not, therefore, eliminate a high degree of competition.[199]

11.165 However, the exclusivity rule is acceptable only within reason. Thus, a rule which prohibited exhibitors at the annual London International Boat Show from exhibiting in other shows in the UK during a period stretching from 7 months prior to the London show to 12 months after it was found to be unacceptable to the Commission.[200] On the other hand a prohibition on exhibitors at the British Dental Trade Association Exhibition from exhibiting elsewhere for 4 months prior to and 1 month after the exhibition was exempted.[201]

11.166 Similarly, discounts given to members of a trade association on the fees for exhibiting are only acceptable within reason. In *London International Boat Show* the Commission objected to the size of discounts given to members of the Ship and Boat Builders National Federation (UK) and required the maximum possible discount to be reduced from 55 per cent to 25 per cent and to be accorded on the basis of the category of space taken by the member and of the seniority of the member within the Federation. In *British Dental Trade Association Exhibition*, a discount of 25 per cent to members was sanctioned, being justified in view of the costs and financial risks incurred by the Association in promoting the exhibition.

11.167 As regards rules governing the allocation of exhibition space (a factor of considerable importance) organisers should consider only objective factors such as: the size and weight of the exhibit; the seniority of the exhibitor within a nationally recognised trade association; the wishes of exhibitors who have occupied the same size in previous years; whether the exhibitor is a manufacturer of the country which hosts the exhibition or is a sole concessionaire for the UK as opposed to a foreign exhibitor, though with regard to this factor care must be taken not to raise unreasonable barriers to foreign exhibits since this would distort trade between domestic and foreign exhibitors.

11.168 If exhibition space is limited, restrictions may be placed on the range of products which may be displayed, in order that customers benefit by seeing as wide a range of products as possible.[202]

11.169 Where an association imposes a penalty for breach of the rules, then the procedure for assessing the alleged breach should comply with the rules of natural justice; there should be adequate appeal procedures for dealers who have been penalised, which might include resource to arbitration.[203]

11.170 The Commission might include notification obligations in any decision granting exemption under Article 85(3). Thus parties may have to report to the Commission details of: all expulsions from the exhibition, other penalties imposed on traders, lists of other exhibitions at which the associations allows members to exhibit, correspondence between associations organising trade fairs.

199 See *Internationale Dentalschau* 1987 OJ L293/58 para. 29; *Sippa* OJ 1991 L60/19 para. 21.
200 [1985] 3 CMLR 622. See also *VIFKA* OJ 1986 C146/9.
201 *British Dental Trade Association* [1989] 4 CMLR 1021; see also *Internationale Dentalshau* OJ 1987 L293/58 where a period of three months before and two after was exempted.
202 *Internationale Dentalschau* 1987 OJ L293/58; *Sippa* OJ 1991 L60/19.
203 *UNIDI No. 2* [1985] 2 CMLR 38 at p. 41, para. 10; *London International Boat Show* [1985] 3 CMLR 622; *VIFKA* OJ 1986 C146/9.

(4) Advertising restrictions in supplier–dealer relations

11.171 It is perfectly legal for suppliers to require dealers to follow the supplier's instructions on advertising,[204] or for the dealers to be required to submit advertisements in advance to the supplier for approach.[205] However, the Commission will be suspicious of a requirement that dealers must submit advertisements on prices and terms and conditions for prior approval. Such a requirement could suggest an attempt by the supplier to control vertical prices and terms.[206]

11.172 In an exclusive dealing contract the dealer may be prohibited from actively advertising outside of his contract territory, though he should retain the contractual right to satisfy unsolicited orders from outside of his territory. Within his contract territory the dealer may be required to accept advertising obligations, for example, with regard to regularity, forum, value (perhaps as a percentage of turnover) etc. The dealer may be required to sell the contract goods under trade marks, or packed and presented as specified by the supplier.[207] The Commission consider that these restrictions do not restrict competition so would not be within Article 85(1).[208] Accordingly, advertising obligations may be accepted by a supplier, for example, with respect to international advertising.

2. *UK Law*

(1) Legal framework: registrability and dispensation under section 21(2)

11.173 Under the RTPA 1976—distinction between goods and services. For inexplicable reasons advertising restrictions concerning goods are apparently not registrable whereas advertising restrictions concerning services are. Section 11(2)(d) RTPA 1976 requires the registration of agreements relating to "the form or manner in which designated services are to be made available, supplied or obtained." No equivalent provision exists for goods. The OFT seemingly takes the view that an agreement concerning the advertising of services is an agreement within section 11(2)(d). On this view, the advertising of a service is a part of its being made available or supplied. Thus, an agreement between X and Y, two travel agents, not to advertise is an agreement containing a restriction on the form or manner in which travel agency services are made available. Since advertising involves bringing the existence of the service to the consumer's awareness, it may arguably be said to be part of the form or manner in which a service is made available, supplied or obtained. Certainly, if X and Y agree to stop granting special discount rates to consumers who present an advert from a newspaper to the seller at the moment the service is purchased, then a restriction on the form/manner of supply has occurred (e.g. "50 pence off hamburgers on presentation of this coupon"). There is no decided case on the registrability of service advertising restriction and given the not entirely clear position parties to agreements might consider furnishing details of agreements on a "fail-safe" basis only. If serious problems arise, parties might seek a declaration of the RPC under section 26 RTPA 1976 as to the registrability of the clause.

11.174 It may be noted that restrictions or trade association rules requiring parties to reserve a certain amount of floor or shelf space for showpieces or demonstrations may fall within

[204] *BMW* [1975] 1 CMLR D44 (Commission Decision).

[205] *IBM Personal Computer* [1984] 2 CMLR 342 at p. 346, para. 10(4).

[206] e.g. Case 86/82 *Hasselblad* v *Commission* [1984] ECR883 at paras. 48, 49 of the judgment.

[207] See Reg. 1983/83/EEC, on block exemption for exclusive dealing OJ 1983 L173/1, Art. 2(2)(c), and Art. 2(3). See also Reg. 1984/83/EEC on block exemption for exclusive purchasing OJ 1983 L173/5 Art. 2(3)(d).

[208] e.g. *Krupps* OJ 1980 L120/26 at p. 28, para. 15 advertising restrictions technically within Art. 85(1) but are excluded on a *de minimis* basis.

sections 6(1)(f) (goods) or 11(2)(e) (services) (areas or places in or from which goods/services are to be supplied, etc) despite their being essentially concerned with advertising. For analysis, see paras 11.163–11.170. Likewise if the service *per se* is advertising (e.g. public relations or advertising agency firms) the restrictions on the provision of that service are registrable.

11.175 The OFT has granted section 21(2) dispensation to a number of services agreement containing advertising restrictions. Many have no real economic impact. Thus, for example, section 21(2) dispensation was accorded in *Outdoor Advertising Council*[209] where the Council recommended a voluntary code designed to conserve energy by restricting the use of electricity for advertising lighting. Under the code users of illuminated signs would, *inter alia*, choose to use electricity to illuminate that sign for one and only one of the following periods: (a) the hours during which the premises are open for business; or (b), the hours between midday and midnight. Compliance with the code was entirely voluntary and hence users were not restricted as to the forms of advertising they adopted. In *Society of Catering and Hotel Management*[210] the Society promulgated a Code of Ethics for the use of total management consultants. The Code was given section 21(2) dispensation after a clause which read, "A member shall not promote his/her professional services through any advertising media", was deleted. A clear case on point is *Association of Average Adjusters*[211] where the OFT gave section 21(2) dispensation to the association rules only after clauses which, *inter alia*, discouraged advertising were removed. Specifically, the OFT objected to clauses

[209] No. S. 571 Register of Restrictive Trade Practices (1977)—Code approved by the Department of the Environment. See for other examples: S. 1399 Register of Restrictive Trade Practice, *British Wood Preserving Association*. Association rules prohibit door to door canvassing by members unless prior notification of the visit has been given in writing through the postal system and agreed by the occupier of the property. Associations seeking to curb what are considered as exploitative, pressure methods of selling will probably be acting in the consumer's favour. Such a rule is restrictive in that it hinders aggressive selling strategies which may differentiat the vigorous from the non-vigorous company. See also No. S. 1280 Register of Restrictive Trade Practices, *Association of Air Courier Services*. Association sought, *inter alia*, to prevent misleading adverts. This is probably not a restriction at all since an obligation to comply with the ordinary law (i.e. on misleading and deceptive advertising) cannot be viewed as "restrictive". The Association also required members to ensure that their advertisements complied with the standards of external bodies, e.g. Advertising Standards Authority; Code of Advertising Practice Committee; Independent Broadcasting Authority; Independent Television Company Authority, and Association of Independent Radio Authorities. An obligation to abide by widely held standards does not restrain a firm's freedom to select the form or substance of adverts. The restriction would rarely be considered significant.

[210] No. S. 657 Register of Restrictive Trade Practices, *Society of Catering and Hotel Management Code of Ethics* (1980). See also, No. S. 1314 Register of Restrictive Trade Practices, *Corporation of Finance Brokers* (1985)—Members agreed to abide by advertising practices issued by the Corporation; No. S 155 Register of Restrictive Trade Practices, *Association of Telecommunication Services* (1985)—Members agreed to abide by advertising codes of practice issued by the relevant authorities and trade associations.

[211] No. S. 1373 Register of Restrictive Trade Practices (1985). An interesting example of restrictive advertising of legal services occurred in the USA. The Department of Justice, Antitrust Division, sent business review letters in September 1984, to the Chief Justices of the higher judicial courts in 40 states in connection with the adoption of the American Bar Association Model Rules of Professional Conduct provisions on fees, solicitation and advertising. These Courts were in the process of adopting the rules. The rules contained restrictions, *inter alia*, on lawyers initiating communications with prospective clients either in person, over the telephone or by mail except in defined and limited circumstances. The Antitrust Division commented cautiously that the rules could be useful in protecting the public from over-zealous lawyers but added that they could restrict the flow of "useful information to consumers of legal services". They added that the rule banned communications to those most in need of legal assistance. The Antitrust Division were also critical of rules restricting the communication of fields of practice and specialisation. They stated: "Such information would assist consumers in deciding which lawyers they may wish to approach about providing a particular legal service and which lawyers they prefer not to consider. In general there is no apparent reason for prohibiting dissemination of truthful information about lawyers efforts to specialise or even claims of specialisation since such communications contain useful consumer information and reduce search costs."

discouraging: (i) "advertising for the purpose of obtaining business in any form and by any medium"; and (ii), "soliciting business". The rules did not prohibit advertising: they simply branded it as a breach of the standards of "fair dealing" and "integrity".

11.176 Agreements restricting the advertising of fees or restricting the choice of advertising media or which prohibit styles of advertising which reasonably disparage rivals or challenge their services will not be suitable for section 21(2) treatment. Such advertising is an integral part of competition. Thus in *Sharman Newspapers*[212] an agreement between Sharman Newspapers and the City of Peterborough Estate Agents Association (CPEAA) was referred, by the OFT, to the RPC. Under the agreement, members of the CPEAA accepted a restriction not to obtain press advertising services for regular "sales by private treaty" or "sales by auction" from newspapers circulating in the same area as the *Peterborough Classified Standard*. This latter paper was owned by the Sharman Newspapers company. In return that company gave discounts on the space purchased by estate agents in membership of the CPEAA. The discounts given entailed, *inter alia*, a 10 per cent allowance on the normal rates where payment for advertising services was made by the last Friday of the month following invoice date. Sharman Newspapers did not give this discount to non-members of the CPEAA. The parties gave undertakings to the RPC that they would not give effect to or enforce the above agreement, or enter into any other agreements to like effect. The agreement was objectionable because it created entry barriers to newspapers who sought to compete in providing property advertising services with Sharman Newspapers. Members of CPEAA were discouraged from placing advertisements with such papers because they were contractually bound *also* to place advertisements with papers belonging to Sharman Newspapers. The incentive to patronise rival papers was hence low.

11.177 A similar case to that of *Sharman Newspapers* occurred in *Solihull Estate Agents Boycott*.[213] The OFT intervened to prevent a group consisting of most of the estate agents in the Solihull area (a wealthy residential area south of Birmingham) who had formed a consortium to produce their own advertising newspaper from agreeing not to advertise in any other newspaper. The OFT objected to this boycott of other advertising mediums for two principal reasons. First, the boycott prevented competition between property advertisers. Secondly, a householder in the area would, if he used any of the estate agents who were party to the agreement, be persuaded not to advertise his property in other local newspapers, a fact which might have reduced the number of potential buyers of the property. In the event, the estate agents terminated the boycott thereby settling the case to the OFT's satisfaction. This case is particularly interesting since it highlight a factual situation in which advertising restrictions may fall under section 11(2)(c) RTPA 1976 ("the extent (if any) to which, or the scale (if any) on which, designated services are to be made available, supplied or obtained.") An agreement between X, Y and Z *not* to obtain advertising services from a particular provider of that services is surely an agree as to the extent to which a services is obtained, i.e. it is an agreement to purchase no advertising services at all and falls squarely therefore within section 11(2)(c). This conclusion is regardless of section 11(2)(d) RTPA 1976 whose application is, as explained above, somewhat uncertain. The case also shows that where the service *per se* is advertising then, as noted above, restrictions imposed upon the availability of that service may be registrable.

11.178 Sections 9 and 18 RTPA 1976—advertising restrictions in distribution agreements. Sections 9(3) and 18 (2) RTPA 1976 require that terms relating exclusively to the goods or services supplied are to be "disregarded" when registrability under the Act is being considered. If the agreement concerns goods distribution it will not in any event be registra-

[212] Nos. 1161 and 1597 Register of Restrictive Trade Practices (unreported judgment of RPC, 1984).
[213] Unreported, December 1985. See generally DGFT Annual Report 1985, p. 25.

ble and recourse to section 9(3) is superfluous. If the agreement concerns services then section 18(2) should permit such restrictions to be disregarded. A restrictive clause concerning advertising is a term relating exclusively to the services provided so may be disregarded.

11.179 Sections 9(3) or 18(2) would not apply to exempt dealer or franchise clubs. Where all of the dealers of a supplier (or the franchisees of a franchisor) agree to abide by the majority decision at a meeting designed to determine how best to promote and advertise the supplier's (or franchisor's) brand or trade mark then an agreement that is registrable under section 11(2)(d) RTPA 1976 might arise where the advertising concerns services. Sections 9(4) and 18(3) RTPA disapply sections 9(3) and 18(2) as between parties at the same level of distribution, i.e. those provisions only effectively apply along the (vertical) supplier–wholesaler–dealer chain.

(2) Trade fairs

11.180 Many trade fair rules will be registrable. If they regulate the extent to which exhibitors may participate in rival fairs this may be a restriction under section 11(2)(b), i.e. restriction on terms or conditions on or subject to which the service of providing exhibition facilities will be supplied. If there are penalties for non-compliance with the rules which, for example, ban exhibitors or result in their being offered less favourable stands, these may be registrable under section 11(2)(e), i.e. restrictions on persons for whom the service of providing exhibition facilities is to be made available or supplied. If the organising trade association will not provide display space to a person who has displayed in a rival fair, this is a restriction on persons to whom services will be supplied. It might also be a restriction under section 11(2)(b), i.e. a restriction on the conditions subject to which the service will be provided—the association impose the *condition* that they will only provide exhibition facilities where exhibitors have not displayed in rival fairs. Where the trade fair attracts a significant number of foreign exhibitors or (more likely) purchasers, then the rules will have to comply with Article 85(1) EC since there will be an effect upon trade between the Member States. Where the Commission has granted exemption under Article 85(3) EC, it has been OFT practice to refrain from referring the agreement to the RPC using the section 21(2)(a) RTPA 1976 procedure whereby the OFT may refrain from taking proceedings in respect of an agreement authorised or exempted under EC law. Thus in *Society of Motor Manufacturers and Traders*[214] no reference was made to the RPC, despite the fact that the trade fair rules contained significant restrictions, because of a formal exemption granted by the Commission. Presumably, a comfort letter given by the Commission would also suffice under section 21(1)(a), it is after all an "authorisation" of sorts which has legal effect in that national Courts are at least bound to recognise it though are not bound by it.

11.181 Where no EC authorisation or exemption exists, parties may have to remove some of the restrictions, e.g. on exhibiting in other fairs, if they wish to benefit from section 21(2) dispensation.

(3) Funding of joint advertising

11.182 Where industry-wide advertising is undertaken, individual members of the association or body undertaking the advertising will have to fund the activity. Usually the extent of an individual firm's contribution is determined by reference to the amount of total value of the product or service supplied. Where the association is advertising goods, these

[214] No. S. 1083 Register of Restrictive Trade Practices (9184) in respect of the EC exemption reported at OJ 1983 L 376/1; [1984] 1 CMLR 611.

schemes are registrable under section 6(4) RTPA 1976 (see section 17(2) for services). This states, in pertinent part:

> "an agreement to make payments calculated by reference—
> (a) to the quantities of goods produced or supplied by him ... being payments calculated, or calculated at an increased rate, in respect of quantities of goods or materials exceeding any quantity specified in ... the agreement, shall be treated ... as a restriction in respect of the quantities of those goods ..."

11.183 Thus, an agreement to pay a sum to an association based upon the amount of a product sold is a restriction as to quantities under section 6(1)(d). There is no reason why such agreements should not be suitable for section 21(2) treatment,[215] provided the association is not used for some covert purpose, e.g. profit pooling where parties pay moneys into a central association which distributes it according to an agreed formula. Profit pooling is a form of market sharing (see para. 8.216).

11.184 Some funding schemes for central advertising are probably registrable under section 11(2)(a) and/or (b) RTPA 1976. Suppliers of services who pay a levy to an association in consideration for central advertising will be purchasers of advertising services. Thus, if purchasers collectively agree as to the prices they shall pay for advertising services this presumably is an agreement registrable under section 11(2)(a). If the purchasers agree as to the terms and conditions upon which the advertising services are to be acquired by them this is registrable under section 11(2)(b). As with goods agreements there is no reason why section 21(2) should not apply.[216]

(4) Competition Act 1980

11.185 Advertising practices carried on by trade associations that are exempt from the RTPA 1976 may be investigated under the CA 1980 (provided of course that the association can be said to be carrying on business so as to satisfy that Act). Likewise, certain practices carried out by economically powerful suppliers may be subject to the CA 1980. One such is the granting of discounts to retailers who reserve a percentage of their display space for the suppliers' goods. This may create an entry barrier for smaller firms seeking advertising outlets for their products.[217] Alternatively, advertising practices may be investigated as part of an investigation into a monopoly situation under the FTA 1973.

11.186 The advertising industry has been involved in a number of investigations under the CA 1980, although the practices complained of have usually has more to do with pricing policies than advertising *per se*. In *Scottish Universal Newspaper Ltd*[218] a free advertising newspaper was used as a predatory device to exclude a new entrant; advertising space was sold at below cost. The anti-competitive conduct was predatory pricing. In *Essex County Newspapers*[219] ECN employed discriminatory criteria for deciding who they would allow to advertise real estate in their newspapers. The OFT concluded that because ECN was

[215] See e.g. No. 3798 Register of Restrictive Trade Practices, Agreement between the Members of the Federation of *Mushroom Spawn Suppliers and the Mushroom Growers' Association* (1981), concerning a levy to provide funds for central publicity. The levy was raised by means of a proportional increase in the prices charged to grocers.

[216] e.g. No. S. 202 Register of Restrictive Trade Practices, Agreement between Organisations representing advertising agencies and media-owning companies to fund the *Advertising Standards Authority* through a surcharge set and administered by the Advertising Standards Board of Finance (1979).

[217] e.g. MMC Report on the *Supply of Frozen Foodstuffs for Human Consumption* HC 674 (1976) at paras. 326–332; MMC Report on the *Supply of Cigarettes and Tobacco* HC 218 (1961).

[218] January 1983.

[219] July 1983.

dominant in the relevant property advertising market, it had the power to affect the relative ability of different property agents to compete in the Colchester area house agency market by its decision on whether or not to accept advertisements. In *Sheffield Newspapers*[220] SN prohibited retailers of their papers from circulating "free-sheets" to customers; it refused to accept advertising copy from those who had advertised or intended to advertise in a particular rival production; and they granted quantity discounts to estate agents who placed a substantial amount of their advertising with the company. The OFT declared these practices to be anti-competitive. SN gave undertakings to the OFT in respect of certain of the practices. The OFT referred the remaining practices to the MMC.[221] The MMC held that the prohibition on retailers circulating "free-sheets" was anti-competitive and contrary the public interest. With regard to the discounts the MMC held that they did not exert a sufficient enough impact upon the market to be anti-competitive. In *British Telecommunications* (*Pricing Policy for the Placing of Advertisements in Yellow Pages*)[222] British Telecommunications (BT) incorporated in the price of the Yellow Pages advertising space a cost component for advertisement creation and campaign planning services which it provided. Hence, it was complained, advertisers were forced to accept BT services as well as advertising space since the two were effectively tied together. Advertising agencies asserted that this created a barrier to them in that it penalised advertisers who wished to hire independent agency services but who were none the less forced to pay for BT services. The OFT concluded that the practice of BT was not economically significant enough to exert anti-competitive consequences.

11.187 Where a dominant concern employs advertising to deter new entry, an anti-competitive practice might arise. If X, a dominant supplier, on learning that Y was considering entry to the market, suddenly offered a plethora of free gifts with its products and/or conducted an aggressive advertising campaign designed to nullify the effects of the rival's introductory campaigns, then this might amount to anti-competitive conduct.[223]

11.188 Probably the most important indications of OFT policy in this field is to be found in their report of 30 October 1985 in *Holmes McDougall Ltd* (restriction of advertisements containing prices). HM is a publishing house which is wholly owned by Lonrho Ltd. It produces, *inter alia*, magazines for outdoors enthusiasts. Consequently it is an important forum for the advertising of the goods and services relating to outdoor activities (climbing, rambling, hill-walking, etc.). In 1983, in response to pressure imposed by the major advertisers in these magazines, HM altered its advertising policy so as to refuse to accept advertisements containing prices and/or price comparisons unless the product or service advertised was own-brand or exclusively imported and only available through the advertiser's own outlets. Despite some conflicting evidence the OFT concluded that these restrictions had the effect of severely discouraging price competition between suppliers of goods and services advertised in HM magazines. In this context the OFT expressed the following principle:

220 October 1981.
221 (1983) Cmnd 8664.
222 October 1984.
223 See MMC report on *Supply of Household Detergents* HC 105 (1966), para. 97—MMC concluded that free gifts can distort competition by artificially creating demand in a manner unrelated to product quality. See *Scottish Universal Newspapers Ltd* (January 1983) OFT investigation under CA 1980. OFT recognised that practices connected with introduction of a new product or service may be anti-competitive (*ibid.*, at p. 39, para. 8.16).

> "The office consider that one of the requirements for any market to work competitively is that consumers must be aware of the prices of goods and services provided by alternative suppliers so that they might make an informed choice. The flow of such information from suppliers to consumers is therefore fundamental to competition and the interference by any supplier in the flow of information from a competing supplier can only be intended to affect competition between those suppliers."

11.189 Holmes McDougall resisted giving undertakings following the OFT's report on the basis that it would lose out to its competitors who were continuing to pursue the same advertising policy. Therefore the DGFT made a monopoly reference under the FTA 1973 to the MMC of the magazine. The MMC's report on *Specialised Advertising Services*[224] and found that there was a complex monopoly situation in favour of all publishers of such specialist magazines. It upheld the conclusions of the OFT's report that this advertising policy operated against the public interest, adopting the view of the OFT that consumers should be able to enjoy an informed choice enabling them to make the choice based on all factors including price.[225]

11.190 The message is clear: providers of advertising services should not impose restrictive conditions on the way in which advertisers present their goods. This does not, however, prevent publishers requiring advertisers to comply with the British Code of Advertising Practice, nor should publishers be prevented from discouraging adverts for defective or dangerous goods or services. The OFT statement also makes it clear that advertisers with purchasing power may act anti-competitively if they use that power to coerce publishers into imposing restrictive advertising rules which happen to suit those advertisers' needs and which will harm competitors.

11.191 Professional advertising restrictions have also been the subject of investigations under the FTA 1973. In a series of reports in 1989,[226] the MMC found that advertising was not itself incompatible with professional status. This was found to be true in *Services of Medical Practitioners* even of the medical profession, despite the unique relationship of doctor and patient. Professional standards require the maintenance of some advertising restrictions, but any restriction on advertising must be justified as being necessary to uphold those standards. It cannot be assumed that any advertising is in itself incompatible. The purpose of advertising is that of enabling consumer choice. This could only be restricted if necessary to uphold professional standards. This assessment is stated by the MMC to involve a balancing of the benefits and detriments in advertising. It might be suggested that the MMC applied what was is in essence a test of proportionality: identifying the legitimate purpose of the maintenance of professional standards and then assessing whether restrictions on advertising went further than was necessary for those purposes. If there are other less restrictive means of achieving a legitimate purpose, then they should be adopted. In *Services of Medical Practitioners* the MMC recommended that rather than preventing a doctor advertising a specialisation, there should be professional rules regulating who can claim a specialisation.

11.192 Professional requirements may, however, entail restrictions beyond those which are required by the British Code of Advertising Practice. For example, in *Civil Engineering*

224 Cm 280 (1988).

225 The MMC's recommendations are given effect by the Restriction on Conduct (Specialist Advertising Services) Order S.I. 1988 No. 1017).

226 *Civil Engineering Consultancy Services* Cm 564 (1989); *Services of Medical Practitioners* Cm 582 (1989); *Professionally Regulated Osteopaths* Cm 583 (1989). Earlier reports on professions were carried out in 1976: *Veterinary Surgeons* Cmnd. 6572 (1976); *Solicitors in England and Wales* HC 557 and 559 (1976). See also *Professional Services* Cmnd 4463 (1970) and paras. 2.62–2.85.

Consultancy Services the MMC accepted that the Code's requirements could be limited by a further provision that advertising should contain nothing which could reasonably be regarded as likely to bring the profession into disrepute. In *Services of Osteopaths*, the MMC indicated that rules to prevent denigration of or claims of superiority over other members of the profession would be acceptable. This could be phrased as a restriction on advertising likely to bring the profession into disrepute. It also stated that it would allow restrictions to protect patients from potentially harmful advertising, which could be on terms that advertising should not be such as to abuse the trust of potential patients or exploit their lack of knowledge.

K. Standards, Quality Control and Description

11.193 Undertakings, invariably under the aegis of a trade association, may seek to standardise the language they use in promoting goods or services. This may help the consumer where it facilitates the making of comparisons between different goods or services. If X, Y and Z all produce a relatively homogeneous product but market their products using different technical, descriptive language and in different size packages, then consumers may make uneducated buying decisions. The disparities in the styles of marketing may hide differences in quality and content of the various brands. Thus, X might sell low grade beans in 500g tins for 50 pence whilst Y might sell high grade beans in 400 g tins for 48 pence. A buyer—P— wishes to purchase lower grade beans at an economy price but purchasers the higher quality beans erroneously thinking them to be better value. P is thus misled due to the lack of conformity between brands as to packing sizes. Alternatively, X and Y might sell products which are relatively similar in very different style packages and using very different labels and descriptions. Buyer P might purchase product X not realising that there is a competing brand Y which might be better value. These differences may not lead to confusion where competing brands are sold in close physical proximity to each other, as when they are sold together on a supermarket shelf. However, where no proximity exists, as when the goods are simply itemised on a product list, then the scope for confusion increases. Thus, lack of conformity in product description or presentation can lead to distortions of the market where buyers make uneducated buying decisions; competition may be enhanced and rendered more efficient where buyers are able to compare more easily the merits of different products.

11.194 Another economic consequence of standardisation is that where packaging is standardised, e.g. where coffee tins are of roughly similar size or cardboard boxes are of roughly similar construction, scale economies may be realised in the production of such packaging. If X, Y and Z all agree on packaging construction and size, then suppliers of such packaging to X, Y and Z may be able to realise scale economies (fewer design lines, greater rationalisation, etc.) which may be passed on to X, Y and Z and ultimately to their customers in lower prices. Standardisation may thus confer considerable benefits on consumers. Conversely, there may be anti-competitive consequences. It is with the problem of differentiating beneficial from anti-competitive standardisation that this section is concerned.

1. EC Law

11.195 Harmonisation measures taken by a trade association, or by undertakings, which do not extend beyond legitimate appellation or quality control may be outside of Article 85(1) EC. The Commission adopts this view with respect to the use of a common label to designate a certain quality where use of the label is available to all competitors on the same conditions.[227] There is no objection to rendering use of the label subject to a one-off or periodic payment to the association. However, the charge should be commensurate with the actual burden suffered by the association with respect to administration, market research, etc. The charge might restrict competition if it acts as a deterrent to use of the label. The association might set a standard that must be met by undertakings using the label.[228] However, there must be no attempt to remove certain qualities of product from the market or enforce standards *generally* on the parties. Parties must remain free to sell lower or higher quality goods than those designated by the label, appellation or trade mark, etc.[229]

11.196 Where the association provides national advertising and promotion on behalf of the label, appellation, trade mark, etc., the parties must remain free to conduct their own advertising.[230] Associations may perform reasonable quality control activities designed to ensure that goods or services using the label, etc. do actually conform to the requisite standard.[231] This is especially important to associations which provide general publicity for the label. Clearly, the integrity of the label, etc., will suffer if goods or services not living up to the requisite standard employ the label and gain the benefit of the association's advertising.

11.197 Article 85(1) is infringed if, with respect to the goods using the label, parties accept restrictions.[232] Thus, there must be no restriction on advertising goods without the label since this distorts competition between non-labelled and labelled goods.[233] It is, however, acceptable to require parties to the agreement to advertise the labelled product. Though, if the obligation were so extensive that in practice compliance with it rendered effective advertising of non-labelled qualities impossible then a breach of Article 85(1) might arise, e.g. parties must expend 85 per cent of their total advertising budget upon the labelled product. Quality or other labels may not be used to hinder parallel imports.[234] It is obvious that the association must not impose selling price restrictions on members, e.g. parties will maintain resale prices of goods with quality labels.[235]

11.198 In the context of distribution networks it is acceptable for suppliers to require goods to be packaged in a certain manner or to have trade marks attached to them by dealers.[236]

2. *UK Law*

(1) Exemption from the Act

11.199 Sections 9(5) (goods) and 18(5) (services) RTPA 1976 require that in determining registrability, no account shall be taken of any term in an agreement providing for the compliance

[227] Notice concerning Agreements, Decisions and Concerted Practices in the Field of Co-operation between Enterprises, OJ 1968 C75/3 [1968] CMLR 5 Art. 8. See *ASBL* [1970] CMLR D31; *VVVF* [1970] CMLR D1 (quality label coupled to sales restrictions operating outside of the EC).

[228] *ASBL* above; *VVVF* above.

[229] *ibid.*

[230] *ASBL* [1970] CMLR D31 at p. D33, para. 10.

[231] *ibid.*

[232] *Transocean Marine Paint I* [1967] CMLR D9; *Transocean Marine Paint II* [1974] 1 CMLR D11.

[233] *ASBL* [1970] CMLR D31.

[234] *Transocean Marine Paint I* [1967] CMLR D9. See generally, Baden-Fuller, "Economic issues relating to property rights in trade marks: export bans, differential pricing, restrictions resale and repackaging" (1981) ELRev 162; *IAZ* v *Commission* [1983] ECR 3369, [1984] 3 CMLR 276.

[235] See e.g. Case 73/74 *Belgian Wallpaper* [1976] 1 CMLR 589; [1975] ECR 1491 at p. 1513 (Trade mark Association, joint vertical price fixing).

[236] See Art. 2(3)(b), Reg. 1983/83/EEC, OJ 1983 L 173/1 on block exemption for exclusive dealing; and Art. 2(3)(c), Reg. 1984/83/EEC, OJ 1983 L173/5 on block exemption for exclusive purchasing.

with: (i) standards of design, dimension, quality or performance; or (ii) arrangements as to the exchange or dissemination of information on such standards. This exemption for standards is not absolute; it applies only to standards approved by the British Standards Institute (BSI), or to standards approved by the Secretary of State under statutory instrument.

(2) Treatment under section 21(2) RTPA 1976

11.200 Where no exemption exists because no approval lies, particulars of agreements concerning product/service standards must be furnished. Such agreements will be registrable under section 6(1)(d) (goods) which covers restrictions on the "descriptions" of goods supplied. With respect to services section 11(1)(d) covers restrictions on the "form or manner" in which services are supplied (the goods and services provisions of the RTPA 1976 are not identical) these sections are broad enough to embrace standardisation agreements. Where the agreement concerns goods (which is the usual case) then section 6(1)(e) might apply. This covers restrictions on processes of manufacture to be applied. If an association seeks to disseminate and promote a standard this might entail adoption of a uniform process of manufacture. In applying section 21(2) the OFT take into account many of the factors discussed above in respect of EC law. Such agreements are often dealt with under section 21(2) RTPA 1976.[237] Occasionally, an agreement specifies standards and also recommends withdrawal of products not conforming to the standards. As a rule such an agreement is unsuitable for section 21(2) treatment because it denies the consumer choice between approved and non-approved qualities. However, where the recommendation to withdraw is made on clear environmental or health grounds it might be acceptable.[238] In *Hard Non-ionic Detergents*[239] the Soap and Detergent Industry Association recommended a

[237] See e.g. No. S. 15 Register of Restrictive Trade Practices, *Building Societies Association* BSA (1984) Document V55 dated 8 March 1985. The BSA in a circular (No. 3056) to members recommended adoption of a Code of Practices on common standards for advertising of deposits and shares. The code was jointly drafted with, *inter alia*, the British Bankers Association. In the circulate the BSA stated: "The principal object of the code is to ensure that when the composite rate arrangements are also applied to banks and other financial institutions, advertisers use a common terminology to describe the various types of rates on offer in printed advertisement. This will assist consumers in making comparisons between advertised rates and avoid the confusion that would result from the different use of different terms to describe the same variable." The OFT did not obtain s. 21(2) dispensation for the code since the BSA were registering too many circulars on a regular basis to give the OFT a chance to assess the overall impact of the recommendations. However, in a letter of the BSA, the OFT indicated that in their view the code was unlikely to contain any significant restrictions. See also, No. 5166, Register of Restrictive Trade Practices, *Soap and Detergent Industry Association Agreement on increasing fill levels*. In 1977 the Department of Prices and Consumer Protection encouraged development of an express agreement on fill levels of heavy duty fabric washing powder packed in "E sizes" (soap and synthetic). The parties agreed on the current weights of different categories of heavy duty fabric washing powder used in the home (e.g. Tide, Surf, Omo, Radiant)—s. 21(2) dispensation given (1984); No. 4681, Register of Restrictive Trade Practices, *Interlocking Paving Association*. Agreement specified a minimum manufacturing standard against which members would negotiate contracts for pre-cast paving blocks. The agreement was designed to provide a common standard in the absence of the approved BSI standard which was still under consideration. The agreement did not in any way impinge on members' discretion as to prices or terms and conditions—s. 12(2) dispensation given (1984); No. 4883, Register of Restrictive Trade Practices, *The Tea Council Catering Tea Grading Scheme* (1982). Agreement between members of the Tea Council concerning graded tea sold in bags. The Council promulgated a Code of Practice under which members would regulate the weight of tea in each tea bag and would label tea bags accordingly to the quality of the tea enclosed. A system of stars (1 star plain tea, 2 stars medium tea, 3 stars quality tea) would be used. The Council would supervise and enforce the standard of tea of those members who wished to comply with the Code—s. 21(2) dispensation given.

[238] Health based justifications for restrictions are expressly provided for under ss. 10(1)(a) (goods) and 19(1)(a) (services) RTPA 1976.

[239] No. 3769 Register of Restrictive Trade Practices (1974). For other cases on health standards see: No. 4868 Register of Restrictive Trade Practices, *British Aerosol Manufacturers' Association*. Members sub

ban on the sale of hard non-ionics in detergents because these non-ionics were a major cause of foaming in sewage works and water courses. The association appreciated that such a ban would have economic repercussions entailing extra costs and processing difficulties for some users. However, the association considered the environmental question paramount. The OFT obtained section 21(2) dispensation for the agreement.

(3) Terms in supplier–dealer agreements: sections 9(3) and 18(2) RTPA 1976

11.201 Restrictions contained in individual agreements between suppliers and dealers relating to descriptions of goods, or packaging, etc., will be exempt from registration under sections 9(3) and 18(2) RTPA 1976 as terms relating exclusively to the goods or services supplied or provided.

(4) Interpretation by the RPC

11.202 The words "description of goods" in sections 6(1)(d) RTPA 1976 (i.e. restrictions on the "quantities or descriptions of goods to be produced, supplied or acquired") means "kinds of goods". There is no equivalent wording in section 11 RTPA 1976 for services, though as noted above section 11(1)(d), which uses quite different wording, is probably broad enough to catch services agreements. There is no guidance from the RPC on this question. The RPC has, however, held that an agreement whereby the parties adopt uniform nomenclature for goods is *not* a restriction caught within section 6(1)(d) RTPA 1976: "what [section 6(1)(d)] is dealing with is restrictions as to the quantities of goods and as to the kinds of goods; not as to the quantities and the nomenclature of goods." The RPC has also held that section 6(1)(c) might cover an "advance agreement as to the contractual definition of particular words which may be used in anticipated contracts."[240] It follows that if X and Y agree to describe goods in a specified manner this will not be registrable under section 6(1)(d). However, if X and Y agree on nomenclature to be used in anticipated contracts this might be registrable under section 6(1)(c). Such a contract should be suitable to section 21(2) treatment.

11.203 In an unreported case in 1969, *National Association of Scaffolding Contractors*[241] the RPC held that a recommendation to members of an association concerning a model form of conditions for the hire, erection and dismantling of scaffolding was in the public interest. The recommendation was pursuant to a governmental report on safety and health in the construction industry, it read: "Hirers and owners of scaffolding should be urged to use the model forms of contract documents among other things to alert both of the parties as to their responsibilities for safety of the scaffold. The contract documents should give ample descriptions of the purpose and detail of the scaffolding including a section on safety."

cont.
scribed to a code of practice concerning the standards for the content, labelling and performance of aerosols containing more than a certain amount of flammable material, and standards and procedures for long-term storage testing of new or codified aerosol products—s. 12(2) dispensation given (1983). No. 5130 Register of Restrictive Trade Practices, *British Soft Drinks Council* (1985)—concerning the compliance of members to an EEC Directive on labelling and minimum durability datemarking of retail packs of food and drink; and, No. 5543 Register of Restrictive Trade Practices, *National Edible Oil Distribution Association* (1985) noted at para 12.317, note 39.3.

240 See *British Waste Paper Association* (1963) LR 4 RP 29 at p. 50. See also *British Furniture Manufacturers' Federated Association* (1966) LR 6 RP. 185 an agreement containing a restriction on members copying the designs of other manufacturers was *not* a restriction upon the "description" or "kinds" of goods to be supplied; *Blanket Manufacturers' Agreement* (1959) LR 1 RP 208, association recommendation that members should not produce blankets of less than a certain quality *was* a restriction on the "description" or "kinds" of goods to be purchased.

241 No. 644, Register of Restrictive Trade Practices.

11.204 The judgment of the RPC in this case supports the general approach of the OFT under section 21(2) to standards, quality control and descriptions, i.e. that restrictions incorporated with safety motives in mind may be acceptable but that restrictions seeking to limit consumer choice may be unacceptable.

(5) Under the CA 1980

11.205 Quality control systems can operate as a barrier to entry justifying investigation under the CA 1980. The OFT has investigated a quality control system as part of a wider investigation into allegedly anti-competitive courses of conduct. In *Wales Tourist Board*[242] the WTB operated an accommodation quality verification system. The OFT investigated whether the WTB was attempting to restrict advertisng by accommodation letting agencies, by only promoting details of accommodation which had passed its scrutiny. As the WTB was found only to operate in the market for promoting tourism, not being in the business of letting property as principal or agent, the OFT rejected the complaint. It considered that the verification system did not operate as a barrier to entry into the accommodation letting market, in the absence of any market power by WTB. From this it can be concluded that if WTB had been supplying accommodation letting services, its verification system would have been subject to scrutiny had it operated as a barrier to entry to that market.

L. Customers, End-User Restrictions

11.206 Restrictions influencing the ultimate customer or end-user may arise in a wide variety of forms and circumstances. Indeed, there appears to be no consistent principles which apply so that every case must be treated on its merits. This section simply highlights some of the problems, it does not purport to be exhaustive.

1. EC Law

(1) Under Article 85 EC

11.207 Restrictions imposed on customers of end-users may often be restrictive since their objective is to limit competition between seller and buyer. The European Court has indicated that clauses in contracts of sale restricting the buyer's freedom to *use* goods supplied in accordance with his own economic interests infringes Article 85. Hence, a contract which imposes upon the buyer an obligation to use the goods supplied for his own needs, not to re-sell the goods in a specified area, and to consult the seller before soliciting business in another specified area infringes Article 85(1) EC.[243]

11.208 The Commission recognises that customer restrictions in distribution agreements may be perfectly acceptable. Regulations 1983/83/EEC and 1984/83/EEC on exclusive distribution and purchasing make clear, in their recitals that such agreements do not always fall within Article 85(1) but, if they do, they warrant exemption. In *Kathon Biocide*[244] the

[242] OFT Report dated 7 March 1991; see Kirkbride [1991] JBL 496.

[243] e.g. Case 319/82 *SCVB* v *Kerpen* [1985] 1 CMLR 511 [1983] ECR 4173, confirmed by the Commission in *Sperry New Holland* OJ 1985 L376/21 at para. 53. *Cementhandelaren* (Case 8/72) [1973] CMLR 7; [1972] ECR 977; *European Sugar Cartel (Sucker Unie)* (Cases 40–48, 50, 54– 56, 111, 113, 114/73) [1976] 1 CMLR 295; [1975] ECR 1663; *Bayo-n-Ox* OJ 1990 L21/71, [1990] 4 CMLR 930.

[244] See Commission Notice pursuant to Art. 19(3) of Reg. 17/62/EEC *Kathon Biocide* OJ 1984 C59, noted *Fourteenth Commission Competition Report* (1984), p. 66, para. 73. See also *Distillers-Victuallers* OJ 1980

Commission issued a comfort letter to market leaders in isothiazolone technology and development who reserved the right to require from buyers an undertaking that only a certain grade of Kathon biocide and no others be used in preparing cosmetic, toiletry and other human contact applications. These users restrictions were justified in the light of health requirements and the existing legislation in some Member States. However, there are dangers in undertakings taking it upon themselves to enforce safety standards using restrictions in contracts. In *Hilti*,[245] the Court of First Instance dismissed an argument that tying the supply of nail gun nail to nail gun cartridges was necessary for safety purposes. Although the argument was not ruled out in appropriate circumstances, there was no evidence here, such as complaints to the appropriate government department, that competitors' nails raised safety problems justifying tying.

11.209 Purchaser restrictions are justifiable, to a degree, in vertical distribution networks. Thus, a supplier may require an exclusive dealer to refrain from actively soliciting customers outside of his territory by direct advertising or the institution of warehousing facilities. Restrictions which go no further than this may claim block exemption under Regulation 1983/83/EEC on exclusive dealing contracts.[246] However, such exemption is unavailable if the supplier prohibits the dealer from accepting unsolicited orders made from outside of his territory. The Commission accepts that dealers may be restricted in their choice of customers to those within their territories. This concentrates the dealer's efforts and helps improve the efficiency of the distribution network. However, the Commission also demand that dealers must remain free to supply parallel importers who come to them from outside of their territory and who intend to take the goods back to another territory where they are priced more highly. The Commission has stated in an explanatory notice to the Regulation that clauses which impede the dealer in his free choice of customers are outside the scope of the block exemption,[247] purchaser restrictions as described above are to be distinguished from restrictions imposed by dealers on consumers. These restrictions, as noted above, will not be acceptable.

(2) Under Article 86 EC

11.210 An undertaking in a dominant position may have an obligation to supply all those customers who make orders. Where no alternative supplies exist refusal by the dominant supplier may put the buyer out of business. Refusal to supply a customer is an abuse of dominance if it is not objectively justified.[248] It will never be justified if the refusal to supply is designed to exclude the customer from the market.[249] Nor may a dominant supplier refuse supplies because the customer promotes a rival brand.[250] However, not every refusal to supply is unlawful. In times of crisis when supply of a product is in very short

cont.
L233/4 (4 September 1980) end-user restrictions given negative clearance because they did not appreciably effect inter-state trade.

245 Case T-30/89 *Hilti* [1991] ECR II-1439 [1992] 4 CMLR 16, paras. 115–119, upholding Commission Decision OJ 1988 L65/19, [1989] 4 CMLR 677; Court of First Instance decision upheld by Court of Justice in C-53/92 P, [1994] ECR I-667, [1994] 4 CMLR 614. See also *Bayo-n-Ox* [1994] 4 CMLR 930, paras. 41–43.

246 Art. 2(2)(c), OJ 1983 L173/1.

247 See Commission Explanatory Notice OJ 1983 C355/7, para. 17.

248 Case 77/77 *Benzine en Petroleum Handelsmaatschappij* v *Commission* [1978] 3 CMLR 174; [1978] ECR 1515; *Boat Equipment* Bull EC 1/80, para. 2118; *Polaroid/SSI Europe, Thirteenth Commission Competition Report* (1983), p. 95, paras. 155–157.

249 Cases 6, 7/73 *Commercial Solvents* [1974] 1 CMLR 309; [1974] ECR 223; *London European/Sabena* OJ 1988 L 317/47, [1989] 4 CMLR 662.

250 Case 27/76 *United Brands* v *Commission* [1978] 1 CMLR 429; [1978] ECR 207 at p. 298.

supply (e.g. supply of oil during the 1973 oil crisis when OPEC countries reduced supplies dramatically to the west)[251] it is not an abuse of dominance for suppliers to rank their customers in order or priority and supply them proportionately with the inevitable consequence that low priority customers receive no or reduced supplies.[252]

It is probably always abusive for a dominant supplier to refuse supplies unless the customer accepts restrictions on the territory in which the goods may be resold[253] or the usage to which the goods may be put.[254] Any collateral condition imposed upon an unwilling customer is likely to be an abuse.[255] In *Telemarketing*,[256] the Court of Justice held that refusal of access to a market ancillary to the market on which the undertaking was dominant could constitute an abuse of Article 86, a view adopted as well by the Court of Justice in *Magill TV Guide*.[257]

2. UK Law

(1) Under the RTPA 1976

11.211 Agreements between persons as to the customers they will or will not supply are registrable under sections 6(1)(f) (goods) and 11(2)(e) (services) as agreements containing restrictions on the classes of persons to whom goods or services will be supplied. Where such agreements aim to divide up a market between parties they will be inappropriate to section 21(2) treatment and will almost certainly be referred to the RPC. The Court has, in the past, taken a dim view of market sharing.[258]

11.212 In *Diazo Copying Materials*[259] the RPC held that a clause in a joint venture agreement which effectively limited one party in its capacity to supply customers was not registrable. Under the agreement HTL manufactured photocopiers to the order of MSL. MSL had an exclusive right to sell the product throughout the world but granted to HTL a non-exclusive non-assignable right to make retail sales in the UK. By this means HTL and MSL imposed restrictions on HTL's ability to seek customers outside of the UK. However, the RPC held that the restrictive term was one which related exclusively to the goods supplied so was therefore to be disregarded under section 9(3) when determining the application of the RTPA 1976. Thus, if joint venture partners wish to impose area or customer restric-

[251] As occurred in Case 77/77 *Benzine en Petroleum Handelsmaatschappij* v *Commission* [1978] 3 CMLR 174; [1978] ECR 1513.

[252] In the *Benzine* case *ibid.* BP rationed fuel amongst its customers giving priority to regular contractual customers, secondly to regular non-contractual customers, and lastly to periodic non-contractual customers. ABG a Dutch joint purchasing co-operative fell into the last category of customer and was accordingly refused supplies of its normal requirements. The European Court, overturning the Commission's decision (for which see [1977] 2 CMLR D1, *Third Commission Competition Report* (1973), pp. 23–25, *Fourth Commission Competition Report* (1974), pp. 17–19), decided that the system set up by BP was justifiable and not an abuse of dominance.

[253] e.g. *Hugins/Liptons* [1978] 1 CMLR D19 overturned on appeal to the European Court for lack of an appreciable effect upon inter-state trade (see Case 22/78 [1979] 3 CMLR 345; [1979] ECR 1869).

[254] Cases 40–48, 50, 54–56, 111, 113, 114/73 *European Sugar Cartel (Suker Unie)* [1976] 1 CMLR 295; [1975] ECR 1663 at p. 2004. (Supplier sold denatured sugar as fodder for animals only and not for consumption by humans.)

[255] Case 27/76 *United Brands* v *Commission* [1978] 1 CMLR 429; [1978] ECR 207 at p. 295.

[256] *Telemarketing* [1985] ECR 3261, [1986] 2 CMLR 558.

[257] Case C-241/91 *RTE & ITP* v *Commission* [1995] ECR I-743.

[258] e.g. *Doncaster and Retford Co-operative Societies Agreement* (1960) LR 2 RP 105. See also No. 2385 Register of Restrictive Trade Practices, *Agreements of the Sunday Newspapers Proprietors No. 2* (RPC 1972). The RPC held to contravene the public interest restrictions in an agreement whereby newspaper proprietors agreed to regulate jointly the wholesalers and retailers they would supply to. Many potential customers (wholesalers and retailers) were refused supplies in accordance with the agreement.

[259] [1984] ICR 429.

tions, *inter se*, it would appear that if they grant one party an exclusive selling right of the joint venture product or service and then that party grant the other a licence to sell restricted as to area, then the agreement is not registrable provided it contains no other registrable restrictions. Many practitioners have doubted whether this ruling is strictly correct. If in doubt a fail-safe furnishing is advisable.

11.213 The OFT scrutinises customer and end-user restrictions carefully. In exceptional cases they will be suitable for section 21(2) treatment. Thus, in *General Council of British Shipping* (GCBS),[260] the GCBS made recommendations to members concerning the carriage of disabled passengers. These recommendations were designed to encourage the adoption of practices and procedures which would enable members to provide for the needs of disabled passengers more effectively. There are very few competition issues here, the market for disabled passengers being small relative to other categories of passenger who do not have special needs. Moreover, the recommendations were clearly in the public interest. In *Independent Marketing Services*[261] the OFT objected to joint-buying consisting of wholesalers in the grocery field who imposed restrictions on participating companies in respect of the supply of goods to members of the public. Similarly in *Chart Information Network Ltd* a restriction on recorded music retailers supplying sales information to competitors of Chart Information Network for the purpose of compiling charts was removed from an agreement with the British Association of Record Dealers in order to avoid a reference to the Restrictive Practices Court.[262] The OFT gave section 21(2) dispensation only after the Group altered its rules to free participating companies to supply whomsoever they pleased. In *Access Consortium*[263] Lloyds Bank, Midland Bank, National Westminster Bank and Williams and Glyn's Bank, agreed that in view of limitations on the processing capacity of the Joint Credit Card Company Ltd which produced bank cards, the number of cards issued by each bank should be limited to an agreed number and that each party would recruit customers only from those holding an existing account with that party. In practice, the operational restraint arising from the Joint Credit Card Company's lack of production capacity did not prevent any party issuing the number of cards it wished nor was there any deterrent effect upon recruitment. The agreement expired by effluxion of time and was formally terminated in 1980. Since the agreement had no restrictive effect in practice and was in any event terminated there would have been no need for further official action. However, it must be very doubtful whether an agreement between oligopolistic competitors to share supplies and limit sales during a period of shortages in supply would ever be suitable for section 21(2) treatment. In the EC context co-operation agreements in crisis times have been condemned by the European Court as illegal market sharing devices.[264]

(2) Under the Competition Act 1980

11.214 The OFT and MMC have concluded that an economically powerful supplier who refused to admit certain categories of customer/dealer to their distribution networks on the basis that the customer/dealer employs new and inventive selling methods that the supplier objects to, may be acting anti-competitively if, in other respects, the customer/dealer meets the supplier's criteria as to qualifications, adequacy of premises and staff, etc.[265] The MMC has said that suppliers must not use selective distribution criteria

[260] No. S. 1179 Register of Restrictive Trade Practices.
[261] No. 3755 Register of Restrictive Trade Practices (1976).
[262] OFT Press Release dated 6 June 1995, [1995] ECLR R-162.
[263] No. S. 256 Register of Restrictive Trade Practices (1976).
[264] See e.g. Cases 29, 30/83 *CRAM* v *Commission* [1984] ECR 1679, [1985] 1 CMLR 688.
[265] See e.g. *Raleigh* (February 1981) OFT Investigation, for MMC Report see HC 67 (1981–82).

to hinder new and innovative dealers obtaining the supplier's brand of goods. In particular, the MMC has considered such customer/dealers as discounts warehouses and multifunction department stores.

M. Tying Clauses[266]

1. *Legal and Economic Framework*

(1) Nature of tying: examples[267]

11.215 Tying occurs where a supplier requires customers to acquire, as a condition of acquiring a main product (the typing product), another product (the tied product) or at least where the supplier conditions sale of the main product to agreement by the buyer that he will not purchase the tied product from any other supplier. Tying can also occur where a supplier encourages customers to acquire a tied product because of some pricing advantage or discount offered. The following are example cases:

Example (a)

11.216 Supplier enjoys a monopoly over widgets. He refuses to sell widgets unless customers also take gidgets from him (two goods tied together).

Example (b)

11.217 Supplier sells widgets and requires purchasers to accept a maintenance/guarantee contract for the servicing of the widget (goods and services tied together).

Example (c)

11.218 Supplier sells widgets at a price which includes provision of maintenance services by supplier. If customer does not want maintenance services the overall price does not change.

Example (d)

11.219 Supplier sells widgets at £X. However, if purchaser also takes gidgets from the supplier at full price then the price of the widgets reduces to £X/2. In this example purchasing both widgets and gidgets operates to effectively tie the products together.

Example (e)

11.220 Supplier sells widgets at £X which includes a built in amount for provision of maintenance services. If customer does not wish maintenance/guarantee services, then the price for the widget is reduced but not by an amount commensurate to the value of the service. Where the price of goods and services combined amounts to £100, good alone to £95, and where the value of the services is £25, then there is a financial incentive on the customer to accept the services. If he rejects the services he still effectively pays for them.

[266] D. Waelbroeck, "The compatibility of tying agreements with antitrust rules: a comparative study of American and European rules" (1987) 7 YEL 39.

[267] See generally, MMC *General Report into Full-Line Forcing and Tie-In Sales* HC 212 (1981); Posner, *Antritrust Law: An Economic Perspective* (1976), pp. 171–184; Scherer and Ross, *Industrial Market Structure and Economic Performance* (3rd edn. 1990), pp. 565–568.

11.221 Complaints are sometimes made by customers of tie-ins which appear unfair to the customer but in reality are natural consequences of the market. Thus, a customer or user of equipment may consider that he is force to accept the servicing facilities of the supplier because there is no alternative in the relevant area of because no competitive servicing facilities have yet emerged to challenge the supplier. These situations do not reflect tying. Though, if the supplier is dominant in the area, then any attempt to charge excessive or discriminatory prices may be challengeable. Alternatively, if the supplier sought to prevent or hinder the entry of new firms to the market for servicing the equipment, e.g. by refusing to make spare parts available, or refusing to license competitors to make spare parts, or refusing to make available servicing and maintenance manuals, then these might represent anti-competitive or abusive practices.

(2) Objections to and justifications for tying

11.222 Suppliers may use tying clauses for a number of reasons:

11.223 (a) Supplier exploits monopoly over widgets and extends it into market for gidgets over which he enjoys no market power. Thus, a manufacturer of a novel type of supercomputer ties sales of the computer to sales of memory thereby extending monopoly power over the company to memory capacity. The supplier, by this practice, may seek to increase his profits. More likely, the intention is to create entry barriers in the market for the tied product.[268]

11.224 (b) Supplier charges different consumers different prices for widgets over which the supplier is dominant on the basis of the intensity of their use of gidgets. For example, the supplier of punchcard machinery and related cards may charge a uniform price to all buyers both for machines and for punchcards. However, by tying punchcard to sale or hire of the machine and by overpricing such cards he is able effectively to charge a higher price for the machine to those purchasers who use it most intensively, i.e. use most punchcards. The objection to this practice is that it is effectively a form of price discrimination.

11.225 (c) Supplier seeks to ensure the standard of performance of product A thereby protecting his reputation and customer goodwill by requiring that product A only be taken in connection with product or service B. Thus, if the supplier of a new type of photocopier required purchasers to also acquire a new formula of ink and/or a maintenance contract with the supplier then this might be explained by the supplier's desire to protect the integrity of the photocopier. Where the supplier uses this as an excuse to erect entry barriers to rival suppliers of ink or maintenance services it may be anti-competitive.[269]

11.226 (d) Supplier supplies product or service A more cheaply if purchaser also takes product or service B where the price reduction relates to economies of scale realised by the supplier. Thus, if a supplier sells bulk storage and handling machinery at a lower

[268] See Scherer *op. cit.* at pp. 565–566: "Suppose, for instance that one copying machine user makes 3,000 copies per month, while another makes 20,000 copies per month. It would be difficult for a company selling only copying machines to price its machines in such a way as to extract more revenue from the more intensive user. But if the machine maker can tie the purchase of special supplies to the purchase of its machine, and if it can price the supplies such as ink (toner) to realise a supra normal profit margin on them, it will be able to extract additional profits from the high volume users."

[269] See also the US Supreme Court's decision in *Eastman Kodak* v *Image Technical Services* 112 S.Ct 2072 (1992), in which the Court rejected an argument that tying-in of maintenance services to the supply of copying machines could not as a matter of law be caught under the Sherman Act without proof of market power in the tying product market. See paras. 13.102–13.103.

than normal price where the customer also purchases chemicals or fertilisers, etc. from him, then the reduced price (which creates an economic tie through the incentive it presents) may be justified by virtue of scale economies in transport of bulky products.

11.227 (e) Supplier may use tying as a means of penetrating a new market. It may be argued that a "pro-competitive use of tying is to redistribute risk. For example, a manufacturer may induce distributors to carry a new product by selling it to them at a low price, while relying on expected sales of some item used in conjunction with the new product to generate his profits. The manufacturer, thus, assumes a greater share of the risk that the new product will be rejected by consumers. If the new product proves very popular, the distributors will require many of the related items, and the manufacturer will receive a large reward. If the new product does not succeed, however, the distributors will require very few of the related items and will have to pay very little. The 'risk sharing' efficiency may apply to a wide range of licensing, franchising, and similar distributional arrangements that involve tying."[270]

2. *EC Law*

(1) Under Article 85 EC

11.228 The practice of tying is referred to as being prohibited under Article 85(1)(e). The Commission, however, has specifically mentioned full line forcing as permissible in the block exemptions on exclusive dealing and purchasing. Hence, suppliers may require exclusive dealers or purchasers to take "complete range of goods". Though in respect of exclusive purchasing agreements, the block exemption only applies where the obligation to take complete ranges of goods relates to goods which are connected to each other by their nature or according to commercial usage.[271] Tying is viewed less favourably however in the context of patent and know-how licences.[272] Full line forcing clauses are also common in franchise agreements where the franchisee is required to purchase a full range of the franchisor's goods.

11.229 Collective tying will violate Article 85(1) and almost certainly be unsuitable for exemption under Article 85(3).[273] Thus, if a trade association recommended to members that they include the price of maintenance and post-sales services in the cost of a machine then this would infringe Article 85(1). Trade associations who perform cost-calculation modelling for members should ensure that in the models and formulae they disseminate they have not artificially tied the costings for different products together.

(2) Under Article 86 EC

11.230 Tying is prohibited by Article 86(d). It appears to be the case that tying by a dominant concern will be almost invariably an abuse of dominance.[274] According to Article 86(d)

[270] See US Department of Justice, Vertical Restraint Guidelines (25 January 1985), at para. 5.1 now withdrawn.

[271] Art. 2(3)(a), Reg. 1983/83/EEC on block exemption for exclusive dealing OJ 1983 L173/1; and Art. 2(3)(a), and 3(c), Reg. 1984/83/EEC on block exemption for exclusive purchasing OJ 1983 L173/5.

[272] See Arts. 2(1)(5) and 4(2)(a) Reg. 240/96. See for analysis paras. 13.18–13.124.

[273] See Commission answer to WQ 1865/83, OJ 1984 C152/12 and 13.

[274] Case 85/76 *Hoffman-La Roche* v *Commission* [1979] 3 CMLR 211; [1979] ECR 461 a para. 111 of judgment; see *IBM Settlement* [1984] 3 CMLR 147; *GEMA I* [1971] CMLR D35. (customers of GEMA, a copyright Society had to pay a royalty fee for uncopyrighted material as well as copyrighted material; this was an abusive extension or power over copyrighted material to unprotected material); *Re. Hilti AG* [1985] 3 CMLR 619.

tying is only an abuse where the tied product or service has no connection with the subject to the contract in terms of its nature and/or commercial usage. Thus, if there is an objectively justifiable relationship between tying and tied products no abuse occurs. The subjective views of the supplier or customer are not decisive on this point. The relationship may be based upon technical or other economically justifiable grounds.

11.231 The Commission apparently does not look too sympathetically upon the technical justification defence especially where a technical relationship between two products can be sustained by a less extreme commercial measure than typing. In *Hilti*[275] the Commission issued a decision condemning tying practices entered into by Hilti, which enjoyed a mixture of patent and copyright protection over cartridge magazines for powder actuated tools (sometimes known as nail guns, they are used in the construction industry to make a wide variety of fixings in various materials). Hilti also enjoyed a dominant position in the market for powder actuated tools, nails for the tools and cartridge magazines. Following complaints by two UK manufacturers of nails for use in powder actuated tools, the Commission intervened to prevent Hilti from tying the supply of nails to that of cartridge magazines. Hilti argued that the tie was necessary for safety reasons. The Commission rejected this as a valid justification for a tie but, as part of an undertaking given by Hilti allowed Hilti to include a legal disclaimer in respect of the safety in the use of its products. The disclaimer read:

> "These cartridges are designed for use in a Hilti tool for the particular purposes recommended by Hilti and for use with direct fastening nails fit for the purpose. The cartridges must not be used for purposes other than those recommended by Hilti nor with direct fastening nails which are not fit for the purposes. Hilti decline all responsibility for loss, damage or injury which might arise through the use of cartridges in guns not manufactured by Hilti or for purposes other than those for which they are recommended by Hilti or with nails which are not fit for the purpose."

11.232 The relevance of this disclaimer is that it indicates the Commission's view that notices, warnings and disclaimers, etc., are preferable alternatives to enforced tying, i.e. a seller can exhort buyers in health/safety/technical ground to purchase a related product but should not force buyers to take the related product. This is not to say that cases of justifiable tying may not still arise. It is pertinent to note further that Hilti undertook: (i) not to discriminate, *inter alia*, by granting special, or withholding normal, discounts against orders for magazines alone as compared with orders for magazines *and* nails; (ii) not to persuade or deceive buyers into believing that purchase of nails was a condition of buying magazines. The Commission's ruling was upheld on appeal by the Court of First Instance.[276] The Court stressed that safety considerations could not have justified tying as that was a disproportionate response to the safety threat. It rejected Hilti's claim that safety considerations had motivated its tying, since there was no evidence that Hilti had taken other steps, such as referring the problem to regulatory authorities, to deal with these alleged safety problems.

11.233 Simply because tying and tied products are technically related, or even interdependent, does not necessarily justify a tie. In *IBM Settlement*[277] IBM, *inter alia*, tied the sale of main memory capacity to that of central processing units (CPUs). Following negotiations, IBM gave the following undertaking to the Commission: "Without prejudice to

275 OJ 1988 L65/19, [1989] 4 CMLR 677.

276 Case T-30/89 *Hilti* [1991] ECR II-1493 [1992] 4 CMLR 16, paras. 115–119; the Court of First Instance decision was subsequently upheld by the Court of Justice in C-53/92 P [1994] ECR I-667, [1994] 4 CMLR 614.

277 Case 60/81 [1984] 3 CMLR 147, see also *IBM* v *Commission* [1981] ECR 2639 at p. 2642.

IBM's freedom to design its CPUs upon announcement of a new System/370 CPU which is to be supplied within the EEC, IBM will offer within the EEC and, upon applications of a customer, will supply that CPU at IBM's option either without any main memory capacity or with only such capacity of main memory as is strictly required in order that reasonable tests of the CPU can be affected." The "unbundling" of memory from CPUs required actual physical changes to the CPUs which hitherto had memory capacity built in to them. However, given that IBM were alleged to control over 70 per cent of the world market for mainframe computers the effect of the bundling was to erect entry barriers to rival producers of memory capacity that is compatible with IBM computers.

3. UK Law

(1) Under the RTPA 1976

11.234 Collective attempts at tying are registrable under sections 6(1)(c) (goods) and 11(2)(b) (services) (i.e. conditions on which goods/services are supplied). Recommendations by trade or service supply associations to members to employ tying terms are likewise registrable. It is most unlikely that collective tying would be suitable for section 21(2) treatment. This at least was the position adopted by the OFT in *Building Societies Association (BSA)*.[278] Under section 101(1) of the Law of Property Act 1925, mortgagees have the power to insure and keep insured against loss or damage by fire any buildings, etc., forming part of the mortgaged property. Building societies hence provided for insurance in their rules which were binding on borrowers. The BSA had, until 1975, recommended to members that insurance be organised by societies through insurers of their choice. The societies thus tied financial services to insurance services. Borrowers were not allowed to arrange own-insurance. Societies would earn commission on introductions to insurers which they did not pass on to borrowers. Following the receipt of complaints from members of the public in respect of these practices, the OFT informed the BSA that the restrictions were significant and inappropriate to sections 21(2) dispensation. The BSA decided to amend their rules so that in 1975 borrowers would be given the choice of three insurance companies plus the option to nominate companies of their own choosing. The would remain free to reject the nomination where they were *un*convinced that: the scope and amount of the cover was equivalent to the societies normal cover; the service was likely to be satisfactory; and that the insurer would keep the society covered should the borrower fail to pay a premium. Moreover, the Society could demand that the policy not be altered without prior notification to the Society.[279] Subsequently, the OFT expressed their concern to the BSA that some societies insisted, as a condition of granting a mortgage, that they should receive some, or all, of the commission payable in respect of linked endowment policies. The OFT indicated that this practice was hard to justify in cases where the society had not arranged the policy. The BSA, in response, recommended that societies stop commission sharing where the borrower arranged his own insurance.[280] As a result of

[278] No. S. 15 Register of Restrictive Trade Practices (1984); See also DGFT Annual Report (1976) at pp. 87, 88, and MMC *General Report into Full Line Forcing and Tie-In Sales* HC 212 (1981) at pp. 27–29, paras. 9.1–9.13. See the view of the European Commission on this case, answer to WQ No. 1965/83, OJ 1984 C 152/12. See also DGFT Annual Report 1982, p. 192. Halifax Building Society agreed that it would no longer insist on its borrowers taking out property insurance through the Society.

[279] No. S. 15 Register of Restrictive Trade Practices (1984); see Circular 1940 and see also Document V.4 dated 7 December 1978 Circular 2233.

[280] *ibid*. Document V.9 dated 19 August 1976 Circular 2038 at paras. 10. The circular stated: "It is often contended that the sharing of endowment commission is justified because building society funds not only make the mortgage possible but also make the sale of the endowment policy possible, that being the real justification for entering the commission sharing arrangement with the broker. Where a broker

these modifications to existing rules and practices, the BSA rules were not referred to the RPC and, ultimately, were given exemption under section 21(2) RTPA 1976.[281] Matters relating to insurance are now dealt with by regulatory bodies set up under the Financial Services Act 1986.[282]

11.235 A form of voluntary tying has been accepted by the RPC. In *Building Employers' Confederation Application*[283] the RPC accepted as being in the public interest, an association scheme whereby members had to offer building services with an insurance scheme to customers, there being, however, no requirement that customers take both service and insurance. The association was seeking to protect purchasers of building and construction services from "cowboy builders". If customers accepted insurance they paid 1 per cent of the contract price or a minimum of £20. The RPC accepted that the scheme was in the public interest and that the restriction—members must not undertake work unless the insurance scheme had been first offered to customers—did not restrict or discourage competition to any material degree. Thus, customers could buy services and insurance together though they had the option of buying the two services separately. There was no price regime whereby the cost of insurance was included in that for the building work, thereby creating an incentive for purchasers of building services to also take insurance; buyer could choose between building work alone at a cheaper price or building work plus insurance at a higher price with the difference accurately accounted for by the cost of the insurance. A scheme such as this whereby services sold only have been sold tied to insurance would probably not have been accepted.

(2) Under the Competition Act 1980

11.236 The OFT has investigated a number of instances of tying under the CA 1980. In *British Telecommunications (Pricing Policy for the Placing of Advertisements in Yellow Pages directories)*.[284] British Telecommunications (BT) sold advertising space in Yellow Pages directories (YP) through specially appointed sales contractors. It charged a price for space which included an element for creation and campaign planning services. Advertising agents complained to the OFT of this tying of space to advertising services: "The advertising agencies' case is

cont.
has already arranged an acceptable policy for an applicant independent of and prior to the mortgage application, the Society should not normally expect a share of the commission."

281 The public interest arguments in respect of the retention of insurance agency (that would have been relevant had the OFT referred the case to the RPC) appear to have been: *For*: (i) continuity and adequacy of cover is assured and the method of payment is convenient for the mortgagor; (ii) the coverage of risk is good and the societies bargaining power has enabled them to negotiate improvements from time to time without increasing premiums; (iii) usually the settlement of claims can be handled expeditiously by local offices of a society and insurance companies who know the standard policies; (iv) administrative scale economies because of block handling of policies may be realised which, along with profits from commission, benefit members of the society. *Against*: (i) independent brokers have special skills and act independently in the best interests of their clients and can therefore give attention to the characteristics of individual properties and to local conditions; (ii) insurance of *some* properties can be better and more cheaply covered by individual treatment; (iii) a borrower should be free to limit the insurance arranged via the agency of a society to the amount of the loan outstanding, insuring the balance of the value of the property where he can obtain the best terms (rather than have to insure to the full replacement value of the property). See MMC General Report, *op. cit.*, at para. 9.11.

282 See paras. 2.133-2.138.

283 [1985] ICR 167. See No. 4620 Register of Restrictive Trade Practices, *Mail Order Association Code of Practice* (1979) Clause 13 of Code; ban on tying of cost of free gifts into cost of main item.

284 10 October 1984. During 1984 the OFT investigated the practice of some landlords in requiring lessees to accept insurers nominated by them, or even in forcing sitting tenants to change to insurers nominated by the landlord. The landlords earned commission in introductions to insurers. See Commission answer to WQ 1865/83, OJ 1984 C 152/12. See also *Austin Rover Corrosion Warranty* DGFT Annual Report 1984, pp. 107, 108. See cases referred to at para 3.29 under the Competition Act 1980.

that BT's sales contractors are placed at an advantage over others who could provide advertising agency services to larger advertisers in that such advertisers which choose to use an alternative provider of such services still have to pay for the agency services offered by the sales contractors because they are included in the rate card price. They argue that there is therefore a financial penalty incurred by all advertisers who wish to exercise choice, and that the presence of this penalty distorts competition in the provision of services to the advertiser between the sales contractor and any others who could provide such services."[285] The OFT concluded that the tie was not anti-competitive being too insignificant in economic terms to have a detrimental effect. It estimated that the cost of BT contractors providing the services in question was less than 4.5 per cent of the total cost of advertising in YP directories. Accordingly, it did not consider that this "small amount" would play any part in advertiser's choice between using an advertising agency to provide services or using its own resources to deal with BT and its contractors. The case demonstrates that for tying to be anti-competitive the supplier of the product or service must significantly affect the market for the tied product or service. In this case, the OFT concluded that advertising agencies were not hindered by the effect of the tie-in on the market for the provision of advertising services.[286]

11.237 The MMC, in monopoly references, has been highly critical of tying practices.[287] However, in its *General Report into Full Line Forcing and Tie-In Sales*[288] it recognised that tying may be more ambiguous in its economic effects and that there can be pro as well as anti-competitive consequences from the practices. In that Report the MMC laid down a number of guidelines that it considered should be used when deciding whether or not to proceed against tying and full-line forcing:[289]

(a) Does the supplier enjoy market power in the supply of the tying good or service? Where there is little market power because, for example, there are alternative goods/services or alternative suppliers available, then the likelihood of tying being anti-competitive is greatly reduced.
(b) What is the structure of the market for the tied product and to what extent is that structure fixed or changing? If there are many supplies of the tied product or service, then customers may be loathe to accept a tie from the main supplier. More importantly, if the tie-in forecloses only a small percentage of the market the effect on competition will be insignificant. This was essentially the case in the *British Telecommunications* case described above.
(c) Where tying indicates simply the attempt by a dominant supplier to stretch his market power into another market then the practice will almost invariably be anti-competitive.

285 *ibid.*, at p. 47, para. 7.10.
286 *ibid.*, at pp. 47–50, paras. 7.11–7.16. The MMC also seem to have adopted a *de minimis* approach on occasion; see the Report on *Supply of Electrical Equipment for Mechanically Propelled Land Vehicles* (1983) HC 21. MMC did not condemn a very informal form of full-line forcing whereby the supplier would negotiate with the buyer on the basis that discounts attached to purchases of ranges of products rather than single products. The tie was very loose and was not apparently considered to have exerted a more than minimal effect (see *ibid.* at para. 998).
287 e.g. MMC Report on the *Supply and Processing of Colour Film* (1966) HC 1. Practice of supplying film on a processing prepaid basis was condemned. The tying of the film to the processing service erected considerable entry barriers to rival providers of processing services; MMC Report on the *Supply of Barristers' Services* HC 512 (1975), Practice whereby a Queens Counsel could not appear without a junior was criticised by the MMC; MMC *Report into Supply of Films for Exhibition in Cinemas* (1966) HC 206. MMC critical of the tying of support films to main feature films.
288 (1981) HC 212.
289 *ibid.*, at pp. 44, 45, para. 13.33.

(d) Is the tying practice operating within the context of exclusive dealing? The anti-competitive effect is likely to be exacerbated where purchasers are contractually prevented from obtaining supplies from elsewhere.[290]

(e) Is there a strong technical justification for the tie as in the case of tying spare parts or maintenance to a main product as a means of protecting both the suppliers reputation and the products integrity? In such cases tying may be justified.

(3) Under the Patents Act 1977

11.238 Certain tying clauses in patent licences are void under the Patents Act 1977. For details see paras. 13.348–13.350.

[290] MMC Report on the *Supply of Petrol to Retailers* in the UK (1965) HC 264.

12 Joint Ventures and Co-operation Agreements

A. Introduction

12.1 In this chapter the following is examined:

Section B.	Legal framework, co-operative and concentrative joint ventures.
Section C.	Joint selling ventures.
Section D.	Joint purchasing.
Section E.	Joint research and development.
Section F.	Specialisation.
Section G.	Rationalisation agreements.
Section H.	Products standardisation.
Section I.	Joint carriage ventures.

B. Legal Framework

12.2 Competition law, of necessity, adopts a pragmatic view of joint ventures. Some are beneficial, others are detrimental to the market. Joint ventures are essentially structural devices to support some other form of activity by parties. Hence each case must be assessed on its merits and these will vary according to the type of co-operation in question. Pragmatism at EC level has become somewhat tempered by a more formalistic approach to joint ventures following the introduction of the new merger control regime.

1. *EC Law*[1]

(1) Joint ventures and merger control

12.3 The fundamental question in deciding how to approach a joint venture from an EC point of view is to determine whether it is to be dealt with under the Merger Control Regulation (MCR)[2] or under Article 85. "Concentrative" joint ventures are dealt with under the MCR whereas "co-operative" joint ventures fall outside the scope of the MCR and are therefore governed by the general provisions of Article 85. Although the Commission has issued a Notice regarding concentrative and co-operative operations for the purposes of the MCR[3] (the "Interface Notice"), it is still easier to state the distinction than it is to explain it.

12.4 The principle behind making the distinction is that of the difference between changes in market structure and in market behaviour. Some joint ventures affect market structure, being equivalent to a merger where the original parties are replaced on the market by the new entity, the joint venture which fulfils all the functions of an autonomous economic entity,[4] and that therefore these ought to be treated as if they were mergers i.e. concentrative. The remaining type of joint ventures are those where the parties remain present on a market or have the capacity to re-enter the market. In such cases, the underlying structure of the market remains the same, though the behaviour of the original parties on the market is altered by the existence of the joint venture.

12.5 The practical implications of the distinction are both substantive and procedural. Substantively, the test for compatibility with the MCR is easier to pass than that under Article 85. Whereas an agreement having only potential to prevent, restrict or distort competition can be caught under Article 85(1), thus requiring exemption, a concentration is only caught by the MCR if it "creates or strengthens a dominant position as a result of which effective competition would be significantly impeded in the common market or in a substantial part of it".[5] The requirements of proof of creation or strengthening of a dominant position and of causation of significant impediments to competition create a much higher threshold for the Commission to overcome before being able to intervene in a concentrative joint venture.

12.6 Procedurally, the MCR offers considerable advantages to notifying parties when compared to those under the older procedures set out in Regulation 17/62. Broadly, the Com-

[1] See generally, F.L. Fine, *Mergers and Joint Ventures in Europe: The Law and Policy of the EEC* (2nd edn, 1994); see also Ritter and Overbury, "An attempt at a practical approach to joint ventures under the EC rules on competition" (1977) CMLRev 601; John Temple Lang, "Joint ventures under EC rules on competition: part I" (1977) *Irish Jurist* 15; John Temple Lang, *EC Competition Policies: A Status Report, in Enterprise Law of the 80s* (Rowe, Jacobs and Joelson, eds.) (1980), pp. 22–26; Verstrynge, "Problèmes relatifs aux filiales communes" (1979) *Cahiers de Droit Europeéen* 13. Brodley, "Joint ventures and antitrust policy" (1982) 95 *Harvard Law Rev.* 1523; Faull, "Joint ventures under the EC competition rules" (1984) ECLR 358; Reynolds, "Extra-territorial aspects of mergers and joint ventures: the EC position" (1985) ECLR 165. V. Korah, "Critical comments on the Commission's recent decisions exempting joint ventures to exploit research that needs further development" (1987) 12 ELRev 18; B. Hawk, "Joint ventures under EC law" [1991] *Fordham Corp L Inst* 557; A.S. Pathak, "The EC Commission's approach to joint ventures: a policy of contradictions" [1991] ECLR 171; F.L. Fine, "EEC anti-trust aspects of production joint ventures" [1992] ECLR 206.

[2] Council Reg. 4064/89 on the control of concentrations between undertakings 1989 OJ L395/1 (corrected text published at 1990 OJ L257/14).

[3] Commission Notice on the distinction between concentrative and co-operative joint ventures under Council Reg. (EEC) No. 4064/89 of 21 December 1989 on the control of concentrations between undertakings, OJ 1994 C385/1; this replaced an earlier notice published at OJ 1990 C203/10. This is referred to as the "Interface Notice".

[4] Art. 3(2), MCR.

[5] Art. 2(3), MCR.

mission must deal with a notified joint venture under the MCR in one month, to decide whether it raises serious doubts as to its compatibility with the common market.[6] If there are serious doubts, the Commission has a further four months within which to investigate before reaching a final decision,[7] but if not the joint venture is cleared. If the joint venture is declared compatible after the full Commission investigation, it is then cleared. These procedures are much quicker than the period taken by the Commission in considering a request for clearance or exemption under Regulation 17/62, where an investigation may continue for many months if not years. Moreover, clearance under the MCR is a one-off decision. There is no limited period of clearance, whereas if an exemption is granted to a co-operative joint venture, it must be limited in duration, thus necessitating the renewal of the application as the period of the exemption comes up for expiry. Ironically, one would have thought that this substantive and procedural imbalance in favour of concentrative joint ventures should, if anything, be weighted in the opposite direction. co-operative joint ventures would in principle seem more benign, not involving any alteration in the structure of a market. The ideal solution would be for no regulatory imbalance to exist. The same level of regulation should apply, lest regulation become in itself a distortion of competition.

12.7 There has been an attempt to redress this regulatory imbalance on the procedural side. The then Competition Commissioner Sir Leon Brittan announced in December 1992[8] that as from the beginning of 1993 "structural" co-operative joint ventures would[9] receive an initial assessment of their compatibility with Article 85 within 2 months of complete notification (as compared with one month under the MCR). If compatible, a comfort letter is issued. If potentially incompatible, then a warning letter is sent and further investigation is carried out under a timetable announced in advance (as compared with a further four months under the MCR). As can be seen, even this does not completely correct the imbalance on the procedural side and it does not affect the substantive issues.

12.8 The Commission has attempted to clarify the substance of the approach to joint ventures under Article 85, if not to redress any imbalance with the MCR, by issuing a Notice explaining the way in which joint ventures are assessed under Article 85[10] (the "CJV Notice"). This is essentially only a restatement of Commission practice which dates, at least in its present form, from the 1983 announcement of the "realistic" approach[11] to analysing potential competition between parties to a joint venture. However, the CJV Notice makes no concession to those who have argued that the assessment of co-operative joint ventures should be dealt with on the same substantive test as concentrative joint ventures.

6 Arts. 6 and 10(1). MCR.

7 Arts. 8 and 10(2). MCR.

8 Commission Press Release IP (92) 1009, [1993] ECLR R-11. Details are given in the Commission's *Twenty-second Report on Competition Policy* (1992), para. 122–124. See also the Commission's *Twenty-third Report on Competition Policy* (1993), paras. 192–197 and 214–217, and *Twenty-fourth Report on Competition Policy* (1994), para. 114.

9 The concept of a structural cooperative joint venture is explained in the revised Form A/B annexed to Reg. 3385/94, OJ 1994 L377/28, as being "one that involves an important change in the structure and organisation of the business assets to the agreement. This may occur because the joint venture takes over or extends existing activities of the parent companies or because it undertakes new activities on their behalf. Such operations are characterised by the commitment of significant financial, material and/or non-tangible assets such as intellectual property rights and know-how. Structural joint ventures are therefore normally intended to operate on a medium-or long-term basis."

10 Commission Notice concerning the assessment of co-operative joint ventures pursuant to Art. 85 of the EEC Treaty OJ 1993 C43/2 (The "CJV Notice").

11 *Thirteenth Report on Competition Policy* (1983), paras. 53–55.

12.9 Unless otherwise stated, throughout this book references to joint ventures are to co-operative joint ventures. This chapter is concerned primarily with those joint ventures which fall under Article 85. It will be noted where a joint venture can or will be dealt with under the MCR (often it will be a matter of choice for the parties), but the wider issues of the MCR, other than those applying specifically to joint ventures are not covered in this work.[12]

(2) Structural and contractual considerations

12.10 Joint ventures affect the structure of a market: Five firms control between them 80 per cent of the market, two of these firms, X and Y, control 23 per cent and 28 per cent respectively X and Y form a joint venture company, XY Ltd. To produce and sell the relevant product, they agree not to individually compete with the joint venture company. The market structure has now changed. Four firms control 80 per cent of the market and one of these firms, XY Ltd, controls 51 per cent which may well be enough to turn it into the market leader. It follows from the fact that joint ventures are evaluated by reference to their economic effect and their legal form, that restrictions on competition may arise not only from express contractual provision but also from the mere existence of the joint venture and of the economic inter-relationship of the parents and parties. Indeed there is a growing tendency (especially in the EC where the structure of the relevant legislation lends itself to effects based analysis) to consider that the economic impact of a venture is more important in the appraisal of an agreement than its contractual or organisational form. Though this tendency is checked somewhat by the existence of block exemptions which adopt a formalistic structure of analysis, i.e. they premise legal conclusions upon the existence or omission of certain clause types.

(3) Economic consequences

12.11 Joint ventures may have consequences which bring them within the scope of Article 85(1) EC. These consequences are particularly acute where the parents are either competitors or have the potential to be competitors. This is further accentuated in the case of co-operation between networks of joint ventures.[13] The CJV Notice spells out some of these consequences. Others are evident from the case law.

12.12 (a) Joint ventures which sell the parent companies' products or services to third parties inevitably distort competition between the parents. Even where the parents retain some selling freedom and the joint venture sells only a percentage of their goods or services, competition between the parents is distorted. In such cases there is a natural tendency for the parents to harmonise their prices and terms and conditions with those of the joint venture since to do otherwise could undermine the viability of the joint venture which may be against the commercial best interests of the parent companies.[14]

12.13 (b) Where the joint venture provides goods or services to the parents, for example, research results or components for the parents' manufacturing process, then there will be a tendency for the parents to align their prices. Clearly where the parents' R&D or other input costs are identical then the overall price will tend to be simi-

[12] In addition to chapters in the standard works, there are a number of specialist monographs now available on the MCR. See Downes and Ellison, *The Legal Control of Mergers in the European Communities* (1991); Cook and Kerse, *EEC Merger Control* (1991); Bos, Stuyck and Wytinck, *Concentration Control in the European Economic Community* (1992).

[13] *Night Services* OJ 1994 L259/20, paras. 49–50.

[14] *Bayer-Gist Brocades* [1976] 1 CMLR D98; *De Laval–Stork* [1977] 2 CMLR D69; *Vacuum Interrupters* [1977] 1 CMLR D67.

lar. This will particularly be the case where the goods or services provided by the joint venture represent a high percentage of total costs since, in such cases, the percentage of overall cost attributable to the individual parents' own efforts will be small compared to the percentage of overall cost attributable to the joint venture.

12.14 (c) Where the joint venture supplies its parents' needs for a particular good or service, this will operate as a barrier to those firms who hitherto had supplied the parents with the good or service. If the parent companies represent major purchasers of the good or service the joint venture may serve to foreclose a significant portion of the demand for those goods or services.

12.15 (d) Where the joint venture sells to third parties and is not in competition with the parents then the very existence of the joint venture might deter the parents from individually entering the market.[15] Though, in many cases the parents may be incapable (for technical or financial reasons) of independent market entry.

12.16 (e) Where the joint venture is between oligopolistic companies it may deleteriously alter the structure of the market by increasing overall concentration and by discouraging market entry.[16]

12.17 (f) Where the joint venture has taken over the operations of one or other of the parents this may indicate an unwillingness by the parents to compete, though it could also indicate an inability of one or both of the parents to remain in business alone.

12.18 (g) Joint ventures may simply represent structural umbrellas beneath which the parents may align their policies. Such concertation between the parties almost inevitably activates Article 85(1) EC. Horizontal restrictions between the parties, *inter se*, are always scrutinised carefully by the Commission.[17]

12.19 Joint ventures may also have pro-competitive consequences which render them suitable for exemption under Article 85(3) EC.[18]

12.20 (a) Joint ventures may facilitate the penetration of a market, increasing competitiveness therein, whereas independently the parents would have been technically incompetent to achieve penetration or at least would have been considerably less efficient at penetration. This is particularly so where the parents combine complementary technology or expertise in a joint venture[19] or where the joint venture enables small and medium sized firms to operate on the scale necessary to enable them to compete on a market dominated by larger undertakings.[20]

12.21 (b) Joint ventures may lead to improved or novel technology where they combine the R&D capacity of two undertakings. Again this is especially true where the

[15] e.g. *GEC–Weir* [1978] 1 CMLR D42; and the American decision *US* v *Penn–Olin Chemical Co 378 US 158* (1964). The Supreme Court held that a joint venture would infringe the antitrust laws (in *casu*, s. 7 Clayton Act) where: (a) it was a reasonable probability that either of the parents would enter the market by constructing plant whilst the other party remained a substantial potential competitor; and (b) that the joint venture was likely to lessen competition substantially. For detailed analysis of this case see Pitofsky, "Joint ventures under the antitrust laws: some reflections on the significance of Penn–Olin" (1969) *Harvard Law Rev.* 1007.

[16] See *Vacuum Interrupters* [1977] 1 CMLR D67 but cf. *United Reprocessors* [1976] 2 CMLR D1.

[17] e.g. *SHV Chevron* [1975] 1 CMLR D68. *Procter and Gamble/Finaf* OJ 1992 C 3/2.

[18] e.g. *Vacuum Interrupters* [1977] 1 CMLR D67; *De Laval–Stork* [1977] 2 CMLR D69; *WANO–ICI* [1979] 1 CMLR 304.

[19] See *Seventh Commission Report on Competition Policy* (1977) p. 115, para. 150. See also *Sixth Commission Report on Competition Policy* (1976), para. 53.

[20] *Transocean Marine Paint Association* [1967] CMLR D9; *BDO Binder BV* [1991] 4 CMLR 242, Press Release IP(91) 602.

parents couple complementary skills together in the joint venture and the advent of new technology helps make the industry more efficient and may benefit the consumer if it improves available products or services and/or increases choice.[21]

12.22 (c) Joint ventures may enable the parents to overcome the financial risks of market entry. A shared risk is, *per se*, a minimised one.[22] Again, the joint venture may be the only way that the parents can effect entry.

12.23 (d) A joint venture may be the most effective way in which the manufacturer of an intermediate product used by both parents may be placed upon a profitable footing. The joint venture by maximising scale economies may reduce the parents' costs which in turn may be passed on to the consumer.[23]

12.24 To be suitable for exemption the joint venture must not eliminate competition in respect of a substantial part of the products in question. Thus, the effectiveness and extent of the residual competition will be an important factor in assessing a joint venture. In this respect ease of entry to the market will be relevant: if new firms can enter the market with ease the threat of potential entry may operate as a disciplining force to existing participants, including any joint ventures.

(4) Legal principles of assessment of joint ventures

12.25 The Commission will first assess whether the agreement creating the joint venture and the operation of the joint venture infringes Article 85(1). It will then assess any additional covenant or agreements (ancillary restraints) that the parties have entered into and determine whether they infringe Article 85(1) or are strictly necessary for the operation of the joint venture.

(5) Article 85(1)

12.26 In the assessment of the joint venture agreement, the Commission's concerns can be divided into four categories: (i) restriction of actual or potential competition; (ii) foreclosure of third parties; (iii) "spillover" effect; (iv) network effect.

12.27 *(i) Restriction of actual or potential competition*[24] This is an area where the Commission's attitude has undergone a certain amount of change. Traditionally the Commission had taken an expansive view of when parties to a joint venture agreement were potential competitors,[25] but there then came a series of indications that the Commission was prepared to take a more economically realistic view. In the *Thirteenth Report on Competition Policy* the Commission set out the criteria it would use in determining whether parties were potential competitors.[26] These criteria have been endorsed and expanded in the CJV Notice.[27] In assessing restrictions of competition between the parents, the Commission conducts its analysis in the following way by reference to the answers to a series of questions posed in each case.

[21] *Elopak/Metal Box–Odin* 1990 OJ L209/15.
[22] *Konsortium ECR 900* [1991] 4 CMLR 832.
[23] e.g. *Carbon Gas Technologie* [1984] 2 CMLR 275.
[24] Generally see *Thirteenth Report on Competition* (point 55) CJV Notice (paras. 18–20)
[25] *KEWA* OJ 1976 L51/15, [1976] 2 CMLR D15 (para. 20); *Vacuum Interrupters (No. 1)* OJ 1977 L48/32, [1977] 1 CMLR D67 (para. 15).
[26] *Thirteenth Report on Competition Policy* (1983) (point 55).
[27] OJ 1993 C43/2.

12.28 *Contribution to the JV* Does each parent company have sufficient financial resources to carry out the planned investment? Does each parent company have sufficient managerial qualifications to run the JV? Does each parent company have access to the necessary input products?

12.29 *Production of the JV* Does each parent know the production technique? Does each parent make the upstream or downstream products himself and does it have the necessary production facilities?

12.30 *Sales by the JV* Is actual or potential demand such as to enable each parent company to manufacture the product on its own? Does each parent company have access to the distribution channels needed to sell the product manufactured by the JV?

12.31 *Risk factors* Can each parent on its own bear the technical and financial risks associated with the production operations of the JV?

12.32 *Access to the relevant market* What is the relevant geographic and product market? What are the barriers to entry into the market? Is each parent company capable of entering that market on its own? Can each parent overcome existing barriers within a reasonable time and without undue effort or cost?

12.33 The key question is whether either of the parties could have entered the market independently. Obviously an important question relates to the relevant timescale in which this market entry is to be assessed. The shorter the timescale required for entry the less likely it is that the parties will be considered potential competitors. In the *Sixth Report on Competition Policy* the Commission indicated that the medium term was the appropriate timescale, but in some recent cases the short term has been deemed more appropriate.[28] In *Konsortium ECR 900*, for example, the reason a short timescale was appropriate was that the joint venture had to meet a tight deadline for a tender. However, the Commission has not followed a consistent economically realistic line and there are several recent decisions where the finding of potential competition has been unlikely and often contradicted by the Commission's Article 85(3) discussion.[29]

12.34 Where the Commission finds that the parent companies are actual or potential competitors it has often gone on to say that the formation of the joint venture inherently restricts that competition.[30] There is also the separate question of restriction of competition (actual or potential) between any of the parents and the joint venture itself.[31] Where this is a problem the Commission has sought to ensure that the joint venture can operate independently of the competing parent. For example, in *Elopak/Metal Box–Odin* the Commission was satisfied that the extensive cross-licensing provisions which would ac-

[28] *Elopak/Metal Box–Odin* OJ 1990 L209/15, [1991] 4 CMLR 832 (para. 25); *Konsortium ECR 900* OJ 1990 L228/31, [1992] 4 CMLR 54 (para. 25).

[29] *KSB/Goulds/Lowara/ITT* OJ 1991 L19/25 [1992] 5 CMLR 55; *IVECO/Ford* OJ 1988 L230/39 [1989] 4 CMLR 40 (potential competition assumed because parties accepted non-compete obligations (para. 24)); but cf. *Konsortium ECR 900* (note 28 above) where the parties were not held to be potential competitors despite a non-compete clause (para. 33); *Eirpage* OJ 1990 L306/22 [1991] 4 CMLR 233 (paras. 11, 14); *Cekacan* OJ 1990 L299/64 [1992] 4 CMLR 406 (paras. 30, 31); *BBC/Brown Boveri* OJ 1988 L301/68 [1989] 4 CMLR 610 (para. 5).

[30] *GEC/Weir* OJ 1977 L327/26 [1978] 1 CMLR D42; *Olivetti/Canon* OJ 1988 L52/51 [1989] 4 CMLR 940.

[31] CJV Notice (paras. 21, 22); *Elopak/Metal Box-Odin* OJ 1990 L209/15 [1991] 4CMLR 832; *Mitchell Cotts/Sofiltra* OJ 1987 L41/31; *Montedison/Hercules (Himont), Seventh Report on Competition Policy* (1987) (point 69); *Du Pont/Merck* IP(91)381 (see [1991] 4 ECLR R-117).

company termination of the joint venture ensured that there would be no collusion between one of the parents and the joint venture.[32]

12.35 *(ii) Foreclosure effects on third parties*[33] The very existence of the joint venture may make the parents less likely to collaborate with third parties and hence foreclose competitive opportunities to those third parties.[34] The strength of the foreclosure factor will depend upon the degree of market concentration and the market position of the parties.[35] Certain types of ancillary restrictions, such as exclusive licensing provisions, can reinforce a foreclosure effect.

12.36 *(iii) "Spillover or "group" effects* The Commission appears to be concerned about two types of spillover effects. First there is the possibility of spillover of co-operation either up or down stream of the permitted co-operation.[36] Secondly, there is the possibility of spillover into adjacent markets.[37] Where the Commission is concerned about either of these two types of anti-competitive effect it may well require the parties to take steps to prevent co-operation in one area lessening competition in another.[38] The Commission's concern over spillover effect is reflected in Article 2 of the R&D block exemption,[39] part (a) of which requires that:

> "the joint research and development work is carried out within the framework of a programme defining the objectives of the work and the field in which it is to be carried out."

12.37 *(iv) Network effect*[40] The network effect occurs where a series of joint ventures are set up throughout the EU, having a common parent or parents. The possibility of co-ordination of behaviour between the joint ventures, and in particular territorial market division, arises. It was the *Optical Fibres*[41] case that highlighted the Commission's concern with this type of restriction on competition. Corning had set up a series of 50/50 joint ventures with national partners in different Member States. The Commission was concerned that at the marketing level, the joint ventures themselves might act in a way that was restrictive of competition, especially as Corning would be in a position to influence the conduct of each joint venture.[42] Before granting an individual exemption for the agreements, the Commission required modifications to Corning's control over the joint ventures.[43]

12.38 *(b) Ancillary restraints*[44] According to the doctrine of ancillary restraints any specific restrictions which are truly ancillary and necessary to a joint venture that does not fall

[32] para. 33.
[33] CJV Notice (paras. 23–25).
[34] GEC/Weir OJ L327/26 [1978] 1 CMLR D42 (paras. 25, 28); *Screensport/EBU Members* OJ 1991 L63/32 [1992] 5 CMLR 273 (para. 63).
[35] *Eirpage* OJ 1991 L306/22 [1991] 4 CMLR 233 (para. 12); *Astra* OJ 1993 L20/23 (para. 17); *Olivetti/Canon* OJ L52/51 [1989] 4 CMLR 940; *KSB/Goulds/Lowara/ITT* OJ 1991 L19/25 5 CMLR 55 (para. 17); for cases where an unconcentrated market has negated the foreclosure see *Mitchell Cotts/Sofiltra* OJ 1987 L41/31 [1988] 4 CMLR 111 (para. 19); *Elopak/Metal Box–Odin* OJ L209/15 [1991] 4 CMLR 832 (para. 27).
[36] *Montedison/Hercules (Himont), Seventh Report on Competition Policy* (1987) (point 69); *KSB/Goulds/Lowara/ITT* OJ 1991 L19/25 [1992] 5 CMLR 55; *Ford/VW* OJ 1993 L20/14 (para. 38).
[37] *Ford/VW*; *Electrolux/AEG* OJ 1993 C 269/4 (point 6).
[38] *Ford/VW* (Art. 2 of Decision).
[39] Reg. 418/85 OJ L53/5, amended by Reg. 151/93 L21/8. See also *Twenty-fourth Report on Competition Policy* (1994), para. 165.
[40] CJV Notice (paras. 27–31).
[41] OJ L236/30.
[42] At para. 45.
[43] At para. 64 *et seq.* For criticism of the decision see Korah (1987) 12 ELR 18, 22–39.
[44] See CJV Notice (paras. 65–76).

within Article 85(1) will also not infringe Article 85(1).[45] Again if the joint venture agreement itself falls within Article 85(1) but benefits from any individual exemption under Article 85(3), then any truly ancillary restraints will also benefit from the exemption.

If the specific restrictions are not genuinely ancillary they must be assessed independently to see if they fall within Article 85(1) or can benefit from an Article 85(3) exemption. The Commission has not given any formal definition of "ancillary restrictions" but it is clear that they are those restrictions without which the existence of the joint venture would be undermined.

12.39 (i) Specific restrictions likely to fall within Article 85(1) as non-ancillary include:

(a) exclusive licensing of technology to the joint venture by the parents;[46]
(b) provision for exclusive use of technology developed by the joint venture by the parents;[47]
(c) restrictions on the joint venture's output;
(d) restrictions likely to lead to market division.

12.40 (ii) Restrictions which have been treated as ancillary[48] include:

(a) non-compete obligations accepted by the parents for the lifetime of the joint venture;[49]
(b) exclusive sourcing or purchasing obligations accepted either by the parents or the joint venture at least for a start-up period;[50]
(c) restriction on the joint venture manufacturing or dealing in competing products;[51]
(d) exclusive relevant know-how licences from each parent to the joint venture with a field of use restriction.[52]

(6) Article 85 (3)

12.41 Despite what appeared to be a change in Commission policy[53] towards assessing the competitive advantages and disadvantages of joint ventures under Article 85(1), it now seems that the Commission has returned to its previous practice of engaging in economic analysis more under Article 85(3) than under Article 85(1).

12.42 Article 85(3) requires that four conditions be met before an individual exemption can be granted. The agreement must:

[45] See e.g. *Elopak/Metal Box-Odin* OJ 1990 L209/15 [1991] 4 CMLR 832; *Twenty-fourth Report on Competition Policy* (1994), para. 166.

[46] *Rockwell/Iveco* OJ L224/19 [1983] 3 CMLR 709; *Optical Fibres* OJ L236/30; *Continental/Michelin* OJ 1988 L305/33 [1989] 4 CMLR 920; In *Mitchell Cotts/Sofiltra* OJ 1987 L41/31 [1988] 4 CMLR 111 it was accepted that a territorial exclusive licence could be treated as ancillary, at least for an initial start-up period (para. 23).

[47] *KSB/Goulds/Lowara/ITT ante* (para. 36); *Olivetti/Canon ante*; *Continental/Michelin ante*.

[48] See Commission Notice Regarding Restrictions Ancillary to Concentrations OJ 1990 C203/5 for guidance by analogy.

[49] *GEC/Weir ante*; *Carbon Gas Technologie* OJ 1983 L367/17 [1984] 2 CMLR 275.

[50] *Fiat/Hitachi* OJ 1993 L20/10 (para. 27); *Rockwell/Iveco* OJ 1983 L224/19 [1983] 3 CMLR 709; *Olivetti/Canon* OJ 1988 L52/51 [1989] 4 CMLR 940.

[51] *Mitchell Cotts/Sofiltra* OJ 1987 L41/31 [1988] 4 CMLR 111.

[52] *Elopak/Metal Box–Odin* OJ L209/15 [1991] 4 CMLR 832.

[53] See *Elopak/Metal Box–Odin ante*; cf. *Eirpage ante*.

(i) contribute to improving the production or distribution of goods or to promoting technical or economic progress; and
(ii) allow consumers a fair share of the resulting benefits; and
(iii) not contain any indispensable restrictions; and
(iv) not eliminate competition.

12.43 However, the fundamental question under Article 85(1) is whether the benefits of the proposed co-operation outweigh the disadvantages. As such the categories used by the Commission are not rigid, and the same benefit can appear under more than one heading.

12.44 *(i) Contribution to technical/economic progress, etc.* Typical benefits include the development of new products[54] or services,[55] new production methods,[56] increased industry capacity,[57] more comprehensive distribution,[58] developing a Community-wide market for products.[59] New products may bring environmental benefits in the shape of greater energy efficiency[60] or pollution control.[61] The Commission has also referred to the benefit of technology being imported into the Community by a joint venture between a non-Community partner and a Community partner.[62]

12.45 *(ii) Fair share of the benefits for consumers* The Commission tends to restate the benefits listed above, such as new products becoming available and the cost improvements due to the co-operation and then goes on to state that these benefits will be passed on to the consumer because the market remains competitive.[63] Consumer benefits can include better safety[64] and better environmental results.[65]

12.46 *(iii) Indispensability* The Commission seeks to ensure that the benefits claimed for the co-operation could not be achieved in a less restrictive manner. It is under this heading that the Commission tends to discuss the issues which it appeared at one stage would be discussed under Article 85(1) relating to potential competition. The following are reasons why a joint venture may be considered indispensable:

(a) the benefits of the co-operation could not have been achieved as quickly if the parties had acted independently;[66]
(b) the joint exploitation allows the minimum efficient scale of production to be reached;[67]

[54] *KSB/Goulds/Lowara/ITT* OJ 1991 L19/25 [1992] 5 CMLR 55; *Optical Fibres* OJ 1986 L236/30; *GEC/Weir* OJ 1977 L237/26.
[55] *Eirpage ante.*
[56] *Ford/VW* OJ 1993 L20/14.
[57] *Ford/VW ante* (para. 25); *Optical Fibres ante; Bayer/BP Chemicals* OJ 1988 L150/35 [1989] 4 CMLR 24; *Rockwell/Iveco* OJ 1983 L224/19 [1983] 3 CMLR 709.
[58] *Ford/Iveco* OJ 1988 L230/39 [1989] 4 CMLR 40 (para. 33).
[59] *Cekacan* OJ 1990 L299/64 [1992] 4 CMLR 406.
[60] *KSB/Goulds/Lowara/ITT ante; BBC/Brown Boveri* OJ 1988 L301/68 [1989] 4 CMLR 610.
[61] *KSB/Goulds/Lowara/ITT ante.*
[62] *Olivetti/Canon ante; BBC Brown Boveri ante.*
[63] *Olivetti/Canon ante; Ford/VW ante.*
[64] *Continental/Michelin* OJ 1988 L305/33 [1989] 4 CMLR 920.
[65] *KSB/Goulds/Lowara/ITT ante.*
[66] *Eirpage ante; KSB/Goulds/Lowara/ITT ante.*
[67] *Ford/VW ante; KSB/Goulds/Lowara/ITT ante.*

(c) the parties have complementary skills which allows the joint venture to achieve results which could not be achieved independently;[68]

(d) the joint venture allows high fixed R&D costs to be spread over a larger output, and as such unit costs can be reduced.[69]

12.47 *(iv) No elimination of competition* Joint ventures can improve the competitive structure of the market,[70] if not in the short term then at least when the co-operation is terminated because there will then be two new competitors.[71] The Commission will try to ensure that on termination of the co-operation both parties are in a position to compete.

12.48 The Commission has often referred to the need to maintain "workable competition",[72] but it is not possible to give this term any precise definition. However, guidance can be taken from the R&D block exemption which gives market share limits of 20 per cent for production joint ventures and 10 per cent for production-to-sales joint ventures. In the CJV Notice the Commission stated that where these limits are exceeded "an exception will be considered only after a careful examination of each individual case".

12.49 In some "structural" joint venture cases the Commission has analysed elimination of competition in terms of strengthening of a dominant position.[73] This is the criterion used by the Merger Control Regulation[74] in the assessment of concentrative joint ventures.

12.50 The Commission is also required to find an effect on trade between Member States in order to apply Article 85(1). Trade between Member States will be affected where the joint venture's production will be marketed in more than one Member State.[75] In *Auditel*[76] trade between Member States was held to be affected where the operation of the joint venture, though confined to a single Member State, influenced marketing decisions concerning products that are traded between states. In *ENI/Montedison*[77] trade between Member States was said to be affected because "as a result of the agreement the whole structure of competition is substantially changed from the point of view both of consumers and of other producers in Italy and the rest of the EEC". Trade between Member States can be affected whether the parties to a joint venture are from the same Member State,[78] different Member States,[79] if one party only is from a Member State,[80] or even if none of the parties is from a Member State.[81]

12.51 Specific restrictions which are indispensable to the operation of the joint venture can be exempted if the joint venture is itself exempted. These have included:

68 *GEC/Weir ante*; *Beecham/Parke-Davis* OJ 1979 L70/11 [1979] 2 CMLR 157.
69 *KSB/Goulds/Lowara/ITT ante*; *Olivetti/Canon ante*.
70 *Ford/VW ante*.
71 *Continental/Michelin ante*.
72 *Bayer/BP ante*; *Enichem/ICI* OJ 1988 L50/18 [1989] 4 CMLR 54.
73 *PRB/Shell*, *Seventh Report on Competition Policy* (point 74); *Fiat/Hitachi* OJ 1993 L20/10 (para. 26).
74 Reg. 4064/89 OJ 1990 L257/14.
75 *KSB/Goulds/Lowara/ITT* OJ 1991 L19/25 [1992] 5 CMLR 55; *Olivetti/Canon* OJ 1988 L52/51 [1989] 4 CMLR 940; *Mitchell Cotts/Sofiltra* OJ 1987 L41/31 [1988] 4 CMLR 111.
76 OJ 1993 L306/50 (para. 23–26).
77 OJ 1987 L5/13 (para. 24); also see UIP OJ 1989 L226/25 [1990] 4 CMLR 749.
78 See e.g. *BP/ICI* OJ 1984 L212/1 [1985] 2 CMLR 330; *ENI/Montedison* OJ 1987 L5/13 [1989] 4 CMLR 444.
79 *Mitchell Cotts/Sofiltra* OJ 1987 L41/31, [1988] 4 CMLR 111.
80 e.g. *Olivetti/Canon* OJ 1988 L52/51 [1989] 4 CMLR 940; *BBC/Brown Boveri* OJ 1988 L301/68 [1989] 4 CMLR 610.
81 *Ansac* OJ 1991 L152/54.

(i) non-compete obligations accepted by the parents;[82]
(ii) exclusive purchasing obligations, at least for an initial start-up period;[83]
(iii) non-exclusive intellectual property licences;[84]
(iv) exclusive manufacturing licence by parents to the joint venture;[85]
(v) obligation on the parents to use their best efforts in selling the joint venture products;[86]
(vi) obligation on the parents to purchase a minimum volume of the joint venture product;[87]
(vii) obligation on the parents to purchase certain quantities of the joint venture product.[88]

(7) Examples

12.52 Some examples[89] may illustrate the Commission's approach. The Commission exempted in *Fiat/Hitachi*[90] a joint venture for the manufacture, distribution and sale of hydraulic excavators, for use in road construction and in mines and quarries, in Western Europe. The market concerned was one which had been in decline during a recession and was now in the process of rationalisation in response, this joint venture being part of that process. Since both parents remained as potential competitors, it was not treated as a concentrative joint venture. It was caught by Article 85(1) because the parties, by granting exclusivity to the joint venture in Western Europe, had thus agreed not to compete with it or with each other in that territory. A ban on active sales by Hitachi into Europe was similarly caught. Exemption for 13 years was granted on the basis that the joint venture would develop better excavators than those currently on offer from the parties. A market share of about 16 per cent, placing the joint venture in fourth place in the European Community market, would not create a dominant position.

12.53 In *Ford/Volkswagen*[91] the Commission exempted an agreement for joint development, engineering and manufacture of a multi-purpose vehicle (MPV) between two of the Community's major car manufacturers, both of whom were held to be capable of producing a MPV on their own.[92] Exemption was granted because of the exceptional circumstances of this market. First, the market was considered to be likely to continue to have only a relatively low volume of sales in the medium term. Thus if both parties were new entrants there would be a risk for them of glutting the market which might deter entry in the first place.[93] Second, neither party was currently in the market in any significant way. Thus the agreement did not remove any actual competition from the market. Third, the market leader was not subject to much significant competition either from within Eu-

[82] *Rockwell/Iveco ante; Optical Fibres ante; Continental/Michelin ante; KSB/Goulds/Lowarra/ITT ante; Eurosport* OJ 1991 L63/32 [1991] 4 CMLR 228.
[83] See note 50.
[87] *Iveco/Ford ante* (para. 36); *Fiat/Hitachi ante* (para. 11); *Olivetti/Digital* OJ 1994 L3091/24 (para. 22).
[84] *Optical Fibres ante.*
[85] *Olivetti/Canon ante* (para. 57); *Fiat/Hitachi* OJ 1991 C206/3 (para. 9).
[86] *Olivetti/Canon ante* (para. 57).
[87] *Olivetti/Canon ante* (para. 57).
[88] *Ford/VW ante.*
[89] See also *Eirpage* OJ 1990 C1990 C249/3; *Cekacan* OJ 1990 L299/64.
[90] 1993 OJ L20/10.
[91] OJ 1993 L20/14.
[92] OJ 1993 L20/14, para. 19.
[93] The Community market was currently 100,000 units a year and minimum capacity for a viable new plant was considered to be 110,000 units a year (para. 15). The plant set up under the joint venture was capable of producing 190,000 units a year in its own right, so even with the joint venture there was a risk of over-capacity.

rope or from Japan, the latter due to its voluntary export restraint to the Community. Thus the sooner a competitor could enter the market, the sooner the market leader (enjoying an average market share in the Community of over 50 per cent) could be subject to effective competition. Fourth, the proposed MPV would be produced in a new and modern plant built in one of the poorest areas of the Community, Portugal, creating directly an estimated 5,000 jobs with a further 10,000 jobs to be indirectly attracted by this investment. Thus the joint venture would assist the reduction in regional disparities within the Community, this being one of the basic aims of the Treaty, as well as promoting the integration of Portugal more closely into the Community. The Commission acknowledged that this latter factor was not sufficient in its own right to justify exemption but was an element that the Commission had taken into account.[94] An important factor in obtaining exemption was that Ford and Volkswagen would market the MPV separately under their respective badges and with different finishes and specifications. This level of visual and technical product differentiation was regarded by the Commission as the minimum necessary[95] to obtain exemption, since it ensured that Ford and Volkswagen would continue to compete for market share against each other.

12.54 The Commission is often more likely to grant an exemption rather than a negative clearance for a joint venture. The former enables it to exercise continuing surveillance on a project, and to review its decision when the exemption comes to an end and the parties seek renewal. Moreover, the Commission may attach conditions and obligations to the exemption decision. However, the Commission has given negative clearance to some joint ventures.

12.55 In *Odin*[96] a joint venture to create new food packaging was granted negative clearance on the basis that the parties concerned were not actual or potential competitors in the new technology concerned. The only means for them to create a new market for the new form of packaging was to combine their respective expertise. The joint venture was set up so that on dissolution, the party not taking over the joint venture's business would be licensed to use the joint venture's technology, thus enabling it to set up in competition if it so wished, and so introducing more competition into the market. In *Konsortium ECR 900*[97] negative clearance was granted to a joint venture between three telecommunications companies to develop, manufacture and supply a pan-European mobile telephone network to national telecommunications bodies. The joint venture was held not to restrict competition as the investment and risk involved in the project, together with the small number of potential purchasers, would have deterred individual bids. In addition, the tender had to be submitted in a short period of time.

12.56 These decisions were heralded at the time by some as marking a move by the Commission to greater use of negative clearance powers, but this has proved to be a false dawn. Both decisions depended on their special facts, enabling the Commission to relinquish the control the grant of an exemption gives. The *Fiat/Hitachi* and *Ford/Volkswagen* decisions indicate that the Commission's formal approach to joint ventures of applying Article 85(1) and using Article 85(3) to exempt remains the rule, though the *Ford/Volkswagen* case indicates a willingness overtly to take criteria other than strictly competition oriented matters into account.

94 The Commission had authorised state aid to the joint venture under Art. 93 EC as well. The market leader unsuccessfully sought to challenge the approval of state aid: Case C-225/91 *Matra* v *Commission* [1993] ECR I-3203.

95 OJ 1993 L20/14, para. 38.

96 [1991] 4 CMLR 832.

97 [1992] 4 CMLR 54.

12.57 The Commission is willing to exempt joint ventures, even in oligopolistic markets, particularly where they are concerned with the creation of new products through R&D. This is considered at paras. 12.114–12.185. It is clear that the Commission takes into account considerations of industrial policy pursuant to Article 130f of the EC Treaty when exercising its powers to grant exemption under Article 85(3).

(8) Concentrative joint ventures under the MCR

12.58 Concentrative joint ventures can qualify as concentrations fall under the MCR. A concentrative joint venture is defined as one "performing on a lasting basis all the functions of an autonomous economic entity, which does not give rise to coordination of the competitive behaviour of the parties among themselves or between them and the joint venture".[98] There are thus three main tests to be satisfied in determining whether a joint venture is concentrative: first, is it a full function autonomous economic entity, secondly, is the joint venture set up on a lasting basis, and, thirdly, does it avoid giving an opportunity for co-ordination between the parents? Only if the answer to all three is yes will the joint venture be regarded as concentrative, i.e. equivalent to a merger, and thus coming within the MCR. The Interface Notice gives some guidance on how to approach these questions.

12.59 What constitutes a full function autonomous economic entity is amplified in the Interface Notice. This sets out the requirement that the joint venture must act as an independent supplier and buyer on the market, rather than being a mere auxiliary to the parents' commercial activities. It must not remain substantially dependent after an initial starting period on the parents for the maintenance and development of its business.[99] Thus a joint venture will not be regarded as having acquired sufficient autonomy if it depends on its parents for technology, research and development, supplies or sales,[100] or if it markets its own products under its parents' trade marks.[101] If the parents provide technology by way of licence, whether the joint venture remains dependent on the licensing parents depends on the terms of the licences. In *Baxter/Nestle*,[102] the parents' licences were limited in time and revocable, whereas in both *Sanofi/Sterling Drug*[103] and *Lucas/Eaton*,[104] permanent licensing arrangements were found to have removed dependency on the parents and thus supported a finding of autonomy.

12.60 A joint venture which remains dependent on its parents for supplies or sales of its products will not be autonomous, but where such agreements to obtain products front or sell products to the parents do not show dependency, as in *Lucas/Eaton*[105] where the agreement to obtain supplies from a parent only represented a small proportion (1–2 percent) of the joint venture's total requirements, there was no reason for regarding such supply arrangements as evidence of lack of autonomy.

12.61 Separate premises are not necessary to show autonomy, but separate ownership of assets will be,[106] though intellectual property may be licensed rather than owned.

12.62 The second requirement is that the joint venture be set up on a lasting basis, further defined in the Interface Notice as being for a sufficiently long time in order to bring

98 Art. 3(2) MCR.
99 para. 15, Interface Notice.
100 *Baxter/Nestle* [1992] 5 CMLR M-33.
101 *Baxter/Nestle* [1992] 5 CMLR M-33; though see *Renault/Volvo* [1991] 4 CMLR 297, para. 5, where industry practice to use parents' badges on a commonly produced vehicle did not prevent a finding of concentration.
102 [1992] 5 CMLR M-33.
103 Case IV/M.072, Decision of 10 June 1991.
104 OJ 1991 C7/7
105 OJ 1991 C7/7.
106 para. 15, Interface Notice.

about a lasting change in the structure of the undertaking concerned.[107] In *BSN-Nestle/Cokoladovny*,[108] an agreement for a minimum period of seven years was treated as satisfying this requirement (though other considerations relating to the likelihood of the joint venture competing with its parents meant that overall it was co-operative), since it involved the privatisation and transfer into a joint venture of a previously state (Czech) owned business. Clearly this was a structural alteration in the market.

12.63 The third requirement, that there be no possibility of co-ordination of the competitive behaviour of the parents *inter se* or between the joint venture and either of the parents, is one which has undergone quite a considerable degree of modification in practice after the Interface Notice was issued and this reflected in the present Interface Notice. This Notice assesses whether a joint venture is co-operative by considering whether there is co-ordination between the parent companies in relation to prices, markets, output or innovation. The co-ordination between parent companies and the joint ventures, although referred to in Article 3(2) of the MCR, is only considered by the Commission to be relevant in so far as it is an instrument for producing or reinforcing co-ordination between the parent companies.[109] This means that co-ordination between one parent and the joint venture does not prevent the joint venture being concentrative, provided it does not lead to co-ordination between that parent and the other parent.[110]

12.64 Finally, the Commission takes the view that the fact that a joint venture leads to co-ordination of the competitive behaviour of the parent companies does not prevent the assumption of a concentration where those co-operative elements are only of minor economic importance in relation to the operation as a whole. However, the *de minimis* rule does not apply if there is an accumulation of minor elements of co-ordination, since this may lead to the operation as a whole being considered co-operative.[111]

(9) Joint ventures and Article 86

12.65 Article 86 may apply where a joint venture reinforces the dominance of the parties on the market or where it artificially creates a dominant undertaking (e.g. a joint venture company) where one did not hitherto exist or where a joint venture in a dominant position abuses that position. However, concentrative joint ventures fall to be considered under the MCR, so Article 86 is now relevant only for co-operative joint ventures. Despite the structural/behavioural justification for the concentrative/co-operative distinction, even a co-operative joint venture can affect market structure. The Court of Justice has on a number of occasions stressed the relevance of protecting market structure:

> "The concept of abuse is an objective concept relating to the behaviour of an undertaking in a dominant position which is such as to influence the structure of a market where, as a result of the very presence of the undertaking in question, the degree of competition is weakened and which, through recourse to methods different from those which condition normal competition in products or services on the basis of the transactions of commercial operators, has the effect of hindering the maintenance of the degree of competition still existing in the market or the growth of that competition."[112]

[107] *Courtaulds/SNIA* OJ 1991 C333/16.
[108] para. 16, Interface Notice.
[109] paras. 17–20, Interface Notice.
[110] For the first application of this analysis, prior to the revision of the Interface Notice, see *Thomson/Pilkington* OJ 1991 C279/19. The Interface Notice gives further examples in paras. 18 and 19.
[111] para. 20, Interface Notice.
[112] Case 85/76 *Hoffman-La Roche* v *Commission* [1979] 3 CMLR 211; [1979] ECR 461 at para. 91 of the judgment. See Paull, "Joint ventures under the EC competition rules" [1984] ECLR 358 at p. 368.

12.66 Elsewhere the Court has stated,

> "Article 86 covers practices which are likely to affect the structure of a market where, as a direct result of the presence of the undertaking in question, competition has already been weakened and which, through recourse to methods different from those governing normal competition in products or services based on trader's performance, have the effect of hindering the maintenance or development of the level of competition still existing on the market."[113]

12.67 The Commission, to date, has not actively used this structural approach to joint ventures. However, the development of the collective dominance theory of Article 86 may lead to situations in which Article 86 could be applied to parents which set up a joint venture, the parents and/or the joint venture being regarded as being collectively dominant. While the joint venture agreements themselves would fall to be considered under Article 85,[114] the subsequent activities of the parents and the joint venture could be challenged under Article 86 as an abuse, Article 86 applying by virtue of their collective dominance. Whereas the Court of First Instance in the *Italian Flat Glass* case emphasised that Article 85 was to apply to agreements, anything taking place beyond the scope of what could be considered as the joint venture agreement or any concerted practice would thus fall to be determined under Article 86. Thus a co-operative joint venture enjoying a technological advantage along with its parents could be considered as occupying a collectively dominant position and thus be subject to Article 86.

(10) Commission procedures for assessing joint ventures

12.68 Notification of a joint venture to the Commission is to be made on form A/B,[115] and the normal timetable applies. However, the Commission has now adopted a "fast track" procedure for dealing with certain "structural" joint ventures.[116] This is an attempt to reconcile the time taken for a MCR decision, a maximum of five months (more usually one month), and that for a Regulation 17 decision or a comfort letter, for which there was no fixed deadline.[117]

12.69 The concept of a structural joint venture is explained in the preliminary notes to Form A/B as being "one that involves an important change in the structure and organisation of the business assets of the parties to the agreement. This may occur because the joint venture takes over or extends existing activities of the parent companies or because it undertakes new activities on their behalf. Such operations are characterised by the commitment of significant financial, material and/or non-tangible assets such as intellectual property rights and know-how. Structural joint ventures are therefore normally intended to operate on a medium or long-term basis. This concept includes certain "partial function" joint ventures which take over one or several specific functions within the parents' business activity without access to the market, in particular research and development and/or production. It also covers those "full function" joint ventures which give rise to co-ordination of competitive behaviour of independent undertakings, in particular between the parties to the joint venture or between them and the joint venture."

12.70 These principles may be illustrated by two of the earliest cases dealt with under the accelerated procedure. In *Alenia/Honeywell*[118] the Commission indicated that a 60/40 JV

[113] Case 322/81 *Michelin* v *Commission* [1985] 1 CMLR 282 at p. 330, para. 70.
[114] Cases T-68, 77 and 78/89 *Italian Flat Glass* [1992] ECR II-1403, [1992] 5 CMLR 302.
[115] See paras. 6.146–6.149.
[116] See para. 12.7.
[117] An average period for a decision or comfort letter for a JV would be one to two years.
[118] *Twenty-third Report on Competition Policy* (1993), para. 216.

between the two firms merited clearance, since the combination of an Italian aeronautical company and a US computer company through a JV to make space satellite components did not involve co-operation between actual or potential competitors in the satellite market. A comfort letter was sent in *Philips/Thomson/Sagem*[119] assuring the parties that a 80/10/10 JV met the conditions for individual exemption. The JV was set up as the first European company capable of making liquid crystal displays in a market dominated by strong Japanese manufacturers and characterised by strong purchasing power on behalf of the consumers of these products, car, telecommunications and consumer electronics manufacturers.

12.71 Under the new approach, the Commission undertakes within two months of complete notification of a structural joint venture, to issue one of three types of letters to the parties:

(a) if it is clear that the agreement does not infringe Article 85(1) or would merit an exemption under Article 85(3) EC, then the Commission will issue a comfort letter;[120]
(b) if the Commission considers that a formal decision needs to be taken, it will send a letter informing the parties of its intention to do so; or,
(c) a warning letter will be sent where the Commission has serious doubts as to the compatibility of the agreement with the competition rules, stating the need for an in-depth examination before a decision can be made.

In cases (b) and (c) the Commission will indicate the envisaged date of the final decision. However, none of the time limits set out are legally binding.

2. UK Law

12.72 Surveys undertaken by the European Commission suggest that a significant proportion of joint venture activity within the EC is set in a national framework.[121] In the UK the OFT and the Department of Trade and Industry (DTI) regularly encounter joint ventures of different types. There are three principal means of control of joint ventures in the UK. First, under section 21(2) RTPA 1976; secondly, under section 29 RTPA 1976; and thirdly under section 568 Income and Corporation Taxes Act 1988 (ICTA).[122] Of these section 21(2) is the most important. If a joint venture is given individual exemption under Article 85(3), then it is likely to be given section 21(1)(a) authorisation by the OFT. If it comes within

[119] *ibid.*, para. 215. The JV was initially notified as concentrative under the MCR. The Commission decided it was not and it was converted at the request of the submitting parties into a notification under Reg. 17/62/EEC.

[120] In a speech given by the then competition commissioner, Sir Leon Brittan, "The future of EC competition policy" (7 December 1992, Centre of European Policy Studies, Brussels, text unpublished), it was indicated that such comfort letters could only be revoked in the most extreme cases and when the conditions of Art. 8 of Reg. 17 have been fulfilled. Art. 8(2), Reg. 17, provides that an individual exemption may only be revoked or amended where there has been a change in facts underlying the exemption, a breach of any obligation accompanying the exemption, where the exemption was procured deceitfully or on the basis of incorrect information, and where the parties have otherwise abused the exemption.

[121] Commission figures from the annual *Reports on Competition Policy* (Annex IV provides statistics on joint ventures for certain years, a practice now apparently discontinued) suggest that although there remain a significant number of purely national joint ventures, approximately 25 per cent in 1990/91 of all joint ventures recorded were cross-border joint ventures, both intra-Community and involving international firms entering into JVs with Community firms. The areas of most activity involving manufacturing are metal, engineering and cars, while in the service sector it is banking, insurance and financial services.

[122] Previously s. 406 Income and Corporation Taxes Act 1970.

one of the block exemptions for R&D or Specialisation agreements relevant in this area (see sections E and F below respectively), then it is in any event non-notifiable for the purposes of the RTPA, which therefore only applies to agreements falling outside the block exemptions.[123]

(1) Registrability under the RTPA 1976

12.73 Many joint ventures and co-operation agreements are subject to the RTPA 1976.[124] There must be at least two parties carrying on business in the UK.[125] Thus, if a UK firm agrees with an American firm not trading in the UK the agreement is not registrable. If the UK firm and the American firm incorporate a jointly owned company in the UK, the agreement will be registrable since there will be two parties carrying on business in the UK.[126] If the RTPA 1976 does not apply because only one party carries on business in the UK, it will become applicable if another party commences business in the UK. If the parties are desirous of avoiding registration, they might incorporate a clause in the agreement providing that the agreement is terminated in the event of two or more parties commencing to carry on business within the UK. Though, as will be shown later in this chapter many joint ventures obtain section 21(2) clearance and hence registration need not necessarily be feared.

12.74 To be registrable the joint venture agreement must contain restrictions of a type listed in sections 6(1)(a)–(f) (goods), or, 11 (2)(a)–(e) (services) (discussed at paras. 1.63–1.69).

12.75 If X and Y form a joint venture company, XY Ltd, and agree not to compete with it, this will be registrable under sections 6(1)(f) (goods) or 11 (2)(e) (services) RTPA 1976 as an agreement containing restrictions on "the persons or classes of persons to ... whom ... goods are to be supplied." If X and Y agree not to compete with XY Ltd they will have to refuse to supply customers who come to them for the product or service rather than to XY Ltd. This might also be a restriction under section 6(1)(d) (for goods) as a restriction on the "quantities or descriptions" of goods to be produced or supplied. If X and Y refrain (or partially refrain) from competing with XY Ltd they are restricted as to the quantities of goods they produce and/or the descriptions (i.e. kinds) of goods they produce (see s.11 (2)(c) for services).

12.76 Often joint venture agreements contain a clause requiring the parents to refer to the joint venture company all enquiries and orders concerning the joint venture activity and goods or services. Such a clause necessarily restricts the parents as to the persons or classes of person to whom they may supply goods. Variations on this theme, for instance where

123 Restrictive Trade Practices (Non-notifiable Agreements) (EC Block Exemptions) Order, S.I. 1996 No. 349, issued under s. 27A RTPA 1976 (added by s. 10 Deregulation and Contracting Out Act 1994). See further paras. 2.250 and following.

124 The principles are essentially the same irrespective of whether X and Y form a joint venture company XY Ltd, or whether they simply conclude an agreement between themselves. In the latter case non-competition clauses may take the form of obligations on one party not to supply the product manufactured by the party who is producing the joint product. See, e.g. No. S.1393 Register of Restrictive Trade Practices, *Legal and General Assurance Society and Forward Trust* (1984) joint venture to promote life assurance and credit services.

125 ss. 6(1) and 11(1)(a) RTPA 1976.

126 e.g. No. 4747 Register of Restrictive Trade Practices, *RTZ and Virginia Chemicals* (1984). VC is a US company manufacturing sodium hydrosulphite by the formate process. RTZ manufactures the product by the zinc process; VC sought a marketing base in Europe, RTZ sought a switch in manufacturing process to the formate process but lacked technical know-how. RTZ and VC incorporated a joint subsidiary in the UK to manufacture sodium hydrosulphite by the formate method. The agreement was registrable because, *inter alia*, RTZ and the subsidiary were incorporated in the UK and hence the two party requirement in s. 6(1) was satisfied.

the parents are restricted from supplying the joint venture good or service other than where the board of the joint venture company so permits, are also registrable.[127]

12.77 An agreement between X and Y as to the prices the joint venture company will charge is registrable under sections 6(1)(a) or 11 (2)(a) RTPA 1976 as restrictions on the prices to be charged, quoted etc. Where X and Y agree as to terms and conditions on which the joint venture company will trade, this is registrable under section 6(1)(c) or 11 (2)(b) as restrictions on terms and conditions of trade. If X and Y agree that the joint venture company will only produce 10,000 tonnes or a specified number of a product, then this will be a restriction as to the quantities of goods to be produced or supplied under sections 6(1)(d) RTPA 1976 or, where the agreement regulates the extent or scale of services to be supplied by a joint venture, section 11(2)(c) RTPA 1976. If X and Y agree that the joint venture company will limit its production to specified kinds of goods leaving the parents to produce and supply other kinds of goods then this is a restriction under section 6(1)(d) as to the "descriptions of goods to be produced".[128] These examples are of course not exhaustive of the restrictions that render joint ventures registrable.

(2) Avoiding registration

12.78 Where it is considered desirable to avoid registration, parties will have to refrain from accepting restrictions listed in sections 6(1) and 11(2) RTPA 1976. Thus, if X and Y wish to institute a joint venture company to manufacture a component they both need, then they would have to avoid the following: (a) clause preventing parents from competing with the joint company in production of the component; (b) clause requiring joint company to supply parents on preferential terms and conditions; (c) clauses restraining joint company's right of free action. Where the parents do not consider it worth while to incorporate a joint venture without such restrictions then particulars should be furnished. Parties should thus consider whether these restraints are necessary and, in particular, whether the commercial realities of the agreement would not mean that the parties would not in any event refrain from competing with the joint company. Failure to furnish particulars renders restrictions in the agreement void and unenforceable in a court of law, thus permitting a party to breach the agreement with impunity.[129] It may be reiterated that if only the joint venture company accepts restrictions leaving the parents unrestrained then the agreement is not registrable since there will not be at least two parties accepting restrictions.

(3) Clauses not registrable

12.79 Certain clauses in a joint venture may be disregarded when registrability is being considered according to sections 9 (goods) and 18 (services) RTPA 1976. Principally, terms relating exclusively to the goods or services supplied may be disregarded. Thus, where X and Y both supply goods or provide services for the joint venture company these may be disregarded. For example, X might supply goods at cost price or agree to provide training services for the staff of the joint venture. Y might provide accounting facilities or secretarial assistance. Agreements between X and Y to provide these goods or services are thus to be disregarded. An agreement between X and Y to license know-how or trademarks or

[127] Similarly, where X and Y agree that their joint venture company will only supply certain categories of customer, or in certain defined territories. These restrictions will render the agreement registrable under s. 6(1)(f) (goods) or s. 11(2)(e)(services).

[128] "Descriptions" in s. 6(1)(d) RTPA 1976 means "kinds"—*British Waste Paper Association* (1963) LR 4 RP 29 at p. 50.

[129] s. 35(1) RTPA 1976.

other intellectual property to the joint venture company does not count as an agreement for the supply of goods or services so is outside the scope of the RTPA 1976.[130] Restrictions on use of the parent licensors intellectual property rights are not legally counted as restrictions on goods or services so are also exempt from the Act.[131] The same conclusion applies to licences granted by a joint venture company to the parents even though the licences contain restrictions on use. This liberal attitude to intellectual property licensing is *not* repeated at the EC level so that an agreement affecting inter-state trade so as to activate Article 85 EC must be prepared to justify licensing clauses. Usually few problems arise in this context.

12.80 Following the decision of the RPC in *Diazo Copying Materials*[132] certain restrictive clauses in agreements between parties to agreements will be disregardable under sections 9(3) and 18(2) RTPA 1976 when registration is being considered. In that case HTL and MSL entered an agreement under which HTL would manufacture using MSL know-how in addition to its own, a new type of photocopying machine and MSL would market, on an exclusive basis, the product throughout the world. This was subject to a non-exclusive, non-assignable right granted to HTL to retain the product and make other disposals of it in the UK. The OFT considered that HTL had accepted a restriction not to sell the product in countries other than the UK. This would make the agreement registrable under section 6(1)(f) RTPA 1976 (restriction "on areas or places ... in ... which, goods are to be supplied ..."). The RPC held that this negative obligation on HTL was within section 9(3) and hence to be disregarded as a term relating exclusively to the goods supplied. It appears to follow from this case that if X and Y wish jointly to manufacture a product and subsequently to limit the selling area of one of them, then they may avoid creating a registrable agreement by granting one of the parties an exclusive distribution right subject to a non-exclusive right to sell in a specified area granted to the other party. By this device, a market-sharing arrangement between the parties, drafted as an agreement granting one party the exclusive right to sell anywhere but subject to a non-exclusive right granted to the other party to sell in a geographically limited area, escapes registration. It is uncertain how far the rule in *Diazo Copying Materials* extends. It has been subject to some debate as to its corrections. The decision of the RPC might have been coloured by the fact that had the clause had been registrable, HTL would have been in contempt of court for breaching an earlier order of the RPC restraining HTL from enforcing any other unregistered agreement. Given that the actual restriction appears to have exerted a minimal effect on competition, the RPC might have felt ill-disposed to holding HTL in contempt of court. A second reason for exercising caution over the decision is the decision of the RPC in *Association of British Travel Agents*[133] in which the RPC held that section 18(6) (and *a fortiori* section 9(6)) which allows restrictions on employees to be disregarded when considering whether an agreement is registrable did not operate to exempt terms that had an obviously restrictive effect. If this were applied to section 9(3) or 18(2) RTPA 1976, then it would severely curtail their usefulness as exempting provisions. A final point on the *Diazo Copying Materials* case concerns the fact that HTL was only restricted from competing with MSL outside of the UK. Within the UK there were no restrictions on competition between the parties and hence it is difficult to see that the RTPA 1976 could have applied since Schedule 3, paras. 6(1) and 9(1) RTPA 1976 exempts from the Act agree-

[130] See paras. 2.202–2.210.
[131] See *Ravenseft Properties* v *Director General of Fair Trading* [1977] 1 All ER 47, and DGFT Annual Report 1976 at p. 36.
[132] [1984] ICR 429.
[133] [1984] ICR 12.

ments having "overseas operation" only. This point seems to have been overlooked by the RPC.

12.81 One final clause type that is worth noting is the procurement clause whereby X and Y agree that XY Ltd (the joint venture company) should perform certain tasks, e.g. in respect of preparing documentation or in obtaining tax relief. It would seem unlikely that XY Ltd has accepted any registrable restriction although he has covenanted to act in a specific way and hence his freedom is curtailed. Likewise, neither X nor Y have accepted registrable restriction. A more difficult case is where X and Y agree with XY Ltd that X shall procure a third party or even a subsidiary controlled by X to supply specified services or goods to XY Ltd. Has X accepted a restriction under the Act? It is possible that X has accepted an implied negative restriction under sections 6(1)(f) (goods) or 11 (2)(e) (services) on the persons who may be supplied, i.e. X has restricted his freedom to supply XY Ltd in favour of the third party or subsidiary. However, the better view is that X has not accepted a registrable restriction since under the agreement X has no inherent right to supply XY Ltd and is merely agreeing to facilitate supply by another person.

(4) Joint ventures and section 21(2) RTPA 1976

12.82 Joint ventures are appropriate to section 21(2) treatment. In assessing whether a restriction is significant or not the OFT take account of three main factors:

(a) Minimum restrictiveness

12.83 The restriction should be the minimum necessary to enable the parties to attain the objectives of their agreement. Thus, the liberty of the parties to sell independently of the joint venture company must be limited only to the extent necessary to enable the joint venture company to market the contract product or service with greatest efficiency. Thus, if X and Y agree not to compete in sales of the contract product with their jointly owned company XY Ltd for 15 years, when it is economically reasonable to expect that XY Ltd will achieve successful market penetration with the contract product within eight years, then the non-competition clause may be "significant". If X and Y agree not to compete with XY Ltd in respect not only of the contract product or service but also in respect of other products or services that have not been the subject of joint R&D, then this will be a significant restriction. The agreement whereby X and Y refrain from competing with XY Ltd is also implicitly a negation of competition between X and Y. Hence, if the non-competition clause applies to products or services other than those the subject of joint production then the clause unjustifiably restrains competition between X and Y and is excessive in relation to the objectives of the agreement, i.e. development and exploitation of a new or improved product.[134]

(b) Extent of residual competition

12.84 The OFT assesses a restriction in the light of the extent of residual competition from competing products or from products which are substitutes on the market. Thus, a definition of the product market is an essential part of section 21(2) analysis. The following examples give an indication of how this test may be applied. In each case X and Y have jointly incorporated a company, XY Ltd, whose shares they hold in equal part. XY Ltd conducts the business of the agreement:

12.85 – X and Y are not competitors but combine complementary abilities and technological skills to produce a new or improved product or service. Since neither X nor Y could

[134] [1984] ICR 12 at p. 51.

individually have created the product or service, the agreement has enhanced competition by adding something to the market that would not otherwise have emerged. The agreement might hence intensify existing competition or create a new product market.[135]

12.86 – XY Ltd provides joint transport facilities for X and Y thereby reducing their carriage costs and ultimately their overall cost.[136] The agreement may enable X and Y to compete more effectively against larger rivals. The agreement thus intensifies competition on the market.

12.87 – XY Ltd undertakes R&D and exploitation of a product that improves upon those manufactured individually by X and Y. XY Ltd sells in a market dominated by oligopolists. The agreement by enhancing competition with oligopolists helps to protect the market structure against the development of conscious parallelism amongst the oligopolists which might harm the consumers interests.[137]

12.88 – XY Ltd undertakes joint R&D and marketing and becomes, through its efforts, the dominant supplier in the UK. However, it is subject to intensive competition from EC and other international firms. Individually X and Y would, at the time of the agreement, have experienced difficulty in competing with the international competition, collectively they are so able. This is a more difficult case under section 21(2). The agreement may well create a dominant firm with regard to the UK market. The agreement between X and Y not to compete, *inter se*, or with XY Ltd negates the potential for X and Y to compete individually on the UK market in the future. However, by forming a joint venture, X and Y have intensified competition on the international market and in so doing may indirectly benefit UK consumers by adding to the choice of products and helping keep prices down. Whether section 21(2) dispensation applies may depend upon the extent to which the OFT accepts that international competition, which may not have a direct bearing on the UK market, is an adequate disciplining force on XY Ltd in its sales to the UK market, i.e. international competitors are able to supply the UK market should XY Ltd prove inefficient or overprice its product or service, etc. In practical terms, X and Y would have to consider the implications of EC law and if necessary notify their agreement to the Commission. Alternatively, if the agreement were of sufficient overall importance to the economy X and Y might consider applying for exemption from registration under section 29 RTPA 1976 on the basis that the agreement was important to the UK economy. Section 29 RTPA 1976 exemption does not affect the need to notify the agreement to the Commission.

12.89 – X and Y in incorporating XY Ltd create a monopolist in the UK and a dominant supplier in the world. This might be the case for a new high-technology product

[135] e.g. No. 7220 *British Urban Development Ltd*, which was registered on 25 August 1988 but not given s. 21(2) directions until 6 April 1993, after the removal of a restriction on shareholders in a joint venture company (formed to promote urban renewal development projects) preventing them from becoming involved in any site in which the joint venture company had identified an interest.

[136] e.g. No. S.466 Register of Restrictive Trade Practices, Agreement between *Cleveland Co Ltd, Texaco Ltd, Gulf Oil (GB) Ltd, Amoco* and *MMM Pipelines Ltd* to establish joint carriage facilities via pipeline for petroleum (1984).

[137] For an analogous case see No. 4747 Register of Restrictive Trade Practices, *RTZ and Virginia Chemicals* (1984). RTZ and VC are rival producers of sodium hydrosulphite. However, they use different production methods. RTZ needed to change its method (the zinc process) to that of VC (the formate process) but did not possess the requisite technology. VC needed a manufacturing and marketing base in Europe. RTZ and VC hence formed a joint production venture controlled mainly by RTZ using VC know-how. The agreement enabled the parties to market sodium hydrosulphite in Europe by the formate method. Without the agreement production might not have occurred.

where XY Ltd is the innovator and seeks to obtain worldwide patent protection for its invention. Individually X and Y might have failed to create the new product. Time might be of the essence where the first company or consortium to produce the product can create legal entry barriers for rivals in the form of intellectual property rights. Such an agreement negates competition between X and Y who are clearly important firms in the UK technically capable of undertaking their own R&D. Restrictions in the agreement, e.g. a non-competition clause, would appear to be significant. However, the joint venture may well be appropriate for section 29 RTPA 1976 treatment. Clearance with the Commission might well also be necessary.

(c) Detriment to third parties

12.90 The interests of the consumer or user are always relevant in determining the "significance" of a restriction.[138] Users and customers are interested in as wide a choice of products or services as possible and in competitive prices and terms and conditions. Consumer choice can suffer where X and Y stop competing with each other in order to create XY Ltd. However, where XY Ltd creates a new or improved product, then the consumer may have benefited. Clearly, where X and Y do not compete but combine complementary skills to create something new or improved, then the consumer enjoys added choice, i.e. the new/improved product or service. Where XY Ltd jointly manufactures a component used by X and Y separately in their own manufacturing processes, the consumer can benefit because the scale economies realised by X and Y through joint production of a component may be passed on to the consumer in low prices. Where the component accounts for a high percentage of total cost such that there is a tendency for X and Y to align their final selling price on the basis of common costs, a greater problem arises, and the extent to which external competition to X and Y exists will be an important indicator of the pressures on X and Y to respond to the market generally, rather than to each other. In some markets especially for high technology or complex products price may not be the central ingredient of competition, pre and post-sales levels of service may be crucial. In these markets the natural alignment of prices between X and Y might not be a hindrance to section 21(2), provided that X and Y compete effectively in non-price matters.

(5) Pending registration and severance clauses

12.91 It is customary in joint venture containing registrable restrictions to include a clause which provides that: "No provision of the arrangement constituted by this agreement and any related understandings between the parties which is such as to make it liable to registration under the Restrictive Trade Practices Act 1976 shall come into effect until the day after that on which particulars thereof are duly furnished to the Director General of Fair Trading in accordance with the said Act." The need for such a suspensory clause has largely been removed by the removal of the requirement that restrictions be registered before they come into effect.[139] It is sufficient in most cases that furnishing of particulars takes place within three months of the agreement being made. It will be recalled that restrictions in unregistered agreements are void and unenforceable[140] and any party who suffers damages as the

[138] See DGFT Annual Report 1980, p. 50; DTI and OFT Document, *Guidelines on the Operation of the Restrictive Trade Practices Act 1976* (1984), Annex C, para. 1; OFT Document, *Restrictive Practices* (1985), p. 31.

[139] By the Deregulation (Restrictive Trade Practices Act 1976) (Amendment) (Time Limits) Order S.I. 1996 No. 347 made pursuant to s. 1 Deregulation and Contracting Out Act 1994. See further paras. 4.35–4.37.

[140] s. 35(1)(a) RTPA 1976.

result thereof may bring action for damages in respect of the agreement.[141] Additionally, it is not uncommon for agreements to contain severance clauses whereby the parties specify that if the restrictions in the agreement have not been cleared by the relevant authorities (formally, the Director General of Fair Trading) by a specified date, then the agreement shall take effect as if the restriction therein were deleted.[142] Such a clause is really only useful in respect of restrictions that the parties do not consider essential and which the parties are unwilling to allow become an obstacle to commencement of the agreement.

(6) Section 29 RTPA 1976: agreements important to the national economy

12.92 The Secretary of State, advised by the DTI, may exempt from registration any agreement that is considered to be of importance to the national economy under section 29 RTPA 1976. The cases exempted by this provision are invariably have been joint ventures.[143] Detailed analysis of the wording of section 29 is given at paras 2.3–2.36. There are no limits to the type of agreement that benefit from section 29. To be considered important to the national economy, agreements will probably have to be involved in a new high-technology field, or be in a field of activity in which the government considers it important to have active UK corporate participation. There is little doubt but that certain agreements, registered in normal fashion under the RTPA, might have benefited from this provision. The advantage of section 29 is that it allows the parties to keep restrictions in their agreements that might have had to be deleted if the parties had wanted to benefit from the section 21(2) procedure; section 29 does not provide that only agreements whose restrictions are not "significant" may obtain exemption. Another advantage is that the DTI gives priority to section 29 agreements and decisions on them may be given within weeks; the "waiting period" under section 21(2) is rarely less than six months for even the most innocuous agreements and may be longer. It should not be overlooked that agreements of a size likely to benefit from section 29 exemption will almost certainly have to be cleared with the European Commission under Article 85 EC. Cases on section 29 RTPA 1976 are discussed throughout this chapter.

(7) Joint ventures and the Fair Trading Act 1973

12.93 Technically, some joint ventures may qualify as mergers within the meaning of the Fair Trading Act 1973. Where X and Y combine their respective capacities and facilities in a joint venture such that one or other or both of the parties ceases to be distinct, then the Secretary of State is empowered to refer the joint venture/merger to the MMC under section 64 FTA 1973. Where X and Y, however, create a new joint venture company so that no enterprise "ceases to be distinct" no reference may be made. In practice, the merger provisions are not used to regulate joint ventures.

12.94 Joint ventures may come under scrutiny in the course of a complex monopoly investigation under the FTA 1973. A proposal by the two main cross-channel ferry operators, P&O and Sealink, to enter into an agreement to provide a joint car ferry service, ostensibly to counter the threat of competition from Eurotunnel, was found to be likely to be against the public interest by the MMC.[144] This decision was reached on the basis that it

[141] s. 35(2) RTPA 1976.

[142] e.g. No.1583 Register of Restrictive Trade Practices, *Structure Testing Systems Ltd* (1984): "Each paragraph above shall be construed as a separate and independent stipulation and if any restriction on the parties therein contained shall be held to be void or unenforceable all other restrictions therein contained shall remain in full force and effect."

[143] e.g. Exempt Register No. 149, *Agricultural Biotechnology* (1984); Exempt Register No. 147, *Systems X* (1982); Exempt Register No. 148, *Rolls-Royce and GEC (Gas Turbine Powered Generating Sets)* (1984)

[144] *Cross-Channel Car Ferries*, Cm 903, 1989.

was difficult to predict what competitive check would be exercised by Eurotunnel on the ferry operators in return for the reduction in competition between the ferry operators resulting from the proposed joint arrangements. Undertakings not to put these arrangements into effect were given to the Secretary of State by the ferry operators.[145] The companies were subsequently released from these undertakings and mergers permitted in view of overcapacity in the cross-channel ferry services and intense competition from Eurotunnel.

C. Joint Selling Ventures

12.95 Where parties agree to pool their collective selling resources through a single selling agency which has the exclusive right to sell the goods and set prices, competition between the parties as to price may be negated. Such agreements are rarely permissible.[146] Where the central agency does not set the prices and where parties are not bound to sell exclusively via the central agency, then the anti-competitive potential is minimised and the relevant authorities may treat the venture sympathetically. Where a joint selling agency is instituted as a means of obtaining fair negotiation terms with a dominant purchaser (nationalised industry, joint-purchasing consortium, monopolist, etc.) then the attitude of the authorities is harder to predict. There is certainly scope for exemption in such cases.

1. EC Law

(1) Under Article 85(1) EC

12.96 Joint sales agencies, which have the exclusive right to export the members' products to the EC and to set selling prices, will invariably be caught by Article 85(1).[147] It is immaterial that the joint sales venture will effect only a small percentage of the target market, especially where that market is oligopolistic or where the exporters are oligopolists in their own market or where excess capacity exists.[148] Article 85(3) will be given in exceptional cases only. The Commission has in the past exempted cases where the joint agency sold exclusively to the national market and/or on markets outside of the EC but where the parties retained freedom to sell on the remainder of the EC market.[149] However the Commission usually takes the view that a joint sales agency which concentrates upon the domestic market can, none the less, affect trade between the Member States so as to activate Article 85(1) EC.[150] This will particularly be the case where the parties hold substantial market shares and through the joint agency may exert a dominant influence on pricing in the market which non-nationals may feel loathe to disturb for fear of a price war. The Commission contend that the size and solidarity of national producers has a direct bear-

[145] DTI Press Notice dated 20 December, 1989.

[146] See CJV Notice, paras. 38 and 60.

[147] e.g. *Cimbel* [1973] CMLR D167; *Central Stikstof* [1979] 1 CMLR 11; *Cobelaz No. 1* [1968] CMLR D45; *Cobelaz No. 2* [1968] CMLR D68, *Comptoir Français de L'Azote* [1968] CMLR D57; *Necomout, Seventh Report on Competition Policy* (1977), p. 94, para. 112. *Hudson's Bay Co/Dansk Pelsdryavlerforening* OJ 1988 L316/43; *Ansac* OJ 1993 L152/54.

[148] e.g. *Floral* [1980] 2 CMLR 285.

[149] e.g. *Cobelaz No. 1* [1968] CMLR D45; *Cobelaz No. 2* [1968] CMLR D68; *Supexie* [1971] CMLR D1.

[150] *CSV* OJ 1976 1192/27; *Kali and Salz* [1974] 1 CMLR D1.

ing on foreign producers willingness to export to that state.[151] Joint sales agencies which seek to combine competitors "in a syndicated" or "complete" fashion by regulating sales patterns will infringe Article 85(1) with almost no chance of exemption. Thus attempts to allocate quotas to the members,[152] or operate equalisation of receipts schemes,[153] or limit the development of new capacity among members, or require members to notify each other when they intend to increase output,[154] etc., will be prohibited under Article 85(1).[155] Furthermore, the Commission is unlikely to exempt an agreement between competitors to use each other as sales agencies.[156]

(2) Exemption under Article 85(3) EC: negative clearance

12.97 Few agreements to harmonise sales efforts will be suitable for exemption. Joint selling ventures which operate only outside of the EC do not fall within Article 85(1).[157] They might, however, if they are sold subject to a ban on reimportation to the EC, in which case Article 85(1) may apply if the ban affects a significant number or amount of the products. Joint sales ventures between small firms may obtain exemption where their combined market share is small, probably under 5 per cent of the total market[158] and where the joint venture enables the parties to compete more effectively with larger competitors.[159] Such cases may not even be within Article 85(1) since they enhance rather than diminish overall competition or at least have only a minimal effect on competition, though the Commission is more likely to decide that such an agreement is subject to Article 85(1) but potentially exemptible under Article 85(3). It will be relevant to ask whether the parties could have exported without the assistance of the joint venture. Only in exceptional cases will joint sales ventures which export be exemptible under Article 85(3). One such case is *UIP*[160] where a film distribution joint venture between three film producers was, after several modifications to the original agreement, granted exemption, initially for five years. The key to this decision seems to have been that there was a declining market,[161] in that cinema audiences were reducing in size, and this was an attempt to rationalise distribution

[151] *Central Stikstof* [1979] CMLR 11 at pp. 36, 37: "The concentration of supplies from two manufacturers of this size and importance on a Community market constitutes an economic unit which discourages foreign manufacturers from pursuing a more active export policy, effectively preventing them altogether from doing so. This danger increases in proportion to the power and solidarity of manufacturers in the country of destination." See also Commission answer to WQ No. 29/72, OJ 1972 C 68/11.

[152] e.g. *Air Forge, Twelfth Report on Competition Policy* (1982), pp. 71, 72, paras. 85, 86—it is incompatible for two large producers to incorporate a joint venture which will obtain orders for goods and share them out between the parents. This amounts to prohibited market sharing.

[153] See paras. 8.216–8.225 on equalisation of receipts schemes.

[154] *Cimbel* [1973] CMLR D167 and especially at p. D184, para. 36.

[155] *Kali and Salz* [1974] 1 CMLR D1.

[156] *SAFCO* [1972] CMLR D83. But cf. Art. 3(b) Reg. 1983/83/EEC OJ 1983 1173/1, block exemption avail. able for non-reciprocal exclusive dealing agreements where one of the parties has a total annual turn. over of not more than ECU100 million. See Art. 3(b) of Reg. 84/83/EEC, OJ 1983 L173/5 in respect of exclusive purchasing. For analysis of these provisions see paras 10.67-68 and 10.163.

[157] *DECA* JO 1964 2761, [1965] CMLR 50; *VVVF* JO 1969 L168/22, [1970] CMLR D1. however, in *Centraal stiksjor Verkoopkantoor NV* [1979] 1 CMLR 11, the Commission, at para. 74, left open the question whether a joint selling venture which consisted only of making specified quantities of products available for sales in non-member states could be held to have an appreciable effect on intra-Community trade.

[158] Under the Notice on Agreements of Minor Importance, OJ 1986 C231/2, parties to an agreement which have less than 5 per cent market share and combined turnover of less than ECU300 million are presumed by the Commission not to be caught by Art. 85(1). But see proposed revisions noted at para. 6.53.

[159] See Notice on Co-operation Agreements, para. II(6), OJ 1968 C75/3.

[160] [1990] 4 CMLR 749.

[161] [1990] 4 CMLR 749, 761 at para. 47.

by combining facilities to reap economies of scale. The final decision whether a film was to be distributed remained with the parent producer rather than the joint venture distributor, hence the joint venture could not by itself co-ordinate producers' distribution policy. Rather, the joint venture operated as a facility which had the right of first refusal to distribute a film, but otherwise no exclusive control over distribution.[162] Finally, although the joint venture would have approximately 22 per cent of the EC market, this would be countervailed by the market power of the exhibitors which actually show the films and which had greater concentrations of market power in their roles as buyers.[163] The joint venture can thus be seen as the minimum necessary to reduce distribution costs in a declining market, while preserving the maximum of competition between the parent producers. In considering an application for renewal of this exemption, the Commission stated that it was concerned that the joint venture did not prevent third parties having equal access to this market on equitable terms.[164]

12.98 Where, however, the parties to a joint venture are not in direct competition with each other, then the joint venture will generally be lawful.[165] In the Commission Notice on Co-operation, the Commission has confirmed this view that consortia of non-competing firms set up for the joint execution of orders do not restrain competition.[166] By non-competing the Commission means firms which will not, in the foreseeable future, compete with regard to the products or services involved in the consortia.[167] Where the parties do compete they may, none the less, enter the agreement where they are otherwise unable (for lack of experience, specialised knowledge, capacity or finances, etc.) to execute the order at all or in time or in accordance with the specified requirements, There may, however, be a restraint of competition if parties agree only to work within the consortia and to curtail their independent activities.

2. *UK Law*

(1) Registrability

12.99 Joint sales agreements are usually registrable under section 6(1)(d) RTPA 1976 as restrictions in respect of the quantities of goods to be acquired by the joint venture.[168] Where X and Y and Z agree to sell exclusively via a joint agency, this will be a restriction under section 6(1)(d) RTPA 1976 as to the quantities (i.e. 100 per cent) to be supplied and perhaps under section 6(1)(f) RTPA 1976 as to the persons or classes of person to be supplied, since the parties, by selling exclusively to the joint agency, impliedly accept negative restrictions on selling to other persons. Where the parties agree to sell only a percentage of output via the agency this will be a restriction under section 6(1)(d) and section 6(1)(f) RTPA 1976 in so far as the parties are limited in their ability to sell to other persons. Where the agency sells on common terms and conditions, this would be a restriction under section 6(1)(a) and (c) on prices and terms and conditions.

162 [1990] 4 CMLR 749, 763 at para. 55.
163 [1990] 4 CMLR 749, 763 at para. 58.
164 *Twenty-third Report on Competition Policy* (1993), para. 147. Film distribution was also investigated in the UK by the MMC under the FTA 1973, and its system of film distribution found largely not to be operating against the public interest: *Films*, Cm 2673 (October 1994).
165 *Wild and Leitz* [1972] CMLR D36; *Machine Outils* [1968] CMLR D23.
166 para. II(5) OJ 1968 C 75/3; [1968] CMLR D1.
167 See paras 12.27-12.34.
168 *British Basic Slag Ltd* (1962) LR 3 RP 178; [1962] 1 WLR 986 at p. 994 (RPC) affirmed [1963] 1 WLR 727 at pp. 738, 744, 745 (CA).

(2) Dispensation under section 21(2)

12.100 Where the joint selling agency is a vehicle for producers to align selling prices and terms and conditions it will be inappropriate for section 21(2) treatment. Where the parties sell through the agency as a means of reducing transport costs but accept no restrictions as to the amount of product they sell via the agency or as to the prices and terms and conditions on which they sell, then there should be no problems under section 21(2).[169] This is particularly so where the parties are small or medium-sized and where scale economies are passed on to consumers. It might well be possible to draft such agreements so as to avoid registration where the parties do not accept restrictions on quantities, prices or terms and conditions. Agreements need only be registered of course where two parties accept restrictions. Thus, if X and Y incorporate XY Ltd as a joint selling agency and in this tripartite agreement only XY Ltd accepts restrictions, then the agreement is not registrable. Where X and Y combine complementary skills and technologies to jointly research produce and sell a product section 21(2) dispensation may well be available. Thus in *Water Injection and Treatment Agreement*[170] BP Trading Ltd and Plenty Group Ltd incorporated Oil Plus Ltd as a joint venture company to produce and market a water injection and treatment package for use in enhanced oil recovery from oil reservoirs. The joint company thus combined Plenty's experience in water filtration and treatment and BP's technological expertise and know-how relating to enhanced recovery of oil from oil reservoirs by means of water injection. One of the clauses of the agreement restricted the parents from competing with the joint venture for a five-year period, subject to Plenty's right to meet the specific filtration requirements of any third party and subject to a right for either parent to supply where a customer bona fide desired the services of a particular parent and not the joint venture. The joint venture was occasioned primarily because neither party had the overall skills to provide effectively the treatment and filtration services. Hence, in the absence of the agreement, the services and related products might not have been produced. In such cases exclusive sales rights (albeit limited to a number of years) may be reasonable adjuncts to joint production. Joint tendering agreements whereby X, Y and Z combine to tender for the supply of goods and/or services may benefit from section 21(2). Such agreements are distinct from collusive tendering cartels whereby X, Y and Z agree as to the prices at which they will all *separately* tender. Thus, in *Taylor Woodrow Construction–Co-operative Wholesale Society-William Steward*[171] the parties agreed to combine forces to tender for supply of goods and services in connection with construction work.

[169] See No. S466 Register of Restrictive Trade Practices, Agreement between *Cleveland Co Ltd, Texaco Ltd, Gulf Oil (GB) Ltd, Amoco* and *MMM Pipelines Ltd* to establish MMM Pipelines as a joint venture company to transport petroleum by pipeline to the Midlands and Manchester areas. Under the agreement the parties incorporated MMM Pipelines to construct, own, operate and maintain a pipeline from Milford Haven to the Midlands and Manchester for transporting petroleum. Esso was the major contributor to share capital (75 per cent) and was the operator of the transportation network. The tariff for transportation was set at a rate which was not in excess of that charged for alternative modes of transport. Third parties were allowed to use the network on terms that were the same as the parties to the agreement. S. 21(2) dispensation was granted in 1954. See also *Freightron US Department of Justice Antitrust Division Business Review Letter* (15 February 1984)—shipping associations incorporated joint venture to solicit and consolidate freight. The venture would solicit and consolidate less-than-container, and less-than-truckload cargo and would obtain rate discounts offered by truckers and railroads on these amounts. The Department of Justice stated that they would not challenge the agreement.

[170] No. 4767 and S.745 Register of Restrictive Trade Practices (1982) (agreement contained registrable goods and services elements).

[171] No. 5301 Register of Restrictive Trade Practices (1983). See also for other agreements involving the same parties No. 5484 (concerning a tender for work on Bridlington Community Hospital); and No. 5485 (concerning a tender for work on Goole Community Hospital). See also No. 3632 Register of Restrictive Trade Practices, *National Electrical Distributors Joint Tendering Scheme* (1979).

The parties possessed different areas of expertise in general building work, mechanical services, and, electrical services. The agreement effectively precluded the parties from making individual tenders but this restriction did not operate where either the joint tender failed to materialise or failed to succeed. Given that the agreement combined complementary expertise and that in the absence of the agreement the parties might have been unable to provide effectively the goods and services sought by the buyer, the restriction was considered insignificant. Indeed, the agreement may have enhanced competition by enabling an additional tender to be added to those already existing.

(3) Exempt agreement under Schedule 3, paras. 6 and 9 RTPA 1976: export agreements

12.101 Agreements containing restrictions which have overseas operation exclusively are not within the scope of the RTPA 1976 under Schedule 3, paras. 6 and 9 RTPA 1976. These provisions are discussed at paras. 2.215–2.221. The *agreement* need not, *per se*, be exclusively concerned with exports; any *restrictions* therein must be. By virtue of section 25 RTPA 1976 export agreements to which Schedule 3, paras. 6 and 9 apply must be registered on a non-public register. This registration duty is for the government's administrative convenience, no legal consequences attach to failure to register. In practice the duty is often flouted. The Schedule 3, paras. 6 and 9 exemptions have very limited value since an export agreement affecting the EC will be subject to Article 85(1) EC which applies strictly to joint export ventures (see above); its only use may be in respect of sales outside of the EC, though these sales should not be accompanied by bans on resale back to the EC, since this might influence the EC market and render the agreement subject to Article 85 EC.

(4) Joint selling and section 29 RTPA 1976: agreements important to the national economy

12.102 A number of agreements involving joint production and marketing have been exempted under this provision. These are dealt with in more depth in the section on R&D below. In *Rolls-Royce and GEC*[172] the parties combined the complementary talents of Rolls-Royce in the manufacture of gas-turbine engines and of GEC in the manufacture of generating sets to produce gas turbine generating sets. These are electricity generators that operate independently of a grid and had considerable export potential. They may be used, for example, in heavy engineering or other operations located in areas remote from organised power sources (deserts, oceans, etc.). Rolls-Royce and GEC jointly developed the product through a joint venture company which had the exclusive right (subject to certain exceptions) to sell the joint product. The agreement was exemptible under section 29 since it enabled the parties to compete effectively on the international market and ensured a British representation in those markets.

12.103 In *Agricultural Biotechnology*[173] an agreement in the field of agricultural biotechnology providing for joint R&D and subsequent marketing was given a five-year exemption under section 29. The agreement was important to the national economy in that it enabled UK firms to participate actively in a highly specialised market considered to be of future importance.

12.104 In *System X*[174] an agreement between British Telecommunications (BT), Plessey (P) and GEC was exempted from registration under section 29. Unlike the other agree-

[172] Exempt Register No.148 (June 1984).
[173] Exempt Register No.149 (June 1984).
[174] Exempt Register No.147 (October 1982).

ments, this did not involve a joint R&D upon which was appended joint marketing and supply. This agreement concerned the planned and co-operative supply of improved telephone exchange equipment to BT for use in the (then) new System X telephone systems. Under the agreement GEC and P shared supplies on an ordered basis for a specified period prior to the resumption of full competitive tendering by GEC and P for supply contracts to BT. In the note prefacing the heads of agreement the parties stated: "BT is considering a revised programme of modernisation and is accordingly examining the practicability of accelerating the rate of development, manufacture and introduction of System X. It is the objective of the parties to this Agreement to achieve changes in the procurement and supply of System X to allow more effective production of equipment in higher volumes at lower cost, with progressively improved features and facilities. This would permit GEC and Plessey to achieve their aim of expansion of export activity." This joint supply agreement was in reality a market sharing agreement between GEC and P and hence registrable under section 6(1)(d) RTPA 1976 as a restriction on quantities to be supplied (i.e. GEC and P divided supplies to BT between them). The agreement was exempted under section 29. A number of reasons may be advanced for this. First, the agreement was only temporary, pending the reintroduction of competitive tendering between GEC and P. Secondly, the agreement covered a transitional period in the development of System X during which BT was seeking to accelerate the introduction of System X. Thirdly, the installation of System X was a nationwide operation, the efficiency of which directly affected consumers and users of telephone services. Fourthly, the technology and products in question had significant export potential as other European states privatised telecommunications sectors and opened their markets to foreign technology and suppliers. There may have been a fifth reason in this particular case in that the UK government did not wish BT to have to face the option of defending a lengthy and potentially reputation-damaging defence of the agreement before the RPC shortly prior to (or even during) the sale of its shares to the public in 1984.

D. Joint Purchasing

12.105 Joint purchasing is not treated the same as joint selling. It may be justified as a means whereby small and medium-sized buyers join forces either to negotiate collectively with a dominant supplier or to purchase in greater quantities so as to earn greater discounts which can then be passed on to consumers. The acceptability or otherwise of joint buying ventures will depend largely upon circumstances.

1. *EC Law*

12.106 The Commission has issued fewer decisions on joint purchasing than on joint selling. The Commission appears to be sceptical about the need for joint purchasing, stating that "the disadvantages often outweigh the possible benefits which can accompany purchasing JVs, particularly those between competing producers".[175] It has stated that exemptions are available "only in exceptional cases and then only if the parents retain the possibility of purchasing individually, i.e. they must not agree to buy only via the purchasing

175 The Commission's policy on joint purchasing is set out in the CJV Notice, paras. 39 and 61. The Commission notes, perhaps ominously, in para. 61 that "no decision has, however, concerned the most important of the purchasing JVs so far".

agency.[176] More specifically the parties should retain the liberty to purchase about 75 per cent of their requirements from other suppliers of their choice.[177] If the parties, in exercising their discretion as to suppliers, thereafter decide independently to purchase a higher percentage of their needs from the agency, this is apparently acceptable.[178] Parties should not restrain their freedom as to the prices and terms and conditions upon which they resell the goods purchased from the agency.[179] Nor should parties accept restrictions on purchasing from other Member States, as such a restriction would amount to a material infringement of Article 85(1) EC.[180] It follows from the above that joint purchasing is perfectly acceptable where contractually the parties retain buying and selling independence from the agency; though buying independence may be limited by up to 25 per cent.

12.107 In every case the respective purchasing power of each individual party to the agreement must be examined. Where parties are economically powerful enough to obtain on an individual basis favourable buying terms from suppliers, the Commission doubts the need for a joint venture.[181] Conversely, where the parties even collectively are small (i.e. between 1 and 5 per cent of total demand is affected by the venture) and the joint venture enables them to obtain quantity discounts which may be passed on to customers, then negative clearance may be available on the basis that the agreement has an imperceptible impact upon completion and/or inter-state trade.[182] Alternatively, where the parties combined have a significant degree of market power, exemption under Article 85(3) may be available where the agreement enables the parties to negotiate reasonable terms with dominant suppliers.[183] An exemption may be possible where the parties have combined to

[176] *SOCEMAS* [1968] CMLR D28; *INTERGROUP* [1975] 2 CMLR D14; *FRUBO* [1974] 2 CMLR D89; Commission answer to WQ No. 676/76, OJ 1977 C50/17. See also Case 61/80 *Co-operative Stremsel* v *Commission* [1982] 1 CMLR 240; [1981] ECR 851—Court condemned a joint production co-operative whose output accounted for 90 per cent of the total output of the product in the Netherlands and who required members, upon payment of financial penalty, to purchases their total requirements from the co-operative. (For Commission decision, see [1980] 2 CMLR 402.)

[177] On the basis of *National Sulphuric Acid* [1980] 3 CMLR 429 where the joint purchasing association was given exemption under Art. 85(3) on condition, *inter alia*, that it reduced its buying requirement for members to 25 per cent. This exemption was renewed for a further ten years in 1989: *National Sulphuric Acid (No. 2)* [1990] 4 CMLR 612, even though in practice nearly all of the members bought all of their requirements of sulphur through the association (para. 9 of the Decision).

[178] *SOCEMAS* [1968] CMLR D28: *National Sulphuric Acid (No. 2)* [1990] 4 CMCA 612, para. 9; the essential point is that parties retain freedom to purchase elsewhere *if they wish*.

[179] *INTERGROUP* [1975] 2 CMLR D14; *National Sulphuric Acid* [1980] 3 CMLR 429. Commission required deletion of clauses restricting the uses to which sulphur purchased via the pool could be put and the customers to whom it could be resold, before they would grant exemption under Art. 85(3) EC. See also *Jernbranchen* [1974] 2 CMLR D73 under Art. 65 (2) of the ECSC Treaty and see for subsequent developments on this case, *Thirteenth Report on Competition Policy* (1983), pp. 86, 87, paras. 130, 131. See also *Stahlring* [1972] CMLR D107 and (renewal of exemption) [1983] 2 CMLR 307, also under Art. 65(2) ECSC.

[180] e.g. *Cementhandelaren* [1973] CMLR D16. In *Re Sugar Beet* OJ 1990 L31/35, [1991] 4 CMLR 629, the commission condemned an agreement favouring domestic suppliers; *Ijsselsentrale* OJ 1991 L28/32.

[181] This is apparently also the current view of the US Department of Justice, see *Shippers Association FAK rates Business Review Letter* (12 February 1985). The Department notified an association of shipping associations that they would not challenge the joint negotiation by the association of freight rates. The Department *stated*, in the business review letter: "collective rate negotiation of the type AISA proposes has the potential to create volume discounts that result in lower freight charges. To the extent this occurs, joint negotiation of FAK [freight all kinds] contracts could be pro-competitive. The Department would challenge collective negotiation of FAK rates, however, if such concerted activity is likely to result in the exercise of market power by shippers over freight rates (monopsony power) in any relevant market."

[182] e.g. *SOCEMAS* [1968] CMLR D28; *Department Stores* [1979] 3 CMLR 637; *INTERGROUP* [1975] 2 CMLR D14.

[183] e.g. *National Sulphuric Acid* [1980] 3 CMLR 429 noted in *Tenth Report on Competition Policy* (1980), pp. 76, 77, paras. 112, 113.

compete with other larger suppliers. In *EEIG Orphe*[184] the Commission indicated in a comfort letter that it would exempt a joint venture through the medium of a European Economic Interest Grouping whereby small and medium-sized pharmaceutical wholesalers combined to purchase in a market dominated by very large wholesalers. A factor that will be relevant will be the extent to which members of the group are in competition with each other. A buying pool which purchases a basic raw material (e.g. sulphur) may act on behalf of a number of different types of buyer who operate in very different markets. A problem of joint buying is that purchasers take the relevant product at similar if not uniform prices. Where the product forms a high percentage of the total costs of the buyer, then this might encourage uniform pricing of the ultimate product. Similar costs lead to similar selling prices. Where the buyers are all producing *different* products such price harmony cannot evolve. Hence the degree of competition between buyers is relevant. The Commission's 75 per cent freedom rule minimises the risk involved, though it does not negative the risk altogether since buyers may voluntarily increase the volume of their purchases through the agency.

12.108 The Court of Justice stated in *Gottrup-Klim*[185] that a provision in an agricultural co-operative purchasing association restricting members from participating in other forms of co-operative purchasing was not caught by Article 85(1) EC, provided it was necessary to ensure that the co-operative functioned properly and maintained its contractual power in relation to producers. The Court considered that the co-operative in question did not exceed such limits, since it was restricted to purchasing only those farm supplies where price would decrease with bulk purchases, and that non-members were entitled to buy from the co-operative, though without the annual discounts available to members. Importantly, the co-operative did not restrict its members from purchasing individually if they so wished.

12.109 Finally, joint purchasing JVs will not be permitted exemption if they exclude other potential purchasers from the market. This is illustrated by a series of cases in the audio-visual sector, where the Commission has intervened to regulate the joint purchasing of film and sports programmes rights.[186] For example, in *EBU/Eurovision*[187] the Commission required the members to grant access to non-members to coverage of television programmes, particularly of sporting events, as a condition of granting exemption. This was to ensure that other broadcasters, not being EBU members, were not excluded from the sporting coverage market.

2. *UK Law*

(1) Registrability under the RTPA 1976

12.110 Group purchasing agreements are common in the grocery market and indeed elsewhere in markets populated by small and medium sized businesses. They frequently involve registrable restrictions. Common clauses which will lead to activation of the RTPA 1976 are as follows: (a) price recommendations: recommendation made by the joint agency (often

[184] *Twentieth Report on Competition Policy* (1990), para. 102.

[185] C-250/92 *Gottrup-Klim Grovvareforeninger* v *Dansk Landbrugs Grovvareselskab* [1994] ECR I-5641.

[186] *Film Purchases by German TV Stations* OJ 1989 L284/36, [1990] 4 CMLR 841; *Screensport/EBU* OJ 1991 L63/32, [1992] 5 CMLR 273; *Eurosport (III)* OJ 1993 C76/8. See *Nineteenth Report on Competition Policy* (1989), para. 33; *Twentieth Report on Competition Policy* (1990), para. 82; *Twenty-second Report on Competition Policy* (1992), paras. 64–66.

[187] OJ 1993 L179/23; see *Twenty-third Report on Competition Policy* (1993), para. 220.

a trade association) as to the prices to be charged for goods covered by special promotions and/or its "own brand" goods are registrable under section 6(1)(b) as restrictions on prices to be recommended or suggested as to the prices to be charged on resale of the goods supplied. These recommendations are common in joint purchasing organisations in the grocery field where members are recommended to charge specified prices for lines of goods marked as "promotions" or "own brands"; (b) geographical selling restrictions on wholesalers: where the joint agency restricts its wholesaler members from supplying or otherwise sponsoring retailers outside a defined area or from supplying or otherwise sponsoring two or more retailers who would be in direct competition with each other, then this is a restriction under section 6(1)(f) RTPA on the persons or classes of persons to whom goods are to be supplied; (c) minimum purchase requirements: clauses requiring members (wholesalers or retailers) to purchase minimum requirements (e.g. 50 per cent of total demand) from the joint agency entail restrictions under section 6(1)(d) RTPA 1976 on the quantities of goods to be acquired; (d) clauses restraining members from joining any other buying group constitute restrictions under section 6(1)(f) RTPA 1976 on the persons or classes of person from whom goods are to be acquired; (e) quotas: clauses allocating quantities purchased by the group to members according to a formula which is not necessarily related to the members actual needs is a restriction under section 6(1)(d) RTPA 1976 on the quantities of goods to be acquired by the members; (f) restrictions on use or sale of product: clauses limiting the uses to which members may put the purchased product, for example, requiring members to use the product for their own needs and prohibiting them from reselling it, may constitute a restriction under section 6(1)(c) on the terms and conditions subject to which goods are to be acquired (i.e. product can be purchased on condition that it is utilised by purchaser and is not resold). It may also be a negative implied restriction under section 6(1)(f), i.e. as a restriction on the persons or classes of person to whom the goods are to be supplied, since the own-use/resale ban clause impliedly prevents sale to other persons;[188] (g) ban on sales to public: clauses in agreements concerning "cash and carry" wholesalers prohibiting direct sale to the public are restrictions under section 6(1)(f) RTPA 1976 on the persons or classes of person to whom goods may be supplied.

(2) Dispensation under section 21(2) RTPA 1976

12.111 The OFT have given a number of dispensations from reference to the RPC under section 21(2). Though in some cases clauses have had to be deleted or modified in order to render the agreement suitable for section 21(2) treatment. Thus in *Land Mark Cash and Carry*[189] the group purchasing agency required members (wholesalers) to feature, for a two-week period, products as promotions when the agency notified the product to the member. The agency in this period would undertake national promotion of the product. The OFT required the agency to modify the mandatory element in the rules so that members were not in future *required* to promote or feature the notified product. The OFT was also concerned to ensure that certain other aspects of the scheme did not operate restrictively. Thus, it required the agency to give an assurance that clauses in the code of practice providing for the provision of information on sales volumes and types to the agency by members and also providing that a member would notify the agency when it intended to expand or extend its operations, were not being used to facilitate the exchange

[188] See e.g. *National Sulphuric Acid Association* [1963] LR 4 RP 169; [1963] 1 WLR 848 at p. 852 where restrictions requiring purchasers to use the elemental sulphur purchased via the pool for their own purposes and prohibiting resale to any person outside of the pool were assumed to be registrable though it is not stated under which provision of s. 6 RTPA.

[189] No. 3686 Register of Restrictive Trade Practices (1977).

of price information and policies or as a means of regulating the commercial expansion of members. Ultimately, section 21(2) RTPA 1976 dispensation was given.[190]

12.112 Recommendations by the agency as to prices for promotions or own-brand goods are usually appropriate to section 21(2) treatment. Though, the recommendation should not bind members nor should members be informed that, though technically free to make their own pricing decisions, they are expected to comply with the recommended price. Ideally, the recommended price should be in the form of a maximum price below which members are free to choose their own price level.[191] Bans on sales to the public imposed on wholesalers are unsuitable for section 21(2) treatment. Though, where such restrictions are imposed on wholesalers by local authorities in the form of conditions in planning permissions in respect of the use of warehouses, this will not represent a bar to section 21(2) treatment. Many local authorities impose such conditions under planning legislation as a means of preventing warehouse areas being converted into retail centres with the traffic and "people" problems that entails.[192] Geographical restrictions on the areas in which a wholesaler member may supply goods to retailers are unsuitable for section 21(2) treatment and indeed will entail reference to the RPC should market sharing clauses not be deleted. In *V.G. Grocery Services Ltd*[193] section 21(2) dispensation was given but only after the purchasing group had abandoned certain restrictions on wholesaler's rights to sell to retailers. In particular, the agency had to delete from the rules restrictions on wholesalers: (a) not to supply goods bearing the trademark of the group save in each member's own territory; (b) not to open or service a wholly owned shop under the VG banner in another wholesaler's territory unless the latter agrees; (c) not to service a VG shop outside a member's own territory unless the company in whose territory the shop is situated has agreed and (when it is a case of a retailer opening another shop in a different territory) unless the member shall have first tried to persuade the retailer to accept servicing from his local wholesaler; and (d) not to canvass or supply VG shops outside a member's territory with products other than grocery products. Clauses requiring members to purchase a minimum requirement from the agency may be suitable for section 21(2) treatment, where the minimum requirement does not significantly restrain the member's freedom to purchase from other suppliers.[194] A large requirement has the effect of foreclosing rival suppliers from the purchasers. Under EC rules the Commission has allowed 25 per cent purchasing requirements.[195] The OFT does not consider as appropriate for section 21(2) dispensation clauses prohibiting members from joining any other buying group, or which impose quotas.[196]

[190] The agency has a legitimate need for information on sales and consumer patterns since this enables the agency to make more educated and efficient buying decisions. It is doubtful whether goods agreements concerning sales and volumes are registrable. See para 9.66. See also No. 3755 Register of Restrictive Trade practices, *Independent Marketing Services*, exchange of information on the availability of stocks in different parts of the country and terms which they have respectively been able to negotiate with manufacturers. Agreements concerning exchange of information of terms and conditions of trade are registrable (see Art. 3(2)(b) S.I. 1969 No. 1842, discussed at paras. 9.18–9.26).

[191] See e.g. No. 4355 Register of Restrictive Trade Practices, *NISA* (1980).

[192] See e.g. No. 3686 Register of Restrictive Trade Agreements, *Keen Cost Centres* (1977); No. 3828 Register of Restrictive Trade Practices, *Trade markets Management Ltd* (1975); No. 3603 Register of Restrictive Trade Practices, *Big 'N' Cash and Carry* (1974).

[193] No. 3 176 Register of Restrictive Trade Practices (1974).

[194] See e.g. No. 4904 Register of Restrictive Trade Practices, *GG Furniture Ltd* (1981).

[195] *National Sulphuric Acid Association* [1980] 3 CMLR 429.

[196] However, it may be permissible to include a restriction on being involved in ownership of a competing business, depending on the market shares of the parties being restricted. In No 11467 register of Restrictive Trade Agreements *United Roofing Contractors plc* (1993), s. 21(2) directions were given for an agreement where shareholder members of a buying group were restricted from being involved in a competing business, except by way of a minority shareholding in a publicly listed business. As this was a highly competitive market, there was no risk of foreclosure of suppliers as a result of this restriction.

12.113 Joint purchasing may thus, perhaps with appropriate modifications, be suitable for section 21(2) RTPA 1976 treatment. In general terms the OFT considers that joint purchasing confers benefits on consumers in that scale economies realised through quantity discounts may be passed on in lower prices. This, in turn, may enhance inter-brand competition. Where, however, the agency counts for a high percentage of total demand this justification is less convincing. In such cases the OFT may adopt a stricter approach to some of the restrictions in the agreement. Where the agency enables the purchasers to negotiate fair terms with a preponderant supplier, the cartel may be viewed as a counterweight to the dominant supplier. In this respect the argument is expressly referred to in section 10(1)(d) RTPA 1976 and has been assessed, and accepted by the RPC in *National Sulphuric Acid Association Agreement.*[197] It is a serious weakness of this absurdly complex legislation that parties may be precluded from justifying certain restrictions on sound economic grounds simply because the OFT feel legally constrained to refuse to hear such arguments on the basis that they are public interest arguments which only the RPC may assess.

E. Joint Research and Development

12.114 Research and development (R&D) is an integral component of competition which relies upon innovation and the creation of new or improved products or services. The introduction of new products or services stimulates competition and benefits the consumer. R&D, whether concerned with innovation or imitation, is thus central in maintaining a dynamic market structure; a dominant firm can, *in extremis*, almost overnight lose its market share because of the introduction of newer, superior or cheaper technology. None the less, the risks inherent in R&D are substantial; it is expensive and there is no guarantee of success. co-operation in R&D reduces the risks and enables innovation to arise where otherwise it would not have, due to the unwillingness or inability of firms to bear individually the risks. Competition authorities thus adopt a favourable attitude towards joint R&D concentrating their efforts on ensuring that parties limit competition between them only so far as is necessary to attain the objectives of the R&D venture.

1. EC Law

12.115 The Commission has always viewed joint R&D favourably. Indeed, the Community is mandated by Article 130f Treaty of Rome, as introduced by the Single European Act and amended at Maastricht, to encourage all undertakings in "their research and technological development activities of a high quality". In Article 4(2)(3)(b) of Regulation 17/62/EEC the Commission has provided that certain types of joint venture are exempt from the need to notify. Agreements having as their *sole* object joint research and development are accordingly exempt. This exemption is, however, narrow: exemption from the need to notify only lies where the joint venture does not entail any restrictions.[198] In addition to this exemption, the Commission has publicly stated that many joint R&D activities do not restrict competition.[199] The Commission has issued a block exemption granting automatic exemption under Article 85(3) to R&D agreements satisfying its terms, which has been

[197] (1963) LR 4 RP 169; [1963] 1 WLR 848.

[198] Art. 4(2)(3)(b), Reg. 17/62/EEC (see para 6.144 for analysis).

[199] Art. II(3) Notice concerning Agreements, Decisions and concerted Practices in the field of Co-operation between enterprises, OJ 1968 C75/3; [1968] CMLR D5. "The Co-operation Notice".

amended[200] in order to extend its application to R&D agreements which include joint distribution of resulting products, subject to market share limits. Finally, the recent CJV Notice stresses that a R&D joint venture will only restrict competition in exceptional cases, for example where it precludes individual activity by each parent in that area or where it would lead to a restriction of competition on the market for the resulting products.[201] The Commission has indicated its willingness in a number of decisions to exempt R&D agreements not coming within the block exemption, and these are discussed at para. 12.185.

(1) Commission Notice on co-operation: research and development

12.116 In a non-binding Notice issued by the Commission in 1968 a favourable attitude is expressed towards the joint implementation, placing and sharing of R&D between parties. In general the notice indicates that pure R&D agreements are not restrictive. Though subsequently the Commission has taken the view that pure R&D agreements incorporating no restrictions on the parties behaviour may, none the less, be caught by Article 85(1) where R&D is central to the development of the market in question and where the market is oligopolistic in structure. The notice thus has application to generally unconcentrated markets.[202] The validity of this notice remains despite enactment by the Commission of the block exemption for categories of R&D agreement.[203] The following summarises the Notice and its interpretation.

12.117 (a) The mere exchange of experience and results serving only for information does not restrict competition and hence falls outside of Article 85(1).

12.118 (b) Joint R&D up to the point of industrial application is not distortive of competition. This also applies to the sharing out of fields of research provided the results are available to all participants. Where no provision as to access to results is arrived at, the agreement is to be treated as a specialisation agreement.

12.119 (c) Where parties to an agreement restrict their own independent R&D activities, this does restrain competition.[204] The same conclusion applies where participation in the joint venture factually inhibits independent research albeit that they remain contractually free to undertake own R&D.[205] For example, the parties might commit 90 per cent of their R&D budget to the joint venture, thereby leaving an insufficient amount to fund own efforts.[206] Where firms do not perform own R&D, any contractual provision reinforcing the inability by a prohibition is a restriction under Article 85(1). It matters not that the firm would, in all probability, have refrained from individual R&D regardless.[207]

[200] Reg. 151/93/EEC amending Regs. 417/85/EEC, 418/85/EEC, 2349/84/EEC and 556/89/EEC, OJ 1993 121/8. For the amended text of the research and development block exemption, see [1993] 4 CMLR 163. For the original text, see Reg. 418/85/EEC, OJ 1985 153/5 on the application of Art. 85(3) to categories of research and development agreements.

[201] CJV Notice, paras. 37 and 59.

[202] *Henkel–Colgate* OJ 1972 L14/14. This philosophy has been carried over into the block exemption in the form of the 20 per cent rule (see para. 8 of the preamble, and Art. 3(2)).

[203] *Fourteenth Competition Policy Report* (1984), p. 38, para. 29, see also para. 2 of the preamble to Reg. 418/85/EEC.

[204] Notice para. 11(3)(3); *Bayer-Gist Brocades* [1976] 1 CMLR D98; *Beecham–Parke Davis* [1979] 2 CMLR 157 at p.167, para. 33; *Vacuum Interrupters* [1977] 1 CMLR D67.

[205] *Eurogypsum* [1968] CMLR D1; *MAN-SA VIEM* [1974] CMLR D123.

[206] Co-operation Notice para. II(3)(3).

[207] See e.g. *Henkel–Colgate* OJ 1972 114/14; *GEC–WEIR* [1978] 1 CMLR D42; *SOPELEM–Vickers* [1978] 2 CMLR 146.

12.120 (d) Where parties to an agreement accept restrictions on the utilisation of R&D results, this may infringe Article 85(1). For example, X and Y undertake joint R&D but X agrees to use the results for certain purposes only, which do not compete with Y's activities. However, it is not a restraint if parties obtain results of the joint R&D only in relation to their contribution.[208] It may be a restraint, however, if parties are excluded from results not commensurate with their contributions.

12.121 (e) Where parties restrain the licensing of results to third parties there may be an infringement of Article 85(1).[209] Though, parties may agree only to license third parties by common agreement or by majority decision.[210] Participation in a R&D agreement restricts competition if it prevents parties from entering co-operation agreements, in particular concerning R&D, with third parties.[211] However, it is clearly permissible to restrain a party to an R&D venture from divulging results to a third party.[212]

12.122 (f) In assessing a joint R&D venture, the structure of the agreement is immaterial, it is the effects that are important.[213]

(2) Framework of the block exemption for categories of research and development agreement: Regulation 418/85/EC[214]

12.123 The Regulation has a limited ambit. It provides block exemption for three types of agreement: (i) joint R&D coupled to joint exploitation and distribution of the results; (ii) joint exploitation and distribution of the results of prior R&D between the same parties; and (iii) joint R&D without joint exploitation or distribution. The Regulation does *not cover*: (a) agreements in concentrated markets (Article 3); (b) agreements for common exploitation of R&D results which have been derived independently by the parties; or (c) agreements whereby the R&D results of one party are to be exploited jointly. Thus in *BP-Kellogg* the parties entered an agreement to develop designs for the construction of ammonia plant using a catalyst developed beforehand by BP. The Commission noted that the agreement was not block exempt in that it gave rise to restrictions on the exploitation of products and processes that had not been *jointly* developed by the parties. However, the agreement was given individual exemption.[215] It is worth pointing out that the Regulation covers joint exploitation whether contemplated in the original R&D agreement or in a later agreement, thus, the parties need not commit themselves to joint exploitation at the outset, they may wait and see whether the fruits of their labours justify the additional co-operation.

208 Co-operation Notice para.II(3): "It is of the essence of joint research that the results should be exploited by the participating enterprises in proportion to their participation. If the participation of certain enterprises is confined to a specific sector of the joint research project or to the provision of only limited financial assistance, there is no restraint of competition—in so far as there has been no joint research at all—if the results of research are made available to these enterprises only in relation with the degree of their participation."

209 *Henkel–Colgate* OJ 1972 114/14; *Rank–SOPELEM* [1975] 1 CMLR D72.

210 Co-operation Notice para. II(3)(7). *Henkel–Colgate* OJ 1972 L14/14. Though when the exemption was renewed, the Commission required either party to be free to license third parties to use the results of the R&D without the other's consent, the requirement of consent being seen as a barrier to entry to what was an oligopolistic market: *Eighth Report on Competition Policy* (1978), paras. 89-90. See also *EMI Electronics–Jungheinrich Seventh Report on Competition Policy* (1977), p. 98, paras. 119, 120.

211 e.g. *Rank–SOPELEM* [1975] 1 CMLR D68.

212 e.g. *ACEC–Berliet* [1968] CMLR D35.

213 Co-operation Notice para. II(3)(8).

214 OJ 1985 153/5 (22 February 1985). For detailed analysis see: White, "Research and development joint ventures under EC competition law" (1985) 16 IIC 663 (author was largely responsible for drafting the Regulation); Venit, "The research and development block exemption regulation" (1985) ELRev 151 ; Korah, *Collaboration in R&D and EC Competition Rules: Regulation 418/85* (1986).

215 OJ 1985 L369/6.

(3) The basic exemption: the ambit of Regulation 418/85/EC: Article 1(definition of terms)

12.124 The Regulation applies the exemption in Article 85(3) to three types of agreement: (a) joint R&D of products or processes and joint exploitation of the results; (b) joint exploitation of the results of R&D products or processes jointly executed pursuant to a *prior* agreement between the *same parties;* and (c) joint R&D of products or processes excluding joint exploitation of results.

12.125 "Research and development of products or processes" is defined in Article 1(2)(a) to mean: acquisition of technical knowledge; the carrying out of theoretical analysis; systematic study or experimentation including experimental production, technical testing of products or processes, the establishment of the necessary facilities and the obtaining of intellectual property rights for the results. None of these activities entail exploitation. It is notable that the "obtaining" of intellectual property rights constitutes research and development. Clearly however the joint licensing of such rights once obtained would constitute exploitation.

12.126 "Contract processes" means processes arising out of the R&D. "Contract products" means products or services arising out of the research and development or manufactured or provided applying the contract processes.[216] Note that, unlike some other block exemptions, services are included. "Exploitation of the results" means: manufacture of the contract products; application of the contract processes; assignment of intellectual property rights; licensing of intellectual property rights; communication to outsiders of know-how required for manufacture or application. It is thus considered that joint exploitation does not include sales of the contract products or the granting of pure sales licences. Though the grant of a manufacturing licence is presumably taken to imply a licence to sell the products manufactured otherwise the grant would be no more than joint subcontracting which is already exempted in Article 1(3)(a).[217] Distribution of the resulting contract products may be covered following the amendments which have been made to the block exemption.[218] This is done by an extension to the whitelist of permissible restrictions[219] rather than by a more extensive interpretation of "joint exploitation".

12.127 "Technical knowledge" means: technical knowledge which is either protected by an intellectual property right or is secret know-how. Thus, technical knowledge does not necessarily have to be protected by intellectual property rights: it may include secret know-how. No definition is given, however, of "secret" know-how. In general case law, "secret knowledge" remains "secret" until such time as it becomes public knowledge.[220] In fields where technology is rapidly advancing the Commission apparently takes the view that "secret knowledge" may become "public" quite quickly.[221] It is "public" when the knowledge becomes accessible to the average expert. This does not mean to say that the

216 *ibid.*, Art. 1(2)(b) and (c). In *Continental/Michelin* OJ 1988 L305/33, [1989] 4 CMLR 920, the Commission stated at para. 32 that the scope of Art. 1 does "not excluded the joint exploitation of technical knowledge that existed before the cooperation began if ... it has become a component part of the joint development to such an extent that it is necessary for the manufacture, use or sale of the [product]. such technical knowledge has become a part of the contract processes and contract products within the meaning of the definitions given in Article 1(2)(b) and (c) of Regulation 418/85".

217 See White, *op. cit.*, n. 214 p. 679.

218 By Reg. 151/93/EEC.

219 Art. 4.

220 See e.g. *Kabelmetal's Agreement* [197S] 2 CMLR D40 at p. D46, case concerning, *inter alia*, protection of secret know-how in a patent licence.

221 cf. *Reuter–BASF* [1976] 2 CMLR D44: "In view of the rapid development of technology in polyurethane chemistry, it may be questioned whether such knowledge has at the present time sufficient economic value to justify its continued protection by an obligation of secrecy."

average expert actually knows of the technology but only that he should have access to it, e.g. because it has been published.

12.128 Research and development is performed "jointly" where the work is: (a) carried out by a joint team, organisation or undertaking; (b) jointly entrusted to a third party; or (c) allocated between the parties by way of specialisation in research, development or production. Where R&D is entrusted under (b) to a third party the Commission notice on sub-contracting will be more relevant in analysing restrictions than will be the block exemption. Such a third party is apparently not a party to the joint venture. The term "specialisation" is undefined. Hence does it cover only reciprocal specialisation or does it also include agreements whereby only one party specialises? Arguably, the latter, wider interpretation applies given that the Regulation (Article 5(1)(f)) clearly contemplates unequal contributions to the joint R&D or exploitation of results. "Exploitation" is joint where the parties collaborate in any way in the assignment or the licensing of intellectual property rights or the communication of know-how. Finally, it should be borne in mind that only agreements between "undertakings," i.e. commercial operators, are covered by the regulation. A university is not necessarily an undertaking (unless it markets its goods or services). Hence an agreement between a company and a university is not necessarily within Article 1 of the Regulation or Article 85 EC. However, as most universities are now marketing their research facilities in an effort to earn revenue, it seems likely that such activity would be sufficient to make that university an "undertaking" for this purpose.

(4) Pre-conditions for the existence of block exemption: Article 2

12.129 Article 2 provides that the exemption only applies where certain positive conditions are satisfied. Paragraphs 4–7 of the preamble explain that these conditions are necessary to ensure that agreements adequately satisfy the conditions of Article 85(3).

12.130 *(a) Formal structure for R&D*

The Commission require that the R&D be performed within the framework of a programme defining the objectives of the work and the field in which it is to be carried out. R&D agreements should hence be in formal contractual form. Many well drafted agreements contain a preamble setting out in general terms, the respective abilities and areas of expertise of the participating firms, the reasons for the joint venture and the field in which the joint venture is to operate. However, too general a framework may lack the necessary degree of specificity.[222] The block exemption does *not* apply to joint R&D schemes with infinite duration and generalised objectives. Where parties can foresee that R&D efforts may continue in respect of a product once joint exploitation of that product has commenced (e.g. concerning modifications, improvements, etc) then it would be wise to make contractual provision for the situation whereby R&D and exploitation proceed in tandem. This should overcome any problems that might arise from an interpretation of some provisions of the regulation which appear to envisage a cut-off point between joint R&D and subsequent exploitation.

12.131 *(b) Access to results*

All parties must have access to the results of the work.[223] The Commission states in paragraph 4 of the preamble that each of the parties should be given the chance to exploit "any

[222] See *GEC/ANT/Telettra/SAT* [1988] OJ C180/3, para. 12(1), where an agreement to carry out five sets of research and development was held in itself to be too widely drawn to satisfy this test, though the Commission was prepared to grant individual exemption.

[223] See *Carbon Gas Technologie* OJ 1983 1376–parties altered agreement to allow fair access as a condition of being granted exemption under Art. 85(3).

of the results that interest it". This must surely be qualified with the proviso that access may be limited by reference to the respective contributions of the parties. If X participates in a narrow part of a wide venture, there is no commercial reason why he should be entitled to access to all other results, however great his "interest" in them. Access should be proportionate to contribution. This has been recognised by the Commission in the Co-operation Notice (see above). However, this interpretation may not be correct since article 5 (1)(f) allows royalties to be charged to counteract the effects of unequal participation. The permissibility of this clause may imply recognition of the strictness (and validity) of the parties' rights to exploit *any* of the results.[224] Where universities or research institutes participate and are not interested in the industrial exploitation of the results, it may be agreed that they are limited in the use of the results to further research only. It may well be that universities and other similar bodies should be treated as sub-contractors in which case the Commission notice on sub-contracting may be referred to.

12.132 *(c) Pure R&D agreements and use of results*

Where the agreement provides only for pure R&D, each party must remain free to exploit independently the R&D results *and* any pre-existing technical knowledge. Presumably a party (X) who wishes to exploit the intellectual property right made available by party (Y) to the scheme should pay royalties. Thus X would pay Y for the use of Y's pre-existing rights.[225] The requirement that background technical knowledge be licensed to the other party may prove problematic given that the other party will enjoy the right to sub-license that background to third parties.

12.133 *(d) Limitation on joint exploitation*

Joint exploitation must be limited to results which are protected by intellectual property rights. Where know-how is concerned, joint exploitation is exemptible only in respect of such know-how results that "substantially contributes to technical or economic progress". Use of these particular words refer to Article 85(3) which allows exemption where, *inter alia*, the agreement contributes to technical or economic progress. The Commission has added the word "substantially" before the requirement. It has not, however, given any guidance on how to quantify substantially. No assistance is given in the preamble which merely repeats the word (Recital 7). Some assistance may be given by the technology transfer block exemption, which also requires that know-how be, *inter alia* substantial in order to benefit from that block exemption.[226] For that purpose, substantial means that the know-how includes information which is of importance for the whole or a significant part of a process, product or service. With both categories (intellectual property and know-how) joint exploitation is further only permissible where it is limited to those R&D results which are "decisive" (i.e. central or essential) for the manufacture of the contract products or the application of the contract process. Hence, joint exploitation can only arise out of an agreement which had joint R&D as its prime objective. Joint exploitation cannot arise from an agreement which had some other objective but which also contained some ancillary provisions on R&D. Thus if X and Y enter a specialisation agreement whereby X will concentrate on widget production and Y will concentrate on gidget production and the agreement contains some ancillary provisions relating to the pooling of any R&D results that might arise in the unlikely event that it is undertaken on a component common to

224 White, *op. cit.*, at p. 681 seems to support this latter interpretation.

225 See *De Laval–Stork* [1977] 2 CMLR D69 royalties chargeable on licences granted following termination of the scheme. The rate of royalty was required to be set at no more than the lowest rate paid by a third party.

226 Art. 10(3) Reg. 240/96; see para. 13.40.

both widgets and gidgets, then X and Y may not obtain block exemption for joint manufacture even of the common component. Such a joint exploitation agreement might have to be notified to the Commission individually.[227]

12.134 *(e) Repealed*

Prior to amendment by Regulation 151/93, the block exemption did not apply if there was any joint distribution or sale. This is now dealt with under the whitelist in Article 4, where provisions exempting joint distribution and sale arrangements have been included.[228]

12.135 *(f) Specialisation*

Where different parties agree to specialise in the production of different results of the joint R&D, then each party must agree to fulfil orders for suppliers from all of the parties. Under Article 5(1)(h) the parties may be required to supply the other parties with minimum quantities of contract products and to observe minimum standards of quality.

(5) Conditions as to market share, duration of exempt agreement: Article 3

12.136 Article 3 lays down market share criteria which must be satisfied if block exemption is to apply to agreements between competitors, or, to agreements which involve joint exploitation irrespective of whether the parties were competitors when the agreement was first entered into.[229] These market share criteria are further limited if distribution of the contract products is to be carried out by one of the parties, one or more joint undertakings or one or more third undertakings. The concern of the Commission is that the Regulation must guarantee that a number of independent poles of R&D can flourish—recital 8 of the preamble. Where R&D co-operation occurs between oligopolists the prospects for independent innovation is curtailed. Further, where the agreement extends to joint exploitation of the results of the R&D, especially with joint distribution then the parties can regulate output of the product, a fact that can lead to anti-competitive results where the parties enjoy market power. Accordingly, the Regulation lays down, in Article 3, three principles which are further qualified in the case of joint distribution.

12.137 (i) Agreements between undertakings which do not compete at the outset of the agreement do not initially pose acute problems and hence there is *no* market share limitation. However, once the R&D results are available for exploitation the parties become actual or potential competitors and accordingly the market share limitation (see below) comes into operation after 5 years from the date of first marketing;

12.138 (ii) Agreements between competitors are exempt provided that at the date the agreement was entered the parties combined held no more than 20 per cent of the market (thus there remains scope for a number of competing joint ventures). The 20 per cent rule applies to R&D agreements whether coupled to joint exploitation or not.

12.139 (iii) In respect of (ii) above (competing undertakings) exemption is not lost simply because the R&D is successful and as exploitation proceeds the 20 per cent threshold is breached since the 20 per cent threshold need only be satisfied "at the time the

[227] See para. 7 of the preamble: "Joint exploitation is not therefore justified where it relates to improvements which were not made within the framework of a joint research and development programme but under an agreement to having *some* other principal objective such as the licensing of intellectual property rights, joint manufacture or specialisation, and merely containing ancillary provisions on joint research and development." See White, *op. cit.*, at p. 682.

[228] Arts. 4(fa)–(fc).

[229] Competing products are those which may be "improved or replaced" by the contract product. See, Venit, *op. cit.*, at p. 159; White, *op. cit.*, at p. 686. See for an example of non-competing parties, *NCB. CEGB* Bull EC 7 and 8/85 paras. 2.1., 3.1.

agreement is entered into". However, the market share condition *is reintroduced* five years after first marketing.

12.140 These three principles are qualified if distribution is carried out by one of the parties, one or more joint undertakings or one or more third undertakings. In such cases, the 20 per cent market share limitation is replaced by a 10 per cent market share limitation.[230] This is because the Commission considers that distribution agreements between competing manufacturers cause more of a concern about co-ordination of activity at a lower level of market power.[231]

12.141 *(a) Rules for non-competing manufacturers*

Where parties on entering an R&D agreement do not compete, the exemption lasts for the duration of the R&D programme. Where the results are jointly exploited the exemption continues for five years from the time the contract products are first put on the market within the Common Market. Thereafter exemption is subject to the market share condition. If X and Y market their contract product in the USA in 1986 but commence European marketing in 1988, then the exemption would have run until 1993 (1988 plus five years). The Regulation is silent as to from when time runs where X and Y commence marketing different products which all derive from the joint R&D at different times. If product A is first marketed in 1986 and product B in 1987, then did exemption last for different periods of time according to which product is being marketed? If X and Y decide to market one product of their R&D in 1986 but continue with R&D on other more complex products intending to market them after 1991, then it would be absurd to deny exemption to the more important fruits of the labour on the basis that time had run from marketing of a less significant product some five years earlier. Accordingly, the preferable interpretation is that the five-year period commences from first marketing of each separate contract product. Where X and Y marketed a product in 1987 but thereafter continued with R&D on the product periodically replacing the product with *improved* models, does the period run from first marketing or from each successive introduction of a new model? Presumably the five-year period ends in 1992 despite the fact that each new model might very substantially alter the style, operation or even nature of the first prototype. The relevant principle presumably is that the five-year period of grace runs from the first time the parties feel confident enough to market the product. If X and Y replace prototype 1 with prototype 2 which is in reality a *different product* (albeit that it is a substitute for prototype 1) then arguably five years runs from prototype 2. Parties might consider drafting separate R&D agreements with respect to each product where this is possible as a means of safeguarding against the equivocality of this provision.

12.142 *(b) Rules for competing manufacturers*

Where manufacturers compete exemption lasts for the same period as for non-competing manufacturers agreements. However, this is only so where, at the time the agreement was entered "the parties' combined production of the products capable of being improved or replaced by the contract products does not exceed 20 per cent of the market for such products in the EC or a substantial part thereof". If the manufacturers have agreed that one of them should distribute the contract products or have set up a joint venture to distribute or have entrusted distribution to a third party, this 20 per cent threshold is reduced to 10 per cent. This quantitative threshold demonstrates the concern of

[230] Art. 3(3a).

[231] See para. 64, CJV Notice.

the Commission that agreements between large competitors threaten the existence of separate poles of research within the community. As such, agreements of this size require individual treatment. The phrase a "substantial part thereof" may cause problems. It requires parties to make an assessment of the relevant geographical market.[232] X and Y might control 5 per cent of the EC market but 60 per cent of the Benelux market where they primarily operate. In the context of Article 86 EC the words "a substantial part" of the EC have been construed in a minimalist, *de minimis*, fashion. Thus, Luxembourg can, *per se*, represent a substantial part of the EC although its population and size are relatively very small.[233] At the end of the formal exemption period block exemption may, none the less, continue for as long as the production of the contract product together with the parties' combined production of other competing goods does not exceed 20 per cent of the total market for such products in the EC or in a substantial part thereof. Products which compete with the contract product are those which are considered by users to be equivalent in view of their characteristics, price and intended use.[234] For example: X produces widgets and controls 5 per cent of the market; Y produces gidgets which compete with widgets and controls 8 per cent of the market. X and Y form a joint venture company, XY Ltd, to produce "widgits" which compete with both widgets and gidgets. After five years of joint exploitation XY Ltd controls about 6 per cent of the widgits market. After 10 years widgits account for 12 per cent of the total market. Thus, the combined market shares of X plus Y plus XY Ltd amounts to 25 per cent and block exemption will have lapsed. Where contract products are components used by the parties for the manufacture of other products, reference is to be made to the markets for such of those latter products for which the components represent a "significant" part. The word significant part is not defined. Significance will hence vary according to circumstances. A component may be a significant part of the main product where it accounts for a high percentage of its weight, size or price. Alternatively, a small, lightweight, cheap, but brilliantly novel component may be significant because it is considered to be so by users or purchasers of the main product.

12.143 *(c) Lapse of block exemption*

Exemption remains where the 20 per cent market share is exceeded during any period of two consecutive financial years by not more than one tenth.[235] Where block exemption does lapse a six-month period of grace continues to apply which commences from the end of the financial year during which it was exceeded.[236] This period enables the parties to adjust to the different legal circumstances and notify their agreement where necessary.

[232] See paras. 6.101–6.102.

[233] *per* Advocate General Warner in Case 77/77 *BP* v *Commission* [1978] 3 CMLR 174; [1978] ECR 1513 at p.1521. See White, *op. cit.*, at p. 686.

[234] See para. 21 of the Commission explanatory notice on exclusive dealing and purchasing (OJ 1983 C355/7) which comments on the user vantage point test: "Only identical or equivalent goods are regarded as belonging to the same product market. The goods in question must be interchangeable. Whether or not this is the case must be judged from the vantage point of the user, normally taking the characteristics, price and intended use of the goods together. In certain cases, however, goods can form a separate market on the basis of their characteristics, their price or their intended use alone. This is true especially where consumer preferences have developed."

[235] Art. 3(4) The same margin applies in the exclusive dealing and purchasing regulations: Art. 5(2), Reg. 1983/83/EEC, OJ 1983 L173/1 on exclusive dealing, and Art. 5(2), Reg. 1984/83/EEC, OJ 1983 L73/5 on exclusive purchasing. See also Art. 3(2), Reg. 417/85/EEC OJ 1985 L53/1 on specialisation agreements which provides the same.

[236] Art. 3(5).

12.144 *(d) Exemption for R&D joint ventures with large market shares*

Notwithstanding the 20/10 per cent limits in the block exemption, the Commission has shown that it is prepared to grant individual exemption to R&D joint ventures with large market shares. In *KSB/Gould/Lowara/ITT*,[237] co-operation between the first and third largest producers of pumps in both the world and the EC was exempted.[238] The Commission takes into account the importance enabling European industry to deal with world competition in assessing the impact on competition of a joint venture in an oligopolistic market.[239]

(6) Permissible restrictions, "white clauses": Articles 4 and 5

12.145 Articles 4 and 5 provide a non-exhaustive enumeration of clauses that may be included in the agreement without loss of exemption. Article 4 clauses are considered to fall within Article 85(1) but to be worthy of exemption under Article 85(3). Article 5 clauses are considered for the currency of the agreement to fall outside of Article 85(1) EC. Recital 11 of the preamble to the Regulation makes it clear that Article 5 restrictions do not necessarily infringe Article 85(1) but that they might do in certain contexts in which case they may be cleared under the block exemption. Restrictions and obligations which are similar in nature to those below but which have a more limited scope are also permitted under Article 4(2) and 5(2). The list of "white clauses" is of course not exhaustive of the clauses that might with sound economic and commercial justifications be incorporated in contracts. However, the inclusion of extraneous clauses which restrict competition prevents operation of the exemption and may necessitate notification under the opposition procedure. For example, in *BP-Kellogg*[240] BP and K entered a joint venture agreement for the development of designs for the construction of ammonia plant using a catalyst developed beforehand by BP. Under this agreement were agreed the following terms which were not in the whitelist in the block exemption: (a) a restriction on BP not to supply the catalyst during the life of the agreement without K's consent; (b) a restriction on K not to commercialise any new ammonia process using iron based catalysts likely to be more commercially attractive than the process using BP's catalyst without informing BP; (c) restriction on K bidding for ammonia plants other than by way of offering the jointly developed process without informing BP. The Commission noted that these clauses were not in the whitelist, "in so far as they give rise to restrictions on the exploitation of products and processes which have not been jointly developed by the parties to the agreement." However, the agreement was individually exempted under Article 85 (3) on the basis that it would promote technical and economic progress especially in the field of energy saving, a factor which would benefit consumers. Furthermore, the market was competitive and the parties would hence be subject to considerable external pressures.

(7) Article 4

12.146 *(a) Restrictions on independent R&D*

Obligations preventing independent R&D by the parties in the field to which the programme relates or in a closely connected field during the currency of the programme are exempt. This ensures that the parties concentrate their efforts on the joint activity thereby maximising the chances of success.[241] However on completion of the programme the

237 OJ 1991 L19/25.

238 See also *Henkel/Colgate* OJ 1972 L14/14; *Continental/Michelin* [1989] 4 CMLR 920.

239 See Recital 10, Reg. 418/85/EEC. *GEC/ANT/Telettra/SAT* [1988] OJ C180/3 could be seen as an example of this justification.

240 OJ 1985 1369/6 criticised in Korah, *op. cit.*, n. 214.

241 e.g. *Carbon–Gas Technologie* OJ 1983 1376 noted *Thirteenth Report on Competition Policy* (1983), pp. 82, 83, paras. 114–118.

exemption lapses if any restraints upon the parties' legal capacity to undertake independent R&D in the same or connected fields is imposed. The regulation fails to address the common situation whereby R&D proceeds after first marketing. Provided this post-marketing R&D is clearly contemplated by the terms of agreement it may be said that the R&D programme is not completed until the end of the post-marketing product improvement/enhancement phase has occurred. Where such R&D is envisaged by the parties it may be wise to expressly provide, perhaps in the preamble to the agreement, that the R&D programme is intended to extend beyond initial development into improvements and enhancement. This should satisfy the requirements of Article 2(a). However, there is also a risk that post-marketing R&D would be seen as ancillary to joint exploitation of the results of the R&D, as the manufacture of products following R&D would be seen as exploitation.[242] It may be that it depends whether marketing could be seen as an essential part of the R&D programme, or whether it would only be part of the normal process of taking into account practical experience in producing and marketing a new product (see Article 6(a) below).

12.147 *(b) Third-party agreements*

Obligations preventing parties from entering agreements with third parties on R&D in the field to which the programme relates or in a closely connected field during the currency of the programme are exempt. The same rationale as in (a) applies.

12.148 *(c) Exclusive purchase, procurement*

Obligations requiring the parties to procure the contract products exclusively from parties, trade associations, joint venture companies and others who are jointly charged with manufacturing the contract product. X and Y might be research institutes without production capacity or X might be a large company with considerable R&D capacity but minimal production capacity and Y might be the opposite. Accordingly they agree with Z (third party) for the manufacture of the R&D product. X and Y may use Z as a joint distributor or seller subject to the market share criteria under Article 3(3a). Hence, an obligation to procure the products exclusively from Z will be acceptable. This clause may be linked to Article 5 (1)(h), see below. There is no requirement that an English clause be incorporated (as there was in earlier drafts). See para. 10.150.

12.149 *(d) Territorial exclusivity for manufacturer*

Clauses prohibiting parties from manufacturing the contract products or applying the contract process in territories reserved for other parties to the joint R&D are exempt. Such clauses require the parties to concentrate their activities in defined locations thus rationalising sales effort and enhancing penetration of the contract product or product or service derived from the contract process, on the market.

12.150 A number of points deserve mention. First, this clause could operate as a territorial restriction on sales and marketing: X and Y have developed a heavy, low cost per unit product which is not easily transportable. The possibility for parallel imports exists in theory though in practice it is unlikely. In such a case the clause might be treated as granting an exclusive territory—see Article 4(f) below. Secondly, it is uncertain whether the regulation exempts restraints on parties being able to license third parties to manufacture the contract product in areas reserved for other parties. Arguably if the parties themselves must respect each other's territories then licensees may also be required to accept the same obligation. A clause requiring participant manufacturers to grant geographically limited li-

[242] *KSB/Goulds/Lowara/ITT* OJ 1991 L19/25, para. 21.

cences only would arguably be a clause exempted under Article 4(2), i.e. a clause of the same type as that covered by Article 4(1)(d) but having a more limited scope than is permitted by the provision. In assessing terms included in an intellectual property licence to a third party the patent and know-how licensing regulations will need to be considered. These have been amended to make them applicable in certain joint venture situations.[243]

12.151 *(e) Field of use restrictions*

Obligations requiring parties to restrict manufacture of the contract product or application of the contract process to one or more technical fields are exempt. However, such a clause is outside the block exemption where two or more of the parties are competitors at the time of entering the agreement.[244] This restriction can only be to "technical fields of application", not to product markets[245] (though product market restrictions *are* now permitted for all technology transfer agreements under the technology transfer block exemption). In such cases the clause restricts the parties' rights of exploitation and individual exemption under the opposition procedure may be necessary. The same questions concerning use limitations in licences to third parties as arise under Article 4(1)(d) arise under Article 4 (1)(e). The same conclusions may be drawn. See Article 6(e) below on customer restrictions. An obligation on parties not to license third parties in each other's field of use has been held to be ancillary to this provision and, though not regarded as exempt as a more limited restriction under Article 4(2), was exempted under the opposition procedure.[246]

12.152 *(f) Exclusive territories*

An obligation prohibiting, for five years from the time the contract products are first put on the market within the Common Market, parties from actively putting the products on the market in territories reserved to other parties is exempt. Such a clause may be buttressed with other clauses preventing, for example, advertising outside of a party's territory, or preventing the establishment of any branch or distribution depot in another party's territory. However, these market division clauses must not be used to prevent parallel imports. Article 4 (1)(f) adds that the clause is only exempt where: "users and intermediaries can obtain the contract products from other suppliers and the parties do not render it difficult for intermediaries and users to thus obtain the products." For example, X sells the contract product in the UK at 10 units; Y sells the contract product in France at 14 units. Wholesaler Z from France wishes to purchase the contract product in the UK and sell it in France at 13 units. The agreement may not prevent X from supplying Z. Does the regulation cover restrictions on the parties appointing dealers to put the products onto the market in other parties territories? The wording of the article refers only to the *parties* themselves accepting restrictions. Arguably Article 4 (2) (similar restrictions of a more limited scope exempted by analogy) brings such a restriction within the block exemption. Presumably if party X appoints a commercial agent to sell for it in another party's area this will infringe the exempt clause since a commercial agent and its principal are legally considered to comprise a single economic unit. It does seem logical that the same should apply where X appoints an exclusive dealer to act for it. At the end of the exempt period restrictions must be ended or the agreement may need to be notified to the Commission (Article 6(f)).

243 Reg. 151/93: for the text of the amended patent licensing and know-how licensing block exemptions, see [1993] 4 CMLR 177 and 195; see further Chapter 13.

244 See *Quantel International-Continuum/Quantel SA* OJ 1992 L235/9, para. 49.

245 Contrast with the technology transfer block exemption, Art. 2(1)(8) Reg. 240/96/EEC, which does permit product market as well as field of use restrictions.

246 *Seventeenth Report on Competition Policy*, para. 31(c).

12.153 *(fa), (fb) and (fc) Exclusive distribution*

Provisions relating to the grant of exclusive distribution rights were inserted by Regulation 151/93. Exclusive distribution of the contract products can be entrusted to one of the parties, provided that it does not distribute competing products manufactured by a third producer. similarly, exclusive distribution rights for the contract products may be granted to a joint undertaking or third undertaking provided that undertaking does not either manufacture itself or distribute competing products. If exclusive distribution rights for the contract products are granted in the whole or a defined area of the common market to more than one joint or third undertaking, then there is an additional safeguard built in through the requirement that exemption is only granted on the basis that users and intermediaries are able to obtain contract products from other suppliers, and that the distributors must not make it difficult for those users and intermediaries to obtain the contract products. This additional requirement is included to prevent the distribution arrangements being used in a way which would set up a distribution network dividing up markets for the contract products and preventing parallel imports.[247]

12.154 *(g) Exchange of information and improvement licences*

Obligations on parties requiring them to communicate experience they have gained in exploitation to each other, and obligations to grant each other non-exclusive licenses for inventions relating to improvements or new applications, are exempt.

(8) Article 5

12.155 *(a) Know-how, technical knowledge*

An obligation requiring parties to communicate patented or non-patented technical knowledge necessary for the performance of the R&D or the exploitation of its results is not within Article 85(1). Article 5(1)(a) is silent as to whether only pre-existing know-how is covered; the provision should be wide enough to cover also subsequently acquired know-how.

12.156 *(b) Limitation on use of know-how*

An obligation not to use any know-how received from another party to the agreement for purposes unrelated to the joint R&D or its exploitation is not within Article 85(1). Since Article 5 clauses are exempted only during the currency of the agreement the restriction lapses with the agreement. The clause may be exempted under the opposition procedure if the restriction is not drafted so as to fall within the Article 6 blacklist.

12.157 *(c) Maintenance of intellectual property rights*

Obligations to obtain and maintain in force intellectual property rights for the contract products or processes escape Article 85(1). This clause is subject to Article 6 (b) (no-challenge clauses). See para. 12.165.

12.158 *(d) Confidentiality*

Obligation to preserve the confidentiality of any know-how received or jointly developed under the R&D programme. This obligation may be imposed even following expiration of the agreement.[248]

[247] See the same rationale under the exclusive distribution block exemption: see para 10.44.

[248] See *European Music Satellite Venture* [1984] 3 CMLR 162, noted *Fourteenth Report on Competition Policy* (1984), pp. 72, 73, para. 86 comfort letter sent to consortium in the UK of the BBC, a merchant banker, and, a concert promoter and musical agent. The parties undertook a feasibility study in respect of the proposed establishment of a new satellite broadcasting company. Under the agreement the parties undertook not to disclose details of the feasibility study for a period of three years after a party ceased to be a shareholder in the venture, See also *ACEC-Berliet* [1968] CMLR D35; *MAN–SAVIEM* [1974] CMLR D123.

12.159 *(e) Legal enforcement of intellectual property rights*

Clauses requiring parties to do the following are acceptable: inform other parties of infringements of their intellectual property rights; take legal action against infringers; assist in any such legal action or share with the other party in the cost thereof. However, such clauses must *not* prevent a party challenging the validity of a right (under Article 6 (b), nor may they utilise intellectual property rights to hinder parallel imports (under Article 6 (h)).

12.160 *(f) Compensation*

Obligation to pay royalties or render services to the other parties to compensate for unequal contributions to the joint R&D or unequal exploitation of its results, are not within Article 85(1). It remains questionable whether an extreme financial arrangement which operates as a disincentive to competition is covered, e.g. where X must pay Y a sum whenever his output exceeds Y's—might not this fall within Article 6(c)?

12.161 *(g) Royalty sharing*

Obligations to share royalties received from third parties with other parties are not restrictive. Royalty pooling is thus exempt. Parties may divide royalties according to extent of participation; this is the implication to be derived from Article 5 (1)(f). Arguably this provision also implies that parties may grant joint licences. The provision could equally imply only the division of the royalties earned by parties in individual licences.

12.162 *(h) Minimum quantities and standards*

Obligations to supply other parties with minimum quantities of contract products and to observe minimum standards of quality are outside of Article 85(1). Such clauses will be relevant, for example, in specialisation agreements where parties manufacture different contract products subject to supply rights held by the other parties.

(9) Non-permissible restrictions, "black clauses": Article 6

12.163 The block exemption only applies to agreements that may be presumed to satisfy the requirements of Article 85(3) EC. The following clause types are of equivocal value in competition terms and if included in agreements entail loss of block exemption.

12.164 *(a) Restrictions on independent R&D*

Clauses which restrict the party's freedom to execute R&D either independently or in co-operation with third parties in a field unrelated to that covered by the joint venture are not automatically exempt. The same applies to the joint venture R&D or connected R&D after completion of the R&D.[249]

12.165 *(b) No-challenge clauses*

The block exemption does not apply where parties are: (i) prohibited *after* the completion of the R&D programme from challenging the intellectual property rights which the parties hold in the common market and which are relevant to the programme, or; (ii) are prohibited from challenging the validity of the rights which the parties hold in the common market and which protect the results of the R&D after expiry of the agreement (i.e. including joint exploitation). Article 6 (b) is silent as to no-challenge clauses in respect of the period up to dissolution of the programme which concern pre-existing rights. Nor does Article 6 (b) address no-challenge clauses concerning intellectual property rights

[249] See Arts. 4(1)(a) and (b).

derived from the R&D which are operative before the end of the agreement (even though the clause applies to the post R&D period). Presumably, these are not prohibited, this is apparently the view of the Commission, though the Regulation is equivocal on the point. As a general rule the Commission has been strict on no-challenge clauses.[250] For analysis of such clauses in patent and know-how licences see paras. 13.32 and 13.104–13.105. In such agreements the position of the Commission has substantially softened.

12.166 *(c) Quotas*

Clauses restricting the parties as to the quantity of the contract products they may manufacture or sell or as to the number of operations employing the contract process they may perform are not automatically exemptible.[251] While clauses controlling a party's output may help ensure a productive output sufficient to facilitate penetration of a new market, such clauses may also unduly hinder parties in their attempts to expand at other parties' expense—see text on Article 5(1)(f) above.

12.167 *(d) Prices*

Clauses restricting parties in their determination of prices, components of prices or discounts when selling the contract product to *third parties* are not automatically exemptible. It is unlikely that joint price fixing will be exemptible even on an individual basis. Article 6(d) does not cover the prices, etc, paid or charged as between the parties themselves, for example, under a specialisation arrangement between the parties.

12.168 *(e) Customer restrictions*

Clauses restricting the customers whom parties may serve are not automatically exemptible. However, Article 6(e) would not apparently apply to a field of use restraint involving rivals that is excluded from the block exemption by Article 4(1)(e) and, consequently, such a restriction could benefit from the opposition procedure (see below). The regulation (unfortunately) fails accurately to distinguish between field of use and customer restraints. Parties should be very careful in drafting field of use restrictions exempt under Article 4(1)(e) to ensure that they cannot be construed as customer restrictions.[252]

12.169 *(f) Exclusive territories*

Clauses prohibiting parties from putting the contract products on the market or pursuing an *active* sales policy for those products in territories of the EC reserved for other parties after the end of the exemption period are not block exempt. Prior to end of the period such restrictions are acceptable (Article 4(1)(f)). Restrictions on fulfilling unsolicited orders, i.e. engaging in passive sales, are not dealt with by the block exemption. The Com-

[250] *Raymond-Nagoya* [1972] CMLR D45; *Davidson Rubber* [1972] CMLR D52; *Kabelmetal* [1975] 2 CMLR D40; *Bayer–Gist Brocades* [1976] 1 CMLR D98. See White, *op. cit.*, at p. 694. This attitude has evidently been relaxed somewhat. No-challenge clauses are now capable of approval under the opposition procedure under the technology transfer block exemption, whereas under the earlier patent and know-how licensing block exemption, such clauses were blacklisted and therefore incapable of block exemption; see para. 13.32.

[251] Though, in the context of intellectual property licences positive obligations on the licensee requiring him to produce a specified number/quantity of the licensed product are unobjectionable, e.g. *Burroughs–Delplanque* [1972] CMLR D67; *Burroughs–Geha* [1972] CMLR D72. Restrictions on quantities are blacklisted in the technology transfer block exemption.

[252] A workable definition of the distinction is that a field of use restriction occurs where the products manufactured by use of the R&D results do not form part of the same product market and a customer restriction occurs where they do—see White, *op. cit.*, p. 692. Contrast with the know-how licensing block exemption, Art. 2(1)(7) Reg. 556/89/EEC, which does permit product market as well as field of use restrictions.

mission's view is that a restriction on passive sales cannot be block exempt and must be notified for individual exemption, for which the opposition procedure is available.[253]

12.170 *(g) Limitations on manufacture*

If the exploitation by the parties of the results of the joint research and development is not provided for or does not take place, then clauses requiring the parties not to grant licences to third parties to manufacture the contract products or to apply the contract processes will not be block exempt. But if there is provision for exploitation or exploitation does in practice happen, then these restrictions will not be caught by the block exemption, since the provisions relating to distribution in Articles 3(a) and 4(f)(a)–(c) will apply.

12.171 *(h) Hindrances to parallel imports*

Clauses which require parties to refuse to meet demand from users or dealers in their territories who intend to market the contract products in other territories in the EC are not block exempt. Parties may not hinder parallel imports: X sells contract product in the UK at 10 units; Y sells the contract product in France at 14 units. Purchaser Z wishes to buy in the UK and sell the contract products in France at 13 units. In the agreement between X and Y neither party shall sell to anyone intending to resell the products outside of their territories. Thus X should refuse to supply Z, this refusal to deal will help X and Y maintain the price differential between the UK and France. The clause preventing supply will not be automatically exemptible. Indeed, it stands little chance of individual exemption under Article 85(3).[254] Parties may refuse to supply users or dealers where they have an objective justification, e.g. the dealer does not meet the selective distribution criteria imposed by the supplier.[255]

12.172 Similarly clauses which make it difficult for users or dealers to obtain the contract products from other dealers within the EC are not exemptible. Thus, if X and Y agree not to provide guarantee or after-sales services to customers located outside their territories, this would hinder the ability of those customers to obtain supplies. In particular, clauses whereby the parties use intellectual property rights to prevent users or dealers marketing contract goods within the EC, where such products have been lawfully put on the market within the EC by another party or with its consent, are not exemptible.

(10) Extension of exemption to agreements containing "grey" clauses not mentioned in the Regulation: the "opposition procedure": Article 7

12.173 The list of "white", permissible clauses expressed in Article 4 and 5 is non-exhaustive. Where an agreement to which the Regulation applies (under Articles 1, 2 and 3) contains restriction that are not expressly permitted (under Articles 4 and 5) but which are not amongst the categories of "black" clauses, then the exemption applies to the agreement if, following notification of the agreement to the Commission, the latter has not opposed exemption within a six month period. Details of the opposition procedure which applies *mutatis mutandis* to specialisation and technology transfer agreements is given at paras. 7.167–7.173.

253 *Seventeenth Report on Competition Policy* (1987), para. 31(d). See *Quantel International-Continuum/Quantel SA* OJ 1992 L235/9, para. 49.

254 But cf. the arguments on the "free-rider" problem discussed at paras. 10.117-10.120. It is possible that in the future the Commission might accept clauses protecting against parallel imports which threaten the existence of an effective distribution network.

255 See paras. 10.349–10.393.

(11) Extension of exemption to connected undertakings: Article 9

12.174 The exemption extends to rights and obligations which parties create for undertaking connected with them. In this respect the market share of the connected undertaking and its general conduct is attributable to that of the parties themselves. A "connected" undertaking is one in which a party to the agreement directly or indirectly: (a) owns more than 50 per cent of the capital or business assets; or (b) has power to exercise more than 50 per cent of the voting rights; or (c) has power to appoint more than half the members of the supervisory board, board of directors or bodies legally representing the undertaking; or (d) has the right to manage the affairs. These criteria are non-cumulative.

12.175 The parent companies or other undertakings who control (as per the criteria above) parties to a joint venture are also "connected undertakings". Thus, if X and Y are parties then A and B who control X and Y respectively are connected undertakings. Parents of parents would also be caught. Thus where Z controls A, and A controls X, then A is a connected undertaking with X. joint venture companies especially incorporated by parties are connected to the parties, despite the fact that neither parent can individually control the joint venture company. Thus if X and Y incorporate XY Ltd and each holds 50 per cent of the shares then XY Ltd is connected to both X and Y.

(12) Withdrawal of exemption: Article 10

12.176 In individual cases the Commission may decide to withdraw the block exemption. It would certainly require a formal decision to withdraw the exemption.[256] Article 10 gives four examples of instances where withdrawal of exemption might occur. These examples are not exhaustive.[257]

12.177 *(a)* The existence of the agreement substantially restricts the scope for third parties to carry out R&D in the relevant field due to limited research capacity else. where. The Commission has not defined "limited research capacity". If X and Y hire as employees or consultants all or a high percentage of the scientists expert in a relevant field, then this might substantially restrict the scope for third party R&D. Likewise, if X and Y control the supply of raw materials necessary to the R&D and restrict the access of third parties to it, then an obstacle to third party R&D exists. However, if X and Y are first in the field and exploit the contract product so that total market demand can be satisfied, then the very existence of the X–Y agreement coupled to a satisfied fixed demand might deter competitive R&D. This would not, however, be related to limitations on research capacity elsewhere since other parties are not denied access to the resources needed for the R&D.

12.178 *(b)* Because of the particular structure of supply, the existence of the agreement substantially restricts the access of third parties to the market for the contract products. The Commission considers that in some cases the very existence of an R&D venture may operate as an entry barrier. This may be the case where demand is fixed and customers of the parties use the contract product for their own manufacturing processes and have adapted those processes to the particular characteristics of the contract product. Competitors who are late arrivals may find that customers are technologically tied to the product of the

256 The Commission recognises this fact in respect of the block exemption for exclusive purchasing and dealing. See para. 24 of the explanatory memorandum on those regulations OJ 1983 C 355/7 (30 December 1983). See para. 10.86 on Art. 6 of Reg. 1983/83/EEC, OJ 1983 L 73/1. See para. 13.114 for the position under the technology transfer exemption; the Commission has on one occasion used this power under the preceding patent licensing block exemption.

257 The power to withdraw exemption is general and is conferred by Art. 7 of Reg. 2821/71/EEC, OJ Spec. Ed.1971 III p. 1022.

parties. Alternatively, demand levels might be such that there is room on the market for only one R&D agreement. In neither of these two examples is it very likely that exemption would be withdrawn. They are economic consequences that are inherently likely in some high technology markets and parties should not be punished for being efficient. In assessing entry barriers the Commission will consider the world wide market context.[258]

12.179 *(c)* Without any objectively valid reason, the parties do not exploit the results of the R&D. A principal tenet of Commission policy on joint R&D ventures is that innovation is essential to economic growth and that if innovation is expedited by co-operation, then that co-operation must be treated favourably. Where the fruits of joint R&D do not materialise, the raison d'être of co-operation disappears.[259] Objectively valid reasons for inertia might include lingering doubts about safety or quality; imminent changes in relevant quality control or standards legislation; or delays due to the time needed to exhaust supplies of old stock.

12.180 *(d)* The contract products are not subject in the whole or a substantial part of the EC to effective competition from identical products or products considered by users as equivalent in view of their characteristics, price and intended use. This situation concerns levels of inter-brand competition.[260] If X and Y jointly create an entirely new product which will replace all substitutes, then there will be no (or diminishing) competition from other brands. In such situations the Commission might consider that it wishes to scrutinise the R&D agreement on an individual basis and perhaps impose conditions (e.g. notification and reporting obligations) in a formal decision granting exemption under Article 85(3) EC. Withdrawal of exemption does not imply that the agreement is anti-competitive, only that it is unsuitable for block exemption. The behaviour of a joint venture company whose product is not subject to effective inter-brand competition may be reviewed under Article 86 EC since the company may well be in a dominant position.

(13) Transitional periods: Article 11

12.181 For agreements notified prior to 1 March 1985 the exemption has retroactive effect from the time at which the agreement satisfied the terms of the regulation. Where the agreement is not exempt from notification under Article 4(2) (3)(b) of Regulation 17/62/EEC (which exempts pure R&D agreements with no restrictions) then the exemption in Regulation 418/85/EEC commences on a date not earlier than the date of notification. In the case of "old" R&D agreements (see para 6.78) which were in existence prior to 13 March 1962[261] and which were notified before 1 February 1963[262] the exemption

[258] para. 10 of the preamble to Reg. 418/85/EEC.

[259] See *Fourteenth Commission Report on Competition Policy* (1984), pp. 37, 38, para. 28: "Although innovative efforts should be regarded as a normal part of the entrepreneurial spirit of individual undertakings, it can not be denied that in many cases the synergy arising out of cooperation is necessary because it enables the partners to share the financial risks involved and in particular to bring together a wider range of intellectual and mental resources and experience, thus promoting the transfer of technology. In the absence of such cooperation, the innovation may not take place at all, or otherwise not as successfully or efficiently. Also, the present situation in the Community demands a more rapid and effective transformation of new ideas into marketable products and processes, which may be facilitated by joint efforts by several undertakings."

[260] See *Amersham–Buchler* OJ 1982 1314 noted *Twelfth Report on Competition Policy* (1982), pp, 70, 71, paras. 83, 84; *VW-MAN* OJ 1983 L376 noted *Thirteenth Report on Competition Policy* (1983), pp. 83, 84, paras. 119–121.

[261] In the case of agreement *subject* to Art. 85(1) EC as a result of the accession of the UK, Ireland and Denmark the date is 1 January 1973, for Greece the date is 1 January 1981, for Spain and Portugal the date is 1 January 1986, and for Austria, Sweden and Finland the date is 1 January 1995.

[262] *ibid.*, 1 July 1973, for Greece the date is 1 July 1981, for Spain and Portugal the date is 1 July 1986, and for Austria, Sweden and Finland the date is 1 July 1995.

applies retroactively from the time at which the agreement satisfied the terms of the Regulation. Where such an "old" agreement was notified prior to 1 January 1967 but was amended prior to 1 September 1985 so as to render it compatible with the block exemption, such amendment being communicated to the Commission prior to 1 October 1985, Article 85(1) shall not apply in respect of the period prior to the amendment. Communication of amendments takes effect from the date of their receipt by the Commission. Where communication is by registered post the date on the postmark is determinative. The same applies to agreements covered by Article 4(2)(3)(b) of Regulation 17/62/EEC.

(14) Currency of block exemption: Article 13

12.182 According to Article 13 the Regulation applies until 31 December 1997.

(15) Relationship with other block exemptions: paragraph 14 of preamble

12.183 Agreements benefiting from block exemption may also, according to paragraph 14 of the preamble take advantage of the provisions of other block exemptions. However, where parties wish exemption under the R&D block exemption the provisions of other block exemptions are only applicable in so far as they do not *conflict* with specific provisions of the R&D block exemption. Paragraph 14 is necessary since it clarifies the obvious confusion that would arise given that the regulation contemplates that an R&D agreement might involve, *inter alia*: patent and know-how licensing within the technology transfer block exemption (Article 1(3) (a) and (b); specialisation (Article 1(3)(a)); exclusive purchasing (Article 4 (1)(c)); exclusive dealing (impliedly under Article 4 (1)(d) and (f)). Where a clause is permitted under the R&D regulation which is not block exempt under another regulation this fact does not affect the application of the R&D regulation. Thus, for instance, a specialisation arrangement under Article 1(3)(a) is exempt under the R&D regulation despite the fact that the agreement exceeds the turnover threshold permitted in the specialisation regulation.

(16) Check list for application of the block exemption

12.184 The Regulation should give automatic exemption to many agreements between small and medium-sized undertakings. A summary of the conditions for application of the exemption is as follows.

Condition 1

Agreement must be of a type described in Article 1, i.e. concerning: joint R&D coupled to joint exploitation of results; joint R&D without joint exploitation; joint exploitation of results of prior R&D between same parties. Exemption extends to connected undertakings as defined in Article 9.

Condition 2

Agreement must satisfy the general conditions in Article 2 concerning: formality of the structure of the R&D programme; access to results; use of results derived from pure R&D agreement; and, specialisation of production.

Condition 3

Agreement must satisfy market share criteria as laid down in Article 3. Criteria depends upon whether parties to the agreement are competing or non-competing and whether exploitation extends to distribution.

Condition 4

Agreement *may* contain restrictions of a type described in Article 4 and 5. These lists are non-exhaustive. See condition 6 below where parties seek incorporation of a restriction not mentioned in Article 4 and 5.

Condition 5

Agreement must *not* contain restrictions of a type described in Article 6.

Condition 6

Where agreement contains restrictions that are not expressly permitted by Articles 4 and 5 (see Condition 4 above) but are *not* prohibited by Article 6 then it may be notified in accordance with the "opposition procedure" in Article 7. Exemption extends to such an agreement six months following notification provided that no "opposition" has been raised.

Condition 7

Block exemption may be withdrawn under Article 10 from any agreement where in a particular case the Commission determines that the criteria in Article 85(3) are not satisfied.

(17) R&D agreements falling outside the block exemption

12.185 Agreements for the development of new products will often qualify for exemption although not falling within the block exemption. The Commission is prepared to grant exemption, even for agreements between competition in oligopolistic markets.[263]

The Commission distinguishes between input joint ventures and production joint ventures in assessing both the direct elimination of competition caused by the agreement and the risk of spill-over effects.[264]

An input joint venture, where the parties collaborate to produce a component for their respective final products, will cause more concern the higher the value of the common component to the parties' products in which it is incorporated. In *Philips/Osram*[265] an exemption was granted for parties to a joint venture to make lead-free glass, even though the parties had a combined market share in excess of 50 per cent as the value of the products was no more than 2–3 per cent of the value of the final product into which it was to be incorporated.

Production joint ventures pose greater spill-over threats and so are examined more critically. Nevertheless, exemptions are available provided that the structure of competition in the industry was not adversely affected.[266] In making the analysis, the Commission is prepared to define the market globally if this is warranted by the nature of the goods or services concerned.[267]

2. *UK Law*

12.186 As a preliminary point, it should be borne in mind that if an agreement comes within the block exemption for R&D, then it is non-notifiable for the purposes of the RTPA, which thus only applies to agreements falling outside the block exemption.[268]

[263] *Twenty-fourth Report on Competition Policy* (1994), paras. 163–177.
[264] *ibid.*, para. 165.
[265] *Philips/Osram* OJ 1994 L 378/37, para. 18.
[266] See the examples given in the *Twenty-fourth Report on Competition Policy* (1994) at paras. 171–174.
[267] e.g. *BT/MCI* OJ 1994 L223/36.
[268] Restrictive Trade Practices (Non-notifiable Agreements) Order, S.I. 1996 No. 349, issued under section 27A RTPA 1976 (added by s. 10 Deregulation and Contracting-out Act 1994).

(1) Registrability under the RTPA 1976

12.187 A number of clauses common in joint R&D ventures fall within the RTPA 1976 thereby rendering the agreement registrable (see paras. 12.73–12.81).

12.188 Non-competition clauses whereby X and Y agree not to compete for a specified period of time with a jointly owned subsidiary, XY Ltd, constitute restrictions under section 6(1)(f)(goods) or section 11(2)(e) (services) RTPA 1976. This conclusion does not change simply because X and Y might retain freedom to compete with XY Ltd in certain defined circumstances. The supply of goods and services by the parties to a jointly owned venture company may constitute disregardable clauses when registration is being considered under sections 9(3) and 18(2) RTPA 1976.[269]

12.189 Clauses requiring the parties to purchase their requirement of the contract product exclusively from the joint venture company may be exempt under Schedule 3(2) RTPA 1976 but only where there are no other relevant restrictions in the agreement.[270]

12.190 Where the joint venture company researches and produces a component that the parents will use in their own production and the parents agree to specialise in their production of goods based on the component, this will be registrable under section 6(1)(d) as a restriction on the description of goods to be produced. For example, XY Ltd (the joint venture company) produces product A which both X and Y use in their own manufacturing processes. X agrees to use product A in the manufacture of gidgets; Y agrees to use product A in the manufacture of widgets. X and Y are restricted as to the kinds of goods they produce. It would appear to be the case that if XY Ltd simply derives research results, i.e. it does not in any way exploit the results then a specialisation agreement may be drafted that is not registrable. Licences for the transfer of intellectual property rights are outside the scope of the RTPA 1976.[271] Thus, if XY Ltd transfer the R&D results in the form of a patent licence or as a know-how licence and include in the licence restrictions on use, then the agreement is not registrable. Thus XY Ltd can license X to manufacture only gidgets, and Y to manufacture only widgets. Likewise, individual licences by X and Y to XY Ltd, of know-how and other relevant patents will be outside the scope of the RTPA 1976.

12.191 Clauses whereby X and Y agree (perhaps in conjunction with XY Ltd once it is incorporated) as to prices and terms and conditions will be registrable under sections 6(1)(a)–(c)(goods) or 11 (2)(a)–(c) (services). Such clauses might relate to sale by the joint venture of the contact product; individual sale by X and Y of the product produced by XY Ltd; or, individual sale by X and Y of the product produced by them from R&D results derived by XY Ltd.

(2) R&D agreements and section 21(2) RTPA 1976

12.192 Many R&D agreements are suitable for section 21(2) treatment. The OFT always asks whether the R&D would have been likely in the absence of the agreement. If X and Y are perfectly capable of undertaking own R&D and the market is such that there exists an incentive for both X and Y to undertake R&D then there is little economic justification for permitting X and Y to combine forces where to do so entails the negation of compe-

[269] See paras. 1.75–1.86 for details. ss. 9(4) and 18(3) RTPA 1976 withdraw the benefit conferred by ss. 9(3) and 18(2) where the term appears in a contract for the supply *of goods between suppliers* (or buyers) *inter se*. However, this withdrawal of benefit does not operate where the term is in a contract for supply which is itself made in pursuance of an agreement that has been registered, or is exempt from registration under ss. 29 RTPA 1976. Thus, even where the parents are in competition with the subsidiary ss. 9(3) and 18(2) may still apply provided the agreement is registered or exempt under s. 29.

[270] See paras. 2.141–2.151.

[271] See paras. 2.202–2.210.

tition between them. Where the financial risks are very high such that individual R&D is prohibitively expensive, then X and Y may be justified in entering an agreement. Where there is pressing need for rapid development of a new product, an agreement between X and Y might be justified on the basis that without it neither X nor Y could have individually marketed the relevant product or service *in time* so might not have bothered. Where X and Y are not competitors and combine their complementary abilities to manufacture a new product, then clearly the agreement is the only means by which X and Y can provide the product or service.[272]

12.193 As noted above, the OFT question whether the R&D would have been likely in the absence of the agreement. It does not ask whether individual R&D would inevitably have occurred without the agreement, the question is rather one of likelihood. Thus, in discussions with the OFT, X and Y need not establish to any degree of certainty that they would not have undertaken own-R&D. It should suffice to show that own R&D would be very difficult, e.g. because of prohibitive cost, high risk, inadequacy of individual facilities, etc.

12.194 Typical examples include agreements between pure scientists (working from universities or other research institutes) and companies able to exploit the results of the R&D. Clearly the scientist has no marketing capacity whereas the company has not the R&D ability. The results of the R&D could not have been exploited without an agreement.[273]

(3) Joint R&D and section 29 RTPA 1976: agreements important to the national economy.

12.195 A number of R&D agreements considered unsuitable for section 21(2) dispensation have been exempted from registration under section 29 RTPA 1976 as agreements important to the national economy. Two in particular directly concern R&D. Exempt agreements must satisfy the criteria listed in section 29. Essentially it must appear to the Secretary of State that the agreement: (a) is calculated to promote commercial ventures of substantial importance to the national economy; (b) is intended to promote efficiency or to create or improve productive capacity; (c) is the only means by which the objectives of the agreement may be realised; (d) contains only such restrictions as are reasonably necessary; and (e) is on balance expedient in the national interest.

12.196 In *Agricultural Biotechnology*[274] the Agricultural Research Council (ARC) and certain agricultural research Institutes which are grant aided by the ARC (the Institutes) entered an agreement with a joint venture company: Agricultural Genetics Co Ltd (AG). Under the agreement ARC and the Institutes granted AG an exclusive option to adopt, develop and market in a territory defined as the whole world all discoveries made by the parties in the field of agricultural biotechnology and processes and products resulting therefrom. Under the agreement, the parties remained free to undertake independent R&D, though specific projects were commenced between the parties which involved AG. There were a number of ancillary restrictions including a provision restricting the right of ARC or the Institutes to enter into any form of agreement or joint venture with third parties which could affect the commercial viability of projects or activities

[272] e.g. No. S. 745 Register of Restrictive Trade Practices, *Water Injection and Treatment Agreement* (1982).

[273] e.g. No. S.960 Register of Restrictive Trade Practices, *Sea Energy Associates Ltd* (1981). Agreement concerned the exploitation of a device invented and developed by a University scientist for extracting electrical energy from the action of ocean waves. See also No. S.1583 Register of Restrictive Trade Practices, *Structure Testing Systems Ltd* (1984) concerning the exploitation of an invention relating to the structural testing of buildings for defects.

[274] Exempt Register No. 149 (11 June 1984).

carried on by AG.[275] The exclusive option enjoyed by AG effectively negated the ability of the parties to market any product themselves without first giving AG the right to decide whether to adopt it. This was clearly a restriction under section 6(1)(f) RTPA 1976 on ARC and the Institutes regarding the persons to whom they could supply their products, i.e. they had to supply to AG should the latter exercise its option to take the product. The registered documents do not indicate why section 21(2) treatment was inappropriate. However, the option clause was probably significant because of the market context. The agreement gave the parties very considerable market power. The option clause prevented competition between potential rivals on an already concentrated market. The agreement was exempted under section 29 RTPA 1976 by the Secretary of State. It was apparently accepted that the agreement was in the interests of the UK in that agricultural biotechnology was an area of technology of considerable future relevance and it was important for the UK to be well represented in the field. It was considered secondary that the agreement artificially gave the parties substantial market power. The level of international competition was another significant factor, the agreement enhanced export potential onto a rapidly developing market at an accelerated rate. The parties had to notify their agreement to the European Commission. Interestingly, a variation to the agreement was made by the parties subsequent to approval having been given by the Secretary of State. This variation, which concerned restraints on the rights of ARC or the Institutes to enter into other agreements or joint ventures with third parties, was amended so that AG would not refuse consent on the ground of demonstrable risk of commercial prejudice.

12.197 In *Rolls-Royce and GEC*[276] the application of section 29 was perhaps more straight forward. Rolls-Royce (RR) and GEC possess specialist expertise which is technologically complementary. They incorporated a jointly-owned and controlled company which was to undertake R&D, supply, installation and commissioning of generating sets or gas turbine drivers for use therein. The principal function of the product is to generate electricity with or without ancillary equipment. The joint company would at the time become dominant within the UK. Both GEC and RR covenanted not to compete with the joint company thus negating the possibility of individual entry by either company into the market for such generating sets. Such individual entry was not impossible. However, the parties claimed that, "GEC and RR intend that such complementary expertise should encourage orderly technical research and development to establish a more effective product range than one which either GEC or RR acting separately could support". The agreement thus expanded the considerable export potential of the product by enabling a wider range of products to be developed. The agreement gave the UK a powerful supplier as representative in a competitive world market. Thus, whereas section 21(2) would almost certainly have been inoperative because of the increase in market concentration the agreement and its restrictions entailed, the agreement benefited from section 29.

12.198 There is inadequate case experience on section 29 to be able to draw detailed conclusions as to its operation. None the less, certain factors seem to be relevant. Briefly, these are: an agreement concerning a high technology product; considerable export potential; the existence of international competition in which it is considered important that UK companies should participate.

275 Such a clause would probably be exempt under Sch.1, para. 13 from the scope of the RTPA. This provision excludes from the Act the services of professional engineers or technologists operating in the field of, *inter alia*, "metallurgy, chemistry, biochemistry or physics or ... any other form of ... technology analogous to those mentioned". The services of professional biochemists and analogous scientists would appear to be excluded from the Act. An agreement which restrains a biochemist's ability to provide biochemistry services in an R&D venture may be excluded from the Act.

276 Exempt Register No.148 (19 June 1984).

F. Specialisation Agreements

12.199 Specialisation agreements occur where X and Y agree to allocate production of certain products between them. They may accompany this with mutual obligations on each party to supply the other with the products specialised in. Thus X and Y give up production in a defined field in favour of the other. Competition between X and Y thus disappears. However, X and Y, by the agreement can set up extended production runs and thereby realise scale economies and a rationalisation of effort. Ultimately, X and Y can supply customers with the full range of products at cheaper prices. Specialisation may occur also where one party agrees simply to run down operations in one field, or, not to invest in new technology in one field, or, not to increase capacity in one field in the light of expanding demand. All of these agreements can lead, sooner or later, to specialisation.

1. EC Law

(1) Under Article 85(1) EC

12.200 Specialisation agreements only infringe Article 85(1) if the parties are competitors; where X and Y are not rivals the agreement will not foreclose competition between them.[277] Where X and Y are potential competitors, then the agreement might infringe Article 85(1) albeit that at the time of entering the X and Y did not compete.[278] They may be potential competitors because they both employ similar technologies or have the requisite skills to enter each others markets. Where future competition is improbable, for example because long-term economic forecasts indicate that the other market is too expensive to enter or the profit forecasts are very unattractive, then no breach of Article 85(1) occurs.

Agreements only infringe Article 85(1) where they have an appreciable effect upon trade between the Member States. Thus, if X and Y agree to concentrate production upon components that are common to them then there may be no effect on customers or competitors.[279] Specialisation agreements may contain restrictions which require one party to purchase from the other party its total requirements of the product in the manufacture of which the other has specialised either for its own use or for sale to third parties. Such restrictions may fall within Article 85(1) if they have a foreclosing effect on third parties.[280] In *BP/ICI*, ICI's obligation "to obtain for five years a large part of its polyethylene" requirements was held to constitute in effect an exclusive supply agreement caught by Article 85(1).[281]

(2) Exemption under Article 85(3)

12.201 The Commission recognises that specialisation agreements contribute towards improving production and distribution of goods since parties can concentrate on manufacturing specific products thus operating more efficiently and being able to sell the goods more cheaply. Provided that inter-brand competition from other suppliers is effective, parties have an incentive to pass on scale economies to consumers and users.[282] The

277 *SOPELEM–Langen* [1972] CMLR D77; *Jaz–Peter II* [1978] 2 CMLR 186.
278 *Machine Outils* [1968] CMLR D23.
279 *MAN–SAVIEM* [1974] CMLR D123; *Clima-Chappee-Buderus* [1970] CMLR D7.
280 *VW/MAN* OJ 1983 L376/11, [1984] 1 CMLR 621.
281 OJ 1984 212/1, [1985] 2 CMLR 330, para. 29.
282 para. 3 of preamble to Reg. 417/85/EEC, OJ 1985 153/1 on block exemption for categories of specialisation agreement. Thus in *Electrolux/AEG* OJ 1993 C269/4, the Commission indicated its willingness to give exemption to an arrangement where leading manufacturers of washing machines and

Commission has issued a block exemption on specialisation.[283] This is discussed below.

(3) Framework of the block exemption for categories of specialisation agreement: Regulation 417/85/EC: Article 1

12.202 The Regulation gives automatic exemption to agreements whereby undertakings accept reciprocal obligations: (a) not to manufacture certain products or to have them manufactured but to leave it to the other parties to have those products manufactured; or (b) to manufacture certain products or have them manufactured only jointly.[284] Thus specialisation can arise through X and Y agreeing negatively (i.e. not to produce a specific product) or positively (i.e. to produce only certain products). Agreements caught by the Regulation need not be notified though where parties are unsure as to exemption they may notify and request a positive decision granting exemption.[285] More likely, the Commission will issue a comfort letter to the parties. The exemption only applies where "reciprocal" obligations are accepted. Thus, where X agrees with Y that X will no longer produce a particular product that Y produces this is not exempt since Y accepts no obligation. Such agreements may be notified though they should benefit from exemption. The Commission has recognised these agreements as being species of specialisation.[286] Though if X and Y are competitors and X refrains from producing Y's product in the hope that Y will respond and refrain from producing X's product this may have the effect of simply reducing competition generally in the markets for the relevant products. The behaviour of X might represent an attempt to foster a form of market sharing by product type. Such an agreement will rarely be acceptable particularly where X and Y are large undertakings and the concerted practice (presuming it evolves) does not seek production improvements thereby.

12.203 The Regulation only covers manufacture. Though, if X and Y also agree to specialise in R&D, this may still benefit from exemption since R&D specialisation is exemptible under Article 1 of Regulation 418/85/EEC on block exemption for R&D agreements. The R&D regulation and the specialisation regulation are *not* mutually exclusive, they can operate concurrently.[287] Indeed where specialisation *and* R&D are sought as concurrent goals parties will find that drafting their agreement so as to fit within the R&D regulation may provide a more permissive form of exemption.

12.204 Exemption should also apply where parties agree to specialise in future, planned production. Article 1 states that exemption lasts for the duration of the agreement. X and Y could agree that they will specialise in production of any future results they derive from a current R&D agreement between them.

12.205 Presumably the exemption only applies where parties actually do specialise their functions. If X and Y agree on specialisation but retain a discretion whether in fact to do so, then the *raison d'être* for exemption has gone, the rationalisation of production, resultant

cont.
dryers agreed to specialise in one of these products and to rely on supplies from the other. This was on the basis that although each was in some markets the market leader for these products, there was effective inter-brand competition from other European and world manufacturers, and that the parties were not combining distribution so remained competitors at the retail, if not the manufacturing, level.

283 *ibid.* This regulation replaced Reg. 3604/82/EEC, OJ 1982 L376/33, which in turn had replaced Reg. 2779/72/EEC, OJ 1972 1292/23, as amended by Reg. 2903/79/EEC, OJ 1977 1338/14. It has been most recently amended by Reg 151/93, OJ 1993 L21/8.

284 *ibid.* Art. 1 and see para. 4 of the preamble.

285 *ibid.* para. 9 of the preamble.

286 See e.g. *Prym–Beka* [1973] CMLR D250, the Commission has accepted that such agreements may be specialisation agreements and hence suitable for Art. 85(3) exemption.

287 Art.1(3)(a) and para.14 of preamble to Reg. 418/85/EEC, OJ 1985 153/5 on block exemption for R&D agreements. See *MAN–SAVIEM* [1974] CMLR D123; *SOPELEM–Langen* [1972] CMLR D77.

scale economies and passed on benefits to consumers are not guaranteed. Accordingly, an *obligation* on X and Y to actually undertake manufacture is within the scope of the exemption. Likewise, obligations on X and Y to produce minimum quantities are exemptible since these only support the obligation to actually manufacture.

12.206 Surprisingly, the Commission makes no mention of the communication of know-how as between the parties. Restrictions on know-how might hence take an agreement outside the exemption in which case the agreement should be notified. See paras. 13.36 and following, for details of know-how licences in technology transfer agreements.

(4) Permissible restrictions, "white clauses": Article 2

12.207 Article 2 lays down permissible restrictions that may be incorporated in an agreement without loss of exemption. With respect to (a)–(c) below exemption also applies where the parties accept restrictions which are similar in type but have a more limited scope. Parties may choose those of the white clauses which suit their needs, the clauses are not mandatory.[288] There is no specific list of black clauses. Instead, it is provided that exemption is not granted if restrictions of competition, other than those specified in the whitelist, are included.[289]

12.208 *(a) Exclusivity*

Obligations on the parties not to conclude other specialisation agreements with third parties in respect of identical or equivalent goods are permissible. An equivalent product is one which is considered by users to be equivalent in view of its characteristics, price and intended use. This is the standard definition employed by the Commission in the various block exemptions. If the restriction *exceeds* this obligation the block exemption lapses, e.g. restriction on entering agreements with third parties in fields other than those covered by the specialisation. If the obligation has more limited scope then it remains exempt, e.g. obligation not to enter specialisation agreement in respect of the contract goods with third parties without the consent of the other parties.[290] An obligation preventing parties from entering specialisation agreements with third parties for products which are not the same as, nor substitutes for, the products covered by the main agreements, goes beyond the scope of the block exemption and would take the agreement outside its protection.

12.209 *(b) Exclusive purchasing*

An obligation on parties to procure relevant products exclusively from another party, a joint venture company or other undertaking responsible for manufacture of the relevant products is permissible where it is coupled to an "English clause" which provides that the exclusive purchase obligation is inapplicable where the relevant products are available from other sources on more favourable terms and the supplier under the main agreement is not prepared to offer the same terms. Thus, if X and Y incorporate XY Ltd to manufacture widgets for them, leaving them to concentrate production on other products, then X and Y can be bound to purchase widgets exclusively from XY Ltd. However, there must also be a clause providing that X and Y can purchase widgets from Z in the event that Z can offer better terms and XY Ltd refuses to match those terms. If this proviso is not added to the exclusive purchase clause then the block exemption does not

288 para. 5 of the preamble to Reg. 417/85/EEC.
289 Art. 2a, Reg. 417/85.
290 This consent of other parties clause was *specifically* exempted under Art. 2(a), Reg. 2779/72/EEC, the precursor to Reg. 417/85/EEC.

apply. The proviso enables parties to purchase from the cheapest source thereby maintaining the drive towards reduced costs. Parties may wish to elaborate upon what is meant by "more favourable terms" or other details. Such elaborations are within the scope of the exemption. The same applies to the exclusive purchase obligation: parties may wish to impose duties on parties to notify the supplier in advance of requirements, or to buy minimum quantities. These should fall within the scope of the exemption. However, any quantitative restriction on purchases will take the agreement outside the block exemption. A maximum purchase obligation coupled with an exclusive purchasing obligation would be equivalent to a quota; to gain exemption, the obligation not to purchase more than a specified amount would have to be removed.[291]

12.210 *(c) Exclusive distribution*

Obligations on the parties to grant other parties exclusive distribution rights of the products they specialise in are permissible. Thus, where X produces widgets and Y produces gidgets, X can make Y exclusive dealer for widgets and Y can make X exclusive dealer for gidgets. The rationale behind this clause is that it enables each of the parties to supply the complete range of products covered by the specialisation agreement. The exclusive dealing provisions, however, must not result in access to the products by third parties (e.g. users, other suppliers, wholesalers, parallel importers) being rendered more difficult. Thus, the dealership provisions must accord with the provisions of Regulation 1983/83/EEC on block exemption for exclusive dealing. Thus, the dealer cannot be given absolute territorial protection: he cannot be prevented from making passive sales of the goods outside of his territory. The dealer may be prevented from undertaking *active* sales promotion outside his area but he must retain the freedom to supply unsolicited orders. As with the R&D block exemption, Regulation 151/93 introduced amendments to the specialisation block exemption to enable it to be used for distribution joint venture arrangements, i.e. where one of the parties, a joint undertaking or a third party is entrusted with distribution. Thus the block exemption now exempts an exclusive distribution right granted to one of the parties for products which are the subject of the specialisation agreement provided that that party does not distribute a third party's competing products.[292] Exclusive distribution rights may also be granted to a joint undertaking or third party provided that it does not manufacture or distribute competing products.[293] Finally, if such exclusive distribution rights are granted to more than one joint undertaking or third party, i.e. if an exclusive distribution network is set up, then exemption is granted on the basis that those distributors do not manufacture or distribute competing products and that the distributors do not make it difficult for users or intermediaries to obtain the contract products.[294]

12.211 *(d) Quality control*

Obligations on parties to supply other parties with relevant products which observe minimum standards of quality are permissible. Standard obligations in respect of products not subject to the specialisation are not exempt. The specialisation agreement is silent as to whether such clauses may be imposed only where such specifications are necessary for a technically satisfactory exploitation of the contract product. It is also silent as to the status of clauses allowing the parties to carry out quality control checks on their partners. Both the necessity and monitoring elements are expressly covered by the patent and know-how

[291] *Perlite, Nineteenth Report on Competition Policy* (1989), para. 39. In this case the agreement was notified under the opposition procedure under Art. 4.

[292] Art. 2(1)(d), Reg. 417/85.

[293] Art. 2(1)(e), Reg. 417/85.

[294] Art. 2(1)(f), Reg. 417/85.

licensing regulations. Does their absence here imply that they are *not* exempt? It is arguable that clauses included in a contract which merely support another clause and are ancillary to it are exempt to the same degree as the main clause. Article 2(3) is not inconsistent with this view since it provides that the exemption remains "notwithstanding that any of the following obligations, *in particular*, are imposed". Article 2(3) then proceeds to exempt quality control, minimum stocks, and, customer and guarantee services. The words *in particular* imply that obligations other than the three types mentioned also be exempted. If this is so then clauses ancillary to those main three should fall within the exemption.

12.212 *(e) Minimum stocks*

Obligations on parties to keep minimum stocks of products and of spare and replacement parts are permissible.

12.213 *(f) Customer and guarantee services*

Obligations on the parties to provide customer and guarantee services for the products subject to specialisation are exempt. Thus, if X and Y produce widgets and gidgets respectively and they make each other exclusive dealer for their respective products, then Y may bind X to providing customer and guarantee services on gidgets as well as on widgets, and vice versa.

(5) Market share threshold, limits on the block exemption: Article 3

12.214 Paragraph 6 of the preamble states: "The exemption must be limited to agreements which do not give rise to the possibility of eliminating competition in respect of a substantial part of the products in question. The Regulation must therefore apply only as long as the market share and turnover of the participating undertakings do not exceed a certain limit." Article 3 lays down these limits. There are two central criteria based upon (a) market share; and (b) turnover. Both apply cumulatively, they are not alternatives.

12.215 *(a) Market share*

Exemption only applies where the aggregated market share of the parties to the agreement does not exceed 20 per cent of the market for the relevant products. The product market is defined as those products subject to the specialisation agreement *and* those products produced independently by the parties which are considered to be the same or substitutes (i.e. users would consider them equivalent in view of their characteristics, price and intended use).[295] The geographical market in which market share is to be assessed is the whole EC or a substantial part thereof. The meaning of "substantial" is unclear, see para. 12.142 for general discussion of "substantial" in the context of the R&D block exemption.

Where the specialisation agreement includes provisions relating to distribution of the contract products by one of the parties, or by one or more joint undertakings or third parties, then the market share limit is reduced to 10 per cent.[296]

A "tolerance" margin exists whereby exemption is not lost where, during any period of two consecutive financial years, the market share is exceeded by not more than one-tenth. Where, because the total market share threshold is breached to an extent not covered by the tolerance period, exemption lapses, then exemption continues to apply for a six-month "tailing off" period which commences from the end of the financial year during which the threshold and tolerance margin were exceeded.

[295] See for Commission thinking on the "consumer vantage" test, para. 21 Commission explanatory Memorandum to the block exemptions on Exclusive dealing and purchasing OJ 1983 C355/7 (30 December 1983).

[296] Art. 3(2), Reg. 417/85.

12.216 *(b) Turnover*

The aggregate annual turnover of all the participants to the agreement must not exceed ECU1,000 million.[297] The "tolerance margin" and "tailing off" provisions noted above apply to turnover also, Where the turnover limit is exceeded but the aggregate market share remains below 20 per cent then the agreement may obtain exemption through the "opposition procedure" (below).[298] Under Article 6, for the purposes of calculating total annual turnover, the turnovers achieved by the parties during the last financial year in respect of all goods and services excluding tax are to be added together. No account, however, is to be taken of dealings between the parties, *inter se*, or between the parties and a third party jointly charged with manufacture. Thus, supplies of goods between X and Y are to be excluded as are supplies of goods between XY Ltd (a joint manufacturing company) and X and Y. If XY Ltd manufactures a component for X and Y, sales by XY Ltd to X, for example, are not to be counted. A party to an agreement is described by the Regulation as a "participating undertaking". These are defined in Article 7 in terms that are, *mutatis mutandis*, the same as the R&D block exemption definition of a "connected undertaking". For details see paras. 12.174–12.175.

(6) Extension of exemption to agreements not satisfying the turnover requirement: the "opposition procedure": Article 4

12.217 Recital 7 of the preamble to the Regulation states that it is "appropriate to offer undertakings which exceed the turnover limits set in the Regulation a simplified means of obtaining the legal certainty provided by the block exemption". An "opposition procedure" is hence available for specialisation agreements involving parties whose aggregate turnover exceeds ECU1,000 million and the tolerance margin. Details of this "opposition procedure" are given at paras. 7.167-7.173.

(7) Withdrawal of exemption: Article 8

12.218 The Commission may, in exceptional circumstances, withdraw the exemption. This can only be done by a formal decision.[299] Withdrawal will occur when the Commission finds that an agreement protected by the Regulation has effects which are incompatible with Article 85(3) EC.[300] The Regulation lists two examples. Clearly, the list is non-exhaustive.

12.219 *(a) Agreement not yielding results*

Where the agreement is "not yielding significant results in terms of rationalisation or consumers are not receiving a fair share of the resulting benefit". Thus, the Commission is concerned to ensure that the agreement does lead to greater efficiency. This means that the "rationalisation" of effort should result in the realisation of greater productive efficiency as producers focus their efforts and scale economies are realised as longer production runs may be carried out. Likewise these "rationalisation" benefits should lead to cheaper products for consumers with suppliers also being able to hold complete ranges

297 Increased from ECU500 million by Art. 1(5), Reg. 151/93.

298 *Fourteenth Report on Competition Policy* (1984), pp. 44, 45, para. 42.

299 See for commentary on analogous provisions in the block-exemptions on exclusive dealing and purchasing, para. 24 of the explanatory memorandum to the exclusive dealing and purchasing regulations, OJ 1983 C 355/7. For analysis see paras. 10.86–10.90 on Art. 6 of Reg. 1983/83/EEC.

300 The power to withdraw an exemption derives from Art. 6 of Reg. 2821/71/EC on the application of Art. 85(3) to categories of Agreement, decision and concerted practice JO 1971 1285/46 (20 December 1971)—the Commission may respond on its own initiative or at the request of a Member State or of natural or legal persons claiming a legitimate interest.

of products thereby increasing consumer service and choice. The benefits arising must occur in a "significant" manner: thus, parties must be able to point to substantial benefits if so challenged by the Commission.

12.220 *(b) Inter-brand competition weak*

Theoretically, the level of competition between the contract goods and other brands should be high given that exemption only lies where the parties combined possess up to 20 per cent (10 per cent if there is to be joint distribution) of the market. Where for some exceptional circumstance inter-brand competition is ineffective, albeit existing, then exemption may be withdrawn.

(8) Currency of block exemption: Article 10

12.221 The period of validity of the Regulation is approximately 13 years: 1 March 1985 until 31 December 1997. The Commission notes that this period is set to facilitate the conclusion of long-term agreements which can have a bearing on the structure of the parties. However, it also notes that if circumstances should change significantly the Commission might make the "necessary amendments".[301] Presumably, it could shorten or extend the period of validity.

(9) Relationship with other block exemptions: paragraph 14 of the preamble to the R&D block exemption

12.222 Recital 14 of the preamble to the R&D block exemption (see above) provides that it may apply contemporaneously with the block exemption on, *inter alia*, specialisation. Thus a specialisation agreement entailing also joint R&D may obtain block exemption for both different elements of the overall agreement. However, in the event of conflict between the two regulations, the block exemption on R&D takes precedence.

(10) Check list for application of the block exemption

12.223 The Regulation should give automatic exemption to many agreements between small and medium-sized undertakings. A summary of the conditions for application of the exemption is as follows:

Condition 1

Agreement must be of a type described in Article 1 involving reciprocal obligations on specialisation of products for manufacture.

Condition 2

Agreement must not include any restrictions other than those described in Article 2 concerning: exclusivity; exclusive purchasing; exclusive distribution; quality control; maximum stocks; and customer and guarantee services. If the agreement contains additional restrictions it may have to be notified. Though clauses that are of a similar type to, or are ancillary to, the main exempt obligations should also be exempt.

Condition 3

The agreement must not exceed either the market share or turnover limits in Article 3 (as elaborated upon by Articles 6 and 7).

301 para. 8 of the preamble to the Regulation.

Condition 4

Where the agreement exceeds the *turnover* limit but otherwise satisfies the terms of the Regulation it may be notified in accordance with the "opposition procedure" in Article 4. Exemption extends to such an agreement six months following notification provided that no "opposition" has been raised.

Condition 5

Agreements exceeding the *market share* limit can never benefit from block exemption, they may obtain individual exemption or otherwise be settled informally by comfort letter upon notification.

Condition 6

Block exemption may be withdrawn from any agreement where in a particular case the Commission determine that the criteria in Article 85(3) are not satisfied.

2. UK Law

12.224 As a preliminary point and as with R&D agreements, it should be borne in mind that if an agreement comes within the block exemption for specialisation, then it is non-notifiable for the purposes of the RTPA, which thus only applies to agreements falling outside the block exemption.[302] Specialisation agreements where registrable are generally suitable for section 21(2) treatment.

(1) Registrability

12.225 Agreements usually contain two principal restrictions. First, on production by the parties of specified products. Secondly, on mutual supply of the relevant products to each other. The first restriction is registrable under section 6(1)(d) or (e) RTPA 1976. If X and Y agree that in future X will concentrate exclusively on production of widgets, and Y will concentrate exclusively on production of gidgets then both have accepted restrictions as to the descriptions (i.e. kinds) of goods they will produce (under section 6(1)(d)), i.e. X will not produce gidgets, and Y will not produce widgets). If X and Y agree that they will apply a particular process that they are both experienced in (perhaps because they have jointly derived the process through joint R&D) to different products, then this is a restriction under section 6(1)(e) on the description of goods to which the process is applied. If, in either example above, only one party accepts the restriction the agreement is not registrable for lack of mutuality, i.e. two parties are not accepting restrictions.

12.226 If X and Y license know-how or patents to each other, restrictions on use of the intellectual property rights are not registrable, e.g. X may only use Y's patents for production of widgets and for nothing else. Restrictions in licences of proprietory rights are not contracts for the supply of goods or services and are accordingly outside the scope of the RTPA 1976. Nor are limitations contained therein considered as legal restrictions.[303] Where in pursuance of a specialisation agreement, X agrees to supply Y with widgets and Y agrees to supply X with gidgets on an exclusive basis this would involve restrictions under section 6(1)(f) on the persons to whom goods are to be supplied, i.e. X and Y must supply only to each other and, therefore, are restricted as to the supply to third

[302] Restrictive Trade Practices (Non-notifiable Agreements) (EC Block Exemptions) Order, S.I. 1996 No. 349, issued under section 27A RTPA 1976 (added by s. 10 Deregulation and Contracting Out Act 1994). See further paras 2.250 and following.

[303] See paras. 2.202–2.210 for details.

parties. Where the agreement contains no other registrable restrictions at all then mutual exclusive dealing obligations *may* be exempt from registration under Schedule 3, para. 2 which exempts exclusive dealing from the Act. However, it is unclear whether mutual exclusive dealing is exempt, i.e. where parties are both supplier *and* exclusive dealer.[304] Where only one party is bound to supply Schedule 3, para 2 applies (provided there are no other restrictions in the agreement).

12.227 Where in pursuance of an agreement X and Y agree to purchase exclusively from each other this entails restrictions under section 6(1)(f) on the persons from whom goods are to be acquired. In this situation X and Y are *not* restricted as to whom they may sell: the restriction is that should either party require the other's product they must take supplies exclusively from that other party. Where no other restrictions at all are included, then exclusive purchasing may be exempt under Schedule 3, para. 2 RTPA 1976 which exempts exclusive purchasing obligations from the Act provided no other restrictions are contained in the agreement. The same proviso applies with respect to *mutual* exclusive purchasing as applies to mutual exclusive dealing (see above).

(2) Specialisation and section 21(2) RTPA 1976

12.228 Specialisation agreements are generally suited to section 21(2) treatment, especially where the parties are small or medium sized. Registrable restrictions may not be "significant" where they enable the parties to rationalise their product and hence produce more cheaply, thereby serving the consumer and intensifying competition on the market.

12.229 Where the parties are not competing but agree to supply, on an exclusive basis, products or services supplied by the other then the agreements, if registrable, should be suitable for section 21 (2) dispensation, In *Legal and General Assurance–Forward Trust*[305] LGA was a provider of life assurance and FT was a provider of credit and loan facilities. The parties agreed that, in order to provide customers with a broader range of services, they would supply the service provided by the other in addition to their own. Hence, both LGA and FT now provided life assurance and credit and loan facilities. There was no restriction on either party commencing provision of the other's service. Hence, the case did not concern specialisation in its usual form. None the less, it does demonstrate that mutual exclusive dealing between suppliers of complementary products or services may be suitable for section 21(2) treatment. The agreement enabled the parties to provide a wider range of services to customers without having to divert effort into actually creating the product or service in question. In this case, there were ancillary restrictions on LGA and FT under which, *inter alia*, LGA would not produce credit advertisements without the prior approval of FI; and LGA and FT agreed to standardise the criteria they would use in deciding whether or not to allow applicants to open accounts.

12.230 In respect of specialisation agreements incorporating exclusive purchase obligations, a contractual device which renders purchasing restrictions of less significance for section 21(2) purposes is the "English clause". In *Croda–Manox*[306] Croda (C) and Manox (M) agreed to specialise in the production of different paints, in particular varieties called "iron blue" and "lake red". C would, for a five-year period, produce "lake red"; M would, for the same period, produce "iron blue". Under the agreement C agreed to purchase its entire requirements of "iron blue" from M: "provided that Croda shall be released from this undertaking if Croda can demonstrate to Manox that equivalent material is available in comparable quantities on a continuing basis from a third party source

[304] See paras. 2.154–2.156 for details.
[305] No. S.1393 Register of Restrictive Trade Practices (1984).
[306] No. 5044 Register of Restrictive Trade Practices (1983).

at lower prices and Manox is unable to agree to supply at such lower prices, or if Manox is unable for any reason to supply for a period of one month". The existence of such a clause means that efficiency need not necessarily suffer in the event of a failing in the joint venture agreement. The agreement in question also contained, *inter alia*, restrictions on C and M producing certain types of paint. Section 21(2) dispensation was given in 1983.

(3) Specialisation and section 29 RTPA 1976

12.231 Where a specialisation agreement is unsuitable for section 21(2) treatment, for example, because the parties combined enjoy a substantial market share and hence restrictions on competition between them are significant, then section 29 RTPA 1976 might apply. Details of the relevant procedures are given at paras 2.3-2.28. Agreements benefiting under section 29 RTPA 1976 are exempt from registration. To obtain exemption, parties must convince the Secretary of State that the agreement is important to the national economy.

12.232 In an early case *Bowater Paper–Reed Paper*[307] Bowater (B) and Reed (R) purchased a company, Donside Paper (DP) to act as a jointly-owned venture company. B and R agreed to concentrate production on different types of paper. DP was to be responsible for formulating a common marketing policy, co-ordinating the parties production of coated papers, and promoting further development of coated paper. It was also to produce paper on its own account and provide extra capacity for the grades produced by B and R. Under the agreement B and R agreed to act as *del credere* agents for each others type of paper. Furthermore, both B and R agreed to act as agents for paper produced by DP. Thus, B and R specialised in different grades of paper and purchased grades they did not themselves produce from each other. With respect to paper produced by DP there was also joint distribution and marketing through DP. With respect to paper produced by B and R, the parties took independent marketing measures. B and R adopted independent price policies but had "regard" to recommendations made by the board of DP as to price differentials between different grades and qualities of coated papers. Since B and R were major producers in the UK, the agreement had a substantial effect on the UK market. Given the size of the parties, the restrictions could hardly be said not to be "significant". However the agreement was exempted from registration under section 29 RTPA 1976. A number of factors were relevant to this decision. Principally, the agreement enabled the parties to bring extra capacity on line more rapidly than would otherwise have been the case. Speed was considered important here since the extra capacity was needed to meet a substantial upturn in demand engendered through the increased use of colour printing by advertisers and consumers and the need for publishers to be prepared to meet competition from colour television. Moreover, rapid introduction of extra capacity was needed to counter increased imports into the UK from Scandinavia, where producers were gearing up to increased output with an expansion of UK sales in mind. In a memorandum submitted in support of their section 29 application the parties stated:

> "Duplication of installations by the British producers must be avoided in the future owing to the scale of investment required and the cost of below capacity operations. If the joint operation can be undertaken it is expected that an initial investment in a new, fast running machine, with a blade coater, will be made in the years 1971–1973. A second machine will probably be called for some three years later, depending on the speed of the growth in demand from publishers for light weight coated mechanical printing and publication papers.

[307] Exempt Register 2 (January 1969) exemption given for six years, extended in 1975 for a further four years. The agreement was terminated by the parties in December 1977.

It is considered that the change-over from uncoated to coated light weight mechanical printing will offer the British paper industry a unique opportunity to recover a share of the market for printing papers which it has lost to foreign manufacturers in the uncoated grades. This opportunity is unlikely to occur again."

12.233 Whether a specialisation agreement of this nature would be exempted today may be questioned. Current thinking on section 29 tends to focus upon the creation of new and improved technology and the desirability of having UK firms competing effectively in such markets. The *Bowater Paper–Reed Paper* agreement, which was given exemption in 1969, was predominantly an expansion of capacity scheme, designed to counter the threat of imports. More recent agreements have had a significant element of technology enhancement in addition to output expansion.[308]

G. Rationalisation Agreements, often Termed "Crisis Cartels"

1. *Legal and Economic Context*

12.234 Basic economic principle teaches that when an industry encounters an unanticipated decline in demand, this will have a depressant effect upon prices, volumes sold and revenues of producers. Consumers will, however, benefit in the short term from the decline in prices. Where the downturn in demand is long term the market will move to readjust. Theoretically, less efficient high cost producers will leave the market leaving the more efficient to satisfy demand. In practice the process of readjustment may be slow and ineffective: the efficient producers might depart leaving the inefficient (who for structural or other reasons are unable to diversify) to satisfy demand. Adjustment might be slow because equipment is durable, dedicated to a single function and difficult to adapt to alternative functions; plant may be outdated but fully depreciated and hence needs only recover its operating costs; labour may be over specialised; redundancy laws might hinder closures and add to exit costs where it entails substantial redundancy payments.

12.235 In certain cases, where it is predictable that market forces might not bring about a restructuring of an industry in an efficient manner, it may well be in the public interest for the restructuring process to be brought about by concerted effort by the market participants; government agencies may also wish to become involved in the scheme. In such cases a rationalisation agreement might be concluded which seeks an orderly reduction of capacity in order to restore the balance between output and demand. In a rationalisation agreement members of an industry agree to reduce capacity. This may be achieved by the total closure of some firms in consideration of departure compensation; alternatively, it may involve controlled reductions in capacity for all participant firms but no departures. Numerous alternatives exist within these frameworks. Compensation, where payable, may be funded by compulsory levys on those remaining or it may be voluntary. Payment of compensation will be made conditional upon evidence that the excess capacity (plant) has been irrevocably destroyed or dismantled. There may be additional restrictions on re-entry to the market or future expansion of capacity coupled to penalty payments levied for breach of the restrictions. Invariably an independent central agency (accountancy firm, merchant banker, etc.) will act as referee and co-ordinator. A successful agreement will lead to the elimination of excess capacity in a swifter manner than could

[308] See cases on s. 29 at paras. 12.195–12.198 (R&D agreements).

have been achieved by the market, an increase in the capacity utilisation of residual plant and an overall increase in prices. The fact that the agreement may enhance prices does not imply exploitation but only a restoration of price levels allowing scope for adequate profit margins and long term viability.

12.236 Rationalisation agreements inevitably require antitrust clearance. Thus, a phased capacity reduction may be akin to a market sharing by volume; a system of closures and compensatory payments likewise represent a form of market division; alternatively firms who simply merge with each other with capacity being shed in the process may need merger clearance.

2. *EC Law*[309]

(1) General position

12.237 The Commission adopts a cautious yet generally favourable view towards agreements to reduce serious structural overcapacity:

> "In a predominantly free market economy such as the Community's, it is up to each undertaking to assess for itself whether and at which point such overcapacity becomes economically unsustainable and to take the necessary measures to reduce it. However, within a given crisis-struck industry, economic circumstances do not necessarily guarantee a reduction of the least profitable surplus capacity. Undertakings which have failed to make the necessary adjustments may have their losses offset within their groups, to the detriment of healthy undertakings and there may be additional distortion from external subsidies."[310]

12.238 In view of the inefficiency of individual action in certain circumstances, the Commission is prepared to accept agreements aimed at co-ordinated reduction of overcapacity and which, otherwise, do not restrain free decision making by the firms involved. Restructuring, however, may *not* occur by price-fixing or quota schemes. The Court of First Instance stressed in *Montedipe*[311] that undertakings must not take private measures to deal with industry wide crises. Furthermore, the Commission have expressed criticism of state aids granted to firms to sustain overcapacity. Such aids are reviewable under Articles 92 and 93. Firms receiving such aid are in danger of being made the victim of Commission decisions addressed to the granting Member State to recover the aid[312] (see paras. 12.279–12.281 for details).

(2) Meaning of structural overcapacity

12.239 The Commission has defined structural overcapacity as existing, "where over a prolonged period all the undertakings concerned have been experiencing a significant reduction in their rates of capacity utilisation, a drop in output accompanied by substantial

[309] See *Twelfth Report on Competition Policy* (1982), pp. 43–45; *Thirteenth Report on Competition Policy* (1983), pp. 53–56; *Fourteenth Report on Competition Policy* (1984), pp. 69–72. These principles were restated in the *Twenty-third Report on Competition Policy* (1993), paras. 84–88. Van Grevenstein, "Restructuring arrangements under EC competition law" (1985) ECLR 56. For the position in Germany see, Stockman, "The role of anti-trust in the face of economic recession: recent developments in Germany" [1984] ECLR 83.

[310] *Twelfth Report on Competition Policy* (1982), p. 43, para. 38. This view has been confirmed in *Synthetic Fibres Agreement* [1985] 1 CMIR 787 at p. 796, para. 30. See also Commission answer to WQ No. 578/84, OJ 1984 C344/5, para. 3.

[311] Case T-14/89 *Montedipe SpA* v *Commission* [1993] ECR II-115

[312] See Commission Notice on State Aids, OJ 1980 C252/2 noted Flynn, (1983) EL Rev 297 and subsequent Commission Notice at OJ 1983 C318/3 on recovery from recipients of aids illegally paid. See also the view of the Court of Justice in Case 70/72 *Commission* v *Germany* [1973] ECR 813 at p. 829.

operating losses and where the information available does not indicate that any lasting improvement can be expected in this situation in the medium-term".[313] Thus four conditions must exist before a rationalisation agreement becomes feasible:

(i) undertakings must already have experienced a significant reduction in the rate of capacity utilisation. Note that such reductions must be existent *and significant;*
(ii) undertakings must already have experienced a drop in output *and* substantial operating losses. Again the real effects must be existent and substantial in degree;
(iii) no *medium-term* prospect of a change in fortunes is foreseeable. Note that the Commission adopts a medium-term analysis and not a short or long-term perspective. How long is medium term will depend on market circumstances;
(iv) the real effects noted in (i) and (ii) above must have been in existence for a prolonged period.

12.240 It appears to be the case that structural over-capacity so defined is an essential precondition for a favourable approach from the Commission; curative agreements are crisis agreements justified only by exceptional circumstances. Thus, in *Synthetic Fibres Agreement*[314] European manufacturers were experiencing a significant disparity in supply and demand which derived from adverse market conditions characterised by weak demand and increased import penetration and the existence of substantial surplus capacity in the industry. By 1977 plant was operating at an average of only 70 per cent of capacity. Profit margins were seriously eroded. To compound the structural problems, firms in some sectors had sought to compete with cheap imports by creating much larger plants which enabled the realisation of scale economies leading to lower prices. These market conditions were considered acute enough to justify curative action by means of an agreement.

(3) Types of rationalisation agreement

12.241 Depending upon the nature of the market crisis in question rationalisation agreements may take a number of forms:

12.242 *(a) Sector agreements*

Agreements between whole sectors of industry to close down excess plant may be condoned. The agreement must contain detailed and binding programmes for each production centre which ensures that overcapacity is irreversibly dismantled and no new capacity is created for the duration of the agreement except for replacement capacities provided for in the restructuring agreement.[315]

12.243 *b) Specialisation between small groups of firms*

Where individual firms desire to take concerted action to reduce over-capacity they may achieve this end by a specialisation agreement whereby each party dismantles production of certain lines whilst concentrating on others.[316]

313 *Twelfth Report on Competition Policy* (1982), p. 43, para. 38.

314 [1985] 1 CMLR 787. The Commission had objected to an earlier agreement on the basis that it would have affected the production and sales policies of the parties. See *Eighth Report on Competition Policy* (1978), para. 42. See also *Twelfth Report on Competition Policy* (1982), paras. 38–41.

315 e.g. *ibid.* See also *Zinc Shutdown Agreement* [1983] 2 CMLR 473—parties not restrained from investing in capacity that was not shutdown in order to modernise it provided capacity not substantially increased thereby. The agreement was later terminated by the parties: Commission Press Release (9 January 1984) IP (84) 8.

316 e.g. *BPCL–ICI* OJ 1984 L212/1 [1985] 2 CMLR 330; see also *Bayer/BP* [1989] 4 CMLR 24, para. 28.

12.244 *(c) Joint capacity utilisation agreements*

Where X and Y have excess capacity they may decide to place their plant at the disposal of the other in order that excess capacity be taken up. The need for either party to individually create new capacity diminishes if they can realise additional output from the other party's plant.[317]

12.245 *(d) Mergers*

X and Y merge their subsidiaries, or take over a third company, with a view to rationalising production between the parties. For details see below on UK rationalisation mergers.

(4) Sectoral rationalisation schemes

12.246 In *Synthetic Fibres Agreement* a sectoral scheme was exempted under Article 85(3) EC. The size of capacity was based upon two assumptions: (i) that capacity had to be operated at 85 per cent to be profitable; (ii) that sales would stabilise at 1981 levels by 1986. On the basis of an appraisal of European and world markets the producers concluded that there was no prospect of a significant upturn in demand between 1982 and 1985. Consequently, the parties decided that increases in capacity would exacerbate the problems being faced and that, conversely, reductions in capacity were required. The parties hence agreed to reduce capacity by an amount that would align a capacity utilisation of 85 per cent with demand. The upshot of this was a calculated reduction in capacity of 354,000 tonnes in the parties' combined production capacity to be effected by the end of 1985. On the basis of this reduction each party drew up its own detailed plan taking as its starting point the capacity it was supposed to have by the end of an earlier proposed 1978 agreement and allowing for any intervening transfers of capacity between signatories or between signatories and non-signatories. In addition the parties undertook to: supply to a central body all relevant data concerning the capacity to be dismantled; accept the right of the central body to make on the spot investigations by independent experts; consult each other in the light of changing market circumstances with a view to identifying appropriate solutions; refrain from selling dismantled plant in Western Europe; refrain from increasing capacity, during the currency of the agreement, of capacity they have determined; pay compensation to other parties in the event of violation of the agreement; permit access to the agreement to any EC or Western European company not already a signatory on terms to be independently negotiated.

12.247 The Commission disallowed certain clauses which had to be deleted from the scheme:

(i) Clause imposing a ban on investment leading to increases of capacity without the consent of all the other parties. The Commission considered that this was too inflexible. The relevant clause was deleted. Increases in parties' capacities was brought under the clause providing for consultations in the event of major changes (e.g. concerning the behaviour of European non-signatories, imports from non-European sources, or the collapse of export markets).

(ii) Clause providing that the Commission would use its good offices in the event of difficulties arising from implementation of the agreement. The Commission declined to act as referee for the parties.

(iii) Clause providing for the transmission of information concerning deliveries to the central body. Such clauses might enable parties to monitor output and deliveries and

[317] *Shell–AKZO* (Rovin) Notice pursuant to Art.19(3) of Reg. 17/62/EEC, OJ 1983 C295/7—case settled by comfort letter. See also *PRB–Shell* Notice pursuant to Art.19(3) of Reg. 17/62/EEC, OJ 1984 C189/2. Parties rationalised production by jointly placing capacity at disposal of joint venture company.

could lead to market sharing. Rationalisation agreements permit of ordered plant closures, they do not permit of co-ordination of sales policies.

(iv) Clause providing that the operation of plant at over 95 per cent of the party's declared capacity would be taken as casting doubt upon the correctness of the original capacity declaration. The clause was criticised for allowing parties to monitor output and deliveries.

12.248 The Commission exempted a sectoral scheme for the Dutch brick industry in *Stichting Baksteen*.[318] Structural overcapacity in this industry had led to stockpiles of bricks amounting to 32 per cent of total sales, 50 per cent more than the norm of 20 per cent stockpiles. Demand for bricks was in decline due to competition from new types of building materials, prices had fallen, production capacity was only being used at 80 per cent capacity and so profits had fallen by 30 per cent in real terms since 1980. The Commission accepted that the forces present on the market were unable individually to make the necessary cuts in capacity to restore an effective competitive structure. This was because there was very little elasticity of demand with respect to price levels in the short or medium term. This was coupled with very little flexibility in the brick production process for reducing capacity. The proposal was for a system of co-ordinated closures of the most inefficient plants together with restrictions on re-utilisation of that capacity. This would also have the advantage of reducing capacity with the minimum of social disruption. What was not permitted were arrangements to fix production quotas backed by a system of fines for not doing so, thus leading to market sharing. Instead, the Commission insisted that the parties refrain from divulging information on individual outputs and deliveries of bricks, either directly or via any intermediary.

(5) Rationalisation schemes between individual firms

12.249 It is possible for a bilateral rationalisation agreement exceptionally to fall outside Article 85(1).[319] In *Enichem/ICI*, para 35, the Commission stated that "bilateral arrangements in sectors suffering from structural overcapacity that lead to radical restructuring and, in particular, to capacity closures, are in line with current Commission policy". *Normally*, however, the Commission regards such agreements as caught by an assets swap through Article 85(1) but suitable for exemption. Thus in *BPCL–ICI*[320] BPCL and ICI sought by a sale of assets and specialisation agreement to rationalise their production and thereby dismantle excess capacity. Under the agreement, ICI sold both its most modern UK low density polyethylene (LDPE) plants to BPCL along with all relevant goodwill and licences for requisite LDPE technology; BPCL sold both its most modern UK polyvinylchloride (PVC) plants to ICI along with all relevant goodwill and licences for requisite PVC technology. ICI retained two LDPE plants on

[318] OJ 1994 L131/15; see also *Twenty-third Report on Competition Policy* (1993), para. 89 and OJ 1993 C34/11. restructuring arrangements were also approved under the ECSC for the steel industry: see *Twenty-third Report on Competition Policy* (1993), paras. 481–482; but this approval was subsequently withdrawn when it became apparent that the firms involved would not meet the objectives set: see *Twenty-fourth Report on Competition Policy* (1994), para. 18.

[319] In *Montedison/Hercules (Himont), Seventeenth Report on Competition Policy* (1987), para. 69, the Commission held that a joint venture, Himont, set up to regroup the parents' assets in the polypropylene sector, fell outside Art. 85(1). Were the same scheme to be followed now, the joint venture would be caught by the MCR as a concentrative joint venture.

[320] *BPCL–ICI* OJ 1984 L212/1; *ENI-Montedision* [1988] 4 CMLR 444; *PRB-Shell* OJ 1984 C 189/2, *Seventeenth Report on Competition Policy* (1987), para. 74; *Enichem-ICI (EVC)* [1989] 4 CMLR 54, [1991] 4 CMLR 327; *EMC-DSM (LVM)* OJ 1988 C18/3; *Bayer-BP Chemicals* [1989] 4 CMLR 24, OJ 1992 C 44/11; *Iveco-Ford* [1989] 4 CMLR 40. In *Enichem/ICI*, para. 35, the Commission stated that "bilateral arrangements in sectors suffering from structural overcapacity that lead to radical restructuring and, in particular, to capacity closures, are in line with current Commission policy".

the continent which formed no part of the agreement. In consequence of the agreement, though not pursuant to any provision therein, the parties closed down remaining plants in the fields they were not specialising in. Furthermore, under the agreement ICI increased its shareholding in an ethylene cracker which hitherto it had owned in equal part with BPCL. This extra capacity allowed ICI to close down its remaining ethylene plant. The result of the agreement was a specialisation of production in the UK with limitations on output through plant closures. The Commission granted Article 85(3) exemption.

12.250 Another variant on rationalisation occurred in *Shell–AZKO (Rovin)*[321] Shell (S) and AKZO (A) manufactured PVC and vinylchloride monomer (VCM). S and A created a joint venture partnership, Rovin, and placed at its exclusive disposal VCM and PVC capacity owned by S and A respectively. Rovin was responsible for co-ordination of production, R&D and world wide marketing and sales. The purpose of the agreement was to achieve a structural improvement of capacity utilisation and a healthier structural situation in the sector concerned which was characterised by over-capacity. By co-ordinating their productions and A could prevent over-capacities and A argued that independently they could not have produced VCM and PVC since they neither manufactured the required prime materials nor possessed production capacity or know-how. Further, they contended that the agreement enabled them to integrate vertical production processes and marketing of the products, thereby facilitating a better match between supply and demand of prime materials, a better utilisation rate of installations and the maintaining of constant quality specifications.[322] The Commission approved the agreement by comfort letter.

12.251 Perhaps the most contractually sophisticated rationalisation scheme was that entered into by ICI and Enichem to create *European Vinyls Corporation (EVC)*.[323] This involved the setting up of a new company, EVC, to operate in the vinyl chloride monomer (VCM) and polyvinyl chloride (PVC) sectors. Initially, the shareholders retained ownership of all the operating assets which were made available for use by EVC under contract. EVC was thus essentially a marketing operation. The Commission granted a five-year exemption for this agreement. Subsequently, the shareholders divested themselves of other interests in the PVC market, as well as transferring downstream manufacturing interests to EVC. The Commission then gave approval to the transfer of production assets to EVC, which meant that EVC had became a fully functioning autonomous economic entity. On the basis that the shareholders removed non-competition covenants between them and EVC, the Commission took the view that no further considerations arose under Articles 85 or 86.

12.252 The net effect of these rationalisation agreements in the thermoplastics sector has been to concentrate production in certain large producers. Thus BP Chemicals leads in LDPE, EVC in PVC and Montedison in polypropylene, each with around 20 per cent of their respective markets.[324] Whether this degree of concentration has solved the problem of overcapacity and the concomitant tendency to cartelisation remains to be seen.

(6) Criteria for exemption under Article 85(3) EC

12.253 Rationalisation schemes must satisfy Article 85(3) EC. Hence it must be established that the agreement: contributes to improving production or distribution or promotes technical or economic progress; allows consumers a fair share of the resulting benefit; does not

[321] OJ 1983 C 295/7 Notice pursuant to Art. 19(3) of Reg. 17/62/EEC, case settled by comfort letter, see Bull EC 5/84, p. 38; *Thirteenth Report on Competition Policy* (1983), para. 71.

[322] *ibid.*, at p. 10, para.15.

[323] *Enichem-ICI (EVC)* [1989] 4 CMLR 54, [1991] 4 CMLR 327.

[324] Butterworths *Competition Law*, Division III, para. 787.

impose restrictions which are not indispensable; does not afford such enterprises the possibility of eliminating competition in respect of a substantial part of the products in question; and has beneficial aspects which outweigh the restrictive aspects.

12.254 *(a) Improving production or distribution, etc.*

Production may improve where capacity reductions lead, in the long-term, to increased profitability and restored competition. In the *BPCL–ICI* case, the agreement allowed the parties to increase loading capacity in the product in which they specialised allowing them to reduce unit costs and realise more efficient production. Furthermore, the closures stemmed loss-making activities and hence released resources for investments which helped promote technical progress. The agreement achieved what market forces could not have (or would have been too slow at achieving) and hence accelerated the tendency to re-establish a supply/demand equilibrium. Similar factors applied in the *Synthetic Fibres Agreement* case where the Commission pointed out that such agreements encouraged specialisation since each signatory would select for closure its least efficient and profitable plant. This specialisation thereby encouraged the adoption of optimum plant size and enhanced technical efficiency. An important additional factor in that case concerned the effect on employment prospects of capacity reductions in recession-hit industries.[325] The Commission are under considerable pressure to make employment an issue.[326] Rationalisation agreements may hence be exempted where, *inter alia*, the co-ordination of closures helps to mitigate, spread and stagger the impact on employment. For example because parties can make provision for retraining and redeployment of redundant workers.

12.255 *(b) Consumers obtain fair share of benefit*

Consumers benefit if, at the end of the agreement, they can rely upon competitive and economically healthy supply structures in the EC without having been deprived during the currency of the agreement of their freedom of choice or the benefits of competition. Consumers benefit where the agreement allows firms to be more cost effective and hence more competitively priced and where it allows firms to release resources from loss-making activities and reinvest in new technology.[327]

12.256 *(c) Restrictions indispensable*

All restrictions must be absolutely necessary to the planned restructuring exercise. The agreement must be strictly limited to reducing surplus capacity; it must not extend to quotas or price-fixing or to the exchange and dissemination of information on deliveries and output.[328] However the exchange and dissemination of information which is designed solely to ensure that agreed closures are being undertaken is admissible. Likewise where

[325] [1985] 1 CMLR 787 at p. 797, para. 37. See also *Twelfth Report on Competition Policy* (1982), pp. 43, 44, para. 39.

[326] See Commission Answers to WQ No. 1723/83 OJ C148; and WQ No. 2182/83 OJ 1984 C158/16 at p. 17, para. 2: "The Commission wishes restructuring plans to be carried out with full account being taken of the social consequences of the decisions envisaged." In *Stichting Baksteen* OJ 1994 L131/15, para. 12, the Commission noted, in expressing its view in favour of the restructuring agreement, that a social plan had been negotiated with trade unions.

[327] *Synthetic Fibres Agreement* [1985] 1 CMLR 787 at pp. 797, 798, paras. 39–41; *BPCL–ICI* OJ 1984 1212/1 at pp. 8, 9, para. 36. Though reduction of excess capacity may also led to a rise in prices for consumers as supply moves more to demand, a concern expressed by third parties in *Enichem–ICI (EVC)* [1989] 4 CMLR 54, para. 21. See also *Synthetic Fibres Agreement* [1985] 1 CMLR 787, para. 41. The Commission regards this as only a short term argument, since in the long term consumers will suffer as industry is unable to make the investment into new R&D: see *Twenty-third Report on Competition Policy* (1993), para. 82.

[328] *Stichting Baksteen* OJ 1994 L 131/15, para. 10,

it is essential that each party adhere rigidly to a closure timetable, pecuniary sanctions may be imposed for violation of the agreement. Provisions allowing for the adjustment of parties obligations in the event of transfers of capacity between themselves are acceptable. The same applies to adjustments caused by the accession of new signatories to the agreement. The duration of the agreement must be the minimum necessary for the technical implementation of the programme of cutbacks. In practice, the period for which exemption has been granted has varied greatly: fifteen years in *BPCL–ICI*; three years in *Synthetic Fibres Agreement*; undetermined period but at least five years in *Shell–AKZO (Rovin)* and in *Stichting Baksteen*,[329] the obligation not to use capacity taken out of production would last for 30 years (though third parties remained free to enter the market). By contrast, the initial agreement in *Enichem-ICI* was exempted for a period of five years only, this being considered the minimum necessary period to assess whether the agreement was achieving its aims or was just a vehicle for co-operation on an already concentrated market. In the event, the joint venture became a full function autonomous economic entity at the end of the five year period, the parents having completed their withdrawal from that market.

12.257 *(d) Elimination of competition, etc.*

Generally these agreements do not eliminate competition to an unacceptable degree. First, competition between the parties remains since the agreement affects plant capacity alone and not marketing; secondly, the agreement is usually made necessary by the existence of strong import competition and other firms not party to the agreement; and thirdly, the agreement is for a limited duration and hence signatories will bear in mind the return to unfettered competition in the future. An interesting manifestation of this view appears in *Synthetic Fibres Agreement* where, in respect of fears expressed by textile manufacturer customers of the parties over the perceived inflationary effect on prices charged the agreement would have, the Commission responded by admitting that prices might increase in the short term but that:

> "This tendency may be expected to be limited by the special features of the synthetic-fibres market where each signatory faces considerable pressure in his pricing from synthetic fibre users, who, because they are now operating on a very competitive market and have difficulties of their own, resist price increases which they regard as unjustified. Users could also switch to other sources of supply in Europe or elsewhere if the signatories tried to charge exorbitant prices."[330]

12.258 In essence the extent of residual supplier competition, and, the effectiveness of purchaser power are relevant factors in assessing both consumer benefits ((b) above) and, elimination of competition. Where the agreement is between a small number of firms and external competition is strong, the Commission seems willing to countenance longer periods of duration.[331]

12.259 *(e) Benefits outweigh disadvantages*

The Commission seems to accept as a rule that an agreement to overcome industry wide structural over-capacity which entails also the possibility of improved plant loading at the *end* of the agreement has beneficial aspects which outweigh harmful aspects.[332]

329 *Synthetic Fibres Agreement* at p. 798, para. 43. *Stichting Baksteen* OJ 1994 L 131/15, para. 39.
330 [1985] 1 CMLR 787, para. 41.
331 e.g. *Shell–AKZO (Rovin)* OJ 1983 C295/7.
332 *BPCL–ICI* OJ 1984 12 12/1 at p. 8, para. 34.

3. *UK Law: Self-Help Levy Schemes*

12.260 The position under UK law is of considerable complexity. Section 568 Income and Corporation Taxes Act 1988 (ICTA 1988 hereafter) provides a rather obscure but, none the less, important form of competition law exemption for rationalisation schemes. The details are given below as are details in respect of the state aid implications of government assistance to rationalisation schemes under the Industry Act 1972.

(1) Text of section 568 ICTA 1988

12.261 "568 (1) Notwithstanding anything contained in section 74 [general rules as to deductions not allowable], but subject to the following provisions of this Chapter, where a person pays, wholly and exclusively for the purposes of a trade in respect of which he is chargeable under Case I of Schedule D, a contribution in furtherance of a scheme which is for the time being certified by the Secretary of State under this section, the contribution shall, in so far as it is paid in furtherance of the primary object of the scheme, be allowed to be deducted as an expense in computing the profits or gains of that trade.

(2) The Secretary of State shall certify a scheme under this section if he is satisfied.

(a) that the primary object of the scheme is the elimination of redundant works or machinery or plant from use in an industry in the United Kingdom; and

(b) that the scheme is in the national interest and in the interests of that industry as a whole; and

(c) that such number of persons engaged in that industry as are substantially representative of the industry are liable to pay contributions in furtherance of the primary object of the scheme by agreement between them and the body of persons carrying out the scheme.

References in this subsection to an industry in the United Kingdom shall include references to the business carried on by owners of ships or of a particular class of ships, wherever that business is carried on, and, in relation to that business, references in this subsection to works or machinery or plant shall include references to ships.

(3) The Secretary of State shall cancel any certificate granted under this section if he ceases to be satisfied as to any of the matters referred to in subsection (2) above.

(4) The Secretary of State may at any time require the body of persons carrying out a scheme certified under this section to produce any books or documents of whatever nature relating to the scheme and, if the requirement is not complied with, he may cancel the certificate.

(5) In this section and section 569, 'contribution', in relation to a scheme, does not include a sum paid by a person by way of loan or subscription of share capital, or in consideration of the transfer of assets to him, or by way of a penalty for contravening or failing to comply with the scheme."

(2) Advantages of section 568 ICTA 1988

12.262 There are two principal advantages of section 568. First, schemes certified under the Act are exempted from the RTPA 1976 by virtue of Schedule 3(1)(2) RTPA 1976. Hence, a rationalisation scheme need not be concerned with the RTPA, though such a scheme may still have to be notified to the Commission. Secondly, certified schemes obtain tax advantages. Payments made under a scheme will be treated as allowable deductions for tax purposes. Though, for companies electing to close, compensation received will be treated for tax purposes as an ordinary trading receipt and will thus be taxable at the applicable rate. An additional advantage is that the government may give aid to the scheme under Industrial Development Act 1982.

(3) Analysis of certification criteria in section 568 ICTA 1988

12.263 Section 568(2)(a)–(c) lays down criteria that must be satisfied if certification is to be given.

12.264 (a) "that the primary object of the scheme is the elimination of redundant works or machinery or plant from use in an industry in the United Kingdom". The scheme must have as its "primary" object industry rationalisation, thus ancillary objectives for the scheme are not ruled out. The word "elimination" is generally understood to be permanent, irrevocable elimination. Thus the excess plant may be destroyed, dismantled or sold to domestic or other buyers who will not put it to use in the relevant market. The government have in these cases expressed concern that plant sold second hand to traders on the international market may find its way back to the UK. Parties may be asked to give guarantees that elimination is permanent. The existence of overseas participation in a scheme is not a bar to certification, provided that their primary object is the elimination of surplus UK capacity. The tax advantages apply to UK companies only. Where international participation occurs, the necessity of obtaining EC clearance may be increased. Restrictions in rationalisation schemes must only go so far as is strictly necessary to achieve effective restructuring. The government apparently consider that the exemption afforded such schemes under Schedule 3 paragraph (1)(2) RTPA 1976 from the strictures of that Act only covers restrictions necessary to achieve the "primary object" of the scheme.[333] Ancillary restrictions, therefore, should be avoided or, if included, registered under the RTPA 1976.

12.265 (b) "That the scheme is in the national interest and in the interest of the said industry as a whole". Schemes will be in the national interest where they are more effective mechanisms for securing orderly restructuring than the market itself. This provision provides few problems in practice, although if in a particular case the government considered that the scheme would be slow in taking effect and would encourage the efficient firms to shut down capacity and the inefficient fir-ms to remain, they may be inclined to question the value of the scheme to the national interest. In general terms, however, the government appears willing to permit the parties to make their own strategic decisions. One important consideration is employment, the "national interest" is generally assumed to be served if without the scheme greater long-term unemployment will result than will occur with the scheme. The principle is "short-term pain for long-term gain". The government's overall view of the scheme will have an effect upon the decision whether to grant aid.

12.266 (c) "that such number of persons engaged in the said industry as are substantially representative of the industry are liable to pay contributions in furtherance of the primary object of the scheme by agreement between them and the body of persons carrying out the scheme."

12.267 The meaning of "substantially representative" depends upon the facts of each case. In *Wire Drawing Industry*[334] the companies participating operated 23 wire-drawing sites and had a combined capacity of 850,000 tonnes per annum. This constituted over 80 per cent of estimated UK capacity and contrasted with a market *demand* within the UK of about 550,000 tonnes per annum. In *Steel Castings: High Alloy Sector (Static Group)*[335] the partic-

[333] Typical "primary object" restrictions that may fall within s. 6 RTPA 1976 include: (i) not to accept new orders after a specified date—s. 6(1)(d) and (f); (ii) to cease production within X months—s. 6(1)(d); (iii) not to sell, transfer or dispose of any mould, pattern or other specified equipment which it owns and which it will not use itself in the future i.e. permanent elimination clause—s. 6(1)(f); (iv) payment of a levy—s. 6(1)(d) or s. 6(4); (v) not to engage in the same business as either a principal or an agent—s. 6(1)(f).

[334] 2 December 1982.

[335] 23 March 1982.

ipants accounted for approximately 95 per cent of the UK open market production of high alloy static castings. Approximately 22 per cent of participating tonnage was closed by the scheme. In *Steel Castings: General Sector*[336] a scheme involving the closure of 10 foundries representing approximately 25 per cent of relevant capacity and funded by contributions from remaining foundries was certified. It has been estimated that between 50–60 per cent of total capacity was involved in the scheme. Part of the reasoning for this was the *specific* exclusion from the scheme of certain categories of producer (e.g. rollmakers who had recently been fined by the Commission for price fixing and whose inclusion in the scheme was hence considered likely to raise governmental opposition); and vertically integrated (then state owned) producers, e.g. British Rail, National Coal Board). However, some firms refused to sign the agreement for want of conviction whilst others thought they could reap the benefits of the scheme without bearing the burdens. The government's "ideal" figure is 80 per cent of total capacity though figures well below this may be acceptable.

(4) Procedure and government involvement: independent surveys

12.268 The government have described section 568 schemes as "self-help levy" schemes. In essence a self-help levy scheme involves the companies in a particular sector or industry in identifying one or several of their number who are willing to close plant or works in exchange for compensation which is funded by the remainder of the industry on the basis of an annual levy. The government require initiative for such schemes to commence with the industry itself. Assistance from government may arise in three main ways. First, by the appointment of independent consultants if appropriate to undertake sectoral studies and to explore the potential for a scheme. Secondly, by the certification of the scheme under section 568. Thirdly, by providing, in exceptional cases, financial assistance under section 7 of the Industrial Development Act 1982.

12.269 The appointment of independent experts to undertake exploratory studies has in the past generally been considered essential. First, independent analysis is considered a more appropriate basis for the government to predicate its decisions upon. Secondly, and more importantly, it is considered as an essential catalyst to bringing about productive discussion between the prospective parties to the scheme.

12.270 During 1982–83 the DTI commissioned five sectoral studies from independent consultants with a view to promoting rationalisation schemes in the markets for: cold-rolled narrow steel strip; bright bars; wire drawings; vehicle suspension springs; and, open-die forgings. The decision as to whether to appoint a consultant is, it is understood, a ministerial one upon the advice of the sponsoring department within the DTI. Invariably the independent consultant has acted as administrator of the scheme (sometimes called the scheme trustee).

12.271 It has been noted that initiative for schemes should derive from industry. Such initiatives may be hard to come by in industries where firms are not used to talking with each other. In *Steel Castings: High Alloy Sector (Static Group)* the scheme arose from discussions between a number of the largest steel founding companies in the UK. The firms contacted merchant bankers Lazard Brothers and Co with a view to their acting as consultants and administrators of a rationalisation scheme. Subsequently discussions occurred with and between the DTI; the Bank of England; the EC Commission; the Steel Castings Research and Trade Association; and financiers. These discussions were engendered by the industry and not the government.

(5) Governmental aid under Industrial Development Act 1982

12.272 Financial assistance may be available under the Industrial Development Act 1982. Details are given below.

12.273 *(a) Level of aid*

The government in exceptional cases, is prepared to accord financial assistance under section 7 Industrial Development Act 1982. Aid is offered depending essentially upon need. In the case of the steel cases (see below) aid was offered towards self-help levy schemes at the set level of 25 per cent of total compensation paid to firms closing all capacity and departing the industry.[337] This assistance, however, was apparently considered to be exceptional and due to the unique problems encountered by the private sector when competing against not only the British Steel Corporation (BSC) but also other vertically integrated companies in other EC and non-EC states (the latter despite anti-crisis measures adopted at the Community level). In practice the government consider the assistance is likely to be approximately 25 per cent of total compensation payments. Financial assistance will not be available in every case. Indeed the government fund for assistance is of limited extent. Under the Industrial Development Act 1982, the amount available has been increased to £1,900 million with power being given to the Secretary of State, on not more than four occasions, by order made with the consent of the Treasury, to increase or further increase the limit by a sum not exceeding £200 million.[338] The Secretary of State may pay or undertake to pay a sum not exceeding £10 million in respect of any one project, though a greater sum may be paid where consented to by a resolution of the House of Commons.[339] In *Wire Drawing Industry* the total cost of the scheme was approximately £24 million, of which the government contributed £6 million, In the *Steel Castings* cases the government contributed approximately £7 million.

12.274 *(b) Criteria for granting aid*

The government may grant aid in accordance with sections 7 and 8 Industrial Development Act 1982. Under section 7(2) aid may be granted:

"(a) to promote the development or modernisation of an industry;
(b) to promote the efficiency of an industry;
(c) to create, expand or sustain productive capacity in an industry or in undertakings in an industry;
(d) to promote the reconstruction, re-organisation or conversion of an industry or of undertakings in an industry;
(e) to encourage the growth of, or the proper distribution of undertakings in, an industry;
(f) to encourage arrangements for ensuring that any contraction of an industry proceeds in an orderly way."

12.275 Section 7(2)(d) clearly justifies aid to rationalisation schemes. Section 7(2)(f) might also be of relevance. Section 8(1) provides that the Secretary of State may, for the purposes described in section 7(2) and with the consent of the Treasury, grant aid where the Secretary of State is satisfied that:

"(a) the financial assistance is likely to benefit the economy of the United Kingdom, or of any part or area of the United Kingdom; and
(b) it is in the national interest that the financial assistance should be provided on the scale, and in the form and manner, proposed; and
(c) the financial assistance cannot, or cannot appropriately, be so provided otherwise than by the Secretary of State."

[336] 11 February 1983.
[337] This assistance was provided under the Private Sector Steel Scheme which is an offshoot of s. 8 Industry Act 1972.
[338] 58(5) Industrial Development Act 1982.
[339] *ibid.*, s.1 8(8).

12.276 Where these rather vague criteria are met, the Secretary of State may provide financial assistance on any terms and conditions and by any description of investment, lending, guarantee or grant.[340] The government generally provide assistance by way of grant of money with a view to enabling self-help levy schemes get started. Thus assistance is calculated on the basis of the minimum necessary to secure industry wide agreement, that being the trigger for activation of the full scheme. Decisions on whether to grant assistance are usually Ministerial decisions with advice from the sponsoring department (i.e. the government department responsible for the industry in question) and from the Industrial Development Unit at the DTI.

12.277 *(c) Industrial Development Advisory Board*

Under section 10 Industrial Development Act 1982 the Board is instituted to advise the Secretary of State on the exercise of powers under section 7 and 8 of the Act. The Board comprises a chairman plus between six and twelve other members selected for their experience of industry, banking, accountancy and finance. Where the Board advises the Secretary of State but the latter rejects the advice, the Board may request the Secretary of State to lay a statement as to the matter before Parliament and the Secretary of State must comply. The organisers of schemes are usually required to be present at Board discussions. In this respect, the independent consultants appointed by the government to survey the market and who subsequently may become employed by the parties as scheme administrator are important as providers of information. Where possible the government prefer such consultants to be retained at this stage by departments rather than by the parties to the scheme. Thus, the transfer of the consultants from government to private employ may take place at a date subsequent to the Advisory Board deliberations.

12.278 Assistance is usually granted on strict terms and conditions designed to facilitate the objectives of the scheme. Thus, the assistance may be granted on clawback terms that it will be repayable should the scheme fail and the "closers" not depart the market. Terms providing for mandatory reporting obligations (e.g. annual reports, copies of accounts, etc.) on the parties or on the administrators may also be imposed. Similarly, terms prohibiting re-entry to the market may be imposed on "closers" receiving compensation as well as terms providing for the permanent closure or disposal of plant. Grant letters are invariably expressed to be subject to the approval of the European Commission to the aid (see below).

(6) Notification of aid schemes to the European Commission

12.279 *(a) Notification*

Under Article 93(3) EC, Member States must notify aid schemes to the Commission for appraisal prior to their taking effect. Failure to notify the scheme is an infringement of Article 93(3) last sentence EC which is directly effective.[341] This reads: "The Member State concerned shall not put its proposed measures into effect until this procedure has resulted in a final decision." Any individual firm, for example a foreign exporter to the UK, who suffers damage as a consequence of the aid may proceed against the government for breach of a directly effective provision of the Treaty.[342] Although the Com-

[340] *ibid.*, ss. 8(2) and 7(3).

[341] See Case 78/76 *Steinike and Weinlig* [1977] 2 CMLR 688; [1977] ECR 595; Cases 91/83 and 127/83 *Heineken Brouwerijen* v *Inspecteur de Vennootschapsbelasting* [1985] 1 CMLR 389 at para. II of the judgment. See Flynn, "State aid and self help" (1983) ELRev 297. On state aids generally, see D. Schina, *State Aids under the EEC Treaty Arts. 92–94* (1987); L. Hancher, T. Ottervanger and P.J. Slot, "EC state aids" (1993).

[342] See *R* v *Attorney General ex parte Imperial Chemicals' Industries plc* [1985] 1 CMLR 588 at para. 67. See also *Garden Cottage Ltd* v *Milk Marketing Board* [1984] 1 AC 13; [1983] 3 CMLR 43. See Commission answer

mission may approve such schemes as being compatible with Article 92 EC, national courts and national authorities have no competence to apply Article 92 EC which lays down exemption criteria for aid schemes.[343] Hence Commission approval is essential.

12.280 *(b) Repayment actions*

There is another reason why Commission approval is essential. Aid granted to individual firms unlawfully in breach of Article 93 EC may be subject to repayment decisions issued by the Commission to the defaulting Member State.[344] The Commission has already issued repayment decisions in respect of aids to firms in crisis industries. Thus, in one case, the Commission required the withdrawal and repayment of aid given by the Belgian government to a synthetic fibre producer.[345] The aid was by way of a capital injection in the form of a BF 550m majority shareholding in an insolvent synthetic fibre producer. The Belgian government appealed the decision to the European Court but subsequently withdrew its appeal, accepted the Commission decision and froze the account holding the tranche of aid. The recipient was forced to repay the aid and interest earned thereon by raising loans on the open market without any government assistance. Moreover, the government withheld subsequent, legal payments of aid in order to offset the benefits gained by the recipient in terms of interest earned on the sums illegally paid as aid.

12.281 *(c) Commission policy*

The Commission is generally sympathetic towards genuine grants of aid to facilitate rationalisation and restructuring. However, it seeks to ensure the aid does not go beyond what is strictly necessary for meeting the needs of the exercise. Furthermore, the aid must be transparent, i.e. open to scrutiny. The Commission adopts a very cautious view of aid to depressed industries since assistance to these sectors can have a distortive effect on competition out of proportion to the size of the aid, e.g. aid to keep open redundant

cont.
to WQ No. 308/84, OJ 1984 C 243/3 at p. 4 para. 2: "The Commission would also stress that, since the procedural rules of Article 93(3) are directly applicable, it is always open to undertakings concerned to bring actions in the national courts to secure the withdrawal of an illegally granted aid."

343 Case 78/76 *Steinike and Weinlig* [1977] 2 CMLR 688, note 170, *supra*.

344 See Case 70/72 *Commission* v *Germany (Kohlegeset)* [1973] ECR 813 at p. 829. See also the Commission notice on unlawful aid grants, OJ 1980 C 252/2 entitled "The notification of state aids to the Commission pursuant to Article 93(3) of the EC Treaty: the failure of the Member States to respect their obligations." See the Commission comment at *Tenth Report on Competition Policy* (1980), para. 162 "any aids implemented by Member States without due notification and adoption of a decision by the Commission are paid illegally and may therefore be subject to a decision that repayment be made on the aid in question." The Commission have reaffirmed this policy in a Communication OJ 1983 C 318/3 which gives a warning to aid recipients that they may have to refund the aid.

345 *Belgian Synthetic Fibre Aid Doc.* 84/111/EEC, OJ 1984 162/18 (3 March 1984) noted *Fourteenth Report on Competition Policy* (1984), pp. 151, 152 and see Commission answers to WQ No. 2442/ 84, OJ 1985 C291/1 and, WQ No. 2030/85, OJ 1986 C142/8,9. See also for another example of a repayment order: *Belgian Ceramic Sanitaryware Aid*, Dec. 83/130/EEC, OJ 1983 191/32 (aid granted by Belgian government to a firm manufacturing ceramic sanitary ware). The Commission, following the refusal of the Belgian government to comply with this decision referred the case to the European Court who confirmed the failure of the Belgian government: Case 52/84 *Commission* v *Belgium* [1986] ECR 89, [1987] 1 CMLR 710. In that case the Court held that a Member State could plead, as a defence, the impossibility of complying with the decision. However, they rejected the argument of the Member State that the impecuniousness of the recipient undertaking constituted impossibility. The Court pointed out that following the issuance of a decision which orders a Member State to effect repayment the Member State was in the position of a creditor of the recipient and as such could commence liquidation proceedings and thereby enforce repayment if necessary. See also Case C-142/87 *Re Tubemeuse: Belgium* v *Commission* [1990] ECR 959, [1991] 3 CMLR 213, noted by Ross (1989) 26 CMLRev 167.

plant which would close if ordinary market forces applied. Thus grantors and recipients of such aid must ensure that it is narrowly defined to stated objectives.[346]

(7) Other competition law problems

12.282 All self-help levy schemes have competition implications. Parties must ensure that agreements are notified to the European Commission either under Articles 65 and 66 of the Treaty of Paris (ECSC) for coal and steel products covered by that Treaty, or under Articles 85 or 86 of the Treaty of Rome (EEC) for all other products. Similarly, parties should be prepared to discuss their schemes in the context of the merger provisions of the FTA 1973. Certified schemes are, as noted above, exempt from the RTPA 1976. The government has the duty under the Treaty of Rome to notify aid schemes. Though, parties may consider ensuring that such notification is made, given that serious consequences may flow for parties as a result of non-disclosure by a government (see above). It is usual practice in cases of self-help levy schemes for the sponsoring department to make informal, direct contact with both the OFT and the DTI General Policy Division (which deals with competition matters).

(8) Major cases certified under section 568 ICTA 1988

12.283 A number of cases concerned with ferrous and other metal industries have been certified. These coupled to a generally sympathetic Commission attitude sparked considerable interest in rationalisation schemes elsewhere in the UK economy.[347] Two examples of major schemes are described below.

12.284 *(a) Wire drawing industry scheme*[348]

The purpose of this scheme was to reduce significantly the excess capacity existing within the non-alloy steel wire drawing industry and thereby to alleviate the heavy burden of prevailing overhead costs. The parties operated 23 wire drawing sites with a combined capacity of approximately 850,000 tonnes per annum. This constituted over 80 per cent of estimated UK capacity and compared with a market demand of only approximately 550,000 tonnes per annum. Under the scheme, seven sites were to cease operations altogether and fourteen others were to rationalise capacity. In total the scheme envisaged a reduction in capacity of some 212,000 tonnes per annum (i.e. 25 per cent of parties existing capacity). The total costs amounted to about £24 million of which government contributions were £6m (25 per cent). The government money derived from the Private Sector Steel Scheme and was intended to assist rationalisation and restructuring schemes. Money was offered towards closure and rationalisation costs (e.g. redundancy payments) and re-equipment and rebuilding projects for "closers" seeking new commercial outlets to invest in.

[346] See Commission answer to WQ No. 2060/82 OJ 1983 C 167/11 concerning aid to the zinc sector. For detailed analysis of Commission policy with regard to steel products see Dec. 257/80/ECSC, OJ 1980 L29/5 (6 February 1980) discussed *Tenth Report on Competition Policy* (1980), p. 134 *et seq.* and see also Dec. 2320/81/ECSC OJ 1981 1228/14 superseding the earlier decision as itself amended by Dec 101 8/85/ECSC OJ 1985 L110/5. See also *Twelfth Report on Competition Policy* (1982), pp, 114—123 for a very detailed account of Commission policy. For rules on "transparency" see Directive 80/723/EEC, OJ 1980 L193/35 (29 July 1980). See also the Commission's Communication to Member States concerning the application of Arts. 92 and 93 and the Transparency Directive to public undertakings in the manufacturing sector, OJ 1991 C273/2, annulled for failure to follow procedure for adoption under Art. 90(3) in Case C-325/91 *France* v *Commission*, [1993] ECR I-3283.

[347] See NEDO Report, *Competition Policy* (1978), p.13 which states that UK competition authorities should take a sympathetic line with, *inter alia*, "temporary cartelisation" in a "declining industry, to facilitate the controlled scrapping of outdated plant and equipment in order to concentrate production in the most efficient plants." See also at pp. 34–37.

[348] 2 December 1982.

12.285 The scheme was administered by Touche Ross and Co. who previously had been appointed by the DTI to review the wire drawing industry and to assist the companies in their restructuring plans. The scheme was certified under the predecessor section 568 ICTA and hence was exempt from the RTPA 1976. Moreover, approval of the European Commission was given without the latter issuing a formal decision under Article 85(3).

12.286 *(b) UK steel castings industry schemes 1982–1983*[349]

Between 1982 and 1983 three schemes in the Steel Castings industry were certified under the predecessor of section 568 ICTA 1988 and granted aid under section 8 Industrial Development Act 1982. The industry suffered from the recession of the 1970s. Participants took measures to shed labour and plant, although the measures were inadequate to secure an effective realignment of supply and demand. Furthermore, there was evidence that economically the wrong plants were closing, i.e. the plants closing were not the least profitable. At the request of major companies in the industry merchant bankers, Lazard Brothers and Co Ltd, were requested to review the market and devise a rationalisation scheme.[350] Negotiations commenced in May 1981 and were concluded in February 1983. The three agreements in question all derived from these negotiations and involved three sectors of the steel castings industry.

12.287 Lazard's reviewed the market and concluded that, despite a degree of product heterogeneity, three broad segments could be discerned premised upon products as produced by a foundry. The segments were: roll-makers accounting for about 6 per cent of industry tonnage; high alloy producers accounting for about 12 per cent of industry tonnage; and all other products—the general sector—accounting for over 80 per cent of industry tonnage. Subsequently, the scheme proposals for roll-makers were abandoned in the light of recent Commission proceedings against participants for price fixing which, it was felt, might prejudice the producer's chances of a sympathetic Commission hearing.

12.288 Under the Lazard's scheme, companies would voluntarily decide to close down (closers) whilst others would remain taking on the closer's customers (openers). The openers would pay a levy out of future income from 1983–88 to fund the immediate closure of closers. For each firm a defined reference value was arrived at. This effectively amounted to the average annual sales turnover in steel castings during the period 1980–82. Openers paid an annual levy based upon 2.5 per cent of the reference value; closers received compensation of 32 per cent of their reference value upon elimination of certain predetermined plants. Additionally, a sum of 4 per cent of reference value was determined to be paid in 1988–89. In total, parties to the schemes paid £13 million over five years. The government paid £8 million under section 8 Industrial Development Act 1982. Approximately 16 per cent of the industry's capacity closed; this amounted to approximately 24,000 tonnes of capacity with a market value of approximately £32 million. It has been estimated that only about 50 per cent of total capacity was involved in the schemes. This is generally considered due to the policy of certain firms to encourage the scheme from the outside and thereby to benefit from it without having to contribute financially to it. The schemes resulted in about 2,400 redundancies. The schemes were notified to the Commission who raised no objections under Article 85(1) (the products were not ECSC products).

[349] *High Alloy Sector (Static Group)* (22 March 1982); *General Sector* (11 February 1983); *FVF—SAC* (31 March 1983). See for a general economic analysis, Baden Fuller, "The wisdom of collective action: an assessment of the Lazard Scheme for restructuring the UK Steel Casting Industry" in *The Economics of Closure and Industry Dynamics* (EARIE, 1984) edited by H. Thomas.

[350] Apparently at the suggestion of the then British Steel Corporation Chairman, Ian MacGregor. SCRATA (Steel Castings Research and Trade Association) was considered practically inappropriate and the government was considered inappropriate for obvious political reasons.

12.289 *(c) High alloy scheme*[351]

The high alloy agreement which was certified as part of the steel castings schemes (above) is worthy of individual attention. The high alloy sector scheme became necessary, as did the other steel schemes, due to the severe economic recession of the 1970s. During the period it was estimated that capacity utilisation stood at about 50–70 per cent. Very serious over-capacity developed and prospects for an upturn in demand were minimal. However, it was considered that demand levels pertaining during 1982 did represent a new, lower base level upon which producers could consolidate. Interestingly, the high alloy sector is not unduly prone to import penetration, nor is it an easily exportable product: at that time approximately 17 per cent of UK production was exported; imports were thought to account for approximately 8–10 per cent of domestic demand. The participants to the scheme manufactured high alloy steel castings (generally containing 11.0 per cent or more chromium with or without other elements). The molten alloy is transformed into castings by pouring it into a static pattern or mould. Alloy castings thus manufactured have a wide range of applications principally as wear and corrosion resistant castings for the chemical and petrochemical industries and as stainless steel castings for the automotive, power generation, pump, valve, oil refining, food plant, and, chemical plant industries. Approximately 5,000 tonnes per annum of the product were placed on the market during the relevant period prior to the scheme with an annual value exceeding £20 million. Companies amounting to approximately 95 per cent of UK open market production participated in the agreement. Of these participants, companies accounting for about 22 per cent of tonnage elected to cease production.

12.290 The scheme proceeded along voluntary lines with participation being determined upon purely commercial criteria. The aim of the agreement was to reduce capacity and concentrate the reduced level of demand in a reduced number of plants. The reconstruction agreement signed by the parties contained extensive provisions designed to ensure minimal disturbance to supply. Thus, for example, the agreement included a three-month closure period coupled to contractual obligations on closing foundries to give detailed information on products and customers to the remaining undertakings. During the three-month period closers were entitled to accept orders provided this did not result in melting taking place on a date after expiry of the three months; this clause facilitated a smoother transition for customers from closing supplier to remaining supplier. Indeed closers and those remaining were contractually bound to co-operate closely to ensure that the transition was smooth and that continuing demand was met satisfactorily.

12.291 The contract obviously included detailed provisions on the payment of compensation for closers. Firms remaining open were bound to pay an annual levy to closers for a five-year period with the larger payments deferred to the later years (thereby enabling the "stayers" to: (a) organise their finances in advance to take account of the foreseeable debt; and (b), reap some rewards from the increase in demand and capacity utilisation the scheme afforded them before having to make payments). The levies were supplemented by the sums paid by the government as aid under section 8 of the Industrial Development Act 1982. Compensation to closers was to be paid in four instalments. Closers received an immediate lump-sum payment to help off-set closure costs; this was followed by single smaller payments paid after 45 months, 51 months and 57 months. To enable the stayers to pay the immediate sums which became due a city finance house agreed to discount promissory notes issued by the stayers.

[351] 22 March 1982.

12.292 As regards other economic consequences the closure of the agreed five foundries entailed 400 of the 1500 workers employed in the sector being made redundant, i.e. over 25 per cent of the sector. The EC Commission was notified of the agreement but raised no objection under Article 85 EC.

4. UK Law: section 29 RTPA 1976

(1) Legal context

12.293 Details of procedure under section 29 are given at paras. 2.3–2.28. The provision exempts agreements from registration where they satisfy the criteria laid down in section 29(2)(a)–(e). A brief survey of these conditions suggests that rationalisation agreements might be suitable candidates for exemption.[352] The first condition requires that the agreement be calculated to promote a scheme of substantial importance to the national economy: rationalisation is certainly important where it leads to eradication of excess capacity and a healthier industrial structure. The second condition requires that the object or main object of the agreement is the promotion of efficiency or the creation or improvement of productive capacity. Clearly, rationalisation reduces capacity so, prima facie, that aspect of this condition is not satisfied. However, rationalisation does aim to enhance long-term efficiency so that the first part of the condition is satisfied. Further, it is arguable that rationalisation while not increasing capacity does "improve" it in the sense that after the agreement has been implemented and it has run its course the capacity demand ratio will have been improved by closer alignment. The third condition requires that the object of the agreement cannot be achieved within a reasonable time except by means of an agreement. This condition is satisfied in that it is a central justification for the agreement that unadulterated market forces would be inadequate to cure the problems of over-capacity.[353] The fourth condition is that the restrictions are reasonably necessary to achieve the desired objective. This causes no problems since it involves questions of drafting rather than of economic substance. The final condition is that the agreement is, on balance, expedient in the national interest. Again, this condition raises no substantive point.[354]

(2) When section 29 useful

12.294 Section 568 ICTA 1988, in view of the related tax advantages, is more important than section 29. However, the former provision only covers schemes involving parties who are "substantially representative of the industry".[355] Where the scheme does not meet these criteria, section 29 might be relevant. Thus an asset-swapping scheme between two companies only such as occurred in *BPCL–ICI* (discussed in relation to EC law) might not meet the substantiality requirements, yet it is deserving of antitrust clearance.

(3) Relationship with EC law

12.295 Exemption under section 29 only clears a scheme under the RTPA 1976. It does not excuse parties from the need to notify to the Commission. Nor, indeed, does it excuse schemes from the merger provisions of the FTA 1973 where relevant.

[352] This was also the view of the NEDO Report *on Competition Policy* (1978), pp. 34, 35.

[353] This has been accepted by the Commission: See *Synthetic Fibres Agreement* [1985] 1 CMLR 787 at paras. 31, 32.

[354] See for a similar Commission balancing act *BPCL–ICI* OJ 1984 L212/1 at p. 8, para. 24.

[355] s. 568(2)(c) ICTA 1988.

5. *UK Law: Rationalisation Mergers*

(1) Legal context

12.296 Firms may undertake rationalisation by way of merger. A scheme certified under section 568 ICTA 1988 (see above) is *not* exempt from the merger provisions of the Fair Trading Act 1973 (FTA 1973 hereafter). Section 64(1) FTA 1973 provides that the Act applies to mergers which either create or strengthen a statutory monopoly (25 per cent or more of specified goods or services supplied by or to the same person in the UK) *or* result in the transfer of assets exceeding £70 million in value.[356] A merger occurs where two enterprises have ceased to be distinct. "Enterprise" means "the activities, or part of the activities, of a business". Accordingly, a full merger between two companies need not occur. A subsidiary of a company or a division may be merged with another firm.

Firms whose rationalisation mergers satisfy these criteria should clear their merger with the OFT. In the past this has not been a problem. Thus in *FVF–SAC*[357] as part of the Steel Castings Scheme, Firth Vickers Foundry Ltd (FVF) (a subsidiary of Johnson and Firth Brown PLC) continued to trade whilst Sheepbridge Alloy Castings Ltd (a subsidiary of Guest Keen and Nettlefolds PLC (GKN)) closed. The closure costs were met in part by GKN and FVF with a contribution from the government under the Industrial Development Act 1982. GKN obtained a 25 per cent interest in the business of FVF. The OFT raised no objections.

(2) Relationship with section 568 ICTA 1988

12.298 There is no reason why rationalisation mergers should not be certified under section 568 thereby obtaining tax reliefs. The merger, however, must constitute a scheme, or at least be part of a scheme, as was the *FVF–SAC* case above which was brought about by the parties in the context of the Lazards Steel Casting Scheme.

(3) government financial assistance

12.299 Finance may be available under the Industrial Development Act 1982. Assistance was provided in the *FVF–SAC* case. Much will depend upon the financial strengths of the parties concerned and, of course, the extent of the government's funding capacity.

(4) Relationship with EC rules

12.300 Rationalisation mergers may be assessed under the Merger Control Regulation or (possibly) under Articles 85 and 86 EC. Where they involve steel and other products governed by the Treaty of Paris (as most of the agreements have), Article 66 ECSC is relevant. Article 66 essentially provides that any transaction leading to an increase in concentration must be authorised by the Commission. A "transaction" includes: "mergers, acquisition of shares or parts of the undertaking or assets, loan, contract or any other means of control". Approval may be given under Article 66(2) ECSC where the increase in concentration does not give the parties power:

> "– to determine prices, to control or restrict production or distribution or to hinder effective competition in a substantial part of the market for those products; or

[356] See S.I. 1984 No. 392 raising the asset value test to £30 million. The asset threshold was subsequently lifted to £70 million on 9 February 1994, in the Merger References (Increase in Value of Assets) Order 1994, S.I. 1994 No. 72.

[357] 31 March 1983.

–to evade the rules of competition instituted under this Treaty, in particular by establishing an artificially privileged position involving a substantial advantage in access to supplies or markets."

In assessing these criteria, the Commission consider the size of the parties and their competitors to the extent that this is justified in order to avoid or correct advantages resulting from unequal competitive conditions. The Commission may impose conditions on authorisations.

12.301 In *British Steel Corporation–TI Group*[358] the Commission approved a merger between BSC and TI whereby the parties regrouped and merged part of their seamless tubes businesses into a joint company called Seamless Tubes Ltd. The merger was intended to rationalise facilities for the manufacture of smaller diameter hotfinished seamless tubes; this would enable the parties to operate more efficiently in the face of competition on a contracting market. The Commission assessed the merger under Article 66(2) ECSC in respect of tube rounds (a Treaty of Paris product), and Article 85 EC in respect of seamless tubes (a Treaty of Rome product). In particular, the Commission was concerned to ensure that the merger gave neither party an artificially privileged position on the international market. The Commission concluded that the merger would not have this effect. The Commission also considered the merger under Article 86 EC but concluded that it did not enhance a pre-existing dominant position. Similarly, in *British Bright Bar Limited*[359] the Commission authorised BSC, GKN and Brymill to incorporate a joint subsidiary, British Bright Bar Ltd, to take over the parties' assets in this sector, to rationalise them and form them into a viable business. The parents would then withdraw from the sector for Bright Bars. The Commission considered under Article 66(2) ECSC, that the merger would not secure the parent companies an artificially privileged position as suppliers of hot-rolled steel bars or producers of bright steel bars (which was an EC product). With regard to Article 86 EC it was held that the merger would not strengthen a pre-existing dominant position. In *Hadfields*[360] the Commission authorised a rationalisation merger between BSC and GKN to take over Hadfields Ltd although the merger made the parents the fourth largest Community producer. However, competition was strong from other EC producers and from imports. It is possible for steel merger to come within the exclusive jurisdiction of the EC Commission under the ECSC, while those products not covered by the ECSC remain the subject of a merger reference to the MMC under the Fair Trading Act 1973. In *British Steel plc/C Walker and Sons (Holdings) Ltd*,[361] the MMC undertook such a limited review and concluded that the proposed merger might be expected not to operate against the public interest. The European Commission also authorised that part of the merger which came within its jurisdiction.[362]

358 *Thirteenth Report on Competition Policy* (1983), p. 99, Bull EC 12/83, para. 2.1.68. See also *Fagersta–Sandvik Tube AB, Thirteenth Commission Report on Competition Policy* (1983), pp. 99, 100. See also Commission answer to WQ No. 86/82, OJ 1982 C 167/118 on the *Cockerill-Sambre merger* (Bull EC 3/82, para. 2.1.27).

359 *Thirteenth Report on Competition Policy* (1983), p. 97, Bull FC 3/83 at p. 45, para. 2.1.84.

360 *Thirteenth Report on Competition Policy* (1983), pp. 97, 98, Bull EC 11/83 at para. 2.1.49. See for another example *Fagersta–Sandvik Tube AB, Thirteenth Report on Competition Policy* (1983), p. 99. The case is notable for the fact that it concerned two then non-EC (Swedish) firms who were deemed to be undertakings under Art. 80 ECSC because they distributed steel products within the EC via Community based subsidiaries.

361 Cm 1028 (1990).

362 *Twentieth Report on Competition Policy* (1990), para. 132.

6. *Section 21(2) RTPA 1976*

12.302 Rationalisation agreements are generally unsuitable for section 21 (2) treatment since restrictions contained therein are unlikely to be insignificant. This will certainly be the case if price fixing or market sharing clauses are included. Though where restrictions are the minimum necessary to facilitate rationalisation and competition outside of the agreement remains strong then section 21(2) dispensation may be available. Parties contemplating such agreements should consider the section 568 ICTA and/or section 29 RTPA 1976 routes before deciding to register their agreements under the normal rules of the RTPA 1976. Parties may wish to consult the OFT and/or DTI and/or Inland Revenue prior to entering any binding agreement.

H. Product Standardisation

12.303 Agreements between competitors to standardise product specifications restrain competition in that they eliminate consumer choice. If X, Y and Z agree to use the same raw materials in the same proportions in the manufacture of their product, then customers may be denied choice between different products produced by X, Y and Z. Further, X, Y and Z will be likely to align prices since their inputs costs will be similar thereby dampening price competition. Conversely, standardisation may be very desirable where customers have to adapt their processes to match the supplier's product. Thus, it is essential, for example, that a standard screw thread be developed if screws and nuts are to be matched. Poorly matched nuts and screws hampered industry and the armed forces during the First World War. To overcome such difficulties industry-wide standardisation programmes are common. Standards may be used in respect of contract terms, abbreviations and symbols, dimensions or quality specifications for materials or equipment, etc. Standards generally fall into two categories, performance standards and design standards. Performance standards prescribe a level of operation to be achieved with the design and materials to be used left to the discretion of the producer. Design standards prescribe the manner in which the product is to be manufactured in terms of raw materials and dimensions. Performance standards are used commonly where a specified level of performance is required, for instance, for health and safety purposes or to secure efficient performance standards. Design standards are used commonly where standardisation is desired, for example, to facilitate interchangeability between different manufacturers products. Where standardisation serves pro-competitive or consumer safety goals it is not problematic.[363] However, where standardisation is a smoke screen designed to hide covert, restrictive activities clearly the opposite applies.[364]

[363] See e.g. US cases: *Maple Flooring Manufacturers Association* v *US 268 US 563* (1925) at p. 566; *Tag Manufacturers Institute* v *FTC* 174 F. 2 452 (1st Cir.1949) at p. 462.

[364] e.g. *National Macaroni Manufacturers' Association* (1964) FTC Dkt 8524, 65 FTC 583 at p. 612. During a period of shortage of durum wheat, an ingredient in the production of macaroni, members of the association agreed that millers would offer a blend of 50 per cent scarce wheat and 50 per cent other wheats. The association also recommended that members avoid producing low quality macaroni. This was held by the Federal Trade Commission to amount to an attempt to lower total industry demand for durum wheat and thereby prevent price competition for the available supplies.

12.304 There are a number of standards organisations at international,[365] European[366] and national[367] levels. As a general principle, compliance with standards set by such bodies is voluntary, but increasingly such standards are being used as legal requirements by national legislation. Where these are not legally required, it may still be the case that compliance is necessary as part of industry practice, or because it is required by a monopolist or monopsonist.

1. EC Law[368]

12.305 Standards can also be used as barriers to free trade in goods and services. Hence an important part of the European Community's programme to complete the internal market has been harmonisation of standards.[369] The Commission is endeavouring to ensure that European standards progressively replace national standards through CEN, CENELEC and ETSI.[370] So far, the only measures it has adopted which relate to the application of competition rules in standard setting have been addressed to public undertakings in the telecommunications sector under Article 90(3) of the Treaty.[371] The Commission has the power to issue a block exemption in respect of agreements relating to "the application of standards or types".[372] It has not to date exercised this power. There is no reason to suppose that genuine product standardisation schemes would encounter competition problems.[373] Thus schemes enabling quality control and approval certification to be applied to products are regarded as eligible for negative clearance, provided that application for approval is open to all on non-discriminatory criteria.[374] However, schemes which lead to price alignment or loss of consumer choice may be in violation of Article 85. Examples of common issues are given below:

(1) Standardisation to achieve product interchangeability

12.306 This has been at issue in the computer markets where common standards are desired to make different brands of computer product compatible with each other. Adoption of common standards was viewed as a means of countering IBM dominance in the field. Indeed, the Commission has viewed the failure by IBM to disclose sufficient information to enable rivals to standardise interface specifications between their computer products and IBM computer products as an abuse of a dominant position by IBM. Implicit in this Commission view is a belief that product interchangeability may be desirable and pro-competitive.[375]

365 International Standards Organisation (ISO); International Electrotechnical Commission (IEC).

366 European Committee for Standardisation (CEN); European Committee for Electrotechnical Standardisation (CENELEC); European Telecommunications Standards Institute (ETSI).

367 British Standards Institute (BSI) in UK; there are equivalent organisations in other EC countries, such as the *Association Française de Normalisation* (AFNOR).

368 See A.N. Vollmer, "Product and technical standardisation under Article 85" [1986] ECLR 388.

369 See para 13.466 for ETSI's interim intellectual property rights policy, which seeks to ensure that standards are adopted in a way that reconciles IPR ownership with preserving access to the market.

370 Commission White Paper on *Completing the Internal Market*, COM(85)310 final, Part 2, s. I.

371 Telecommunications Terminal Equipment directive 88/301/EEC [1991] 4 CMLR 922; Telecommunications Services Directive 90/388/EEC [1991] 4 CMLR 932; see also Commission Notice of 6 September 1991 clarifying the application of Community competition rules to the market participants in the telecommunications sector [1991] 4 CMLR 946.

372 Art. 1(a) of Reg. 2821/71/EEC, OJ 1971 L285/56 (29 December 1971).

373 See *First Report on Competition Policy* (1970), para. 39.

374 *German Pasta Manufacturers' Agreement*, OJ 1986 C266/5 (notice of intention to grant negative clearance); *APB* OJ 1990 L18/35 (negative clearance granted).

375 *IBM Settlement* case [1984] 3 CMLR 147 (though no formal decision to this effect was adopted).

12.307 Thus the Commission granted an exemption to an agreement between major manufacturers of computers to use and develop an open industry standard for operating systems software in *X/Open Group*,[376] even though there were provisions restricting access to these standards. The agreement to develop a common standard for use in operating systems software was only open to those manufacturers either with sufficient turnover to be able to contribute to the programme or to those who could provide some other significant contribution to the programme. This restricted competition as non-members would not have the immediate access to the new standards, thus giving members a springboard advantage in developing new systems. It also restricted competition in that membership for those without sufficient turnover depended on a vote by the existing members and so there could be discrimination as to who should be a member. However, the Commission regarded these restrictions as exemptible as they were necessary to ensure only those who could make a substantial contribution to the success of the project could become members and the group needed to be restricted to such firms in order for the project to be viable. This exemption depended on the results of the co-operation being made available for use in the industry as soon as possible[377] and on annual reports on refusals of applications for membership being made to the Commission.

(2) Standardisation to promote consumer welfare

12.308 An agreement between manufacturers to refrain from using a particular raw material or design feature may be permissible where the standardisation is to eradicate a dangerous raw material or defective design feature. The agreement, if it infringes Article 85(1) at all, should satisfy Article 85(3) since it improves technical progress (i.e. renders safer) and benefits the consumer (decreased risk of physical injury or breakdown of product).

12.309 An agreement to standardise labels and descriptions of contents may allow consumers to make choices between different products in a more educated manner (see paras. 11.195–11.198). An agreement to standardise traffic lights for example or colour codes on electrical goods may be permissible where it reduces consumer/user confusion and minimises the risk of injury. Standardisation to defeat fraud may also be acceptable.[378]

12.310 Agreements to improve consumer convenience may be permissible under Article 85(3) EEC. In *Uniform Eurocheques*[379] the Commission exempted a scheme for standardising the

[376] [1988] 4 CMLR 542. Also see *Philips/Matsushita–D2B* [1991] OJ C220/2.

[377] [1988] 4 CMLR 542, 555, Art. 2 of the Decision.

[378] See Commission answer in respect of a question concerning an agreement between IBM and STET (a company in which the Italian state is principal shareholder): WQ No.1414/84, OJ 1985 C93/97. See *Association of Data Processing Service Organisation (ADAPSO)* US Department of Justice Antitrust Division Business Review Letter (7 January 1986). ADAPSO represented most of the leading developers of microcomputer software for commercial use. It sought to develop voluntary industry standards for a hardware based software protection system. According to ADAPSO, the unauthorised use of software cost the industry US$1.3 billion in lost revenues between 1981 and 1984 and an estimated US$800 million in 1985. The standards ADAPSO sought to develop were based on a protection of software system employing three hardware devices: (i) a "lock" embedded in the software; (ii) a lightweight "key ring" that will plug into the computer; (iii) a "key" which will plug into the key ring. The standardisation programme would be kept to the minimum necessary to achieve the objective. Thus the scheme did not cover the entire software protection system, only these central elements. Nor did the scheme seek to exclude other means of software protection mechanism. The Department of Justice gave clearance on the basis that the scheme was not anti-competitive. They stated: "It would appear to be in the interest of the vast majority of ADAPSO members to ensure that the standards ultimately developed will promote rather than impair competition in the development and production of software protection systems." Further they stated: "to the extent that the standards lead to improved protection of software their effect should be pro-competitive; more and better software should be available to consumers."

[379] OJ 1985 L35/43. See also the subsequent decision exempting the agreement relating to production and finishing of Eurocheque cards: *Uniform Eurocheques* OJ 1989 L36/16.

international use and clearing of Eurocheques. Agreements which came into force in 1981 governed the system. They provided, *inter alia*, that no commission could be charged at the time of encashment of a Eurocheque by the foreign cashier or retailer. Foreign banks received a standard rate of commission payable when the cheque was reimbursed to it by the clearing centre responsible for the accepting banks area. Moreover, issuing institutions gradually adopted a standard format for the guarantee card and the cheque. The fixing of standard commission rates clearly breached Article 85(1). However, the Commission decided that the benefits for consumers outweighed any detriments. Bearers of Eurocheques may draw them in local currency in any Member State and in some non-Member States. Moreover, they can often be used directly in payment to traders who benefit from the guarantee up to a certain amount. The system rationalises and improves the efficiency of the central clearing system and it accelerates the reimbursement of cheques to accepting banks. The setting of a standard rate of commission was accepted as a necessary consequence of the scheme.

(3) Standardisation to safeguard the environment

12.311 Standardisation agreements may be entered into to promote reuse and recycling of materials. The Commission has emphasised that while it can exempt an agreement which has a favourable impact on the environment, it can only do so if it meets the conditions for an exemption laid down in Article 85(3).[380] In *Spa Monopole/GDB*,[381] the Commission initiated infringement proceedings under Articles 85 and 86 EC against a German mineral water standardisation agreement, which specified certain types of standard refillable bottles for use on the German market to comply with German environmental legislation. In the view of the Commission, refusal to allow non-German companies access to the same pool of standard bottles operated as a barrier to entry to the German market, since supermarkets and other retailers were not in practice likely to operate two different schemes for refillable bottles. Proceedings were terminated when access to non-German water producers was allowed, on condition that the bottles used must be exported only to Germany (to prevent the pool of bottles being depleted) and that the label attached to the bottles must make clear the original of the mineral water and where it was bottled.[382]

(4) Dubious standardisation

12.312 Standardisation which serves a covert, restrictive purpose will infringe Article 85(1).[383] If manufacturers agree to standardise their products so as to avoid using low quality raw materials, or less than the state of the art components, then the consumer loses choice and is almost certainly required to pay more because of the elimination of lower quality products from the market. Standardisation thus allows producers to force consumers/users to acquire a quality of product or service that may be excessive when compared with their needs. Standardisation must not be used to encourage aligned prices (producers all use similar raw materials) or eliminate grades of product or service from the market.[384]

380 *Twenty-third Report on Competition Policy* (1993), para. 91. See for example *BP/Montedipe, Twenty-third Report on Competition Policy* (1993), Annex III, para. 5.

381 *Twenty-third Report on Competition Policy* (1993), paras. 169 and 240.

382 Similar problems have arisen with other environmental recycling and reusing schemes, since the first scheme may quickly become the accepted scheme for that state and therefore, de facto, other potential competitors have to have access to that scheme in order to compete. See the *DSD* scheme, *Twenty-third Report on Competition Policy* (1993), para. 168, and the *IFCO* scheme, *Twenty-third Report on Competition Policy* (1993), para. 169. The Commission observed, para. 170, that the issues raised are similar to those involved in access to other essential facilities: see para 11.127.

383 See Commission's Notice on Cooperation Agreement, OJ 1968 C75/3, at para. II(2).

384 See e.g. *Crousse–Hinds Co.* FTC Dkt 4610, 46 FTCs 1114 (1950).

2. UK Law

12.313 Agreements to comply with standardisation schemes may be exempt from registration under sections 9(5) and 18(5) RTPA 1976. In respect of other agreements the OFT may provide section 21(2) dispensation where the scheme does not, as with EC law, allow the participants to fix or align prices or unduly reduce consumer choice.

(1) Sections 9(5) and 18(5) RTPA 1976

12.314 Section 9(5) (goods provision) reads:

"no account shall be taken of any term by which the parties or any of them agree to comply with or apply, in respect of the production, supply or acquisition of any goods or the application to goods of any process of manufacture.
(a) standards of dimension, design, quality or performance; or
(b) arrangements as to the provision of information or advice to purchasers, consumers or users being either standards or arrangements for the time being approved by the British Standards Institute or standards or arrangements prescribed or adopted by any trade association or other body and for the time being approved by order of the Secretary of State made by statutory instrument."

12.315 Section 18(5) is, *mutatis mutandis*, the same as section 9(2).[385] A number of agreements have been exempted under these provisions by the Secretary of State, e.g. concerning safety precautions for veterinary products,[386] pesticides,[387] tobacco products, small arms (guns),[388] and a number of standards and information agreements relating to the electricity industry, as a consequence of the breakup of the nationalised industry into a number of separate generation, transmission and distribution companies.[389]

12.316 An example is the tobacco order.[390] Under this order the Secretary of State approved standards and arrangements relating to the provision of information to consumers, purchaser and users of tobacco products. The standards were incorporated in two documents entitled, "Tobacco Product Modification and Research" and "Tobacco Product Advertising and Promotion and Health Warnings". These were drawn up at the request of the government between the tobacco industry and the Department of Health and Social Security. The documents provide for standardisation of the information and advice given to consumers and agreements relating thereto. Thus cigarette producers may agree to standardise the government health warnings that appear on cigarette packets.

(2) Under section 21(2) RTPA 1976

12.317 The OFT have accorded section 21(2) treatment to a number of non-authorised agreements. Thus, an agreement to improve environmental safety by the elimination of a chemical which causes foaming in sewage works and water-courses from production of synthetic detergents has been accepted.[391] Similarly, an agreement to standardise product

[385] See paras. 1.96–1.98 and 1.104.
[386] S.I. 1969 No, 226 Sch. 1.
[387] *ibid.*, Sch. 2.
[388] S.I. 1984 No. 2031 concerning "standards of dimension, design quality or performance and arrangements as to the provision of information or advice to purchasers, consumers or users, contained in Decision XV-7 (as amended by Decision XVI-4) taken pursuant to the Convention for the Reciprocal Recognition of Proof Marks for small arms done at Brussels on 1 July 1969 by the Permanent Inter. national Commission for the Reciprocal Recognition of proof marks for small arms."
[389] Restrictive Trade Practices (Standards and Arrangements) Order 1990, S.I. 1990 No. 888; Restrictive Trade Practices (Standards and Arrangements) (Services) Order 1991, S.I. 1991 No. 1897.
[390] S.I. 1983 No. 382.
[391] No. 3769 Register of Restrictive Trade Practices, *Hard Non-ionic Detergents* (1974).

quality thereby facilitating consumer choice has been accepted.[392] Also accepted under section 21(2), is an agreement for the standardisation of cheque cards and guarantee amounts by banks which improved consumer convenience. Under this agreement, the banks agreed to standardise the form and use of the card.[393] A similar scheme was exempted under Article 85(3) EC in respect of Eurocheques.[394]

12.318 Agreements to standardise products because of technical specifications needed by a dominant purchaser are suitable for section 21(2) treatment. In *Plessey-GEC (5005 Crossbar)*[395] Plessey and GEC standardised the products they were contracted to supply to the Post Office. Given the desirability of the purchaser being able to acquire uniform and interchangeable products section 21(2) was clearly appropriate. Where the consumer is a monopolist the OFT is more likely to assume that it is able to negotiate fair standards without their intervention. Agreements to protect quality may be acceptable where the agreement does no more than discourage use of defective raw materials or inputs. Thus, an agreement between the British Wool Marketing Board and producers of sheep dips and powders providing for a voluntary ban on the manufacture and supply of dips and powders which had the effect of discolouring wool, was given section 21(2) dispensation.[396]

I. Joint Carriage Ventures[397]

12.319 The joint provision of carriage services is generally considered not to be anti-competitive since it enables parties to realise economies which may be passed on. Where the agreement has an ulterior motive, then restrictions on competition might arise.

1. EC Law

12.320 The Commission Notice on co-operation states that agreements which have as their *sole* object the joint use of production facilities and storing and transport equipment, do not restrict competition because they are confined to organisation and technical arrangements for the use of the facilities.[398] There may be restrictions on competition where the parties do not

[392] No. 4883, Register of Restrictive Trade Practices, *The Tea Council: Catering Tea Grading Scheme* (1982).

[393] No. S.271 Register of Restrictive Trade Practices, *Cheque Guarantee Cards Scheme* (1983). Another "convenience" case is No. 3868 Register of Restrictive Trade Practices, "And the *Best of British Campaign*" (1978)–Firms standardised the guarantees they gave on Hi-Fi equipment and made the guarantees transferable between themselves so that they would each honour guarantees provided by the other parties. See also No. S.412 Register of Restrictive Trade Practices, *AA* and *RAC–Agreement whereby the AA and RAC standardised telephone boxes on new main roads*. They also agreed as to siting and provision of new boxes. Under the agreement members of either organisation could use the facilities provided by the other; and No. 5543 Register of Restrictive Trade Practices, *National Edible Oil Distributors Association* (1985) Association recommended to members that they join a scheme whereby a "NEODA" logo could be attached to certain packages of edible oil complying with specifications. The logo was designed to represent a "guarantee of confidence". The agreement hence concerned product standardisation and joint use of a mark.

[394] *Uniform Eurocheque* OJ 1985 L35/43.

[395] No. 3784 Register of Restrictive Trade Practices (1984).

[396] No. 4508 Register of Restrictive Trade Practices, *British Wool Marketing Board* (1979).

[397] This book does not deal with agreements in any of the Transport sectors, for which see R. Greaves, *Transport Law of the European Community* (1991). See also Commission Decision of 24 February 1993 relating to tariff structures in the combined transport of goods OJ 1993 L73/39.

[398] In *Ansac* OJ 1991 L152/54, the Commission, in finding a US Webb–Pomerene natural soda ash export cartel infringing Art. 85(1), stressed, at para. 30, that it would have been willing to give favourable consideration to arrangements limited to joint transport and storage facilities.

bear the cost of utilisation of the installation or equipment themselves, or if agreements are concluded concerning the establishment or running of a joint enterprise.[399] Thus, if X, Y and Z all agree only to use the shipping facilities provided by a joint venture company, XYZ Ltd, and provide that in times of demand for carriage services exceeding supply capacity they will share out carriage capacity between them and not hire alternative forms of transportation, then this may restrain competition since it may hinder the parties' selling ability. Similarly, if X, Y and Z share warehousing facilities but agree that X will pay for 80 per cent of the running costs of the facility, this may restrain competition where X, Y and Z all use the facility equally.

2. *UK Law*

12.321 The OFT has taken an equally permissive attitude towards carriage-sharing ventures.[400]For example, they have given section 21(2) dispensation to an agreement between major oil companies for the joint transportation of petroleum through a jointly-owned pipe line.[401] Similarly, it has given dispensation to joint use of warehousing facilities.[402] As with EC law, the OFT is concerned to ensure that a participants' contribution to the running costs of a facility are commensurate with utilisation. Thus, a fixed agreement to share costs equally may be inappropriate where there is not roughly equal use of the facility. If X, Y and Z share a transport system but utilise the system to varying degrees, an agreement whereby costs are shared equally, in effect, entails subsidisation of intensive users by less intensive users. Where X, Y and Z are competitors such a scheme would come close to being akin to an equalisation of receipts scheme whereby producers selling locally (and using the transport system least) compensate those who sell at a distance (on export markets) and use the system most.

[399] OJ 1968 C75/3; [1968] CMLR D1.

[400] e.g. No. 3363 Register of Restrictive Trade Practices, *Bournemouth Wholesalers Newspaper Deliveries* (1978)—two wholesalers share cost of joint delivery and transport system.

[401] No. S.466 Register of Restrictive Trade Practices Agreement between *Cleveland Co Ltd, Texaco Ltd, Gulf (Oil) GB Ltd, Amoco* and *MMM Pipelines Ltd* (1984).

[402] No. S.172 Register of Restrictive Trade Practices, *Import Clearance Services at Heathrow* (1978).

13 Intellectual Property Licensing

A. Introduction

13.1 Intellectual property ("IP") licences are a particularly common form of commercial agreement. They form both transactions in their own right and ancillary agreements to other transactions such as joint ventures and distribution agreements. Thus licensing agreements may have to be assessed for compatibility with competition law both independently and as part of a wider arrangement. The more general aspects are covered elsewhere in this book and this chapter will concentrate specifically upon the compatibility of licensing arrangements with competition law. EC law also regulates the way in which IP rights may be exercised under the provisions in the Treaty relating to free movement of goods and services, Articles 30–36 and 59–66, and this is summarised below.

The following are discussed in this chapter:

Section B.	The relationship between free movement of goods and services and intellectual property rights under EC law.
Section C.	Patent and know-how licensing in EC law: general considerations.
Section D.	The technology transfer block exemption: Reg. 240/96.
Section E.	The patent licensing block exemption: Regul. 2349/84.
Section F.	The know-how licensing block exemption: Reg. 556/89.
Section G.	Patent and know-how licensing in UK law.
Section H.	Copyright licensing in EC law
Section I.	Copyright licensing in UK law.
Section J.	Software licensing in EC law.
Section K.	Software licensing in UK law.
Section L.	Trade mark licensing in EC law.
Section M.	Trade mark licensing in UK law.

Section N. Licensing intellectual property to sub-contractors.
Section O. The duty to license intellectual property rights

13.2 Under EC law, there are broadly three potential regimes which might apply to an IP licence: the technology transfer block exemption,[1] other block exemptions relating to distribution and franchising,[2] and the general provisions of Articles 85 and 86 as they apply to agreements not coming within any of the block exemptions. There are similarly separate categorisations under UK law for different types of intellectual property licences under the provisions of Schedule 3 of the RTPA.[3] It is necessary to fit an agreement within one of the paragraphs granting exemption under that Schedule; the paragraphs cannot be used cumulatively however.[4] Guidance is given in this chapter as to whether an agreement falls within a particular block exemption. However some more general and introductory comments are called for at this stage. It has been argued that the approach to categorising IP licences is based on the misconception that it is possible to identify one type of intellectual property right as always predominant in a transaction, and that other intellectual property rights can therefore be characterised as ancillary. This fails to understand the way in which intellectual property rights operate in a cumulative way. An item of machinery may, for example, perform a patented process, require extensive know-how to be constructed, employ designs protected by design right, use copyrighted software as part of its function, and be used to make trade marked goods. How then does one ascertain which is the predominant element of intellectual property? Often the intellectual property rights are complementary and cumulative rather than hierarchical in their relative significance.

13.3 It has been suggested that there is no objective answer to this dilemma and that relative importance must therefore depend on the intention of the parties to the agreement.[5] The problems with this are that first the Commission seems to purport to apply an objective test[6] and that secondly it may not be possible to ascertain what is the true intention of the parties. Indeed the parties themselves as opposed to their lawyers are not likely to concern themselves with questions as to what type of intellectual property protects their technology. From a lawyer's standpoint, the best response is to make use of recitals in agreements to seek to characterise the transaction in a particular way in order to take advantage of the most advantageous legal regime for the parties. Care must be taken not to transgress the letter or spirit of the EC provisions when doing so.

[1] Commission Reg. (EC) No. 240/96 of 31 January 1996 on the application of Art. 85(3) of the Treaty to certain categories of technology transfer agreements. This replaced the Patent Licensing Block Exemption Reg. 2349/84, and the Know-how Licensing Block Exemption Reg. 556/89. A cross-referenced text is at [1996] ECLR 204 i–xii, see Robertson, "Technology transfer agreements: an overview of how Regulation 240/96 changes the law" [1996] ECLR 157.

[2] See Chapter 10 above.

[3] See paras. 2.165–2.211.

[4] See paras. 2.212–2.214.

[5] Korah, *Know-how Licensing Agreements and the EEC Competition Rules Regulation 556/89* (1989) at p. 76.

[6] But see *Moosehead* OJ 1990 L100/32; [1994] 4 CMLR 391, where an agreement licensing use of certain know-how to brew a trade marked brand of lager was characterised as a trade mark agreement on the basis that the parties' "principal interest" lay with the mark, rather than the know-how to brew a distinctive tasting lager (if there is such a thing).

B. The Relationship between Free Movement of Goods and Services and Intellectual Property Rights under EC Law[7]

13.4 The goal of the European Community Treaty is the creation of a single market.[8] Intellectual property rights present two particular problems in achieving this goal. First, they are granted on a national rather than EC wide basis, and have an inherent capacity for territorial division of the EC market along national lines. Secondly, they confer upon the holders exclusive rights, which may then be exploited anti-competitively, either unilaterally or in licensing agreements.

13.5 The first of these problems can be tackled at source by replacing national IP rights with EC-wide rights. This solution has so far only been attempted in the field of patent and trade mark laws, and thus far with limited success. A Community Patent Convention was agreed in 1975 but has not yet been ratified to bring it into effect. If it does come into effect, it will enable one patent to be obtained for the whole of the EC. It will, however, exist alongside rather than replace national patents. There has been a greater advance in trade marks with the adoption of the Community Trade Mark Regulation,[9] which is based on the same principle of creating a Community-wide right co-existing with national rights and which came into operation in 1996. Other than these, EC law has concentrated upon approximation and harmonisation of national laws,[10] accepting that the doctrines to be found in the case law of the Court of Justice as a remedy to the second problem are, at least for the time being, a workable compromise.

13.6 The Court of Justice has developed two main doctrines as a means of reconciling EC law on free movement with national IP rights: (i) the existence/exercise distinction; and (ii) the exhaustion of rights principle.

(1) The existence/exercise distinction

13.7 Article 30 EC sets out the principle of free movement of goods within the Community.[11] Article 36 EC states that Article 30 does not, however, apply to restrictions for the protection of intellectual property, provided these do not constitute a means of arbitrary discrimination or a disguised restriction of trade between Member States. Article 222 of the EC Treaty provides that the Treaty "shall in no way prejudice the rules in Member States governing the system of property ownership". It becomes necessary to reconcile the competing objectives of, on the one hand, free movement of goods throughout the EC, and on the other hand the protection of the rights of IP owners, inherent in which is the right to prevent the circulation of goods in breach of such rights.

[7] See generally, Cornish *Intellectual Property* (3rd edn. 1996) pp. 31–39 and 644–655; Wyatt and Dashwood's *cont.*
European Community Law (3rd edn. 1993), Chapter 20; G. Marenco and K. Banks, "Intellectual property and the Community rules on free movement: discrimination unearthed" (1990) 15 ELRev 224.

[8] See in particular Arts. 2, 3(c) and 7a of the Treaty.

[9] Reg. 40/94, OJ 1994 L11/1. The Community Trade Mark Office is situated in Alicante, Spain. Community trade marks have been available since 1 April 1996.

[10] See Robertson, "Recent developments in EEC intellectual property legislation" (1992) 12 YEL 175 and subsequent annual surveys in the YEL.

[11] Art. 30 EC states that "[q]uantitative restrictions on imports and all measures having equivalent effect shall ... be prohibited between Member States". Measures having equivalent effect have been defined by the Court of Justice in Case 8/74 *Procureur du roi* v *Dassonville* as being capable of including "all trading rules enacted by Member States which are capable of hindering, directly or indirectly, actually or potentially, intra-Community trade" [1974] ECR 837, [1974] 2 CMLR 436. Art. 59 EC on services has been similarly extensively interpreted.

13.8 The Court of Justice has, in a long line of cases,[12] done so by drawing a distinction between the existence and the exercise of IP rights. The Treaty has been declared not to affect the existence of IP rights, thus enabling member states to enact and maintain in force their own IP laws.[13] However, IP owners may only exercise those rights in ways which are compatible with the other provisions of the Treaty. In deciding what constitutes a valid exercise of an IP right, the Court has narrowed the concept of what is protectable to its "specific subject matter". This is an attempt to identify what is the core of an IP right justifying protection. For example, the specific subject matter of a patent right is defined as "the guarantee that the patentee, to reward the creative effort of the inventor, has the exclusive right to use an invention with a view to manufacturing industrial products and putting them into circulation for the first time, either directly or by the grant of licences to third parties, as well as the right to oppose infringements".[14] Thus IP rights may be used in ways which are proportionate to their specific subject matter, but beyond that will be subject to restrictions to ensure the free movement of goods.

13.9 Rules on free movement therefore limit the ways in which IP rights may be exercised, either by limiting the scope for unilateral action by the IP right owner (hence overlapping with Article 86 EC), or by limiting the provisions which may be included in licences by IP owners (and so overlapping with Article 85 EC). Where there is such an overlap, the Court of Justice has ruled in the *Magill TV Guide* case[15] that the competition rules apply to the exclusion of any inconsistent exercise of intellectual property rights.

(2) The exhaustion of rights principle

13.10 This principle derives from the control on the exercise of IP rights by EC law, in the field of parallel imports. Were it not for EC law, an IP owner, X, could in most situations prevent imports from state B into state A of goods protected by X's IP rights in state A. This would be the case even if X had sold those goods or licensed their sale in state B. This is because whatever the rights granted in state B, the rights in state A are entirely separate and entitle X to control those goods in state A (depending always on the particular provisions of state A's legislation). This state of affairs would enable X to sell goods protected by IP rights throughout the EC, but prevent them being imported back into state A, thus maintaining rigid territorial market division, contrary to the basic goal of market integration.

13.11 To remedy this, the Court of Justice set out the principle of exhaustion of rights. This states that an IP owner's rights to control a product's distribution only apply until that product is sold either by the IP owner or with its consent,[16] and is reflected in the definitions given by the Court of the specific subject matter of IP rights. For example, the definition of the specific subject matter of a patent cited above refers to putting patented products "into circulation for the first time, either directly or by the grant of licences to third parties", indicating that once this has been done, any further attempt to use the patent right to control the products will fall outside the scope of the specific subject matter. The same principle applies to other IP rights.

[12] Commencing with Case 78/70 *Deutsche Grammophon* v *Metro* [1971] ECR 487, [1971] CMLR 631.

[13] Case 144/81 *Keurkoop* v *Nancy Kean Gifts* [1982] ECR 2853, [1983] 2 CMLR 47. However, the Court will declare incompatible with the Treaty provisions of national law which discriminate between Member States: Case 434/85 *Allen and Hanbury's* v *Generics* [1988] ECR 1245.

[14] Joined cases 15 and 16/74 *Centrafarm* v *Sterling Drug* [1974] ECR 1147, [1974] 2 CMLR 480, para. 9.

[15] Joined cases C-241 and 242/91 P *RTE and ITP* v *Commission* [1995] ECR I-743; see Robertson (1995) 111 LQR 588.

[16] Case 78/70 *Deutsche Grammophon* v *Metro* [1971] ECR 487, [1971] CMLR 631; for the most recent statement of this principle, see C-9/93 *IHT Internationale Heiztechnik GmbH* v *Ideal-Standard GmbH* [1994] ECR I-2789.

13.12 As result, any attempt by an IP owner to control dealings in a product after sale by it or by its licensee by relying upon IP rights will be met by the objection that the IP owner's rights were exhausted by the sale, and hence the IP rights may no longer be exercised over those products. The IP owner must then turn to contractual means to control dealings, subject to the limitations on such contracts imposed by competition law (to be discussed below), as well as to more general problems raised by contract law, such as privity.

C. Patent and Know-how Licensing in EC Law: General Considerations[17]

1. *Legal Context*

13.13 The principal consideration in respect of patent and know-how licensing in EC law is now the block exemption for certain categories of technology transfer agreement: Regulation 240/96.[18] This grants automatic exemption under Article 85(3) to various types of licence satisfying the criteria laid down in the Regulation. It also proceeds along certain basic lines, in particular it follows the reasoning of the Court of Justice in *Nungesser* v *Commission* (*Maize Seed*).[19] From this case three broad principles may be derived which are relevant to the Regulation.[20] First, a certain degree of protection is necessary for technology owners (licensors) and licensees to create a favourable climate for the transfer of new technology throughout the EC and simultaneously to stimulate and reinforce the R&D activities of firms which generate advanced techniques and new products; secondly, a balance must be struck between maintaining effective competition in the EC and protecting the monopoly-based rights of holders of intellectual property; and thirdly, a law designed to regulate patent and know-how licensing must recognise the importance of legal security for contract partners.

2. *The Preceding Block Exemptions*

13.14 Until 1 April 1996, two different regimes existed for licensing patents and know-how. These different regimes were unified in the 1996 Technology Transfer Regulation. However, because the transitional provisions of the 1996 Regulation permit agreements in the force as of the date of coming into force of the 1996 Regulation, to remain in force until they naturally terminate, the old regimes for patents and know-how remain of considerable relevance. For this reason they are examined in this chapter in addition to the new 1996 Regulation. The "old" Regulations are also relevant in that the case law under the old provisions will remain at least relevant to understanding the 1996 Regulation and in many cases, where the policy in relation to a particular clause has not changed, critical.

[17] See J.S. Venit, "In the wake of *Windsurfing*: patent licensing in the common market" [1986] *Fordham Copr L Inst* 521.

[18] See note 1.

[19] Case 258/78 [1983] CMLR 278; [1982] ECR 2015; and Commission Decision [1978] 3 CMLR 434 discussed Korah (1983) *Antitrust Bulletin* 699.

[20] See *Fourteenth Report on Competition Policy* (1984), pp. 40–42, paras. 31–35.

3. *Exclusive Licences and the Application of Article 85(1): "Open" and "Closed" Licences*

13.15 In *Nungesser* v *Commission* the Court held that certain types of exclusive licence did not fall within Article 85(1).[21] To be excluded, the licence would have to be "open", i.e. a licence whereby the licensor agrees not to compete with the licensee in the licensed territory and not to grant additional licences for that territory, but which does not, however, afford the licensee absolute territorial protection, i.e. protection from competition by other licensees and parallel importers. A licence which seeks to protect the licensee from competition is a "closed" licence and is subject to Article 85(1) EC.[22]

13.16 "Open" exclusive licences do not, therefore, require notification. Though, caution should be adopted when considering the "open"–"closed" distinction since the Court itself did not draw a black and white division between the concepts. The Court apparently viewed only certain types of "open" licence as outside the scope of Article 85(1). The criteria for the non-applicability of Article 85(1) would appear to be as follows:

(a) the product is new on the market and users and consumers are unfamiliar with it;
(b) the product requires exclusivity to provide the licensee a degree of protection which is necessary to encourage the licensee to accept the licence and help off-set research and development costs;
(c) the possibility of competition from other licensees and parallel importers remains; and
(d) the licence is not concluded for an unduly long period of time.

13.17 The Commission has subsequently applied these considerations in negotiations with parties to licences.[23] It is important to appreciate from the outset that the principles in *Nungesser* v *Commission* are considered to be of general application to all intellectual property rights and not just patents. Indeed, the case itself concerned plant breeders' rights which are a *sui generis* species of intellectual property.[24] It will be recognised that these criteria may not be equated with precise rules. They demonstrate a pragmatic approach to the problem of affording inventors the economic security that is essential to the creative process. For a licensee to enter a high risk venture there must exist some sort of cushioning protection from competition. The Court, however, has refused to allow absolute territorial protection (the "closed" licence). Precisely what degree of protection is to be allowed remains unanswered. The Commission's approach can be illustrated by *Becton Dickinson/Cyclopore*.[25] In this case, Cyclopore (which operated under a patent licence from the Université Catholique de Louvain) exclusively licensed a medical supply company, Becton Dickinson to manufacture and sell tissue culture products from membranes exclusively supplied by Cyclopore. The Commission required the parties to allow Cyclopore to sell its membranes to other potential manufacturers of

[21] [1983] CMLR 278; [1982] ECR 2015 at para. 58 of the judgment.
[22] *ibid.*, at para. 53 of the judgment. "Closed" licences are well established as falling within Art. 85(1) EC: Case 51/75 *EMI Records* v *CBS United Kingdom* [1976] 2 CMLR 235; [1976] ECR 811; Case 28/77 *Tepea BV* v *Commission* [1978] 3 CMLR 392; [1978] ECR 1391.
[23] See *Knoll-Hille Form, Thirteenth Report on Competition Policy* (1983), p. 91, where these conditions were held not to have been satisfied.
[24] Under Art. 8.1(h) of Reg. 240/96, plant breeders' certificates are treated as patents for the purpose of the block exemptions.
[25] *Twenty-third Report on Competition Policy* (1993), para. 241.

tissue culture products after five years, thus enabling a degree of cushioning from competition for Becton Dickinson, but ensuring third party access after the transitional period. The Commission in the technology transfer block-exemption have sought to draw more sharply defined lines.

D. The Technology Transfer Block Exemption: Regulation 240/96

1. Introduction

13.18 Regulation 240/96[26] makes a number of changes to the regime for patent and know-how licensing agreements, which are considered in the following paragraphs, and there then follows at para. 13.36 a comprehensive commentary on the provisions of the block exemption.

The new block exemption makes four principal changes to the existing regime:

(i) As already explained, it creates a single block exemption to cover both patents and know-how licences.
(ii) The list of permissible restrictions of competition, the so-called "whitelist", which may be imposed upon a licensee is extended.
(iii) The list of impermissible restrictions of competition, the so-called "blacklist", which may be imposed upon a licensee is reduced.
(iv) There is greater opportunity for getting the European Commission to authorise licences not falling completely within the terms of the block exemption.

These will be dealt with in turn.

(1) A single legal regime

13.19 A certain amount of rigidity is inevitable in a system using block exemptions. There are now three possible outcomes for patent and know-how licensing agreements. Either the agreement is not caught by Article 85(1), and thus does not require exemption, whether block or individual or the agreement is caught by Article 85(1), and is exempted by the Technology Transfer Block Exemption Regulation or the agreement is caught by Article 85(1), and is not exempted by the Technology Transfer Block Exemption Regulation, and therefore requires individual exemption or at least a comfort letter. The further step which hitherto existed of considering whether a licence is subject to the Patent or the Know-how Block Exemption Regulation has been removed because, the technology transfer block exemption covers the combined area of both the earlier Regulations (pure patent,[27] pure know-how[28] and mixed patent and know-how licences, including those containing ancillary provisions relating to other IP rights such as trade marks, design rights and copyright "especially software protection").[29] To some extent, the simplification is only on the surface: there remain different rules as to the permissible duration of territorial restrictions

[26] See note 1.
[27] The definition of patent has been extended to include semi-conductor topography rights, supplementary protection certificates and plant breeders' certificates—see Art. 8(1), Reg. 240/96.
[28] The definition of protectable know-how remains the same—see Art. 10(1)–(4) which repeats the requirements that it be secret, substantial and identified, these being set out previously in Reg. 556/89.
[29] Recitals 4–6, Reg. 240/96.

depending upon whether the agreement is a pure patent licensing agreement, pure know-how licensing agreement or a mixed patent and know-how agreement.

13.20 Although the classification of agreements has been simplified by doing away with the concept of know-how which is only ancillary to licensed patents (hitherto covered by the patent licensing block exemption) and know-how which is more than ancillary (hitherto covered by the know-how licensing block exemption) the new Regulation has introduced a new complication in the concept of "necessary" patents, which is of relevance to mixed patent and know-how agreements. "Necessary" patents are defined in Article 10(5) as

> "patents where a licence under the patent is necessary for the putting into effect of the licensed technology in so far as, in the absence of such a license, the realisation of the licensed technology would not be possible or would only be possible to a lesser extent or in more difficult or costly conditions. Such patents must therefore be of technical, legal or economic interest to the licensee".

The concept of necessary patents is relevant in calculating the permissible length of territorial restrictions in mixed agreements in the following way.

13.21 In a pure patent licensing agreement, a licensee may be restricted from actively selling into the licensor's or another licensee's territory for the duration of the licensed patents in each territory, but can only be completely prevented from making all sales (including passive or unsolicited sales) for the first five years that the licensed product is placed onto the common market by one of the licensees. In a pure know-how licensing agreement, a licensee may be restricted from actively selling into the licensor's or another licensee's territory for the ten years from when the licensed product was first put on the common market by any licensee. This period is halved to five years for a restriction on a licensee from making all sales including passive or unsolicited sales. In a mixed patent and know-how licensing agreement, a licensee may be restricted from actively selling into the licensor's or another licensee's territory either for ten years from the date that the licensed product is placed on the common market by one of the licensees, or if longer, for the duration of the licensed necessary patents in each territory. As with pure licences, the licensee can only be completely prevented from making all sales (including passive or unsolicited sales) for the first five years that the licensed product is based on to the Common Market by one of the licensees.

13.22 Similarly, the licensor may be restricted from licensing others in the territory or exploiting the licensed technology in the territory itself:

(a) in the case of a pure patent licensing agreement, for the duration of the patents in so far as they continue in force;

(b) in the case of a pure know licensing agreement, for ten years from the date that the licensed product is first placed on the Common Market by one of the licensees; and

(c) in the case of a mixed licensing agreement, for the longer of ten years from the date that the licensed product is first placed on the Common Market by one of the licensees, and the duration of the licensed necessary patents in each territory.

13.23 So despite the apparent simplicity of one single regime for both pure and mixed agreements, the lengths of territorial protection are now open to an assessment of the "necessity" of patents. In practical terms, appropriate recitals may be included to demonstrate that the parties regarded licensed patents as fulfilling this requirement of necessity, although strictly speaking such expressions cannot be conclusive and it is ultimately subject to determination by the courts.

13.24 The purpose behind the concept of "necessary patents" is, presumably,[30] to prevent improvement patents continually being obtained to provide continuous protection against active marketing. But it ignores that many products move on in development incrementally and through improvement patents. How then is one to tell at which point a new product has been developed which can set the ten year period running again? In any event, no territorial protection is permitted if a patent ceases to be valid or expires or if the know-how ceases to be secret, substantial and identified. Moreover, the licensor may under Article 2(1)(16) validly reserve a right to terminate the agreement if a licensee seeks to challenge the necessity of a necessary patent, as a means of evading restrictions during the term of a necessary patent. The end result is that the Commission's suspicions about the ability of parties to use patents as a means of evading limitations on territorial restrictions has considerably reduced the level of legal certainty for both parties.

(2) Changes to the "whitelist"

13.25 The "whitelist" of obligations considered not to be generally restrictive of competition in Article 2 has been extended. There is little major change from the whitelist contained in the know-how licensing block exemption, though it does mark further liberalisation compared with the original patent licensing block exemption.

13.26 There are two changes in practical terms: a welcome simplification of the rules on licensing back of improvements under Article 2(1)(4), and some less significant changes in royalty calculations under Article 2(1)(7). Other than these changes, although the whitelist looks longer than in the know-how licensing Block exemption, the extra paragraphs in fact reflect drafting changes more of presentation than of substance. For example, some paragraphs which were previously exemptions to blacklisted clauses, such as the right to terminate in the even of challenge by a licensee to the validity of the licensed patents,[31] have been moved out of the blacklist and into the whitelist.

13.27 The licensing back rules in the previous block exemption Regulations were a mess. The patent licensing block exemption was too simplistic, requiring all licences of improvements to be non-exclusive.[32] The know-how licensing block exemption, on the other hand, was too complicated in its attempt to allow exclusive licensing back of improvements on an equitable basis between licensor and licensee.[33] The new block exemption permits:

> "an obligation on the licensee to grant to the licensor a licence in respect of his own improvements to or his new applications of the licensed technology, provided:
> – that, in the case of severable improvements, such a licence is not exclusive, so that the licensee is free to use his own improvements or to license them to third parties, in so far as that does not involve disclosure of the know-how communicated by the licensor that it still secret,
> – and that the licensor undertakes to grant an exclusive or non-exclusive licence of his own improvements to the licensee."

13.28 Unlike the know-how licensing block exemption, there is now no need to deal specifically with the right to use improvements after the termination of the licence in order to come within the block exemption. The only question that affects the content of a licensing back clause now is whether the licensee's improvements are severable from the licensor's know-how. If they are, the licensee must remain free to use or to license them else-

[30] No Recital elaborates the need for the concept.
[31] Art. 2(1)(15), Reg. 240/96.
[32] Art. 2(1)(1), Reg. 2349/84.
[33] Art. 2(1)(4), Reg. 556/89.

where; if not, the licensor can demand an exclusive licence to use them as they depend upon that licensor's know-how. Article 3(6) of the Regulation refuses exemption if the licensee is obliged to assign rights to improvements or new applications.

13.29 The licensing back rules now at least have the virtue of comprehensibility restored after the know-how licensing block exemption. Whether requiring such a free flow of information will hinder licensing activity is another question, depending in any particular case on whether the concept of severable know-how is capable of meaningful application. As to the calculation of royalties, the earlier block exemptions did not permit royalties to be calculated for a period going beyond the duration of licensed patents[34] or a period going past the time when the licensed know-how ceased to be secret,[35] although the royalty payments—though not the calculations—could take place over the whole life of the agreement. Now, under Article 2(1)(7), royalties can be calculated over the length of the agreement provided that, in the case of patents, this is in order to facilitate payment.[36] This change is a small relaxation of the existing rules, but it remains doubtful whether there is really any legitimate interest in the Commission continuing to impose restrictions on royalty calculation.

(3) Changes to the "blacklist"

13.30 The blacklist under the new block exemption is considerably shorter than either of its predecessors. This is partly due to the exemptions to the earlier blacklist is now being moved to the whitelist. The main changes in the blacklist are the removal of the blacklisting of tying-in clauses, no-challenge clauses and automatic prolongation of duration by inclusion of improvements.

(a) Tying-in clauses

13.31 Tying-in clauses are now specifically whitelisted provided that they are necessary for a technically proper exploitation of the licensed technology or ensure that the product meets accepted minimum specifications.[37] Previously, tying-in clauses not meeting these requirements were blacklisted.[38] The practical significance of the change is that such a clause may be notified under the opposition procedure discussed below and receive exemption: this was not previously possible, because agreements containing blacklisted clauses have never been capable of exemption under the opposition procedure.

(b) No-challenge clauses

13.32 No-challenge clauses have been treated in a similar way. Under the earlier block exemptions, a clause preventing a licensee from challenging the validity of the licensor's patent or the secrecy of its know-how was blacklisted, subject to the proviso that the licensor could nevertheless reserve the right to terminate in the event of such challenge.[39] The new Regulation now specifically whitelists the reservation of the licensor's rights to terminate the event of challenge.[40] No-challenge clauses themselves may be exempted under the opposition procedure, discussed below, and are no longer specifically blacklisted.

[34] Art. 3(4), Reg. 2349/84.
[35] Art. 3(5), Reg. 556/89.
[36] See Recital 21, Reg. 240/96.
[37] Art. 2(1)(5), Reg. 240/96.
[38] Art. 3(9), Reg. 2349/84 and Art. 3(3), Reg. 556/89.
[39] Art. 3(1), Reg. 2349/84 and Art. 3(4), Reg. 556/89.
[40] Art. 2(1)(15), Reg. 240/96.

(c) Automatic prolongation by inclusion of improvements

13.33 The earlier block exemptions blacklisted clauses by which agreements were automatically prolonged by the inclusion of new improvements, unless the licensee had the right to terminate on expiry of the initial duration and then at least annually (in the case of the patent licensing block exemption)[41] or at least every three years (in the case of the know-how licensing block exemption).[42] Such clauses are now no longer blacklisted. What is blacklisted is the situation where the duration of a territorial restriction on licensor or licensee is extended through automatic prolongation.[43] This extends the existing prohibition on using separate agreements of the same technology to extend the duration of a territorial restriction.[44] However, under Article 8(3), the block exemption will only apply if the licensee has the right to terminate on the expiry of the initial term and at least every three years thereafter. So, though no longer on the blacklist, the rules on automatic prolongation continue to have effect. It is unclear whether an agreement with an automatic prolongation provision would be able to take advantage of the opposition procedure; given the wording of Article 8(3), it is thought not.

(4) Improvements to the opposition procedure

13.34 The technology transfer block exemption provides that agreements within the block exemption, but containing restrictive clauses not specifically mentioned in the block exemption and not containing any of the specifically blacklisted clauses, can be notified for exemption under an opposition procedure set out in Article 4.[45] This enables exemption to be granted four months after notification, unless the Commission raises opposition to exemption within that period. This is two months shorter than under the former Regulations and, to that extent, represents an improvement on the opposition procedure which applied previously.

13.35 The Commission has sought to encourage more use of the opposition procedure by setting out two specific examples of possible occasions for the use of the procedure in Article 4(2):

(i) tying-in clauses going beyond the limits permitted elsewhere in the block exemption i.e. not being necessary for a technically satisfactory exploitation of the licensed technology and not being necessary for conformity to quality standards; and
(ii) no-challenge clauses.

This was not an option available for either of those types of clauses under the earlier Regulations, since, as explained above, the clauses were specifically blacklisted and therefore outside the scope of the opposition procedure. Presumably, this change of policy indicates a readiness on the part of the Commission to exempt such clauses, at least in appropriate cases.[46] However, it must be observed the opposition procedure has not been hitherto widely used.[47]

41 Art. 3(2), Reg. 2349/84.
42 Art. 3(10), Reg. 556/89.
43 Art. 3(7), Reg. 240/96; see also Art. 8(3).
44 Art. 3(10), Reg. 2349/84 and Art. 3(1), Reg. 556/89.
45 See Recital 25, Reg. 240/96.
46 See paras. 13.101–13.105.
47 See paras. 7.172–7.173.

2. The Basic Exemption: Article 1

(1) Scope

13.36 Article 1 exempts patent licensing agreements, know-how licensing agreements and mixed agreements, to which only two undertakings are party. The Regulation extends beyond patents and includes[48] further: utility models; *certificats d'utilité* and *certificats d'addition* under French law; topographies of semiconductor products;[49] supplementary protection certificates or medicinal products;[50] and plant breeders certificates.[51] Applications are also covered even if, although not made at the time of the agreement, they are subsequently made within the time limits set down in relevant national laws or international conventions.[52]

13.37 The block exemption has introduced a new concept of "necessary" patents. These are defined in Article 19(5) as "patents where a licence under the patent is necessary for the putting into effect of the licensed technology in so far as, in the absence of such a licence, the realisation of the licensed technology would not be possible or would only be possible to a lesser extent or in more difficult or costly conditions. Such patents must therefore be of technical, legal or economic interest to the licensee." "Necessary" patents is used as a concept in calculating the length of territorial restrictions which may be imposed on licensors and licensees, discussed at paras. 13.20–13.24. While necessity is a legal test, parties may assist their case on demonstrating necessity by inclusion of appropriate recitals in an agreement.

13.38 Unlike patents which are subject to definition both by international conventions and in national legislation, there is no accepted definition of know-how which could have been adopted for the purposes of the know-how block exemption. Accordingly it was necessary for the block exemption to define what is meant by know-how. The block exemption gives a tripartite definition of know-how: know-how must be (a) secret, (b) substantial and (c) identified.[53]

13.39 (a) "Secret" is defined as meaning "that the know-how package as a body or in the precise configuration and assembly of its components is not generally known or easily accessible, so that part of its value consists in the lead which the licensee gains when it is communicated to him; it is not limited to the narrow sense that each individual component of the know-how should be totally unknown or unobtainable outside the licensor's business."[54] So it seems that a compilation of know-how, the individual components of which are known but not the way in which they are assembled, would qualify as secret. Difficulties exist with the ascertaining what is meant by "generally known" or "easily accessible". It may well be that this is another way of expressing the English concept of public domain which determines whether

[48] Art. 8(1), Reg. 240/96. Under Art. 1(1)(b) of Reg. 19/65/EEC, JO 1965, pp. 533–65 (6 March 1965) the Commission has general legislative competence to provide block-exemptions for industrial property rights, including: patents, utility models, designs or trade marks, or the rights arising out of contracts for assignment of, or the right to use a method of manufacture or knowledge relating to the use or to the application of industrial processes.

[49] Protection is granted in the UK under the Design Right (Semiconductor Topographies) Regulations 1989, S.I. 1989 No. 1100.

[50] SPCs are granted in the UK under the Patents (Supplementary Protection Certificate for Mechnical Products) Regulations 1992, S.I. 1992 No. 3162, implementing EC Council Regulation 1768/92/EEC.

[51] Plant Varieties Act 1983.

[52] Art. 8(2), Reg. 240/96.

[53] Art. 10(1), Reg. 240/96.

[54] Art. 10(2), Reg. 240/96.

know-how remains protectable as confidential information under English law. If so, then this is to be decided by looking at knowledge in the relevant industry. In practice, who would take a licence of know-how if it was not secret?

13.40 (b) "Substantial" is further defined as meaning "that the know-how includes information which must be useful, i.e. can reasonably be expected at the date of conclusion of the agreement to be capable of improving the competitive position of the licensee, for example by helping him to enter a new market or giving him an advantage in competition with other manufacturers or providers of services who do not have access to the licensed secret know-how or other comparable secret know-how".[55] Despite the verbosity of this requirement, its most notable feature is its superfluity, a throwback to the earlier more suspicious Commission view of know-how as a subterfuge for anti-competitive collusion, since what licensee would take a licence of know-how which was not "useful"?

13.41 (c) "Identified" is further defined as meaning that "the know-how is described or recorded in such a manner as to make it possible to verify that it satisfies the criteria of secrecy and substantiality and to ensure that the licensee is not unduly restricted in his exploitation of his own technology, to be identified the know-how can be set out in the licence agreement or in a separate document or recorded in any other appropriate form at the latest when the know-how is transferred or shortly thereafter, provided that the separate document or other record can be made available if the need arises".[56] In practice, this is the most onerous requirement, since know-how often depends on demonstration of the technology as much as it can be recorded in an appropriate form. Again, this requirement seems to be included more for the convenience of the Commission in verifying the application of the block exemption rather than being required as a means of preventing a breach of Article 85(1).

13.42 The Regulation covers agreements between a licensor and a licensee. It also covers agreements between a licensee and a sub-licensee. Further, agreements for the assignment or acquisition of rights where the risks associated with exploitation are borne by the assignor are covered. Thus, agreements whereby the assignor earns a royalty dependent upon the turnover of patented products attained by the assignee, or the quantity of such products manufactured, or the number of operations carried out employing the patented invention, are all exempt. Also covered are agreements in which rights or obligations are assumed by undertakings connected with the parties.[57] Thus, an assignment of the licensee's rights to a wholly owned subsidiary of the licensee is perfectly acceptable.

13.43 With regard to the geographical scope of an agreement, exemption applies to a licence which contains obligations relating not only to territories within the Common Market but also to non-Member States.[58] However, agreements for territories other than the EC which have effects within the Common Market are subject to the Regulation.[59] Thus, an agreement between X (a British firm) and Y (a Norwegian firm) whereby Y is licensed to manufacture and sell products resulting from X's patent may be subject to EC

[55] Art. 10(3), Reg. 240/96.
[56] Art. 10(4), Reg. 240/96.
[57] Art. 6(3), Reg. 240/96 "Connected undertakings" is defined in Art. 12.
[58] Though where the licence affects a non-EC state there may be no effect on inter-State trade and hence no cause for Art. 85 to apply. See e.g. *Raymond–Nagoya* [1972] CMLR D45: licence between German licensor and Japanese licensee for licences in Japan and other states in the Far East—negative clearance given.
[59] para. 7 of the preamble.

law if X imposes on Y an obligation to refrain absolutely from supplying customers situate outside Japan the patent product. If customers and users in the EC have difficulty in obtaining the patent product in the EC and are prevented from acquiring it from the Japanese licensee, then the EC market has been affected.

13.44 The exemption does not apply to agreements concerning sales alone. Such agreements, if exempt, fall within Regulations 1983/83/EEC and 1984/83/EEC on block exemption for exclusive purchasing and distribution. Thus if X (patentee) licenses Y to distribute, on an exclusive basis, the product X has manufactured within a given area, the agreement must satisfy Regulation 1983/83/EEC.

13.45 As noted above, the Regulation exempts only bilateral agreements. Though where a number of legal persons form a single economic unit they may enter a licence as one party.[60]

(2) Relationship with licences of other intellectual property rights

13.46 The block exemption includes the licensing of intellectual property rights other than patents, and in particular trade marks, design rights and copyright, especially software protection, when such additional licensing contributes to the achievement of the objects of the licensed technology and is only ancillary to the patents and know-how. An attempt to present what is in substance a trade mark or software licence as a know-how licence will not comply with the block exemption: EC law looks at the substance rather than the form of an agreement.[61]

3. Permissible Restrictions: Article 1 (White Clauses)

13.47 Article 1 enumerates restrictions which may be incorporated safely into patent licences without endangering the exemption. The word "technology" is used to mean the subject-matter of the patents and know-how being licensed. These "white clauses" are examined below. A clause of more limited scope than that specified below is, according to Article 1(5), stated to be exempt with the clause specified. If the clause in question goes beyond that noted below it is not exempt.

(1) Exclusive territories (Article 1(1)(1), (2))

13.48 Article 1(1)(1) permits: "an obligation on the licensor not to license other undertakings to exploit the licensed technology in the licensed territory". Article 1(1)(2) permits: "an obligation on the licensor not to exploit the licensed invention in the licensed territory himself". Thus the licensor can grant the licensee an exclusive territory and covenant not to compete with the licensee in that territory. Paragraph 10 of the preamble explains the Commission's policy on exclusivity clauses. Such clauses are not necessarily contrary to Article 85(1) where they are concerned with the introduction and protection of a new technology in the licensed territory by reason of the scale of the research which has been undertaken and of the risk that is involved in manufacturing and marketing a product which is unfamiliar to users in the licensed territory at the time the agreement is made. Paragraph 10 also refers to the increase such a licence may create in the competitiveness of the undertakings concerned resulting from the dissemination of innovation within the Community. This may also be the case where the agreements are concerned with the introduction and protection of a new process for manufacturing a product which is already

[60] Case 170/83 *Hydrotherm* v *Andreoli* [1985] 3 CMLR 224 in respect of analogous situation under the exclusive distribution regulation.
[61] *Moosehead/Whitbread* OJ 1990 L100/32; [1991] 4 CMLR 391.

known. This is, in reality, an affirmation of the judgment of the Court of Justice in *Maize Seed*.[62] To the extent that an exclusivity clause does not satisfy these economic criteria, for example where the product is not "new",[63] it will now be exempt, none the less, under Article 1. The exemption applies irrespective of the size of the undertakings in question. The Commission (reluctantly) dropped size limitations from drafts of the Regulation.[64]

13.49 The exemption of these obligations on the licensor is however limited in time. The time limits depend upon whether the agreement is a pure patent, pure know-how or mixed licensing agreement. For a pure patent agreement, the obligation may be imposed on the licensor to the extent that and for as long as the licensed product is protected by parallel patents in the relevant licensees' territories.[65] For a pure know-how agreement, the obligation may be imposed on the licensor for not more than ten years from the date when the licensed product is first put on the market within the common market by one of the licensees.[66] It is important to note that time starts to run from the date of first marketing by any licensee. A standard period of ten years in a licensing agreement entered into with a number of licensees each marketing at different times would, except for the first to market, fall foul of this provision. For a mixed agreement, the obligation may be imposed on the licensor for the longer of two periods: either the period of protection permitted for a pure know-how agreement, or the period of protection permitted for a pure patent agreement, provided that the patents used in that calculation are "necessary" patents.[67] The definition of "necessary" patents is considered at paras. 13.20-13.24.

(2) Non-competition clauses (Article 1(1)(3))

13.50 Article 1(1)(2) permits the licensor to covenant not to compete with the licensee in the latter's territory. Article 1(1)(3) permits: "an obligation on the licensee not to exploit the licensed technology in the territory of the licensor within the Common Market".

13.51 The exemption of these obligations on the licensor is limited in time. The time limits depend upon whether the agreement is a pure patent, pure know-how or mixed licensing agreement. For a pure patent agreement, the obligations may be imposed on the licensee to the extent that and for as long as the licensed product is protected by parallel patents in the licensor's territory.[68] For a pure know-how agreement, the obligation may be imposed on the licensee for not more than ten years from the date when the licensed product is first put on the market within the common market by one of the licensees (not, note, by the licensor).[69] It is important to note that the time runs from the date of first marketing by any licensee (see para. 13.49).

13.52 For a mixed agreement, the obligation may be imposed on the licensee for he longer of two periods, either the period of protection permitted for a pure know-how agreement or the period of protection permitted for a pure patent agreement, provided that the patents used in that calculation are "necessary" patents.[70] The definition of "necessary" patents is considered at paras 13.20–13.24 above. It will be observed that the licensor is entitled to a greater degree of protection from his licensees than he is permitted, under the Regula-

[62] Case 258/78 *Nungesser* v *Commission (Maize Seed)* [1982] ECR 2015; [1983] CMLR 278 at para. 58 of the judgment. See Turner, "Competition and the Common Market after maize seed" (1983) ELRev 103.
[63] See for example, *Velcro/Aplix* OJ 1985 L233/22, [1989] 4 CMLR 157, para. 43.5.
[64] See Commission draft Technology Transfer for Block Exemption Regulation, OJ 1994 C178/3.
[65] Art. 1(2), Reg. 240/96.
[66] Art. 1(3), Reg. 240/96.
[67] Art. 1(4), Reg. 240/96.
[68] Art. 1(2), Reg. 240/96.
[69] Art. 1(3), Reg. 240/96.
[70] Art. 1(4), Reg. 240/96.

tion, to confer on licensees *inter se* (as to which see the analysis of the passive sales ban in Article 1(1)(5) at para. 13.54 below).

(3) Protection for licensees against each other (Article 1(1) (4), (5) and (6))

13.53 The Commission recognises that licensees require a degree of protection from each other. Licensees protected from competition, *inter se*, may focus their efforts in a more intensive manner thereby maximising the chances of effective exploitation and utilisation of the patent. However, the Commission and indeed the Court of Justice have refused to countenance absolute territorial protection whereby licensees are protected from *all* competition, in particular from parallel importers.[71]

13.54 The Regulation hence lays down strict rules for exclusivity and protection of licensees from each other. At the extreme under Article 1(1)(6) the licensor may grant licensees protection from any competition from other licensees for up to five years from the time the product is first "put on the market" within the EC by a licensee. Protection in this sense means protection from "active" *and* "passive" competition. "Active" competition occurs where a licensee in one territory markets the goods in the territories of other licensees; undertakes specific advertising aimed at those territories; or establishes any branch or maintains any distribution depot in those territories. "Passive" competition occurs where a licensee simply responds to unsolicited requests from users or resellers established in other territories. Article 1(1)(6) does not, however, allow the licensor to prohibit the licensee from supplying any customer in his own territory who intends to export the goods for resale to another licensee's territory, i.e. a parallel importer.

13.55 Article 1(1)(4) exempts obligations on the licensee not to manufacture or use the licensed product, or use the licensed process in territories within the common market licensed to other licensees. This obligation does not, however, prevent one licensee manufacturing in his own territory and selling the licensed product over the border in another licensee's territory. The Commission adopts a more liberal view of restraints on *manufacture* than they do with restraints on *sale*. Article 1(1)(5) exempts obligations partially preventing sales outside of the territory. The provision allows the licensor to prohibit the licensee from undertaking "active" selling (as defined above) outside of his territory. The obligations in Article 1(1)(4) and (5) do not prevent competition from parallel importers: X who is situate in the UK which is served by L1 travels to France which is served by L2. X purchases the licensed product from L2 and takes it back to the UK for sale there in competition with L1. It may well be that L2 is considerably cheaper or produces better quality goods or provides better terms and conditions than L1 so that it is commercially viable for X to purchase in France for export to the UK. Clauses exempt under Articles 1(1)(4) and (5) are valid for the following periods.

13.56 In the case of pure patent agreements, the obligation may be imposed upon the licensee to the extent that and for as long as the licensed product is protected by parallel patents in the other licensees' territories.[72] For a pure know-how agreement, the obligation may be imposed on the licensee for not more than ten years from the date when the licensed product is first put on the market within the common market by one of the licensees.[73]

13.57 For a mixed agreement, the obligation may be imposed on the licensee for the longer of two periods: either the period of protection permitted for a pure know-how agreement

[71] See Case 258/78 *Nungesser* v *Commission (Maize Seed)* [1982] ECR 2015; [1983] CMLR 278 at para. 61 of the judgment approving, Cases 56 and 58/64 *Consten and Grundig* v *Commission* [1966] CMLR 418; [1966] ECR 299.

[72] Art. 1(2), Reg. 240/96.

[73] Art. 1(3), Reg. 240/96.

or the period of protection permitted for a pure patent agreement, provided that the patents used in that calculation are "necessary" patents[74] (see paras. 13.20–13.24).

13.58 If a licensor wishes to protect licensees he may impose an obligation on licensees not to put the licensed product on the market in territories licensed to other licensees under Article 1(1)(6) noted above but only for a period of five years from the date when the product is first "put on the market" by a licensee. It is to be observed that the restriction applies in relation to territories of other licensees. The clause does not refer to the licensor's territory: that is covered by Article 1(1)(3) which permits a restriction to be imposed on the licensee not to exploit the licensed technology in the licensor's territory. This restriction is permitted for a longer duration than the ban on passive exploitation under Article 1(1)(6). The phrase "put on the market" is not defined. Paragraph 5 of the Preamble defines "exploitation" in wider terms as including manufacture, use or putting on the market. This latter concept may presumably be construed to mean first commercial marketing, it would probably exclude experimental sales for market research purposes. At the end of this period licensees must be free to supply the product in the territories of other licensees in response to unsolicited requests from users or resellers (parallel importers) situated in those territories (i.e. "passive" sales).[75] Thus L1 in the UK may be required to refuse to satisfy an unsolicited order from a buyer in Germany for up to five years. Though if the buyer travels to the UK to buy or place his order through an agent or intermediary in the UK, the licensor cannot prevent L1 from supplying the buyer. Article 1(6) thus falls short of absolute territorial protection, though it may give considerable protection in practice where the goods are bulky and of relatively low value, i.e. not easily exportable.

13.59 Under no circumstances can the licensor attempt to *prevent* absolutely parallel imports; see Article 3 (1) below.

(4) Trade marks (Article 1(1)(7))

13.60 This provision exempts, "An obligation on the licensee to use only the licensor's trade mark or get up to distinguish the licensed product during the term of the agreement, provided that the licensee is not prevented from identifying himself as the manufacturer of the licensed product." Article 1(1)(7) does not expressly exempt a pure trade mark licence.[76] The trade mark licence must be ancillary to the licence and must not be used to extend the effects of the licence beyond the life of the licensed patents or after the know-how has ceased to be secret or substantial or to permit territorial exclusivity.[77] The licensee must not be prevented from identifying himself as the manufacturer of the licensed product.

(5) Production licences (Article 1(1)(8))

13.61 A licence may be limited to enabling the licensee to limit his production of the licensed product to the quantities he requires in manufacturing his own products and to selling the licensed product only as an integral part of, or a replacement part for, his own products, or otherwise in connection with sale of his own product. Where this is done, the licensee must remain free to determine the level of his own production. The licence cannot be used as a means of restricting the licensee's output. Such a licence can only

[74] Art. 1(4), Reg. 240/96.

[75] See *Maize Seed* [1978] 3 CMLR 434 at p. 455 (Commission decision)—Commission recognise that export bans may be acceptable where the exclusivity is needed to protect small or medium-sized undertakings in their attempts to penetrate new markets or promote new products provided that parallel imports are not impeded at the same time. See Korah, *op. cit.*, note 5 at pp. 40–44.

[76] See in the context of the previous know-how block exemption *Moosehead* OJ 1990 L100/32 [1991] 4 CMLR 391, discussed at para. 13.408.

[77] *Velcro/Aplix* OJ 1985 L233/22, [1989] 4 CMLR 157, para. 48.5.

continue for the life of any licensed patents or for as long as any licensed know-how remains secret and substantial.

4. Permissible Clauses not Generally Falling within Article 85(1): Article 2 (White Clauses)

13.62 Article 2 lists typical licence clauses that are generally not considered to fall within Article 85(1). Where such clauses are within Article 85(1) because of particular economic or legal circumstances, they will be automatically exempt under Article 85(3) even if no restrictions of the type exempted by Article 1.[78] Exemption is also given to an obligation similar to but of more limited scope than those set out in Article 2(1).[79] The list is given by the Commission for purposes of legal certainty but none the less is not exhaustive. Article 2(1) provides that Article 1 shall apply notwithstanding the presence of any of the following contractual obligations.

(1) Non-disclosure of know-how

13.63 Article 2(1)(1) permits obligations on the licensee not to divulge know-how communicated by the licensor. This obligation may extend beyond expiry of the agreement, until such time as the know-how enters the public domain. At that time a restriction on the licensee might unduly restrict him vis a vis competitors who are free to do as they please with the know-how. A not uncommon clause provides that know-how shall remain secret until such time as the licensee proves it has entered the public domain. In practice this can be an onerous and expensive burden of proof. Such a clause is not specifically in either the "white" or "black" categories of clause which might suggest that adoption of such a clause renders the licence potentially notifiable to the Commission probably using the opposition procedure. However, it is arguable that such a clause is *within* the ambit of the "white" obligation and hence also exempt.

(2) Prohibition on sub-licensing or assignment

13.64 Article 2(1)(2) permits obligations on the licensee not to grant sub-licences or assign the licence. It follows that a clause laying down conditions under which a licensee may sub-license is also exempt. This is a less restrictive version of the ban on sub-licensing so is included on the "more limited scope" rule (Article 1(5)).

(3) Post-expiry of the agreement exploitation

13.65 Article 2(1)(3) permits an obligation to be imposed on the licensee not to exploit the patent after termination of the agreement in so far as the patent is still in force. Recital 20 explains that such a clause is a normal feature of licensing since otherwise the licensor would be forced to transfer his know-how or patents in perpetuity. It will of course be permissible to grant a licence for a period less than the lifetime of the patent. It restrains competition however if the obligations in the agreement extend beyond expiry of the patent. When the right to protection expires, restrictions on the use of that right are likewise no longer protected.[80]

[78] Art. 2(2), Reg. 240/96.

[79] Art. 2(3), Reg. 240/96.

[80] It is unclear whether the exemption also applies to a clause restraining the licensee from using technology which has ceased to be protected by patent or know-how due to action by the licensee. Since the licensor may terminate an agreement in such circumstances, and may require the licensee to continue paying royalties under Art. 2(1)(7), it seems arguable that restraining the licensee for such period as would, in the absence of the licensee's action, have applied is a more limited restriction and therefore exempted under Art. 2(3), Reg. 240/96. Arts. 3(4) of Reg. 2349/84 and 3(1) of Reg. 556/89 exempted such a restriction.

13.66 However, there is no objection to an obligation on the licensee to pay royalties following expiration of the patent, where the royalties arose for payment in instalments and these have not yet finished. Thus, if X licenses Y a patent for five years but, as a kindness to Y, staggers the payment of royalties over a seven-year period, this is exempt under Article 2(1)(7) (see para. 13.74).

13.67 Where the licence includes provisions for the licensing of trade marks these, being ancillary to the main grant, must expire with the licence. If they exceed the licence the agreement becomes one for the licence of a trade mark and hence is not exempt.

(4) Improvements and communication of experiences (grant/licence back clauses)

13.68 Article 2(1)(4) permits obligations on the parties to exchange details of experience gained in exploiting the licensed invention. An obligation on the licensee to swap experience with other licensees is not exempt unless it complies with Article 5(1)(1). Adoption of such a clause, however, might render use of the opposition procedure appropriate. Nor is an obligation on a licensee to assign to the licensor ownership of improvements.[81]

13.69 Exemption is only granted under Article 2(1)(4) to licensing such obligations which are mutual. A licensor may only require a licensee to license back improvements if the licensor himself undertakes to grant an exclusive or non-exclusive licence of his own improvements to the licensee. The license back obligation on the licensee may only be non-exclusive, leaving the licensee free to license to third parties, unless the improvements are not severable from the licensed technology. In that latter case, the licensee may be restricted for licensing the improvements to third parties because to do so would involve a disclosure of the licensed technology.

13.70 Finally, licence back provisions which thereby extend the final duration of the agreement must allow either party to terminate at the end of the initial term and every three years thereafter or must allow the licensee to refuse such improvements.[82]

(5) Minimum quality and procurement obligations

13.71 Article 2(1)(5) permits obligations to be imposed on the licensee to observe minimum quality requirements including technical specifications for the licensed product. However, such obligations must be necessary either (a) for a technically satisfactory exploitation of the licensed invention or (b) for ensuring that the product of the licensee conforms to the minimum quality specifications that are effective to the licensor and other licensees. An ancillary obligation on the licensee to allow the licensor to perform monitoring checks (e.g. audits, reporting obligations, retention of records etc) is equally permissible. With respect to minimum quality the Commission has stated that such clauses do not restrain competition because they are "... only designed to allow an adequate and technically adequate exploitation of the rights conferred by patents on their holder".[83] In decided cases the Commission has accepted as non-restrictive, obligations on the licensee to manufacture, so as to render the licensed product compatible with the licensor's own products[84]

[81] Art. 3(6), Reg. 240/96; see para. 13.97.

[82] Art. 8(3), Reg. 240/96; see para. 13.33.

[83] *Burroughs–Delplanque* [1972] CMLR D67; *Burroughs–Geha* [1972] CMLR D72. *Campari* [1978] 2 CMLR 397.

[84] *Raymond–Nugoya* [1972] CMLR D45. But for a case deciding that an obligation on the licensee to manufacture according to the licensor's technical specification restricted competition see *Video Cassette Recorders* [1978] 2 CMIR 160, the obligation prevented licensees from changing to the manufacture and distribution of competing systems.

and to manufacture employing all due care and attention.[85] Licensees may be required to comply with design plans and drawings.

13.72 Article 2(1)(4) also permits an obligation on the licensee to procure goods or services from the licensor or from an undertaking designated by the licensor. However, this obligation is *only* exempt in so far as such products or services are necessary, either (a) for a technically satisfactory exploitation of the licensed invention or (b) for ensuring that the product of the licensee conforms to the minimum quality specifications that are applicable to the licensor and other licensees. In *Vaessen–Moris*[86] the Commission refused exemption to a patent licence containing a purchase obligation on a licensee of a process and device used in sausage meat manufacture. The obligation was on the licensee also to purchase casings from the patentee. The Commission decided that the clause prohibited the licensee from purchasing casings from other suppliers at more favourable prices. Moreover, the tie-in between patent licence and casings supply was not essential to the proper exploitation of the patent since casings provided by rival suppliers were perfectly adequate for use with the patented process and device. It would appear that the Regulation merely follows earlier Commission policy on tying within patent licences, i.e. that it is justifiable and not restrictive where the tied product or service (e.g. maintenance) is reasonably necessary for satisfactory exploitation of the patent. The tied product or service need not necessarily be essential to the patent; ties are justified in lesser circumstances. No definition is given of "technically satisfactory exploitation" but it is clearly a lesser nexus than necessity.[87]

(6) Infringement clauses (excluding no-challenge clauses)

13.73 Article 2(1)(6) permits obligations on the licensee: (a) to inform the licensor of infringements of the patent of misappropriation of the know-how; (b) to take legal action against an infringer; (c) to assist the licensor in any legal action against an infringer. However, "no-challenge clauses" are *not* exempt. These prohibit the licensee from challenging the validity of the patents or the secrecy of the know-how covered by the agreement during its currency and are considered at paras 13.104–13.105.

(7) Royalty calculation

13.74 Article 2(1)(7) exempts an obligation on the licensee to continue paging royalties over the duration of the agreement, even though the patents may have expired or the know-how has ceased to be secret, provided that, in relation to patent royalties, this is to facilitate payment and, in relation to know-how, that the know-how did not cease to be secret due to the licensor's ration. Royalty obligations for expired patents and non-secret know-how not falling within these categories are seen as being no more than a fetter on the competitiveness of licensees and as such are not block exempt.

(8) Field of use restrictions

13.75 Article 2(1)(8) permits an obligation on the licensee to restrict his exploitation of the licensed invention to one or more technical fields or product markets covered by the licensed technology. The licensor may thus restrict the licensee's use to a major or minor field of application. The licensor may thus grant different licences to different licensees limiting their use of the invention to fields in which they are experienced or have greatest production capacity. In some industries (e.g. chemicals, drugs) a single product can have

[85] *Davidson Rubber* [1972] CMLR D52.

[86] [1979] 1 CMLR 511. See also *Campari* [1978] 2 CMLR 397.

[87] Tying-in may also be an abuse of a dominant position: see Case T-30/89 *Hilti* OJ 1990 L100/32 [1992] 4 CMLR 16; CFI decision upheld by ECJ in Case C-53/92 P, [1994] ECR I-667, [1994] 4 CMLR 614.

multifarious uses. There is no obligation on a patentee to give licensees carte blanche in their use of the patent or know-how. The same principle applies to other intellectual property rights. Such restrictions are economically logical as enabling patentees to license firms in the field of use or product market that the firm is best able to exploit. Article 2(1)(8) is subject to Article 3(5) (a black clause). Unfortunately the divide between the two provisions is unclear so that where white becomes black is unpredictable. This point is examined below in connection with Article 3(5) in para. 13.96.

(9) Minimum royalties, production quantities or number of operations

13.76 Article 2(1)(9) permits an obligation on the licensee to: (a) pay a minimum royalty; (b) produce a minimum quantity of the licensed product; (c) carry out a minimum number of operations exploiting the licensed technology.

(a) Minimum royalties

13.77 The obligation to pay minimum royalties is rarely within Article 85(1) even where the royalties demanded are considered to be excessive by the licensee since Article 85(1) is not appropriate for curing or redressing commercial misjudgments.[88] Though, it will restrict competition where the licensee has to pay royalties on its own unprotected products; such an obligation has no connection with the licensed patent (see para. 13.74 above). Where the licensed product is an integral component of a larger product sold by the patentee and the royalty is based upon the sales price of the whole product, then the obligation to pay a royalty on an unprotected product may be legitimate.[89] In more general terms royalties may cause problems in a number of situations which warrant brief mention. Thus differential royalties whereby the licensee pays more if he exports than if he sells domestically may be viewed as attempts by the licensor to discourage exports. Similarly a scale of royalty payments which increases as the licensee's output increases may also be viewed as an attempt by the licensor to limit the licensee to his domestic territory. Conversely sliding scales whereby royalties decrease as output increases are acceptable since they do not deter production and are compatible with "best endeavours" clauses which are frequently inserted in licences.

(b) Minimum quantities

13.78 Obligations of this nature protect the licensor against under-use by the licensee and perhaps against the threat of compulsory licensing. If the latter fails to meet the quantitative requirement he will be liable for breach of contract to the licensor. The clause minimises the risk for the licensor. Article 2(1)(3) only applies to minima not maxima; the Commission view maxima limitations as curbs on productivity which are not exemptible.[90]

[88] e.g. *AOIP–Beyrard* [1976] 1 CMLR D14. See *IGR Fourteenth Report on Competition Policy* (1984), p. 76 where a trade association which holds its members' patents charges excessive royalties this will infringe Art. 85(1) EC.

[89] In *British Leyland* v *T.I. Silencers* [1980] 1 CMLR 598 it was held by the High Court that the extension of the obligation to pay royalties to an unprotected product is not an abuse of Art. 86 EC where the extension merely is a device for calculating royalties on the protected rights; see also UARCO *Fourteenth Report on Competition Policy* (1984) at p. 77 which appears to confirm this view.

[90] See Art. 3(5) of the Reg.; *Fourth Report on Competition Policy* (1974), para. 31; and also the *Maize Seed* case [1978] 3 CMLR 434 at p. 451 (Commission); and Case 258/78 [1983] CMLR 278; [1982] ECR 2015 at para. 32 of the judgment (Court of Justice). For a case where a minimum quantity clause ("to produce in sufficient quantity to satisfy the demand") was held to be exemptible on the basis that it optimised exploitation see *Burroughs-Delplanque* [1972] CMLR D67.

(c) Minimum number of operations

13.79 Minimum numbers of operations may be treated in the same way as minimum quantities. The same proviso as to maxima applies.

(10) Most favoured licensee's terms

13.80 Article 2(1)(10) permits obligations on the *licensor* to grant the licensee any more favourable terms that the licensor may grant to another undertaking after the agreement is entered into. It is possible that such a clause might restrain competition though where it does it will *still* be block exempt:

> "The licensor's obligation to extend to the original licensee any more favourable terms subsequently granted to other licensees would not in general dissuade the licensor from granting further licences to third parties. In specific cases, however, particularly where the market situation was such that the only way to find other licensees was to grant them more favourable terms than those granted to the first licensee, this obligation could be an obstacle to the granting of further licences and therefore constitute an appreciable restriction of competition."[91]

13.81 What is not covered by the block exemption is an obligation on the licensor to include a particular term or terms in its other licences. Such an obligation could be found to inhibit a licensor's ability to grant further licences and would thus be caught under Article 85(1), requiring exemption under the opposition procedure (see para. 13.101).

(11) Identification of patentee on licensed product

13.82 Article 2(1)(11) permits obligations on the licensee to mark the licensed product with an indication of: (a) the licensor's names or (b) the licensed patents (but not, apparently, both). If the patentee does not intend to commence marketing the licensed product himself until after expiry of the licence agreement, then he may wish to have his name or mark associated with the product from first marketing onwards thereby facilitating post-contract marketing. The Commission recognises that obligations on the licensee to allow identification of the patentee on the product by a distinctive mark may have "only the aim of facilitating a control by [the patentee] of the quality and quantity of the products covered by the agreement".[92]

(12) Construction of facilities for third parties

13.83 The licensee may be restricted under Article 2(1)(12) from using the licensor's technology to construct facilities for third parties. However, the licensee may not be restricted from increasing his own capacity or setting up his own additional facilities on normal commercial terms. Recital 24 explains that a licensee may legitimately be so restricted since the purpose of the agreement is not to permit the licensee to give other producers access to the licensors technology while it remains secret or protected by patent.

[91] See *Davidson Rubber* [1972] CMLR D53 at para. 18; *Glashersteller* Bull EC 8/70 at p. 68; and *Henkel-Colgate* OJ 1972 L 14/14.

[92] *Burroughs-Delplanque* [1972] CMLR D67 at section II of the decision; and *Burroughs-GEHA* [1972] CMLR D72 at Sect. II of the decision. But cf. *Windsurfing* [1984] 1 CMLR 1 (Commission), Case 193/83 [1986] ECR 611, [1986] 3 CMLR 489, paras. 79 and 101 where the Court held that an obligation on a licensee to affix to the patented product a notice identifying the patentee restricted competition because it induced confusion in consumers who might believe that the patent extended to articles that were not patent protected. The question of Art. 85(3) was not discussed.

(13) Second source of supply

13.84 The licensee may be limited under Article 2(1)(13) to supplying only a limited quantity of the licensed product to a particular customer. However, this is only permitted where the licence was granted in order that the customer might have a second source of supply inside the licensed territory. If the customer is himself the first licensee, then this restriction on the record licensee is only permitted where the customer is himself the first licensee, then this restriction on the record licensee is only permitted where the customer is himself to manufacture the licensed product or to have them manufactured by a subcontractor.

(14) Reservation of patent rights

13.85 Article 2(1)(14) exempts the reservation by the licensor of the right to exercise his patent rights to oppose the exploitation of the licensor technology by the licensee outside the licensed technology. This is subject to whatever limits may be imposed by EC and on the exercise of those patent rights (see paras 13.4–13.12). The provisions is silent as to know-how. So far as equivalent or comparable rights exists under national law to cover know-how, there is, by parity of reasoning to the case of patent rights, no reason why such a clause should be held to restrict competition and hence prejudice block exemption.

(15) Termination on challenge to validity

13.86 While a no-challenge clause may only be exempted by use of the opposition procedure (see para. 13.101), block exemption is available under Article 2(1)(15) for a reservation by the licensor of a right to terminate the agreement if the licensee challenges either the secret and substantial nature of the know-how or the validity of the licensed patents.[93] The right to terminate arises if the licensee challenges the licensed patents. Thus, the licensor may terminate if the challenge is to a field under the patent which is not actually licensed to the licensee. For instance a pharmaceutical patent may cover a number of different formulations or processes only one of which is licensed to the licensee. If the licensee challenges one of the non-licensed processes this is still a challenge to "the licensed patent".

The Regulation does not expressly whitelist a right for the licensor to terminate if the licensee challenges the know-how on the basis that it is not "identified" in an appropriate form notwithstanding that the requirement to identify know-how is a constituent of the definition of know-how provided for under Articles 10(1) and (4). The rationale for this is (presumably) that a challenge to the substantiality or secrecy of the know-how is a challenge to the very *raison d'être* of the agreement from the licensor's perspective. A challenge to the know-how's identification may only be a challenge as to the scope of the licence e.g. who is responsible for an improvement—licensee claims he developed the improve and points to the fact that it is not covered in the written (identified) specifications of the know-how.

(16) Termination on challenge to necessity

13.87 The licensor may also reserve the right under Article 2(1)(16) to terminate the licence agreement if a licencee raises the claim that a patent is not necessary and thereby seeks to evade territorial restrictions imposed for the duration of such necessary patents (see paras 13.20–13.24). There is no explanation of the phrase "raises the claim". Plainly, issuing

[93] See also the English licensee estoppel rule: Robertson, "Is the licensee estoppel rule still good law? Was it ever?" [1991] EIPR 373.

judicial proceedings amounts to raising a claim. Conversely, questioning the scope of the patent or raising questions only as to its value of conducting research with a view to deciding whether its necessity can be challenged, may fall short of the conduct which may amount to "raising the claim". A written, unequivocal statement that the patent is not necessary would satisfy the requirement.

(17) Best endeavours

13.88 The licensor may not require licensee to use only his technology. However, he may come close to such an obligation by requiring the licensee to use his best endeavours (and, *a fortiori*, reasonable endeavours) to manufacture and market the licensed product,[94] and such an obligation is exempted under Article 2(1)(17).[95] Competition by the licensee may also be inhibited as explained in the next paragraph.

(18) Termination of exclusivity

13.89 If an exclusive licensee does compete with the licensor in respect of R&D, production, use or distribution of competing products, the licensor may terminate that licensee's exclusivity and may cease licensing improvements to it. Competition in these respects may trigger the licensor's right to terminate exclusivity where it occurs, competes on his behalf against the licensor or with undertakings corrected with the licensor (as to which see the definition in Article 10(14)). The Regulation also covers the case where the case where the licensee competes in the prescribed manner with "other undertakings" who presumably are neither the licensor nor undertakings connected with the licensor. This extension might cover the case where the licensee enters into competition with a competitor of the licensor and thereby becomes a potential competitor or the licensor. The licensor may not exploit the technology in (say) Germany. The licensee sets up in Germany in competition with undertakings those selling products which are interchangeable with those of the licensor.

5. Non-permissible Restrictions: Article 3 (Block Clauses)

13.90 Exemption is not given automatically for certain clauses. Incorporation of these clauses gives rise to the need to notify; the "opposition procedure" is *not* available to licences containing such clauses. However, individual exemption granted following notification in the usual manner may be available. It should be noted at this stage that the blacklist comprises a number of clauses whose exemptibility or otherwise depends upon the existence or non-existence of other factors. Such clauses must hence be seen within the context of previous case law on the subject.

(1) Prices and discounts

13.91 No exemption lies under Article 3(1) where, "one party is restricted in the determination of prices components of prices or discounts for the licensed products". The restric-

[94] For example, it has been held in the High Court that an implied term in a contract to use best endeavours in the context of that contract need not be inconsistent with a company being at liberty to promote competing products provided it treated the other at least as well as it treated its competitors: *Ault & Wiborg Paints* v *Sure Service* The times, 2 July 1983. But see Stephen J in the High Court of Australia, *Transfield Pty Ltd* v *Arlo International* [1981] RPC 141, 150 where an express term requiring licensee's use of best endeavours to sell the licensed product was held to mean that competing products could not be sold if that would prejudice sales of the licensed product. And note the dictum of Lawrence J in *Sheffield District Rly Co* v *Great Central Rly Co* (1911) 27 TLR 451, 452: "We think 'best endeavours' means what the words say; they do not mean second-best endeavours."

[95] But see the Commission's powers to withdraw the benefit of the block exemption in cases of *de facto* exclusivity under Art. 7(4), considered at para. 13.117 below.

tion is usually imposed upon the licensee in the form of a fixed sale price but a restriction on the licensor would equally be caught. Such a clause always restricts competition and is unlikely to receive individual exemption.

(2) Non-competition clauses

13.92 Article 3(2) provides that no exemption lies where "one party is restricted from competing with the other party, with undertakings connected with the other party or with other undertakings in respect of research and development, production, use or distribution of competing products without prejudice to the provisions of Articles 2(1)(17) and (18) (see paras 13.88-13.89). No restrictions on competition may be imposed on either party after the termination of the agreement.[96]

(3) Creation of obstacles to parallel imports

13.93 According to Article 3(3) no exemption lies where,

> "one or both of the parties are required without any objectively justified reason:
> (a) to refuse to meet orders from users or resellers in their respective territories who would market products in other territories within the Common Market;
> (b) to make it difficult for users or resellers to obtain the products from other resellers within the Common Market, and in particular to exercise intellectual property rights or take measures so as to prevent users or resellers from obtaining outside or from putting on the market in the licensed territory products which have been lawfully put on the market within the Common Market by the licensor or with his consent;
> or do so as a result of a concerted practice between them."

These provisions act as a counterweight to Article 1(1)(4)–(6) which permits licensors to limit the extent to which licensees compete with each other. Thus, irrespective of Article 1 the licensees must be free to supply customers in their own territories who are intending to parallel import the goods into the territory of another licensee. Thus licensees may not be prohibited from supplying exporters. Likewise attempts by either party to bring actions for infringement of the patent or of other proprietary rights licensed as ancillary to the main patent (e.g. trade marks), will render the agreement not automatically exempt. The Commission has reinforced its objections to attempts to prevent parallel imports by repeating the wording of Article 3(3) in Article 7(3). This provision allows the Commission to withdraw an exemption that would otherwise exist where the parties seek to hinder parallel imports.

(4) Restrictions on supplying end users

13.94 Article 3(4) denies exemption where before the grant of the licence the parties were already competing manufacturers, and after the grant of the licence one of them is restricted, within the same technical field of use or within the same product market, as to the customers he may serve. The article does not state whether the relationship between licensor and licensee *before* the agreement must be one of *actual* competition or whether *potential* competition suffices. The tenor of the article suggests actual competition only. This article covers, in particular, restrictions on supplying certain classes of user, employing certain forms of distribution of, with the aim of sharing customers, using certain types of packaging for products. This is stated to be without prejudice to articles 1(1)(7) and 2(1)(13) (see paras 13.60 and 13.84 above).

[96] Case 320/87 *Ottung* v *Klee* [1989] ECR 1177 [1990] 4 CMLR 915, para. 18.

13.95 Restrictions of the type referred to in this Article would in any event be block exempt, as they would go further than what is permitted under Article 2(1)(8). The purpose of this provision is somewhat obscure, and paragraph 23 of the preamble sheds little light upon it. Its main practical effect is to deny the possibility of block exemption through the opposition procedure for such restrictions accepted by competing manufacturers (see para. 13.101), whereas such restrictions between non-competition might obtain exemption in that way.

(5) Limitations on quantity or number of operations

13.96 Article 3(5) provides that no exemption exists where "the quantity of licensed products one party may manufacture or sell or the number of operations exploiting the licensed technology he may carry out are subject to limitations save as provided in Article 1(1)(8) and Article 2(1)(13)." Whereas the licensor may impose minimum requirements on the licensee maximum requirements may not be imposed; see paras 13.61 and 13.84 for details. Limitations on production may have the same effect as an export ban and are accordingly equally unacceptable.

(6) Assignment back of improvement patents

13.97 No exemption lies under Article 3(6) where, "the licensee is obliged to assign whole or in part to the licensor rights to improvements to or new applications of the licensed technology". Clauses providing for compulsory assign-back are viewed by the Commission as potential evidence of exploitation by the licensor of unequal bargaining power i.e. the licensee accepts such restrictions reluctantly in order to secure the licence.

(7) Prohibitions on licensing

13.98 No exemption lies under Article 3(7) where the licensor is required for periods going beyond those exempted in Articles 1(2) and (3) not to license other undertakings to exploit the licensed technology in the licensed territory. Similarly, no exemption is granted where any party is restricted beyond the periods exempted in Articles 1(2), (3) and (4) from exploiting the licensed technology in the territory of another party or of other licensees. This provision merely buttresses the provisions of Articles 1(2), (3) and (4), discussed in paras. 13.19–13.24 above.

(8) Automatic extension of the agreement

13.99 Article 8(3) provides that exemption applies to licences whose initial duration is automatically prolonged by the inclusion of any new improvements, whether potential or not, communicated by the licensor, provided that the licensee has the right to refuse such improvements or each party has the right to terminate the agreement at the expiry of the initial term of an agreement and at least every three years thereafter.

13.100 Although this provision appears, somewhat oddly, in Article 8 rather than in the black-list , it must be complied with in order to have the benefit of the block exemption.

6. Extension of Exemption to Licences not Expressly Covered: The "Opposition Procedure" Article 4

13.101 Article 4(1) extends the exemption to agreements whose clauses are not expressly covered by Articles 1 and 2 (the white clauses) but which contain no clauses prohibited by Article 3 (black clauses). Agreements of this nature may be notified to the Commission in accordance with the "opposition procedure" outlined in Article 4 and thereby may receive accelerated treatment. In essence, exemption automatically extends to the agreement if no opposition to it has been raised within a four-month period commencing from the date of notification. Details of the "opposition procedure" are given at paras. 7.167–7.173.

13.102 Two specific situations are specified in the block exemption for the possible application of the opposition procedure. The first is where the licensee is obliged at the time the agreement is entered into to accept quality specifications or further licences or to procure goods or services not necessary for a technically satisfactory exploitation of the licensed technology or for ensuring that the production of the licensee conforms to the licensor's and other licensees' quality standards.[97]

13.103 It is difficult to speculate as to what justifications might be sufficient to ensure exemption is granted by the Commission, as hitherto the Commission has regarded tying-in as strictly blacklisted. It is suggested that where such provisions are included as an alternative to charging royalties, where royalty calculation is otherwise difficult to monitor, then (in the absence of any foreclosing effect of the tying-in) the Commission ought to grant exemption.

13.104 The second situation mentioned in the block exemption as a possible candidate for exemption under the opposition procedure is where the licensee is prohibited from contesting the secrecy or substantiality of the licensed know-how or the validity of a licensed patent.[98]

13.105 Similarly, in respect of such no-challenge clauses, there is a problem in determining the Commission's likely attitude. It is suggested that one likely justification for a no-challenge clause would be where an economically weak licensor enters into a licence agreement with a correspondingly powerful licensee. In such circumstance, a licensor might be deterred from licensing by the risk of having to prove its ownership of its technology through expensive infringement proceedings.

7. *Types of Licence not Exempt: Article 5*

13.106 The Regulation is not all embracing. It expressly excludes from its application certain categories of agreement. Agreements with Article 5 thus cannot benefit from the opposition procedure.

(1) Patent pools

13.107 The Regulation does not apply, "to agreements between members of a patent or know-how pool which relate to the pooled technologies" under Article 5(1)(1). To this Article 5(2)(2) provides an exception for pooling agreements where the parties are not subject to any territorial restriction with regard to the use of the pooled technologies. Such pools are regarded as promoting the dissemination of technology. Otherwise the Commission is generally unsympathetic to patent pooling where the patentees hold significant market power and objects that, first, pooling eliminates competition between the parties as regards technical innovation, and secondly, by concentrating a substantial "package" of know-how in the parties hand's pooling encourages purchasers to deal with the pool to the exclusion of other suppliers. The pool hence creates entry and expansion barriers.[99] Likewise, an agreement between undertakings jointly to purchase and exploit certain patents which are essential to the operation of a certain market restricts competition where the resultant pool excludes from the relevant market firms not belonging to the group. Such pools may be acceptable where they are willing to grant licences free of restriction and

97 Art. 4(2)(a), Reg. 240/96.
98 Art. 4(2)(b), Reg. 240/96.
99 *Concast–Mannesmann, Eleventh Report on Competition Policy* (1981), p. 62, para. 93.

on reasonable terms to all other manufacturers in the Community.[100] A pool that requires members to surrender their rights upon leaving but which allows remaining members to retain the rights they have enjoyed in respect of the departing members' patents infringes Article 85(1) EC. Such a pool deters exit from it and hence hinders the freedom of firms to develop technology without having to share it with competitors.[101]

(2) Licences in the context of a joint venture

13.108 Although it is stated in Article 5(1)(2) that the block exemption does not apply "to licensing agreements between competing undertakings who hold interests in a joint venture or between one of them and the joint venture, if the licensing agreements relate to the activities of the joint venture", it is stated in Article 5(2)(1) that in such cases block exemption is available to such agreements

> "under which a parent undertaking grants the joint venture a patent or a know-how licence, provided that the licensed products and the other goods and services of the participating undertakings which are considered by users to be interchangeable or substitutable in view of their characteristics, price and intended use represent:
> – in case of a licence limited to production not more than 20%
> – in case of a licence covering production and distribution not more than 10% of the market for the licensed products and all interchangeable or substitutable goods and services."

13.109 The benefit of the block exemption is not lost either of these market share limits is exceeded by up to one-tenth for up to two consecutive financial years, and if this limit is breached, then the block exemption continues for six months beyond the end of the year in which it was breached (Article 5(3)).

(3) Reciprocal licences

13.110 The Regulation does not apply under Article 5(1)(3) to "agreements under which one party grants the other a patent and/or know-how licence and in exchange the other party, albeit in separate agreements or through connected undertakings, grants the first party a patent trade mark or know-how licence of exclusive sales rights, where the parties are competitors in relation to the products covered by those agreements." It should be noted that no exemption ties even in respect of a non-exclusive reciprocal licence. The sales right must, however, be exclusive for the Regulation to be inapplicable.

13.111 The Regulation does not thus extend to reciprocal licensing between competitors. The Regulation certainly precludes reciprocal licences between actual competitors. Since competition is generally assumed to include its potential form then, originally, a reciprocal licence between potential rivals is precluded from block exemption. Reciprocal licensing between non-competitors would appear to be exempt. In deciding whether reciprocal licences exist the Commission will not examine the form of the licences; rather it examines the overall effect. Thus if L1 and L2 exchange licences using two separate licensing agreements the Commission may view the agreements conjunctively as a single scheme, not disjunctively as two separate licences which may each be exempted. Under Article 5(2)(2) however block exemption *does* apply to reciprocal licences where the parties are not subject to any territorial restraint within the EC on the manufacture, use or putting on the market of the products covered by the agreement or on the use of the licensed processes.

[100] *IGR Stereo Television, Eleventh Report on Competition Policy* (1981), pp. 63, 64, para. 94.
[101] *Video Cassette Recorders* [1978] 2 CMLR 160.

(4) Sham agreements

13.112 Articles 5(4) and (5) confirms that the block exemption cannot be used for either licensing agreements containing provisions relating to intellectual property rights (other than patents) which are not ancillary[102] and to agreements entered into solely for the purpose of sale.[103] Recital 8 makes it clear that the purpose of the block exemption is to "facilitate the dissemination of technology and the improvement of manufacturing processes". For this reason the exemption applies only to know-how (as defined) and patents which are necessary. Other forms of agreements involving IP rights do not necessarily serve these stated ends and do not therefore warrant *automatic* exemption

8. Withdrawal of Exemption: Article 7

13.113 The Commission may, in exceptional cases, withdraw the block exemption from a particular case by formal decision where it considers that an agreement has effects that are incompatible with Article 85(3) or 86 EC. The following are examples of cases where exemption might be withdrawn; the enumeration is not exhaustive.

(1) Inter-brand competition ineffective

13.114 Exemption may be withdrawn under Article 7(1) where, "the effect of the agreement is to prevent the licensed products being exposed to effective competition in the licensed territory from identical goods or services or from goods or services considered by users as interchangeable or substitutable in view of their characteristics, price and intended use". This is stated as being particularly likely to occur "where the licensee's market share exceeds 40%".[104] The Commission considers as significant, in assessing a licence, the extent to which the parties are subject to competition from competing brands or substitutes. Where such competition is effective, it will act as a pressure on the licensor and licensee to behave competitively; strong inter-brand competition is hence a form of guarantee for the consumer. It does not follow that exemption will be withdrawn in every case where inter-brand competition is weak. X might invent and patent a revolutionary new product which has no substitutes which he licenses to Y. Simply because X is innovative and efficient is no reason to deny him exemption. If X abused his market power, then the abuse in conjunction with the lack of inter-brand rivalry might warrant withdrawal of exemption. Such a case might be suitable for review under Article 86 EC as well. In *Tetra Pak (No. 1)*[105] acquisition by a dominant undertaking of a company holding the benefit of an exclusive patent licence, which was within the terms of the block exemption, was regarded by the Commission as an abuse of that dominant position contrary to Article 86, since it prevented potential competitors from gaining access to new technology which would have exposed the dominant undertaking to actual competition.[106] The Commission intimated that it would use its powers of withdrawal whereupon the dominant undertaking renounced exclusivity to terminate the abuse. Subsequent proceedings before the Court of First Instance confirmed that Article 86 can apply to behaviour notwithstanding that it relates to agreements sanctioned under Article 85(3) or a block exemption.[107]

[102] Such licensing agreements must be assessed under the general principles relevant to such agreements and considered in this chapter.

[103] Such agreements may take advantage of the block exemption for exclusive distribution, 1983/83/EEC, or exclusive purchasing, 1984/83/EEC: see Chapter 10.

[104] The Commission's draft of the block exemption had included several other market share tests, all of which were ultimately dropped, see OJ 1994 C178/3.

[105] *Elopak* v *Tetra Pak* [1990] 4 CMLR 47.

[106] *ibid.*, at p. 71, para. 45.

[107] Case T-51/89 *Tetra Pak* v *Commission* [1990] ECR II-309 [1991] 4 CMLR 334.

(2) Refusal by the licensee to meet unsolicited demands (passive competition)

13.115 Exemption may be withdrawn where, "without prejudice to Article 1 (1)(6), the licensee refuses, without any objectively justified reason, to meet unsolicited orders from users or resellers in the territory of other licensees". Article 1(1)(6) makes it clear that licensees *may* refuse to meet unsolicited demands from outside of their territory for a limited period of five years from first marketing by any licensee within the EC. In circumstances other than Article 1(1)(6) (e.g. after the five-year period has elapsed) it will be rare for a refusal to be objectively justified. The Commission does not accept that the "free-rider" problem is a proper justification for refusal to supply. This problem is discussed at paras. 10.117–10.120 on distribution in connection with Regulation 1983/83/EEC. Essentially, licensees may contend that they need protection from parallel importers who sell at prices lower than those of the authorised licensee. Such parallel importers can afford to charge low prices because they need not provide comprehensive promotion and pre-sales services such as are provided by the licensee. Indeed, so the argument runs, parallel importers rely upon customers being able to exploit the licensee's services (displays, testing facilities, advice of sales staff, etc.) but make the actual purchase from the parallel importer. Thus, the parallel importer "free rides" on the sales services provided by the licensee. Ultimately, the licensee may have to reduce the sales services he provides in order to bring his prices into line with those of the parallel importer thereby threatening the licensor's reputation which may be present in the form of a trade mark or other designation on the product. The Commission, while accepting that free-riding is a problem, does not consider that it is so prevalent as to justify measures to prevent parallel imports which are perceived as healthy forms of competition.

(3) Parties create obstacles to parallel imports

13.116 Exemption may be withdrawn where one or both of the parties seeks to create obstacles to parallel imports. The wording of Article 7(5) which is to this effect the same, *mutatis mutandis*, as Article 3(3) is discussed above at para. 13.93. Reference may be made thereto for analysis. Under Article 3(3), any agreement which seeks to hinder parallel imports is automatically outside the scope of the block-exemption. Therefore Article 7(3) is really only of importance where there is no agreement to hinder imports, but where one party acts unilaterally to do so.

(4) *De facto* non-compete

13.117 Exemption may be withdrawn under Article 7(4) in circumstances where the parties were competing manufacturers at the date of the grant of the licence and obligations on the licensee to product a minimum quantity, exempted under Article 2(1)(9) (see para. 13.79) or to use his best endeavours under Article 2(1)(17) (see para. 13.88) have the effect of preventing the licensee from using competing technologies. This stresses that *de facto* exclusivity may be a reason for the Commission's intervention, if the parties were originally competitors. A minimum quantity obligation, by forcing the licensees to concentrate the entirety of its efforts on the licensed technology, and on best endeavours obligation drafted so as to be breached where the licensee does otherwise than concentrate wholly on the licensed technology are tantamount to *de facto* exclusivity.

9. Meaning of "Connected Undertakings": Articles 6(3) and 10(14)

13.118 Article 6(3) states that the Regulation shall apply to licensing agreements in which rights or obligations of the licensor or the licensee are assumed by undertakings connected with them. Article 10(14) defines a "connected undertaking". The definition is exactly the same as that used in the block-exemption on exclusive dealing Regulation 1983/83/EEC. This is discussed at paras. 10.73–10.76 to which reference may be made. In essence a connected undertaking is one in which a party to the agreement directly or indirectly exercises effective control (i.e. *de jure* or *de facto* control). Furthermore, it includes parents and subsidiaries of such connected undertakings.

10. Transitional Periods and Duration of Block Exemption: Articles 11 and 13

13.119 Articles 6–8 cover agreements already in force at the time the Regulation.

(1) Transitional periods

13.120 Agreements exempted under the earlier patent and know-how licensing block exemptions continue to have the benefit of these block exemptions after the entry into force of the technology transfer block exemption.[108] The patent licensing block exemption, having expired at the end of 1995,[109] was extended for a further three months,[110] to 31 March 1995.[111] The know-how licensing block exemption was repealed with affect from 1 April 1996.[112] Agreements coming into force from 1 April 1996 are therefore subject to the technology transfer block exemption.

(2) Duration of the Regulation

13.121 The Regulation became operative on 1 April 1996 and continues until 31 March 2006.

11. Confidentiality on the Part of the Commission: Article 9

13.122 Information received by the Commission under the opposition procedure may only be used for the purposes of the Regulation, i.e. deciding whether exemption lies or not. The Commission and national authorities (who are involved in the opposition procedure) are prohibited from disclosing information acquired by them under the Regulation of the kind covered by the duty to maintain professional secrecy. The obligation to protect professional secrecy is a generally accepted principle of community law which is given concrete expression by Article 214 EC which applies the obligation to details of companies business relations and their cost components. Unauthorised disclosure by the Commission could render the latter subject to a claim for damages before the European Court under Article 215(2) EC (liability of the Community for non-contractual liability).[113] It is most unlikely that authorities in the Member States could be liable under Article 215 EC unless they were viewed as agents of the Commission, but see para. 13.221.

13.123 It should be appreciated, as a proviso to the above, that the authorities are not prevented from publishing general information or surveys which make use of such information but which do *not* contain information relating to particular undertakings or associations of undertakings, i.e. the authorities may use the data collected in a general way.

[108] Art. 11(3), Reg. 240/96.

[109] It was originally due to expire at the end of 1994, Art. 14, but was twice extended until the end of 1995, due to the failure of the Commission to agree the terms of the technology transfer block exemption: see Reg. 70/95 OJ 1995 L12/13 and Reg. 2131/95, OJ 1995 L214/6.

[110] One month retrospectively.

[111] Art. 11(2), Reg. 240/96.

[112] Art. 11(1), Reg. 240/96.

[113] Art. 215(2) EC reads: "In the case of non-contractual liability, the Community shall, in accordance with the general principles common to the laws of the Member States, make good any damage caused by its institutions or by its servants in the performance of their duties."

12. Check List for Determining whether the Technology Transfer Block Exemption Applies

13.124 The check list below is an overview only: it is *not* a substitute for proper analysis of the text of the Regulation itself.

Condition 1 (rights licensed)

If other intellectual property rights are being licensed as well as patents and know-how, are those rights more than ancillary to the patents or know-how? If the answer to this question is yes, then the block exemption does not apply and reference should be made to the relevant parts of this chapter dealing with the licensing of such rights.

Condition 2 (agreements exempt)

Agreement must be of a type described in Article 1 of the Regulation. Account should be taken of Articles 6(1) and (2) which extend exemption to agreements that are effectively the same as the licence described in Article 1. The Regulation covers agreements involving undertakings "connected" to the parties to the licence (Article 6(3)). The Regulation may *not* apply to: patent pools; licences derived from some joint ventures; and reciprocal licences (Article 5).

Condition 3 (white clauses)

The agreement may legitimately contain clauses listed in Article 1. These are, in summary, clauses: granting exclusivity to the licensee; obliging the licensor not to compete with the licensee; protecting licensees from competition from each other; obliging the licensee to use the licensor's trade mark.

Condition 4 (white clauses)

Agreements containing clauses listed in Article 2 cause no problem. These clauses do not generally restrict competition, but where they do Article 2 extends the exemption to them. The permissible clauses may concern the following:

(i) non-disclosure of know-how;
(ii) prohibition on assignment or sub-licensing;
(iii) post-term use ban;
(iv) licensing back;
(v) minimum quantity specifications;
(vi) tying-in if necessary for technically proper exploitation;
(vii) tying-in if necessary for minimum quality specifications;
(viii) assistance in legal proceedings;
(ix) royalty calculation;
(x) restriction on exploitation to a technical field of application;
(xi) restriction on exploitation to a product market;
(xii) minimum royalty payment;
(xiii) minimum performance;
(xiv) most favoured licensee;
(xv) marking product with licensor's name or patent;
(xvi) non-use for construction of facilities for third parties;
(xvii) secured source of supply only;

(xviii) licensor's reservation of rights outside territory;
(ixx) termination in event of challenge to validity;
(xx) best endeavours; and
(xxi) termination of exclusivity.

Condition 5 (black clauses)

Under no circumstances can block-exemption be claimed for licences containing clauses outlined in Article 3. The "black" unacceptable clauses concern the following:

(i) excessive non-competition clauses;
(ii) royalty payments in respect of unprotected rights;
(iii) limitations on quantity or number of operations;
(iv) prices and discounts;
(v) customer restrictions
(vi) assignment back of improvement patents;
(vii) prohibitions on passive sales; and
(viii) creation of obstacles to parallel imports.

Condition 6 (extension of exemption by opposition procedure)

Agreements of a type generally caught by the Regulation (Condition 2 above) which contain clauses which are not expressly permitted by Articles 1 and 2 but which, conversely, are not expressly prohibited by Article 3 may obtain automatic exemption by use of the opposition procedure in Article 4, in particular no-challenge and tying clauses.

Condition 7 (withdrawal of exemption)

In exceptional cases the Commission might, by formal decision, withdraw exemption from an agreement. The Commission might issue such decisions in the following cases, among others:

(i) where inter-brand competition is ineffective;
(ii) where licensee refuses to meet unsolicited demands; and
(iii) where parties create obstacles to parallel imports.

E. The Block Exemption for Patent Licensing: Regulation 2349/84

13.125 As explained above the technology transfer block exemption confirms the continued applicability of the earlier patent and know-how block exemptions which thus remain of considerable importance. Regulation 2349/84/EEC[114] lays down criteria which if met enable a patent licence to claim automatic exemption from the prohibition in Article 85(1) under Article 85(3). It now applies to agreements which were in force prior to 1 April 1996. Patent licensing agreements coming into force on or after 1 April 1996 are governed by the technology transfer block exemption.

[114] OJ 1984 L219/15, as amended by Reg. 151/93, OJ 1993 L21/8. The amended text is printed at [1993] 4 CMLR 177.

1. The Basic Exemption: Article 1

(1) Scope

13.126 Article 1 exempts patent licensing agreements, whether combined with know-how licences or not, to which only two undertakings are party. Patent licensing agreements are defined widely as: "agreements whereby one undertaking, the holder of a patent (the licensor), permits another undertaking (the licensee) to exploit the patented invention by one or more means of exploitation afforded by patent law, in particular manufacture, use or putting on the market."[115] A patent licence need not necessarily be confined to these three activities. The Regulation mainly concerns the licensing of, and application for, patents which includes licenses issued in respect of national patents of the Member States, Community patents,[116] and European patents granted for Member States.[117] However, the regulation extends beyond patents and includes further: utility models; applications for registration of utility models; *certificats d'utilité* and *certificats d'addition* under French law; and applications for *certificats d'utilité* and *certificats d'addition* under French law. Additionally, the exemption applies to agreements for the exploitation of an invention if an application is made in respect of the invention for the licensed territory within one year from the date when the agreement was entered into.[118] Two questions arise in respect of the definition above of a patent licence. First, what does "putting on the market" mean? It certainly includes sales and presumably also includes hiring out, swapping, giving, leasing, etc. It probably does not extend to the disposal on the market for market research purposes since the notion of putting on the market is generally assumed to connote placement in commercial quantities. Secondly, what does "afforded by patent law" mean? There being no Community law on patents, it must imply national law. Thus the notion of exploitation may be left to be determined by domestic laws.

13.127 The Regulation covers agreements between a patentee and a licensee. It also covers agreements between a licensee and a sub-licensee. Further, agreements for the assignment or acquisition of rights where the risks associated with exploitation are borne by the assignor are covered. Thus, agreements whereby the assignor earns a royalty dependent upon the turnover of patented products attained by the assignee, or the quantity of such products manufactured, or the number of operations carried out employing the patented invention, are all exempt. Also covered are agreements in which rights or obligations are assumed by undertakings connected with the parties.[119] Thus, an assignment of the licensee's rights to a wholly owned subsidiary of the licensee is perfectly acceptable.[120]

13.128 With regard to the geographical scope of an agreement, exemption applies to a licence which contains obligations relating not only to territories within the Common Market but also to non-Member States.[121] However, agreements for territories other than the EC which have *effects* within the Common Market are subject to the Regulation.[122] Thus, an agreement between X (a British firm) and Y (a Czech firm) whereby Y is licensed to manufacture and sell products resulting from X's patent may be subject to EC law if X imposes on Y an obligation to refrain absolutely from supplying customers situ-

[115] Recital 2.

[116] See the Community Patent Convention of 15 December 1975, OJ 1976 L17/1.

[117] Munich Convention on the grant of European Patents of 5 October 1973.

[118] Recital 4 and Art. 10.

[119] Recital 6 and Art. 11.

[120] See definition of "connected undertakings" in Art. 12.

[121] Though where the licence affects a non-EC state, there may be no effect on inter-State trade and hence no cause for Art. 85 to apply: see *Raymond-Nagoya* [1972] CMLR D45.

[122] Recitals 4 and 5.

ate outside the Czech Republic with the patent product. If customers and users in the EC have difficulty in obtaining the patent product in the EC and are prevented from acquiring it from the Czech licensee, then the EC market has been affected.

13.129 The exemption does not apply to agreements concerning sales alone. Such agreements, if exempt, fall within Regulation 1983/83/EEC on block exemption for exclusive distribution.[123] Thus if X (patentee) licenses Y to distribute, on an exclusive basis, the product X has manufactured within a given area, the agreement must satisfy Regulation 1983/83 and not Regulation 2349/84.

13.130 As noted above, the Regulation exempts only bilateral agreements. Though where a number of legal persons form a single economic unit they may enter a licence as one party.[124] In addition the Regulation does *not* cover: patent pools; reciprocal licensing whereby X licenses Y his patents and Y licenses X his patents;[125] reciprocal distribution agreements whereby X makes Y exclusive dealer for his patented products and Y makes X the exclusive dealer of his patented products. The block exemption was amended to enable it to be applicable to some joint ventures,[126] and details are given on the section on joint ventures below. Furthermore, the Commission refrained from extending the Regulation to licensing agreements in respect of plant-breeders' rights.[127]

(2) Relationship with know-how and trade marks

13.131 Patent licences often include provisions concerning know-how and trade marks. Such mixed agreements allow the effective transfer of complex technology containing both patented and non patented elements. Agreements of this nature are covered by the Regulation in defined circumstances. As regards know-how, exemption applies where the technical knowledge is secret and helps the licensee to exploit more effectively the patent. Provisions in the patent licence concerning the communication of know-how are exempt only in so far as the licensed patents are necessary for achieving the objects of the licensed technology and as long as at least one of the licensed patents remains in force.[128] However, mixed agreements not exempted under the patent block exemption may be exempt under the know-how block exemption. The know-how block exemption applies where the licensed patents are not necessary for the achievement of the object of the licensed technology containing both patented and non-patented elements, or where regardless of whether the licensed patents are so necessary, the agreement extends to territories where there is no patent protection and accordingly no exemption under the patent block exemption.

13.132 Where patent licences contain ancillary provisions relating to trade marks, exemption applies with the proviso that the trade mark licence must not be used to extend the effects of the patent licence beyond the life of the patents. These ancillary licences enable the patent licensee to identify himself within the contract territory as the manufacturer of the licensed product. This avoids the difficulty of the licensee having to enter a new trade mark licence with the licensor when the licensed patents expire in order not to lose the goodwill attaching to the licensed product.[129]

[123] See paras. 10.11–10.92.
[124] Case 170/83 *Hydrotherm* v *Andreoli* [1984] ECR 2999, [1985] 3 CMLR 224.
[125] Though reciprocal agreements which do not involve any territorial restrictions within the EC are within the block exemption: Recital 8 and Art. 5(2)(3).
[126] By Reg. 151/93, OJ 1993 L21/8.
[127] Although the Commission applied the same principles: Roses, *Fifteenth Report on Competition Policy* (1985), para. 80. Breeders' rights *are* now covered under the technology transfer block exemption.
[128] Recital 9. See *Boussois/Interpane* [1988] 4 CMLR 124.
[129] Recital 10 and Art. 1(1)(7).

2. *Permissible Restrictions: Article 1 (White Clauses)*

13.133 Article 1 enumerates restrictions which may be incorporated safely into patent licences without endangering the exemption. These "white clauses" are examined below. A clause of more limited scope than that specified below is, according to Article 1(3), stated to be exempt with the clause specified. If the clause in question goes beyond that noted below it is not exempt. Articles 1(1)(1)–(6) all grant exemption "in so far" as and "as long as" the patents remain in force. These words hence qualify the exemption. It is not clear why the Commission has used two phrases and whether they mean the same thing. It is believed that the phrases mean that where A licenses a number of patents to B, A may enter the licensees market on expiry of a single patent only in respect of the product subject to the expired patent. Exclusivity remains for the other patents.

(1) Exclusive territories (Article 1(1)(1), (2))

13.134 Article 1 (1)(1) permits: "an obligation on the licensor not to license other undertakings to exploit the licensed invention in the licensed territory, covering all or part of the Common Market, in so far and so long as one of the licensed patents remains in force". Article 1(1)(2) permits: "an obligation on the licensor not to exploit the licensed invention in the licensed territory himself in so far and as long as one of the licensed patents remains in force". Thus the licensor can grant the licensee an exclusive territory and covenant not to compete with the licensee in that territory.[130]

13.135 Paragraph 11 of the preamble explains the Commission's policy on exclusivity clauses. Such clauses are not necessarily incompatible with competition rules where they are concerned with the introduction of a new technology in the licensed territory by reason of the scale of the research which has been undertaken and of the risk that is involved in manufacturing and marketing a product which is unfamiliar to users in the licensed territory at the time the agreement is made. This may also be the case where the agreements are concerned with the introduction and protection of a new process for manufacturing a product which is already known. The Commission continues to indicate that clauses satisfying these criteria may not even fall within Article 85(1). This is, in reality, an affirmation of the judgment of the Court of Justice in *Maize Seed*.[131] To the extent that an exclusivity clause does not satisfy these economic criteria, for example where the product is not "new", it will now be exempt, none the less, under Article 1. The exemption applies irrespective of the size of the undertakings in question.

13.136 According to Article 1(2) the exemption in Article 1(1)(2) applies only where the licensee manufactures the licensed product himself or has it manufactured by a connected undertaking or by a sub-contractor. The exclusivity allowed under this provision may be very effective in the case of bulky, low value goods whose characteristics do not encourage parallel imports; however, such exclusivity may not be so valuable where the goods are small, light and high value. See Articles 1, 1(4)–(6) below.

13.137 For extension of the exclusivity and the concomitant cushioning of the licensee from the licensor by the addition of new patents to the agreement see the commentary on Article 3(2) below.

(2) Non-competition clauses (Article 1(1)(3))

13.138 Article 1(1)(2) permits the licensor to covenant not to compete with the licensee in the latter's territory. Article 1(1)(3) permits: "an obligation on the licensee not to exploit

[130] After expiry of the patent, such exclusivity would infringe Art. 85(1): *Velcro/Aplix* OJ 1985 L 233/22.
[131] Case 258/78 *Nungesser v Commission (Maize Seed)* [1982] ECR 2015, [1983] CMLR 278, para. 58.

the licensed invention in territories within the Common Market which are reserved for the licensor, in so far and as long as the patented product is protected in those territories by parallel means". The Commission explains, in paragraph 12 of the preamble, that these clauses are economically desirable in that they focus the efforts of the parties on certain areas and afford the parties a degree of security "they make patentees more willing to grant licences and licensees more inclined to undertake the investment required to manufacture, use and put on the market a new product or to use a new process, so that undertakings other than the patentee acquire the possibility of manufacturing their products with the aid of the latest techniques and of developing these techniques further. The result is that the number of production facilities and the quantities and quality of goods purchased in the Common Market are increased." The non-competition clause may only be included in the licence in so far as it relates to territories in which the licensor has patent protection and has not granted any licences. Where several patents have been licensed the clause is operative so long as one of the licensed patents remains in force, but not beyond.

13.139 Under Article 1(2), Article 1(1)(3) only applies where the licensee manufactures the licensed product himself or has it manufactured for him by a connected undertaking or sub-contractor.

(3) Protection for licensees against each other (Article 1(1) (4), (5) and (6))

13.140 The Commission recognises that licensees require a degree of protection from each other. Licensees protected from competition, *inter se*, may focus their efforts in a more intensive manner thereby maximising the chances of effective exploitation and utilisation of the patent. However, the Commission and the European Courts have refused to countenance absolute territorial protection whereby licensees are protected from *all* competition, in particular from parallel importers.

13.141 The Regulation hence lays down strict rules for exclusivity and protection of licensees from each other. At the extreme under Article 1(1)(6) the licensor may grant licensees protection from any competition from other licensees for up to five years from the time the product is first "put on the market" within the EC. Protection in this sense means protection from "active" *and* "passive" competition. "Active" competition occurs where a licensee in one territory markets the goods in the territories of other licensees; undertakes specific advertising aimed at those territories; or establishes any branch or maintains any distribution depot in those territories. "Passive" competition occurs where a licensee simply responds to unsolicited requests from users or resellers established in other territories. Article 1(1)(6) does not, however, allow the licensor to prohibit the licensee from supplying any customer in his own territory who intends to export the goods for resale to another licensee's territory, i.e. a parallel importer.

13.142 Article 1(1)(4) exempts obligations on the licensee not to manufacture or use the licensed product, or use the patented process or the communicated know-how in licensed territories other than his own. This obligation is exempt in so far, and as long, as the licensed product is protected in those territories by parallel patents. This obligation does not, however, prevent one licensee manufacturing in his own territory and selling the licensed product over the border in another licensee's territory. The Commission adopts a more liberal view of restraints on *manufacture* than they do with restraints on *sale*. Article 1(1)(5) exempts obligations partially preventing sales outside of the territory. The provision allows the licensor to prohibit the licensee from undertaking "active" selling (as defined above) outside of his territory. The obligations in Article 1(1)(4) and (5) do not prevent competition from parallel importers: X who is situate in the UK which is served by L1 travels to France which is served by L2. X purchases the licensed product from L2 and takes it back to the UK for sale there in competition with L1. It may well be that L2 is considerably cheaper or produces better quality goods or provides better terms and conditions than L1 so that it is commercially viable for X to purchase in France for export to the UK. Clauses exempt under Articles 1(1)(4) and (5) are valid for the duration of the agreement.

13.143 If a licensor wishes to protect licenses further and prohibit even passive sales it may do so under Article 1(1)(6) noted above but only for a period of five years from the date when the product is first "put on the market" by either the licensor or licensee. The phrase "put on the market" is not defined. Paragraph 2 of the Preamble defines "exploitation" in wider terms as including manufacture, use or putting on the market. This latter concept may presumably be construed to mean first commercial marketing, it would probably exclude experimental sales for market research purposes. At the end of this period licensees must be free to supply the product in the territories of other licensees in response to unsolicited requests from users or resellers (parallel importers) situated in those territories (i.e. "passive" sales). Thus L1 in the UK may refuse to satisfy an unsolicited order from a buyer in Germany for up to five years. Though if the buyer travels to the UK to buy or place his order through an agent or intermediary in the UK, the licensor cannot prevent L1 from supplying the buyer. Article 1(6) thus falls short of absolute territorial protection, though it may give considerable protection in practice where the goods are bulky and of relatively low value, i.e. not easily exportable.

13.144 Under no circumstances can the licensor attempt to *prevent* parallel imports; see Article 3 (1) below.

13.145 According to Article 1(2) exemption in Article 1(1)(5) and (6) (but not Article 1(1)(4)) only applies where the licensee manufactures the licensed product himself or has it manufactured by a connected undertaking or sub-contractor.

(4) Trade marks (Article 1(1)(7))

13.146 This provision exempts, "An obligation on the licensee to use only the licensor's trade mark or the get up determined by the licensor to distinguish the licensed product, provided that the licensee is not prevented from identifying himself as the manufacturer of the licensed product." Article 1(1)(7) does not expressly exempt a pure trade mark licence.[132] The trade mark licence must be ancillary to the patent licence and must not be used to extend the effects of the patent licence beyond the life of the patent or to permit territorial exclusivity. The licensee must not be prevented from identifying himself as the manufacturer of the licensed product.

3. Permissible Clauses not Generally Falling within Article 85(1): Article 2 (White Clauses)

13.147 Article 2 lists typical licence clauses that are generally not considered to fall within Article 85(1). Where such clauses are within Article 85(1) because of particular economic or legal circumstances, they will be automatically exempt under Article 85(3). The list is given by the Commission for purposes of legal certainty but none the less is not exhaustive. Article 2(1) states that Article 1 shall apply notwithstanding the presence of any of the following obligations.

[132] See in the context of the know-how block exemption, *Moosehead/Whitbread* [1991] 4 CMLR 391.

(1) Purchase or procurement obligations

13.148 Article 2(1)(1) permits an obligation on the licensee to procure goods or services from the licensor or from an undertaking designated by the licensor. However, this obligation is *only* exempt in so far as such products or services are necessary for a "technically satisfactory exploitation of the licensed invention." In *Vaessen–Moris*[133] the Commission refused exemption to a patent licence containing a purchase obligation on a licensee of a process and device used in sausage meat manufacture. The obligation was on the licensee also to purchase casings from the patentee. The Commission decided that the clause prohibited the licensee from purchasing casings from other suppliers at more favourable prices. Moreover, the tie-in between patent licence and casings supply was not essential to the proper exploitation of the patent since casings provided by rival suppliers were perfectly adequate for use with the patented process and device. It would appear that the Regulation merely follows earlier Commission policy on tying within patent licences, i.e. that it is justifiable and not restrictive where the tied product or service (e.g. maintenance) is reasonably necessary for satisfactory exploitation of the patent. The tied product or service need not necessarily be essential to the patent; ties are justified in lesser circumstances. No definition is given of "technically satisfactory exploitation" but it is clearly a lesser nexus than necessity.

(2) Minimum royalties, production quantities or number of operations

13.149 Article 2(1)(2) permits an obligation on the licensee to: (a) pay a minimum royalty; (b) produce a minimum quantity of the licensed product; (c) carry out a minimum number of operations exploiting the licensed invention.

(a) Minimum royalties

13.150 The obligation to pay minimum royalties is rarely within Article 85(1) even where the royalties demanded are excessive since Article 85(1) is not appropriate for curing or redressing commercial misjudgments. Though, it will restrict competition where the licensee has to pay royalties on its own unprotected products; such an obligation has no connection with the licensed patent.[134] Where the licensed product is an integral component of a larger product sold by the patentee and the royalty is based upon the sales price of the whole product, then the obligation to pay a royalty on an unprotected product may be legitimate.[135] In more general terms royalties may cause problems in a number of situations which warrant brief mention. Thus differential royalties whereby the licensee pays more if he exports than if he sells domestically may be viewed as attempts by the licensor to discourage exports. Similarly a scale of royalty payments which increases as the licensee's output increases may also be viewed as an attempt by the licensor to limit the licensee to his domestic territory. Conversely sliding scales whereby royalties decrease as output increases are acceptable since they do not deter production and are compatible with "best endeavours" clauses which are frequently inserted in licences.

[133] [1979] 1 CMLR 511. See also *Campari* [1978] 2 CMLR 397.

[134] *AOIP/Beyrard* [1976] 1 CMLR D14. See IGR, *Fourteenth Report on Competition Policy* (1984) at para. 76: a trade association which holds its members patents and charges excessive royalties will infringe Art. 85(1).

[135] In *British Leyland* v *TI Silencers* [1980] 1 CMLR 598, the High Court held that the extension of the obligation to pay royalties for an unprotected product is not an abuse contrary to Art. 86 EC where it was merely a means of calculating royalties on patented rights; see also UARCO, *Fourteenth Report on Competition Policy* (1984) at para. 77.

(b) Minimum quantities

13.151 Obligations of this nature protect the licensor against under-use by the licensee and perhaps against the threat of compulsory licensing. If the latter fails to meet the quantitative requirement he will be liable for breach of contract to the licensor. The clause minimises the risk for the licensor. Article 2(1)(3) only applies to minima not maxima; the Commission view maxima limitations as curbs on productivity which are not exemptible.[136]

(c) Minimum number of operations

13.152 Minimum numbers of operations may be treated in the same way as minimum quantities. The same proviso as to maxima applies.

(3) Field of use restrictions

13.153 Article 2(1)(3) permits an obligation on the licensee to restrict his exploitation of the licensed invention to one or more technical fields covered by the licensed patent. The licensor may thus restrict the licensee's use of the patent to a major or minor field of application. The licensor may thus grant different licences to different licensees limiting their use of the invention to fields in which they are experienced or have greatest production capacity. In some industries (e.g. chemicals, drugs) a single product can have multifarious uses. There is no obligation on a patentee to give licensees carte blanche in their use of the patent. The same principle applies to other intellectual property rights. Such restrictions are economically logical as enabling patentees to license firms in the field of use that the firm is best able to exploit. Article 2(1)(3) is subject to Article 3(7) (a black clause). Unfortunately the divide between the two provisions is unclear so that where white becomes black is unpredictable. This point is examined below in connection with Article 3(7).

(4) Post-expiry of the agreement exploitation

13.154 Article 2(1)(4) permits an obligation to be imposed on the licensee not to exploit the patent after termination of the agreement in so far as the patent is still in force. It will of course be permissible to grant a licence for a period less than the lifetime of the patent. It restrains competition however if the obligations in the agreement extend beyond expiry of the patent. When the right to protection expires, restrictions on the use of that right are likewise no longer protected.[137]

13.155 However, there would appear to be no objection to an obligation on the licensee to pay royalties following expiration of the patent, where the royalties arose for payment in instalments and these have not yet finished. Thus, if X licenses Y a patent for five years but, as a kindness to Y, staggers the payment of royalties over a seven-year period, this should be exempt. Article 2(4) it may be noted speaks only of exploitation of the patent and not payment in respect of exploitation.[138]

13.156 Where the patent licence includes provisions for the licensing of know-how and/or trade marks these, being ancillary to the main grant, must expire with the licence for the patent. If they exceed the licence for the patent the agreement becomes one for the licence of know-how or a trade mark and hence is not exempt.

[136] Art. 3(5).

[137] *Davidson Rubber* [1972] CMLR D53 at para. 18; *Henkel Colgate* OJ 1972 L14/14.

[138] See Art. 3(4) which implies that this is acceptable and see also Art. 3(2) which condones the analogous situation of royalties being paid by a licensee for use of secret know-how even though the related patents have expired. See also UARCO, *Fourteenth Report on Competition Policy* (1984), para. 77.

(5) Prohibition on sub-licensing or assignment

13.157 Article 2(5) permits obligations on the licensee not to grant sub-licences or assign the licence. It follows that a clause laying down conditions under which a licensee may sub-license is also exempt. This is a less restrictive version of the ban on sub-licensing so is included on the "more limited scope" rule (Article 2(2)). This principle applies to all forms of intellectual property, it is the holders right to determine with whom he shares his rights. The prohibition is necessary often as a safeguard for the patentees secret know-how.

(6) Identification of patentee on licensed product

13.158 Article 2(1)(6) permits obligations on the licensee to mark the licensed product with an indication of: (a) the patentee's name; (b) the licensed patent; or (c), the patent licensing agreement. If the patentee does not intend to commence marketing the licensed product himself until after expiry of the licence agreement, then he may wish to have his name or mark associated with the product from first marketing onwards thereby facilitating post-contract marketing.

(7) Non-disclosure of know-how

13.159 Article 2(1)(7) permits obligations on the licensee not to divulge know-how communicated by the licensor. Recital 9 defines know-how somewhat nebulously "communicated technical knowledge [which] is secret and permits a better exploitation of the licensed product". No explanation of the meaning of "better exploitation" is given. The Commission is unlikely to impose a qualitative link such that the know-how must improve the product to a certain degree. This obligation may extend beyond expiry of the agreement. It is generally presumed that such an obligation remains valid until such time as the know-how enters the public domain. At that time a restriction on the licensee might unduly restrict him vis a vis competitors who are free to do as they please with the know-how.[139] A not uncommon clause provides that know-how shall remain secret until such time as the licensee proves it has entered the public domain. In practice this can be an onerous and expensive burden of proof. Such a clause is not specifically in either the "white" or "black" categories of clause which might suggest that adoption of such a clause renders the licence potentially notifiable to the Commission probably using the opposition procedure. However, it is arguable that such a clause is *within* the ambit of the "white" obligation and hence also exempt.

13.160 It is notable that the Article refers only to technical know-how thereby excluding economic and commercial know-how (e.g. customer lists, sales assessments, etc). Restrictions on disclosure of commercial know may arguably be *within* the concept of technical data and hence exempt, or, *analogous* to technical data and hence exempt. It will be recalled that the whitelist in Article 2 is *not* exhaustive so that other restrictions not specified therein may be equally exempt.

(8) Infringement clauses (excluding no-challenge clauses)

13.161 Article 2(1)(8) permits obligations on the licensee: (a) to inform the licensor of infringements of the patent; (b) to take legal action against an infringer; (c) to assist the licensor in any legal action against an infringer. Obligation (b) may be imposed on licensor and/or licensee. However, "no-challenge clauses" are *not* exempt. These prohibit the licensee from challenging the validity of the patents covered by the agreement during its currency.

[139] *Burroughs-Delphanque* [1972] CMLR D67; *Kabelmetal* [1975] 2 CMLR D40 at para. 8(iv).

13.162 Until recently the Commission did not consider such clauses as ever suitable for exemption under Article 85(3). In *Vaessen–Moris* the Commission, confirming earlier decisions, stated of a no-challenge clause:

> "it is not a requirement imposed by the patent. Rather it constitutes a contractual restriction of competition in that it deprives the sub-licensee of the possibility, which is available to everyone else, of removing an obstacle to his freedom of action in the commercial field by means of an action for revocation of the patent. This is no less the case where the relevant authority examines an application for novelty and degree of inventiveness before granting a patent, since such an examination does not affect the right of undertakings which might profit from such non-existence of the patent to oppose it or bring actions for its revocation. Even if it is the licensee or sub-licensee who is best placed to attack the patent on the basis of information given to him by the licensor, the public interest in the revocation of patents which ought not to have been granted requires that the licensee and the sub-licensee should not be deprived of this possibility."[140]

13.163 Incorporation of a no-challenge clause expressly entails loss of block exemption under Article 3(1) unless it can be argued that the no-challenge clause does not come within Article 85(1) at all, as the Court of Justice ruled in *Bayer* v *Sullhöfer*.[141] The emphasis is on assessing the licensee's competitive position in the light of the restriction rather than the concern to ensure that invalid patents do not remain registered which characterised the Court's and Commission's previous decisions. Though see commentary below on the licensor's right to terminate the licence in the event of challenge. Under the technology transfer block exemption no-challenge clauses are no longer blacklisted and many obtain exemption through the opposition procedure thus revealing a relaxation of the older strict view.

(9) Minimum quality

13.164 Article 2(1)(9) permits obligations on the licensee to observe minimum quality requirements for the licensed product. However, such obligations must be necessary for a technically satisfactory exploitation of the licensed invention. An ancillary obligation on the licensee to allow the licensor to perform monitoring checks is equally permissible. With respect to minimum quality the Commission stated that such clauses do not restrain competition because they are "only designed to allow an adequate and technically adequate exploitation of the rights conferred by patents on their holder".[142] In decided cases the Commission accepted as non-restrictive, obligations on the licensee to manufacture, so as to render the licensed product compatible with the licensor's own products[143] and to manufacture employing all due care and attention.[144] Licensees may be required to comply with design plans and drawings.

[140] [1979] 1 CMLR 511, para. 14. The Commission seem to have followed the decision of the US Supreme Court in *Lear* v *Adkins* 395 US 653; see Robertson [1991] EIPR 373 "Is the licensee estoppel rule still good law? Was it ever?"

[141] Case 65/86 *Bayer* v *Sullhöfer* [1988] ECR 5249, [1990] 4 CMLR 182: the Court held that a no-challenge clause would not, when seen in its legal and economic context, constitute an appreciable restriction of competition if it was royalty free or if the technology was technically outdated so that the licensee did not in fact use the patented process.

[142] *Burroughs/Delphanque* [1972] CMLR D67; *Burroughs/Geha* [1972] CMLR D72; *Campari* [1978] 2 CMLR 397.

[143] *Raymond/Nagoya* [1972] CMLR D45. But for a case deciding that an obligation on the licensee to manufacture according to the licensor's technical specification restricted competition, see *Video Cassette Recorders* [1978] 2 CMLR 160, where the obligation prevented licensees from changing to the manufacture and distribution of competing systems.

[144] *Davidson Rubber* [1972] CMLR D52.

(10) Improvements and communication of experiences (grant/licence back clauses)

13.165 Article 2(1)(10) permits obligations on the parties to exchange details of experience gained in exploiting the licensed invention. An obligation on the licensee to swap experiences with other licensees is not exempt—Article 5(1)(3). Adoption of such a clause however might render use of the opposition procedure appropriate. As regards obligations on the parties to grant one another licences in respect of improvements and new applications Article 2(1)(10) says these are not restrictive. The provision covers only improvements and new applications not new patentable inventions. With regard to improvement and new applications grant backs, they are not restrictive so long as they are not exclusive.

13.166 Improvement licences must not be used, however, artificially to extend the life of the agreement. An agreement which is to remain current "for the life of the most recent original or improvement patent, whether or not already held", restrains competition. The clause enables the licensor to extend unilaterally the duration of the agreement. It has restrictive consequences where combined with other restraints on competition, e.g. exclusivity, export bans, no-challenge clauses, non-competition clauses. Thus, the improvement patent licence should not extend beyond the currency of the last patent granted at the time the licence was first entered.[145] See paras 13.173-13.179. If the licensee is obliged to permit the licensor to register the licensee's improvements in the licensor's name or in joint names, this will almost certainly be treated as if it were an exclusive licence. The same applies if the licensor is also obliged to grant back to the licensee royalty free licences.

13.167 It appears that for both communications of experience and improvement licences obligations must be mutual, i.e. on licensor and licensee.[146] Article 2(1)(10) seems to require this duality, though precisely why is unclear since an obligation on the licensee to grant back improvement licences may be offset by his having to pay reduced royalties, i.e. the obligation may merely be a function of the consideration paid for the licence. Despite the requirement of duality there would appear to be no reason to suggest that the terms of licences granted by licensor and licensee should necessarily be identical. The licensor should not however become legally entitled to hold the rights to the licensees invention.

(11) Most favoured licensee's terms

13.168 Article 2(1)(11) permits obligations on the *licensor* to grant the licensee any more favourable terms that the licensor may grant to another undertaking after the agreement is entered into. It is possible that such a clause might restrain competition though where it does it will *still* be block exempt:

> "The licensor's obligation to extend to the original licensee any more favourable terms subsequently granted to other licensees would not in general dissuade the licensor from granting further licences to third parties. In specific cases, however, particularly where the market situation was such that the only way to find other licensees was to grant them more favourable terms than those granted to the first licensee, this obligation could be an obstacle to the granting of further licences and therefore constitute an appreciable restriction of competition."[147]

13.169 What is not covered by the block exemption is an obligation on the licensor to include a particular term or terms in its other licences. Such an obligation could be found to inhibit a licensor's ability to grant further licences and would thus be caught under Article 85(1).

145 *AOIP/Beyrard* [1976] CMLR D14; *Velcro/Aplix* OJ 1985 L233/22.
146 *Davidson Rubber* [1972] CMLR D52; *Kabelmetal* [1975] 2 CMLR D40.
147 *Kabelmetal* [1975] 2 CMLR D40, para. 8(i).

4. Non-permissible Restrictions: Article 3 (Black Clauses)

13.170 Exemption is not given automatically for certain clauses in a licence would disqualify the agreement from the benefit of the block exemption. As such to be exempt it would have to be exempted under the 1996 Technology Transfer Block Exemption Regulation. It should be noted at this stage that the blacklist comprises a number of clauses whose exemptibility or otherwise depends upon the existence or non-existence of other factors. Such clauses must hence be seen within the context of the case law on the subject.

(1) No-challenge clauses

13.171 Article 3(1) denies exemption where: "The licensee is prohibited from challenging the validity of licensed patents or other industrial or commercial property rights within the Common Market belonging to the licensor or undertakings connected with him, without prejudice to the right of the licensor to terminate the licensing agreement in the event of such a challenge." No-challenge clauses have already been noted above. Article 3(1) extends to rights other than just patents. It is thought that Article 3(1) does not however apply to an agreement by the licensee to recognise the confidentiality of the licensor's know-how provided that it does not restrict the licensee subsequently from challenging the secrecy of that know-how.

13.172 It is pertinent here to add that according to Article 3(1) no consequences attach to a licensor's termination of the licensee's licence should the latter decide to challenge the former's rights. Incorporation of a no-challenge clause in a post 1 April 1996 licence would permit the parties to invoke the opposition procedure under the 1996 Technology Transfer Regulation, as to which see Article 4(2)(b) considered at para. 13.104.

(2) Extension of the agreement beyond expiry of patent

13.173 Article 3(2) provides that no exemption lies where:

> "the duration of the licensing agreement is automatically prolonged beyond the expiry of the licensed patents existing at the time the agreement was entered into by the inclusion in it of any new patent obtained by the licensor, unless the agreement provides each party with the right to terminate the agreement at least annually after the expiry of the licensed patents existing at the time the agreement was entered into, without prejudice to the right of the licensor to charge royalties for the full period during which the licensee continues to use know-how communicated by the licensor which has not entered into the public domain, even if that period exceeds the life of the patents."

13.174 Agreements which last for the lifetime of a patent or for a shorter period do not generally infringe Article 85(1). On expiry of patent rights, the Court of Justice has held that an agreement may only escape being caught by Article 85(1) if the licensee's obligation to pay royalties is subject to the licensee's right to terminate on reasonable notice.[148] What is a reasonable period depends on the agreement's legal and economic context according to the Court of Justice, hence making this means of escaping Article 85(1) somewhat unclear in practice. It cannot be assumed automatically that the twelve month periods referred to in Article 3(2) would be reasonable in every case. Conversely, Article 3(2) provides that no exemption lies where the licensor attempts to restrict the licensee once the initial intellectual property has expired.

13.175 However, it is notable that Article 3(2) lays down no absolute rule. Exemption may still be claimed provided that the agreement does not "automatically" extend beyond

[148] Case 320/87 *Ottung* v *Klee* [1989] ECR 1177, [1990] 4 CMLR 915, para. 13.

expiry of the first patents. Thus, the agreement may be prolonged provided the parties include termination clauses which may be activated at regular periods of 12 months or less. Further, according to Recital 20, Article 3(2) does *not* affect the right of the parties to extend their contractual relationship by entering into new agreements concerning new patents. However this does not permit contractual provision in the initial licence for such additions, nor should parties enter an unwritten understanding or other concerted practice which is to the same effect.

13.176 Where there is a legal doubt over the validity of the patent, it is not uncommon for royalties to be based primarily on use of the know-how and not the patented invention. This minimises the economic risk to the licensor of a successful challenge to the patent.

13.177 Where the original licence is based upon the grant of *several* patent rights, then the wording of Article 3(2) implies that the agreement prima facie lapses (subject to permissible extension by inclusion of termination clauses) when the last of the originally licensed patent rights expires.

13.178 The most common situation envisaged by Article 3(2) above is extension of the agreement by inclusion of improvement patents. The Commission has hitherto condemned a clause providing that the agreement would remain in force, "for the life of the most recent original or improvement patent, whether or not already held".[149] The Regulation adopted a less strict line and allows such clauses, where ameliorated by periodic termination clauses.

13.179 With respect to the imposition of royalty obligations after expiry of the patent see paras. 13.183–13.184.

(3) Non-competition clauses

13.180 Article 3(3) provides that no exemption lies where "one party is restricted from competing with the other party, with undertakings connected with the other party or with other undertakings within the Common Market in respect of research and development, manufacture, use or sales, save as provided in Article 1 and without prejudice to an obligation on the licensee to use his best endeavours to exploit the licensed invention." The Commission does not consider non-competition to be exemptible and a similar approach is found in the technology transfer block exemption (see Article 3(1)):

> "A non-competition restriction could prevent a licensee from extending his product range and closely bind his future to that of a licensed patent. Consequently, a licensee so tied might have to go out of business when the licensed technology becomes obsolete. Non-competition prohibitions can have the effect of not only strengthening a monopoly position of a patentee, but also of weakening competition between manufacturers of substitute products. A licensee might no longer have worthwhile prospects in carrying out independent development. Accordingly, the Commission regards non-competition provisions as covered by Article 85(1). Possibilities of exemption under Article 85(3) could only arise in special situations, particularly cases relating to specialisation agreements."[150]

13.181 The Court of Justice has also expressed the view that a non-competition covenant on termination of an agreement will be caught by Article 85(1), subject to the reservation that this depends on the legal and economic context in which the agreement was concluded.[151]

13.182 However, note that Article 3(3) is without prejudice to the licensee's duty to use best endeavours, i.e. the licensor has a valid interest in ensuring full exploitation by the licensee.

[149] *AOIP/Beyrard* [1976] 1 CMLR D14.
[150] *Fourth Report on Competition Policy* (1974), para. 30.
[151] Case 320/87 *Ottung* v *Klee* [1989] ECR 1177, [1990] 4 CMLR 915, para. 18.

How this may be ensured where the licensee carries dual obligations is uncertain. This provision does not prevent the inclusion of "best endeavours" clauses; it may well be up to national courts to reconcile the conflicts that may arise. Adoption of minimum performance criteria might provide a solution.[152] However even these clauses might be problematic if they are set at such a level that the licensee must concentrate exclusively on the licensed technology to the disadvantage of other, rival processes. This might be the case where the obligation on the licensee is so large as to encompass all or most of the demand. The Commission consider that national courts must reconcile the inherent conflicts in this provision. In Recital 21 it states that the blacklist includes:

> "restrictions on the freedom of one party *to compete* with the other and in particular involve himself in techniques other than those licensed, since such restrictions impede technical and economic progress. The prohibition of such restrictions should however be reconciled with the legitimate interest of the licensor in having his patented invention exploited to the full and to this end to require the licensee to use his best endeavours to manufacture and market the licensed product."

(4) Royalty payments in respect of unprotected rights

13.183 No exemption lies where "the licensee is charged royalties on products which are not entirely or partially patented or manufactured by means of a patented process, or for the use of know-how which has entered into the public domain otherwise than by the fault of the licensee or an undertaking connected with him". Clauses providing for royalties should be limited to protected rights only. Thus they may cover fully and/or partially protected products manufactured by a patented process and know-how until such time as it enters the public domain.

13.184 Where the licensee has, by default, allowed the know-how to enter the public domain the obligation to pay royalties remains presumably until such time as the know-how might reasonably have been expected to become public. This time period may, in the Commission's opinion, be quite short in cases of rapid technological advance: "In view of the rapid development of technology in polyurethane chemistry, it may be questioned whether such know-how has at the present time sufficient economic value to justify its continued protection by an obligation of secrecy."[153] Article 3(4) continues to provide that the preceding text (above) is "without prejudice to arrangements whereby, in order to facilitate payment by the licensee, the royalty payments for the use of a licensed invention are spread over a period extending beyond the life of the licensed patents or the entry of the know-how into the public domain".

(5) Limitations on quantity or number of operations

13.185 Article 3(5) provides that no exemption exists where "the quality of licensed products one party may manufacture or sell or the number of operations exploiting the licensed invention he may carry out are subject to limitations." Whereas the licensor may impose

[152] For example, it has been held in the High Court that an implied term in a contract to use best endeavours in the context of that contract need not be inconsistent with a company being at liberty to promote competing products provided it treated the other at least as well as it treated its competitors: *Ault and Wiborg Paints* v *Sure Service*, *The Times*, 2 July 1983. But see Stephen J in the High Court of Australia, *Transfield Pty Ltd* v *Arlo International* [1981] RPC 141, 150, where an express term requiring licensee's use of best endeavours to sell the licensed product was held to mean that competing products could not be sold if that would prejudice sales of the licensed product. Note the dictum of Lawrence J in *Sheffield District Rly Co* v *Great Central Rly Co* (1911) 27 TLR 451, 452: "We think 'best endeavours' means what the words say; they do not mean second best endeavours".

[153] *Reuter/BASF* [1976] 2 CMLR D44.

minimum requirements on the licensee maximum requirements may not be imposed; see Article 2(1)(2) above for details. Limitations on production may have the same effect as an export ban and are accordingly equally unacceptable.[154] An equivalent clause is blacklisted in the technology transfer block exemption (see para. 13.96).

(6) Prices and discounts

13.186 No exemption lies under Article 3(6) where, "one party is restricted in the determination of prices components of prices or discounts for the licensed products." The restriction is usually imposed upon the licensee in the form of a fixed sale price but a restriction on the licensor would equally be caught. This restriction is still blacklisted under Article 3(1) of the Technology Transfer Block Exemption Regulation.

(7) Customer restrictions

13.187 No exemption lies under section 3(7) where, "one party is restricted as to the customers he may serve, in particular by being prohibited from supplying certain classes of user, employing certain forms of distribution or, with the aim of sharing customers, using certain types of packaging for the products, save as provided in Article 1(1)(7) and Article 2(1)(3)". Recital 23 states unhelpfully that non-permissible obligations "include restrictions imposed on the parties regarding prices, customers or marketing of the licensed products or regarding the quantities to be manufactured or sold, especially since restrictions of the latter type may have the same effect as export bans". Article 1(1)(7) essentially permits obligations on the licensee to use only the licensor's trade mark or get up as determined by the licensor to distinguish the licensed product. Article 2(1)(3) is more problematic: it provides that an obligation on the licensee to restrict his exploitation of the licensed invention to one or more technical fields of application is not generally restrictive of competition. If X licenses Y to use his patent for certain specific technical uses only, then this will inevitably limit Y's capacity to supply certain customers who are interested in products other than those Y is permitted to produce but which derive from the patent. The effect of a field of use restriction may hence be to restrain the licensee as to customers. However, it appears that this is accepted as an inevitable consequence and does not threaten the exemption. Precisely where the divide between Articles 2(1)(3) and 3(7) lies is unclear; if the parties misuse Article 2(1)(3) and disguise customer restrictions as field of use restrictions the Commission might treat the clause as a customer restraint.[155]

13.188 The Regulation makes it clear that customer restrictions may take a number of forms. Thus, restrictions on categories of user, e.g. only wholesalers, are not exempt. Likewise restrictions on the forms of marketing, e.g. only through specialist retailers and non multi-function supermarkets, are not exempt. Equally restrictions on the packaging used which have as their object the sharing of customers are not exempt.

(8) Assignment back of improvement patents

13.189 No exemption lies under Article 3(8) where, "the licensee is obliged to assign wholly or in part to the licensor rights in or to patents for improvements or for new applications of the licensed patents". Clauses providing for compulsory assign-back are viewed by the Commission as potential evidence of exploitation by the licensor of unequal bargaining

[154] *Maize Seed* [1978] 3 CMLR 434, para. 25(f).

[155] In *France/Sualmo, Ninth Report on Competition Policy* (1979), at paras. 114–115, a restriction on a licensee sub-licensing diesel engine technology based on whether it was for civilian or military use was removed after the Commission objected to it as a customer restriction. The position has altered somewhat in the technology transfer block exemption: see Art. 3(4) thereof.

power i.e. the licensee accepts such restrictions reluctantly in order to secure the licence. The Commission complains that the licensor obtains an unjustified competitive advantage by such terms. This provision must be read in the light of Article 2(1)(10) which permits a *mutual* obligation on the parties to grant to each other on a non-exclusive basis improvement licences and to communicate to each other experience gained. It should be noted that Article 2(1)(10) does not cover anything other than reciprocal obligations. A clause which requires the licensee to grant non-exclusive improvement licences to the licensor and through him to all other licensees may not be restrictive where the licensee is at that time the *only* licensee.[156] It may conversely be restrictive if the licensee in question is not the sole licensee and by the clause he is forced to share his improvement with rival licensees.

13.190 Although Article 3(8) only refers to assignments, it would seem that the same principles should apply to licences. For example, obligations to license on a reciprocal but exclusive basis would appear to be caught by Article 85(1) since outside *Maize Seed* type situations non-reciprocal exclusivity will be caught.

(9) Excessive tying clauses (package licensing of patents)

13.191 No exemption lies, under Article 3(9) where, "the licensee is induced at the time the agreement is entered into to accept further licences which he does not want or to agree to use patents, goods or services which he does not want, unless such patents, products or services are necessary for a technically satisfactory exploitation of the licensed invention." As with compulsory grant-back obligations (above) the Commission perceive tying as evidence of exploitation by the licensor of superior bargaining power.

13.192 Tying is considered not to restrain competition where it is related to quality control but is considered to be restrictive, and unsuitable for exemption, where it has no reasonable connection to quality control.[157] In *Campari* (a case on trade marks) the Commission accepted a tying clause that sought to maintain the quality of the licensed product and thereby the licensor's reputation:

> "According to information provided by the parties, the standards enforced do not oblige the licensees to obtain supplies of albumin or bitter orange essence from any particular source, but only to choose between different products on the basis of objective quality considerations. This does not, however, apply to the colouring matter and the herbal mixtures, where the licensor's legitimate concern to ensure that the product manufactured under licence has the same quality as the original product can be protected only if the licensees obtain all their supplies from it."[158]

The fact that the case concerned trade marks does not affect the principle that tying may be legitimate to protect the quality of an ultimate product.

13.193 The tie-in alluded to in Article 3(9) need not be a strict contractual requirement, i.e. licensee *must* take product X in conjunction with licence; the provision speaks of licensees being "induced". Thus in *Complaint in Plastics Industry*[159] patentees granted licences royalty free if certain non-patented products were purchased from them but charged a royalty if the products were purchased from rival suppliers. The parties amended their practice before the Commission issued any decision. Thus, it may be a tie-in if the licensee is

[156] *Kabelmetal* [1975] 2 CMLR D40, para. 8(iii).
[157] *Vaessen/Moris* [1979] 1 CMLR 511.
[158] [1978] 2 CMLR 397, 409.
[159] Bull EC 11/61, at p. 11.

not *required* to purchase a secondary product, service, etc. from the licensor but does so because of economic "persuasion".

(10) Prohibitions on passive sales

13.194 No exemption lies under Article 3(10) where, "without prejudice to Article 1(1)(5), the licensee is required, for a period exceeding that permitted under Article 1(1)(6), not to put the licensed product on the market in territories licensed to other licensees within the Common Market or does not do so as a result of a concerted practice between the parties". This provision merely buttresses the provisions of Article 1(1)(5) and (6) for discussion of which see above.

(11) Creation of obstacles to parallel imports

13.195 According to Article 3(11) no exemption lies where,

> "one or both of the parties are required:
> (a) to refuse without any objectively justified reason to meet demand from users or resellers in their respective territories who would market products in other territories within the Common Market;
> (b) to make it difficult for users or resellers to obtain the products from other resellers within the Common Market, and in particular to exercise industrial or commercial property rights or take measures so as to prevent users or resellers from obtaining outside, or from putting on the market in, the licensed territory products which have been lawfully put on the market within the Common Market by the patentee or with his consent;
> or do so as a result of a concerted practice between them."

13.196 These provisions act as a counterweight to Article 1(1)(4)–(6) which permits licensors to limit the extent to which licensees compete with each other. Thus, irrespective of Article 1 the licensees must be free to supply customers in their own territories who are intending to parallel import the goods into the territory of another licensee. Recital 13 links this provision to the requirement in Article 85(3) EC that consumers be allowed a fair share of the resulting benefit resulting from an improvement in the supply of the licensed products on the market:

> "To safeguard this effect ... it is right to exclude from Article 1 cases where the parties agree to refuse to meet demand from users or resellers within their respective territories who would resell for export, or to take other steps to impede parallel imports, or where the licensee is obliged to refuse to meet unsolicited demand from the territory of other licensees (passive sales). The same applies where such action is the result of a concerted practice between the licensor and the licensee."[160]

13.197 Thus licensees may not be prohibited from supplying exporters. Likewise attempts by either party to bring actions for infringement of the patent or of other proprietary rights licensed as ancillary to the main patent (e.g. trade marks), will render the agreement not automatically exempt. The Commission has reinforced its objections to attempts to prevent parallel imports by repeating the wording of Article 3(11) in Article 9(5). This provision allows the Commission to withdraw an exemption that would otherwise exist where the parties seek to hinder parallel imports.

[160] Recital 13 ostensibly conflicts with Art. 1(1)(b), in that the latter permits restrictions on passive sales whereas the former could be seen as excluding them. Recital 13 may be reconciled by limiting it to the period following that specified in Art. 1(1)(6).

5. Extension of Exemption to Licences not Expressly Covered: The "Opposition Procedure" Article 4

13.198 Article 4(1) extended the exemption to agreements whose clauses are not expressly covered by Articles 1 and 2 (the white clauses) but which contain no clauses prohibited by Article 3 (black clauses). Agreements of this nature could be notified to the Commission in accordance with the "opposition procedure" outlined in Article 4 and thereby may receive accelerated treatment. In essence, exemption automatically extends to the agreement if no opposition to it was raised within a six-month period commencing from the date of notification. Given the expiry of the block exemption for agreements concluded after 1 April 1996 it is no longer available for use in respect of new licences.

6. Types of Licence not Exempt: Article 5

13.199 The Regulation is not all embracing. It expressly excludes from block exemption certain categories of agreement. In Recital 8 of the preamble the Commission explained the rationale: "Since the experience so far acquired is inadequate, it is not appropriate to include within the scope of the Regulation patent pools, licensing agreements entered into in connection with joint ventures if certain market share limits are exceeded, reciprocal licensing or distribution agreements, or licensing agreements in respect of plant breeder's rights."

(1) Patent pools

13.200 The Regulation does not apply, "to agreements between members of a patent pool which relate to the pooled patent." The Technology Transfer Regulation does not apply to patent or know-how pools either (Article 5(1)(1)). The Commission are unsympathetic to patent pooling where the patentees are economically powerful. It objects that, first, pooling eliminates competition between the parties as regards technical innovation, and secondly, by concentrating a substantial "package" of know-how in the parties hand's pooling encourages purchasers to deal with the pool to the exclusion of other suppliers. The pool hence creates entry and expansion barriers.[161] Likewise, an agreement between undertakings jointly to purchase and exploit certain patents which are essential to the operation of a certain market restricts competition where the resultant pool excludes from the relevant market firms not belonging to the group.

13.201 Such pools may be acceptable where they are willing to grant licences free of restriction and on reasonable terms to all other manufacturers in the Community.[162] A pool that requires members to surrender their rights upon leaving but which allows remaining members to retain the rights they have enjoyed in respect of the departing members' patents infringes Article 85(1) EC. Such a pool deters exit from it and hence hinders the freedom of firms to develop technology without having to share it with competitors.[163]

(2) Licences in the context of a joint venture

13.202 The block exemption was amended to enable it to be applicable to joint ventures.[164] Although it is stated that the block exemption does not apply "to patent licensing agreements

[161] *Concast/Mannesmann, Eleventh Report on Competition Policy* (1981), para. 93.
[162] *IGR Stereo Television, Eleventh Report on Competition Policy* (1981), para. 94.
[163] *Video Cassette Recorders* [1978] 2 CMLR 160.
[164] Reg. 151/93 OJ 1993 L21/8.

between competitors who hold interests in a joint venture or between one of them and the joint venture, if the licensing agreements relate to the activities of the joint venture",[165] it is stated that in such cases block exemption is available to such agreements

> "under which a parent undertaking grants the joint venture a patent licence, provided that the contract products and the other products of the participating undertakings which are considered by users to be equivalent in view of their characteristics, price and intended use represent:
> – in case of a licence limited to production not more than 20%
> – in case of a licence covering production and distribution not more than 10% of the market for all such products in the Common Market or a substantial part thereof".[166]

13.203 The benefit of the block exemption is not lost either of these market share limits is exceeded by up to one-tenth for up to two consecutive financial years, and if this limit is breached, then the block exemption continues for six months beyond the end of the financial year in which it was breached.[167]

(3) Reciprocal licences

13.204 The Regulation does not apply, "to agreements under which the parties, albeit in separate agreements or though connected undertakings, grant each other reciprocal patent or trade mark licences or reciprocal sales rights for unprotected products or exchange know-how, where the parties are competitors in relation to the products covered by those agreements".[168]

13.205 The Regulation does not thus extend to reciprocal licensing between competitors (e.g. between licensees). Reciprocal licensing between non-competitors would appear to be exempt. In deciding whether reciprocal licences exist the Commission will not examine the form of the licences; rather they examine the overall effect. Thus if L1 and L2 exchange licences using two separate licensing agreements the Commission may view the agreements conjunctively as a single scheme, not disjunctively as two separate licences which may each be exempted.

13.206 Under Article 5(2)(b) however block exemption *does* apply to reciprocal licences where the parties are not subject to any territorial restraint within the EC on the manufacture, use or putting on the market of the products covered by the agreement or on the use of the licensed processes.

(4) Plant breeders' rights

13.207 The Regulation does not apply to, "licensing agreements in respect of plant breeders' rights".

7. *Withdrawal of Exemption: Article 9*

13.208 The Commission may, in exceptional cases, withdraw the block exemption from a particular case by formal decision where it considers that an agreement has effects that are incompatible with Article 85(3) or 86 EC. The following are examples of cases where exemption might be withdrawn, but are not exhaustive.

165 Art. 5(1)(2).
166 Art. 5(2)(a).
167 Art. 5(3).
168 Art. 5(1)(3).

(1) Arbitration awards leading to restrictive settlements

13.209 The Regulation provides that exemption may be withdrawn where restrictive consequences derive from an arbitration award. A clause requiring parties to submit disputes to arbitration has been held not to restrain competition.[169] However, arbitration schemes may be a device for maintaining a restrictive agreement and hence the Commission is cautious of them. The existence of an arbitration clause in a licence is not a bar to scrutiny by the Commission.[170] The Technology Transfer Regulation does *not* include this example in the list in Article 7 of that Regulation governing clauses where exemption may be withdrawn.

(2) Inter-brand competition ineffective

13.210 Exemption may be withdrawn where, "the licensed product or the services provided using a licensed process are not exposed to effective competition in the licensed territory from identical products or services or products or services considered by users as equivalent in view of their characteristics, price and intended use". The Commission considers as significant, in assessing a licence, the extent to which the parties are subject to competition from competing brands or substitutes. Where such competition is effective, it will act as a pressure on the licensor and licensee to behave competitively; strong inter-brand competition is hence a form of guarantee for the consumer. It does not follow that exemption will be withdrawn in every case where inter-brand competition is weak. X might invent and patent a revolutionary new product which has no substitutes which he licenses to Y. Simply because X is innovative and efficient is no reason to deny him exemption. If X abused his market power, then the abuse in conjunction with the lack of inter-brand rivalry might warrant withdrawal of exemption. Such a case might be suitable for review under Article 86 EC as well. In *Tetra Pak (No. 1)* acquisition by a dominant undertaking of a company holding the benefit of an exclusive patent licence, which was within the terms of the block exemption, was regarded by the Commission as an abuse of that dominant position contrary to Article 86, since it prevented potential competitors from gaining access to new technology which would have exposed the dominant undertaking to actual competition.[171] The Commission intimated that it would use its powers under Article 9, whereupon the dominant undertaking renounced exclusivity to terminate the abuse. The Commission took a decision to enable subsequent proceedings before the Court of First Instance to take place which confirmed that Article 86 can apply to behaviour notwithstanding that it relates to agreements sanctioned under Article 85(3) or a block exemption.[172]

(3) Licensee fails to effectively exploit licence: termination rights

13.211 Exemption may be withdrawn where, "the licensor does not have the right to terminate the exclusivity granted to the licensee at the latest five years from the date the agreement was entered into and at least annually thereafter if, without legitimate reason, the licensee fails to exploit the patent or to do so adequately". Exclusivity clauses in licences are not, *per se*, restrictions under Article 85(1), where they are necessary to facilitate the market penetration of a new product; such clauses help overcome the risks inherent in marketing new products and, accordingly, may ultimately lead to increased, not reduced, levels of competition if a new product is successfully launched. However, if the licensee proves

169 *Burroughs/Delphanque* [1972] CMLR D67, D71; *Davidson Rubber* [1972] CMLR D52, D60.
170 *Pentacon, Eighth Report on Competition Policy* (1978), para. 119.
171 [1990] 4 CMLR 47, para. 45.
172 T-51/89 *Tetra Pak* v *Commission* [1990] ECR II-309, [1991] 4 CMLR 334.

ineffective as a vehicle for exploitation of the invention the licensor may wish to seek a more effective undertaking to grant a licence to. Indeed, successful penetration of the market may depend upon the licensor being able to switch licensees. Legally, if the desired fruits of the licence do not materialise, and show no prospect of so doing, then the criteria for exemption under Article 85(3) have not been satisfied: no improvements in distribution or technological progress have been realised, consumers have not benefited from new products and increased choice. Article 9(3) hence permits the Commission to withdraw exemption where Article 85(3) has not been satisfied[173] and there is no possibility of the failure being rectified by a switch of licensees. It follows that licensors would be prudent to include in the agreement a clause entitling them to terminate the licence at the end of five years and thereafter at yearly intervals if exploitation by the licensee is inadequate. To this end the parties will need to predetermine what they consider to be an "adequate" exploitation and they may wish to incorporate their conclusions in the licence itself. This ground for withdrawal was excluded from the Technology Transfer Regulation list in Article 7 thereof.

(4) Refusal by the licensee to meet unsolicited demands (passive competition)

13.212 Exemption may be withdrawn where, "without prejudice to Article 1(1)(6), the licensee refuses, without objectively valid reason, to meet unsolicited demand from users or resellers in the territory of other licensees". Article 1(1)(6) makes it clear that licensees *may* refuse to meet unsolicited demands from outside of their territory for a limited period of five years from first marketing within the EC. Recital 12 justifies Article 1(1)(6) on the basis that it enables the licensee to focus his efforts on his own territory in the security of absolute protection for a period of years from other licensees. By this "the number of production facilities and the quantity and quality of goods produced in the Common Market are increased". Thus, Article 1(1)(6) and paragraph 12 of the preamble constitute one "objectively valid reason" for a refusal to meet unsolicited demands. In circumstances other than Article 1(1)(6) (e.g. after the five-year period has elapsed) it will be rare for a refusal to be objectively justified. The Commission does not accept that the "free-rider" problem is a proper justification for refusal to supply. Essentially, licensees may contend that they need protection from parallel importers who sell at prices lower than those of the authorised licensee. Such parallel importers can afford to charge low prices because they need not provide comprehensive promotion and pre-sales services such as are provided by the licensee. Indeed, so the argument runs, parallel importers rely upon customers being able to exploit the licensee's services (displays, testing facilities, advice of sales staff, etc.) but make the actual purchase from the parallel importer. Thus, the parallel importer "free rides" on the sales services provided by the licensee. Ultimately, the licensee may have to reduce the sales services he provides in order to bring his prices into line with those of the parallel importer thereby threatening the licensor's reputation which may be present in the form of a trade mark or other designation on the product. The Commission, while accepting that free-riding is a problem, does not consider that it is so prevalent as to justify measures to prevent parallel imports which are perceived as healthy forms of competition.

(5) Parties create obstacles to parallel imports

13.213 Exemption may be withdrawn where one or both of the parties seeks to create obstacles to parallel imports. The wording of Article 9(5) which is to this effect the same, *mutatis mutandis*, as Article 3(11) is discussed above. Reference may be made thereto for analysis.

[173] An argument that failure to exploit automatically leads to withdrawal of the block exemption was rejected by the Arnhem District Court: see *Twenty-third Report on Competition Policy* (1993), Annex V, para. 121.

Under Article 3(11), any agreement which seeks to hinder parallel imports is automatically outside the scope of the block-exemption. Therefore Article 9(5) is really only of importance where there is no agreement to hinder imports, but where one party acts unilaterally to do so.

8. Meaning of "Connected Undertakings": Articles 11(3) and 12

13.214 Article 11(3) states that the Regulation shall apply to patent licensing agreements in which rights or obligations of the licensor or the licensee are assumed by undertakings connected with them. Article 12 defines a "connected undertaking". The definition is exactly the same as that used in the block exemption on exclusive dealing.[174] In essence a connected undertaking is one in which a party to the agreement directly or indirectly exercises effective control (i.e. *de jure* or *de facto* control). Furthermore, it includes parents and subsidiaries of such connected undertakings.

9. Transitional Periods and Currency of Block Exemption: Articles, 6, 7, 8 and 14

13.215 Articles 6–8 cover: agreements already in force at the time the Regulation became operative; "old agreements"; and, accession agreements. Article 13 concerns the duration of the Regulation itself. Recital 26 reads:

> "The Regulation should apply with retroactive effect to patent licensing agreements in existence when the Regulation comes into force where such agreements already fulfil the conditions for application of the Regulation or are modified to do so (Articles 6 to 8). Under Article 4(3) of Regulation No. 19/65/EEC, the benefit of these provisions may not be claimed in actions pending at the date of entry into force of this Regulation, nor may it be relied on as grounds for claims for damages against third parties."

(1) Existing agreements, retroactivity

13.216 For two very specific categories of agreement exemption under the Regulation applied retroactively from the time at which the conditions for application of the Regulation were fulfilled. These two types of agreements are: (a) agreements existing on 13 March 1962 and notified before 1 February 1963. This group of agreement will be very small in number due to the obvious historical nature of the category; (b) agreements (whether notified or not) to which Article 4(2)(2)(b) of Regulation 17/62/EEC applies. This provision exempts from the need to notify bilateral agreements which only, "impose restrictions on the exercise of the rights of the assignee or user of industrial property rights—in particular patents, utility models, designs or trade marks—or of the person entitled under a contract to the assignment, or grant, of the right to use a method of manufacture or knowledge relating to the use and to the application of industrial processes."

13.217 As regards all other agreements notified before the Regulation came into force, the exemption applied retroactively from the time at which the conditions for application of this Regulation were fulfilled, or from the date of notification, whichever was the later. Thus many of the two thousand agreements notified to the Commission and pending a Commission response prior to the Regulation became exempt on its enactment.[175]

[174] Arts. 4(2) and (3), Reg. 1983/83/EEC.

[175] *Fourteenth Report on Competition Policy*, para. 35.

(2) "Old agreements"

13.218 An "old agreement" is one existing on 13 March 1962 (the date when Regulation 17/62/EEC—the main legislative instrument on competition procedure—came into force) and notified to the Commission prior to 1 February 1963 (the period of grace provided for notification by the Council in Regulation 17/62/EC as amended). For "old" agreements and agreements to which Article 4(2)(2)(b) of Regulation 17/62/EEC applied which were notified before 1 January 1967, the rules were quite generous. Where such agreements were amended so as to comply with the Regulation before 1 April 1985 *and* these amendments were communicated to the Commission before 1 July 1985, the prohibition in Article 85(1) was inapplicable in respect of the period prior to the amendment. The notification took effect from the time of its receipt by the Commission. Where the notification was sent by registered post it becomes effective on the date shown on the postmark of the place of posting.

(3) Accession agreements

13.219 As regards agreements caught by Article 85 as a result of the accession of the UK, Ireland and Denmark, Articles 6 and 7 apply except that the relevant dates are: 1 January 1973 instead of 13 March 1962; and 1 July 1973 instead of 1 February 1963 and 1 January 1967. Where Greece is concerned the date changes are: 1 January 1981 instead of 13 March 1962; and, 1 July 1981 instead of 1 February 1963 and 1 January 1963. Where Spain and Portugal are concerned the date changes are: 1 January 1986 instead of 13 March 1962; and 1 July 1986 instead of 1 February 1963 and 1 January 1967. Where Austria, Finland and Sweden are concerned the date changes are: 1 January 1995 instead of 13 March 1962; and 1 July 1995 instead of 1 February 1963 and 1 January 1967.

(4) Duration of the Regulation

13.220 The Regulation became operative on 1 January 1985 and initially applied until 31 December 1994, i.e. 10 years. It was then extended for two successive periods of six months,[176] expired on 31 December 1995 and was then given the kiss of life by Article 11(2) of the technology transfer block exemption which was not adopted until 31 January 1996 for a further three months. It finally expired, after its three curtain calls, on 31 March 1996, though continues, by virtue of Article 11(3) of the technology transfer block exemption, to apply to those agreements in force on that date. While legal certainty normally precludes retrospective legislation, it is thought that the particular circumstances of this case mean that the retrospective application of Regulation 2349/84 does not offend that principle; rather it promotes legal security for those whose agreements were caught by the patent licensing block exemption and whose agreements continued in force at the beginning of 1996.

10. Confidentiality on the Part of the Commission: Article 13

13.221 Information received by the Commission under the opposition procedure may only be used for the purposes of the Regulation, i.e. deciding whether exemption lies or not. The Commission and national authorities (who are involved in the opposition procedure) are prohibited from disclosing information acquired by them under the Regulation of the kind covered by the duty to maintain professional secrecy.[177] The obligation to pro-

[176] Commission Regs. 70/95, OJ 1995 L12/13 to 30 June 1995 and 2131/95, OJ 1995 L214/6, to 31 December 1995.

[177] Case C-67/91 *Direccíon General de Defensa de la Comptencia* v *Asociación Española de Banca Privada* [1992] ECR I-4785.

tect professional secrecy is a generally accepted principle of EC law which is given concrete expression by Article 214 EC which applies the obligation to details of companies business relations and their cost components. Almost certainly, unauthorised disclosure by the Commission would render the latter subject to a claim for damages before the Court of First Instance under Article 215(2) EC (liability of the Community for non-contractual liability). It is most unlikely that authorities in the Member States could be liable under Article 215 EC, unless they were viewed as agents of the Commission, but might be liable under the principles laid down in *Brasserie du Pêcheur.*[178]

13.222 It should be appreciated, as a proviso to the above, that the authorities are not prevented from publishing general information or surveys which make use of such information but which do *not* contain information relating to particular undertakings or associations of undertakings, i.e. the authorities may use the data collected in a general way.

11. Check List for Determining whether the Patent Block Exemption Applies

13.223 The check list below is an overview only: it is *not* a substitute for proper analysis of the text of the Regulation itself.

Condition 1 (does the patent block exemption still apply?)
Was the agreement in force on or before 31 March 1996? If not, and it came into force more recently, the technology transfer block exemption is applicable.

Condition 2 (patents or know-how?)
If know-how is being licensed as well as patents, do the patents cover all the licensed territory, and is the know-how no more than ancillary to the patents? if the answer to either of these questions is no, then the patent block exemption does not apply and reference should be made to the know-how block exemption.

Condition 3 (agreements exempt)
Agreement must be of a type described in Article 1 of the Regulation. Account should be taken of Articles 10 and 11 which extend exempt) the Regulation to agreements that are effectively the same as the patent licence described in Article 1. The Regulation covers agreements involving undertakings "connected" to the parties to the licence (Article 12). The Regulation does *not* apply to: patent pools; licences derived from some joint ventures; reciprocal licences; and, plant breeders' rights (Article 5).

Condition 4 (white clauses)
The agreement may legitimately contain clauses listed in Article 1. These are, in summary, clauses: granting exclusivity to the licensee; obliging the licensor not to compete with the licensee; protecting licensees from competition from each other; obliging the licensee to use the licensor's trade mark.

[178] Joined Cases C-46 and C-48/93 *Brasserie du Pêcheur SA* v *Germany and R* v *Secretary of State for Transport ex parte Factortame Ltd* [1996] 1 CMLR 889; Case C-392/93 *R* v *HM Treasury ex parte British Telecommunications Plc* [1996] 2 CMLR 217; Case C-5/94 *R* v *MAFF ex parte Hedley Lomas* [1996] 2 CMLR 391.

Condition 5 (white clauses)

Agreements containing clauses listed in Article 2 cause no problem. These clauses do not generally restrict competition, where they do Article 2 extends the exemption to them. The permissible clauses may concern the following:

(i) purchase or procurement;
(ii) minimum royalties, minimum quantities or minimum number of operations;
(iii) restrictions on technical use: field of use restrictions;
(iv) post expiry of the agreement exploitation;
(v) prohibition on sub-licensing or assignment;
(vi) identification of patentee on licensed products;
(vii) non-disclosure of know-how;
(viii) infringement clauses (excluding no-challenge clauses);
(ix) minimum quality;
(x) improvement and communication of experience (grant/licence-back);
(xi) most favoured licensee's terms.

Condition 6 (black clauses)

Under no circumstances can block-exemption be claimed for licences containing clauses outlined in Article 3. The "black" unacceptable clauses concern the following:

(i) no-challenge clauses;
(ii) extension of the agreement beyond expiry of patent;
(iii) excessive non-competition clauses;
(iv) royalty payments in respect of unprotected rights;
(v) limitations on quantity or number of operations;
(vi) prices and discounts;
(vii) customer restrictions;
(viii) assignment back of improvement patents;
(ix) excessive tying clauses (package licensing of patents);
(x) prohibitions on passive sales; and
(xi) creation of obstacles to parallel imports.

Condition 7 (extension of exemption by opposition procedure)

Agreements of a type generally caught by the Regulation (Condition 3 above) which contain clauses which are not expressly permitted by Articles 1 and 2 but which, conversely, are not expressly prohibited by Article 3 may obtain automatic exemption by use of the opposition procedure in Article 4.

Condition 8 (withdrawal of exemption)

In exceptional cases the Commission might, by formal decision, withdraw exemption from an agreement. The Commission might issue such decisions in the following cases, amongst others:

(i) where arbitration awards result in restrictive settlements;
(ii) where inter-brand competition is ineffective;
(iii) where the licensee fails to effectively exploit the licence and no termination rights belong to the licensor;
(iv) where licensee refuses to meet unsolicited demands; and
(v) where parties create obstacles to parallel imports.

F. The Block Exemption for Know-how Licensing: Regulation 556/89

13.224 Regulation 556/89[179] lays down criteria which if met enable a know-how licence to claim automatic exemption form the prohibition in Article 85(1) under Article 85(3). It now applies to agreements which were in force prior to 1 April 1996. Know-how licensing agreements coming into force on or after 1 April 1996 are governed by the technology transfer block exemption.

1. The Basic Exemption: Article 1

(1) Scope

13.225 Article 1 exempts know-how licensing agreements for both "pure" know-how and for know-how combined with patents, "mixed agreements". However, a mixed agreement which comes within the ambit of the patent block exemption is subject to that block exemption and cannot come within the terms of the know-how block exemption. Ancillary provisions relating to trade marks and other intellectual property rights are also exempted.

13.226 Only agreements between two parties are exempted. Parties for these purposes can be interpreted as meaning economic entities or units. The licensor need not be the developer of the know-how:[180] agreements between licensee and sub-licensee are therefore exempted, but not, for example, a tripartite agreement between licensor, licensee and sub-licensee. Further agreements for the assignment or the acquisition of rights where the risks associated with exploitation are borne by the assignor are covered.[181] Thus agreements where the assignor earns a royalty dependent upon the turnover of products made using the know-how or the patents attained by the assignee, or the quantity of such products made, or the number of operations carried out employing the know-how or patents, are all exempt. Also covered are agreements in which rights or obligations are assumed by undertakings connected with the parties.[182] Thus an assignment of the licensee's rights to a wholly owned subsidiary of the licensee is perfectly acceptable.

13.227 With regard to the geographical scope of an agreement, exemption applies to a licence which contains obligations relating not only to territories within the Community but also to non-Member States. However, agreements for territories other than the Community which have effects within the Community are subject to the Regulation.[183] Hence, a restriction imposed on a licensee in a non-EC territory not to export to the Community where there were no alternative sources of supply within in the Community could be said to have an effect within the Community and thus the licensor and licensee could

[179] OJ 1989 L61/1. For a commentary on the Regulation, see Korah *Know-how Licensing Agreements and the EEC Competition Rules: Regulation 556/89* (1989). It was subsequently amended by Regulation 151/93, OJ 1993 L21/8, and the amended text is reproduced at [1993] 4 CMLR 195. The principal decisions adopted by the Commission prior to adopting this block exemption were: *Campari* [1978] 2 CMLR 397; *Boussois/Interpane* [1988] 4 CMLR 124; *Rich Products/Jus-Rol* [1988] 4 CMLR 527; *Delta Chemie/DDD* [1989] 4 CMLR 535.

[180] Art. 6(1).

[181] Art. 6(2).

[182] Art. 6(3).

[183] Recital 4.

find their agreement caught by Article 85(1) notwithstanding that neither had a presence within the Community.[184]

13.228 The exemption does not apply to agreements concerning sales alone, unless the supply of the licensed product by the licensor to the licensee is merely a prelude to the licensee commencing production itself.[185] The same applies under the technology transfer block exemption.

13.229 Nor does the exemption apply in situations where each of the parties would be both a licensor and a licensee, such as know-how exchanged further to patent pooling arrangements, as well as reciprocal licensing arrangements between competitors unless there are no territorial restrictions imposed on distribution.[186]

13.230 The block exemption was amended to enable it to be applicable to some joint ventures,[187] and details are given at paras 13.307-13.308.

13.231 If the know-how relates to marketing in the context of franchising, the agreement is subject to the franchising block exemption.[188]

(2) Relationship with patents and other intellectual property rights

13.232 "Pure" know-how agreements clearly fall to be considered under the know-how block exemption. But often know-how agreements contain provisions relating to patents, trade marks, and copyrights such as design rights and software. It is therefore in respect of pre-April 1996 licences of importance to identify the relevant block exemption. The principle is that the patent block exemption applies to pure patent licences and to patent licences containing provisions relating to know-how which is no more than necessary for achieving the objects of the licensed technology. Provisions relating to trade marks and other intellectual property rights will be covered provided that they are no more than ancillary to the agreement.[189]

13.233 If the know-how or other intellectual property rights are more extensive, then the patent block exemption cannot apply and consideration must then be given to the application of the know-how block exemption. The know-how block exemption will apply where the licensed patents are not necessary for the achievement of the objects of the licensed technology containing both patented and non-patented elements, or where regardless of whether the licensed patents are so necessary, the agreement extends to territories where there is no patent protection and accordingly no exemption under the patent block exemption.[190]

13.234 There are several significant differences between the types of clauses which may be permitted under the block exemptions, the know-how block exemption generally being the more permissive. If a restriction is permitted under the know-how block exemption but falls outside the patent block exemption, it will be crucial to determine which block exemption applies. It must always be borne in mind that unlike the RTPA where careful drafting can be used to achieve the outcome desired due to the formalistic nature of

[184] This should be read in the light of the Court of Justice's judgment in Joined Cases 89, 104, 114, 116, 117 and 125–129/85 *Åhlström* v *Commission (Wood Pulp)* [1988] ECR 5193, [1988] 4 CMLR 901, which limits Art. 85's application to those agreements which are implemented within the EC, arguably a narrower jurisdiction than if it were to apply to those agreements which have effects in the EC.

[185] recital 5.

[186] Art. 5.

[187] Reg. 151/93, OJ 1993 L21/8. The amended text is reproduced at [1993] 4 CMLR 195.

[188] Recital 5; see Reg. 4087/88 on block exemption for franchising agreements, discussed at paras. 10.270–10.315.

[189] Recital 9, Reg. 2349/84.

[190] Recital 2.

that legislation, under the block exemptions, it is the substance which matters. It is not possible in theory to deem something to be a know-how licence agreement when in fact the agreement is to license a patent where the accompanying know-how is no more than ancillary to the patented technology.

(3) Definition of know-how

13.235 Unlike patents which are subject to definition both by international conventions and in national legislation, there is no accepted definition of know-how which could have been adopted for the purposes of the know-how block exemption. Accordingly it was necessary for the block exemption to define what is meant by know-how. Earlier drafts of the block exemption had adopted quite narrow definitions; the final text was criticised widely as being too restrictive but seems not to have provoked many problems in practice as far as reported cases are any guide. The block exemption gives a tripartite definition of know-how: know-how must be (a) secret, (b) substantial and (c) identified.[191]

13.236 (a) "Secret" is defined as meaning "that the know-how package as a body or in the precise configuration and assembly of its components is not generally known or easily accessible, so that part of its value consists in the lead-time the licensee gains when it is communicated to him; it is not limited to the narrow sense that each individual component of the know-how should be totally unknown or unobtainable outside the licensor's business."[192] So it seems that a compilation of know-how, the individual components of which are known but not the way in which they are assembled, would qualify as secret. Difficulties exist with the ascertaining what is meant by "generally known" or "easily accessible". It may well be that this is another way of expressing the English concept of public domain which determines whether know-how remains protectable as confidential information under English law. If so, then this is to be decided by looking at knowledge in the relevant industry. In practice, who would take a licence of know-how if it was not secret?

13.237 (b) "Substantial" is further defined as meaning "that the know-how includes information which is of importance for the whole or a significant part of (i) a manufacturing process or (ii) a product or service, or (iii) for the development thereof and excludes information which is trivial". Such know-how must thus be useful, i.e. can reasonable be expected at the date of conclusion of the agreement to be capable of improving the competitive position of the licensee, for example by helping him to enter a new market or giving him an advantage in competition with other manufacturers or providers of services who do not have access to the licensed secret know-how or other comparable secret know-how.[193] Despite the verbosity of this requirement, its most notable feature is its superfluity, a throwback to the earlier more suspicious Commission view of know-how as a subterfuge for anti-competitive collusion, since what licensee would take a licence of know-how which was not "useful" or was only "trivial"?

13.238 (c) "Identified" is further defined as meaning that "the know-how is described or recorded in such a manner as to make it possible to verify that if fulfils the criteria of secrecy and substantiality and to ensure that the licensee is not unduly restricted in his exploitation of his own technology. To be identified the know-how can be set out in licence agreement or in a separate document or recorded in any other

[191] Art. 1(7)(1).
[192] Art. 1(7)(2).
[193] Art. 1(7)(3).

appropriate form at the latest when the know-how is transferred or shortly thereafter, provided that the separate document or other record can be made available if the need arises."[194] In practice, this is the most onerous requirement, since know-how often depends on demonstration of the technology as much as it can be recorded in an appropriate form. Moreover, subsequent improvements covered by agreement must also be identified in this way.[195] This requirement seems to be included more for the convenience of the Commission in verifying the application of the block exemption rather than being required as a means of preventing a breach of Article 85(1).

2. *Permissible Restrictions: Article 1 (White Clauses)*

13.239 Article 1 enumerates restrictions which may be incorporated into know-how licences without endangering the exemption. These "white clauses" are examined below. A clause of more limited scope is also covered by the same exemption.[196] If a clause goes beyond what is permitted in Article 1 it is not exempt under the know-how block exemption. The exemption is only granted on the condition that the know-how together with subsequent improvements communicated under the agreement is identified and only for as long as the know-how remains secret and substantial.[197]

(1) Exclusive territories (Article 1(1) (1), (2))

13.240 Article 1(1) (1) permits: "an obligation on the licensor not to license other undertakings to exploit the licensed technology in the licensed territory"; and Article 1(1) (2) permits "an obligation on the licensor not to exploit the licensed technology in the licensed territory himself". Thus the licensor can grant the licensee an exclusive territory and covenant not to compete with the licensee in that territory.

13.241 Recital 6 explains the Commission's policy on exclusivity clauses. Such clauses are not necessarily incompatible with competition rules where they are concerned with the introduction and protection of a new technology in the licensed territory, by reason of the scale of the research which has been undertaken and of the increase in the level of competition, in particular inter-brand competition, and in the competitiveness of the undertakings concerned resulting from the dissemination of innovation within the Community. This may be the case for example where the agreement is concerned with the introduction and protection of a new process for manufacturing a product which is already known. This Recital in effect affirms the *Nungesser (Maize Seed)* judgment.[198] Where an exclusivity clause does not satisfy the criteria in Recital 6, for example where the product is not "new", it will be exempt, none the less, under Article 1.

13.242 The exemption under Article 1(1) (2) for a restriction on the licensor from exploiting the licensed technology in the licensed territory only applies if the licensee (or its connected undertaking or subcontractor) manufactures or proposes to manufacture the licensed product itself.[199]

[194] Art. 1(7)(4).
[195] Art. 1(3).
[196] Art. 1(6).
[197] Art. 1(6).
[198] Case 258/78 *Nungesser* v *Commission (Maize Seed)* [1982] ECR 2015, [1983] CMLR 278.
[199] Art. 1(5).

13.243 These exemptions under Article 1(1) (1) and (2) are limited in time to ten years from the date of signature of the first licence agreement entered into by the licensor for that technology in that licensed territory. This is the longest period of exemption allowed under the block exemption. It should be contrasted with the position under the patent block exemption where the equivalent exemptions could last until the expiry of each of the licensed patents. The difference is explained by the limited period of protection granted by a patent. Since know-how is potentially perpetual, the Commission is unwilling to grant potentially perpetual exclusivity.

13.244 However, if there is patent protection for the licensed technology in a licensed territory which is for longer in duration than this ten year period, then that period of patent protection may be substituted for that territory.[200]

13.245 For the extension of exclusivity through the addition of new know-how, see the commentary on Article 3(10) at para. 13.301.

(2) Non-competition clauses (Article 1(1) (3))

13.246 The obverse of Article 1(1) (2) is exempted by Article 1(1) (3) which permits "an obligation on the licensee not to exploit the licensed technology in territories within the common market which are reserved for the licensor".

13.247 This exemption is subject to two of the same limitation as apply to Article 1(1) (1) and (2), namely that it only applies if the licensee (or its connected undertaking or subcontractor) manufacturers or proposes to manufacture the licensed product itself and that it may only be granted for the same ten year period (subject to additional patent protection), as are discussed above.

13.248 In addition it is important to note the territories reserved to the licensor is defined[201] as meaning territories where the licensor has not granted any licences and which the licensor has expressly reserved to itself.

(3) Protection for licensees against each other (Articles 1(1) (4), (5) and (6)

13.249 The Commission recognises that licensees require a degree of protection from each other. Licensees protected from competition, *inter se*, may focus their efforts in a more intensive manner thereby maximising the chances of effective exploitation and utilisation of the licensed technology. This recognition is reflected in the wording of Recital 6 which expressly states that the increase in the level of competition may be a factor in deciding that exclusivity need not be caught by Article 85(1). However, the Commission and the European Courts have refused to countenance absolute territorial protection whereby licensees are protected from *all* competition, in particular from parallel importers.[202]

13.250 There are three types of territorial exclusivity which the Commission distinguishes in order to give different treatment to them: (a) exclusive manufacture or use in Article 1(1) (4), (b) exclusive selling rights with protection from actively marketed but not unsolicited parallel imports in Article 1(1) (5), and (c) exclusive selling rights with absolute territorial protection from parallel imports in Article 1(1) (6).

13.251 (a) Under Article 1(1) (4) a licensor may require a licensee "not to manufacture or use the licensed product, or use the licensed process, in territories within the common

[200] Art. 1(4).
[201] Art. 1(7)(12).
[202] Case 258/78 *Nungesser v Commission (Maize Seed)* [1982] ECR 2015, [1983] CMLR 278, at para. 61 of the judgment, approving Joined Cases 56 and 58/64 *Consten and Grundig v Commission* [1966] ECR 299, [1966] CMLR 418.

market which are licensed to other licensees." This exemption lasts for a period of no more than ten years from the date of signature of the first licence agreement entered into by the licensor within the EC (rather than just the licensed territory) for that licensed technology.[203] As before, if there is relevant patent protection for that territory which extends beyond that period, then the duration of that patent protection may be substituted.[204]

13.252 (b) Under Article 1(1) (5) a licensor may require a licensee "not to pursue an active policy of putting the licensed product on the market in the territories within the common market which are licensed to other licensees, and in particular not to engage in advertising specifically aimed at those territories or to establish any branch or maintain any distribution depot there". This allows a licensee to sell licensed products in other licensees' territories provided those sales are unsolicited or passive to use the wording of the block exemption. This exemption lasts for a period of no more than ten years from the date of signature of the first licence agreement entered into by the licensor within the EC (rather than just the licensed territory) for that licensed technology.[205] As before, if there is relevant patent protection for that territory which extends beyond that period, then the duration of that patent protection may be substituted.[206] It only applies if the licensee (or its connected undertaking or subcontractor) manufactures or proposes to manufacture the licensed product itself.[207]

13.253 (c) If the licensor requires to grant its licensees absolute territorial protection form parallel imports form each other then under Article 1(1) (6) a restriction may be imposed on a licensee "not to put the licensed product on the market in the territories licensed to other licensees within the common market". This exemption only lasts for no longer than five years from the date of signature of the first licence agreement entered into by the licensor within the EC in respect of the same licensed technology. As before, if there is relevant patent protection for that territory which extends beyond that period, then the duration of that patent protection may be substituted.[208] It only applies if the licensee (or its connected undertaking or subcontractor) manufactures or proposes to manufacture the licensed product itself.[209]

13.254 Some general comments may be made about the exemptions for restrictions on marketing. First, the licensor may not impose any restrictions on a licensee with a view to preventing or hindering a third party being supplied where that third party is known or suspected to be exporting those products into other licensees' territories.[210]

13.255 Secondly, the restrictions examined here are only concerned with relations between the licensees; a licensee can be restricted from selling at all into the licensor's territory under Article 1(1) (3) and vice versa under Article 1(1) (2) subject to the limitations noted above.

13.256 Thirdly, the licensor may not be able to accept an obligation in response to a licensee which wants a guarantee that similar restrictions will be imposed on all other licensees. The status of such a "most favoured licensee" clause is unclear: see para. 13.277.

[203] Art. 1(2).
[204] Art. 1(4).
[205] Art. 1(2).
[206] Art. 1(4).
[207] Art. 1(5).
[208] Art. 1(4).
[209] Art. 1(5).
[210] Arts. 3(12) and 7(5).

13.257 Fourthly, the permissible restrictions in the know-how block exemption go further than their counterparts in the patent block exemption[211] since the periods of protection are not dependent on the patents continuing in force. The duration of the restrictions under the know-how block exemption may continue notwithstanding the expiry of relevant patents until the expiry of the periods of time exempted under Article 1(2), and if any patents continue for longer than those periods, so does the exemption under Article 1(4). So the period of exemption can never be shorter than it would have been under the patent block exemption and may well be longer.

(4) Trade marks (Article 1(1) (7))

13.258 This provision exempts "an obligation on the licensee to sue only the licensor's trade mark or the get-up determined by the licensor to distinguish the licensed product during the term of the agreement, provided that the licensee is not prevented from identifying himself as the manufacturer of the licensed products". A pure trade mark licence can not be exempted under the block exemption and will have to seek individual exemption.[212]

(5) Limited production licences (Article 1(1) (8))

13.259 Whereas the patent block exemption did not exempt limitations on a licensee's production, Article 1(1) (8) of the know-how block exemption provides that a licensee may be limited to using the licensed technology only for the purposes of incorporation as an integral part of its products or as spare parts for its own products. However, the licensee must remain free to determine the level of its own production. Although this is listed in Article 1 as a restriction which could come within Article 85(1), it has been argued that it must fall outside Article 85(1) and therefore would not render notifiable an agreement otherwise exempt under the patent block exemption.

3. Permissible Clauses not Generally Falling within Article 85(1): Article 2 (White Clauses)

13.260 Article 2(1) lists typical licence clauses that are generally not considered to fall within Article 85(1). Where such clauses are within Article 85(1) because of particular economic or legal circumstances, they will be automatically exempt under Article 85(3). The list is given by the Commission for purposes of legal certainty but none the less is not exhaustive. Article 2(1) states that Article 1 shall apply notwithstanding the presence of any of the following obligations. Article 2(2) states that the exemption shall apply to any restriction coming within Article 2(1) even if unaccompanied by a restriction caught under Article. This is further clarified by Article 2(3) which states that restrictions of more limited scope than those set out in Article 2(1) may also take the benefit of the exemption under Article 2(2). The restrictions listed in Article 2(1) will now be dealt with in numerical order.

(1) Non-disclosure of know-how

13.261 Under Article 2(1)(1) the licensee may be required not to divulge know-how communicated by the licensor both during the agreement and thereafter. It is uncertain whether

211 Arts. 1(1)(1)–(6), Reg. 2349/84.

212 *Moosehead/Whitbread* OJ 1990 L100/32, [1991] 4 CMLR 391. The Commission refused to accept an argument that the know-how block exemption could apply to an agreement whereby a Canadian brewery exclusively licensed a UK brewery to use its know-how to brew its brand of lager for the UK market, apparently taking the view that all there is to British brewed lager nowadays is the brand name and that this was the core of the agreement, not the brewing know-how which was subsidiary: see para. 13.408.

know-how in this context must be understood as know-how as it is defined under the block exemption ie being secret, substantial and identified. If it is, a clause restricting disclosure of know-how not meeting those criteria e.g. non-identified know-how or trivial know-how, would not come within Article 2(1)(1). While it would be unusual for a licensor to seek to prevent disclosure of know-how not meeting these first two of these criteria, the third criterion must always be borne in mind in mind in practice. A contrary interpretation would be that Article 2(1) (1) allows the restriction of the disclosure of any know-how whether or not still secret substantial and identified. This interpretation is, it is submitted, the better one since Article 2(1)(3) discussed below finds it necessary to qualify a restriction on exploitation as relating only to secret know-how, a qualification which would not be necessary if that were already inherent in the definition of know-how.

13.262 A further matter for consideration is the status of a clause requiring a licensee to demonstrate that know-how is no longer secret before release from this obligation. Like the patent block exemption, there is no indication in the know-how block exemption as to how such a clause would be treated. As Article 2(1) is not exhaustive, such a clause could in any event escape Article 85(1).

(2) Prohibition on sub-licensing or assignment

13.263 Article 2(1) (2), like the corresponding provision under the patent block exemption,[213] permits obligations on the licensee not to grant sub-licences or assign the licence. Hence conditions on what may be included in sub-licences should in principle be exempt under Article 2(2), since if a licensee can be restricted from sub-licensing at all, more limited restrictions on what may be included in a sub-licence should also be covered.

(3) Post-expiry of the agreement exploitation

13.264 Article 2(1) (3) permits an obligation to be imposed on the licensee not to exploit the licensed know-how after the termination of the agreement in so far as and for so long as the know-how is still secret. Although this makes no mention of any proviso relating to know-how ceasing to be secret due to unauthorised disclosure by the licensee, it seems that this is a legislative oversight possibly caused by carrying over the wording the equivalent provision in the patent block exemption[214] without sufficient regard for the different nature of know-how. The better view is, it is submitted, that such a provision would not bring this restriction within Article 85(1).

13.265 It should be noted that under Article 7(6) the Commission reserves the right to withdraw the benefit of the block exemption should the operation of the post-term use ban prevent the licensee from working an expired patent which can be worked by all other manufacturers. Because parallel patents often expire at different times, there is an ambiguity here: does this mean only manufacturers in that licensee's territory, or does it mean all manufacturers wherever located? It is submitted that the former is the more likely interpretation given since it is less restrictive of the licensee.

(4) Improvements and communications of experience (grant/license back clauses)

13.266 Article 2(1) (4) is considerably more extensive than the corresponding provision under the patent block exemption[215] and can generally be considered to give greater considera-

[213] See para. 13.157.
[214] See para. 13.154.
[215] See paras. 13.165–13.167.

tion to the licensee than is the case under the patent block exemption. However the Technology Transfer Regulation has now modified the position further.

13.267 An obligation on the licensee "to communicate to the licensor any experience gained in exploiting the licensed technology and to grant him a non-exclusive licence in respect of improvements to or new applications of that technology" will fall outside Article 85(1) subject to the two following conditions:

> "(a) the licensee is not prevented during or after the term of the agreement from freely using his own improvements, in so far as these are severable from the licensor's know-how, or licensing them to third parties where licensing to third parties does not disclose the know-how communicated by the licensor that is still secret; this is without prejudice to and obligation on the licensee to seek the licensor's prior approval to such licensing provided that approval may not be withheld unless there are objectively justifiable reasons to believe that licensing improvements to third parties will disclose the licensor's know-how, and
> (b) the licensor has accepted an obligation whether exclusive or not, to communicate his own improvements to the licensee and his right to use the licensee's improvements which are not severable from the licensed know-how does not extend beyond the date on which the licensee's right to exploit the licensor's know-how comes to an end, except for termination of the agreement for breach by the licensee; this is without prejudice to an obligation on the licensee to give the licensor the option to continue to use the improvements after that date, if at the same time he relinquishes the post-term use ban or agrees, after having had an opportunity to examine the licensee's improvements, to pay appropriate royalties for their use."

13.268 The main practical difficulty with the provision lies in determining criteria to determine whether improvements, *ex hypothesi* not yet made, are in fact severable. It should be noted that reciprocal exclusive licenses will be caught by Article 85(1) and fall to be considered under the blacklist .

(5) Minimum quality and tying in

13.269 Article 2(1) (5) permits obligations on the licensee to observe minimum quality requirements for the licensed product or to obtain goods or services from the licensor or the licensor's nominee where necessary for: (a) a technically satisfactory exploitation of the licensed technology, or (b) ensuring that the production of the licensee conforms to the quality standards that are respected by the licensor and other licensees. The licensor's freedom to impose quality standards and tying obligations to ensure conformity with quality standards is wider than that permitted under the patent block exemption.[216] In order to come within the exemption it will be necessary for the licensor to demonstrate that such quality standards are not only provided for contractually but are in practice observed.

(6) Infringement clauses (excluding no-challenge clauses)

13.270 Article 2(1) (6) like its counterpart in the patent block exemption[217] permits obligations on the licensee:

(a) to inform the licensor of misappropriation of the know-how or of infringements of the licensed patents, or
(b) to take legal action against such misappropriation or infringement, or
(c) to assist the licensor to take such legal action.

[216] See para. 13.148.
[217] See paras. 13.161–13.163.

However, a no-challenge clause, if caught by Article 85(1), is not exempt. The licensee must remain free to challenge the validity of the licensed patents or to contest the secrecy of the know-how provided it has not in some way contributed to its disclosure. A no-challenge clause may not be incorporated without losing the benefit of the block exemption, though it is possible for a licensor to reserve the right to terminate in the event of challenge.[218]

13.271 However, it may be possible to argue that a particular no-challenge clause is not within Article 85(1) on the strength of the Court of Justice's ruling in *Bayer* v *Süllhöfer* that a no-challenge clause would not, when seen in its legal and economic context, constitute an appreciable restriction on competition if it was a royalty free licence or if the technology is technically outdated so that the licensee does not in fact use the patented process.[219] The emphasis on assessing the licensee's competitive position in the light of the restriction rather than the concern to ensure that invalid patents do not remain registered (which characterised the Court's and Commission's previous decisions) could be applied to know-how occupying a similar economic function. Ultimately, it is far safer to rely upon Article 3(4) and include a right to terminate in event of challenge rather than rely on trying to argue that the *Bayer* v *Süllhöfer* principles apply.

(7) Royalty payments

13.272 Article 2(1) (7) adopts a less restrictive approach than that under the patent block exemption in permitting methods of calculation of royalties. The Technology Transfer Regulation now adopts flexible rules for patent and know-how licences: see Recital 21 and Article 2(1)(7). Under the know-how block exemption, a licensee may be required to continue paying royalties until the end of the term of the agreement notwithstanding that the know-how has become publicly known, unless the disclosure of the know-how was due to the licensor's action.

13.273 This contrasts with the licensor's more limited ability under the patent block exemption to require payment of royalties for know-how only for so long as it has not entered into the public domain other than through the licensee's action; a clause requiring payment for use of publicly known know-how would be blacklisted under the patent block exemption. The only exceptions under the patent block exemption to this are if the payments relate to patents still in force or if the royalty payments though calculated for use of secret know-how are spread over a longer period to facilitate payment by the licensee.[220]

13.274 This provision is subject to quite detailed comment in Recital 15 where the Commission acknowledges that practically to do otherwise would lead to licensors seeking higher initial payments for know-how licences to lessen their exposure to subsequent premature disclosure. Importantly, the Commission warns that in cases where it is clear that the licensee would have been able and willing to develop the know-how itself in a short period of time and in comparison to that period of time the period of continuing payments for know-how is excessively long, the Commission may exercise its power to withdraw the benefit of the exemption under Article 7 of the block exemption.[221]

(8) Field of use and product market restrictions

13.275 Article 2(1) (8) allows a licensor to limit a licensee's exploitation of the licensed technology either to one or more technical fields of application, as is the case with the patent block ex-

218 Art. 3(4).
219 Case 65/86 *Bayer* v *Süllhöfer* [1988] ECR 5249, [1990] 4 CMLR 182, paras. 17 and 18.
220 See para. 13.183.
221 Art. 7(7); see para. 13.312.

emption, or to one or more product markets. The Technology Transfer Regulation permits field of use and product market restrictions for both patent and know-how licences: see Article 2(1)(8). As has already been explained in the context of the patent block exemption blacklist [222] the first distinction is not easy to draw in practice, even if there were any consensus as to what the phrase "technical field of application" means it is not a recognised term of art in patent law. The second may be easier in practice, though definition of product market will be crucial. It may be possible to adopt the same restrictive analysis of product markets that the Commission has done in its case law in applying Article 86 EC. But in many industries it is impossible to say whether items are different products or the same products produced to different customer specifications. If the latter then a restriction to supplying only particular specifications will amount to a customer restriction which is blacklisted.[223]

(9) Minimum royalties

13.276 Article 2(1) (9) virtually repeats the equivalent provision of the patent block exemption[224] in allowing the licensor to require the licensee:

(a) to pay a minimum royalty,
(b) to produce a minimum quantity of the licensed product, and
(c) to carry out a minimum number of operations exploiting the licensed technology.

However, there is one additional point to take into account under the know-how block exemption. The Commission reserves the right to withdraw the benefit of the block exemption under Article 7 should the licensee have been competitors prior to the grant of the licence and the minimum quantity requirements effectively prevent the licensee from using competing technologies.[225]

(10) Most favoured licensee's terms

13.277 Article 2(1) (10) permits a restriction on the *licensor* to grant the licensee any more favourable terms that the licensor may grant to another undertaking after the agreement is entered into. This is the same as under the patent block exemption.[226] What is not covered by this block exemption is an obligation on the licensor to include a particular term or terms in its other licensor's ability to grant further licences and would thus be caught under Article 85(1). The same provision is found in Article 2(1)(10) of the Technology Transfer Regulation.

(11) Identification of licensor on licensed product

13.278 Article 2(1) (11) permits the licensor to require the licensee to mark the licensed product with the licensor's name. Nothing is mentioned about marking details of any patentee's name or licensed patent. As such provisions are referred to in the whitelist in the patent block exemption,[227] then it will normally be the case that such obligations would not be caught within Article 85(1). Furthermore, Article 1(1) (7) permits the licensor to require the licensee only to use the licensor's trade mark on the licensed product, subject to the licensee being able to identify itself as manufacturer.

222 See para. 13.153.
223 Art. 3(6).
224 See para. 13.150.
225 Art. 7(8).
226 See para. 13.168.
227 See para. 13.158.

(12) Prohibition on construction of facilities for third parties

13.279 Article 2(1) (12) permits the licensor to require the licensee not to use the licensed know-how to construct facilities for third parties. The purpose of this provision, not related to any provision of the patent block exemption, is to prevent third party access to the licensor's secret know-how. However, it is expressly provided that it cannot prejudice the licensee's right to increase the capacity of its own facilities or to set up additional facilities for its own use on normal commercial terms including payment of royalties.

4. Non-Permissible Restrictions: Article 3 (Black Clauses)

13.280 Exemption is not given automatically for certain clauses. Inclusion of such clauses means that an agreement is not exempt unless either the agreement is notified or it falls within the scope of the Technology Transfer Regulation. The blacklist comprises a number of clauses whose exemptibility or otherwise depends upon the existence or non-existence of other factors. Such clauses must hence be seen within the context of previous case law on this subject.

(1) Post-term use ban

13.281 Article 3(1) denies exemption to a clause which would prevent a licensee form continuing to use the licensed know-how after the termination of the agreement where the know-how has become publicly known, other than by the licensee's action in breach of the agreement. This does not prevent a clause restricting post-term use of secret know-how.

13.282 The principles are the same as those which apply under the patent block exemption.[228]

13.283 If a post-term use ban is included, it will also be necessary to take account in any grant back or licence back clause the provisions of Article 3(2) (c) analysed in the next section.

(2) Impermissible improvements and communications of experience (grant/licence back clauses)

13.284 Article 3(2) sets out at length grant back and licence back provisions that are blacklisted. These are where the licensee is required:

(a) to assign in whole or in part to the licensor rights to improvements to or new applications of the licensed technology;

(b) to grant the licensor an exclusive licence for improvements to or new applications of the licensed technology which would prevent the licensee during the currency of the agreement and/or thereafter from using his own improvements in so far as these are severable form the licensor's know-how, or from licensing them to third parties, where such licensing would not disclose the licensor's know-how that is still secret; or

(c) in the case of an agreement which also includes a post-term use ban, to grant back to the licensor, even on a non-exclusive and reciprocal basis, licences for improvements which are not severable form the licensor's know-how, if the licensor's right to use the improvements is of a longer duration than the licensee's right to use the licensor's know-how, except for termination of the agreement for breach by the licensee.

[228] See para. 13.154.

13.285 The recitals give no assistance in unravelling this intricate provision, nor any justification for limiting the licensor's freedom to include grant back and licence back clauses to a greater extent than is done under the patent block exemption. Moreover, this provision must be read in the light of Article 2(1)(4).[229] Finally, there is no case law to provide assistance.

13.286 Reading the white and black clauses together, the following (unsurprisingly) grey picture emerges as to the sort of clause which may be exempted. First, grant back clauses: Article 3(2) (a) makes it clear that a requirement on the licensee to assign ownership of improvements to the licensor is blacklisted and will not benefit from an exemption.

13.287 Secondly, exclusive licence back clauses: if a licensor seeks an exclusive licence of improvements, the effect of Articles 3(2) (b) and 2(1)(4) is to blacklist such a provision unless the licensee remains free to use its own improvements, provided they are severable from the licensor's know-how and to license them to third parties. The licensor may reserve the right to require its consent to licensing third parties but such consent may only be refused if licensing would disclose the licensor's know-how. Moreover, if there is a post-term use ban on the licensee the licence back provision will be blacklisted if it applies to improvements which are not severable from the licensor's know-how and the licensor's right to sue the improvements is of a longer duration than the licensee's right to use the licensor's know-how.

13.288 If a provision manages to escape being thus blacklisted, it does not gain automatic exemption under the whitelist unless the following further obligation is accepted by the licensor: to license back to the licensee use of its own improvements under the detailed provision of Article 2(1)(4)(b). Failing such a provision, such a clause will not qualify under the block exemption.

13.289 Thirdly, a non-exclusive licence back clause will not be blacklisted except where there is a post-term use ban on the licensee. In such a case, the licence back provision will be blacklisted if it applies to improvements which are not severable from the licensor's know-how and the licensor's right to use the improvements is of a longer duration than the licensee's right to use the licensor's know-how. A non-exclusive licence back clause escaping blacklist ing under Article 3(2)(c) will not be automatically exempted unless it complies with the provisions of Article 2(1)(4), and in the absence of such compliance will require notification for exemption under the opposition procedure.

(3) Tying and quality specifications

13.290 Under Article 3(3) there is no exemption where the licensee is required to accept quality specifications or further licences or is to procure goods or services which the licensee does not want. There are two exceptions to this. First, if such provisions are necessary for a technically satisfactory exploitation of the licensed technology. Secondly, if such provisions are necessary for ensuring that the production of the licensee conforms to the quality standards that are respected by the licensor and other licensees. These provisions are the converse of the whitelisted provisions in Article 2(1)(5).[230]

13.291 The reference to the licensee accepting quality specifications or goods which it does not want seems somewhat vague. Will it be open to a licensee to argue that an apparent willingness to submit to such provisions did not represent what the licensee really wanted? Recital 17 states that the requirement to take such specifications or goods will not cause the block exemption to be lost if it can be shown that the licensee wanted such specifications, licences, goods or services for reasons of its own convenience, which equally seems

[229] See paras. 13.266–13.268.

[230] See para. 13.269.

to let the matter of compatibility with the block exemption rest with the whim of the licensee. In practice this provision has not caused material difficulties.

13.292 The licensor's freedom to impose quality standards and tying obligations to ensure conformity with quality standards goes further than that which is permitted under the patent block exemption.[231] In order to come within this it will be necessary for the licensor to demonstrate that such quality standards are not only provided for contractually but are in practice observed. It is possible to argue that the patent block exemption is more generous to a licensor since it requires that the licensee be induced into accepting further licences, goods or services, whereas the blacklisted provision in the know how block exemption applies irrespective of this element of causation. Alternatively, it may well be that everything turns on whether the licensee can be said to have "wanted" the additional specifications, licences, goods or services. The Technology Transfer Regulation expressly places tying obligations in the category of clauses suitable for treatment under the opposition procedure (see Article 4(2)(9)).

(4) No-challenge clauses

13.293 No exemption lies under Article 3(4) where the licensee is prohibited from contesting the secrecy of the licensed know-how or from challenging the validity of the licensed patents. However, the licensor may reserve itself the right to terminate an agreement in the event of such a challenge. This reflects the position under the patent block exemption.[232] As has been noted,[233] it is possible to argue that some no-challenge clauses are not caught by Article 85(1) at all on the strength of the Court of Justice's decision in *Bayer* v *Süllhöfer*,[234] but realistically it is far safer including the right of termination acknowledged by Article 3(4) as compatible with the block exemption. The Technology Transfer Regulation removes no-challenge clauses from the blacklist and makes them expressly suitable for treatment under the opposition procedure (see Article 4(2)(b)).

(5) Royalty payments in respect of unprotected rights

13.294 Article 3(5), which is similar to the corresponding provision of the patent block exemption,[235] removes the benefit of the block exemption for a restriction where the licensee is charged royalties on goods or services which are not entirely or partially produced by means of the licensed technology or for the use of know-how which has become publicly known by the action of the licensor or connected undertaking. It is the converse of Article 2(1)(7) and the effect of these provisions is that royalties may continue to be calculated as payable despite the know-how falling into the public domain except where this is due to the action of the licensor. This goes further than the net effect of the patent block exemption which only allows royalties to be continued to be calculated once the know-how is in the public domain if this was due to the licensee's action.

(6) Customer restrictions

13.295 No exemption lies under Article 3(6) where one party (i.e. either licensee or licensor) is restricted within the same technological field of use or within the same product market as to the customers it may serve, in particular by being prohibited from supplying certain classes of user, employing certain forms of distribution or, with the aim of sharing cus-

[231] See para. 13.148.
[232] See para. 13.171.
[233] See para. 13.271.
[234] Case 65/86 *Bayer* v *Süllhöfer* [1988] ECR 5249, [1990] 4 CMLR 182
[235] See para. 13.183.

tomers, using certain types of packaging for the products. This is expressed to be without prejudice to the provisions of Article 1(1)(7) relating to licensee's use of the licensor's trade mark and Article 4(2) relating to limited licences to ensure a customer a second source of supply within a licensed territory. These prohibitions on inclusion of customer restrictions have to be seen in the light of the permissible restrictions on licensees to different technical fields of application or product markets under Article 2(1)(8). The problems of defining when a technical field of applications or product market restriction becomes a customer restriction have already been discussed[236] and this Article does nothing to clarify the point. Nor do the Recitals give any assistance. Similar problems arise under the patent block exemption which is more restrictive since the licensor may not limit the licence to a particular product market but only to a particular technical field of application. The Technology Transfer Regulation now permits product market restrictions for both patents and know-how licences.

(7) Limitations on quantity or number of operations

13.296 Exemption is refused under Article 3(7) where either party is restricted as to the quantity of the licensed products it may manufacture or sell or the number of operations exploiting the licensed technology it may carry out. This is expressed to be without prejudice to the permissible restrictions under Article 1(1)(8) relating to limited licences for licensee's use in its own production relating to limited licences to ensure a customer a second source of supply within a licensed territory. These provisions render the know-how block exemption more permissive in allowing such restrictions than its counterpart under the patent block exemption.[237]

(8) Prices and discounts

13.297 No exemption lies under Article 3(8) where either licensor or licensee is restricted in the determination of prices, components of prices or discounts for the licensed products. This is the same as under the patent block exemption: any provision relating to any type of price fixing is highly unlikely to receive exemption under EC law.

(9) Non-competition clauses

13.298 Article 3(9) refuses exemption where one party is restricted from competing with the other party, undertakings connected to that party or any other undertakings in the Common Market in respect of research and development, production, use or distribution of competing products. This is expressed to be without prejudice to an obligation on the licensee to use its best endeavours to exploit the licensed technology. To this extent this blacklist provision repeats the position under the patent block exemption. As with that provision, the permissible best endeavours clause in effect can restrict one party from dealing in competing products since that may give grounds for the other to argue that it is not using its best endeavours to promote the licensed products.[238]

13.299 Article 3(9) proceeds to allow the licensor to impose additional restrictions not found in the patent block exemption should the licensee engage in competing activities. In such a case, the licensor may terminate the licensee's exclusivity, cease communicating improvements to the licensee and require the licensee to prove that the licensed know-how is not used for the production of goods and services other than those licensed. No

[236] See para. 13.153.
[237] See paras. 13.151–13.152.
[238] See para. 13.182.

standard of proof is specified; it may be argued that it cannot be so heavy as to make it impossible for a licensee to engage in competing activities.

13.300 Finally, the Commission under Article 7(8) reserves the right to withdraw the benefit of block exemption if the parties were competitors prior to the grant of the licence and this obligation has the effect of preventing the licensee from using competing technologies. There is no equivalent provision under the patent block exemption.

(10) Extension of agreement beyond initial duration

13.301 No exemption is available under Article 3(10) if the initial duration of the licensing agreement is automatically prolonged by the inclusion in it of any new improvements communicated by the licensor. This reflects the position under the patent block exemption.[239] However, exemption is available in two cases, which go further than the patent block exemption. First, if the licensee has the right to refuse such improvements. There is no equivalent provision to this effect in the patent block exemption. Secondly, if each party has the right to terminate the agreement at the end of the initial term and at least every three years thereafter. Under the patent block exemption, the right to terminate after expiry of the initial term has to be annual. It should be noted that this provision only relates to extending the agreement beyond its initial term. It does not allow the periods under Article 1(1) for which an agreement may be exempted to be extended.

(11) Prohibitions on licensing and exploitation

13.302 Article 3(11) refuses exemption to any provision where the licensor is required, albeit in separate agreements, for a period exceeding that permitted under Article 1(2) not to license other undertakings to exploit the same technology in the licensed territory, or a party is required for periods exceeding those permitted under Articles 1(2) or 1(4) not to exploit the same technology in the territory of the other party or of other licensees. Therefore it can be seen that this provision buttresses the provisions of those Articles discussed above. There is an equivalent provision in the patent block exemption.[240]

(12) Creation of obstacles to parallel imports

13.303 According to Article 3(12) no exemption lies where one or both of the parties are required:

(a) to refuse without any objectively reason to meet demand from users or resellers in their respective territories who would market products in other territories within the common market; or,

(b) to make it difficult for users or resellers to obtain the products from other resellers within the common market, and in particular to exercise intellectual property rights or take measures so as to prevent users or resellers from obtaining outside, or from putting on the market in the licensed territory products which have been lawfully put on the market within the common market by the licensor or with his consent.

These prohibitions also apply although there is no requirement to act in that way, the parties do so as a result of a concerted practice between them. This provision effectively repeats its counterpart in the patent block exemption.[241] Moreover, these provisions are repeated as grounds under which the Commission may withdraw the benefit of the block exemption under Article 7(5).

[239] See para. 13.173.
[240] See para. 13.194.
[241] See para. 13.195.

5. Extension of Exemption to Licences not Expressly Covered: The "Opposition Procedure", Article 4

13.304 Article 4(1) extended the exemption to agreements whose clauses were not expressly covered by Articles 1 and 2 (the white clauses) but which contained no clauses prohibited by Article 3 (black clauses). Agreements of this nature could be notified to the Commission in accordance with the "opposition procedure" outlined in Article 4 and thereby could receive accelerated treatment. In essence, exemption automatically extended to the agreement if no opposition to it had been raised within a six-month period commencing from the date of notification.

6. Types of Licence not Exempt: Article 5

13.305 The Regulation is not all embracing. Article 5 expressly excludes from the block exemption certain categories of agreement. It largely repeats the position under the patent block exemption.[242]

(1) Patent and know-how pools

13.306 Under Article 5(1) the block exemption does not apply to agreements between members of a patent or know-how pool which relate to the pooled technologies.

(2) Licences in the context of a joint venture

13.307 The block exemption was amended to enable it to be applicable to joint ventures.[243] Although it is stated that the block exemption does not apply "to know-how licensing agreements between competitors who hold interests in a joint venture or between one of them and the joint venture, if the licensing agreements relate to the activities of the joint venture",[244] it is also stated that in such cases block exemption is available to agreements

> "under which a parent undertaking grants the joint venture a know-how licence, provided that the contract products and the other products of the participating undertakings which are considered by users to be equivalent in view of their characteristics, price and intended use represent:
> – in case of a licence limited to production not more than 20%
> – in case of a licence covering production and distribution not more than 10% of the market for all such products in the Common Market or a substantial part thereof."[245]

13.308 The benefit of the block exemption is not lost where either of these market share limits is exceeded by up to one-tenth for up to two consecutive financial years. If this limit is however breached, then the block exemption continues for six months beyond the end of the financial year in which it was breached.[246]

(3) Reciprocal licences

13.309 Under Article 5(1)(3) the block exemption does not apply to agreements under which one party grants the other a know-how licence and the other party, albeit in separate agreements or through connected undertakings, grants the first party a patent, trade mark or know-how licence or exclusive sales rights, where the parties are competitors in relation to products covered by those agreements.

242 See para. 13.199.
243 Reg. 151/93, OJ 1993 L21/8; the amended text is printed at [1993] 4 CMLR 195.
244 Art. 5(1)(2).
245 Art. 5(2)(a).
246 Art. 5(3).

13.310 The key points to bear in mind are: first that this does not apply to reciprocal licences between non-competitors; secondly that whether licences are reciprocal is a matter of substance, not of form; and thirdly, that Article 5(2) creates a proviso to the foregoing, viz. that reciprocal licences between competitors can come within the block exemption provided that the parties are not subject to any territorial restriction within the common market on the manufacture, use or putting on the market of the products covered by the agreements or on the use of licensed technologies. These provisions largely repeat the equivalent provisions under the patent block exemption.[247]

(4) Other intellectual property licences

13.311 Article 5(1)(4) provides that the block exemption does not apply to agreements including the licensing of intellectual property rights other than patents (in particular trade marks, copyright and design rights) or the licensing of software except where these rights or the software are of assistance in achieving the object of the licensed technology and there are no obligations restrictive of competition other than those also attached to the licensed know-how and exempted under the know-how block exemption.

7. *Withdrawal of Exemption: Article 7*

13.312 The Commission may, in exceptional cases, withdraw the block exemption from a particular case by formal decision where it considers that an agreement has effects that are incompatible with Article 85(3). There are eight grounds set out in Article 7 on which the Commission gives notice that it may withdraw the benefit of the block exemption, though these are not exhaustive. The first five repeat the equivalent provisions of the patent block exemption and so are only summarised here.[248]

(1) Arbitration awards leading to restrictive settlements

13.313 Exemption may be withdrawn under Article 7(1) if the restrictive effects result from an arbitration award.

(2) Inter-brand competition ineffective

13.314 Exemption may be withdrawn under Article 7(2) where the effect of the agreement is to prevent the licensed products from being exposed to effective competition in the licensed territory from identical products or products considered by users as equivalent in view of their characteristics, price and intended use.

(3) Licensee fails to effectively exploit licence: termination rights

13.315 Article 7(3) allows the Commission to withdraw the benefit of the block exemption if the licensor does not have the right to terminate the exclusivity granted to the licensee at the latest five years from the date the agreement was entered into and at least annually thereafter if, without legitimate reason, the licensee fails to exploit the licensed technology or to do so adequately.

(4) Refusal by the licensee to meet unsolicited demands (passive competition)

13.316 Exemption may be withdrawn under Article 7(4) where the licensee refuses, without objectively valid reasons, to meet unsolicited demand from users or resellers in the territory of

[247] See paras. 13.204–13.206.
[248] See para. 13.208.

other licensees. This is expressly stated to be subject to Article 1(1)(6) which allows licensees to refuse to meet unsolicited demands for licensed products from outside its territory for a period of up to five years from the date of signature of the first licence agreement fro that technology entered into by the licensor in the common market.

(5) Parties create obstacles to parallel imports

13.317 Under Article 7(5) exemption may be withdrawn where one or both of the parties seeks to create obstacles to parallel imports. As such a provision or concerted practice is already blacklisted under Article 3(12), this power is really only of importance where one party seeks to hinder parallel imports unilaterally.

(6) Restrictions on using expired patents

13.318 The Commission may withdraw the exemption under Article 7(6) if there is a post-term use ban exempted under Article 2(1)(3) which prevents the licensee from working an expired patent which can be worked by all other manufacturers.

(7) Payment of royalties for publicly known know-how

13.319 Under Article 7(7) the Commission may withdraw the exemption if the period for which the licensee is obliged to continue paying royalties after the know-how has become publicly known by the action of third parties substantially exceeds the lead time acquired because of the head start in production and marketing and this obligation is detrimental to competition in the market. This relates back to Article 2(1)(7) which provides that normally an obligation to continue paying royalties for publicly known know-how will be treated as a white clause.

(8) Preventing licensee from using competing technologies

13.320 Article 7(8) allows the Commission to withdraw the block exemption if the parties were already competitors before the grant of the licence and obligations on the licensee to produce a minimum quantity as referred to in Article 2(1)(9) or to use its best endeavours as referred to in Article 3(9) have the effect of preventing the licensee from using competing technologies.

8. Transitional Periods and Currency of Block Exemption: Articles 8, 9, 10 and 12

13.321 Articles 8–10 cover: agreements already in force at the time the Regulation became operative; "old agreements"; and accession agreements. These provisions repeat those set out in Articles 6-8 respectively of the patent block exemption and reference is made to paras 13.215-13.219 for commentary on them.

13.322 Article 12 concerns the duration of the Regulation itself. The Regulation became operative on 1 April 1989 and was due to apply until 31 December 1999. As with the patent block exemption, it was superseded by the technology transfer block exemption with effect from 1 April 1996 and so now only applies to agreements already in force on 31 March 1996.

9. Confidentiality of the Part of the Commission: Article 11

13.323 As with the patent block exemption, information received by the Commission under the opposition procedure may only be used for the purposes of the Regulation, ie deciding whether exemption lies or not. For further commentary, see paras 13.221-13.222 above.

10. *Check List for Determining whether the Know-how Block Exemption Applies*

13.324 The check list below is an overview only: it is *not* a substitute for proper analysis of the text of the Regulation itself.

Condition 1 (does the patent block exemption still apply?)

Was the agreement in force on or before 31 March 1996? If not, and it came into force more recently, the technology transfer block exemption is applicable.

Condition 2 (patents or know-how?)

If both know-how and patents are being licensed, do the patents cover all the licensed territory, and is the know-how no more than ancillary to the patents? If the answer to either of these questions is no, then the patent block exemption does not apply and reference should be made to the know-how block exemption. Otherwise the patent block exemption applies, not the know-how block exemption.

Condition 3 (agreements exempt)

Agreement must be of a type described in Article 1 of the Regulation. Account should be taken of Article 6 which extends the Regulation to agreements that are effectively the same as the know-how and mixed licences described in Article 1. The Regulation covers agreements involving undertakings "connected" to the parties to the licence (Article 6(3)). The Regulation does *not* apply to: know how pools, licences derived from some joint ventures, reciprocal licences, and other intellectual property licences (Article 5).

Condition 4 (white clauses)

The agreement may legitimately contain clauses listed in Article 1. These are, in summary, clauses of no more than the specified duration: granting exclusivity to the licensee; obliging the licensor not to compete with the licensee; protecting licensees from competition from each other; obliging the licensee to use the licensor's trade mark; and limiting the licensee to production for its own use.

Condition 5 (white clauses)

Agreements containing clauses listed in Article 2 cause no problem. These clauses do not generally restrict competition, where they do Article 2 extends the exemption to them in any event. The permissible clauses may concern the following:

(i) non-disclosure of know-how;
(ii) prohibition on sub-licensing or assignment;
(iii) post-expiry of the agreement exploitation;
(iv) improvement and communication of experience (grant/licence back);
(v) minimum quality;
(vi) infringement clauses (excluding no-challenge clauses);
(vii) royalty payment throughout term of agreement;
(viii) field of use and product market restrictions;
(ix) minimum royalties, minimum quantities or minimum number of operations;
(x) most favoured licensee's terms;
(xi) identification of licensor on licensed product; and
(xii) prohibition on construction of facilities for third parties.

Condition 6 (black clauses)

Under no circumstances can block exemption be claimed for licences containing clauses outlined in Article 3. The "black" clauses concern the following:

(i) post-term use ban;
(ii) impermissible improvements and communications of experience (grant/licence back clauses);
(iii) executive tying clauses;
(iv) no-challenge clauses;
(v) royalty payments in respect of unlicensed products;
(vi) customer restrictions;
(vii) limitations on quantity or number of operations;
(viii) prices and discounts;
(ix) excessive non-competition clauses;
(x) automatic extension of agreement beyond initial term;
(xi) prohibitions on passive sales; and
(xii) creations of obstacles to parallel imports.

Condition 7 (opposition procedure)

Agreements of a type generally caught by the Regulation (Condition 3 above) which contain clauses which are not expressly permitted by Articles 1 and 2 but which, conversely, are not expressly prohibited by Article 3 may obtain automatic exemption by use of the opposition procedure in Article 4.

Condition 8 (exception withdrawal)

In exceptional cases the Commission might, by formal decision, withdraw exemption from an agreement. The Commission might issue such decisions in the following cases, amongst others:

(i) where arbitration awards results in restrictive settlements;
(ii) where inter-brand competition is ineffective;
(iii) where the licensee fails to effectively exploit the licence and no termination rights belong to the licensor;
(iv) where license refuses to meet unsolicited demands;
(v) where a party or parties create obstacles to parallel imports;
(vi) post-term use ban prevents licensee working an expired patent;
(vii) royalty payment for publicly known know-how substantially exceeds lead time gained; and
(viii) minimum quantity requirements prevent a previously competing licensee from using competing technologies.

G. Patent Licensing in United Kingdom Law

13.325 Agreements caught by Article 85(1) EC and exempt under block exemption Regulation 240/96, its predecessors, Regulations 2349/84/EEC and 556/89/EEC, are non-notifiable for the purposes of the RTPA, which therefore only applies to agreements falling outside those block exemptions.[249] Patent licences are not regulated in the UK to the extent that they are in EC law. Prima facie licences are exempt from the RTPA 1976. They are, however, subject to the CA 1980 though there is no case expressly on point to date.[250]

1. Under the RTPA 1976

13.326 Schedule 3, paras. RTPA 1976 exempts from application of the Act licences and other disposals of patents and registered designs. For details see paras. 2.181-2.187. Patent pools however are not exempt from registration.

13.327 Regardless of Schedule 3, para. 5 RTPA 1976 it is generally accepted that licences of proprietary rights are not registrable. First, the licensing of a proprietary interest does not amount to a supply of services or goods for the purposes of the RTPA 1976.[251] Secondly, a licence imposing limitations on the licensee is not legally to be counted as restrictive. The licensee has no inherent right to utilise the proprietary rights and hence a licence, albeit one limited in scope, constitutes a grant of rights and not a restriction on existing rights.[252]

13.328 A licence is not registrable if only one party accepts relevant restrictions. Thus, if only the licensee is subject to restrictions, the agreement need not be registered. When considering registrability no account is to be taken of any term which relates exclusively to the goods or services concerned.[253]

13.329 Know-how licences containing clauses unrelated to the know-how will require registration in the usual fashion. Thus, in *Croda-Manox*[254] C and M entered a specialisation agreement under which they transferred capacity to each other in the fields of production that they were not specialising in. They also transferred know how to each other in respect of that capacity. The agreement was given section 21(2) dispensation.

13.330 In practice very few licensing agreements are furnished to the OFT for registration. Where they are furnished this is often done on a "fail-safe basis" whereby the parties do not necessarily accept that their agreement is within the Act.

2. Under the Competition Act 1980

(1) Legal context

13.331 The terms of licensing agreements not subject to the RTPA 1976 are subject to the Competition Act 1980 (CA 1980). To date the OFT and MMC have dealt with copyright questions but not directly with other forms of intellectual property. The principal issue in these cases has been whether the refusal to grant a licence has been anti-competitive. In respect of patents, refusal to license is expressly covered, not by the CA 1980, but by section 48 of the Patents Act 1977 which makes provision for compulsory licences. This is examined below. As regards tying clauses in patents these also are covered by the Patents Act 1977 and are discussed below.

[249] Restrictive Trade Practices (Non-notifiable Agreements) (EC Block Exemptions), Order, S.I. 1996 No. 3490, issued under section 27A RTPA 1976 (added by s. 10 Deregulation and Contracting Out Act 1994). See further paras. 2.250 and following.

[250] But see the Ministerial Statements made in connection with the Competition Bill HC Committee Rep. (22 November 1979) cols. 383–385.

[251] *Ravenseft Properties* v *Director General of Fair Trading* [1977] 1 All ER 47 (QBD), DGFT Annual Report (1976), p. 36.

[252] *ibid.*

[253] ss. 9(3) and 18(2) RTPA 1976. Discussed generally at paras. 1.75–1.86.

[254] No. 5044 Register of Restrictive Trade Practices (1983).

13.332 As regards other clauses in licences there is scant guidance to assist in predicting the likely attitude of the OFT or MMC. However, the MMC has stated in respect of proceedings under the CA 1980 that where there is relevant EC law on a point this will be relevant in its reckoning.[255] Hence it may be useful to refer to Regulation 240/96/EC (discussed at paras. 13.18-13.124) on block-exemption for patent and know-how licensing as an indicator of how the MMC may approach specific clauses. Though in general terms it is predictable (based on past record) that the MMC will take a more relaxed view of vertical restraints and give greater credence, than does perhaps the Commission, to arguments premised upon the inventor's right to control licences as being part of the reward for successful creativity.

13.333 The power to investigate terms and conditions, for example tying, in patent licences is unaffected by the provisions of the Patents Act discussed at paras 13.348-13.350.[256]

13.334 There is no doubt but that the anti-competitive use of know-how is subject to the CA 1980.

(2) Follow-up action after an adverse report by the MMC

13.335 Where the MMC concludes adversely that a course of conduct by a patentee is anti-competitive and against the public interest then the powers in section 51 Patents Act 1977 may be exercised. Under section 51(2A)[257] of the Act, the appropriate Minister may apply to the Comptroller General of Patents, Designs and Trade marks for relief. The Comptroller may give relief where he is satisfied that the public interest is being harmed by one or more of three things:[258]

(a) any conditions in a licence or licences granted under any patent by its proprietor restricting the use of the invention concerned by the licensee; and
(b) any conditions in a licence or licences granted under the patent by its proprietor restricting the right of the proprietor to grant other licenses under the patent; or
(c) a refusal by the proprietor to grant licences under the patent on reasonable terms.

13.336 The curative action that the Comptroller may take will consist of the exercise of one or more of three options:

(a) cancellation of any condition(s) in the licence;
(b) modification of any condition(s) in the licence; and,
(c) the entering onto the register of patents[259] that licences under the patent are to be available as of right.

13.337 Under section 51(3) Patents Act 1977 prior to an application to the Comptroller the relevant Minister must publish a notice describing the nature of the proposed application and the Minister must consider any representation which is made to him within 30 days of the notice by persons whose interests may be affected by the proposed application. Parties may use this as an opportunity to persuade the Minister as to the appropriate course of action to be taken. The Minister, though bound to *consider* representations, is *not* bound to concur with them.

[255] MMC Investigation into *Sheffield Newspapers* (1983) Cmnd 8664, pp. 54, 55, para. 7.12.
[256] See Statement of Minister concerning cl. 16 competition, Bull HC Committee Rep. (13 December 1979) cols. 673–675. Cl. 16 became s. 14 CA 1980.
[257] Inserted into the Patents Act 1977 by s. 14(1) Competition Act 1980.
[258] s. 51(5A) inserted by s. 14(3) Competition Act 1980.
[259] As defined by s. 32 Patents Act 1977.

(3) General attitude of the MMC

13.338 The MMC in general investigations under the FTA 1973 has considered patents on a number of occasions.[260] Its analysis has generally been somewhat superficial though a number of policy indications may be tentatively drawn from reports which may be relevant under the CA 1980 or the Patents Act 1977. In *Colour Film*[261] the MMC indicated that control over patents may have no significant competitive consequences where competitors were also successful in producing comparable products. Thus, the level of inter-brand competition is pertinent. Where rivals are producing effective substitutes there may be a case for arguing the *de minimis* defence, i.e. restrictive effects not significant. In *Flat Glass*[262] the dominant concern licensed its patents selectively (albeit quite generously) and required licensees to grant non-exclusive improvement licences to it; the patentee also granted non-exclusive royalty free improvement licences to licensees. The MMC did not criticise the selective patenting, indeed it praised the dominant concern for its inventiveness. One of the most express statements by the MMC which has implications for patent pooling agreements is found in *Reprographic Equipment*.[263] Rank Xerox owned, by 1975, in excess of 2,250 patents. There was evidence that the company took out patents designed to extend the scope of existing patents and also took out patents that were open to the objection that they were obvious and trivial. The MMC stated:

> "A large portfolio of patents impedes and delays the emergence of competition. The mere cost of technical examination of a large portfolio of patents is intimidating. As the Committee of Experts on Restrictive Business Practices of the OECD said in 1972 in their report on Restrictive Business Practices Relating to Patents and Licences: 'A large company, or particularly a combination of large companies, holding hundreds or thousands of patents relating to important technology may be able to exercise dominance in an industry and subject it to excessive conditions or royalties. The tremendous number of patents held by large companies may in itself, prevent a testing of their validity in the courts'."[264]

13.339 In this context failure to license the patents had anti-competitive effects. Competitors experienced considerable difficulties in developing substitutes and this hindered their expansion. No undertakings were sought from Rank Xerox because in July 1975 the US Federal Trade Commission's consent Order had required its US parent company to grant worldwide licences on its copier patents. As a result, by the time the copier market was investigated again by the MMC in its report on *Indirect Electrostatic Photocopiers*,[265] Rank Xerox's market share had been reduced from 90 per cent to 31 per cent and there were now eleven other firms in the UK with significant market shares.

(4) Compulsory licensing under section 48 of the Patents Act 1977

13.340 The Comptroller General of Patents, Designs and Trade marks has power to grant compulsory licences at the end of three years after a British patent has been granted.[266] The Comptroller may settle the terms of the licence as he sees fit[267] and this may include a com-

[260] e.g. MMC General Reports on: *Industrial and Medical Gases* HC 83 (1956), pp. 13–15, paras. 32–37, and p. 92, para. 251; *Cigarette Filter Rods* HC 335 (1969), pp. 49–51, paras. 158–165; *Chlordiazepoxide and Diazepam* HC 197 (1973), pp. 58, 59, paras. 197–199.

[261] HC 1 (1966), p. 101, para. 248.

[262] HC 83 (1968), p. 72, para. 244.

[263] HC 47 (1976), pp. 93–95, paras. 384–392.

[264] *ibid.*, at p. 94, para. 387.

[265] Cm 1693, 1991.

[266] s. 48(1) Patents Act 1977.

[267] Section 48(4). See on the Comptroller's powers, *R* v *Comptroller General of Patents, Designs and Trade Marks, ex parte Gist-Brocades NV* [1986] 1 WLR 51 at pp 62, 63 (HL).

pulsory licence that is exclusive of the patentee and which revokes other licences.[268] Compulsory licences are rarely applied for and granted. This is ascribed to the fact that they are granted only at the discretion of the Comptroller and, more pertinently, that there is no principle that once one of the grounds for compulsory licensing laid out in section 48(3) is made out, there arises a general expectation that the application will be granted unless exceptional circumstances also exist.[269] However, these grounds are qualified by the application of Article 30 EC, as confirmed by the Court of Justice's ruling in *Commission* v *UK (Compulsory Patent Licences)*.[270] Essentially, in sections 48(3)(a)–(c), the references to the UK should be modified to take account of patented products being made elsewhere in the EC.[271] There are five grounds in section 48(3)(a)–(e) which may justify the granting of compulsory licenses. These are as follows:

13.341 (a) "Where the patented invention is capable of being commercially worked in the United Kingdom, that it is not being so worked or is not being so worked to the fullest extent that is reasonably practicable." The provision may be pleaded where the patent has been exploited outside the UK but not in the UK, with UK demand being met by imports. Since the Court of Justice's ruling in *Commission* v *UK (Compulsory Patent Licences)*, this provision cannot be used to grant a compulsory licence where a patented invention is being worked elsewhere in the EC. The Courts have rejected arguments under this provision based upon the restraining of output by the patentee as a means of maximising monopoly profits. They have declined to examine whether lower prices would stimulate demand.[272] However, the courts will apparently take account of arguments that demand levels remain unsatisfied at the prevailing price.[273]

13.342 (b) "Where the patented invention is a product, that a demand for the product in the United Kingdom—(i) is not being met on reasonable terms, or (ii) is being met to a substantial extent by importation." Since the Court of Justice's ruling in *Commission* v *UK (Compulsory Patent Licences)*,[274] this provision cannot be used to grant a compulsory licence where demand is being met by importation from the EC. With respect to the first ground it would appear that compulsory licences may be granted where the patented products are supplied in the UK at price levels which are a burden to the consumer and are unreasonable.[275]

13.343 (c) "Where the patented invention is capable of being commercially worked in the United Kingdom, that it is being prevented or hindered from being so worked—(i) where the invention is a product, by the importation of the product; (ii) where the invention is a process, by the importation of a product obtained directly by means of the process or to which the process has been applied." As with section 48(3)(b), since the Court of Justice's ruling in *Commission* v *UK (Compulsory Patent Licences)*,[276] this provision cannot be used to grant a compulsory licence where the importation forming the basis for the complaint is from the EC.

13.344 (d) "That by reason of the refusal of the proprietor to grant a licence or licences on reasonable terms—(i) a market for the export of any patented product made in the

[268] s. 49(2).
[269] Cornish, *op. cit.*, note 7, at pp. 256–258.
[270] Case C-30/90 *Commission* v *UK* [1992] ECR I-829, [1992] 2 CMLR 709.
[271] s. 48 is due to be amended by Statutory Instrument to reflect this ruling.
[272] e.g. *Kent's Patent* (1909) 26 RPC 666.
[273] e.g. *Kamborian's Patent* [1961] RPC 403.
[274] Case C-30/90 *Commission* v *UK* [1992] ECR I-829, [1992] 2 CMLR 709.
[275] See *Robin Electric-Lamp Co's* petition (1915) 32 RPC 202.
[276] Case C-30/90 *Commission* v *UK* [1992] ECR I-829, [1992] 2 CMLR 709.

United Kingdom is not being supplied, or (ii) the working or efficient working in the United Kingdom of any other patented invention which makes a substantial contribution to the art is prevented or hindered, or (iii) the establishment or development of commercial or industrial activities in the United Kingdom is unfairly prejudiced." This ground is based upon the public interest need to ensure the adequate exploitation of patents. Thus, if a patentee refuses to license a master patent to another who holds a derivative patent for an improvement, then the refusal has hindered the working of another patent under section 48(3)(d)(ii). This provision is subject to section 48(7) whereby any compulsory licensee must be prepared to cross-license his own patent on reasonable terms. One relevant question is what is meant by "reasonable terms". The Courts have taken the view that the patentee enjoys considerable freedom as to choice of price or royalty and this freedom is only substantively curtailed by the limit of the licensees willingness to pay.[277]

13.345 (e) "That by reason of conditions imposed by the proprietor of the patent on the grant of licences under the patent, or on the disposal or use of the patented product or on the use of the patented process, the manufacture, use or disposal of materials not protected by the patent, or the establishment or development of commercial or industrial activities in the United Kingdom, is unfairly prejudiced." The essence of this provision is the unfairness ground, ie. the restrictions imposed on the licensee must unfairly prejudice the ability of the licensee to exploit the patent. In common with other grounds in section 48(3), attempts by the patentee to wring excessive profits from the licensee do not appear to be "unfair".[278]

13.346 In addition to the grounds listed above in section 48(3)(d), the Comptroller, in deciding whether or not to grant a compulsory licence, must bear in mind overriding factors.[279] First, to ensure full exploitation rapidly; secondly, to ensure that the patentee receives reasonable remuneration from the patent; and thirdly, to ensure that anyone working or developing an invention in the UK is protected from unfair prejudice. These factors are to be assessed as at the time of making the application.[280] In addition to these three broad objectives the Comptroller will consider certain narrower objectives, i.e.[281] the nature of the invention; the time that has elapsed since grant of the patent; the extent to which the patentee or licensee has already exploited the invention; and the ability of the applicant to properly exploit the patent including any financial and operating risks to him.[282]

(5) Compulsory licensing and the free movement of goods: patentee's right to prevent imports

13.347 In *Pharmon BV* v *Hoechst AG*[283] the Court of Justice stated that the exhaustion principle did not apply to a compulsory licence. H held the patent in Germany for a process for the manufacture of the drug furosemidum. Parallel patents were held in the UK and Holland. In 1972 DDSA obtained a compulsory licence in the UK under section 41 of the Patents Act 1949 (now repealed by Schedule 3 paragraph 2(c) Patent Act 1977) for

[277] e.g. *Kamborian's Patent* [1961] RPC 403; *Brownie Wireless Application* (1929) 44 RPC 457; *Robin Electric Lamp Co's Petition* (1915) 32 RPC 202.

[278] *Kamborian's Patent* [1961] RPC 403; *Colbourne Engineering Co's Application* [1954] 72 RPC 169.

[279] s. 50(1) Patents Act 1977, See Cornish, *op, cit.*, at pp. 256–258.

[280] *McKecbnies Application* (1934) 51 RPC 461—the patentee may not seek to fend off an application by last minute activity giving an impression of effective exploitation.

[281] s. 50(2).

[282] See *Brownie Wireless Application* (1929) 46 RPC 457 at p. 473.

[283] Case 19/84 [1985] ECR 2281 [1985] 3 CMLR 775.

production of furosemidum valid only in the UK and subject to an export prohibition. In breach of this condition, DDSA exported the drug to Holland where H commenced infringement proceedings against DDSA. The Court first reaffirmed that Articles 30–36 EC prohibit the application of national legislation which grants a patent holder the power to prevent the importation and distribution of a product which has lawfully been placed on the market of another Member State by the patent holder himself with his consent or by a person with whom he has close legal or economic links. However, the Court held that the same rule did *not* apply when the importation and marketing related to a product which had been manufactured in the exporting Member State by the holder of a compulsory licence under a parallel patent held by the holder of a patent in the importing Member State. The explanation being that when a Member State grants a compulsory licence the patentee cannot be deemed to have consented to the acts carried out by the compulsory licensee.[284] Thus H was entitled to succeed against DDSA. The terms and conditions in the compulsory licence were irrelevant to this decision, hence the fact that the compulsory licensee breached the terms of the compulsory licence was not relevant. Whether this rule applies to all types of compulsory licence is unclear. There may well be a distinction between compulsory licences ordered *against* the wishes of the patentee (for example under the section 48 Patents Act 1977 procedure) and compulsory licences ordered with the consent of the patentee, for example where the patentee has arranged for his patents to be subject to licences of right (see under Section 46 Patents Act 1977 where, in return for reduced renewal fees a patentee procures the registration of his patents as licences of right which enables all third parties to obtain licences subject only to agreement or settlement of appropriate terms and conditions). In this latter case, although licences are compulsorily granted, the patentee having no discretion, it cannot realistically be stated that the licences are involuntary.[285]

(6) Tying clauses in patent licences: section 44 Patents Act 1977

13.348 Under section 44 Patents Act 1977 certain clauses in contracts for the supply of patented products; licences to work a patent; or contracts relating to any such supply or licence, are void.[286] The prohibited clauses are as follows:

(a) clauses requiring the purchaser or licensee to purchase or acquire from the supplier, patentee or nominee of either, "anything other than the product which is the patented invention," i.e. a secondary product.

(b) clauses prohibiting the purchaser or licensee from taking competing technology whether in the form of patented or unpatented articles or processes.

13.349 While a prohibited term remains in the agreement it constitutes a defence to *any* proceedings for infringement commenced by the patentee.[287] The Act does not provide an exemption for technically necessary ties, though there is such an exemption in the EC technology transfer block exemption[288] so that a licence complying with the EC

[284] Applying the principle in Case 187/80 *Merck* v *Stephar* [1981] ECR 2063 that the substance of a patent right lay essentially in according the inventor an exclusive right of first marketing to enable him to obtain the reward for his creativity. This principle has been reaffirmed by the Court of Justice in Joined Cases C-267-268/95 *Merck & Co. Inc* v *Primecrown Ltd*, judgment of 5 December 1996.

[285] See *R* v *Comptroller General of Patents, Designs and Trade Marks, ex parte Gist-Brocades NV* [1986] 1 WLR 51 at pp. 54, 55, 67, 68. The compulsory licence in *Pharmon BV* v *Hoecht AG* was granted under section 41 Patents Act 1949 which provided (before its repeal) that licences of food or pharmaceutical products would be granted almost as of right. Licences were to be granted irrespective of the wishes of the proprietor.

[286] e.g. *Huntoon* v *Kolynos* [1930] 1 Ch 528 (CA).

[287] s. 44(3) Patents Act 1977.

[288] Art. 2(1)(5), Reg. 240/96/ECE.

Regulation despite the exemption contained therein, may not be safe from section 44 in so far as that provision conflicts with the Regulation. Such a conflict might arise where a licence between a licensor and licensee both situate in the UK which has potential to affect inter-state trade contains a tie that is void under the Patents Act but exempt under the Regulation. There is, however, an exemption under the Patents Act where the patentee is willing to supply the patented product or grant a licence without the tie clause on reasonable terms. Furthermore, the purchaser or licensee must be entitled under the contract or licence to escape the tie by giving three months' notice in writing, though such a party must also be prepared to pay compensation to the supplier/patentee. "Compensation" means, in the case of a contract to supply, a lump sum or rent for the residue of the term of the contract, and in the case of a licence, a royalty for the residue of the licence. The actual sum is determined by an arbitrator appointed by the Secretary of State.[289]

13.350 Section 44 applies in a formalistic manner; only contracts or licences incorporating formal ties or prohibitions are void. Hence, where the tie or prohibition is informal, the clause is valid. Thus, inducements and incentives may be used as substitutes for formal clauses. For example, a licence whereby the licensee accepts an inducement (e.g., a reduction in royalty obligations, or automatic grant of royalty-free improvement patents taken out by the patentee) not to take alternative supplies from a competitor of the patentee is not within section 44.[290] Likewise, a clause whereby the licensee is given an inducement to take an additional product or service from the patentee should also be outside of section 44. The scope of section 44 was examined in *Chiron Corp* v *Organon Teknika (No 3)*.[291] A clause requiring a licensee to obtain supplies or raw material for the manufacture of a patented pharmaceutical was held to be caught by section 44(1)(b), as was an amendment to the agreement which would have allowed the licensee to obtain the raw material for the manufacture of products for the UK market, but still require purchase of the raw material for manufacture of products to be supplied outside the UK. An argument that s. 44 did not apply as the patent had not been granted at the date of the agreement was rejected, since the agreement in question provided for the grant of a licence upon issue of the patent applied for.

H. Copyright Licensing in EC Law

1. *Legal Context*

13.351 Due to the diversity of the areas in which copyright measures may be exploited, there is no one statement of the application of competition law to copyright licensing. A number of measures have been put forward for the harmonisation of various aspects of copy-

[289] s. 44(4)(b).

[290] See, e.g. *Tool Metal* v *Tungsten Electric* (1955) 72 RPC 209 (HL) at pp. 218—221 but cf. dissent at pp. 214 *et seq*. See also *Hunters Patent* [1965] RPC 416 at pp. 426, 427 where the Irish Supreme Court rejected the legality of a licence to use the patented machinery only in contracts for the supply of the other (tied) product (bottle tops). In this licence there was no restriction only a permission to use. See also *Sarason* v *Frenay* [1914] 2 Ch 474 (CA).

[291] [1994] FSR 202, Patents Court (Aldous J), upheld by the Court of Appeal [1996] FSR 153.

right law throughout the Community. Of particular importance for licensing agreements is the Software Directive,[292] now implemented in the UK,[293] and this topic is dealt with separately below.

13.352 The Commission considers that the principles applicable to patent licensing are equally relevant to copyright licensing.[294] Hence the technology transfer block exemptions may be a useful guide to the policy of the Commission towards different clause types. In particular, the list of "black" unacceptable clauses in Article 3 should be taken note of. In most cases the list of obligations which are stated prima facie to fall outside of Article 85(1) will apply also to copyright. However, simply because the block exemptions may be used as a guide does *not* mean that copyright licences complying with it are necessarily exempt from notification to the Commission.

13.353 Although design rights are increasingly being treated separately from the main body of copyright law,[295] the law stated in this and the subsequent section is applicable to design rights unless otherwise stated.

2. *Exclusive Licences: Open and Closed Licences*

13.354 The principles in *Nungesser* v *Commission*[296] discussed at paras. 13.13–13.17 are relevant here. Indeed the Commission has informally applied the principle that certain types of open exclusive licence are not within Article 85(1) to copyright. In *Nungesser*, it will be recalled, the Court ruled that open exclusive licences are outside of Article 85(1) where they involve new products created through substantial R&D where exclusivity was needed to facilitate market penetration. In *Knoll-Hille Form*[297] the licensor granted various intellectual property rights, and in particular copyright, to a licensee. The licence prohibited the licensor from granting further licences in the licensee's territory and from exploiting its rights there (exclusivity and non-competition clause). The licensee was prohibited from selling outside of its territory. Both licensor and licensee held significant market positions. The Commission doubted whether the *Nungesser* case applied: "Neither the newness of the products concerned nor the amount of investment involved seemed to indicate that the exclusivity granted was indispensable to launching the products in the relevant market, at any rate not for the length of time originally envisaged (eight years)."[298] Thus the provisos that attach to the open exclusive licence exception were being applied by the Commission. Given the broad spectrum of copyright protection, it is difficult to generalise about the attitude the commission will take to exclusivity in copyright licences. One broad distinction does seem to have emerged: that between performance related copyrights and product related copyrights. Where performance is the means of

[292] Council Directive 91/250/EEC of 14 May 1991 on the legal protection of computer programs. OJ 1991 L122/42

[293] Copyright (Computer Programs) Regulations 1992 (S.I. 1992/3233).

[294] e.g. *Twelfth Report on Competition Policy*, *Neilson–Hordell/Richmark* (1982), p. 73; *Sixth Report on Competition Policy*, *BBC–Valley Printing* (1976), para. 163; *Sixth Report on Competition Policy*, "*Old Man and the Sea*" (1976), para. 163; *Ninth Report on Competition Policy*, *Ernest Benn Ltd* (1979), para. 118; *Eleventh Report on Competition Policy*, *STEMRA* (1981), p. 66; Cases 55, 57/80 *Membran and K—tel International* v *GEMA* [1981] ECR 147; *Dutch Books* [1977] 1 CMLR D2.

[295] See Cornish, *op. cit.*, Chapter 14. For examples, see the creation of a new unregistered design right in UK law under Part III, ss. 213 *et seq*, Copyright, Designs and Patents Act 1988. At EC level, see proposals to harmonise Community design right law by directive, OJ 1993 C345/14, and to introduce a new Community design right, OJ 1994 C37/20.

[296] Case 258/78 [1983] 1 CMLR 278; [1982] ECR 2061.

[297] *Thirteenth Report on Competition Policy* (1983), p. 91.

[298] *ibid.* at para. 144. *Quaere*: was the Commission implying that for a lesser period the restrictions might have been within the *Nungesser* principle?

exploitation being protected by copyright, it seems that a greater degree of territorial protection will be allowed than in situations where exploitation is through a copyright product. Thus in *Coditel II*[299] the Court of Justice held that an exclusive copyright licence of a film was not necessarily caught by Article 85(1).[300]

3. *Other Clauses in Copyright Licences*

13.355 That the Commission view copyright licences in much the same way as they do patent and know-how licences is apparent from *Neilson–Hordell/Richmark*.[301] The Commission intervened following a complaint by a licensee against certain clauses included in a settlement terminating earlier copyright infringement proceedings. In question were four clauses: no-challenge clause; non-competition clause; clause requiring the payment of royalties on unprotected products; and a clause requiring the licensee to transfer the title of any copyright in any improvement made to the licensed product to the licensor. In the light of Commission opposition, the parties voluntarily deleted all the above clauses. The Commission stated that usually such clauses were prohibited by Article 85(1) and were inappropriate for exemption under Article 85(3). The fact that the clauses formed part of a settlement agreement terminating earlier proceedings was immaterial.

13.356 Where the copyright holder enjoys a dominant position, terms in a licence which are unfair and exploitative may constitute an infringement of Article 86 EC. However, simply because a firm owns intellectual property does not *necessarily mean that it holds a dominant position*;[302] the level of competition from substitute products must be considered. For a dominant concern to tie products together will, in the absence of a technical justification, almost certainly amount to a breach of Article 86. Thus, the Commission considered that the practice of IBM—who was alleged to be dominant in a part of the computer market—in "bundling", first, the price of main memory with that of central processing units, and secondly, the price of operating systems with that of central processing units, was an infringement of Article 86 EC.[303]

13.357 The Commission adopted a similar stance in the *Magill TV Guide* case[304] in which it was held that a refusal to license use of copyright protected TV programme listings was an abuse of a dominant position by each of the three broadcasters owning those copyrights. The Court of First Instance upheld this decision,[305] as did the Court of Justice[306] (see paras. 13.458–13.463).

299 Case 262/81 *Coditel* v *Cine Vog Films* [1983] 1 CMLR 49; [1982] ECR 3381.

300 *ibid.*, at para. 15 of the judgment. The Court indicated that in certain economic circumstances such a licence might infringe Art. 85(1): (i) where the exclusive licence created artificial and unjustifiable economic barriers; (ii) where royalties charged exceeded a fair return on investment; (iii) where the exclusivity was for an undue period of time; and (iv) where in general terms the licence restricts competition (*ibid.*, at para. 19). In *ARD/Turner Entertainment Co* OJ 1989 L284/36, the Commission applied this proviso in requiring changes to be made to a licence agreement between a German broadcasters' association and a US film library in order to enable third party broadcasters in Germany to apply for licences to broadcast those films at times which did not clash with those of association members. The features of the original agreement that the Commission had objected to were the large number of films licensed under it, the long duration of the licences and the duration of the selection period for those films. All three factors were said to impede third party access.

301 *Twelfth Report on Competition Policy* (1982), p. 73.

302 Case 24/67 *Parke-Davis* v *Probel* [1968] CMLR 47; [1968] ECR 55.

303 See *IBM Settlement Case* [1984] 3 CMLR 147. See also the *Microsoft* settlement, considered at para. 13.403.

304 *Magill TV Guide* [1989] 4 CMLR 757.

305 Cases T-69, 70 and 76/89 *RTE, BBC and ITP* v *Commission* [1991] ECR II-485, 535 and 575 [1991] 4 CMLR 586, 669 and 745.

306 Joined Cases 241 and 242/91P *RTE and ITP* v *Commission* [1995] ECR I-743 122.

4. Protecting Exclusive Territories: Free Movement of Goods and Services

13.358 The principles concerning free movement of goods and the exhaustion principle apply to copyright as well as to patents. See paras 13.4-13.12 for an overview of the question. Thus in *Membran and K-tel International* v *GEMA*[307] the Court emphasised that sound recordings, even where incorporating protected musical words, are products subject to the rules on the free movement of goods. Thus, the owner of an exclusive right to produce records under national law cannot use that law to prevent the importation of records which have been lawfully marketed in another Member State by the owner himself or with his consent. An exception to the general rule on exhaustion is the performance field as regards re-transmission by cable television.[308]

5. Compulsory Licensing

13.359 In the *IBM Settlement* case,[309] following protracted negotiations between IBM and the Commission, the former agreed to make available certain proprietary information concerning the interfaces between its computers and plug-compatible machines and those of competitors. The basis of the settlement between IBM and the Commission was Article 86 EC. The Commission considered that the refusal to disclose the relevant data, which was needed by competitors to ensure that their machines were efficiently plug-compatible with IBM's, was designed to enhance IBM's alleged world dominance over the mainframe computer market. Without a formal decision being taken, nor IBM having admitted either dominance or abuse, the company agreed to license competitors with relevant data. Whilst neither party relied upon issues of intellectual property the data in question related to copyrighted designs and hence the case is a signal indicator of Commission policy. Where a holder of copyright enjoys a dominant position and refusal to license creates entry and expansion barriers to rivals, then such refusal may constitute a breach of Article 86 EC. The same may apply to the inadequate licensing of the proprietary right. For a copyright holder to be dominant there would have to be an absence of substitutes or alternatives to the copyrighted product (i.e. lack of inter-brand competition).

13.360 A question mark exists in respect of the legal competence of the Commission to enforce compulsory licences in view of the Berne Convention of 1886 as amended by the Brussels Revision of 1948 (coming into force 1951) and the Paris Revision 1971 (coming into force 1974). The Berne Convention and its relevant provisions are discussed at greater length in paras. 13.378–13.382 in respect of UK law where it has become a "live" issue and reference thereto should be made for details of the Convention. In brief, the Convention precludes the possibility of compulsory copyright licensing other than in limited circumstances provided for in the Brussels and Paris Revisions. The question that is thus to be asked is whether the Community (which is not a signatory to the Convention) is bound by the Convention given that all of the Member States *are* signatories to the Convention. To what extent does an International Treaty acceded to by all the Member States bind the Community?

[307] Cases 55, 57/80 [1981] ECR 147; See also, Case 78/80 *GEMA* [1985] 2 CMLR 1 *Deutsche Grammophon* v *Metro* [1971] CMLR 631; [1971] ECR 487. See generally *Copinger and Skone James on Copyright* (13th edn. 1991, Supp. 1994), paras. 14,30–14.95.

[308] See Case 62/79 *Coditel I* [1981] 2 CMLR 362; [1980] ECR 883.

[309] [1984] 3 CMLR 147; Bull EC 10/84 App. 4. See also *"Old Man and the Sea"* [1977] 1 CMLR D121 one publisher held the licence for a book for the whole of the EC and sub-licensed its rights for the whole of the Community excepting the UK and Eire. However, it failed to make copies available in Eire. Following Commission intervention the publisher appointed a sub-licensee for Eire.

13.361 The Court of Justice decided in *Magill TV Guide*[310] that the Community was not bound by the Convention, and the Convention did not therefore limit the powers of the Community. While this clarifies the question of the legal competence of the Commission as a matter of Community law, it does not resolve the question of whether the Member States are individually responsible for a breach of the Convention as a matter of public international law.

I. Copyright Licensing in United Kingdom Law

1. *Under the RTPA 1976*

13.362 Prima facie copyright licences are exempt from registration under the RTPA 1976 by virtue of Schedule 3, paragraph 5A of the Act and design right licences are similarly exempt under Schedule 3, paragraph 5B. This is discussed at paras 2.194–2.200. However, restrictions may become registrable if they extend beyond the currency of the legal protection granted the copyright. Agreements that do become registrable are generally suitable for section 21(2) treatment, though account may be taken of the degree of market power enjoyed by the copyright holder when assessing the economic effect of any restrictions.[311] See the expression of policy of the OFT in the *Ford Motor Company* case below. In this as in the previous section, the law relating to copyright in general is to be taken as also applicable to design rights.

2. *Under the Competition Act 1980*

13.363 Copyright licensing is subject to the CA 1980. In particular, refusals to license copyright have proven a major issue. As regards terms and conditions in licences, these will be subject to the Act and some cautious guidance as to what may be considered anti-competitive may be found in the discussion above concerning EC law which itself refers to the block exemption on patent licensing for guidance.

(1) Refusal to license: when anti-competitive

13.364 In two cases both resulting in references to the MMC, the OFT have considered the question of refusal to license. In both cases, they have enunciated the principle that a refusal to license, though perfectly legal, may none the less be anti-competitive under the CA 1980 when the copyright holder is not subject to effective inter-brand competition.

13.365 In *Ford Motor Company*[312] the OFT stated:

[310] Joined Cases 241 and 242/91P *RTE and ITP* v *Commission* [1995] ECR I-743, [1995] 4 CMLR 718, paras. 83–87. On the application of Art. 234 EC, see, Case 10/61 *Commission* v *Italy* [1962] ECR 1. On the relationship between EC law and the Berne Convention and Revisions generally see Gillian Davies and Hans Hugo Von Rauscher auf Weef, *Challenges to Copyright and Related Rights in the European Community* (1983), Chapter 2.

[311] See, e.g. No. 5079 Register of Restrictive Trade Practices, *W and T Manufacturing (Birmingham) Ltd* and *J and L Randall Ltd* (1984).

[312] 21 March 1984 (OFT Report). See also the MMC Report in the same case (1985) Cmnd 9437 at p. 31, para. 6.3; and OFT Report *British Broadcasting Corporation* and *Independent Television Publications Ltd* (*The publication of programme information*) (13 December 1984), p. 59, para. 8.3.

"Copyright confers on one person (the owner of the right) the exclusive right to control the supply of a particular good (a good made to the registered design of the owner or copied from work in respect of which he owns the artistic copyright) and to prevent all unauthorised persons from supplying that particular good to the market. To the extent that this right is exercised competition in the supply of the good in question is restricted. Prevention of other persons from supplying a particular good is however, unlikely to amount to an anti-competitive practice in markets where there are substitutes for the good or where substitutes may be freely developed by others.

The effects on competition arising from the exercise of copyright therefore depend on the market in which the particular good is supplied. Where there are reasonable substitutes for the particular good or alternative designs or developments can be made, the exclusive rights of supply do not confer monopoly rights in the market and the exercise of copyright is unlikely to have an anti-competitive effect."[313]

13.366 Thus, the level of actual and potential inter-brand competition is a central factor. The actual level of competition will be determined by considering the extent to which substitutes are available or could be developed for the copyright product. Thus, for example, where the product is replacement body parts for Ford vehicles, there may be no substitutes by the very nature of the product.[314] Conversely, where the product is a recording of a Beethoven symphony, the fact that there may be a dozen or more competing recordings made in the past few years denies the copyright holder any degree of market power.[315] Likewise, the author and copyright holder of a reference book on competition law is subject to competition from other authors and copyright holders of reference books on competition law.

(2) Refusal to license and excessive royalty payments

13.367 A copyright holder might in principle agree to grant licences but in practice refuse unless the licensee agrees to pay an exorbitant royalty fee. The (intended) effect of this policy may be to discourage prospective licensees. In effect this policy is indistinguishable from one of blanket refusal to license. In *Ford Motor Company* the OFT stated: "A refusal by Ford to license unless a royalty fee is paid, appropriate to the circumstances of the case, would not constitute conduct which was restricting or likely to have the effect of restricting or preventing competition."[316] They continued to suggest that a royalty fee would be anti-competitive if it were set at a level such that no competitor would be prepared to enter the market. The OFT did not lay down appropriate levels though they did note that British Leyland demanded a fee of 7 per cent of selling price of copyrighted products.[317] Where patents were concerned, the OFT accepted that royalty payments vary considerably but stated that rates' between 20–25 per cent of gross sales price were usual where R&D costs were high and rates of approximately 10 per cent were normal where R&D costs were lower. Obviously, it is open to holders of intellectual property rights to plead unusually high R&D costs justifying higher than normal royalty fees. However, the opinion of the OFT is that demands in excess of the figures given above *may* be anti-competitive. The view of the MMC is generally in line with that of the OFT. Interestingly,

[313] *ibid.*, at pp. 37, 38, paras. 8.4, 8.5.

[314] *ibid.*, at p. 38, paras. 8.7, 8.8. But cf. the judgment of the HL in *British Leyland Motor Corporation* v *Armstrong* [1986] AC 577. House of Lords held that there was no copyright in spare motor parts and hence manufacturers of spares could copy BL spares without infringing the copyright.

[315] In a monopoly investigation under the FTA 1973, *The Supply of Recorded Music* Cm 2599 (June 1994), the MMC found that CD prices in the UK were sufficiently competitive and therefore made no adverse findings.

[316] *ibid.*, at p. 40, para. 8.14.

[317] *British Leyland* v *TI Silencers* [1981] 2 CMLR 75 at p. 81.

the MMC have accepted the "free-rider" argument that unless a licensee pays a royalty fee which realistically reflects the R&D costs of the licensor, then the licensee may "free-ride" on the R&D efforts of the licensor with whom he may be in competition.[318] Furthermore, the MMC accepts that "there is a public interest in the provision of an adequate reward for innovation throughout industry."[319] A proper royalty fee would respect this principle; enable the licensor to recover its R&D costs yet not be such as to create an unfair entry barrier to rival suppliers.

13.368 In the event, Ford agreed to license third parties to manufacture or sell Ford replacement body parts at a 2 per cent royalty. Following a House of Lords ruling that Ford did not have design rights in those parts[320] and so could not prevent third party manufacture or sale, Ford was released from those undertakings.[321]

13.369 In *BBC and ITP*[322] (publication of programme information) the OFT investigated the refusal by BBC and ITP to grant licences, concerning copyrighted information relating to programme schedules, to other potential suppliers of such information (magazines, journals, etc.). By refusing to license, BBC and ITP sought to protect their respective markets for the *Radio Times* and the *TV Times*. When considering appropriate royalty fees, both companies indicated that royalties should be such as to compensate for any *loss* of profits that would result from compulsory licences.[323] The OFT rejected this view that royalty payments should be connected to profit margins and reaffirmed the position adopted in *Ford Motor Company* that royalty fees should bear a relation to production costs and should not be so high as to deter market entry by potential suppliers.[324] This view was accepted by the MMC in its subsequent report.[325] However, although the MMC found that the refusal to license was anti-competitive, it did not hold that it was against the public interest.[326]

13.370 The Broadcasting Act 1990 has now addressed the specific issue of publication of programme information, and provides for the publication and licensing of use of such information[327] subject to payment of a licence fee to be adjudicated in default of agreement by the Copyright Tribunal. The Tribunal may make such order as it may determine to be reasonable in the circumstances.[328]

13.371 The most recent expression of MMC views in this area is to be found in its report into *Video Games*[329] issued under the FTA 1973, though it may be taken as applicable under the Competition Act 1980 as well. The Report concerned the licensing practices of the two major video games manufacturers within the UK, Sega with 38 per cent of the combined console and games software market and Nintendo which has just less than 25 per cent. Both sold consoles cheaply but obtained higher profit margins on the sup-

318 MMC Report above at p. 38, para. 6.34.

319 *ibid.*, at p. 41, para. 6.50.

320 *R v Registered Designs Appeal Tribunal ex parte Ford Motor Co. Ltd.* [1995] 1 WLR 18.

321 (1995) 11 Fair Trading 4.

322 13 December 1984.

323 *ibid.*, at p. 63, para. 8.19.

324 *ibid.*, at pp. 63, 64, paras. 8.20, 8.21.

325 *BBC and ITP.* Cm 9614 (1985).

326 See T. Frazer, "Unchanging times: the Monopolies and Mergers Commission Report on the BBC and ITP" [1986] ECLR 96.

327 Sch. 17 broadcasting Act 1990; see *Copinger and Skone James on Copyright* (13th edn, 1991, Supp. 1994) paras. 10.127–10.132.

328 Sch. 17 para. 5(1) Broadcasting Act 1990. In the first proceedings under this provision, the Copyright Tribunal ruled on a dispute between the BBC and Independent Television Publications Ltd on the one hand and the newspaper and magazine industry on the other (1992) 15 IPN June 1992, p. 1.

329 Cm 2781 (1995). See M. Williams, "Sega, Nintendo and after-market power: the MMC Report on video games" [1995] ECLR 310.

ply of games. About 40 per cent of games software was supplied by them, the remaining 60 per cent being supplied by third party software publishers under copyright licences. It was the terms of these copyright licences which attracted the MMC's attention. The MMC summarised the situation thus:

> "The practice of refusing licences except to those accepting certain conditions, together with the technical features designed to prevent the production of unlicensed software, affects competition by limiting the numbers of games produced to be played on the two companies' machines. The conditions imposed enable the companies to control the numbers and timing of such games published and to influence their price. Some technical features segregate markets and thus discourage the import of software. These practices thus prevent, restrict or distort competition ... compared with a situation in which such controls were not applied."[330]

13.372 The MMC described the licensing system as "an effective barrier to entry into the video games market in the UK except with the approval of [Nintendo] or [Sega], since the other existing suppliers' sales of hardware to provide a platform for games publishing are tiny."[331] In particular, the MMC objected to the requirement that third parties obtain cartridges for games from Sega and Nintendo and their nominated suppliers, since it regarded this as being the biggest factor in raising the cost of games, thereby allowing Sega and Nintendo to charge more for their own games and reduce the price of their hardware, thus making it more difficult for other companies to enter the market.

13.373 Sega and Nintendo put forward three principal justifications for their business strategy:

(i) that control was necessary for brand image. The MMC rejected this on the ground that the same necessity did not appear to be apparent in the analogous computer industry.
(ii) that as they owned the rights to the consoles, they should be able to control what was used on those consoles. This was rejected on the ground that it was not clear why video games should be any different from other types of products in facing competition from complementary products.
(iii) that the system provided a reasonable return for their initial R&D investment. This was rejected on the basis that the IPR owned by Sega and Nintendo related to the microchips used in the games cartridges, and royalties on those could be collected directly from the cartridge manufacturers rather than by requiring games makers only to buy through Sega and Nintendo.

13.374 Essentially, the MMC investigation concluded that Sega and Nintendo were not driven to use this system for business reasons, and could obtain an adequate reward for their innovation while still allowing third parties to produce games software on different terms.

13.375 The MMC made a series of recommendations relating to the licensing system to the Secretary of State (responsible for taking action as a consequence of the Report), based upon the licensing provisions of section 51 Patents Act 1977 and Section 144 Copyright Designs and Patents Act 1988. The MMC's recommendation was that software publishers should be licensed to produce games for Sega and Nintendo formats on payment of an appropriate royalty, to be agreed or settled by the Copyright Tribunal. The MMC recommended the removal of all licence conditions as to number of games produced, prior approval of games concepts or programs, prior approval of packaging, manuals, advertising and publicity material, and cartridge manufacturing.

[330] para. 2.32.
[331] para. 2.48.

(3) Remedies available following an adverse MMC Report

13.376 Following an adverse MMC Report the Secretary of State may exercise any of the powers laid down in Part 1 of Schedule 8 to the FTA 1973.[332] Alternatively or additionally he may, "Prohibit a person named in the order from engaging in any anti-competitive practice which was specified in the report or from pursuing any other course of conduct which is similar in form and effect to that practice".[333]

13.377 Moreover, if a MMC Report has specified as matters operating against the public interest either conditions included in a copyright licence by a copyright owner to restrict a licensee's use of a work, or a condition restricting the right of the copyright owner to grant other copyright licences, or the refusal of a copyright owner to grant licences on reasonable terms, then part of Schedule 8 to the FTA 1973 is to read as including the power to cancel or modify those conditions. Instead or in addition, there is also to be read into the provision the power to provide that licences of right for the copyright be available, the terms of such licences to be determined in default of agreement by the Copyright Tribunal.[334]

(4) Whether Parliament has power under international law to provide for compulsory licensing of copyright

13.378 Section 144(3) of the Copyright Designs and Patents Act 1988 restricts the Minister's exercise of powers under section 144 only to cases where he or she is satisfied that such exercise would not contravene any convention to which the UK is a party.

13.379 Due account has therefore to be taken of the Berne Convention for the Protection of Literary and Artistic Works 1886 and also of the Brussels Revision of 1948 (coming into force 1951) and the Paris Revision 1971 (coming into force 1974).[335] The Berne Convention is the oldest existing international treaty on copyright and is adhered to by more than 70 states, including all the EC states. Though not all of the Member States of the EC have as yet ratified the latest Revision.

13.380 Article 2(1) of the Convention defines "literary and artistic works". The definition embraces all literary productions whatever their form.[336] Article 7 of the Brussels Revision lays down that the term of the author's copyright for literary works shall be his lifetime plus 50 years after his death. No derogations from the author's right to prevent unauthorised copyings are allowed for. There are, however, two derogation provisions which provide for compulsory licensing for broadcasting and public performance of literary and artistic works; and for recording of musical works (Article 11(2) and 13(2) respectively of the Brussels Revision). Both of these exceptions are relatively narrow. No other exceptions are provided for in that Revision. The UK has adhered to the Paris Revision.[337] One relevant provision of the Paris Revision is Article 9(2). This reads:

[332] s. 10(2)(b) CA 1980.

[333] s. 10(2)(a) CA 1980.

[334] s. 144 Copyright Designs and Patents Act 1988; this section was introduced as a consequence of the *Ford Motor Company* MMC report highlighting the lack of such a power under Part 1 of Sch. 8 FTA 1973.

[335] See *Copinger and Skone James on Copyright* (13th edn, 1991, Supp. 1994), Chapter 17 for analysis of the various conventions and revisions. See also pp. 851 *et seq.* for text for Berne Convention as amended by Paris Revision 1971. See, Gillian Davies and Hans Hugo Von Rauscher auf Weeg, *op. cit.*, n. 310, Chapter 2.

[336] para. 2.6(a) of the "Guide to the Berne Convention" (WIPO) provides that, "literary and artistic works" includes "almanacs, year books, programmes, guides etc. irrespective of their contents, their length, their purpose (entertainment, education, information, discussion, advertisement, propaganda etc.) and their form (manuscript, typescript, printing)."

[337] With effect from 2 January 1990.

> "It shall be a matter for legislation in the countries of the Union to permit the reproduction of such works in certain special cases, provided that such reproduction does not conflict with a normal exploitation of the work and does not unreasonably prejudice the legitimate interests of the author."

13.381 Article 9(2) would permit of compulsory licences in respect of reproduction but only as provided in the Article. Hence, first, there must be a "special" case thus implying that no *general* right to enforce compulsory licences may be enacted into national law. Secondly, the reproduction must not conflict with normal exploitation of the work. Thirdly, reproduction must not unreasonably prejudice the legitimate interests of the author. The meanings of "normal exploitation" and "unreasonably prejudice the legitimate interests" are undefined. However, they appear to deny national law the right to enforce compulsory licences where such inhibits the inherent right of the holder to prevent unauthorised usage.[338] Though perhaps the concepts of normality and reasonableness may be assimilated with competition theory such that it is abnormal and unreasonable to refuse to grant licences in an anti-competitive manner.

13.382 The MMC has reserved its full opinion on the implications of the Berne convention though in its Report on *BBC and ITP* in September 1985 it appears, implicitly, to have recognised the limitations it imposes.[339] It does indicate, however, that the Convention has no application to copyright laws on industrial design (which was at issue in the *Ford Motor Company* case).

13.383 To conclude this section, one point concerning the relevance of the EC position on compulsory licensing to UK law requires mentioning. The EC is not bound by the Berne Convention (see para. 13.361). Article 234 EC could complicate the UK position. Article 234 EC concerns international obligations accepted by the Member States prior to entry into force of the EC Treaty. Article 234(2) provides that: "To the extent that such agreements are not compatible with this Treaty, the Member States or States concerned shall take all appropriate steps to eliminate the incompatibilities established. Member States shall, where necessary, assist each other to this end and shall where appropriate, adopt a common attitude." As the EC does not accept the Berne Convention, at least in so far as it conflicts with antitrust policy, then Article 234(2) EC may raise an obligation on Member States to "eliminate the incompatibilities established." This might be construed as requiring Member States to give priority to competition policy over Berne Convention policy, i.e. to curing anti-competitive refusals to license by compulsory licensing regardless of the implications of the Berne Convention. Though one final complexity should be added which is that Article 234 EC would only impinge on cases where the refusal to license affected inter-state trade so as to activate Articles 85 or 86 EC. Where the licensor's refusal involves domestic repercussions only then Article 234 EC would not apply, nor would Articles 85 or 86 and Berne would prevail.

[338] See Official Report of the Stockholm meeting as quoted in the Whitford Committee Report Cmnd 6732, para. 60: "If it is considered that reproduction conflicts with the normal exploitation of a work, reproduction is not permitted at all. If it is considered that reproduction does not conflict with the normal exploitation of the work, the next step would be to consider whether it does not unreasonably prejudice the legitimate interests of the author. Only if such is not the case would it be possible, in certain special cases, to introduce a compulsory licence, or to provide for use without payment. A practical example might be photocopying for various purposes. If it consists of producing a very large number of copies it may not be permitted, as it conflicts with the normal exploitation of the work. If it implies a rather large number of copies for use in industrial undertakings, it may not unreasonably prejudice the legitimate interests of the author provided that, according to national legislation, an equitable remuneration is paid. If a small number of copies is made photocopying may be permitted without payment particularly for individual or scientific use."

[339] *ibid.*, para. 6.43.

3. Non-derogation from Grant: Spare Parts

13.384 The House of Lords in *British Leyland Motor Corporation* v *Armstrong Patents*.[340] In that case the Court held that British Leyland (BL) could not prevent the direct copying of spare parts by manufacturers of spare parts by reference to copyright law. This negation of copyright power will be of central importance in future to manufacturers who are refused a licence by a proprietor of copyright to copy a design for the manufacture of spare parts for use with a product manufactured by the proprietor. The House of Lords based their judgments upon the concept of non-derogation from grant which is applied in the law of property and in patent law. This concept they extended to the law of copyright with particular reference to spare parts needed in repair. Lord Templeman stated:

> "I see no reason why the principle that a grantor will not be allowed to derogate from his grant by using property retained by him in such a way as to render property granted by him unfit or materially unfit for the purpose for which the grant was made should not apply to the sale of a car."

Applying this principle Lord Templeman stated:

> "The principle applied to a motor car manufactured in accordance with engineering drawings and sold with components which are bound to fail during the life of the car prohibits the copyright owner of the drawings from exercising his copyright powers in such a way as to prevent the car from functioning unless the owner of the car buys replacement parts from the copyright owner or his licensee. BL own the car and the copyright in a drawing of an exhaust pipe fitted to the car. BL sell the car and retain the copyright. The exercise by BL of their copyright in the drawing will render the car unfit for the purpose for which the car is held. BL cannot exercise their copyright so as to prevent the car being repaired by replacement of the exhaust pipe."

13.385 It is unclear how far the simple proposition that no copyright rests in spare parts extends. In the case the Court was ruling on the manufacture of exhaust pipes a product which is "bound to fail during the life of the car" (Lord Templeman) and "whose value rests exclusively in its utility and function" (Lord Bridge). Does the judgment apply narrowly to spare parts which by their nature: (i) have a longevity inevitably shorter than that of the main product; and (ii) are utilitarian and functional. Alternatively, was the Court laying down a general principle that copyright never subsists in spare parts irrespective of the nature of the spare part. From the tenor of the judgments there are certainly grounds for arguing that the wider view prevails. Lord Templeman thus stated:

> "I see no reason to confer on a manufacturer the right in effect to dictate the terms on which an article sold by him is to be kept in repair and working order."

The *Ford Motor Company* case discussed above reflects the competition issues inherent in the refusal to license spare parts. The judgment of the House of Lords will have eased potential licensees' problems who may perform reverse engineering on the spare part they wish to copy and produce. There is no need to apply to the proprietor for a licence to copy the proprietor's drawings and plans.

13.386 One obvious difficulty with the judgment lies in the fact that the Court refrained from defining a "spare part" and since this concept is the effective boundary line of the spare

[340] [1986] AC 577. The case related to the 1988 Act's predecessor, the Copyright Act 1956. While the specific issue of spare parts is now dealt with by Part III of the 1988 Act, the principles enunciated in that case remain relevant.

parts exception this is unfortunate. Thus, as mentioned above, does the exception apply only to spare parts whose longevity is *inevitably* exceeded by that of the main product and which are utilitarian and functional, or, does it apply to *any* component of the main product which might (or might not) require repair before the "death" of the main product irrespective of the relative importance of the component to the whole. It will require future case law to clarify the precise scope of this exception.

13.387 It has been argued that the principle of non-derogation from grant can be applied to computer systems suppliers. In *Digital Equipment Corporation* v *LCE Computer Maintenance Ltd*,[341] an argument that this principle applied to allow third parties to use the plaintiff's diagnostic software in the repair and maintenance of the plaintiff's hardware was considered by the judge to "raise interesting questions" and was not struck out under RSC Order 18 Rule 19.

13.388 In a judgment in the High Court of Hong Kong, *Canon* v *Green*,[342] it was held that the principle of non-derogation from grant only applied to enable the repair of goods, meaning "to restore the good condition by renewal or replacement if decayed or damaged parts". Moreover, the principle of non-derogation did not apply to patents for which there had always been acknowledged by law a right to repair.[343] In the case it was held that non-derogation did not entitle a third party to make spare toner cartridges for photocopiers, although it did entitle it to supply spare parts for broken for worn cartridges.

J. Software Licensing in EC Law[344]

1. *Legal Context*

13.389 In the UK computer software is protected under copyright law.[345] Elsewhere in the EC computer software has been dealt with in a variety of ways which have not always made it so easy as in the UK to protect computer software through copyright.[346]

13.390 This has therefore been an area which cried out for harmonisation of laws. The response was the Software Directive.[347] Recital 1 states as one its reasons for being implemented that computer programs are not clearly protected in all Member States by existing legislation and that such protection, where it exists, has different attributes. Recital 7 and Article 1(1) state the general principle that Member States are to protect computer programs as literary works within the meaning of the Berne Convention.

341 Unreported judgment of Mervyn Davies J in the Chancery Division, 22 May 1992.

342 *Canon Kabushiki Kaisha* v *Green Cartridge Co (Hong Kong) Ltd* [1995] FSR 877, Rogers J. Upheld by the Privy Council on 30 April 1997.

343 *Sirdar Rubber Co Ltd* v *Wallington Weston and Co* (1907) RPC 539, 543 per Lord Halsbury "You may prolong the life of a licensed article but you must not make a new one under the cover of repair."

344 See I.S. Forrester, "Software licensing in the light of current EC competition law considerations" [1992] ECLR 5; T.C. Vinje, "Compliance with Article 85 in software licensing" [1992] ECLR 165.

345 s. 3(1) Copyright Designs and Patents Act 1988 extends the definition of a literary work as including a computer program for the purposes of being granted copyright protection under the Act.

346 German law in particular requires a higher degree of author creativity than UK law; see the *Inkasssoprogram* case No 1ZR 52/83 (1985). It has been estimated that prior to the EC Software Directive only 15% of computer programs in circulation in Germany attracted copyright protection.

347 Council Directive 91/250/EEC of 14 May 1991 on the legal protection of computer programs [1992] OJ L122/42.

13.391 Member States were required to alter their national laws before 1 January 1993[348] and so national laws should reflect the position under the Directive as from that date. National courts are under a duty to interpret national law in accordance with the Directive as from that date.[349] Thus even though the directive is addressed at Member States, its provisions will apply to licensing agreements between private businesses. Accordingly, the Software Directive can be taken as authoritative guidance as to restrictions which may be included in software licences.

13.392 Software licensing can be treated as a form of copyright licensing under EC law,[350] thus reflecting what has thus far been the situation under UK law.[351] To that extent, the comments at paras. 13.351–13.388 apply. However, there are a number of provisions in the Software Directive which require additional comment.

2. *Restricted Acts and Exceptions to Restricted Acts*

13.393 The Software Directive sets out in Article 4 a number of restricted acts, these being acts which only the copyright holder in the software (the "rightholder") may do or authorise to be done. These are:

(a) the permanent or temporary reproduction of computer program by any means and in any form, in part or in whole. Moreover, insofar as loading, displaying, running, transmission or storage of the computer program necessitates such reproduction, such acts shall be subject to authorisation by the rightholder;

(b) the translation, adaptation, arrangement and any other alteration of a computer program and the reproduction of the results thereof. This is stated to be without prejudice to the rights of the person who alters the program; and,

(c) any form of distribution to the public, including the rental of the original or any copies thereof. The matter of exhaustion of rights is dealt with expressly: the first sale in the Community of a copy of a program by the rightholder or with his or her consent shall exhaust the distribution right within the Community of that copy, with the exception of the right to control further rental of the program or a copy thereof.

13.394 There are four exceptions under the software directive to the general principle that the rightholder has the right to prohibit any of these restricted acts. These exceptions are set out in Articles 5 and 6, and only the first may be excluded by an appropriate contractual provision. It must be borne in mind that these restrictions are in addition to other restrictions applicable under the main body of copyright licensing law.

13.395 (i) If the acts referred to in paragraphs (a) and (b)[352] above are necessary for the use by a lawful acquirer of the computer program in accordance with its intended purpose, including for error correction, then the acquirer has the right to carry out such acts, unless there is specific contractual provision to the contrary.[353]

[348] Art. 10(1) Directive 91/250/EEC.

[349] Case C-106/89 *Marleasing* [1990] ECR I-4133 [1992] 1 CMLR 305.

[350] In turn, the principles relevant to patent and know-how licensing are applicable: see Commission's *Sixth Report on Competition Policy* (1976) para. 162 and *Thirteenth Report on Competition Policy* (1983), para. 88.

[351] See para. 13.404.

[352] Arts. 4(a) and (b) Directive 91/250/EEC.

[353] Art. 5(1) Directive 91/250/EEC. Implemented by s. 50C Copyright Design and Patents Act 1988. Under English contract law's strict doctrine of privity, it may well not be possible for such a restriction to be placed on any subsequent acquirer other than the initial licensee: see *Chitty on Contracts* (27th edn. 1994) paras. 18-065–18-075.

13.396 (ii) It is not permissible to restrict a person having the right to use a computer program from making a back-up copy of that program insofar as it is necessary for the use of that program.[354] This thus applies to all legitimate users of a piece of software, not just the lawful acquirer of the program.

13.397 (iii) It is provided that[355] the person having the right to use a copy of a computer program shall be entitled to observe, study or test the functioning of the program in order to determine the ideas and principles which underlie any element of the program if that is done while performing any of the acts of loading, displaying, running, transmitting or storing the program which he is entitled to do. This right may not be limited by any contractual provision.

13.398 (iv) Article 6 of the software directive is concerned with ensuring the interoperability of computer programs. It introduces a right to reproduce the software code and translate its form within the meaning of paragraphs (a) and (b) above if this is indispensable in order to obtain the information necessary to achieve the interoperability of an independently created computer program with other computer programs.[356] this right may not be restricted by the rightholder, but it is subject to three conditions, as well as limitations on the use of information so obtained. The conditions are:

– the acts of reproduction and translation are performed by the licensee or by another person having a right to use a coy of a program, or on their behalf by a person authorised to do so;[357]
– the information necessary to achieve interoperability has not already been made available to the persons wishing to do these acts;[358] and,
– these acts are confined to the parts of the original program which are necessary to achieve interoperability.[359]

The limitations on use of information so obtained are that the information shall not be:

– used for goals other than to achieve the interoperability of the independently created computer program;[360]
– given to others, except where necessary for the interoperability of the independently created computer program;[361] or,
– be used for the development, production or marketing of a computer program substantially similar in its expression, or for any other act which infringes copyright.[362]

13.399 Article 6 acknowledges the point made in para. 13.361 that this article could be interpreted in such a way as to be inconsistent with the Berne convention's restrictions on providing for compulsory licensing. Therefore it provides that[363] nothing in that Article is to be interpreted in such a way as to allow its application to be used in a manner which unreasonably prejudices the rightholder's legitimate interests or conflicts with a normal exploitation

354 Art. 5(2) Directive 91/250/EEC implemented by s. 50A Copyright Designs and Patents Act 1988.
355 Art. 5(3) Directive 91/250/EEC. Not implemented by the Copyright, Designs and Patents Act 1988, not being an act restricted under UK law.
356 Art. 6(1) Directive 91/250/EEC implemented by s. 50B Copyright Designs and Patents Act 1988
357 Art. 6(1)(a) Directive 91/250/EEC.
358 Art. 6(1)(b) Directive 91/250/EEC.
359 Art. 6(1)(c) Directive 91/250/EEC.
360 Art. 6(2)(a) Directive 91/250/EEC.
361 Art. 6(2)(b) Directive 91/250/EEC.
362 Art. 6(2)(c) Directive 91/250/EEC.
363 Art. 6(3) Directive 91/250/EEC.

of the computer program, a point to be borne in mind when considering how such limitations and conditions can be written into a licence.

13.400 This provision reinforces the position that the Directive is not exhaustive, but rather that it adds new restrictions to be taken into account. In practice the interoperability provisions in Article 6 are likely to provoke controversy. In this particular respect, Recital 27 warns that the provisions of the Directive are without prejudice to the application of competition rules under Articles 85 and 86 of the Treaty if a dominant supplier refuses to make information available which is necessary for interoperability.

13.401 Beyond the principles set out with respect to copyright as well as to patent and know-how licences, it is possible to identify some other common restrictions which would bring a software licence within Article 85(1). A designated machine or site clause is probably only compatible with Article 85(1) if necessary to measure a true level of royalties for use of the software. If such a clause instead is intended to prevent a rival manufacturer competing to supply hardware compatible with that software, then it is a restriction of competition contravening Article 85(1). Restrictions on third party maintenance are hard to justify, in the light of Article 5(1) and Recital 18 of the Software Directive.[364]

13.402 Restrictions on systems integration depend on a case by case analysis, in the light of Article 5(1) of the Software Directive. Restrictions on reverse engineering and decompilation are governed by Articles 5(3) and 6 of the software Directive, and in any case are likely to contravene Article 85(1) and seem highly unlikely to benefit from Article 85(3) individual exemption.

13.403 The application of Article 86 as well as of US antitrust was illustrated by the proceedings brought jointly by the European Commission and Antitrust Division of the US Department of Justice in *Microsoft*,[365] relating to its licensing practices for its MS-DOS and Windows software. Three types of conduct were condemned by the competition authorities. First, Microsoft's practice of requiring licensees to pay a licence fee based upon the numbers of personal computers old by a licensee irrespective of whether the licensed software was used was held to restrict competition, since it meant that any computers using rival software would cost more since it would have to bear the cost of a Microsoft licence. The settlement prohibited Microsoft from requiring such licence fees or lump sum fees, and from requiring minimum purchases of Microsoft's software. Thus a purchaser is able to obtain and pay for only what it needs, giving rival manufacturers the ability to supply as well. Secondly, unreasonably long licences were held to foreclose new entrants and thus to restrict competition. Licences going beyond the normal lifetime of most operating system products were held to be unreasonably long. Rather, Microsoft should have allowed purchasers the opportunity, at the end of the lifetime of an operating system, to look elsewhere for competing supplies. Thus Microsoft agreed not to enter into contracts for a term of more than one year's duration. Thirdly, confidentiality agreements entered into with independent software firms testing new Microsoft products were held to be anti-competitive since they restricted unreasonably the ability of such firms to do work for Microsoft's competitors. The agreements went further than was necessary to protect Microsoft's confidential information.

364 See also in US law, *Eastman Kodak* v *Image Technical Services*, 112 S Ct 2072, 199 L Ed 2d 265 (1992).

365 Commission Press Release IP/94/653, (1994) 1 CPN 17. The settlement between Microsoft and the European Commission was made in a settlement dated 15 July 1994. The US investigation is reported at (1994) 67 ATRR 106 and was due to be settled by a consent decree. However, somewhat unexpectedly, the judge refused assent to the terms of the consent decree on the basis that its scope was too narrow and did not constitute an effective antitrust remedy, as required by the Tunney Act. The Department of Justice successfully appealed: *US* v *Microsoft Corp* 56F.3d 1448 (DC Cir 1995) and a consent decree was subsequently entered.

K. Software Licensing in United Kingdom Law

13.404 The only specific provision in UK law for software licensing to date has been in the implementation of the Software Directive, which as lead to the amendment of the Copyright, Designs and Patents Act 1988.[366] This follows the Software Directive relatively faithfully, and must be interpreted in accordance with the Directive as far as possible.[367] Reference is thus made back to paras13.393-13.400, where the UK legislation is cross referenced.

13.405 Other than that, there are not specific provisions relating to software licensing and so the general considerations relating to copyright licensing set out in above will apply.

L. Trade Mark Licensing in EC Law

1. Legal Context

13.406 Trade mark licensing raises many of the same issues as are raised by patent know-how and copyright licensing. The decision of the Commission in *Compari*[368] indicates that it will treat clauses in trade mark licences in much the same way as clauses in patent and know-how licences. Hence, Regulation 240/96/EEC may be a useful guide to Commission thinking.

13.407 With respect to the technology transfer block exemption, trade mark licences incorporated into patent licences which are ancillary to the grant of the patent may be exempted under that Regulation. Article 1(1)(7) of the Regulation permits, "an obligation on the licensee to use only the licensor's trade mark or get up to distinguish the licensed product during the term of the agreement provided that the licensee is not prevented from identifying himself as the manufacturer of the licensed product." It should be stressed that the trade mark licence is ancillary to that of the patent and know-how licence and it may not be used to extend the effects of the licence beyond the life of the patents or secrecy of the know-how.

13.408 In *Moosehead*,[369] the Commission decided that an agreement whereby a Canadian brewery licensed a British brewery to produce its trade marked brand of lager using its know-how was primarily a trade mark licence rather than a know-how licence, since the principal interest of the parties lies in the exploitation of the trade mark rather than of the know-how. This test, though undoubtedly right given the sad state of the British lager market, may not be one that could easily be applied to other types of mixed licence.

2. Exclusive Licences: Open and Closed Licences

13.409 It may be assumed that the principles derived from *Nungesser v Commission*[370] apply equally in theory to exclusive trade mark licences.[371]

[366] Amendment was made by the Copyright (Computer Programs) Regulations 1992 (S.I. 1992 No. 3233), pursuant to s. 2 European Communities Act 1972.

[367] Case C-106/89 *Marleasing* [1990] ECR I-4135, [1992] 1 CMLR 305; C-91/92 *Dori* [1994] ECR I-3325.

[368] [1978] 2 CMLR 397.

[369] OJ 1990 L100/32 [1991] 4 CMLR 391.

[370] Case 258/78 [1983] 1 CMLR 278; [1982] ECR 2061.

[371] See Joliet, "Territorial and exclusive trade mark licensing under the EC law of competition" (1984) IIC 21 at p. 31; and, "Trade mark licensing agreements under the EC law of competition" (1983) 5

13.410 However, in practice the Commission seems to reluctant to apply *Nungesser* to trade mark licences. In *Moosehead*, exclusivity was held to fall within Article 85(1) since "the exclusive character of the licence has as a consequence the exclusion of third parties, namely the five other large brewers in the territory, from the use as licensees of the Moosehead trade mark, in spite of their potential interest and their ability to do so".[372] This statement bears no relation to the reality that no lager brewer would contemplate developing and marketing a new brand in competition with one of its rivals. Established brands might be different, though there is no evidence that this is the case. Therefore, little weight can be placed on the *Nungesser* principle in practice when it comes to trade mark licensing.

3. *Other Clauses in Trade Mark Licences*

13.411 It was stated above that the treatment of trade mark licences may be expected to follow that of patent and copyright licensing. The decisions of the Commission in *Campari*[373] and *Moosehead*[374] support this view. In those cases the Commission held that the following clauses fell outside of Article 85(1) or were exemptible under Article 85(3). There is no block exemption for trade mark licensing agreements.[375] However, the decisions of the Commission in *Campari*[376] and *Moosehead*[377] indicate that they will treat clauses in trade mark licences on the same principles as apply to patent and know-how licences.

(1) Quality control measures

13.412 In *Campari*, a clause whereby the licensor granted licences only in respect of certain of the licensee's plants which were capable of guaranteeing the quality of the product was cleared, as were restrictions not going beyond what was necessary for quality control.

13.413 A clause permitting the licensor to veto any change in the place of manufacture in cases where the new establishment might adversely affect the product quality was also outside of Article 85(1) since "the maintenance of quality is referable to the existence of the trade mark right".[378]

(2) Compliance with licensor's specifications

13.414 An obligation to follow the licensor's instructions relating to the manufacture of the product and the quality of the ingredients is not restrictive. So in *Moosehead*, a restriction whereby the licensee agreed that the quality of the lager and the type and quality of the raw materials was to comply with the licensor's specifications was cleared.[379]

(3) Exclusive purchase of certain products from licensor

13.415 An obligation to purchase certain secret raw materials from the licensor is another legitimate quality control measure and falls outside of Article 85(1). In both *Campari* and *Moosehead*, obligations to purchase in the former case a secret mixture of herbs and colouring

cont.
Northwestern Journal of International Law and Business 755. But cf. "Everling, zur neueren EuGH-Rechtsprechung zum wettbewerbsrecht" (1982) Eur. 301 at p. 310.

372 [1991] 4 CMLR 391, 397 para. 15.
373 [1978] 2 CMLR 397.
374 OJ 1990 L100/32; [1991] 4 CMLR 391.
375 C.D. Ehlerman of DGIV has indicated that the Commission is considering or has considered a trade mark licensing block exemption, (1994) 1 CPN 2, 4.
376 [1978] 2 CMLR 397.
377 OJ 1990 L100/32; [1991] 4 CMLR 391.
378 [1978] 2 CMLR 397 at II(C); [1991] 4 CMLR 391, 398 para. 15.2.
379 [1991] 4 CMLR 391, 398 para. 15.2.

matters and in the latter the licensor's particular strain of yeast were held to fall outside Article 85(1). However, in *Campari*, the Commission had objected to an obligation on the licensees to purchase certain non-secret materials (bitter orange essence and albumin) and the agreements were amended to remove this obligation.[380]

(4) Confidentiality of know-how licensed with trade mark

13.416 An obligation prohibiting the licensee from divulging the manufacturing process to third parties does not infringe Article 85(1). Obligations to this effect in *Campari* and *Moosehead* were cleared.[381]

(5) Prohibition on assignment

13.417 A clause prohibiting the licensee from assigning or sub-licensing the trade mark does not restrain competition. The licensor, by use of such a clause, merely safeguards its freedom to select its licensees.[382]

(6) Prohibition on exports outside of EC

13.418 A ban on licensees supplying outside of the EC was held in *Campari*[383] not to infringe Article 85(1) where supplementary economic factors, such as the accumulation of trade margins and of excise duties and taxes levied by importing countries as well as the duties charged on crossing the EC borders, rendered reimportation unlikely. It need not be proved that reimportation is impossible. This assessment applies also to States with which the EC has entered into free trade agreements, though in such cases, given the diminished level of trans-frontier burdens, reimportation is inherently more likely and hence prohibitions on supply to such states might indirectly affect intra-EC trade. Where the effect on such trade is marginal a *de minimis* rule may be assumed. Commission clearance however would be a prudent precaution.

(7) Promotional obligations

13.419 An obligation on the licensee to take measures for promoting the relevant product does not prima facie infringe competition. Thus, clauses requiring licensees to maintain continuous contact with customers and to spend a standard minimum sum on advertising are not restrictive.[384]

13.420 An obligation on the parties jointly to agree a marketing policy was held in *Moosehead* to fall outside Article 85(1).[385] An advertising restriction may be restrictive where the sum in question prevents the licensee from engaging in other activities or carrying on their own advertising.[386] An analogous provision is included in Article 2(3)(c) of the block exemption on exclusive dealing.[387]

(8) Exclusive territories and ban on "active" exports

13.421 See the commentary concerning *Nungesser* v *Commission* above relating to exclusive territories. Where such a clause does fall within Article 85(1) it may be exemptible under

[380] [1978] 2 CMLR 397, 402 para. 22. See also Art. 2(1) Reg. 2349/84; Art. 2(1)(5) Reg. 556/89 and Art. 2(1)(5) Reg. 240/96.
[381] *Campari* [1978] 2 CMLR 397, 409 para. 63; *Moosehead* [1991] 4 CMLR 391, 398 para. 2.
[382] See *Campari* [1978] 2 CMLR 397, 409 para. 65.
[383] [1978] 2 CMLR 397, para. 60
[384] See *Campari* [1978] 2 CMLR 397, 409 para. 64.
[385] [1991] 4 CMLR 391, 396 para. 10.
[386] *Campari* [1978] 2 CMLR 397, para. 64.
[387] Reg. 1983/83/EEC, OJ 1983 L173/1. See also Art. 2(3)(c) of Reg. 1984/83/EEC OJ 1983 L173/5 on block exemption for certain categories of exclusive purchasing.

Article 85(3) provided the licensee is permitted to meet unsolicited orders from outside of his territory.[388]

(9) Ban on dealing in competing products, "no-dualling" clauses

13.422 An obligation on the licensee not to carry products which compete with those licensed (i.e. a no-dualling clause) infringes Article 85(1) but may in appropriate cases be exempted under Article 85(3). Such a clause contributes to improving distribution of the licensed product by concentrating sales efforts, encouraging the build up of stocks and shortening delivery times.[389] Analogous provisions may be found in Article 2(2)(a) of Regulation 1983/83/EEC on exclusive dealing and Article 2(2) of Regulation 1984/83/EEC on exclusive purchasing. In *Campari* the Commission stated:

> "The restriction on the licensees freedom to deal in other products at the same time as the products here in question prevents the licensees from neglecting Campari in the event of conflict between the promotion of Campari sales and possible interest in another product. Although a non-competition clause in a licensing agreement concerning industrial property rights based on the result of a creative activity, such as a patent, would constitute a barrier to technical and economic progress by preventing the licensees from taking an interest in other techniques and products, this is not the case with the licensing agreements under consideration here. The aim pursued by the parties, as is clear from the agreements taken as a whole, is to decentralise manufacture within the EC and to rationalise the distribution system linked to it, and thus to promote the sale of Campari-Milano's Bitter, manufactured from the same concentrates provided by Campari-Milano, according to the same mixing process and using the same ingredients, and bearing the same trade mark as that of the licensor."[390]

13.423 In *Moosehead* the Commission held that a restriction on producing or promoting within the licensed territory "any other beer identified as a Canadian beer" could be exempted under Article 85(3) because "of the existence of many similar competing beers" which meant that "the parties to the agreement will not have the possibility of eliminating competition in respect of a substantial part of the products in question".[391]

13.424 In view of the fact that "no-dualling" clauses are generally forbidden by the Commission in patent know-how licences and that this has been confirmed in the block-exemptions, a degree of caution should be exercised in relying upon *Campari* as indicating permissiveness by the Commission to such clauses, though the readiness of the Commission to take account of interbrand competition in *Moosehead*, albeit under Article 85(3) rather than 85(1), is encouraging. Licences incorporating such a clause may need to be notified.

(10) No-challenge clauses

13.425 Prior to the *Moosehead* decision, the generally held view was that an obligation on the licensee not to challenge the legal validity of the licensor's trade mark is a serious infringement of Article 85(1) and is unsuitable for exemption.[392] The Commission's decision in

388 *Campari* [1978] 2 CMLR 397 at para. 76. Criticised, Joliet, *op, cit.*, at p. 30, 31. Case 56, 58/64 *Consten and Grundig* v *Commission* [1966] CMLR 418; [1966] ECR 299. *Moosehead* [1991] 4 CMLR 391, 397 para. 15. See also Art. 2(2) Reg. 1983/83.

389 *ibid.* para. III (2).

390 *Campari, ibid.*, at para. 73.

391 [1991] 4 CMLR 391, 400 para. 16.2.

392 e.g. Penneys [1978] 2 CMLR 100 noted *Seventh Report on Competition Policy* (1977), sp. 110; Toltecs-Dorcet [1983] 1 CMLR 412. But there may be scope for exemption of trade mark delimitation agreements, see, Case 35/83 BAT Cigaretten-Fabriken GmbH v Commission [1985] 2 CMLR 470; Waelbroeck, "Les conventions de limitation des Marques face au droit Communautaires" (1985) Cahiers de Droit 402. R. Subiotto, "Moosehead/Whitbread: industrial franchises and no-challenge clauses relating to licensed trade marks under EEC competition law" [1990] ECLR 226.

Moosehead marks a softening of this absolute condemnation of no-challenge clauses.[393] A distinction is drawn between challenging the ownership and the validity of a licensed trade mark. A clause restricting a challenge to the ownership by the licensor of the trade mark will not be caught by Article 85(1), since "[w]hether or not the licensor or licensee has the ownership of the trade mark, the use of it by any other party is prevented in any event, and competition would not thus be affected".[394] By contrast, a restriction on challenging the validity of the trade mark will be caught by Article 85(1), since "it may contribute to the maintenance of a trade mark that would be an unjustified barrier to entry in a given market".[395] In this particular case, the restriction on challenging validity was held to fall outside Article 85(1) as it was so new to the lager market in the licensed territory, and so its maintenance did not constitute in practice an appreciable barrier to entry to the market. Therefore, for new trade marks, a no-challenge clause may fall outside Article 85(1) all together if the trade mark does not constitute a barrier to entry. If it is sufficiently well-known to be regarded as a barrier to entry, then only a restriction on challenging ownership, not validity, will be cleared under Article 85(1); a restriction on challenging validity will be caught and, given previous case law, is unlikely to be given exemption under Article 85(3). Problems will arise, however, in assessing when a new trade mark becomes sufficiently well-known to present a barrier to entry, and thereby bringing a previously cleared restriction within Article 85(1). So a cautiously drafted no-challenge clause should be limited in duration for the earlier years of an agreement, bringing the restriction on challenge on validity to an end after a specified period when it can be assumed that the mark will have become sufficiently well-known to constitute a barrier to entry.[396]

4. *Protecting Exclusive Territories: Free Movement of Goods*

13.426 It has already been noted[397] that there are restrictions over the extent to which holders of intellectual property rights may bring infringement proceedings to prevent parallel imports and protect the integrity of geographical territories. The general principle applicable to patents is that patent rights cannot be used by the patentee to restrain subsequent dealings in patented goods placed on the market by the patentee or with its consent.

13.427 It was held by the Court of Justice in *Hag (No. 1)*[398] that a trade mark owner could not oppose subsequent dealings in trade marked goods in the additional case where the goods being imported, although not marketed by the trade mark owner or with its consent, were marked with a trade mark having a common origin to that of the trade mark owner's mark. In that case the *Hag* trade marks had originally been owned by the same company but following post Second World War sequestration had ended up in the ownership of different companies across the common market. This ruling, though affirmed in *Terrapin* v *Terranova*[399] had no doctrinal basis in Community law, rather being founded upon a seeming antipathy to the trade mark rights as being somehow less worthy of protection than other intellectual property rights. It has now overturned in *Hag (No. 2)*.[400]

[393] *ibid.*

[394] [1991] 4 CMLR 391, 398 para. 15(4)(a) first indent.

[395] [1991] 4 CMLR 391, 398 para. 15(4)(a) second indent.

[396] It is also arguable that a well-known trade mark constitutes a barrier to entry: see Baden Fuller, "Economic issues relating to property rights in trade marks" [1981] ELRev 162.

[397] See paras. 13.4–13.12.

[398] Case 192/73 *Van Zyulen Freres* v *Hag* [1974] ECR 731; [1974] 2 CMLR 127.

[399] Case 119/75 *Terrapin* v *Terranova* [1976] ECR 1039; [1976] 2 CMLR 482.

[400] Case 10/89 *SA CNL-Sucal NV* v *Hag GF AG* [1990] ECR I-3711 [1990] 3 CMLR 575; For comment see Rothnie [1991] EIPR 24; Metaxas-Marangidis [1991] ELRev 128.

13.428 Accordingly, proceedings may be instituted by a national trade mark rights owner to prevent imports bearing a similar mark owned elsewhere in the Community where those imports have not been placed on the market by the national trade mark rights owner or with its consent. However, the Court of Justice has noted two limitations on this position. First, where the mark owner uses national proceedings in a selective, discriminatory manner, then this might amount to arbitrary discrimination or a disguised restriction or trade under Article 36 EC. Secondly, the infringement action must only be in respect of foreign marks which bear a close nexus to the mark sought to be protected. The decision of a domestic court on this nexus is apparently not determinative; the Commission and Court may take a different view.[401]

5. Trade Mark Assignments

13.429 Trade marks may be assigned as well as licensed.[402] Where this involves a mere transfer of ownership there is little problem for competition law. Problems do occur, however, where there is a division of ownership by assignment. Where different undertakings following an assignment own the same mark in different territories, this may amount in effect to market sharing. The Court of Justice took this view in *Sirena* v *Eda*,[403] holding an assignment to be caught by Article 85 in view of its continuing effect, notwithstanding that it had been entered into well before the Treaty had come into effect.[404]

13.430 The Commission adopted this approach in *Chiquita/Fyffes*.[405] Chiquita had sold off the Fyffes business and trade mark, but had retained the right to prevent Fyffes using the "Fyffes" trade mark in mainland Europe for 20 years, although after three years it has agreed to cease use itself of the Fyffes name. Fyffes thus were free to sell under that name only in the UK and Ireland, Chiquita relying on contractual and trade mark rights to prevent sale in mainland Europe. The Commission objected under both Articles 85 and 86 to what it saw as market division through the assignment of trade marks and use of trade mark rights. The case was settled when Chiquita dropped its opposition to Fyffes imports under that name.[406]

13.431 How valid the Commission's approach remains is in doubt following the Court of Justice's decision in *Ideal Standard*.[407] It held that an agreement dividing trade mark rights between different owners in separate Member States by assignment was effective to entitle one to use trade mark infringement proceedings to block the other's imports, provided it was not part of a wider market sharing agreement caught by Article 85 EC.

13.432 In this case, a mark ("Ideal Standard") had been in the common ownership of the US owned American Standard group, but had been assigned with heating business in France to a third party which had sold it on to IHT. American Standard still owned the Ideal Stan-

[401] The Commission have confirmed this. *Toltecs–Dorcet* [1983] 1 CMLR 412. For judgment of the Court of Justice see Case 35/83 *BAT Cigaretten–Fabriken GmbH* v *Commission* [1985] 2 CMLR 470 [1985] ECR 363.

[402] The limitations on the trade mark assignment imposed by the UK's Trade Marks Act 1938, s. 22 *et seq.*, have been lifted by the Trade Marks Act 1994.

[403] Case 40/70 *Sirena* v *Eda* [1971] ECR 69, [1971] CMLR 260.

[404] The consequence of this ruling would have been to declare void an assignment entered into some thirty years previously, and, perhaps unsurprisingly, the Italian court which had referred the case refused to be drawn to this conclusion: see [1975] 1 CMLR 409.

[405] Commission's *Twenty-second report on Competition Policy* (1992), paras. 168–176.

[406] One can contrast this with the approach of Vinelott J in the parallel High Court case of *Fyffes* v *Chiquita Bands Inc* [1993] FSR 8. He robustly took issue with the Commission's view, observing that "Chiquita introduced a new competitor into the EEC which was free to trade under the Fyffes name in the United Kingdom and to trade in any part of continental Europe under any name except Fyffes in competition with Chiquita. Thus far, the transaction, far from restricting competition, promoted it".

[407] Case C-9/93 *IHT Internationale Heiztechnik GmbH* v *Ideal-Standard GmbH* [1994] ECR I-2789.

dard trade mark in Germany through its German subsidiary. The German subsidiary made sanitary ware and though it had ceased making heating equipment had retained the trade mark rights. IHT imported heating equipment into Germany and was met with trade mark infringement proceedings. The Court of Justice upheld Ideal Standard's right to bring trade mark proceedings as being justified under Article 36 EC.

13.433 The Court referred to its ruling in *Hag II* that essential function of a trade mark was to give consumers the right to identify origin. It rejected an argument that since the assignment was voluntary, then the trade mark owner had to accept that weakening of his rights, saying that since trade marks were territorial, the fact of territorial division had to be accepted. French law (the law of the assignment) permits partial assignments ie for some goods, not other. German law does not. The Court held that by allowing imports from France of goods under the trade mark, that would be exporting French trade mark law which allows co-existence of different products under the same mark to German law which does not. Such a change in law could not be made by case law, said the Court of Justice, but only by a Directive or Regulation under 100a.

13.434 The *Ideal Standard* ruling marks a considerably more relaxed approach to trade marks than has been evident in the Court's previous case law,[408] as well as being more relaxed than the Commission settlement in *Chiquita/Fyffes*. Doubts will however still remain as to when an assignment does form part of a wider market sharing agreement. It is not unusual for businesses to seek to concentrate their business efforts upon particular geographical areas and to sell their business not located in those areas. Is a withdrawal from a particular market to be characterised as market sharing? Or does market sharing contemplate a more active role in allocating customers or quotas for sales? It is submitted that the latter is the better approach, since to adopt the former would be to condemn most sales of part of a business as market sharing and this cannot be consistent with the result in *Ideal Standard* which was to permit just such an arrangement.

6. Trade Mark Delimitation Agreements

13.435 Trade mark delimitation agreements often resemble trade mark licence agreements, and to the extent that clauses are included of the type that have already been discussed, reference should be made to para. 13.406-13.434. A trade mark delimitation agreement is essentially an agreement whereby businesses using similar trade marks agree to restrict their use of those trade marks to avoid confusion. Provided that an agreement does no more than that, it will fall outside Article 85(1), but in a series of decisions the Commission has held that delimitation agreements going further than that may be caught[409] a view which has been upheld by the Court of Justice.[410]

[408] The Court stated in Case 40/70 *Sirena* v *Eda* [1971] ECR 69 at para. 7 that "a trade mark is distinguishable ... from other rights of industrial and commercial property, inasmuch as the interest protected by the latter are usually more important, and merit a higher degree of protection, than the interests protected by an ordinary trade mark".

[409] *Sirdar/Phildar* [1976] 1 CMLR D93; *Penney* [1978] 2 CMLR 100, *Toltecs/Dorcet* [1983] 1 CMLR 412, on appeal to ECJ sub nom Case 35/83 *BAT* v *Commission* [1985] ECR 363, [1985] 2 CMLR 470; *Syntex/Synthelabo* [1990] 4 CMLR 343; *Hershey/Schiffers*, unreported, see Press Release IP(90)87; see also the Court of Appeal decision in *Apple Corps* v *Apple Computer Inc* [1991] 3 CMLR 49,73 (Neill LJ), 82 (Nicholls LJ).

[410] Case 35/83 *BAT* v *Commission* [1985] ECR 363, [1985] 2 CMLR 470, para. 33: "agreements known as 'delimitation agreements' are lawful and useful if they serve to delimit, in the mutual interest of the parties, the spheres within which their respective trade marks may be used, and are intended to avoid confusion or conflict between them. That is not to say, however, that such agreements are excluded from the application of Article 85 of the Treaty if they also have the aim of dividing up the market or restricting competition in other ways."

13.436 In order to escape Article 85(1), a trade mark delimitation agreement must satisfy the following criteria:

13.437 (a) the agreement must not be a disguised means of partitioning the common market. In assessing this, the Commission will consider whether there was a serious risk of confusion between the trade marks. If there is no, as in *Sirdar/Phildar*[411] then the agreement will be caught by Article 85(1) and will not be capable of exemption. In *Toltecs/Dorcet*,[412] a delimitation agreement entered on the ground of supposed confusion between those two marks for cigarettes was held to contravene Article 85(1) as one of the marks, Dorcet, was not in use, was indeed liable to be struck off the register for non-use, and there was thus no actual likelihood of confusion. The only effect of the agreement was then to prevent imports of the cigarettes bearing the other mark, Toltecs. If there is a serious risk of confusion, then the next criterion must be considered.

13.438 (b) the agreement must not divide the common market, unless there are no other less restrictive solutions. Thus in *Syntex/Synthelabo*,[413] where Synthelabo had sought to agree not to market their pharmaceutical products in the UK, the Commission was unwilling to exempt such a restriction of competition since less restrictive methods could have been adopted such as the clear labelling of products. The agreement was amended to allow marketing of products throughout the Common Market by both parties and the file closed, details of the actual agreement as to delimitation not being divulged.

M. Trade Mark Licensing in United Kingdom Law

1. *Under the RTPA 1976*

13.439 Trade mark licences are exempt from the RTPA by virtue of Schedule 3(4) RTPA 1976. This is examined at paras. 2.173–2.180 and reference thereto may be made for discussion. Even where a licence contains terms which are not expressly covered by Schedule 3(4) the RTPA 1976 does not apply provided the restriction concerns the actual trade mark.

2. *Under the Competition Act 1980*

13.440 Terms in licences which have an anti-competitive effect may be subject to the CA 1980. As with patents, know-how and copyright (above) EC law may be of some guidance value. Where compulsory licensing is concerned, the Secretary of State does not have power, contrary to the provisions for copyright under the Copyright Designs and Patents Act 1988, to issue an order compelling licensing in respect of trade marks.

411 [1976] 1 CMLR D93.

412 *Toltecs/Dorcet* [1983] 1 CMLR D93; on appeal to ECJ *sub nom* Case 35/83 *BAT* v *Commission* [1985] ECR 363, [1985] 2 CMLR 470.

413 [1990] 4 CMLR 343.

N. Licensing Intellectual Property to Sub-contractors

13.441 In the conduct and performance of works by a contractor the hiring of independent sub-contractors is commonplace. Often the sub-contractor will employ technology protected by intellectual property rights of the contractor; licensing problems are hence raised.

1. *EC Law: The Sub-contracting Notice*

13.442 The Commission has issued a Notice concerning its assessment of certain manufacturing sub-contracting agreements in relation to Article 85(1)EC.[414]

> "Sub-contracting agreements" are defined as "agreements under which one firm, called 'the contractor', whether or not in consequence of a prior order from a third party, entrusts to another, called 'the sub-contractor', the manufacture of goods, the supply of services or the performance of work under the contractor's instructions, to be provided to the contractor or performed on his behalf ..."[415]

The Notice discusses a number of varieties of clause. These are described below. For discussion of other clause types see the discussion in the sections above.

(1) Limitations on use of technology by sub-contractor

13.443 Clauses whereby technology or equipment provided by the contractor may not be used for purposes other than the sub-contracting agreement and/or may not be made available to third parties do not fall within Article 85(1). The same applies to clauses requiring the sub-contractor to supply the goods, services or work resulting from use of the technology only to the contractor or on his behalf. The basic principle is that the contractor is entitled to safeguard the economic value of his particular technology or equipment and is hence entitled to restrict the sub-contractor to a utilisation of the technology/equipment which is the minimum necessary to enable the sub-contractor to operate effectively. Article 85(1) is not breached *provided that* the technology/equipment is necessary to enable the sub-contractor under reasonable conditions to operate in accordance with the contractor's instructions. To this extent the sub-contractor is providing goods, services or work in respect of which he is not an independent supplier in the market. The proviso is satisfied where performance of the subcontracting agreements makes *necessary* the use by the subcontractor of:

(a) intellectual property rights owned by the contractor or at his disposal, e.g. patents, utility models, copyrighted designs, registered designs;
(b) know-how of the contractor or at his disposal;
(c) studies, plans or documents accompanying the information given which have been prepared by or for the contractor; or,
(d) dies, patterns or tools and accessory equipment that are distinctively the contractors which even though not covered by industrial property rights nor containing any secret elements permit the manufacture of goods which differ in form,

[414] OJ 1979 C1/2 supplementing the Commission notice on cooperation between Enterprises OJ 1968 C75/3. See also Commission answer to WQ No. 1092/79, OJ 1980 C74/36 outlining the Commission's involvement in sub-contracting policy.

[415] *ibid.*, para. 2. Exclusive manufacturing and supply arrangements between joint inventors are *not* covered by the Notice: Bramley-Gilbert, *Tenth Report on Competition Policy*, para. 128. It is believed that the subcontracting of R&D work *does* fall outside of Art. 85(1), see White, "Research and development joint ventures under EC competition law" (1985) IIC 663 at p. 680 n. 29.

function or composition from other goods manufactured or supplied on the market.

13.444 The Notice states however that Article 85(1) is breached where the restrictions noted above are imposed on a sub-contractor who has independent capacity to provide the sub-contracted goods or services. In such cases the restrictions could deprive the sub-contractor of the possibility of developing his own business in the fields covered by the agreement.[416]

(2) Other permissible clauses[417]

13.445 Article 85(1) is not infringed in respect of the following clauses.

(a) Confidentiality

13.446 Undertakings by either party not to divulge secret or confidential information or other know-how so long as it has not become public knowledge.

(b) Restriction on use of know-how after expiry of agreement

13.447 An undertaking by the sub-contractor not to use, even after expiry of the agreement, know-how or other secret information received during the currency of the agreement whilst that know-how or secret information is not in the public domain. Restrictions on the use of know-how gained other than through the agreement may be restrictive.

(c) Non-exclusive improvement grants

13.448 Undertakings by the sub-contractor to pass on to the contractor on a non-exclusive basis any technical improvements made during the currency of the agreement are not restrictive. The same applies in respect of licences for improvement patents taken out by the sub-contractor for the term of the patent held by the contractor.

(d) Exclusive improvement grants

13.449 Where in (c) above the improvement is only effective in conjunction with the contractor's know-how or patent then the sub-contractor may be required to grant an exclusive licence to the contractor. Such a clause is declared not to restrain competition on the basis that it is *de minimis*.

(e) Trade marks

13.450 The contractor may prohibit the sub-contractor from using the contractor's trade mark, trade name or get up in respect of goods, services or work not supplied to the contractor.

(3) Prohibited clause: research and development

13.451 Any clause limiting the sub-contractor's right to dispose of the results of his own R&D restrains competition. In such situations the sub-contracting relationship does not displace the ordinary rules on disposal of intellectual property rights and know-how.[418]

[416] See Commission answer to WQ Nos: 2015/82, 2016/82, 2017/82, OJ 1983 C189/7.
[417] *ibid.*, Commission Notice paras. 3, 4.
[418] *ibid.*, para. 4.

2. UK Law

13.452 There are no special rules on intellectual property licensing in sub-contracting agreements. Hence the rules described above in respect of patents, copyright, trade marks and know-how apply.

O. The Duty to License Intellectual Property Rights

1. EC law: Article 86 EC

13.453 The duty not to abuse a dominant position imposed by Article 86 EC may require positive steps to be taken to avoid the abuse. Such steps may include the grant of a licence. The Commission has the powers to require the grant of a licence. The Commission has informally settled cases on the basis that a dominant undertaking license its IP rights.[419]

13.454 It was conventionally thought that the essence of the ownership of any property right is the right to prevent others using that property, and that technology protected by intellectual property rights fell within this general principle.

13.455 That was the apparent position of the Court of Justice in two virtually identical cases concerning motor vehicle spare parts decided in 1988: *Volvo*[420] and *Renault*.[421]

13.456 In both cases national legislation granted industrial design copyright protection to car components, thus preventing other manufacturers from making compatible spare parts without a licence, which neither car maker was prepared to grant. The Court of Justice rejected an argument put forward in both cases that the refusal to grant licences is as an abuse of the car makers' dominant positions. It did however acknowledge that the exercise of the intellectual property rights could be an abuse and gave three examples of such an abuse: (i) where there was an arbitrary refusal to supply spare parts to an independent repairer; (ii) where there was unfair pricing of spare parts; or, (iii) where there was a refusal to continue to supply spare parts for a model of motor vehicle of which many were still in circulation.

13.457 None of these examples of abuse involved a duty on the part of the dominant undertaking to license use of the intellectual property rights in question; each relates to the use of products protected by intellectual property rights.

13.458 From this one might conclude that Court would not hold that there was an abuse which could only be remedied by a licence of intellectual property rights. However, this is precisely what both the Court of First Instance and Court of Justice held in the *Magill TV Guide* case. The case arose after an attempt by a TV listings guide publisher to print a weekly advance guide to all programmes capable of reception on the island of Ireland. The copyright owners brought successful interim injunction proceedings in the Irish High Court restraining publication in breach of their copyright. The publisher then complained to the Commission which decided that each of the broadcasters was abusing its dominant position.[422] The Commission's decision seems to be founded upon two objections. Firstly, the Commission noted that the broadcasters did license daily newspapers to print the day's

[419] See *IBM Settlement* [1984] 3 CMLR 147, concerning copyright protected interface information relating to computers.

[420] Case 238/87 *Volvo* v *Erik Veng (UK) Ltd* [1988] ECR 6211, [1989] 4 CMLR 122.

[421] Case 53/87 *CICRA and Maxicar* v *Renault* [1988] ECR 6039, [1990] 4 CMLR 265.

[422] OJ 1989 L78/43.

or the coming weekend's listings. Therefore the broadcasters were indulging in discriminatory licensing.[423] Secondly, the broadcasters were using their monopolies in broadcasting to establish monopolies in the neighbouring markets for TV listings guides. The broadcaster's appeal to the Court of First Instance was rejected.[424] The Court upheld the right of the Commission to order the copyright licences necessary to bring the infringement of Article 86 to an end.

13.459 Although the position was then altered in the UK, since the Broadcasting Act 1990 required UK programming authorities to license on terms, in the absence of agreement, to be decided by the copyright Tribunal set up under the Copyright, Designs and Patents Act 1988, two of the broadcasters appealed to the Court of Justice.[425]

13.460 The Court of Justice, in a surprisingly brief judgment, found an abuse on three, more limited, grounds, based upon its observation at paragraph 53 of its judgment that the broadcasters "were the only sources of the basic information on programme scheduling which is the indispensable raw material for compiling a weekly television guide". First, the Court found that the refusal to license copyright "prevented the appearance of a new product, a comprehensive weekly guide to television programmes, which the [broadcasters] did not offer and for which there was a potential consumer demand".[426] This suggests that any infringer of an intellectual property right, provided it can allege that the right owner is the only source of the material required to create a new product, is entitled to defend infringement proceedings by pointing to the consumer demand for the infringing product as demonstrated that the demand is not being met by that the right owner and thus justifying its infringement in order to meet that demand. If this is right, the existence of the intellectual property right is severely limited, as it may only be exercised against those infringers who have not succeeded in meeting new consumer demand.

13.461 Secondly, the Court stated that there was "no justification for such refusal either in the activity of television or in that of publishing television programmes.[427] Implicit in this statement is the view that intellectual property owners in the broadcasters' position may only prevent infringement if it is justifiable to do so, though the criteria relevant to such a justification are not elaborated upon in the judgment.

13.462 Finally, it was held to be an abuse for the broadcasters to reserve "to themselves the secondary market of weekly television guides by excluding all competition on that market ... since they denied access to the basic information which is the raw material indispensable for the compilation of such a guide."[428] While it is appreciated in national law that certain intellectual property rights should not be used to extend the monopolies they confer into neighbouring areas, as the anti-tying provisions under section 44 Patents Act 1977 illustrate, the Court of Justice has in effect developed this into a general dominance.

13.463 The Court of Justice gave no further guidance on the application of Article 86 to intellectual property rights, confining itself largely to the facts of the case. Particularly disap-

[423] The Commission indicated in *Tiercé Ladbroke (B)/PMU-DSV-French "sociétés de courses", Twenty-third Report on Competition Policy* (1993), Annex III, para. 17, that discriminatory licensing might constitute discrimination caught by Art. 86 EC.

[424] Case T-69, 70 and 76/89 *RTE, BBC and ITP* v *Commission* [1991] ECR II-485 *et seq.*, [1991] 4 CMLR 586 *et seq.*; see Robertson, "Compulsory copyright licensing under EEC law?" (1992) 108 LQR 39.

[425] Joined Cases C-241 and 242/91P *RTE and ITP* v *Commission* [1995] ECR I-743 [1995] 4 CMLR 718.

[426] *ibid.*, para. 54.

[427] *ibid.*, para. 55.

[428] *ibid.*, para. 56.

pointing was its refusal to consider the existence/exercise distinction drawn under Article 36 and applied by the Court of First Instance.

2. EC Law: Article 85 EC

13.464 The Commission has intimated that, outside of Article 86, infringement of Article 85 by a patentee does not give a third party a right to obtain a licence.[429] However, licensing has been required as an obligation tied to grant of an exemption under Article 85(3). In *EBU/Eurovision* exemption was granted to a joint venture running a satellite TV sports channel subject to it granting access on reasonable terms to non-members. This form of copyright licensing was regarded as necessary by the Commission to prevent the joint venture members using their position to foreclose the sports events broadcasting market.[430]

13.465 The exemption was subsequently annulled by the Court of First Instance on the basis that the Commission had not adequately considered whether the rules of the EBU were sufficiently objective and to enable them to be applied uniformly and in a non-discriminatory manner *vis-à-vis* non-members.[431]

13.466 Similarly, the European Telecommunications Standards Institute (ETSI) notified an interim policy on intellectual property rights which the Commission proposed to exempt.[432] This policy sought to ensure where an intellectual property right existed over technology which it was proposed to adopt as a European Standard that the owner of that right would agree to grant irrevocable licences on fair, reasonable and non-discriminatory terms. This is considered necessary to prevent adoption of a standard creating a *de facto* monopoly for the intellectual property right owner.

3. EC Law in UK Courts

13.467 Actions based upon Article 85 or 86 before the UK courts are apparently more hopeful. The Court of Appeal has held that no injunction may be granted at full trial against an unauthorised user where the licence on offer to that user is held to infringe Article 85.[433] The unauthorised user may, however, be required to pay reasonable royalties to the patentee.[434] Thus a third party may indirectly obtain a licence by unauthorised use coupled with subsequent payment of reasonable royalties. Such a tactic is not without its difficulties. The UK courts have stressed that in order to rely upon Articles 85 or 86 by way of defence to infringement proceedings, there must be a sufficient nexus between the relief sought and the alleged breach.[435] This requirement of nexus was considered by Ferris J in

[429] *Kalwar/Plast Control* v *Kabelmetal, Twelfth Report on Competition Policy* (1982), p. 73.

[430] OJ 1993 L179/23, paras. 51 and 71.

[431] Joined Cases T-528, 542, 543 and 546/93 *Métropole Télévision SA* v *Commission*, [1996] 5 CMLR 386

[432] OJ 1995 C76/5.

[433] See also *Holleran and Evans* v *Thwaites plc* [1989] 2 CMLR 917, where an interlocutory injunction was granted to restrain a landlord issuing a notice to quit to a tenant as a means of forcing the tenant to accept a new tenancy which was arguable in breach of Art. 85(1).

[434] *British Leyland* v *TI Silencers* [1981] FSR 213. See also *ICI* v *Berk Pharmaceuticals* [1981] 2 CMLR 712; *Lansing Bagnall* v *Buccaneer Lift Parts* [1984] 1 CMLR 224; *Pitney Bowes* v *Francotyp-Postalia* [1989] 3 CMLR 446; *Ransburg-Gema* v *Electrostatic Plant Systems* [1990] FSR 287 (Aldous J at p. 293, "for there to be a defence under Article 86, it must be pleaded that the plaintiff is in a dominant position and that the relief claimed would involve an abuse of a dominant position affecting trade between Member States. If such is pleaded properly and proved, the court is precluded from granting the relief, because to do so would produce a result which could be contrary to the Treaty.").

[435] See Oliver LJ in *British Leyland* v *Armstrong* [1984] 3 CMLR 102 (this point not considered before the House of Lords decision, [1986] AC 577). This is also the approach of the Commission: see *Kalwar/Plast Control* v *Kabelmetal, Twelfth Report on Competition Policy* (1982), p. 73.

IBM v *Phoenix International (Computers) Ltd*,[436] in which the plaintiff sought to restrain use of its trade mark. He noted that there had been cases in which defences based upon Article 86 had been allowed to go on trial.[437] Applying the approach of those cases, he considered whether, if the plaintiff were successful in pleading infringement of its intellectual property rights, the defendant would have any ground for restraining exercise of those rights under Article 86. In this case he held not, striking out a defence based upon Article 86 and observing that there had not yet been a successful defence based upon Article 86.[438] In the absence of the requisite nexus, it will not be possible to use either Article 85 or 86 as a means of defence to infringement proceedings, and hence as a way of indirectly obtaining a licence.

13.468 It is possible to argue that there is, in any particular market protected by intellectual property rights, a market for licences under those intellectual property rights, and hence to argue that a refusal to grant such a licence is an abuse of a dominant position. Whether such a market exists is a matter of fact, not of law.[439] If it does, then it may be possible to argue that refusal to license constitutes an abuse, for example, if it is a discriminatory refusal.

4. Under UK law

13.469 The position has already been covered at paras 13.363-13.366 in the case of firms in a dominant position. The MMC's Report under the FTA 1973 into *Historical on-line database services*[440] confirms that in a competitive market, a refusal to license others to use copyright protected information is not anti-competitive and therefore cannot be against the public interest.

[436] [1994] RPC 251.

[437] *Lansing Bagnall* v *Buccaneer Lift Parts* [1984] 1 CMLR 224; *Pitney Bowes* v *Francotyp-Postalia* [1989] 3 CMLR 446; *Digital Equipment Corp* v *LCE Computer Maintenance Ltd*, judgment of Mervyn Davies J, 22 May 1992, unreported.

[438] Ferris J refused at [1994] RPC 251, 273, to hold that trade mark rights were inherently different from other intellectual property rights: "To assert the passing off or trade mark cases are in a different category from other intellectual property cases would, I think, fail to recognise the true impact of what has been said on Article 86 as a defence in intellectual property cases since *ICI* v *Berk Pharmaceuticals Ltd*. I think that the matter must depend upon a consideration of nature of the right asserted, the nature of infringement of that right which is alleged and the nature of the supposed abuse. The one clear rule, it appears to me, is that there must be some nexus between the infringement complained of and the abuse which is said to constitute a defence to the claim for infringement."

[439] *Intergraph Corp* v *Solid Systems CAD Services Ltd*, [1995] ECC 53, 69-71 per Ferris J, interpreting the judgment of Aldous J in *Chiron Corporation* v *Murex (No. 2)* [1993] FSR 324.

[440] *Historical on-line database services*, Cm 2554 (May 1994).

14 Trade Association Membership

A. Introduction

14.1 In this chapter the following are discussed:

Section B.	Membership fees: analysis of when fees and levies may breach EC competition rules and other general EC law. Consideration of the scope of the exemption in UK law.
Section C.	Rules for membership: analysis of legality of imposing strict conditions for admission to membership.
Section D.	Inter-member exclusive dealing: closed systems. Analysis of association rules requiring members to only trade with other members or with members of other approved trade associations.
Section E.	Guilt by membership: consideration of when a member can be liable under competition law for activities undertaken by the association.

1. EC Law[1]

14.2 EC competition laws applies in practice to the activities of trade associations. Trade associations have always been looked upon with suspicion by antitrust authorities. They operate at all levels of the market and regulated substantial portions of industry. Traditionally, trade associations set prices and terms and conditions and, not uncommonly, imposed a form of "closed shop". However, over time, trade associations have modified and moderated their activities and competition authority have come to recognise that they serve valid and valuable objects in the market place. In particular, trade associations, nowadays: provide an umbrella under which members of an industry may meet to discuss is-

[1] See generally P. Watson and K. Williams, "The application of the EEC competition rules to trade associations" (1988) 8 YEL 121; *Butterworth's Competition Law*, Volume 1, tab. III (section on trade associations).

sues of general importance; provide a vehicle whereby the industry's views may be disseminated to government or to regulatory authorities; provide a mechanism for harmonisation of technical standards; provide administrative facilities for the collection and dissemination of relevant market data; undertake market research, etc. Most trade associations represent voluntary bodies. However, over time, some trade associations have acquired predominant status within an industry to the extent that non-membership, or conversely expulsion from membership, can severely prejudice the ability of a trader in the market place. Often, trade associations are delegated special responsibilities by government.[2] Trade associations may own or operate important national or regional markets or facilities such as auctions.[3] Furthermore, trade associations may control or operate markets such as commodities and futures markets.[4]

14.3 The Court of Justice has, on many occasions, reviewed the activities of trade associations and usually found them wanting since they have been found to involve themselves in the price mechanism in the market place.[5] However, the Court of Justice has also recognised that the activities of trade associations are, in principle, subject to the "rule of reason". In *Gottrup-Klim*[6] the Court of Justice was concerned with the rules of a cooperative purchasing association which included among its constitutional documents a provision the effect of which was to forbid the members the right to participate in other forms of organisation or cooperative which were in direct competition with the association in question. It was alleged before the national court that the prohibition on memfbers participating in competing associations fell within the prohibition in Article 85(1). The Court stated that the compatibility of the statutes of such an association could not be assessed in the abstract but would depend upon the particular clauses in the statutes and the economic conditions prevailing on the markets concerned. The Court observed that in a market where produce prices varied according to the volume of orders the activities of cooperative purchasing associations could, depending upon the size of their membership, constitute a significant counterweight to the contractual power of large producers and make way for more effective competition.[7] The Court stated further that where certain members of two competing cooperative purchasing associations belonged to both associations simultaneously the result might be to make each association less capable of pursuing its objectives for the benefit of the remainder of its members, especially where the members

2 See e.g Case 123/823 *BNIC* v *Clair* [1985] ECR 391; Case 136/86; *BNIC* v *Aubert* [1987] ECR 1789.

3 See e.g. *Cauliflowers* OJ 1978 L21/23; [1978] 1 CMLR D66; *Bloemenveilingen Aalsmear* OJ 1988 L262/27; [1989] 4 CMLR 500.

4 See e.g. the London futures markets case: *Baltic International Freight Futures Exchange Limited (BIFFEX)* OJ 1987 L22/24; *London Meat Futures Exchange Limited (LMEFL)* OJ 1987 L19/30; *London Grain Futures Market (LGFM)* OJ 1987 L19/22; *London Potato Futures Association Limited (LPFAL)* OJ 1987 L19/26; *The GAFTA Soyabean Meal Futures Association Limited (SOMFA)* OJ 1987 L19/18; *Petroleum Exchange of London (IPE)* OJ 1987 L3/27; *London Cocoa Terminal Market Association (LCTMA)* OJ 1985 L369/28; *Coffee Terminal Market Association of London (CTMAL)* OJ 1985 L369/31; *London Sugar Futures Market (LSFM)* OJ 1985 L369/25; *London Rubber Terminal Market Association (LRTMA)* OJ 1985 L369/34.

5 See e.g. Case T-29/92 *SPO* v *Commission* [1995] ECR II-289 where the CFI condemned the joint fixing of price increases which all undertakings participating in a tendering procedure were to include in their price tenders. The prices were to be disseminated to the companies trade association which was entrusted with the duty of sharing the information among all of the relevant undertaking submitting tenders. The purpose of the arrangement was to make it possible to ensure that the contract awarder bore, on a flat rate basis, the calculation costs incurred by all of the participants in the tendering procedure. The Court observed that such an arrangement constituted the fixing of part of the price and thereby restricted competition between undertakings as regards their calculation costs and led, ultimately, to an increase in prices.

6 Case C-250/92 *Gottrup-Klim* v *DLG* [1994] ECR I-5641.

7 *ibid.*, para. 32, p. I-5687.

concerned were themselves cooperative associations with a large number of individual members. The Court concluded that:

> "It follows that such dual membership would jeopardise both the proper functioning of the co-operative and its contractual power in relation to producers. Prohibition of dual membership does not, therefore, necessarily constitute a restriction of competition within the meaning of Article 85(1) of the Treaty and may even have beneficial effects on competition. Nevertheless, a provision in the statutes of a co-operative purchasing association, restricting the opportunity for members to join other types of competing co-operatives and thus discouraging them from obtaining supplies elsewhere, may have adverse effects on competition. So, in order to escape the prohibition laid down in Article 85(1) of the Treaty, the restrictions imposed on members by the statutes of co-operative purchasing associations must be limited to what is necessary to ensure that the co-operative functions properly and maintains its contractual power in relation to producers."[8]

14.4 In considering whether or not the statutes were necessary to achieve the legitimate objects of the association in question the Court identified, as matters for the national court to investigate, whether the penalties were non-compliance with the statutes were disproportionate to the objective they pursued and whether the minimum period of membership was unreasonable. In this regard the Court examined whether the restriction only covered products in respect of which a direct relationship existed between sales volume and price. The Court also considered whether members of the association were free to purchase products outside of the association provided that such transactions were carried out otherwise than through a competing consortium or association.

14.5 In the light of *Gottrup-Klim* it is clear that the rules of trade associations are to be viewed in their context and it is not possible to say without a detailed analysis of the surrounding economic considerations that any particular rule, even if it confers a fetter upon the individual economic freedom of members, constitutes a restriction distortion or prevention of competition within the meaning of Article 85(1). It is important also to note that in *Gottrup-Klim* the Court of Justice was asked whether the association in question, which as explained above carried out purchasing in its own name on behalf of its members, held a dominant position within the market in question. According to the national court, the association held a market share of circa. 36 per cent of the Danish fertiliser market and 32 per cent of the Danish market in plant protection products. The Court stated that while an undertaking which holds market shares of that size might, depending on the strength and number of its competitors, be considered to be in a dominant position, those market shares in themselves did not constitute conclusive evidence of the existence of a dominant position. The Court stated that so far as concerns the concept of abuse of a dominant position that neither the creation nor the strengthening of a dominant position were, *per se*, contrary to Article 86.[9]

14.6 The Court went on to observe that the activities of cooperative purchasing associations could encourage more effective competition on some markets if the conditions imposed on the members were limited to what was necessary to ensure that the cooperative functioned properly and maintained its contractual power in relation to producers and, provided such conditions were met, no abuse of a dominant position would arise.[10]

14.7 A trade association set up to promote standards in an industry or to enable small and medium sized undertakings to develop sufficient expertise to break into a new market

[8] *ibid.*, paras. 34 and 35, pp. I-5687, 5688.
[9] *ibid.*, para. 49, p. I-5691.
[10] *ibid.*, paras. 50–52, p. I-5691.

might not be caught by Article 85(1) EC provided membership is open on a non-discriminatory basis, it does not create any barriers to entry to undertakings from other Member States and it is not a facade behind which prohibited collusion takes place. Thus in *Retel 1988*[11] the Commission indicated that it would regard such an association, set up by Dutch private telecommunications equipment suppliers, as not caught by Article 85(1), since it observed the foregoing principles. The trade association promoted competition since its purpose was to give the consumer confidence to use private suppliers rather than the state PTT which had previously had the legal monopoly over the supply of such equipment. By way of contrast, the Commission insisted that several objectionable features be removed from a Dutch elevator manufacturers and repairers trade association in *NVL*.[12] These included minimum tariff setting, standard delivery terms, and restrictions on members' advertising and information exchange provisions.

2. *UK law*

14.8 Most control of trade associations is carried out by the OFT using its powers under the RTPA 1976, though it is possible that the CA 1980 could also apply. The last substantive case to be argued on its merits before the Restrictive Practices Court, *ABTA*,[13] dealt with a trade association of travel agents and is discussed below.[14]

B. Membership Fees

14.9 Trade associations usually gear their fee structures to the members' ability to pay, though a floor and ceiling fee might also be imposed to prevent too great a disparity between small and large members. Care must be taken to ensure that fee structures are not used in an anti-competitive manner. If Association X accounts for 90 per cent of the firms in the market and imposes a fee structure which operates to deter new members, this might be viewed as an attempt to create entry barriers to new entrants since membership of the

[11] OJ 1991 C121/2.
[12] OJ 1994 C231/5, [1994] 5 CMLR 682.
[13] [1984] ICR 12.
[14] In *Jetclub Limited* v *The Association of British Travel Agents Limited* (judgment of Laddie J, 13 March 1996) the Plaintiff (Jetclub Limited) was a member of ABTA. The Association sought to amend its articles of association. Prior to the changes the rules of the association permitted members to employ agents to provide travel agency services to the public. As a result of certain developments in the market the Association sought to amend the rule so as to require travel agents only to use employees in order to provide travel agency services to members of the public. The effect of the rule change was to curb the activities of certain travel agents who were using networks of agents, largely working from home, to sell their holidays. Jetclub represented a travel agent who used agents extensively and submitted that it was, or would be, severely prejudiced by the rule change. Jetclub sought an interlocutory injunction upon the day of the Extraordinary General Meeting (EGM) pursuant to which the new article of association was to be inserted. At first, the Plaintiff alleged that the rule change would bring the association into breach of a prior order of the RPC. However, at the hearing this averment was not pursued. Instead the member alleged first, that the alteration to the articles of association was not proposed bona fide for the benefit of the company as a whole; secondly, that the proposed change was outwith the Association's power (i.e. it was *ultra vires*) as set out in the memorandum of the association. The learned Judge concluded that neither submission was arguable and, *inter alia*, declined the application for an interlocutory injunction. The application was rejected upon its merits and not upon the basis that, given appropriate facts, such allegations made by a member could not succeed in principle. The case shows that where an association is a company and its members shareholders then members will acquire rights by virtue of company law in their capacity qua-shareholders in addition to any rights they may hold under UK or EC competition law.

association might be perceived as essential for any serious trader. Where the fee demanded is prohibitively high this might deter new firms or at least increase their entry costs. Similarly, the data collected about fees can be used restrictively. Where the fee paid is calculated by reference to a well-known formula based upon firm size (for example turnover, total billings, payroll, etc.) dissemination of such data to members will give them information about their rival's capacity that might otherwise be considered confidential. Thus, the amount of fees paid and the figures upon which they are based should not be disclosed.

1. *EC Law*

(1) Under Article 86 EC

14.10 There is very little guidance on Commission policy towards membership fees imposed by dominant associations. In *BRT* v *SABAM* the Court ruled that a copyright society which managed the copyright of its members (authors, composers) could not impose obligations on members which exceeded the limits absolutely necessary for the attainment of the legitimate objectives of the association.[15] On this basis fees should be related to the value of services provided and perhaps the ability of the member to pay. The imposition of excessive or unfair terms may infringe Article 86(a) EC which prohibits the imposition of unfair trading conditions.

14.11 If an association which enjoyed a *de facto* monopoly, for example, a copyright society in a single Member State, were to discriminate in the fees demanded from members according to non-justifiable criteria, this would almost certainly infringe Article 86 EC.[16] If the fees were set so as to exclude a certain type of firm from membership, then this might also represent an abuse of dominance. This might particularly be so where membership of the association were important to commercial success and/or where the association was seeking to exclude firms employing new and innovative methods from entering the market.

14.12 It might well be an abuse of dominance for an association to impose excessive fee demands on applicants who compete with the existing membership when reasonable fees are imposed on applicants who do not compete.[17]

(2) Under Article 85 EC

14.13 Trade association fee structures which differentiated in an unobjective fashion between categories of competing members might infringe Article 85(1) if the level of fee and the amount of the difference between different categories of fees were sufficient to give rise to a more than *de minimis* effect on competition. Where an association sets fees upon some quantitative criteria such as each members turnover and compiles statistics based upon data used to calculate a member's fees, that data should not be disseminated to the membership in any individualised form which permits members to identify the fees paid by other members. Such data might assist members to learn of confidential matters relating to other firms. See Chapter 9, for further details of this question.

[15] Case 127/73 *BRT* v *SABAM* [1974] 2 CMLR 238; [1974] ECR 313 at para. 11 of judgment. See also per Advocate General Mayras at [1974] ECR 313 at p. 325: "an undertaking occupying a dominant position is prohibited from exceeding a limit of fairness, and the measures which it chooses to attain its object must be the least restrictive possible".

[16] e.g. on grounds of nationality. In this respect see Art. 6(1) EC.

[17] See e.g. the US decision in *Associated Press* v *US* 326 US 1 (1945), see also *US* v *Allied Florists Association of Illinois* (1952–53) Trade Cases para. 67.433 at 68. 170 (ND Illinois 1953); and *US* v *Republic Steel Corp.* (1952–53) Trade Cases para. 67.510 at 68.497 (ND Ohio 1953).

(3) Under Articles 9–17 EC: import/export charges

14.14 Where a statute or other legislative instrument *requires* traders to belong to an association and pay a membership fee as a condition of being allowed to import or export goods, the fee might be prohibited under Articles 9–16 EC. These prohibit all customs duties on imports and exports and all measures of equivalent effect. These provisions are directly effective and may be pleaded before the national court as the basis of an action for restitution of the fee paid. The Court of Justice has in other contexts condemned: fees charged by a national agricultural intervention agency for the issue of import licences;[18] fees charged on all imports and exports to off-set the cost of compiling statistical records the availability of which is alleged to benefit the traders;[19] and fees charged to defray the cost of health and sanitary inspections.[20] The Court has, however, stated that in exceptional cases a charge may be justified where it is in consideration for some service provided and where it doe.s not exceed either the value or the cost of the service.[21] Thus, an association set up by government to provide publicity and advertising might be justified in imposing a charge on exporters.[22]

14.15 It should be stressed that for Articles 9–17 EC to apply the charge must be levied in accordance with a governmental requirement and the fee must legally count as a charge of equivalent effect to a customs duty.

2. UK Law

(1) Under the RTPA 1976

14.16 An obligation on any party to an agreement to make a payment based upon the quantity of goods or services supplied is viewed as registrable under section 6(1)(d) for goods (restriction on quantity of goods supplied) and section 11(2)(c) for services (restriction on extent to which services supplied).[23] Thus, prima facie, membership fees based upon turnover or other analogous quantitative criteria are registrable. However, the Act expressly excludes (in sections 6(4) and 17(2) RTPA 1976) membership fees from sections 6(1)(d) and 11 (2)(c) where the payments consist of bona fide subscriptions for membership of the association. Thus, where member X pays £500 membership per annum based upon an annual turnover of £1m and Y pays £1,000 on the basis of a £2 million annual turnover the obligation to pay according to turnover is not registrable. This exemption only applies to bona fide subscriptions. Where members pay a fee for services rendered, for example national advertising performed by the association, then any agreement as to fees paid for the services may become registrable as a restriction on the prices to be paid for services obtained under section 11(2)(a) RTPA 1976.

14.17 It is difficult to know precisely where a bona fide subscription ends and a consideration for services rendered commences. If the association charges a membership fee and a separate fee to cover advertising or other services rendered, then the membership fee

[18] *Germany* v *Commission* (Cases 52 and 55/65) [1967] CMLR 22; [1966] ECR 159. Such fees cannot be justified under Art. 36 EC: Case 29/72 *Marimex* v *Italian Tax Administration* [1973] CMLR 486; [1972] ECR 1309, but cf. Case 46/76 *Bauhuis* v *Netherlands* [1977] ECR 5.

[19] e.g. Case 24/68 *Commission* v *Italy* [1971] CMLR 611; [1969] ECR 193.

[20] e.g. Case 39/73 *Rewe-Zentralfinanz* v *Landwirtschaftskammer* [1977] 1 CMLR 630; [1973] ECR 1039; Case 35/76 *Simmenthal* v *Italian Minister of Finance* [1977] 2 CMLR 1; [1976] ECR 1871.

[21] *Rewe-Zentralfinanz* (above) [1973] ECR 1039 at p. 1044.

[22] See *Apple and Pear Development Council* v *Lewis* (Case 222/82) [1983] ECR 4083, but cf. *Cadskey* v *Instituto Nazionale per il Commercio Estero* (Case 63/74) [1975] 2 CMLR 246; [1975] ECR 281. For a case where the Commission condemned under Art. 85(1) EC an association whose members paid a levy which was used to fund export promotion see *Milk Production Fund* [1985] 3 CMLR 101 especially at paras. 38, 39.

[23] ss. 6(4) and 17(2) RTPA 1976 respectively.

and the service charge are differentiated and only the former is exempted from the Act. However, if the association charges a single subscription fee which is calculated to cover the cost of all services rendered then the fee might be exempt although in economic effect it is indistinguishable from the first example. The exemption in the Act refers only to a bona fide subscription for membership. It is arguable that a "subscription" that includes a cost component for services rendered goes beyond mere membership. Where an association is doubtful as to the registrability of its membership fee structure they might consider furnishing details to the OFT on a fail safe basis.

(2) Under the CA 1980

14.18 Presumably under the CA 1980, the practice of a trade association in using membership fees in an anti-competitive manner is reviewable by the OFT and MMC where the fees are exempt from the RTPA 1976. It would have to be established as a preliminary question that the association satisfied the criteria of section 2(1)CA 1980.

C. Rules for Membership

14.19 An association may set membership requirements that seek to control the type of firm operating in the market. Thus, membership might be restricted to firms enjoying a minimum number of qualified staff, or having a floor space in excess of a specified minimum, or have stocking capacity of a certain level. Where association membership is a valuable commercial asset, as it may be where the association provides commercial data or other trade advantages, the membership rules may exert a significant influence over the market.

1. EC Law

(1) Under Article 85 EC

14.20 Trade association rules are treated as an agreement between members to comply with the rules.[24] Thus, stipulations in the articles of association imposing strict conditions on membership are deemed to have been agreed by the members. The Commission has, on this basis, condemned, under Article 85(1), rules which require members to own their business premises and not rent them.[25] A potential market entrant seeking association membership is hence prevented from leasing premises. This rule adds to market entry costs and makes the entrant more expensive and less competitive in the long run. It follows that membership rules should not lay down criteria designed to exclude different forms and methods of trading.[26] Prima facie, it is the right of each trader to decide how they will trade and the right of the customer to decide who they choose to do business with. It is not the right of an association to make these decisions.

[24] e.g. *FEDETAB* (Cases 209–215, 218/78) [1981] 3 CMLR 134; [1980] ECR 3125 at paras. 85—89 of the judgment. See *Society of Lloyd's* v *Clementson* [1995] 1 CMLR 695, 704 *et seq. per* Sir Thomas Bingham MR.

[25] *Stoves and Heaters* [1975] 2 CMLR D1 at D9, paras. 36—38. *Donck* [1978] 2 CMLR 194; *Gas Water Heaters* [1973] CMLR 231; see also, *Groupement d'Exportation du Leon* [1978] 1 CMLR D 66 at para. 33, association rule that dealers doing business with members had to own a packaging centre within a catchment area was held to infringe Art. 85(1) EC. The Commission decided that the rule was designed to hinder entry into the dealer's market and thus protect members' customers from further competition. The rule was moreover superfluous in that many goods were sold pre-packed to dealers.

[26] For an early exposition of this principle see *Convention Faience* Bull EC 5/64 at p. 53 *et seq*. See also *Krups* [1980] 3 CMLR 274 in respect of dealership associations run by a single supplier. See also *BNSBA and BNCBA, Twenty-second Report on Competition Policy*, p. 416.

14.21 In some cases entry rules *MAY* impose strict conditions where they are necessary to protect the reputation of the industry or the interests of consumers. Thus, the rules of an association of wine producers which only admits to membership firms whose production methods meet certain recognised technical standards, would probably be suitable for exemption under Article 85(3) EC, provided the rules actually applied were the minimum necessary to meet the standards.[27] Conditions may be excessive where they extend to personal characteristics of the trader (age, years experience, etc.) and not to objectively determined minimum qualifications needed to carry out the trade in a reasonable manner. Rules permitting a majority of members or all members to govern admission may restrict competition.[28]

14.22 Some guidance on entry conditions to trading floors and futures markets and indeed to trade associations more generally may be gained from the Commission's attitude towards the applications for exemption and negative clearance in the London futures cases.[29] These associations administer the various futures markets and provide organised facilities for the conclusion of contracts for purchase and sale of the commodities. From these cases a number of indicators concerning Commission thinking on rules for entry to international trading markets may be noted.

(a) Limits on the number of members

14.23 A limit may be placed on the number of members allowed to become floor members which is related to the practical maximum for the orderly conduct of business. Limits on the total number of persons who can trade in any capacity should be avoided; the market and not the association should determine the number of suppliers and purchasers. Where fixed limits are imposed on any category of membership there should exist a mechanism whereby the numbers can be varied to suit fluctuating market conditions; rigidity should be avoided. The association should ensure that membership criteria are based upon strictly objective criteria. The relevant criteria for membership should be available freely from the association. Membership, being regarded as an asset, should be transferable, subject to the transferee satisfying the membership criteria.

(b) Capital requirements

14.24 A financial requirement representing a reasonable minimum that could be expected from a solvent, stable trader is acceptable. This requirement protects the reputation of the market as a secure place to do business. An unduly high requirement will distort competition by erecting entry barriers to perfectly capable and reputable traders.

(c) Experience

14.25 Rules requiring traders to have had a certain number of years experience, or requiring potential members to prove that they have a bona fide and continuing interest in the production or sale of the relevant commodity may also be acceptable as guarantees of the reputation and security of the market.

[27] e.g. *Cauliflowers* OJ 1978 L21/23.

[28] cf. *Belgian Central Heating Association* [1972] CMLR D130.

[29] e.g. *Baltic International Freight Futures Exchange* OJ 1987 L222/24; *GAFTA Soya Bean Meal Futures Association* 1987 L19/18; *London Grain Futures Market* OJ 1987 L19/22; *London Potato Futures Association* OJ 1987 L19/26; *London Meat Futures Exchange* OJ 1987 L19/30; *London Petroleum exchange* OJ 1987 L3/27; *London Sugar Futures Market* OJ 1985 L369/25; *London Cocoa Terminal Market* OJ 1985 L365/28; *London Coffee Terminal Association* OJ 1985 L369/31; *London Rubber Terminal Market Association* OJ 1985 L369/34.

(d) Physical presence rules

14.26 A requirement that a member trade form an office located in the city of the market in question and established for that purpose is, again, an acceptable requirement designed to weed out unreliable traders and provide security for the market and its participants. Rules laying down the size (floor space, employees etc) of the "presence" should be avoided though a requirement that "presence" be genuine and not simply a sham name plate should be acceptable.[30]

(e) Composition of managing bodies

14.27 Wherever possible managing bodies should be comprised of members who roughly represent the spread of interests involved in the market. A fair representation helps ensure that the competitive balance existing between the interests is not distorted by unrepresentative decisions of the managing body.

(f) Appeal procedures

14.28 Refusal of membership may well constitute an absolute entry barrier to a market. As such, any decision of a body deciding membership should be subject to review by another body. It will be a matter for discussion with the Commission whether appeal to another body within the market is acceptable or whether an independent appeal board should be instituted. In general appeals should be to independent bodies and ultimately to the ordinary courts. Indeed, in principle it is incompatible with EC law to preclude by contract the power of the courts to enforce EC law.[31] Similar rights of appeal should apply to decisions on expulsion, suspension, transfers of membership and other decisions influencing a trader's capacity to do business. Relevant bodies should always give reasons for their decisions since this is a minimum safeguard for an adversely affected member who wishes to appeal the decision.

(g) Membership of other organisations

14.29 Rules requiring that members belong to organisations such as the International Commodities Clearing House (ICCH) and that members must register their contracts with the ICCH who in return for a fee guarantee performances of the contract, are acceptable. Such a rule, yet again, is a device aimed at securing market efficiency and security. In appropriate circumstances it is not a breach of Articles 85 or 86 for the rules of any association to prohibit members from belonging to rival associations.[32]

30 See e.g. *Centraal Bureau voor de Rijwielhandel* OJ 1978 L20/18, [1978] 2 CMLR 194, where the Commission condemned a trade association's regulation establishing a system for the distribution and servicing of bicycles and related goods in the Netherlands. The system established by the association was open to all undertakings which obtained the status of recognised dealers, and in practice 80 per cent of Dutch bicycles were sold through this system. The Commission held that some of the requirements for recognition were unlawful, including the requirement that the dealers do business in the Netherlands and satisfy conditions as to stocks premises and presentation, since these were a barrier to entry for importers of bicycles in the Netherlands. These are matters for a selective distribution network rather than a trade association. Similarly restrictive conditions were condemned by the Commission in another Dutch trade association for crane-hire: *SCK/FNK* OJ 1994 L117/30.

31 See Case 246/80 *Broekmuelen* [1981] ECR 311; Case 102/81 *Nordsee* [1982] ECR 1095; Case C-393/92 *Alemlo* [1994] ECR I-1477; *Society of Lloyd's* v *Clementson* [1985] 1 CMLR 693, 711 where the Master of the Rolls stated that even statutory exclusions or ousters cannot serve to preclude the operation of Article 85(1). See for an example of the Commission condemning inadequate appeal provisions: *CBR* OJ L20/18 at para. 28.

32 See e.g. Case C-250/92 *Gottrup-Klim* [1994] ECR I-5641.

(2) Under Article 86 EC

14.30 It is rare that Article 86 EC would be applied to trade association rules since Article 85 EC has traditionally been viewed as the most appropriate regulator of the constitutions and rules of associations of competitors. However, Article 86 might be applied where an association provides a unique function in the market, for example, a copyright society holding the copyrights of its members and licensing them on their behalf.[33]

(3) Under Articles 30–36 EC: compulsory membership

14.31 Statutory requirements that traders belong to an association as a pre condition of import or export will almost inevitably be unlawful under Articles 30 (imports) or 34 (exports) EC. The Court of Justice has stated in respect of exports: "it is contrary to the freedom of commercial transactions for national legislation to make the exportation of the products in question conditional on the exporter's being affiliated to a public body or a body approved by an official authority."[34] There is no reason to believe that a different rule would apply to imports. It makes no difference that membership is as of right, i.e. a formality since no *DE MINIMIS* rule exists under Articles 30–36 EC.[35] Compulsory membership may, in exceptional cases, be justified under Article 36 which permits governmentally imposed trade restrictions where justified on the basis of "public morality, public policy or public security; the protection of health and life of humans, animals or plants; the protection of national treasures possessing artistic, historic or archaeological value; or the protection of industrial or commercial property." However, the restriction chosen by the government must be the minimum necessary to achieve the desired objective under Article 36 EC. Thus, if a trader can establish that the interest described in Article 36 could be protected by a measure less restrictive of trade than compulsory affiliation, then the compulsory affiliation rule is unlawful under Article 30 EC.

2. *UK Law*

(1) Under the RTPA 1976

14.32 In *Association of British Travel Agents*[36] (ABTA hereafter) the RPC was asked, *inter alia,* to assess the membership rules of ABTA against the public interest. Membership of ABTA is almost essential in the travel industry.[37] Thus, the membership conditions of the association act as effective entry requirements to the travel market. The RPC considered that many of these rules were overly restrictive. In particular, ABTA imposed requirements as to staffing and premises which many small traders would have found costly to meet. With regard to the premises requirements the RPC stated that they: "impose a rigid structure on the industry which is not responsive to customer demand so that there is a danger that ... the industry will become fossilized. If the premises requirements continue

[33] e.g. Case 121/73 *BRT* v *SABAM* [1974] ECR 313; *GEMA* JO 1971 L134/15; 22/79 *Greenwich Film Production* v *SACEM* [1979] ECR 3279; 7/82 *GVL* v *Commission* [1983] ECR 483; *GEMA* OJ 1982 L94/22; 402/85 *Basset* v *SACEM* [1987] 1747, [1987] 3 CMLR 173; see an Art. 86 Case C-250/92 *Gottrup-Klim* [1994] ECR II-5641.

[34] Case 29/82 *Van Luipen* [1983] 2 CMLR 681; [1983] ECR 151 at para. 9 of the judgment; Case 94/79 *Vriend* [1980] 3 CMLR 473; [1980] ECR 327.

[35] Case 11/84 *Van der Haar* [1985] 2 CMLR 566 Court held that Art. 30 was not subject to a *de minimis* rule, unlike Art. 85 EC. See Oliver, *Free Movement of Goods in the European Community* (3rd edn.), para. 6.25 *et seq.*

[36] [1984] ICR 12.

[37] *ibid.*, at p. 19D.

to be enforced, the public will be denied the free choice of premises which should be theirs and the possibility (not necessarily the probability) of new, better and cheaper forms of marketing."[38]

14.33 With regard to staffing requirements the RPC stated: "they may raise costs needlessly, and discourage technological and other forms of inventiveness. They stifle new forms of competition."[39]

14.34 The concern of the RPC with restrictive entry requirements would appear to be two fold. First, restrictive rules may create entry barriers and thereby have a deterrent effect on potential entrants; and secondly, such rules artificially maintain the status quo thereby hindering the introduction of innovative and technologically advanced ideas. It should be added that these undesirable effects are only likely to occur where the association enjoys considerable market power, i.e. membership is at a premium. Where this is not the case the incentive for traders to join the association and comply with its rules is weak and, as such, traders enjoy greater freedom to make their own decisions.

(2) Under the Competition Act 1980

14.35 Even if rules do not fall under the RTPA, they may nevertheless be objected to by the OFT under the CA 1980. Thus the British Equestrian Trade Association was persuaded by the OFT to drop its requirement that manufacturers of body protectors joint the BETA in order to obtain approval for their goods.[40]

D. Inter-Member Exclusive Dealing (Closed Systems)

14.36 Where membership of an association is a sine qua non to being able to conduct trade with other members or other traders, then membership may be essential to commercial success. Thus, association rules banning members from dealing with non-members create significant entry barriers to the market. Likewise where a buyers' association agrees with a sellers' association that members will deal only with members of the other association, then entry barriers are erected to non-members and a premium is placed upon membership.

1. EC Law

14.37 Trade associations which operate or encourage closed systems infringe Article 85(1) and the systems will rarely be suitable for exemption under Article 85(3) EC. The Commission object that closed systems represent unreasonable restraints on the sources of supply available to members, and, unreasonable entry barriers to non-members.[41] Moreover, such

[38] *ibid.*, at p. 42H.

[39] *ibid.*, at p. 44A.

[40] DGFT Annual Report 1992, p. 30. See also DGFT Annual Report 1994, pp. 44–45 in relation to the Association of British Insurers. In that case a problem arose because consumers appeared to be under a misconception as to whom they were required to deal with, rather than an actual restriction. The remedy was increased consumer information.

[41] e.g. *Convention Faience* Bull EC 5/64 at p. 53; *VCH* [1973] CMLR D16; *GISA* [1973] CMLR D125; *Bomée–Stichting* [1976] 1 CMLR D1; *ASPA* [1970] CMLR D25; *FEDETAB* [1978] 3 CMLR 524 (Commission decision); *VBBB and VBVB* [1982] 2 CMLR 344 at paras. 39, 40 (Commission Decision); *Groupement d'Exportation du Leon* [1978] 1 CMLR D66 at paras. 33, 34. Rules that strengthen the mutuality also restrict competition. For example, a rule whereby members of a dealer's association could only deal with suppliers from the supplier's association as principals was, held the Commission, designed to

systems solidify distributional patterns which make them less responsive to change.[42] The Court of First Instance upheld the Commission's condemnation in *Hudson's Bay*[43] of a Danish auction association's rules which compelled its members to sell their entire production to a subsidiary set up by the association. The Commission had found that members were prevented from exporting part of their production and that the agreement was aimed at limiting market entry by competitors by monopolising the supply and sale of the products in Denmark. On the other hand, a rule requiring members of a purchasing cooperative only to buy through their association may well be held not to restrict competition under Article 85(1), provided it is restricted to what is necessary to ensure that the cooperative functions properly and maintains its purchasing power in relation to producers.[44]

14.38 Exclusive dealing agreements whereby one association agrees with another association that members of the former will only sell through members of the latter are *NOT* within the block exemption for exclusive distribution in 1983/83/EEC.[45]

2. UK Law

(1) Under the RTPA 1976

14.39 Trade association exclusive dealing is registrable under sections 6(1)(f) and 11 (2)(e) as a restriction on the persons or classes of persons who may be supplied to or purchased from. Such agreements are generally assumed to be unsuited to section 21(2) treatment and unlikely to be accepted as in the public interest by the RPC. However, this assumption is not entirely correct since the RPC has accepted a major closed system run by a powerful association as discussed below.

(2) Under section 21(2) RTPA 1976

14.40 As a general rule trade association exclusive dealing will not be suitable for section 21(2) treatment since the restrictions may not be said to be insignificant. Thus in *South West Herts Coach Operators Association*[46] the OFT gave section 21(2) dispensation to an association's membership conditions only after a clause which provided that inter-hire would take place "within the Association whenever possible unless an emergency occurs" was deleted.

cont.
prevent non-members gaining access to the suppliers by using admitted dealers as their agents: *Motor Assessors* Bull EC 7 and 8/85 at p. 38.

42 e.g. *Bomée–Stichting* [1976] 1 CMLR D1 at D6, para. 23: "The effect of these restrictions is to consolidate existing distribution structures and the positions of the undertakings concerned on the relevant markets in such a way that new market entrants and firms which refuse to accept the Bomee conditions ... find it difficult to penetrate the market. The Bomée system makes it particularly difficult for market positions to be modified by the free play of competition."

43 Case T-61/89 *Dansk Pelsdryavlerforening* v *Commission* [1992] ECR II-1931, Commission decision *Hudson's Bay/Dansk Pelsdryavlerforening* OJ 1988 L316/43. See also *Bloemenveilingen Aalsmeer* OJ 1988 L262/27 (condemned of auction association's activity) and *Bloemenveilingen Aalsmeer II*, OJ 1989 C83/3, Commission indicating that it would take a favourable view following amendments.

44 Case C-250/92 *Gøttrup-Klim Grovvareforening* v *Dansk Landbrugs Grovvarelleskab* [1994] ECR I-5641; [1996] 4 CMLR 191, at paras. 28–40. See also the *Twenty-fourth Report on Competition Policy* (1994), para. 17.

45 See e.g. Case 126/80 *Salonia* v *Poidomani* [1982] 1 CMLR 64.

46 No. S.292 Register of Restrictive Trade Practices (1977). See also, No. S.598 Register of Restrictive Trade Practices, *Pontefract and Castleford Transport Association* (1980).

(3) Position of the RPC

14.41 While is remains true to say that trade association exclusive dealing will rarely be in the public interest it is also true that such systems may be acceptable in exceptional cases. In *ABTA*[47] the RPC was required to assess against the public interest a scheme operated by ABTA where tour operator members could only deal with travel agent members and vice versa, i.e. members could only deal with members. ABTA consists of about 2,400 members divided into two broad categories: tour operators and retail agents (travel agents). ABTA's dominance over the industry is almost complete, membership is viewed as a licence to trade. The RPC commented "exclusion from ABTA in its present form, if it does not amount to a denial of such a licence, is at the very least a severe handicap."[48] The exclusive dealing provisions derived from the association's articles of association which prohibited members from dealing with non-members. This was subject to a few limited exceptions. This provision was labelled the "stabilizer" by the association. Despite the objections of counsel for the OFT, the RPC accepted that "stabilizer" was in the public interest. To belong to ABTA applicants had to satisfy certain financial criteria which had been imposed as a result of the collapse of certain travel companies which had caused great inconvenience to travellers and which had received considerable adverse publicity. Furthermore, members had to comply with a code of conduct which was also designed to maintain standards. The RPC stated:

> "In order to survive, stabilizer, too, has to fulfil the conditions of one of the gateways in section 19(1) of the Act of 1976. We are satisfied that it does so. The financial safeguards, whether considered in conjunction with the other arrangements and operations such as the codes of conduct stripped of their vices, and the many non-restrictive benefits referred to in this judgment, or whether considered in isolation, are important, specific and substantial benefits to the purchasers and would-be purchasers of foreign inclusive tours. Stabilizer ensures that the safeguards are contributed to by a wide membership and that ABTA's requirements are adhered to. If stabilizer were to be removed, the compulsive force of this sanction would decline and the benefits of the safeguards would be lost. So the financial safeguards result from the maintenance of the stabilizer restrictions. The conditions of section 19(1)(b) of the Restrictive Trade Practices Act 1976 are accordingly satisfied."[49]

14.42 It is notable that the RPC indicated that although "stabilizer" was in the public interest it could, nonetheless, be improved by incorporating a more flexible set of exceptions into it.[50] Under the articles of association, ABTA could exempt members from the restrictions on dealing with traders outside of the association. The RPC considered that, hitherto, ABTA had granted dispensation in an arbitrary manner.[51] However, the RPC refused to lay down strict guidelines for ABTA to apply. Instead the Court stressed that: (a) dispensation should not be granted in an arbitrary manner; and (b) ABTA should employ criteria relating to the consumer's interest only, for that was the paramount consideration justifying stabilizer in the public interest.[52] Thus, ABTA should not act as a "recruiting sergeant" refusing dispensation simply because ABTA wished to maintain its membership numbers.[53]

14.43 Following *ABTA* trade association exclusive dealing may be in the public interest where membership to the association confers benefits on the consuming public. Probably, there

[47] [1984] ICR 12.
[48] *ibid.*, at p. 17G.
[49] *ibid.*, at p. 46C, D.
[50] *ABTA (No. 2)* [1985] ICR 122 at pp. 130, 131.
[51] [1984] ICR 12 at p. 47E, G.
[52] [1985] ICR 122 at p. 131A, B.
[53] *ibid.*, at p. 131C.

must exist exceptional circumstances (for instance the need to provide financial security for the public) before the restrictions will be acceptable. It should be added that simply because the RPC might accept a closed system does *NOT* imply that such systems are suitable for section 21(2) treatment. It will almost certainly be the case that even the most meritorious of schemes will have to justify themselves before the RPC.

E. Guilt by Membership

14.44 Members of an association which infringes competition rules run the risk of being implicated in the association's unlawful activities by mere fact of membership. In one American case the Court commented that membership *PER SE* was not evidence of collusion but they added:

> "Thus, the issue is reduced to whether a member who knows or should know that his association is engaged in an unlawful enterprise and continues his membership without protest may be charged with complicity as a confederate. We believe he may. Granted that his mere membership does not authorize unlawful conduct by the association, once he is chargeable with knowledge that his fellows are acting unlawfully his failure to disassociate himself from them is a ratification of what they are doing. He becomes one of the principals in the enterprise ..."[54]

14.45 "Guilt by membership" is an important issue in EC law where the fines that may be imposed may be very considerable in extent. It is perhaps less pressing in UK law though members of associations subject to court orders or injunctions may risk being in contempt of court if they become implicated in association conduct that infringes a Court order. Contempt of court is punishable by gaol and/or fines.[55]

1. *EC Law*

(1) Basic principle

14.46 According to the Court of Justice in *FEDETAB*[56] a member of an association may be liable for concerted practices with other members where the association rules provide that its decisions shall be binding on members. In such a case a member may be liable even though it did not *specifically* agree to follow such decisions where it does *in fact* comply with those decisions. The fact that the member asserts that its behaviour was due to compelling market forces rather than the decision is immaterial (or perhaps more accurately contrary to the reasonable implications to be drawn from the fact of the members compliance).[57] In *FEDETAB* the Court made the additional comment that the association acted in the name of its members who "took part in the adoption and observance of the said measure through the intermediary of their trade association".[58] Precisely what relevance is to be accorded this dictum is unclear. It is unlikely that mere innocent membership would suffice to raise an implication of involvement. However, if a member either takes part in the

54 *Phelps' Dodge Refining Corp* v *FTC* 139 F. 2d 393 (2d Cir. 1943). See also *Boyle* v *US* 40 F. 2d 49 at p. 51 (7th Cir. 1930).
55 See paras. 5.69–5.86.
56 Joined Cases 209–215, 218/78 [1980] ECR 3125, [1981] 3 CMLR 134; at paras. 90, 91 of the judgment.
57 In *Lloyd's Underwriters' Association* OJ 1993 L4/26, the Commission held that the absence of sanctions for failure to respect a price fixing agreement, other than disapprobation, did not prevent the agreement falling within Art. 85(1). The Court of Justice has stated in Case 45/85 *Verband der Sachversicherer* v *Commission* [1987] ECR 405, paras. 26–32, that a recommendation described by an association as non-binding fell within Art. 85(1).
58 *ibid.*, at para. 91.

adoption of a measure or complies with it subsequent to its adoption then this apparently will imply involvement.

(2) Fines[59]

14.47 In determining whether to impose fines and, if so, the amount, the Commission may consider, *inter alia,* the extent of participation in the infringement. The different roles of members and their respective degrees of complicity should be reflected in the fine. Hence, a member whose complicity is primarily through membership rather than through active involvement should receive a lesser fine than a member who actively participated in the infringement.[60] A trade association can be fined even if individual members are also fined.[61] Whether it will be fined separately depends on the role it has played in the infringement.[62] If the trade association has not played an active role, it will not generally be fined, even in cases where the association may have been used by its members to further the effect of the infringement.[63]

(3) Practical considerations

14.48 Given that the threat of fines is not a remote one, members may wish to take steps to minimise the risks of guilt by membership. To this end, members might consider departing any association meeting or discussion during which conduct they consider likely to infringe competition rules is proposed or considered. Departure from the meeting might be accompanied by a statement that the member is departing as a result of the nature of the discussions in question. Where such a statement can be minuted it may help to disassociate the member from any subsequent unlawful behaviour. Where the association refuses to minute the departure and/or the reasons for the departure the member should prepare its own note and send it to the association. The Court of First Instance has stated on several occasions that once it is established that an undertaking is a regular participant in meetings which have been held to constitute a concerted practice caught by Article 85(1), it is for the undertaking to adduce evidence that it was not party to any prohibited concerted practice, and that evidence simply that, for example, prices actually achieved on the market did not agree with those set by the meeting is insufficient rebuttal. The undertaking must ensure that the other members of the association understand that it will not comply with the anti-competitive agreement. Advice of this nature is commonly given in the USA. It is relevant also under EC rules.

2. UK Law

14.49 UK Competition law does not impose the same threat of financial sanction that EC law does. Situations in which guilt by membership may pose serious problems are hence

[59] See paras. 7.44–7.67. See Kerse, *EC Antitrust Procedure* (3rd edn. 1994), Chapter 7.

[60] See, e.g. the position of Firma Schiffer in *Floral* [1980] 2 CMLR 285 at p. 301, para. 77.

[61] *Roofing Felt* OJ 1986 L232/15, upheld on appeal 246/86 *Belasco* v *Commission* [1989] ECR 2117, [1991] 4 CMLR 96; *Navewal/Anseau* OJ 1982 L167/39, upheld on appeal Joined Cases 96–102, 104, 105, 108 and 110/82 *IAZ International Belgium* v *Commission* [1983] ECR 3369.

[62] 89/85 etc. *Ahlstrom* v *Commission (Wood Pulp)* [1993] ECR I-1307, [1993] 4 CMLR 407; *Hudson's Bay/Dansk Pelsdryavlerforening* OJ 1988 L316/43, upheld on appeal T-61/89 *Dansk Pelsdryavlerforening* v *Commission* [1992] ECR II-1931; *Avewal/Anseau* OJ 1982 L167/39, upheld on appeal Joined Cases 96–102, 104, 105, 108 and 110/82 *IAZ International Belgium* v *Commission* [1983] ECR 3369.

[63] *Welded Steel Mesh Cartel* OJ 1989 L260/1, [1991] 4 CMLR 13. Case T-3/89 *Atochem* v *Commission* [1991] ECR II-1177, paras. 52–54 and 100.

more limited. Where an association enters an agreement that is registrable under the RTPA 1976, then it may become subject to a prohibitive court order. However, in such cases it will primarily be the association and not the members which must appear before the Court. Moreover, the Court has no power to impose fines. However, "guilt by membership" may be a problem for a firm who becomes or is a member of an association subject to a Court order. Under section 2 RTPA 1976 the RPC may make an order against, *inter alia*, "the persons party to the agreement who carry on business within the United Kingdom". Members of associations are, by virtue of sections 8 (goods) and 16 (services) RTPA 1976, deemed to be parties to agreements made by a trade association and to accept recommendations made by the association. Thus, members of associations are subject to court orders. Breach of such an order is contempt of court which is punishable by gaol or fine. The OFT and the RPC have, in recent years, adopted an increasingly strict attitude towards alleged contempt cases and a number have been brought to trial. Heavy fines have been levied. Gaol is a very real possibility for defaulting individuals. Thus, members of associations should ensure that their conduct does not infringe any outstanding court orders. If they find that it does they should take immediate steps to disassociate themselves from the conduct and have their opposition formally recorded.[64]

[64] See paras 5.87–5.88 for further discussion on contempt cases.

Index